5/98

D0222335

An Encyclopedia
of the History of
Classical Archaeology

An Encyclopedia
of the History
# of Classical Archaeology

Edited by
Nancy Thomson de Grummond

A–K

GREENWOOD PRESS
Westport, Connecticut

Library of Congress Cataloging-in-Publication Data

An encyclopedia of the history of classical archaeology / edited by
   Nancy Thomson de Grummond.
       p. cm.
    Includes bibliographical references and index.
    ISBN 0–313–22066–2 (alk. paper : set). — ISBN 0–313–30204–9
   (alk. paper : A–K). —ISBN 0–313–30205–7 (alk. paper : L–Z)
    1. Classical antiquities—Encyclopedias. 2. Art, Classical—
   Encyclopedias. 3. Architecture, Classical—Encyclopedias.
    4. Excavations (Archaeology)—Mediterranean Region—Encyclopedias.
    5. Archaeology and history—Mediterranean Region—Encyclopedias.
    I. De Grummond, Nancy Thomson.
   DE5.E5   1996
   938'.003—dc20   94–29838

British Library Cataloguing in Publication Data is available.

Library of Congress Catalog Card Number: 94–29838
ISBN: 0–313–22066–2 (set)
         0–313–30204–9 (A–K)
         0–313–30205–7 (L–Z)

First published in 1996

Greenwood Press, 88 Post Road West, Westport, CT 06881
An imprint of Greenwood Publishing Group, Inc.

Printed in the United States of America

The paper used in this book complies with the
Permanent Paper Standard issued by the National
Information Standards Organization (Z39.48–1984).

10 9 8 7 6 5 4 3 2 1

*In memory of
Louise Ponder Thomson (1913–1994)
and
Alfred Valerie Thomson (1913–1993)*

Contents

Preface

I entered upon it, as one does on a country newly discovered; without any paths made and generally much embarrassed. Had any work of this kind been published . . . I certainly could have made this much more perfect, with extremely less pains; whereas all I can beg for it now is, that the difficulty of making one's way almost everywhere, may be duly considered; and that the many imperfections and errors which that must occasion, may meet with the indulgence that the case deserves.

—J. Spence, Introduction to *Polymetis* (1747)

Since this is the first time an encyclopedia of the history of classical archaeology has been prepared, it is appropriate to begin by describing the scope and methodology of the work. It is necessary to explain first what is understood by "classical archaeology." The expression is used here to mean basically the study of the visual remains of the ancient classical lands, Greece and Italy. Greek and Roman material is central; but also included here are the prehistoric or proto-historical cultures of the Bronze Age Aegean and of the Etruscans, which have a relationship of continuity and overlapping with the succeeding cultures in Greece and Italy, respectively, and the study of which is often inseparable from the historical Greek and Roman periods. Also included are manifestations of these cultures outside Italy and Greece proper; in France, for example, Roman arches, amphitheaters and aqueducts that were known, reused, admired and studied are of significance for the history of the study of classical remains. Greek temples and sites in Asia Minor were noted from the fifteenth century, and the story of their systematic recovery and study in the nineteenth century constitutes an important chapter in the history of archaeology. But other related archaeological spheres—Egyptian, Near Eastern, Phoenician, Celtic, Scythian, and New World—are referred to only in passing, for to treat these fully would have meant to write a very different book.

As for the word "archaeology," some today apply the term only to the rigorously systematic and scientific aspects of the discipline that have grown up in connection with purposeful excavation in the field. A book like Glyn Daniel's *A Short History of Archaeology* (1981) is based on the idea that archaeology is properly the science of excavating and interpreting excavated evidence and that it reaches its greatest purity when the study is completely prehistoric; inscriptions and literary traditions are considered far less relevant for the discipline. Advocates of this approach have given little attention to those who studied antiquities prior to the advent of scientific fieldwork. Bruce Trigger's recent work, *A History of Archaeological Thought* (1989), shows an awareness of scholarly study of classical remains prior to the nineteenth century but allots a quite small amount of space to early classical archaeologists. For a just survey, one must go back more than one hundred years to the work of C. B. Stark, *Systematik und Geschichte der Archäologie der Kunst* (1880), approximately half of which is devoted to archaeology of the fifteenth to eighteenth centuries.

In this encyclopedia the Middle Ages, Renaissance and seventeenth and eighteenth centuries are treated as periods to be taken seriously for their archaeological study of the visual remains of antiquity. This approach constitutes one of the principal ways in which the work differs from the studies of Daniel, Trigger and others who have, in recent years, written on the history of archaeology. Included here are the biographies of travelers, collectors, artists and scholars whose activities made a difference in knowledge of the sites and monuments in their own day and in the history of archaeological scholarship. Scholars such as Peiresc and Bellori were on the cutting edge of research on antiquities in the seventeenth century and were passionately committed to the exchange of knowledge; we still follow some of their basic methodology and even conclusions. Travelers of the fifteenth century such as Buondelmonti and Ciriaco of Ancona made valuable records of the status of sites and monuments in their day and thus enlarge our own view. Artists like Alberti and Vasari reported on antiquities excavated in their time (Alberti himself attempted an underwater excavation at Nemi), and their reports help us to recover the context of artifacts and monuments under study today.

In addition, here the reader will find entries on famous monuments as seen, changed and interpreted through time; obvious inclusions are the Parthenon, the Mausoleum of Halikarnassos, the Colosseum and the Pantheon, which were visited and studied during the Renaissance and later (for some monuments there are continuous records from the Middle Ages). There are entries on major works of art, such as the *Laocoon* group, the Farnese *Herakles* and the Aldobrandini *Wedding,* which were excavated during the Renaissance and seventeenth century (albeit with an intent and by techniques that are considered very limited today), as well as works that were known throughout the Middle Ages and later, such as the Capitoline *Wolf.* Studying the "biographies" of these works, we understand how they came to be the way they are today and are better able to conjecture what they were like originally. The different restorations of the missing parts of the *Laocoon* group, which make a critical difference in our interpretation of its style and subject matter, can be traced from the sixteenth century. The seventeenth-century report that the Portland Vase was discovered in a sarcophagus is of great interest for our understanding of the usage and meaning of this unusual artifact. Besides such major monuments, many others are included; clearly, not every building or statue or artifact that has been studied through the centuries can have an entry of its own, though a quite large number of works are at least mentioned (the index may be consulted to locate those that do not have an entry). In selecting sites, monuments and statuary for individual entries, an attempt has been made to choose the items that have had a strong impact on classical studies and that have a rich historical past. These are often works that have, or have had, an important place also in the history of art or architecture; for this, perhaps the encyclopedia may be criticized, since New Archaeology in the twentieth century believes that the discipline should not be concerned with the beauty of excavated materials. To this the answer is that in reconstructing antiquity, the basic task of archaeology, it is appropriate to try to see with the eyes of the ancients, who cared a great deal about the beauty of their monuments. In this sense, those who practiced the Old Archaeology were much closer to understanding antiquity than are some scholars today.

Other considerations in selection of materials and viewpoints are listed by the following categories.

ARTISTS

Art historians may consult this work for information about the study and imitation of antiquity by artists of the Renaissance and later periods. Since the number of artists who worked within the ''classical tradition'' is vast (Michael Greenhalgh has surveyed them in *The Classical Tradition in Art,* 1978), it is impossible to include them all; an attempt has been made to determine which artists should have priority, with the operative criterion that the artist should demonstrate some concrete evidence of study of the visual remains of classical antiquity. Thus, artists who did sketchbooks and created a repertory of illustrations of such material, even though they may be minor figures in the history of art, are certainly appropriate subjects for entries. For artists who simply show a style that has an ''antique'' feeling, it is sometimes difficult, if not impossible, to determine how they contributed to archaeological knowledge in their time. With great reluctance the decision was made to eliminate certain key artists of the Renaissance who left no drawing or written record of the study of specific antiquities and whose painted or sculptured works reveal relatively little data about antiquities visible in this period.

SCHOLARS

The omission most regretted relates to humanist scholars and philologists who were powerfully influential in their time but whose scholarly output reveals little or no involvement with archaeological material. Those who collected manuscripts and studied and wrote ancient history are borderline cases and are normally excluded if there is little or no evidence of serious study of at least inscriptions and/or coins for their own sakes. The decision was made to omit paleography as well as papyrology, disciplines that are more properly the sphere of philologists. It is not that this encyclopedia intends to promote categorization, only that from a practical point of view, some things must be omitted, and since histories of classical scholarship have normally given heavy emphasis to research on texts and literary criticism (e.g., J. E. Sandys, *A History of Classical Scholarship,* 3rd ed., 1958; Ulrich von Wilamowitz-Moellendorff, *A History of Classical Scholarship,* 1982), information may be sought there rather than in these pages.

Scholars living today, however significant their place in the history of archaeological scholarship, have not been included.

SITES

It has been especially difficult to explain to potential readers and contributors what the encyclopedia would do in regard to sites. Those who were asked to write about sites thought immediately of the *Princeton Encyclopedia of Classical Sites* and wanted to know what more needed to be done. The present reference work differs from the *Princeton Encyclopedia,* above all, in its attempt to give fuller coverage to the history of the study of sites. Dates when excavations took place, who directed the work, what results were obtained and what conclusions were drawn, what significance the finds had for the development of scholars' understanding of the site and the culture represented—these are the matters that were recommended to the contributors. In a way, the sites have "biographies" like those of artists, travelers and scholars, including information about what happened at the site in antiquity and what happened to it in later periods, as well as an evaluation of its contribution to our archaeological knowledge.

The selection of sites has been extremely difficult. Again, the number of possibilities is enormous, as demonstrated by the *Princeton Encyclopedia* itself. Further, each site seems important to the person who digs it or studies it. Emphasis was given to those sites that have a longer or more prominent history of visitation and excavation and to those that seem to have generated important changes in archaeological thinking. Some attempt has been made to take into account geographical distribution and, by including sites in areas outside Greece and Italy, to give some idea of the development of classical archaeology in other countries.

ABOUT THE BOOK

A word is in order about the history of this encyclopedia of the history of archaeology. The idea to do the work was not my own; when first invited to be a coeditor, I replied that I would love to look up things in such a work but was unable to commit to such a large undertaking. When approached a second time, my resolve weakened, and my enthusiasm for the project was so strong that I agreed to serve as coeditor as well as coauthor of a certain percentage of the articles, especially those that had to do with my own area of Etruscan studies and with the development of classical archaeology in the seventeenth century, a subject that had been part of my dissertation. With the help of an advisory board (see Acknowledgments, later in Preface), a master list was drawn up (it had 748 entries), and a list of some fifty potential contributors was compiled. Editorial and authorial duties were divided and invitations sent out.

Then the entries began to come in, and a remarkable phenomenon developed. Authors had been asked to supply suggestions for cross-references in the encyclopedia, and almost every entry submitted listed one or more cross-references that did not appear on the master list. The master list thus began to expand, and more contributors were invited. At this point my coeditor withdrew, and I determined to continue the work; on two occasions I sought a new coeditor, inviting colleagues whom I considered ideal for the job. They were not so rash as I had been, and no collaborator was secured.

Today, some fifteen years later, the list of entries numbers 1,125, and the number of contributors 171. My editors at Greenwood, urging practicality, have nevertheless graciously acquiesced as the work expanded well beyond what they had envisioned. In the final months of completing the manuscript, I continued to discover entries that should be on the list, and no doubt reviewers will likewise note (I hope without being overly indignant) that omissions have occurred. A limit had to be drawn, however arbitrary it might seem, and thus some entries of potential importance have been omitted. Others that might seem in retrospect of lesser significance were contributed early and would have been excluded unfairly.

Other matters became evident as entries were completed and compared. Each individual contributor had his or her own style of presenting the information requested. As editor, I recommended a rewrite if a contributor had not included enough of the appropriate historical material, and I requested condensation when too much purely descriptive material was given. But, on the whole, it seemed desirable to let each scholar have some latitude in self-expression and to avoid an excessively standardized or sterilized form for entries.

Thus, normally each entry begins with a brief identifying phrase and ends with a bibliography of approximately four items. But there is considerable variation among entries, depending, first of all, on whether the subject is a site or monument, scholar or traveler, or yet another kind of entry in which a topic is the focus (e.g., underwater archaeology), and depending further on the way in which the author organized the material. All entries have some kind of historical content, but this is often combined with descriptive material that helps to identify or explain the subject, with opinions of archaeologists of the past and present and with references to achievements in archaeological scholarship. These do not necessarily follow a standard order or predetermined balance from entry to entry.

The bibliographies were intended to serve several purposes. They often show what sources an author used, though they are not meant to substitute for footnotes to an entry, and they also show which sources the author recommends for further study. Works that are especially rich in illustration are marked by a + mark before the listing of the author and title of the book. An attempt was made to keep these bibliographies short (about two to four items), but contributors were concerned lest they might prove insufficient, and in some cases, for longer entries on weighty topics, I have allowed an increase. In addition, as press time drew nearer, many authors kindly updated entries that had been written in the early years, and they were allowed to insert new and important bibliography. On the whole, whenever bibliographies were trimmed, I have been partial to listings that are recent, that themselves contain abundant, up-to-date bibliography, that are well illustrated and that are in the English language.

Within entries, an asterisk is used before a name or topic to indicate a cross-reference to a separate entry. The asterisk would be redundant for ''Rome'' and ''Athens'' and is therefore omitted.

Articles that are unsigned were written by the editor. No articles, signed or unsigned, were written after 1994, and many entries were completed considerably before that date. In some articles the bibliographies do include items published in 1995 or forthcoming. Under no circumstances are contributors of the articles to be held accountable for the timeliness of their scholarship; the editor alone is responsible in this matter.

For whom was *An Encyclopedia of the History of Classical Archaeology* written? A broad spectrum of users of this reference tool is envisioned. Obviously, it is meant for readers of the English language; thus, quotations from other languages are regularly translated into English, and archaeological terms that are derived from other languages, especially Latin and Greek, have been replaced with equivalent English terms when possible or have been ''translated'' in the text.

It is hoped that the encyclopedia will be of use to students and researchers in a variety of fields, especially archaeology, classics, history, topography, art history and architectural history. The history of archaeology is a discipline that is comparatively new; some of its results have only recently become more available and mostly remain to be integrated into various other areas of scholarship. A fine example of what may be accomplished lies in R. T. Ridley's work *The Eagle and the Spade: The Archaeology of Rome During the Napoleonic Era, 1809–1814* (1992), a detailed study of Napoleon's effect on the monuments of the city of Rome, a work of the utmost significance for those studying the programs of Napoleon and, more specifically, the political uses to which he put archaeological research. Equally fascinating is the analysis of exploitation of archaeological projects and Roman revival architecture by Mussolini and Hitler, published recently by A. Scobie, *Hitler's State Architecture, The Impact of Classical Antiquity* (1990). Another recent work on the history of archaeology in the city of Rome is the richly illustrated survey by Claude Moiatti, *The Search for Ancient Rome* (1993). For Greece, the companion volume in the same series is *The Search for Ancient Greece* by Roland and Françoise Etienne (1990).

Another area that has recently received attention is the history of the discovery, collecting and study of Greek and Roman sculpture. The information is critical for art historians of the Renaissance and Baroque, and they are the ones who have made the most significant contributions in assembling the data and in integrating them into a context. The *Census of Works of Antique Art Known in the Renaissance,* conducted for many years by Phyllis Bober and Ruth Rubinstein at the Warburg Institute of the University of London and the Institute of Fine Arts at New York University, has reached fruition in their rich volume of *Renaissance Artists and Antique Sculpture: A Handbook of Sources* (1986). Similar material, with a different interpretive approach, may be found in the now-classic catalog of F. Haskell and N. Penny, *Taste and the Antique: The Lure of Classical Sculpture, 1500–1900* (1981). Their aim is to reveal significant aspects of the history of taste over the span of some four centuries by cataloging the ancient sculptures that were most popular and most influential. In citing information about the find spots of famous sculptures and in quoting opinions of critics and scholars about these pieces, Haskell and Penny have created a fabric often interwoven with archaeological scholarship and immensely useful for those who wish to understand a piece of sculpture through its ''biography.'' Not many scholars working on Greek and Roman sculpture today concern themselves with this kind of background. A rare exception is Brunilde Ridgway, who has published searching studies of Greek sculpture from the Archaic to the Hellenistic, in which she frequently takes into account the history of study of a particular work of art. Her review of this history, not only in the Renaissance but also, or especially, in nineteenth-century scholarship, has led to a healthy deconstruction of the edifice of attributions to Pheidias, Polykleitos, Skopas, Lysippos and others made by German scholars of the last century. Retracing their steps, she has made far-reaching conclusions.

Curators and researchers in museums have been in position to contribute much to the history of archaeology in their study of object proveniences; it is hoped that entries in the encyclopedia can serve as ready reference for this kind of information and that the bibliographies will provide access to fuller detail than could be incorporated gracefully into the brief format adopted for the entries.

It is hoped, above all, that the encyclopedia will be useful to teachers and students of classical archaeology. New textbooks in Greek and Roman art by John Pedley (*Greek Art and Archaeology,* 1992) and by Andrew and Nancy Ramage (*Roman Art,* 1995) include some discussion and illustrations that will give students a taste of the material that is waiting to be studied. But, on the whole, very little of the information on the history of archaeology found in this encyclopedia is regularly included in the classroom; students of classical archaeology are given little exposure to the roots of the discipline. An exception is the case of Heinrich Schliemann, whose name is known to most students; unfortunately, what seems to continue to fascinate is the idea that he had a unique dream of proving the truth of the poems of Homer and that he fulfilled it with an uncanny ability to locate archaeological sites. He continues to be lionized as a great archaeologist, in spite of the books and articles by William Calder and David Traill that dispel the myths promoted by Schliemann about himself and his own importance. In these pages one may consult the entry on Frank Calvert, who actually ascertained the location of Troy and suggested it to Schliemann, and the entry on Troy itself, where it is noted that many travelers had believed in the truth of the Homeric poems long before Schliemann. In the eighteenth century Dawkins had visited the Troad, Homer in hand, and had even invented a form of ethnoarchaeology, studying the modern inhabitants of the area in order to understand Homeric society. It is hoped that such entries can help to sift out the facts of the history of archaeology. No doubt much that is reported in this encyclopedia will, and rightly should be, subject to scrutiny and revision, as more archaeologists join in the study of our fascinating past. Most of all it is hoped that the mere existence of this work will create awareness of the long tradition of this discipline and the richness of the perspective gained by reviewing the discovery and study of specific monuments and sites as well as general trends in the history of archaeological scholarship.

ACKNOWLEDGMENTS

There are very many whom I wish to thank. First are the kind colleagues who consented to act as advisers in the earliest stage of the encyclopedia, in planning the master list and in suggesting the names of potential contributors for the various entries. Though they must certainly not be held responsible for the final shape of this volume, I wish to acknowledge the many wonderful suggestions made by Phyllis Pray Bober, Larissa Bonfante, William M. Calder III, Philipp Fehl, David Ridgway and Homer A. Thompson. My sincere thanks for similar advising at a later date goes to Elizabeth McGraw, Marjon van der Meulen and Ruth Rubinstein, who generously shared their rich knowledge of Renaissance and Baroque scholarship, and to Katherine Geffcken, who consulted on several crucial points. Brunilde S. Ridgway characteristically gave up her own time to help other authors, reading many entries and making valuable suggestions for entries on Greek sculpture. Larissa Bonfante, as usual, helped with every bibliographical question I asked her, as well as many that I did not. Francesca Ridgway (related to David but not Brunilde) gave much welcome advice on Etruscan entries. L. Richardson, jr, provided unfailing support, moral as well as scholarly, in regard to Roman archaeology, especially topography; Ronald Ridley willingly shared the burden of entries on Rome and its archaeologists. William Calder III poured forth information from his fund of knowledge of German archaeological scholarship. Jack Davis and Philip Betancourt made helpful suggestions for Bronze Age Aegean archaeology, and so did Robert Koehl, who also advised generally on potential authors for other entries on Greek archaeology. No one helped me or cheered me more than Judith Binder, unless it was Norma and Bernard Goldman, faithful correspondents who kept me laughing and believing that the encyclopedia would surely be finished one day. Elfriede R. Knauer energized me with her own total commitment to quality in scholarship. I was inspired by Phyllis Lehmann, with her rare ability to move skillfully and easily back and forth between antiquity and Renaissance.

Many of these colleagues also wrote multiple entries for the encyclopedia. I am so very grateful to them for that and to others who valiantly wrote entry after entry in their special areas, sometimes in several areas. I will restrict my mention of names to those who wrote seven or more: James Anderson, Barbara Barletta, Clifford Brown, John Camp, Mortimer Chambers, Glenys Davies, W. W. de Grummond, Ann Gunter, A. Trevor Hodge, Peter Holliday, Fred S. and Diana E. E. Kleiner, Carol Mattusch, Emeline Hill Richardson, David Thompson, David A. Traill, and Shellie Williams.

Finally, I wish to express my gratitude to those who aided in the construction of this book, whether retyping manuscripts, filing, Xeroxing, editing, searching bibliography, confirming references, corresponding, indexing, or helping in some other way. I think of Deborah Halsted at the beginning and Melissa Moss, Dara Helser and Diane Kampert at the end, of Claudette Gatlin all along. I wish to thank Sharon Loucks Wichmann, who provided an enormous boost in the middle years of the project, with her varied talents as author, editor, secretary. I was delighted when Joann McDaniel agreed to prepare the Select Bibliography for the History of Classical Archaeology and wish to record now my warm appreciation for her work on this assignment. I thank Rochelle Marrinan, who transformed my working habits by providing computer support, and Elizabeth de Grummond, who did a wonderful job on the cross-references, thereby also getting training for the day when she will edit the second edition of the encyclopedia. I thank Patty Grandy for effective prayer for the completion of the work, and, I am grateful to Louise Thomson for the kind of support that only a mother can give.

I reserve a special place to thank my editor at Greenwood, Cynthia Harris. In all the years she has been associated with the project, she has truly never said a discouraging word and always seemed to have an unquestioning faith that the book would be delivered. For this steadfast confidence and her genuine enthusiasm, which kept me going on, I wish to express my deep gratitude.

The entire undertaking has provided a great lesson in humility for me. On the one hand, I have never learned so much on any other project I have attempted; on the other, I have not failed so much in learning at any other time in my life. The scope of the subject is so large that even today I am not sure of its limits. For many years, I have kept the book from the hands of the publishers, haunted by the specters of reviewers, feeling ashamed to let it go with the many omissions I knew of or simply suspected, feeling the need to check and check again the hundreds of entries completed, and often noting with horror the errors that existed. In effect, I have spent much of my "free" time for the last quarter of my life on this manuscript. I often felt deeply moved as I reviewed the history of archaeological scholarship and the lives of its practitioners. With Joseph Spence, I trembled over the reception of an untried publication; his fears turned out to be quite well founded, in light of the fury with which Lessing later attacked him. With John Leland, who was assigned in 1533 to do a survey of antiquities throughout the realm of England, I agonized that the enormous amount of material would never be gathered together and properly arranged for publication. His torment over the work was so intense that he was forced to give it up; it is reported that his antiquarian research overtaxed his brain and that the insane scholar had to be turned over to his brother for safekeeping. A fairly well-known case of scholarly overwork in modern times is that of Rostovtzeff, who suffered a mental collapse after the completion of *The Social and Economic History of the Hellenistic World* (1941). Others were able to endure unimaginable deprivation and pressure as they devoted their lives to the tasks they had assumed. I was inspired by Tommaso Fazello (d. 1570), who, to further his studies of ancient Sicily, cut back on the amount of time he wasted eating, so that he had only one meal a day; by Janus Gruter (d. 1627), who always stood upright and vigilant while he worked; by Bernard Montfaucon (1741), who, for the last forty-six years of his life, normally spent thirteen hours a day studying or writing. Again and again I was reminded of the humanity of the archaeologists of the past, of their failures and successes, and was compelled to continue the quest to publish this work about their work. In the end it was for them—and, of course, for the contributors who have waited so patiently for their entries to appear—that I was able to finish the encyclopedia.

—Nancy Thomson de Grummond

Bibliographical Abbreviations

AA	*Archäologischer Anzeiger*
AAA	*Athens Annals of Archaeology*
ActaArch	*Acta Archaeologica* [Copenhagen]
Aerial Atlas of Crete	*The Aerial Atlas of Ancient Crete*, ed. J. W. Myers—E. E. Myers—G. Cadogan (Berkeley, 1992)
AfrIt	*Africa Italiana*
AIRF	*Acta Instituti Romani Finlandiae*
AJA	*American Journal of Archaeology*
AJP	*American Journal of Philology*
AM	*Mitteilungen des Deutschen Archäologischen Instituts, Athenische Abteilung*
AnatSt	*Anatolian Studies. Journal of the British Institute of Archaeology at Ankara.*
ANRW	*Aufstieg und Niedergang der römischen Welt*
AnnInst	*Annales Institutorum*
AntK	*Antike Kunst*
AntP	*Antike Plastik*
Archäologenbildnisse	*Archäologenbildnisse, Porträts und Kurzbiographien von klassischen Archäologen deutscher Sprache*, ed. R. Lullies—W. Schiering (Mainz am Rhein, 1988)
ArchCl	*Archeologia Classica*
ArchDelt	*Archaiologikon Deltion*
ArchEph	*Archaiologike Ephemeris*
ArchEspArq	*Archivo Español de Arqueologia*

ArchEspArt	*Archivo Español de Arte*
ArchJ	*Archaeological Journal*
ArtB	*Art Bulletin*
ArchRep	*Archaeological Reports*
ASAtene	*Annuario della Scuola Archeologica di Atene e delle Missioni italiane in Oriente*
AttiMGrecia	*Atti e Memorie della Società Magna Grecia*
BABesch	*Bulletin Antieke Beschaving*
BCH	*Bulletin de Correspondance Hellénique*
BdA	*Bollettino d'Arte*
Beazley—Ashmole	J. D. Beazley—B. Ashmole, *Greek Sculpture and Painting to the End of the Hellenistic Period* (London, 1966)
Berve—Gruben	H. Berve—G. Gruben, *Greek Temples, Theaters and Shrines* (New York, 1963)
BICS	*Bulletin of the Institute of Classical Studies,* University of London
Bieber	M. Bieber, *The Sculpture of the Hellenistic Age,* rev. ed. (New York, 1961)
BIM	*Boletin de Information Municipal,* Valencia
BiogJahr	*Biographisches Jahrbuch und Deutscher Nekrolog*
Bober—Rubinstein	P. P. Bober—R. Rubinstein, *Renaissance Artists and Antique Sculpture: A Handbook of Sources* (London, 1986)
BMon	*Bulletin Monumental*
BMMA	*Bulletin of the Metropolitan Museum of Art*
Briggs—Calder	*Classical Scholarship: A Biographical Encyclopedia,* ed. W. W. Briggs—W. M. Calder III (New York, 1990)
BSA	British School at Athens, *Annual*
BU	*Biographie Universelle*
BullCom	*Bulletino della Commissione Archeologica Comunale di Roma*
BurlMag	*Burlington Magazine*
CIG	*Corpus Inscriptionum Graecarum*
CIL	*Corpus Inscriptionum Latinarum*
Coarelli	F. Coarelli, *Guida Archaeologica di Roma,* 2nd ed. (Rome, 1975)
CR	*Classical Review*

CRAI	*Comptes Rendus de l'Académie des Inscriptions et Belles Lettres*
CVA	*Corpus Vasorum Antiquorum*
DAB	*Dictionary of American Biography*
DBF	*Dictionaire de Biographie Française*
DBI	*Dizionario Biografico degli Italiani*
DialAr	*Dialoghi di Archeologia*
DNB	*Dictionary of National Biography*
DOP	*Dumbarton Oaks Papers*
EAA	*Enciclopedia dell'Arte Antica, Classica e Orientale*
EC	*Enciclopedia Cattolica*
EI	*Enciclopedia Italiana*
EPRO	*Études preliminaires aux religions orientales dans l'empire romain*
EWA	*Encyclopedia of World Art*
FGrHist	F. Jacoby, *Fragmente der griechischen Historiker* (Berlin, 1923–)
GBA	*Gazette des Beaux-arts*
GGA	*Göttingische gelehrte Anzeiger*
Gnomon	*Gnomon*
GRBS	*Greek, Roman and Byzantine Studies*
Greenhalgh, *Survival*	M. Greenhalgh, *The Survival of Roman Antiquities in the Middle Ages* (London, 1989)
Haskell—Penny	F. Haskell—N. Penny, *Taste and the Antique: The Lure of Classical Sculpture, 1500–1900* (New Haven, CT, 1981)
Helbig	W. Helbig, *Führer durch die öffentlichen Sammlungen klassischer Altertümer in Rom,* 4th ed., ed. H. Speier, 1–4 (Tübingen, 1963–72)
IJNA	*International Journal of Nautical Archaeology and Underwater Exploration*
ILN	*Illustrated London News*
IstForsch	*Istanbuler Forschungen*
IstMitt	*Mitteilungen des Deutschen Archäologischen Instituts,* Abteilung Istanbul
JdI	*Jahrbuch des Deutschen Archäologischen Instituts*
JEA	*Journal of Egyptian Archaeology*
JHS	*Journal of Hellenic Studies*
JRS	*The Journal of Roman Studies*

JSAH	*Journal of the Society of Architectural Historians*
JWAG	*Journal of the Walters Art Gallery*
JWarb	*Journal of the Warburg and Courtauld Institutes*
Kleiner, *Roman Sculpture*	Diana E. E. Kleiner, *Roman Sculpture* (New Haven, CT, 1992)
Klio	*Klio.* Beiträge zur alten Geschichte
Lanciani, *Destruction*	R. Lanciani, *The Destruction of Ancient Rome* (London, 1899; repr. New York, 1980)
Lanciani, *Storia degli scavi*	R. Lanciani, *Storia degli scavi di Roma e notizie intorno le collezioni romane di antichità,* 1–4 (Rome, 1902–12; "Edizione integrale," ed. L. M. Campeggi, Rome, 1989–92).
LIMC	*Lexicon Iconographicum Mythologiae Classicae* (Zürich, 1974–)
Ling, *Roman Painting*	R. Ling, *Roman Painting* (Cambridge, 1991)
Lullies—Hirmer	R. Lullies—M. Hirmer, *Greek Sculpture,* rev. ed., tr. M. Bullock (New York, 1960)
MA	*Le Moyen âge*
MAAR	*Memoirs of the American Academy in Rome*
Meded	*Mededeelingen van het Nederl. Historisch Instituut te Rome*
MEFRA	*Mélanges de l'École Française de Rome, Antiquité*
MelRome	*Mélanges d'Archéologie et d'Histoire de l'Ecole française de Rome*
MemLinc	*Memorie. Atti della Accademia Nazionale dei Lincei, Classe di scienze morali, storiche e filologiche*
MGH	*Monumenta Germaniae Historica*
Michaelis	A. Michaelis, *A Century of Archaeological Discovery,* tr. B. Kahnweiler (London, 1908)
MittFlor	*Mitteilungen des Kunsthistorischen Instituts in Florenz*
MJb	*Münchener Jahrbuch der bildenden Kunst*
MonAnt	*Monumenti Antichi*
MonPiot	*Monuments et Mémoires. Fondation E. Piot*
MonPitt	*Monumenti della pittura antica scoperti in Italia*
MSNAF	*Memoires de la Societé Nationale des Antiquaires de France*
Nash	E. Nash, *A Pictorial Dictionary of Ancient Rome,* rev. ed., 1–2 (London, 1968)
NBG	*Nouvelle Biographie Generale*
NCAB	*National Cyclopaedia of American Biography*

NDB	*Neue Deutsche Biographie*
Pastor, *History of the Popes*	L. von Pastor, *History of the Popes* 1–40 (London, 1938–)
NSc	*Notizie degli Scavi di Antichità*
OpAth	*Opuscula Atheniensia*
OpRom	*Opuscula Romana*
PBSR	*Papers of the British School at Rome*
PECS	*Princeton Encyclopedia of Classical Sites,* ed. R. Stillwell (Princeton, NJ, 1976)
Pfeiffer	R. Pfeiffer, *History of Classical Scholarship from 1300 to 1850* (Oxford, 1976)
Platner—Ashby	S. B. Platner—T. Ashby, *A Topographical Dictionary of Ancient Rome* (London, 1929)
Pliny, *NH*	Pliny the Elder, *Natural History*
Pollitt, *Hellenistic Age*	J. J. Pollitt, *Art in the Hellenistic Age* (Cambridge, 1986)
Porträtarchiv	*Der Archäologe: Graphische Bildnisse aus dem Porträtarchiv Diepenbroick,* catalog of exhibition (Münster, 1983)
PP	*La Parola del Passato*
ProcBrAc	*Proceedings of the British Academy*
RA	*Revue Archéologique*
RACrist	*Rivista di Archeologia Cristiana*
RBN	*Revue Belge de Numismatique*
RE	*Real-Encyclopädie der Altertumswissenschaft,* ed. A Pauly—G. Wissowa
RendPontAcc	Atti della Pontificia Accademia Romana di Archeologia, Rendiconti
RepKunstW	*Repertorium für Kunstwissenschaft*
RhM	*Rheinisches Museum für Philogie*
Richardson, *New Topographical Dictionary*	L. Richardson, jr, *A New Topographical Dictionary of Ancient Rome* (Baltimore, 1992)
Richter, *Sculpture and Sculptors*	G.M.A. Richter, *The Sculpture and Sculptors of the Greeks,* 4th ed. (New Haven, CT, 1984)
Ridgway, *Hellenistic Sculpture* I	B. S. Ridgway, *Hellenistic Sculpture,* 1, *The Styles of ca. 331–200* B.C. (Madison, WI, 1990)
Ridgway, *Fifth Century Styles*	B. Ridgway, *Fifth Century Styles in Greek Sculpture* (Princeton, NJ, 1981)
Ridley, *Eagle and the Spade*	R. T. Ridley, *The Eagle and the Spade: The Archaeology of Rome During the Napoleonic Era, 1809–1814* (Cambridge, 1992)

RM   *Mitteilungen des Deutschen Archäologischen Instituts,*
                                    Römische Abteilung

RQ   Renaissance Quarterly

Sheard   W. S. Sheard, *Antiquity in the Renaissance,* catalog of
                                    exhibition (Northampton, MA, 1978–79)

StEtr   Studi Etruschi

Steingräber   S. Steingräber, *Città e necropoli dell'Etruria* (Rome,
                                    1981)

Stewart, *Greek Sculpture*   A. Stewart, *Greek Sculpture: An Exploration* (New
                                    Haven, CT, 1990)

Stoneman, *Land of Lost*   R. Stoneman, *Land of Lost Gods, The Search for*
Gods   *Classical Greece* (London, 1987)

StRom   *Studi Romani*

TAD   *Turk Arkeoloji Dergisi*

TAPS   *Transactions of the American Philosophical Society*

Thieme-Becker   *Allgemeines Kunstlerlexikon,* ed. U. Thieme—F.
                                    Becker

Travlos   J. Travlos, *Pictorial Dictionary of Ancient Athens*
                                    (New York, 1971)

Tsigakou, *Rediscovery*   F.-M. Tsigakou, *The Rediscovery of Greece: Travel-*
                                    lers and Painters of the Romantic Era (New Rochelle,
                                    NY, 1981)

Valentini—Zucchetti   R. Valentini—G. Zucchetti, *Codice topografico della*
                                    città di Roma, 1–4 (Rome, 1940–53)

Weiss, *RDCA*   R. Weiss, *The Renaissance Discovery of Classical An-*
                                    tiquity, 2nd ed. (Oxford, 1988)

ZfK   *Zeitschrift für Kunstgeschichte*

An Encyclopedia
of the History of
Classical Archaeology

A

ABYDOS. Greek city in Mysia (northwest Asia Minor) on the Hellespont, ca. 6km north of modern Çanakkale.

Strabo (13.590–1) records its later history as a Milesian colony founded in the time of the Lydian Gyges, whose possessions included the Troad. During Xerxes' invasion of Greece in 480 B.C., Abydos was at one end of the Persian bridge across the Hellespont. The city fell under Athenian rule, assessed at four talents by the Delian League in 454/3 B.C. In 411 B.C. Abydos went over to the Spartans, then remained under Persian rule until its liberation by Alexander in 334 B.C. The city surrendered to Philip V in 200 B.C. and became a free city under Rome. Until late Byzantine times it was the toll station of the Hellespont.

The site of Abydos was first identified in 1675. R. *Wood visited the area in 1750 and observed that it was the location of the bridge of Xerxes; R. *Chandler (1764) romantically recalled the ancient tale of Leander's swimming across the Hellespont to be with his beloved, Hero, and in 1810 Lord *Byron actually reenacted the chilly swim, starting at Sestos and coming ashore at a point at Abydos claimed as four miles distant.

Abydos was visited and briefly described by other travelers through the nineteenth century. Since the early twentieth century the area has been a restricted military zone; there is now little to be seen aboveground of the ancient city.

BIBLIOGRAPHY

+M.G.F.A. Choiseul-Gouffier, *Voyage pittoresque de la Grèce* 2 (Paris, 1822), 449; W. Leaf, *Strabo on the Troad* (Cambridge, 1923), 116–33; J. M. Cook, *The Troad* (Oxford, 1973), 55–57.

ANN C. GUNTER

ACADEMIA HERCULANENSIS (REALE ACCADEMIA ERCOLA-NESE; ACCADEMIA DI ERCOLANO). Academy formed in 1755 by

Charles III, king of *Naples and later of Spain, for the purpose of publishing the finds excavated at *Herculaneum.

The academy consisted of fifteen members (among the founders were A. Mazzocchi, J. Martorelli and B. Galieni) who met every two weeks to pass around and discuss three objects that had been excavated since the last committee meeting. All present then wrote about the objects, and the reports were collated by a secretary to produce a definitive description. These analyses were published in the series of volumes of *Antichità di Ercolano,* which began to appear in 1757, sumptuously illustrated and bound. A projected volume on the marble sculpture was never published. The publication of the finds from Herculaneum served to ignite the interest in classical motifs in architecture, painting, furniture and clothing that swept Europe and America during the period of Neoclassicism.

Inactive from 1799 to 1816, the academy was revived in 1817 as part of the Società Reale Borbonica. It was amalgamated with the Reale Accademia di Belle Arti in 1861.

BIBLIOGRAPHY

+*Le Antichità di Ercolano esposte,* 8 vols. (Naples, 1757–92); W. Leppmann, *Winckelmann* (New York, 1970), 175–76.

ACCADEMIA DEI LINCEI (ACCADEMIA NAZIONALE DEI LINCEI).

Italian academy of letters and science; among its distinguished publications are many relevant to classical archaeology.

The Accademia dei Lincei was founded in Rome on 17 August 1603 by four noblemen, three of them Italian and one Dutch: Prince Federico Cesi, Count Anastasio de Filiis, Francesco Stelluti (a nobleman from Fabriano) and the Dutch physician Jan Heck, from Deventer. The last was a Catholic who had fled Holland because of Protestant persecutions. All were very young; Cesi, the initiator, was but eighteen years old. They dedicated themselves to the study of nature, letters and philosophy with the purpose of exalting the wonders of God's creation.

They were joined in 1610 by G. B. Della Porta and in 1611 by Galileo Galilei, who brought great renown to the academy. From this year Galileo always added *Lynceus* to his signature. (*Lynceus* means "pertaining to the lynx," an animal noted for its keen sight.) The first publication of the academy was, in fact, Galileo's pamphlet on sunspots, *Istoria e dimostrazioni intorno alle macchie solari* (1613). When Galileo provoked the wrath of the Church by defending the Copernican heliocentric doctrine, the Accademia supported him fully.

With the death in 1630 of Cesi, the most active and influential member of the academy, the first period of the Accademia dei Lincei came to an end. After that, there were several attempts to revive it, but without success. It was finally reestablished in 1795 and was accorded a grant of 2,500 lire by Napoleon. It was suppressed by Pope Gregory XVII after the liberal uprising of 1830; temporarily revived again in 1838, it was suppressed in 1840, to be reestablished yet again under the liberal Pope Pius IX, with a new charter that excluded letters and philosophy for reasons of religious orthodoxy. In 1875 the prime minister of the new Italian State, Quintino Sella, founded the Accademia Nazionale dei Lincei, announcing by its title that the body was formally independent of the papacy, which sponsored its own Accademia Pontificia dei Nuovi Lincei. In 1939, the Accademia Nazionale was replaced by the Accademia d'Italia, but it was restored after the fall of Fascism in 1944.

Since that date the Accademia Nazionale dei Lincei has resumed and enlarged its activity, regularly issuing publications on classical archaeology and other subjects in its *Rendiconti, Memorie,* and *Notizie degli Scavi.* It has arranged many scholarly conventions and lectures by foreign and Italian scholars and counts among its members many prominent archaeologists. Included are P. *Orsi, G. *Lugli, G. Q. *Giglioli, R. *Bianchi Bandinelli, D. *Levi, P. Romanelli, P. Zancani-Montuoro, S. Moscati and M. Pallottino.

The Accademia dei Lincei, originally founded over 390 years ago, is the oldest academy in Europe still operating today.

BIBLIOGRAPHY

B. Odescalchi, *Memorie istorico-critiche dell'Accademia dei Lincei del principe Federico Cesi* (Rome, 1806); S. Carutti, *Breve storia dell'Accademia dei Lincei* (Rome, 1883); G. Gabrieli, "Il carteggio linceo della vecchia Accademia di F. Cesi," *MemLinc* ser. VI, 7 (1930), fasc. 1–4; R. Morghen, *The Accademia Nazionale dei Lincei in the Life and Culture of United Italy in the 368th Anniversary of Its Foundation* (Rome, 1974).

GIULIANO BONFANTE

ACCADEMIA DI ERCOLANO. See ACADEMIA HERCULANENSIS.

ACCADEMIA ETRUSCA. Italian academy of arts and sciences, founded at Cortona, with a special emphasis on the Etruscan culture of the city's past.

The organization was preceded by the Società degli Occulti (Society of the Occult), a small group formed approximately one year earlier. A donation to this society by Abbot Onofrio Baldelli, consisting of his collection of antiquities and his library, gave impetus to the founding of an academy with clearly defined interests, the *Accademia etrusca delle antichità, ed inscrizioni* (Etruscan Academy of Antiquities and Inscriptions). On 29 November 1727 the notary Barbi registered the group of seventeen learned men, among whom the leaders were the brothers Ridolfino, Filippo and Niccolò Marcello Venuti of Cortona and the Florentine senator Filippo *Buonarroti. They were joined by representatives of the ancient families of the city. The academy was created in an environment of long-standing artistic and cultural traditions, characteristic of the Tuscany of the last of the *Medici and in a context, on one hand, broader than that of the eighteenth-century Enlightenment and, on the other hand, more specialized, since it concerned Etruscan archaeology, the so-called *Etruscheria.

The aims and the character of the academy were inspired by a truly scientific seriousness. If the name *Etrusca* and the title of the president, *Lucumo* (a word of Etruscan derivation meaning "prince" or "leader"), signify that the preferred field of activity was Etruscan, the academy did not, in fact, limit itself to this; its motto, taken from Lucretius, was *obscura de re lucida pango* ("I reveal clear things about an obscure matter").

The statutes admitted forty effective members in Cortona and one hundred corresponding members, both Italians and foreigners. Thanks to the relations that its more authoritative representatives had with the cultural world in general, the academy rapidly acquired a remarkable renown. Not only elevated figures of the Church and the diplomatic world were named among its *Lucumones,* who normally held office for one year, but also among its members were scholars and intellectuals like Anton Francesco *Gori, Ludovico Antonio Muratori, Scipione *Maffei, Bernardo Tanucci, Voltaire and *Winckelmann.

The academicians gathered periodically in the rooms allotted to them by Gian Gastone de' Medici in the Palazzo Casali, where their seat is located even today. Their meetings were referred to as *Notti Coritane* (Cortona Nights) and featured news reports, reading of letters from correspondents and discussion of various subjects. These were recorded and issued in a publication called *Notti Coritane,* of which thirteen volumes are preserved. From 1735 to 1791 the academy also published the *Saggi di dissertazione* in nine volumes—studies on a variety of antiquarian subjects going beyond the purely Etruscan.

The donation by Baldelli, followed soon by other gifts, gave birth to the academy museum and library, which were, from the beginning, its two main institutions. By 1750 the museum had already attained such distinction as to merit publication in a large volume by Gori and others, *Museum Cortonense.* After the middle of the nineteenth century more gifts and purchases increased the prestige of the museum. Among other things there were the tomb called the Tanella di Pitagora; the famous Cortona Lamp, purchased in 1851, an outstanding work in bronze of the fifth century B.C. (about which D'Annunzio wrote a splendid sonnet); and an encaustic painting on slate of the Muse *Polyhymnia,* which was considered at first an ancient classical work but is more likely an imitation of the eighteenth century. Other important acquisitions included a significant collection of Egyptian antiquities, gathered by the apostolic delegate in Egypt, the Cortonese Guido Corbelli, and, in more recent times, the collection of antiquities and art objects of the family Tommasi Baldelli, as well as a series of works by the Futurist painter Guido Severini, which the artist's family left to his native city.

The original library of the academy was united in 1778 with the municipal one, into which flowed manuscripts, parchments and bound volumes that came, in part, from the convents suppressed in 1870 by the Italian State.

The official organ of the Accademia Etrusca was at first the journal *Polimnia* (1927–33). Since 1934 this function has been served by the *Annuario;* it has been accompanied since 1970 by *Note e Documenti* for shorter writings. In 1985, the "Year of the Etruscans," a special exhibition on the academy was held at the Palazzo Casali.

BIBLIOGRAPHY
P. Barocchi—D. Gallo, eds., *L'Accademia etrusca* (Milan, 1985).

ACCADEMIA NAZIONALE DEI LINCEI. See ACCADEMIA DEI LINCEI.

ACCADEMIA ROMANA. See ROMAN ACADEMY.

ACQUAROSSA. Etruscan Archaic habitation site on the hill of S. Francesco, 6km north of *Viterbo.

First developed in the later seventh century B.C., Acquarossa was destroyed before 500 B.C. and never inhabited again. The site was first reported by Luigi Rossi Danieli in 1908 but remained unexcavated until a team from the *Swedish Institute in Rome, under the direction of Carl Eric Östenberg, began work there in 1966. The king of Sweden, *Gustavus VI Adolphus, was a regular participant in the project. Excavations continued annually until 1978, exploring a number of sectors on the hill (A–R).

Zone F was found to be a center for the settlement, featuring monumental buildings with stone walls, colonnaded porticoes and architectural terracottas. As at Etruscan *Murlo, scholars have debated whether the center functioned as a palace or as a sacred area. Acquarossa is also important for yielding the remains of about fifty houses, providing an abundance of evidence about Etruscan domestic architecture, as well as local ceramics and utensils of daily life. Some of the finds are on display at the Rocca Albornoz, *Viterbo.

BIBLIOGRAPHY
+C. E. Östenberg, *Case etrusche di Acquarossa* (Rome, 1975); +S. Stopponi, ed., *Case e palazzi d'Etruria* (Milan, 1985), 41–58; +*Architettura etrusca nel Viterbese, Ricerche svedesi a San Giovenale e Acquarossa, 1956–1986* (Rome, 1986).

ACRAGAS. See AKRAGAS.

ADAM FAMILY. Scottish family of architects.

ROBERT ADAM (1728–92)—one of the most prolific and versatile architects and designers in European Neoclassicism—was the creative driving force in promoting a stylistic revolution based on archaeological sources. As the leader of a family firm, he and his brothers JOHN ADAM (1721–92) and JAMES ADAM (1732–94) trained under their father WILLIAM ADAM (1689–1748), the leading architect of his time in Scotland. Their younger brother WILLIAM ADAM (1738–1822) later joined them to head the largest contracting business of the age.

Robert was educated at Edinburgh University, where he was friends with several other brilliant young men, including David Hume and Adam Smith. His *Grand Tour, mainly in Italy, between 1754 and 1758 (he was followed by James in 1760–63), was to prove of crucial importance in the formation of the Adam Style, which was later to be disseminated by an efficient business as well as the new processes and synthetic materials of the early Industrial Revolution. The ornamental vocabulary of classical antiquity was to be applied throughout an unprecedented range of media from façades, interior decorative schemes in plasterwork and stucco (with a novel concern for color) and furniture to metalwork, textiles and ceramics, all with a particular influence on the American Federal Style.

The sheer impact of Rome (described by Adam as his "Holy See of pleasurable antiquity"), together with the discoveries at *Herculaneum, was reinforced by the catalytic effects on his imagination of the teachings of *Piranesi. Countering the astringent theories of the early Greek Revival, Piranesi vigorously advocated the need for a flexible system of modern design based on a wide-ranging use of antique sources that embraced not only Etruscan culture (*Etruscheria) and Late Imperial Rome, but also ancient Egypt and Greece. A lifelong friendship was signaled by Piranesi's dedication to the Scot of his ambitious archaeological folio, *Il Campo Marzio dell'antica Roma* (1762). Living in the intellectually lively neighborhood of Piazza di Spagna, Adam also became acquainted with Robert *Wood, who had recently published his *Ruins of Palmyra* (1753), as well as the quarrelsome French architect C. L. Clérisseau. *Winckelmann seems to have made less of an impression on him.

Abandoning a projected book revising *Desgodetz, in 1757 Adam decided to survey and publish the remains of Diocletian's marine palace at Spalato (*Split) in Dalmatia, before returning to Britain. Owing to local political difficulties, this had to be accomplished in five weeks, with the aid of Clérisseau and a team of draftsmen. The book, flawed by conflicting tensions between reasonably accurate recording and picturesque Piranesian images, was finally published in 1764 as *The Ruins of the Emperor Diocletian's Palace at Spalatro [sic] in Dalmatia,* dedicated to George III. Adam was to observe how important it was for him to study this well-preserved example of residential architecture, as opposed to the wide range of sacred and public buildings available in Rome.

Starting his practice in London in 1758, Robert swiftly developed a fashionable reputation with a series of major country house commissions, applying his idiosyncratic style to largely interior schemes—represented by Keddleston Hall (1760–70), Syon House (1761–69), Osterley Park (1761–80), Kenwood House (1764–79) and Harewood House (1765–72). The 1770s saw a series of skillfully designed town houses in London, inspired by antique spatial planning and characterized by an increasing refinement and delicacy of ornament. The monumental influence of Spalato was to recur in the immensely influential speculative housing scheme, the Adelphi, overlooking the Thames (1768–72). In reaction to rival designers such as Chambers and Wyatt, Adam later carried out a number of highly controversial ideas, notably demonstrated by his Etruscan Style, partly inspired by Sir William *Hamilton's vases publications and Herculaneum (e.g., the Etruscan Dressing Room, Osterley Park, ca. 1775). An exceptional sequence of neomedieval castles, chiefly in Scotland (e.g., Culzean Castle, 1777–90), was to be distinguished by the play of abstract geometrical forms, thought to have been indirectly inspired by the Roman military architecture of Hadrian's Wall. Ultimately, the theoretical justification and illustration of the Adams's achievement were to be effectively summed up in their own folio, *Works in Architecture* 1 (1773), 2 (1779) and 3 (1822).

BIBLIOGRAPHY

J. Fleming, *Robert Adam and His Circle in Edinburgh and Rome* (London, 1962); E. Harris, *British Architectural Books and Writers: 1556–1785* (Cambridge, 1990); D. King, *The Complete Works of Robert and James Adam* (Oxford, 1991); I. G. Brown, *Monumental Reputation: Robert Adam and the Emperor's Palace* (Edinburgh, 1992); J. Wilton-Ely, *Piranesi as Architect and Designer* (New Haven, 1993).

JOHN WILTON-ELY

AD GALLINAS ALBAS. See VILLA OF LIVIA.

ADLER, JOHANN HEINRICH FRIEDRICH (1827–1908). German architect and archaeologist.

Adler studied at the Berlin Bauakademie, where he remained as teacher (from 1859) and later as professor (1863–1903). From 1874 to 1881 he directed the German excavations at *Olympia with Ernst *Curtius and designed the original museum there (1883). Among his Berlin students was his future son-in-law, W. *Dörpfeld, whom he sent in 1876 to assist at Olympia. Besides his contributions to the volumes of *Olympia* (1892–97), he wrote a number of short architectural studies, including *Das Pantheon in Rom* (1971), *Das Mausoleum zu Halikarnass* (1900) and the remarkable introduction to Schliemann's *Tiryns* (1886). He was among the first in Germany to see the importance of Schliemann's excavations.

BIBLIOGRAPHY

H. Riemann, s.v. "Adler, Johann," *NDB* 1 (1953), 71; A. Kurzwelly, "Adler, Friedrich," in Thieme-Becker, 1 (1907), 84–85.

DAVID A. TRAILL

ADRIA (ADRIAS, ATRIA). Pre-Roman town located on a lagoon on the coast of the Adriatic Sea in northeast Italy; flourishing port from the mid-sixth century to late fourth century B.C.

Ancient sources disagree as to the foundation of Adria, attributing it variously to Greeks and Etruscans, although modern evidence suggests a probable Venetic origin. During the sixth century B.C. it became an Etruscan center for the importation of Greek products into Northern Italy and thereby for the diffusion of Greek culture. According to Strabo (5.1.7), the harbor town was built entirely of timber, laid out on canals with ferries and bridges to accommodate traffic. In the second half of the fourth century B.C., Adria was occupied by the Gauls, and in Roman times it became a *municipium.* The harbor evidently had begun to silt up in the first century A.C., and Adria was eventually superseded by *Aquileia.

The site was first explored in the Renaissance, and a drawing of 1662 shows a Roman theater and other buildings. Excavation was undertaken by three members of a local family, Ottavio Bocchi (1697–1749), Francesco Girolamo Bocchi (1748–1810) and Francesco Antonio Bocchi (1821–88). Their collection of vases, jewelry, inscriptions and glass was housed in the Museo Bocchi, which in the early twentieth century was donated to the Italian government and became the Museo Civico di Adria.

The entire area of the ancient city was covered over by the flooding of rivers. Beginning in 1938, systematic excavations have been conducted under very difficult conditions, resulting in the discovery of pilings of houses from the ancient city, disposed on a regular network of canals and *insulae* (blocks) similar to those found at nearby *Spina. From the town site came numerous significant specimens of red- and black-figure vase painting by Attic Greek masters (Lydos, Brygos Painter, Makron, Douris, Achilles Painter, Polygnotos). Cemeteries of the fourth century B.C. and later have also been found.

BIBLIOGRAPHY
G. Ghirardini, "Il Museo Civico di Adria," *Nuovo Archivio Veneto* 9 (1905); G. Brusin, s.v. "Adria," *EAA* 1 (1958), 72–73; G. Fogolari—B. M. Scarfi, *Adria Antica* (Adria, 1970); S. Steingräber, *Città e necropoli dell'Etruria antica* (Rome, 1983), 556–58.

AEGAE. See VERGINA.

AEGINA. See AIGINA.

AGORA, Athens. Greek civic center and marketplace located on the sloping ground northwest of the Athenian *Akropolis.

Used as a cemetery and for habitation in the Bronze and Dark Ages, the area was given over for public use in the Archaic period. The earliest civic buildings, dating to the first half of the sixth century B.C., were built along the west side of the square, which thereafter remained the administrative and political center for centuries. By the late sixth century, the square itself was formally delineated by a series of marble boundary stones. Also in use by 500 B.C. were a fountainhouse and lawcourt (?) along the south side, an altar of the Twelve Gods within the square, a sanctuary of Aphrodite to the northwest and other administrative buildings along the west. These were all badly damaged or destroyed by the Persians in 480 B.C. and rebuilt or replaced thereafter.

By the end of the fifth century, the west side consisted of a new Bouleuterion (Senate), the old Bouleuterion (used to house archives), the Tholos (Senate dining chamber), the Royal Stoa (seat of the king archon) and the Stoa of Zeus Eleutherios, perhaps used by the lesser archons known as Thesmothetes. The south side still had the old fountainhouse and lawcourt (?), along with South Stoa I (a commercial building with dining rooms) and a building that served as one of the mints of Athens, for the striking of bronze coins. At the northwest corner there were the earliest elements of a complex that may have served as lawcourts. Along the north was the Stoa Poikile, the Painted Stoa famed for its philosophers and paintings. Above the square to the west was a handsome Doric temple of marble usually identified as the *Hephaisteion.

To the southwest of the Agora lay a large residential and industrial district, in which was found a large building tentatively identified as the state prison. In the fourth century, a temple of Apollo Patroos and a new monument of the Eponymous Heroes were added to the west side, and a fountainhouse was built at the southwest corner. The third century B.C. was difficult for Athens; either at war or under Macedonian control, it had few resources for building activity. The only exception in the Agora is a large building just north of the Hephaisteion, identified as an arsenal.

With the help of Hellenistic monarchs, a revival occurred in the second century B.C., and the appearance of the old square was altered dramatically. It was now enclosed on all sides by monumental colonnades of the kind in fashion in the big cities of Asia Minor. In the Agora, the huge Middle Stoa (ca. 180 B.C.) was built across the square, effectively dividing it in two. A second South Stoa was built to replace South Stoa I, which further defined the southern square. Along the east, the *Stoa of Attalos II (159–138 B.C.) was constructed, a large market building with two stories and forty-two shops. Finally, a new Metroon (archives) was built and given a colonnaded façade in an attempt to spruce up the appearance of the old building along the west side.

The attack on Athens by Sulla in 86 B.C. left many Agora buildings damaged, and little was done until Augustan times, when there was a major building program. A new marketplace was constructed to the east (*Roman Agora), and the old Greek square was filled with buildings. Taking up the center was a huge odeion donated by Agrippa, son-in-law of Augustus. Several other buildings were erected in the square as well; old Classical temples at depopulated Attic sites (*Sounion, Thorikos, Acharnai) were dismantled, brought in and re-erected—in whole or in part—in the old square. At least four such reuses can be detected. The city flourished in the second century A.C., especially under Hadrian, and to the Agora were added a library, a nymphaion and a basilica. In addition, the old odeion was rebuilt as a lecture hall with a new façade of sculpted giants and tritons.

In A.D. 267 the city was destroyed in a raid by the Heruli, and the old Agora was demolished. In refortifying the city during the reign of Probus (A.D. 276–82), the Athenians enclosed a much smaller area that ran east of, and did not include, the Greek Agora. The fortification wall, which runs along the Panathenaic Way, is built almost entirely of pieces of Agora buildings destroyed in A.D. 267. The area of the square, insofar as it was refurbished, was damaged again during Alaric's attack in A.D. 395. A revival in the early fifth century led to the construction of a large gymnasium complex on the site of the old square— perhaps one of the universities of Athens—and the houses of wealthy philosophers were built on the slopes above. This new flourishing of philosophy was halted in A.D. 529, with the decree of Justinian forbidding any pagan to teach philosophy at Athens, effectively ending all significance of the city. The physical decline was hastened in A.D. 582/3 by the arrival of the Slavs. There are slight signs of activity in the seventh century, then a total Dark Age in the eighth and ninth centuries, before the area of the Agora was used for houses once again in the tenth century, becoming a residential district in use until modern times.

The excavations that have brought to light this long and complicated history of the heart of Athens continue today. The earliest work was carried out by the *Greek Archaeological Society in 1859, 1871, 1907–8, 1910 (under Kourouniotes) and 1912 (under Kastriotes). In 1890–91, less formal work was done during the extension of the Athens-Peiraeus railroad, which passes through the north part of the site. From 1891 to 1898 some excavation was conducted by the *German Archaeological Institute under the direction of W. *Dörpfeld. Since 1930 the excavation of the area has been undertaken by the *American School of Classical Studies at Athens under the direction of T. L. *Shear, Sr. (1930–45), H. A. Thompson (1945–68), T. L. Shear, Jr. (1968–1993) and J. McK. Camp (1994–   ), the funds coming largely from J. D. Rockefeller and the Ford, Mellon, Rockefeller and Packard foundations. Also carried out were the reconstruction of the Stoa of Attalos (1953–56) and the landscaping of the Agora park under R. Griswold (1954).

BIBLIOGRAPHY

R. E. Wycherley, *The Athenian Agora, 3, Testimonia* (Princeton, NJ, 1957); H. A. Thompson—R. E. Wycherley, *The Agora of Athens* (Princeton, NJ, 1972); H. A. Thompson, *The Athenian Agora* (Athens, 1976); J. Camp, *The Athenian Agora* (London, 1986); Idem, *The Athenian Agora Guide,* 4th ed. (Athens, 1990).

JOHN McK. CAMP II

AGOSTINI, LEONARDO (1593–ca. 1669). Italian antiquarian, specializing in numismatics and glyptics.

A native of Grosseto, Agostini established himself in Rome during the pontificate of Urban VIII, serving as antiquarian to the *Barberini family under the recommendation of Cassiano dal *Pozzo. When the Barberini were in exile from Rome (1646–50), he corresponded with them, sending the latest archaeological news, in letters now preserved in the Vatican Library (Ms. Barb. Lat. 6455).

Agostini resumed his work on the Barberini antiquities when they returned, continuing to acquire objects and arrange the collection so that it emerged as the best organized of all Roman museums. In 1655, he became commissioner of antiquities (*Commissario delle Antichità) in Rome and Latium for Pope Alexander VII and directed important excavations in the *Forum Romanum, the Forum of Trajan (*Imperial Fora) and baths near S. Lorenzo in Panisperna.

His original specialty and early publication were in the field of numismatics, but he is remembered, above all, for his pioneering studies of carved gems. His *Le Gemme antiche figurate,* in two parts and with a separate volume of annotations for each part, was issued at Rome in 1657 and 1669. The illustrations were done by G. B. Galestruzzi, and G. P. *Bellori assisted with the annotations. The gems are arranged by subject matter, and the scholarly commentary em-

Portrait of *Leonardo Agostini*, engraving from L. Agostini, *Le Gemme antiche figurate* (1685). (The Warburg Institute, University of London.)

phasizes the identification of themes and the resulting classification of the pieces. The work was much valued and was reprinted by P. S. *Bartoli in 1686 and again in 1702 and 1707–9 (edited by P. A. *Maffei).

BIBLIOGRAPHY

A. Furtwängler, *Die Antiken Gemmen* (Leipzig, 1900), III, 405–6; R. Barabesi, "L'antiquario Leonardo Agostini e la sua terra di Bocchegiano," *Maremma* 3 (1926–27), 148–89; "Agostini, Leonardo," *DBI* 1 (1960), 464–65.

AGRIGENTO. See AKRAGAS.

AGRIGENTUM. See AKRAGAS.

AGUSTÍN (AGOSTÍN, AUGUSTINO, AUGUSTINUS), ANTONIO (1517–86). Spanish scholar of canon and Roman law and Roman antiquities.

A prodigy, entering the university of Alcala at nine, Agustín gained a doctorate in civil law at Salamanca in 1534, moving then to Bologna and graduation as jurisconsult in 1541. Converted to *Alciatus's humanistic methods at Bologna, he went to Florence and Venice to investigate manuscripts of Justinian's *Corpus Iuris,* of which he soon became a famous editor and commentator. He was appointed auditor of the Roman Rota in 1544, and there he pursued his interests in classical philology and antiquities, forming lasting friendships with *Panvinio, *Ligorio, Delfini, Pantagato, Sigonio and Fulvio *Orsini. He edited Varro's *De lingua latina* in 1557 and Verrius Flaccus and Festus in 1559 and for the next three decades passionately collected evidence on Roman archaeology. His judicious *Dialogues on Medals, Inscriptions, and Other Antiquities (Diálogos de medallas, inscriciones y otres antiguedadas),* posthumously published in 1587, bears eloquent testimony to his critical acumen, but his letters give the liveliest sense of his skeptical approach to problems of authenticity and Greek and Roman numismatics, epigraphy and history. Agustín had a profound knowledge of the ancient world and collected more than 830 important Greek and Latin manuscripts. He died as archbishop of Tarragona.

BIBLIOGRAPHY

F. de Zulueta, *Don Antonio Agustín* (Glasgow, 1939); C. Mitchell, ''Archaeology and Romance in Renaissance Italy,'' in *Italian Renaissance Studies,* ed. E. F. Jacob (London 1960), 455–83; E. Mandowsky—C. Mitchell, *Pirro Ligorio's Roman Antiquities* (London, 1963); C. Flores Sellés, *Epistolario de Antonio Augustín* (Salamanca, 1980); M. Crawford, ed., *Antonio Agustín between Renaissance & Counter-Reform* (London, 1993).

ROBERT W. GASTON

AIGAI. See VERGINA.

AIGINA (AEGINA). Greek island dominating the Saronic Gulf between Attika and the Peloponnese.

At the modern harbor town on the northwest coast, a prehistoric settlement (Final Neolithic through Late Mycenaean) flourished on the Kolonna headland, later occupied by a sanctuary during the period of the prosperous city-state founded by Dorians from the Argolid. Aigina's early activity in shipping and trade financed Greece's first coinage and challenged the growth of Athens, its enemy through classical times. After the Persian Wars its power declined under Athens and Sparta but prospered under Pergamon and Rome. Aigina was a refuge during postantique raids by Goths, Herulians, Avars and Saracens until the population withdrew inland in the ninth century. After the Greek War of

Independence, the harbor town revived as the first capital of the new state (1827–29) and home to Greece's first modern museum and coinage.

Early European visitors, including *Chandler (1765) and *Dodwell (1805), drew the remains at Kolonna, the temple of Aphaia, and noted antiquities in the town. The most important modern exploration began in 1811 as an architectural study under *Cockerell, *Haller von Hallerstein, John Foster and Jacob Linckh, at the Doric temple of Aphaia in northeast Aigina, then misidentified as that of Zeus Panhellenius. In twenty days they cleared the temple and discovered unexpected sculptural fragments of Parian marble. Two pediments of Greeks and Trojans revealed to modern eyes the preclassical style, polychrome statues and the quality of lost Aiginetan bronze sculpture. Casts were made by *Fauvel, and the fragments were moved to Athens, then to Zante and Malta; despite fierce competition from British and French national collections, the pediments were sold to J. Martin von *Wagner for *Ludwig of Bavaria in 1813. The fragments were shipped to Rome in 1815 for restoration in Carrara marble by *Thorvaldsen and reached the Munich *Glyptothek for display in a neoclassical room in 1828. After damage in 1944, the controversial neoclassical additions were removed for a modern restoration, exhibited since 1972.

Exploration of Aigina increased after Greek independence, including a visit by the *Expédition scientifique de Morée in 1829 and an official survey of the rock-cut tombs by Ludwig *Ross in 1832. Greece's first archaeologist, A. Mustoxydis, explored the Mount Oros sanctuary, identified as that of Zeus Panhellenius by L. *Curtius's finds in 1904. The *Greek Archaeological Service under Stais (1894) and Keramopoullos (1904) excavated in the town, Kolonna sanctuary and necropolis of Aigina, as well as the Aphaia sanctuary. Necropolis plunder produced the prehistoric "Aigina Treasure" acquired by the *British Museum in 1893 and a collection of Protoattic vases now in Berlin. In 1901, a Bavarian expedition led by A. *Furtwängler reopened excavations at the Aphaia sanctuary in search of new fragments of the Munich pediments; they found the remains of a third pediment, contemporary with the west pediment found in 1811 but never installed. An inscription identified Aphaia's temple, elements from an earlier temple emerged and surrounding structures, as well as the island's two other sanctuaries, were explored. Interrupted by World War I, German investigations were renewed by Gabriel Welter from 1925 to 1940 and scantily published in brief reports. Since 1966, an Austrian expedition under Hans Walter at Kolonna publishes prehistoric through Byzantine material. A third Munich investigation at the Aphaia sanctuary, under Dieter Ohly (1966–79) and Klaus Vierneisel (1979–   ), is producing new studies of the architecture and related finds.

BIBLIOGRAPHY

+R. Chandler, *The Antiquities of Ionia* (London, 1797), II, 15–19; +A. Blouet, *Expédition scientifique de Morée* (Paris, 1833), 21–33; +C. Cockerell, *The Temples of Jupiter Panhellenius at Aegina and of Apollo near Phigaleia in Arcadia* (London, 1860); +A. Furtwängler, *Aegina: Das Heiligtum der Aphaia* (Munich, 1906); +G. Welter, *Aigina*

(Berlin, 1938); +H. Walter, ed., *Alt-Ägina,* 1–4 (Munich, 1974–91); +D. Ohly, *Die Aegineten* (Munich, 1976); R. Higgins, *The Aegina Treasure: An Archaeological Mystery* (London, 1979); E.-L. Schwander, *Der Ältere Poros-tempel der Aphaia auf Ägina* (Berlin, 1985).

SARAH P. MORRIS

AINSLEY, SAMUEL JAMES (ca. 1810–74). British artist (draftsman, etcher, and lithographer).

Ainsley made three tours (1842–44) of Etruria as the traveling companion and artistic collaborator of G. *Dennis and was in Etruria on several subsequent occasions until at least 1857. His pleasing and accurate sketches of several Etruscan sites are the ideal complement to the verbal descriptions in Dennis's *Cities and Cemeteries of Etruria* (1848); no mean draftsman himself, Dennis also acknowledges his debt to Ainsley's notes. A projected work on the rock-cut cemetery at Sovana, announced in an enthusiastic and informed article in the *Gentleman's Magazine* (1843), did not materialize. Ainsley bequeathed his Etruscan drawings and watercolors to the *British Museum; admirably cataloged by Binyon, they still constitute a valuable documentary resource of which modern Italian field-workers (notably, those concerned with the rock cemeteries of Middle Etruria) have made good use.

BIBLIOGRAPHY

L. Binyon, *Catalogue of Drawings by British Artists* 1 (London: British Museum, 1898), 3–14; D. E. Rhodes, *Dennis of Etruria* (London, 1973), 35–40; +E. Colonna di Paolo— G. Colonna, *Norchia* 1 (Rome, 1978), 441–43; +B. Origo Crea, ed., *Etruria svelata: I Disegni di S.J. Ainsley nel British Museum* (Rome, 1984).

DAVID RIDGWAY

AKRAGAS (ACRAGAS; AGRIGENTO; AGRIGENTUM). Greek colony in *Sicily.

Akragas was founded as part of the westward expansion of *Gela under the leadership of Aristonoos and Pystilos (Thucydides 6.4.4; Strabo 2.72). Although evidence exists for contact and perhaps occupation of this area by the seventh century B.C., the colony was not officially established until ca. 582 B.C. The power of Akragas grew under its tyrants, especially Theron, who, in conquering *Himera, provoked the war with *Carthage that ended in Greek victory in 480 B.C. In 406 the Carthaginians conquered Akragas and destroyed its buildings. Subsequently abandoned, Akragas was refounded under Timoleon (ca. 340 B.C.) but in the third century fell under the control of Carthage and then Rome. It continued to exist as a Roman city and later a Christian community until the Arab invasion of A.D. 825. By 1130 the name had become transformed to Girgenti, which it remained until 1927. At that time it took its current name, Agrigento.

An early and important topographical description of Akragas is provided by T. *Fazello in *De rebus siculis* (1558). G. M. Pancrazi, in his *Antichità siciliane* *spiegate* (1751–52), included illustrations and a report on archaeological exploration of the Olympieion, the enormous temple of Zeus dating to the sixth century B.C., which features giant figures (Telamones) as structural supports on the exterior. Excavations were carried out in several parts of the city in 1835–36 under D. LoFaso Pietrasanta, Duca di Serradifalco. During this same period (eighteenth and nineteenth centuries), clandestine operations in the cemeteries plundered numerous tombs, especially yielding coins and vases.

Modern investigations of Akragas began in the cemeteries in 1899 and elsewhere in 1916. The first extensive exploration of the site was undertaken by P. Marconi in 1925–32. His excavations provided information concerning occupation of the site from the prehistoric through the Roman periods. The resulting monograph discussed topography, architecture, sculpture and minor arts, with special emphasis on the many religious buildings. Marconi's researches were continued, although intermittently, by later excavators, including G. Cultrera, G. Ricci and I. Bovio Marconi. More extensive excavations were resumed in 1953–58 to the west and south of the Olympieion, in the sanctuary of the Chthonic Deities and in the Hellenistic and Roman quarter. The most recent work has been in the area of San Nicola. These researches are significant for the evidence they provide of civic and domestic life in Akragas.

In 1967 the Museo Archeologico Nazionale (now Regionale) of Agrigento was established near the church of San Nicola, and in it were consolidated remains from Akragas that had been housed from 1864 in the Museo Civico and new finds that had been housed in the Antiquarium of Villa Aurea at Agrigento. The body of material provides evidence of life within the province of Agrigento from prehistoric through Roman times. Besides an excellent series of Greek vases—especially Attic and Italian fabrics—there are terracottas recovered by Marconi in the sanctuary of Chthonic Deities that illustrate stylistic development from Archaic through Hellenistic times. Among the stone sculptures are the ''Ephebe of Agrigento,'' found near the temple of Demeter, parts of Telamones from the Olympieion, and carved sarcophagi.

BIBLIOGRAPHY

+P. Marconi, *Agrigento* (Florence, 1929); P. Griffo, ''Ultimi scavi e ultime scoperte in Agrigento,'' *Quaderni di Archeologia, Arte, Storia, Agrigento* 3 (1946), 5–34; +Idem, *Agrigento, nuovissima guida ai monumenti e agli scavi* (Agrigento, 1961); J. A. deWaele, *Acragas graeca* (Nijmegen, 1971); +P. Griffo, *Il Museo archeologico regionale di Agrigento* (Rome, 1987).

BARBARA A. BARLETTA

AKROPOLIS, Athens. Rocky hill and citadel in the heart of ancient Athens (156m above sea level), site of the city's most important temples—the *Parthenon and the *Erechtheion—as well as the smaller *Temple of Athena Nike and the monumental entranceway of the *Propylaia, all built in the fifth century B.C.

The Akropolis was inhabited by ca. 5000 B.C. in the Neolithic period and shows continuous occupation in prehistoric times. It was first fortified in the Mycenaean age (thirteenth century B.C.). The building of temples on the site began in the sixth century B.C. with the Hekatompedon (570–566 B.C.) and the "Old Temple" of Athena (529–520 B.C). A reworking of the hill in the early fifth century was halted by the razing of the Akropolis by the Persians in 480 B.C., succeeded, in turn, by a complete new scheme of rebuilding (beginning 448 B.C.), culminating in the construction of some of the most famous buildings in Greece.

In Hellenistic and Roman times, only minor building activity occurred. The temples of the Akropolis survived the Middle Ages virtually intact, thanks to their conversion to Christian churches. The Akropolis again became important strategically at the time of the Crusades, and under the Venetians the hill was newly fortified in 1401. When *Ciriaco of Ancona visited Athens in the 1430s, he found the Propylaia converted into a palace for the ruling duke of Athens and even found private homes on the Akropolis (he stayed in one of these). Ciriaco copied inscriptions there and made his famous drawings of the Parthenon pediments at this time (known in copies by Giuliano da *Sangallo). Copies were also made at the bidding of the Marquis de *Nointel, upon his visit to the Akropolis in 1674. These were to prove immensely valuable records, after the notorious shelling of the Akropolis by the Venetian *Morosini in 1678.

Numerous visitors came to the Athenian Akropolis in succeeding centuries, from the travelers *Spon and *Wheler to the architects *Stuart and *Revett and the avid collector Lord *Elgin and his agent *Lusieri. Not until Greece became an independent free state in 1830 were the first excavations conducted, west of the Propylaia. In 1833, Turkish troops holding the hill were withdrawn, and a garrison of Bavarian soldiers guarded the Akropolis. Ludwig *Ross began clearing away debris and uncovered the inscribed architrave of the temple of Roma and Augustus (seen by Ciriaco in 1444).

In the years 1834–36, between the southeast corner of the Parthenon and the south wall of the Akropolis, Ross found and identified Persian destruction fill of 480 B.C. and proclaimed its significance for dating black- and red-figure pottery. He also found graves with coins of Justin (A.D. 518–27) and Justinian (A.D. 527–65), the earliest relevant evidence for determining the date of the conversion of the Erechtheion and Parthenon into churches. The area between the Erechtheion and Parthenon was excavated by K. S. Pittakis in 1837–39, and a Mycenean wall behind the southwest wing of the Propylaia was unearthed. In succeeding years the medieval and Turkish structures on the Akropolis were demolished (1842–45), and Pittakis built a high, long wall out of ancient and mainly Byzantine marbles as a display (1844–49; demolished in 1888). He excavated the interior and the south side of the Parthenon, the north porch of the Erechtheion, the Roman monumental stairway to the Akropolis and the area northeast of the Propylaia.

In 1852–53, *Beulé conducted extensive excavations west of the Propylaia. He discovered the prehistoric rock-cut footholds, the retaining wall of the Archaic ramp and the third century A.C. outwork with gate that bears his name. Intermittent investigations in the second half of the nineteenth century turned up various finds, such as the *Calfbearer and the *Kritios Boy, as well as a boat lamp dedicated to Athena in the Erechtheion, the only object found in situ inside an Akropolis temple. Truly systematic excavation of the Akropolis had to wait for the appointment of P. *Kavvadias as ephor-general in 1885. From that year until 1890, he and G. Kawerau worked feverishly, and all the surface soil was excavated to bedrock. *Dörpfeld served as architect to the project and left valuable plans of the whole area. The greatest discoveries were the "Old Temple" of Athena just south of the Erechtheion; Archaic limestone pedimental sculpture, including the "*Bluebeard"; the stele of the Mourning Athena; and the Persian destruction fill at the north wall of the Akropolis, containing Archaic sculpture, inscriptions and statue bases, which was at once understood to be fill brought in to raise the ground level in stages during construction of the wall. During this period, P. Wolters established a basis for dating vases by means of exact systematic observation of the finds and recording stratification.

In 1898, the civil engineer N. Balanos began what was to be a far-reaching program of restoration of the monuments of the Akropolis; he worked on the Parthenon (1898–1902, 1923–33), the Erechtheion (1902–9) and the Propylaia (1909–17). Using techniques that ultimately had disastrous results, he employed iron clamps to hold together ancient fragments and to attach new marble repairs, and he employed long, thick iron beams to bring stability. In later years the rusting and swelling of the iron broke up the marbles and caused terrible damage. Balanos was also criticized for rebuilding more of the various structures than was allowed by the evidence and for reusing in a random way blocks of marble that he found lying around on the Akropolis.

During this period Bert Hodge *Hill did a pioneering investigation of the Older Parthenon (1910), followed by a study of the columns of the Older Parthenon—fifty-nine in all—by A. Tschira (1938). W. Kolbe excavated at the little stairway in the Older Parthenon retaining wall and at a nearby Mycenaean wall.

A. *Orlandos succeeded Balanos in 1940 and applied his background in architectural history as he directed work on the Akropolis over the next twenty years. In 1975 was founded the Committee for the Preservation of the Acropolis Monuments, to coordinate interdisciplinary work by architects, surveyors, draftsmen, archaeologists, geologists, physicists, chemists, conservators and technicians. Rapid progress has already been achieved on all fronts. In connection with the work of saving the four classical buildings and inventorying the thousands of fragments formerly heaped up in dumps, the various teams have made dramatic new discoveries about the monuments and the site, including two previously unknown classical temples. (See also *Akropolis Museum, Athens.)

BIBLIOGRAPHY

P. Kavvadias—G. Kawerau, Die Ausgrabung der Akropolis vom Jahre 1885 bis zum Jahre 1890 (Athens, 1906); J. A. Bundgard, The Excavations of the Athenian Akropolis,

1882–1890 (Copenhagen, 1974); *The Acropolis at Athens: Conservation, Restoration and Research, 1975–1983,* tr. J. Binder (Athens, 1985).
JUDITH BINDER AND NANCY THOMSON DE GRUMMOND

AKROPOLIS MUSEUM, Athens. Greek museum, containing finds from the *Akropolis, Athens, and other sites in the city.

During the Greek War of Independence (1821–31) Chevalier Andreas Mustoxydis advised Colonel Leicester Stanhope, representative of the London Committee to aid the Greek cause, that a museum for antiquities should be founded in Greece. In 1824 Stanhope persuaded Odysseus Androutsos, commander of the Akropolis fortress, to convert the *Parthenon into a museum. By 1834, hundreds of sculptures and inscriptions were on display in the *Propylaia, which served as a gallery for over fifty years.

In September 1834 Athens was made the capital of Greece, and antiquities from all over Greece were transferred to the Akropolis. In 1835 the mosque in the Parthenon became a storeroom for antiquities on the recommendation of Leo von *Klenze, who drew up plans for a National Archaeological Museum on the Akropolis. By 1835 a ramshackle wooden Turkish house, east of the *Erechtheion, was in use as a museum. In 1837 many antiquities were transferred from the first National Museum on the island of *Aigina to this museum. From 1842 onward the *Temple of Athena Nike and the Parthenon served as sculpture galleries. In 1844 K. S. Pittakis requested permission to build a museum on the Akropolis site chosen by von Klenze. In 1861 Breton noted antiquities on show in the Turkish House, such as finds from the Persian destruction layer excavated in 1836, antefixes, the Byzantine floor mosaic from the Parthenon, wooden plugs (*empolia*) from the Erechtheion columns, a pot of minium (vermilion), chunks of worked ivory (from *Athena Parthenos?), carbonized objects and vases found in the *Peiraeus.

The present Akropolis Museum was built 1865–74. Casts of the Parthenon sculptures sent by the *British Museum in 1846 were transferred there from a depot in lower Athens. By 1877 the collections in the Turkish House had been distributed among the Akropolis Museum, Central Museum and Ministry of Education. By 1881 the museum housed many finds from the Asklepieion and the *Theater of Dionysos and, subsequently, finds from the *Temple of Olympian Zeus, Syntagma Square and other sites in lower Athens. In 1886 P. *Kavvadias began organizing the museum workrooms and displays; as new finds from his large-scale Akropolis excavations (1885–90) demanded museum space, he had the Akropolis inscriptions and bronzes transferred to the National Museum. The Akropolis vase fragments, temporarily sent to the National Museum for study, have remained there ever since.

In 1887–88 G. Kawerau built a second Akropolis Museum behind the first one; ''das kleine Akropolis Museum,'' where the votive reliefs were displayed, was demolished in 1953, when the museum was enlarged and remodeled. By 1964 all of the museum galleries were open again. The glory of the Akropolis

Museum is the Archaic and Classical sculpture from the five temples of Athena on the Akropolis, the Archaic *Korai, the *Kritios Boy, the *Calfbearer and the *Blond Boy.

In 1976 and again on 1 February 1983, the government announced that a new Akropolis Museum, uniting all of the Akropolis finds, was to be constructed below the Akropolis opposite the Theater of Dionysos.

BIBLIOGRAPHY

F. de Saulcy, *RA* 2 (1845), 269–77; A. Milchhöfer, *Die Museen Athens* (Athens, 1881), 45–62; P. Kavvadias—G. Kawerau, *Die Ausgrabung der Akropolis vom Jahre 1885 bis zum 1890* (Athens, 1906), 1–16, 44–6; M. Brouskari, *The Akropolis Museum*, tr. J. Binder (Athens, 1974).

JUDITH BINDER

AKROTIRI. See THERA.

ALARI-BONACOLSI, PIER JACOPO. See ANTICO.

ALBACINI, CARLO (birth date unknown–d. 1807). Highly successful Roman sculptor-restorer; pupil of Bartolomeo *Cavaceppi.

Albacini was active from the 1770s to the 1790s: he restored the *Farnese family collection for the king of Naples (late 1780s–'90s), worked for Catherine the Great and restored antique marbles for the *Vatican and for numerous British collectors, especially those buying through Thomas *Jenkins, such as *Townley and *Blundell. He also created some modern works, copies of famous pieces in Roman collections; his studio was visited and commented on by both *Canova and *Goethe. In 1783 he was elected a member of the Accademia di San Luca.

Albacini was probably responsible for making plaster casts of the majority of the Greek and Roman portrait busts, numbering about 255, that were sold to the Board of Trustees for Manufactures in Edinburgh in 1838, by Filippo Albacini, the artist's son. Some 154 of the busts survive today and are in the care of the National Galleries of Scotland, in Edinburgh.

BIBLIOGRAPHY

A. de Franciscis, "Restauri di Carlo Albacini a statue del Museo Nazionale di Napoli," *Samnium* 1 (1946), 96–110; +G. Vaughan, "Albacini and His English Patrons," in *Plaster and Marble, The Classical and Neo-Classical Portrait Bust (The Edinburgh Albacini Colloquium)*, ed. G. Davies; *Journal of the History of Collections* 3.2 (1991), 183–98 (papers by Smailes, Davies, de Grummond and Howard in same issue).

GLENYS DAVIES

ALBANI FAMILY. A papal family whose ancestral site was Urbino; famous for its library and collections of antiquities and works of art.

GIOVANNI FRANCISCO, Pope Clement XI (1649–1721), had a long career in the Church, becoming cardinal in 1690. At first only in minor orders, he was ordained priest shortly before his election to pope (1700). Although he had drawn up regulations against nepotism, two of his nephews became cardinals.

Cardinal ALESSANDRO (1692–1779), nephew to Clement IX, played a more prominent part than any other member of the family in the collection of antiquities. He was born in Urbino; bad eyesight, suffered from his youth and later resulting in total blindness, forced him to abandon a military life for a career in the Church. He received as guests in Rome the brothers of George III, the dukes of York, Gloucester and Cumberland. As host to many Britishers in Rome, as agent for their collections, he entertained Richard Wilson, Thomas *Jenkins, Robert and James Adam (*Adam family) and James Barry. He became a member of the *Society of Antiquaries of London (1761).

Alessandro began his antiquarian interest early, having planned as a youth the foundation of an antiquarian society. He supported excavation, it was said, "turning up the whole soil of Rome," at the same time "without excessive scruples about the manner of making acquisitions." He also accepted as a gift from the Jesuits (1729) the fragments of an obelisk (*obelisks) that had originally adorned the temple of Isis in the Campus Martius; in 1739 he presented the restored obelisk, surmounted by a cross and the Albani coat of arms, to the city of Urbino.

Alessandro Albani acquired as town residence the palace on the Tiber corner of the Quattro Fontane. Antiquities were kept here until the building of the Villa Albani near Porta Salaria (see later in this entry) . Especially famous was the library, begun by Clement, increased by Alessandro and presided over by *Winckelmann. The most famous manuscript was a collection of over a hundred folio volumes, made up of two parts. The core was the *Museum Chartaceum,* essentially a group of drawings of Roman antiquities, put together by Cassiano dal *Pozzo. By the time the Albani acquired the group, there had been added to it other drawings originally chosen by *Domenichino, then acquired by Maratta. In 1703 Clement bought the collection, which passed to Alessandro on his death. After lengthy negotiations engineered by James Adam, the collection was sold to George III, to the mortification of Winckelmann, and is now at Windsor.

The palace passed ultimately to the Principe del Drago. In the courtyard still is a Roman inscription naming Drusus. At the foot of the stairs is a magnificent porphyry lion with a hieroglyphic inscription. The Albani arms are to be seen on the doors upstairs.

From 1743 to 1763 Alessandro was occupied with the construction of the villa on Via Salaria. While the library remained in the city palace, the sculptures, with Winckelmann as guide, were famous in all Europe. Despite papal bounty, Alessandro was frequently short of funds, and he developed a connoisseur's shrewdness in equivocal transactions. In 1728 he sold some thirty pieces to Frederick Augustus, king of Poland, including the recumbent *Son of Niobe.* In 1733 a major part of the Albani collection was sold to Clement XII, who gave it to the *Capitoline Museums, Rome. Many items of the group would be considered of minor aesthetic value today; indeed, only two of them (the *Antinous* from *Hadrian's Villa and the *Juno* from the *Cesi family collection) were included by the French in the more than one hundred statues sent from Rome to Paris under *Napoleon's treaty. By far the most valuable part consists of the portraits of members of the Roman imperial families and a large number of "philosophers," including poets, dramatists and orators.

The collection formed by Alessandro that passed to his heirs suffered near disaster in the Napoleonic troubles at the end of the century. GIOVANNI FRANCESCO ALBANI had become a cardinal as early as 1747. Claiming that he was active in anti-French activities toward the end of the century, Napoleon had the villa confiscated and the collection sent to Paris. A large group of statues was exhibited in Paris with other Napoleonic loot. After 1815, when other acquisitions were being returned to their owners, the Albani family was financially unable to pay the expenses of restitution. Some considerable part remained in Paris and is today in the Musée du *Louvre, including numerous portraits and anonymous busts. *Ludwig I of Bavaria purchased several items now in the Munich *Glyptothek. Among the most famous of this group are the *Diomedes, Peace* and portraits of *Lucius Verus* and *Commodus*. The only work of major value to return to Rome was the relief of *Antinous* from Hadrian's Villa, used as an overmantel in a room named after it to this day. A recent catalog of the remaining collection includes over 400 items, mostly sculpture.

In 1866 the Villa Albani and all its remaining contents were acquired by the *Torlonia family. It may be visited today by request to the Torlonia administration.

BIBLIOGRAPHY

Notice des statues, bustes et bas-reliefs de la Galerie des Antiques du Musée Napoléon (Paris, 1811); J. Fleming, "Cardinal Albani's Drawings at Windsor: Their Purchase by James Adam for George III," *Connoisseur* (December 1958), 164–69; L. Lewis—G. Sofri, "Albani, Alessandro," etc. *DBI* 1 (1960), 595–98; L. Lewis, *Connoisseurs and Secret Agents in Eighteenth Century Rome* (London, 1961); H. Beck—P.C. Bol, eds. *Forschungen zur Villa Albani, Antike Kunst und die Epoche der Aufklärung* (Berlin, 1982); C. Pietrangeli, *Le Collezioni private romane attraverso i tempi* (Rome, 1985), 14–15, 22; +P. C. Bol, ed., *Forschungen zur Villa Albani, Katalog der antiken Bildwerke,* 1–3 (Berlin, 1989–1992).

ALBERTI, LEANDRO (1479–ca. 1552). Italian theologian, historian and geographer.

Born in Bologna, Leandro Alberti entered the Dominican order there in 1493; afterward he served in posts in Bologna and Rome and also was assigned as a companion to the general of his order on travels in *Sicily and Southern Italy.

Alberti wrote biographies, sermons and historical works but is remembered, above all, for his *Descrittione di tutta Italia, nella quale si contiene il sito di essa, l'origine et la signoria delle città et de' castelli* (Bologna, 1550). This work, prepared along the same lines as the *Italia illustrata* of Flavio *Biondo and imitating it quite closely in some passages, deals in colorful language with the geography, topography and history of Italy. Alberti draws heavily from classical authors, whom he sites with accuracy, as well as from his contemporaries (although they were not always trustworthy, e.g., *Annio da Viterbo). The *Descrittione* is rich in antiquarian information, much of it culled by Alberti personally in his travels or obtained from local authorities from the towns he describes. His interest in the ancient origins and founding of towns is relevant for those interested in classical scholarship in the Renaissance, and his description of landscapes in the sixteenth century, many of which are much changed today, may give us a closer idea of their nature in antiquity. The book is generally regarded as the best description of Italy written during the sixteenth century and in its own time was highly regarded and reprinted many times.

BIBLIOGRAPHY

R. Almagià, "Alberti, Leandro," *EI* 2 (1929), 180–81; A. L. Redigonda, "Alberti, Leandro," *DBI* 1 (1960), 699–702; V. Bracco, *L'Archeologia classica nella cultura occidentale* (Rome, 1979), 72–73.

ALBERTI, LEON BATTISTA (1404–72). Italian Renaissance artist, architect and author.

Of all fifteenth-century Italians, Leon Battista Alberti perhaps most nearly achieved the Renaissance ideal of "the universal man." The Genoa-born son of an exiled Florentine patrician, Alberti received the education appropriate to a humanist scholar (under Gasparino Barzizza at Padua and at the University of Bologna). His career was devoted to rediscovering, propagating and surpassing the achievements of classical antiquity. His thorough knowledge of Latin and his skillful use of classical literary forms were demonstrated in 1424, when he published *Philodoxeus*. This play, actually his own creation, was acclaimed by his contemporaries as an ancient masterpiece. In the 1430s and 1440s, Alberti wrote and published a number of classically inspired essays and treatises dealing with a wide variety of civic, social and philosophical topics (e.g., *De iure, Della famiglia, Intercoenales, Della tranquillità dell'anima, Momus*). During this period, perhaps through contact with the Florentine mathematician Paolo Toscanelli and with the artists *Brunelleschi and *Donatello, Alberti began to devote considerable attention to the visual arts. Although examples of his sculpture and painting are either known or mentioned, most of his artistic endeavors at this time were theoretical (*De statua, De pictura*).

Alberti's *Descriptio urbis Romae,* dating from the early 1440s, was a landmark in archaeological topography. The system of making a map of imperial Rome described in this survey illustrates his knowledge of Ptolemaic cartography and the newly formulated rules governing proportional relationships. In 1446, he attempted to raise two ancient Roman ships from the bottom of Lake *Nemi, south of Rome, an episode described in his *Navis.*

Alberti had entered papal service in Rome as a secretary in the early 1430s and became an artistic adviser to popes Eugenius IV, *Nicholas V and *Pius II. In 1452, he presented his monumental and highly influential treatise on architecture, *De re aedificatoria,* to Nicholas V. The main intent of this work was to modernize Vitruvius, to extol the merits of ancient architecture and to explain how the principles of rational Roman urban planning could be put to contemporary use. The plans Alberti formulated at this time for renovating and rebuilding the Basilica of Saint Peter's and the Vatican district never came to fruition.

His architectural career, for which Alberti is best remembered, began in 1450, when he was asked by Sigismondo Malatesta to transform the medieval church of San Francesco in Rimini into a humanistic mortuary. The resulting Tempio Malatestiana, left unfinished in 1468, is a testimony to Alberti's antiquarian interests. For the façade, he designed a classicizing screen based on the *Arch of Augustus in Rimini and the *Arch of Septimius Severus and the *Arch of Constantine in Rome. The arched flanks of the Tempio recall the rhythm of a Roman aqueduct. If completed as intended, it is probable that the nave would have opened into a great *Pantheon-like rotunda.

His works in Florence during the 1450s and 1460s for Giovanni Rucellai (façade of Santa Maria Novella, Shrine of the Holy Sepulcher in San Pancrazio) combine traditional Tuscan architectural elements with classical quotations. The façade of S. Maria Novella draws on the Arch of Septimius Severus and the *Basilica Aemilia as well as the Pantheon. His connection with the façade of the Rucellai Palace is questionable.

Alberti is mentioned in the *Commentaries* of Pope Pius II as the "scholar and very clever archaeologist" who guided the pope through the Alban hills on a tour of antiquities. Alberti accompanied Pope Pius to Mantua in 1459 and, while there, received a commission from the Marquis Federico Gonzaga for the church of San Sebastiano. The unfinished façade, articulated by pilasters and an architrave that breaks into the pediment, has been reconstructed by Rudolf Wittkower as an illusionary temple front. For this Alberti may have been inspired by the Tomb of Annia Regilla near Rome (second century A.C.), the *Arch of Tiberius at Orange or the vestibule of Diocletian's Palace at *Split. A more plausible and accessible source may have been the third-century tomb of the Cercenii on the *Via Appia Antica. The lower façade, with its series of round-headed and square-headed openings, shows detailed parallelism with the Roman theater at *Orange and provides part of the circumstantial evidence that Alberti may have visited Roman remains in Provence. The ground plan of San Sebastiano also relates to the cruciform plan of the tomb of the Cercenii, as well as to the Greek Library in *Hadrian's Villa at Tivoli.

The church of Sant'Andrea in Mantua was designed by Alberti and begun in 1471. Here, Alberti combined temple front and triumphal arch motifs for the façade and carried this conception into the interior to articulate the entrances of the major and minor chapels opening off the nave. The great, aisleless nave of Sant'Andrea is barrel-vaulted in a manner that brings to mind the side aisles of the *Basilica of Maxentius and Constantine in Rome.

Alberti is recorded as giving a guided tour of the *Forum Romanum to Lorenzo de' Medici (*Medici family) and other courtiers in the fall of 1471. He died the following spring in Rome.

BIBLIOGRAPHY
J. Gadol, *Leon Battista Alberti, Universal Man of the Early Renaissance* (Chicago, 1969, repr. 1973); R. Wittkower, *Architectural Principles in the Age of Humanism,* 4th ed. (New York, 1973, reissued 1988); C. Westfall, *In This Most Perfect Paradise: Alberti, Nicholas V, and the Invention of Conscious Urban Planning in Rome, 1447–55* (University Park, PA, 1974); +F. Borsi, *Leon Battista Alberti* (Milan, 1975); P. W. Lehmann, "Alberti and Antiquity: Additional Observations," *ArtB* 70 (1988), 388–400.

CHARLES RANDALL MACK

ALBERTINI, FRANCESCO (fl. 1493–1510). Florentine priest and antiquarian; author of an important guidebook to Rome, *Opusculum de mirabilibus novae et veteris urbis Romae* (Rome, 1510).

Little is known of Albertini's life. He was a pupil of *Ghirlandaio, and it has even been conjectured that he may have been the author of the drawings of Roman antiquities in the *Codex Escurialensis, from the workshop of Ghirlandaio. He wrote a guidebook to Florence, *Memoriale di molte statue e pitture della città di Firenze* (Rome, 1510), showing his knowledge of, and interest in, the arts of his own time.

In 1502, Albertini went to Rome as a chaplain for Cardinal Fazio Santoro. There he composed his *Opusculum de mirabilibus,* intended as an up-to-date guide to the city of Rome, taking the place of the medieval *Mirabilia urbis Romae.* The work is divided into two parts, the first being a description of the ancient city, adapted from medieval guides, and the second, a description of the modern city. Albertini's guidebook was superior to earlier works in its rich quotations from classical texts, inscriptions and coins and in its inclusion of the latest information about excavations, discoveries and collections. The author was widely read and knowledgeable in the opinions of his contemporaries (he refers to *Biondo, *Leto, *Poggio, *Alberti and many others). The work was immensely popular and went through five editions between 1510 and 1523.

BIBLIOGRAPHY
A. Schmarsow, ed., *De mirabilibus novae urbis Romae* (Heilbronn, 1886); R. Valentini— G. Zucchetti, *Codice topografico di Roma* 4 (Rome, 1953), 457–546; J. Ruysschaert, "Albertini, Francesco," *DBI* 1 (1960), 724–25; Weiss, *RDCA,* 84–86.

ALBRECHT V (1528–79). Collector, duke of Bavaria from 1550.

Albrecht succeeded the co-regents Wilhelm IV and Ludwig X, who built, in the Italian style, the Stadtresidenz at Landshut. This project set the tone for Albrecht's own humanist ambitions. He turned to similar sources for the design for his Stadtresidenz in Munich; Jacopo *Strada provided measured drawings of the Ducal Palace and the Palazzo del Te in Mantua. Substantially transformed by his successor, Wilhelm V (1586–1600), the original shape of the Antiquarium is known from a dated drawing. The Hall of Antiquities in the Munich Residenz, which was built in the years following the completion of the *Kunstkammer* (1569–71), was designed to house those purchases of statues and busts made by various agents, including Nicolò Stoppio and Jacopo Strada, during the years

1566–70. Advice on these and related matters was sought from Max Fugger and Otto, cardinal of Augsburg. The latter wrote disapprovingly in 1569 of Strada's purchase in Venice for 7,000 ducats of the Loredano collection, maintaining that the duke would be better served by such experts as Tommaso dei Cavalieri and Gerolamo *Garimberto. While an inventory of the latter's collection was sent to Munich, there is nothing to indicate that a purchase resulted. The impressive, although uneven, collection of busts and small-scale statuary now on display in the Hall of Antiquities dates back to Albrecht V but includes, as well, works added by Wilhelm V.

BIBLIOGRAPHY

J. Stockbauer, *Die Kunstbestrebungen am Bayerischen Hofe unter Herzog Albert V und seinem Nachfolger Wilhelm V* (Vienna, 1874); E. Hubala, "Ein Entwurf für das Antiquarium der Münchner Residenz—1568," *MJb* 3 (1958–59), 128–46; R. von Busch, *Studien zu deutschen Antikensammlungen des 16. Jahrhundert* (Tübingen, 1973); E. Weski—H. Frosien-Leinze, *Das Antiquarium der Münchner Residenz* 1–2 (Munich, 1987); D. J. Jansen, "Jacob Strada et le commerce d'art," *Revue de L'Art* 77 (1987), 11–21.

CLIFFORD M. BROWN

ALCIATUS, ANDREAS (ALCIATI; ALCIATO, ANDREA; 1492–1550).

Italian jurisconsult, historian, epigrapher and numismatist.

Acclaimed during his lifetime as one of the most influential European jurisconsults because of his role in directing the study of jurisprudence back to its Roman sources, Alciatus in our time is best known as the inventor of the Renaissance emblem book, into which he incorporated his wide knowledge of classical civilization.

Alciato's contributions to our understanding of antiquity began during his student days in Milan under the guidance of Giano Parrasio. In 1504–5, while he was writing a history of Milan (*Rerum patriae Andreae Alciati I. C. celeberrimi libri IIII,* Milan, 1625), he began to collect local inscriptions. The result was a *Sylloge* of inscriptions of Milan and its environs that still exists in manuscript form only, although he considered it ready for publication in 1518–19, and, as late as 1542, his Paris printer, Christian Wechel, was eager to publish it. That copies of the manuscript were available to Alciato's contemporaries we know from Theodor *Mommsen's list of them (*CIL.* V.II). Each text was preceded by an introduction indicating the exact location of the original and its historical significance. So superior was Alciato's method to that of earlier collectors of local inscriptions, such as Benedetto Giovio and Konrad *Peutinger, that Mommsen, praising him for his learning and diligence, credited him with being the founder of epigraphy. According to Dante Bianchi, his work became the source for all later epigraphists. Roberto Weiss noted that without the help of epigraphy, the history of Milan by Alciato would have been quite different and that subsequently "the historian or philologist who presumed to dispense with epigraphic evidence did so at his own risk."

Portrait of *Andreas Alciatus*, engraving from A. Alciati, *Opera omnia* (1617). (V. Callahan.)

An interpretation of a sum of sesterces in the text of the *Monumentum Plinianum* led to Alciato's correspondence with Benedetto Giovio. Alciato wrote a brief essay showing the modern equivalents of ancient coins (*De re nummaria antiquorum ad recentia tempora redacta compendiosa ratiocinatio* [printed in

F. Argelati, *De monetis Italiae,* Milan, 1750, app. 23–28]) and a study of ancient metrology (*Libellus de ponderibus et mensuris,* composed 1522–27, printed in Hagenae, 1530). As Costanzo Landi demonstrated in his treatise on Roman coins, a number of Alciato's emblems derived their subject matter from his numismatic interests.

BIBLIOGRAPHY

C. Landi, *Veterum numismatum romanorum explicationes* (Lyons, 1560); D. Bianchi, "L'opera letteraria e storica di Andrea Alciato," *Archivio Storico Lombardo* 20 (1913), 46–57; P. E. Viard, *André Alciat* (Paris, 1926); Weiss, *RDCA,* 152–53.

V. W. CALLAHAN

ALDOBRANDINI WEDDING. Section of a Roman fresco (2.42m × .92m) representing an ancient wedding.

The painting has been identified as an example of the Third Pompeian Style and dated to the period of Augustus (31 B.C.–A.D. 14). Excavated in Rome ca. 1604, most probably on the Esquiline Hill in the Gardens of Maecenas, the fresco came into the possession of Cardinal Pietro Aldobrandini, from whom it received its name. It is today located in a room named for it in the Vatican Library.

Except for the paintings of the Golden House (*Domus Aurea) of Nero, discovered in the Renaissance, this was for a century the best example known of large-scale ancient painting (*Roman wall painting). As such, it influenced the painters of the seventeenth and eighteenth centuries who came to Rome to study, as well as intellectuals, historians, aestheticians and archaeologists.

The first published account of the fresco appeared in Federico Zuccaro's *Idea de' pittori, scultori e architetti,* whose dedication is dated 1607. The exact date of discovery is not known but is thought to be 1604 or 1605. Nor is it certain where the painting was discovered; Zuccaro notes that it was found "on the hill of Santa Maria Maggiore in the Gardens of Maecenas"; all reliable sources place the spot on the Esquiline. Cardinal Aldobrandini mounted the fresco on one wall of an open portico built especially for its display in his palazzo and gardens of Monte Magnanapoli.

Early scholarship and artistic influences were dependent on firsthand knowledge or copies of the famous painting. Through his correspondence with *Peiresc many years later, Peter Paul *Rubens was able to obtain a copy in color of the painting he had studied in Rome, 1606–7. In 1622–23, fresh and lively pen-and-ink sketches were made by Anthony Van Dyck during his trip to Italy. A drawing by *Pietro da Cortona served as a basis for two engravings; two drawings exist in the dal *Pozzo-Albani collections in the *British Museum; and *Poussin painted a copy in oil that is perhaps the one seen today in the Galleria Doria-Pamphili, Rome.

Susanna Maria von Sandrart (in 1683) and P. S. *Bartoli (in 1693) engraved more accurate versions of the Aldobrandini Wedding that differed from the Doria copy, causing difficulties for early scholars. An influential copy was the watercolor by Heinrich Meyer executed in Rome in 1796, given to *Goethe and preserved to the present day at Weimar; it was the basis for the engraving illustrating the earliest monograph on the painting, by K. A. Böttiger in 1810. References to the fresco occur repeatedly in the writings of *Winckelmann, who saw in it all the qualities he idealized as uniquely Greek—monumental calm, dignified gesture and restrained emotion. The painting justified his theories on Greek art and was used to validate his premise that Roman art at its best imitated the classic qualities of Greek art.

The influence of Winckelmann's theories on Goethe and others helped form the ideas of nineteenth-century neoclassicism and established the persistent belief that works of Roman art such as the Aldobrandini panel disclosed lost masterpieces of Greek culture. Neoclassicism as promoted in England by Robert Adam and his brothers (*Adam family) brought with it copies of the Aldobrandini Wedding, such as the one executed on the wall of the dining room of Syon House or another used as part of a design for a chimneypiece in Saint-James's Palace. These were published and widely disseminated in *The Works of Robert and James Adam* (1773).

In 1811, agents for *Napoleon attempted to secure the famous painting from the *Borghese (and Aldobrandini) family; instead, through the work of the dealer Vincenzo Nelli and Antonio *Canova, it came into the Vatican collection. In 1838, Pope *Gregory XVI formed a small but exquisite collection of ancient paintings as a counterpoint to more recent paintings then being installed. The renowned panel was its chief jewel then; today, having been overshadowed by discoveries at *Pompeii and *Herculaneum and afflicted by a long scholarly controversy over its interpretation (still unsettled), it suffers from ever-increasing neglect.

BIBLIOGRAPHY

B. Nogara, *Le nozze Aldobrandini e i paesaggi nella Vaticana e nei Musei Pontifici* (Milan, 1917); L. Vlad Borelli, s.v. "Nozze Aldobrandini," *EAA* 5 (Rome, 1963), 569–70; W. Handrick, "Die 'Aldobrandinische Hochzeit,' Kopie eines antiken Gemäldes in Goethes Kunstsammlung," *Goethe, Neue Folge des Jahrbuchs der Goethe-Gesellschaft* 25 (1963), 143–66; P. H. Von Blanckenhagen—B. Green, "The Aldobrandini Wedding Reconsidered," *Archäologischer Anzeiger* 82 (1975), 83–98; B. U. DuRette, *The History and Interpretation of the Aldobrandini Wedding: Bacchus, Fertility and Marriage in the Time of Augustus*, diss., Florida State Univ. (Tallahassee, 1992).

B. UNDERWOOD DURETTE

ALDROVANDI (ALDROANDI), ULISSE (1522–1605). Italian Renaissance scientist and humanist scholar.

This renowned Bolognese naturalist, likened by contemporaries to Pliny or Aristotle, was at the same time a classical scholar of considerable stature, well versed in the literature and the archaeology of antiquity, an adviser on art theory to Cardinal Paleotti and a correspondent of the Grand Dukes of Tuscany and other rulers and learned men of the day, as well as a patron of painters and

Portrait of *Ulisse Aldrovandi*, attributed to Agostino Carracci, engraving from U. Aldrovandi, *Ornithologia* (1599). (Westfälisches Landesmuseum für Kunst und Kulturgeschichte, Münster, Porträtarchiv Diepenbroick. Photo: R. Wakonigg.)

engravers (among them, Jacopo Ligozzi) to produce final renderings of his detailed studies of flora and fauna. Because the bulk of his researches remains in manuscript, preserved, for the most part, in the University and Biblioteca Comunale (Archiginnasio) of Bologna, supplemented by volumes of letters and illustrative material in Florence and Modena, his place in the history of ideas is obscured. Even more misleading in this respect is the fact that—save for his *Ornithologia* (1599), the *De animalibus insectis* (1602) and one work of his youth—dates of posthumous publications edited by others (e.g., *Musaeum Metallicum,* 1648; *Dendrologia,* 1665) are often taken at face value by modern authors. The same flaw affects the history of archaeological discovery when the date of his youthful inventory of Roman collections, *Delle Statue di Roma . . .* is taken as coincident with the Ziletti editions, Venice, 1556, 1558 or 1562 (cf. infra).

As far as his scientific research is concerned, the Enlightenment greatly admired its exhaustive character and reliance on detailed observation and dissection and his pioneering work in embryology and in botany (Linnaeus may have been influenced in his own taxonomy, to judge by plant names that preserve the memory of Aldrovandi). As late as Darwin, Ulisse won praise for his *Ornithologia* as a reliable document on domestic breeds of fowl and pigeons, while the book's value continues today for students of the history of gastronomy in recipes developed from Apicius and other sources, classical, medieval and Renaissance. In the eighteenth century, the regard of Buffon, however, was tempered by impatience with Aldrovandi's encyclopedic humanism, which led him "uncritically" to allow fabulous creatures in his *syntaxis animalium* since they existed in the writings and arts of the past. Buffon did not appreciate the tradition of Renaissance polymaths, concerned for universal history interpreted in moralizing Christian context, nor the philological bias of Ulisse's contribution— which he thought would gain by being reduced to a tenth of its length.

For Aldrovandi, with degrees in philosophy and medicine, his studies were natural *philosophy,* and under that rubric he lectured at Bologna on fossils, plants and animals from 1555/6 to his retirement in 1600 and founded the Commune's *Orto Botanico* or his own Musaeum. He dealt with no phenomenon of the sublunary world—animal, vegetable or mineral—without exploring its every facet: etymology and everything the ancients had written about it; its virtues or drawbacks in human use, including the religious and magical; and its significance in emblems and hieroglyphs, in history and legend. As a result, his autograph manuscripts and copies are a historiographical thesaurus for archaeologists and historians of art. Among antiquarian topics treated in extenso are the nature and propriety of *grottesche,* ancient funerary rites, customs of dining in antiquity, weights and measures, types and names of vessels and musical instruments of the Muses. Antiquity for him, of course, meant Greek, Roman, Hebrew, "Chaldaean," Egyptian, Etruscan and Indian of the New World. For his so-called *Biblologia,* he considered every aspect of the development of human language and writing from such topics as the communication of dolphins and Adam's first speech or Cadmus bringing letters to Athens down to technical matters (types of papyrus, the invention of other writing materials) and the development of libraries and academies (Noah, surprisingly, having founded the first in Vetulonia).

Aldrovandi's *Delle statue antiche che per tutta Roma in diversi luoghi . . . si veggono* (Venice, 1556, and other eds.), published as a supplement to Lucio Mauro's treatise on the topography and antiquities of Rome, dates in actuality from 1549–50, as may be learned from both internal evidence and his autobiography, written in 1586 (Bologna, Bib. Univ. Misc. 97, ca. 647–70). He recalls his enrollment in the University of Padua at the beginning of 1548 and leaving for Rome twenty months later to spend the next eighteen months there. He is silent on the reason for the latter *giorni straordinari,* although we know it was to answer charges of heresy (''Lutheranism'') brought against him and a small group of fellow students in a process initiated at Bologna during June 1549. Amnesty came with the accession of Pope *Julius III, but Ulisse stayed on, ostensibly to clear his name. Thus, visits to Roman collections began in the latter part of 1549, while actual writing occupied much of 1550; a first private printing allegedly appeared in 1553 to serve his *laurea dottorale.*

In a letter of 1576 to a brother, Aldrovandi writes of his description of Roman collections, referring to this *compendiosa historia, non lasciando alcuna statua, che . . . da me non fosse diligentemente delineata et descritta.* Though the catalog is not as complete as claimed, every significant collection of midcentury is included (if one uses the editions of 1558 or 1562, which correct a number of omissions in that of 1556); it embraces not only statues, torsos and fragments but also reliefs and some inscriptions, as well as minor antiquities in the studios of such connoisseurs as Cardinal *Carpi or Gerolomo *Garimberto. He frequently gives find spots, and his predisposition to logical order aids in recovering iconographic programs that often governed the installation of antique sculptures in *vigne* and statue gardens.

Even without the drawings that seem to have been planned originally, Aldrovandi's guide to ninety-odd private collections is uniquely valuable to archaeologists and art historians. The undersigned is presently preparing an annotated, illustrated edition of *Delle Statue.*

BIBLIOGRAPHY

A. Balducci et al., *Studi intorno alla vita e alle opere di Ulisse Aldrovandi* (Bologna, 1907); G. Montalenti, s.v. ''Aldrovandi, Ulisse,'' *DBI* 2 (1960), 118–24 (with error citing the date of the *Statue* as 1542); *Aldrovandi on Chickens: The Ornithology of Ulisse Aldrovandi (1600), Volume II, Book XIV,* tr. and ed. L. R. Lind (Norman, OK, 1963); A. Adversi, ''Nuovi appunti su Ulisse Aldrovandi bibliofilio, bibliotecario e bibliografo, e sua inedita *Bibliologia,*'' *La Bibliofilia: Rivista di storia del libro e di bibliografia,* ed. A. Ridolfi, 68 (1966), 51–90, with bib.

PHYLLIS PRAY BOBER

ALEANDRO, GIROLAMO (1574–1629). Italian cleric, poet, humanist and antiquarian.

In Rome Aleandro served as a clerical secretary for twenty years, first to Cardinal O. Bandini and then to Cardinal Francesco Barberini (cf. *Barberini family). Along with Cassiano dal *Pozzo from the Barberini household, he took a keen interest in scholarship on classical antiquities known or discovered in his time and kept up a lively correspondence with *Peiresc, *Rubens and other members of the international archaeological community. Through Peiresc, he was familiar with the *Calendar of 354 and numerous antique gems (e.g., the *Gemma Augustea, the *Gemma Tiberiana). He wrote a number of learned treatises, most of which went unpublished; an exception was his *Antiquae tabulae marmoreae Solis effigie symbolisque exculptae. . . explicatio* (Rome, 1616).

BIBLIOGRAPHY
R. S. Magurn, *The Letters of Peter Paul Rubens* (Cambridge, 1955), 450 and passim; A. Asor-Rosa, "Aleandro, Girolamo," *DBI* 2 (1960), 135–36.

ALESSANDRO DI MARIANO FILIPEPI. See BOTTICELLI, SANDRO.

ALEXANDER AND BUCEPHALUS. See QUIRINAL HORSE TAMERS.

ALEXANDER AZARA. Marble herm portraying Alexander the Great, a Roman copy made in the second century A.C., probably based on a Greek original of the fourth century B.C.

It may be derived from a portrait of *Alexander* by Lysippos, known from literary sources (cf. Pliny, *NH* 34.63; Plutarch, *On the Fortune or Virtue of Alexander* 2.2). The piece has played an important part in iconographic studies of Alexander the Great because it is inscribed in Greek with his name. The herm was discovered in 1779 in a Roman villa near *Tivoli by José Nicolás Azara, a Spanish diplomat, along with a group of herms from the same workshop, dating to the period of Hadrian or later. The herm owes part of its fame to the fact that it was later presented to *Napoleon by Azara. It is presently in the *Louvre (see also *Prado, Madrid).

BIBLIOGRAPHY
+Richter, *Portraits of the Greeks,* III, 255; A. Herrmann, in *The Search for Alexander, An Exhibition* (Boston, 1980), 99–100; R. R. R. Smith, *Hellenistic Royal Portraits* (Oxford, 1988), 62, 155; Ridgway, *Hellenistic Sculpture* I, 123.

ALEXANDER, DYING. Approximately lifesize marble head of Hellenistic style, showing a male with long locks, open mouth and head turned so that his eyes look up toward heaven.

The head is mounted on a modern bust. The piece may be identical with a head of Alexander the Great observed by *Aldrovandi in 1550 in the collection of Cardinal Rodolfo Pio da *Carpi in Rome. Certainly by 1579 it was in the collection of the *Medici in Florence. Soon afterward it went into the *Uffizi, where it remains today.

The identification of the individual as Alexander the Great may have been based on the observation of Plutarch (*Life of Alexander* 4.1; *On the Fortune or Virtue of Alexander* 2.2.) that Lysippos alone was able to capture the essential characteristics of Alexander—the leonine hair, the melting gaze and the head turned toward heaven. Aldrovandi declared that the head owned by Pio da Carpi showed Alexander on his deathbed, and this interpretation remained the most common one, though others suggested different moments in the life of Alexander when he expressed great pain. The sculpture was regarded as one of the most authoritative representations of Alexander and was frequently referred to as a diagnostic comparison for other proposed portraits of him. But in the nineteenth century, *Amelung identified the figure as a dying giant, copied from the Pergamene school (cf. *Great Altar, Pergamon), and this identification now prevails.

The Baroque pathos of the head obviously appealed to many artists, and the type, with head twisted, mouth open and anguished expression, recurs in many sculptures and paintings of the sixteenth and seventeenth centuries, for example, *St. Sebastian* by Sodoma (Uffizi, before 1531); the *Rape of the Sabines* by *Giambologna, set up in Florence by 1583; the *Milo of Crotona* by *Puget, in the Louvre; and the *Daniel* by *Bernini, in the Chigi Chapel, S.M. del Popolo, Rome.

BIBLIOGRAPHY
Bieber, 119–20; E. Schwarzenberg, "From the *Alessandro Morente* to the *Alexandre Richelieu*," *JWarb* 32 (1969), 398–405; Haskell—Penny, 134–36.

ALEXANDER MOSAIC. One of the largest (5.82m × 3.13m) and most significant examples of mosaic from the ancient world, representing Alexander the Great in battle against the Persian king Darius III.

Found in 1831 as the floor covering of a room in the House of the Faun at *Pompeii, it is usually considered to have been made around 100 B.C. as a copy or imitation of a lost monumental painting of Alexander in battle, created in the late fourth or early third century B.C. The original is frequently attributed to Philoxenos of Eretria, on the basis of a passage in Pliny saying that he painted a "Battle of Alexander against Darius."

Immediately after the discovery of the mosaic, a drawing was made of it by the German archaeologist W.J.K. Zahn (the drawing is now in Weimar, Goethe-National Museum). The drawing documents the state of the mosaic, which already had large areas that had been ruined in antiquity. Some areas had been filled in with plaster; others had been repaired with cubes or *tesserae* that are distinctly larger than the tiny ones used throughout the rest of the mosaic. (The *Alexander* Mosaic is done by the technique known as *opus vermiculatum*, featuring *tesserae* as small as one millimeter on a side.)

The drawing was sent by Zahn to *Goethe, who, at the age of eighty-two, took a great interest in the work. The house in which it was found was at that time widely nicknamed the "House of Goethe," in memory of the visit Goethe paid to it in 1787. Zahn noted that the subject of the mosaic was a battle of Alexander against Darius, and Goethe made several observations on the nature of the representation, comparing it with a *Battle of Constantine* (presumably the one by *Giulio Romano in the Vatican).

By the time of Heinrich *Brunn's *Geschichte der griechischen Kunstler* (1859), the mosaic was routinely linked with Philoxenos. Other scholars have noted that Aristeides did a *Battle with Persians* (Pliny, *NH* 35.99) and that Helen, daughter of Timon, did a *Battle of Issos.* From an early date there was discussion about which battle was represented. In Goethe's circle, Arbela was suggested; besides Arbela and Issos, Gaugamela and the battle of the Granikos River have been mentioned. Pollitt articulates a widespread sentiment that the battle is a generalized representation of Alexander and Darius, meant to transcend a particular time and place. C. Nylander (1977) focused debate on the question of who is the hero in the scene, since Darius is fleeing and Alexander is off to the left. A much-damaged figure of a Persian rider near the center of the scene, being killed by Alexander, was actually the most conspicuous figure and may provide a clue to understanding the scene.

The mosaic is today in the *Museo Nazionale at Naples.

BIBLIOGRAPHY

+A. Niccolini et al., "Musaico scoperto in Pompeii il 24 di ottobre 1831," *Real Museo Borbonico* 8 (1832), text to pl. 36–45; +B. Andreae, *Das Alexandermosaik aus Pompeii* (Recklinghausen, 1977); B. Ridgway, "Court Art and Hellenistic Art: The Role of Alexander the Great," *Archaeological News* 11 (1982), 43–44; Pollitt, *Art in the Hellenistic Age,* 45–46.

ALEXANDRIA. Harbor city on the Nile Delta in Egypt, founded by Alexander the Great in 332–331 B.C.

The city was laid out on a grand scale by the Macedonian architect Deinokrates and enriched with important public buildings throughout the period of the Ptolemies (323–30 B.C.). Among the most famous in antiquity were the library, which by the first century B.C. contained 700,000 items, and the Mouseion, a center of scholarly and artistic activity; both were placed in the royal quarter of the city, but the specific locations have not been discovered. The mausoleum containing the body of Alexander was located at the principal intersection of the city, placed there probably by Ptolemy I Soter, and the body was venerated for centuries. (Augustus visited it in 30 B.C. and is said to have knocked off Alexander's nose.) The building disappeared by the fourth century A.C. and has never been rediscovered.

After the death of Cleopatra, the last of the Ptolemies, the city was enlarged by Augustus and remained the principal center of Roman Egypt. By the late third century, local attempts at rebellion were repressed by wholesale destruction, first by Aurelian (A.D. 272) and then by Diocletian (A.D. 294–95). A monolithic granite column (height 26.85m) was erected in honor of Diocletian in A.D. 197 and is one of the rare monuments of ancient Alexandria that has remained visible to travelers through the centuries. *Ciriaco of Ancona saw it in the fifteenth century and noted its popular name, the "Pillar of Pompey," which he pronounced erroneous on the basis of the inscription on it (which, however, he read incorrectly as referring to Deinokrates rather than Diocletian).

Thorough devastation of the city was carried out in the reign of Theodosius (A.D. 379–95) when the Patriarch Theophilos, in his campaign to abolish paganism, ordered the destruction of all pagan buildings, shrines, statues and even books. In A.D. 641 the city fell into Arab hands.

The famous lighthouse of Alexandria, completed under Ptolemy II Philadelphos in 279 B.C. on the island of Pharos and regarded as one of the wonders of the world, has almost completely disappeared. (Fragments of Aswan granite thought to be from its court lie in the sea near the site.) Frequently damaged and restored during the Arab period, it was utterly destroyed by an earthquake in the fourteenth century. Its site is covered by a fort built in 1480 by the Mameluke Sultan Kait Bey.

L. F. S. *Fauvel visited Egypt in 1789 and 1792 and made a plan of the city at that time, as well as drawings of tombs and sculptures (some now traced to the Museo Archeologico in Venice). He climbed to the top of the Pillar of Pompey, leaving behind his signature on an iron plate. *Napoleon's expedition to Egypt (1799) was of considerable importance in the study of the antiquities of Alexandria. Among other things the Pillar of Pompey was finally correctly identified, and an officer of Napoleon unearthed the famous Rosetta Stone during the rebuilding of the Fort of St. Julien at Rashid (Rosetta), some 60km east of Alexandria.

Throughout the nineteenth and twentieth centuries, necropoleis have come to light in many parts of the city—at Kom-el-Shugafa, Moustapha Pasha, Hadara and Anfushy—containing paintings, sculpture and vases. In 1960, the excavation of tombs in the Wardian quarter yielded a painted tomb of the Roman period with a representation of oxen at a water wheel; the pastoral subject and impressionistic style were immediately linked with long-standing arguments that there existed a particular "Alexandrian style" in painting.

The leading scholar on ancient Alexandria in modern times was Achille Adriani (1905–82), whose long years of work in Egypt were especially devoted to the Graeco-Roman Museum of Alexandria, where many of the finds from the city are housed.

BIBLIOGRAPHY
E. M. Forster, *Alexandria, A History and a Guide* (London, 1922; reissued 1961); J. Marlowe, *The Golden Age of Alexandria* (London, 1971); S. Shenouda, s.v. "Alexandria," *PECS*, 36–38; N. Bonacas—A. Di Vita, eds., *Alessandria e il mondo ellenistico-romano, Studi in onore di Achille Adriani, Studi e materiali, Istituto di Archeologia, Università di Palermo* 4–6 (Rome, 1983–84); +G. Steen, ed., *Alexandria, the Site and the History* (New York, 1993).

ALFÖLDI, ANDREAS (ANDREW; 1895–1981). Hungarian archaeologist, historian, numismatist, epigrapher.

Andreas Alföldi was born near Budapest, in a village close to the Roman site of *Aquincum. As a boy he was already fascinated by the Roman ruins and objects (especially coins) discovered in the area. In 1913 he became an assistant at the Museum of Aquincum, a post he held while enrolled at the University of Budapest. His work was interrupted by World War I, in which he served as an infantryman. Wounded early and sent to the hospital to recover from an infected ankle, he quietly continued his studies, receiving his doctorate at Budapest in 1918.

In the following thirty years, Alföldi held a number of positions of distinction in Hungary: assistant at the Hungarian National Museum, Budapest (1918–23); professor of ancient history at Debrecen (1923–30); chair of ancient history and chair of archaeology of the Hungarian territories, at Budapest (1930–47). The political situation made these years difficult, and finally Alföldi was able to leave Hungary, along with his family and some of his books. He was professor successively at Bern, Basel and, finally, Princeton, where he arrived in 1955 and remained until his death. He was a member of numerous learned societies and academies (*Society of Antiquaries, Institut de France, *Pontificia Accademia Romana di Archeologia, *Accademia dei Lincei, Swedish, Danish, Hungarian, Bulgarian academies) and received several honorary degrees (Utrecht, Ghent, Bonn, Paris).

Alföldi's publications spanned sixty-seven years and numbered over 300 items (including some two dozen books). They manifest an amazing variety of topics: the archaeology and history of the ancient province of Pannonia; late Roman civilization; Roman history, ritual, clothing, numismatics, epigraphy. Many have become classics in their sphere; in German, there are two key works on Roman ceremony and dress: *Die Ausgestaltung des monarchischen Zeremoniells am römischen Kaiserhofe* (1934) and *Insignien und Tracht der römischen Kaiser* (1935); in English, there are *The Conversion of Constantine and Pagan Rome* (1948) and *Early Rome and the Latins* (1965; given originally as the Jerome Lectures at Ann Arbor).

At his death he was working on a study on Julius Caesar (a volume on the coinage had appeared in 1974). His wife, Elisabeth Alföldi-Rosenbaum, herself an expert on Roman portraiture, arranged for the publication of Alföldi's remaining writings on Caesar, before her own death in 1992.

BIBLIOGRAPHY

J. F. Gilliam, "Andrew Alföldi," *AJA* 85 (1981), 514–15; G. Alföldy, "Andreas Alföldi," *Gnomon* 53 (1981), 410–14; A. Alföldi, *Caesariana: gesamellte Aufsätze zur Geschichte Caesars und seiner Zeit,* ed. E. Alföldi-Rosenbaum (Bonn, 1984).

ALGARDI, ALESSANDRO (1598–1654). Italian sculptor and restorer of ancient sculpture.

Born in Bologna, Algardi departed at the age of about twenty for Mantua, there to work for Duke Ferdinando Gonzaga. He was assigned various tasks in the ducal collection of gems, cameos, medals, bronzes and marbles, including the fitting of handles and a foot on an antique cameo vase carved with a *Sacrifice* *of Isis.* *Bellori reports the amusing story that while displaying the precious vase, Algardi dropped it but was able to recover immediately and catch it before it dashed upon the floor. During this period the artist may have obtained experience in the restoration of ancient marbles, an area in which he demonstrated great competence later in Rome.

In 1625 Algardi arrived in Rome and remained there the rest of his life. He is said to have gone in the company of *Poussin to copy the *Belvedere *"Antinous"* and no doubt had countless opportunities to study ancient marbles. Hired by Cardinal Ludovico Ludovisi (*Ludovisi family) to do restorations in his collection of ancient sculptures, Algardi's first effort (1626) was an imaginative statue of a *Torchbearer,* for which he created a new head and limbs to add to an ancient torso; he also did minor restorations on the Ludovisi *Minerva* and *Mercury.* (The Ludovisi marbles are today in the collections of the Museo Nazionale delle *Terme, Rome.) In 1628, Algardi repaired a *Seasons* Sarcophagus of Antonine date that had been in the Palazzo dei Conservatori since 1509, adding the heads of a panther, a lion and seahorses, as well as parts of the figures. For Camillo Pamphili he also restored many antiquities, of which the only recorded specimen is a *Faun* or *Infant Bacchus* made of *rosso antico* marble (1645), now in the Palazzo Doria-Pamphili. A rather unusual "restoration" was made with a Roman cuirassed torso of the first century A.C., for which *Bernini carved a portrait head and Algardi produced arms, legs and drapery, to create a memorial portrait of Carlo Barberini (1630; now Palazzo dei Conservatori).

Many of Algardi's original sculptures display his knowledge of antiquity in their themes, compositions and selected motifs. His image of the child *Sleep* in black marble (1635–36; Rome, Borghese Gallery) recalls numerous Roman Cupids and features the traditional gesture of antique sleeping figures with one arm raised back over the head. His most archaeological production is to be seen in the stucco reliefs of the Villa Pamphili, Rome (1645–46), designed by Algardi after careful study of ancient stuccos at *Hadrian's Villa at Tivoli. The rich array of antique themes, selected by the Pamphili to celebrate their ancestry, may be seen in the Gallery of Hercules and the Gallery of Roman Customs; in the latter, the *Battle of Romans and Dacians* closely imitates the Trajanic battle reliefs on the *Arch of Constantine, while medallions of *A Triumph of an Emperor* and other themes show study of Roman coins.

BIBLIOGRAPHY

O. Raggio, "Alessandro Algardi e gli stucchi di Villa Pamphili," *Paragone* 251 (1971), 3–38; +B. Palma, *Museo Nazionale Romana, Le Sculture* 1,4, *I Marmi Ludovisi, Storia della Collezione* (Rome, 1983); +J. Montagu, *Alessandro Algardi* 1–2 (New Haven, CT, 1985).

ALMA-TADEMA, SIR LAWRENCE (1836–1912). Popular Victorian painter of sentimental classical subjects, member of the British Royal Academy (1879) and subscriber of the *British School at Athens.

Born at Donrijp in Friesland, Alma-Tadema became a naturalized British citizen in 1873, when he Anglicized his Christian name (Laurens). He resided in a London house decorated with reproductions of classical art, architecture and furniture. An immensely successful and wealthy man, he was knighted by Queen Victoria (1899), was appointed to the Order of Merit by King Edward VII (1905) and was given the Gold Medal by the Royal Institute of British Architects for his promotion of architecture through painting (1906).

Alma-Tadema was known for his convincing representation of marble and for his archaeological accuracy, realized through his travels to classical sites and his study of the monuments. He also possessed a substantial library of works on classical archaeology and 167 massive albums of drawings, prints and photographs of antiquities, now in the Birmingham University Library. Also at Birmingham, in the City Art Gallery, is his painting *Pheidias and the Parthenon* (1868), which is a good example of the artist's concern for archaeological accuracy. The painting shows the northwest corner of the *Parthenon frieze carefully copied from the actual sculpture and rendered in all its polychromatic glory.

BIBLIOGRAPHY
V. G. Swanson, *Alma-Tadema: The Painter of the Victorian Vision of the Ancient World* (New York, 1977); R. A. Tomlinson, "The Acropolis of Athens in the 1870's: The Evidence of the Alma-Tadema Photographs," *BSA* 82 (1987), 297–304; Idem, "A Photograph of Olympia in the Alma-Tadema Collection," *BSA* 84 (1989), 353–54; R. Ash, *Sir Lawrence Alma-Tadema* (New York, 1990).

ANN M. NICGORSKI

AL MINA. Trading center at the mouth of the Orontes River in Syria.

Sir Leonard Woolley, searching for the port of entry connecting the Minoan-Mycenaean Aegean with western Asia, deduced it would have to be on the north Syrian coast, situated where there would be good anchorage and easy access to the interior. He selected (1936) a coastal location at the mouth of the Orontes (called locally Tal Shiekh Yusuf) and excavated ten levels to hardpan.

Al Mina proved to be a major trading center manned by Greeks from Euboia and Cypriots, with a ceramic sequence extending from the last quarter of the ninth century B.C. (Level X) to 375–320 B.C. (Level II). From the latest period were discovered significant remains of warehouses and shops. It is possible that the earliest occupation, of which little more remained than the floors of some huts, may have been earlier, but no Bronze Age Mycenaean material was recovered. However, Woolley had discovered a significant commercial entrepôt that served as the gateway for Iron Age interchange between Greece and Syro-Hittite and Assyrian Asia. He suggested that Al Mina probably was the Posideion that Amphilochos was said to have founded.

The finds are today in the Antakya Museum, the *British Museum and other museums in Britain.

BIBLIOGRAPHY
C. L. Woolley, "Excavations at Al Mina (Sueidia), I, II," *JHS* 58 (1938), 1–30, 133–70; J. D. Beazley, "The Excavations at Al Mina, Sueidia, III," *JHS* 59 (1939), 1–44; S.

Smith, "The Greek Trade at Al Mina," *AJ* 22 (1942), 87–112; J. Boardman, *The Greeks Overseas,* 2nd ed. (London, 1980), 38–54.

BERNARD GOLDMAN

"ALTAR OF DOMITIUS AHENOBARBUS," Rome. A group of Roman reliefs, commonly referred to as belonging to the Altar of Domitius Ahenobarbus; but these reliefs are not necessarily from an altar, nor are they properly associated with any member of the Domitii.

Three panels depict a Roman Republican religious ceremony; nine other panels depict a mythological marine procession and are carved in a different, Hellenistic style.

During the excavation for the foundation of the church of S. Salvatore in the southernmost part of the *Campus Martius, the architect F. Peparelli found and extracted 110 pieces of marble. In the bill for these operations (dated 12 June 1639), nos. 72–74 and 91–92 are listed as missing. Meanwhile, a marble relief in three pieces had been installed in the cortile of the new Palazzo Santa Croce, diagonally across from the church. By 9 February 1639, another relief, consisting of nine pieces, was installed there. Although the number of sculptures in Palazzo Santa Croce does not correspond precisely with the missing pieces in the inventory, it is generally assumed that the sculptures came from under S. Salvatore. The reliefs remained in the Palazzo until 1811, when they were bought by Napoleon's uncle, Cardinal Fesch, for 1,500 scudi. Fesch was forced to sell them in 1816 following the Hundred Days War. The longer frieze was purchased by Leo von *Klenze for the new Munich *Glyptothek. Eight years later the shorter frieze went to the *Louvre.

*Furtwängler was the first modern scholar to recognize the connection between the Munich and Paris reliefs. He suggested that they came from the ancient building, a temple, excavated beneath the church of S. Salvatore in 1837. Recent scholarship has concentrated on identifying that temple and the sacrificing official in the Paris relief, in order to secure the date of these early examples of Roman historical relief sculpture. The theory that the building was the temple of Neptune vowed by Gnaeus Domitius Ahenobarbus, ca. 42 B.C., gave rise to the now-discarded identification of the reliefs as part of the "Altar of Domitius Ahenobarbus." Another suggestion, made recently, connects the monument with the naval victories in the Greek east of Mark Antony, grandfather of the more famous general and orator (A. Kuttner).

BIBLIOGRAPHY

+H. Kähler, *Seethiasos und Census: die Reliefs aus dem Palazzo Santa Croce in Rom* (Berlin, 1966); +F. Coarelli, "L'Ara di Domizio Enobarbo," *DialAr* 2 (1968), 302–68; T. P. Wiseman, "Legendary Genealogies in Late Republican Rome," *Greece and Rome* 21 (1974), 153–64; A. Kuttner, "Some New Grounds for Narrative: Marcus Antonius's Base (The *Ara Domitii Ahenobarbi*) and Republican Biographies," in P. Holliday, *Narrative and Event in Ancient Art* (New York, 1993), 198–229; +Kleiner, *Roman Sculpture,* 49–51.

PETER HOLLIDAY

Photograph of *Walther Amelung*. (Deutsches Archäologisches Institut, Rome, Inst. Neg. 92.955.)

AMELUNG, WALTHER OSKAR ERNST (1865–1927). German archaeologist and art historian; served 1921–27 as first secretary of the *German Archaeological Institute at Rome.

Born in Stettin (Szezecin), son of a wealthy insurance executive and an actress of French descent, Amelung studied at Tübingen under *Rohde and at Leipzig, briefly under *Overbeck; and in Munich he found his teacher, Heinrich *Brunn, who directed his dissertation (1888) on the personification of nature in Hellenistic vase painting. After an interval of professional acting, he returned to scholarship. A wealthy bachelor, he traveled widely in classical lands with Paul *Arndt and others. He decided in 1895 to reside permanently in Rome and catalog the *Vatican collections of ancient sculpture. Two volumes containing over 1,900 pieces appeared (1903, 1908). He lived as a private scholar in Rome until 1915, leading tours, writing authoritative guides, and translating Sophokles's "Theban Trilogy," adding a tragedy on Laios's rape of Chrysippos. His *Antigone* was successfully produced at Berlin in 1921. He wrote numerous articles on Greek clothing for the *Realencyclopädie*. During his unhappy exile in Berlin (1915–21), he restored the museum's cast collection for F. Noack and adopted a young Hamburg businessman, in whose arms he would die.

During World War I, the Italian government expropriated the German embassy and archaeological institute. Only by the intervention of Benedetto Croce was the great library saved. In 1921 the institute appointed Amelung as first secretary to restore it from its ruins. The amiable, tactful scholar proved a brilliant choice. On 30 October 1924 the new library opened in Via Sardegna. Only the French boycotted the reception.

*Wilamowitz saw in Amelung's restriction to sculpture the start of decline in contrast to the wide expertise of C. *Robert or *Furtwängler. Amelung sought the individual in sculpture with no interest in the questions of suprapersonal development of form in the sense of *Riegl or Wölfflin. Art remained the manifestation of lofty thoughts in a creative personality; art history was a logical, unbroken chain of individual efforts.

BIBLIOGRAPHY

H. Bulle, *BiogJahr* 228 (1930), 69–100, with bib.; L. Curtius, *Deutsche und Antike Welt* (Stuttgart, 1950), 172; H. Diepolder, "Amelung, Walther Oskar Ernst," *NDB* 1 (Berlin, 1953), 245–46; L. Wickert, "Beiträge zur Geschichte des Deutchen Archäologischen Instituts 1879 bis 1929," *Das Deutsche Archäologische Institut: Geschichte und Dokumente* 2 (Mainz, 1979), 163; R. Lullies, in *Archäologenbildnisse*, 160–61.

WILLIAM M. CALDER III

AMERICAN ACADEMY IN ROME. Center in Rome for American scholars and artists, especially for the study of the city of Rome itself and of the classical tradition.

The academy is a privately funded institute, chartered by an act of Congress of the United States, situated on the Janiculum Hill. With its School of Classical Studies and its School of Fine Arts, it provides facilities for research and creative work for students of the ancient Greek and Roman world, including philologists, historians, archaeologists, art historians and other students of medieval, Renaissance, Baroque and modern Italy, as well as sculptors, musicians and writers of poetry and prose.

Charles Follen McKim (1847–1909), inspired by the cooperation of artists at the Chicago World's Fair (World's Columbia Exposition) of 1893, devoted himself to founding an academy for artists and architects in Rome, modeled on the great *French Academy in the Villa Medici, with a curriculum to be based on the copying of classical models, the so-called atelier system of study. By 1894, the American School of Architecture in Rome had been founded, and rooms were rented in the Palazzo Torlonia on Via Condotti. In 1895 the Villa Aurora on the Pincio was rented, near the French Academy. In the same year the American School of Classical Studies in Rome was opened, through the initiative of the *Archaeological Institute of America. The classical group, directed by William Gardner Hale of Chicago, also resided for a while in the Villa Aurora but then moved to other quarters, and the two schools were not to be reunited until 1909.

The School of Architecture changed its name to the American Academy in Rome, and in 1905 the U.S. Congress incorporated the academy as a national institution, in spite of the opposition of House Speaker Joe Cannon. In 1909 the academy received the Villa Aurelia on the Janiculum, a bequest of Clara Jessup Heyland of Philadelphia, and soon, due to the enthusiastic support of J. P. Morgan, it was possible to purchase much surrounding land, which the academy still owns, and a number of houses and villas. The present main academy building was constructed in the 1910s by the firm of McKim Mead and White under the supervision of *Stevens, one of their former architects, who was director of the architecture students at the new academy.

In 1912, the two schools were officially merged, and in 1914 the American Academy opened the doors of the new building on the Janiculum. A new director, Jesse Benedict Carter, reigned. A classicist, dynamic and abrasive, a brilliant speaker and a figure of Roman society who entranced J. P. Morgan and irritated the architects by his aggressiveness and excessive spending, Carter dominated the early years of the joint academy. He died of sunstroke in 1918, working for the Italian war effort, and was succeeded by the cautious and conservative architect Gorham P. Stevens.

The academy continued to grow and be a center for society. Painters, sculptors and musicians added to the atmosphere. Women had been a part of the classical school from the beginning, although the new building was, in fact, not planned to accommodate them, and it was not until the 1940s that women were fully included in residential life at the academy.

In 1914 Thomas Spencer Jerome died, bequeathing one-third of his library to the academy as well as a sum of $45,000 to establish a lectureship in his name. (The Jerome Lectures are delivered both at the academy in Rome and at the University of Michigan at Ann Arbor.) The classicists dominated during the 1920s. Tenney Frank did his seminal work on the quarries that supplied the stone for Rome's major buildings, still an indispensable aid for dating the development of the ancient city. In the 1930s, young artists and musicians of distinction (e.g., Elliott Carter) began to appear at the academy again. The summer school began in 1923 and within twenty years, under the direction of Henry Rowell, became a secure part of the academy's contribution to a wider knowledge of the ancient world, providing enrichment for teachers and graduate students.

Slowed by World War II, the American Academy rebounded, and the classical school undertook excavation of the Roman Republican colony at *Cosa in 1948. The early publications, under the direction of Frank *Brown and including major publications in the *Memoirs of the American Academy,* by Emeline Hill Richardson and L. Richardson jr, brought attention to the academy. Excavation at Cosa has recently been resumed (Elizabeth Fentress is investigating a medieval component), and publication continues, with a new volume on houses at the site by Vincent Bruno and Russell Scott (1993), and another on lamps by Cleo Fitch and Norma Goldman. The site of Cosa, with a fine museum, was donated in 1981 to Italy.

Brown also excavated in the Regia, in the *Forum Romanum, and in recent years the academy has been active in the Forum again (R. Scott in the Atrium Vestae) and on the slope of the Palatine (E. Hostetter). A summer program in archaeology, begun in 1992, introduces graduate students to sites, theory, method and actual fieldwork.

BIBLIOGRAPHY

L. Valentine—A. Valentine, *The American Academy in Rome, 1894–1969* (Charlottesville, VA, 1973); F. Yegül, *Gentlemen of Instinct and Breeding, Architecture at the American Academy in Rome, 1894–1969* (New York, 1991).

E. C. KOPFF

AMERICAN NUMISMATIC SOCIETY. America's leading organization for the study of numismatics, especially of the ancient classical civilizations.

The American Numismatic Society was founded as the American Numismatic and Archaeological Society by a group of New York collectors in 1858. It was incorporated in 1865 but lacked a permanent home until 1908, when it moved to its present quarters in uptown Manhattan; its academic orientation was enhanced by the membership and later presidency (1916–41) of E. T. *Newell.

The society's purpose is the dissemination of knowledge of coins and medals, and it maintains a collection, library and exhibition to serve its 2,200 members and the public. Its collection of 1 million items is one of the world's largest, with particular strengths in classical and Islamic coins; its library is definitive in the field. The society published the first of 162 *Numismatic Notes and Monographs* in 1921. Its publications also include *Numismatic Studies,* of which seventeen have appeared; *Museum Notes,* first an irregular and now an annual journal, begun in 1946; *Numismatic Literature,* a semiannual abstract bibliography; and *Ancient Coins in North American Collections,* covering small public and private collections. The society also participates in the international *Sylloge Nummorum Graecorum.*

Nearly 400 people have completed the Graduate Seminar in Numismatics, held annually since 1952. The society also supports dissertation research with an annual fellowship.

BIBLIOGRAPHY

H. L. Adelson, *The American Numismatic Society 1858–1958* (New York, 1958).

WILLIAM E. METCALF

AMERICAN SCHOOL OF CLASSICAL STUDIES AT ATHENS. Center in Greece for American research on the archaeology, history and literature of ancient Greece.

The American School of Classical Studies at Athens (ASCSA) was founded in 1882 as the brainchild of Charles Eliot *Norton, also the founder of the *Archaeological Institute of America, who considered that the proper place to study the monuments and culture of the ancient Greeks was in Greece itself. Seven students and a director spent the first year of study in rented quarters opposite the *Arch of Hadrian on Amalias Street in a situation that served the school until a permanent structure could be secured. In 1884 the Greek government offered to donate to the school a sizable tract of land on the south slope of Mt. Lykabettos, which was adjacent to the site already presented to the *British School of Archaeology. Construction was delayed until 1887 because of lack of funds, but in April 1888 the school moved into its permanent home on Souidias Street.

The school has functioned continuously as the American archaeological research institution in Greece, with only two interruptions. From 1918 to 1920, it served as the headquarters of the American Red Cross Commission to Greece. During World War II the property of the school was transferred to the control of the Swiss and Swedish Red Cross commissions.

The research capabilities of the ASCSA were significantly enhanced in 1922 with the donation by the distinguished Greek diplomat Joannes *Gennadius of his magnificent library, which focused on the whole range of Greek history from ancient to modern times. The gift was made, as Gennadius stated in his bequest, in "confident hope that the American School in Athens may thus become a world center for the study of Greek history, literature and art, both ancient, Byzantine and modern." Through generous funding by the Carnegie Foundation, a neoclassical marble structure called the Gennadeion was constructed to house the collection and was dedicated in 1926.

From its beginning, the ASCSA was involved in archaeological investigation. The first excavation conducted by the school, directed by Walter Miller, a student, was in the theater at the Attic site of Thorikos in 1886. The theaters of *Sikyon (1887–92) and *Eretria (1891–95) were also among the early archaeological missions of the school. The first major excavation of a classical site was at the *Argive Heraion, directed by Charles *Waldstein from 1892 to 1895. The publication of the site, the school's first major excavation report, appeared in two volumes between 1902 and 1905.

The most prominent excavations conducted by the school are at *Corinth and the *Agora in Athens. The excavation of Corinth began in 1896 and marked the first archaeological investigation of a large Greek city. Exploration of the city continues to the present day, serving as the teaching excavation for the students of the School. In 1925 the ASCSA was given permission to conduct excavations in the area of Athens where the ancient agora was believed to lie. Excavation began in 1931, funded in large part by John D. Rockefeller, Jr., and directed by T. Leslie *Shear, Sr. This excavation, which continues to the present day, has provided scholars and lay people alike a wealth of information concerning the political and commercial center of ancient Athens.

Some of the other major sites excavated under the auspices of the ASCSA from 1900 to the present include Halai (1911–23), Korakou (1915–16), Eutresis (1924–27, 1958), Prosymna (1925–28), *Olynthos (1928–38), Athenian *Pnyx (1931–37), *Samothrace (1938–present), *Pylos (1939, 1952–67), *Lerna (1952–57), *Isthmia (1952–62, 1967–78, 1989–present), *Keos (1960–68), Halieis (1962, 1965–79), Franchthi Cave (1967–76), *Messenia (1962–68), *Nemea (1964, 1974–86), *Kommos (1976–present) and Kavousi (1899, 1987–present).

BIBLIOGRAPHY
L. E. Lord, *History of the American School of Classical Studies at Athens, 1882–1942* (Cambridge, MA, 1947); L. S. Meritt, *History of the American School of Classical Studies at Athens, 1939–1980* (Princeton, NJ, 1984).

MICHAEL HOFF

AMNISOS (KARTEROS). Bronze Age Minoan site, located 7km east of Herakleion near the ancient Amnisos (now Karteros) River; harbor town for *Knossos and location of the cave of the birth goddess Eileithyia.

The cult cave of Eileithyia, mentioned by Homer as visited by Odysseus (*Odyssey* 19.188), was identified in 1888 by J. Hazzidakis and excavated in 1929–30 by S. *Marinatos. It was found to contain stalagmites—manifestations of the Cretan pillar/tree cult—and a simple altar, with pottery belonging to the Late Minoan (LM) III period and later.

On the sea, an important villa of the LM IA period was excavated by Marinatos in 1932. The two-story building is famous for its frescoes representing formal gardens with white lilies and red irises, thought to have religious connections. The house featured massive outer walls of dressed ashlar masonry. Next to the site is an open-air early Greek sanctuary with numerous votive offerings and inscriptions dedicated to Zeus Thenatas.

BIBLIOGRAPHY
D. J. Blackman, s.v. "Karteros," *PECS,* 437–38; J. W. Graham, *The Palaces of Crete,* rev. ed. (Princeton, NJ, 1987), 68–69; J. Schäfer et al., *Amnisos* 1–2 (Berlin, 1992).

COSTIS DAVARAS

AMPURIAS. See EMPORION.

ANATOLIA. The area known as Asia Minor in classical antiquity; modern-day Turkey.

The methodical investigation of classical remains in Asia Minor began with travelers for the *Society of Dilettanti in the mid-eighteenth century, who published records of their journeys (*Antiquities of Ionia*, 1769–1840). Early travelers and scholars were guided principally by the descriptions of sites and regions preserved in Greek and Roman authors. By the early nineteenth century, attention was increasingly directed east and south of coastal Asia Minor. The Frenchman Charles *Texier traveled extensively (1833–37) and published descriptions and drawings of sites and monuments. Lycia and Caria were areas of early interest. In 1838–40 and 1843–44 Charles *Fellows investigated several sites in Lycia, in particular, *Xanthos, and acquired for the *British Museum a number of its monuments, including the Nereid Monument and the Harpy Tomb. The British Museum also acquired sculptures from the site of the *Mausoleum at Halikarnassos and from *Knidos and *Didyma through the work of C. T. *Newton (1846, 1856–58).

The period from ca. 1870 to 1914 saw the beginning of systematic excavations at several major sites, including *Ephesos (British, 1845, 1869–74, 1904–5; Austrian, from 1898), *Miletos and Didyma (French, 1872–73; German, from 1899) and *Pergamon (German, from 1878). While interest centered on the great cities of Ionia and Mysia with their extensive Hellenistic and Roman remains, earlier Greek and native Anatolian cultures were not neglected. *Assos in Aeolis was studied by an American expedition, 1881–83. The sculptures from *Trysa (Gölbaşi) in Lycia were acquired for Vienna. By this time considerable quantities of sculpture and architectural fragments from sites in Asia Minor had reached European and American museums, a transfer enlarged by the addition of the *Great Altar of Pergamon to the Berlin Museum in 1882.

This period saw, as well, the first research into preclassical cultures, initially a classical undertaking. Between 1871 and 1890 H. *Schliemann endeavored to locate and then excavate Homer's *Troy at Hissarlık in northwestern Asia Minor, revealing an important prehistoric sequence beneath remains of Greek and Roman date.

Few investigations of classical antiquity resumed until after World War II. By that time the Turkish Historical Society had firmly established the importance of prehistoric and early historic cultures in Anatolia (including Alaca Hüyük, from 1935; Pazarlı, 1937). The American expedition to Alişar Hüyük also recovered Phrygian remains during a principally Bronze Age investigation (1927–32). This period saw, as well, the reexcavation of Troy (1932–38) by an American team interested primarily in the Bronze Age levels.

In the decades since World War II systematic excavations at several of the classical and Roman cities of western Asia Minor, including Ephesos, Miletos and Didyma, *Priene and Pergamon, have resumed and are still in progress. New emphases include further elucidation of the Archaic period and the relationships between the east Greek settlements and native Anatolian cultures (British and Turkish excavations at Old *Smyrna, 1948–51, Turkish from 1966). Expeditions have returned to, or commenced in, such regions of early exploration as Lycia (Xanthos, *Letoon, *Elmalı), Caria (*Aphrodisias, Hierapolis, Halikarnassos, Knidos) and Lydia (*Sardis). They have been concerned with investigating preclassical occupation and have revealed significant evidence of Bronze Age habitation, in particular, Minoan and Mycenaean settlements and cemeteries. *Gordion, the capital of Phrygia, was extensively excavated by an American team from 1950 to 1973, continuing an initial exploration in 1900 by an Austrian expedition. In southern Anatolia the Hellenistic and Roman cities of Pamphylia have been the focus of Turkish campaigns, still in progress (*Perge, *Side, from 1946 to 1947). Cilicia is better known from lengthy excavations at Tarsus (American, 1934–39, 1947–48) and Anemurium (Canadian, from 1965). To the east and southeast, Hellenistic and Roman occupation in the areas of Cappadocia and Commagene has also been a major focus of recent field research.

BIBLIOGRAPHY

Michaelis, esp. 166–204; M. J. Mellink, "Anatolia: Old and New Perspectives," *Proceedings of the American Philosophical Society* 110 (1966), 111–29; +H. Metzger, "Perspectives nouvelles dans le domaine de l'archéologie classique en Asie Mineure," *RA* (1967), 344–61; +M. J. Mellink, "Archaeology in Asia Minor," annual reports in *AJA* 59–97 (1955–93; titled "Archaeology in Anatolia" from 1985).

ANN C. GUNTER

ANDREA DA PONTADERA. See PISANO, ANDREA.

ANDREA DE VICENTIA. See MANTEGNA, ANDREA.

ANDRONIKOS, MANOLIS (1919–92). Greek archaeologist, leading figure in the discovery of the antiquities of Macedonia.

Born at Prousa (modern Bursa), Manolis Andronikos moved with his family in 1922 to Thessaloniki, the city that would remain the center of his personal and professional life. In 1936 he joined the team excavating under K. A. Rhomaios at the Hellenistic Palace at *Vergina. During World War II, Andronikos fled Greece and served in the Free Greek forces in the Middle East, eventually returning to Thessaloniki to join the Archaeological Service. Having received his doctorate in 1952, he proceeded to Oxford for two years to study with J. D. *Beazley, returning to a lectureship at the University of Thessaloniki in 1957. There he achieved the rank of full professor in 1964.

Andronikos excavated at a number of sites in Macedonia and Chalkidike but is best known for his spectacular discovery of an unplundered Macedonian tomb at Vergina in 1977. Identifying it as the *"Tomb of Philip II," king of Macedon and father of Alexander the Great, he dated it to the third quarter of the fourth century B.C. His controversial claims, accepted by some, disputed by others, were presented by Andronikos in comprehensive final form in *Vergina: The Royal Tombs and the City* (Athens, 1987).

BIBLIOGRAPHY
E. Borza, "Manolis Andronikos, 1919–1992," *AJA* 96 (1992), 757–58.

ANKARA, MUSEUM OF ANATOLIAN CIVILIZATIONS. Collection of Anatolian antiquities.

The museum is located on the citadel in Ankara and housed in the Kurşunlu Han and Mahmut Paşa Bedesten (covered bazaar) built between 1464 and 1471 by Mahmut Paşa, grand vizier to Mehmed the Conqueror. It was designed to hold antiquities recovered from the excavations of native Anatolian cultures undertaken by the Turkish Historical Society beginning in the 1930s. The collection consists principally of excavated finds from sites in central Turkey, representing occupation from the Palaeolithic through Greek and Roman periods. It includes outstanding works of art from Neolithic Çatal Hüyük and Chalcolithic Hacılar, Early Bronze Age Alaca Hüyük and Middle Bronze Age Kültepe. Also displayed are sculptures and small finds from the Hittite capital, Boğazköy-Hattuša, and objects from the Phrygian capital, *Gordion. The central gallery contains relief sculptures from Hittite Alaca Hüyük and the Neo-Hittite sites of Malatya, Zincirli, Carchemish and Sakçegözü, installed in their original architectural arrangement. Objects from Urartian sites of eastern Turkey are also represented.

BIBLIOGRAPHY
+H. G. Güterbock, *Guide to the Hittite Museum in the Bedesten at Ankara* (Istanbul, 1946); +R. Temizer, *Museum of Anatolian Civilizations* (Ankara, 1981).
ANN C. GUNTER

ANNIO DA VITERBO (ANNIUS OF VITERBO; GIOVANNI NANNI; 1432?–1502). Dominican friar; Italian scholar and antiquarian specializing in Etruscan and early Roman studies.

Annio was born at *Viterbo and entered the Dominican convent there early in his life. He studied in Florence, pursuing the laureate in theology, and subsequently held teaching and administrative positions in Viterbo and Genoa and at the Vatican in which he was able to display his erudition in theology, philosophy, astrology, grammar and antiquarian studies.

His magnum opus, the *Antiquitates,* was printed at Rome in 1498 with the privilege from Annio's protector, Pope Alexander VI (Borgia). Almost from the beginning his extravagant scholarship was condemned as false by many reputable scholars. He claimed to have discovered ancient texts and inscriptions that were, in fact, his own fabrications, such as a Latin tract "by Fabius Pictor" on the history of early Rome, published complete with a fanciful map of the Archaic city. Annio contrived gibberish inscriptions that he claimed to be Etruscan, publishing them with confident translations into Latin. Most outrageous of all were his works on the history of his native city Viterbo, which he identified as a cradle of civilization founded by Osiris. His motives were partly political; flattery was directed, for example, toward the *Farnese at Viterbo, when Annio reported that the family was brought to Tuscany by the Etruscan founder-figure Tyrrhenus.

His campaign to glorify Viterbo had already begun in 1493, when Alexander VI and his court were staying there. Annio arranged for an excavation to take place at the locality of Cipollara before the very eyes of the court; naturally, the results were exciting. As sculptures of "Cybele," "Electra" and others were disinterred, Annio was able to begin "reading" the inscriptions and lecturing on the spot. The sculptures were actually Etruscan sarcophagi; these were subsequently displayed in the Palazzo dei Priori in Viterbo but are now lost.

His success with Alexander VI may be gauged by the fact that he was evidently consulted for themes for paintings by Pintoricchio—showing Isis, Osiris and Apis—in the decoration of the Borgia apartments in the Vatican. His ideas on the history of Viterbo were also taken up in his hometown in the council hall of the Palazzo Comunale, where Annio himself was portrayed, along with Hercules, Tyrrhenus and other illustrious citizens of Viterbo.

Not all members of the Borgia family favored Annio da Viterbo. In 1502 he died of a poison supplied by Cesare Borgia.

BIBLIOGRAPHY

R. Weiss, "Traccia per una biografia di Annio da Viterbo," *Italia Medioevale e Umanistica* 5 (1962), 425–41; Weiss, *RDCA,* passim; G. Baffioni—P. Mattiangeli, *Annio da Viterbo, Documenti e ricerche* (Rome, 1981); A. Emiliozzi, *Museo Civico di Viterbo: Per una storia delle raccolte archeologiche comunali* (Viterbo, 1985).

ANONIMO MAGLIABECHIANO. See ANONYMUS MALIABECHIANUS.

"ANONIMO MORELLIANO." See MICHIEL, MARCANTONIO.

ANONYMOUS EINSIDLENSIS. See EINSIEDELN ITINERARY.

ANONYMUS MALIABECHIANUS (ANONIMO MAGLIABECHIANO). Treatise on the topography of Rome written in the early fifteenth century.

The author is unknown and thus is referred to as *Anonymus* and is called *Maliabechianus* after the provenience of one of the manuscripts of the treatise in the Biblioteca Nazionale in Florence. (There are two other manuscripts of the work, in the Vatican Library and in the Marciana Library in Venice.) The title of the work, as given in the Vatican manuscript, is *Tractatus de rebus antiquis et situ urbis Romae* (Treatise on Ancient Things and the Site of the City of Rome).

The *Tractatus* was written after 1411, as is clear from the reference to the restoration of the corridor from the Vatican to *Castel Sant'Angelo made by the Antipope John XXIII in that year. The spirit of the work moves beyond the old medieval guide, *Mirabilia urbis Romae, in that the author pays little attention to churches and relics and omits some of the more fantastic legends of the *Mirabilia.* Of special value is his use of the contemporary popular names for many of the monuments. Nevertheless, he shows nothing of the critical sense of *Poggio Bracciolini or Flavio *Biondo, who examined the traditional stories and identifications and drew new conclusions.

The work describes the walls, gates, bridges and streets of Rome, as well as the triumphal arches, baths, palaces, columns, temples. The ancient authors cited include Ovid, Suetonius, Solinus, Eutropius, Cassiodorus, all medieval favorites. There is no awareness shown of the new humanistic scholarship on ancient authors.

BIBLIOGRAPHY
Valentini—Zucchetti IV, 101–50; Weiss, 60–61.

ANTICO (ALARI-BONACOLSI, PIER JACOPO; ca. 1460–1528). Italian goldsmith and bronzist; artist patronized by the *Gonzaga family.

Probably a native of Mantua, Pier Jacopo Alari-Bonacolsi, better known as "Antico," was at work there by 1479. For Gianfrancesco Gonzaga (d. 1496), he made bronze portrait medals in a Roman style, as well as silver and gilt vessels and bronze statuettes copying famous sculptures in Rome (e.g., the *Marcus Aurelius* Equestrian Statue, the *Quirinal *Horse Tamers*). Documents reveal that Antico had been in Rome in 1495 and returned in 1497. By 1499 he had completed for Bishop Ludovico Gonzaga—Gianfrancesco's younger brother—reductions of the *Belvedere *Apollo* (example in the Galleria Giorgio Franchetti alla Ca d'Oro, Venice) and the *Spinario* (example in the Wrightsman Collection, New York).

In 1501, Antico executed his first commission for Isabella d'*Este (a *Spinario*); from then until his death he was constantly at her service as artist, friend and adviser on antiquities. In 1519, when Isabella was planning her new Studiolo and Grotta in the Gonzaga palace, she commissioned Antico to make copies of some of the bronzes he had earlier created for Bishop Ludovico. His success with the commission was due, as has been shown by R. E. Stone, to a highly sophisticated technique of exact replication that had been mastered by Antico.

Antico seems to have chosen his own name at an early date, indicating his desire to work in an antique manner. Among his original creations that reveal the same exquisite technique as his copies are the bronze Gonzaga Vase (decorated with a *Triumph of Neptune* and other classical motifs) and a number of statuettes with antique subject matter and style (a *Cupid* in the Bargello, Florence; a *Hercules* in the *Museo Arqueológico Nacional, Madrid, and so on). There is documentary evidence that Antico was skilled in working marble and did restorations of ancient marble sculpture, but confirmation of these documents is rare; A. Nesselrath discovered the signature of ANTICUS MANTUANUS as restorer on the base of one of the Quirinal *Horse Tamers.* It is not possible to ascertain Antico's role, but his sensitivity as an archaeological restorer may be judged by the way he added appropriate parts to his bronze of the Belvedere *Apollo* (the hands, which were missing from the marble statue) and took others

away (the tree trunk, which likely would not have been part of the original
bronze *Apollo*).

BIBLIOGRAPHY

+A. Radcliffe, "Antico and the Mantuan Bronze," *Splendours of the Gonzaga*, ed. D.
S. Chambers—J. T. Martineau (London, 1981), 46–49; R. E. Stone, "Antico and the
Development of Bronze Casting in Italy at the End of the Quattrocento," *Metropolitan
Museum Journal* 16 (1981), 87–116; A. Nesselrath, "Antico and Montecavallo," *Burl
Mag* 124 (1982), 353–57.

ANTIKENSAMMLUNGEN, Munich. German collections of Greek vases,
Greek and Roman bronzes and terracottas, Greek and Etruscan metalwork, and
ancient glass; Attic vase painters of the sixth and fifth centuries B.C. are especially well represented.

Two projects of Duke *Albrecht V of Bavaria provided the roots for the
Munich Antikensammlungen. Albrecht collected curiosities, including small-
scale antiquities (coins and bronzes), which he brought together in a *Kunstkammer* (constructed 1563–67). Albrecht also provided for an *antiquarium* in the
ducal Residenz, a room devoted to the display of Roman portrait busts (many
bearing fanciful identifications) as a series of illustrious men. By the time the
bronzes of the *Kunstkammer* were united with the portrait busts in 1808, Albrecht's collection had been transformed. It had suffered losses during the Thirty
Years' War and through neglect but had also been enriched through new finds
and through the acquisition of the antiquities collection of Elector Karl Theodor
of the Palatinate (1803).

The Königliches Antiquarium was decisively enhanced in the nineteenth century through the addition of the private collection of King *Ludwig I of Bavaria.
Ludwig's *antiquarium* included Etruscan goldwork from the *Canino collection,
gold and silver objects from the Lipona collection, ancient glass and Etruscan
bronzes from the *Dodwell collection and Greek terracottas from the Fogelberg
collection. Ludwig also assembled an astounding collection of Greek vases,
through the purchase of newly excavated objects and established collections
(Panettieri, Canino, Lipona). Ludwig's vase collection was displayed in the Alte
Pinakothek, beginning in 1841, in rooms decorated in imitation of Etruscan
burial chambers.

The *antiquarium* was exhibited for a few years (1869–72) in the museum
building known since 1919 as the Neue Staatsgalerie, which had been built by
Georg Friedrich Ziebland (1838–48) to complement the *Glyptothek on the
Königplatz. The collection was subsequently transferred to the Neue Pinakothek,
where it resided for about fifty years. After World War I, the *antiquarium* joined
the vase collection in the Alte Pinakothek, where they together formed the Königliches (later, Staatliches) Museum Antiker Kleinkunst. The artworks owned
by Ludwig became the property of the Bavarian state (1923) in the wake of the
deposing of the Wittelsbach dynasty.

In the twentieth century the holdings of the Antikensammlungen were enriched through private bequests, including the collections of Paul *Arndt (1908), James *Loeb (1933) and Hans von Schoen (1964). Antiquities acquired by the Bayerischer Verein der Kunstfreunde (Bavarian Society of Friends of Art) came into the possession of the museum in 1939. Serious losses of Etruscan vases occurred during World War II due to bombing. In 1967, the Museum Antiker Kleinkunst found a home in the newly restored Neue Staatsgalerie. Since the reopening of the Glyptothek in 1972, all of the ancient art in the Bavarian state collections can now be viewed in the two buildings on the Königplatz. Founded in 1971, the Verein der Freunde und Förderer der Glyptothek und der Antiken-sammlungen (Society of Friends and Patrons of the Glyptothek and the Anti-kensammlungen) supports public programs, conservation work and new acquisitions.

BIBLIOGRAPHY
H. Diepolder, s.v. "Monaco," *EAA* 5 (1963), 146–49; D. Ohly, *Die Antikensammlungen am Königplatz in Munchen,* 2nd ed. (Waldsassen, [1968]).

ELIZABETH C. TEVIOTDALE

ANTIKYTHERA YOUTH (BALLPLAYER). Over-lifesize Greek bronze statue of a nude youth (Athens, *National Archaeological Museum; height 1.96m), one of many finds from an ancient shipwreck discovered in 1900 off the island of Antikythera, between Kythera and Crete.

A sponge fisher first reported the find, telling that he had seen ghostly, rotting bodies of humans and horses on the ocean floor. A salvage crew from the University of Athens, assisted by the Greek navy, worked the site for nearly a year.

The best-known piece from the wreck, the youth is restored from many frag-ments, and portions of it are still missing, including the base of the neck, a large area above the hips and part of the left thigh. The statue was cast in pieces and the original divisions are evident. Eyes, teeth and nipples were inset. The well-muscled youth stands on his left foot, the right trailing behind. He is sometimes referred to as the *Ballplayer,* because the right hand appears to have been cupped around an object. *Bieber suggested that he was Paris holding the golden apple, while Svoronos argued for Perseus with the head of Medusa. Usually considered to fall within the later Polykleitan tradition, and sometimes compared to works by Lysippos, the statue is most often dated to the third quarter of the fourth century B.C.

BIBLIOGRAPHY
J. N. Svoronos, *Das Athener National Museum* 1 (Athens, 1908), 18–29; R. Carpenter, *Greek Sculpture* (Chicago, 1960), 44, 161–63, 170–73; C. Karouzos, "To chronikon teis anasustaseos tou chalkinou neou ton Antikutheiron," *ArchEph* (1969), 59–79; P. C. Bol, *Die Skulpturen des Schiffsfundes von Antikythera, AthMitt* Beiheft 2 (1972), 18–24.

CAROL MATTUSCH

ANTIOCH-ON-THE-ORONTES. City in northwestern Syria on the Orontes River at modern Antakya, Turkey. Greek tradition ascribed its founding variously to Argives, Cretans, Heraclids and Eleans. The earliest historical sources indicate that it was founded in 300 B.C. by Seleucus I, together with the harbor settlement Seleucia Pieria. Antioch became the principal cultural and commercial city of the eastern Mediterranean, rivaled only by *Alexandria. It was at the western end of the trade routes that led by caravan from Asia through the upper Tigris-Euphrates valley. In 64 B.C. Antioch was brought under Roman control. It was an important administrative center of the eastern Roman provinces and strategic point in the defense of the empire against threats from Parthia. Antioch remained important during the later Roman Empire, when the Sasanian Persians advanced against the eastern Roman provinces. The city was attacked in A.D. 540 by Chosroes II. The Arab invasion of A.D. 628 ended the Graeco-Roman history of the city.

The monuments of ancient Antioch are known, in part, from descriptions preserved in the writings of ancient authors, including Strabo, Libanius, John Chrysostom, Malalas and Procopius. Most have been destroyed by a number of earthquakes or through removal or reuse in subsequent construction. From 1932 to 1939 an American team led by William A. Campbell excavated at Antioch, as well as in the suburb Daphne and at the seaport Seleucia Pieria. These and topographical studies have revealed that the city was laid out in a grid arrangement whose major axis was a great colonnaded street. Parts of the enclosure wall, which originally extended a length of 18km, are preserved. Other surviving monuments include an amphitheater and baths. The excavations also brought to light a number of floor mosaics from private houses in Daphne and Antioch (studied by Doro *Levi). These constitute an important corpus of mostly figured mosaics, dating from the second through early sixth centuries A.C.

BIBLIOGRAPHY

+Antioch on the Orontes, the Excavations, 1–5 (1934–72); +D. Levi, Antioch Mosaic Pavements (Princeton, NJ, 1947); G. Downey, A History of Antioch in Syria from Seleucus to the Arab Conquest (Princeton, NJ, 1961); J.H.W.G. Liebeschuetz, Antioch: City and Administration in the Later Roman Empire (Oxford, 1972).

ANN C. GUNTER

ANTIQUARIO FORENSE (MUSEO DEL FORO), Rome. Museum in Rome displaying antiquities discovered in the *Forum Romanum.

The museum is located at the southeast corner of the Forum, in the fifteenth-century cloister of S. Francesca Romana constructed over the ruins of the Hadrianic *Temple of Venus and Roma. In 1900 the cloister was designated by G. *Boni as the repository for finds from the Forum and the *Palatine. Materials from Boni's own excavations—the Forum necropolis, the *Temple of Vesta, the *Lapis Niger, the Cloaca Maxima and the Regia—were put on display there, as well as the remains of the important frieze from the Republican phase of the *Basilica Aemilia, first constructed in 179 B.C. Portions of the frieze, which shows stories of early Rome, were found in various excavations beginning in 1900.

BIBLIOGRAPHY
E. Gjerstad, *Early Rome* 3 (1960); Helbig, 4th ed., II, 795–850; I. Iacopi, *L'Antiquario forense* (Rome, 1974); Coarelli, 100–101.

ANTIQUARIO PALATINO (ANTIQUARIUM OF THE PALATINE), Rome. Museum of antiquities established in the former convent of the Sisters of the Visitation, erected over part of the site of the Domus Augustiana on the *Palatine Hill, Rome.

The museum contains objects found on the Palatine from 1870 on, from the excavations of *Boni, Romanelli, Vaglieri and others. Also displayed are paintings from some of the houses around the Palatine (Aula Isaica, House of the Griffins, Domus Transitoria) and reconstructions of some of the eighth-century B.C. huts discovered by Puglisi. In recent years the museum has been closed for rearranging.

BIBLIOGRAPHY
S. M. Puglisi, "Gli abitatori primitivi del Palatino attraverso le testimonianze archeologiche e le nuove indagini stratigrafici sul Germalo," *MA* 41 (1951), 1–146; Helbig, 4th ed., II, 850; Coarelli, 159–61.

APHRODISIAS. Ancient city in Caria (southwest Asia Minor) located at modern Geyre.

Historical sources link Aphrodisias in sympolity with the nearby city of Plarasa beginning in the late second century B.C. By the Early Imperial period Aphrodisias had gained importance as a center for the worship of Aphrodite and home of a major sculptural school. The emperor Augustus especially favored the city and has left his affection inscribed on the wall of its theater: "Aphrodisias is the one city from all of Asia I have selected to be my own." During Early Christian times it became known as Stauropolis and served as seat of the bishopric of Caria.

The ancient site was described by *Texier and was included in the 1840 volume of *Antiquities of Ionia.* It was investigated by the French, under Paul Gaudin and Gustav Mendel (1904–5), and the Italians, under G. Jacopi (1937), but both expeditions were short-lived and beset by problems. Since 1961 an American expedition, formerly under the direction of Kenan *Erim, has conducted annual campaigns, still in progress under R.R.R. Smith and C. Ratté.

These expeditions have revealed a lengthy prehistoric occupation extending from the early third millennium B.C. on the "acropolis," a habitation mound. A settlement of the Archaic period (seventh–sixth centuries B.C.) is also attested. The city remains date principally to Late Hellenistic and Roman Imperial times. Among the major monuments are the temple of Aphrodite, built in the first century B.C., a well-preserved stadium (first century A.C.) and odeion (second century A.C.). The Hellenistic-Roman theater has yielded extensive epigraphical documents, including imperial letters. The agora is flanked by the baths of Hadrian and the Early Imperial Sebasteion with spectacularly rich sculptural decoration.

Aphrodisias was enclosed by walls first constructed in the second century A.C. and rebuilt in the fourth century and Byzantine period. In the fifth century A.C., the temple of Aphrodite was converted to a Christian basilica. From this period also dates the complex west of the odeion, identified as the bishop's residence. The city was devastated by Tamerlane the Great in 1402.

BIBLIOGRAPHY

G. Mendel, in *CRAI* (1906), 178–84; G. Jacopi, "Gli scavi della Missione Archeologica Italiana ad Afrodisiade," and L. Crema, "I monumenti architettonici afrodisiensi," *MonAnt* 38 (1939–40); J. M. Reynolds, *Aphhrodisias and Rome, Documents from the Excavation of the Theatre at Aphrodisias*, JRS Monographs 1 (London, 1982); +K. T. Erim, *Aphrodisias, City of Venus Aphrodite* (New York, 1986); C. Roueché—J. M. Reynolds, *Aphrodisias in Late Antiquity*, JRS Monograph 5 (Cambridge, 1989); C. Roueché—K. T. Erim, eds., *Aphrodisias Papers, Recent Work on Architecture and Sculpture*, JRA Suppl. 1 (Ann Arbor, MI, 1990).

ANN C. GUNTER

APHRODITE OF MELOS. See VENUS DE MILO.

APOLLO SAUROKTONOS. Greek bronze statue of the fourth century B.C. by Praxiteles (Pliny, *NH* 34.69–70; Martial 14.172); traditionally associated with a Roman marble statue type of Apollo in the act of attacking a lizard.

The most famous of the few marble copies of the statue known is that in the *Louvre (height 2.5m; other important copies are in the *Vatican and the Villa Albani), which was in the *Borghese family collection, probably already in 1650. The Louvre piece was acquired by *Napoleon in 1807, displayed in the Musée Napoléon by 1812 and has remained in Paris to the present. *Winckelmann was the first to link the Borghese copy with the description in Pliny; he was followed by E. Q. *Visconti and others, who debated the meaning of the unusual iconography, according to which Apollo was attacking the lizard with an arrow (the dart is absent in the Louvre copy). The theme is probably playful but was taken seriously at the time. Visconti suggested that Apollo was cleansing the air of putrid impurities, while T. B. Éméric-David argued (1824) that the god was not killing the reptile but merely stimulating it to wake it from hibernation. W. Fröhner observed (1884), a little apologetically, that the creature was useful in ancient pharmacology. Robertson noted (1975) that the lizard may be regarded as an ill-omened creature and that the killing of it by Apollo could allude, presumably in an amusing way, to the heroic theme of Apollo's slaying the Python.

BIBLIOGRAPHY

+G. E. Rizzo, *Prassitele* (Milan, 1932), 39; Robertson, *Greek Art*, 388; Haskell—Penny, 151–53; Ridgway, *Hellenistic Sculpture*, I, 91, 105; *LIMC* II, 378 (E. Simon).

APOXYOMENOS ("SCRAPER"). Greek bronze statue of an athlete scraping himself clean after exercise; now lost, the work was created by Lysippos in the second half of the fourth century B.C.

The statue was a favorite of the Roman people when it was brought to Rome and set up outside the Baths of Agrippa (Pliny, *NH* 34.61). The emperor Tiberius was so fond of the figure that he had it moved into his own bedroom, but the populace demanded that it be returned.

A Roman marble statue of an athlete scraping himself in the *Vatican is often cited as a copy of the statue by Lysippos. Discovered in Trastevere in 1849, it was restored by P. Tenerani (the inclusion of a die in the right hand was erroneous and is now removed) and first published by E. *Braun. *Michaelis summarized the nineteenth-century opinion that the work was a key monument in the study of Lysippos and Greek sculpture in general, because of its innovative canon of slender proportions and smaller head and its development of the figure in the round—a view still held by many scholars. In fact, as Ridgway has observed, the head is so small as to be disconcerting, and the statue lacks the quality that is to be expected of the work of Lysippos. Various *apoxyomenoi* are mentioned in literary sources, and the Vatican statue may be a reflection of a work by some other artist.

BIBLIOGRAPHY

Michaelis, 71–72; +Bieber, 31–32; Ridgway, *Hellenistic Sculpture,* I, 74–76.

AQUEDUCTS. Aqueducts did exist in Greece, sometimes reaching a high degree of sophistication (*Pergamon) but reached their zenith as the monument most supremely characteristic of Roman civilization. Studies normally concentrate on the actual aqueducts, omitting urban delivery networks and questions of hydraulics; they are based on the archaeological monuments and the account of Frontinus (and, rather less, Vitruvius, Book 8).

Typical aqueduct lengths are 50km (*Nimes), 66, 75 (*Lyons), 60–90 (Rome), 123 (*Carthage). Many cities had two or more aqueducts, and Rome had eleven (total daily discharge ½–1 million m³): two—the Alsietina and the Traiana, serving the Janiculum—came in from near Lake Bracciano, to the west, and the other nine all came from the east, drawing water from the Anio valley and the Sabine hills. Their dates are Appia, 312 B.C.; Anio Vetus, 272; Marcia, 144; Tepula, 125; Julia, 40 (or 33?), Virgo, 19; Alsietina, 2; Claudia, A.D. 47; Anio Novus, 52; Traiana, 109; Alexandria, ca. 226. Since the water was of varying quality (the best was the Marcia), the channels were kept separate even when following the same route, to the extent of up to three being carried, one on top of the other, on the same set of arches.

For perhaps 90% of its length, the average aqueduct ran at ground level or just below, in a cement-lined masonry channel. Bridges and the inverted siphon were used to cross valleys, especially in Gaul. These great bridges are some of the most striking Roman monuments existing, with two or even three tiers of arches carrying the conduit. The greatest is the *Pont du Gard (France); others are at *Segovia, *Tarragona (Spain), Cherchell (Mauretania), *Aspendos (Turkey) and Ponte Lupo and Ponte San Gregorio (Rome). Remains of siphons, less striking, are to be seen in the southwest suburbs of Lyons and also at Aspendos. Approaching the city across a plain, the aqueduct often had to run on a continuous arcade to maintain water level. This is particularly to be seen in the Roman Campagna and also at Carthage, Minturnae, Caesaraea (Israel), *Mérida (Spain). Arriving at the city (at Rome, by the *Porta Maggiore), the aqueduct ran into a distribution tank, *castellum divisorium* (best preserved examples at *Pompeii and *Nîmes), from which radiated the lead pipes of the urban network.

After the fall of Rome, the fate of the aqueducts, infrequently maintained, if at all, varied. That at Segovia is still in service, and in the nineteenth century there were several proposals, notably by the French in North Africa, to reopen or adapt Roman aqueducts for modern use, but little came of them. At Rome, in spite of restoration by Belisarius after the siege of the Goths A.D. 537 and in the eighth century by Hadrian I, by about 900–1000, failure had become general. Though the aqueducts were remarkably neglected by the artists and antiquarians of the Renaissance, from the sixteenth century the popes tried sporadically to restore the system. Though often incorporating parts of the ancient network, the result was really a virtually new creation. In 1570 the Virgo was rebuilt as the Aqua Vergine by Pius IV and Pius V, extensively masking the ancient construction, changing to a different and nearer source; it was cut short to deliver its waters at what was later (1762) to become the fountain of Trevi, instead of at the *Campus Martius. In 1583–87 *Sixtus V built the Acqua Felice (still in use), which drew on the springs of the Alexandriana and was carried on top of the arches of the Marcia and Claudia. Others were the Acqua Paola (1611, Paul V) and the Acqua Pia (1870, Pius IX), which used the springs of the Marcia.

Because of their nature, aqueducts have seldom required excavation in the orthodox sense, and study has usually been a question of mapping and tracing their routes. At Rome, the work of Raffaele *Fabretti (1680), though uneven, is the first real survey, and Rodolfo *Lanciani's topographical study of Frontinus (1880) is the foundation of modern scholarship. More recently, the largely complementary work of *Van Deman (1934) and *Ashby (1935) at Rome has reinforced in aqueduct studies the emphasis on dating and topography that has been their hallmark ever since.

BIBLIOGRAPHY

G. de Montauzan, *Les Aqueducs antiques de Lyon* (Paris, 1909); T. Ashby, *The Aqueducts of Ancient Rome* (Oxford, 1935); R. J. Forbes, *Studies in Ancient Technology* (Leiden, 1955), I, 149–94; P. Grimal, *Frontin, Les aqueducs,* ed. Budé (Paris, 1961); P. Pace, *Gli Aquedotti di Roma e il De aquaeductu di Frontino* (Rome, 1983); +A. T. Hodge, *Roman Aqueducts and Water Supply* (London, 1992); D. Crouch, *Water Management in Ancient Greek Cities* (New York, 1993).

A. TREVOR HODGE

AQUILEIA. Roman colony founded in 181 B.C.; modern Italian town in the province of Udine in the Veneto.

Rich archaeological remains reveal the presence of the Romans (including imperial patronage; Augustus, Tiberius and Marcus Aurelius were among the Roman emperors who visited Aquileia), as well as the splendid early Christian culture in this area, dating from the third and fourth centuries A.C. The city was an easy mark for barbarian invaders (beginning with Alaric in 401), and it sank into oblivion in the early Middle Ages, until a revival began in the ninth century under the rule of church patriarchs.

The extensive ancient city underwent heavy destruction from the barbarians, and it suffered further from periodic earthquakes. After long abandonment, the ancient part of Aquileia became a quarry for the builders of the medieval city, so that only foundations of the Roman structures remained.

The cemeteries of Aquileia were rich, and luxury objects probably from burials attracted the attention of early collectors. In the sixteenth century the *Grimani enriched their famous gem collection with items from Aquileia, and other wealthy Venetians sought antiquities during the seventeenth and eighteenth centuries. The canon G. D. Bertoli was an exceptionally responsible collector and observer who studied Aquileian antiquities in order to place them in a historical context; his *Le Antichità di Aquileia* (Venice, 1739) featured gems, glass, pottery, lamps, sculpture and objects from daily life.

In the eighteenth century, during the period when Aquileia was under Austrian domination, numerous inscriptions and objects were excavated, often with little method, and the finds carried away from Aquileia, most often to Vienna. More systematic excavations were undertaken at Aquileia in the late nineteenth and early twentieth centuries, uncovering numerous elements of the ancient city— fortifications, granaries, the forum, an amphitheater, a circus and port installations on the river Natissa. Mosaics from the early Roman colony and imperial city, as well as from the early Christian churches, constitute a continuous series that has made Aquileia one of the most important sites for the study of ancient mosaics. The rich necropolis is famed for its fine objects of glass, amber and other luxury materials.

The Museo Archeologico Nazionale, founded in 1882 in the Villa Cassis Faraone, is the chief repository of the city's treasures. Refurbished in 1955, it features carefully chosen objects and modern didactic displays. The centenary of the museum was celebrated with two special volumes of *Antichità Altoadriatiche* (vols. 23–24, 1983–84) that review the museums and antiquities of Aquileia in the light of the latest European and American scholarship.

BIBLIOGRAPHY

G. B. Brusin, *Gli Scavi di Aquileia* (Udine, 1934); V. Scrinari, s.v. "Aquileia," *EAA* 1 (1958); L. Bertacchi, s.v. "Aquileia," *PECS,* 79–80.

AQUINCUM. Site of a Roman legionary camp and city on the west bank of the Danube, today in Budapest (Old Buda), Hungary.

Aquincum was a tribal center of the Eravisci before the arrival of the Romans. Tiberius first stationed a division (*ala*) there; reconstructed in the time of Domitian, the camp thereafter long housed the Second Legion (*Legio II Adiutrix*). In A.D. 106 Aquincum became administrative capital of Pannonia Inferior and received municipal status in 124, colonial in 194. Two fortresses were built on the opposite bank of the river, one of which (*contra Aquincum*) later became the nucleus of the city of Pest. Under continual pressure from the Sarmatians in the fourth century, Aquincum was overrun by the Germans and Huns in the fifth, though a Roman community still subsisted.

Excavations undertaken by J. Schönwisner of Pest University in 1778 and continued intermittently by the Hungarians through the nineteenth century (S. Német in the 1820s; E. Sacken in the 1850s) and the twentieth century, especially since 1947, have revealed extensive settlement, though destruction has been heavy, and the Roman military site lies under a populous section of the modern city. A military and a civilian amphitheater are known, and remains can be seen of the governor's palace, waterworks, a marketplace, workshops, numerous private houses, over a dozen baths, part of the main streets (*cardo* and *decumanus*), a sanctuary of Fortuna and several Mithraea and early Christian churches. Statues, tombstones, floor mosaics and fragments of wall paintings are on display; especially well known is the portable organ (ca. A.D. 220; the only one of its kind extant), the bronze portions of which are found in the modern and attractive museum of Aquincum built on the site (opened in 1894).
BIBLIOGRAPHY

B. Kuzsinszky, *Aquincum, Ausgrabungen und Funde* (Budapest, 1934); J. Szilágyi, s.v. "Aquincum," *RE,* suppl. 11 (1968), cols. 61–131; A. Mócsy, *Pannonia and Upper Moesia* (London, 1974); S. K. Póczy, s.v. "Aquincum," *PECS,* 80–81.

W. W. DE GRUMMOND

ARA GRIMANI. See GRIMANI ALTAR.

ARA PACIS AUGUSTAE, Rome. Roman altar, erected 13–9 B.C., to commemorate Augustus's triumphal return from Spain and Gaul and his restoration of peace to the world (*Res gestae* 12).

The altar was built on the eastern edge of the *Campus Martius on the Via Flaminia (the modern Via del Corso), the road taken by Augustus when he entered Rome from the north. The monument consists of the sacrificial altar surrounded by marble precinct walls richly decorated on both sides with reliefs (the exterior with figural scenes and a scroll frieze, the interior with a re-creation of the original wooden precinct walls and garlands).

Today the tufa foundations of the altar remain 6m beneath the Palazzo Ottoboni Fiano Almagià (formerly, the Palazzo Peretti). Sections of the precinct walls were discovered on the Via in Lucina north of the Piazza Colonna during the sixteenth century. Agostino Veneziano sketched one of the panels of the scroll frieze prior to 1536; today that piece is missing. During construction work on the Palazzo Peretti in 1568, additional sections of the precinct wall were discovered and purchased for the *Medici collections. The slabs were sawed in half along their longitudinal axis, and most were sent to Florence (including the "Tellus" relief and sections of the southern procession). The first panel of the northern procession was acquired by the *Vatican and was presented to the Italian state in 1954. It is now set into the reconstructed monument along with its inner side, which had been sawed away, and was discovered separately in the church of Il Gesù in 1899 as the tombstone of a certain Monsignor Poggi, who had died in 1628. Four garland panels and two scroll pilasters are still immured in the garden façade of the Villa Medici in Rome and have been replaced on the reconstructed monument in plaster. Whereas the Florence and Vatican fragments were restored, the penultimate panel of the northern procession remains in the *Louvre, replaced on the altar with a plaster cast. During an operation to reinforce the foundations of the Palazzo Ottoboni in 1859, further fragments were discovered, including the Aeneas relief and the head of Mars from the counterpanel. This piece was sent to Venice but was later returned to Rome.

F. von *Duhn first suggested that the known fragments could belong to the Ara Pacis in 1879. E. *Petersen followed in 1902 with the first reconstruction of the entire monument. An excavation in 1903 revealed details of the ground plan; all the fragments discovered at that time were collected in the Museo delle *Terme and partly reconstructed. G. Moretti oversaw further excavations from 1937 to 1938; he experimented with the most modern techniques (hydraulic engineer G. Rodio froze the groundwaters to permit digging) and brought forth additional sections of the actual altar.

In 1938 the Ara Pacis was reconstructed near its former site and now stands by the Tiber next to the *Mausoleum of Augustus. It was rotated ninety degrees from its original orientation: in antiquity one entered the enclosure from the west, today from the south. Mussolini ordered this transposition to fit the monument into a new architectural ensemble juxtaposing Imperial and fascist Rome (*see* *Fascism, archaeology under).

Modern scholarship on the Ara Pacis is formidably complex, reflecting the richness and importance of the monument as the centerpiece of art of the age of Augustus. The long reliefs on the north and south sides, showing processions of important personages from the retinue of Augustus, have provided a fertile field for iconographers and historians (e.g., M. Torelli, J. Pollini), with Augustus's portrait agreed upon by all but with some debate over the identity of Agrippa, Livia, Tiberius, Julia and other members of the imperial court. Especially controversial are the two children in the procession who seem to wear foreign dress and have been identified alternatively as foreign princes (C. B. Rose) or the grandsons of Augustus, Gaius and Lucius. Among the mythological/allegorical reliefs on the east and west, the most controversial is that of a goddess of fertility who was originally called Tellus, "Earth," during the Renaissance, when the relief was thought to represent the elements of the universe. Recent attempts to identify her as Pax Augusta (N. T. de Grummond), Venus, Italia and others have led to discussion of the multivalence of images on the

Ara Pacis and in Augustan art (Karl Galinsky). The setting of the Ara Pacis has received new examination as the result of the excavations by E. Buchner in the adjacent area of the great Solarium or sundial of Augustus (1979–81).

BIBLIOGRAPHY
+G. Moretti, *Ara Pacis Augustae* (Rome, 1948); +E. Simon, *Ara Pacis Augustae* (Tübingen, 1967); G. Koeppel, "Die historischen Reliefs der römischen Kaiserzeit V: Ara Pacis Augustae 1–2," *Bonner Jahrbücher* 187 (1987), 101–57; 188 (1988), 97–106; P. Holliday, "Time, History, and Ritual in the Ara Pacis Augustae," *ArtBull* 72 (1990), 542–57; K. Galinsky, "Venus, Polysemy and the Ara Pacis," *AJA* 96 (1992), 457–75; Kleiner, *Roman Sculpture,* 90–99, 119.

PETER HOLLIDAY

ARA PIETATIS AUGUSTAE, Rome. Monumental Roman altar, modeled on the *Ara Pacis Augustae, vowed by Tiberius in A.D. 22 but not erected until 43 under Claudius.

A series of reliefs known since the early sixteenth century was first attributed to this altar in 1907 by Sieveking; previously they had been thought to be part of the Ara Pacis. Recently they have been reattributed to the Ara Gentis Iuliae. The reliefs, once part of the collection of Cardinal Andrea della *Valle (della *Valle family), depict a procession with a *flamen,* sacrifices, and two temple façades. In 1584 the reliefs were purchased by Cardinal Ferdinando de' Medici (*Medici family), along with the rest of the della Valle-Capranica collection, and set into the interior garden façade of the cardinal's new villa on the Pincio; missing sections of the reliefs were "completed" with poor restorations. Casts of the Villa Medici reliefs—minus the Renaissance additions—are today in the *Museo della Civiltà Romana, where the sacrifices and the temple façades have been combined into two unified panels. Other fragments, including a third temple façade, attributed to the same altar, were found in 1923 and 1933 near the church of S. Maria in Via Lata; these reliefs are today housed in the Palazzo dei Conservatori (*Capitoline Museums). Many of the "Ara Pietatis" reliefs were probably reused in the Arcus Novus of Diocletian, which stood in the Via Lata.

BIBLIOGRAPHY
+M. Cagiano de Azevedo, *Le Antichità di Villa Medici* (Rome, 1951), 9–23, 56–64; L. Cozza, "Ricomposizione di alcuni rilievi di Villa Medici," *BdA* 43 (1958), 107–11; H. P. Laubscher, "Arcus Novus und Arcus Claudii, Zwei Triumphbögen an der Via Lata in Rom," *Nachrichten der Akademie der Wissenschaften in Göttingen* (1976), 73–77, 108; M. Torelli, *Typology and Structure of Roman Historical Reliefs* (Ann Arbor, 1982), 66–88.

FRED S. KLEINER

ARAUSIO. See ORANGE.

ARCHAEOLOGICAL INSTITUTE OF AMERICA. Principal organization within the United States and Canada for the advancement of world archaeology, especially of Greece, Italy and the Mediterranean.

When Charles Eliot *Norton and eleven Boston scholars founded the Archaeological Institute of America (AIA) in May 1879, their stated goals included the support of archaeological expeditions and the publication of research reports. Through these endeavors Norton hoped to awaken American interest in classical studies, a field previously dominated by European scholars. To further this aim, he suggested enlarging American museum collections with objects acquired by the institute through excavation.

Throughout its history the AIA has emphasized various of these goals as the situation and times permitted. During its early years it proved possible to raise funds sufficient to support two major excavations, as well as several small independent expeditions. In 1881 Joseph T. Clarke and Francis H. Bacon started work on a promising city site at *Assos in northwest Turkey. After three seasons' work, the excavators returned with several prize pieces, among them the frieze blocks from an Archaic temple that now form part of the collection of the *Museum of Fine Arts, Boston. Some years later, in 1910, Richard Norton (Charles's son) led an institute excavation at the North African site of *Cyrene. Beset by problems ranging from the assassination of the assistant director to the outbreak of war between Turkey and Italy, the expedition was forced to withdraw. Not until the 1960s was work on the site resumed under the sponsorship of several American universities.

In addition to mounting its own excavations, the AIA has sponsored many independent scholars working at various Mediterranean sites. Under the institute's aegis, W. J. Stillman investigated remains at *Knossos and *Gortyn in 1881, and F. *Halbherr undertook further work on inscriptions at Gortyn in 1894 and 1895. In the late 1930s the institute supported Hetty *Goldman's work at Tarsus, and local societies of the AIA have independently helped underwrite excavations at such places as *Nemea and *Mycenae.

Recognizing that excavation without publication is little more than the destruction of man's heritage, the institute has always maintained that the publication of excavation reports and research results was one of its primary obligations. From the time of its introduction in 1885, the *American Journal of Archaeology* (AJA) has earned an international reputation for its valuable contribution to scholarship. Through its quarterly editions, the *AJA* serves as a vehicle for the swift reporting of excavations results, as well as a forum for the introduction of research work. As membership in the institute soon grew beyond an academic core, the value of a more popular periodical oriented toward the well-informed layperson was quickly recognized. In 1914 the institute brought out a magazine entitled *Art and Archaeology*. Despite its popularity it was discarded twenty years later as too much an art magazine and not fostering the institute's archaeological aims. Recognizing the wisdom in maintaining a broad base of support, the AIA reintroduced a popular periodical in 1948, calling it *Archaeology*. Published bimonthly, *Archaeology* contains a blend of scholarly and nontechnical articles that enlighten a widening circle of armchair archaeologists. In contrast to the classical focus of the *American Journal of Archae-*

ology, Archaeology reports on all periods and areas of humankind's past. Among other publications of the institute are thirteen monographs that appeared between 1948 and 1973 in a series on archaeology and the fine arts, cosponsored by the College Art Association. Since 1944 the institute has administered the publications of the International Committee on the *Corpus Vasorum Antiquorum.* Recently a new series of monographs and colloquia was initiated under the editorship of B. Ridgway and E. Will.

When Charles Norton founded the AIA, one of his primary goals was the establishment of American schools in Greece and Italy where future scholars could live in the land, study the ancient monuments and through these experiences uniquely enhance their later teaching. Under the guidance of John Williams White, a committee of the institute first elicited support for the venture from Harvard, Yale, Johns Hopkins, Cornell and Brown and in October 1882 opened the *American School of Classical Studies in Athens. Thirteen years later another school of classical studies was established in Rome; in 1913 it merged into the *American Academy.

By the time of its centennial the institute had grown from a single Boston society to a group of eighty-five local societies with over 7,000 members throughout the United States and Canada. From its very beginnings, the AIA has sought ways of encouraging the scholar and enlightening the layperson. Honor and distinction in archaeological achievement are annually recognized through the award of a Gold Medal for Distinguished Archaeological Achievement. Though widely scattered, all members of the local societies are kept informed of the most recent archaeological developments through a program of traveling lecturers, highlighted by a special Norton Lectureship that brings outstanding American and foreign scholars to the local societies. An annual meeting for the general membership provides numerous sessions for archaeologists to present the latest results of their excavations, as well as their research on a wide range of topics.

BIBLIOGRAPHY

C. E. Norton, "The Work of the Archaeological Institute of America: An Address at the Opening of the First General Meeting of the Archaeological Institute of America," *AJA* 4 (1900), 1–16; Idem, "The Founding of the School at Athens," *AJA* 7 (1903), 351–56; V. Dort, "The Archaeological Institute of America, Early Days," *Archaeology* 7 (1954), 195–201; P. S. Sheftel, "The Archaeological Institute of America, 1879–1979: A Centennial Review," *AJA* 83 (1979), 3–17.

PHOEBE S. SHEFTEL

ARCHAEOLOGICAL SOCIETY. See GREEK ARCHAEOLOGICAL SOCIETY.

ARCHAIOLOGIKE HETAIREIA. See GREEK ARCHAEOLOGICAL SOCIETY.

ARCHANES. Major site on *Crete for Bronze Age Minoan culture.

The modern village of Epano Archanes, ca. 10km south of *Knossos, covers a rich and important Minoan settlement. Sir Arthur *Evans recognized that the site was the equivalent of Acharna in the classical period; in 1922 he excavated there a monumental circular well-house. In 1970 A. Lebessi discovered a unique Middle Minoan terracotta model of a house or shrine at Archanes.

The main explorers of Archanes are Yannis Sakellarakis and Efi Sakellaraki, who have been working in the area since 1964. Their discoveries have been made in three localities: Tourkoyeitonia, where the remains of a large palatial structure have been found; Phourni, a cemetery; and Anemospilia, the site of a Minoan religious building, where the excavators believe they have found evidence of human sacrifice. The cemetery, including material dating from the Early Minoan to the Sub-Minoan, is one of the largest and richest of the Bronze Age Aegean culture, with many unique features. Among the finds are gold jewelry, fine seals, ivory plaques with various representations, terracotta burial containers and a great amount of pottery, as well as imported Cycladic marble figurines and goods from Egypt.

BIBLIOGRAPHY

C. Davaras, *Guide to Cretan Antiquities* (Park Ridge, NJ, 1976), 17; Y. Sakellarakis, "Drama of Death in a Minoan Temple," *National Geographic Magazine* 159 (February 1981), 205–23; Y. Sakellarakis—E. Sakellaraki, in *Aerial Atlas of Ancient Crete*, 51–62.

COSTIS DAVARAS

ARCH AT ORANGE. Roman honorary or *"triumphal" arch, the earliest preserved true triple-bay arch in the Roman world, with elaborate relief decoration consisting of battle scenes, piles of arms, armor, and prows, and captives bound to trophies.

Although its date has been disputed, it is now usually thought to have been erected under Tiberius between A.D. 20 and 26. Always visible since its erection, the arch was made part of the fortifications of *Orange in the thirteenth century under Raymond de Baux, prince of Orange, and was known as the "Tour de l'Arc" or "Chateau de l'Arc" in succeeding centuries. The thirteenth-century crenellations added to the arch's attic were removed in 1721, and repairs and restorations were carried out in the late eighteenth and early nineteenth centuries, especially by Auguste Caristie after 1824. The monument was repaired once again between 1950 and 1957 prior to the publication of a definitive scientific study by Robert Amy and others. Frequently chosen as a subject by artists, the Orange arch appears in many prints and drawings of the seventeenth, eighteenth and nineteenth centuries, and was painted for Louis XVIII in 1787 by Hubert *Robert as one of a group of Provençal antiquities with the theater at Orange and *Les Antiques* of St-Rémy-de-Provence (cf. *Arch at St-Rémy and *Monument of the Julii).

BIBLIOGRAPHY

+R. Amy et al., *L'Arc d'Orange, Gallia,* suppl. 15 (Paris, 1962); P. Gros, "Pour une chronologie des arcs de triomphe de Gaule Narbonnaise," *Gallia* 37 (1979), 55–83; Idem,

"Une hypothèse sur l'Arc d'Orange," *Gallia* 44 (1986), 191–201; J. C. Anderson, jr., "The Date of the Arch at Orange," *Bonner Jahrbücher* 187 (1987), 159–92.

FRED S. KLEINER

ARCH AT ST-RÉMY. Single-bay Roman honorary or *"triumphal" arch, decorated with Victories in the spandrels and large reliefs of captives on the piers, probably erected ca. A.D. 10–20 as the gateway to Glanum (*Glanon).

Together with the neighboring *Monument of the Julii, the two "Antiques" have long been the emblem of St-Rémy-de-Provence. The arch, which lacks its original attic and the upper parts of the piers, was given a protective roof in the eighteenth century. The gate is first mentioned in 1343 and was known during the Renaissance as the *Portail Sarazin,* the *Arc du trésor* (an allusion to an alleged treasure buried beneath it) or the *Arc du Sex* (a name borrowed from the inscription of SEX(tus) on the Monument of the Julii). The arch was a popular subject of drawings and prints of the seventeenth, eighteenth and nineteenth centuries and was recorded by Jean-Honoré Fragonard in 1760 and painted by Hubert *Robert in 1787.

BIBLIOGRAPHY

+H. Rolland, *L'Arc de Glanum, Gallia,* suppl. 31 (Paris, 1977); P. Gros, "Pour une chronologie des arcs de triomphe de Gaule Narbonnaise (à propos de l'arc de *Glanum*)," *Gallia* 37 (1979), 55–83; Idem, "Note sur deux reliefs des 'Antiques' de Glanum," *Revue Archéologique de Narbonnaise* 14 (1981), 159–72.

FRED S. KLEINER

ARCH OF AUGUSTUS, Rimini. Roman honorary or *"triumphal" arch, commissioned in 27 B.C. by the emperor Augustus to mark the terminus of the restored Via Flaminia.

Inserted into the western wall of ancient Arminium (Rimini), this single arch is closer in form and concept to a city gate. It was incorporated into subsequent fortification systems and is still crowned by late-medieval Ghibelline brick crenellations. The arch is notable for its undersized, decorative pediment, relatively broad central opening, and complex sculptural program, including spandrel medallions and sculptured keystones. Possibly it had a crowning statue of Augustus (Dio Cass. 53.22). Well known in the Renaissance, the arch probably inspired *Alberti's fifteenth-century façade for the nearby Tempio Malatestiano.

BIBLIOGRAPHY

+M. Brighenti, *Illustrazione dell'arco di Augusto in Rimini* (Rimini, 1825); G. A. Mansuelli, "L'arco di Augusto in Rimini," *Emilia romana* (Florence, 1945), II, 109–99; +P. G. Pasini, *L'Arco di Augusto* (Rimini, 1974); S. De Maria, "La porta augustea di Rimini nel quadro degli archi commemorativi coevi, Dati strutturali," *Studia Archaeologica* 21 (1979), 73–92.

DIANE FAVRO

ARCH OF AUGUSTUS, Susa. Freestanding stone monument commemorating the bestowal of Roman municipal rights on local Alpine tribes in 9/8 B.C.

The arch rises 14m over the road leading into ancient Segusio. Above the single arched opening winds a continuous frieze, preserved on three sides. Executed in a naive provincial style, the frieze reliefs depict ceremonies formalizing the agreement between the Romans and the tribal ruler Cottius. The bronze attic inscription announcing the pact has disappeared. Remotely located, the arch was not carefully examined until the late nineteenth century, when the lively, archaizing reliefs attracted the attention of European scholars.

BIBLIOGRAPHY

+E. Ferrero, *L'Arc d'Auguste à Suse* (Turin, 1901); +F. Studniczka, "Über den Augustusbogen in Susa," *JdI* 18 (1903), 1–24; +B. M. Felleti Maj, "Il fregio commemorativo dell'arco di Susa," *RendPontAcc* 23 (1961), 129–53; S. De Maria, "L'apparato figurativo nell'arco onorario di Susa, Revisione critica del problema," *RivIstArch* 1 (1977), 44–52.

DIANE FAVRO

ARCH OF CLAUDIUS, Rome. Lost single-bay Roman honorary or *"triumphal" arch spanning the Via Lata near the present-day Palazzo Sciarra erected in A.D. 51/52 to commemorate Claudius's conquest of Britain; the arch was part of the Aqua Virgo aqueduct, which crossed the Via Lata at this point.

Some have thought that the arch is represented in abbreviated form on the reverses of Claudian coins, but the coins are earlier in date. The arch was torn down no later than the ninth century. Part of the dedicatory inscription and architectural and relief fragments believed by some to come from the lost arch were found in 1562, 1641, 1869 and 1925 and are now in the Palazzo dei Conservatori (*Capitoline Museums). Recently, other reliefs in the Villa Medici, the *Louvre and Hever Castle have been attributed to the monument, but almost all the attributions have been disputed, and the original appearance of the arch is uncertain. The earliest finds were recorded by Flaminio *Vacca, and a— probably fanciful—reconstruction of the arch was drawn by Pirro *Ligorio. Drawings of part of the arch's battle frieze and two male relief heads, possibly from the arch, were made by Pierre *Jacques in 1577.

BIBLIOGRAPHY

+F. Castagnoli, "Due archi trionfali della via Flaminia presso piazza Sciarra," *BullComm* 70 (1942), 58–73; H. Laubscher, "Arcus Novus und Arcus Claudii, Zwei Triumphbögen an der Via Lata in Rome," *Nachrichten der Akademie der Wissenschaften in Göttingen* (1976), 78–101; G. M. Koeppel, "Two Reliefs from the Arch of Claudius in Rome," *RM* 90 (1983), 103–9; S. De Maria, *Gli Archi onorari di Roma e dell'Italia romana* (Rome, 1988), 280–82.

FRED S. KLEINER

ARCH OF CONSTANTINE, Rome. Triple-bay Roman honorary or *"triumphal" arch erected at the beginning of the Via Triumphalis between A.D. 312 and 315 in honor of Constantine's *decennalia* (25 July 315) and military victory over Maxentius at the *Milvian Bridge (28 October 312).

Despite its fourth-century dedication, only part of the arch was made at that time. Much of the relief sculpture and even some of the architectural members come from earlier monuments, possibly destroyed in fires of A.D. 287 and 307 or perhaps never finished. Constantinian in date are the spandrels with Victories, Seasons and river gods; the keystone figures; the column pedestals with Victories and Roman soldiers and captured barbarians; the tondi with Sol and Luna; and the frieze, which depicts Constantine's departure from Milan, the siege of Verona, the battle of the Milvian Bridge, the emperor's entrance into Rome, his address from the rostra to the Roman people and a *congiarium.*

The reused material includes four sections of the "Great Trajanic Frieze," in which two of Trajan's heads have been recarved as Constantine. The Trajanic reliefs, purported to come from the Forum of Trajan, were already recognized as part of a continuous frieze in the Renaissance and were reconstructed on paper by Giuliano da Sangallo and later by P. S. *Bartoli and Luigi Rossini. Casts of the panels were recombined to form a frieze for the Mostra Augustea (1937) and are now in the *Museo della Civiltà Romana. Eight figures of Dacian prisoners, perhaps also from the Forum of Trajan, surmount the eight projecting columns of the arch. Eight tondi with scenes of hunting and sacrifice probably come from a lost private monument of Hadrian; a number of heads were recut to portray Constantine and Licinius. Eight relief panels from a lost arch of Marcus Aurelius are embedded in the attic; the panels depict scenes of *adventus* and *profectio, liberalitas* and submission, *adlocutio* and *lustratio, rex datus* and prisoners.

In the early Middle Ages, the arch belonged to the monks of S. Gregorio, who incorporated it as a tower into their battlements. The arch later became part of the castle of the Frangipani and was known in the late Middle Ages and the Renaissance as the Arcus Trasi. These later constructions around the arch caused damage to many of the relief sculptures, and other damage may have been done by deliberate pillaging of the monument. Already in 1498–99 it was necessary to restore the arch. In 1536 *Paul III had the column pedestals exposed by removing the earth that had accumulated over the centuries. Restorations are also documented in 1570 and again in 1733 under Clement XII, when the eight imperial heads in the Aurelian panels were added, and those of the eight Dacians above the columns were restored by Pietro Bracci. In 1805 under Pius VII the arch was finally freed from all later accretions. A scaffolding was erected against the arch in 1931 and again in 1936, allowing L'Orange and von *Gerkan to examine the structure and the reliefs closely and allowing Faraglia to produce the first full set of photographs of the monument. Scaffolding was reerected recently in order to clean and protect the arch from the effects of pollution, thus giving scholars a chance to study anew the remarkable combinations of preexisting monuments.

During the long history of the arch, its form and that of the later structures around it have been recorded by many artists, including *Botticelli, Perugino, Pinturicchio, the artist of the *Codex Escurialensis, Giuliano da Sangallo, Antonio da *Sangallo the Younger, *Serlio, Antoine *Desgodets, *Bellori and *Piranesi, among others. Many of the representations show a second attic in the form of a parapet, which suggested to Magi that the Arch of Constantine was not crowned by the customary statuary group. The lost parapet is included in the model of the arch now on display in the Museo della Civiltà Romana.

The reuse of earlier reliefs beside new ones on the arch has been a subject of controversy from the Renaissance to the present day. In a letter of 1519 to *Leo X, *Raphael praised the architecture of the monument and its reused sculpture but described the Constantinian reliefs as "most absurd, without art or any good design" ("sciocchissime, senza arte o disegno alcuno buono"). Francesco Milizia, an influential Neoclassical theorist, condemned the mixing of reliefs from various eras and considered the arch a corruption not only of art but of the heart (1725–28). The negative judgment of the Constantinian reliefs on the arch is epitomized by Bernard Berenson's *The Arch of Constantine or the Decline of Form* (New York, 1954). However, the interest of fourth-century artists in hierarchical forms, frontal figures and symbolic spatial relationships is now viewed as a valid expression of the period and as a prelude to the art of the Middle Ages.

BIBLIOGRAPHY

+H. P. L'Orange—A. von Gerkan, *Der Spätantike Bildschmuck des Konstantinsbogens* (Berlin, 1939); +A. Giuliano, *L'Arco di Costantino* (Milan, 1955); F. Magi, "Il coronamento dell'arco di Costantino," *RendPontAcc* 29 (1956–57), 84–110; I. Iacopi, *L'Arco di Costantino e le Terme di Caracalla,* Itinerari dei musei, gallerie e monumenti d'Italia 113 (Rome, 1977); S. De Maria, *Gli Archi onorari di Roma e dell'Italia romana* (Rome, 1988) 203–11, 316–9; +Kleiner, *Roman Sculpture,* 444–55.

                                                                DIANA E. E. KLEINER

ARCH OF HADRIAN, Athens. Monumental stone arch set up to honor Hadrian (A.D. 117–38) at the boundary of his "New Athens" (*Novae Athenae*).

The freestanding structure made of Pentelic marble is in two stories. The lower story features a semicircular arch (twenty feet, four inches wide) that was originally flanked by Corinthian columns (now missing), and the upper story has three bays articulated by Corinthian columns, the central bay topped by a triangular pediment. The monument is in excellent condition except for the missing columns on the first story and a thin stone sheath that once stood in the central bay in the upper story—removed, it is said, by Queen Amalia, wife of Otho (ruled 1832–62), to make the monument more picturesque.

The identity of the monument and its connection with Hadrian seem to have been secure always, probably due to the fact that the arch bears two Greek inscriptions making clear its function in dividing the old city of Athens from the new part built by Hadrian. On the west the inscription reads, "This is Athens, the city of Theseus"; on the east, the side of the new town, "This is the city of Hadrian and not of Theseus." *Ciriaco of Ancona copied the inscriptions in the fifteenth century. The Prussian soldier J. G. Transfeldt (d. 1685) had no doubt about the identity of the monument, nor did *Spon and *Wheler, whose

Arch of Hadrian, engraving designed by James Stuart, from J. Stuart–N. Revett, *The Antiquities of Athens* 3 (1794).

modest description and schematic engraving were published in 1682. *Stuart did a handsome drawing of the arch, still useful for study purposes, showing the sheath in the upper story before it was removed. *Dodwell (1819), unmoved by Stuart's drawing, characterized the arch as ''a monument which has not much architectural merit.'' Ippolito *Caffi has left an oil painting of the Arch of Hadrian (1844; Venice, Ca' Pesaro).

The arch is located at the northwest corner of the precinct of the *Temple of Olympian Zeus, which was completed and dedicated by Hadrian in A.D. 131/2. Scholarly opinion has been divided over whether the arch was erected on that occasion (as argued by J. Travlos and J. B. *Ward-Perkins) or whether it was set up later by his successor, Antoninus Pius (as proposed by H. Thompson, F. Sear).

BIBLIOGRAPHY

W. Judeich, *Topographie von Athen* (Munich, 1931), 381–82; P. Graindor, *Athènes sous Hadrien* (Le Caire, 1934), 228–29; +Travlos, 253–57.

ARCH OF SEPTIMIUS SEVERUS, Leptis Magna.

ARCH OF SEPTIMIUS SEVERUS, Leptis Magna. Roman honorary or *''triumphal'' arch with four faces, erected in the hometown of Septimius Severus, presumably for his African tour in A.D. 203.

Located at the crossing of the southern *cardo* and *decumanus,* this marble monument rises over 16m tall and, though hastily constructed, is remarkable for its steep, broken pediments, shallow interior dome and complex sculptural program. The deeply carved narrative reliefs on the four attic faces are punctuated with hieratic images of the emperor and his family. The carving techniques, subject matter, and frontal posing indicate Eastern craftsmen, probably from Asia Minor. An Italian team excavated the arch at *Leptis Magna in the 1920s, and in 1949, members of the *British School at Rome executed measured drawings. Subsequent research has focused on the reliefs, now housed at the Tripoli Museum. Though perhaps overly decorated, this Severan arch stands as one of the most magnificent tetrapylons in the Roman world; it has not yet been published as it deserves in an individual monograph.

BIBLIOGRAPHY

+R. Bartoccini, ''L'Arco quadrifonte dei Severi,'' *AfrIt* 4 (1931), 32–152; +J. B. Ward Perkins, ''The Arch of Septimius Severus at Lepcis Magna,'' *Archaeology* 4 (1951), 226–31; +R. Bianchi Bandinelli—E. V. Caffarelli—G. Caputo, *The Buried City, Excavations at Leptis Magna* (New York, 1966), 31–41, 67–70.

                                                                      DIANE FAVRO

ARCH OF SEPTIMIUS SEVERUS, Rome.

ARCH OF SEPTIMIUS SEVERUS, Rome. Roman *''triumphal'' arch with three openings, dedicated in A.D. 203 in honor of the emperor Septimius Severus and his sons Caracalla and Geta, at the northwest end of the Roman Forum (*Forum Romanum).

In 1199 Pope Innocent III gave one-half of the arch to the church of SS. Sergio e Bacco (built originally on the Rostra and totally removed by 1812).

The other half belonged to the Ciminius family, who turned their possession into a feudal stronghold. The arch is listed in the eighth-century *Einsiedeln Itinerary and the twelfth-century *Mirabilia. These entries were elaborated in the thirteenth-century *Graphia Aureae urbis Romae. The thirteenth-century redaction, the Miracole de Roma, attempted to correlate the inscription with the historical reliefs and to make an aesthetic assessment, an approach followed by the Iter Romanum of Giovanni *Dondi and the anonymous Tractatus de rebus et situ urbis Romae (ca. 1411).

The drawing in the *Codex Escurialensis after D. *Ghirlandaio shows the arch free from any encumbering church and buried to the level of the column bases (1491). Drawings by Marten van *Heemskerck in Berlin of the Roman Forum feature the arch (1535), and S. *Serlio published further plans and elevations with measurements in his Architettura (1556). Jan Brueghel's drawings of 1594 in the collection of the Duke of Devonshire, Chatsworth, show the east façade and the north end of the pier of the arch buried up to the column bases with tower and battlements still present. Suaresius published a monograph on the arch with plates originally drawn by *Pietro da Cortona (1676), a study that was incorporated into the publication of P. S. *Bartoli and G. P. *Bellori (1690).

In 1520, Pope *Leo X had the arch freed from some of the earth fill around it. In 1535 Pope *Paul III excavated the street through the central bay, and in 1536 the entire area was replanned for the triumph of Charles V. The tower was removed from the north pier in 1636. Major excavations were begun by Pope *Pius VII in 1803 under the direction of C. *Fea.

BIBLIOGRAPHY

Lanciani, Ruins and Excavations of Ancient Rome, 282–85; +R. Brilliant, Arch of Septimius Severus in the Roman Forum, MAAR 29 (1967); +Nash, I, 126–30; Kleiner, Roman Sculpture, 329–32.

                                                    PETER HOLLIDAY

ARCH OF THE ARGENTARII, Rome. Monumental Roman gate, erected near or at the entrance to the Forum Boarium in A.D. 204 by the argentarii et negotiantes boarii huius loci to the emperor Septimius Severus and his family.

The dedicatory inscription was modified three times, after the murders of Geta, Septimius Severus's younger son; Plautilla, wife of the emperor's older son, Caracalla; and Plautianus, Plautilla's father. The extensive relief decoration includes large vertical panels of Roman soldiers with Parthian captives and the Severan family sacrificing. Of the original six figures in the two sacrificial panels of the bay, only Septimius Severus, his wife, Julia Domna, and Caracalla survive; the figures of Geta, Plautilla and Plautianus were removed after their murders in accord with the damnatio memoriae each suffered.

The earliest known drawings of the gate appear in the late-fifteenth-century Sienese sketchbooks of Giuliano da *Sangallo; the monument was also drawn in the sixteenth century by Marten van *Heemskerck and Giovanni Antonio *Dosio, among others. These drawings show the gate much as it is today, stand-

ing next to, and partly covered by, the church of S. Giorgio in Velabro. Part of
the wall at the southwest corner of the church was removed in 1871 to uncover
more of the east pier of the gate.

BIBLIOGRAPHY
+D.E.L. Haynes—P.E.D. Hirst, *Porta Argentariorum* (London, 1939); +M. Pallottino,
L'Arco degli Argentari, Monumenti romani 2 (Rome, 1945); S. De Maria, *Gli Archi
onorari di Roma e dell'Italia romana* (Rome, 1988), 185–89, 307–9.

FRED S. KLEINER

ARCH OF THE GAVII, Verona. Single-bay Roman honorary arch with
smaller arches also on the short ends, a rare example of a *quadrifrons* of rectangular plan.

The arch was erected on the ancient Via Postumia and has been variously
dated to the early or mid-first century A.C. It is rather austere in appearance and
without figural decoration, save for the statues (now lost) of four members of
the *gens Gavia* that were set into niches on the two façades. Inscriptions give
the names of the members of the rich and influential local family to whom the
arch was dedicated, as well as the name of the architect, L. Vitruvius Cerdo, a
freedman.

In the Middle Ages the arch became a gate in the fortified walls of *Verona
and appears as such in the sixteenth-century plans of the city. At that time the
lower part of the monument was below ground level, and shops had been installed in the arch. In 1805 the arch was dismantled; it was reconstructed in
1932 on its present site, based on the detailed drawings of Andrea *Palladio.
Other valuable records of the arch's appearance were made by Baldassare *Peruzzi, Antonio da *Sangallo the Younger, Sebastiano *Serlio and Giovanni Car-
oto. The arch has influenced the form of several later Italian monuments; most
striking is the use of the Arch of the Gavii as the model for Florio Pindemonti's
1542 altar in the Veronese church of S. Anastasia.

BIBLIOGRAPHY
+A. Avena, *L'Arco dei Gavi ricostruito dal Comune di Verona* (Verona, 1932); +G.
Tosi, "L'Arco dei Gavi," in *Palladio e Verona,* ed. P. Marini (Verona, 1980), 34–49;
+G. Tosi, *L'Arco dei Gavi a Verona* (Rome, 1982); S. De Maria, *Gli Archi onorari di
Roma e dell'Italia romana* (Rome, 1988), 169–71, 331–33.

FRED S. KLEINER

ARCH OF THE SERGII, Pola (Pula), Croatia. Roman honorary arch erected
at Pola in the first century B.C. by one of the town's foundation families.

The arch commemorated members of the Sergii family who were civil and
military functionaries—Gaius Sergius, Lucius Sergius and Lucius Sergius Lepidus, who, as we know from one of the inscriptions on the attic, was a tribune
in the twenty-ninth legion, which was disbanded by Augustus shortly after the
Battle of Actium in 31 B.C. On the basis of this inscription and an examination

of the younger Sergius's career, as well as stylistic analysis of the sculptured decoration, the date of the arch can be placed between 25 and 10 B.C.

The arch consists of a single, shallow bay, with a pair of engaged Corinthian columns on either side. The exterior decoration includes a rich vegetal pattern carved on the impost pilasters, Victory figures in the spandrels and a frieze with an alternating design of arms and trophies, garlands held up by Erotes and scenes of racing chariots. The vegetal decoration is continued inside, on both sides of the actual passageway, and a panel at the top of the vault depicts a serpent borne by an eagle. The iconography of the relief sculpture serves to confirm the funerary nature of the arch. Privately erected arches commemorating families are rare. In this aspect the Arch of the Sergii is akin to the *Arch of the Gavii at Verona.

The monument is not mentioned in a single ancient text. Only with the renewed interest in classical studies in the Renaissance did writers begin to record it. *Ciriaco of Ancona was the first of many commentators on the arch, including Fra Giovanni *Giocondo, Konrad *Peutinger and Antonio de Ville (*Descriptio portus et urbis Polae,* 1633). For most of these writers the structure itself had secondary importance; they were chiefly interested in the inscriptions found on the arch. Exceptionally penetrating were the observations of Gianrinaldo Carli (*Delle antichità italiche* [Milan, 1788]), who stands apart in not calling the monument a triumphal arch. He rightly called it a funerary arch and, in addition, correctly transcribed from the inscription the number of the tribune's legion (others had failed to do so). Carli also studied the measurements and proportions of the arch in comparison with the precepts of Vitruvius and concluded that it possessed numerous discordances. He argued, as well, for the anterior date for the monument of 31 B.C., after which the legion was disbanded.

Many drawings and engravings were made of the arch. It was "discovered," admired and drawn throughout the Renaissance by architects such as Sebastiano *Serlio, Giovanni Maria Falconetto (1468–1535), G. B. da Sangallo and Andrea *Palladio, who all saw in the arch a model for the theoretical studies of their treatises. Palladio, it seems certain, even visited Pola and personally measured the Arch of the Sergii.

The arch was also reproduced by numerous artists, especially of the seventeenth and eighteenth centuries, who took pleasure in it as a prime example of the ancient "fragment." An engraving by *Piranesi (*Alcune vedute di archi trionfali ed altri monumenti . . .* [Rome, 1765]) offers a romantic "archaeological" interpretation typical of the period. The most precise representations are those by Francesco Monaco for Carli's book.

The first true academic study of the arch was done in the nineteenth century by Luigi Rossini (*Gli Archi trionfali, onorari e funebri degli antichi Romani* [Rome, 1836]). The inscriptions have continued to interest scholars of this century (*Mommsen, Bruna Forlati Tamaro, Hermann Dessau, A.H.M. Jones), but no detailed study of the entire monument appeared before Gustavo Traversari's book in 1971.

BIBLIOGRAPHY
C. D. Curtis, "Roman Monumental Arches," *Supplementary Papers of the American School of Classical Studies in Rome* 2 (1908), 37–38; +A. Gnirs, *Pola, Ein Führer durch die antiken Baudenkmäler und Sammlungen* (Vienna, 1915), 105–9; I. A. Richmond, "Commemorative Arches and City Gates in the Augustan Age," *JRS* 23 (1933), 149–51; +G. Traversari, *L'Arco dei Sergi* (Padua, 1971).

CHERYL L. SOWDER

ARCH OF TITUS, Rome. Roman *"triumphal arch," dedicated to the deified emperor Titus after his death in A.D. 81.

The arch, revetted entirely with Pentelic marble, stood on the highest point of the Via Sacra in Rome. In the passageway (twenty-six feet high), relief panels with excerpts, as it were, of Titus's triumph over Judea in A.D. 70 face each other. On the side near the *Palatine Hill is shown the parading of spoils from the temple in Jerusalem (seven-branched candelabrum, offering table, trumpets), while on the facing panel, Titus, crowned by Victory, stands in the triumphal chariot accompanied by lictors, officials and divinities. In the very top of the coffered vault is a relief showing the deified emperor seated on the back of an eagle, ascending to the heavens.

The monument is praised for its well-balanced, "classic" proportions. An almost exact replica was built in the *Arch of Trajan at Benevento (A.D. 114). In the medieval period the structure was known as the *arcus septem lucernarum* (arch of the seven lamps) because of the menorah in one of the panels. In the twelfth century the Frangipani, one of the most influential families of the time, incorporated the arch into a fortified passage connecting their possessions on the Palatine Hill, by way of S. Maria Nuova, with their palace on the site of the *Temple of Venus and Roma. At that time the passageway was partly obstructed by a chamber built into the upper part of it, destroying portions of the reliefs. Engravings by Hieronymus *Cock (1551) still show a series of buildings cutting across the top of the Velia (the projecting spur of the Palatine) with battlements on top of the arch but with the passageway now fully open again. In a view from the *Capitoline Hill drawn in the seventeenth century by Gaspare van *Wittel, this series of buildings persists, as do the battlements, but now, across the open square of the *Forum Romanum, the Arch of Titus is linked to the *Arch of Septimius Severus by a tree-lined alley. A close-up view of the monument by Alò Giovannoli (1615–19) documents its ruinous state.

When Giuseppe *Valadier was commissioned to reconstruct it in 1822, he took it down completely and rebuilt it on the remaining foundations, restoring the missing parts, using the Arch of Trajan at Benevento as a model. As a contrast to the marble of the ancient portion, Valadier used travertine for the new parts—the first instance of such scientific restoration.

Since the later nineteenth century, the panel reliefs have elicited much interest among art historians and archaeologists. Their "pictorial" or "illusionistic" quality, which succeeds in giving the impression of figures moving about freely

Arch of Titus, drawing by M. van Heemskerck, Berlin, Kupferstichkabinett. (© Bildarchiv Preussischer Kulturbesitz, Berlin, 1994. Photo: J. P. Anders, 79 D 2a.)

in space, led *Wickhoff and other scholars to see in them a close relationship
to monumental painting and to value them as masterpieces, even as the acme
of Roman relief sculpture.

BIBLIOGRAPHY

+F. Magi, "Ancora sull'Arco di Tito," *RM* 84 (1977), 331–47; M. Pfanner, *Der Titus-bogen, Beiträge zur Erschliessung hellenistischer und kaiserzeitlicher Skulptur und Architektur* 2 (Mainz, 1983).

GERHARD M. KOEPPEL

ARCH OF TRAJAN, Ancona. Single-bay Roman honorary or *"triumphal"
arch with engaged Corinthian columns, dedicated in A.D. 115 in honor of Trajan
on the occasion of the construction of a new mole in the Adriatic port city.

The arch was devoid of figural decoration, save for the lost statuary group
once on the attic. Some have thought that the monument is depicted (prospec-
tively) on the *Column of Trajan, although others believe the Trajanic relief
reproduces an Augustan arch at Brindisi. The Ancona arch unquestionably appears in a 1510 general view of the city's port painted by Andrea Lilli for the
Palazzo of Alessandro Nembrini in Ancona and was documented many times
in succeeding centuries (e.g., by Luigi Rossini in 1834) as the chief ancient
landmark of Ancona. Restoration work is recorded in 1667 and again in 1893.
In the 1930s neighboring edifices and an eighteenth-century crenellated wall
were cleared in order to isolate the monument; at the same time, excavations
were conducted to expose the original foundations of the arch. The monument
is, nevertheless, still approached by the staircase built before it in 1859.

BIBLIOGRAPHY

+G. Bevilacqua, *Sul porto e sull'arco di Traiano in Ancona* (Ancona, 1889); +E. Galli,
"Per la sistemazione dell'Arco di Traiano in Ancona," *BdA* 30 (1936–37), 321–36; A.
Campana, "Gianozzo Manetti, Ciriaco e l'arco di Traiano ad Ancona," *Italia Medioevale
e Umanistica* 2 (1959), 483–504; S. De Maria, *Gli Archi onorari di Roma e dell'Italia
romana* (Rome, 1988), 132–33, 150–51, 227–28.

FRED S. KLEINER

ARCH OF TRAJAN, Benevento. One of the best-preserved Roman honorary
or "triumphal" arches in the world, erected on the Via Traiana ca. A.D. 114
(the exact date is disputed) and modeled on the *Arch of Titus in Rome.

The arch is the earliest standing arch with superimposed relief panels celebrating the emperor on both façades; the rich decoration also includes Victories,
water deities and Seasons in the spandrels, three reliefs in the bay, composite
capitals and an elaborate cornice. In the Middle Ages the arch formed part of
the Langobard fortification of *Benevento and was referred to as the Porta Aurea. The monument's relief sculptures and architectural details already served
as models in the twelfth century for the figural panels of the bronze doors and
the cornice of the façade of the Cathedral of Benevento, and later, in the fifteenth
century, for the Arch of Alfonso d'Aragona in Naples. The inscription on the
attic was transcribed first in 1437 by *Ciriaco of Ancona and later by other

Renaissance humanists. The arch was a favored subject for sketches, prints and paintings and was recorded by, among others, Giuliano da *Sangallo (1488), Sebastiano *Serlio (1540), Gian Paolo *Panini (ca. 1740–50), Giuseppe Piermarini (1770), Giovanni Battista *Piranesi (1773), Luigi Rossini (1836) and Luigi *Canina (1840). Casts of the relief panels were made by A. L. *Frothingham in 1893 and for the Mostra Augustea della Romanità of 1937; they are now exhibited in the *Museo della Civiltà Romana. The arch is discussed in the groundbreaking late nineteenth-century studies of Roman sculpture by Philippi and *Wickhoff and figures prominently today in studies of the official relief sculpture of the Roman Empire.

BIBLIOGRAPHY

F. J. Hassel, *Der Trajansbogen in Benevent, Ein Bauwerk des römischen Senates* (Mainz, 1966); +M. Rotili, *L'Arco di Traiano a Benevento* (Rome, 1972); K. Fittschen, "Das Bildprogramm des Trajansbogens in Benevent," *AA* 87 (1972), 742–88; S. De Maria, *Gli Archi onorari di Roma e dell'Italia romana* (Rome, 1988), 128–32, 148–49, 232–35.

FRED S. KLEINER

"ARCO DI PORTOGALLO," Rome. Single-bay Roman honorary or *"triumphal" arch that once spanned the Via Lata (now Via del Corso) at the corner of the Via della Vite.

The arch has been variously dated and for a long time was thought to be an Antonine monument, but it is most likely a structure of the Late Antique period incorporating spolia of earlier monuments, including two relief panels of Hadrianic date commemorating the apotheosis of Sabina. The name "Arco di Portogallo" dates from the sixteenth century, when the Portuguese ambassador resided nearby in the Palazzo Fiano. The arch was demolished in 1662 by the order of Pope Alexander VII to permit widening of the Corso for horse racing; a marble plaque commemorates the removal of the arch. The appearance of the arch is known from drawings and prints by Giovanni Antonio *Dosio, Pirro *Ligorio, Carlo Fontana (who was responsible for dismantling the arch) and others. The reused Hadrianic reliefs are today in the Palazzo dei Conservatori (*Capitoline Museums) in Rome and have recently been restored.

BIBLIOGRAPHY

+S. Stucchi, "L'Arco detto 'di Portogallo' sulla via Flaminia," *BullComm* 73 (1949/50), 101–22; +E. La Rocca, *Rilievi storici capitolini* (Rome, 1986), 21–37; S. De Maria, *Gli archi onorari di Roma e dell'Italia romana* (Rome, 1988), 221–22, 324–25.

FRED S. KLEINER

ARELATE. See ARLES.

AREZZO (ARRETIUM). Etruscan and Roman city.

In the sixth century B.C., Arezzo was a small town on a low hill overlooking the valleys of the Arno and the Chiana, but by the third century it had become one of the richest and most powerful Etruscan cities. The *Chimaera*, discovered in 1553 with a number of small bronze figures, is a masterpiece of Late Classical bronze casting and perhaps the best known and handsomest of all Etruscan ex-votos.

An earlier deposit was discovered by Francesco Leoni in 1869 near the Fonte Veneziana ontside the city. It contained some 200 small bronze figures, male and female, with other votive material of the sixth century B.C. Some of these can still be recognized in the museums of Arezzo and Florence. A third votive deposit, recently discovered near the Roman amphitheater, include male and female terracotta heads of the late second and early first centuries B.C., classicizing in style and showing a relationship with Roman sculpture of the Late Republic.

In 1918 Luigi *Pernier excavated in the Via Catona, north of the Fortezza, remains of the mud-brick city walls recorded by Vitruvius. With them, he found large fragments of fine Hellenistic architectural terracottas in a style based on the Pergamene, probably debris from a temple on the arx (the present Fortezza). In 1948 Early Classical terracotta temple revetments were found near the amphitheater, parts of a raking cornice decorated with figures of warriors in high relief, so far unique.

Except for the mud-brick walls and the terracotta temple revetments, little is known of the Etruscan city proper; the sanctuaries outside the walls, from which the *Chimaera* came, and the ex-votos of the Fonte Veneziana and the terracotta heads found near the amphitheater define its limits. Arezzo's Roman period is documented by quantities of fine *Arretine pottery manufactured there in the first century B.C. and first century A.C.; a charming bronze Minerva found in a well in 1554; a Roman copy of a Greek fourth-century statue; the Roman amphitheater, on the ruins of one of whose curving walls the sixteenth century monastery of S. Bernardo was built, now the Museo Archeologico Mecenate; and the many marble statues and reliefs now in that museum.

BIBLIOGRAPHY

G. Dennis, *Cities and Cemeteries of Etruria,* 2nd ed. (London, 1878), II, 379–93; +C. Lazzeri, "Arezzo etrusca, Le origini della città e la stipe votiva alla Fonte Veneziana," *StEtr* 1 (1927), 113–27; +P. Bocci Pacini, "La stipe di via della Società Operaia ad Arezzo," *Santuari d'Etruria* (Milan, 1985), 179–85; +S. Haynes, *Etruscan Bronzes* (London, 1985), 105–8.

EMELINE HILL RICHARDSON

ARGIVE HERAION (HERAEUM). Greek sanctuary of the goddess Hera, located ca. 7km northeast of *Argos, Greece.

The principal remains of the site belong to an early temple on an upper terrace, perhaps of the seventh century B.C., and a later temple on a lower terrace to the south, belonging to around the middle of the fifth century B.C. Associated structures include a massive wall of conglomerate boulders tentatively dated to the Geometric period supporting the upper terrace and a monumental stairway leading up to the lower terrace, as well as porticoes and several large unidentified structures.

The Argive Heraion was a site of major religious importance from a very early date. An often-anthologized terracotta model of a shrine (now National Museum, Athens) suggests that there may have been a structure on the site by the eighth century B.C. The remains of a stone foundation with widely spaced columns (evidently supporting a wooden superstructure) seem to belong to the seventh century B.C. and the Archaic period. This may be the setting for the dramatic tale told by Herodotos (1.31) of how the two youths Kleobis and Biton pulled the chariot of their mother, a priestess of Hera, all the way from Argos to the Heraion, then went inside the Heraion to lie down and sleep eternally. The temple burned in 423 B.C. and was replaced by the new temple, probably already under way on the lower terrace. The latter, a Doric structure designed by the Argive architect Eupolemos and containing a gold and ivory statue of Hera by Polykleitos, was still standing when Pausanias (2.17) visited the site in the second century A.C.

The Argive Heraion was not known to the travelers of the seventeenth and eighteenth centuries but was rediscovered in 1831 by General Thomas Gordon, who dug there in 1836. In 1854, A. R. Rangabe and C. Bursian excavated at the temple. *Schliemann made soundings in 1874, but large-scale, comprehensive excavation was not carried out until the campaigns of the *American School of Classical Studies under Charles *Waldstein (1892–95). Preclassical remains on the slopes of the acropolis at Prosymna were investigated by C. *Blegen (1925–28). The stratigraphy of the site was studied in 1949 in a joint international effort by J. L. *Caskey of the American School and P. Amandry of the *French School in Athens. Recently, Christopher Pfaff of the American School has done a thorough documentation of the architectural remains of the fifth-century temple and a new reconstruction.

BIBLIOGRAPHY

+C. Waldstein et al., *The Argive Heraion,* 1–2 (Boston, 1902–5); J. L. Caskey—P. Amandry, "Investigations at the Heraion of Argos, 1949," *Hesperia* 21 (1952), 165–221; +R. A. Tomlinson, *Argos and the Argolid* (Ithaca, 1972), 33–34, 230–46; A. Foley, *The Argolid 800–600* B.C.*, An Archaeological Survey, Studies in Mediterranean Archaeology* 80 (1988), 172; C. A. Pfaff, *The Argive Heraion: The Architecture of the Classical Temple of Hera,* diss., New York University, 1992.

ARGOS. Greek city in the northeast Peloponnesus, located in the Argolid plain ca. 5km from the sea.

Rich in a legendary past, Argos has yielded remains from the Neolithic and Bronze ages and shows evidence of long, continuous habitation. Devoted to the goddess Hera (cf. *Argive Heraion), the city is associated with the mythical figure of Io as mother of the Argive royal family and the hero Perseus, as well as with Diomedes, who ruled Argos at the time of the Trojan War. After the Dorian invasion, Argos was governed by the tyrant Pheidon (probably seventh century B.C.) and experienced its period of greatest strength. Engaged in bitter rivalry with *Sparta, Argos dominated the northeast Peloponnesus until its defeat by Sparta in 546 B.C. An attack on the city by the Spartans under Kleomenes was thwarted by the leadership of the poetess Telesilla, who armed the women and slaves of Argos when the regular army had been massacred. In the fifth and fourth centuries, Argos was allied with Athens against Sparta and then with Macedon. Though the city had declined from its greatest days, it continued to flourish into the period of the Roman Empire (Pausanias, 2.18–24, recorded various monuments in the second century A.C.) and to survive into the Middle Ages.

The city was disposed between two acropolis hills, the Aspis and the Larissa. Because of extensive later habitation, it is not possible to understand how the city was laid out in any period of antiquity. The sites of several temples have been identified—the temple of Pythian Apollo and of Athena Oxyderkes on the west of the Aspis, the temple of Aphrodite near the Larissa. The best-preserved monument of Argos is the great theater, with some ninety tiers of seats still intact (end of the fourth century B.C.).

When the French traveler Des Morceaux visited Argos around 1668, he noted that many of the contemporary houses were built with ancient materials but that it was not possible to identify any ancient monuments. The prevaricator *Fourmont reported, in 1732, the presence of a huge subterranean gallery under the Larissa, cut through a dark-colored stone full of petrified shells. The first plan of the site, a simple sketch, was made by Colonel *Leake (1806), and an only slightly better one was made by the *Expédition Scientifique de Morée. Leake noted the presence of a fortification wall stretching from the Larissa, but by 1833, according to L. *Ross, it had been torn down. The whole town was sacked and burned by Ibrahim Pasha during the War for Independence.

Modern investigation of Argos began early in the twentieth century, with the Dutch scholar Wilhelm Vollgraff, working for the *French School at Athens. He continued his investigations for some years, clearing the theater in 1930. In 1953, the French, under the direction of Paul Courbin, discovered the famous Panoply Grave, containing hoplite armor of the Geometric period.

BIBLIOGRAPHY
W. Vollgraff, "Fouilles d'Argos," *BCH* 31 (1907), 139–84; R. A. Tomilinson, *Argos and the Argolid* (Ithaca, 1972); A. Foley, *The Argolid, 800–600 B.C., An Archaeological Survey* (Göteborg, 1988).

ARLES (ARELATE). City in southern France, a Roman colony in antiquity.

Arles was probably established as a trading post by Greeks from Massalia (*Marseilles), but its early history is obscure. It was founded as a *colonia* by Caesar in 46 B.C., from which period may date the amphitheater. The structure is almost a twin of that at *Nîmes—two tiers of arches, 21,000 seating capacity, 136m × 107m—and, like it, was rebuilt in the Middle Ages, first as a fortress, then as a self-contained village of 200 houses and a church. Restoration began in 1825.

Alongside the amphitheater is the theater (Augustan), of 10m diameter and

Amphitheater at Arles, with houses built around and in the arena, engraving of 1686. (Museon Arlaten, Arles.)

capacity 7,000; *cavea,* orchestra (of red and green marble) and curtain pit are well preserved. Here in the seventeenth century was found the *Venus* of Arles (now in the *Louvre).

Other antiquities include the Baths of Constantine, a three-sided cryptoporticus (11m × 76m) surrounding the forum and probably used for grain storage, and the Alyscamps ("Champs-Elysées," or Elysian Fields), a cemetery of Roman and later date, laid out along the line of the Via Aurelia as it entered the city there to join the Via Domitia. Leaving the city to the west, the Domitia crossed the Rhône on a permanent pontoon bridge, which accommodated the river level as it varied with floods. This was one of the only two Roman bridges on the Rhône (the other was at Vienne); there is now little trace, but it was locally celebrated, and a mosaic picture of it survives in the Square of the Corporations, *Ostia. Alongside it, an underwater siphon of lead pipes laid on the riverbed (remains are in the Musée Lapidaire) delivered water from the Arles aqueduct (source, Les Alpilles) to the west-bank suburb, the modern Trinquetaille.

BIBLIOGRAPHY

L. A. Constans, *Arles antique* (Paris, 1921); F. Benoit, "Le sanctuaire d'Auguste et les cryptoportiques d'Arles," *RA* 39 (1952), 31–67; Idem, "Le developpement de la colonie d'Arles et la centuriation de la Crau," *CRAI* (1964), 156–69; J. P. Clébert, *Provence antique* (Paris, 1970), II, 155–71; P. MacKendrick, *Roman France* (London, 1971), 61–64; J. M. Rouquette, *Arles Antique (Guides archéologiques de la France)* (Paris, 1989).

A. TREVOR HODGE

ARMENINI, GIOVAN BATTISTA (1530–1609). Italian painter and writer, best known for his treatise on art, *De' veri precetti della pittura,* published in three volumes in 1587.

Armenini provides a discourse on Mannerist art theory, giving regulations and precepts for the art of painting grounded in his own wide travels in Italy and study of monuments ancient and modern. He ardently recommends drawing from ancient models and in one passage provides a roll call of the famous pieces of his day worth studying: *Laocoon, *Belvedere *Apollo, *Belvedere Torso, *Venus Felix, *"Cleopatra," *Nile River God, *Marcus Aurelius* Equestrian Statue, *Pasquino,* and *Quirinal Horse Tamers,* as well as the reliefs on the *Arch of Titus and *Arch of Constantine and on the *Column of Trajan and *Column of Marcus Aurelius. It is remarkable that he refers students to existing casts of these sculptures and asserts that there were large collections of casts in Milan, Genoa, Venice, Mantua, Florence, *Bologna, Pesaro, Urbino, Ravenna and elsewhere. While he may not be taken completely literally, the passage provides important evidence on the increasing significance of casts in archaeological and artistic study. Armenini was also concerned to locate pictorial sources from the ancient world and was one of the first to take an interest in antique mosaics.

BIBLIOGRAPHY
J. Schlosser Magnino, *La Letteratura artistica,* 2nd ed. (Florence, 1956), 384–85; G. Previtali, "Armenini, Giovan Battista," *DBI* 4 (1962), 238–39; Haskell—Penny, 16–17.

ARNDT, PAUL JULIUS (1865–1937). German collector, art dealer and private scholar.

Paul Arndt was born in Dresden, son of a wealthy Mecklenburg merchant. He studied in Leipzig with J. *Overbeck and in Munich with H. *Brunn, under whom he gained his doctorate in 1887 with a dissertation on Greek vases. He became assistant to Brunn and later to Adolf *Furtwängler, whose Munich appointment he did much to encourage.

First and always a wealthy amateur who loved Greek art, Arndt never habilitated nor sought a university career. From practical experience he developed a remarkable ability to detect forgeries. His extensive library and expertise were always available to the deserving young, such as Ludwig *Curtius. Museums at Munich, Copenhagen (*Ny Carlsberg Glyptotek), Budapest and Yale owe many of their finest pieces to him. His unique collection of ancient gems was purchased by Crown Prince Rupprecht of Bavaria in 1918 and is today in Munich (Staatliche Münzsammlung).

Arndt's publications, largely in journals, catalogs and corpora (e.g., *Denkmäler griechischer und römischer Skulptur*), stress Greek and Roman portraits and sculpture; they are ignored at peril. He was a pioneer in the use of photography in art research. Half-Jewish, he died, like his friend James *Loeb, just before the worst persecutions began. But almost fifty years passed before his life was written.

BIBLIOGRAPHY
L. Curtius, *Deutsche und Antike Welt: Lebenserinnerungen* (Stuttgart, 1950), 195–98; R. Lullies, in *Archäologenbildnisse,* 158–59; P. Zazoff—H. Zazoff, *Gemmensammler und Gemmenforscher: Von einer noblen Passion zur Wissenschaft* (Munich, 1983), 212–39.

WILLIAM M. CALDER III

ARNOLFO DI CAMBIO (ca. 1245–ca. 1310). Italian sculptor and architect.

Born at Colle Val d'Elsa, Arnolfo di Cambio went to work as an assistant of Nicola *Pisano and was early exposed to Roman remains at *Pisa that provided inspiration for his style, as well as particular iconographic motifs. By 1277 he was at work in Rome itself and thus would have been able to see and absorb the lessons of classical monuments there. Later, he settled in Florence as chief architect of Florence cathedral (1296ff.).

Though Arnolfo left no drawings or descriptions of antiquities, his sculptures provide indirect evidence of close study of ancient monuments at an early date, well before the Renaissance. The influence of a second-century battle sarcophagus from Pisa has been seen in the plasticity and the articulation of the figures done by Arnolfo for the Arca of St. Dominic (S. Domenico Maggiore, Bologna;

completed by 1267). The *Madonna Enthroned* on the tomb of Cardinal Guillaume de Braye (d. 1282; tomb in San Domenico, Orvieto) has the dress and features of a Hellenistic matron, perhaps under the influence of Etruscan sculpture; her tiara, earrings and necklace all recall Etruscan Hellenistic examples. In addition, the Virgin of the *Nativity* from the façade of Florence cathedral reclines in the manner of deceased figures on the lids of Etruscan ash urns.

One of the most remarkable connections of Arnolfo with classical antiquity is suggested by the bronze statue of *St. Peter* enthroned in the basilica of St. Peter's (Vatican), the famous image whose feet have been worn smooth by the loving and pious touch of pilgrims. According to an ancient legend, the statue was made from the bronze of a statue of Capitoline Jupiter as a thank offering from Pope Leo I after the halt of the advance of Attila in 452, and many scholars have approved a Late Antique date for the work. Another school of thought attributes the work to Arnolfo and notes that the formula for the bronze alloy is consistent with a thirteenth-century date. Stylistic arguments in favor of Arnolfo reveal how often his documented works may be compared convincingly with Late Antique/Early Christian works. Whatever the origin of the bronze, it is closely related to a statue in the Grotte Vaticane that shows, by general consent, an ancient marble figure of a philosopher converted into St. Peter by the addition of keys and a gesture of benediction and by the substitution of a bearded head of St. Peter for the original. The bearded head is widely attributed to Arnolfo and thus suggests his direct manipulation of ancient statuary.

BIBLIOGRAPHY

M. Salmi, "Il problema della statua bronzea di S. Pietro nella Basilica Vaticana," *Commentari* 11 (1960), 22–29; +J. Pope-Hennessy, *An Introduction to Italian Sculpture* 1 *Italian Gothic Sculpture,* 2nd. ed. (London, 1972), 180–83; K. Christian, "Arnolfo and Antique Sculpture," ch. 5 of *Arnolfo di Cambio's Sculptural Project for the Duomo Façade in Florence: A Study in Style and Context,* unpub. diss., New York University, 1989; +E. Carli, *Arnolfo* (Florence, 1993).

ARRETINE WARE. Red-gloss ceramic vases, mass-produced during the principate of Augustus (31 B.C.–A.D. 14) and slightly later.

Arretium (*Arezzo) was the principal, though not only, center of manufacture, and such vases were exported to all parts of the empire. The finest Arretine vases, decorated in relief, were made in a mold and were often decorated in the interior with intaglio designs or stamped in sequence with units of molded relief, sometimes with the potters' names. "Plain wares," made on the wheel without molds, were also produced at Arezzo and later at other centers.

Arretine relief vases were the finest, most luxurious Roman ceramic tableware. Often called "poor man's silver," they reflect the archaizing Augustan taste in the minor arts for terracotta imitations of chased metal and marble. The shapes, mixed styles, repertory of Greek and Augustan foliage patterns and great variety of mythological, genre and specific subjects—Bacchic rites and triumphs, Seasons, grape harvesting, Satyrs, erotic groups, banquets, hunts, and Alexander the Great slaying a lion (by Perennius)—were borrowed mainly from Hellenistic silver *repoussé* vases and neo-Attic reliefs. Arretine ware belongs to the broader category of red-gloss vases known as *terra sigillata* (originally so-called because it was decorated by means of a *sigillum,* "stamp"), but what sets it apart is its high aesthetic quality, formal elegance and, in more elaborate designs, delicate modeling that evokes qualities of atmosphere and realistic landscape usually absent in neutral backgrounds of Greek reliefs.

Arretine ware was superseded by a similar, coarser pottery made in Gaul, yet it retained its prestige in the account of *Isidore of Seville in the seventh century and through frequent discoveries of fragments, such as those recorded by Ristoro d'Arezzo in 1282, who likened them to "sacred relics" when they came into "the hands of sculptors or artists or other connoisseurs," and by Giovanni Villani (d. 1348). Other large finds of Arretine ware and kilns made during the late fifteenth century were described by Marco Attilio Alessi and *Vasari, whose grandfather Giorgio, later called *vasaio* ("vasemaker"), found a kiln, four complete vessels and many fragments about a mile from Arezzo. The vessels were presented to Lorenzo de' Medici, a gift that gained Vasari's ancestors the favor of the *Medici family. Artists such as *Giovanni da Udine and *Giulio Romano were influenced by specific motifs and the relief modeling of Arretine vases.

In the eighteenth century, Francesco Rossi discovered two pottery workshops near Arezzo at Cincelli, one of which belonged to P. Cornelius. Later, in 1779, excavations in the same area unearthed the remains of a potter's wheel, kilns, vats, molds and stamps (today in the museum at Arezzo). Such discoveries were widely publicized by A. F. *Gori and Francesco Inghirami, who included the first engraved colored illustration of Arretine pottery in volume 5 of his *Monumenti Etruschi* (1824).

Modern studies of Arretine and other Italian-type *sigillata* ware begin with the work of H. Dragendorff, who studied fragments of red gloss excavated at Tübingen on the Rhine in comparison with material from Arezzo (1895) and with Siegfried Loeschcke, who constructed a typology of "services" of dinnerware (each service had a bowl, platter, plate and cup) on the basis of his finds at the Roman legionary camp of Haltern (1907). These finds were crucial for dating, since the camp at Haltern was abandoned in A.D. 9 (rather than A.D. 16, as Loeschcke thought). In 1968, Howard Comfort published the *Corpus vasorum arretinorum, A Catalogue of the Signatures, Shapes and Chronology of Italian Sigillata,* a fundamental work begun by A. Oxé in 1912 and interrupted twice by world wars. Also in 1968, C. Goudineau published his influential typology of *terra sigillata* plain wares from the well-recorded stratigraphy at *Bolsena. The results of various typological studies on plain wares during the century have been collated and digested in the authoritative work compiled by ten collaborators, *Conspectus formarum terrae sigillatae italico modo confectae* (1990).

BIBLIOGRAPHY
+C. Alexander, *Arretine Relief Ware, The Metropolitan Museum of Art,* CVA, fasc. 9 (Cambridge, MA, 1943); +G. H. Chase, *A Catalogue of Arretine Pottery,* enlarged ed. (Cambridge, MA, 1975), 4–7; T. Yuen, "Giulio Romano, Giovanni da Udine, and Raphael: Some Influences from the Minor Arts of Antiquity," *J Warb* 42 (1979), 263–72; E. Ettlinger et al., eds., *Corpus formarum terrae sigillatae italico modo confectae* (Bonn, 1990).

TOBY YUEN

ARRETIUM. See AREZZO.

ARRINGATORE (AULE METELI). Lifesize bronze Etruscan statue (1.79m) of the late Hellenistic period (ca. 100–75 B.C.).

The sculpture became a part of the *Medici collections under Cosimo I in 1566, shortly after the *Chimaera* of Arezzo, and is now in the Archaeological Museum in *Florence. It is thought to have been found in the vicinity of *Perugia (though some gave as its provenance the Sanguineto Valley, near Lake Trasimene).

Early identifications of the statue named him as a *Consul,* or as *Scipio Africanus;* *Gori called him an Etruscan *Haruspex* (priest). The statue actually depicts Aule Meteli, represented with all the insignia of a Roman citizen of distinction: the high-laced shoes (*calcei*) of the Roman citizen, the gold ring, the tunic with vertical stripes (inlaid in a darker color) and the bordered *toga praetexta* of a magistrate. The inscription on the border of his toga, however, gives his names and titles in the Etruscan language. Aulus Metellius (as his name would have been in Latin) was evidently a native Etruscan and a magistrate in his own Etruscan city, which at this period would have been under Roman control. This statue, cast of seven separate parts, was apparently dedicated in a local sanctuary. The name by which the statue has long been known, the *Arringatore* ("orator"), derives from the gesture of the (correctly restored) right hand, raised to command attention for the orator's speech.

BIBLIOGRAPHY
+T. Dohrn, *Der Arringatore, Bronzestatue im Museo Archeologico von Florenz* (Berlin, 1968); M. Cristofani, "Per una storia del collezionismo nella Toscana granducale, I: I grandi bronzi," *Prospettiva* 17 (1979), 4–15; A. Maggiani, in *La Città degli Uffizi* (Florence, 1982), 37.

LARISSA BONFANTE

ARROTINO (SCYTHIAN SLAVE; "GRINDER"). Lifesize marble statue of a crouching male figure, perhaps a Roman copy of a Hellenistic Greek original of the Pergamene school (second century B.C.).

The sculpture represents a nude male with a cloak thrown over his shoulders, crouching on one knee and gazing upward as he sharpens a knife (whence the Italian popular name *Arrotino,* "knife-grinder").

It has been argued that the sculpture was already known in the late fifteenth century and that it was used by *Ghirlandaio as a model for a disrobed figure in his *Baptism of Christ* in Florence, S. Maria Novella. But the first real documentation of the work comes in a drawing by van *Heemskerck made in Rome between 1534 and 1536. *Aldrovandi saw it in the collection of Niccolo Guisa in Rome in 1550, and in 1551, the piece went to P. Soderini. It was purchased by the *Medici in 1578 and kept in Rome in the Villa Medici until 1677, when it was moved to Florence. It was placed in the *Uffizi and has remained there (except for a brief trip to Palermo to escape the predations of the French, 1800–3) until the present day.

The statue, if a copy, is the only one known of the type and is of overall high quality. These factors constitute background for the bold theory, first proposed by *Sandrart in the seventeenth century but followed by some twentieth-century scholars, that the work is a Renaissance imitation of ancient art, to be attributed to *Michelangelo. Most scholars, however, believe that it is indeed ancient and that it should be paired with a sculpture of the flayed Marsyas known in a number of copies, one of which was in the Medici collection in Rome in the sixteenth century at the time the *Arrotino* was acquired. This interpretation, which sees the figure as the Scythian slave who served Apollo and flayed Marsyas, was, in fact, first advanced by *Agostini at that time but was ignored by many. It has recently been infused with new life by A. Weis, who dates the Uffizi *Arrotino* to the second half of the first century A.C., and argues for the existence of another knife-grinder, dressed in oriental garb, created in the Late Hellenistic period. A number of bizarre interpretations have been suggested through the centuries for the admittedly strange figure: that he was a barber overhearing a conspiracy against Julius Caesar or a conspiracy by Catiline; that he was the Roman augur Attus Navius, who succeeded in cutting a whetstone with a razor; or that he was the servant Milichus, who sharpened a knife for his master to use to murder Nero.

BIBLIOGRAPHY
Bieber, 110–11; Haskell—Penny, 154–57; Bober—Rubinstein, 75–76; A. Weis, *The Hanging Marsyas and Its Copies: Roman Innovations in a Hellenistic Sculptural Tradition* (Rome, 1992).

ARSE. See SAGUNTUM.

ARTEMISION. See TEMPLE OF ARTEMIS.

ARTEMISION GOD. Early Classical Greek over-lifesize bronze statue (*National Archaeological Museum, Athens; height 2.09m), discovered by sponge divers amid the debris of an ancient shipwreck near Cape Artemision, Euboia, in 1926.

In 1928 the site was further investigated by archaeologists. Also recovered were two Hellenistic bronze sculptures of a horse and boy jockey; some pottery of the first century B.C.; and a portion of the ship's hull.

The statue, universally regarded as a masterpiece, belongs to the type of the striding, attacking god or hero that first appeared in Greece in the Archaic period. The legs are spread far apart, the long slender arms gracefully extended. Since the weapon of the deity is missing, it has been debated whether he is Zeus hurling the thunderbolt or Poseidon with the trident. It is generally agreed that the statue dates to about 460 B.C.; it has been attributed to some of the most famous artists of the Early Classical period, including Onatas, Kalamis and Myron. The artist was a master in the medium of cast bronze and created a magnificent contrast of polished flesh, textured hair and beard, and inlaid eyes.

BIBLIOGRAPHY

C. Karouzos, "Ho Poseidon tou Artemisiou," *Deltion* 13 (1930–31), 41–104; G. Mylonas, "The Bronze Statue from Artemision," *AJA* 48 (1944), 143–60; Ridgway, *Severe Style in Greek Sculpture,* 62–64; R. Wunsche, "Der Gott aus dem Meer," *JdI* 94 (1979), 77–111.

CAROL MATTUSCH

ARTEMIS OF EPHESOS. Cult statue of Artemis at the sanctuary of *Ephesos in Ionia, whose temple numbered among the seven wonders of the ancient world and whose cult challenged St. Paul and Christianity (*Acts* 19.23).

Preserved only in ancient reproductions and descriptions, the original statue was attributed to the Amazons and survived seven restorations of the temple from the seventh century B.C. through Roman times (Pliny *NH* 16.79). Copies were transported by Phokaian colonists to Massilia (*Marseilles) around 600 B.C. (Strabo 4.1.4) and by Xenophon to Elis in the fourth century (*Anabasis* 5.3.12). Hellenistic and Roman representations in sculpture, coins and gems illustrate a wooden statue, under lifesize, in elaborate gold clothing and jewelry, a high *polos* (headdress) and veil, with rows of breastlike bulbs across her chest, an attribute common to other Anatolian deities. These reproductions survived the demise of Ephesian cult and statue and were rediscovered in Rome in the Renaissance, providing rich decorative and symbolic motifs first attested in the work of *Raphael. His antiquarian interests and supervision of antiquities for *Leo X acquainted him with many copies of Ephesian Artemis. The example of the type in the Capitoline Museums was described in 1514 by Claude Bellièvre of Lyons and is reflected in the decoration of *Raphael's Vatican Logge. The painter incorporated the goddess into his Vatican Stanza della Segnatura frescoes, where Artemis figures serve as throne supports for the figure of *Philosophy* above the *School of Athens* (1508–11). His pupils, including *Giulio Romano, painted *grottesche* versions of her into the Vatican Loggia (1518–19) and allegorical ones in the Gonzaga's Palazzo del Te in Mantua (1525–35). The Baroque imagination, as in William Hogarth's *Introduction to the Harlot's Progress* (1733) or Tiepolo's ceiling fresco for the Würzburger Residenz (1756), exaggerated her pagan aspects, especially the attributes mistaken for breasts. Her European popularity lasted through Victorian and Pre-Raphaelite tastes and encouraged forgeries of ancient copies; her exotic iconography continues to absorb scholarship.

Grottesche with *Artemis of Ephesos*, engraving after painting by the school of Raphael, Vatican Loggie, 1518–19. (S. P. Morris.)

BIBLIOGRAPHY
D. Hogarth, *Excavations at Ephesus: The Archaic Artemisia* (London, 1908), 323–38; +H. Thiersch, *Artemis Ephesia, Eine archäologische Untersuchung* 1, *Katalog* (Berlin, 1935); +R. Fleischer, *Artemis von Ephesus und verwandte Kultstatuen aus Anatolien und Syrien, EPRO* 35 (Leiden, 1973); *Supplement* in *Studien zur Religion und Kultur Kleinasiens (Festschrift Karl Dörner), EPRO* 66 (Leiden, 1978), 324–58; *LIMC* II, 755–63 (R. Fleischer).

SARAH P. MORRIS

ARTEMIS OF VERSAILLES (DIANE CHASSERESSE). Over-lifesize marble statue of Artemis at the hunt, striding forward with head turned sharply to her right.

The statue has been restored with a stag at her feet, but the creature should be a dog instead. The marble is traditionally thought to be a Roman copy of a Greek original of the fourth century B.C., perhaps created by Leochares as a pendant for the *Belvedere *Apollo,* whose striding pose and turned head mirror the Artemis. Another school of thought, represented by E. Simon, attributes it to Praxiteles, on the basis that the depiction of Artemis on the run was an innovation in the representation of a goddess parallel to Praxiteles' bold choice of nudity for Aphrodite in the *Knidian statue. K. D. Morrow's analysis of the footwear on this and the many replicas and variants of the statue suggest a later date, perhaps even in the second century B.C.

The work is important as one of the rare sculptures outside Rome that acquired a reputation as a classical masterpiece during the Renaissance/Baroque eras. The find spot of the Artemis has not been recorded, but it was displayed at Fontainebleau by 1586, and earlier it may have been at the chateau of Meudon. In 1602 it was newly restored by Barthélemy Prieur and moved to the *Louvre. Prieur also made a bronze copy of the work to remain at Fontainebleau, on a fountain adorned with spouting stags' heads. *Louis XIV had the marble Artemis moved to the Grande Galerie at Versailles, but it returned to Paris in 1798 to go on display in the Musée Central des Arts (now the Musée du Louvre).

In the seventeenth century, the work was believed to represent the *Artemis of Ephesos. But the cult figure of the Ephesian temple is radically different, and this identification of the Versailles figure was refuted in the early eighteenth century. In Rome *Panini included the statue in a *capriccio* showing the sacrifice of Iphigenia at the shrine of Artemis (Holburne of Menstrie Museum, Bath). Numerous copies of the statue from the seventeenth, eighteenth and nineteenth centuries attest to its popularity during that era, but the work is widely ignored today.

BIBLIOGRAPHY
Bieber, 63; S. Favier, "À propos de la restauration par Barthélemy Prieur de la 'Diane à la Biche,' " *Revue du Louvre* 20 (1970), 71–77; Haskell—Penny, 196–98; Ridgway, *Hellenistic Sculpture,* I, 93–94; *LIMC* II, 645 (L. Kahil) and 805–6 (E. Simon).

ARUNDEL, THOMAS HOWARD, EARL OF (1585–1646). English statesman, collector and patron of the arts.

COMES   ARUNDELIUS

A P.P. Rubenio memoriter designatum non coram. J.L.Krafft fec.aqua forti

Portrait of *Thomas Howard, 2nd Earl of Arundel*, etching by J. L. Krafft after P. P. Rubens, Oxford, The Ashmolean Museum. (Museum.)

Arundel was born at Romford in Essex at a time when his family fortunes had sunk to a very low ebb. His grandfather, the fourth duke of Norfolk, had been beheaded for treason, and his father, Philip (d. 1595), was deprived of the Arundel title and spent the last ten years of his life imprisoned in the Tower of London. In 1604 James I restored Thomas Howard to the Arundel title; a Howard was not to be restored to the dukedom of Norfolk until 1652, but it could be claimed that both Arundel's public career at court as well as his private antiquarian and artistic tastes were directed toward that end. Arundel, as earl marshal of England, came to personify traditional values of order and sobriety in public life and drew inspiration for this role from the world of Greece and Rome, where, it was felt, these values were exemplified.

Arundel's fortunes changed dramatically in 1606, when he married Alatheia Talbot, the daughter of the Earl of Shrewsbury, who was one of the richest men in England. Arundel had also been a close companion of Henry, Prince of Wales, sharing his intellectual and sporting interests. With hindsight, we can see that the prince's death in 1610 prevented Arundel from achieving the absolute success in politics he doubtless wished for, but at the time it appeared but a temporary setback.

In 1613 Arundel traveled to Italy in the company of Inigo Jones, visiting Venice, Florence and Rome. In Rome, Arundel's host was Vincenzo *Giustiniani, a patron and collector of the first rank. Arundel's Roman Catholicism doubtless caused the Roman authorities to regard him as a potentially sympathetic friend at the English court. Probably for this reason, he was allowed not only to excavate the ruins of several houses at Rome but to take away the ancient Roman statues he found—statues that may even have been planted for him to find. Arundel's excavations in Rome, however, stand at the beginning of a long tradition of British archaeological investigations abroad, a tradition that has its present-day representatives in the *British School of archaeology at Rome, Athens and elsewhere. Since there was clearly a limit to the extent to which a foreigner could be allowed to remove ancient remains from Rome, Arundel coped with the problem in two ways: he had some statues made *all'antica,* and he encouraged his agents to explore the Aegean on his behalf, a notion he evidently picked up in Venice, where collections of antiquities came, for the most part, from the East.

By 1618, Arundel had built sculpture and picture galleries at Arundel House on the Strand in London; views of them appear in the backgrounds of Daniel Mytens's portraits of the earl and countess painted in that year. Ten statues are visible in the sculpture gallery, some of them apparently part of the gift of Lord Roos, who in 1616 "gave the Earl of Arundel all the statues he brought out of Italy at one clap." Many more were to come the earl's way in the next two decades. Thus, when Joachim *Sandrart visited Arundel House in 1627, even the garden was "resplendent with the finest ancient statues in marble, of Greek and Roman workmanship." Many of these were acquired by William Petty, Arundel's loyal agent in Turkey, who endured shipwreck and imprisonment in his search for antiquities for his master's collection. Assisted at first by Sir Thomas *Roe, Petty was able to gather some 200 marbles from the Greek islands and cities of Asia Minor. The first academic result of Petty's activities was the publication of thirty-nine Greek and Latin inscriptions in John Selden's *Marmora Arundelliana* in 1628. The most celebrated item in the work was the *Marmor Parium, a Greek chronological table.

Arundel's influence on his contemporaries was considerable. He was a patron of P.P. *Rubens and Van Dyck and in 1636 persuaded the sculptor François Dieussart to come to England from *Bernini's Rome. Arundel House was a meeting place for a group that found their intellectual roots in the Italian intellectual tradition of classical scholarship. In 1637 Arundel's librarian, Franciscus *Junius, wrote *De pictura veterum,* clearly outlining links between aesthetic pursuits and social and political values. Even the taste of Arundel's political enemy and collecting rival, the Duke of *Buckingham, owed something to this. King Charles I testified to "a Royall liking of ancient statues, by causing a whole army of old forraine Emperors, Capitaines and Senators all at once to land on his coasts, to come and doe him homage, and attend him in his palaces of St James and Sommerset House." There was another side of the coin, however, and it might justly be claimed that the competitive spirit in which patronage and collecting were conducted in Caroline England, competitiveness generated by no one more than Arundel himself, was, in no small part, responsible for the deluge that engulfed the British Isles in the 1640s and 1650s. Arundel himself died a political exile in Padua in 1646, and his collections were dispersed. Most of the surviving sculpture is now in the *Ashmolean Museum at Oxford.

BIBLIOGRAPHY

M.S.F. Hervey, *Thomas Howard Earl of Arundel* (Cambridge, 1921); D.E.L. Haynes, *The Arundel Marbles* (Oxford, 1975); K. Sharpe, "The Earl of Arundel, His Circle and the Opposition to the Duke of Buckingham, 1618–1628," in *Faction and Parliament, Essays in Early Stuart History,* ed. K. Sharpe (Oxford, 1978), 209–44; D. J. Howarth, *Lord Arundel and His Circle* (New Haven, 1985); *The Earl and Countess of Arundel: Renaissance Collectors* (*Apollo* Magazine Publ., 1995).

MICHAEL VICKERS

ASHBY, THOMAS (1874–1931). British archaeologist.

Educated at Winchester and Christ Church, Oxford, Ashby settled in Rome in 1897. In 1898 he began exploration of the antiquities in the Campagna, often with Rodolfo *Lanciani. He was the first "scholar" of the *British School at Rome (1901), its assistant director from 1903 and director (1905–24). Between 1902 and 1910 he published a series of papers on the topography of the classical Campagna while continuing his research there. He resigned from the British School in 1924 but continued to be active in Roman archaeology until his death in a fall from a train outside London in 1931.

Ashby published articles on prints and drawings of Roman antiquities and a book on the Campagna (1927) that revised his earlier studies, and he collaborated with S. B. *Platner on a topographical dictionary of ancient Rome (1929); his last years were devoted to a definitive study of the Roman *aqueducts, which was published in 1935. Ashby had collected an extensive library on Rome and its environs, many important prints, drawings and photographs, and a virtual museum of artifacts gathered principally from the Campagna. The artifacts, including an important collection of brick stamps, were donated to the *American Academy in Rome; upon his death the prints and drawings were deposited in the Vatican Libraries, and his books, manuscripts and photographs remain at the British School. The clarity and accuracy of Ashby's topographical work remain unsurpassed, and the importance of his publications on the classical Campagna becomes more manifest as that area disappears beneath Rome's modern sprawl. The topographical dictionary is still indispensable.

BIBLIOGRAPHY

T. Ashby, "The Classical Topography of the Roman Campagna," *BSR* 1 (1902), 125–285; 3 (1905), 1–212; 4 (1907), 1–159; 5 (1910), 213–432; Idem, *The Roman Campagna in Classical Times* (London 1927, repr. 1970); Idem, with S. B. Platner, *A Topographical Dictionary of Ancient Rome* (Oxford, 1929; repr. Rome, 1965); Idem, *The Aqueducts of Ancient Rome* (Oxford, 1935); V. Scott—T. Martinelli, *Thomas Ashby: un archeologo fotografa la Campagna Romana tra '800 e '900* (Rome, 1986).

JAMES C. ANDERSON, JR.

ASHMOLE, ELIAS (1617–92). English antiquary, numismatist, alchemist and herald.

In Anthony Wood's eyes, Elias Ashmole was "the greatest virtuoso and curioso that ever was known or read of in England before his time." The career through which Ashmole had graduated to this preeminent position brought him from fairly modest beginnings in Lichfield, Staffordshire. Early legal training in London and a propitious marriage led to his appointment to the Commission for Excise (of which he was ultimately to become comptroller). The Civil War took him to Oxford, where he combined a position as one of the King's Gentlemen of Ordnance with studies at the university. A second marriage to a rich and well-connected widow helped to cushion the years of Royalist eclipse and enabled Ashmole to cultivate his developing interests in astrology, alchemy and antiquarian studies.

Under the latter category, Ashmole's tastes lay in heraldry, books and manuscripts and numismatics. So skilled did he become in matters of heraldry that shortly after the restoration of Charles II, Ashmole was appointed Windsor Herald. One of his particular interests in this field was in the Order of the Garter, on which he published a definitive history in 1672. Although many of his books and manuscripts were destroyed by fire in 1679, over 2,000 volumes—the contents of which reflected Ashmole's interests as just outlined—were eventually inherited by the University of Oxford, many others being sold elsewhere. In the field of physical antiquities, coins and medals particularly drew Ashmole's attention; again, several thousands of his specimens were lost in the disastrous fire that destroyed his chambers in 1679, but others survived or were later acquired by him and were ultimately presented to his university. (Oxford had previously honored Ashmole with a doctorate for a catalog of Roman coins in the Bodleian Library collection, which he had produced between 1658 and 1666.)

From 1650, Ashmole developed an acquaintance with John Tradescant the Younger at Lambeth (*Tradescant family). In the following years and in cooperation with Dr. Thomas Wharton, Ashmole produced a catalog of Tradescant's famous museum collection, which was published in 1656—the first example in England of such an enterprise. In gratitude for Ashmole's cooperation, Tradescant left him the entire collection by deed of gift, and in 1675 Ashmole took charge of his inheritance. In turn, this was offered to the University of Oxford, to be housed in a new purpose-built institution that opened in 1683—the *Ashmolean Museum.

BIBLIOGRAPHY

C. H. Josten, *Elias Ashmole 1617–1692* (Oxford, 1966); M. Welch, ''The Foundation of the Ashmolean Museum,'' in *Tradescant's Rarities. Essays on the Foundation of the Ashmolean Museum, 1683, with a Catalogue of the Surviving Early Collections,* ed. A. MacGregor (Oxford, 1983), 40–58; M. Hunter, introduction to *Elias Ashmole (1617–1692), The Founder of the Ashmolean Museum and His World, A Tercentenary Exhibition, 1683–1983* (Oxford, 1983).

ARTHUR MacGREGOR

ASHMOLEAN MUSEUM, Oxford. The oldest public museum in the English-speaking world, founded over 300 years ago in 1683.

The nucleus of the Ashmolean Museum was the ''closet of rarities'' formed by the royal gardeners, John Tradescant and his son (*Tradescant family), in London during the early seventeenth century. These passed into the possession of Elias *Ashmole, who presented them to Oxford University in 1683. They were housed in an elegant building near the Sheldonian Theatre, which served as the center of Oxford University's scientific teaching until the reforms of the nineteenth century. Geological, ethnographic and manuscript collections were then transferred to more specialized institutions, leaving miscellaneous curiosities behind in the Ashmolean. The energy and foresight of A. J. (later Sir Arthur) *Evans, coupled with the financial and political support of Charles Drury Fortnum, transformed the institution during the 1890s. All the university's art and antiquarian collections were brought together on a new site in Beaumont Street within and behind the University Galleries, a Neoclassical building designed by C. R. *Cockerell and built in 1845 to house the *Arundel collections of Greek and Roman sculpture and inscriptions and the university's pictures. In 1908 the museum was given the name it still bears: the Ashmolean Museum of Art and Archaeology.

The Ashmolean today comprises five departments: Antiquities, Western Art, Eastern Art, the Heberden Coin Room, and the Cast Gallery. The Cast Gallery possesses more than 250 casts of Greek and Roman sculpture. The Coin Room was created in 1921 and has rich collections of Greek, Roman, Byzantine, Islamic and European coins and medals. Eastern Art concerns itself with the material culture of Islam, India and the Far East and possesses a comprehensive collection of shards from Japanese kiln sites. Western Art is devoted to medieval, Renaissance and later European art, with notable collections of drawings by *Raphael, *Michelangelo and Samuel Palmer.

The collections in the Department of Antiquities cover wide chronological and geographical areas, and their contents reflect the interests of British archaeologists over the past century or so. There are good representative collections of Egyptian, Near Eastern, European prehistoric, Cypriot, Greek, Etruscan, Roman, Anglo-Saxon and British medieval antiquities, but the department's main

The *Ashmolean Museum*, Oxford, designed by C. R. Cockerell, drawing by F. Mackenzie, 1848. Oxford, The Ashmolean Museum. (Museum.)

strength lies in its important assemblages of excavated material. The following are perhaps the most noteworthy: the prehistoric Egyptian antiquities, the protodynastic material from Hierakonpolis and the finds from el Amarna, *Naukratis and Nubia; from the Near East, finds from Jericho, Kish, Nimrud, *Al Mina and Deve Hüyük; from Central Europe, some remarkable Early Iron Age grave groups; material given by the Cyprus Exploration Fund; from the Greek world, finds from Sir Arthur Evans's excavations at *Knossos in *Crete and at *Gela in Sicily, material from Artemis Orthia at *Sparta and important Scythian and Thracian grave groups; and Anglo-Saxon jewelry and pottery from England and the Continent. Among the remaining Tradescant "rarities" are "Powhatan's Mantle" (a seventeenth-century Native American cloak of caribou hide and cowrie shells), wampum belts and tomahawks. Significant archival material includes Evans's Knossos excavation records and the photographs taken by the pioneer archaeological aerial photographer Major G.W.G. Allen in the 1930s.

BIBLIOGRAPHY

A. MacGregor, ed., *Tradescant's Rarities: Essays on the Foundation of the Ashmolean Museum, 1683, with a Catalogue of the Surviving Early Collections* (Oxford, 1983); *Summary Guide to the Department of Antiquities,* Ashmolean Museum, 2nd ed. (1951); *Treasures of the Ashmolean* (Oxford, 1970); *Annual Report of the Visitors of the Ashmolean Museum* (1901–); *Treasures of the Ashmolean Museum* (Oxford, 1990).

MICHAEL VICKERS

ASINE, Argolis, Greece. Prehistoric, Hellenistic and Roman settlement on the coast of Greece, ca. 8km southeast of Nauplion; first mentioned by Homer, Il. 2.560 (Catalogue of Ships), later by Strabo and Pausanias.

In modern times, Asine was first correctly identified by E. *Curtius (1852), thereafter visited and described by H. *Schliemann (1886) and J. G. *Frazer (1898). Small-scale excavations were carried out by I. K. Kofiniotis around 1900. The first map of the site was made by L. Renaudin (of the *French School in Athens) in 1920. On the initiative of the crown prince of Sweden (later King *Gustavus VI Adolphus), Swedish excavations started in 1922 and were continued in 1924, 1926 and 1930. Directors were Axel W. *Persson and Otto Frödin. The excavations were unusually careful for their time, and practically all potsherds were kept (a large number were given to Sweden and are now kept in Uppsala). The most important results concern the prehistoric periods, since Asine turned out to have been more or less continuously inhabited from Early Helladic (EH) times to ca. 700 B.C. Rich pottery material characterized the phases of Early and Middle Helladic (MH); of special historical interest was a horizon of destruction between EH III and MH (questioned by later research, especially because of observations by J. L. *Caskey at *Lerna). Both the settlement of the "Lower City" and the necropolis of chamber tombs on the slopes of Barbouna Hill yielded especially plentiful finds from the Late Helladic (LH) IIIC period. The Mycenaean pottery was studied by A. *Furumark, who based many of his conclusions in *Mycenaean Pottery* (1941) on this material. Of special interest was also the Protogeometric cemetery with its cist tombs, containing, among other things, handmade, so-called Dorian pottery. Among the later finds were Hellenistic houses and graves and a well-preserved Roman bath. On the top terrace of Barbouna Hill, building remains were found that could plausibly be interpreted as the temple of Apollo Pythaieos, according to Pausanias, the only building spared when the Argives destroyed Asine ca. 700 B.C.

During a second period of major excavation, E. Protonotariou-Deilaki in 1969 and C.-G. Styrenius and S. Dietz in 1970–74 excavated in a field to the east of the acropolis, while in 1971–78, I. and R. Hägg explored the lower slopes of Barbouna Hill. The most important finds are, east of the acropolis: (1) a MH cemetery of cist graves around a stone tumulus, (2) early Mycenaean settlement remains, (3) a continuous habitation through Protogeometric and Geometric; and in the Barbouna area: (4) an extramural MH cemetery, (5) a LH IIB-IIIA settlement, (6) circular platforms and other buildings with large quantities of pottery of the Late Geometric period, apparently connected with funerary ceremonies, and (7) a cemetery of Hellenistic tile graves, often with Charon's obols in the mouths of the dead.

BIBLIOGRAPHY

A. W. Persson—O. Frödin—A. Westholm, *Asine, Results of the Swedish Excavations, 1922–1930* (Stockholm, 1938); *Asine* 2, *Results of the Excavations East of the Acropolis, 1970–1974* (Stockholm, 1976–); I. Hägg—R. Hägg, eds., *Excavations in the Barbouna Area at Asine* (Uppsala, 1973–).

ROBIN HÄGG

ASPALATHOS. See SPLIT.

ASPENDOS. Graeco-Roman city in Pamphylia (southern Asia Minor), ca. 30km east of modern Antalya on the Eurymedon River.

Greek sources record that Aspendos was founded by Argive settlers, perhaps part of a group led by Mopsos following the Trojan War. The Athenian Kimon won a victory over Persian land and naval forces in 469 B.C. at the Eurymedon, at that time navigable from the Mediterranean. For part of the fifth century B.C., Aspendos was a member of the Delian League. The city resisted Alexander in 333 B.C. and in the Hellenistic period met with rival claims of the Ptolemies and the Seleucids. In 190 B.C. Aspendos came under Roman domination.

Aspendos was visited by *Texier and A. Schönborn and then was systematically explored in 1885 by an Austrian expedition financed by Count K. Lanckoronski, with the archaeological work carried out by E. *Petersen and G. *Niemann. Their results were presented in a handsome publication on Pamphylia and Pisidia, with the architectural drawings by Niemann. Of the ruins, which date principally from the Roman period, the most impressive is the theater, the best-preserved example in the ancient world, built in the second century A.C. to the design of a local architect, Zeno. West of the theater are remains of the agora, a bouleuterion (?), basilica and nymphaeum. Other well-preserved monuments are a Roman aqueduct and a stadium.

BIBLIOGRAPHY

+K. Lanckoronski, *Die Stadte Pamphyliens und Pisidiens* (Vienna, 1890), I, 85–124, 179–84; +J. B. Ward Perkins, "The Aqueduct at Aspendos," *PBSR* 23 (1955), 115–23; G. E. Bean, *Turkey's Southern Shore* (London, 1968), 67–77; +H. Lauter, "Die hellenistische Agora von Aspendos," *BJb* 170 (1970), 77–101; H. Brandt, "Kulte in Aspendos," *IstMitt* 38 (1988), 237–50.

ANN C. GUNTER

ASPERTINI, AMICO (1474–1552). Italian artist, known particularly for his drawings after classical antiquities.

Born in Bologna, Amico Aspertini was at work in Rome by 1500; he is thought to have made a second trip there between 1531/32 and 1534. These trips gave him ample opportunity to study and make copies of classical remains. His artistic production is especially associated with his native Bologna and embraces works in painting, sculpture, graphics and book illustration. Early biographical notices by *Vasari and others depict Amico as eccentric in the extreme and as working at frenzied speed, to the extent that he would simultaneously use one hand to paint shadows and the other to paint light. He is reported to have sought everywhere to make copies of antiquities, both good things and bad.

Three sketchbooks of antiquities by Amico Aspertini have been preserved, one in Schloss Wolfegg, Württemberg, dating to his first trip to Rome, ca. 1500–3, and two in the *British Museum, London, the first dating from his postulated Rome trip in the 1530s and the second somewhat later.

The Wolfegg Codex preserves the twenty-nine leaves of a sketchbook (perhaps half of it is lacking) bound into pages before use and therefore created specifically as a book in which the artist might make his drawings. Some compositions extend from one page to the next. All subjects are drawn from works of art existing in Rome, and there is frequent duplication of subjects in the Wolfegg Codex and London I. The album contains numerous scenes of battles and trophies, including some from the *Column of Trajan and *Trophies of Marius. The drawings are in pen and ink, often washed with bistre, on vellum.

London I features fifty vellum leaves of a complete sketchbook, with the drawings mostly in pen and ink, supplemented by a brown wash. Again the drawings extend over double folios. Included are numerous famous statues of the early sixteenth century [the *Laocoon, the *"Cleopatra" and the Tiber (*Nile and Tiber) from the *Vatican Belvedere; the *Quirinal Horse Tamers; the della *Valle family Pan figure] and many reliefs from sarcophagi. London II differs markedly from the two earlier sketchbooks in that it is not devoted exclusively to antiquities. The miscellaneous array of drawings includes views of ruins, sketches for compositions, copies made from Renaissance paintings and engravings and from architectural pattern books and images of antiquities radically transformed. What was originally forty-two paper leaves have been cut apart and rebound. Five of the sheets are in pen and brown ink and watercolor, and most of the remainder are in black chalk and bistre wash.

A development may be seen from the Wolfegg Codex, which shows a preoccupation, typical of the Quattrocento, with antiquarian details and motifs, to the first London sketchbook, which shows a greater interest in grand compositional effects. Aspertini reveals a distinct preference for scenes of intense action and conflict, with densely entangled forms and expressive distortion of the human figure. His own personal style shows affinity with some of the Roman battle sarcophagi he copied, especially those of the Antonine period (second century A.C.) and of later antiquity in general. His drawings of antiquities are often quite unarchaeological, especially in London I, in which he departs from the original scenes and creates his own permutations of the antiquities he is imitating.

Individual classical motifs, decorative schemes and compositions are quoted or alluded to in the paintings of Aspertini. For example, in his fresco of San Frediano changing the course of a river (San Frediano, Lucca; ca. 1508–9), the artist borrowed effectively from a relief on Trajan's Column of soldiers building a bridge. Grisaille pilasters framing the San Frediano frescoes show the use of a system remarkably like one seen in wall paintings of the Second Pompeian Style (e.g., the *Odyssey Landscapes). Later works by Aspertini show a less literal approach to antiquity and a tendency to develop formal values absorbed through long years of study.

BIBLIOGRAPHY

+P. P. Bober, *Drawings After the Antique by Amico Aspertini: Sketchbooks in the British Museum,* Studies of the Warburg Institute, 21 (London, 1857); Sheard, no 22; +G. Schweikhart, *Der Codex Wolfegg, Zeichnungen nach der Antike von Amico Aspertini* (London, 1986); Bober—Rubinstein, esp. 451–52.

ASSOS. Ancient city located in northwest Asia Minor (modern Turkey) on the southern coast of the Troad, facing the island of Lesbos.

Assos was founded according to tradition by Aeolian settlers from Lesbos. In the sixth century B.C. it came under Lydian, then Persian, domination. A contributing member of the Delian League in the fifth century B.C., Assos subsequently fell to Seleucid and Pergamene control. Together with the other Attalid possessions, the city came under Roman rule in 133 B.C.

Assos was visited by nineteenth-century travelers, including *Texier and *Fellows. The site was excavated by an American team (1881–83) sponsored by the *Archaeological Institute of America (AIA) and under the direction of J. T. Clarke. Many of the finds are in the *Museum of Fine Arts, Boston, and some documentation remains in the archives of the AIA. Assos has recently been under reinvestigation by Turkish archaeologists.

The earliest datable remains at Assos are assigned to the sixth century B.C. and include a major monument on the acropolis, a temple to Athena Polias (540–

530 B.C.). From the fourth century and Hellenistic period date the well-preserved fortifications, extending some 3km in length and enclosing an area to the north of the acropolis as well as two ancient harbors to the south. South of the acropolis are remains of the Hellenistic agora, below which are a Greek theater and a Roman bath. West of the agora, inside the main gate in this area, stands a Hellenistic gymnasium. The necropolis of Greek and Roman times is located along the roads leading west from the city gate.

BIBLIOGRAPHY

J. T. Clarke et al., *Investigations at Assos* (Cambridge, MA, 1902–21); +F. Sartiaux, *Les Sculptures et la restauration du temple d'Assos en Troade* (Paris, 1915); R. Merkelbach, *Die Inschriften von Assos,* Inschriften griechischer Städte aus Kleinasien, 4 (Bonn, 1976); *Ausgrabungen in Assos,* ed. Ü. Serdaroğlu—R. Stupperich—E. Schwertheim, Asia Minor Studien 2 (Bonn, 1990); *Ausgrabungen in Assos 1990,* ed. Ü. Serdaroğlu—R. Stupperich, Asia Minor Studien 5 (Bonn, 1992).

ANN C. GUNTER

ATHENA LEMNIA. Greek sculpture of the goddess Athena, created by Pheidias, one of the most admired works of art in antiquity.

Little is known of the appearance and precise date of creation of the statue. Three ancient authors identify the *Lemnia* by name (Pausanias 1.28.2; Lucian, *Imag.* 4; Aristeides, *Orat.* 50), revealing that the statue, signed by Pheidias, stood on the *Akropolis in Athens and was called "Lemnia" after the citizens of Lemnos who dedicated it. Three other ancient passages may refer indirectly to the *Lemnia* (Pliny, *NH* 34.54; Himerius, *Orat.* 21.4, 30.44); if so, it could be said that the statue was bronze, was also known as "The Fair," was made before the *Athena Parthenos,* and had reddish cheeks and no helmet. A date of ca. 450 B.C. for the creation of the statue has been proposed, but the evidence for such a date is not conclusive.

In 1893 *Furtwängler published as the *Athena Lemnia* a statue composed of an Athena torso in Dresden, which had come in 1728 from the *Chigi collection, and the famous head in *Bologna, which had been purchased by Pelagio Palagi from the Venetian antiquarian Sanquirico. The head had been identified as a young man or an Amazon. Furtwängler's reconstruction, resting on the indirect reference stating that the *Lemnia* did not wear a helmet, has been generally accepted. Recently, however, Hartswick has challenged the physical evidence for Furtwängler's reconstruction, arguing that the literary references are the only means for a reconstruction of the *Lemnia* but that they are too few and too ambiguous to serve as identification from the extant Athena types, and that the Palagi head is a classicizing creation incompatible with a fifth-century date.

BIBLIOGRAPHY

A. Furtwängler, *Meisterwerke der griechischen Plastik* (Leipzig, 1893), 3–45; Idem, *Masterpieces of Greek Sculpture* (London, 1895), 3–26; K. J. Hartswick, "The Athena Lemnia Reconsidered," *AJA* 87 (1983), 335–46; C. Morigi Govi—G. Sassatelli, eds., *Dalla Stanza delle Antichità al Museo Civico* (Bologna, 1984), 208–9; H. Protzmann, "Anti-

quarische Nachlese zu den Statuen der sogenannten Lemnia Furtwänglers in Dresden,''
Jahrbuch der Staatlichen Kunstsammlungen Dresden 1984 (pub. 1987), 7–22.

KIM J. HARTSWICK

ATHENA PARTHENOS. Colossal gold and ivory cult statue of Athena for the *Parthenon, Athens, made by Pheidias and dedicated in 438/7 B.C.

The statue was forty feet tall, with the skin made of ivory and the drapery in gold. The drapery, worth forty talents, was removable, according to Thucydides, in case of need (2.13.5). It was removed once for weighing and then was removed for good by the Athenian tyrant Lachares in the early third century B.C. (Pausanias 1.25.7). The later history of the *Athena Parthenos* is uncertain, but it may have been taken to Constantinople (*Byzantium) around the time of the decrees of Theodosius II (A.D. 435) that all pagan shrines and temples should be closed or converted to Christian churches. Nothing more is heard of the statue.

The marble Varvakeion *Athena* (discovered 1859, identified by C. *Lenormant; *National Archaeological Museum, Athens; height with base 1.105m) is probably one of the most accurate Roman copies of the Parthenos; its appearance tallies with Pausanias's description of the chryselephantine statue (1.24.5–7). The goddess bears her weight on her right foot, her left one relaxed. She wears a peplos, an aegis (ivory on the original) and a helmet decorated with a sphinx between griffins. In her right hand she holds a Nike (supported by a column in the copy), and with her left she holds her shield upright at her side, within which is a coiled serpent, Erichthonius. Pliny (*NH* 36. 181) reported that the statue stood twenty-six cubits in height and that the shield had an Amazonomachy on the outside and a Gigantomachy on the inside, with a Centauromachy on the goddess's sandals. Evidently, Pheidias included portraits of himself and his friend Perikles in the Amazonomachy (Plutarch, *Perikles* 31).

The literary sources and the surviving copies have provided evidence for various scholarly reconstructions of the magnificent sculpture. Benoit Loviot, after winning the Prix de Rome, did a drawing project (1879–91) with a brilliantly colored reconstruction of the Parthenon and the cult statue. His watercolors, showing the head of the Athena emerging through an opening in the temple roof, became widely known after they were exhibited in the Paris Salon (1880). Loviot's rendering of the richly painted cult statue and temple reflects the theories of *Hittorff, who had first proposed polychromy for Greek temples in 1851.

In modern times, two notable reconstructions have been made of the *Athena Parthenos*. In the 1950s a four-foot-high model of the cult statue was installed in the *Royal Ontario Museum, Toronto. A full-size replica was erected in 1990 in Nashville, Tennessee, inside the cella of the full-scale reproduction of the *Parthenon (made of concrete) that was built there in 1931.

BIBLIOGRAPHY

S. Karouzou, *National Archaeological Museum Collection of Sculpture: A Catalogue* (Athens, 1968, repr. 1974), 68–69; J. Boardman, *Greek Sculpture: The Classical Period*

(London, 1985), 110–12; *Paris, Rome, Athens: Travels in Greece by French Architects in the 19th and 20th Centuries* (Paris, 1982).

CAROL MATTUSCH

ATHENIAN TREASURY, Delphi. Greek storehouse, erected during the Archaic period to hold religious offerings made by the Athenians at *Delphi.

The earliest all-marble building in the great sanctuary of Delphi, the little treasury takes the typical form of a small temple with two Doric columns *in antis,* a shallow porch and a single main chamber. It was built of Parian marble and richly adorned with sculpture, including pedimental groups and metopes. Of the sculptures only the largely fragmentary metopes survive; they depict the deeds of Herakles and Theseus and combats of Greeks and Amazons.

Prior to the French excavations of the late nineteenth century, the building was known to exist through two literary references: Xenophon in the *Anabasis* (5.3.4) mentions an Athenian Treasury at Delphi where an offering was made, and Pausanias records it (10.11.5), in his tour of the site in the second century A.C., as located just before the Stoa of the Athenians. The latter was excavated and identified by an inscription in 1880. The treasury was uncovered in the French excavations of 1893, and its placement below the stoa, as well as inscriptions on its walls, provided a clear identification; it is the only one of the treasuries at Delphi whose identity is in no way disputed. Its date, however, has been hotly contested, ranging from as early as about 510–500 B.C. to 490–480 B.C. Recent scholarship has tended to support the later date.

So much of the fabric of the treasury was recovered that it was immediately recognized that it could be largely rebuilt. Reconstruction was begun, partially funded by the municipality of Athens, ten years after its discovery. Four campaigns sufficed to reerect most of the building, using ancient blocks as well as modern Pentelic marble, and the work was completed in 1906.

BIBLIOGRAPHY

M. G. Colon, *Inscriptions du Trésor des Athéniens, Fouilles de Delphes* 3.2 (Paris, 1909–13); +J. Audiat, *Le Trésor des Athéniens, Fouilles de Delphes* 2 (Paris, 1933); +P. de la Coste-Messelière, *Sculptures du Trésor des Athéniens, Fouilles de Delphes* 4.4 (Paris, 1957); S. Morris, *Daidalos and the Origins of Greek Art* (Princeton, NJ, 1992), 294–95.

WILLIAM R. BIERS

ATHENS, Greece. Ancient city-state and capital of the modern Hellenic Republic.

Inhabited as early as the Neolithic period, Athens was especially prominent from the eighth to the fourth century B.C., producing during the fifth century some of the greatest monuments of European civilization. Serious study of the monuments of Athens began at a relatively late date (cf. *Rome); it was not until the eighteenth century that Athenian antiquities began to receive their due.

From the start, investigations of ancient Athens were motivated and shaped by the longing to identify the physical remains with famous monuments and sites described by ancient authors and linked to the deeds of gods and heroes and famous men and women. Numerous ancient authors from the fifth century B.C. to the fifth century A.C. provided such *testimonia;* most important was Pausanias, whose ten books on travel in Greece included information on some 447 monuments, sites and place names of Athens, as well as observations on the Athenian people and the cults, history and personalities of ancient Athens. Inscriptions, collected from the fifteenth century onward, added to the great mass of written evidence about the antiquities of the great city.

Travelers' and clerics' accounts—mostly patchy—provide some information about Athens during the Middle Ages and Renaissance. In 1102 the Anglo-Saxon pilgrim Saewulf described his visit to the Christian church created in the *Parthenon. "Here," he wrote, "is a church of the blessed Virgin Mary which has a lamp that burns always and never wants oil." Michael Choniates (1183) noted that the Lykeion (Lyceum) of Aristotle and the Peripatos of Plato had vanished without a trace and that sheep grazed on the ruins of the Stoa Poikile that had once flanked the *Agora. He called the *Monument of Lysikrates the "Lamp of Demosthenes," a name that endured for centuries. It was not until 1395 that a connected, eye-witness description of Athens was made, by Niccolò da Martoni. Around the same time, the *Arch of Hadrian was mentioned by Chaucer in his *Knight's Tale,* as being built by Duke Theseus. The indefatigable traveler *Ciriaco of Ancona visited the city in 1436 and recorded inscriptions and other antiquities.

In the late seventeenth century, a more continuous sequence of activities is discernible in Athens. Around 1670 the Capuchin monks generated a map of the city, a peculiar mixture of ground plan and bird's eye view. Important records of the city's past were made by the Marquis de *Nointel, who visited Athens in 1674 with his entourage including Jacques Carrey, who painted the first panorama of Athens; the anonymous Flemish artist who made extensive drawings of the Parthenon sculptures (formerly referred to as the Carrey Drawings); and Jean Giraud, author of the so-called Anonymus Nointelianus, an account of the antiquities of Athens in their present state. Nointel had a Catholic mass read in the fifth century B.C. temple of Artemis Agrotera on the Ilissos River, from which time the Greek clergy regarded the church as desecrated, let it fall into ruin and disposed of it as building material.

J. G. Transfeldt (1674) correctly identified the *Temple of Olympian Zeus and the Monument of Lysikrates, whose inscription he first correctly read. In 1676, Jacob *Spon, who visited Athens in the company of George *Wheler, produced the first scientific treatment of the topography of Athens, rightly linking the ancient sources to his own observations. His pioneer work remained authoritative for almost a century. In 1687, the Venetians under Francesco *Morosini captured the lower town, bombarded the *Akropolis, and exploded the Turkish powder magazine in the Parthenon. For the first time concerted action was taken to remove antiquities to Europe, including a horsehead from the west pediment of the Parthenon.

The eighteenth century saw Athens become well known to cultured Europeans, especially as a result of the projects of the *Society of Dilettanti. Their famous members, James "Athenian" *Stuart and Nicolas *Revett, worked from 1751 to 1754 recording the monuments of Athens. Stuart did the text, plans, views and sculpture; Revett measured and drew up the architecture. The *Antiquities of Athens* (the first volume of which appeared in 1762) was an epoch-making work and is still indispensable. Interest in collecting antiquities gathered strength with the advent of L.F.S. *Fauvel, the French consul in Athens from 1803, who tirelessly excavated and gathered up sculptures. He was surpassed, however, by the agents of Lord *Elgin, whose original interest in taking plaster casts (e.g., of the *Hephaisteion, 1800) and making drawings soon evolved into the removal of the Parthenon sculptures. In 1821, William Martin *Leake produced his landmark study, the *Topography of Athens.*

During the Greek War of Independence, the Klepsydra, the classical spring house high on the northwest Akropolis slope, was rediscovered by K. Pittakis and was cleared and cleaned, to provide the Akropolis with a water supply. Pittakis, becoming superintendent of the antiquities of Athens, reported in 1832 that the Turks had left only sixty houses standing in Athens. Basically a little village, Athens was declared the capital of Greece for romantic historic reasons. The German architect Leo von *Klenze was commissioned by the government to revise the plan of Athens.

All over Athens were many fragments of inscriptions, architecture and sculpture. Conspicuous monuments of the city beside the Parthenon included the *Erechtheion and the *Propylaia on the Akropolis and the Hephaisteion overlooking the area of the Agora, which still lay largely hidden. The Temple of Olympian Zeus still showed sixteen columns standing, and the nearby Arch of Hadrian was virtually intact. On Mouseion Hill, the *Monument of Philopappos could be seen; but the popular Monument of Lysikrates was at this time covered with debris, after the burning of the adjacent Capuchin monastery during the War of Independence. The *Tower of the Winds survived, in good condition, its usage by the Turks for religious purposes; while in the *Roman Agora, the gate of Athena Archegetis was visible.

With the founding of the *Greek Archaeological Society and the *Greek Archaeological Service and under the jurisdiction of an important new law framed by G. L. Maurer in 1834 to regulate archaeology, enormous projects of clearing and excavation were launched. The Parthenon and the Akropolis, in general, were cleared and restored under L. *Ross and K. Pittakis; and Ross and others reconstructed the *Temple of Athena Nike (1835). A variety of new operations of clearing and/or excavation began: on the Akropolis north slope (1842–43, 1848, 1859, 1861), the Areopagus (1842–43), the Odeion of Herodes Atticus (1846, 1858), the Temple of Olympian Zeus (1861), the Akropolis south slope (1864) and the stoa of Eumenes (1864). Pittakis battled constantly to save inscribed stones; by 1860 he had published 4,158 inscriptions, hoping to spread knowledge of them throughout the civilized world. Antiquities assembled on the Akropolis were housed in a new museum, constructed between 1865 and 1874.

The second half of the nineteenth century brought new evidence about Athens in the time of Hadrian, as the Hadrianic reservoir on the hill of Lykabettos was cleared and the great aqueduct of Hadrian was reconditioned to function properly to bring water into the city (1871). In 1885–86, excavations in the library of Hadrian established the ground plan. Meanwhile, exploration of the banks of the Ilissos River yielded information about various cult places along its course. The location of the sanctuary of Apollo Pythios on the right bank was ascertained in 1872; a portion of the altar, dedicated by the younger Peisistratos, was seen and identified in a courtyard southwest of the Temple of Olympian Zeus and purchased by the Archaeological Society. Some 205 stone finds from the Royal Gardens were handed over by King George in 1884, and were taken to the *National Archaeological Museum in Athens.

During this period an increasing number of foreign scholars became involved in the study of Greece in general and Athens in particular, and the city became the base for institutes and schools that promoted a vigorous intellectual atmosphere and provided for the training of students, who would in turn study the antiquities of the city and the country. The *French School was founded first (1846), followed by the *German Archaeological Institute (1874), the *American School of Classical Studies (1882), and the *British School (1886). These schools sponsored a number of important excavations.

A. N. Skias of the Greek Archaeological Society uncovered what was left of the Temple of Artemis Agrotera, including fragments of its frieze, on the left bank of the Ilissos. In the same period, excavations were conducted at the Temple of Olympian Zeus (1883, 1886–1901) and at the *Theater of Dionysos (1859, 1861–67, 1886–89). Extensive work on the Akropolis south slope (1876–78) yielded information about the Asklepieion and related inscriptions. Frequent campaigns in the area of the *Kerameikos produced numerous tombs and identified the Dipylon Gate and the Sacred Gate (1863–70, 1873–74).

Ambitious excavations by Dörpfeld in the valley between the Areopagus and the *Pnyx produced a wide range of material chronologically, from graves of the Geometric period to the sixth-century B.C. precinct of the healing hero Amynos to Roman houses with mosaics. He also unearthed a fountain house that he thought (erroneously) was the Enneakrounos mentioned by Pausanias, and the aqueduct of the Peisistratids. A great number of terracotta molds, inscriptions and sculptures were excavated.

In the study of Athenian topography, E. *Curtius became a key figure, with his *Sieben Karten zur Topographie von Athen* (1868) and his *Atlas von Athen* (1878), prepared with J. A. Kaupert, containing the first precise topographical survey of the city. A. Milchhoefer gathered the ancient literary sources on Athens to be published along with Curtius's general work *Die Stadtgeschichte von Athen* (1891).

In 1899 a new law was passed giving the state absolute jurisdiction over all antiquities everywhere—on public, private and church property, in rivers and harbors and at the bottom of the sea. The Greek Archaeological Society continued to sponsor projects in Athens, uncovering the odeion of Perikles under P. Kastriotis (1914–27) and A. *Orlandos (1928–31); they found evidence of the destruction of Athens at the time of Sulla (86 B.C.) as well as an altar in the shape of an omphalos and a marble statue of the so-called *Omphalos Apollo,* but the entire interior of the building was left unexcavated. In 1930 the American School of Classical Studies began to sponsor the excavations in the Agora, with T. L. *Shear, Sr. as director (some investigation had been done previously by the German Archaeological Institute and the Greek Archaeological Society). At the same time O. *Broneer explored the upper north slope of the Akropolis, finding stratified deposits from Neolithic times to the end of the Bronze Age; a Mycenean stairway and spring were noted, as well as significant finds of arrowheads from the Persian attack of 480 B.C., a black-figured krater by Exekias, and 190 ostraka with the name of Themistokles inscribed.

In this period Greek excavations under K. Kourouniotis, financed by P. Aristophron, were carried out from 1929 to 1940 in the section west of the city that had been identified as the Academy since the eighteenth century (but without confirmation). Exploration was resumed in 1955 by P. Stavropoullos for the Greek Archaeological Society, with finds ranging from the Neolithic through Early, Middle and Late Helladic, as well as material from the Geometric, Archaic and later. An apsidal house of the Early Helladic was termed the "House of Hekademos (=Akademos)" by Stavropoullos, and a complex of the Hellenistic or Roman period was interpreted as a gymnasium. North and east of these was found an Academy boundary stone of ca. 500 B.C. *in situ,* near the intersection of Aimonos Street and Tripoleos Street (1966).

The Roman Agora also was under excavation by Kourouniotis and Stavropoullos (1930–31) and later by the *Italian School of Archaeology, under whom the south colonnade of the market was reerected (1942). The American work in the older Agora was highlighted by the reconstruction of the *Stoa of Attalos (1953–56), under the supervision of H. A. Thompson.

In addition to the Agora and Academy mentioned above, the most important excavations carried out from 1945 to the present are: the Pankrates sanctuary on the Ilissos (1952–54); the Akropolis South Slope including the sanctuary of Nymphe and the house assigned to the Neo-Platonic philosopher Proklos (1955–59); the Panhellenion (1956–58); the sanctuary of Artemis Aristoboule (1958); the sanctuary of Aphrodite Pandemos (1960); excavations between the Olympieion and the Ilissos (1960–62); the site of Epikouros's Garden (1968); excavations at the Center for Akropolis Studies with remains from prehistoric times to the Ottoman period (1984–95).

BIBLIOGRAPHY

J. G. Frazer, *Pausanias's Description of Greece* 1–6 (London, 1898); W. Judeich, *Topographie von Athen,* 2nd ed. (Munich, 1931); P. Graindor, *Athènes sous Hadrien* (Le Caire, 1934); S. H. Weber, *Voyages and Travels in Greece . . . made Previous to the*

Year 1801 (Princeton, 1953); +J. Travlos, *The Pictorial Dictionary of Ancient Athens* (London, 1971); +*The Akropolis at Athens: Conservation, Restoration and Research, 1975–1983,* tr. J. Binder, publ. by the Committee for the Preservation of the Acropolis Monuments (Athens, 1985).

JUDITH BINDER AND NANCY THOMSON DE GRUMMOND

ATRIA. See ADRIA.

AUGSBURG (AUGUSTA VINDELICUM). Roman provincial settlement; probably the site of a legion area camp in the period of Augustus (31 B.C.–A.D. 14); later the capital of the province of Raetia.

The outstanding figures in the early history of the city's archaeology were Konrad *Peutinger and Marcus Welser (1558–1614). Peutinger collected Roman coins and stone monuments and published Roman inscriptions (1505 and 1520). Welser collected antiquities and published a history of Roman Augsburg (1594).

The Antiquarium Romanum (the later Maximilianmuseum) was established in 1822. Johann Nepomuk von Raiser (1768–1853) was a key figure in the founding of the museum and also published a corpus of local Roman antiquities (1820). In 1917/18, thousands of early Roman objects (military equipment, ceramics and coins) were found in a gravel pit at Oberhausen (ca. 2km northwest of the later Roman city). This discovery, above all, has led to speculation about the presence of at least one Roman legion in the area. Although no buildings of the provincial capital survive aboveground, Ludwig Ohlenroth (1892–1959) published a reconstruction plan of the city in the 1950s based on scattered subterranean evidence. The Römisches Museum (situated in the former Dominican church of St. Magdalena) opened in 1966 and houses many of the objects formerly displayed or stored at the Maximilianmuseum.

BIBLIOGRAPHY

G. Ulbert, s.v. "Augusta Vindelicum," *PECS* 121–22; G. Gottlieb, *Das Römische Augsburg mit einer Bibliographie [zum römischen Augsburg] von Gerd Rupprecht* (Munich, 1981); W. Kuhoff, "Römische Archäologie," *Augsburger Stadtlexikon: Geschichte, Gesellschaft, Kultur, Recht, Wirtschaft,* ed. W. Baer et al. (Augsburg, 1985), 311.

ELIZABETH C. TEVIOTDALE

AUGUSTA EMERITA. See MERIDA.

AUGUSTA TREVERORUM. See TRIER.

AUGUSTA VINDELICUM. See AUGSBURG.

AUGUSTUS OF PRIMA PORTA. Over-lifesize statue (2.08m) of the emperor Augustus, found at the *Villa of Livia located at Prima Porta, on the outskirts of Rome.

The statue, of Parian marble, depicts Augustus standing with his right hand raised; he wears a handsome "muscled" cuirass carved with the theme of the return of the Roman legionary standards by the Parthians, which took place in 20 B.C. Scholarly debates over the statue include whether the Roman general depicted receiving the standard is Tiberius; whether Augustus's right hand was empty (E. Simon) or held a sprig of laurel (H. Kähler) or carried a replica of a legionary standard (P. Zanker); whether the statue is a copy in marble of an original in bronze (as most now believe); whether the statue dates soon after the return of the standards (Zanker, G.M.A. *Hanfmann, Simon), or whether it shows Augustus deified and thus dates to the time of his death in A.D. 14 or later (Kähler, B. Andreae).

The statue was excavated on 20 April 1863, on the eve of Rome's birthday, and word of its discovery spread immediately. Wilhelm Henzen, secretary of the *Instituto di Correspondenza Archeologica, was among those who thronged to Prima Porta to see the work. Unfortunately, the exact find spot was not recorded. The piece may have originally stood on a terrace of the villa, overlooking the Tiber River.

The work was in excellent condition. Though it had experienced a fall and had been restored in antiquity (the raised right arm and the lower left leg were reattached with iron pins), almost all parts were recovered in the excavation. The restoration by the sculptor P. Tenerani involved reinsertion of the head and neck in the cavity framed by the border of the cuirass and attachment of the plinth to a modern base; most significantly, it involved restoration of the forefinger of the left hand and all the fingers of the raised right hand, leaving cause for dispute over the meaning of Augustus's gesture. There were many traces of paint remaining, including red, blue, rose, gold, brown; the scene on the cuirass was originally painted in rich detail.

After restoration the great statue was placed in a niche in the Braccio Nuovo of the Museo Chiaramonti, *Vatican Museums (where it may be seen today). Pius IX immediately paid a visit to the new acquisition and praised the head, the armor and the drapery.

The *Augustus* of Prima Porta is regarded as "the quintessential example of imperial Roman statuary" (B. Andreae) and is frequently anthologized and reproduced in popular contexts. Lifesize and smaller reproductions of the statue have been available since soon after its discovery; in the late nineteenth century, plaster casts could be ordered from the London firm of D. Brucciani. Modern copies have been erected in various public settings: appropriately, in front of the Forum of Augustus in Rome and near Augustus's harbor of Classis at Ravenna; less so, at Caesar's casino at Atlantic City, New Jersey.

BIBLIOGRAPHY

E. Simon, "Zur Augustusstatue von Prima Porta," *RM* 64 (1957), 46–68; H. Kähler, *Die Augustusstatue von Primaporta,* Monumenta Artis Romanae (Cologne, 1959); G. Daltrop, "Augustus of Prima Porta," in *The Vatican Collections, the Papacy and Art* (New York, 1982), 208; P. Zanker, *The Power of Images in the Age of Augustus,* tr. A. Shapiro (Ann Arbor, 1988), 187–92.

AULE METELI. See ARRINGATORE.

AURELIAN WALL, Rome. Late Roman fortification of the city of Rome.

The 18-km defensive circuit was begun by the emperor Aurelian (A.D. 270–75); originally, it was at least 6m high and 3.5m wide with nearly 400 square towers, eighteen main gates and additional smaller ones. The building of this brick-faced concrete wall reflected the uncertain defenses of the empire in the later third century, and its models seem to have been provincial fortifications in the Hellenistic East, such as those at Tyana and *Palmyra.

First repaired under Maxentius (A.D. 306–12), the walls were thickened and doubled in height under Honorius (A.D. 401–3), whose work is especially evident in the marble refacing of the towers of the Porta San Sebastiano. Subsequent repairs, additions and alterations to the wall were executed under Theodoric (509–10), Belisarius (537–47), the popes Hadrian I (772–95) and Leo IV (846), the Roman Senate in 1157, and various Renaissance and later pontiffs, most notably popes *Paul III (1534–49: southeast and southwest portions of the wall), Pius IV (Porta Pia, built 1561–64 by *Michelangelo near the Aurelian Porta Nomentana), and Urban VIII, who destroyed a section of the original circuit for a new line of defense on the right bank of the Tiber (1642–44). The Aurelian wall remained the defensive wall of Rome until 1870, when it was breached by Garibaldi's forces near the Porta Pia. Somewhat less than two-thirds of the circuit stands today.

BIBLIOGRAPHY

+I. Richmond, *The City Wall of Imperial Rome* (Oxford, 1930); +Nash II, 86–103; M. Todd, "The Aurelianic Wall of Rome and Its Analogues," *Roman Urban Defenses in the West*, ed. J. Maloney—B. Hobley (London, 1983); +L. Cozza, "Osservazioni sulle mura aureliane a Roma," *Analecta Romana* 16 (1987), 25–52.

LAETITIA LA FOLLETTE

AUXERRE, DAME D' (LADY FROM AUXERRE). Greek sculpture of a *kore* ("maiden"; cf. *korai*), dated 625–600 B.C.; regarded as a key example of early Greek art, exemplifying the Daedalic style.

The figure measures 75cm (with base) and shows a standing female in a "tube" dress; according to E. Harrison, part of the garment was pulled over her shoulders to create a capelike effect. B. Ridgway and others argue that the lady wears a true cape of Daedalic style. The provenance of the statue is unknown, but analysis of the limestone shows it to be of a Mediterranean type, comparable to samples from Prinias and Taranto. The work is first recorded in the 1890s as belonging to the Parisian sculptor Bourgoin; it was sold at auction in 1895 for the sum of one franc to Louis David, the caretaker of the Municipal Theater in Auxerre. The piece was kept in the theater until 1908, when it was moved to the Auxerre Museum; soon afterward it was seen there by M. *Collignon and transferred to the *Louvre, its present location. Hodge has demonstrated that suspicions about its authenticity have no grounds for support.

BIBLIOGRAPHY
C. Rolley, "La Provenance de la Dame d'Auxerre," *BCH* 88 (1964), 444–45; E. Harrison, "Notes on Daedalic Dress," *Journal of the Walters Art Gallery* 36 (1977), 37–48; *Greek Art of the Aegean Islands* (New York, 1979), 134–35; B. Ridgway, "The Fashion of the Elgin Kore," *Getty Museum Journal* 12 (1984), 29–58; A. Trevor Hodge, "The Auxerre Goddess: A Cautionary Tale," *Echos du Monde Classique,* n.s. 6 (1987), 87–197.

AYIA TRIADA. See HAGIA TRIADHA.

B

BAALBEK (BAALBEC; HELIOPOLIS). Hellenistic town and Roman colony located in modern-day Lebanon.

Named Heliopolis at the time it was dominated by the Ptolemaic dynasty of Egypt (third century B.C.), Baalbek stands on an ancient tell, strategically located between Emesa and Damascus, ca. 70km northeast of Beirut. The visible Roman monuments were begun soon after the establishment of the colony Julia Augusta Felix Heliopolitana (ca. 16 B.C.); the city flourished especially in the second and third centuries A.C. The most grandiose of all Roman temples preserved, that of Jupiter Heliopolitanus (late first–second centuries A.C.; never completed) features a columned propylaeum opening onto a hexagonal forecourt and a large rectangular arcaded court; the temple proper rests on a huge podium and has ten columns across the front with nineteen on a side (six of the original columns are still standing). Nearby are an octastyle temple, perhaps of Bacchus (second century A.C.) and a striking circular temple of Venus, elegantly small and with an entablature that features Baroque curves and countercurves.

In the late fourth century, the great temple of Jupiter was partially demolished in favor of a Christian church, then was transformed into Arab fortifications in the seventh century. Further damage was done by two major earthquakes in the twelfth and eighteenth centuries.

The Jewish traveler Benjamin of Tudela visited the ruins ca. 1170, and in the sixteenth century the site was reported by the French botanist Pierre Belon (in the Near East, 1546–49). In 1757, Robert *Wood published his illustrated account of his journey with James Dawkins, *The Ruins of Baalbec*. Kaiser Wilhelm II, having visited the site in 1898, ordered R. *Koldewey and W. Andrae, the German Mesopotamian archaeologists, to survey the site and then had Otto Puchstein lead a team in clearing and restoring the temple area (1902–5); the work was completed and published by T. *Wiegand and K. Wulzinger. Beginning with the French Mandate in Lebanon (1920) and after World War II under the direction of Maurice Chehab for the Lebanese Department of Antiquities, the primary concern has been clearing and consolidating the three Roman imperial temples.

BIBLIOGRAPHY

T. Wiegand, ed., *Baalbek, Ergebnisse der Ausgrabungen und Untersuchungen in den Jahren 1898–1905,* 1–3 (Berlin, 1921–25); P. Collart—J. Coupel, *L'Autel monumental de Baalbek* (Beyrouth, 1951); +F. Ragette, *Baalbek* (London, 1980).

BERNARD GOLDMAN

BABELON, ERNEST (1854–1923). French numismatist; conservator of the Cabinet des Médailles of the Bibliothèque Nationale, Paris, 1892–1923.

Babelon's life was dedicated to his work in archaeology, particularly, the field of numismatics. On completion of his studies at the Collège de France, he took a position at the Cabinet and remained there until his death. In 1902 he established the chair of numismatics at the college and occupied it until 1923. After participating in excavations at *Carthage, he published the results (1883) and wrote, as well, on glyptics (1894); cameos of the Bibliothèque Nationale (1897); and, with Adrien Blanchet, a catalog of the bronzes at the Bibliothèque (1895). His major work, *Traité des monnaies grecques et romaines* (5 vols., 1901–32), was conceived as a summation of all ancient numismatics. The realization of the *Traité* was beyond the powers of one man, and the work was completed by his son Jean only after Babelon's death. A volume of *Description historique et chronologique des monnaies de la république romaine* (1885–86) was criticized for using an unscientific alphabetical arrangement (later revised by H. *Grueber).

With Bischoffsheim, he founded the Societé Française des Fouilles Archéologiques and served as its president, and alone he established and edited the *Revue Numismatique.* His numerous articles for that publication are gathered in four volumes titled *Mélanges numismatiques.*

BIBLIOGRAPHY

D. Le Suffleur, *Ernest Babelon* (n.d.); A. E. Dieudonne, *L'Oeuvre numismatique d'Ernest Babelon* (Paris, 1924); J. Nostos, "Babelon, Ernest," *DBF* 4 (1948), cols. 997–99; E. E. Clain-Stefanelli, *Numismatics, An Ancient Science, A Survey of Its History* (Washington, DC, 1965), 43.

SHARON WICHMANN

BAHRFELDT, MAX VON (1856–1936). German numismatist; one of the first "modern" students of Roman coinage.

By 1878 Bahrfeldt recognized crucial linkages between the Mars/Eagle gold and the early symbol denarii and, in 1883, the association of both with the sextantal bronze. His "Nachträge und Berichtigungen" to *Babelon's alphabetical compilation recognized both the nuances of Republican coinage and its importance as a historical source, and his corpus of Republican gold remains fundamental. He edited *Numismatisches Literaturblatt,* a basic bibliographical tool, for over fifty years. Bahrfeldt was a career military officer and his role in World War I led to a death sentence in absentia; his scholarship was often ignored in the non-German (particularly British) community.

BIBLIOGRAPHY

M. Bahrfeldt, *Die Römische Goldmünzenprägung während der Republik und unter Augustus* (Halle, 1923); K. Pink, *Numismatische Zeitschrift* 69 (1936), 95; G. R. Gaettens, *Blätter fur Münzfreunde* (1936), 409–15; W. Jesse, ''Bahrfeldt, Max von,'' *NDB* I (1953), 543.

WILLIAM E. METCALF

BAIAE. The foremost Roman resort in Italy, built along a small curving bay, the ruins of an ancient volcano, facing east over the gulf of Pozzuoli.

Baiae became famous for its mineral waters and therapeutic baths by the time of Sulla. Its territory was a favorite site for sumptuous villas by the time of Julius Caesar and continued so at least to the mid-second century. Julius Caesar, Crassus and Cicero all had villas there. Under Augustus, a large part of Baiae became imperial property and the site of a palatium. Caligula closed the mouth of the bay with a pontoon bridge; Nero arranged the assassination of Agrippina there; and Hadrian died there. Throughout history it was notorious for its licentiousness and extravagance of life. Remains of villas, tombs and thermal establishments dot the area very thickly, the most impressive constructions being three large, domed buildings called Tempio di Diana, Tempio di Mercurio and Tempio di Venere.

Between 1941 and 1954 extensive excavations were carried out in the middle of the site, first under the direction of I. Sgobbo, later under A. *Maiuri. Large parts of a sequence of four thermal establishments have been recovered, the Terme di Mercurio, a complex including a high terrace more than 100m long, Terme dell'Acqua Rogna (or di Sosandra) and Terme di Venere. All date in their present form from the mid-second century but include older construction and underwent subsequent modification. They extend in an arc for a continuous length of ca. 300m and a depth of 140m and rise to a height of ca. 40m above sea level. They were luxurious edifices arranged on a succession of terraces stepping down the slope to the sea and including rooms of interesting shape, roofing and lighting on every level. These seem to have been, in part, hotels, in part, watering places. Since much of ancient Baiae has now sunk below sea level, due to bradyseism, these edifices may possibly have continued considerably beyond the area at present uncovered. Despite the superb quality of its architecture, Baiae has produced comparatively little in the way of sculpture and carved architectural members.

BIBLIOGRAPHY

J. H. D'Arms, *Romans on the Bay of Naples* (Cambridge, MA, 1970); R. F. Paget, ''From Baiae to Misenum,'' *Vergilius* 17 (1971), 22–38; M. Borriello—A. D'Ambrosio, *Baiae-Misenum, Forma Italiae,* Regio I, 14 (Florence, 1979), 35–98; *I Campi Flegrei nell'archeologia e nella storia, Atti dei Convegni Lincei* 33 (Rome, 1977), 227–328 (esp. G. De Angelis d'Ossat, ''L'architettura delle 'terme' di Baia,'' 227–74; P. Mingazzini, ''Le terme di Baia,'' 275–81; I. Sgobbo, ''I templi di Baia,'' 283–321); P. Amalfitano—G. Camodeca—M. Medri, eds., +*I Campi Flegrei* (Venice, 1990), 183–237.

L. RICHARDSON, JR

BALLPLAYER. See ANTIKYTHERA YOUTH.

Portrait of *Baccio Bandinelli*, engraving by Nicolo della Casa, published by A. Lafréry. (Westfälisches Landesmuseum für Kunst und Kulturgeschichte, Münster, Porträtarchiv Diepenbroick. Photo: R. Wakonigg.)

BANDINELLI, BACCIO (1493–1560). Italian sculptor.

Born in Florence, Baccio Bandinelli was patronized by the *Medici family and created a number of works for them in Florence and Rome. He was first in Rome in 1514 and lived at the Vatican from 1517 to 1521/22, when *Leo X was pope. Thereafter he returned to Rome a number of times and had ample opportunity to study the ancient statuary there. He made a drawing of the *Belvedere *Apollo* (Biblioteca Ambrosiana, Milan), a work that inspired and informed his statue of *Orpheus* (1516/17) for the courtyard of the Medici Palace in Florence. His drawing of the figure of ''Amor'' (*Louvre, Paris) from the ''*Bed of Polykleitos*'' is one of several references he made to this figure in his art; the *Dead Christ* carved by Baccio Bandinelli for his own tomb in SS. Annunziata, Florence, shows in mirror image, somewhat awkwardly, the hanging arm and lolling head of "Amor." Best known of his imitations of the antique is his magnificent full-size copy of the *Laocoon,* commissioned in 1520 and evidently originally intended as a gift for Francis I but kept by the Medici and today in the *Uffizi in Florence. The vitality of the original is conveyed well. The often-disputed right arm of Laocoon is shown half-raised (as it probably was in a wax arm restored by Bandinelli for Clement VII in the early 1520s), instead of fully extended, as was preferred in other proposed restorations of the group beginning ca. 1550, or pulled all the way down, as has now been proved the arm was actually positioned.

Although enviably successful, patronized by the Medici and knighted with the order of St. James, Bandinelli was also sometimes ridiculed in his own day. His would-be magnum opus, the *Hercules and Cacus* before the Palazzo Vecchio in Florence (1534), failed signally to capture the drama of the ancient passage in Vergil's *Aeneid* (8.193–267), from which the story is drawn, and was fiercely criticized and lampooned.

BIBLIOGRAPHY

+J. Pope-Hennessy, *An Introduction to Italian Sculpture* 3, *Italian High Renaissance and Baroque Sculpture,* 2nd ed. (London, 1970), 362–66; *Porträtarchiv,* no. 4; Bober—Rubinstein, esp. 452; R. Ward, *Baccio Bandinelli, 1493–1560, Drawings from British Collections,* catalog of exhibition (Cambridge, Fitzwilliam Museum, 1988).

BANTI, LUISA (1894–1978). Italian archaeologist and art historian, specialist in Etruscan studies.

Analytical precision and a concrete historical sense, rather than pure art appreciation, were already apparent in the exemplary studies of Luisa Banti on the Hagia Triadha tholos (1930–31) and *Luni* (1937). Employment in the Vatican Library (1930–40) and on the Italian excavations in *Crete preceded appointments as assistant in history of religions (Rome), as chair of archaeology (Pavia, 1948) and Etruscology (Florence, 1950–65; with intervals in American universities) and as director of the Istituto di Studi Etruschi (1965–72). Her contributions include major treatments of Etruscan painting and bronzework (discussing the reception of Greek myth in Etruria) and a brilliant Etruscan synthesis.

BIBLIOGRAPHY

L. Banti, *Il Mondo degli Etruschi,* 2nd ed. (Rome, 1969), *The Etruscan Cities and Their Culture* (London, 1973); *Studi in onore di Luisa Banti* (Florence, 1965; with bib. of LB); G. Camporeale, "Luisa Banti," *StEtr* 47 (1979), ix–xv.

F. R. SERRA RIDGWAY

BARBERINI FAMILY. A papal family known for its patronage of the arts.

In 1623 the election of MAFFEO BARBERINI as pope (Urban VIII, 1568–1644) initiated one of the grossest examples of papal nepotism but provided the background for unrivaled patronage of the arts. Urban himself is known for his commissions to *Bernini, of which the baldachino with the twisted columns in the crossing of St. Peter's is one of the best known. The bronze for the canopy, or part of it, is supposed to have come from the beams of the *Pantheon and gave rise to the epigram *Quod non fecerunt barbari, fecerunt Barberini* ("What the barbarians didn't do, the Barberini did").

Urban acted so closely with other members of his family in patronage that it is difficult to tell just what individual is responsible. He made cardinals of his brother ANTONIO and two nephews, FRANCESCO and ANTONIO. Another nephew, TADDEO, became ancestor of later generations of the family. Urban initiated plans for an imposing family palace, begun by Carlo *Maderno and continued by Borromini and Bernini.

The ancestral estates of the counts of Tusculum at Palestrina (*Praeneste) passed through marriage to the *Colonna family and, in turn, were acquired by Urban, who presented them to his brother CARLO. An Etruscan tomb on the estates later yielded the objects of the so-called *Barberini Tomb, now a rich treasure in the *Villa Giulia in Rome. The museum in the palace today contains the great *Barberini Mosaic of the *Nile,* found in the lower section of the *Sanctuary of Fortuna.

The Roman palace has now passed to the state and serves many purposes; the Galleria Nazionale d'Arte Antica does not contain ancient art, as the name would imply, but primarily paintings of the Italian Renaissance. Adjoining the Palazzo Barberini are the remains of a Mithraeum, with a fresco of Mithras killing the bull. For nearly a century (ca. 1627 until a date not known but presumably near the opening of the tapestry shop at S. Michele by Clement XI, about 1714), the palace housed a private tapestry factory. Among the sets woven there was a series on the life of Constantine the Great, designed by *Pietro da Cortona to match another group of tapestries that Cardinal Francesco Barberini had received from the French crown; these were designed by P. P. *Rubens. The major portion of the set is now in the Philadelphia Museum of Art, though some pieces are still in the Barberini collections. In the Salone of the palace is the ceiling painting by Cortona, depicting the apotheosis of the Barberini. In addition to the obvious symbols of the family and allegories of the triumph of the Church, many scenes are taken from classical mythology; examples include *Hercules and the Harpies, Vulcan, Janus,* the *Titans* and *Minerva.*

The Barberini collected an impressive library, much of which came from the Strozzi library at Florence. Cassiano dal *Pozzo was librarian, though his own collection of drawings passed to the *Albani and for the most part is today at Windsor. The library, now in the Vatican, possessed the manuscript of Giuliano da *Sangallo, containing drawings of ancient objects then known and including portions of the manuscripts of *Ciriaco of Ancona, the early traveler to Greece. The humanist *Aleandro served as secretary to Cardinal Francesco and was an ardent participant in the study of antiquity.

Among the most famous objects once belonging to the family was the glass cameo cut vase (*Portland Vase) with white scenes on a dark blue background, illustrating some mythological scenes not yet conclusively deciphered. The vase was popularly, but probably erroneously, supposed to have been found in the sarcophagus of Alexander Severus (*Capitoline Museums). James *Byres engineered its acquisition by Sir William *Hamilton; it later passed to the Duchess of Portland and, after being broken by a madman and restored, is displayed today in the *British Museum. For a long time it continued to be called the Barberini Vase.

Although the family were great patrons of the arts, and motifs of antiquity appear throughout works commissioned by them, they made no really significant collections of antiquities comparable to the collections of other papal families. Some of their objects remain in the palace, for instance, a lion from *Hadrian's Villa on the landing of Bernini's stairs. Some examples of ancient sculpture are now in the portions of the palace occupied by the Circolo delle Forze Armate. A few objects are in the Capitoline; some are in the Vatican. Perhaps the finest of the objects belonging to the family is the *Barberini *Faun,* discovered during renovation of *Castel Sant'Angelo and acquired by Cardinal Francesco. It was sold to *Ludwig of Bavaria in 1814 and is now in the Munich *Glyptothek.

The coat of arms of the family consists of the famous three golden bees on a blue field, omnipresent in Rome, especially on the defensive walls of Trastevere and on Urban's tomb in St. Peter's.

BIBLIOGRAPHY

D. DuBon, *Tapestries from the Samuel H. Kress Collection, The History of Constantine the Great, Designed by Peter Paul Rubens and Pietro da Cortona* (Aylesbury, 1964); M. Lavin, *Seventeenth-Century Barberini Documents and Inventories of Art* (New York, 1975); +A. Negro, *Guide rionali di Roma: Rione II-Trevi,* 1 (Rome, 1980); +Haskell—Penny, passim.

BARBERINI FAUN. Hellenistic marble statue of a drunken, sleeping *Faun* (height 1.78m), today in the *Glyptothek, Munich.

The sculpture, probably of Pergamene origin, adorned the Mausoleum of Hadrian (*Castel Sant'Angelo); a hole in the rock below the left arm demonstrates that it once served for a fountain.

During Urban VIII's work on the Castel Sant'Angelo, the torso was found in the moat, where it had doubtless been hurled upon the invading Goths in 537. On 15 May 1627 it was carried to the Palazzo Barberini.

Its first restoration, attributable to Arcangelo Gonelli, is recorded by an engraving in H. Tetius, *Aedes Barberinae* (1642), which shows the *Faun* lying supine. This incorrect position was changed by Giuseppe Giorgetti and Lorenzo Ottone (1679), who set the torso diagonally upon a rock carved with foliage and panpipes, and modeled stucco limbs incorporating the original marble fragments. A 1738 inventory attributes this restoration to *Bernini, and later his name was associated also with the horizontal restoration. Although he cannot have executed either version, he may have provided the designs: the 1679 base was typical of his manner.

STATVA D'VN BACCO ritrouato sotto_l'Pontificato d'Vrbano VIII. tra le rouine della
Mole Adriana nello scauar il terreno per far le fondamenta delle nuoue fortificazione
del Castello S. Angelo.
Nel Palazzo Barberino.

The Barberini *Faun*, as restored by G. Giorgetti and L. Ottone, engraving from D. de Rossi— P. A. Maffei, *Raccolta di statue antiche* (1704). (The Warburg Institute, University of London.)

Financial difficulties under the French occupation compelled the Barberini in 1798 to sell the *Faun* to the sculptor Vincenzo Pacetti, who at once replaced the stucco legs with marble, drawing the right foot farther in; by 1738 the right arm was described as marble, and Pacetti does not appear to have touched this. His attempts to sell the statue were frustrated by the Barberini, who repossessed it after a complex lawsuit (1804) and sold it to *Ludwig I of Bavaria; its export was vigorously resisted, but in 1820 it arrived in Munich. Immediately the carving of the rock was simplified. In the 1960s the torso was stripped of all restorations, and its angle slightly altered; the marble limbs have now been replaced, except for the left arm.

The *Faun* has always been appreciated: the discovery of the torso was noted as important, and *Poussin in 1644 was the first of many to comment on its quality. It was engraved for D. de Rossi and P. A. *Maffei's *Raccolta di statue* (1704), Volpato copied it in biscuit porcelain, and Pacetti sold several casts of his restored marble.

BIBLIOGRAPHY

A. Furtwängler, *Beschreibung der Glyptothek König Ludwig's I zu München* (Munich, 1900), 199–206; J. Paul, "Antikenergänzung und ent-restaurierung: Bericht über die am 13. und 14. Oktober 1971 im Zentralinstitut für Kunstgeschichte abgehalten Arbeitstagung," *Kunstchronik* 25 (1972), 85–112; O. Rossi Pinelli, "Artisti, falsari o filologhi?" *Ricerche di storia dell'arte* 13–14 (1981), 41–56; J. Montagu, *Roman Baroque Sculpture: The Industry of Art* (London, 1989), 163–69.

JENNIFER MONTAGU

BARBERINI MOSAIC (PALESTRINA MOSAIC). Roman floor mosaic with Nilotic subject matter found at *Praeneste (Palestrina), in the lower zone of the *Sanctuary of Fortuna.

The date of the mosaic is much disputed, but it may have been laid at the time when Sulla restored the city, soon after 82 B.C. Alternative theories date the work to the reign of Hadrian (A.D. 117–38) or even as late as the third century A.C. The semicircular mosaic, ca. 6.5m wide and 5.25m high, shows the *Nile* at the time of inundation. The upper portion represents the rise of the river in Ethiopia, with its exotic animals and dark-skinned inhabitants, and beneath is the lower Nile, a marshy area with temple complexes, towers and huts, peopled by soldiers and civilians.

The earliest description of the mosaic is found in a collection of papers in the Palestrina archives, dated between 1588 and 1607. The mosaic lay in an ancient basilica-like structure, which at that time had been incorporated into the Bishop's Palace of the nearby cathedral of St. Agapito. The first serious investigation of the work dates to 1614, when Prince Federico Cesi examined it "by torchlight and with water poured over [the mosaic] to aid visibility." Cesi's account was passed on to Francesco Stelluti, one of the founders, along with Cesi, of the *Accademia dei Lincei, and was subsequently published by G. M. Suares (Suaresius) in his *Praenestes antiquae libri duo* (in vol. 2, 1655).

Suares also noted the existence of eighteen copies after the mosaic made for Cassiano dal *Pozzo, while the work was in the possession of the *Barberini family. These had been presumed lost by many scholars but have recently been rediscovered by H. Whitehouse in the dal Pozzo material at the Royal Library, Windsor Castle. There are actually nineteen copies extant, done in ink and watercolor (Windsor Portfolio Pf. Z 19201–219); they were probably made between 1626 and 1637 and, according to Baldinucci, were made by Pietro *Testa. The copies are of critical importance for evaluating the original appearance of the mosaic, which has been much damaged and often restored in the dreary history of its trips back and forth between Palestrina and Rome.

The mosaic was first moved piecemeal to Rome in 1624–26 by Andrea Peretti, archbishop of Palestrina; soon afterward it passed to Cardinal Lorenzo Magalotti, who, in turn, gave the mosaic to his nephew Cardinal Francesco Barberini. Magalotti kept back one segment, which has made its way today to *Berlin. In the early 1640s, the mosaic was returned to Palestrina and set up in the Palazzo Barberini by an expert in mosaic, Giovan Battista Calandra. Studied by Athanasius *Kircher and *Gori, among others, it remained there until 1853, when it was again taken to Rome for restoration, to be returned in 1855. During World War II, the mosaic was stored in Rome and subsequently was carefully analyzed and restored, in an operation documented by S. Aurigemma. In the mid-1950s the work was returned to Palestrina, where it may now be seen on the wall in the Museo Nazionale Prenestino.

BIBLIOGRAPHY

G. Lumbroso, *L'Egitto dei greci e dei romani,* 2nd ed. (Rome, 1956); G. Gullini, *I mosaici di Palestrina, Archeologia Classica,* suppl. vol. 1 (Rome, 1956); S. Aurigemma, ''Il restauro di consolidamento del Mosaico Barberini, condotto nel 1952,'' *RendPontAcc* ser. III, 30–31 (1957–59), 41–98; +H. Whitehouse, *The Dal Pozzo Copies of the Palestrina Mosaic,* Bar. suppl. ser. 12 (Oxford, 1976).

BARBERINI TOMB. Luxurious burial made at *Praeneste in the seventh century B.C., the first of the great Orientalizing tombs discovered at the site (1855; cf. *Bernardini Tomb).

Of the circumstances of the find, practically nothing is known. The excavation was undertaken by Giorgi for the prince Barberini. The contents of the tomb, having been separated from any bones or ceramic material in the grave, were kept in the Barberini library, mixed in with objects of later date. The homogeneity of the group is generally accepted and dictates its present display in the *Villa Giulia museum.

The tomb was said to be a trench (*fossa*) with a covering of stones partly lying directly on the corpse and partly above it in a corbeled pattern. The burial held a treasure of gold jewelry, silver and bronze vessels, a bronze throne, shields, cauldrons, tripods, fittings for a chariot and much carved ivory. Among the finds were at least two Oriental imports, a silver-gilt Phoenician bowl and a bronze cauldron decorated with protomes of lions and griffins, along with its conical hammered bronze stand.

BIBLIOGRAPHY

+C. D. CURTIS, ''The Barberini Tomb,'' *MAAR* 5 (1925), 9–52; +I. Strøm, *Problems Concerning the Origin and Early Development of the Orientalizing Style* (Odense, 1971), 157–59; *Civiltà del Lazio primitivo* (Rome, 1976), 214–15.

EMELINE HILL RICHARDSON

BARBERINI VASE. See PORTLAND VASE.

BARBO, PIETRO. See PAUL II.

BARTOLI, PIETRO SANTI (SANTE; 1635–1700). Italian engraver, painter and antiquarian; one of the leading figures in a circle of artists, patrons and scholars in seventeenth century Rome who were deeply interested in the study of classical antiquity.

*Poussin was the foremost artist in this circle, while patrons included Cardinal Francesco Barberini (*Barberini family), Cassiano dal *Pozzo (whose *Museum Chartaceum* comprised a vast collection of drawings after the antique), Cassiano's nephew Carlo Antonio dal Pozzo and Cardinal Camillo Massimi, like dal Pozzo, a friend and patron of Poussin. Bartoli's closest link was with G. P. *Bellori, scholar and antiquarian (and biographer of Poussin), who contributed the learned commentary to many of Bartoli's illustrations.

Bartoli was himself both artist and antiquarian. He was born at Bertola, near Perugia, but soon moved to Rome, where he was a pupil first of Le Maire, then (apparently) of Poussin himself. His biographer, Pascoli, stresses the influence Poussin had on Bartoli, asserting that Poussin first encouraged Bartoli to make copies of "the most famous works of art, both antique and modern," directing the young artist's attention to the *Laocoon,* the *Belvedere *Apollo,* the *Belvedere *Torso* and the *"*Antinous.*" Bartoli soon acquired such facility in copying that even Poussin (Pascoli tells us) could hardly distinguish his work from the original.

Though his early training was as a painter, it is chiefly as an etcher/engraver that he is celebrated. His practice in copying stood him in good stead for the work for which he is now remembered: illustrating the statues and monuments of classical Rome. The volumes of prints after classical sculpture (often with commentary by Bellori) were frequently reprinted. They include *Colonna Traiana* (1665), which Pope Alexander VII eagerly perused on publication, and *Colonna Antoniana* (1672). A selection of famous works appeared in *Admiranda romanarum antiquitatum* (1675[?]; 2nd ed., 1693). The accuracy of Bartoli's copies has been debated; Misson wrote that "we cannot always be certain that the antique venerable Figures he has engraved have not been mightily embellished by his tool," and *Winckelmann observed that Bartoli "has made everything of indifferent merit appear to belong to a flourishing age of art." However, Bellori praises his "most exact art," and it seems that—while his treatment is inevitably colored by some of the artistic preconceptions of his age—Bartoli took fewer liberties than some of his predecessors. Sometimes modifications (such as the "restoration" of a broken head) would be noted in the commentary (e.g., *Admiranda* 37). Pascoli praises Bartoli's ability to "imitate exactly every manner," but Milizia, while commending him for having "engraved the monuments of antiquity," nonetheless feels that the design of his prints, while deriving from the antique, "yet is not the antique."

Bartoli's interests were not confined to sculpture. After Bellori's death in 1696, he became papal antiquarian and antiquarian to *Christina, the queen of Sweden. His interests in other aspects of classical antiquity are shown in his illustrations of funeral lamps, *Le Lucerne sepolcrali* (1691) and of coins and gems in *Nummophiliacum reginae Christianae* and *Museum Odescalchum* (1742 and 1747). But perhaps his most remarkable contribution—again with Bellori— was the publication of copies of antique paintings and mosaics. There was a growing interest in antique painting (*Roman wall painting) in seventeenth-century Rome—to some extent an extension of the Renaissance interest but with a different emphasis and approach. Thus, Bellori and Bartoli turned to the figure paintings of the *Domus Aurea, rather than to the *grottesche* decorations. More paintings were rapidly being discovered, with the construction of roads and buildings; there existed a desire to record these while they were accessible and a special concern that the study should be scientific and systematically comprehensive.

Bartoli expresses his enthusiasm for this task in the preface to *Gli Antichi sepolcri* (1697), where he describes how, from an early age, he was "fired with enthusiasm for beauty" and how, with Bellori, he went around studying classical remains. His love of antiquity impelled him to try to record what he saw, "with the utmost accuracy." Although corpulent in build, he was tireless in exploring the sites, as Pascoli says, "to search for, discover, and draw the remains of antiquity." Bartoli and Bellori both lament the ravages of inexpert excavations, and a part of their mission was to record the works of art before they were destroyed.

The prints after antique paintings appeared in various volumes, the first illustrating the Tomb of the Nasonii (see *Tomb of Ovid), on the Via Flaminia: *Le Pitture antiche del Sepolcro de' Nasonii* (1680). Next came *Gli Antichi sepolcri* (1697) and, lastly, a volume published posthumously, *Le Pitture antiche delle grotte di Roma* (1706); here Francesco Bartoli, son of Pietro, took over his father's role, and Bellori was succeeded by M. A. de la *Chausse. In addition to the prints, there are watercolor copies of antique paintings and mosaics, made chiefly under auspices of Massimi. These works (some of which were also engraved) were highly prized and later much sought after (especially in eighteenth-century Britain). Important collections are at Eton (including the "Baddeley Codex"), Holkham and Windsor Castle. A leather-bound volume containing watercolors by Bartoli and bearing the Massimi coat of arms has recently come to light in Glasgow; this is probably the volume once owned by Dr. Richard Mead. The Comte de *Caylus owned watercolors by Bartoli (now in the Bibliothèque Nationale, Paris), which were published in a facsimile edition in 1757, with an explication by *Mariette. Caylus acknowledges Bartoli's initiative in making such copies but feels they have too much of his personal "manner" to be strictly accurate.

In 1677 Bartoli made for Massimi watercolor copies of the illustrations to the *Vatican Vergil; the facsimile copy containing these is now in the British Museum (MS. Lansdowne 834). In the same year appeared Bartoli's engravings of all but the first illustrations in the Vatican Vergil, together with illustrations from the Roman Vergil. Both drawings and engravings have recently been analyzed by D. H. Wright, in his study of the Vatican Vergil, together with a group of related pen-and-ink drawings and watercolors in the Royal Library, Windsor Castle—also probably by Bartoli.

In addition to his studies of the antique, Bartoli made copies of the work of artists of the Renaissance and of the seventeenth century; he also worked, with his father-in-law, Grimaldi, in the Borghese Palace. He traveled widely, making visits to France and Holland. It is, however, above all for his contributions to the study of classical antiquity that he is now remembered. His watercolors and prints—of classical sculpture, painiting, gems and coins—bear witness to his great diligence and zeal in attempting to make a record of classical civilization that would be both as full as possible and artistically valuable. Bartoli's achievements earned him not only renown and wealth but also the right to be buried near Nicolas *Poussin, in S. Lorenzo in Lucina.

BIBLIOGRAPHY

L. Pascoli, *Vite de' pittori scultori ed architetti perugini* (Rome, 1732), 228–33; A. Petrucci, "Bartoli, Pietro Santi," *DBI* 6(1964), 586–88; +C. Pace, "Pietro Santi Bartoli: Drawings After Roman Paintings and Mosaics in Glasgow University Library," *PBSR* 147 (1979), 117–55; Haskell—Penny, 22; M.-N. Pinot de Villelom, "Fortune des fresques antiques de Rome au 18e siècle: P. S. Bartoli et le Comte de Caylus," *GBA* 116 (October, 1990), 105–15; +H. Joyce, "Grasping at Shadows: Ancient Paintings in Renaissance and Baroque Rome," *ArtB* 74 (1992), 219–46; M. Pomponi, "Alcune precisazioni sulla vita e la produzione artistica di Pietro Santi Bartoli," *Storia dell'Arte* 27 (1992), 195–225.

                                                                                    CLAIRE PACE

BASILICA AEMILIA (BASILICA PAULLI), Rome. Building on the northeast side of the *Forum Romanum called in antiquity Basilica Paulli but known today as the Basilica Aemilia.

The building stretches behind the Tabernae Novae on a stepped platform straddling the Cloaca Maxima. It replaced the Basilica Aemilia et Fulvia of 179 B.C., which, in turn, was a replacement for what was probably the earliest basilica in Rome, a nameless one built between 210 and 193 B.C.

Pliny (*NH* 36.24.102) considered the Basilica Paulli one of the four most beautiful buildings in Rome; its columns of Africano marble with white marble bases and capitals were especially admired. Parts of a frieze in white marble decorated with reliefs showing scenes of early Roman history (*Tarpeia,* the *Rape of the Sabines,* now in the *Antiquario Forense) have been reconstructed from many small fragments and are an important monument of Late Republican art. But their place in the building and that of many splendid architectural elements are uncertain and debated.

The basilica was partly demolished when Alaric sacked Rome (A.D. 410), but a significant portion was still standing in the Renaissance. The façade of the elegant Doric front on the Argiletum was drawn by Giuliano da *Sangallo (cod. Vat. Barb. Lat. 4424, fol. 26) before it was removed by *Bramante (before 1507); it exercised a powerful influence on much architecture of the High Renaissance (*Alberti's façade for Santa Maria Novella, Florence; S. Biagio at Montepulciano, designed by Antonio da Sangallo the Elder).

The remains of the forum side were excavated by G. *Boni at the end of the nineteenth century, and these excavations were extended by A. Bartoli in the 1930s, but the northeast front, where a shallow second aisle is introduced beyond the aisle around the nave, is still, in large part, buried under the Via dei Fori Imperiali and very poorly understood. Excavations under the floor to trace the history of building on the site were conducted by G. Carettoni in the 1940s.

BIBLIOGRAPHY

G. Carettoni, *NSc* (1948), 111–28; +Nash, I, 174–79; P. W. Lehmann, "The Basilica Aemilia and S. Biagio at Montepulciano," *ArtB* 64 (1982), 124–31.

L. RICHARDSON, JR

BASILICA JULIA, Rome. Roman business house, located on the southwest side of the *Forum Romanum, filling the area between the *Temple of Castor and the *Temple of Saturn.

The basilica was begun by Julius Caesar, probably about 54 B.C., to replace the Basilica Sempronia of 170 B.C. and to balance the Basilica Paulli (*Basilica Aemilia) on the opposite side of the Forum. It was dedicated unfinished in 46 and completed by Augustus. After a fire it was rebuilt and rededicated in A.D. 12 in the names of Augustus's grandsons Gaius and Lucius, but the original name persisted. Damaged by fire in A.D. 283, the basilica was restored by Diocletian in 305 and again was damaged in 410 in the sack of Alaric. Soon after, it received its final recorded restoration and continued in use. In the eighth century, a church was located in the northwest end, but by the ninth century, dismantling had already begun. *Bramante salvaged worked blocks for the building of the Palazzo Giraud (Torlonia) in the sixteenth century.

A huge building, 101m long and 49m wide, the Basilica Julia had a central nave 82m long and was surrounded by two vaulted aisles of two stories, each 7.50m wide. The façade was embellished with engaged orders, Tuscan in the lower story, Ionic above. At the back was a row of tabernae, presumably used as government offices, with others in a second story. It was notable for its façade of blocks of white marble and seems to have been the first basilica to use arches and vaults, but the nave was roofed with a trussed gable.

The size and location of the Basilica Julia, unknown to *Nibby in 1826, had been established before *Canina's map of 1850. Canina reported on excavations here in 1849, but the building was not cleared until excavations in 1870–72 and 1883. Very little of the building is to be seen today; only the podium, with some of its steps, remains, with some arches in brick of the Diocletianic restoration at the west corner and a specimen reconstruction of an arch of the façade in modern travertine.

BIBLIOGRAPHY

H. Jordan, *Topographie der Stadt Rom in Alterthum* I.2 (1885), 384–95; +Nash, I, 186–89; Richardson, *New Topographical Dictionary,* 52–53.

L. RICHARDSON, JR

BASILICA OF MAXENTIUS (BASILICA OF CONSTANTINE; BASIL-
ICA CONSTANTINIANA: BASILICA NOVA), Rome. The last of the great
secular basilicas of ancient Rome, begun by Maxentius but finished, with modifications, by Constantine after 313.

The basilica stood north of the Sacra Via on the lower slopes of the Velia,
in an area earlier occupied by the Horrea Piperataria of Domitian. Its concrete
platform was 100m long, 65m wide. There were three aisles, each side aisle
divided into three equal barrel-vaulted chambers that opened their whole width
to the nave and communicated with one another by generous archways. The
central nave was 80m long, 25m wide and originally 35m high. The roof was
divided into three cross-vaulted sections and supported on four massive piers
on each side, in front of which stood eight monolithic columns of Proconnesian
marble. One column survives, now standing in Piazza di S. Maria Maggiore
(taken there in 1614), its shaft 14.50m high. All ceilings were of concrete, deeply
coffered, with large octagonal and small square coffers. The façades were generously lit by round-headed windows in sets of three in two stories in each side
aisle chamber, while big triple-light clerestory lunettes of the type familiar from
imperial bath architecture lit the nave.

The original entrance was from the east through a shallow narthex approached
up a paved street off the Sacra Via, but having only two doors in this front, one
on the axis of the nave and one on the axis of the side aisle to the south, that
to the north aisle being suppressed because of the interference of part of the
*Domus Aurea. A third door opened at the south end of the narthex. At the
west end of the nave opened a semicircular apse 20m in diameter covered by a
half-dome ornamented with hexagonal coffering. This was evidently used as a
setting for a colossal seated statue of Constantine, an acrolith, parts of which
were found here in 1486 and are now displayed in the courtyard of the Palazzo
dei Conservatori (*Constantine I).

Constantine changed and spoiled the architectural concept of the building by
adding a new approach and a second apse on the minor axis. In the new approach, a broad stair led up from the Sacra Via to a shallow porch supported
on four porphyry columns in front of three double doors replacing the windows
originally here. The apse, opening out of the north side, was screened from the
rest of the building by a pair of columns that must have carried a straight
epistyle.

Numerous niches for statuary are provided throughout the building, and more
statuary probably decorated the exterior. The floor was richly paved with colored
marble in patterns reminiscent of the *Pantheon pavement, and marble veneer
seems to have covered the walls up to the springing of the vaults. The vaults
and exterior were presumably finished with stucco.

The building was a triumph of engineering, as well as design, showing a bold
use of brick-faced concrete and an ingenious system of flying buttresses to
support the vaults of the central nave. Concern for the stability of the fabric,
however, led the builders to add an enormous buttress at the northwest corner.

The basilica belongs in the architectural tradition of the great imperial baths, its nave being the largest of all such cross-vaulted halls. Although its proper identity was early lost, and by the sixth century it was called *templum Romae,* it has excited interest and admiration throughout history. The north aisle still survives in relatively good condition, though the south aisle and nave collapsed, probably in the earthquake of 847. Already in the fifteenth century the plan was sketched, and Buddensieg was able to catalog studies of it by at least thirty artists before the end of the sixteenth century. It was an inspiration for many architects of the High Renaissance, notably *Bramante, *Raphael and *Michelangelo. Its influence is clearly seen in the new basilica of St. Peter.

BIBLIOGRAPHY

A. Minoprio, "A Restoration of the Basilica of Constantine, Rome," *PBSR* 12 (1932), 1–25; T. Buddensieg, "Die Konstantinsbasilica in einer Zeichnung Francesco di Giorgio," *MJb* 3rd ser. 13 (1962), 37–48; Richardson, *New Topographical Dictionary,* 51–52.

L. RICHARDSON, JR

BASSAI (BASSAE). Site in Arcadia, Greece, location of a renowned temple to Apollo Epikourios, built in the late fifth century B.C.

Bassai was a place of active cult from ca. 625 B.C. until 350 B.C., with visitors continuing to come occasionally into Roman times. The temple of Apollo standing on the site today is the fourth and last of the temples to the god erected there. It was designed by Iktinos, the architect of the *Parthenon, for the citizens of Phigalia, who wished to thank Apollo for help in a plague. Apart from its spectacular location and excellent preservation, the temple is important for its use in the cella of a single Corinthian capital (the earliest known), along with engaged Ionic columns, and for its splendid sculptured frieze, with a *Centauromachy* and an *Amazonomachy,* which ran around the interior of the temple.

The temple, unknown for many centuries, was discovered by the French architect Joachim Bocher in 1765. (When he later revisited the site, he was murdered for some brass buttons he was wearing, believed to be gold.) The picturesque site was extolled by W. M. *Leake (there in 1805), and the temple was drawn by *Dodwell in 1806. In 1811–12 an international band of archaeologists led by Charles *Cockerell and *Haller von Hallerstein explored its ruins; under the direction of Haller (Cockerell was away in Sicily), the crew unearthed the sculptured frieze, which was sold to the *British Museum. The Corinthian capital, which was sketched by Haller and later published by Cockerell, was lost. Among the other members of the expedition were P. O. *Brøndsted and the baron von *Stackelberg. An oil on canvas of the temple by Edward *Lear (1854–55) is in the Fitzwilliam Museum, Cambridge.

Excavation and restoration of the walls of the cella and the columns and architrave were carried out under P. *Kavvadias from 1902 to 1908. (Fragments thought to be from the Corinthian capital were found in the excavation.) The first complete and detailed plans of the temple and site were made by F. A. Cooper.

The *Temple of Apollo* at Bassai, painting by Edward Lear, 1854–55, Cambridge, Fitzwilliam Museum. (Reproduction by permission of the Syndics of the Fitzwilliam Museum, Cambridge.)

BIBLIOGRAPHY
F. A. Cooper, *The Temple of Apollo at Bassai: A Preliminary Study* (New York, 1978); *Pausanias, Guide to Greece,* rev. ed., tr. and ann. P. Levi, (Harmondsworth, 1979), II, 474; Tsigakou, *Rediscovery,* 22–23, 262–64; Stoneman, *Land of Lost Gods,* 188–91; F. A. Cooper, *The Temple of Apollo Bassitas,* 2, 4 (Princeton, NJ: 1992–   ).

BATH (AQUAE SULIS). Roman settlement, celebrated for its hot springs, associated with the Celtic god Sul and, by assimilation, with Minerva.

A Corinthian temple with four columns on the façade, dedicated to Sulis (or Sul) Minerva, stood in a colonnaded courtyard (53m × 74m), adjacent to the springs; the earliest remains date shortly before A.D. 100. They show conflation of Roman and Celtic elements, notably in the famous male gorgonhead from the temple. The sacred spring stood between the temple and the great bathing establishment, which, from perhaps the late first century on, was in continual use for 300 years or more.

The springs were associated with the monastery that arose there later, and Bath flourished in Saxon times, only to be ravaged when it joined in revolt against King William II. In the Norman period, the medicinal efficacy of the spring waters was promoted. Geoffrey of Monmouth (twelfth century) tells in his *Historia regum Britanniae* of the curing, in pre-Roman times, of Prince Bladud's leprosy and of his subsequent construction of bath buildings in gratitude. John *Leland (sixteenth century) left a description of ancient carvings.

By the eighteenth century, the town was a haven for antiquarians as well as fashionable patients and tourists. When the Pump Room was rebuilt in 1790, many Roman sculptured stones were discovered, including the gorgonhead. Excavation was recorded, beginning in 1864, by James Thomas Irvine and, in the 1870s, by his friend Richard Mann, who, working under the direction of Major Charles Davis, the city engineer, in 1879 discovered the Roman reservoir under the medieval baths. From 1963, exploration was conducted by the new Bath Exploration Committee; and from 1978, active excavation could be undertaken by the Bath Archaeological Trust. The Roman baths and temple complex, together with associated sculpture and inscriptions and other artifacts, have been extensively cleared and are open to the public.

BIBLIOGRAPHY
S. Lymons, *Reliquiae Romano-Britannicae,* 1 (London, 1813); F. Haverfield, *Victoria County History of the County of Somerset,* ed. W. Page, 1 (London, 1906), 219–88; B. Cunliffe, ed., *Excavations in Bath 1950–1975* (Bath, 1979); B. Cunliffe, *Roman Bath Discovered,* 2nd ed. (London, 1984).

W. W. DE GRUMMOND

BATHS OF CARACALLA (THERMAE ANTONINIANAE), Rome. Roman imperial bath complex.

The Baths of Caracalla, or the Thermae Antoninianae, as the name was recorded in the *Mirabilia urbis Romae,* were among the Seven Wonders of Rome in the fifth century. Occupying an area of ca. 120,000m² (ca. thirty acres), they are the second largest and the best-preserved imperial thermae in Rome. The monumental complex, with its *natatio* (swimming pool), *frigidarium* (cold room), *tepidarium* (warm room) and *caldarium* (hot room), represents the culmination of formal and fully symmetrical thermal planning introduced by Apollodorus in the *Baths of Trajan. The design of the bath block is developed by the crossing of two principal axes: the north-south axis of the *natatio-frigidarium-tepidarium-caldarium* and the east-west axis of the internalized *palaestrae* (exercise grounds) on both sides of the *frigidarium.* The *caldarium* was a circular structure roofed by a tall, concrete dome 35m in diameter.

The construction of the baths started under Septimius Severus in A.D. 206 and was completed by Caracalla in 216–17. Work on the precinct continued under Elagabalus and was finished by Severus Alexander. Various parts of the gigantic structure, especially the subterranean service units and galleries, were restored under Aurelian and Constans. In 365, statue bases carrying dedications to the emperors Valentinian I (364–75) and his brother Valens were set up by C. Rufus Volusianus, the prefect of Rome. The baths were restored for the last time by Theodoric early in the sixth century but fell into disuse soon after A.D. 537, when the aqueducts of Rome were damaged by the Goths.

During the sixteenth century, especially under Pope *Paul III of the *Farnese family, the building and its grounds were thoroughly ransacked for statuary and art objects. The great majority of the Farnese collection was taken to the archaeological museum in Naples (*Museo Nazionale). Among the well-known pieces are the *Farnese *Hercules,* its pendant the *Weary Hercules* (or the *Hercules Latinus*), *Achilles and Troilos,* the *Punishment of Dirce* (*Farnese *Bull*) and a colossal *Athena.*

Fortunately, interest in the building was not restricted to random treasure hunts. Among the notable architects and artists who measured, sketched and studied the impressive structure were Giuliano da *Sangallo, *Francesco di Giorgio, *Dosio, Fra *Giocondo, Baldassare *Peruzzi, Sebastiano *Serlio and *Palladio. The first modern study of the Baths of Caracalla was undertaken by G. A. *Blouet, a Prix de Rome winner from the *French Academy.

Blouet conducted a series of test excavations and published the results in a sumptuous folio volume in 1828. This was followed by the restoration studies of the complex by the Russian architect S. A. Ivanoff in 1847–48 and the subsequent joint publication in 1898 with the collaboration of the noted archaeologist C. *Hülsen. The baths became the center of many small-scale excavations in the nineteenth century (1824–29, 1868, 1870–72, 1878–81). In 1900–1 and 1911–12, the subterranean service zone of the southwest front of the bath block was investigated; some of these galleries had been converted to house a Mithraeum and a water-powered mill. Investigations and restorations of the southwest peribolus structures, especially the rectangular hall identified as a library, have been undertaken in recent years.

BIBLIOGRAPHY
+D. Krencker et al., *Die Trierer Kaiserthermen* (Augsburg, 1929), 270–74; E. Brödner, *Untersuchungen an der Caracallathermen* (Berlin, 1951); +Nash II 434–41. +W. Heinz, *Römische Thermen* (Munich, 1983), 124–41; I. Nielsen, *Thermae et balnea* (Aarhus, 1990), 53–54; F. Yegül, *Baths and Bathing in Classical Antiquity* (Cambridge, MA, 1992), 146–62.

FIKRET K. YEGÜL

BATHS OF CONSTANTINE (THERMAE CONSTANTINIANAE), Rome. The last of the great Roman Imperial baths in Rome.

The baths were constructed during the reign of Constantine (ca. A.D. 315) in the aristocratic quarter of the Quirinal Hill. The site of the Baths of Constantine appears to have been severely restricted by topography and the existing city fabric. The design was therefore developed in the north-south direction as a response to the narrow site, and internalized *palaestrae* (exercise grounds), the hallmark feature of imperial baths, were omitted. The expressive use of curves in the overall design seems consistent with Late Antique planning. Little remains of the Baths of Constantine today. From the sixteenth century onward, the building of houses and palaces covered the ruins of the complex on top of the Quirinal Hill.

The northern part of the baths was destroyed ca. 1570 for the construction of the Palazzo della Consulta; the southern half, with its major vaulted halls, was completely demolished in 1605–21 to make room for the Palazzo Palavicini-Rospigliosi of Cardinal Scipione *Borghese. Works of art of high quality found on the site include two over-lifesize statues of *Constantine* and his son *Constans* (now exhibited at the entrance to the *Capitoline Hill); two fine bronzes, the *Bronze Boxer* and the *Hellenistic Ruler* at the Museo Nazionale delle *Terme; and two river gods, *Nile* and *Tiber* (set flanking the stairway of the Palazzo Senatorio on the Capitoline). The two colossal statues, probably the Dioscuri, set up in the Piazza Quirinale (*Quirinal *Horse Tamers*), also come from the site. They may have been erected inside the baths by the prefect Petronius P. Magnus Quadratianus, who restored the building in 443.

The plan of the Baths of Constantine was recorded by Sebastiano *Serlio and *Palladio. Some of the details of these plans were confirmed by minor excavations in the nineteenth and twentieth centuries. These excavations also uncovered architectural remains (including wall and vault frescoes) of private houses dating from the late first to the third centuries A.C.

BIBLIOGRAPHY
G. Bendinelli, "Le antiche pitture Rospigliosi-Pallavicini nel Museo Nazionale Romano," *BdA* 5 (1925–26), 147–62; D. Krencker et al., *Die Trierer Kaiserthermen* (Augsburg, 1929), 282–83; Nash II 442–7; T. L. Lorenz, "Montecavallo, ein Nymphaeum auf den Quirinal," *Meded* (1979), 43–57; F. Yegül, *Baths and Bathing in Classical Antiquity* (Cambridge, MA, 1992), 169–72.

FIKRET K. YEGÜL

BATHS OF DIOCLETIAN (THERMAE DIOCLETIANI), Rome. Roman imperial bath complex.

According to an eighth-century copy of the building inscription, the largest of the imperial thermae in Rome was begun by Maximian in A.D. 298 and dedicated to his coregent Diocletian. The gigantic complex was finished in record time between May 305 and July 306. Its bricks uniformly carry stamps of the Diocletianic period. The complex occupies the high ground northeast of the Viminal Hill, serving the residents of this quarter as well as the Quirinal and the Esquiline hills. The area inside the precinct is 120,000m², the same as the *Baths of Caracalla, but the bath block is larger. The baths may have stopped functioning by the fifth century. In 1561, Pope Pius IV gave a large section of the colossal establishment to the Carthusian monks of S. Croce in Gerusalemme in order to establish a monastery. In building Villa Peretti Montalto (1586–89), Pope *Sixtus V demolished roughly one-fifth of the existing ruins, using explosives.

Prints and drawings by sixteenth-century artists, such as Marten van *Heemskerck, É. *Du Pérac, G. A. *Dosio and the Anonymous Destailleur, reveal that some of the heated halls along the southwest side of the bath block still retained their vaulting and colonnaded façades. In *Vedute di Roma* (ca. 1748) and *Antichità Romana* 1 (1756), *Piranesi gives general views of the complex as well as an impressive drawing of the wall of the *natatio* (swimming pool), displaying a rich, aedicular façade.

In 1561, *Michelangelo converted the *frigidarium* (cold room), which had been preserved intact with its great triple cross-vaults and eight colossal red granite columns, into the church of S. Maria degli Angeli. The design was altered by Vanvitelli, who rotated the axis of the church ninety degrees. Large-scale urban development and construction of the Termini train station in the 1860s demolished most of the remaining portions of the peribolus, whose great semicircular exedra was retained in the familiar curved façade of the adjoining Piazza dell'Esedra. An energetic restoration campaign championed by *Lanciani was started in 1889 and continued into 1908–11. The main objective was to restore the east *palaestra* (exercise ground) and the group of halls southwest of S. Maria degli Angeli in order to house the Museo Nazionale Romano delle *Terme.

Like the Baths of Caracalla, Diocletian's baths became the subject of a spectacular exercise in historical reconstruction, by E. Paulin, the winner of the Prix de Rome in architecture in 1875. Besides the numerous test trenches opened by Paulin, no large-scale excavations have been conducted in the Baths of Diocletian. In more recent years, minor probes inside the complex have revealed the existence of an extensive vaulted service level under the hypocaust and have borne out the accuracy of sixteenth-century drawings of the heating system.

BIBLIOGRAPHY

+E. Paulin, *Restoration des monuments antiques, Thermes de Diocletian* (Paris, 1890); D. Krenker et al., *Die Trierer Kaiserthermen* (Augsburg, 1929), 279–82; +Nash, II, 448–

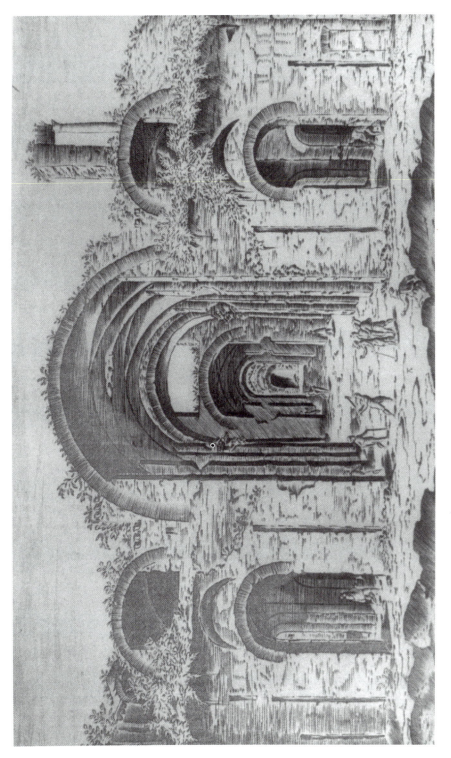

The *Baths of Diocletian*, Rome, engraving by É. Du Pérac, from *I Vestigi dell'antichità di Roma* (1575).

53; C. B. Salvetti, "Il sottosuolo delle terme di Diocleziano nel sec. XVI nei disegni della Biblioteca d'Arte nel Museo di Stato di Berlino," *StRom* 18 (1970), 462–66; F. Yegül, *Baths and Bathing in Classical Antiquity* (Cambridge, MA, 1992), 163–69.

FIKRET K. YEGÜL

BATHS OF TITUS (THERMAE TITI), Rome. Roman imperial bath complex.

Modest in scale and experimental in nature, the Baths of Titus (dedicated in A.D. 80) display all the essential elements of imperial thermae and represent the last stage before their finalization in the *Baths of Trajan. Of particular importance is the cross-vaulted *frigidarium* (cold room), probably the first appearance of this monumental type in bath architecture.

The complex, which occupied a rectangular area of ca. 105m × 120m on the southeast edge of the Oppian Hill, west of the Esquiline wing of Nero's *Domus Aurea, was started under Titus and finished in considerable haste in order to be dedicated with the *Colosseum in A.D. 80. Barely a generation after their construction, the Baths of Titus were eclipsed by the much grander bathing complex Trajan built immediately to the northeast, higher on the Oppian Hill. The building was abandoned in the fourth century, and an annex office for the prefecture of the city was built on the site. By the middle of the sixteenth century the ruins had completely disappeared. The reconstructed plan is known to us from a sketch by *Palladio (identified as the "Thermae of Vespasian").

In 1895, excavations north of the Colosseum revealed the remains of an impressive brick portico and wide stairs that can still be seen today. The portico had obviously provided a monumental approachway from the south and connected the baths with the valley of the Colosseum.

BIBLIOGRAPHY
R. Lanciani, *BullCom* 23 (1895), 110–15; D. Krencker et al., *Die trierer Kaiserthermen* (Augsburg, 1929), 265–66; +Nash, II, 469–71; F. Yegül, *Baths and Bathing in Classical Antiquity* (Cambridge, MA, 1992), 139–42.

FIKRET K. YEGÜL

BATHS OF TRAJAN (THERMAE TRAIANI), Rome. The large bathing establishment dedicated by Trajan on the Oppian Hill, which covered, in part, the remains of Nero's *Domus Aurea.

The date of construction of the baths is disputed: St. Jerome's *Chronicle,* and hence various early medieval sources, attribute it to Domitian, but the evidence of brick stamps and other inscriptions shows that most construction was carried out between A.D. 104 and 109. It is possible that the intent to build, and perhaps the design of the building, belonged to Domitian and his architect, Rabirius, but the execution of the plan and the visible remains are clearly Trajanic and are ascribed to his architect, Apollodorus, by Cassius Dio (69.4.1). This building provided the model upon which later monumental bath complexes were designed. Trajan's baths were supplied with water, at least in part, by the Aqua

Traiana, which was dedicated just two days after the baths were opened to the public (in A.D. 109, on 22 and 24 June, respectively). The baths remained in use, to some extent, into the fourth or early fifth centuries A.C. In medieval times the ruins were plundered repeatedly for building material but retained their correct name until the sixteenth century, when they were erroneously labeled "Thermae Titianae."

In 1506 the statuary group of *Laocoon and his sons, now in the *Vatican Museums, was discovered between the baths and their well-preserved water reservoir to the northeast, the so-called Sette Sale (actually, a series of nine interconnected water storage chambers). During the sixteenth and seventeenth centuries, several drawings and plans of the extant ruins were made, but by the end of the eighteenth century, most of the complex had disappeared, leaving visible only the exedrae on the northeast and southwest corners of the eastern palaestra. A fragment of the Marble Plan (*Forma Urbis Romae) that shows part of the baths was identified by R. *Lanciani in 1886, and minor excavations were reported in 1886 and 1913. From 1931 to 1935 a major but rapid campaign of excavation and partial restoration was undertaken under G. *Calza, A. Muñoz and I. Gismondi, and in 1976 the baths were further restored. Excavation in the Domus Aurea beneath the baths may bring to light more information on their date and structure; at present, both the architectural plan and the date of the complex remain controversial.

BIBLIOGRAPHY

Platner—Ashby, 534–36; +Nash, II, 472–76; H. Bloch, "Aqua Traiana," *AJA* 48 (1944), 339–41; K. De Fine Licht, "Untersuchungen an der Trajansthermen zu Rom," *Analecta Romana,* Suppl. 7 (1974); J. Anderson, "The Date of the *Thermae Traiani,*" *AJA* 89 (1985), 499–509.

JAMES C. ANDERSON, JR.

BEAZLEY, Sir JOHN DAVIDSON (1885–1970). English archaeologist and art historian.

Born at Glasgow of Anglo-Scottish parents, Beazley studied classics at Balliol under Cyril Bailey and Pickard-Cambridge. The men whose books molded him were Paul Hartwig, Friedrich Hauser and especially Adolf *Furtwängler. Early a classicist, poet and frequenter of Bloomsbury, he rigorously renounced these interests to concentrate on Attic vase painting, especially red-figured but later also black-figured. He possessed a keen eye for style and an astonishing visual memory, together with the discipline to labor long on often unpromising material. His goal was to isolate individual styles and establish the connections of artists to one another. His lifework culminated in *Attic Black-Figure Vase-Painters* (Oxford 1956) and *Attic Red-Figure Vase-Painters* (2nd ed. Oxford, 1963). In the latter alone he identifies almost 800 artists. He also made lasting contributions to the study of sculpture and gems and Etruscan mirrors and vases.

BIBLIOGRAPHY

B. Ashmole, "Sir John Beazley 1885–1970," *ProcBrAc* 56 (1970), 443–61; M. Robertson, "John Davidson Beazley," *Gnomon* 43 (1971), 429–32; *Select Exhibition of Sir*

John and Lady Beazley's Gifts to the Ashmolean Museum 1912–1966 (Oxford, 1967), 177–88, with bib.; D. von Bothmer, "J. D. Beazley," in Briggs—Calder, 1–6.

WILLIAM M. CALDER III

BECATTI, GIOVANNI (1912–73). Italian archaeologist and art historian.

Born in Siena and educated at Rome University, Becatti began his archaeological career in 1938 in the *Ostia Superintendency, moving in 1953 to the chair in Milan and later succeeding R. *Bianchi Bandinelli in Florence (1957) and Rome (1964), as well as in the direction of the *Enciclopedia dell'Arte Antica.* After early publication of Etruscan monuments, Becatti's main interests were centered on Ostia, where he conducted masterly excavations and published numerous monuments and classes of finds to 1969. As an art historian, his perceptive studies ranged from the outstanding *Arte e gusto negli scrittori latini* (1951) to jewelry, from the essays on Pheidias and the Master of Olympia to Roman sculpture and mosaics. A visiting professor at Princeton and Chicago, Becatti was universally respected for his quiet and helpful disposition no less than for the unassuming but profound quality of his scholarship.

BIBLIOGRAPHY

A. Adriani, "Giovanni Becatti," *Studi Miscellanei* 22 (Rome, 1976), 1–12; *Biografie e bibliografie degli Accademici Lincei* (Rome, 1976) 723–27.

F. R. SERRA RIDGWAY

BECKER, WILHELM ADOLF (1796–1846). German archaeologist and novelist.

Born at Dresden, student of Hermann at Leipzig, Becker became professor of archaeology there in 1836. Abandoning his teacher's narrow *Wortphilologie* and inspired by Boettiger's *Sabina,* he wrote two historical novels, *Gallus* (1838) and *Charikles* (1840) about boys of the Augustan and Periklean periods. A massive apparatus of footnotes and appendixes supported the naive narrative and, with archaeological and literary testimonia, introduced readers to "the private antiquities" of the ancients. Both were constantly reprinted and expanded throughout the nineteenth century (in bowdlerized English translations as well). *Wilamowitz attests their popularity among schoolboys at a time when classical instruction was arid and grammatical.

BIBLIOGRAPHY

C. Bursian, *Geschichte der classischen Philologie in Deutschland von den Anfängen bis zur Gegenwart* (Munich, 1883), 582–83; U. von Wilamowitz-Moellendorff, *Erinnerungen 1848–1914,* 2nd ed. (Leipzig, 1929), 62, n. 1; H. Riikonen, "Die Antike im historischen Roman des 19. Jahrhunderts: Eine literatur— und kulturgeschichtliche Untersuchung," *Commentationes Humanarum Litterarurm* 59 (1978), 61–64.

WILLIAM M. CALDER III

BEGER, LORENZ (1653–1705). German librarian and scholar; specialist in numismatics and glyptics.

Beger was the most active and versatile antiquarian in Germany in the second

LAURENTIUS BEGER
SERENISSIMI ELECTORIS PALATINA
ANTIQUARIUS ET BIBLIOTHECARIUS
ÆTATIS UÆ XXXII

Portrait of *Lorenz Beger*, anonymous engraving (1685). (Westfälisches Landesmuseum für Kunst und Kulturgeschichte, Münster, Porträtarchiv Diepenbroick. Photo: R. Wakonigg.)

half of the seventeenth century. Born in Heidelberg, he served as librarian (from 1675) to the prince Karl Ludwig von der Pfalz and was conservator of a collection of coins and other antiquities originally amassed for Karl Ludwig by Ezechiel Spanheim. Beger published many items from the collection in his *Thesaurus ex Thesauro Palatino selectus* (Heidelberg, 1685), arranging the gems according to mythological themes and sorting the coins into issues of Greek rulers, Greek coins from city-states and colonies and Roman imperial issues. He also published some sculptures, including an early bronze statue of *Hermes* or *Apollo* found in 1507 at Constanz.

Beger was appointed in 1693 to oversee the library, coin cabinet and art and curio collection in Berlin of Frederick I, king of Prussia. He was instrumental in acquiring for the king the collection of G. P. *Bellori in Rome and bringing it to Berlin, thus creating one of the most important collections of antiquity in Northern Europe.

These were years of great productivity for Beger. He issued a series of monographs on mythological themes in ancient art, including studies of Meleager (1696); the Trojan War (1699; among the monuments consulted were the *Tabulae Iliacae); as well as Alcestis; Sisyphos and Ixion; Odysseus; and Hercules (1703–5). Of greatest significance was his three-volume *Thesaurus Brandenburgicus selectus* (Cologne, 1696–1701), containing coins, gems, statues, busts, vases and lamps. The work has been described as the most important work on archaeology to come out in Germany before the time of *Winckelmann, and Beger has been credited with first establishing Berlin as a center for the study of classical antiquities. His status is made clear by the fact that he is presented as the first entry in *Archäologenbildnisse, Porträts und Kurzbiographen von klassischen Archäologen deutscher Sprache* (1988), issued by the *German Archaeological Institute to commemorate German archaeologists from the seventeenth to the twentieth centuries.

BIBLIOGRAPHY
Stark, esp. 112–13, 157–59; *Porträtarchiv,* no. 47; *Archäologenbildnisse* 1–2.

BELLAY, JEAN DU (1498–1560). Collector of antiquities, French ecclesiastic.
Jean du Bellay was archbishop of Paris and was appointed cardinal in 1535. He was governor of Paris for Francis I but fell into political disfavor. Afterward he moved to Rome and purchased a house near the *Campus Martius. A few of the statues kept there were recorded by *Aldrovandi, but the bulk of his collection was to be found in his villa near the exedra of the *Baths of Diocletian in Rome. Statues decorated the paths of his gardens and were displayed in his casino. J. J. *Boissard described the collection during his visit to Rome and illustrated a dozen sculptures in his *Antiquitates* (1598). Pirro *Ligorio mentioned a herm with *Sappho* owned by the cardinal and an oval relief supposedly depicting *Aristotle,* which was illustrated by Fulvio *Orsini in his *Imagines* (1570).

After the death of du Bellay, an inventory of his collection was drawn up by the French sculptor Claude Lusinier. Some of the antiquities were acquired by the Cardinal d'Este (see *Este family). When Caterina Nobili-Sforza purchased du Bellay's villa in 1593, there were still statues, columns and fragments to be found. She reserved these for herself when she disposed of the property in 1594.

BIBLIOGRAPHY
A. Bertolotti, *Artisti francesi in Rome* (Rome, 1886), 40–44; Lanciani, *Storia degli scavi* II (1903), 138–44; III (1907), 263; C. Hülsen, *Göttinger Gelehrte Anzeiger,* 176 (1914), 289.

MARJON VAN DER MEULEN

BELLINI FAMILY. Family of painters from Venice, of whom the earliest was JACOPO (1390s–1470/71); his sons were GENTILE (1429–1507) and GIOVANNI (ca. 1430–1516).
Trained under Gentile da Fabriano, Jacopo Bellini first worked in his master's

manner, that is, the International Style of the Late Gothic. He may have traveled to Florence with Gentile and there developed the interest in linear perspective that manifests itself in many of his drawings and paintings. Jacopo's knowledge of antiquities is seen in his albums of drawings, one in the *Louvre, Paris (in various techniques, retouched, on parchment), and the other in the *British Museum, London (in leadpoint, unretouched, on heavy paper), datable to the 1440s and 1450s.

In the Louvre album are two sheets with detailed drawings of antiquities. There is a drawing of a sestertius of Domitian, with an image of the defeated *Germany* on the reverse (GERMANIA CAPTA), as well as blank circles into which other coins might be inserted, and a number of altars or grave markers with inscriptions (with beautiful lettering, but sometimes adapted from other monuments). In the British Museum album there are many sheets with wistful Arcadian fantasies, often with nudes and a varied array of Bacchic characters.

Many of Jacopo's paintings contain representations of ancient objects or monuments he had seen or invented. On his buildings in elaborate perspective, careful scrutiny reveals statues, plaques, coins and reliefs, often chosen to convey a Roman atmosphere in stories of Christ set at the time of the Caesars. In his Louvre drawing of *Christ Led Before Pilate,* the archway imitates the *Arch of the Sergii at Pola on the Dalmatian coast, possibly known to Jacopo from a personal visit. No doubt many of the altars and reliefs he depicted were locally visible in Padua and the surrounding area.

Jacopo owned marbles, reliefs and casts, as is evident from his wife's will, but nothing specific is known about them.

Gentile, through his mother, inherited his father's drawings and thus owned an archive in which he might study antiquities. He, too, had a personal collection of ancient pieces, including a bust of *Plato* and a torso of *Venus,* attributed to Praxiteles, which Isabella d*'Este sought to buy. (These also may have come from his father.)

Relatively little evidence of his utilization of classical motifs is to be seen in his paintings. The ambitious canvas of *St. Mark Preaching at Alexandria* (Brera, Milan; 1504 and following, completed by Giovanni Bellini) reveals his knowledge of ancient and contemporary *Alexandria, perhaps derived from consulting a manuscript of the travels of *Ciriaco of Ancona. The painting contains monuments perhaps to be identified as the Column of Diocletian (the ''Pillar of Pompey''), the obelisk moved from Heliopolis to Alexandria by Augustus, and the Pharos (Lighthouse). Gentile's knowledge of the appearance of such antiquities was no doubt affected by his journey to Constantinople (*Byzantium) (1479–80), where he worked for the sultan Mehmed II and was able to view monuments like the Column of Theodosius the Great, the Column of the Goths and the obelisk erected by Theodosius in the hippodrome.

Giovanni, half-brother of Gentile and illegitimate son of Jacopo, was the most celebrated of the three painters; he has left only a modest record of his interest in classical antiquities. Drawings or paintings of ancient monuments are exceedingly rare. In this respect Giovanni contrasts not only with his father but also with his brother-in-law *Mantegna, whose art is intensely archaeological. Giovanni's patrons commissioned sacred subjects and portraits but seldom requested classical themes, and these, such as they are, occur mainly in his later years, around the end of the fifteenth century and the beginning of the sixteenth, when humanism began to make greater gains in Venice.

Giovanni Bellini's baffling *Allegories* in the Accademia, Venice (1480s–90s), include a few classical elements—nudity, vaguely antique drapery, a decorated "altar" resembling one in Jacopo's Paris album, a Bacchic figure—and his *Feast of the Gods* (National Gallery, Washington, DC), commissioned by Isabella d'Este and finished after his death in 1516, is based on texts of Ovid and a fourteenth-century commentary on Ovid. Here, as P. Fehl demonstrated, Bellini did not intend to depict ideal images of the antique gods, but rather country folk at a feast.

Bellini's most archaeological painting is his *Continence of Scipio* (National Gallery, Washington, DC), prepared as a pendant to Mantegna's *Triumph of Scipio* and, like it, done in a grisaille that creates the effect of a classical relief and contains a wall plaque imitating an ancient inscription.

BIBLIOGRAPHY

+P. W. Lehmann, *Cyriacus of Ancona's Egyptian Visit and Its Reflections in Gentile Bellini and Hieronymus Bosch* (Locust Valley, NY, 1977); +B. Degenhart—A. Schmitt, *Jacopo Bellini, The Louvre Album of Drawings,* tr. F. Mecklenberg (New York, 1984); +R. Goffen, *Giovanni Bellini* (New Haven, CT, 1989); +C. Eisler, *The Genius of Jacopo Bellini* (New York, 1989).

BELLORI, GIOVANNI PIETRO (1613–96). Roman antiquarian, collector and critic of the arts.

Bellori's interest in ancient civilization, literature, numismatics, poetry and the visual arts was formed by Francesco Angeloni, who became his second father and of whose household he was officially a member by 1634. Angeloni was secretary to Cardinal Ippolito Aldobrandini, and through him Bellori was introduced to the most prominent antiquarians and collectors of his day. He also studied drawing with *Domenichino and was a close friend of many artists, including *Poussin, Canini, Duquesnoy, Dufresnoy and Maratta.

Upon his death in 1652, Angeloni made Bellori his universal heir. The will was contested, however, and Angeloni's collection of antiquities and works of art was dispersed. Bellori set about forming his own collection along the same lines. After Bellori's death his collection of antiquities was purchased by Frederick I of Prussia and then by Augustus III of Saxony. Ultimately, it was transferred to Vienna, where it was studied by *Winckelmann. In building his collection, Bellori was assisted by Leonardo *Agostini, a *marchand-amateur.* Agostini introduced him to Carlo di Tommaso Strozzi, keeper of antiquities in Florence, and through Strozzi, Bellori advised the *Medici in their purchases of antiquities. Bellori, in turn, contributed annotations to Agostini's *Le Gemme* *antiche figurate* (Rome, 1657) and edited a second edition of this work in 1686. Bellori was made commissioner of the antiquities of Rome and its environs (*Commissario delle Antichità) by Clement X in 1670 (after having assisted the elderly Agostini perform the same task under Alexander VII), a post he held until 1694. He served as antiquarian and librarian to *Queen Christina of Sweden from ca. 1680 until her death in 1689.

Bellori's first independent publication was his *Icones et segmenta illustrium e marmore tabularum quae Romae adhuc extant* (Rome, 1645). This included engravings by F. Perrier and was the model for later works for which Bellori supervised the production of engraved illustrations of the highest quality, providing detailed explanations of his own. After the appearance of his influential *Le Vite de' pittori, scultori e architetti moderni* in 1672 Bellori concentrated upon the publication of his antiquarian studies, in which the illustrations by Pietro Santi *Bartoli (who succeeded him as keeper of antiquities at the Vatican in 1694) provide the essential complement to Bellori's texts. Among the most important of these joint publications are the studies of the *Column of Trajan (1665), the *Column of Marcus Aurelius (1672), the paintings in the Tomb of the Nasonii (*Tomb of Ovid) on the Via Flaminia (1680), ancient lamps from the catacombs (1691) and the *Admiranda romanarum antiquitatum ac veteris sculpturae vestigia* (1691).

Bellori brought to his antiquarian studies the same selective critical standards, concern for accurate description and interest in iconography that informed his writings on more contemporary art. He chose to write about what he considered the outstanding remains of antiquity and wrote from his direct experience. In 1661 he traveled to Palestrina (*Praeneste) Montecassino, Capua, *Naples, Vesuvius, the *Tomb of Vergil, Sorrento and *Capri as the companion of M. Parisot, the personal representative of *Louis XIV. In 1668 he took the opportunity to study the reliefs of Trajan's Column at first hand when scaffolding was erected to make plaster casts for the King of France. The illustrations for the book on the Tomb of the Nasonii were based on drawings made during the excavations in order to provide the most accurate record possible. Like Cassiano dal *Pozzo, Bellori devised categories for the cataloging of minor objects as a basis for their comparative study. To his *Nota delli musei, librerie, galerie et ornamenti di statue e pitture ne' palazzi, nelle case, e ne' giardini di Roma* (published anonymously in 1664) Bellori added an appendix entitled *Delli Vestigi delle pitture antiche dal buon secolo de' Romani*. According to C. *Hülsen, this discussion of the ancient paintings then existing in Rome, together with excavation drawings, and notes on the quality, state of conservation, and subjects of the paintings, is the first treatment of the subject. Bellori was also interested in oriental studies and published a biography of the traveler Pietro della Valle (1586–1652) in 1662.

Bellori the antiquarian is inseparable from Bellori the critic of contemporary art. He praised those artists, from *Raphael to Annibale *Carracci, Domenichino, Poussin, and Maratta, who in his view perpetuated the tradition of the ancients. In this he was deeply influenced by Poussin, who persuaded him to model his biographies on the *Imagines* of Philostratus. In 1664 Bellori delivered his lecture, *L'Idea del pittore, dello scultore et dell' architetto,* to the Academy of St. Luke in Rome, in which he urged artists to form their idea of the beautiful from a selection of the most beautiful natural models, reconstituted and perfected by the intellect. For this he found support in the process by which Zeuxis was said to have made his statue of Helen and in recent appeals to that process by *Alberti, Leonardo, Raphael and Guido *Reni. Bellori's lecture was derived in great part from Franciscus *Junius's *De pictura veterum* (1637). Junius had also sought to establish a modern tradition based on antiquity, but Bellori's lecture exerted a more powerful influence upon the academic tradition, especially in France, because it was published as an introduction to *Le Vite* in 1672.

Bellori was secretary of the Academy of St. Luke (1669–72), delivered the prize-giving address at the pro forma union of the French and Roman academies in 1677 and became rector of the Roman Academy of St. Luke in 1678. In 1689 he was nominated an honorary member of the Académie Royale de Peinture et Sculpture.

For Bellori, as for Poussin, the ancient past provided an example of moral virtue and a foundation for a modern classical tradition that sought to avoid the twin excesses of naturalism and fantastic novelty.

BIBLIOGRAPHY

E. Panofsky, *Idea: Ein Beitrag zur Begriffsgeschichte der älteren Kunsttheorie, Studien der Bibliothek Warburg* 5 (Leipzig, 1924), tr. J. J. S. Peake, *Idea: A Concept in Art Theory* (Columbia, SC, 1968); K. Donahue, "The Ingenious Bellori," *Marsyas* 3 (1945), 107–38; +K. Donahue, "Bellori, Giovanni Pietro," *DBI* 7 (1965), 781–89; +G. P. Bellori, *Le Vite de' pittori, scultori e architetti moderni,* ed. E. Borea, with an introduction by G. Previtali (Turin, 1976); E. Cropper, "*La più bella antichità che sappiate desiderare:* History and Style in Giovan Pietro Bellori's *Lives,*" in *Kunst und Kunsttheorie 1400–1900,* ed. P. Ganz et al., *Wolfenbütteler Forschungen* (Wiesbaden, 1991), 145–73.

ELIZABETH CROPPER

BELOCH, KARL JULIUS ALWIN (1854–1929). German historian of antiquity.

Beloch, born in Prussia, lived mainly in Italy and taught ancient history in the University of Rome, 1879–1929. His many books are crowned by his vast *Griechische Geschichte* (2nd ed., 4 vols. in 8, 1912–27), which reaches 217 B.C. A volume of special studies accompanies each volume of narrative. Beloch's main interest was in economic history and population (his *Die Bevölkerung der griechisch-römischen Welt,* 1886, is still not superseded) rather than in great personalities. His work is more modern and original than the comparable history of *Busolt but probably not superior to it in responsible judgment.

BIBLIOGRAPHY

S. Steinberg, ed., *Die Geschichtswissenschaft der Gegenwart in Selbstdarstellungen,* 2 (Leipzig, 1926), 1–27; A. Momigliano, "Beloch, Karl," *DBI* 8 (1966), 32–45; L. Polverini, *Annali della Scuola Normale Superiore di Pisa,* Cl. di Lett. e Filosofia, ser. 3, 9 (1979), 1429–62; with bib.

MORTIMER CHAMBERS

BELVEDERE "ANTINOUS" (HERMES). Lifesize marble statue (1.95m) of a beardless nude male standing figure, with a mantle tossed over the proper left shoulder.

The work is a Roman copy of the time of Hadrian (A.D. 117–38) of a Greek bronze original created possibly within the circle of Praxiteles (late fourth century B.C.). It is now believed to represent Hermes (Mercury).

The identification of the work as Antinous, the lover of Hadrian, was partly conventional, since this label was frequently given to statues of unknown nude youths, but it may also be based on the find spot of the piece, reported to be a garden near *Castel Sant'Angelo, the tomb of Hadrian. The statue was acquired by Pope *Paul III, probably in 1543, and was installed in the Belvedere court by 1545. (An alternative tradition reports the statue discovered at S. Martino ai Monti and acquired by *Leo X.) *Aldrovandi is the first on record to call it Antinous (1549–50); *Cavalieri published an engraving (by 1584), identifying the figure as Milo or Antinous. Later, *Winckelmann rejected the theory that it portrayed Antinous and proposed, instead, Meleager, while *Mengs argued for a youthful Hercules, and E. Q. *Visconti, who won the day, suggested Mercury.

The statue was admired enormously for centuries. Artists drew from it and treated it like a canon for its proportions: Parmigianino and Hendrick *Goltzius copied it, and *Poussin made measured drawings, which were used by *Bellori in his *Lives* of the artists. Largillière's portrait of Charles *Le Brun (1686; *Louvre, Paris) shows him as president of the Royal Academy of Painting and Sculpture with a copy of the *"Antinous"* for inspiration. William Hogarth cited the work as the ultimate in bodily proportions.

Like most other antique sculptures considered canonical in the Renaissance and Baroque periods, the *"Antinous"* has faded. In the eighteenth century, scholars began to collate the other versions of the original and ultimately have ranked several other copies as superior to this one—above all, the Farnese *Hermes* (*Sassi family) in the *British Museum (recently loaned to the National Gallery, London), but also copies in the *National Archaeological Museum, Athens, and the Ludington collection, Santa Barbara.

BIBLIOGRAPHY
Helbig, I, 4th ed., 190; H. Brummer, *The Statue Court in the Vatican Belvedere* (Stockholm, 1970), 210–14; Haskell—Penny, 141–43; Bober—Rubinstein, 58; Ridgway, *Roman Copies,* 85.

BELVEDERE APOLLO. Ancient marble statue of the god Apollo, long of surpassing popularity; now considered to be a Roman work carved in the second century A.C.

This famous sculpture is named after the hilltop Villa Belvedere of Pope

Innocent VIII (cf. *Vatican Museums), in which *Julius II established a statue court and garden, not long after his election in 1503. The court, with niches let into the surrounding walls for the principal statues, was, and still is, presided over by the *Apollo*. The report that the statue was found in the late fifteenth century on property on the old road to Marino that belonged to Cardinal Giuliano delle Rovere (later, Julius II) is plausible, and the tradition that the cardinal placed it in the sculpture garden of his residence at SS. Apostoli in Rome was recently vindicated by Deborah Brown. From this garden Julius transferred it to the Belvedere, no later than 1509. In its history the *Apollo* was absent from the court for a brief time when it was taken in triumph to Paris in 1798 by *Napoleon (to be returned in 1816) and again in 1983–84, when the newly restored sculpture was the glory of a Vatican exhibition sent to New York, Chicago and San Francisco.

The statue shows Apollo in an avenging action that yet reveals him as the god of poetry and leader of the Muses. Made of Parian marble, the over-lifesize figure (height 2.25m) was no doubt once enlivened by color; traces of paint possibly have survived in the splendidly coiffed hair, which we may imagine with locks shining brightly in the color of gold. The extended left arm, with hand now missing, probably held a large bow of gilded metal. The right hand, missing along with the forearm, may have held an arrow or a wreath of laurel or perhaps both. Fragments of Apollo's sacred laurel leaves can still be discerned near the top of the tree trunk that serves the statue as a support. The meticulously worked sandals and their laces perhaps also were the color of gold.

Modern archaeology rather coldly calls the work a Roman copy of ca. A.D. 130–40 but makes up for this diminution of a much-celebrated work of art by attributing the presumed original to Leochares. All the praise that modern criticism feels it must withhold from the "copy" may thus with impunity be lavished on the unknown but still "Classical" original behind it. In 1934, R. *Bianchi Bandinelli pointed out, in what still remains a minority opinion, that the attribution to Leochares (first proposed by F. Winter in 1892) is based on wishful thinking rather than tangible evidence. Bianchi Bandinelli, calling into court a comparable but passionately animated head of Apollo now in Basel, argued, instead, that the Belvedere *Apollo* was a frigid copy of a Hellenistic original of the third if not the second century B.C. He thus denied the work's cherished aura of classical perfection and balance and replaced it (in its putative original) with another ideal, the expression of hot-blooded life that is traditionally attributed to Hellenistic art. It may, however, be more fruitful not to think of the Belvedere *Apollo* as a copy at all but rather as a work of creative imitation (for Roman use) in which a number of characteristic aspects of Apollo's divinity that had already been well defined and perfected in Classical and Hellenistic art and poetry are harmoniously combined into one living image.

An approach of this kind perhaps will provide a bridge to a better understanding of the immense delight, love and gratitude with which the Belvedere *Apollo* was viewed and celebrated by artists, poets and the art-loving public alike, virtually from the time the statue was found to nearly the end of the nineteenth century. Franz *Wickhoff identified as one of the earliest adaptations of the statue in a Renaissance work of art the seated and conspicuously nude figure in Signorelli's *Moses Reading the Law to the Israelites* in the Sistine Chapel (1482–83). The beautiful youth, who represents the Bible's "stranger among the Israelites," listens with intense longing to Moses' words of revelation. Here, as in later interpretations of the Belvedere *Apollo* in art, the statue is comprehended as a flexible figure, in its iconography as much as in its form. Its appearance depends on the situation to which it is adapted, but it is always used as a guide to the representation of supreme beauty in body and in soul. *Raphael, in the Vatican Stanza della Segnatura (1508–12), both quotes the work and combines it with other well-established representations of Apollo, as he shows the god in different aspects of his being. The Belvedere figure guides the hand of *Michelangelo in the painting of his nude figures (*ignudi*) on the Sistine Ceiling (1508–12) and, in an entirely different aspect of the statue's poetical potential, in his representation of Christ in the Sistine *Last Judgment* (completed 1541). For *Dürer, the Belvedere *Apollo* is the source of his own renderings of Apollo and also of his Adam (engraving of *Adam and Eve,* 1504). In *Rubens's Marie de' Medici Cycle (1621–25), in the painting of the *Government of the Queen,* Apollo springs into life and action directly from the statue. The *Apollo,* in turn, always has received its own enlivenment from the light reflected back upon it by various interpretations in art, music and poetry.

*Winckelmann's famous paean on the statue soon became canonical. The figure, remarkably enough, is also the anchoring point of his biologically conceived view of the history of art and civilization, published in 1764. The origins of modern archaeology are thus linked to the appreciation of the Belvedere *Apollo.*

The revelation of the *Parthenon sculptures by *Elgin in the early nineteenth century made the Belvedere *Apollo* pale in the eyes of the *cognoscenti,* but it was not until the respect for imitation in the arts (and in manners) as a source of greatness or distinction was eroded that the Belvedere statue came to be despised, derided and even hated. In the 1950s and 1960s, professors and students in academies of art vented their spleen on the plaster casts of the work within their reach, but their hammer blows really were directed at the original, which in their eyes was itself "only a copy." Lethargy and cultural relativism have since allowed the Belvedere *Apollo* to reside in peace at the Vatican Museum, where, in a new, carefully pondered and successful restoration, the work continues to move and delight countless visitors.

BIBLIOGRAPHY

E. Morani, *Stanze sopra le statue di Laocoonte, di Venere et d'Apollo* (Rome, 1539); R. Bianchi Bandinelli, "Apollo del Belvedere," *La Critica d'Arte* 1 (1935), 3–9; +H. H. Brummer, *The Statue Court in the Vatican* (Stockholm, 1970); +*The Vatican Collections: The Papacy and Art,* catalog of exhibition (New York, 1982), 14–25, 57–63, 200–203; D. Brown, "The Apollo Belvedere and the Garden of Giuliano delle Rovere at SS.

Apostoli," *JWarb* 49 (1986), 235–38; D. R. Coffin, *Gardens and Gardening in Papal Rome* (Princeton, NJ, 1991).

PHILIPP FEHL

BELVEDERE PIGNA, Vatican. Roman sculpture of a pinecone cast in bronze.

The *Pigna* is first mentioned in the **Mirabilia urbis Romae* (1144), by which time it had been incorporated into a fountain formerly in the atrium of the Constantinian church of St. Peter's. Four meters high, the *Pigna* is composed of three parts: the body, cast in Roman times and dated on epigraphical evidence between the first century B.C. and the second century A.C.; the pinnacle, associated with repairs under Clement XI (1700–21); and a bronze basin added in post-Roman times. The most important of the inscriptions, not all of which are ancient, is that of the signature of the artist, "P(ublius) Cincius P(ublii) l(ibertus) Salvius fecit," a graffito incised three times with minor variations around the convex base molding of the pinecone.

The pinecone's function is uncertain, but in the late eighth century, probably upon the restoration of the Aqua Traiana by Hadrian I (772–95), it was moved to St. Peter's from the Campus Martius, where it left its name on seven churches and the *rione* (district.) At this time, the scales of the *Pigna* were pierced, and the basin was added so that water (est. cap. 9,700 liters or 900 liters/hr) could squirt out the scales as described in the *Mirabilia*. The fountain's appearance is preserved in drawings and engravings by Simone di Tommaso, *Francisco d'Ollanda, G. A. *Dosio and G. B. de' *Cavalieri. Under Paul V (1608–10), the *Pigna* was moved to the Cortile della Pigna, one of the three courts that subdivide *Bramante's Cortile del Belvedere, where, by 1615, it decorated the great niche. Under Clement XI the niche was embellished, and the *Pigna* was restored and mounted on a capital from the Baths of Severus Alexander. The *Pigna* inspired several other medieval fountains, such as *Charlemagne's at Aachen (ca. 800) and two in the Basilica of Basil I (d. 886) in Constantinople.

BIBLIOGRAPHY

+G. Maggi-Mascardi, *La Grande veduta del Tempio e del Palazzo Vaticano* (Rome, 1615) folio IV; +C. D'Onofrio, *Le Fontane di Roma* (Rome, 1986), 22, 27–31; +S. Angelucci, "Il restauro della pigna vaticana," *Bollettino dei Monumenti, Musei e Gallerie Pontificie* 6 (1986), 5–49; I. di Stefano Manzella, "Le iscrizioni della pigna vaticana," *BollMonMusGalPont* 6 (1986), 65–78.

LAETITIA LA FOLLETTE

BELVEDERE TORSO. Fragmentary marble sculpture of an over-lifesize male torso, dating to the first century B.C., frequently identified as Hercules.

Inscribed on the statue's rocky base is the name of the artist, Apollonios of Athens, the son of Nestor, who lived in Rome at the end of the Republican period and who may have modeled this work after an earlier Hellenistic Greek sculpture. The figure, seated on a boulder, shows intense action of the musculature as it leans forward with a twist of the shoulders. Over the left thigh is

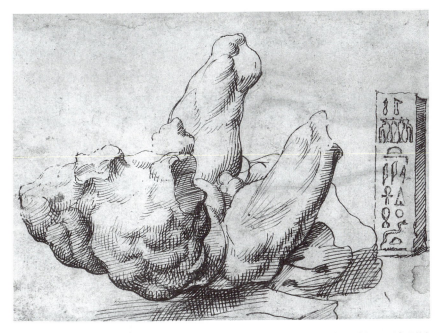

Belvedere *Torso*, drawing by M. van Heemskerck, Berlin, Kupferstichkabinett. (© Bild-archiv Preussischer Kulturbesitz, Berlin, 1994. Photo: J. P. Anders, 79 D 2.)

draped part of the skin of a feline, often interpreted as the lion skin of Hercules; traditionally, the torso has been understood as Hercules resting after completing his labors. Other interpretations of the iconography identify the figure as Poly-phemos, sitting on the shore and turning his lovesick gaze to the sea nymph Galatea, or Marsyas defeated and bound by Apollo (or even playing his pipes) or Philoktetes waiting on Lemnos.

The torso is first referred to in a comment on its inscription attributed to *Ciriaco of Ancona, who was in Rome in 1424 and again between 1432 and 1434; in that period the piece was in the collection of the *Colonna family, located on the lower Quirinal Hill near SS. Apostoli. By ca. 1500, the work seems to have come into the possession of the sculptor Andrea *Bregno, also living on the Quirinal. The next information comes from drawings by *Heems-kerck (ca. 1532–35), revealing that the torso was lying on the ground in the Belvedere court of the *Vatican. How it was obtained for the papal collections is not known, but evidently soon afterward it was set upright on a base and remained in the courtyard until the time of Clement XI (1700–21), when it was moved to a small adjoining room. In the 1770s it was placed in the ''round vestibule'' of the new Museo Pio-Clementino, and in 1797 it went to France for the glory of *Napoleon, to be displayed in the Musée Central des Arts in

Paris. It was returned to the Vatican in 1816 and remains there today, in the Atrio del Torso, adjoining the courtyard.

The statue, greatly admired through the centuries and one of the few Renaissance favorites that retain a high reputation today, was originally something of a connoisseur's piece. It was never restored, and so was sought out and studied, especially by the learned or by artists who were able to restore it mentally or in their own works of art. *Michelangelo was one of the greatest admirers of the Belvedere *Torso,* and his praise undoubtedly increased its prestige. Numerous drawings and copies were made through the centuries, sometimes suggesting partial or complete restoration (e.g., in a portrait by Bernardino Licinio in the Villa Borghese; in small bronzes of the sixteenth century), and casts were regularly displayed in the art academies (*French Academy in Rome; Royal Academy in London). P. P. *Rubens, the *Carracci and numerous other artists of the seventeenth century were excited by the Baroque style of the torso and the lessons it taught about power in the human body. *Winckelmann, in spite of his prejudices against late works, was rapturous about the Belvedere *Torso* and attempted to date it a century earlier than is generally accepted today. In modern times, Rhys *Carpenter made an astute examination of the piece, challenging the centuries-old identification as Hercules and arguing for Marsyas (1941).

BIBLIOGRAPHY

R. Carpenter, "Observations on Familiar Statuary in Rome," *MAAR* 18 (1941), 84–93; H. H. Brummer, *The Statue Court in the Vatican Belvedere* (Stockholm, 1970), 142–52; Haskell—Penny, 311–14; Bober—Rubinstein, 166–68, *LIMC* VI, 375 (A. Weis).

BEMBO, PIETRO (1470–1547). Leading humanist of the Italian Renaissance; poet, scholar, collector, cardinal.

Pietro Bembo, born of a noble Venetian family, resided successively at Ferrara, where he wrote *Gli Asolani,* his celebrated dialogue on love; Urbino (1506–12), where he became friends with Baldassare Castiglione, who immortalized Bembo as a participant in *The Courtier* (*Il Cortegiano*); and Rome, where he served as papal secretary to *Leo X (until 1519). He then settled at Padua in 1522, in a palace that remained his major residence until the end of his life, although he was called to Rome as cardinal by *Paul III in 1539.

Bembo's interest in classical antiquity was philological and archaeological. He produced critical studies on the plays of Terence and Vergilian poetry and himself wrote poetry and Ciceronian letters in Latin. His collection at Padua was a source of immense pride, containing sculptures said to be of Parian marble and Corinthian bronze; ancient earthenware pottery and glass vessels; coins; engraved gems set in rings; marble busts of emperors and one of *Brutus;* a bronze head of *Antoninus Pius;* a marble *Sleeping Cupid.* Visitors praised his illuminated manuscripts of Terence and Vergil, which were later sold to Fulvio *Orsini and are in the Vatican Library today (*Vatican Vergil). His most curious item was the bronze tablet known as the *Mensa Isiaca* (or *Tabula Isiaca*), decorated with Egyptianizing motifs, made in the Antonine period (second century

A.C.). The piece was sold by Bembo's son Torquato in 1592 to Vincenzo I Gonzaga, duke of Mantua, and then went to Carlo Emanuele I of Savoy (1630). It is in the Museo Egizio of Turin today. He also owned paintings by Jacopo Bellini (*Bellini family), *Mantegna, *Raphael, Sebastiano del Piombo and Giulio Campagnolo.

Throughout his life Bembo had many connections with his native Venice. His portrait was painted by *Titian, and he served the press of Aldus Manutius well, not only in print but also by providing a gold coin of the emperor Titus, with a reverse with a dolphin entwined around an anchor, a motif to be selected by Aldus as his press's device.

BIBLIOGRAPHY

+E. Scamuzzi, *La Mensa Isiaca del Regio Museo di Antichità a Torino* (Rome, 1949); C. Dionisotti, "Bembo, Pietro," *DBI* 8 (1966), 133–51; Weiss, *RDCA* 198, 201–2; S. Eiche, "On the Dispersal of Cardinal Bembo's Collection," *Mitteilungen des Kunsthistorischen Institutes in Florenz* 27 (1983), 353–59.

BENAKI MUSEUM, Athens. Greek museum featuring art objects from, or related to, Greece in all periods—ancient, Byzantine and modern.

The collection was formed personally by Antony Benaki over a period of ca. thirty-five years and set up in 1931 in the three-storied mansion that had belonged to his parents, on the corner of Leoforos Vasilissis Sofias and Odhos Koumbari. Benaki donated the museum to the Greek nation but continued to organize, maintain and enrich the collection until his death in 1954. Among the classical antiquities, the Greek jewelry is of most importance.

BIBLIOGRAPHY

Musée Benaki, Athènes, Guide (Athens, 1936); *Benaki Museum, A Short Guide,* 2nd ed. (Athens, 1960).

BENEVENTO (BENEVENTUM). Latin colony in Southern Italy founded in 268 B.C. following the Romans' final battle with Pyrrhus, fought nearby in 275.

The site was an ancient Samnite settlement said to have been originally called Malventum (perhaps in Oscan Maloeis or Malieis), which may have been the chief town of the Hirpini. It was always an important road center in south-central Italy, situated on a low ridge above the confluence of the rivers Calore and Sabato. Main roads led west to Rome through Calatia and Capua (Via Appia), east to Brundisium, through Venusia and Tarentum (Via Appia), or later through Aequum Tuticum, Aecae and Canusium (Via Traiana), north to Aesernia through Saepinum and Bovianum Undecimanorum and south to Salernum and Abellinum.

The colony flourished and became a *municipium* inscribed in the tribe Stellatina following the Social War. It received a veteran colony in 42 B.C., after which it was called Colonia Iulia Concordia Augusta Felix Beneventum. In A.D. 571 it became a Lombard duchy and entered the period of its greatest power and prosperity. Within little more than a century and a half, the dukes of Benevento had extended their dominion over most of Southern Italy, from Isernia and Siponto to Cosenza and Brindisi. Benevento's power declined after the middle of the ninth century but was not extinguished until late in the eleventh century.

The most important monument of antiquity is the *Arch of Trajan, also called Porta Aurea, erected at the head of the Via Traiana by order of the Senate of Rome in A.D. 114. Other monuments are a poorly preserved theater; a crypto-porticus that may belong to the forum; the badly destroyed Arco del Sacramento, a single-bay arch stripped to its core of concrete faced in part with brick; parts of at least five bridges, almost all much rehandled in the course of time and all but the least important, the Ponticello on the Via Traiana, heavily damaged in World War II; and some lesser constructions. A number of interesting Roman reliefs, including several funerary busts, are built into the campanile of the ca-thedral (beginning of the thirteenth century). A remarkable number of Egyptian and Egyptianizing monuments, including parts of two obelisks and numerous statues and sculptures of animals in granite and diorite, attest to flourishing cults of the Egyptian gods in Beneventum, especially of Isis Pelagia and of Osiris Canopus and Isis. This is the largest concentration of such material in Italy outside Rome, in part, certainly due to Domitian's building and furnishing of a new temple of Isis here in A.D. 88–89. Unfortunately, no architectural remains of any sanctuary have ever been identified. The archaeological material is dis-played in the Museo del Sannio, arranged in the twelfth-century cloisters of the church of S. Sofia, itself a fascinating building dedicated in 760.

BIBLIOGRAPHY

+A. Meomartini, *I Monumenti e le opere d'arte della città di Benevento* (Benevento, 1889, repr. 1979); M. Schipa, s.v. "Benevento," *EI* 6 (1930); H. W. Mueller, *Il Culto di Iside nell'antica Benevento* (Benevento, 1971); E. T. Salmon, s.v. "Beneventum," *PECS* 149; B. Zevi, *Guida a Benevento* (Bari, 1979).

L. RICHARDSON, JR

BENNDORF, OTTO (1838–1907). German-Austrian excavator, art historian and academic organizer.

Born at Greiz in Vogtland, Benndorf studied at Bonn under F. G. *Welcker, O. *Jahn and F. Ritschl; he habilitated at Göttingen in 1868 under F. Wieseler. He taught briefly at Schulpforte, where the young Friedrich Nietzsche was among his pupils. He became associate professor (*Extraordinarius*) for archae-ology at Zurich in 1869 and progressed rapidly to posts in Munich (1871) and Prague (1872), succeeding A. *Conze in the Vienna chair in 1877. He founded the department of archaeology and epigraphy there and assembled a large col-lection of casts for teaching purposes.

Benndorf excelled in epigraphy and in 1890 founded *Tituli Asiae Minoris,* a collection flourishing today. He early participated in excavations, sharing in the second Austrian expedition to *Samothrace with Conze in 1875. In 1881–82 he excavated at *Trysa (Gjölbaschi) in Lycia and shipped to the *Kunsthistorisches

Museum in Vienna 167 crates of sculpture that may be seen on display there today. In 1895, with Carl *Humann, he undertook the first archaeological expedition to *Ephesos. In 1898 he founded the Austrian Archaeological Institute. Unasked, he supported Jane *Harrison for the Yates Professorship at London in 1888 and 1896.

Among Benndorf's many publications must be noted *Die Metopen von Selinunt* (1873), *Reisen in Lykien und Karien* (1884) and *Das Heroon von Gjölbaschi-Trysa* (1889). He died in Vienna at the age of sixty-eight.

BIBLIOGRAPHY

U. von Wilamowitz-Moellendorff, *Erinnerungen 1848–1914,* 2nd ed. (Leipzig, 1929), 81; H. Kenner, in *Archäologenbildnisse,* 67–68; S. L. Gilman, ed., *Begegnungen mit Nietzsche,* 2nd ed. (Bonn, 1987), 48–50; W. M. Calder III, ed., "The Cambridge Ritualists Reconsidered," *Illinois Classical Studies Supplement* 2 (Atlanta, 1991), 44.

WILLIAM M. CALDER III

BENZO D'ALESSANDRIA (BENCIUS ALEXANDRINUS; second half thirteenth century–post-mid-1329). Italian humanist, scholar and encyclopedist, associated especially with *Verona, where he was head of the chancery of Cangrande della Scala.

The archaeological interests of the chancellor and scholar Benzo d'Alessandria are known to us chiefly through his extensive encyclopedia, only part of which has survived and still less of which is available in print. For our purposes the most relevant portion of the encyclopedia, published as a separate unit by J. R. Berrigan, deals with the cities of Northern Italy. Among those that Benzo treats, it is not surprising that Milan receives the most lengthy as well as the most original handling.

Despite his adherence to the same encyclopedic tradition to which Vincent of Beauvais belonged, Benzo's so-called *Chronicon* repeatedly has caught the attention of modern scholars interested in the origins of the Renaissance. Two important reasons for this attraction are what Roberto Weiss described as Benzo's "scholarly curiosity and his exceptional critical powers, especially in the discussion of historical sources and legends." What seems more debatable, however, is how we should interpret the archaeological details that his encyclopedia includes. The attentive scholar incorporated a wide variety of personal observations in his text, recorded during excursions in the northern half of the peninsula made apparently at various times throughout his life. Among the monuments he records are the *"Regisole" at Pavia and the "Laberinthum" (Amphitheater) at Verona. Given the sheer quantity and variety of these observations, it is difficult to assess the motivation behind Benzo's remarks on classical remains that he includes. One may wonder, in other words, whether his recordings of ancient inscriptions and his ability to distinguish between classical and medieval buildings and artifacts indicate an interest in antiquity for its own sake on Benzo's part or simply an encyclopedist's passion for accurate detail.

What lends weight to the former possibility is the chancellor's keen appetite for classical literature as well. His frequent borrowings from Roman authors are drawn, in some cases, from the most reliable and complete manuscripts (as opposed to anthologies) of the original texts themselves. These include, for example, Catullus, the *Historia Augusta* and Ausonius. Therefore, even though Benzo's achievements as a humanist undoubtedly overshadow whatever contribution to the knowledge of the ancient world he may have made, he deserves attention nonetheless for an understanding of antiquity that was unusual in his day.

BIBLIOGRAPHY

J. K. Hyde, "Medieval Descriptions of Cities," *Bulletin of the John Rylands Library* 48 (1966), 308–40; E. Ragni, "Benzo d'Alessandria," *DBI* 8 (1966), 723–28; J. R. Berrigan, "Benzo d'Alessandria and the Cities of Northern Italy," *Studies in Medieval and Renaissance History* 4 (1967), 125–92; Weiss, *RDCA* 21, 24–26.

ANDREW P. McCORMICK

BÉRARD, JEAN (1908–57). French historian and archaeologist.

Jean Bérard is best known for a major synthesis: *La Colonisation grecque de l'Italie méridionale et de la Sicile dans l'antiquité, L'histoire et la légende* (1941; 2nd ed., 1957). This book propounded the fundamental distinction between two periods in Graeco-Italian relations. The first is the heroic age preserved by legend; the second is represented by the historical colonial movements in the eighth century B.C. and following centuries. Central to Bérard's work was the thesis that the second period owed much to the first, in the important sense that the historical colonists were familiar with the Western exploits of their legendary counterparts. In less prudent hands, this approach could have been disastrous; Bérard's capacity for clear and informed thinking in both the literary and the archaeological dimensions prepared the way for much subsequent exegesis, notably of the growing material evidence from his legendary period—for example, Mycenaean finds in Sicily vis-à-vis Minos and Herakles. Bérard professed ancient history successively at Bordeaux, Nancy and the Sorbonne. The Centre Jean Bérard (attached to the Institut Français in Naples) perpetuates his memory, and its series of Colloques and *Cahiers* bears witness to the continuing French commitment to his field of study.

BIBLIOGRAPHY

M. Pallottino—D. Adamesteanu, review of *La Colonisation . . . ,* 2nd ed., *ArchCl* 10 (1958), 323–32; J. Bérard, *L'Expansion et la colonisation grecques jusqu'aux guerres médiques* (Paris, 1960); E. Manni, "Hommage à la mémoire de Jean Bérard," *Bulletin de l'Association Guillaume Budé* 1 (1977), 79–89.

DAVID RIDGWAY

BERLIN, ANTIKENSAMMLUNG. Important German collection of ancient architecture, sculpture, minor arts and inscriptions now housed in the *Pergamon Museum on the Museum Island and in the Antikenmuseum at Schloss Charlottenburg.

Among the highlights of the collection are the *Great Altar from Pergamon (second century B.C.), the market gate from *Miletos (ca. A.D. 130), an Attic *kore* holding a pomegranate (the "Berlin Goddess," ca. 575 B.C.; purchased 1925), a lifesize marble, enthroned goddess (ca. 480 B.C.; purchased 1916), a Roman marble statue of a girl playing dice (second century; formerly in the collection of Cardinal Melchior de Polignac), a bronze figure of a *Praying Boy* (probably Roman after a Greek original; purchased by King Frederick II of Prussia in 1747) and the name vase of the Berlin Painter (an Attic red-figure amphora; ca. 490 B.C.). Except for the last mentioned, these are all currently housed in the Pergamon Museum.

The art collections of the electors of Brandenburg and the kings of Prussia provided the roots for the Königliche (later Staatliche) Museen, of which the Antikensammlung forms a part. The holdings of the electors of Brandenburg included the collections of Gerrit Reynst (acquired 1671) and Giovanni Pietro *Bellori (acquired 1698). Under Frederick II, the Prussian royal collection expanded its holdings of ancient art through the acquisition of the collections of de Polignac (by purchase, 1742), of the margravine Wilhelmine of Ansbach-Bayreuth (through inheritance, 1758) and of Philipp von *Stosch (by purchase, 1764).

In August 1830, after more than thirty years of planning, a public museum was opened in Berlin to display works from these collections. This building, eventually known as the Altes Museum, was built on plans by Karl Friedrich *Schinkel and included galleries for the display of antiquities and a plaster casting studio. In 1841, the Prussian king purchased the Museum Island, a tract of land behind the Altes Museum bounded on the northeast by the River Spree and on the southwest by a canal. The first building to be erected on this land was the Neues Museum, designed by August Stüler, which opened in 1859 and housed a part of the archaeological collection and plaster casts of antique statuary.

The purchase of the Museum Island and the expansion into the Neues Museum were precipitated by a substantial increase in the holdings of the museums. In the realm of ancient art, several important purchases were made during the first half of the nineteenth century, including three collections of Greek vases (Bartholdy, 1827; Koller, 1828; Dorow-Magnus, 1831). The period immediately following the Franco-Prussian War was marked by important excavations at *Olympia (beginning 1875) and at *Pergamon (directed by Carl *Humann; 1878–86). This was only a beginning, however, and the last decade of the century saw the initiation of Prussian excavations at sites along the west coast of Asia Minor, including *Magnesia (1890–93), *Priene (1895–99) and *Miletos (1898–1914), mostly under the direction of Humann and Theodor *Wiegand. These excavations yielded many important acquisitions for the Antikensammlung.

A new museum designed by Fritz Wolff was erected on the Museum Island in 1902, principally to house the antiquities from Pergamon. This structure, the old Pergamon Museum, had stood for only six years when it was razed to make space for a larger Pergamon Museum designed by Alfred Messel. The central portion of the new Pergamon Museum, which housed large-scale finds from the excavations in Asia Minor, was opened in 1930. At this time, the holdings of the Antikensammlung were displayed in three museum buildings as follows: sculpture, glass (including the collection of Maria vom Rath acquired in 1913), jewelry and gems in the Altes Museum; the *Fayûm mummy portraits (acquired in 1929) and vases in the Neues Museum; architectural reconstructions and inscriptions in the Pergamon Museum.

The World War II history of the Berlin Antikensammlung begins with the removal of all of the small-scale sculpture and minor arts and most of the lifesize sculpture to the vault of the imperial mint in October 1939. The Pergamon Altar was at first protected with wood and sandbags but was later also transferred to the vault at the mint (January–March 1941). Between August 1941 and September 1942, the objects in the vault were moved to two antiaircraft artillery towers in the city. The market gate from Miletos, which remained in the Pergamon Museum, was badly damaged in an air raid in early 1945. It became apparent by that time that Berlin not only would be subject to bombing raids but would be a battlefield. Although many of the artworks stored in the artillery towers were removed from the city to mines in central Germany in March and early April, the most precious ancient sculptures (including the friezes of the Pergamon Altar) remained in the artillery tower in the zoo district. After the city was taken, the Soviets removed all of the artworks remaining in this tower to the Soviet Union.

After the division of Germany, the artworks from the Berlin museums in the American sector were brought to the Landesmuseum Wiesbaden, and those stored in the British sector were transferred to Schloss Celle by the occupation forces. Both included objects from the Antikensammlung. While housed at Schloss Celle, about 200 gold objects (originally from the collection of Friedrich Ludwig Gans and given to the museum in 1912) were stolen sometime in 1946–47 and never recovered.

The artworks stored at the Landesmuseum Wiesbaden and at Schloss Celle were returned to West Berlin in 1957–58. The objects from the Antikensammlung were not displayed until 1960, when the Antikenmuseum opened in a reconstructed guardhouse of Schloss Charlottenburg. Artworks removed from the city by the Soviets in 1945 were returned to East Berlin in 1958–59. In recent times the holdings of the Antikensammlung have been housed in two buildings as follows: most of the small-scale works in the Antikenmuseum; and most of the large-scale sculpture and architecture in the Pergamon Museum. With the reunification of Germany, the Berlin antiquities collections are being reorganized yet again.

BIBLIOGRAPHY

K. Schifner, ed., *Staatliche Museen zu Berlin,* ed. (Leipzig, 1963); I. Kühnel-Kunze, *Bergung–Evakuierung–Rückführung: Die Berliner Museen in den Jahren 1939–1959,* Jahrbuch Preussischer Kulturbesitz, Sonderband 2 (Berlin, 1984); E. Rohde, s.v. ''Berlin,

Staatliche Museen, Antiken-Sammlung,'' *Bildhandbuch der Kunstsammlungen in der DDR,* ed. G. Stelzer—U. Stelzer (Gütersloh, 1985), 91–101.

ELIZABETH C. TEVIOTDALE

BERNARDINI TOMB. Wealthy burial made at *Praeneste in the seventh century B.C., one of the "princely tombs" of the Orientalizing period.

The style and luxury of the objects as well as the presence of actual Oriental imports ally the tomb with the *Barberini Tomb (Praeneste) and with rich Etruscan tombs at *Cerveteri (*Regolini-Galassi Tomb) and elsewhere. A trench tomb (*fossa*) lined and roofed with stone slabs, the Bernardini Tomb contained gold jewelry decorated with granulation, silver and gold tableware and objects of amber, ivory and iron. Three silver-gilt bowls, one with a Phoenician inscription, were imports, probably from Cyprus; also imported were a bronze cauldron and stand (similar to ones in the Barberini Tomb) and a hemispherical bowl of blue glass. Among the bronzes are cast figures of men and animals in a lively local style, the earliest bronze sculpture from Latium and the ancestors of Etruria's Orientalizing bronzes.

The tomb was discovered in 1876 by the brothers Bernardini. Though the precise spot was lost (an attempt to relocate the burial site in 1918 was unsuccessful), an account made by the excavators to *Helbig has been preserved, along with a sketch of the original placement of many of the finds. The grave goods were acquired by the Italian state for 70,000 lire and were placed in the Museo Kircheriano (cf. Athanasius *Kircher). They are today in the *Villa Giulia.

BIBLIOGRAPHY

C. D. Curtis, "The Bernardini Tomb," *MAAR* 3 (1919), 9–90; +I. Strøm, *Problems Concerning the Origin and Early Development of the Etruscan Orientalizing Style* (Odense, 1971), 150–54; +*Civiltà del Lazio primitivo* (Rome, 1976), 221–46; +F. Canciani—F.-W. von Hase, *La Tomba Bernardini di Palestrina* (Rome, 1979).

EMELINE HILL RICHARDSON

BERNINI, GIAN LORENZO (1598–1680). Italian sculptor, architect and painter; the foremost exponent of Baroque art in Italy.

Although the object of Neoclassical ire and despair, Bernini nevertheless represents a genuine strain of classical culture that is more visual and instrumental than literary or learned. A child prodigy, he spent his boyhood learning to carve after ancient statues—the *Laocoon,* *Belvedere *Apollo,* *Belvedere "Antinous"* and *Belvedere *Torso*—and the paintings of *Michelangelo, *Raphael and *Giulio Romano. Thus, later antique sculpture and the example of modern painting became the means by which he disciplined the technical facility and expressiveness inherited from his sculptor father to the new naturalism of the seventeenth century.

Both sources can be traced in the *Goat Amalthea Nursing the Infant Jupiter and a Young Satyr* (Galleria Borghese, Rome), possibly done when he was no more than eleven or twelve years old. Its compact composition and the active but firm figures point to the modern masters, whereas the realistic handling of the surfaces recalls Hellenistic carving and confirms Bernini's later remark that in his youth he turned to antiquity as to an oracle. The lighthearted exuberance of this work is characteristic of his early exercises in the *all'antica* idiom of the time and can also be seen in the impudent Eros sticking out his tongue at the inebriated protagonist of the *Faun Teased by Cupids* (Metropolitan Museum, New York).

Altogether more serious were the statues with classical subjects that Bernini executed between 1618 and 1626. Coinciding with his few known restorations of ancient sculpture (the *Borghese *Hermaphrodite* and *Ludovisi *Ares*), these four lifesize groups were commissioned, with one exception, by Cardinal Scipione *Borghese for his Roman villa, and they were clearly intended to emulate the most famous of the cardinal's antiquities. They are therefore more studied, and their sources are more overt, although increasingly subordinated to an interest in vivid illustration. In the first of the groups, *Aeneas, Anchises and Ascanius* (Galleria Borghese, Rome), Aeneas is based on Michelangelo's *Resurrected Christ,* but he bears Anchises on one shoulder as on Roman coins and wears the lion skin described by Vergil. In the last, the *Apollo and Daphne* (Galleria Borghese, Rome), the idealized god depends on the Belvedere *Apollo,* while the stagelike plinth and one principal view derive from such ancient works as the *Ludovisi *Gaul Killing Himself and His Wife.* But the physical and psychological energy with which Ovid's narrative is brought to its climax looks to the Farnese Ceiling by Annibale *Carracci; the virtuosity of the carving, which transforms Daphne to leaf and twig before our eyes goes far beyond the subtle realism of the *Borghese *Fisherman* that had guided his hand when representing Anchises's aging flesh.

After 1624, Bernini's energies were absorbed ever more exclusively by the Church, and there followed a series of still-brilliant monuments that illuminated seventeenth-century papal Rome. Yet with only a brief interlude in the 1630s, when his work took on a deliberate, neoclassical equilibrium, antiquity continued to play the fructifying role it had earlier. The playful freedom inspired by his first representations of ancient fable, though now more robust and often expounding emblematic messages, lived on in the marine deities of his fountains and in the settings he designed for Egyptian *obelisks. When appropriate, he turned archaeologist in order to dress his *St. Longinus* (Vatican, St. Peter's) in Hellenistic leather armor and to base the features of his *Constantine* (Vatican, St. Peter's) on early descriptions or to assimilate those of *Louis XIV to representations of Alexander the Great. More typically, however, the classical source with which he began was transfigured by a passionate vision and can be recovered only in those rare instances—*Daniel* (Rome, S. Maria del Popolo) or the *Angel with the Superscription* (S. Andrea delle Fratte, Rome)—when preparatory drawings survive. A similar expressive deformation occurs in his architectural designs, which, if superficially classicizing, are used to structure and focus a dramatic figural composition so that painting, sculpture and architecture fuse into a single, emotionally charged whole that implicates the viewer. Thus, in the face of such ecstatically spiritualized works as the Teresa Chapel (S. Maria della Vittoria, Rome) or the *Cathedra Petri* (Vatican, St. Peter's), one can only agree with the Abbé de la Chambre, the artist's friend and eulogist, that Bernini took an entirely different path from that of the ancients, while still recognizing, as did the Abbé, that antiquity furnished the guideposts that Bernini used to chart the custom of his times and the taste of his century.

BIBLIOGRAPHY

R. Wittkower, "The Role of Classical Models in Bernini's and Poussin's Preparatory Work," *Studies in Western Art, Acts of the Twentieth International Congress of the History of Art* (Princeton, NJ, 1963), 41–50; O. Raggio, "A New Bacchic Group by Bernini," *Apollo* 108 (1978), 406–17; I. Lavin, *Bernini and the Unity of the Visual Arts* (New York, 1980); +R. Wittkower, *Gian Lorenzo Bernini. The Sculptor of the Roman Baroque,* 3rd rev. ed. (Oxford, 1981).

GEORGE C. BAUER

BERNWARD OF HILDESHEIM, SAINT (ca. 960–1022). German bishop of Hildesheim, famed for his learning and patronage of the arts.

Bernward was a participant in the imperial chapel and chancellery and in 987 was named one of the tutors of the seven-year-old Holy Roman Emperor Otto III. With the queen mother Theophano, he traveled to Rome in 1001.

By 993, Bernward was established as bishop of Hildesheim, and soon afterward he began to commission the many and varied works of art that have brought him a reputation as a distinguished patron. He sponsored works in many different materials—silver, ivory, stone, bronze—and of many different genres—illuminated books, reliquaries, wall paintings, doors, candlesticks. He revived the art of casting metal in lost wax, a technique used for one of Bernward's most remarkable projects, the column of Hildesheim (ca. 1000–10). The twelve-foot bronze column, cast in a single hollow shaft, was designed to support a crucifix and is decorated with twenty-four scenes of the ministry of Christ, sculpted in a spiral of continuous relief moving from bottom to top. The column is a surprising imitation of the Roman Imperial *Column of Trajan and the *Column of Marcus Aurelius, which Bernward must have seen in Rome. There are striking parallels of imagery (e.g., each sequence of narrative starts with a river god—the Danube on Trajan's Column and the Jordan on Bernward's), but the figure style on the Hildesheim column reveals Ottonian formulas and is not nearly so naturalistic as the style of the Roman reliefs. Yet another index of Bernward's observant attitude toward classical antiquity is given by his practice of having his name stamped on building tiles in the Roman manner.

BIBLIOGRAPHY

F. J. Tschan, *Saint Bernward of Hildesheim,* 1–3, University of Notre Dame Pub. in Medieval Studies (1942–52); W. Berges, "Bernward," *NDB* 2 (1955), 143–44; +R. Wesenberg, *Bernwardinische Plastik: Zur ottonischen Kunst unter Bischof Bernward von*

Hildesheim (Berlin, 1955); W. Oakeshott, *Classical Inspiration in Medieval Art* (London, 1959), 67, passim.

BERRETINI, PIETRO. See PIETRO DA CORTONA.

BEULÉ, CHARLES ERNEST (1826–74). French archaeologist and politician.

Sent around midcentury to the *French School at Athens, Beulé conducted excavations in 1852 at the *Akropolis, in Athens. He discovered and restored the entrance to the Akropolis at the west, near the base of the hill, still known today as the "Beulé Gate." Upon his return to France, he published his results, as well as other studies in the history of Greek art, architecture and topography. Succeeding to the chair of archaeology of the Bibliothèque imperiale, he next undertook excavations at *Carthage (duly published in 1861). In 1860 he became a member of the Académie des inscriptions et belles-lettres and two years later was elected perpetual secretary of the Académie des beaux-arts. His focus became strongly political, and he occupied himself with many, largely minor governmental disputes until his death in 1874.

BIBLIOGRAPHY

Stark, passim; M. Prevost, "Beulé, Charles-Ernest," *DBF* 6 (1954), cols. 362–3.

BIANCHI BANDINELLI, RANUCCIO (1900–75). Italian archaeologist and art historian, specialist in Roman and Etruscan studies.

Descended from the ancient landed aristocracy of the Senese, Bianchi Bandinelli never abandoned the deep-rooted attachment to his origins that inspired early monographs on the Etruscan centers of *Clusium* (1925) and *Suana* (1929). A wide-ranging teacher of classical art history in Italy and abroad, he was converted to militant communism after World War II and occupied numerous influential positions in the academic, administrative and political fields. Meanwhile, from his university chairs (successively in Florence and Rome), Bianchi Bandinelli directed the new generation of Italian archaeologists toward the reinterpretation of ancient artistic phenomena in the light of Marxist social doctrine.

BIBLIOGRAPHY

R. Bianchi Bandinelli, *Storicità dell'arte classica* (Florence, 1943; 2nd ed., 1950); Idem, *Dal diario di un borghese* (Turin, 1948); Idem, *Hellenistic-Byzantine Miniatures of the Iliad* (Olten, 1955); Idem, *Rome: The Centre of Power* and *Rome: The Late Empire* (London, 1970, 1971).

F. R. SERRA RIDGWAY

BIANCHINI, FRANCESCO (1662–1729). Italian polymath, active as a scientist, archaeologist and historian.

Born at Verona, Bianchini was educated at Bologna, then at Padua, where he studied theology, anatomy, botany, mathematics, physics and astronomy. In 1689 he moved to Rome to study languages (Hebrew, Greek and French), history and archaeology. Having taken orders in 1699, he was made canon by Pope Alexander VIII and served as librarian for the pope's nephew, Cardinal Pietro Ottoboni. Clement XI gave him various assignments, including one as "president" of antiquities, with a charge to create a museum with inscriptions and other items relative to the history of the Church. Bianchini compiled a manuscript listing (1706–7) of the inscriptions and works of art that were assembled, which serves as a record of the brief display of the Museo Ecclesiastico (dispersed in 1716).

In his capacity as "president," Bianchini oversaw excavations on the *Palatine Hill conducted by the *Farnese family and the discovery of the columbarium of the slaves and freedmen of Livia (*Columbaria) on the *Via Appia. He published the latter in his *Camere ed iscrizioni sepulchrali de' liberti, servi ed ufficiali della casa di Augusto scoperte nella via Appia* (1727, repr. 1991).

As a scientist, Bianchini is noted for having spent eight years traversing Tuscany, Romagna and Lombardy, attempting to establish a meridian line from one side of Italy to the other. As a historian, he is known for having written a universal history supported by information from monuments and the arts, *Istoria universale provata con monumenti e figurata con simboli degli antichi* (Rome, 1697).

BIBLIOGRAPHY

Stark, 32, 109, 117, 180, 191; S. Rotta, "Bianchini, Francesco," *DBI* 10 (1968), 187–94.

BIEBER, MARGARETE (1879–1978). German-born archaeologist and classicist.

Margarete Bieber is best known for important books on the ancient theater (*The History of the Greek and Roman Theater,* 1939; revised 1961), ancient Greek dress (*Griechische Kleidung,* 1928; *Entwicklungsgeschichte der griechischen Tracht,* 1934; revised 1967) and Hellenistic sculpture (*The Sculpture of the Hellenistic Age,* 1955; revised 1961). She belonged to the "heroic" generation of archaeologists who brought the German scholarly tradition to American universities when they fled *Hitler's racial laws in the 1930s. A child of the nineteenth century, she published her doctoral dissertation for the University of Bonn in 1907; her last book, *Ancient Copies,* appeared in 1977.

She was the first woman to receive the prestigious travel fellowship of the *German Archaeological Institute (1909; one of her colleagues was G. *Rodenwaldt). After teaching in Berlin, 1916–18 (Erwin Panofsky was a student), she became, at Giessen, the second woman professor in Germany. Forced to leave in 1933, she was called to teach at Barnard, in Columbia University's Department of Fine Arts, with William *Dinsmoor and Meyer Schapiro. She became an American citizen in 1939. After her retirement in 1948, she went on to teach at Princeton University and the New School for Social Research, as well as Columbia's Barnard College and newly founded School of General Studies.

Bieber's practical, interdisciplinary approach was congenial to the pragmatic

American tradition; in her teaching and in her writing she often made intelligible the more abstract ideas of German scholars, such as *Kaschnitz von Weinberg. Her books reflect her concern with teaching (*German Readings in the History and Theory of Fine Arts,* 1946; often revised and reprinted) and with the wider cultural aspects of ancient art and archaeology (*Laocoon: The Influence of the Group Since Its Rediscovery,* 1942). In *Ancient Copies* (1977), she tackled the problem of the relationship of the Roman copyists to the Greek statues that served as their models—a remarkably modern approach, but one reflecting her lifelong interest in the actual work of art, from her catalog of the sculpture of the Kassel Museum (1915) to the various "excavations in American museums" she carried on in America. In 1974, when she was ninety-five years old, the *Archaeological Institute of America awarded her its Gold Medal for Distinguished Archaeological Achievement.

BIBLIOGRAPHY

L. Bonfante (Warren)—R. Winkes, *Bibliography of the Works of M. Bieber, For her 90th Birthday* (New York, 1969); +L. Bonfante, "Margarete Bieber (1879–1978): An Archaeologist in Two Worlds," in *Women as Interpreters of the Visual Arts,* ed. C. Sherman (Westport, CT, 1981), 239–74.

LARISSA BONFANTE

BIONDO, FLAVIO (BLONDUS FLAVIUS FORLIVIENSIS; 1392–1463). Italian papal notary and apostolic secretary, philologist, historian and antiquarian.

Born in Romagna (Forlì), Biondo was tutored by Giovanni Ballestreri and studied grammar, literature and rhetoric. Early in his life he was offered employment by ruling families such as the Sforza. Caused to emigrate from his native city, he came back in 1427, when Romagna was returned to papal administration, and young Biondo was employed by the governor-legate Domenico Capranica. Later he served the Barbaro family of Bergamo and Giovanni Vitelleschi in Ancona, but he transferred in 1433 to the papal Curia, having been appointed notary of the chamber and later, apostolic secretary by Eugenius IV (Condulmer, 1431–47). Biondo served the pope as diplomatic emissary and was involved in the complicated proceedings aiming at the unification of the Latin and Greek churches. Under Nicholas V, grave calumnies were raised against Biondo, causing him to abandon his office and to wander within the Italian states; this migratory period happened to open his eyes to geography's working in concert with history. In his fifties, Biondo emerged as a first-rate humanist and famous historian who dedicated his works to popes and rulers.

Biondo already had caught the attention of the learned establishment with his first writings, in spite of the authority enjoyed by his slightly elder colleague *Poggio Bracciolini. In 1453 Biondo composed the treatise *De verbis romanae locutionis* in defense of the opinion that the "volgare" (modern Italian used by Dante and still developing) derived directly from the Latin. He served the Roman Curia until 1447 and during that time turned to the writing of history, beginning the huge *Historiarum ab inclinatione Romani Imperii, Decades III*, covering medieval Italian and European history in a broad objective manner, founded on sources laboriously collected.

After digressions into ancient history, Biondo turned back to his previous theme to add new "decades" to the original *Decades III*. The work was completed in 1453. At the same time, under the impact of the imposing remains of Imperial Rome, he composed the *Roma instaurata* in three books (1444–46), a topographic description of the city in the late Imperial era. Biondo consulted with all possible sources: ancient authors (including Frontinus and Anastasius), epigraphy and identified ruins, as well as the Constantinian catalogs of regions at hand. Addressing the popes and the scholarly establishment, he suggested restorations and the freeing of monuments that had been built into later structures.

Biondo's migratory years resulted in the *Italia illustrata* (1453), a contemporary geographic description of the political partitions of the peninsula, including historic geography, starting from antiquity. It was based on classical authors, medieval chronicles, local information and personal observations of communities and architecture. This work was kept current by successive corrections and amendments.

In 1457–59 Biondo turned again to ancient history and produced the *Roma triumphans,* a description of Roman public and private institutions and of social and religious life in the Roman Empire. This work, in ten books, he dedicated to Pope *Pius II (Enea Silvio Piccolomini).

Biondo was a talented and industrious historian with a remarkable eye for sources, able to arouse curiosity among scholars and a pioneer in the field of Roman archaeology and topography.

BIBLIOGRAPHY

F. Biondo, *De Roma instaurata Libri tres* (Venice, 1510); A. Masius, *Flavio Biondo, sein Leben und seine Werke* (Leipzig, 1879); P. Buchholz, *Die Quellen der Historiarum Decades von Flavius Blondus* (Leipzig, 1881); B. Nogara, *Scritti inediti e rari di Flavio Biondo* (Rome, 1927); R. Weiss, "Biondo Flavio archeologo," *Studi Romagnoli* 14 (1963), 335–41; M. Fubini, "Biondo, Flavio," *DBI* 10 (1968), 536–59.

CHRISTOFFER H. ERICSSON

BJÖRNSTÅHL, JACOB JONAS (1731–79). Swedish scholar and traveler, professor of Oriental languages and Greek at Uppsala and Lund universities, 1776–79.

After having studied Hebrew, Greek and other languages at Uppsala and won a reputation as a thoroughly learned scholar, Björnståhl set out on a journey to the Continent as the teacher of two young noblemen (1767) and spent years in France, Italy and other countries. In 1776 he was appointed professor and ordered by King *Gustavus III to make a scholarly exploration journey to the Near East. The years 1776–79 he spent in Turkey, Smyrna, Constantinople and Greece (especially Thessaly), where he copied ancient inscriptions, studied manuscripts and wrote extensive diaries and letters (posthumously published). He died in Salonica without having returned to Sweden. His collection of rare books and manuscripts he willed to Uppsala University library.

BIBLIOGRAPHY

+K. V. Zettersteen, "Björnståhl, J. J.," *Svenskt biografiskt lexikon* 4 (1924), 722–26.

ROBIN HÄGG

BLACAS D'AULPS, DUC DE. Title of father (LOUIS CHARLES PIERRE CASIMIR; d. 1839) and son (PIERRE LOUIS JEAN CASIMIR; d. 1866) of French nobility known for their collection of antiquities.

The elder Duc de Blacas, serving as French ambassador in Rome, was one of the founding members, in 1828, of the *Instituto di Corrispondenza Archeologica and honorary president of the new organization. Known as a distinguished connoisseur, he gathered a collection of antiquities (many from the *Strozzi family) that included coins, gems and Greek vases. The younger Duc de Blacas inherited from his father the collection and an abiding interest in archaeology. He published an essay on coins of Vespasian and a study on excavations of funerary vases near Albano and began the translation, later completed by J. de Witte, of *Mommsen's history of Roman coinage. Upon his death his collection was purchased by the *British Museum for the equivalent of 1,200,000 francs. Included was the Roman glyptic masterpiece, the Blacas Cameo, an exquisitely carved portrait of Augustus (diadem restored in medieval times).

BIBLIOGRAPHY

Stark, 265, 286, 301; A. Furtwängler, *Die Antiken Gemmen* (Berlin, 1900), III, 316; Roman d'Amat, "Blacas d'Aulps," *DBF* 6 (1954), col. 548.

BLEGEN, CARL WILLIAM (1887–1971). American archaeologist, best known for his excavation and publication of Bronze Age sites, especially at *Troy and *Pylos.

Blegen held degrees from Augsburg Seminary (in Minneapolis, where he was born), the University of Minnesota and Yale; he studied also at Oxford and Cambridge, Hebrew Union College, Jewish Institute of Religion, the University of Athens and the *American School of Classical Studies in Athens, to which he was attached from 1910 until 1927, first as student, later as secretary, assistant director, and finally, acting director, returning in 1948–49 as director. He served as professor of classical archaeology at the University of Cincinnati, 1927–57, and had considerable influence as a teacher. He excavated and published several important sites in the 1920s and 1930s: *Korakou, A Prehistoric Settlement near Corinth* (1921); *Zygouries, A Prehistoric Settlement in the Valley of Cleonae* (1928); *Acrocorinth,* with R. *Stillwell, O. *Broneer and A. Bellinger (1930); *Prosymna, The Helladic Settlement Preceding the Argive Heraeum,* with his wife, Elizabeth Blegen (1937). But his greatest publications came later: the four-volume publication of *Troy,* with J. L. *Caskey, M. Rawson, J. Sperling and C. Boulter (1950–58), followed by *Troy and the Trojans* (1963); and the three-volume *Palace of Nestor at Pylos in Western Messenia,* with M. Rawson, M. L. Lang, W. Taylour and W. P. Donovan (1966–73; completed before Blegen's death, except for printing), preceded by *A Guide to the Palace of Nestor,* with M. Rawson (1962). He collaborated with A.J.B. *Wace in developing a systematic chronology for mainland Greece in the Bronze Age. In 1965 Blegen became the first recipient of the Gold Medal for Distinguished Archaeological Achievement, awarded annually thereafter by the *Archaeological Institute of America.

BIBLIOGRAPHY
AJA 70 (1966), 182; *New York Times,* 26 August 1971; *Who's Who in America* 37 (1972–73), 285.

W. W. DE GRUMMOND

BLOND BOY. Greek Archaic sculpture of a youth, head made of Parian marble, 0.245m high, excavated by *Kavvadias northeast of the *Akropolis Museum, Athens.

The head was found in good condition, and though it is uncertain whether the stratum in which it was found in pre-Persian, it is usually dated to ca. 480 B.C. When it was discovered in 1887, the hair still exhibited the bright yellow ocher color from which the work derives its name. Fragments of the torso had been excavated earlier (1896) near the north wall of the *Akropolis. *Furtwängler suggested Hegias as the sculptor, based on comparisons with the *Apollo* of Mantua, and Dickins and others have compared it stylistically with the Euthydikos Kore. Its conformity to abstract theories of proportion was recognized by *Carpenter. According to E. B. Harrison, the youth may be identified as *Theseus* or *Apollo.*

BIBLIOGRAPHY
G. Dickins, *Catalogue of the Acropolis Museum* (Cambridge, 1912), 248–250; +H. Payne—G. Young, *Archaic Marble Sculpture from the Acropolis* (New York, 1950), pl. 113–115; R. Carpenter, *Greek Sculpture* (Chicago, 1960), 90–96; +G.M.A. Richter, *Kouroi, Archaic Greek Youths* (London, 1960), 149; E. B. Harrison, in *Early Greek Cult Practices* (Stockholm, 1988), 247–54.

SHARON WICHMANN

BLOUET, GUILLAUME ABEL (1795–1853). French architect and antiquarian; a leader of the scientific expedition to the Morea (1828).

Blouet was born in Paris. He studied architecture and was admitted to the École d'architecture in 1814. In 1821 he won the Prix de Rome and left Paris for a five-year stay in the eternal city. The *Baths of Caracalla were of special importance in his research in Rome; he made test excavations there and published a full account of his restoration of the building in a work issued with state funds, *Restauration des thermes d'Antonin Caracalla à Rome* (Paris, 1828–30).

Returning to Paris (1826), he was soon designated by the Institut de France as the director for architecture and sculpture of the *Expédition scientifique de

Morée. He excavated at the *Temple of Zeus at *Olympia, finding some of the metopes of the labors of Herakles; he published the results of these and other investigations in *Expédition scientifique de Morée,* 3 volumes (Paris, 1831–38).

Back in Paris again, he undertook a number of architectural projects for the state, such as the completion of the Arc de Triomphe de l'Étoile (1836) and restoration at the chateau of Fontainebleau (1848 and following). Professor of the theory of architecture at the Académie des beaux-arts (from 1846), member of the Institut de France (1850) and president of the Societé centrale des architects (1844), after a long and distinguished career Blouet died in 1853. He endowed the École des beaux-artes with an annuity of 1,000 francs to be used for the student who held the Grande médaille d'emulation (an honor he himself won in 1825).

BIBLIOGRAPHY

Académie des beaux-arts, Funeraille de M. Blouet, discours de M. Raoul-Rochette, de M. A.-L. Dumont, de M. Caristie (Paris, 1853); "Blouet, Guillaume-Abel," *NBG* 6 (1855), col. 263; M.-L. Blumer, "Blouet, Guillaume-Abel," *DBF* 6 (1954), cols. 721–22.

BLÜMNER, HUGO (1844–1919). German-Swiss archaeologist and philologist.

Born in Berlin, a policeman's son, Blümner studied archaeology at Bonn under Otto *Jahn, of whose *"monumental philology" he became one of the most successful practitioners. After several years' teaching at Breslau and Königsberg, in 1887 he succeeded Karl Dilthey as professor of classics at Zurich. He wrote books on the domestic antiquities of the Greeks and the Romans (1881, 1911), but his most influential publications are two. First is his *Technologie und Terminologie der Gewerbe und Künste bei Griechen und Römern* (4 vols., 1874–87; repr. 1969). In this masterpiece of organization and accurate erudition, he employs all available literary and archaeological evidence to elucidate his theme, often providing, along the way, the definitive commentary on a vase or a passage. His three-volume critical text and commentary of Pausanias (1896–1910), done with Hermann Hitzig, is far more competent linguistically than *Frazer's although weaker in topography and religion. In 1891 he wrote a book on the metaphorical language of Bismarck.

BIBLIOGRAPHY

O. Waser, *Biographisches Jahrbuch für die Altertumswissenschaft* 41 (1914), 1–44; "Blümner, Hugo," *NDB* 2 (1955), 320; H. P. Isler, in *Archäologenbildnisse,* 86–87.

WILLIAM M. CALDER III

BLUNDELL, HENRY (1724–1810). English landowner and art collector, of Ince Blundell Hall, Lancashire.

A Roman Catholic, educated by the Jesuits in France, Blundell showed no interest in collecting antiquities in his early life; it was only in 1776, when he was fifty-two, that he made his first visit to Rome (with further visits in 1782–

83, 1786 and 1790). Under the influence of Charles *Townley, he began buying classical sculptures, acquiring the core of his collection from old Roman collections such as those of the d'*Este and *Mattei in the 1770s and 1780s, at first using Thomas *Jenkins as an agent, but later preferring the former Jesuit John Thorpe. From ca. 1800, he purchased rather from sales of other British collections.

Blundell acquired a large number of pieces (599 by 1810), including statues, busts, cinerary urns and reliefs. The collection included both restored antiquities and modern copies, restored/made by the major sculptors and restorers of the day, such as *Albacini, *Cavaceppi, *Piranesi and *Canova. Few pieces are of major importance, but the collection is typical of the market and English taste in the last quarter of the eighteenth century. Blundell was not a scholar or connoisseur, but his collection was one of the largest of its kind in private hands. He published an *Account* of his collection in 1803 and the two-volume *Engravings* in 1809–10. At first the sculpture was embedded in the walls of the stairs and corridors of his house, but when the collection grew, Blundell built the "Garden Temple" (1792) and the "Pantheon" (1801–10) for its display. After his death, the collection remained relatively intact and was recorded by *Michaelis (1882) and by B. Ashmole in a selected catalog of 1929; it passed to the city of Liverpool in 1959 and is no longer housed at Ince Blundell Hall. A full catalog in several volumes is currently being compiled.

BIBLIOGRAPHY

A. Michaelis, *Ancient Marbles in Great Britain* (Cambridge, 1882), 333–415; G. Vaughan, "Henry Blundell's Sculpture Collection at Ince Hall," in *Patronage and Practice: Sculpture on Merseyside,* ed. P. Curtis (Liverpool, 1989), 13–21; E. Southworth, "The Ince Blundell Collection: Collecting Behaviour in the Eighteenth Century," in *Plaster and Marble, The Classical and Neo-Classical Portrait Bust (The Edinburgh Albacini Colloquium), Journal of the History of Collections* 3.2 (1991), 219–34; J. Fejfer—E. Southworth, *The Ince Blundell Collection of Classical Sculpture, 1, The Portraits,* pt. 1 (London, 1991), introd.

GLENYS DAVIES

BOCCACCIO, GIOVANNI (1313–75). Major Italian poet and humanist scholar; early enthusiast of ancient geography and epigraphy.

The son of a Tuscan merchant, Boccaccio passed his childhood in Florence and at the age of about fifteen was sent to Naples to learn business. It is related that he underwent a fundamental change in his life and interests at the time of a visit to the burial place believed to be the *Tomb of Vergil and henceforth devoted himself to literature and humanist pursuits.

Various passages in Boccaccio's writings, especially in his treatises in Latin, reveal his interest in, and knowledge of, ancient monuments. In his *De montibus, silvis, fontibus, lacubus, fluminibus, stagnis seu paludibus,* a geographical dictionary of mountains, forests, springs, lakes, rivers and ponds, he included references to ancient ruins associated with such features. He notes the ruins of

*Fiesole and the remains of an Etruscan colony at *Adria, and he describes Mount Vesuvius and the eruption that covered the city of *Pompeii (which he dated wrongly, however, to the reign of Nero). Boccaccio's references to the city of Rome are scant, but it is not surprising that he should show little knowledge of the city, for at the time he lived, Rome had been abandoned by the papacy and had shrunk pitifully. In the *Decameron* (5.3), he observed that Rome "is now the tail, as it was once the head, of the world."

Boccaccio studied ancient coins and noted their historical usefulness in his discussion of the empress Faustina in the *De claris mulieribus* (ch. 96). He was interested in inscriptions, both Latin and Greek, and copied these into his notebooks, such as the well-known "zibaldone" in the Laurentian Library, Florence. He carefully copied the Greek lettering of an inscription he came across at San Felici ad Ema, outside Florence, creating the earliest known copy of a Greek inscription by a Western scholar. He supported Leonzio Pilato, a teacher of Greek whom *Petrarch and Boccaccio prevailed upon to make the first Latin translation of the poems of Homer for a humanist readership.

BIBLIOGRAPHY

C. C. Coulter, "Boccaccio's Archaeological Knowledge," *AJA* 41 (1937), 397–405; Weiss, 43–47.

BÖCKH (BOECKH), AUGUST (1785–1867). German Hellenist and epigraphist.

Born at Karlsruhe into a family of distinguished civil servants and clergymen, Böckh studied at Halle (1803–6) under F. A. *Wolf and F. D. E. Schleiermacher. In 1807 he became associate professor (*Extraordinarius*) at Heidelberg and in 1811 was appointed to the newly founded university at Berlin, where he taught for fifty-six years. He developed the "historical-antiquarian" approach to antiquity, stressing objects rather than the narrow "word philology" of his great adversary, Gottfried Hermann. He embraced the *Totalitätsideal* and progressed from Plato and Pindar to fundamental works on ancient science, music, chronology, weights and measures and his masterpiece, *Die Stattshaushaltung der Athener* (ed. M. Fränkel, 2 vols. [Berlin, 1886]), which influenced Karl Marx and Wilhelm Dilthey.

In 1815, acting on a suggestion of Niebuhr, Böckh convinced the Berlin Academy and the Prussian government to support a corpus of all Greek and Latin inscriptions. After initial difficulty, *Corpus Inscriptionum Graecarum* (*CIG*) was completed in four volumes (1828–59), with Roehl's index appearing in 1877. It included 9,926 inscriptions in over 3,000 folio pages arranged geographically. Böckh founded modern Greek epigraphy and in part, therefore, was a decisive figure in the transition from romanticism to historicism. On the one-hundredth anniversary of his birth, Ernst *Curtius called him "the King of Scholarship."

BIBLIOGRAPHY

M. Hoffmann, *August Boeckh* (Leipzig, 1901); A. Boeckh, *On Interpretation and Crit-*

icism, tr. and ed. J. P. Pritchard (Norman, OK, 1968); B. Schneider, "August Boeckh: Altertumsforscher, Universitätslehrer und Wissenschaftsorganisator im Berlin des 19 Jahrhunderts," *Staatsbibliothek Preussischer Kulturbesitz Ausstellungskataloge* 26 (Berlin, 1985); A. Horstmann, *Antike Theoria und moderna Wissenschaft: August Boeckh's Konzeption der Philologie* (Frankfurt, 1992).

WILLIAM M. CALDER III

BODE, ARNOLD WILHELM VON (1845–1929). German art historian and museum director.

First a lawyer, Bode later studied art history at Berlin, Vienna and Leipzig. In 1872 he became assistant for sculpture and painting in the *Berlin museums; in 1883 he became director of the sculpture department, in 1890 of the painting gallery. In 1905 Bode succeeded Richard Schöne as general director. His publications emphasize Renaissance and Rembrandt, but his interests were far wider. He was a successful fund-raiser, a friend of the imperial family, an indefatigable traveler and buyer. He recognized only J. P. Morgan as a rival. Against great odds he secured the construction of the Kaiser Friedrich Museum, the Pergamon Museum and the Dahlem Museum. His powerful personality earned him the title of the "Museum's Bismarck." The Bode Museum bears his name.

BIBLIOGRAPHY

W. von Bode, *Mein Leben,* 1–2 (1930).; L. Justi, "Bode, Arnold Wilhelm v.," *NDB* (1953), 347–48; U. Kultermann, *Geschichte der Kunstgeschichte: Der Weg einer Wissenschaft* (Frankfurt, 1981), 247–50.

WILLIAM M. CALDER III

BOETHIUS, AXEL (1889–1969). Swedish archaeologist, authority on Roman topography and architecture.

Boethius was educated at Uppsala, Berlin and the *British School in Athens; in his youth he assisted in excavations at *Mycenae. In 1925, he was chosen by then crown prince *Gustavus Adolphus (VI) as the first director of the *Swedish Institute in Rome, a post from which he influenced two generations of Swedish archaeologists in Italy. He was professor of classical archaeology at Göteborg University (1934–55) and its rector (1946–51), retiring afterward to Italy for the rest of his life.

Boethius's distinguished reputation as a scholar and teacher is based especially on the breadth of knowledge and the infectious enthusiasm he communicated to those who studied with him or consulted him personally. His longer publications are relatively few but of recognized significance: *The Golden House of Nero; Some Aspects of Roman Architecture,* the published version of his Jerome Lectures, delivered in Rome, 1960; and his segment of the Pelican book on *Etruscan and Roman Architecture,* coauthored with J. B. *Ward-Perkins; his portion later appeared as *Etruscan and Early Roman Architecture* (1978, revised by R. Ling and T. Rasmussen).

BIBLIOGRAPHY
"Prof. Axel Boethius," *London Times,* 10 May 1969, 10; J. B. Ward-Perkins, in *Etruscan and Roman Architecture* (Harmondsworth, 1970), xxv.

SHELLIE WILLIAMS

BOISSARD, JEAN JACQUES (1528–1602). French antiquarian, draftsman and poet.

Boissard was born in Besançon. After study at the University of Louvain, he proceeded to Germany and then to Italy (1556), where he entered the service of Cardinal Carlo Caraffa in Rome. To the years when he was in Rome belongs the gracious anecdote of how Boissard secured an invitation with friends to see the sculpture garden of Cardinal da *Carpi on the Quirinal Hill and remained hiding in the bushes while the others left. Then he began feverishly to copy all the antiquities and inscriptions that were visible. Interrupted by nightfall, he began again the next morning, only to be discovered at work by Cardinal da Carpi. Moved by Boissard's devotion to antiquity, the cardinal invited him to breakfast and told him to copy whatever he wished.

Boissard's claims of wide travel in Greece, Jerusalem and Syria during this period have been doubted. Leaving Rome and making his living as a tutor, he was able to travel, collect and draw in France, Germany and Italy. In Padua in 1576 he purchased 200 portraits from Lentulus Ventidius. He amassed a fine collection of antiquities but had to abandon it at his sister's house in Montbeliard when he took flight for religious reasons to Metz, where he then died. The collection was pillaged by the Lorraines.

Boissard's works, besides his Latin epigrams and epistles, include studies in the "illustrious lives" tradition, illustrated with portraits (*Icones et vitae virorum illustrium,* Frankfurt, 1592–99, with illustrations by Theodore de Bry), as well as a collection of illustrations of Roman sites, ruins and inscriptions, entitled *Romanae urbis topographia et antiquitates,* 6 vols. (Frankfurt, 1597–1602). A sketchbook survives in the Royal Library in Stockholm (Cod. Holmiensis, S. 68, 1559). Boissard has been criticized for his methods of "restoring" ancient monuments in his drawings, by adding pieces from unrelated monuments or evidence from literary sources. He was especially prone to follow this procedure with illustrations for publication; but he has also left numerous sketches that record quite faithfully the condition of monuments.

BIBLIOGRAPHY
"Boissard, Jean-Jacques," *NBG* 6 (1855), cols. 449–50; R. d'Amat, "Boissard, Jean-Jacques," *DBF* 16 (1954), cols. 833–34; Mandowsky—Mitchell, 27–8; Bober—Rubinstein, 453.

BOLOGNA (FELSINA; BONONIA). City in Northern Italy important for its Villanovan, Etruscan and Roman settlements.

Extensive remains of the *Villanovan culture, including huts and cemeteries dating from the Iron Age (ninth–seventh centuries B.C.), have been discovered in Bologna. Habitation was continuous until the fourth century B.C., during a period when the city was the Etruscan capital of the area, known as Felsina (Pliny, *NH* 3.5). In 189 B.C., the Latin colony of Bononia was founded, connected to Rimini by the Vie Aemilia Lepidi and to Arezzo by the Via Flaminia. Antony and Octavian recolonized it, and Bononia was recorded afterward among the major cities of Italy during the Imperial age. The orthogonal urban plan created under Augustus is still discernible in the city today, with the Via Aemilia connecting to the *cardo maximus,* the present-day Vie Rizzoli and Ugo Bassi.

Records of the rediscovery of ancient remains begin in 1513, when a marble cuirassed torso, perhaps of Nero, was discovered in Piazza dei Celestini. The sculpture is in the present-day Museo Civico Archeologico, along with the rich Bolognese patrimony of objects that have been excavated or collected through the centuries. The inception of museography in Bologna may be traced to the scientist Ulisse *Aldrovandi, who bequeathed his collection of things from nature (*naturalia*) and objects made by man (*artificialia*) to his native city at his death in 1605. Aldrovandi's systematic assemblage of botanical, zoological and geological material, along with ethnographic and archaeological material, set a scientific tone for the Bolognese museological and archaeological tradition.

The next important addition was the collection of antiquities gathered by the Marchese Ferdinando Cospi (1606–86), who had been raised at the *Medici court in Florence and had assembled his own museum of *naturalia* and antique objects, especially those from daily life rather than the sphere of monumental art. The famous *Patera Cospiana,* actually an Etruscan mirror found in a burial at *Arezzo, was acquired by Cospi in 1644. The next important group of antiquities came from the scientific collections of Count Luigi Ferdinando Marsili (1658–1730); the finest piece, however, the *Faun with the Stain* (on its face), did not remain in Bologna but went to the *Albani collection (Rome), then to the Musée *Napoléon (Paris) and finally to the *Glyptothek (Munich). In the nineteenth century were added the collections of the artist Pelagio Palagi (1775–1860), encompassing thousands of objects, especially Egyptian and classical, amassed over a forty-year period. The best-known piece is the head sometimes believed to represent the *Athena* Lemnia.

The nineteenth century was also the period of the pioneering excavations of *Gozzadini near Villanova and at *Marzabotto and of *Zannoni at the Certosa cemetery, resulting in a dramatic increase in knowledge of prehistoric Italy. In 1870 came the impetus to unite objects from these excavations with material from the earlier collections, at the time divided between the University of Bologna and the Comune, when Bologna was selected as the venue for the Fifth International Congress of Anthropology and Prehistoric Archaeology. The combining of the collections began in 1871, with the Museo Civico finding its permanent home in the Palazzo Galvani in 1881. The spirited interest in Italian prehistory during this period may be gauged by the enthusiastic reception given to the "Carnival of the Etruscans" in 1874, which included a spectacular parade of hundreds of citizens costumed as Etruscan musicians, soldiers, nobles, lictors, royalty and gods; costumes, weapons, musical instruments and other accoutrements were based on careful archaeological research.

In 1878 Edoardo *Brizio became the director of the antiquities section of the museum, and he brought to the collections a rigorous organization that may still be seen today and wrote the first guide to these objects. Other leading figures who have supervised the antiquities since Brizio include G. Gherardini, P. *Ducati, L. Laurenzi, Mario Zuffa and Rosanna Pincelli. The excavations and numerous publications of G. Mansuelli have played an important role in modern scholarship. Most recently, Cristiana Morigi Govi, as director of the Museo Civico Archeologico, has issued a new guide to the antiquities, exactly one-hundred years after Brizio, and has published rich documentation on the work of her predecessors, so that the inspiring history of archaeology at Bologna is more accessible than that of most other Italian cities.

BIBLIOGRAPHY

G. Mansuelli, s.v. "Bononia," *PECS* 158; +C. Morigi Govi—D. Vitali, eds., *Il Museo Civico Archeologico di Bologna* (Bologna, 1982), 9–23; +C. Morigi Govi—G. Sassatelli, eds., *Dalla Stanza delle Antichità al Museo Civico* (Bologna, 1984); G. Bermond Montanari, ed. *La Formazione della città in Emilia Romagna* (Bologna 1987).

BOLOGNA, GIOVANNI. See GIAMBOLOGNA.

BOLSENA (VOLSINII NOVI). Site of an Etruscan-Roman city in Italy, located on the northeast shore of the Lake of Bolsena, along the ancient Via Cassia; probably the ancient city called Volsinii Novi (new Volsinii) by the Romans.

Historians report that the Etruscan city of old Volsinii (Veteres) was sacked in 265–264 B.C. and the inhabitants resettled at Volsinii Novi. Excavations at Bolsena, begun by the *French School at Rome under R. Bloch in 1946, provide considerable evidence for settlement after 264 B.C. For some time, the French excavators argued that this was the original site of Volsinii, but most scholars now believe that this is new Volsinii and that the old city was at *Orvieto.

In 1905 at the locality of Pozzarello a small sanctuary was discovered, with altar, well and votive offerings, leading to the claim that this was the famous sanctuary of Nortia, Etruscan goddess of fate, said to have been located at old Volsinii. But in 1961 a squared cippus was found there, with an inscription to the god Selvans, suggesting another cult deity. Another sanctuary, sometimes described as a temple (third century B.C.) was found at Poggio Casetta.

The French investigations uncovered a series of terraces where habitation was present. The locality of Poggio Mercatello yielded the most abundant remains of the Roman period, including a forum, baths, theater and amphitheater.

BIBLIOGRAPHY

E. Gabrici, "Scavi nel sacellum della Dea Nortia sul Pozzarello," *MonAnt* 16 (1906), cols. 170–239; R. Bloch, *Recherches archéologiques en territoire Volsinien de la pro-

tohistoire a civilisation étrusque (Paris, 1972); +*Fouilles de l'École française de Rome á Bolsena (Poggio Moscini)* (Paris, 1968–85); Steingräber, 286–92.

BOMARZO (POLIMARTIUM). Italian town, site of Etruscan and Roman habitation in antiquity.

The place is famous, above all, for its Renaissance pleasure gardens, the "Parco dei Mostri," created for the eccentric antiquarian and humanist prince Vicino Orsini in the third quarter of the sixteenth century. In the garden are bizarre sculptures, buildings and inscriptions that imitate antique and exotic monuments, some derived from the *Hypnerotomachia Poliphili* of F. *Colonna. There is abundant evidence of Etruscan influence, including a stone imitation of an Etruscan tomb intentionally carved in ruins.

An Etruscan painted tomb belonging to Vel Urinates, known by the sixteenth century but now destroyed, was recorded in drawings by Vincenzo Campanari (*Campanari family; now in the British Museum, unfortunately damaged during World War II). The area of Bomarzo and *Viterbo was visited in the seventeenth century by Athanasius *Kircher, who reported entering the "grottoes" of cave-dwelling "Troglodytes," in reality, Etruscan tombs carved with furniture for the use of the deceased in the afterlife.

In the nineteenth century the *Borghese family excavated—or rather, plundered—numerous Etruscan tombs in the area of Bomarzo. The rich contents were sold off and now repose in many European museums—in Berlin, Munich, Paris, London and the Vatican. The bronzes, especially a series of fine mirrors, have a measure of fame. Locally, an Etruscan collection was formed by the canon Luigi Vittori, author of *Memorie archeologico-storiche sulla città di Polimarzio, oggi Bomarzo* (1846). *Dennis also visited Bomarzo in the nineteenth century and left a detailed description of the Grotta Dipinta, that is, the painted tomb of the Urinates family.

BIBLIOGRAPHY

S. Settis, "Contributo a Bomarzo," *Bollettino d'Arte* 51 (1966), 17–26; J. P. Oleson, "A Reproduction of an Etruscan Tomb in the Parco dei Mostri at Bomarzo," *ArtB* 57 (1975), 410–17; M. P. Baglione, *Ricognizioni archeologiche in Etruria* 2, *Il Territorio di Bomarzo* (Rome, 1976); Steingräber, 300–1.

BONI, GIACOMO (1859–1925). Italian archaeologist.

Boni conducted numerous excavations in Rome, especially in the *Forum Romanum, where he discovered the *Lapis Niger and the Archaic cemetery. He was the first classical archaeologist in Italy to attach importance to *stratigraphical excavation.

Born in Venice, Boni, an orphan, attended a commercial school. When he was nineteen, he took part in the restoration of the Doge's Palace, disagreeing profoundly with the architect, Forcinelli. Subsequently, he campaigned to protect Venetian monuments from overly zealous restorers and to preserve their historical character. This led to correspondence with Ruskin, William Morris and

Philip Webb and his enrollment at the Venice Academy to study architecture. He became a corresponding member of the Royal Institute of British Architects in 1885, the year of his first excavation at St. Mark's Cathedral.

In 1888, Boni was appointed secretary to the Calcografia in Rome. Shortly afterward he became an inspector of monuments and was instrumental in the creation of a photographic archive at the Ministry of Education. In 1892, he joined L. Beltrami and G. Sacconi in excavations outside the *Pantheon. Six years later, he was made director of excavations in the Forum. He worked on a prodigious scale and, at his best, was a careful observer of stratigraphy. In 1899 he dug in front of the Temple of Caesar, in the *Temple of Vesta and near the *Arch of Septimus Severus, where he found the Lapis Niger. The following year, he excavated at the Comitium and the Regia and demolished S. Maria Liberatrice to reveal the remains of S. Maria Antiqua. He also investigated the Lacus Iuturnae and the Horrea Agrippina. In 1902 he discovered the Archaic cemetery. Subsequent excavations included parts of Trajan's Forum (*Imperial Fora) and the *Servian Wall and the foundations of the cathedral tower in Venice, which had collapsed in 1906.

After visiting Tripoli to advise on the conservation of the Arch of Marcus Aurelius, Boni served in World War I, inventing a camouflage uniform for use in snow and waterproof boots based on the Roman *caliga.* An active supporter of fascism, he became a senator in 1923.

BIBLIOGRAPHY

G. Boni, *NSc* (1899–1906, 1911); E. Tea, "Boni, Giacomo," *EI* 8 (1930), 402–3; P. Romanelli, "Boni, Giacomo," *DBI* 12 (1970), 75–7.

DAVID WHITEHOUSE

BORGHESE (CAFFARELLI-BORGHESE), SCIPIONE (1576–1633). Italian cardinal, patron of the arts, most prominent collector in the *Borghese family.

Scipione was the son of the sister of Camillo Borghese (Pope Paul V) and was allowed to use the name and arms of the family. He was appointed cardinal in 1605 by Paul V and was thus assured of an income to support his collecting ambitions. Scipione started collecting antique statues in and around Rome as soon as he was appointed cardinal. Little is known about the provenance of the marbles. Many may have been newly excavated, such as the *Borghese *Hermaphrodite,* probably discovered in 1608 near S. Maria della Vittoria. Others may have come to light in Frascati during construction to enlarge and beautify Caravilla, purchased by Scipione in 1607. (The villa, situated on an ancient Roman site said to have belonged to Lucullus, was extensively expanded and modified by Flaminio Ponzio.)

Some marbles were derived from private collections, such as the *Standing Hermaphrodite* from the *Savelli and a *Silenus with Infant Bacchus* (*Borghese *Faun*) from Carlo Muti. Four pieces were acquired from the da *Carpi collection

(*Hercules* Piccolomini, *Pallas, Child with Duck,* and an altar). The *"Dying Seneca"* (*Borghese *Fisherman*) previously belonged to the duke of Altemps. Scipione also acquired the cabinet of Cardinal Sacrati, but the most important purchase was made in 1607, when 273 sculptures were secured from the estate of Tiberio *Ceoli for 7,566 scudi.

Scipione resided in the Palazzo Campeggi on the Via Alessandrini, purchased in 1608 by Giovanni Battista Borghese. The marbles were transferred to this palazzo. In 1613 Scipione Francucci wrote a lengthy poem on the Galleria of Borghese in which several sculptures are mentioned. The provenance of the *Centaur with Cupid* is not known, but it was already copied by P. P. *Rubens (between 1605 and 1608). Rubens also drew the statue group *Venus with Mars* (provenance unknown), the *"Dying Seneca,"* the *Borghese Vase and the *Borghese *Hermaphrodite* (*Sleeping*). In 1611 the famous *Borghese *Gladiator* was found in Anzio, together with a statue group of two soldiers and a female riding a horse.

In 1608 Scipione started purchasing property on the Pincio Hill, and in 1612 the construction of the lavish mansion of the Villa Borghese was started. A multitude of reliefs was used to decorate the exterior. Many of these were drawn for the dal *Pozzo "Paper Museum" and are still in situ.

Scipione also had a summer residence built on the Quirinal Hill, his *giardino,* close to the papal summer residence, in 1611. In the façade of the Casino di Aurora were installed a number of sarcophagus reliefs, such as the *Rape of Proserpina* and the *Death of Adonis,* both formerly in the Ceoli collection. Portrait busts were placed in niches. On 30 May 1616 the property, still unfinished, was sold to the duke of Altemps, most likely to reduce Scipione's debt. The villa, now owned by the Pallavicini, still has the reliefs.

In 1621 Pope Paul V passed away, and the Palazzo Borghese came into possession of Marcantonio Borghese. Scipione moved from his palazzo in the Borgo Nuovo to the Palazzo Borghese and reorganized the collections. The gallery on the ground floor of the palazzo was used to display all the paintings, while the Villa Pinciana was to hold all the sculptures. In 1625, 200 loads of statues were delivered to the villa. When Scipione died in 1633, the entire inheritance fell to Marcantonio. The collection was described in several monographs: the first was by L. Leporeo, followed by Jacomo Manilli in 1650 and E. Q. *Visconti in 1796.

BIBLIOGRAPHY

F. Noack, "Kunstpflege und Kunstbesitz der Familie Borghese," *RepKunstW* 50 (1929), 191–230; C. H. Heilman, "Die Entstehungsgeschichte der Villa Borghese in Rom," *MJb* 3rd ser., 24 (1973), 97–158; +P. Moreno, "Formazione della raccolta di antichità nel Museo e Galleria Borghese," *Colloqui del Sodalizio,* 2nd ser., 5 (1975–76), 125–43; +L. de Lachenal, "La collezione di sculture antiche della famiglia Borghese e il palazzo in Campo Marzio," *Xenia* 4 (1982), 49–117.

MARJON VAN DER MEULEN

BORGHESE ARES (MARS). Over-lifesize Roman marble copy (2.12m) in the style of Greek art of the end of the fifth century B.C., once the property of the *Borghese family.

The image shows a nude warrior wearing helmet and baldric with sword. He assumes the graceful "Attic" stance, opening diagonally to his right. Some twenty-one replicas of the type are known; the warrior is usually shown without a beard.

In Roman times the Borghese type was often combined with a figure of Venus, and the pair was then adapted for a portrait of husband and wife or emperor and empress. One such group, in which the god is bearded, was also in the Borghese collection (P. P. *Rubens made a drawing) and was called *Venus with Mars.* That version, today in the *Louvre, is thought to show ideal portraits of Sabina and Hadrian.

The *Ares,* acquired by Scipione *Borghese in 1607 from the collection of Tiberio *Ceoli, was sold to *Napoleon in 1807 and is also now in the Louvre. *Winckelmann identified it as Mars, noting the unique ring around the right ankle of the figure and interpreting it as part of the chains worn by the god when he was caught with Venus. E. Q. *Visconti, followed by Clarac, believed the figure was Achilles. Some modern scholars see the figure as Ares and accept the conjecture of A. *Conze that it is a copy of the cult statue created by Alkamenes in the later fifth century for the temple of Ares described by Pausanias (1.8.4) in the Athenian *Agora. K. Hartswick has proposed a completely different interpretation of the type as a classicizing creation of the period of Augustus. The ring on the Borghese copy has not been satisfactorily explained.

BIBLIOGRAPHY

W. Frohner, *Notice de la sculpture antique du Louvre,* 4th ed. (1878), 161; B. Freyer, "Zum Kultbild und zum Skulpturenschmuck des Arestempels auf der Agora in Athen," *JdI* 77 (1962), 211–20; Bieber, *Ancient Copies,* 43–44; Ridgway, *Roman Copies,* 68; K. Hartswick, "The Ares Borghese Reconsidered," *RA* (1970), 227–83.

BORGHESE DANCERS. Neo-Attic relief sculpture of the first century B.C., now in the *Louvre.

This relief depicts five elegantly clad maidens, hands linked in the dance, garments pressed closely against their bodies; they move to left and right in rhythmic contrapposto before a precinct wall subdivided by Corinthian pilasters. With a pendant representing three maidens decorating a candelabrum, it was purchased in 1807 by *Napoleon among other antiquities of the Villa Borghese (*Borghese family) inherited by his brother-in-law, Camillo Borghese, from collections assembled by Cardinal Scipione *Borghese in the early seventeenth century.

The Borghese *Dancers,* interpreted in the past as the Horae (Hours) and Graces, serve as an instructive lesson in the vagaries of changing taste. Although often cited as a source for *Mantegna's *Parnassus* (the dancing Muses), its popularity truly began in *Raphael's circle (Vatican Logge, Fossombrone sketchbook), the best-known reflection being Lorenzetto's bronze relief of *Christ and the Adulteress* in the Cappella Chigi in S. Maria del Popolo. The relief is also quoted in façade paintings by Polidoro.

We do not know its location in the Renaissance, but the fluttering, calligraphic draperies of the maidens who bring garlands and fruits to adorn a candelabrum in the companion piece were vastly admired during the quattrocento, and a sketchbook drawing attributed to *Ghirlandaio's circle (*Codex Escurialensis) records that it was studied in the piazza of Old St. Peter's. From the sixteenth through the eighteenth centuries, the more classicizing *Dancers* seem to have been thought better exemplars, much admired by *Poussin—who recommended a bronze copy made for Louis XIII—and by *Winckelmann. In modern times, however, both reliefs have been relegated to Louvre storerooms.

The *Maidens with Candelabrum* is much restored (the heads, in particular, being Renaissance work), but enough of the original background remains to show they shared the same precinct wall, here terminating in the façade of a small Corinthian temple.

BIBLIOGRAPHY

W. Fuchs, *Die Vorbilder der neuattischen Reliefs, JdI* Ergänzungsheft 20 (Berlin, 1959), 64; P. Bober, "The Census of Antique Works of Art Known to Renaissance Artists," *Renaissance and Mannerism: Studies in Western Art,* Acts of the Twentieth International Congress of the History of Art (Princeton, NJ, 1963), II, 88–89; Haskell—Penny, 195–96; +Bober-Rubenstein, 95.

PHYLLIS PRAY BOBER

BORGHESE FAMILY. A papal family known in Siena from the thirteenth century, related to St. Catherine; famed for its collection of works of art and antiquities.

A branch of the family moved to Rome in the sixteenth century, where CAMILLO (1552–1621), the future Pope Paul V, was born. Paul was interested in the arts but was not himself a great collector. Through the collecting activities of his brother, GIOVANNI BATTISTA (1554–1609), and the largesse offered his nephews, the Borghese came to rank, along with the *Farnese, the *Ludovisi and the *Medici, as one of the greatest collecting families.

The antiquities owned by Giovanni Battista were inventoried at his death in 1610 and included some one hundred statues, dozens of portrait busts, several sarcophagi, and numerous vases. Most of these had been acquired from Giovanni Paolo della Porta, including the *Orestes and Pylades* group and the *Borghese Dancers*. In 1625 Scipione *Borghese, the son of Paul's sister, transferred the sculptures to his villa outside the Porta Pincio, where they joined his own collection of sculptures.

On the death of Scipione (1633), the younger MARCANTONIO (1601–58) left intact the decoration of the exterior of the villa, but the interior was significantly transformed. (Many ceiling paintings date from this period.) In the latter part of the eighteenth century, the collection was enriched when excavation was undertaken with the help of Gavin *Hamilton on the family farm at Pontarno on Via Praenestina. Among the ruins of ancient Gabii, numerous statues and inscriptions were found.

As the shadow of the French Revolution fell on Rome, the Borghese were sympathetic to the Roman republic of 1798. CAMILLO BORGHESE (1775–1832), now scion of the family, returned to Rome in 1802 from exile. Presented to *Napoleon in 1803, he later met Pauline Bonaparte and married her, moved to Paris and became a French citizen and prince of the imperial family. Napoleon in 1807 began negotiations for the purchase of the Borghese collection of antiquities. The entire collection, a total of 523 pieces, was bought for 13 million francs: 159 statues and groups, 160 busts and herms, 170 bas-reliefs, vases, sarcophagi, sphinxes, thirty columns and four tables of precious marble, all installed in the Musée Napoleon (*Louvre), many to be published by E. Q. *Visconti. After the fall of Napoleon, the collection, with the exception of a few pieces reclaimed because the total price was never paid, remained in Paris. It contains some of the most famous antiquities of all time: *Borghese *Gladiator,* *Borghese *Faun,* *Borghese *Hermaphrodite,* *Borghese Vase, a colossal bust of *Antinous* and the colossal heads of *Lucius Verus* and *Marcus Aurelius.* Some of the other famous items of the collection are the *Diana* of Gabii, the *Borghese *Ares,* *Apollo Sauroctonus,* *Crouching Aphrodite,* altar of twelve gods, three Mithraic reliefs, two Bacchic rhytons, ''Dying Seneca'' (*Borghese Fisherman), many portraits of the Roman imperial family from Gabii and many sarcophagi.

As Napoleon's fortunes worsened, Camillo broke with him and tried to recover the family's works of art, succeeding only with those that had not been paid for. The villa in Rome was enlarged by Luigi *Canina, who began a new collection as the result of excavations undertaken at Montecalvo, Rieti and elsewhere. To Canina we owe the Egyptian propylaea, the two obelisks with inscriptions by Sir William *Gell and the propylaea planned as the principal entrance.

In the latter part of the nineteenth century, the wealth of the family declined, particularly as a result of land speculation when Rome became the capital of united Italy. The manuscripts and archives of the family were acquired for the Vatican by Leo XIII. Ultimately, the Villa Borghese and its contents became the property of the state, along with the pictures in the Palazzo Borghese.

In more recent years the family has recovered something of its former property. GIAN GIACOMO BORGHESE (1889–1954), with a degree in electrical engineering, was a pilot in World War I. He was active in fascist circles, having taken part in the activities at Milan in 1919 opposing the socialists; he served as governor of Rome during a large part of World War II (1939–43) and was involved in much archaeological activity on the *Capitoline Hill and neighboring areas. He can be credited with the discovery of the Temple of Apollo Sosianus and with paving the Campidoglio according to the plan of *Michelangelo.

BIBLIOGRAPHY

Comptes Rendus de l'Académie des Inscriptions et Belles-Lettres (Paris, 1937); +G. Q. Giglioli, ''Il Museo Borghese,'' *Capitolium* 18 (1940), 753–88; B. Di Porto, ''Borghese,

Camillo,'' *DBI* 12 (1970), 586–87; +Haskell—Penny; L. de Lachenal, ''La collezione di sculture antiche della famiglia Borghese e il palazzo in Campo Marzio,'' *Xenia* 4 (1982), 49–117; C. Pietrangeli, *Le Collezioni private romane attraverso i tempi* (Rome, 1985), 8–9, 21–22; G. S. Panofsky, ''Tommaso della Porta's 'Castles in the Air,' '' *JWarb* 56 (1993), esp. 149–52.

BORGHESE FAUN (SILENOS WITH THE INFANT BACCHUS). Over-lifesize marble statue (1.90m) showing a satyr holding a baby; one of several good copies (others in Munich and the Vatican) of a lost Greek original of the late fourth century B.C. usually attributed to Lysippos.

The vine-wreathed satyr is shown with beard and bristling locks, cuddling the child tenderly as he leans against a tree trunk.

The statue was reportedly discovered by Carlo Muti along with the *Borghese Vase in the *Gardens of Sallust, probably by 1569, and was in the *Borghese family collection by 1613. It was bought for *Napoleon in 1807, along with the majority of the Borghese collection, and is today in the *Louvre, Paris.

The figure was frequently referred to as a faun, that is, a satyr, an identification that was made more explicit by reference to Silenos, who was the tutor of the youthful Bacchus. The creature is neither fat nor conspicuously bald and thus may simply be a satyr, tending the child Bacchus. A rather grisly identification made in the seventeenth century saw him as Saturn and the happy baby as an unsuspecting child about to be devoured by his father.

The statue enjoyed great popularity for many centuries, though it has fallen from favor, along with other copies that were beloved in the Renaissance and seventeenth century. Among the many modern replicas, the best known is the fine bronze on the grand staircase in the *Uffizi Gallery, Florence, cast for Cardinal Ferdinando de' Medici (*Medici family) in the 1570s (shown in the Villa Medici, Rome, until its transfer to Florence, 1787).

BIBLIOGRAPHY
F. P. Johnson, *Lysippos* (Durham, NC, 1927), 184; Bieber, 37; Haskell—Penny, 306–7; L. de Lachenal, ''La collezione di sculture antiche della famiglia Borghese e il Palazzo in Campo Marzio,'' *Xenia* 4 (1982), 64; LIMC III 480 (C. Gasparri); Ridgway, *Hellenistic Sculpture* I 180, 101.

BORGHESE FISHERMAN (DYING SENECA). Marble under-lifesize figure of standing, bent old man, probably a fisherman, an exceptionally fine copy of a Hellenistic type (ca. 200–150 B.C.).

The statue, made of black marble with a (restored) light-colored loincloth, lacks its legs below the upper calves and has parts of the left thigh and the face and arms restored.

The statue was long believed to represent the Stoic philosopher and dramatist Seneca, whose image was also identified in a famous portrait-bust type (*Pseudo-Seneca) well known in the sixteenth century and later. P. P. *Rubens was especially influential in popularizing this identification; he studied and drew the figure in the *Borghese family collection in Rome and combined it and a portrait head of "Seneca" that he owned to create a painting of the *Dying Seneca* committing suicide in his bath (Munich, Alte Pinakothek). *Winckelmann demolished the identification as Seneca, pointing out several other versions of the type in which the old man held a basket or pail. The theory that he is a fisherman, first proposed by E. Q. *Visconti and still widely accepted today, would restore the figure with a fishing pole in his right hand and a bucket in his left. The association with statuettes of fishermen noted by Visconti is discounted by R. C. Häuber, who sees the Borghese statue as a nude old man suffering from rheumatism.

Even before the figure was dissociated from Seneca, it was regarded as "unbeautiful" and was never copied as ornamental sculpture in the same way as "Famous Statues" such as the *Belvedere *Apollo,* the *Farnese *Hercules* and others.

This statue is probably identical with the "Seneca of black marble" first recorded in 1594 by Flaminio *Vacca as having been found in Rome on an estate between S. Matteo and S. Giuliano and may have been seen by Rubens in the Borghese collection before he left Rome in 1608. In any case, it certainly belonged to Scipione *Borghese by 1613 and was placed in the Villa Borghese by 1625. The display of the restored statue included a large vase of African marble in which "Seneca" seemed to stand, letting his blood run into his bath. *Napoleon purchased the piece in 1807, along with most of the Borghese collections, and took it to Paris by 1811. It may be seen today in the *Louvre.

BIBLIOGRAPHY

Bieber, 142; +W. Stechow, *Rubens and the Classical Tradition* (Cambridge, MA, 1968), 28–31; Haskell—Penny, 303–5; R. C. Häuber, "The Statue of the Pseudo-Seneca/Fisherman in the Louvre—A Falsifying Restoration of the 16th Century" (abstract of paper), *AJA* 96 (1992), 359.

BORGHESE GLADIATOR (WARRIOR). Over-lifesize marble sculpture, signed by the artist Agasias, son of Dositheos, of Ephesos.

The figure, now lacking its shield and sword, assumes a defensive posture, leaning and stretching tautly as he turns dramatically in space. The statue is possibly a late Hellenistic adaptation (the letter forms of the inscription date to ca. 130 B.C.) or copy from a bronze original of the school of Lysippos (early third century B.C.).

The sculpture was discovered at Nettuno, near Anzio, in 1611, and underwent restoration before entering the collection of Scipione *Borghese. It remained on view at the Villa Borghese (cf. *Borghese family) until 1807, when it was purchased by *Napoleon, along with the majority of the Borghese collections, and taken to Paris. It remains today in the *Louvre.

Of the roll call of "Famous Statues" from antiquity admired during the seventeenth and eighteenth centuries, the Borghese *Gladiator* tops the list. *Perrier included four views of it in his engravings of "noble . . . statues" (1638), and it was described as "the most famous statue of all that antiquity hath left" when a copy of it was installed for the fourth Earl of Pembroke at Wilton in the seventeenth century. *Mengs, *Winckelmann and many other connoisseurs were lavish in their praise of the work, which was seen as a male figure type that mediated between the overly soft *Belvedere Antinous and the massively muscular *Farnese Hercules. A staggering number of copies and casts of it were made, leading eventually to an interdiction by Prince Borghese in the late eighteenth century against taking molds from the sculpture. The work was valued especially by artists and art instructors as a model of correct anatomy, and casts were regularly studied in academies and schools of art in Europe and America in the eighteenth and nineteenth centuries.

The original widespread and persistent identification of the figure as a gladiator was challenged sharply in the eighteenth century, when Winckelmann proposed that it represented, instead, a warrior or hero. Others suggested specific names: Telamonian Ajax or Ajax, son of Oileus, or else Leonidas of Sparta (all by *Fea), or Telamon himself (E. Q. *Visconti). *Bieber (1961) calls the work a "fighting warrior," and today there seems to be little interest in any more precise identification of this once surpassingly popular work of art.

BIBLIOGRAPHY
Bieber, 162; Haskell—Penny, 221–23; +L. de Lachenal, "La collezione di sculture antiche della famiglia Borghese e il palazzo in Campo Marzio," Xenia 4 (1982), 64–65; Ridgway, Hellenistic Sculpture I 83, 103.

BORGHESE HERMAPHRODITE. Lifesize marble sculpture of a sleeping Hermaphrodite (1.47m), probably a Roman copy of a lost Hellenistic original, once the property of the *Borghese family.

Pliny (NH 34.80) mentions a bronze "noble Hermaphrodite," possibly the prototype for the Borghese piece, by the sculptor Polykles (perhaps Polykles of Athens, who flourished in the second century B.C.). The figure is shown stretched out in a restless turning pose that reveals male characteristics from one side and female from the other; this aspect always intrigued visitors who saw the piece. The lifelike mattress upon which the Hermaphrodite rests is a seventeenth-century restoration by *Bernini or possibly his father, Pietro.

The Hermaphrodite type was already known in the fifteenth century, having been described by *Ghiberti from a (now lost) version he had seen in Rome. The statue belonging to the *Borghese was first known in the early seventeenth century; a drawing of it attributed to P. P. *Rubens may have been made before Rubens's departure from Rome in 1608. *Maffei claimed much later that the sculpture was found in the area of S. Maria della Vittoria when the foundations for the church were being dug, that is, in 1608. The sculpture's ancient setting thus may have been in or near the *Baths of Diocletian.

The Hermaphrodite was subsequently presented to Scipione *Borghese, probably in the 1620s, and is recorded as on display in the Villa Borghese by 1638. The room in which it was placed was redecorated in the late eighteenth century by Buonvicini, with paintings of the Ovidian story of Salmacis and Hermaphroditus. Among the artists inspired by the sculpture was *Velazquez, as may be seen in his sensuous Rokeby *Venus* (Prado); *Canova's *Sleeping Nymph* in the Victoria and Albert Museum (London) also reveals its influence.

*Napoleon purchased the *Hermaphrodite* in 1807, along with the greater part of the Borghese statuary and by 1812 had it on display in the Musée Napoleon; at present it is in the *Louvre. Another version that may be seen today in the Villa Borghese came into the Borghese collection only in the eighteenth century, and should not be confused with the more famous "Borghese *Hermaphrodite.*"

BIBLIOGRAPHY

Bieber, 125, 146; Haskell—Penny, 234–36; Bober—Rubinstein, 130; *LIMC* V 276–77 (A. Ajootian); Ridgway, *Hellenistic Sculpture,* I, 330–31.

BORGHESE VASE. Great marble vase (1.71m high) in the shape of a krater or mixing bowl for wine, probably created by a neo-Attic artist of the first century B.C.

The vessel has a relief going around the exterior featuring Dionysos, Satyrs, maenads and a drunken Silenos.

The vessel was first recorded in the garden display of Carlo Muti in Rome in 1594, having been discovered, evidently, in the Gardens of Sallust. By 1645 it was in the Villa Borghese (*Borghese family). One of the most admired specimens of antique marble vases, it was ascribed by some to Pheidias and was copied or adapted many times in marble as well as in bronze, jasperware and silver. In 1807 the Borghese Vase was purchased, along with most of the Borghese antiquities, by *Napoleon and went on display in Paris between 1808 and 1811; it remains in the *Louvre today.

Two ancient marble replicas of the vase were discovered in 1907 in the shipwreck at *Mahdia, which may date to shortly after the time of Sulla in the first century B.C.; they are now in the Musée du Bardo, Tunis. The *Medici Vase in the Uffizi Gallery is also very similar to the Borghese Vase.

BIBLIOGRAPHY

A. Merlin—L. Poinssot, *Cratères et candelabres de marbres trouvés en mer près de Mahdia* (Tunis, 1930), 23 ff.; Bieber, 184–85; Haskell—Penny, 314–15.

BORGHESI, BARTOLOMEO (1781–1860). Italian numismatist and epigraphist.

A precocious student, Borghesi became a prolific writer on coins and Latin inscriptions. In 1821 he moved to the Italian Republic of San Marino. Here, a greatly honored public figure, he was visited by many scholars, including Theodor *Mommsen, whom he encouraged in his efforts to found a Corpus of Latin Inscriptions (*CIL*). Mommsen, in a work of 1852, calls him "teacher, patron, friend" (*magister, patronus, amicus*) and repeats this in *CIL,* volumes 9–10. Borghesi's collected works in ten volumes were published by order of Napoleon

III (Paris, 1862–97). In 1981 his bicentenary was celebrated in Italy with a colloquio.

BIBLIOGRAPHY
A. Campana, "Borghesi, Bartolomeo," *DBI* 12 (1970), 624–43.

†ARTHUR E. GORDON

BOSCOREALE, BOSCOTRECASE. Subdivisions of the modern town Torre Annunziata, located to the north and northwest of *Pompeii.

Finds from three different villas in this area, covered over by the eruption of Vesuvius in A.D. 79, have significance for the history of archaeology.

At the Roman villa rustica called "La Pisanella" was found in 1895 the hoard of precious items known as the Boscoreale Treasure. In the cistern of a room with wine presses were found the skeleton of the possessor and some 1,000 gold coins, four gold bracelets, earrings, a gold chain and 103 pieces of silverware. Many of the pieces seem to belong to the period of Augustus (31 B.C.–A.D. 14). The silver, including a spectacular patera with the image of a goddess dressed in elephant headdress (depicting Alexandria, perhaps, or Cleopatra) and a pair of cups ornamented with skeletons as mock philosophers, was purchased and donated to the *Louvre by Baron Rothschild. Other finds from Boscoreale (including bronze furnishings and utensils) are in Berlin and the Field Museum, Chicago.

In 1900, a villa thought to have belonged to P. Fannius Synistor was excavated by Vincenzo de Prisco on the property of Francesco Vona. The paintings, cut from the walls and framed in wood, were auctioned, with most going to the *Metropolitan Museum of Art in New York. Some remained in the *Museo Nazionale, Naples, and a few went to the Louvre and museums in the Netherlands and Belgium. The well-preserved frescoes are considered among the most important examples of the Second Pompeian Style. The subjects of the numerous frescoes include landscapes and townscapes as well as a cycle of figure painting perhaps based on an earlier Hellenistic series.

The third villa, "of Agrippa Postumus," was discovered in 1903 at Boscotrecase during the construction of a train line from Naples around the base of Mt. Vesuvius. It was excavated by the owner of the land, Cavaliere Ernesto Santini, with the help of the archaeologist Matteo Della Corte. In 1926, M. I. *Rostovtzeff conjectured that the villa was imperial and belonged nominally to the infant son of Agrippa, born in 11 B.C., just after Agrippa's death. The paintings from four bedrooms are celebrated examples of the Third Pompeian Style; they are today in the Metropolitan Museum of Art (three rooms) and Museo Nazionale, Naples (one room). The villa itself was completely covered over by a new eruption of Vesuvius in 1906.

BIBLIOGRAPHY
+R. Héron de Villefosse, *Le Trésor de Boscoreale, MonPiot* 5, fasc. 1–2 (1899); H. F. De Cou—F. B. Tarbell, *Antiquities from Boscoreale in the Field Museum of Natural History* (Chicago, 1912); +P. W. Lehmann, *Roman Wall Paintings from Boscoreale in*

the Metropolitan Museum of Art (Cambridge, MA, 1953); +M. L. Anderson, "Pompeian Frescoes in the Metropolitan Museum of Art," *BMMA,* Winter 1987/88; +*Il Tesoro di Boscoreale,* Catalog of Exhibition (Milan, 1988); +P. H. von Blanckenhagen—C. Alexander, *The Augustan Villa at Boscotrecase* (Mainz, 1990).

BOSIO (BOSIUS, BOSSIUS), ANTONIO (1575–1629). Italian scholar, founder of Christian archaeology.

Justly called the "Columbus" of the Roman catacombs, Bosio was born in Malta and educated in Rome under the guidance of his uncle, the historian Giacomo Bosio. Even before graduating in law (1594), Antonio joined *Chacón, Winghe, Ugonio and l'Heureux in recording the architecture, wall decoration and inscriptions from the basilicas and the few known catacombs. In 1578 a richly decorated catacomb fortuitously had come to light on the Via Salaria, a stimulus to Roman scholars fighting criticism from Protestant opponents to sacred images. In 1593 Bosio began his own series of often risky excavations, resulting in discovery of the major underground cemeteries outside the walls of Rome. He made a systematic compendium of ancient texts that afforded clues to the locations of catacombs, but most of their original entrances eluded him.

Bosio employed artists to draw important burial chambers in situ and made accurate site plans of the multilevel corridors and ground plans and elevations of related surface buildings. He died in Rome while preparing his *Roma Sotterranea* for publication. Severano completed and edited the manuscript, which appeared as a well-illustrated folio in 1634. An amplified Latin version by Aringhi (1651 and later editions) took Bosio's work to a wider European readership. The engravings influenced many artists and were superseded as archaeological illustrations only by G. B. *De Rossi's plates in the nineteenth century.

Bosio's research laid the foundations of Christian archaeology, combining careful ecclesiastical scholarship with meticulous observation of the physical evidence. The early Church's cult of martyrs was thoroughly documented for the first time in the *Roma Sotterranea.* Bosio's sober presentation of the catacombs on the consular roads and of the Vatican cemetery reinforced Catholic claims for historical primacy, but centuries of bitter dispute about the historical value of his evidence were to follow.

BIBLIOGRAPHY

A. Valeri, *Cenni biografici di Antonio Bosio con documenti inediti* (Rome, 1900); G. Ferretto, *Note storico-bibliografiche di archeologia cristiana* (Vatican City, 1942); N. Parise, "Bosio, Antonio," *DBI* 13 (1971), 257–59.

ROBERT W. GASTON

BOSPORUS CIMMERIUS (CIMMERIAN BOSPORUS). Territory in the south of Russia, on the straits between the Black Sea and the Sea of Azov, containing numerous towns, settlements and cemeteries of the Greek and Roman periods.

The native populations of Scythians, Sauromatians, Sarmatians, Maeotians and others interacted with the colonizing Greeks and the Romans to create a unique cultural blend. From the fifth century B.C. onward, this area was part of the Bosporan kingdom, the capital of which was located at Pantikapaion (modern Kerch), on the west side of the strait. Among other important sites are Phanagoria, Gorgippia (modern Anapa) and Hermonassa, all on the east side, on the Taman peninsula.

Since the early nineteenth century, Russian archaeologists have studied the history and culture of the Bosporan kingdom. In 1816 the first excavations were made at Kerch, and from 1830, large-scale, planned excavations were conducted annually around Kerch and on the Taman peninsula. The majority of the rich finds were sent to the Hermitage Museum, St. Petersburg. In this period there was great interest in mound tombs (''kurgans'') and their furnishings. Among the most spectacular discoveries were the Royal Kurgan near Kerch (fourth century B.C.), with its fine stone masonry creating a corbeled dome and dromos for entrance, and the nearby tomb of Kul Oba (also fourth century B.C.; discovered 1830), having a similar structure and containing remarkable objects such as the gold temple frontlets with the head of *Athena Parthenos* and the ivory veneer engraved and tinted with scenes from Greek mythology. A number of painted underground tombs (''catacombs'') were found near Kerch, such as the tomb of Alcimus (discovered 1867), with its plastered walls painted with a scene of the *Rape of Persephone* and imitation masonry like that of the First Pompeian Style. Numerous examples were found in tombs of the Bosporus of the elegant gilded Greek red-figured pottery known as Kerch ware (surveyed authoritatively in 1901 by B. V. Farmakovsky). The accumulated knowledge and perception of the Bosporan kingdom by the time of the early twentieth century may be gauged by the epoch-making publication of E. H. Minns, *Scythians and Greeks, A Survey of Ancient History and Archaeology of the Euxine from the Danube to the Caucasus* (Cambridge, 1913) and the publications of *Rostovtzeff.

Much nineteenth-century excavation was under the supervision of an Imperial Archaeological Commission (founded in 1859). Under the Soviet regime, a comprehensive study was started in 1932 by the Bosporan Archaeological Expedition, with guidance from V. F. Gaidukevich of the Kerch Archaeological Museum. More emphasis was now given to settlement archaeology and to economic aspects of the Bosporan kingdom. In 1945, systematic excavation of Pantikapaion under V. D. Blavatsky focused on the fortified acropolis of Mt. Mithridates, followed by an expedition of the Pushkin Museum of Fine Arts in Moscow (from 1959 under the direction of I. D. Marchenko; from 1977 under V. P. Tolstikov). A large, rectangular complex, with a paved central court fronting a two-story colonnade of the Doric and Ionic orders, has been identified as a Hellenistic palace.

In the Taman peninsula, while numerous rich Scythian burials were uncovered in the nineteenth century, it was under the Soviets that the Greek settlements were studied. At Phanagoria, excavated by Blavatsky from 1936, large public buildings and rich private homes were found, dating from the sixth/fifth centuries B.C. and following. Later, the work at Phanagoria was carried on by the Institute of Archaeology, Moscow, by V. S. Dolgorukov, and from 1989, by A. A. Zavoykin, resulting in the discovery of twelve houses of wattle and mud brick (fifth century B.C.) and elegant Hellenistic buildings featuring polychrome plastered walls and architectural terracottas. A. K. Korovina published 338 graves from Phanagoria, dating from the fourth century B.C. to the fourth century A.C., excavated in 1964–65.

At Hermonassa, one of the largest sites on the Taman peninsula, excavations have uncovered a Greek colony founded in the sixth century B.C. Recent work has been carried out by the Pushkin Museum under Korovina and S. I. Finogenova. Gorgippia, also founded in the sixth century B.C., has been unearthed by a joint expedition of the former Academy of Science of the U.S.S.R, (now the Academy of Science of Russia) and the Krasnodar Archaeological Museum under E. M. Alexeyeva. She published the results of excavations made from 1973 to 1984, as well as various studies of the history, economy and religion of the city. Nearly 7,000m^2 of streets, houses and workshops within the town of Gorgippia have been discovered, as well as another zone of 4,000m^2 on the sea, revealing eleven building periods.

The most sensational recent finds in the Bosporan kingdom were made in the 1980s by E. A. Savostina in the Yubileynoe area near Phanagoria. Two fine Attic marble grave stelai of the fourth century B.C., showing warriors in action or at rest, were found reused as building stone in a Roman villa of the first century B.C.–first century A.C. Also discovered were impressive limestone reliefs of local workmanship depicting an *Amazonomachy*.

BIBLIOGRAPHY

A. Mongait, *Archaeology in the USSR,* tr. D. Skvirsky (Moscow, 1959); +J. G. F. Hind, "Greek and Barbarian Peoples on the Shores of the Black Sea," *ArchRep* 30 (1983–84), 71–97; +M. J. Treister—Y. G. Vinogradov, "Archaeology on the Northern Coast of the Black Sea," *AJA* 97 (1993), 521–63.

BOTTICELLI, SANDRO (ALESSANDRO DI MARIANO FILIPEPI; 1444/ 45–1510). Italian painter.

Born in Florence, Botticelli responded to the ancient world in terms formulated by writers and artists of his native city. For example, *Alberti's treatise *On Painting* praised descriptions of wind-blown draperies, and Filippo Lippi and Antonio *Pollaiuolo demonstrated the possibilities of line and movement. Botticelli was able to appreciate these features in neo-Attic reliefs of figures with streaming hair and clinging or fluttering vestments and incorporate them into his own works, such as the *Birth of Venus* (Uffizi, Florence). Alberti also suggested to painters the theme of *Calumny,* as depicted in a lost painting by Apelles, and his description, together with Lucian's original account of the work, provided a source for Botticelli's *Calumny* (Uffizi).

Called to Rome in 1481 to help decorate the Sistine Chapel, Botticelli immediately showed his reaction to Roman monuments by including an accurate representation of the *Arch of Constantine in his painting of the *Punishment of Korah, Dathan and Abiram*. But such full and literal renderings are rare; he usually borrowed and transformed only details from ancient works. The painter used the motif of the *Venus Pudica* in his *Birth of Venus,* and the statue of the *Hora of Autumn* in the Uffizi may have inspired his Flora in the *Primavera* (Uffizi). A variation on the *Quirinal *Horse Tamers* appears in Botticelli's *Adoration of the Magi* (National Gallery, Washington, DC). Sarcophagi provided motifs for a centaur in the *Pallas* (Uffizi) and the composition of the *Mars and Venus* (National Gallery, London), as well as for the central Grace in the *Primavera*. Botticelli also studied ancient gems in the collection of the *Medici family. Wind gods from the *Farnese Cup fly again in the *Birth of Venus,* while a gem with *Marsyas and Apollo* (*Museo Nazionale, Naples) hangs from a necklace in a *Portrait of a Lady* in Frankfurt; another with a *Triumph of Bacchus* (Museo Nazionale, Naples) provides a prototype for an engraving of *Bacchus and Ariadne.*

BIBLIOGRAPHY

E. Tietze-Conrat, "Botticelli and the Antique," *BurlMag* 47 (1925), 124–29; T. E. S. Yuen, "The Tazza Farnese as a Source for Botticelli's 'Birth of Venus' and Piero di Cosimo's 'Myth of Prometheus,' " *GBA* 74 (1969), 175–77; A. Luchs, "A Maenad from Pisa in the Primavera," *MittFlor* 24 (1980), 369–70; +R. Lightbown, *Sandro Botticelli* (London, 1989).

JONATHAN NELSON

BOULOGNE, JEAN. See BOLOGNA, GIOVANNI.

BOURBON FAMILY. One of the most important ruling houses of Europe; reigned in Naples and Sicily (1735–1860), giving impetus to excavations at *Pompeii and *Herculaneum and to the formation of the collection now in the *Museo Nazionale di Napoli.

CARLO DI BORBONE (DON CARLOS, later CHARLES III of Spain; 1716–88) launched Bourbon power in Italy, ruling first as duke of Parma, by virtue of being the son of ELISABETTA of Parma (ISABELLA; 1692–1766), powerful wife of PHILIP V of Spain (ruled 1700–46) and heir to the *Farnese family fortunes. In 1734 he conquered the kingdom of Naples-Sicily and ruled there until 1759, when he became king of Spain and yielded the throne to his eight-year-old son, FERDINAND IV of Naples (1751–1825). The Marchese Bernardo Tanucci served as regent until Ferdinand reached his majority in 1767; Tanucci's power was then extinguished through the influence of Ferdinand's wife, Maria Carolina of Austria. After the interlude of the Parthenopean Republic (1798–99) and the Napoleonic rule of Naples (1806–16), the king returned as FERDINAND I of the Kingdom of the Two Sicilies.

During this period occurred the most important of the Bourbon archaeological and museological ventures. In 1738 Charles renewed excavations at Herculaneum (first discovered in 1709) under control of the court, and in 1748 he began work at Pompeii. O. Bayardi was commissioned to produce a catalog of the finds from Herculaneum, which appeared in 1755 as *Catalogo degli antichi monumenti.* During the regency of Tanucci, the Royal Herculanean Academy (*Academia Herculanensis) was founded to study and publish the finds in an exclusive series of folio volumes, *Le Antichità di Ercolano,* 8 vols. (1757–96), at first intended only for presentation as gifts. From 1750, the finds were carried to Charles's royal palace at nearby Portici, where they were jealously reserved for the king and a few select visitors. Nothing was for sale, and visitors were not allowed to make sketches or take notes, nor could casts be made of the statuary. Among the antiquities in the palace were the two *Balbus* equestrian statues, the *Seated *Hermes,* the *Drunken Faun,* and the *"Aristides,"* all discovered at Herculaneum. Antique wall paintings (*Roman wall painting) from Pompeii and Herculaneum, such as the images of *Achilles and the Centaur Chiron* and *Theseus,* were among the most novel works to be seen, since previously, very little of ancient figure painting was known (cf. *Aldobrandini Wedding). Also on display were bronzes, lamps, terracottas, objects of glass, coins, cameos, mosaics, papyri (from the *Villa of the Papyri; in addition, some sixty bronze statues were found there). Much of the collection came from Herculaneum, with fewer items from Pompeii and also from *Stabiae.

Ferdinand next determined to consolidate and move the Farnese collections of antiquities to Naples, an undertaking (1787–1800) that meant the transfer of some of the most famous sculptures in Europe—the *Farnese *Herakles,* the *Farnese *Flora,* the *Farnese *Bull* and others—out of the city of Rome to a new center for the study of antiquity. The collection included many splendid carved gems that had once belonged to the *Medici family, such as the *Farnese Cup; these had come to the Farnese in 1538, and in 1600 the gem cabinet of Fulvio *Orsini had been added to the Farnese holdings. The pope and others in Rome objected strenuously, but the move was carried out. Before the sculptures were moved, they were cleaned and restored by Carlo *Albacini, the whole operation being supervised by the German Jacob Philipp Hackert (1737–1807), antiquarian and court painter to Ferdinand. The Farnese antiquities were first placed in the royal villa on the hill of Capodimonti, while a third royal residence, at Caserta, contained copies in marble of other celebrated statues, such as the *Castor and Pollux* of San Ildefonso, the *Medici *Venus* and the *Belvedere "Antinous." The Farnese *Bull* was set apart to be displayed in the Villa Reale at Chiaia, as the centerpiece of a fountain.

The atmosphere for the study of antiquities at Naples in these years was enhanced by the presence of Sir William *Hamilton, established in the city from 1764 as the representative of the king of England. The Bourbon displays and Hamilton's extraordinary collections of *Greek vases attracted some of the leading painters of neoclassicism, for example, Angelica *Kauffman and Wilhelm *Tischbein, as well as many scholars. *Winckelmann made a total of four visits to Naples, the first in 1758, when he was coldly received by court scholars and assistants, who severely restricted his access to the antiquities. After his visit of 1762, scarcely more satisfying, he unleashed a vicious attack on the work at Herculaneum, in his "Open Letter on the Discoveries Made at Herculaneum" (1762) and his "Report on the Most Recent Discoveries Made at Herculaeum" (1764). Vilifying court scholars O. Bayardi, C. Paderni and J. Martorelli, as well as director of excavations Alcubierre, he sent the word around Europe in his carefully planned exposé that the excavations were being carried out by incompetent blunderers. He was thereafter completely excluded from the sites for a time and missed out on major discoveries at Pompeii in 1764 (the temple of Isis, the large theater). But by 1767, Tanucci and Winckelmann had both softened, and the latter enjoyed greater access to the discoveries, even receiving a complimentary copy of the fifth volume of Le Antichitá di Ercolano.

Advised by Hackert, Ferdinand had laid plans from 1787 to install his antiquities in a museum that was to be created from one of the older buildings of the University of Naples, the Palazzo dei Vecchi Studi. The gradual transfer of works of art was interrupted by the French invasions, and Ferdinand departed for Palermo with eighteen cases of sculpture, as well as many other objects. Upon his return from exile in 1816, he resumed his plan and soon announced the renaming of the old palazzo as the Real Museo Borbonico. By 1822, the antiquities from Portici had been moved here, along with the objects brought back from Palermo.

Ferdinand's successors, FRANCIS I (ruled 1825–30) and FERDINAND II (ruled 1830–59) did relatively little for the collection, although excavations did continue at Pompeii; the most notable acquisitions for the museum were the *Dancing Faun (1830) and the *Alexander Mosaic (1843) from Pompeii. During this era an ambitious catalog was prepared, the Real Museo Borbonico, in sixteen volumes (1824–57).

The last Bourbons, regarded as increasingly weak and corrupt, set the scene for Garibaldi's triumphal entry into Naples in 1860 and the absorption of the city into a unified Italy. The Museo Borbonico was then renamed the Museo Nazionale di Napoli.

BIBLIOGRAPHY

+A. De Franciscis, Il Museo Nazionale di Napoli (Naples, 1963); W. Leppmann, Winckelmann (New York, 1970); +Haskell—Penny, 74–78, 153–54, 158–61, 267–69; F. Haskell, "Art Patronage and Collecting in Bourbon Naples During the 18th Century," in The Golden Age of Naples, catalog of exhibition (Detroit Institute of Arts, 1981).

BRADFORD, JOHN SPENCER PURVIS (1918–75). English historian and archaeologist, pioneer in the study of archaeological sites from the air.

An Oxford-trained historian already active in archaeology, Bradford was engaged in aerial reconnaissance for military purposes in Italy between 1943 and 1945. Many of his aerial photographs "were noted . . . as important for archaeological study when peace came." A postwar series of articles in Antiquity (1946–50) duly demonstrated the potential of "air archaeology" in the study of

Etruscan topography and Roman centuriation; in addition, they revealed hundreds of unsuspected Neolithic ditched villages on the Tavoliere plain around Foggia, Apulia. Bradford expounded these revolutionary findings in *Ancient Landscapes* (1957); tragically, incurable illness prevented him from taking any further part in their development.

BIBLIOGRAPHY

G. E. Daniel, editorial, *Antiquity* 49 (1975), 246–47; *Antiquity* 50 (1976), 3–4.

DAVID RIDGWAY

BRAMANTE, DONATO (DONATO DI PASUCCIO D'ANTONIO; 1444–1514). Italian Renaissance architect.

According to Andrea *Palladio, "Bramante was the first to bring to light good and beautiful architecture which from the time of the ancients to his day had been forgotten." Bramante was born near Urbino, and began his career as a painter. By the time he arrived in Milan, ca. 1480, he had turned his attention to architecture. His Milanese projects (San Satiro, Santa Maria presso San Satiro, Santa Maria delle Grazie, cloisters of San Ambrogio) and the Pavia Cathedral reveal his respect for late antiquity and the Carolingian renascence, his knowledge of Vitruvius and his interest in the recent accomplishments of Michelozzo, Filarete and *Alberti, as well as his association with Leonardo da Vinci. In keeping with the neo-Platonic spirit of his day, Bramante sought to reconcile the engineering principles of the Middle Ages with the Renaissance architectural aesthetics of *il modo antico.*

This is especially true of his most important projects executed in Rome after 1500. His cloister at Santa Maria della Pace used a classically correct entablature and sequence of orders. His Tempietto, begun in 1502, at San Pietro in Montorio is a peripteral rotonda inspired by the circular temples in the *Forum Boarium (Rome) and at *Tivoli and, most probably, by Nero's Macellum Magnum of the Caelian Hill. It is likely that an annular colonnade reminiscent of the "Maritime Theater" at *Hadrian's Villa or the Early Christian church of San Stefano Rotondo was intended.

With the accession of Pope *Julius II, Bramante began a series of projects at the Vatican. The concept of parallel corridors linking the papal palace to the Belvedere gallery of antiquities was inspired by the plan of a Roman circus (e.g., that of Maxentius), the Palatine *Stadium of Domitian, the Hadrianic *poikile* at Tivoli and the *Temple of Fortuna Primigenia at Palestrina (*Praeneste). Bramante's plans for a new St. Peter's are subject to conflicting interpretation. Initially, he may have intended a centralized design with vaults inspired by the *Basilica of Maxentius and Constantine. The now vanished Palazzo Caprini ("House of Raphael") utilized the shop-front idea of ancient Roman apartment houses. Bramante's name is connected with the *Antiquarie prospettiche romane,* a pamphlet in verse celebrating the ancient ruins of Rome.

BIBLIOGRAPHY
+C. Baroni, *Bramante* (Bergamo, 1944); +O. Förster, *Bramante* (Vienna, 1956); A. Bruschi, *Bramante architetto* (Bari, 1969); Idem, *Bramante* (London, 1977).
                                                                CHARLES RANDALL MACK

BRANCHIDAE. See DIDYMA.

BRASCHI, GIANNANGELO. See PIUS VI.

BRAUN, EMIL AUGUST (1809–56). German archaeologist and administrator; directing secretary of the *Instituto di Corrispondenza Archeologica.

Born in Gotha, Emil Braun studied art history and mythology at Göttingen with K. O. *Müller (1829). He also studied at Munich (1830), Leipzig (1832) and Dresden (1833) before accepting an assignment as a secretary at the *Berlin Museum from E. *Gerhard. In 1833 he accompanied Gerhard to Rome, where he was given a minor post in the Instituto di Corrispondenza Archeologica. Braun eventually worked his way up to the prestigious job of first secretary of the Instituto (1840), a role he kept until his death in 1856. He also served as editor of the *Bulletino dell'Instituto* from 1835 until his death.

Especially in his early years at the Instituto, Braun was immensely effective. He had a number of gifts that suited him well for his position—a natural ability as a speaker, a great zeal for work, an extraordinary knowledge of ancient monuments. He was also well known for his ability to search out new, unpublished antiquities in private collections or on the art market.

Unfortunately, Braun's attitude toward research and the archaeological institute changed when he was around forty. He became fiercely opinionated, spouting overbold conjectures in rhetorical language, and, at the same time, seemed hasty and careless in his work. He would leave Rome for a month at a time (chiefly for England), neglecting his duties to the point that the Instituto was critically disorganized by the time of his death in 1856.

Of the many publications he left behind, mainly in articles and monographs issued by the Instituto, none are considered particularly noteworthy today.
BIBLIOGRAPHY
K. Schauenburg, "Braun, Emil August," *NDB* 2 (1955), 548–49; H. G. Kolbe, in *Archäologenbildnisse,* 31–32.

BRAURON. Greek sanctuary lying in the Livadi plain on the east coast of Attika.

The sanctuary, dedicated to Artemis Brauronia, was established at the base of a crescent-shaped hill that was occupied in Neolithic times and during the Bronze Age. According to the foundation myth, Artemis, angered at the killing of a pet bear, sent a plague or famine that ended only when the Athenians dedicated their daughters to a period of service to the goddess. The young girls, between the ages of ten and fifteen, wore yellow robes and imitated bears; they are depicted on specially made ritual cups found at the sanctuary. Iphigenia, too, was worshiped in the sanctuary, and vestments of those who died in childbirth were dedicated to her (Euripides, *Iph. Taur.* 1462–67).

Excavations were carried out in the 1950s by J. Papademetriou, who brought to light a wealth of votive material in the form of mirrors, rings, gems and pottery, much of it found in a sacred spring and now on display in the site museum. The earliest votives suggest that the cult dates back to the eighth century B.C. Of the buildings in the sanctuary, the remains of a small Doric temple dating to ca. 500 B.C. were uncovered, as well as a Doric stoa with projecting wings and dining rooms behind, dated to ca. 420 B.C. (partially restored in the 1960s), and a well-preserved stone bridge of the fifth century B.C. The untimely death of Papademetriou in the 1960s brought the excavations to a sudden halt, and the rest of the sanctuary has not been cleared, though an inscription calls for repairs to the following buildings: the temple, a Parthenon, *oikoi,* an *amphipoleion,* a gymnasium, a *palaistra,* and stables. The sanctuary went out of use in the late fourth century B.C., apparently flooded by the Erasinos River, though it should be noted that Pausanias (I.33.1), writing in the second century A.C., reports having seen an ancient wooden idol of Artemis at Brauron.

BIBLIOGRAPHY

J. Papademetriou, "The Sanctuary of Artemis at Brauron," *Scientific American* 208 (1963), 111–20; C. Bouras, *Ē Anastēlōsis tēs Stoǎs tēs Bravrōnos* (Athens, 1967); J. Kondis, "Artemis Brauronia," *Deltion* 22 (1967), 156–206, 221–26; L. Kahil, "L'Artemis de Brauron: Rites et Mystère," *AntK* 20 (1977), 86–98.

JOHN McK. CAMP II

BREGNO, ANDREA (ANDREA DA MILANO; 1421–1503). Lombard sculptor, collector of antiquities.

Andrea Bregno owned a small but important group of antiquities, including sarcophagi reliefs, an altar of Augustus and, in all likelihood, the *Belvedere Torso* (earlier in the possession of Prospero Colonna; see *Colonna family). He resided in Rome in a house at the foot of Monte Cavallo in Via della Dataria. Amico *Aspertini recorded several of Bregno's reliefs, and an anonymous sketchbook of the early sixteenth century depicts some of his statues.

BIBLIOGRAPHY

C. Robert, "Ueber ein dem Michelangelo zugeschriebenes Skizzenbuch auf Schloss Wolfegg," *RM* 16 (1901), 208–43; W. Friedländer, "Bregno, Andrea," Thieme-Becker, 4 (1910), 566–68; P. Bober, *Drawings After the Antique by Amico Aspertini* (London, 1957), 11; A. Schmitt, "Römische Antikensammlungen im Spiegel eines Musterbuchs der Renaissance," *MJb* 21 (1970), 107–14; Haskell—Penny, 311–16; Bober—Rubinstein, 166–67, 471.

MARJON VAN DER MEULEN

BRENDEL, OTTO J. (1901–73). German American art historian and archaeologist.

Born at Nuremberg, Bavaria, after apprenticeship to Frederik *Poulsen (Copenhagen), Brendel took his doctorate in 1928 under Ludwig *Curtius at Munich. In 1938 he emigrated to the United States and taught at Washington University, St. Louis (1938–41), the University of Indiana (1941–56) and Columbia University (1956–73). His work centered on the art of Rome and Etruria and is characterized by the sensitive, stylistic analysis of masterpieces and the application of literary evidence to their elucidation in the manner of Curtius. His *Etruscan Art,* prepared for press by Emeline Richardson (1978), remains authoritative. A selection of special studies is available in *The Visible Idea* (Washington, DC, 1980). His most influential book has been *Prolegomena to the Study of Roman Art* (2nd ed., New Haven, CT, 1979), a thoughtful and stimulating introduction to modern study of the subject. In breadth of knowledge and profound humanism, it reveals much of the man.

BIBLIOGRAPHY

W. M. Calder III, "Biographical Note," *In Memoriam Otto J. Brendel: Essays in Archaeology and the Humanities,* ed. L. Bonfante—H. von Heintze (Mainz, 1978), x–xi, with bib.; S. Settis, " 'Inegualianze' e continuità: un immagine dell'arte romana," in O. J. Brendel, *Introduzione all'arte romana, Saggi* 650 (Turin, 1982), 161–200; W. M. Calder III, in *Archäologenbildnisse,* 283–84.

WILLIAM M. CALDER III

BRITISH MUSEUM, London. Oldest and greatest of the world's universal museums, with an important collection of classical antiquities.

The British Museum was founded by Act of Parliament in 1753 to unite in one national institution the Harleian manuscripts, the Cotton Library and the collection of books and antiquities assembled by Sir Hans *Sloane (1660–1753). The lamps, pots, gems, sculptures and inscriptions from the Sloane Collection were the foundation of the British Museum's collection of Greek and Roman antiquities, now one of the richest in the world.

True to its eighteenth-century foundation, the British Museum remains the example, par excellence, of the universal museum. Although founded primarily as a library of manuscripts and printed books, the collection of antiquities has grown steadily almost from the beginning, so that a Department of Antiquities, separate from the library, became necessary as early as 1807, while the Department of Greek and Roman Antiquities achieved independent status in 1861.

The methods by which the collection was built up have varied over the years. At first the museum was largely dependent either on the generosity of donors or on occasional grants from Parliament for specific purchases. The first great collection of classical antiquities purchased in this way had been assembled by Sir William *Hamilton while British ambassador in Naples. Hamilton was a compulsive collector who more than once found it necessary to sell in order to raise funds to buy more. His "First Collection," acquired by the British Museum in 1772 for £8,410, included 730 vases, 175 terracottas, 300 items of glass, 600 bronzes and 6,000 coins. Important gifts in the eighteenth century included marble reliefs presented by M. Duane and T. Tyrwhitt in 1772 and a bronze portrait head of *Sophocles* given by Lord Exeter in 1760.

There were few marble sculptures in the Hamilton collection, but this gap was amply filled in 1805 by the purchase for £20,000 of a large collection assembled by Charles *Townley. Among his sculptures were many fine Roman portraits and sarcophagi, as well as copies of earlier Greek works, including a celebrated version of Myron's *Discobolos* from *Hadrian's Villa. A few Greek original sculptures, including the fifth-century B.C. Athenian grave relief of Xanthippos, had found their way into Townley's collection, but as in the other English private collections of its day, Greek sculpture was chiefly represented by Roman copies, which had been thought by connoisseurs since the Renaissance to be a true guide to Greek taste. This view was challenged after the first exhibition in London of the Elgin Marbles, including sculptures from the *Parthenon, in 1807. *Elgin's offer to sell his collection to the government was eventually accepted following an inquiry by a Select Committee of the House of Commons into the authority by which Elgin had obtained the collection and the circumstances under which it was granted, as well as the importance of acquiring it for the public and its value. Following the Select Committee's report, the collection was acquired by Act of Parliament in 1816 for £35,000.

Meanwhile, in 1814 the *Bassai Frieze had been purchased with funds made available by the Prince Regent, and Charles Townley's collection of small antiquities, including bronzes, lamps, pottery and sealstones, joined the Townley marbles in the British Museum. An even more notable collection of small antiquities was bequeathed to the museum in 1824 by Richard Payne *Knight, who, like Townley, had been a trustee of the museum. The bronzes and coins in this bequest raised the museum's collections to the highest international standing in those fields.

As the nineteenth century progressed, a new method of acquisition was increasingly practiced: excavation on behalf of the trustees. The pioneer of this method was Charles *Fellows, who had discovered the deserted site of *Xanthos in Lycia in 1838 and who offered to advise the trustees on ancient sculptures to be collected there. The Ottoman government readily gave permission for the removal of sculptures, which included the so-called Harpy Tomb and Nereid Monument. In 1846 the Ottoman government gave further permission to remove from the Castle at Bodrum (ancient *Halikarnassos) a series of marble reliefs, originally from the *Mausoleum, which had been reused to decorate the castle by the Knights of St. John in the early sixteenth century.

The arrival of the Mausoleum sculptures in London raised a great deal of interest, not least in the mind of C. T. (later, Sir Charles) *Newton, then an assistant in the Department of Antiquities. Newton's later appointment as H. M. vice-consul in Mytilene gave him many opportunities for archaeological research in places like *Miletos and *Knidos, but his greatest achievement was to lead the expedition that found the original site of the Mausoleum and brought to London many of its surviving sculptures. His assistant at the Mausoleum, Lieutenant R. Murdoch Smith, was himself fired with enthusiasm for archaeology, and in 1860–61 he was able to excavate at *Cyrene together with Commander E. A. Porcher RN. Among the finds with which they enriched the British Museum's collections were the marble cult statue of Apollo and a bronze head of a North African.

Newton meanwhile had returned to the British Museum as keeper of the new Department of Greek and Roman Antiquities. The trustees were still able to benefit from the archaeological activities of members of the consular service: George *Dennis excavated in *Sicily in 1862–63 and in Benghazi in 1866–68, and A. Biliotti explored the rich cemeteries of Kameiros (1864) and Ialysos (1868) in *Rhodes, as well as conducting supplementary excavations on the site of the Mausoleum. In 1869, after a seven-year search, John Turtle Wood at last found the site of the *Temple of Artemis at *Ephesos, where he continued to dig until 1874, further enriching the collections, especially with sculptures.

Meanwhile, the museum had not ceased to acquire private collections. Purchases included vases and bronzes excavated on the property of the Prince de *Canino (1837); a collection made in Greece and Asia Minor by Thomas Burgon (1842); several lots of Etruscan antiquities from Campanari (*Campanari family) between 1837 and 1847; a group of Etruscan sarcophagi at the Blayds Sale (1849); a collection of vases, gems and bronzes formed by two successive ducs de *Blacas, bought on the death of the second in 1867; and many objects of Italian provenance bought from Castellani (*Castellani family) between 1865 and 1884. Important bequests included the collections of Sir William Temple (1856), James Woodhouse (1866) and Sir A. Wollaston Franks (1897).

From 1894 to 1896, excavations were conducted at Amathus, *Kourion and Salamis in *Cyprus with funds bequeathed by Miss E. T. Turner, but opportunities to collect by excavation in classical lands were now diminishing. One-third of the finds from these excavations in Cyprus were deposited in the Cyprus Museum; when *Hogarth conducted further excavations at Ephesos in 1904–5, all the most important finds remained in Turkey, and only minor duplicates were sent to London. The Greek government presented a collection of over 400 objects in 1912 in exchange for a cast of the *Erechtheion Caryatid and, as late as 1923, presented some duplicates from excavations conducted by the *British School at Athens. Recently only Egypt, Bulgaria and Cyprus have permitted the acquisition of material from officially authorized excavations.

During the twentieth century acquisitions have, in general, tended to come singly or in small groups, like the gems bought at the Story Maskelyne sale at Sotheby's in 1921 and the bronzes bought at the Fouquet sale in Paris in 1922. Important acquisitions since World War II include the *Portland Vase, which had been on loan to the museum from 1811, and a bronze head found in Cyprus in 1856, long at Chatsworth and eventually acquired by the museum in 1958. In recent years the rate of acquisition has slowed down, since the policy of the trustees is not knowingly to acquire objects that they have reason to believe have been clandestinely excavated or illegally exported from their country of origin. It is occasionally possible to buy objects from old collections, like the black-figured amphora signed by Andokides as potter from the Castle Ashby sale, and to obtain interesting items from excavations, such as the painted wooden panel acquired in 1971 as part of the British share of the finds at Saqqâra. It seems likely that, in the future, the efforts of the curatorial staff will be concentrated less on acquisition and more on exhibition, interpretation and publication of this incomparable collection.

BIBLIOGRAPHY

E. Miller, *That Noble Cabinet: A History of the British Museum* (London, 1973); +B. F. Cook, *Greek and Roman Art in the British Museum* (London, 1976); +D. E. Strong, *Catalogue of Carved Amber in the Department of Greek and Roman Antiquities, British Museum* (London, 1966); +D. M. Bailey, *Catalogue of Lamps in the British Museum,* 1–3 (London, 1975, 1980, 1988); +D. B. Harden, *Catalogue of Greek and Roman Glass in the British Museum,* 1 (London, 1981); +S. E. C. Walker, *Catalogue of Roman Sarcophagi in the British Museum* (London, 1989); L. Burn, *The British Museum Book of Greek and Roman Art* (London, 1991).

B. F. COOK

BRITISH SCHOOL AT ATHENS. British institution founded in 1886, primarily to promote the study of Greek archaeology and Greek language and literature of all periods.

The centenary of the school in 1986 was marked by celebrations in Greece and Britain and by an appeal.

The school is situated in the Kolonaki district of Athens, on the lower slopes of Mt. Lykabettos, next to the *American School of Classical Studies. It is administered in Athens by a director and assistant director, who are responsible to the managing committee based in London.

The foundation of the school was the result of a "plea" by Professor R. C. Jebb in the *Fortnightly Review* in May 1883. This was followed by a meeting summoned by the Prince of Wales (later, King Edward VII), at which a committee was formed to collect funds and take practical steps to establish the school.

The first building (now the director's house) was completed in 1886, on land given by the Greek government. It was designed by F. C. *Penrose, an expert on Greek architecture, who became the school's first director (1886–87). This building provided accommodation for a director and space for a library and meetings. In 1897 a residential student hostel was built. This has since been extended several times—most recently in 1986–87 in connection with the school's centenary—mainly to accommodate the expanding library (at present about 65,000 volumes, including periodicals) and other research collections. In addition to its normal holdings, the library also includes the books of the nineteenth-century historian and philhellene George Finlay, which were bequeathed to the school. Apart from these two main buildings, a group of rooms erected by the Swedish Red Cross during World War II was subsequently (1949–50) converted into an annex to the hostel, with a staff flat (1965–66) on the upper story. A storeroom block (1958–59) has now been adapted for use as a laboratory (1973–74; see later in entry).

In 1921–22, Sir Arthur *Evans, excavator of the Minoan palace at *Knossos, offered his Villa Ariadne and estate at Knossos to the school, and the transfer was formally completed four years later. In 1952, the Villa Ariadne and estate were given by the school to the *Greek Archaeological Service, but the school retained a smaller building complex (the "Taverna") as an excavation headquarters, with hostel accommodation and a working library. A curator's house was built in 1970. In 1963–64 a research museum (not open to the public) was constructed by the school and furnished by the Greek Archaeological Service, primarily to house the copious shard material from Evans's excavations. An extension to this is now planned.

The early years of the British School at Athens were rich in archaeological discovery, with several excavations in the Aegean and on *Cyprus, including work on *Melos (Phylakopi), in *Crete, at *Sparta and Megalopolis. The investigations of Sir Arthur Evans at Knossos, although not, in fact, sponsored by the school, were first published in the school's *Annual,* and the relationship was close. Space precludes any comprehensive list, but three-quarters of a century's work at *Mycenae cannot pass unnoticed. Subsequent years have seen continued or renewed work at Knossos and other early centers of activity (Sparta, Melos, other sites on Crete) and excavation in Attika, Epiros and Macedonia, at *Perachora, on *Chios, *Ithaka and Lesbos and, more recently, Euboia (*Lefkandi), where spectacular discoveries are centered on the earliest monumental Greek building yet unearthed. The school has also occasionally been involved in work outside Greece—in Libya (Tocra) and Turkey (Old *Smyrna), as well as Cyprus.

Although excavations of all periods are perhaps the most tangible evidence of the activities of the school, they do not adequately represent their chronological or thematic range, which includes research in the language, history and literature of all periods, in aspects of geology, geography, botany, zoology, social anthropology, traditional crafts, painting and music. This approach continues the catholic tradition established by the early students.

Many of these researches ultimately find publication in the *Annual of the British School at Athens,* which has appeared continuously since the first volume (1894–95). The school also publishes a series of supplementary volumes—chiefly, but not exclusively, excavation reports.

Modern trends toward the use of scientific techniques for the elucidation of archaeological problems have been reflected in the opening (1974) of the Marc and Ismene Fitch Research Laboratory and the later additions of a petrological section (1979) and an upper story (1988) to house environmental work and reference collections. Particular interests of the staff have been the identification of local clay types (crucial for tracing the origins of ancient pottery) and the use of physical methods in archaeological prospection. The Fitch Laboratory publishes a series of occasional papers in archaeological science.

The school has played an increasingly direct educational role in recent years, with the establishment (1973) of an annual course on ancient Greek topography and archaeology for undergraduates and a similar program for schoolteachers of classical subjects.

Since 1986, bursaries endowed by the centenary appeal fund have been offered to Greek and Cypriot scholars for periods of studies in Britain. A society of Friends of the British School at Athens was established in Greece in 1987–88, and its activities extended to Britain in 1991–92.

BIBLIOGRAPHY

G. A. Macmillan, "A Short History of the British School at Athens, 1886–1911," *BSA* 17 (1910–11), ix–xxxviii; D. Powell, *The Traveller's Journey Is Done* (London, 1943); idem, *The Villa Ariadne* (London, 1943); Lady Helen Waterhouse, *The British School at Athens: The First Hundred Years* (London, 1986); E. Hogan, ed., *Anaskafes,* (n.d. [ca. 1987]).

R.L.N. BARBER

BRITISH SCHOOL AT ROME. Principal British institution in Italy for the study of archaeology, history and the fine arts.

The establishment of the British School at Rome arose from an initiative by the *British School at Athens in 1899. The first director was appointed in 1900, rooms were leased in the Palazzo Odescalchi and the school opened in 1901. It was intended to serve "as a training ground for students fresh from the Universities . . . a centre round which more mature students may group themselves . . . a source of information and advice." The first volume of *Papers of the British School at Rome* appeared in 1902.

In 1910, the commissioners of the London Exhibition of 1851 approached the school with a view to expanding its activities by providing for practicing students of architecture, painting and sculpture facilities comparable to those offered by the American, French and other foreign academies in Rome. The following year, the municipality offered the school the site then occupied by the British pavilion at the International Exhibition of Fine Art in the Valle Giulia, on condition that the much-admired façade (designed by Sir Edwin Lutyens) was preserved and that the building was used exclusively for cultural purposes. The pavilion was rebuilt in permanent materials incorporating Lutyens's façade, and the new premises opened in 1915.

Meanwhile, in 1912, a Royal Charter of Incorporation had empowered the council of the school to maintain a hostel, studios and library in Rome and to award scholarships for "the promotion of the study of Archaeology, History and Letters, Painting, Sculpture and the Allied Arts." The school consists, therefore, of the following faculties: archaeology, history and letters, architecture, painting, sculpture and printmaking. Its income is derived mostly from public funds, the British Academy acting as intermediary.

The school has had thirteen directors: G. McN. Rushforth (1901–2), H. (later, Sir Henry) Stuart *Jones (1903–5), T. *Ashby (1906–25), B. Ashmole (1925–

28), A. Hamilton Smith (1928–30 and 1932–33), I. (later, Sir Ian) A. *Richmond (1930–32), C. G. Hardie (1933–36), C. A. Ralegh Radford (1936–45), J. B. *Ward-Perkins (1945–74), D. B. Whitehouse (1974–84), G.W.W. Barker (1984–88), R. Hodges (1988–95) and A. Wallace-Hadrill (1995–   ).

Despite the distinguished work of Rushforth in S. Maria Antiqua, of Stuart Jones on the *Catalogue of Ancient Sculptures in the Municipal Collections of Rome* (1912) and of Eugènie *Strong (assistant director, 1908–25) on numerous aspects of Greek and Roman art, the first quarter-century of the school's existence was dominated by Thomas Ashby—"scholar," assistant director and director for nineteen years—who made major contributions on the ancient topography of Rome and the Roman Campagna.

Two other important aspects of the life of the school in this period were the publication of the first supplementary monographs (by T. Borenius on *The Picture Gallery of Andrea Vendramin* [1923] and by G. Barraclough on *Papal Notaries and the Papal Curia* [1934]) and the program of measured drawing and architectural reconstruction in the tradition of the École des beaux-arts. The latter resulted in a distinguished series of contributions to *PBSR*, beginning with H. C. Bradshaw's work on *Praeneste (1910) and ending with A. Minoprio's survey of the *Basilica of Maxentius (1932).

Ian Richmond had taken part in the program while a student at the school, collaborating with R. A. Cordingly in a reconstruction of the *Mausoleum of Augustus (*PBSR,* 1927) and with W. G. (later, Lord) Holford in a study of Roman *Verona. His magisterial *The City Wall of Imperial Rome* appeared in 1930, the year in which he succeeded to the directorship of the school.

The period between the departure of Richmond in 1932 and World War II saw a pause in practical archaeology. In other fields, however, distinguished results were achieved. A. D. Trendall arrived as a "scholar" in 1934, remained at the school as librarian and in 1936 published *Paestan Pottery,* the first in a series of monographs that transformed our knowledge of the pottery of Magna Graecia.

The postwar period was the age of John Ward-Perkins (1912–81). He came to the school in 1946 and occupied the directorship until retirement in 1974. Ward-Perkins was an exceptionally wide-ranging scholar whose interests and publications extended from archaeological survey (especially in south Etruria, the area north of Rome) to Roman architecture (*Etruscan and Roman Architecture,* written with Axel *Boëthius, appeared in 1970 and will remain the standard work of reference for a generation or more) and medieval archaeology.

BIBLIOGRAPHY

"A British School in Rome," *Quarterly Review* (July 1900), 183–98; British School at Rome, *Annual Report* (London, 1901–); E. Strong, "La formazione delle accademie e scuole straniere di Roma," *Capitolium* (May 1928), 94–111; T. P. Wiseman, "The First Director of the British School," *PBSR* 49 (1981), 144–63; T. P. Wiseman, *A Short History of the British School at Rome* (London, 1990).

DAVID WHITEHOUSE

BRIZIO, EDOARDO (1846–1907). Italian archaeologist, art historian and pre-historian.

Born at Turin, the versatile Brizio had a brilliant early career studying and excavating at *Pompeii and in the *Forum Romanum (Rome). In Rome he frequented the *German Archaeological Institute, where he learned the approach to Greek art history involving formal stylistic analysis espoused by H. *Brunn. He completed his training with a trip to Greece (1874).

At the age of thirty he was called to the University of Bologna to assume the chair of archaeology and numismatics. There he taught the brand of Greek art history he had learned from the Germans and became immersed in the question of the prehistoric populations of Italy, especially as related to *Bologna. He made many enemies, disagreeing with *Gozzadini about *Villanovan culture (for Brizio the Etruscans were not Villanovan but came to Italy from the east after the Villanovan period) and *Marzabotto (Brizio correctly identified the site as a town and not a necropolis); quarreling with *Zannoni about his views on finds from the Certosa; and carrying on a bitter feud with W. *Helbig, who insisted that the Etruscans came from the north, not the east.

Brizio's productivity was immense. He served as ex officio director of the Museo Civico of Bologna and conducted intensive excavation in Bologna, Marzabotto, Verucchio, Montefortino and elsewhere. More than 150 of his publications were the prompt reports he issued on his excavations.

BIBLIOGRAPHY

G. Sassatelli, ''Edoardo Brizio e la prima sistemazione dell'archeologia bolognese,'' *Dalla Stanza delle Antichità al Museo Civico* (Bologna, 1984), 381–400.

BRØNDSTED, PETER OLUF (OLE; 1780–1842). Danish archaeologist and philologist.

Born in Jutland, P. O. Brøndsted studied theology and philology at Copenhagen. After a period in Paris (1808–10), he went to Italy, where he met Otto Magnus von *Stackelberg and *Haller von Hallerstein. With them and his brother-in-law Georg Koes and the Swabian landscape painter Jacob Linckh, Brøndsted set off for a tour of Greece and Asia Minor. With Linckh and the Scot Walsingham, he conducted excavations at *Keos in the sanctuary of Apollo at Kartheia, becoming the first Dane to excavate on Greek soil. The results were described, along with his travels and other research, in his twelve-volume *Voyages dans la Grèce, accompagnes de recherches archéologiques* (Paris, 1826–30). Brøndstedt also assisted in the excavations at *Bassai, directed by Haller von Hallerstein (1812).

Brøndstedt returned to Copenhagen in 1813 to serve as professor of Greek philology at the university. In 1818, assigned as envoy from the Danish king to the papal court, he took full advantage of the opportunity to visit Southern Italy, Sicily and the Ionian islands. He also prepared at this time a monograph on the Praenestine *cista* or toilette box that had belonged to *Ficoroni (*Ficoroni Cista), issued later as *De cista aenea Praeneste reperta* (1834). He next visited England

Portrait of *Peter Oluf Brøndsted*, woodcut. (Westfälisches Landesmuseum für Kunst und Kulturgeschichte, Münster, Porträtarchiv Diepenbroick. Photo: R. Wakonigg.)

(1826) and finally settled for good in Copenhagen in 1832, becoming director of the royal cabinet of antiquities and coins and, eventually, rector of the university. Brøndsted also published translations into Danish of the plays of Aischylos and Sophokles.

He died in a fall from a horse at the age of sixty-one.

BIBLIOGRAPHY

Stark, 260–62; P.-L. Moller, "Broendsted, Peter Oluf," *NBG* 7 (1855), col. 472; *Porträtarchiv,* no. 139; A. Rathje—J. Lund, "Danes Overseas—A Short History of Danish Classical Archaeological Fieldwork," *Acta Hyperborea* 3 (1991), 18–21.

BRONEER, OSCAR THEODORE (1894–1992). Swedish American archaeologist.

Born in Bäkebo, Sweden, Oscar Broneer worked in his youth as a woodcutter. Emigrating to the United States at the age of nineteen, he soon attended college and took up the study of Greek and Latin literature and Greek archaeology. His studies led him to the *American School of Classical Studies in Athens, where he concentrated on the archaeology of *Corinth and *Isthmia. Broneer received his Ph.D. from the University of California, Berkeley, in 1932, with a dissertation on the Roman odeum at Corinth.

He spent many years of his life in Greece but also did much research and teaching in the United States, first at the Institute for Advanced Study, Princeton (1939–45), and later at the University of Chicago (1948–60). His many books and articles report on his excavations at Corinth and Isthmia, where he discovered the temple of Poseidon and its Early Archaic predecessor, as well as on his work at Amphipolis and on the *Akropolis, Athens.

A member of the *German Archaeological Institute and the Royal Swedish Academy of History and Antiquities in Stockholm, Broneer was honored by the *Archaeological Institute of America with its Gold Medal for Distinguished Archaeological Achievement in 1969. He died at Ancient Corinth at the age of ninety-seven.

BIBLIOGRAPHY

"Bibliography of Oscar Theodore Broneer," *Hesperia* 43 (1974), 393–400; E. R. Gebhard, "Oscar Theodore Broneer, 1894–1992," *AJA* 96 (1992), 543–46.

BRONZE ATHENA BY PHEIDIAS ("ATHENA PROMACHOS"). Greek colossal bronze statue of Athena, estimated to have stood between thirty and fifty feet in height, created by Pheidias and erected on the *Akropolis, Athens, ca. 455 B.C.

Often incorrectly called a *Promachos,* or *Warlike Athena,* this figure was, in fact, not striding but standing, as can be seen from representations on Roman coins (second century A.C.).

The *Athena* was still in place in the second century A.C., when Pausanias (1.28.2) reported that the tip of her spear and the crest of her helmet could be seen by sailors coming into port by way of *Sounion. Evidently, during later antiquity, the statue was moved to Constantinople (*Byzantium). Placed in the forum there, she was destroyed during a riot and fire by citizens who believed that her hand, outstretched toward the west, was beckoning to Crusaders to besiege the city.

All that survives today in Athens are part of the base and fragments of the overseers' records for the production of the statue. Covering a nine-year period, these important records from the fifth century B.C. document payments for four overseers, their secretary and a servant, as well as the purchase of copper, tin, silver, coal, firewood for the furnace, clay, hair and perhaps wax.

BIBLIOGRAPHY

W. B. Dinsmoor, "Attic Building Accounts IV: The Statue of Athena Promachos," *AJA* 25 (1921), 118–29; R.J.H. Jenkins, "The Bronze Athena at Byzantium," *JHS* 67 (1947), 31–33; A. E. Raubitschek, *Dedications from the Athenian Akropolis* (Cambridge, MA, 1949), 199–200 (no. 172); C. Mattusch, *Greek Bronze Statuary: From the Beginnings Through the Fifth Century B.C.* (Ithaca, 1988), 166–72.

CAROL MATTUSCH

BROUGHTON DE GYFFORD. See HOBHOUSE, JOHN CAM.

BROWN, FRANK EDWARD (1908–88). American classical scholar; Latinist and Roman archaeologist.

Born in LaGrange, Illinois, Frank Brown pursued his graduate studies at Yale University as a pupil of M. *Rostovtzeff. His career began with a study of the Augustan phase of the Regia in Rome, from which he removed the Fasti Capitolini, earlier thought to have adorned its walls. From 1932 to 1937 he worked at *Dura-Europos on the Euphrates, first as staff member, then for the last two seasons as director, when he was responsible for the excavation of the palace of the Dux Ripae, the Roman military commander of this stretch of the frontier, and the stratigraphic excavations of the Hellenistic levels of the Seleucid foundation.

In 1947, Brown was appointed professor in charge of the Classical School of the *American Academy in Rome and initiated excavations at *Cosa/Ansedonia, a Latin colony on the coast of central Etruria. Its exploration and publication, first the temples on the arx, then the forum and the houses, occupied Brown until his death. He also supervised the design and construction of the site museum for Cosa.

From 1952 to 1963 he was Thatcher Professor of Latin at Yale; in 1963 he returned to the American Academy and served as director from 1965 to 1969. Brown was invited by the Archaeological Superintendency at Rome to complete his work on the Regia (1964–66), where he was able to carry excavation to the earliest occupation of the site at the end of the Orientalizing period and to demonstrate a sequence of six Republican building periods. In 1979 he served the American Academy as the Jerome Lecturer, from which resulted his book *Cosa: The Making of a Roman Town* (1980).

BIBLIOGRAPHY
R. T. Scott, ''Frank Edward Brown, 1908–1988,'' *AJA* 92 (1988), 577–79.

L. RICHARDSON, JR

BRUNELLESCHI, FILIPPO (BRUNELLESCO LIPPI, FILIPPO DI SER; 1377–1446). Italian Renaissance architect.

The well-educated son of a prosperous Florentine notary, Filippo Brunelleschi began his artistic career as a goldsmith and sculptor. After losing the famous competition for the doors of the baptistery in Florence (1401; cf. *Ghiberti) Brunelleschi traveled to Rome, where he immersed himself in a study of the ancient ruins and shifted his interests from sculpture to architecture. His first major project, upon returning to Florence, was to design and superintend the completion (1420–36) of the great cupola of the Florence Cathedral, which, despite its Gothic form, betrays his interest in Roman engineering methods. The buildings with which he began the new style of Renaissance architecture—the Hospital of the Innocents (begun 1419), the Old Sacristy at San Lorenzo (1418–28), the church of San Lorenzo (begun 1419), the Pazzi Chapel at Santa Croce (begun 1429)—all show a determined effort to express the rational principles of design he had noted in the monuments of ancient and Christian Rome. Brunelleschi's close association with Florentine mathematicians and humanists (e.g., Nicolo dei *Niccoli, Paolo Toscanelli) is evidenced by his use of Euclidean geometry in preparing his plans and elevations (e.g., façade of the Hospital of the Innocents, Pazzi Chapel). For the Pazzi Chapel, he intended a pedimented temple front based, in all likelihood, upon the third-century Roman tomb of the Calventii on the Via Appia Antica. His use of pendentives in such projects as the Old Sacristy and the Pazzi Chapel may imply a knowledge of Early Christian and Byzantine forms and a familiarity with medieval examples in the Veneto or in Tuscany itself. On the other hand, Brunelleschi might have found his inspiration in two second-century tombs along the Via Nomentana north of Rome (the so-called Sedia del Diavolo and another near Casale dei Pazzi).

A stay in Rome during the early 1430s intensified his respect for Roman architecture, and Brunelleschi returned to Florence with a new appreciation for spatial manipulation and structural massing. The impact of *Hadrian's Villa at Tivoli and the *Temple of Minerva Medica is found in Brunelleschi's designs for Santa Maria degli Angeli (begun 1434), Santo Spirito (begun 1436) and the lantern and exedrae of the Florence Cathedral. In these late works, Brunelleschi abandoned his earlier planar delineation of wall surfaces and made use of plastic volumes and flowing spaces.

In his use of proportions and ratios, his understanding of the integrity of the classical orders and, finally, his recognition of the active use of wall mass, Brunelleschi shows his respect for the monuments of antiquity. Recent scholarship has stressed his debt to other sources as well, to medieval, Byzantine and, even, Islamic prototypes. It should be remembered that even if he did accept the exemplar of some postclassical buildings, he did so because he saw in them a common concern for the anthropomorphic and universal harmonies of ancient architecture. This dedication to the classical statement established Brunelleschi as the first architect of the antique revival and as the father of Renaissance art in general.

BIBLIOGRAPHY

H. Burns, "Quattrocento Architecture and the Antique: Some Problems," *Classical Influences on European Culture, A.D. 500–1500*, ed. R. Bolgar, (Cambridge, 1971), 269–87; M. Horster, "Brunelleschi und Alberti in ihrer Stellung zur römischen Antike," *MittFlor* 17 (1973), 29–64; +E. Battisti, *Filippo Brunelleschi* (Milan, 1976); C. Bozzoni—G. Carbonara, *Filippo Brunelleschi: saggio di bibliografia, 1436–1976* (Rome, 1977).

CHARLES RANDALL MACK

BRUNN, HEINRICH VON (1822–94). German archaeologist and museum director.

Born at Wörlitz, a clergyman's son, Brunn studied archaeology and philology at Bonn (1839–43) under F. G. *Welcker and F. Ritschl. His dissertation dated Greek artists before Alexander and contained two oft-cited remarks: "sine philologiae lumine caecutire archaeologiam" (without the light of philology archaeology is blind) and "in critica arte malo errare via et ratione, quam sine ratione verum invenire" (in scholarship I prefer to err rationally than to discover truth intuitively). Although a specialist in later years, Brunn always adhered to Welcker's *Totalitätsideal,* and his understanding of art was occasionally impeded by his adulation of method. From 1843 to 1853 he worked at the *German Archaeological Institute in Rome under Emil *Braun, befriended T. *Mommsen and did epigraphical fieldwork for Ritschl. In 1846 appeared his programmatic study on the Farnese *Hera* and, soon after, numerous articles. In 1853 his epoch-making *Geschichte der griechischen Künstler,* vol. 1 (2 in 1859), established the chronology for Greek art history. After three unhappy years at Bonn, he returned in early 1857 to Rome as second secretary of the institute under Henzen.

At Easter 1865, he became professor of archaeology at Munich, a post he held until his death thirty years later, and conservator of the royal coin collection. In 1888 he was made director of the *Glyptothek (his guide to its collection had appeared in 1868). In 1888 he also began, with F. Bruckmann, his influential *Denkmäler griechischer und römischer Skulptur in historischer Anordnung.* He made Munich a center of archaeological study second only to Berlin and assembled a famous collection of casts there (destroyed in 1944). Of his many students, his successor, Adolf *Furtwängler, and, ironically, Julius Langbehn, "the Rembrandt German," were his most famous. He preferred articles to books (*Kleine Schriften,* 3 vols. 1898–1906), publishing mostly stylistic studies of sculpture and vase paintings. His *Griechische Kunstgeschichte,* 2 vols. (1893–97), remains unfinished. He was the first scholar to treat Hellenistic art seriously. Brunn played a major role in changing archaeology from the ancilla of philology to an independent historical discipline. Like *Winckelmann, he never visited Greece.

BIBLIOGRAPHY

A. Flasch, *Heinrich von Brunn: Gedächtnissrede,* ed. A. Furtwängler (Munich, 1902); L. Wickert, *Theodor Mommsen: Eine Biographie,* 2, *Wanderjahre Frankreich und Italien* (Frankfurt am Main, 1964), 75–95; E. Buschor, "Heinrich Brunn," *Geist und Gestalt: Biographische Beiträge zur Geschichte der Bayerischen Akademie der Wissenschaften vornehmlich im zweiten Jahrhundert ihres Bestehens,* 1, *Geisteswissenschaften,* ed. F. Baethgen (Munich, 1959), 274–76.

                                                    WILLIAM M. CALDER III

BRUNS, GERDA (1905–70). German archaeologist.

Gerda Bruns was born in Drulingen and attended gymnasium at Göttingen. Although archaeology was considered a male pursuit, she studied classical archaeology along with Egyptology and Greek philology at Göttingen, Berlin, Vienna and Munich and in 1929 was promoted at Munich by P. Wolters, with a study on the origin of representations of Artemis. At this same time she prepared an inventory of casts of gems for the Archaeological Seminar of Heidelberg University, initiating her study of glyptics, a field in which she would later make significant contributions with her studies of Roman state cameos of the fourth century A.C. (1948) and of the onyx vase formerly in Mantua, now in the Herzog Anton Ulrich-Museum at Braunschweig (1950).

With a travel stipend, Bruns departed for Turkey (1930) to work at the *German Archaeological Institute in Istanbul on the topography and geography of Asia Minor; encouraged by *Wiegand, she participated in the excavations at *Pergamon. Returning to Germany, she took on the assignment of publishing writings left behind by her teacher Wolters on the sanctuary of the Kabeiroi at Thebes (volume 1 appeared in 1940). During this period, she held various posts at museums—at the Landesmuseum Kassel, at Braunschweig and at the Staatliche Museen at Berlin, where she eventually became keeper of the antiquities section (from 1945). She was well known for her precision in documentation of the contents of the Berlin collection and for her publications on the *Great Altar of Pergamon and on the terracottas, bronzes and luxury objects in the museum, issued as part of a series, *Kunstwerke aus den Berliner Sammlungen,* for which she served as editor (1946–49).

In spite of illness in her last years, she twice directed further excavations in the sanctuary of the Kabeiroi at Thebes. She died at Berlin in 1970.

BIBLIOGRAPHY

E. Rohde, in *Archäologenbildnisse,* 295–96.

BUCCHERO. Class of Etruscan pottery, fired in a kiln with reduced oxygen so that it is black throughout.

The earliest type, *bucchero sottile* (early seventh–early fifth centuries B.C), is a thin-walled ware usually decorated with incised designs. The later type, *bucchero pesante* (early sixth–fourth centuries B.C.), has thicker walls and is normally decorated with stamped or modeled reliefs and/or plastic ornamentation.

The term "bucchero" is derived from the Spanish "bucaro," which was first applied to a similar black pottery from Central and South America. During the nineteenth century such pre-Columbian vases were imported into Europe, where they were much admired. At this time, interest in Etruscan antiquities was intense, and the term "bucaro" (adopted in Italian as "bucchero") was easily and naturally applied to the similar Etruscan pottery. Nevertheless, some failed to understand the value of this ware, as noted by George *Dennis at *Vulci, where he saw workers under instructions to save Greek vases only, smashing bucchero pottery they had excavated.

In the twentieth century, bucchero has been studied especially by G. Camporeale, N. Ramage and T. B. Rasmussen.

BIBLIOGRAPHY

D. Lollini, s.v. "Bucchero," *EAA* 2 (1959), 203–10; M. Del Chiaro, "Etruscan Bucchero Pottery," *Archaeology* 19 (1966), 98–103; N. Ramage, "Studies in Early Etruscan Bucchero," *BSR* 38 (1970), 1–61; M. F. Briguet, in *Etruscan Life and Afterlife,* ed. L. Bonfante (Detroit, 1986), 152–55, 173.

ANN M. NICGORSKI

BUCKINGHAM, GEORGE VILLIERS, FIRST DUKE OF (1592–1628).

English statesman, favorite of James I and Charles I; collector of classical antiquities, second in England in his time only to the Earl of *Arundel; one of the first to bring the classical world to the aristocracy of England.

In the autumn of 1624, Buckingham started collecting classical antiquities by asking Sir Thomas *Roe, ambassador to the Ottoman Empire, to buy classical objects for him. In 1625–26, Roe's intermediaries were sent to Greece and to the western coast of Turkey, especially Ankyra and Proussa. The few heads and reliefs they sent back were rejected by the duke, who observed that he was not "courting . . . [antiquity] in a deformed or misshapen stone." A new, unnamed agent sent to Roe in 1627 a "few good statues," which were accepted by Buckingham.

Meanwhile, Roe tried unsuccessfully to obtain six reliefs from the Golden Gate in *Constantinople. To do this, he bribed a Turkish Imam with £500 to renounce the reliefs as sacrilege to the laws of Islam, so that he could buy them at a low price. But the nearby Turkish garrison was superstitious about the reliefs and threatened to kill anyone who tried to remove them.

During the same period, Balthazar Gerbier and Michel Lebond, the duke's collectors in Europe, were much more successful. They may be credited with gathering most of the duke's ancient collection, including the items acquired from Peter Paul *Rubens. This collection, the largest bought by Buckingham, was purchased for 100,000 florins. The duke himself had started negotiations with Rubens in 1625, and Gerbier finished the transactions in 1626–27. Although the collection contained many different kinds of items (including paintings by Rubens), the majority of the antiquities were gems and statues. Rubens reserved some of his favorite gems from the sale, but the duke received, among others, a cornelian with *Apollo and Marsyas* and cameos of *The Three Graces,* a *Hermaphrodite in a Lionskin,* a bust of *Julia* and two heads of *Alexander the Great.* Many of Buckingham's stones are today in the Bibliothèque Nationale, Paris. Most of the statues had been bought earlier by Rubens from Sir Dudley Carleton, who gathered them in Italy in 1615–16. Among these were portraits of *Drusus Major, Caesar* and *Brutus* and a figure of *Bacchus.*

The duke did not enjoy his collection for long; immensely unpopular, he was assassinated in 1628. The collection was left to his infant son, the second duke of Buckingham. Twenty years later, when the heir fled into exile with the royal court, the new government seized all he left behind. At this time, most of the collection was scattered, including the statues. The duke carried the gems to the Continent, selling most of them in Antwerp in 1649. After the restoration of the monarchy in 1660, he was able to regain some of his collection; but it was permanently dissolved in 1687, when the duke died without heirs.

BIBLIOGRAPHY

+M. van der Meulen, *Petrus Pavlus Rubens Antiquarius, Collector and Copyist of Antique Gems* (Alphen aan den Rijn, 1975), 26 and passim; R. Lockyer, *Buckingham: The Life and Political Career of George Villiers, First Duke of Buckingham, 1592–1628* (London, 1981); +D. Howarth, *Lord Arundel and His Circle* (New Haven, CT, 1985); +J. Muller, *Rubens: The Artist as Collector* (Princeton, NJ, 1989).

PHILIP J. TRAINA

BUDAPEST, FINE ARTS MUSEUM (SZÉPMÜVÉSZETI MÚZEUM). Museum of Hungary with the most significant collection of Greek, Roman and Etruscan antiquities.

Created by a resolution of the Hungarian Parliament in 1896, the Szépmü-vészeti Múzeum opened its doors in 1906 in a building on the Pest side of the city, featuring a neoclassical façade adorned with a pediment copied from the *Temple of Zeus at Olympia. At first, among all the works of art from different periods in the museum, there were only plaster casts of ancient sculpture and no original antiquities. In 1908 a major acquisition was made of 135 antique marble statues from the collection of the Munich archaeologist Paul *Arndt. Five years later, 650 terracotta items from the same collection were bought for the museum.

For a long time, the collection contained only these Greek and Roman sculptures. Then a law enacted in 1934 stipulated that the Budapest museum should be the repository of all classical antiquities in Hungary that were discovered outside the boundaries of the country. Works excavated in Hungary were allowed to be placed in museums near the site, as in the case of the Museum of *Aquincum, in Budapest itself. Another exception occurred in the case of the Déri Múzeum at Debrecen, which was created to hold the large and diverse collection amassed by Frigyes Déri (1852–1924), with materials ranging through many periods and locations in Europe and Asia.

As a result of the law, a large number of pieces, some 4,000 in all, are now displayed in the Department of Graeco-Roman Antiquities. These include Greek vases (there are vases painted by Exekias and the Andokides Painter), bronzes, jewelry and objects of daily life. One of the most important pieces in the Roman collection is a relief sculpture from the period of Augustus, showing *The Battle of Actium.*

BIBLIOGRAPHY

G. S. Reed, "Fine Arts Museum, Budapest," *Art Museums of the World,* ed. V. Jackson (New York, 1987), I, 473–83; J. G. Szilágyi, *Corpus Speculorum Etruscorum, Hongrie-Tchécoslovaquie* (Rome, 1992), 13–15.

BUDÉ (BUDAEUS), GUILLAUME (1467–1540). French diplomat, royal librarian and classical scholar.

Budé was the main stimulus for the revived study of Greek in France. He was a favored civil servant of Francis I (1515–47) and proposed to him the creation of a college for the study of Greek, Latin and Hebrew that would be more progressive than the University of Paris; this Collegium Trilinguae, founded in 1530, became the Collège de France, still the leading research academy in France. As the first royal librarian, Budé assembled a collection of manuscripts at Fontainebleau, which was moved to Paris and formed the nucleus of the Bibliothèque Nationale. His name also survives in the Association Guillaume Budé, which publishes the "Budé" Greek and Latin texts, with facing translations.

As a scholar, he achieved most fame with his *Libri V de Asse et partibus eius* (1514), a treatise on ancient coins and measures, in which archaeological data played a part. His *Commentarii linguae Graecae* (1529) collected many lexicographic notes, and his *Annotationes in XXIV libros Pandectarum* (1508) advanced the study of Roman law. He corresponded widely with such personages as Thomas More and *Erasmus, who called him "le prodige de la France." Budé's works were collected after his death (4 vols., Basel, 1557).

BIBLIOGRAPHY

G. Rebitté, *G. Budé* (Paris, 1846), E. de Budé, *Vie de G. Budé* (Paris, 1884).

MORTIMER CHAMBERS

BUFALO, DEL (BUFALI) FAMILY. Family in Rome known for its collections of antiquities.

The earliest pieces acquired were brought together by ANGELO BUFALO in the fifteenth century. There were numerous inscriptions in the Bufalo house in Rione Colonna, which was inhabited by ANTONIO, while a second house in Rione Trevi housed a *Hercules* and a puteal (well-head) with sculptured decoration. STEFANO DEL BUFALO expanded the collection, and his "statue-garden" became quite famous. Moreover, his palace was adorned with frescoes by Polidoro that were related to ancient sculptures. *Aldrovandi's report on the collection covers no less than four pages and is not even exhaustive; a drawing by *Dosio depicts an additional three statues.

In 1562, PAOLO DEL BUFALO sold off ten pieces, of which six sculptures (including the puteal and the famous *Atlas* now in Naples) went to Alessandro Farnese (see *Farnese family). Cardinal Hippolytus of Ferrara purchased eleven sculptures in 1572 (of which several were acquired by Ferdinand de' Medici (*Medici family). Pierre *Jacques studied the collection, and a drawing of a relief with *Graces* appears in the Codex Pighianus (*Pighius). Achilles Statius illustrated three herms from the collection in his *Illustrium virorum . . . vultus* (1569).

BIBLIOGRAPHY

R. Lanciani, *Storia degli scavi* 1 (1902), 104–5; 3 (1907), 193; P. G. Hübner, *Le Statue di Roma* 1: *Quellen und Sammlungen* (Leipzig, 1912), 83–84; C. Hulsen, "*Le statue di Roma* von P. G. Hübner," *GGA* 176.5 (1914), 289–90; H. Wrede, *Der Antikengarten der del Bufalo bei der Fontana Trevi, Trierer Winckelmannsprogramm* 4 (1982).

MARJON VAN DER MEULEN

BULWER-LYTTON, EDWARD GEORGE EARLE, FIRST BARON LYTTON (1803–73). Victorian politician (Colonial Secretary, 1858–59), popular historian (*Athens, Its Rise and Fall,* 1836), sub-Byronic poet and prolific novelist and playwright.

Bulwer-Lytton's best-selling historical novel, *The Last Days of Pompeii* (1834), was dedicated to Sir William *Gell, whose *Pompeiana* (1817–32) guaranteed a market for this stilted melodrama. Though set in a Roman context of

Portrait of *Filippo Buonarroti*, bronze medal, 1731. London, British Museum. (The Warburg Institute, University of London.)

the first century A.C., "which the visitor . . . sees at this day," *Last Days* celebrates the virtues of its Greek hero and heroine. The local archaeological detail complements the classical paintings of *Alma-Tadema and does not compensate for the lack of historical imagination; Bulwer-Lytton's characters are "Englishmen in fancy dress" (Jenkyns).

BIBLIOGRAPHY
A. Christensen, *Edward Bulwer-Lytton: The Fiction of New Regions* (Georgia, 1978); R. Jenkyns, *The Victorians and Ancient Greece* (Oxford, 1980), 82–85, 316–18.

DAVID RIDGWAY

BUONARROTI, FILIPPO (1661–1733). Italian archaeologist, specialist in Etruscan studies.

A native of Florence and a descendant of *Michelangelo, Buonarroti was formed in the antiquarian atmosphere of Rome in the second half of the seventeenth century, under the influence of the brand of research and publication of *Bellori and *Bartoli. Appointed secretary and keeper of the museum and library of the Vice Cardinal Gaspare Carpegna, he issued a volume on the coins of the collection (1698); his interest in inscriptions was stimulated by his close association with the epigraphist R. *Fabretti. He made frequent excursions into the countryside in search of antiquities and had the opportunity to conduct an excavation in Etruscan tombs at Civita Castellana.

Returning to Florence in 1700, Buonarroti was entrusted with the family collection of antiquities, to which he added Etruscan antiquities that were given to him, including an entire set of Hellenistic urns found at Poggio a Moro near *Chiusi. He took on public offices, including that of senator, at the behest of Grand Duke Cosimo III and no longer had opportunity for wide-ranging explorations. He continued to publish on archaeological topics, his most notable and enduring effort being his annotation of the *De Etruria regali* of Thomas *Dempster, published by Sir Thomas Coke (1723–26) and dedicated to Cosimo III. The Dempster text, written approximately one hundred years earlier and largely from a philological point of view, was considerably enriched by the archaeological commentary of Buonarroti and the ninety-three engraved plates prepared by Coke; it enjoyed a sensational success and was an important factor in the passion for Etruscan archaeology that developed in the eighteenth century (*Etruscheria).

BIBLIOGRAPHY

M. Cristofani, *La Scoperta degli etruschi, Archeologia e antiquaria nel '700* (Rome, 1983), 23–36; D. Gallo, ed., *Filippo Buonarroti e la cultura antiquaria sotto gli ultimi Medici,* catalog of exhibition (Florence, 1986); *Les Étrusques et l'Europe*, catalog of exhibition (Paris, 1992), 284–85, 382.

BUONDELMONTI (BONDALMONTI), CRISTOFORO (ca. 1390–post-1423). Traveler, cartographer, member of an eminent Florentine family.

Buondelmonti was born in Florence, ca. 1390; the date of his death is unknown, but he was still alive in *Rhodes in 1423. No contemporary sources mention him, and the following facts are known only from his own statements.

He left Florence before 1410 and went to Rhodes to study Greek, reaching the island ca. 1414. While there, he took Holy Orders. From Rhodes, he traveled to *Crete, the Greek islands and Constantinople (*Byzantium), staying at length in Crete and Constantinople. During his travels, he made descriptions and maps and collected codices, some of which are preserved in the Biblioteca Medicea-Laurenziana in Florence.

Reflecting his travels to Crete in 1415 and 1416, he wrote his *Descriptio insulae Candiae* in 1417, dedicating it to Nicolo dei *Niccoli. He made an abridged edition in 1422. Of prime importance was his *Liber insularum archipelagi,* dedicated to Cardinal Giordano Orsini in 1420 (presumably, this was a second, enlarged edition since he had previously sent Orsini a shorter manuscript). This enlarged manuscript is lost, but he made an abridgment of it, again in 1422. Many redactions, abridgments, excerpts, even translations into Italian and Greek of this manuscript are preserved in Italian libraries (Rome: Biblioteca Apostolica Vaticana; Florence: Biblioteca Medicea-Laurenziana, Biblioteca Nazionale Centrale, Biblioteca Riccardiana; Venice: Biblioteca Nazionale Marciana; Ravenna: Biblioteca Comunale; Padua: University Library; Milan: Biblioteca Ambrosiana; Genoa: Ansaldo Collection; Naples: Biblioteca Nationale; Palermo: Biblioteca Nazionale) and other countries (Paris: Bibliothèque Nationale; London: *British Museum, Holkham Hall; Marburg: Westdeutsche Bibliothek; Madrid: Escorial; Vienna-Lainz: Jesuit Residenz; Istanbul: Sérail

Library; Athens: Gennadius Library). The earliest views or maps of Constantinople appear in numerous fifteenth-century copies of this codex. No complete catalog or comparative study of these manuscripts exists.

Characteristic of Buondelmonti's approach was his interest in monuments. Among the artistic conventions animating his maps of cities and islands are turreted walls, schematic temples, churches, monasteries and broken columns implying antique ruins.

Buondelmonti was the founder of Renaissance cartography and the first archaeological traveler—the first voyager known to have both described and recorded ancient monuments.

BIBLIOGRAPHY

E. Jacobs, "Cristoforo Buondelmonti, Ein Beitrag zur Kenntnis seines Lebens und seiner Schriften," *Beträge zur Bücherkunde und Philologie August Wilmanns zum 25. Marz 1903 gewidmet* (Leipzig, 1903), 313–40; +G. Gerola, "Le vedute di Costantinopoli di Cristoforo Buondelmonti," *Studi Bizantini e Neoellenici* 3 (1931), 249–79; +R. Almagià, *Planisferi, carte nautiche e affini dal secolo XIV al XVIII esistenti nella Biblioteca Apostolica Vaticana, Monumenta Cartographica Vaticana,* 1 (Vatican City, 1944), 105–17; P. W. Lehmann, "Theodosius or Justinian? A Renaissance Drawing of a Byzantine Rider," *ArtB* 41 (1959), nn. 7, 84–87, 91.

PHYLLIS WILLIAMS LEHMANN

BUSCHOR, ERNST (1886–1961). German archaeologist and art historian.

Born at Hürben bei Krumbach of humble parentage, Buschor was won for archaeology at Munich in 1907 by Adolf *Furtwängler, on whose career he modeled his own. He wrote his dissertation under Paul Wolters (1912). After military service and a year (1919) at Erlangen, he became professor of archaeology at Freiburg and (1921) first secretary of the reopened *German Archaeological Institute at Athens. He was professor (*Ordinarius*) at Munich (1929–59). From 1925 to 1961 he was director of the German excavations at *Samos. He wrote numerous pioneer works on Archaic Greek art, the finds at Samos, vase painting, the ''Severe style'' and ancient portraiture. He considered his greatest effort his translation into German of the tragedies of Aischylos, Sophokles and Euripides. His genius and charisma are repeatedly attested.

The subjectivity of his interpretation, his often inscrutable language, his influence and his cooperation with National Socialism make him the most controversial figure in the recent history of the discipline. An honest biography is desperately needed.

BIBLIOGRAPHY

E. Buschor, *Von griechischer Kunst: Ausgewählte Schriften,* ed. Franz Willemsen, 2nd ed. (Munich, 1963), 233–37 (incomplete bibl.); E. Homann-Wedeking, *Gnomon* 38 (1966), 221–24 (with portrait but often inaccurate). W. Schindler, "Ernst Buschor," in Briggs—Calder, 13–16.

WILLIAM M. CALDER III

BUSOLT, GEORG (1850–1920). German historian of ancient Greece.

Born in the small East Prussian village Mühle Keppurren and trained at the

Albertus-University, Königsberg, Busolt was professor of ancient history at the universities of Kiel (1879–97) and Göttingen (1897–1920). His major works are two monumental handbooks. His *Griechische Geschichte* (2nd ed., 3 vols. in 4, 1893–1904) narrates Greek history to 404 B.C. (it was planned to reach 338 B.C.), with stupendously full citations of all sources, ancient and modern. For the prehistoric era he carefully studied the results of excavations; progress has made this part of his work obsolete, but for the period ca. 700–404 B.C., it remains indispensable. His *Griechische Staatskunde* (2 vols., 1920–26; vol. 2, ed. by H. Swoboda) is an equally colossal encyclopedia of Greek constitutional practices. Busolt was not the most original of historians, but his accuracy, mastery of detail and sober judgment assure that scholars will continue to use his books above and beyond any others of their kind.

BIBLIOGRAPHY

H. Degener, *Wer Ist's,* ed. 8 (Leipzig, 1922), 217; C. Krollmann, ed., *Altpreussische Biographie,* 1 (Königsberg, 1941), 97; K. Jordan, in *Geschichte der Christian-Albrechts-Universität Kiel 1665–1965,* vol. 5, Part 2 (Neumünster, 1969), 68; M. Chambers, *Georg Busolt, His Life in His Letters, Mnemosyne* Suppl. 112 (1990).

MORTIMER CHAMBERS

BYRES, JAMES (1734–1817). Scottish architect, antiquarian and guide, known for securing copies of Etruscan tomb paintings at an early date.

The son of a Jacobite exile, James Byres went to Rome from France in 1756 to study painting (under Rafael *Mengs) and architecture. Between 1764 and 1792, he combined the profession of leading cicerone to the visiting nobility with dealings in antiquities and art. Edward *Gibbon recalled that his guide in Rome had been ''Mr. Byres, a Scotch antiquary of experience and taste; but, in the daily labour of eighteen weeks, the powers of attention were sometimes fatigued.'' A lesser patron regarded what seems to have been Byres's ''regular course'' of six weeks at three hours per day as sufficient ''to visit all the churches, palaces, villas, and ruins worth seeing, in or near Rome.'' As a dealer, Byres's clients included Sir William *Hamilton, to whom he sold the *Portland Vase ca. 1780, and the Duke of Rutland, for whom he acquired and exported Poussin's *Seven Sacraments* in 1785—a necessarily discreet transaction that ranks as one of the major coups of eighteenth-century art dealing.

At an early stage in his antiquarian career, Byres conceived the project of publishing an account of the Etruscan antiquities at Corneto (*Tarquinia), accompanied by engraved illustrations of the antiquities themselves. Considerable interest had followed the excavations conducted at Corneto in 1761 by Thomas *Jenkins, the first Englishman to visit the painted tombs and Byres's principal rival in ''the guidance of the taste and expenditures of our English cavaliers.'' Both *Piranesi and *Winckelmann were aware of Byres's plan, and by 1766 he had commissioned his associate Christopher Norton to engrave the plates. As it turned out, Byres did not succeed in attracting the subscribers necessary to achieve publication. The plates alone were finally edited by Frank Howard under

Portrait of *James Byres*
by A. von Maron,
Rome, Accademia di S.
Luca, 1791. (Deutsches
Archäologisches Insti-
tut, Rome. Inst. Neg.
66.752.)

the title *Hypogaei, or Sepulchral Caverns of Tarquinia, the Capital of Antient Etruria* in 1842—the year in which George *Dennis made the first of several visits to Etruria with a view to "supplying the deficiencies" of Mrs. Hamilton Gray's *Tour to the Sepulchres of Etruria in 1839* (1840: one result of the *Campanari family's 1837 Etruscan exhibition in London).

Hypogaei is an important source of information and has been used extensively by students of Etruscan painting from F. *Weege onward. Of the tombs illustrated, three (Biclinio, Ceisinie and Tappezzeria) are otherwise unknown, and two (Cardinale and Mercareccia) have been badly damaged since the eighteenth century.

Witold Dobrowolski established in 1978 that the drawings used by Norton to engrave the plates were executed by a young Polish painter, Franciszek Smu-glewicz, who also seems to have obtained various portrait commissions through Byres's good offices. Byres's own part in the enterprise thus emerges as that of the impresario. There is no proof that he ever completed the text intended to accompany the illustrations; the surviving notes indicate that he would have treated the ancient state of Italy in its Mediterranean setting. This startlingly modern approach to the Etruscans may have prompted Byres's 1766 tour of *Sicily and Malta, regions seldom penetrated by his compatriots and clients on the *Grand Tour.

BIBLIOGRAPHY

B. Skinner, *Scots in Italy in the 18th Century* (Edinburgh, 1966); +H. Möbius, "Zeich-nungen etruskischer Kammergräber und Einzelfunde von James Byres," *RM* 73–4 (1966–67), 53–71; +B. Ford, "James Byres, Principal Antiquarian for the English Visitors to Rome," *Apollo* (June 1974), 446–61; +W. Dobrowolski, "The Drawings of Etruscan Tombs by Franciszek Smuglewicz and His Cooperation with James Byres," *Bulletin du Musée National de Varsovie* 19 (1978), 97–119; D. Ridgway, "James Byres and the Ancient State of Italy," *Atti II Congresso Internazionale Etrusco, Firenze 1985* (1989), I, 213–29.

DAVID RIDGWAY

BYRON, GEORGE GORDON, SIXTH BARON (1788–1824). English Romantic poet, whose early passion for history and classical antiquity culminated in his desire to preserve Greece's ancient relics and restore its liberty.

Inspired by his Celtic ancestry during turbulent years at Harrow and Cambridge, Lord Byron was also well versed in Homer, Plato and Thucydides and contemporary travelers and scholars such as *Leake, *Gell and *Gibbon. In 1809 the poet journeyed to Greece and Turkey, where he spent nearly two years exploring ancient sites, including Athens, *Marathon, *Sounion, *Salamis, *Olympia and the Troad (*Troy). Although he did not keep an accurate record of his travels, through his letters and poetry, Byron described the spirit, if not the archaeological remains, of the sites. He was prone to a dashing Romantic response to Greek antiquity (like Leander, he swam the Hellespont at *Abydos), but at times his letters from Greece have a surprisingly flippant, slightly cynical tone. Other evidence for his travels is provided by his companion, John Cam *Hobhouse, who kept a journal of their trip, *A Journey Through Albania and Other Provinces of Turkey,* which recorded many of the gravestones, columns and bits of architecture that Byron alluded to in his poetry.

In one of his more notable Greek poems, *Childe Harold's Pilgrimage,* Canto 2, he described Marathon as the "vanished Hero's lofty mount," preserved only as a "rifled urn." By the time he visited the mound, it had been violated by *Fauvel and Lord *Elgin's sailors, who had dug there looking for pottery. Byron specifically denounced Elgin for his removal of the *Parthenon sculptures, calling him a "dull spoiler" who "tore down those remnants with a Harpy's hand." An acquaintance of Byron, Lord Sligo, noted, "Relics of ancient art only appealed to Byron's imagination among their original and natural surroundings. For collections and collectors he had a contempt that was unreservedly expressed." The poet himself, however, is criticized for carving his name on a column on the temple of Poseidon at Sounion and transporting marbles and skulls from sarcophagi to England.

Byron was particularly interested in topography and its relationship with archaeological remains. Near Troy he saw the "tombs of her destroyers," "large mounds of earth like the barrows of the Danes." Often he would wander across the Athenian *Akropolis for hours, composing verses replete with his love for the land and his concern for its current plight. While staying in Athens, he had the pleasure of using the *Monument of Lysikrates as his scriptorium.

Byron left Greece in 1811, but he returned in 1823 as an agent on the London Committee for Greek Independence, charged with forwarding supplies and money to the philhellenic partisans in the war against the Turks. Although the liberation of the Greeks had concerned him since his first trip to Greece, he had not taken an active role in the struggle until, in exile from England and tired of Italy, he sought adventure and a heroic, soldier's death. The English poet was accepted by the Greeks for his worldly manners, literary fame and, most important, his money. But as a soldier Byron did not have any great success and was always torn among various internal factions.

Byron can be regarded as a sincere philhellene whose primary love for the ancient glory of the Greeks made him a prominent figure in the Greek democratic restoration. His death on 19 April 1824 caused great astonishment and grief throughout Greece. His place in Greek history and the devotion of the people to him are marked by a statue of the poet that now graces central Athens.
BIBLIOGRAPHY
H. Spender, *Byron and Greece* (London, 1924); H. Nicolson, *Byron, The Last Journey* (London, 1948); P. G. Trueblood, ed., *Byron's Political and Cultural Influence in Nineteenth-Century Europe* (Atlantic Highlands, NJ, 1981).

ANNE J. LYONS

BYZANTIUM (CONSTANTINOPLE; ISTANBUL), Turkey. City in northwest Turkey, site of a Greek settlement and later a Roman city; capital of the Eastern Roman (Byzantine) Empire.

The settlement was founded as Byzantium by Greeks from Megara sometime in the seventh century B.C. The strategic location on a height overlooking the straits of the Bosporus, at the mouth of the Black Sea and between Europe and Asia, was coveted by the Persians (they held Byzantium in the late sixth and early fifth centuries B.C.), Philip II of Macedon (he besieged it in 340–339 B.C.) and Roman emperors. Septimius Severus nearly destroyed the city after a two-year siege against his rival Pescennius Niger but then undertook its reconstruction. Constantine realized the enormous potential of the location when he defeated Licinius in a land battle near Byzantium (A.D. 324) and chose the site both as a seat of government and as a kind of victory monument. Calling the city "New Rome," he celebrated its founding in 330. Soon afterward it came to be called Constantinople.

Relatively little of the Greek or Roman city survives. Spread out over seven hills, like Rome, the ancient remains lie under the modern Turkish city of Istanbul, making it impossible to recover the town plan of the Greek, Roman or Constantinian city. The most conspicuous ancient monuments are of the Late Antique/Early Byzantine phase. Septimius Severus began the famed Hippodrome, which was enlarged and finished by Constantine. An aqueduct of the time of Valens (364–78), the obelisk base of Theodosius I (379–95) in the

Hippodrome and the massive fortification walls of Theodosius II (408–50) are the most impressive ancient remains. From the period of Constantine survives the great porphyry column, taken from Delphi and placed in the forum, which once supported a statue of Constantine in the guise of Apollo.

Most important for the study of ancient monuments was the practice of Constantine of bringing great works of art from Rome and other cities to adorn the new capital. In the Hippodrome were sixty statues brought from Rome, including one of Augustus, as well as a four-horse chariot, which had perhaps come from Chios or may be derived from a group made by Lysippos and dedicated at Delphi in the fourth century B.C. (the horses are now in Venice; *Horses of San Marco). Certainly from Delphi was the famous "Serpent Column" (still today in the Hippodrome), the bronze tripod monument dedicated in 479 B.C. by the Greek victors of Plataia. The three serpents may have had their heads as late as ca. 1682, when they were illustrated by George *Wheler, but by 1700 they were removed, reportedly by Polish ambassadors at Constantinople.

Statues were procured for Constantinople from many other cities—Nikomedia, Nikopolis, Caesarea, *Sardis, Tralles, Tyana, *Antioch, *Smyrna. From the *Temple of Artemis at Ephesos came a bronze door adorned with panels showing the *Battle of Gods and Giants,* reused as a door to the Senate House. Outside the Senate was placed a colossal *Bronze *Athena,* possibly the statue by Pheidias from the *Akropolis in Athens. The great gold and ivory *Zeus of Olympia by Pheidias was taken to Constantinople after the closing of the Olympic Games in 394. It was placed in the palace of Lausus, a retainer of Theodosius I, along with the Lindian *Athena* of Skyllis and Dipoinos, the *Knidian *Aphrodite* of Praxiteles, the Samian *Hera* of Lysippos and Bupalos, and the *Opportunity* by Lysippos.

Unfortunately, the palace of Lausus was burned down in 475, and all the statuary was destroyed. Such conflagrations were frequent in the hectic political climate of Constantinople in the fifth and sixth centuries. The city has also suffered periodically from earthquakes. But the worst destruction wrought on the treasures of Constantinople came in 1204, when warriors of the Fourth Crusade from the Latin West got sidetracked from their mission to the Holy Land and became embroiled in Byzantine politics. In support of an exiled candidate for the throne, they sacked the city with a plundering fury scarcely seen before or since. Bronzes were melted down or carried away; it was then that the *Horses* of San Marco were taken to Venice (along with the porphyry relief group of the *Tetrarchs,* third century A.C.; still attached to the south side of San Marco). Treasuries were plundered for their jewels, gems and precious metals; it has been conjectured that the *Gemma Tiberiana may have gone west at this time. The Bronze *Athena* was a casualty of the conflict, although she actually fell while the invaders were still in the harbor, destroyed by a mob that thought the statue seemed to be beckoning to the army to enter the city.

The Greek historian Nicetas Choniates (ca. 1150–1213) later wrote a lament, *De signis,* describing eighteen of the sculptures that had been damaged or destroyed. They included the colossal *Seated Herakles* by Lysippos (which was "thrown over" by the invaders), a *Bellerophon and Pegasos,* a *Helen,* a group of *Paris Giving the Apple to Aphrodite* and an *Eagle Killing a Serpent,* set up by Apollonios of Tyana to frighten snakes away from Constantinople. The presence of such pagan statuary in the city was justified in various ways in the Middle Ages. A popular explanation was that the images were brought to the city by Constantine to show the follies of pre-Christian religion. Sometimes the works were explained as allegorical; at other times ancient identifications were changed outright into Christian ones (e.g., in the case of an equestrian statue of *Bellerophon* that came to be called *"Joshua"*). Often, ancient statuary was seen through a mist of superstition that gave magic powers to the images. A statue of Aphrodite was supposed to provide a test of the virginity of a female viewer, who, if impure, would experience her skirts flying up to expose her.

*Ciriaco of Ancona visited Constantinople, as did *Buondelmonti, who reported his observations in his *Liber insularum archipelagi* (1420); some codices include a plan of the city, but these are not consistent with each other. By the fifteenth century, much had vanished from Constantinople, and the Byzantine humanist scholar Manuel Chrysoloras commented on how many pedestals with inscriptions, but without statuary, remained. He noted the presence of reliefs on the Golden Gate of Theodosius I, representing the *Labors of Herakles* and the *Punishment of Prometheus.* These were still in evidence in the seventeenth century, when *Arundel's agents, Thomas *Roe and William Petty, sought vainly to secure them. By 1795 they had disappeared.

After the Turkish conquest of Constantinople in 1453, pilgrims, ambassadors and other visitors continued to come to the city for periods of varying length. P. Gyllius (1490–1555) discussed the antiquities of the city in his *De topographia Constantinopoleos et de illius antiquitatibus* (Lyons, 1561), noting, among other things, that the *Herakles* of Lysippos was still to be seen. Drawings of the city and its monuments were made by various artists, of whom perhaps most notable was the Dutch artist Melchior Lorichs, who produced a panorama of the city and drawings of the obelisk base of Theodosius and of the base of the column of Constantine. *Spon and Wheler also wrote accounts of their visit in the seventeenth century. Roe, *Choiseul-Gouffier, *Nointel and *Elgin all served in ambassadorial positions from which they were able to pursue their interest in antiquities in Constantinople and in other parts of the ancient Greek world.

The Istanbul Museum of Antiquities, containing finds from Constantinople as well as other sites in Turkey, began as a collection of works of art assembled by Fethi Ahmed Pasha in the mid-nineteenth century and soon was known as the "Imperial Museum." In 1881, Osman Hambi-Bey became director of the museum and oversaw its emergence as an archaeological collection of significance, with the acquisition of the well-known Phoenician and Greek sarcophagi discovered in 1887 in Sidon (especially the "Alexander Sarcophagus"). He also initiated legislation that made antiquities found in Turkey the property of the state, being therefore illegal to export. New space was added to the Museum of Antiquities, so that 4,500 m² were available for the displays. A catalog covering the classical sculptures was compiled by G. Mendel, *Catalogue des sculptures grecques, romaines et byzantines,* 1–3 (1912–14).

In the twentieth century there have been several campaigns of investigations in the Hippodrome. Excavations made by E. Mamboury and T. *Wiegand in 1918 and S. Casson in 1927 showed the plan of the curved end of the stadium and suggested that the entire Hippodrome measured ca. 450 feet in length. In the years 1948 to 1951, during construction for the Palace of Justice in Istanbul, parts of the vaulted substructure of the Hippodrome from the period of Septimius Severus were discovered.

BIBLIOGRAPHY

C. Mango, ''Antique Statuary and the Byzantine Beholder,'' *DOP* 17 (1963), 53–76; W. MacDonald, s.v. ''Byzantium,'' *PECS,* 177–79; G. Becatti, s.v. ''Costantinopoli,'' *EAA* 2 (1959), 880–919; Stoneman, *Land of Lost Gods,* 1–18.

C

CAFFI, IPPOLITO (1809–66). Italian landscape painter.

Born at Belluno in the Veneto, Caffi was a precocious draftsman. At age twelve he was apprenticed to two local artists; by age sixteen (1825) he was working with Pietro Paoletti at Padua. Between 1827 and 1829 he studied in Venice and in 1835 published a useful guide to perspective rendering, *Lezioni di prospettiva pratica.*

Caffi traveled a great deal in Italy, Europe and the Near East. His numerous paintings of the famous monuments of Athens, *Constantinople, Egypt and, especially, Rome are valuable documents that capture the sites they portray with accuracy and a dramatic sensitivity to light. He is one of the last great painters to produce cityscapes in the tradition of van *Wittel and Canaletto, but with a vibrant impressionism. His magnificent views of Rome, now mostly in the Museo di Roma and the Ca' Pesaro, provide a vivid record of the city's appearance in the last century.

BIBLIOGRAPHY

M. Pittaluga, *Il Pittore Ippolito Caffi* (Venice, 1971); G. Perocco, *Ippolito Caffi 1809–1866* (Venice, 1979).

RICHARD DANIEL DE PUMA

CALENDAR OF 354 (CALENDAR OF FILOCALUS). A richly illustrated pagan calendar, designed for a codex for use in Rome in A.D. 354, now known only in copies.

The scribe Furius Dionysius Filocalus signed his name on the title page but is otherwise famous for his inscribed epigrams for the tombs of martyrs, commissioned by Pope Damasus (366–84). The calendar is the earliest and only known work of Filocalus in the codex medium. Moreover, it is the earliest-dated codex with full-page illustrations, as well as the only codex manuscript that can be securely dated to the fourth century. It is indeed unfortunate that the original fourth-century codex is lost, as is its Carolingian copy, last seen and described in a letter of 1620 by the French antiquarian *Peiresc. This Carolingian manuscript has several Renaissance copies, however, and the best of these, executed under Peiresc's supervision, was sent to Cardinal Girolamo *Aleandro in Rome and is now in the Vatican Library (Barb. lat. 2154). A copy was evidently known to P. P. *Rubens as well.

The numerous copies of the calendar attest to the widespread interest in it. Several editions were published during the Renaissance and seventeenth century, the most noteworthy being those by I. Cuspianus (1473–1529), Aegidius Bucherius (1634) and Henschenius (1675). T. *Mommsen was the first modern scholar to collate all the copies and to re-create the contents of the lost fourth-century original. J. *Strzygowski was the first to study and publish all the illustrations.

The calendar, with the representations of each month on the page facing its corresponding text of pagan holidays, formed the nucleus of the original codex; each month is illustrated by a full-page drawing of a single figure surrounded by appropriate attributes, alluding either to seasonal activities, such as a hunter for October, or to pagan celebrations, such as a tonsured priest of Isis for November. In addition to these, there are illustrations of the astrological signs of the planets, personifications of four great cities of the empire and portraits of the consuls of the year 354, Constantius II and the Caesar Gallus. The second part of the codex contained a series of lists without illustrations, three of a secular nature and four with Christian information. Of these, the Deposition of Christian Martyrs constitutes a virtual Christian calendar to set against the official one of pagan festivals.

The recipient of the calendar must have been an aristocratic Christian, as the Christian contents and the formulaic Christian dedication to a certain Valentinus indicate. The apparent contradiction of this pagan calendar designed for a Christian by a Christian artist had long perplexed scholars; only in 1953 was H. Stern able to interpret imperial anniversaries that reflected the reality of religious life in post-Constantinian Rome, where, clearly, the pagan calendar was still of great importance for the everyday life of the people of the city.

BIBLIOGRAPHY

+J. Strzygowski, "Die Calenderbilder des Chronographen vom Jahre 354," *Jdl, Ergänzungsheft* 1 (Berlin, 1888); T. Mommsen, "Chronographus Anni CCCLIIII," *MGH AuctAnt*, 9, *Chronica Minora Saec. IV–VII* (Berlin, 1892), 13–148; +H. Stern, *Le Calendrier de 354, Étude sur son texte et ses illustrations* (Paris, 1953); +H. Stern, "Les calendriers romains illustrés," *ANRW* Sec. II, vol. XXII.2 (Berlin, 1981), 431–75; M. R. Salzman, *On Roman Time: The Codex Calendar of 354 and the Rhythms of Urban Life in Late Antiquity* (Berkeley, 1990).

MICHELE R. SALZMAN

CALFBEARER (MOSCHOPHOROS). Greek Archaic sculpture of a bearded male figure carrying a calf on his shoulders, found on the *Akropolis, Athens (*Akropolis Museum; Hymettian marble; height 1.65m).

The greater part of the statue was discovered in 1864 during digging of foundations for the Akropolis Museum; the base of *poros* limestone with a foot attached was discovered under the direction of P. *Kavvadias in 1887 in the same region. Winter noted the connection between base and torso, and additional portions of the thighs were joined by Schrader almost down to the knees. The plinth has a dedicatory inscription, [P]ONBOΣ..., (Rhombos?), and it is thought, therefore, to be the representation of a worshiper bringing a sacrifice to Athena. Dated ca. 570–550 B.C., it demonstrates some of the earliest Eastern influence in Attica in the treatment of the inlaid eyes. When it was excavated, traces of blue paint were still visible on the body of the calf.

BIBLIOGRAPHY

G. Dickins, *Catalogue of the Acropolis Museum* (Cambridge, 1912), 156–58; H. Schrader, *Die Archaischen Marmorbildwerke der Akropolis* (Frankfort, 1939), 278–81; +H. Payne, *Archaic Marble Sculpture from the Acropolis* (New York, 1950), pl. 2–4; +R. Lullies, *Greek Sculpture* (New York, 1957), pl. 22–23.

SHARON WICHMANN

CALLIPYGIAN VENUS. See FARNESE VENUS.

CALVERT, FRANK (1828–1908). Anglo-Levantine geologist, diplomat and archaeologist.

Frank Calvert was the most distinguished of a family of British expatriates prominent in the Dardanelles and the Troad throughout the nineteenth century. Besides varied commercial interests, he was, at different times, the British and American consul at the Dardanelles. A geologist and paleontologist of some note, he was, and is, best known for his unrivaled knowledge of the sites and monuments of the Troad. He acted as host and cicerone to innumerable European visitors. He excavated Hanai Tepe and numerous tombs and built up a fine collection of antiquities. After excavating the "Tumulus of Priam" on the Balli Dagh (1863) and reading Charles Maclaren's books on Troy (1822 and 1863), he decided that Hissarlık must be the site of *Troy. He was the first to excavate there, discovering the Hellenistic temple of Athena and pottery dating back to the Archaic period. Lacking funds to continue, he persuaded *Schliemann to take up the task. In February 1873 he astutely noted that Schliemann's excavations revealed no sign of occupation for the period 1800–700 B.C.

BIBLIOGRAPHY

E. Meyer, *Briefe von Heinrich Schliemann* (Berlin, 1936), 86–90; J. M. Cook, *The Troad* (Oxford, 1973), 35 and passim; A. C. Lascarides, *The Search for Troy 1553–1874* (Bloomington, IN, 1977), 63–65; M. Robinson, "Pioneer, Scholar, and Victim: An Appreciation, of Frank Calvert (1828–1908)," *AnatSt* 44 (1994), 153–68; +S. Allen, "Finding the Walls of Troy: Frank Calvert, Excavator," *AJA* 99 (1995), 379–407.

DAVID A. TRAILL

CALZA, GUIDO (1888–1946). Italian archaeologist.

Noted for his excavations at *Ostia, Calza began working there in 1912 and in 1913 became director. In thirty years of work at the site, Calza identified and investigated many notable structures, including the fourth–century B.C. *castrum*, the Forum, Forum Baths, the ''Pantheon,'' and the storehouse of Epagathos and Epaphroditos (*Horrea Epagathiana et Epaphroditiana*). He also excavated the Isola Sacra necropolis of Ostia and the harbor at *Portus. Excavations were conducted on an unprecedented scale from 1938 to 1941 in preparation for the world exhibition planned for 1942. Calza was able to continue his work until September 1943, when the Germans ordered the evacuation of the site within twenty-four hours. Under most difficult conditions, Calza maintained contact with Ostia and succeeded in minimizing damage to the site.

In 1945, Calza opened a new museum in Ostia. In the same year he became superintendent of the *Forum Romanum and Palatine in Rome. He began work on a comprehensive volume about Ostia, which he left unfinished at his death.

BIBLIOGRAPHY

G. Calza, *La Necropoli del Porto di Roma nell'Isola Sacra* (Rome, 1940); H. Bloch, ''Necrology,'' *AJA* 50 (1946), 407–8.

JOHN L. KISSINGER

CAMBRIDGE RITUALISTS. Group of scholars from Cambridge University who united evidence from sociology, anthropology and archaeology to develop a theory of Greek religion as ritual.

The so-called Cambridge Ritualists were four British scholars, three at Cambridge—Jane Ellen *Harrison (1850–1928), A. B. *Cook (1868–1952) and F. M. Cornford (1874–1943)—and one at Oxford—Gilbert Murray (1866–1957). In a series of publications in the years before World War I, the most important of which were Harrison's *Themis* (1912), Cornford's *From Religion to Philosophy* (1912), Murray's *Four Stages in Greek Religion* (1912), Cornford's *The Origin of Attic Comedy* (1914) and part one of Cook's *Zeus* (1914), they put forward an imaginative reconstruction of Greek religion as a special case of a general theory of ''primitive'' religion. Basing themselves on the comparative anthropology of *Frazer, the collectivist sociology of Durkheim and the vitalist psychology of Bergson, they rejected earlier views that simply imposed modern Western individualist religious categories on primitives and, as a result, found their behavior confused and foolish. The Ritualists, instead, asserted that the Greeks were more like primitives than like ourselves and might be understood only if we assumed that the group and not the individual was the significant socioreligious unit. Specifically, they claimed that the central element in Greek religious life was a ritual representation of death and resurrection, inherently dramatic in character, that derived from prehistoric agricultural fertility magic. They further asserted that this ritual paradigm underlay and determined much else, for example, the forms of Greek drama and of the Olympic games. Visual evidence, especially from Greek vase painting, was important for the formulation of these ideas.

Ironically, they are now remembered by classicists mainly for their theory of the ritual origins of drama. This theory, which was roundly attacked from the moment of its enunciation, is today upheld publicly by no one. It was rejected mainly because, as its proponents acknowledged, the record was too spotty, and therefore the Greek evidence needed to clinch the argument simply did not exist; in its place the Ritualists offered comparative ethnographic data drawn from other cultures that, to classicists, at any rate, were of dubious relevance. It is worth noting that, although rejected by their classical colleagues, the Ritualists' ideas have been, and continue to be, influential in postclassical literary criticism.

BIBLIOGRAPHY
G. F. Else, *The Origin and Early Form of Greek Tragedy* (Cambridge, MA, 1965); E. E. Evans-Pritchard, *Theories of Primitive Religion* (Oxford, 1965); Robert Ackerman, "J. G. Frazer Revisited," *American Scholar* 47 (1978), 232–36.

ROBERT ACKERMAN

CAMPANA (CAMPANA DI CAVELLI), GIOVANNI PIETRO, Marchese (1808–80). Italian collector, excavator and entrepreneur.

Born in Rome, Campana began his career as an assistant to the director of the bank of the Monte di Pietà of Rome. He advanced rapidly, and with increasing wealth he was able to begin collecting antiquities, a pursuit he followed passionately until 1857, when he suffered a catastrophic reversal of his fortunes. Besides purchasing objects, he conducted excavations at a number of sites, in Rome at tombs on the Via Latina (in the Vigna Codini; cf. *columbaria), as well as at *Ostia, *Veii, *Cerveteri, *Vulci and Ruvo. Among his Etruscan discoveries were the seventh-century Campana Tomb at Veii, named for him; the sixth-century painted terracotta slabs from Cerveteri, now known as the Campana Plaques; specimens of the sixth-century Caeretan hydriai, a class of pottery previously unknown; and the remarkable Tomb of the Reliefs at Cerveteri (fourth century B.C.).

Campana was a close friend of Emile *Braun, directing secretary of the *Instituto di Corrispondenza Archeologica, and was himself a corresponding member of the organization. He cut an elegant figure in Roman society, entertaining scholars and artists and donating to charity and to the poor. Befriended by popes, he became treasurer of the Pontifical Academy (*Pontificia Accademia Romana) of Archaeology. Through his English wife, Emily Rowles, he had ties with Napoleon III of France.

As he often purchased collections in bulk, Campana also resold items that duplicated what he already had or that were inferior. He was thus a central figure in a quite large traffic of antiquities. From 1838, the Campana gallery was celebrated for its richness and variety; it was not, in fact, a single collection, but several, of which the ancient marbles were displayed in Campana's villa near the Lateran, while the finest Greek vases, the bronzes, the Renaissance sculptures and the paintings were set up in his palazzo in the Via del Babuino. Many scholars viewed his antiquities, and a number of Greek vases were published by *Welcker, *Gerhard, *Brunn, *Michaelis, *Overbeck, *Petersen, *Conze, O. *Jahn and others. He personally published some of the items in his collection, such as the terracotta bas-reliefs now known as *Campana Reliefs, excavated by him in and around Rome; many of these were restored, sometimes questionably. The two volumes of *Museo Campana, Antiche opere in plastica* appeared in 1851, with 120 plates. The marble sculptures were published in 1856 by a French scholar, Henry d'Escamps, in *Description des marbres antiques du Musée Campane.* As for the excavations conducted by Campana through the years, he published little and made only brief reports to various learned societies.

Campana rose to be director of the Monte di Pietà, and from this eminence he began to engage in the activity that would lead to his disastrous fall: he borrowed money from the bank, leaving as pledge a large number of works from his personal collection. In 1857, an investigation revealed that all the assets of the Monte di Pietà were tied up in the collection and that, in addition, there was an enormous deficit of 1 million scudi. The arrest of Campana shocked the archaeological world and outraged the public. He was sentenced to twenty years in prison, but the sentence was commuted, under pressure from Napoleon III. Campana had to give up his collection to the government and went off into exile. The vast collection was inventoried in the *Cataloghi del Museo Campana* [1858], and it was sold off in lots to the *British Museum, the *Capitoline Museums, the Archaeological Museum at *Florence, the Musée Cinquentenaire at Brussels; almost 600 pieces went to the czar of Russia, but the greatest part of the collection was acquired by Napoleon III (not without polemics) for the *Louvre. Known as the Musée Napoleon III, this group of antiquities included the Campana Reliefs, about 300 marbles and 3,400 vases.

Campana lived out his days in relative obscurity, traveling about to Naples, Paris and even back to Rome, vainly seeking legal action to recover some of his resources from the Monte di Pietà.

BIBLIOGRAPHY
S. Reinach, *Equisse d'une histoire de la collection Campana* (Angers, 1904–5); Michaelis, 72–76; N. Parise, "Campana, Giovanni Pietro," *DBI* 17 (1974), 349–55; M. F. Briguet, *Le Sarcophage des époux de Cerveteri du Musée du Louvre* (Florence, 1989), 22–37.

CAMPANA RELIEFS. Terracotta relief slabs, mass-produced during the Late Roman Republic and Early Empire (ca. 50 B.C.–A.D. 150); mostly found in Rome and named for their collector, Marchese G. P. *Campana.

Ornamental in function, the reliefs were hung around an *impluvium* or on the upper walls of buildings in a system akin to that of revetment plaques of Etruscan temples. The majority were cast from molds, painted in unfired polychrome pigments and often joined together to form friezes, attached to the walls by plugs or nails. They have a standard size, ca. eighteen inches long and nine to twelve inches high, and are usually bordered with egg-and-tongue bands and palmette or acanthus moldings that recall ornamental motifs of Greek vases.

The plaques cover a wide field of mythological and Roman subjects and were largely derived from Classical and Hellenistic art and neo-Attic Augustan reliefs. Favorite subjects were the exploits of Hercules and Theseus, the infant Jupiter protected by the Curetes, Amazonomachies, Bacchic triumphs and revels, Seasons, combats and contests, landscapes and emblems.

Owing partly to their modest material and wide diffusion, a number of the reliefs were accessible and may have transmitted motifs to Renaissance artists. The terracotta frieze of the *Marriage of Thetis and Peleus* was well known; Sodoma owned a plaque of it, depicting *Winter* and *Hercules and the Cretan Bull* (?), figures copied separately in engravings by Giovanni Antonio da Brescia and other sixteenth-century artists and in a sketch by Sebastiano del Piombo (Windsor Castle). A plaque of *Mars and Venus* appears in a fifteenth-century North Italian drawing in the Ambrosiana, Milan, and an engraving by Marcantonio *Raimondi. That of a satyr-flutist and two maenads is copied in an engraving by Antonio Veneziano. Motifs of the figure of *Winter* and the *Infancy of Bacchus* are employed in *Giulio Romano's frescoes in the Palazzo del Te in Mantua.

Campana's collection of these reliefs was displayed to an interested public in Rome in the mid-nineteenth century; doubts were soon raised because of his methods of restoration (he had his own pottery and employed the skillful restorer Pennelli). The collection was subsequently sold to the *Louvre to help pay Campana's debts. More recently, important specimens of Campana reliefs have been excavated by G. Carettoni at the temple of Apollo on the *Palatine Hill in Rome.

BIBLIOGRAPHY

+H. von Rohden—H. Winnefeld, *Architektonische römische Tonreliefs der Kaiserzeit* (Berlin, 1911); +A. H. Borbein, *Campanareliefs typologische und stilktitische Untersuchungen* (Heidelberg, 1968); G. Carettoni, ''Terracotte 'Campana' dallo scavo del tempio di Apollo Palatino,'' *RendPontAcc* 44 (1971–72), 123 ff.; T. Yuen, ''Giulio Romano, Giovanni da Udine and Raphael: Some Influences from the Minor Arts of Antiquity,'' *JWarb* 42 (1979), 263–72.

TOBY YUEN

CAMPANARI FAMILY. Italian excavators and entrepreneurs, involved principally with Etruscan archaeology in the earlier nineteenth century.

VINCENZO CAMPANARI of Toscanella and his three sons, CARLO, SECONDIANO and DOMENICO, sponsored excavations at various Etruscan sites in northern Latium (*Vulci, *Bomarzo, Tuscania, Poggio Buco, Ischia di Castro) between 1828 and 1845. In 1834 Vincenzo struck an agreement with authorities at the Vatican concerning excavation in papal territory at Vulci, resulting in a sharing of research and an orderly division of the finds. He observed that there was a need for an Etruscan museum at Rome, and, in fact, soon afterward *Gregory XVI opened the Museo Gregoriano Etrusco (1837), including materials that had been excavated by the Campanari.

A few months later (1837), the Campanari opened the first Etruscan traveling exhibition, in a spectacularly successful venue in London's Pall Mall. The show included reconstructions of Etruscan painted tombs, using watercolor copies of the paintings as well as actual sarcophagi, vases, weapons and other grave goods. Some eleven tomb groups were carefully reconstructed in order to give a clear idea of how an Etruscan burial looked when excavated. A catalog of the show was prepared by Secondiano, *Etruscan and Greek Antiquities Now Exhibited at no. 121, Pall Mall, Opposite the Opera Colonnade* (1837), and when the show closed, the trustees of the *British Museum purchased the greater part of the material. It became the nucleus of the museum's Etruscan collection.

Among the visitors to the exhibition was Elizabeth Caroline Hamilton Gray, who was thoroughly taken by the Etruscans and resolved to include Etruscan sites on her approaching tour to Italy. As a result of seeing the show, she was at least somewhat prepared for the experience she would later write up as a *Tour to the Sepulchres of Etruria* (1840). The Campanari show and the book of Mrs. Hamilton Gray created a favorable climate for the Etruscans that led directly to the publication of James *Byres's *Hypogaei or Sepulchral Caverns of Tarquinia* (1842), some eighty years after his drawings were made, and to the investigations of George *Dennis, who wrote the Etruscan classic of the century in *The Cities and Cemeteries of Etruria* (1st ed., 1848).

BIBLIOGRAPHY
G. Colonna, ''Archeologia dell'età romantica in Etruria: I, Campanari di Toscanella e la tomba dei Vipinana,'' StEtr 46 (1978), 80–117; F. Buranelli, *Gli Scavi a Vulci della Società Vincenzo Campanari, 1835–1837* (Rome, 1992); *Les Étrusques et L'Europe*, catalog of exhibition (Paris, 1992), 313, 330, 334–35, 420–21.

CAMPANIAN TOMB PAINTING. Tombs with interiors painted with figured scenes and other motifs have been found at a number of sites in Southern Italy.

Many such paintings were discovered during the nineteenth century at Capua and at other sites in Campania. F. *Weege published a catalog of the known paintings in 1909; some had already been lost by then, and even fewer survive today. Other examples had been found in Samnium, Apulia and around *Paestum (Poseidonia) in Lucania, just south of Campania. Recent excavations have added many well-preserved painted tombs to the earlier examples, and they are now housed principally in the museums of Naples and Paestum.

A few paintings date to the fifth century B.C.; the best known is the diver's tomb, found at Paestum in 1968. It was painted ca. 480 B.C. and is important in the history of Greek free painting. The majority, however, belong to the fourth century B.C., to the period when the previously Greek communities were dominated by the ''Oscans,'' people originally from the inland areas of Italy. Although this chronological outline was established by the end of the nineteenth century, only in recent years has it been possible to attempt a more precise chronology for the paintings, based on the evidence of datable grave goods rather than stylistic considerations alone. This evidence confirms that the majority of the tombs belong to the second half of the fourth/early third centuries B.C. and has made it possible to place examples more precisely within that period.

The paintings provide important evidence for the character of society in Southern Italy in the fourth century B.C., a period when it was subject to a number of diverse influences. Although the paintings are clearly influenced by Greek and Etruscan painting traditions, they also, as Weege showed, have a vigorous native Italian, or Oscan, element: this is noticeable especially in the armor of the warriors, which is neither Greek nor Etruscan. Later, Nicolet used the tomb paintings to illustrate the existence of a flourishing elite class in fourth-century Campania, the *equites Campani*. This class commissioned the paintings and is represented in them as horse-riding warriors and well-dressed and bejeweled women. More recent studies have considered further the question of status in the paintings and the evidence they provide for local funerary customs and beliefs.

BIBLIOGRAPHY

+F. Weege, "Oskische Grabmalerei," *Jdl* 24 (1909), 99–141; C. Nicolet, "Les *Equites Campani* et leurs représentations figurées," *MEFRA* 74 (1962), 463–517; +A. Greco Pontrandolfo, "Segni di trasformazioni sociali a Poseidonia tra la fine del V e gli inizi del III sec. a.C.," *DialAr,* n.s. I, 2 (1979), 27–50.

GLENYS DAVIES

CAMPORESE, GIUSEPPE (1763–1822). Italian architect and restorer of monuments.

Camporese was a leading pontifical architect who collaborated with Michele Simonetti at the *Vatican in the Museo Pio-Clementino and designed the Sala della Biga. He was a fervent supporter of the Republic (1798–99), being one of the aediles. He collaborated with Zappati in clearing the *Arch of Septimius Severus (1803–4) and with Stern and Palazzi in building the first *Colosseum buttress (1805). With Giuseppe *Valadier, he was the leading architect for all the archaeological undertakings during the French occupation (1809–14), being especially associated with the excavations in the Colosseum, *Domus Aurea and Forum of Trajan (*Imperial Fora). He should be remembered above all, however, for his brilliant dismantling and restoration of the remaining columns of the *Temple of Vespasian (1811).

BIBLIOGRAPHY

F. Gasparoni, *Biografia di Giuseppe Camporese* (Rome, 1836); M. Fischer, "Camporese, Giuseppe," *DBI* 17 (1974), 587–89. +R. T. Ridley, *The Eagle and the Spade: The Archaeology of Rome During the Napoleonic Era,* 1809–1814 (Cambridge, 1992).

R. T. RIDLEY

CAMPO SANTO, Pisa. One of the buildings in the Pisa cathedral complex, now a peaceful, cloistered museum.

The Campo Santo was, in origin, a cemetery, begun in the late thirteenth century because burial accommodation around the cathedral was becoming over-crowded. It gradually acquired a large collection of antiquities, particularly Roman sarcophagi. Most of these had been reused for later burials, some in the Campo Santo itself, but many were transferred there from other sites in Pisa, including the cathedral. The present collection includes Roman sarcophagi of all periods, from one of the earliest garland sarcophagi (that of Tebanianus, consul in A.D. 87) to early Christian examples. Some of these were partially recut in medieval times, and many were given new inscriptions. These record their reuse for members of the noble families of Pisa from the eleventh century onward, but particularly in the fourteenth century. It is disputed where they were acquired, but probably some were found locally while others were imported from the area of Rome, especially *Ostia.

This early taste for Roman sculpture also had its influence on local artists. The Campo Santo collection includes medieval imitations of Roman sarcophagi (e.g., the sarcophagus signed by Biduino of the mid-twelfth century), and Roman sarcophagi influenced the relief sculpture by Nicola and Giovanni *Pisano of the pulpits in the baptistery and cathedral at Pisa. The collection also contains other stone items: of particular interest are two inscribed decrees of the Roman colony of Pisa honoring the dead heirs of Augustus, Lucius and Caius Caesar, found at Pisa in 1603/4 and 1609.

BIBLIOGRAPHY

P. Lasinio, *Raccolta di sarcofagi, urne e altri monumenti di scultura nel Campo Santo di Pisa* (Pisa, 1814); H. Dütschke, *Die antiken Bildwerke des Campo Santo zu Pisa* (Leipzig, 1874); +P. E. Arias—E. Cristiani—E. Gabba, *Camposanto monumentale di Pisa, Le Antichità* (Pisa, 1977).

GLENYS DAVIES

CAMPUS MARTIUS, Rome. A vast plain north of the city of Rome, below the Pincian, Quirinal and Capitoline hills.

On the east it was delimited by a major highway, the straight Via Flaminia. Toward the west, east, and southeast, this state-owned region was surrounded by the Tiber. In all, the ill-defined ancient borders of the Campus Martius en-compassed approximately 250 hectares, originally replete with swamps, streams and volcanic pools. Vulnerable to both frequent flooding and attack, the low-lying campus was sparsely inhabited during the Early Roman Republic, serving as an extramural area reserved for activities prohibited within the sacred city limits or *pomerium.* These included burials, the worship of foreign or dangerous deities and the meetings of foreign ambassadors and assemblies with military associations. Here Roman troops executed military maneuvers and worshiped the powerful war god Mars, after whom the campus was named.

The Campus Martius developed rapidly once state projects provided improved drainage and relatively stable riverbanks. In the Late Republic and Early Empire, sumptuous public structures were erected, connected by shady porticoes and lush landscaping. The flatness, openness and natural beauty of the Campus Martius also made it ideal for recreational pursuits, including running, swimming and chariot races. Rome's residents flocked to this large, grassy field, happy to escape the dense environment of the walled city.

In contrast to the irregular, organic arrangement of Rome proper, the central Campus Martius had a well-ordered plan. Unfettered by preexisting construction or space limitations, new buildings in this open field were sited at right angles to one another, forming an orthogonal layout, based on the east-west orientation of early Republican temples. The zone soon became the showplace of the capital, praised by many writers; Strabo, who visited Rome in 7 B.C., declared that "the Campus Martius . . . affords a spectacle that one can hardly draw away from" (5.3.8).

In the Imperial period, the recreational and religious aspects of the Campus Martius were stressed. Many magnificent entertainment structures appeared, including the *Theater of Pompey (55 B.C.), *Stadium of Domitian (ca. A.D. 90) and the first of the imperial baths, the Thermae Agrippae (25 B.C.). Among the grand new temples were several dedicated to members of the imperial family, such as that to the Divine Hadrian (A.D. 165) and the enigmatic temple to "all the gods," the *Pantheon (25 B.C./A.D. 126).

The Campus Martius also continued as a prime burial site for well-known citizens, who favored its prominent location. This was the first section of Rome seen by visitors entering from the north along either the Tiber or Via Flaminia. No wonder Augustus selected this region for his monumental *Mausoleum (27 B.C.) and famous altar to Peace (*Ara Pacis Augustae; 13–9 B.C.).

During the Late Empire and Early Middle Ages, as Rome declined in size and importance, the dwindling populace abandoned the famous seven hills and gathered in the well-watered Campus Martius. The emperors in residence at Constantinople made feeble attempts to preserve the region's pagan monuments, yet these structures were soon adapted to new uses or quarried for their valuable materials (*Codex Theodosianus* 14.14.1). Nevertheless, the historical importance of the classical buildings in the Campus Martius was increasingly recognized. The region was featured in medieval guidebooks not only because of its proximity to the Vatican and important early churches, such as San Lorenzo in Lucina (fourth century), but also because of its still-visible ancient structures. Medieval representations of the campus were likewise dominated by ancient monuments, especially the Pantheon.

During the Renaissance, the Campus Martius remained densely occupied. As the economy improved, many elaborate palaces were erected, and in the process numerous ancient ruins and artworks were unearthed. For example, Renaissance workers discovered fragments of Domitian's Stadium in 1511 and the Ara Pacis in 1568. Many well-known artists, including Baldassare Peruzzi and Sebastiano

*Serlio, scoured the region, making detailed drawings of its ancient remains. *Piranesi published a monograph on the Campus Martius.

Despite important discoveries in the Campus Martius over the centuries, its overall layout is still uncertain. The zone was not closely examined as a whole until the twentieth century, and only in the 1930s were major monuments, such as the Mausoleum of Augustus, freed of subsequent encumbrances. Large-scale exploration has been hindered by the region's dense occupation and high-water table. Technological advancements have made excavations more feasible, yet they remain extremely expensive. Recently, valuable conclusions have resulted from closely correlating the available archaeological data with representations on the fragmentary third-century marble map, the *Forma Urbis Roma.* Using this approach, Gatti proved in the 1960s that the Circus Flaminius (220 B.C.) had been incorrectly located for centuries, and, in the 1970s, Buchner correctly located the Sundial of Augustus (10 B.C.). Such discoveries will stimulate further exploration in this fertile, enigmatic Field of Mars.

BIBLIOGRAPHY

+F. Castagnoli, "Il Campo Marzio nell'antichità," *MemLinc,* 7:1 (1946), 93–193; G. Marchetti Longhi, "Nuovi aspetti della topografia dell'antico Campo Marzio di Roma," *MélRome,* 82 (1970), 117–58; +E. Buchner, "Solarium Augusti und Ara Pacis," *RM* 83 (1976), 319–65; +Filippo Coarelli, *Roma* (Bari, 1980), 265–309; +R. E. A. Palmer, "Studies of the Northern Campus Martius in Ancient Rome," *TAPS,* 80.2 (1990), 1–64.

DIANE FAVRO

CANCELLERIA RELIEFS. Two large Roman relief sculptures (height, 2.1m, length, ca. 6m; Museo Pio-Clementino, Vatican), carved from seven slabs of Luna marble.

Frieze B is best interpreted as the "Arrival" (*adventus*) of Vespasian in A.D. 70. On Frieze A, probably representing a "Departure" (*profectio*), the figure of Domitian was recarved as Nerva. The reliefs were found by chance in 1937–39 under the Palazzo della Cancelleria Apostolica on the Corso Vittorio Emanuele (in the ancient Campus Martius) during a nonarchaeological excavation of what turned out to be the tomb of Aulus Hirtius (consul in 43 B.C.) located beneath the palace. Some of the slabs were stacked against the tomb, as if in a mason's yard. The reliefs were probably set there to be diverted to new uses after the death of Domitian (hence the recarving following his *damnatio memoriae*). The right outer panel of Frieze A was kept in the Capitoline Museum until 1956, when the Italian government and the city of Rome presented it to Pope Pius XII in honor of his eightieth birthday. The reliefs are fundamental for our understanding of the stylistic development of Roman art, but their dating is controversial, ranging from the Domitianic to the Antonine periods.

BIBLIOGRAPHY

+F. Magi, *I Rilievi del Palazzo della Cancelleria* (Rome, 1945); +J. M. C. Toynbee, *The Flavian Reliefs from the Palazzo della Cancelleria* (Newcastle upon Tyne, 1957); +E. Simon, "Zu den flavischen Reliefs von der Cancelleria," *JdI* 75 (1960), 132–356;

Memorial to *Luigi Canina* (d. 1856), dedicated by Algernon, 4th Duke of Northumberland, Rome, SS. Luca and Martina. (Deutsches Archäologisches Institut, Rome. Inst. Neg. 69.169.)

+A. M. McCann, "A Re-Dating of the Reliefs from the Cancelleria," *RM* 79 (1972), 249–76; Kleiner, *Roman Sculpture*, 191–92.

PETER HOLLIDAY

CANINA, LUIGI (1795–1856). Italian architect and archaeologist.

The youthful Canina studied first at Turin (1815–18) and then at Rome, from the beginning developing his talents as an architect along with his interest in classical antiquity. He was received into the Academy of St. Luke in 1822 with a presentation piece on the *Colosseum that included a description of the monument and some fifteen illustrations. As architect for the *Borghese family (from 1825), he designed additions for the Villa Borghese that showed his study of Egyptian, Greek and Roman architecture; with his monumental propylaea at the principal entrance to the villa on the Via Flaminia (influenced by the temple of Poseidon at *Sounion), Canina emerged as a leading new exponent of ambitious neoclassical architecture in Rome, comparable to L. von *Klenze in Munich.

Canina moved in international circles, including among his friends the Englishmen T. L. Donaldson and C. R. *Cockerell, as well as the Europeans in Rome with whom he collaborated in the early activities of the *Instituto di Corrispondenza Archeologica. In Rome, he received many honors, including the award of merit from the Academy of St. Luke, the presidency of the *Capitoline Museums and elevation to the Roman nobility.

Throughout his life he continued to practice architecture—in Rome, in Turin and in England (to which he made three trips). As an archaeologist he was involved in excavations on the Esquiline (1848–50) that led to the discovery of the *Odyssey landscapes, and he directed work on the Via Appia near the *Tomb of Caecilia Metella and Boville (1850–53). He excavated and did research in the countryside around Rome and in southern Etruria and issued publications on Cere, Tuscolo and *Veii; his *Antica Etruria marittima* (Rome, 1846–51) is still consulted by Etruscan specialists.

Canina's most ambitious project was an all-embracing study of ancient architecture—Egyptian, Greek and Roman—using both literary and archaeological sources and dealing with the historical, theoretical and practical aspects of ancient architecture, as well as describing individual monuments. The three volumes of *L'Architettura antica descritta e dimostrata con i monumenti* were issued at Rome between 1830 and 1844. The work has been criticized as having elements of fantasy but represents a courageous attempt to make a far-ranging synthesis during a period of increasing specialization in scholarship.

BIBLIOGRAPHY

G. Bendinelli, *Luigi Canina, le opere, i tempi* (Alexandria, 1953); P. Pelagatti, "Canina, Luigi," *EAA* 2 (1959), 308; W. Oechslin, "Canina, Luigi," *DBI* 18 (1975), 96–101.

CANINO, LUCIEN (LUCIANO) BONAPARTE, Prince of (1775–1840). Brother of *Napoleon; owner and excavator of property at Canino, in the Etruscan necropolis of *Vulci.

Estranged from his brother and living as an exile in Italy, Lucien Bonaparte became a favorite of Pope *Pius VII, who bestowed upon him lands near *Viterbo and the title of Prince of Canino. After a reconciliation with Napoleon and the collapse of the family fortunes, he retired to his estate in the country, where he devoted himself to literary pursuits and to archaeological excavations.

In 1828 peasants plowing found the remains of an Etruscan tomb on his property, and soon afterward the Prince of Canino undertook excavations in the area. Within four months he had excavated from the plot of three–four acres more than 2,000 artifacts, the most significant of which were *Greek vases. The vases sold with astonishing speed to collectors all over Europe, including William I of Holland (now in the *Rijksmuseum van Oudheden, Leiden) and *Ludwig I of Bavaria. E. *Gerhard described the remarkable find in a report for the Prussian *Official Gazette,* noting that Canino employed large bands of laborers and that he had set up three tents on the site, "into which poured the incessant stream of newly found vases or vase fragments still covered with damp soil." Many vases were restored on the spot, in a tent occupied by the prince and his family. Others were sent to experienced restorers at Musignano. Among the numerous important Greek vases was the famed cup of Exekias with the *Ship of Dionysos* (now in the *Antikensammlungen, Munich), which Canino interpreted, with the help of his chaplain, as Noah discovering wine. Gerhard's lucid account of the vases became a fundamental publication for the study of Greek vase painting. Canino produced two catalogs of the works excavated: *Catalogo di scelte antichità etrusche trovate negli scavi del principe di Canino, 1828–29* (Viterbo, 1829) and an expanded version, *Museum étrusque de Lucien Bonaparte, prince de Canino, Fouilles de 1828 à 1829, Vases peints avec inscriptions* (Viterbo, 1829).

Canino also first opened the enormous tumulus at Vulci known as the Cucumella in 1829. Later discoveries were made on the property under the supervision of the Princess of Canino (Alexandrine de Bleschamps) after the death of her husband. George *Dennis lamented the way in which the excavations were conducted by the princess's foreman, who carried a gun to make sure his laborers stole nothing and who instructed the crew to destroy unfigured black pottery, as if it were junk. From the excavations of the Canino family and on adjacent lands by the *Campanari and others came Greek vases that were later sold to the *Vatican and *British Museum and other major museums of Europe.

Portraits of Canino and his wife by François-Xavier Fabre are preserved in the Museo Napoleonico, Rome.

BIBLIOGRAPHY
Michaelis, 62–64; G. Dennis, *Cities and Cemeteries of Etruria,* 3rd ed. (London, 1883), 447–48, 450–52; F. Bartoccini, ''Bonaparte, Carlo Luciano,'' *DBI* 11 (1969), esp. 549–50; *Les Étrusques et l'Europe,* 326–27, 397.

CANISTRIS, OPICINO DE (1296–1350/52). Italian cleric, early humanist scholar.

Only since his identification in 1927 as the author of an anonymous description of Pavia has Opicino de Canistris begun to receive the attention he deserves. Born to a family of modest means, Opicino's life was plagued by difficulties almost from the start. His preparation for an ecclesiastical career was frequently interrupted by either his family's financial difficulties or the political disturbances with which Pavia was afflicted at the time. He was frequently bored with his studies; his two abiding interests were writing and drawing. Through the development of these two skills he was at least able to survive, despite an ill-fated clerical career and a host of physical and psychological complaints.

Aside from a string of spiritual and theological texts that have all been lost, Opicino is also responsible for three other works that have survived. In addition to his wholly unoriginal *Tractatus de preeminentia spiritualis imperii,* completed in 1329, there are the *Libellus de descriptione Papie* as well as two volumes of drawings that illustrate his geometrical, astronomical and geographical interests. While the *Libellus* has been edited twice, the drawings have been published only in part. Inspired by a variety of visual sources and possibly intended to curry favor with the pope, Opicino's drawings create, in H.-J. Becker's words, "a complicated figurative language, laden with symbols and word games."

In neither the *Libellus* nor his drawings do any antiquarian interests Opicino might have had play an important role. Nevertheless, the cleric does provide an interesting description of the *"Regisole" atop the pillar before the cathedral in Pavia, as well as a fanciful explanation for, and drawing of, the same. He also mentions the older tombs (along with their epitaphs) and statuary of which his town could boast. Furthermore, despite the restrictions of the visual and rhetorical models he meant to imitate, fascination with the world is clearly evident on Opicino's part. Thus, the cleric's personal circumstances and both the literary and artistic traditions he embraced must not be forgotten in any comprehensive evaluation of his work. It can be said, however, that Opicino's powers of observation and novel adaptation of much older forms bespeak a certain originality for his day.

BIBLIOGRAPHY

+F. Gianani, *Opicino de Canistris l'Anonimo ticinese* (Pavia, 1927); +R. Salomon, *Opicinus de Canistris: Weltbild und Bekenntnisse eines Avignonesischen Klerikers des 14. Jahrhunderts* (London, 1936); Weiss, *RDCA* 26–27; H. J. Becker, "Canistris, Opicino de," *DBI* 18 (1975), 116–19.

ANDREW P. McCORMICK

CANOVA, ANTONIO (1757–1822). Italian neoclassical sculptor and administrator for the arts and archaeology.

Born at Possagno near Venice, Canova was known early for his portraiture and marble statuary with classical themes (*Eurydice,* 1773, and *Orpheus,* 1776, now in the Museo Correr, Venice; *Daedalus and Icarus,* 1778, Museo Correr). In 1779 he visited Rome, where he met Gavin *Hamilton and grew ever more interested in classical antiquity. He then proceeded to *Naples, *Herculaneum, *Pompeii and *Paestum. Returning to Rome (1781), Canova launched a career packed with commissions and administrative assignments that would give him a reputation as the greatest living sculptor and the supreme arbiter of taste in the fine arts.

When Pius VII (1800–23) returned the papacy to the *Vatican after the French invasion, he found a difficult job to do in the museum, which had been stripped of its finest treasures for *Napoleon's collections in Paris. In 1802 he appointed Canova as inspector general of the fine arts for life and acquired three of his works to help fill up the Belvedere court—the *Perseus* and the pair of *Pugilists.* Named superintendent of the Vatican and *Capitoline museums, Canova oversaw the replenishing of the Vatican, as many new acquisitions were made. In the same year, Napoleon begged Canova to accept the directorship of the Musée Napoleon in Paris, but the artist refused.

When the French soon afterward took over the administration of Rome (1808–14), Canova remained in power as director of museums and as head (Principe) of the Academy of St. Luke. The latter position turned out to be very important for archaeology, since the new French bureaucracy appointed the council of the academy to take charge of preservation of the ancient monuments of Rome. Important repairs were made at this time to the *Temple of Vespasian, the *Colosseum and the *Pantheon. Canova advised on these and many other projects.

In 1815, at the fall of Napoleon, Canova was dispatched to Paris to negotiate recovery of the world-famous antiquities and paintings that had been plundered by the French. Supported by the Allies and escorted by a platoon of Austrian soldiers, he initiated the return of a large, though not complete, consignment of paintings and sculptures, including the *Belvedere *Apollo,* the *Belvedere *Torso* and the **Laocoon.* For his role in the negotiations, he was subsequently made Marquis of Ischia by Pius VII (though by no means did all find his mission completely satisfactory).

From Paris he proceeded to London, where he viewed the marbles brought from Athens by Lord *Elgin. He had already seen drawings of them in 1803 and had gained a reputation for great sensitivity to the handling of antiquities by telling Elgin that the sculptures were so important that they should not be altered by restoration. He now expressed his realization that many of the works he had admired in Rome in the past were but copies, while the Parthenon sculptures were originals with a natural greatness, lacking affectation, exaggeration or hardness.

Practically every sculpture created by Canova bears some relation to the classical antiquity he revered and served. His subjects, apart from portraits (of Napoleon, his family and others) and sculptures for tombs of the popes, were largely mythological. The early *Theseus and the Minotaur* (1781–82; London, Victoria and Albert Museum) is a pastiche, only partially successful, of several well-known statues in the Belvedere, with the legs of the *Laocoon,* the trunk of the famous *Torso* and the head of the *"Antinous."* The *Perseus* utilizes the pose of the *Apollo,* appropriately enough since it was intended to replace the latter in the Belvedere courtyard. His portraits also reveal strong classical underpinnings; *Pauline Borghese* was shown reclining on a Pompeian-style couch in the guise of Venus Victorious (ca. 1807; Rome, Borghese Gallery), while *Napoleon* was depicted in heroic nudity (1811; Milan, Brera) and *George Washington* in Roman armor (1820; destroyed by fire). None of his sculptures may be described as archaeologically precise (nor did he intend them as such), but he did leave several re-creations of antique paintings inspired by discoveries at Herculaneum (Possagno, Gipsoteca Canoviana). These small canvases represent nymphs, Muses, philosophers and poets, with the figures in bright colors set on a shallow stage space and against a dark monochrome background; careful attention is given to authenticity in costume and furniture.

Canova died in Venice and was buried in his native Possagno, in a temple designed by his own hand to imitate the *Pantheon.

BIBLIOGRAPHY
M. Pavan, "Canova, Antonio," *DBI* 18 (1975), 197–219; S. Howard, "The Antiquarian Market in Rome and the Rise of Neoclassicism: A Basis for Canova's 'New Classics,' " in *Transactions of the Fourth International Congress on the Enlightenment* (Oxford, 1976), I, 185–96; +D. Finn—F. Licht, *Canova* (New York, 1983); C. Pietrangeli, *I Musei Vaticani, Cinque secoli di storia* (Rome, 1985); R. T. Ridley, *The Eagle and the Spade, Archaeology in Rome During the Napoleonic Era, 1809–1814* (Cambridge, 1992).

CAPGRAVE, JOHN (1393–1464). English chronicler and hagiographer, born at Lynn in Norfolk.

Capgrave entered the priesthood, took the degree of Doctor of Divinity at Oxford (where he was lecturer in theology), joined the order of Augustinian Hermits and spent most of his life in the Augustinian house at Lynn, of which he eventually became prior. He was also provincial of his order in England and regarded as one of the most learned men of his time in that country. Most of his works are theological, including sermons, commentaries and lives of saints. He also produced historical works, including a *Chronicle of England* from the creation (unfinished), and a collection of biographies of famous men named Henry (written 1446–53).

Between 1447 and 1452, probably during the jubilee year of 1450, Capgrave journeyed to Rome and wrote a description of the city in English, entitled *Ye Solace of Pilgrimes,* based on his notes of the trip. This work was believed lost until a manuscript at Oxford (Bodleian MS. 423) was correctly identified as Capgrave's in 1911. While Capgrave derived much of his information on ancient monuments from the **Mirabilia,* he was nonetheless an accurate observer. He was in the habit of copying inscriptions and lists of relics, and where these have survived, he is letter-perfect. Thus, his testimony to inscriptions that have disappeared is important. His physical descriptions of the monuments appear to be from direct observation rather than adopted from earlier sources. At the same time, there is a wealth of medieval legend preserved in the *Solace* that is of antiquarian interest.

BIBLIOGRAPHY
C. A. Mills, *Ye Solace of Pilgrimes: A Description of Rome, ca.* A.D. *1450, by John Capgrave* (Oxford, 1911); Valentini—Zucchetti IV, 330–49; Weiss, *RDCA,* 74–75.

JAMES C. ANDERSON, JR.

CAPITOLINE BRUTUS. Lifesize bronze portrait head of a bearded man dating to the Roman Republican period.

This striking work was unearthed early in the sixteenth century, probably in Rome. Antiquarians of the time promptly attached to it the name of the legendary founder and first consul of the Roman Republic, Lucius Junius Brutus. *Aldrovandi's account (1549–50) of the ancient statues of Rome is the earliest written reference to the piece, but van *Heemskerck drew the head between

1532 and 1536. The piece was bequeathed by Cardinal Rodolfo Pio da *Carpi to the city of Rome in 1564 and was kept on the Capitol from the end of the sixteenth century; from 1627 onward it was in the Sala della Lupa in the Palazzo dei Conservatori (*Capitoline Museums). It was ceded by Pope *Pius VI to France in 1797 and was featured in *Napoleon's triumphal procession in Paris (July 1798), where it remained until October 1815. The head was returned to Rome in 1816 and again displayed in the Palazzo dei Conservatori.

The fame of this piece has been largely dependent on its identification with the Republican hero. Aldrovandi's citation presupposes this attribution. Gallaeus later published supporting evidence, comparing its features with those found on an inscribed coin (then in the collection of Fulvio *Orsini) minted by Marcus Junius Brutus, the tyrannicide. Cardinal da Carpi's bequest may have been prompted by the ancient references to a bronze statue of Brutus on the Capitoline (Dio Cassius 42.45; Plutarch, *Life of Brutus* 1). By the seventeenth century it was suggested that the head was a fragment of this very statue. *Piranesi patriotically depicted the head as part of the initial letter of his polemical *Della magnificenza ed architettura de' Romani* (1761). The head was further celebrated during the turbulence of the French Revolution: J. L. *David lent a copy of the piece to be displayed during a performance of Voltaire's *Brutus* (November 1790). The head was one of only two works (along with a bust of Marcus Brutus) specifically named to be surrendered to Napoleon in 1796.

*Winckelmann held reservations about the identity of the head. Upon its return to Rome, E. Q. *Visconti also questioned whether it portrayed Brutus; he left the question open but emphasized the accepted fact that the head and attached bust did not belong together. Some twentieth-century scholars have acknowledged that the head may have been an idealized portrait of Brutus. However, recent scholarship has been most concerned with its date, place of origin and role in the history of the genre. *Kaschnitz and R. *Bianchi Bandinelli identified the head as the prime exemplar of the central Italic vocabulary that set and remained the standard for all subsequent Roman portraiture. Dohrn catalogs the head as a central Italian work inspired by Greek portraiture of the first half of the third century B.C.

BIBLIOGRAPHY
G. Kaschnitz von Weinberg, "Studien zur etruskischen und frührömischen Porträtkunst," *RM* 41 (1926), 133–211; +R. Bianchi Bandinelli, "Il 'Bruto' Capitolino scultura etrusca," *Dedalo* 8 (1927), 5–36; Helbig, 4th ed., II, 268–70; +Haskell—Penny, 163–4.

                                                              PETER HOLLIDAY

CAPITOLINE CAMILLUS (ZINGARA; THE GYPSY; THE SACRIFICER). Roman bronze of the mid-first century A.C. representing a helper at sacrificial rites, now in the *Capitoline Museums.

This lifesize male figure (height 1.41m), with unrestored silver eyes and in excellent condition, wears fine sandals and a large tunic characteristic of the

Claudian era; the hairstyle is also reminiscent of the same era: wavy, parted in the middle and rolled into a band. The left arm hangs casually by the side and may have held a dipper. The right hand is outstretched as if it once held a patera. At some point the piece was apparently colored black; traces of the color are found on the head, tunic and legs. Because a number of antique copies and variations of the "server" theme have been preserved, it is assumed that there was a common prototype for them, but this *camillus* is the best work of all those extant. Its original location is unknown.

The first record of the bronze was made by "Prospettivo Milanese" around 1490, but it is believed to have been part of the collection donated to the Palazzo dei Conservatori by *Sixtus IV in 1471. The statue was moved to the Capitoline wing by the early eighteenth century, but it was returned to the Conservatori late in the nineteenth century. Well into the eighteenth century there was controversy about the gender of the statue, partly because of its physical beauty, as well as debate on whether it represented a *camillus* or a *zingara* (gypsy). Scholarly opinion today generally classifies it as a male, a *camillus*.

The piece was popular during the Renaissance and was admired or commented upon by Andrea *Fulvio, *Cellini and Paolo Alessandro *Maffei. Copies were made for the gardens of Fontainebleau; other copies were made for collections in France and elsewhere. The Villa Borghese (*Borghese family) and the Palazzo Farnese (*Farnese family) have excellent examples. Marble copies and plaster casts were made for a number of European and English collections through the eighteenth century.

BIBLIOGRAPHY

+H. Stuart Jones, *A Catalogue of the Ancient Sculptures Preserved in the Municipal Collections of Rome: The Sculptures of the Palazzo dei Conservatori* (Oxford, 1926), 47–48; Helbig, II, 270–72; +Haskell—Penny, 168–69; Bober—Rubinstein, 224–25.

                                                                JUDY WAGNER

CAPITOLINE FAUN (THE MARBLE FAUN; LEANING SATYR; ANAPAUOMENOS). Marble lifesize copy (1.705m) of a lost Greek original of a young Satyr leaning against a tree.

The original, dating to the fourth century B.C. and attributed to Praxiteles, was evidently one of the most popular of ancient sculptures, for more than one hundred copies of it are known today. Other good replicas besides the one in the *Capitoline Museums are in the *Glyptothek, Munich, and the Torlonia Museum, Rome. The best torso, found on the *Palatine Hill, Rome, in excavations conducted for Napoleon III and now in the *Louvre, conveys the subtlety of modeling associated with Praxiteles.

The provenance of the Capitoline *Faun* is debated (*Fea said it was found on the Aventine Hill; another early report claimed it was excavated at Lanuvium). It was given to the museum by Pope Benedict XIV in 1753. *Winckelmann raised the possibility that the satyr statue type was connected with Praxiteles, specifically on the basis of a passage in Pliny the Elder (*NH* 34.69)

referring to a famed *nobilem Satyrem* by the artist. But he paid little attention to the Capitoline version, and it was only with Nathaniel Hawthorne's novel *The Marble Faun* (published in 1860) that the piece became truly world-famous. In his fantasy novel Hawthorne created the character of Donatello, a youth who physically resembled the Capitoline *Faun* so much as to seem himself to be such a creature. The tale, which depicts the loss of innocence in the "faun" as he commits murder and the concurrent acquisition of moral knowledge, held enormous romantic appeal for artists and travelers in Rome for many decades.
BIBLIOGRAPHY
Bieber, 17–18; Haskell—Penny, 209–10; +E. Bartman, *Ancient Sculptural Copies in Miniature* (Leiden, 1992), 51–101.

CAPITOLINE HILL (CAMPIDOGLIO), Rome. The hill of two crests dominating the *Forum Romanum at its northwest end.

The Capitoline is steep on all sides, approached on the Southeast from the forum by the Clivus Capitolinus, a road that winds in sharp switchbacks, and on the northwest by a similar road from the *Campus Martius, otherwise only by stairs. The precipitous cliffs toward the Tiber were known as the Tarpeian Rock, and from their crest criminals condemned of capital crimes were hurled to their death.

The long history of the hill begins with traditions assigned to the eighth century B.C. Its earliest use was the establishment there of the Asylum in the saddle between the crests, a place where Romulus welcomed all who desired a change in their lives and gave them citizenship in a new polity. The summit of the hill was the fortified citadel of Rome, supposedly as early as the time of Romulus, and after the conclusion of peace with the Sabines and inclusion of them in the city, their king, Titus Tatius, had his house on the higher crest. There were also numerous temples on the hill, including that of Jupiter Feretrius, founded by Romulus.

The lower crest was chosen by Tarquinius Priscus as the site for his great temple of Jupiter Optimus Maximus (sixth century B.C.), and this entailed removal of numerous other shrines to make space, notably that of Saturn. The hill supposedly took its name from a human head of remarkable preservation discovered during digging for the foundations of the temple under Tarquinius Superbus. The temple was of three cellas, Jupiter being flanked by Juno and Minerva, forming the Capitoline triad, and was of Etruscan character, frontal, raised on a platform, with wide-spaced columns and a spreading roof; it was regarded as the nerve center of Roman religion. Here the consuls were inaugurated on the first of January, the triumphal procession ended and the triumphator presented his crown to Jupiter, and the Sibylline books were kept in a stone chest. The temple of Jupiter burned in 83 B.C., A.D. 69 and A.D. 80, but the first two times it was restored along the lines of the original architecture. Domitian's rebuilding, however, was lavish and had Corinthian columns.

The other crest of the hill was eventually crowned with the temple of Juno

Moneta, vowed by Camillus and dedicated in 344 B.C.; it was the site of the mint of Rome throughout the Republican period and the place where the sacred Libri Lintei were kept, one of the great sets of annalistic records of Rome. The temple is presumably buried under the church of S. Maria in Aracoeli (dating from the sixth century), but no trace of it has ever been found.

The tradition that the Capitoline is the sacred heart of Rome and its empire has been responsible in more recent times for the designing by *Michelangelo in the sixteenth century of a new Piazza del Campidoglio, bounded on three sides by buildings; as early as the twelfth century a Senate House was built on the ruins of the ancient Tabularium, the state archives building erected under Sulla in the early first century B.C. Adjacent to the redesigned Palazzo del Senatore are the Palazzo dei Conservatori, on the right, and the Palazzo del Museo Capitolino, on the left. The Conservatori was expanded in 1925 (Museo Nuovo) and again in 1950–52 (Braccio Nuovo). With the ramp of the "Cordonata" that leads up to the piazza, it is one of the world's greatest architectural jewels. Sculptures were brought in, as well, to adorn the hill, including the *Marcus Aurelius Equestrian Statue that stood in the center of the piazza (brought from the *Lateran in 1538 and now removed indoors; cf. *Capitoline Museums). The colossal statues of the Dioscuri with their mounts (discovered in 1560 near the Capitol) were placed on the balustrade at the front of the piazza, one in 1585 and the other in 1590, at which time the *"Trophies of Marius" were also erected on the balustrade.

The chief excavations here were carried out in 1919 following the razing of large portions of Palazzo Caffarelli; these exposed the remains of the temple of Jupiter. In the late 1930s excavations under Piazza del Campidoglio and the Palazzo del Senatore discovered the well-preserved temple of Vediovis, as well as a complex of streets and shops. Otherwise, excavations have been confined to the base of the hill.

BIBLIOGRAPHY

G. Lugli, *Roma antica, il centro monumentale* (Rome, 1946), 1–53; J. S. Ackerman, *The Architecture of Michelangelo* (London, 1961), I, 54–74; II, 49–66.

L. RICHARDSON, JR

CAPITOLINE MUSEUMS (MUSEI CAPITOLINI), Rome. Collection of paintings and classical antiquities, the oldest public museum in the world; major repository of important examples of Graeco-Roman sculpture.

The museum on the Capitoline Hill (Campidoglio) was begun in 1471, when Pope *Sixtus IV gave a collection of monumental bronzes from papal holdings at the Lateran to the Palace of the Conservators of the city of Rome (Palazzo dei Conservatori). With the famous *Spinario (Boy Removing a Thorn) and the image that came to be known as the *Capitoline Wolf, were donated the *Capitoline Camillus and a colossal head, hand and globe of a figure identified as *Constantius II. To these sculptures Sixtus soon added a colossal gilded bronze statue of Hercules excavated in the *Forum Boarium, and along with these were shown two pieces that had long been on the Capitoline Hill, the marble ossuary of Agrippina the Elder, brought from the *Mausoleum of Augustus in the thirteenth century and used as a measuring standard, and a fragmentary marble group of a *Lion and Horse,* which stood on the steps of the adjacent Palazzo Senatorio.

Under Pope Innocent VIII the collection was enriched by the colossal marble head of *Constantine* and parts of the limbs of the statue found in the *Basilica of Constantine in the *Forum Romanum in 1486. All in all, this collection of the late fifteenth century constituted a splendid ensemble, the best display of antiquities to be seen in Rome at the time. Soon other distinguished pieces were added: in 1515 the *Marcus Aurelius* Panels were donated by *Leo X, and in 1564 the *Capitoline *Brutus* arrived from the collection of Cardinal Rodolfo Pio da *Carpi. The most important piece of all, the *Marcus Aurelius* Equestrian Statue, was brought from the Lateran to the Capitol in 1538, with the plan to make it the focal point of a redesigning of the Piazza del Campidoglio and the municipal palaces by *Michelangelo. The Capitoline Hill and its monuments were seen and described at this stage by *Aldrovandi in 1550. Soon afterward came a major addition from the Vatican collections, twenty-seven marbles that had been rejected by Pius V (1566–72) as part of his austerity reforms, in which he concealed or eliminated "idols" from the Vatican.

Michelangelo's new Palazzo dei Conservatori had been begun in 1562 and was completed by Giacomo Della Porta in 1582, while the Palazzo Senatorio was reworked with alteration of Michelangelo's design by Della Porta (1582–1605). The balustrade at the front of the Capitoline Hill was adorned in 1583 with the colossal *Dioscuri,* and in 1590 the *"Trophies of Marius"* were erected near them by Della Porta. The twin of the Palazzo dei Conservatori, called the Palazzo Nuovo (today, the Museo Capitolino), was constructed across the Campidoglio from it (completed 1655). The famous "speaking statue" of the *Marforio* was permanently established in the fountain court of the Palazzo Nuovo at this time.

The collection in the Capitoline was lifted to an entirely new level in the eighteenth century, when Pope Clement XII purchased 408 sculptures from Cardinal Albani (*Albani family) and brought these to the Palazzo Nuovo, opening it up officially as the Museo Capitolino in 1734. The collection now included a number of images of philosophers and Roman Imperial portraits and some of the most appealing statuary excavated at *Hadrian's Villa in the eighteenth century—the Capitoline *Antinous,* the two centaurs discovered by Furietti in 1736 and the *Faun* in *rosso antico* discovered the same year. Some time before 1737, Clement acquired the *Dying Trumpeter (Gladiator)* from the heirs of the *Ludovisi family, and in 1752 was added the *Capitoline *Venus,* presented by Pope Benedict XIV; he donated the *Capitoline *Faun* in 1753.

A number of the best pieces on the Capitoline Hill were seized by *Napoleon and hauled away to Paris in 1797 (*Spinario, Brutus, Dying Gladiator, Antinous, Venus*), but these were returned and incorporated into a reorganized Capitoline

Museum in 1816. In 1866, the *Castellani collection was added to the Conservatori, and in 1876 a new museum was formally opened, called the Museo del Palazzo dei Conservatori. Here were displayed many finds from recent excavations in Rome.

In 1925 was added the Museo Nuovo Capitolino, the former Palazzo Caffarelli, where the *Instituto di Corrispondenza Archeologico had once had its seat (1829), subsequently inherited by the *German Archaeological Institute. The overflow from the Conservatori was placed here, and incorporated into the displays were the massive walls of the podium of the Archaic temple of Jupiter Optimus Maximus, which stood on the spot in the late sixth century B.C. The Braccio Nuovo was added in 1950–52 to display sculptures from the most recent excavations. Perhaps the most conspicuous change on the Capitoline in recent years was the removal of the *Marcus Aurelius* Equestrian Statue from the center of the Campidoglio for restoration (1981) and the return of the cavalier, not to that spot, but to the interior courtyard of the Museo Capitolino.

BIBLIOGRAPHY

+H. Stuart Jones, *A Catalogue of the Ancient Sculptures Preserved in the Municipal Collections of Rome, The Sculptures of the Musei Capitolini* (Oxford, 1912); +Idem, *A Catalogue of the Ancient Sculptures Preserved in the Municipal Collections of Rome, The Sculptures of the Palazzo dei Conservatori* (Oxford, 1926); Helbig, II, 3–576; Haskell—Penny, 8–9, 15, 63–66.

CAPITOLINE VENUS. Lifesize marble statue of Venus (Aphrodite) represented nude, with her hands modestly placed in front of her body.

The statue is regarded as a Roman copy of a Greek bronze original (third or second century B.C.) that was itself created as an imitation of the *Knidian *Aphrodite* of Praxiteles.

The sculpture is recorded by P. S. *Bartoli as having been excavated during the pontificate of Clement X (1670–76), along with some other statuary inside an antique building, near the church of S. Vitale, Rome. Found in the gardens of the Stazi family, the *Venus* belonged to them until purchased in 1752 by Benedict XIV, who presented it to the *Capitoline Museum. It was ceded to the French in 1797, taken to Paris for *Napoleon and displayed there, then returned to the Capitoline in 1816.

Frequently compared with the *Medici *Venus,* which also seems to imitate the Knidia, the Capitoline goddess was considered inferior at first. But during the eighteenth century the Capitoline *Venus* was preferred by *Winckelmann and others because of its excellent state of preservation, and it was regarded as an especially significant addition to the triumph of Napoleon. In modern times its reputation is uneven. Though given special attention by its display in its own room in the Capitoline, this *Venus* was described by Bieber as "much harsher" and "severe" of face in comparison to the Medici statue and by Martin Robertson as having a "fifth-century coldness of features" that makes it less close to the Knidia. Recent scholarship describes the Capitoline *Venus* as an Aphrodite of the *Pudica* ("modest") type, perhaps created in Asia Minor.

BIBLIOGRAPHY
B. Felletti-Maj, "Afrodite Pudica," *ArchCl* 3 (1951), 48–54, 62–65; +Bieber, 20; Robertson, 548–54; Haskell—Penny, 318–20; Ridgway, *Hellenistic Sculpture* I, 355–56.

CAPITOLINE WOLF (ARCHAIC SHE-WOLF, LUPA CAPITOLINA).

Etruscan/Roman bronze of the fifth century B.C., most likely representing the wolf that suckled Romulus and Remus.

The teats are a restoration of uncertain date, and the twins, probably made by Antonio Pollaiuolo, date somewhere between A.D. 1471 and 1473. The wolf is thought to be done in the manner of the Etruscan sculptor Vulca, to whom the work is even sometimes attributed.

Several classical authors mention a sculpture of the *She-Wolf* with twins, but there appears to have been more than one such group. Livy (10.23) says that in 295 B.C. Cnaeus and Quintus Ogulnius placed under the *Ruminal Fig Tree* at the base of the Palatine Hill a group that they had cast from the bronze of fines placed upon usurers. It is uncertain whether Livy means they added some twins to an already existing sculpture or commissioned the whole group. Cicero (*Catil.* 3.7; *Divinat.* 1.13; 2.20) mentions a group on the Capitoline in 65 B.C. that was struck by lightning, torn from its base and partially melted. The reference has led many to speculate that the Capitoline *Wolf* is from that group because there is evidence of extensive fire damage to the hind legs. But Cicero also states that the statue had been gilded, and the wolf shows no traces of ever having been so treated. Maxentius issued coins that show another group of the *She-Wolf* and twins, on top of the temple of Roma. There is also evidence that a wolf was placed on a pedestal in the *Forum Romanum near the *Lapis Niger, beneath which Romulus was thought to be buried.

The Capitoline *She-Wolf* emerges in the early tenth century. At that time Pope Sergius III rebuilt the *Lateran and placed several ancient bronzes (including the *Spinario and *Marcus Aurelius) in the piazza before the palace. Somehow, the *She-Wolf* became the symbol of papal judicial authority. Benedict of Mt. Soracte relates how executions occurred at the "Place of the Wolf." The last such execution, in 1438, was recorded in a painting, complete with wolf, in the transept of the Lateran basilica. It was subsequently destroyed, but not before a copy was made for the papal archives. In 1471 *Sixtus IV established a museum at the Palazzo dei Conservatori (*Capitoline Museums) and donated several antique bronzes, among them the *She-Wolf*. The twins were added soon thereafter.

The group enjoyed immense popularity throughout the Renaissance, as is evidenced by the numerous reproductions dating to that period. A particularly fine half-scale *She-Wolf* in the Kress Collection, Washington National Gallery, probably dates to the late fifteenth century. It has been suggested that the work is of Sienese origin, since the motif of the *She-Wolf* had been adopted by that city as an emblem in the Middle Ages. The motif of wolf and twins can be found in the work of various masters, such as the *Romulus and Remus* in the

Palazzo Magnani, Bologna, by Ludovico *Carracci and the *Romulus and Remus* of P. P. *Rubens, now in the Capitoline.

In the sixteenth century, the wolf was connected with the passages in Livy and Cicero, and its precise relationship to these references was debated for centuries, along with its aesthetic merit. The wolf was admired during the Renaissance, but later visitors to Rome regarded it as a relic rather than an object of beauty. *Mommsen confessed that he was more moved by this "horrible" sculpture than by the many beautiful things displayed around it. *Winckelmann had the perspicacity to identify the work as Etruscan. Today the Capitoline *She-Wolf* holds a secure place in the history of art in Archaic Italy. Further, the motif of the wolf with twins has an unparalleled popularity as the emblem of Rome, the Eternal City.

BIBLIOGRAPHY

H. Stuart Jones, *A Catalogue of the Ancient Sculpture Preserved in the Municipal Collections of Rome: The Sculptures of the Palazzo dei Conservatori* (Oxford, 1926), 56–58; E. K. Gazda—G. M. A. Hanfmann, "Ancient Bronzes: Decline, Survival, Revival," in *Art and Technology: A Symposium on Classical Bronzes,* ed. S. Doeringer—D. G. Mitten—A. Steinberg (Cambridge, 1970), 245–70; Sheard, no. 17; Haskell—Penny, 335–37.

STEPHEN C. LAW

"CAPO DI BOVE." See TOMB OF CAECILIA METELLA.

CAPPELLARI DELLA COLOMBA, MAURO. See GREGORY XVI.

CAPRI (CAPREAE). A rugged limestone island of dramatic beauty but scant water, the southern boundary of the Bay of Naples, geologically a continuation of the Sorrentine peninsula, its ancient name, Capreae, of disputed origin.

Capri was inhabited from Paleolithic times and in historic time was Greek in character (traditionally, a colony of the Teleboi of Acarnania) rather than Italic. Graves containing Italiote vases of the fourth century B.C. have been found, and the use of Greek in inscriptions continued beside Latin in the Roman period. In the time of Augustus the island was a dependency of Naples. Under Augustus the whole island was made imperial property, the island of Ischia being given to Naples in compensation. It was a favorite resort of Augustus and became the retreat of Tiberius during the last ten years of his life. Thereafter it passed out of favor, though it still remained an imperial property. We last hear of it in A.D. 182 as the place of exile for Lucilla, the sister of Commodus, and Crispina, his wife.

The archaeology of Capri is mainly concerned with the identification and exploration of the twelve villas Tacitus (*Ann.* 4.67) ascribes to Tiberius there. Three survive in sufficiently good state to be appreciated. The most impressive, the Villa Iovis, crowns the eastern height of the island, from which it has a commanding view in all directions. It was plundered in the early nineteenth century and completely excavated from 1932 to 1935. Centered around a core of enormous cisterns, it consists of an entrance wing with service quarters toward the land side, a commodious bath wing, a splendid set of state apartments with a hemicyclical belvedere commanding the view toward the sea and an imperial residence above a long loggia, or *ambulatio.* The upper parts of the complex have disappeared with time, possibly taking important apartments with them. The whole fronted on the land side over terraces and gardens in which there were other buildings, including a great lighthouse.

The villa of Damecuta, on gentle slopes under Anacapri on the northwest promontory of the island, was excavated between 1937 and 1948. It consists of a long double *ambulatio,* the narrower outer walk covered by a colonnade, the inner provided with alcoves for seats, with a suite of state apartments fronting on a curving belvedere at the west end and a small private suite at the east. Other detached buildings of the villa are scattered over the higher slopes for a distance of more than 200m, and it is possible that the famous Grotta Azzura was converted into a nymphaeum belonging to this villa. It was abandoned after the eruption of Vesuvius in A.D. 79, as drifts of volcanic material found in the excavation attest.

The Palazzo a Mare on the sea west of the Marina Grande extended for 800m along the shore but has been so exploited and abused in the course of time that little remains today but evidence of terracing and ruined cisterns. At the east end are ruins of port installations, concrete piers built out into the sea, and at the west end are the remains of fishponds and a nymphaeum known as the Bagni di Tiberio. The design of the villa suggests that it was essentially a combination of park and gardens in which were scattered pavilions and buildings unconnected with one another. It is generally believed to have been built by Augustus.

Other ruins are scattered here and there over the island, especially numerous over the saddle where the modern town of Capri is located, but none seem to have been of equal importance with those already described.

The beauty of the island and the romantic appeal of its history have exerted a strong influence on Northern European artists and travelers since the nineteenth century, but the ancient remains have never been properly studied.

BIBLIOGRAPHY

+A. Maiuri, *Capri: storia e monumenti* (Rome, 1956); A. Andrén, *Capri from the Stone Age to the Tourist Age* (Göteborg, 1980), 6–88; S. De Caro—E. Greco, *Campania* (Rome, 1981), 109–18.

L. RICHARDSON, JR

CARNUNTUM. Site of Roman legionary fortress, in the northeast corner of modern Austria ca. 40km east of Vienna, between Petronell and Deutsch-Altenburg.

As early as A.D. 14 or 15 the Fifteenth Legion (*Legio XV Apollinaris*) was stationed at the spot, near an earlier Celtic settlement. Carnuntum became the chief city of the province of Pannonia Superior under Trajan (A.D. 98–117), and the civilian town was granted municipal status by Hadrian (A.D. 117–38). Later in the second century, the Roman stronghold was of central strategic importance in the Marcomannic wars, and Marcus Aurelius composed some of his *Meditations* in residence there. Septimius Severus, proclaimed emperor in Carnuntum by his soldiers (A.D. 193), made the city a colony (*Colonia Septimia Carnuntum,* 194). Throughout the third century Carnuntum remained prosperous and influential, but after the early fourth century, decay set in, and the Romans had already largely withdrawn from Carnuntum before the surrender of the region to the Huns in 433.

The Roman monument known as the *Heidentor* (dated perhaps as early as the late second century A.C., but more likely third century or later), today comprising two piers joined by a vault standing ca. 14m (though it was once taller), has always been visible. Two amphitheaters, one near the camp, the other in the civilian settlement, have been excavated in whole or in part, as have the remains of small houses and larger structures, including a bath complex and the so-called palace. Excavation (begun in 1877) continues, and there is an excellent small museum on the site; other artifacts from Carnuntum are displayed in Deutsch-Altenburg and in Vienna.

BIBLIOGRAPHY

E. Swoboda, *Carnuntum, seine Geschichte und seine Denkmäler,* 4th ed. (Vienna, 1964); A. Mócsy, *Pannonia and Upper Moesia* (London, 1974); R. Noll, s.v. "Carnuntum," *PECS,* 198–99.

W. W. DE GRUMMOND

CARO, ANNIBAL (1507–66). Poet and burlesque writer, secretary to Pier Luigi Farnese (1543–47) and to Cardinal Alessandro Farnese (1547–63; *Farnese Family.*).

Though not primarily a scholar, Caro was much interested in Hellenistic literature. He translated Longus and Theocritus and also, in verse, the *Aeneid* (Venice 1581).

Caro's modest collection included several small antique sculptures and classical manuscripts. A considerable numismatic authority, Caro corresponded with many antiquarians, including Pier Vettori and Fulvio *Orsini, and wrote an iconographic treatise, now lost, on coins. He frequently advised his patrons on artistic matters and devised several schemes for fresco cycles, though, interestingly, he usually derived the images from vernacular handbooks, such as *Cartari's Imagini,* rather than directly from classical literature or coins.

BIBLIOGRAPHY

F. Sarri, *Annibal Caro* (Milan, 1934); A. Greco, *Annibal Caro, Culture e Poesia* (Rome, 1950); C. Mutini, "Annibale Caro," *DBI* 20 (1977), 497–508; C. Robertson, "Annibal Caro as Iconographer: Sources and Method," *JWarb* 45 (1982), 160–81.

CLARE ROBERTSON

CARPENTER, RHYS (1889–1980). American archaeologist and art historian.

Trained at Columbia and, as a Rhodes Scholar, at Oxford, Carpenter taught classical archaeology at Bryn Mawr College, 1913–55. He concentrated on Greek sculpture and architecture (*The Aesthetic Basis of Greek Art,* 1921; *The Sculpture of the Nike Temple Parapet,* 1929; *The Humanistic Value of Archaeology,* 1933). He was director of the *American School of Classical Studies, Athens, 1927–32. He also worked in Rome and wrote *Observations on Familiar Statuary in Rome* (1941). He could challenge canonical views with great originality. In *Folk Tale, Fiction and Saga in the Homeric Epics* (1946), he theorized that Homer was influenced by European folk motifs. In *Discontinuity in Greek Civilization* (1966), he sought to account for various migrations and catastrophes in ancient history through climatic changes. He received the Gold Medal for Distinguished Archaeological Achievement from the *Archaeological Institute of America in 1969.

BIBLIOGRAPHY

M. J. Mellink, "Rhys Carpenter," *AJA* 84 (1980), 260; *Hesperia* 38 (1969), 123–32 (bibl.).

MORTIMER CHAMBERS

CARPI, GIROLAMO DA (1501–56). Italian artist from Ferrara, resident in Rome, ca. 1549–53.

Two compilations of drawings of antiquities have been attributed to da Carpi, preserved today in the Rosenbach Foundation, Philadelphia, and the Biblioteca Reale, Turin. They date from his period in Rome and provide valuable evidence about antiquities that were known there by the mid-sixteenth century. The drawings, numbering several hundred (and augmented by drawings sporadically preserved in other collections) were evidently made largely from other artists' sketchbooks, especially artists of the circle of *Raphael, such as *Giulio Romano, Polidoro da Caravaggio and Perino del Vaga. Girolamo attempted to imitate the draftsmanship as well as reproduce the antique models of a wide range of motifs from sarcophagi and other reliefs and from freestanding statuary. Among the well-known works continued in his sketchbook are the *Venus Felix, the *Marforio, the *Capitoline *Camillus,* the *Quirinal *Horse Tamers,* the *"Cleopatra" in the Belvedere, the *Alexander Dying and the Cesi "Roma".

BIBLIOGRAPHY

N. Canedy, *The Roman Sketchbook of Girolamo da Carpi* (London, 1976); Bober—Rubinstein, 458.

CARPI, RODOLFO PIO DA (1500–64). Collector of antiquities, one of the wealthiest ecclesiastics in Rome; sent on diplomatic missions to the courts of the German emperor and the French kings, from whom he later obtained pensions.

Da Carpi was made cardinal in 1536. He resided first in the Palazzo Ricci (Palazzo Firense) but moved to the Palazzo Palavicini in the *Campus Martius around 1547. He amassed one of the largest collections of antiquities in Rome. *Aldrovandi describes at length the busts, reliefs and bronzes kept in the Palazzo

Palavicini, among them a large head of *Alexander Dying.* Da Carpi donated his famous bronze bust of the *Capitoline *Brutus* to the city of Rome. *Pighius wrote a treatise, *Themis seu de lege divina,* based on a female herm with a relief in da Carpi's collection, interpreting it as the goddess with her three daughters, *Justice, Order* and *Peace.* Seven busts were published by A. Statius, *Inlustrium virorum vultus* (1569), including a curious bust of Euripides and a blind Homer. *Orsini published two busts in his *Imagines* (1570).

In the 1540s the cardinal constructed the Villa da Carpi on the Quirinal Hill, with a statue garden containing courtyards, walkways and a ''giardino segreto'' or private garden, as well as grottoes and fountains. It so impressed Aldrovandi that he referred to it as ''an earthly paradise.'' On display was a fabulous array of statues and inscriptions, which attracted artists such as *Dosio, Pierre *Jacques, G. da *Carpi and *Giambologna. Humanist scholars were keenly interested in the antiquities: the Codex Pighianus (*Pighius) shows several altars and funerary *cippi;* *Smetius transcribed a number of inscriptions and *Boissard published a number of monuments; four plates in G. B. De Rossi, *Insigniores statuae urbis Romae* (1619) illustrate statues standing in the garden.

After da Carpi's death in 1564, Cardinal Giulio della Rovere purchased the villa. In 1578 it changed ownership again, when it was acquired by Cardinal Alessandro Sforza. His nephew sold the property to Cardinal Francesco Barberini in 1625. The *Barberini family built their new palace and a garden on the site of the old villa. A few statues remained, but the majority had been dispersed in 1600, when they went from the da Carpi collection to the Montalto, *Borghese and *Giustiniani family collections.

BIBLIOGRAPHY

Lanciani, *Storia degli scavi,* 3 (1907), 176–85; 4 (1912), 87–90; C. Hülsen, *Göttinger Gelehrte Anzeiger,* 176 (1914), 291; +C. Hülsen, *Römische Antikengärten* (Heidelberg, 1917), 43–84.

MARJON VAN DER MEULEN

CARRACCI FAMILY. Italian family of painters and engravers from Bologna, consisting of LUDOVICO (1555–1619) and his two younger cousins, the brothers AGOSTINO (ca. 1557–1602) and ANNIBALE (1560–1609).

The Carracci are associated with an ideal naturalistic style of painting developed through the study of *Raphael, classical antiquity and North Italian (especially Venetian) painting.

The Carracci studied and worked together in Bologna prior to 1595, when Annibale, and then Agostino, transferred to Rome. In 1582 they formed their much-discussed academy, known by 1590 as the Accademia degli Incamminati (Academy of the Progressives), where they pursued the study of art and various intellectual subjects. While much emphasis was put on acquiring knowledge of the human body to be applied in art, there were also scholarly sessions for studying math, history, science and literature, conducted by scholars such as the Bolognese naturalist and antiquarian U. *Aldrovandi. There is little surviving evidence of direct study of classical antiquity from these years, but the trio collaborated to create an important series of fresco decorations with classical subjects for Bolognese palaces (the cycles of *Jason* and *Aeneas,* Palazzo Fava, 1583–90; the cycle of *Romulus and Remus,* Palazzo Magnani, ca. 1590; myths of *Hercules,* Palazzo Sampieri, 1593–94).

Agostino, the most intellectual of the three, mastered Latin thoroughly and moved in circles of scholars and gentlemen interested in math, philosophy, poetry, rhetoric and other subjects of the traditional liberal arts. Ludovico showed little enthusiasm for scholarship or antiquity (apart from a splendid fresco of *Romulus and Remus with the She-Wolf* in the Palazzo Magnani, derived from images of the nursing scene on Roman coins) and was not inclined to move to Rome; he spent only a brief time there, 1602–4, and then returned to Bologna.

The most significant contact with archaeological study and ancient monuments occurred when Annibale was commissioned to decorate rooms in the Palazzo Farnese in Rome. The *Farnese family collection of antiquities was at its height, and Annibale was able to study at firsthand the famed *Farnese *Hercules* (now in the *Museo Nazionale di Napoli) and other sculptures that were to influence him profoundly, both in a general way and in specific motifs. For Cardinal Odoardo Farnese, he decorated first a Camerino (1595–96) with themes of Hercules and other heroes. The adviser for the iconographic content of the paintings was Fulvio *Orsini, librarian to Cardinal Farnese and intimately acquainted with classical archaeology, having his own collection for reference as well as that of the Farnese. Annibale was assigned to do a painting of *Hercules Bearing the Globe for Atlas,* in which he closely imitated the sculpture that was identified then as *Hercules* but later was called the Farnese *Atlas.*

The next commission, for the grand gallery of the Palazzo Farnese (1597–1600) was planned to create a magnificent setting for the display in niches of Farnese antiquities, six busts and ten standing figures (including an *Apollo* and *Bacchus* and a number of female figures). These were installed soon after the completion of the room but were removed in the eighteenth century, when the Farnese collection was transferred to Naples by the *Bourbon family.

The vibrant frescoes of the Farnese Gallery, focusing on mythological themes of love, show Annibale's total absorption of the lessons of ancient sculpture in Rome, from the *Laocoon* to the *Belvedere *Apollo* to antique Bacchic sarcophagi and reliefs. Though few drawings of antiquities by the Carracci survive, a measure of the care with which they studied them is provided by an anecdote told by G. B. Agucchi, the prelate known for his treatises on the theoretical basis for Annibale's ideal naturalism and its roots in antique sculpture. The brainy, long-winded Agostino was expatiating on the beauty of the *Laocoon,* while Annibale remained silent and withdrawn. Chided by his brother for taking no interest in the subject, Annibale seized a piece of chalk and from memory drew a perfect copy of the sculpture on the wall. This bent for memorization of antiquities is cited also by G. P. *Bellori, who admired Annibale above all artists of his time; he relates how Annibale meditated on the *Atlas* figure and made more than twenty studies to arrive at his own conception of the *Hercules* in the Farnese Camerino.

Annibale Carracci asked, and at his death his request was granted, to be buried in the *Pantheon, near the tomb of Raphael.

BIBLIOGRAPHY

+J. R. Martin, *The Farnese Gallery* (Princeton, NJ, 1965); G. P. Bellori, *The Lives of Annibale and Agostino Carracci,* tr. C. Enggass, with foreword by R. Enggass (University Park, PA, 1968); +D. Posner, *Annibale Carracci* (New York, 1971); +*Annibale Carracci e i suoi incisori,* catalog of exhibition (Rome, 1986), 180–83, 197–98.

CARTARI, VINCENZO (1531?–after 1569). Italian humanist scholar and mythographer.

Almost nothing is known of Cartari's life, except that he was born in Reggio Emilia and that he spent his entire life working for the *Este family.

His writings reveal that he received a humanistic education. His first publication was a translation of Ovid's *Fasti* (Venice, 1551), which was shortly followed by an exposition, *Il Flavio intorno ai Fasti Volgari* (Venice, 1553). Set in the form of a dialogue, this work was really intended as a learned discourse on classical ceremonies and religion.

Cartari's most important work, however, was his *Imagini dei Dei degli antichi* (Venice, 1556). A manual aimed explicitly at artists, the book describes the appearances of all the "classical" gods, although many bizarre Oriental and Egyptian divinities are included among them. Although Cartari insists that his images derive from "worthy ancient authors," in practice, he relies extensively on late antique writers, such as Martianus Capella and Fulgentius. He also owes much to two modern mythographic handbooks: from Boccaccio's *Genealogia deorum* he takes his method of exegesis, as well as much information; but he borrows still more from L. G. Giraldi's *De deis gentium:* whole sections follow this work closely, and the material is organized in a similar way, discarding Boccaccio's genealogical arrangement. Cartari describes many classical works of art and ancient coins, but here he relies exclusively on literary sources, such as Pausanias and Philostratos, and possibly on contemporary numismatic manuals.

The *Imagini* quickly established its usefulness; it was a major source, for example, around 1560 for Veronese's frescoes at the Villa Barbaro at Maser and in 1562 for an iconographic scheme by Annibal *Caro for the Villa Farnese at Caprarola. In 1571 a much expanded second edition was published with woodcuts by B. Zaltieri, which, despite their mediocre quality, were influential. Many subsequent editions and translations were printed, and the *Imagini* continued to be employed for programs, as well as single figures of gods and personifications, well into the seventeenth century.

BIBLIOGRAPHY

M. Palmi, "Vincenzo Cartari," *DBI* 20 (1977), 793–96; J. Seznec, *La Survivance des dieux antiques,* 2nd ed. (Paris, 1980); T. Puttfarken, "Bacchus und Hymenaeus in der

Villa Maser," *MittFlor* 34 (1980), 1–19; P. Tinagli Baxter, in *Giorgio Vasari, Principi, letterati e artisti nelle carte di Giorgio Vasari* (Arezzo, 1981), 183–85.

CLARE ROBERTSON

CARTHAGE. City in Tunisia with important Phoenician, Roman, Byzantine and Arab phases of occupation.

The site is located on a peninsula stretching into the Gulf of Tunis. Modern occupation has taken its toll on the ancient monuments, either plundering them for decorative and building materials or destroying them to make room for new construction. Most pre-1970 excavation was undertaken by members of either the French military or priesthood. Generals were interested in understanding Roman territorial control and administration as a model for French rule in North Africa; the French fathers were interested in excavating the remains of Christian monuments to further their efforts to convert the Muslim population. In the 1970s, a new international program of excavation was begun that has both re-covered a wealth of new archaeological material and helped conserve the antiquities from the depredations of modern development.

Punic Carthage vied with Rome during the third and second centuries B.C. for control of the western Mediterranean; this conflict eventually culminated in the devastation of the city by Roman forces (146 B.C.). The site that had been cursed in perpetuity by its Roman conqueror, Scipio Aemilianus, was refounded as a Roman colony under Augustus and later became capital of the province of Africa; it was soon embellished with all the important public monuments that characterized the Roman urban landscape.

Though few Roman monuments are well preserved today, the urban grid system is still traceable on the ground and in aerial photographs. The center point of the grid that divided the city into four quarters of almost equal size was located atop the acropolis of Byrsa. Public and private monuments were sited within the rectangular insulae created by the grid.

The circus is located on the edge of town, in the southwest quadrant, with the amphitheater situated farther north; the odeum and theater are placed back-to-back on the summit of the plateau still farther to the north. Despite the poor state of preservation of these buildings, it is clear that they were among the largest and most lavishly decorated such monuments in the Roman provinces. The best-preserved building is the imposing Antonine bath complex, whose seaside location allowed it to use the Mediterranean as its cold plunge. The public water supply was ensured both by the aqueduct from Zaghouan, a ben-efaction by Hadrian, and by a huge complex of cisterns at La Malga in the northwest quadrant. The man-made circular harbor that served the Punic fleet was monumentalized as a shrine during the Roman era, while the rectangular harbor to its south continued as a commercial venue.

The wealth of the Roman city is best seen in the elaborate private homes located on the slope of the Odeum Hill. Planned around large central peristyles, these houses are lavishly decorated with floor and wall mosaics made in the local workshops and utilizing the colored stones from local quarries.

The only fortification wall known for the city is the Theodosian wall built ca. 425 in response to the threat of Vandal invasions, which, in fact, overtook the city in 439. After the Byzantine reconquest in 533, Carthage became a famous Christian capital. Several large and important basilicas, including Damous el Karita, the church of St. Cyprian and the Dermech basilicas, date from this period.

BIBLIOGRAPHY

A. Audollent, *Carthage roman* (1901); G. C. Picard, *Carthage* (1964; French edition, 1956); +J. G. Pedley, ed., *New Light on Ancient Carthage* (1980); A. Ennabli, ed., *Pour sauver Carthage: Exploration et conservation de la cité punique, romaine et byzantine* (UNESCO/INAA, 1992); S. Lancel, *Carthage: A History* (1995).

NAOMI NORMAN

CARTOCETO BRONZES. Group of monumental Roman bronze statues.

Fragments of the over-lifesize gilt bronze group of two equestrians and two standing females were discovered by a farmer cleaning a threshing ground near Cartoceto di Pergola (Marche) in 1946 and entered the Museo Nazionale delle Marche in Ancona. The statues were found dumped in a funnel-shaped pit in a secluded area, otherwise totally sterile archaeologically. Evidently willfully destroyed before burial, they posed an immense problem for restorers in modern times. Parts were first exhibited in Ancona in 1959. The heads of the horses were shown together with the traveling exhibition of the *Horses* of San Marco in 1979. Further restoration was performed, and the group, together with a copy of one of the horsemen, went on show in Florence temporarily in 1987. One of the equestrians and the two women were shown in a special exhibition near the findspot at Pergola in 1989. To prevent their return to the Ancona museum, the statues were sequestered by the local authorities and have been inaccessible for years.

The ensemble was interpreted by Sandro Stucchi in 1960 and again in 1987 as an imperial family group, consisting of a presumed central figure ("Tiberius"; now missing), flanked on his right by the well-preserved female figure ("Livia") and the better-preserved of the two equestrians ("Drusus Caesar," elder son of Germanicus and Agrippina Major) and on his left by the now-fragmentary female figure ("Agrippina Major") and the horseman whose portrait is missing ("Nero Caesar," younger son of the same couple). As a date, Stucchi proposed sometime between A.D. 23 and 29. In 1988 Stucchi jettisoned the presumed missing figure of Tiberius, whom he now saw represented in the headless equestrian. Coarelli (1990) suggested that the group might represent the family of Marcus Satrius from Sentinum. In 1992 and 1993, J. Pollini advanced members of the family of the Domitii Ahenobarbi.

Taking into consideration the telling iconographical details ("Persian" saddle blankets, breast straps with marine theme and *phalerae* with Mars, Venus and

Quirinus), an alternate interpretation proposed is that the group may rather be a memorial of Augustus's successful dispatch of his grandson Lucius Caesar to the East, peacefully to reassert Roman supremacy over the Parthians in A.D. 2. It may have comprised Augustus, framed by his mother, Atia, and his consort Livia and by two horsemen, one his adoptive father, Caesar, the other his grandson Lucius.

BIBLIOGRAPHY

S. Stucchi, "Gruppo bronzeo di Cartoceto: Gli elementi al Museo di Ancona," *BdA* 45 (1960), 7–44; Ministero per i Beni Culturali e Ambientali, Soprintendenza ai Beni Archeologici della Toscana, *Bronzi dorati da Cartoceto, un restauro* (Florence, 1987); idem, *Il Gruppo bronzeo tiberiano da Cartoceto* (Rome, 1988); E. R. Knauer, "*Multa Egit Cum Regibus et Pacem Confirmavit, The Date of the Equestrian Statue of Marcus Aurelius*," *RM,* 97 (1990), 277–306; I. Bergemann, *Römische Reiterstatuen, Ehrendenkmäler im öffentlichen Bereich* (Mainz, 1990), 50–54; E.R. Knauer, "Brüchstück einer bronzenen Satteldecke in Bonn," *Bonner Jahrbücher* 192 (1992 [1993]), 241–60; J. Pollini, "The Cartoceto Bronzes: Portraits of a Roman Aristocratic Family of the Late First Century B.C.," *AJA* 97 (1993).

E. R. KNAUER

CASA DEI CRESCENTII (CRESCENZI), Rome. Medieval house built with *spolia,* or remnants of ancient Roman monuments.

This unusually elaborate medieval structure stands between the *Theater of Marcellus and Santa Maria in Cosmedin, an area beside the Tiber River densely occupied in the Middle Ages. Although incomplete, the Casa dei Crescentii is outstanding among the many medieval houses of Rome due to the wealth of *spolia* and the ornate elevations.

The ground floor and part of one upper story survive; the original height is unknown. The surviving parts are built of reused Roman bricks. On the ground floor, the façade is decorated with eight rectangular pilasters, which alternate with seven engaged columns. The columns are surmounted by two rows of bricks set diagonally to simulate capitals. Above each column is a bracket supporting an entablature consisting mainly of fragments of antique marble friezes. The upper story had an arcaded loggia such as occurs elsewhere in Rome (e.g., in the medieval house in Vicolo dell'Atleta). An inscription above the door records that the house was built by a certain Nicolaus, the son or descendant of Crescens, and a certain Alberic.

The inscription, which is embellished with the head of a lion, has been likened to the inscription above the door of the Torre di Pandolfo near the mouth of the river Garigliano; this tower (destroyed in 1943) was built between 961 and 981. Modern opinion, however, favors a later date for the Casa dei Crescentii, perhaps in the twelfth century.

BIBLIOGRAPHY

P. Fedele—B. M. Apolloni, *Il Centro di Studi di Storia dell' Architettura* (Rome, 1940); C. Cecchelli, "La Torre di Pandolfo Capodiferro al Garigliano ed uno scomparso cimielo della sua raccolta,'' *Archivio della Società* 70 (1951), 1–26; R. Krautheimer, *Rome, Profile of a City, 312–1308* (Princeton, NJ, 1980), 197–98.

DAVID WHITEHOUSE

CASA DI LIVIA. See HOUSE OF LIVIA.

CASKEY, JOHN LANGDON (1908–81). American archaeologist and classicist.

Caskey's work established a sound stratigraphical basis for the chronology of pre-Mycenaean periods in southern Greece and in the *Cyclades; he served as director of the *American School of Classical Studies at Athens (1949–59) and professor at the University of Cincinnati (1959–79).

''Jack'' Caskey devoted most of his career to the excavation and study of three prehistoric sites: *Troy (in collaboration with *Blegen), *Lerna in the Argolid and Ayia Irini on *Keos. He took special pride in his lucid prose style. A meticulous concern for accuracy and an untimely death prevented completion of final reports on work at Lerna and Ayia Irini, but his plentiful preliminary studies and essays on Neolithic and Bronze Age Greece have considerably influenced the field. In 1980 Caskey was awarded the Gold Medal for Distinguished Archaeological Achievement by the *Archaeological Institute of America.

BIBLIOGRAPHY

AJA 85 (1981), 182; M. J. Mellink, ''John Langdon Caskey (1908–1981),'' *The American Philosophical Society Year Book 1982* (Philadelphia, 1983), 454–59; G. Cadogan, ''John L. Caskey,'' *The End of the Early Bronze Age in the Aegean,* ed. G. Cadogan (Leiden, 1986), 1–4.

JACK L. DAVIS

CASSON, STANLEY (1889–1944). British Hellenist and archaeologist.

Attracted to anthropology while at Oxford, Casson contributed incisively to many areas of Hellenic study. As assistant director of the *British School at Athens (1919–22), he completed the *Catalogue of the Acropolis Museum* 2 (1922) and turned to historical geography in *Macedonia, Thrace and Illyria* (1926). In Oxford, where he was reader from 1927, his notable works on Greek sculpture were not limited to style: technical processes were examined in detail, and Casson's vigorous exposition extended to the modern period, too, as did his writing on larger historical issues for a wider public in the years preceding the war in which he died—in Greece—on active service.

BIBLIOGRAPHY

J. L. Myres, ''Stanley Casson: 1889–1944,'' *BSA* 41 (1940–45), 1–4.

DAVID RIDGWAY

CASTEL SANT'ANGELO (MAUSOLEUM OF HADRIAN), Rome. Monumental Roman tomb, built for the emperor Hadrian (117–38), later converted into a prison and fortress of the popes.

View of *Castel Sant'Angelo* (the Mausoleum of Hadrian), Rome, drawing from the Codex Escurialensis, before 1508, Madrid, Escorial. (Deutsches Archäologisches Institut, Rome. Inst. Neg. 2321.)

  The Mausoleum of Hadrian, begun in the emperor's lifetime, was completed and dedicated in A.D. 139 by his successor, Antoninus Pius. Hadrian and his wife, Sabina, were buried there, as well as successive emperors and their families into the time of Caracalla. The original exterior featured a huge square base, faced with Parian marble (85m on a side and ca. 10m high), supporting a cylindrical drum of travertine limestone and tufa (diameter 68m; original height ca. 21m). Inside the drum an entrance corridor and spiral ramp led upward to the burial chamber of Hadrian, a square chamber 8m on a side and ca. 10m high. On top of this was a mound of earth covered with vegetation and featuring statuary on the peak, seemingly a huge four-horse chariot, perhaps guided by Hadrian. Other statuary graced the exterior, including colossal representations of horses and men.

  The mausoleum was strategically located on the Tiber River in front of a bridge built by Hadrian (the Pons Aelius, now Ponte Sant'Angelo, retaining three original arches). The situation naturally led to the decision, made by the time of Honorius (A.D. 403), that the tomb should serve as a fortress. The fortified bridgehead was besieged by the Goths in A.D. 537, with the defenders heaving marble statuary down on the attackers.

  Theodoric (A.D. 493–526) was the first to use the mausoleum as a prison, a purpose it was to serve often during the later Middle Ages and the Renaissance. By the eighteenth century, it had a little church atop it, S. Angelo de Castro S. Angeli, commemorating the vision of Pope Gregory the Great (590) of St. Michael sheathing his sword, from which the "Castle of the Holy Angel" gets its name. The mausoleum is mentioned in the *Einsiedeln Itinerary (ca. 800) and in the twelfth-century *Mirabilia, where it is described as adorned with bronze statuary, including two gilded bronze peacocks that later were moved to the forecourt of the old church of St. Peter's and even later to the courtyard of the *Belvedere Pigna, where they remain today.

The mausoleum became a papal stronghold in 1277, when Nicholas III built the long, elevated wall that connected Castel Sant'Angelo with the Vatican. *Cola di Rienzo took refuge there in 1347, and Stefano Porcari (*Porcari family) was hanged there in 1453. Clement VII took his stand against Charles V in the fortress during the great Sack of Rome in 1527, and Urban VIII (1623–44) improved the defenses with new cannon, made from bronze stolen from the roof of the *Pantheon.

The exterior was modified from time to time. A drawing from the *Codex Escurialensis (late fifteenth century) shows part of the podium still in place, but crenellations, a corbel table and a corner bastion all serve to give the tomb a very different appearance. Pius IV (1559–65) created other bastions and a moat, and Urban VIII modified these (restored in 1933–34 to the project of Pius IV).

The interior was vastly changed through the centuries, with many rooms being converted or constructed entirely new for papal usage. *Bramante built the Loggia of *Julius II, and Antonio da *Sangallo the Younger constructed the Loggia of Paul III (1543). Painters of the generation after *Raphael—*Giulio Romano, Perino del Vaga, Giovanni da *Udine, Polidoro da Caravaggio—contributed a great deal to the decorations, with painting and stuccos featuring *grottesche. Much of the interior is used a museum today, for works of art and material connected with the defense of the fortress. Two huge subterranean chambers contain eighty-four storage jars for oil, garrison provisions that could also be poured down on attackers.

Reconstructions of the Hadrianic tomb were attempted as early as the fifteenth century by *Ciriaco da Ancona and Filarete (his appears on the bronze doors of St. Peter's). In modern times, M. Borgatti, who played a major role in restoring the monument after it ceased to be a prison in 1901, generated an authoritative model that is on display with models of Castel Sant'Angelo at the time of Alexander VI (1492–1503) and Urban VIII, along with related architectural fragments in the Museo della Storia Romana del Mausoleo.

BIBLIOGRAPHY
+M. Borgatti, Castel Sant'Angelo in Roma (Rome, 1931); +Nash, II, 44–48; M. T. Boatwright, Hadrian and the City of Rome (Princeton, NJ, 1987), 161–75; Richardson, New Topographical Dictionary, 249–51; Castel Sant'Angelo nelle stampe della Collezione d'Amelio, catalog of exhibition (Rome, 1992); Castel Sant'Angelo, La Memoria fotografica, 1850–1904, catalog of exhibition (Rome, 1993).

CASTELLANI FAMILY. Italian family famed for its skill in gold working and jewelry and for its study and collecting of antiquities.

FORTUNATO PIO CASTELLANI (1794–1865) began trading in 1814 as a manufacturing jeweler and goldsmith in Rome. In 1826, he read a paper to the *Accademia dei Lincei on his successful chemical achievement of the *giallone* ("deep yellow") color characteristic of ancient gold, and subsequently he created imitations of gold artifacts that were being found in the Etruscan cemeteries and at *Pompeii and *Herculaneum. These exercises culminated in his foundation around 1840 of a school where young goldsmiths could absorb the style and methods of their ancient counterparts.

Fortunato Pio retired from business in 1853. Following the political imprisonment in the same year of his eldest son, ALESSANDRO (1823–83), direction of the family firm and fortunes passed to his second son, AUGUSTO (1829–1914). Unable to prevent the sale by the Vatican of the *Campana collection to Napoleon III in 1860, Augusto and his father resolved to spend part of their trading surplus on their own collection of antiquities, particularly jewelry. Meanwhile, Alessandro, by 1860 exiled from the Papal States, opened a branch of the firm in Paris and later transferred his commercial and antiquarian activities to Naples, lecturing and exhibiting widely in France, Great Britain and the United States on the family theme of antique jewelry and its revival.

Fortunato Pio's third son, GUGLIELMO (1836–96), was a potter, as was Alessandro's son TORQUATO (1846–1931); like the jewelry produced by their better-known relatives, their output was influenced by ancient models.

As a distinguished scholarly collector, Augusto moved easily in archaeological and antiquarian circles in Rome. In addition to managing the family business, he was for a time honorary director of the *Capitoline Museums, for which he secured a number of important pieces; many of them were restored by his son ALFREDO (1856–1930) and published by Augusto in the *Bullettino Comunale* between 1874 and 1889. Alfredo inherited the family collection of Greek, Etruscan and Italiote vases, bronzes, ivories, coins, gems and ancient and modern jewelry; he donated it in memory of his father to the *Villa Giulia Museum in 1919.

BIBLIOGRAPHY

Augusto Castellani, *Gems: Notes, and Extracts,* tr. Mrs. J. Brogden (London, 1871); Alessandro Castellani, *Antique Jewelry and Its Revival* (Philadelphia, n.d. [1876]); A. E. Gordon, *The Inscribed Fibula Praenestina* (Berkeley, 1975), 65–75; G. Bordenache Battaglia et al., "Castellani, Famiglia," *DBI* 21 (1978), 590–605.

DAVID RIDGWAY

CASTIGLIONE, SABBA DA (1480–1554). Italian writer, early visitor to the Greek islands of the Aegean as a member of the Order of the Knights Templar of St. John.

Born in Milan, Sabba took orders early and was assigned to duty against the Turks at *Rhodes. He was devoted to Isabella d'*Este, marchioness of Mantua, and before leaving Italy had visited her and pledged to send her some antiquities from the Greek islands. He reported that there were many fine sculptures lying neglected on Rhodes and also on *Delos, which he visited in 1506, but that he was uneasy about removing anything without permission from his order. Isabella managed to obtain the appropriate sanction, and eventually Sabba secured for her a number of marbles, including a statuette from *Naxos (lacking head and limbs), a torso from Delos and three heads from Cos. Most remarkable were the pieces from the newly discovered *Mausoleum of Halikarnassos, including two heads of Amazons and a marble group of a sea god clasping a nymph in his arms. Sabba proposed to Isabella the astonishing scheme of moving the entire Mausoleum (which he never succeeded in visiting) to Mantua but abandoned the idea when he was relieved of duty in Rhodes in 1508.

Sabba returned to Italy and was active in Rome until 1516 and near Faenza until his death in 1554. During this period there is no further evidence of his collecting activities or of his connection with Isabella d'Este.

BIBLIOGRAPHY
J. Cartwright, *Isabella d'Este* (London, 1903), II, 14–19; J. Petrucci, "Castiglione, Sabba da," *DBI* 22 (1979), 100–106.

CASTOR AND POLLUX (SAN ILDEFONSO GROUP; THE DECII; ORESTES AND PYLADES). Roman marble group of two lifesize nude youths (max. height 1.58m) in a classicizing style.

The heavily restored figures are wearing garlands and appear before an altar, toward which the youth on the right guides a torch; a statuette of a female appears on the far right of the statue base. Many theories about their identity have been offered through the centuries. *Winckelmann argued that the sculptures showed Orestes and Pylades (not among the Taurians, but before the tomb of Agamemnon), while *Perrier, *Caylus and others thought the pair were Publius Decius and his son preparing to sacrifice themselves in battle, as described by Livy (8.9; 10.28). The most frequently proposed identification is that of Castor and Pollux, but even today there is no general agreement on the subject matter. The smooth surfaces of the figures, virtually empty of detail, suggest a date in the first century B.C., during the ardently classicizing age of Pasiteles.

The group was probably discovered in 1621 or 1622 in the *Gardens of Sallust on the Pincio, going immediately into the *Ludovisi family collections. Subsequently it was owned by Cardinal Massimi (*Massimi family); from 1678 to 1689 by Queen *Christina of Sweden; by Cardinal Azzolini; by the Odescalchi; and finally by Philip V of Spain (acquired 1724). In 1839 it was taken to the *Prado, where it remains today. A cast of the pair remained in Rome, in the *French Academy, and others were made from it upon request (e.g., for *Louis XIV, for *Goethe). The *Castor and Pollux* group was ranked with the finest classical statuary known during the seventeenth and eighteenth centuries, and even in the nineteenth century, when many works fell from grace, the group retained much of its popularity, especially in Germany. Recent scholarship and art criticism, however, show little interest in the statues.

BIBLIOGRAPHY
A. Blanco, *Museo del Prado: Catalogo de la escultura*, I, *Esculturas clasicas* (Madrid, 1957), 30–32; *Christina Queen of Sweden: A Personality of European Civilization*

(Stockholm, 1966), 433–34, 438; Haskell—Penny, 173–75; E. Simon, "Kritirien zur Deutung 'Pasitelischen' Gruppen," *JdI* 102 (1987), 291–309.

CAUSEUS, MICHAEL ANGELUS. See CHAUSSE, MICHEL-ANGE DE LA.

CAVACEPPI, BARTOLOMEO (ca. 1716–99). Italian sculptor; once Europe's best-known restorer of classical antiquities.

Cavaceppi repaired (as well as copied, cast, collected, displayed and sold) many thousands of ancient sculptures when their decorative renovation was still much in vogue. He was recognized as an accomplished technician from his youth and was trained in the late Baroque and academic traditions of Rome. These stylistic and rhetorical approaches influenced and sustained his original work and renovations through most of his life.

Cavaceppi's activities as a restorer began in the 1730s for the newly founded Capitoline Museum, under the direction of Carlo Napolioni, conservator for his lifelong patron, Cardinal Alessandro Albani (*Albani Family), the Hadrian of his century, Rome's protector of the arts and its *reparateur en chef* of antiquities. First through Albani and then independently, Cavaceppi worked for the papal and private collectors of Italy. Eventually he also served hosts of foreigners (mainly from north of the Alps), who, during a mounting furor for antiquities and the *Grand Tour, came in droves to Rome, then still the art capital of the world. Cavaceppi supplied single examples and whole galleries of works to them, their agents and his fellow entrepreneurs and restorers. There are works from his studio in virtually every major collection of ancient sculptures that acquired pieces in his day.

Through Albani he became the colleague of J. J. *Winckelmann, often referred to as the father of modern archaeology and art history. After Winckelmann's death, working with Rome's new commissioner of antiquities, G. B. *Visconti, and the papal treasurer, Cardinal Braschi (later, *Pius VI), Cavaceppi helped *Clement XIV to establish the Pio-Clementino galleries (*Vatican Museums). Cavaceppi's prodigious wealth, ambition and holdings were invested in the Museo Cavaceppi (also an art academy of sorts), established in the center of Rome, where the sculptor was visited by two generations of influential artists, thinkers and grandees who wished to see, study and buy famous art and antiquities. His huge collections of fragments, restorations, copies, casts, models, coins, bronzes, paintings and folios of drawings (whose chronological arrangement was much admired by, and presumably influenced, Winckelmann) were bequeathed to the art academy of Rome, which unfortunately never received them.

Cavaceppi's earliest work was pictorial and loaded with fanciful attributes in ways compatible with the narrative, emblematic and hermeneutic interests of Baroque taste and learning. Affected by discoveries at *Pompeii and the sober historicism of Winckelmann and other midcentury antiquarians, Cavaceppi made

Studio of Bartolomeo Cavaceppi, illustrating ancient fragments, restorations, copies and sketches in process and on display, from B. Cavaceppi, *Raccolta d'antiche statue*, 2 (1769). (S. Howard.)

his restorations more modest and archaeologically responsible. His last (and preferred) manner avoided repair altogether, anticipating the position of *Canova and others against restoring the Parthenon fragments during the *Elgin controversy. Cavaceppi published his theories in three volumes with 180 large plates of sculptures restored and for sale. (The last volume also had a self-serving open letter and autobiographical sketch addressed to his patron Frederick the Great, ostensibly written to describe Winckelmann's last days in Germany while traveling with Cavaceppi in 1768.) Despite his recorded ideals, Cavaceppi was often capricious and misleading in his work, making fakes, pastiches and massively restored or reworked sculptures that showed little of antiquity and much of fashionable conventions about the antique. Nonetheless, his renovations and inventions, made under the constraint of classical models and antiquarian patronage, helped to determine notions of classical art and establish neo-classicism as the first style of the modern age.

BIBLIOGRAPHY

+B. Cavaceppi, *Raccolta d'antiche statue busti bassirilievi ed altre sculture ristaurate*, 1–3 (Rome, 1768–72); M. Cagiano de Azevedo, *Il Gusto nel restauro* (Rome, 1948); +S. Howard, *Bartolomeo Cavaceppi, Eighteenth-Century Restorer* (Chicago, 1958; New York, 1982); idem, *Antiquity Restored* (Vienna, 1990); *Bartolomeo Cavaceppi*, ed. M. G. Barberini (Rome, 1995).

S. HOWARD

CAVALIERI, GIOVANNI BATTISTA DE' (JOANNES BAPTISTA DE CAVALLERIIS; 1525?–1601). Author of a collection of 200 engravings of antique statues, *Antiquae statuae urbis Romae;* published in sections between ca. 1561 and 1594, when the third and fourth books were printed.

Although not of high quality, these engravings serve to document the holdings of many of the major (*Farnese, *Cesi, *Este, *Vatican Belvedere) and some of the minor (Capranica, *Valle, *Garimberto) Roman collectors. The Cavalieri plates were frequently republished, being the model for many of the subsequent publications, all of which were intended for a popular market. The editions of Vaccaria, Marcucci and De Rossi contain those changes of provenance that chart the movement of a number of the statues from one collection to another. Thus, the designation "Villa Borgesia" replaces the older text, "In Musaeo Garimberto," on several plates, thereby documenting the dispersal of a portion of that collection for which Cavalieri provided some twenty-five plates. Furthermore, the present location of some of these pieces can be established upon this visual evidence.

BIBLIOGRAPHY

T. Ashby, "Antiquae Statuae Urbis Romae," *PBSR* 9 (1920), 107–58; E. Mandowsky, "An Unknown Drawing for Cavalieri's 'Antiquarum Statuarum Urbis Romae,'" *GBA* 45 (1955), 313–20.

CLIFFORD M. BROWN

CAYLUS, ANNE CLAUDE PHILIPPE, COMTE DE (1692–1765). French antiquarian and artist, known for developing a historical approach to the periods and styles of ancient cultures.

Born in Paris, Caylus traveled in his youth to Italy and to Asia Minor with the French ambassador to Constantinople. In 1716 he visited *Smyrna, *Ephesos and Colophon, as well as the Troad, but never made it to mainland Greece. His early travels also included tours of Holland and England, where he visited various collections, churches and convents.

Caylus returned to Paris for good, where he moved in the circle of P. J. *Mariette, Watteau and Crozat and where he became a skilled engraver. He turned his talents to the reproduction of 1,500 Roman imperial gold coins and carved gems from the king's collection (completed after 1729), the plates for which are today in the *Louvre. Admitted as a member of the Royal Academy of Painting and Sculpture and the Académie des inscriptions et belles-lettres, Caylus came to play a major role in documenting ancient monuments and to dominate the study of antiquity in his country. He encouraged young artists (e.g., Hubert *Robert and *Vien, whom he "discovered") to make reproductions or imitations of ancient landscapes and objects, and he himself did reconstructions of lost monuments, such as the paintings in the Lesche of the Knidians at *Delphi (described by Pausanias 10, 25–31) and the *Mausoleum of Halikarnassos.

From 1744 to 1765, Caylus gave some fifty lectures at the Académie des inscriptions. He had an especial interest in ancient techniques, processes and materials, and among his published lectures were important ones on obsidian and papyrus, as well as on the process of mummification, with which he himself had actually experimented. The most famous result of his researches was the rediscovery of the technique of encaustic, or painting on wax, which he demonstrated to the academy with a painting of the head of *Minerva* by Vien. His arguments were disputed by the followers of Diderot, a bitter enemy of Caylus, but modern scholarship has confirmed his conclusions.

The Comte de Caylus was one of the first to analyze in a sound way the differences among Greek, Roman, Etruscan and Egyptian works of art, and as such he was an important forerunner of *Winckelmann. His great work, the *Recueil d'antiquités egyptiennes, étrusques, grècques, romaines, et gauloises,* appeared in seven volumes between 1752 and 1767. In it he drew attention to the tastes and styles of different cultures, including even the art of Persepolis (his was the first illustration of such material), Gaul, Cyprus, Malta and Sardinia. Caylus also prepared a collection of ancient paintings with plates hand-colored after designs by P. S. *Bartoli, of which only thirty specimens were published.

He died after a long and difficult illness, faithfully attended by Mariette and still reviled by Diderot, in 1765.

BIBLIOGRAPHY

E. de Goncourt—J. de Goncourt, *Portraits intimes du XVIIIe s.* 2 (1858), 10–42; S. Rocheblave, *Essai sur le Comte de Caylus* (Paris, 1889); P. Leguay, "Caylus (A.-C.-P.

de Tubières, Comte de)," *DBF* 7 (1950), cols. 1518–21; E. Lissi, "Caylus, A.C.P., Comte de," *EAA* 2 (1959), 447–48.

CELLINI, BENVENUTO (1500–71). Italian sculptor and goldsmith; author of a famous autobiography, his *Vita* or *Life,* and *Due trattati,* treatises on goldsmithing and sculpture.

Born in Florence, Cellini was trained as a goldsmith and worked as a sculptor. In 1517, on his way to Rome, he lost his way and ended up at *Pisa, where he spent two years working with a goldsmith at the cathedral and studying classical *Roman sarcophagi. In 1519 he arrived in Rome and began to study antiquities there. His *Life* describes bizarre scenes of witchcraft in the *Colosseum and mentions the regular discovery of medals and carved gems in Rome. Cellini engaged in the sale of these objects, and he describes an emerald dolphin head, a topaz *Minerva,* a cameo of *Hercules Binding Cerberus* and a bronze medal of *Jupiter,* among others. In 1532 he traveled to Naples, where he also viewed antiquities.

Cardinal Ippolito d'Este commissioned a copy of the **Spinario* through Cellini, which he gave to Francis I in December 1540, and around this time Cellini began work in France at Fontainebleau for the king. Cellini's rival, *Primaticcio, set up a bronze foundry to cast copies of major antique sculptures. Cellini established his own foundry nearby to cast high-quality copies of a few classical statues from models he made while he was in Rome, as well as to cast new works. The most extraordinary of these was his *Nymph of Fontainebleau,* created to represent the genius of the palace above the main entrance. This bronze lunette, now in the *Louvre, depicts a nymph resting her hand on a water jug, surrounded by animals that rival antique animal portrayals. In 1543 he made his famous gold and enamel *Salt Cellar of Francis I.* In his *Life,* he describes it as depicting the Sea and the Earth reclining next to a basin for salt, surrounded by details including seahorses and a small temple for pepper. The oval base is decorated with a relief of alternating trophies and deities, and the serene figures impart a sense of monumentality surprising in a work on such a small scale.

The majority of Cellini's monumental sculpture is in Florence. He was familiar with the *Medici family collection of ancient bronzes, particularly, the *Minerva,* discovered in 1541, and the **Arringatore,* acquired in 1566. His colossal bronze bust of Cosimo I de' Medici (1547) was based on a colossal statue of Julius Caesar in the Palazzo dei Conservatori. His elaborate bronze group of *Perseus* (1552) owes a great deal to his interest in Etruscan art and classical masks; the statue of Perseus may be based on a small Etruscan bronze known to Cosimo I.

Cellini's interest in antiquity tended toward the esoteric or exotic, and he showed a preference for more obscure works. In addition, antiquity was a source not only of style but also of technique. In his *Due trattati* he stated his belief that bronzes must be chased in the manner of the ancients. He viewed antiquity as an inspiration to contemporary art rather than as an end in itself. The aim was to surpass antiquity or improve it; thus, antique objects could be utilized in the creation of new works.

In restoring a torso of Greek marble from Palestrina, Cellini determined that it should represent *Ganymede,* and he added all the missing body parts and an eagle. In his autobiography he mentions, but makes no claim to have restored, the Etruscan *Chimera.* He does, however, mention statuettes found in *Arezzo that Cosimo I enjoyed cleaning with the use of goldsmithing chisels; Cellini was given the job of restoring them. For one of these restorations, now located in the Archaeological Museum in *Florence, Cellini fashioned a horse for an antique bronze rider to create *Alexander and Bucephalus.*

Cellini used classical subject matter and style in creating his small bronzes and medals and his lifesize bronze and marble sculpture. He was one of the finest sculptors working in the Mannerist style, and his *Life* presents an invaluable portrait of the world of art and the uses of antiquity in the sixteenth century.

BIBLIOGRAPHY

B. Cellini, *The Autobiography of Benvenuto Cellini,* tr. J. A. Symonds (New York, 1927); C. Avery—S. Barbaglia, *L'Opera completa del Cellini* (Milan, 1981); J. Pope-Hennessey, *Cellini* (New York, 1985).

C. NAUMER

CELTIS (CELTES), CONRADUS (CONRAD; KONRAD; also C. C. PRO-TUCIUS; real name CONRAD PICKEL or BICKEL; 1459–1508). German poet and humanist.

Born near Würzburg, Celtis left home at age seventeen to study at Cologne (1477) and then at Heidelberg (1484) with Rudolph Agricola. He continued to wander, to Leipzig and then to Rome (1486), where he took part in the *Roman Academy of Pomponio *Leto. His first book of poetry, *Ars versificandi et carminum,* was published to great acclaim in 1486, and Celtis returned in triumph to Germany the following year. At Nuremberg he received the poet's crown, his nation's first, at the hands of the Holy Roman Emperor Frederick III.

Celtis's later years were spent at a number of posts or on visits at Cracow, Prague, Vienna, Ratisbon, Heidelberg, Buda, Mainz, Ingolstadt, Vienna. Sometimes called ''the arch-humanist''(*Der Erzhumanist*) for his promotion of classical studies, Celtis founded humanist societies in Germany (Sodalitas Rhenana), Poland (Sodalitas Litteraria Vistulana) and Hungary (Sodalitas Litteraria Hungarorum). He thus played a major role in stimulating the study of classical literature and antiquities in these lands outside Italy.

Celtis continued to publish volumes of poetry (especially lyric) with great success, as well as an edition of Tacitus's *Germania* (1500) and an edition of the works of Hroswitha of Gandersheim, Germany's first woman poet, whose tenth-century plays Celtis discovered during his searching of libraries for unknown works. He also discovered the *Tabula Peutingeriana, a rare map based on an antique model, and later bequeathed it to K. *Peutinger, for whom it is only incidentally named. Celtis was a friend and patron of *Dürer at Nuremberg.

BIBLIOGRAPHY
Sandys, II, 259; L. Forster, ed., with tr. and comment, *Selections from Conrad Celtis, 1459–1508* (Cambridge, 1948); H. Rupprich, "Celtis (Bickel), Konrad (C. C. Protucius)," *NDB* 3 (1956), 181–83.

CEOLI (CEVOLI; CEULI), TIBERIO (d. 1605). Wealthy Italian banker, collector of antiquities.

In 1576, Tiberio Ceoli acquired the palazzo of Cardinal Ricci di Montepulciani, constructed in 1542 by Antonio da *Sangallo in the Strada Giulia on the corner of Vicolo del Cefalo in Rome (now, Palazzo Sacchetti). Included in the sale were a number of statues. He acquired a collection of bronze statues from Giuliano Cesarini. The collection became well known and was highly recommended by visitors to Rome. Twelve of his marble sculptures were copied by Andrea Boscoli (1553–1606) during his visit to the city (1580–90). Others are illustrated in Girolamo Franzini's woodcuts (1599) and De *Cavallieri's engravings (1594). A drawing of a sarcophagus with the *Adonis* theme occurs in the dal *Pozzo album in Windsor.

After Tiberio's death, 273 of his marbles were purchased by Cardinal Scipione *Borghese (19 December 1607) and removed four days later. Ten of his statues are pictured in Philip Thomassin, *Antiquarum statuarum urbis Romae* 1 (1618) as then in "aedibus Card. Burghesij."

BIBLIOGRAPHY
R. Lanciani, *Storia degli scavi* 3 (1907), 108; C. L. Frommel, *Der Römische Palastbau der Hochrenaissance* 2 (Tübingen, 1973), 294–95; L. de Lachenal, "La collezione di sculture antiche della famiglia Borghese e il palazzo in Campo Marzio," *Xenia* 4 (1982), 52–55, 84–6.

                                                    MARJON VAN DER MEULEN

CERVETERI (CAERE). Modern Italian town coinciding topographically with ancient Caere (Etruscan *Chai[s]re, Cheri;* Greek *Agylla*), an important member of the Etruscan League of twelve peoples.

Situated between *Veii, *Tarquinia and Faliscan territory, Caere was famous for its prosperity, culture, naval strength, alliance with *Carthage, excellent relations with the Greeks (especially of Ionia), treasury at *Delphi, and—later— for helping Rome at the time of the Gallic attack (386 B.C.).

The city area is still virtually unexplored, but offical excavations began there in 1983. The (largely unpublished) cemeteries provide an unbroken sequence from the ninth century B.C. to the Early Empire and bear witness to conspicuous affluence between ca. 700 and ca. 500 B.C.; they constitute a major source of knowledge about Etruscan art and culture. The material from the *Regolini-Galassi tomb (*Vatican Museums), found intact in 1836, revealed the splendors of the Etruscan Orientalizing period; other erratic but extensive nineteenth-century excavations enriched many collections, notably the *Campana, which was subsequently split among the *Capitoline Museums (the Aristonothos krater), the *Louvre (painted terracotta slabs) and other European museums. Toward the end of the century, Caeretan material (e.g., the Sarcofago degli Sposi, with its famous representation of a married couple) began to reach the new *Villa Giulia Museum.

Early twentieth-century exploration of Caere is associated primarily with the name of Raniero Mengarelli, who opened the Banditaccia cemetery to the public. There, monumental tumuli afford exceptionally detailed evidence for Etruscan funerary architecture and, indirectly, for civil and domestic building, too; the rich grave goods (Villa Giulia) include numerous Attic vases. Bureaucratic difficulties prevented Mengarelli from publishing his findings definitively. After World War II, research continued at a slower pace. From 1957, much important information has been provided by the *Lerici Foundation's geophysical surveys and excavations. The Museo Nazionale Cerite (Castello Ruspoli) was opened in 1967, as was a new sector of the necropolis. Contemporary research is hampered alike by clandestine operations and by the nonexistent or inadequate publication of official discoveries. Several recent specialist studies confirm the significance of Caere in the production of fine bronzes (L. *Banti), painted slabs (F. Roncalli) and figured sarcophagi of terracotta (M.-F. Briguet) and of various ceramic categories; the cultural effects of contact with the early Greek colonists have been assessed by G. Colonna.

Knowledge of Caere's principal port, *Pyrgi, is limited essentially to the well-known sanctuary revealed by excavations conducted from 1957 to date.

BIBLIOGRAPHY

G. Dennis, *Cities and Cemeteries of Etruria,* 3rd ed. (London, 1883), I, 227–97; +L. Pareti, *La Tomba Regolini-Galassi* (Rome, 1947); Various authors, *Caere: scavi di Raniero Mengarelli, MonAnt* 42 (1955); +*Gli Etruschi e Cerveteri: Catalogo della mostra* (Milan, 1980); *Gli Etruschi di Cerveteri* (Modena, 1986); H. Blanck, *La Tomba dei Rilievi di Cerveteri* (Rome, 1986).

F. R. SERRA RIDGWAY

CESARINI FAMILY. Prominent family at Rome during the Renaissance; owners of an important collection of ancient sculpture.

In actuality an offshoot of the Montenari, the Cesarini claimed descent from Julius Caesar. The family's legendary genealogy strongly influenced their sense for the Latin past as well as their contemporary loyalties. From the fifteenth through the seventeenth centuries, they even-handedly served Rome both as cardinals of the Church and as Gonfalonieri of the people. In the annals of classical archaeology two members stand out: GIULIANO II (1466–1510), apostolic protonotary, cardinal from 1493; and the son of Cardinal ALESSANDRO (d. 1542), GIANGIORGIO, who left Clelia Farnese a widow in 1585.

On his birthday in the spring of 1500, Giuliano dedicated a *diaeta statuaria* annexed to the palace built by his uncle, the famous cardinal who died at the

Battle of Varna in 1444, flanking the Via Papale on the site of the former Via de'Cesarini and the present Largo Argentina (named for the papal diarist, Burkhard, who came from Strassburg—Argentoratum—and lived in a tower acquired by the Cesarini on the site of today's Teatro). This statue garden, instead of those often cited, established the first private museum of ancient sculpture liberally opened to the public. *Albertini visited in 1509, while Claude Bellièvre during 1512–14 took time to describe certain antiquities, including a bust of *Cato.* In 1549, *Aldrovandi listed the major contents of palazzo and garden in his day.

In the second half of the cinquecento, Giangiorgio developed a *palazzetto* and *vigna* adjacent to S. Pietro in Vincoli, where the *lex hortorum* (or regulation for its use) once again invited friends and students to repose in contemplation of select antiquities. The bulk of these sculptures passed into Farnese hands (*Farnese family) and thence to Naples, although some were bought for the *Ludovisi family collection in the early seventeenth century (today at the *Terme Museum, Rome).

In addition to eighteen portrait heads of ''philosophers'' discovered at the *Baths of Diocletian and purchased by Giangiorgio (Flaminio *Vacca, *Memorie,* no. 105), sold by his brother to the Farnese, famous statues from his collection in Naples include the *Venus Kallipygos* and a *Satyr Carrying the Infant Bacchus* on his shoulder.

BIBLIOGRAPHY

U. Aldrovandi, *Delle statue antiche che per tutta Roma* . . . (Venice, 1556), 221–24; F. Sansovino, *Della origine et de' fatti delle famiglie illustri d'Italia,* 2nd ed. (Venice, 1609), 330–33; Lanciani, *Storia degli scavi* II (1903), 133–35; P. G. Hübner, *Le Statue di Roma,* Römische Forschungen der Bibliotheca Herziana, 2 (Leipzig, 1912), I, 87.

                                                                                        PHYLLIS PRAY BOBER

CESI FAMILY. Prominent family in Rome during the Renaissance, known for its carefully arranged museum and garden of antiquities.

The family could boast no fewer than five cardinals, but two of these were especially important in developing the collection. PAOLO EMILIO CESI (1481–1537) became cardinal in 1517 and soon afterward purchased the property in the Vatican Borgo, where the family was to have its palazzo, library, museum and garden. He acquired hundreds of funerary monuments, some pertaining to the ancient *gens* Caesia. *Heemskerck has left a view of the back wall of the garden during this period, with various statues and sarcophagi standing along it. After the cardinal's death his brother FEDERICO (1500–65) continued collecting antique statues. He obtained monuments from eight different churches in Rome, as well as from other private collections (Colocci, *Chigi, Caffarelli, Mellini) and from new excavations around Rome.

*Aldrovandi's description of the property of the mid-sixteenth century (''one seems to be entering paradise'') aids in a reconstruction of the display in the palace and garden, and there is also a painting by Hendrick van Cleef done late in the century. The cortile of the palazzo housed inscriptions, sepulchral altars and urns, while portrait busts were on display in the studio of the palace. The famed basalt bust of *Scipio Africanus,* the herm of *Sokrates* and a double herm identified as *Thucydides* and *Herodotus* were among the many well-known Cesi portraits. In the garden were a fountain with a *Silenus* pouring from a wineskin and, in the rear, the eye-catching group of a seated *Roma Triumphant* on a base with a relief of *Dacia Weeping* and flanked by two captives of the Farnese type (*Farnese Captives). Other well-known pieces from the Cesi collection are the colossal head of the Ludovisi *"Juno"* (now identified as the younger Antonia) and a standing figure of *Juno* that *Michelangelo supposedly pronounced "the most beautiful thing there is in all of Rome."

Partly due to its proximity to St. Peter's and the Vatican, the garden attracted a record number of artists; *Francisco d'Ollanda, Pierre *Jacques, *Dosio and Girolamo da *Carpi have all left drawings of items in the collection, and *Cavalieri and Franzini both published prints of the Cesi statuary.

When GIOVANNI FEDERICO CESI, Duke of Aquasparta, took over the property in the early seventeenth century, he had little appreciation for the monuments. In 1622 one hundred pieces were sold to the *Ludovisi family (today, in the *Terme Museum, Rome). Part of the palace and garden was destroyed when Bernini built the colonnade in front of St. Peter's (1655–1667). In the eighteenth century, the *Albani family acquired the palace and many of the sculptures, including the *Roma.* The inscriptions were miserably neglected, some being consigned to the lime burner or used for house foundations and others scattered to various collections.

BIBLIOGRAPHY
D. Gnoli, "Il Giardino e l'antiquario del Cardinale Cesi," *RM* 20 (1905), 267–76; Lanciani, *Storia degli scavi* IV (1912), 107–17; C. Hülsen, *Römische Antikengarten, Abhandlungen der Heidelberger Akademie der Wissenschaften, philos.-hist. Klasse* 4 (1917), 1–35; Bober—Rubinstein, 472.

MARJON VAN DER MEULEN

CESNOLA, LUIGI PALMA DI (1832–1904). Italo-American soldier, diplomat and archaeologist; director of the *Metropolitan Museum of Art (1879–1904).

Born into the aristocracy in Rivarolo, Italy, Cesnola was trained as a military officer. In 1860 he came to New York, where he married in 1861. In the Civil War he distinguished himself as a Northern cavalry officer, attaining the rank of colonel, though he later affected the title of general.

While serving as U.S. consul in Cyprus from 1865 to 1877, he claimed to have excavated at about fifty sites, notably Dali, Atheniu (Golgoi), *Paphos, Amathus and *Kourion (Curium), discovering sixty-five necropoleis and some 60,000 tombs. About two-thirds of the 35,000 objects he found he sold to the Metropolitan Museum, of which he became director in 1879, a post he held until his death.

His *Cyprus* (New York, 1879) contains a lively account of these excavations. Gaston Feuardent, an art dealer, accused him in *Art Amateur* (August 1880) of "deceptive alterations and unintelligent restorations" of some of the antiquities. This charge prompted heated exchanges. Eventually, Feuardent sued for libel and lost, but the trial testimony supported the allegation that Cesnola had had substantial restorations made. W. J. Stillman and M. Ohnefalsch-Richter renewed the attack with charges of confused provenances, fraudulent restorations and nonexistent deposits. Others even alleged that the "finds" had been purchased all over the Levant. While subsequent excavations and Sir John *Myres's study of the collection have confirmed the Cypriot nature of most of the pieces, Cesnola's accounts of how and where they were found should be treated with skepticism. Probably he acquired many of them from villagers and invented provenances for them. Most scholars now regard his reports of a temple of Aphrodite at Golgoi and of the temple vaults at Kourion, where he claimed to have found a spectacular treasure, as figments of his imagination. The Kourion Treasure itself, a hodgepodge of wildly different styles and periods, appears to have been assembled by Cesnola in an attempt to eclipse *Schliemann's "Treasure of Priam."

BIBLIOGRAPHY

W. J. Stillman, *Report on the Cesnola Collection to the American Numismatic and Archaeological Society* (New York, 1885); M. Ohnefalsch-Richter, *New York Times,* 16 May 1893, 1; J. L. Myres, *Handbook of the Cesnola Collection* (New York, 1914); E. McFadden, *The Glitter and the Gold* (New York, 1971), with bib.

DAVID A. TRAILL

CHACÓN (CIACONIUS; CIACCONI), ALONSO (ALFONSO; 1540–99). Spanish cleric and antiquarian scholar; an early investigator of the Christian catacombs of Rome.

Chacón was born in Baeza (Andalusia) and took Holy Orders as a Dominican friar in 1548. In 1553 he transferred to Seville, where he developed his major cultural interests. In this period he corresponded with the diligent antiquarian-archaeologist Ambrosio de Morales (at Alcalá), who cited Chacón for providing information on Andalusian epigraphical and archaeological material in his *Las Antiguedades de las ciudades de España* (1575).

Called to the Vatican by Pius V in 1566, Chacón moved to Rome for the rest of his life. In his first years there he lodged in the palace of Cardinal Francesco Pacheco, as he took up the study of the history of the early Church and the antiquities associated with it. He wrote the commentary for the first publication of engravings of the reliefs on the *Column of Trajan, initiated and executed by Girolamo Muziano (*Historia utriusque belli Dacici a Traiano Cesare gesti ex simulacris, quae in eiusdem columna Romae visuntur collecta,* 1576). Along with O. *Panvinio and Cardinal Cesare Baronio, he participated in the wave of interest in Christian antiquities in the middle and later years of the sixteenth century. Chacón was the principal explorer of the catacombs of the Giordani cemetery, discovered in 1578 in a sand quarry on the Via Salaria. His unpublished records of the paintings and inscriptions of the Giordani and other catacombs were later valuable to A. *Bosio and G. B. *De Rossi for their own publications on the catacombs.

BIBLIOGRAPHY

Stark, 105; Lanciani, *Storia degli scavi* 4 (1912), 85, 197, 206, 211; E. Josi, "Le pitture rinvenute nel cimitero de Giordani," *Rivista di Archeologia Cristiana* 5 (1928), 167–227; S. Grassi Fiorentino, "Chacón, Alonso," *DBI* 24 (1980), 352–56.

CHALKIS (CHALCIS). Greek city of the island of Euboia, located at the narrowest point of the Euripos channel between Euboia and mainland Boiotia.

Though Chalkis, along with its nearby rival *Eretria, has claims to be one of the most important of Greek settlements in the Iron Age and one of the first Greek cities to send colonists to Italy in the eighth century (*Pithekoussai, *Cumae), relatively little is known of its monuments. The city was well fortified (traces of the citadel are visible on aerial photographs), and it controlled the fortified bridge built across the Euripos in 410 B.C. The fortress was dismantled by the Romans in 146 B.C., and during the early Byzantine period the city site was moved closer to the bridge. The older, deserted site was quarried to build the new town, which today has taken the name Chalkis.

In 1436 *Ciriaco of Ancona visited the area, and many of the well-known travelers of the nineteenth century—*Dodwell, *Leake, *Ross and others—commented on the topography. *Lear made a drawing of the Turkish fortified bridge that stood over the Euripos in the nineteenth century (now demolished). G. A. Papavasiliou made a major contribution to topographical studies (1889–1913), and recently the literary sources on Chalkis and its topography have been investigated by the Dutch scholar S. C. Bakhuizen, who argues that the Chalcidians exploited nearby iron deposits in the Early Iron Age.

A class of black-figured pottery known as "Chalcidian" ware was associated with the site of Chalkis by A. Rumpf (*Chalkidischen Vasen,* 1927), on the basis of inscriptions on the vases in the Chalcidian alphabet. But no vases of this category have appeared at Chalkis, and other scholars have argued for a workshop at *Cerveteri or elsewhere in Italy.

BIBLIOGRAPHY

S. C. Bakhuizen, *Chalcis-in-Euboea, Iron and Chalcidians Abroad* (Leiden, 1976); Idem, *Studies in the Topography of Chalcis on Euboea* (Leiden, 1985).

CHAMPIONNET, JEAN-ÉTIENNE (1762–1801). French professional soldier.

Championnet was born at Valence and rose to prominence in the armies of the revolution; he distinguished himself in numerous campaigns, notably that of Alsace (1793). In 1798 he was in command of the so-called Army of Rome and pressed with his army to Naples (23 January 1799), where he founded the short-lived Parthenopean Republic (January–June 1799). During his brief period of power he ordered the excavation of the houses numbered VIII ii 1–5 at *Pompeii, which then received his name. It is more particularly applied only to VIII ii 1.

BIBLIOGRAPHY
Michaelis, 19.

L. RICHARDSON, JR

CHANDLER, RICHARD (1738–1810). English antiquarian and explorer.

Chandler was born in Hampshire and educated at Winchester and Oxford, where he made evident his scholarly acumen in his magisterial publication of his university's antiquities, *Marmora Oxoniensia,* which appeared in 1763. The following year he was introduced to the *Society of the Dilettanti and invited to lead a mission of discovery "to some parts of the East," with *Smyrna as headquarters. Chandler was accompanied by Nicholas *Revett, architect (James *Stuart's associate in Athens in the 1750s), and William *Pars, artist, and for two years they explored, first the western regions of Turkey, principally the Ionian coast, then Greece. On returning to England, Revett and Chandler published in handsome fashion the architectural discoveries (1769), while Chandler brought forth the inscriptions (1774) and the journal of their travels (1775, 1776), to which Revett added many critical notes in the edition of 1825. In 1779 Chandler accepted a benefice from his college, and from then until his death his calling was that of a country parson, his life enriched by family and scholarship.

Chandler's achievements were considerable. He was an accurate reporter, and his description of Greek lands is the most significant made in the eighteenth century. Indeed, he is the sole source for some material now lost; moreover, his writing is effective and, in places, moving. Even as invited by his patrons, he set down "whatever can fall within the notice of curious and observing travellers."

BIBLIOGRAPHY
W. Wroth, "Chandler, Richard," *DNB* 10 (1887), 40–41; R. Chandler, *Travels in Asia Minor 1764–1765,* ed. and abr. E. Clay (London, 1971); D. Constantine, *Early Greek Travellers and the Hellenic Ideal* (Cambridge, 1984), 108–209.

C.W.J. ELIOT

CHARBONNEAUX, JEAN (1895–1969). French archaeologist and administrator, known for his contributions to the study of Greek art and to the archaeology of Bronze Age *Crete.

Charbonneaux, a native of Genlis, fought in World War I on the front in Macedonia, where he won the *croix de guerre.* After his discharge he returned to the Greek area as a member of the *French School at Athens. His first publications were on the French excavations at *Delphi, but he soon turned to preclassical Greece, and, in collaboration with F. Chapouthier, he published the first report on *Malia (1928). There followed a number of studies on Aegean art and civilization, including his survey, *L'Art égéen* (1929).

From 1926 to 1965, Charbonneaux was employed at the *Louvre, first as conservator, then as head of the department of Greek and Roman antiquities. In this capacity he was in charge of an enormous amount of Greek and Roman material that, in effect, drew his attention away from Bronze Age Greece. Henceforth he was most occupied with publishing objects in the museum, making new acquisitions and teaching an annual course at the École du Louvre.

Charbonneaux's bibliography reveals his predilection for sculpture, manifest in numerous shorter articles and in authoritative surveys such as *La Sculpture grecque archaique* (1939) and *La Sculpture grecque classique* (2 vols., 1943) as well as museum guides such as *La Sculpture grecque et romaine au Musée du Louvre* (1963). His interests extended to the modern sculpture of Rodin and Maillol. Portraiture of the Hellenistic and Roman periods provided another focus for his research.

Much honored at home and abroad, Charbonneaux had just been elected president of the Académie des inscriptions et belles-lettres at the time of his death. He died tragically as the result of injuries received in an automobile accident in 1969.

BIBLIOGRAPHY

"Bibliographie de Jean Charbonneaux," *RA* (1968), 5–10; P. Devambez, "Jean Charbonneaux (1895–1969)," *RA* (1969), 119–20.

CHARIOTEER OF DELPHI. Early Classical Greek lifesize bronze statue (height 1.8m), discovered with other fragments of a bronze chariot group in 1896, in excavations at *Delphi directed by Théophile *Homolle for the *French School.

The statue was found in fill behind the Ischegaon, a retaining wall built after the landslides of 373 B.C. The inscribed base identifies the group as a dedication by Polyzalos of Gela, which establishes a date of approximately 474 B.C. The dating derived from study of the context corresponds well with Homolle's date, pronounced at the first sight of the upper part of the statue, in the early fifth century B.C.

The draped figure stands motionless, feet together, arms raised to hold the reins, a sophisticated variation on the traditional Archaic type of *kouros* (*korai* and *kouroi*). The statue has been attributed to Pythagoras of Rhegion, to Kalamis of Athens, to the workshop of Kritios and to various other mainland, South Italian and Sicilian artists and schools.

The sculpture was cast in pieces that were joined mechanically. Only the left arm is missing. Scholarly attention was at one time focused on the technique by which the statue was cast, and sand casting was postulated, but it is now universally accepted that the statue is a lost wax casting. Inset eyes are rimmed with bronze lashes, the teeth are of silver and the fillet on the head is inlaid with a copper meander pattern.

One of the most famous Greek bronzes preserved, the *Charioteer* was of great importance in establishing the stylistic characteristics of the Severe style, now usually more broadly defined as Early Classical. The statue is illustrated in practically every handbook on Greek art. During the 1970s, when a traveling exhibition of Greek antiquities was first proposed, a poster appeared in Athens showing a cracked and broken Delphi *Charioteer,* intended as a warning against attempting to ship national treasures out of Greece. In 1992–93, the *Charioteer* was pointedly not included in *The Greek Miracle,* an exhibition of fifth-century Greek sculpture shown in Washington and New York.

BIBLIOGRAPHY

K. Kluge, "Die Gestaltung des Erzes in der Archaisch-Griechischen Kunst," *JdI* 44 (1929), 1030; R. Hampe, *Der Wagenlenker von Delphi,* Denkmäler griechischen und römischen Skulptur (Munich, 1941); F. Chamoux, *L'Aurige de Delphes, Fouilles de Delphes,* 4.5 (Paris, 1955); C. Mattusch, *Greek Bronze Statuary: From the Beginnings Through the Fifth Century B.C.* (Ithaca, 1988), 128–35.

CAROL MATTUSCH

CHARLEMAGNE (KAROLUS MAGNUS; CHARLES THE GREAT; ca. 672–814).

Frankish king and emperor of Western Europe, described as "Augustus, crowned by God, the great and peace-bringing emperor of the Romans," at his coronation on Christmas Day 800 by Pope Leo III.

Charlemagne brought order in a time of political chaos, combining a policy of imperial expansion through military success with a conscious renewal (*renovatio*) of the ideas and forms that characterized the Roman Empire, including its latest phases. He insisted on the need for an education based on Roman authors and the proper use of Latin and also encouraged the study of the Greek language, which he himself knew how to read.

Charlemagne's revival of education included the establishment of schools throughout his domain. He gathered scholars and scribes from all over Europe to develop learning centers in which antique manuscripts and ivories were copied. No specific original models are known to us, but the illustrations in Charlemagne's *Coronation Gospels* (Vienna, Kunsthistorisches Museum) or his personal gospel book still in the Cathedral Treasury (Aachen) strongly suggest the presence of Greek, Roman and Byzantine manuscript paintings in the royal libraries.

Charlemagne placed in charge of his own Palace School at Aachen the English scholar Alcuin (735–804), who taught and practiced the imitation of Roman authors. Succeeding Alcuin at the Palace School was the German noble Einhard (ca. 770–840), who was an expert in architecture as well as the arts and crafts and who was charged with supervising the construction of new buildings for Charlemagne. Einhard advised his students to read Vitruvius's books on architecture written in the first century B.C., telling them that they could better understand the text if they studied the appearance of works made in their own time "in imitation of ancient models." The degree of classicism possible under his instruction may be gauged by the design of a reliquary in the shape of a *"triumphal arch"; the "Einhard Reliquary," known today only in a drawing made in the seventeenth century (Paris, Bibliothèque Nationale), featured a dedicatory inscription in the attic in antique style, and a single arched opening with a coffered vault recalled in a remarkable way some of the arches that would have been known in southern France in Einhard's day. The surfaces of the arch pylons were decorated with figural representations having many Roman echoes. Einhard's writings were no less classical, especially his biography of Charlemagne, which in style and content imitated Suetonius's *Lives of the Twelve Caesars.*

In the architecture of the Carolingian period, there was an intentional revival of the Constantinian T-basilica plan, for example, at St. Denis and Centula (St. Riquier), while the Palatine Chapel at Aachen (begun 792, designed by Odo of Metz) was influenced by the centralized structure of S. Vitale in Ravenna. The building features columns and capitals removed from Roman basilicas, transported across the Alps with the permission of the pope and reemployed to support and decorate the aisles. Charlemagne encouraged artists to reproduce some of the capitals and friezes in stucco; the copies are still standing next to their ancient models in the chapel at Aachen. His imitation of monuments of combined Roman/Christian significance may be seen in his fountain at Aachen based on the famous *Belvedere Pigna.

Charlemagne also brought back from Ravenna a monumental gilt bronze equestrian statue of Theodoric (now lost), which he placed on display in the courtyard of the Palatine chapel and which inspired a small bronze equestrian statue believed by many to represent Charlemagne (Louvre). Additionally, Charlemagne minted coins with portraits based directly on Roman models. At his death, he was buried in a pagan sarcophagus decorated with scenes from the *Rape of Proserpina,* which can be seen today at Aachen.

Carolingian art frequently shows the reuse of ancient gems, for example, in a reliquary for the Palace School of Charles the Bald (840–77), which had as crowning element an intaglio representing Julia, daughter of the emperor Titus (now, Paris, Cabinet des Médailles), and the Cross of Lothair II (d. 869; Aachen, Cathedral Treasury), with a fine antique cameo of Augustus at the intersection of the bars of the cross.

BIBLIOGRAPHY

J. Adhémar, *Influence antique dans l'art du Moyen Age francais* (London, 1939); E. Panofsky, *Renaissance and Renascences in Western Art* (Stockholm, 1960); D. A. Bullough, *The Age of Charlemagne* (New York, 1966); R. Krautheimer, ''The Carolingian Revival of Early Christian Architecture,'' *Studies in Early Christian, Medieval and Renaissance Art* (New York, 1969); J. Hubert—J. Porcher—W. F. Volbach, *The Carolingian Renaissance* (New York, 1970).

JEANINE STAGE

CHAUSSE, MICHEL-ANGE DE LA (MICHAEL ANGELUS CAUSEUS; ca. 1660–1724). French diplomat, antiquarian, numismatist, student of glyptics. The Parisian-born de la Chausse traveled to Rome in a diplomatic capacity and, serving as French consul, spent the rest of an uneventful life there. He dedicated himself to the study of antiquity, giving special attention to gems and coins. His most enduring contribution to classical scholarship was his *Romanum Museum sive Thesaurus eruditae antiquitatis,* first issued at Rome (2 vols., 1690) and dedicated to Louis Auguste de Bourbon. With 170 plates, it provided a corpus of antiquities that gave special emphasis to gems, the first general work to do so. Included were statuary, portraits, bronze objects, mirrors, lamps, vases. It enjoyed two subsequent editions (1707, 1746) and was translated into French with commentary by J. Roche (*Le Cabinet Romain ou recueil d'antiquités,* Amsterdam, 1706). Though the authenticity of some of the objects reproduced was suspect, *Graevius nevertheless did not hesitate to reproduce the majority of the material in his great *Thesaurus* (in vols. 5, 10 and 12; 1694–99). *Montfaucon also borrowed from the *Romanum Museum.*

De la Chausse produced a monograph on gems, *Le Gemme antiche figurate* (Rome, 1700), with engraved plates of 200 gems, by P. S. *Bartoli. In addition, he completed the project begun by Bartoli and G. P. *Bellori to publish the newly discovered Tomb of the Nasonii (*"Tomb of Ovid"). The first edition, in Italian (1706), was considerably enlarged and translated into Latin by de la Chausse and Francesco Santi Bartoli as *Picturae antiquae cryptarum romanarum et sepulchri Nasonum* (Rome, 1738).

BIBLIOGRAPHY

A. de Lacaze, "La Chausse, Michel-Ange de," *NBG* (1859), col. 521; P. Zazoff—H. Zazoff, *Gemmensammler und Gemmenforscher* (Munich, 1983), 40–42; *Porträtarchiv,* no. 52.

CHERON, ELISABETH SOPHIA (1648–1711). French artist and antiquarian.

Settled in Paris, E. S. Cheron, known also by her married name of Madame Le Hay, published a book on the gems of the cabinet of Louis XIV and other collectors, *Pierre antiques gravées tirées des principaux cabinets de la France* (1709). Praised for her skill in painting, poetry, music and the liberal arts, Cheron produced some of her own engravings of the gems and, in other cases, supplied the designs for other capable engravers. Her book created a sensation and provoked acrimonious debate because she had "translated" the gems into images like paintings, with a rich ambience and with skillful effects of light and shadow. Cheron's designs were acceptable for reuse by *Montfaucon, but even in *Mariette's time (1750) the correctness of her approach was a subject for discussion.

BIBLIOGRAPHY

A. Furtwängler, *Die Antiken Gemmen* 1 (Vienna, 1900), 408–9; P. Zazoff, *Gemmensammler und Gemmenforscher, von einer noblen Passion zur Wissenschaften* (Munich, 1983), 45–46.

CHIARAMONTI, BARNABA GREGORIO. See PIUS VII.

Portrait of *Elisabeth Sophia Cheron*, engraving, frontispiece from E. S. Cheron, *Pierres antiques gravées* (1711).

CHIFFLET (CHIFLETIUS), JEAN JACQUES (1588–1660). French doctor, numismatist and antiquarian.

In his youth Chifflet spent years traveling throughout Europe, visiting libraries, museums and collections of antiquities. Serving as a magistrate in Besançon and later as court physician to Philip IV of Spain, he moved within the learned circle of P. P. *Rubens, Valavez and *Peiresc and was interested in coins and gems and in ecclesiastical archaeology. His publications include a study of the iconography of Sokrates on gems and a work on the winding sheet of Christ, in which he argued that the original was in Besançon—*De linteis sepulchralibus Christi* (Antwerp, 1624; he includes for comparison a reproduction of a sculpture in Rubens's collection of a child wrapped in swaddling clothes). He was the author of an inventory of Rubens's gems made at the painter's death.

BIBLIOGRAPHY

Stark, 121, 147; R. S. Magurn, *The Letters of Peter Paul Rubens* (Cambridge, 1955), 453; M. van der Meulen, *Petrus Paulus Rubens Antiquarius* (Aalphen an den Rijn, 1975), 28–29 and passim; *Porträtarchiv*, 178–79.

CHIGI FAMILY. Noble Italian family established in Rome in the sixteenth century; collectors of antiquities.

The immensely wealthy Sienese banker AGOSTINO CHIGI (d. 1520) furnished his Transtiberine villa (later called the "Farnesina") and garden with numerous antiquities. The Chigi collection included a porphyry bust of *Caligula*, a *Caracalla*, a *Daphnis and Pan* and a *"Psyche" Crouching*. The *Psyche* was in Chigi's garden and was of special interest because it echoed the "Psyche" theme painted in the loggia of the Farnesina by *Raphael and his workshop. Profligate heirs sold off the Chigi collection to Ippolito d'Este (*Este family) and to the *Farnese family.

BIBLIOGRAPHY

Lanciani, *Storia degli scavi* 2 (1903), 177–79; Haskell—Penny, 49, 62, 264; Bober—Rubinstein, 472–73.

CHIGI VASE. Greek pitcher (oinochoe) of the Protocorinthian style, dating ca. 650–625 B.C., decorated in an early black-figured technique with scenes of the hunt, warfare and myth (the *Judgment of Paris*).

The small vase (26cm high) was excavated by R. *Lanciani in a partially plundered Etruscan tomb at Formello (near *Veii) on the property of Prince Mario Chigi in 1882. Taken to the Palazzo Chigi in Rome, it was reconstructed from many fragments. Today it forms part of the Chigi Collection in the *Villa Giulia, Rome.

BIBLIOGRAPHY

E. Ghirardini in *NSc* (1882), 413–17; +*CVA*, Villa Giulia, fasc. 1, pl. 1–4; P. E. Arias, *A History of Greek Vase Painting*, tr. B. B. Shefton (London, 1962), 275–76.

CHIMAERA OF AREZZO. Large-scale Etruscan bronze statue created ca. 400 B.C.

Originally conceived as part of a group, with Bellerophon on horseback about to slay the famous monster—part lion, part goat, with a snake for a tail—the statue was found at *Arezzo, an Etruscan city famous for its bronzework. The sculpture combines a powerful, realistic style with Archaistic features, such as the stylization of the lion's mane. The *Chimaera* was at some time dedicated in an Etruscan sanctuary: the formula *tinscvil,* inscribed on its right front leg, means "gift to Tinia (Zeus)," or "sacred gift."

The bronze was discovered in Arezzo on 15 November 1553, purchased by Cosimo I de' Medici (*Medici family) and brought to Florence, where it was placed by *Vasari in the *sala* of *Leo X in Palazzo Vecchio, as a symbol of the monsters conquered by Cosimo I when he created the duchy of Tuscany or Etruria. One of the most famous of Etruscan monuments, the *Chimaera* attracted the attention of artists and scholars (e.g., *Titian, Pietro Aretino, Montaigne) from the sixteenth century on. It is often stated that Benvenuto *Cellini restored the sculpture, but there is no evidence to support this statement. On the contrary, unpublished accounts in the Archivio di Stato, Florence (Fabbriche Medicee VIII, c. 15 recto) show that a payment was made on 11 June 1558 to Francesco di Luigi Ottonaio for attaching the (original) legs of the *Chimaera.* The tail was added by the sculptor F. Carradori in 1784, following a suggestion by Luigi *Lanzi. The *Chimaera* is presently in the Museo Archeologico, *Florence, inv. no. 1.

BIBLIOGRAPHY

W. Amelung, *Führer durch die Antiken in Florenz* (Munich, 1897), 253–55; W. L. Brown, *The Etruscan Lion* (Oxford, 1960), 155–57; +M. Pallottino, "Vasari e la Chimera," *Prospettiva* 8 (1977), 4–6; M. Cristofani, in *Palazzo Vecchio, Committenza e collezionismo medicei* (Florence, 1980), 21–22.

LARISSA BONFANTE

CHIOS. Greek island located 8km from the west coast of Turkey, opposite the Izmir peninsula.

Serious archaeological interest in Chios began with Fustel de Coulanges (1856). Konstantinos Kourouniotis in 1914–15 excavated a late sixth-century B.C. cemetery at Latomia and the temple of Apollo at Kato Phana. Winifred *Lamb, of the *British School at Athens, continued work at Kato Phana in 1934, tracing Early Archaic activity in the sanctuary and documenting three churches above the temple. The Archaic pottery convinced her that "Naukratite" white-slipped ware was made on Chios.

In 1938, Edith Eccles from the British School unearthed Neolithic and Early Bronze remains in the cave at Ayio Gala. British excavations (1952–55) directed by Sinclair Hood and John Boardman at Emporio revealed, south of the harbor, occupation from the earliest Aegean Neolithic into Early Bronze. The pottery sequence continues through the sixteenth century B.C. and includes Late Mycenaean. North of the harbor, the settlement of ca. 700–600 B.C. had a walled acropolis with an Athena sanctuary and chief's megaron; southwest of the harbor, votives attest worship from the Protogeometric through Hellenistic periods, succeeded by an Early Roman basilica and a sixth-century church. Boardman also excavated an Athenian fortress of 412 B.C. at Delphinion and a classical farmhouse at Pindakos.

BIBLIOGRAPHY

W. Lamb, "Excavations at Kato Phana in Chios," *BSA* 35 (1934–35), 138–64; +J. Boardman, *Excavations in Chios, 1952–1955, Greek Emporio, BSA* suppl. 6 (1967); +S. Hood, *Excavations in Chios, 1938–1955, Prehistoric Emporio and Ayio Gala,* 1–2, *BSA* suppls. 15 (1981) and 16 (1982). J. Boardman—C. E. Vaphopoulou-Richardson, eds., *Chios, A Conference at the Homereion in Chios* (Oxford, 1986).

JANE BURR CARTER

CHIUSI (CLUSIUM). Modern Italian town coinciding topographically with ancient Clusium (Etruscan Clevsin, Camars), an important member of the Etruscan League of twelve peoples.

Situated in the fertile Tuscan hinterland near Lake Trasimene, Clusium is traditionally noted for its role in the early history of Rome, in the days of King Porsenna, and its special relationship with the Gauls in the Po Valley, invited to Clusium by Arruns. The city still flourished after the Roman conquest (295 B.C.) and has continued to do so until the present day.

Local interest in the "classical" past favored antiquarianism (S. *Tizio declared that he had seen an inscribed urn containing Porsenna's ashes); early collections were recorded in the archives of the Florentine galleries from 1585 and contributed to eighteenth century *Etruscheria. Systematic (as distinct from scientific) excavation in the early nineteenth century yielded numerous tombs, notably, the Hellenistic Tomba del Granduca (1818) and the first painted tombs (1826), leading to the formation of the Bonci Casuccini collection (the largest of its kind at the time, acquired in 1863 by the Palermo Museum; still unpublished) and to the dispersal to European museums of an incalculable patrimony—especially of Attic vases, for which Chiusi is a prime source. The Florentine A. *François was responsible for more scientific excavations (1840–53: Tomba della Scimmia; the *François Vase), resumed officially by the Società Colombaria (1858–60) and the Commissione Municipale: the finds went to the new museums of Florence (1870) and Chiusi (1871). Private and clandestine plundering persisted.

After the important Chiusine chapters in G. *Dennis, *Cities and Cemeteries of Etruria* (1848; 3rd ed. 1883), the only overall study of the city and its territory is that by R. *Bianchi Bandinelli (1925); interest has since declined, and the museum has recently been extensively robbed. Typically Chiusine categories of material that have received treatment only recently are the "canopic" urns (R. D. Gempeler, 1974) and stone cinerary statues of the Classical period (M. Cristofani, 1975); the Archaic gravestones with figured bas-reliefs and the painted tombs had already attracted attention in 1938 (E. Paribeni) and 1939 (Bianchi Bandinelli); and Archaic stone statuary was discussed by A. Hus in 1961. Individual items assessed include the ivory Pania pyxis (Cristofani, 1971). Epigraphic studies (A. Prosdocimi; Cristofani) have demonstrated the Chiusine origin of the Venetic alphabet, confirming the traditional links between Clusium and the north.

Chiusine territory contains the Archaic center explored by Bryn Mawr College at Poggio Civitate (*Murlo).

BIBLIOGRAPHY

+F. Inghirami, *Etrusco Museo Chiusino* (Florence, 1833–34); +R. Bianchi Bandinelli, "Clusium," *MonAnt* 30 (1925), 209–578; +A. Minto, *Il Vaso François, AttiAcc La Colombaria, Studi* (Florence, 1960); +J.-R. Jannot, *Les Réliefs archaïques de Chiusi* (Rome, 1984).

F. R. SERRA RIDGWAY

CHOISEUL-GOUFFIER, MARIE GABRIEL FLORENT AUGUST, COMTE DE (1752–1817). French nobleman, diplomat and collector of antiquities.

Choiseul-Gouffier first traveled to Greece in 1776 as a member of the French Scientific Expedition to the Mediterranean. Returning to France, he was elected in 1779 as a member of the Académie des inscriptions and the Académie français and published as appropriate for this status his *Mémoire sur l'hippodrome d'Olympie* (1784). From notes and drawings made during his travels he compiled his three-volume work, *Voyage pittoresque de la Grèce* (1782–1802), with illustrations largely by J. B. Hilaire.

Named by Louis XVI as ambassador to Constantinople in 1784, Choiseul took in his retinue the artist *Fauvel, who acted as his agent in Athens and elsewhere in the copying and acquisition of antiquities. Ever competing with British agents, especially those of Lord *Elgin, Fauvel acquired for Choiseul a number of casts and original marbles, including a slab of the *Parthenon frieze and a metope from the building that had been dug up among the ruins. These were shipped back to France, but unfortunately the count did not get to enjoy his treasures. When the French Revolution occurred, he lost his post, and many of his marbles were seized by the new government. Choiseul-Gouffier subsequently went into exile in Russia, where he became a librarian for the czar. Returning from exile in 1802, the count bought a villa near Paris and attempted to recover his collection. He did succeed in reclaiming most of his sculptures taken by the government (though his slab from the Parthenon frieze remained in the *Louvre) but was unsuccessful in trying to regain a number of crates that had remained at the port at Peiraeus awaiting shipping. Included among the sculptures were a second Parthenon metope and the statue later named the Choiseul-Gouffier *Apollo*. These finally sailed for France on a frigate of *Napoleon's in 1803, but, ironically, the ship was seized by the English, and the cases ended up at the Customs House in London, eventually to be claimed by *Elgin himself. A bizarre and touching meeting between these two European noblemen took place at Barèges in 1803, during the period when Elgin was being detained by

Portrait of *M.G.F.A. Comte de Choiseul-Gouffier*, engraving by M. F. Dien. (Westfälisches Landesmuseum für Kunst und Kulturgeschichte, Münster, Porträtarchiv Diepenbroick. Photo: R. Wakonigg.)

the French government. The outcome was that Choiseul-Gouffier joined the effort to get Elgin released, and Elgin wrote to Lord Nelson begging that the count be allowed to buy back his Parthenon metope. Later, when Elgin had taken possession of the pieces in London, he offered to return them to the count, but Choiseul-Gouffier never claimed them before his death in 1817. His heirs decided to sell the antiquities he did have, and though some pieces went to the British Museum, Choiseul-Gouffier's first Parthenon metope was sold to the Louvre.

BIBLIOGRAPHY

Stark, 256; W. St. Clair, *Lord Elgin and the Marbles* (London, 1967); Tsigakou, *Rediscovery*, 195, 201; *Porträtarchiv*, nos. 285–86.

CHRISTINA (KRISTINA) (1626–89). Queen of Sweden.

Sweden's involvement in European foreign policy in the early seventeenth century was, to a large extent, directed toward the Catholic Counter-Reformation in Germany. After successfully conquering parts of Poland for Sweden, Queen Christina's father, King Gustavus II Adolphus, launched an attack against the German Catholics and the House of Hapsburg. Through his death in the battle at Lützen in 1632, the Protestant cause lost one of its most prominent leaders, and the heir to the throne in Sweden, his only child, Christina, was only six years old.

Queen Christina of Sweden, engraving by R. Nanteuil, after S. Bourdon, 1654. (Westfälisches Landesmuseum für Kunst und Kulturgeschichte, Münster, Porträtarchiv Diepenbroick. Photo: R. Wakonigg.)

The queen received a thorough education, which prepared her for the role as monarch, but her intellectual interests went far beyond those of politics. Foreign scholars such as Descartes were invited to the court in Stockholm, and the queen actively supported the arts, literature and science. In addition to collecting books and paintings, she acquired ancient statues and coins from Italy, Germany and Holland. Unfortunately, most of the statues were destroyed when the Royal Palace in Stockholm burned in 1697, but the few pieces that were rescued became part of the collections of King *Gustavus III.

Although the Swedish conservative elements disapproved of the queen's cultural interests, they were not prepared for the ultimate expression of how stifling she found the Swedish intellectual and spiritual climate. She shocked the country and the whole world by abdicating after ten years' reign and by leaving Sweden for Italy and Rome, where she converted to Catholicism.

In Rome Queen Christina was received by Pope Alexander VII, and she soon became involved with church politics as a friend and adviser to the popes. Her own ambitions for power were manifested in attempts to secure the kingdom of Naples and, later, the throne in Poland, but without success. Instead, she came to spend most of her time in Rome, where she became the focal point of the cultural life in the city. Although her financial situation was at times precarious, she supported musicians such as Scarlatti and Corelli, and she founded the learned Accademia Reale (later renamed Arcadia), which held its meetings at her home in the Palazzo Riario (now Palazzo Corsini). She added to her collections of books, paintings, tapestries, gems and coins through purchases and even conducted excavations in Rome to replace the marble statues she had left behind in Sweden.

Contemporary descriptions attest to the variety and high quality of Queen Christina's collections, which, upon her death, she bequeathed to her longtime friend Cardinal Azzolino. Later the collections were bought by Livio Odescalchi (*Odescalchi family), a relative of Pope Innocent XI, but in the eighteenth century they were scattered all over Europe, when the books and manuscripts were sold to the Vatican, the paintings to France, the coins to the Bibliothèque Nationale in Paris and the sculptures to Philip V of Spain (*Prado, Madrid).

The enigma of Queen Christina's personality as a queen, a scholar and a mystic, and her profound impact on the cultural life in Rome are reflected in many contemporary documents that illustrate the events of her life. Her years in Sweden are known through portraits by S. Bourdon and others, and the dramatic abdication at Uppsala castle in Sweden was recorded in a sketch by W. Swidde, while her triumphant entry into Rome through the Porta del Popolo, remodeled for the occasion by *Bernini, was commemorated in medallions and prints. The queen's visits to different parts of Rome and her official reception on the Campidoglio were all recorded, and when she died in 1689, she was buried in St. Peter's, where in 1702 a monument designed by Carlo Fontana was raised in her honor.

In the twentieth century much attention has been given to Queen Christina's interest in religion and the psychological reasons for her abdication and conversion. Of particular interest to art historians are the studies of the history of the queen's collections and the extent to which they can be traced today. Of the over one hundred ancient statues that were displayed in the Palazzo Riario, less than half are now in the Prado Museum. The works that remained in Sweden include a head of *Anakreon,* originally owned by Nicolas *Rockox and drawn by Peter Paul *Rubens, and a Julio-Claudian head, previously identified as *Galba* and perhaps identical with one drawn by Rembrandt. The results of the international interest in Queen Christina were presented in an extensive exhibit at the National Museum in Stockholm in 1966. (See also *Castor and Pollux; *Faun with Kid.)*

BIBLIOGRAPHY

F. Boyer, "Les antiques de Christine de Suède a Rome," *RA* 35 (1932), 254–67; +*Stockholm, Nationalmuseum, Christina Queen of Sweden* (Stockholm, 1966); A. Andrén, "Ur antiksamlandets historia," *Stockholm, Nationalmuseum, Antiken* (Stockholm, 1967), 19–32; +G. Masson, *Queen Christina* (London, 1968); C. D'Onofrio, *Roma val bene un'abiura* (Rome, 1976); C. Callmer, *Königin Christina, ihre Bibliothekare und ihre Handschriften* (Stockholm, 1977); *Porträtarchiv,* no. 42.

INGRID E. M. EDLUND

CIAMPOLINI, GIOVANNI (ca. 1466–1505). Italian collector, connoisseur and dealer of antiquities, one of the earliest in Renaissance Rome; friend of the humanist Poliziano.

Ciampolini displayed his large collection in his house in the via Balestra near Campo dei Fiori. Some pieces may have been excavated in his *vigna* on the Aventine Hill. Fra *Giocondo transcribed thirty-one inscriptions in his collection, and eight statues and several sarcophagi are recorded in the sketchbooks of *Aspertini, the *Codex Escurialensis and the dal *Pozzo albums. After the death of his son Michele, his statues and vases were sold in 1520 to *Giulio Romano for 180 gold ducats and transported to Mantua in 1524.

BIBLIOGRAPHY

R. Lanciani, "La raccolta antiquaria di Giovanni Ciampolini," *BullComm* 27 (1899), 101–15; C. Robert, "Über ein dem Michelangelo zugeschriebenes Skizzenbuch auf Schloss Wolfegg," *RM* 16 (1901), 209–43; A. Schmitt, "Römische Antikensammlungen in Spiegel eines Musterbuchs der Renaissance," *MJb* 21 (1970), 114; L. Fusco-G. Corti, "Giovanni Ciampolini (d. 1505), A Renaissance Dealer in Rome and His Collection of Antiquities," *Xenia* 21 (1991), 7–46.

MARJON VAN DER MEULEN

CICHORIUS, CONRAD (1863–1932). German archaeologist and classical philologist.

Born at Leipzig, Cichorius studied there under the philologists Otto Ribbeck and Curt Wachsmuth and at Berlin under *Mommsen. He was professor of ancient history at Breslau (1900–16) and Bonn (1916–28). His interests within Roman history and literature were catholic but always specialized and strongly philological; see *Römische Studien* (1922). He was a problem solver who avoided the long view. He partly anticipated the prosopographical approach of Münzer and Syme. His masterpiece, *Die Reliefs der Trajanssäule,* in four volumes (1896–1900), remains the basis for all subsequent work on the *Column of Trajan. It led to his *Die römischen Denkmäler in der Dobrudscha: ein Erklärungsversuch* (1904), a work concerned with Roman monuments in Rumania and owing much to Mommsen. His works provide models of precise learning that will always merit the attention of the connoisseur.

BIBLIOGRAPHY

H. Braunert, "Conrad Cichorius 1863–1932," *150 Jahre Rheinische Friedrich-Wilhelms-Universität zu Bonn 1818–1968: Bonner Gelehrte Beiträge zur Geschichte der Wissenschaften in Bonn Geschichtswissenschaften* (Bonn, 1968), 340–50; F. Bobu Florescu, *Die Trajanssäule: Grundfragen und Tafeln* (Bonn, 1969), 10–11.

WILLIAM M. CALDER III

CIMMERIAN BOSPORUS. See BOSPORUS CIMMERIUS.

CINERARIA. Containers to hold the cremated remains of the dead.

Ordinary domestic jars could be used, but in the classical world many cineraria were made for this specific purpose in a variety of materials and shapes. The tombs around Rome yielded many cineraria of Early Imperial date: the marble versions, often inscribed and richly decorated in relief, were collected and studied from the sixteenth century onward. Drawings of such cineraria are to be found in the sixteenth-century collections of drawings made by *Pighius and *Boissard and in the dal *Pozzo-Albani collection. Examples also went into the major seventeenth-century collections (e.g., *Giustiniani, *Mattei) and were subsequently published in *Galleria Giustiniani* (1631), *Monumenta Mattheiana* (1776–79) and other works. Many illustrations of Roman cineraria also appear in *Montfaucon's iconographic study *L'Antiquité expliquée* (1719–24) and *Piranesi's *Vasi, Candelabri* (1778). Piranesi's captions in the latter show many of the cineraria were sold to Northern Europeans, and, indeed, many cineraria found their way into the stately homes of Britain and the collections of Europe during the eighteenth and nineteenth centuries. Piranesi shows a preference for cineraria in the form of vases rather than boxes, and this preference is reflected in the neoclassical taste for decorated stone vases based on the Roman originals.

The eighteenth century also saw collections of Hellenistic Etruscan cineraria; most notable is *Guarnacci's remarkable collection of alabaster urns at *Volterra. Etruscan cineraria were rather more limited in their appeal and did not penetrate northern European collections in such numbers.

BIBLIOGRAPHY

+H. Brunn—G. Körte, *l Rilievi delle urne etruschi,* 1–3 (Rome, 1870–1916); A. Michaelis, *Ancient Marbles in Great Britain* (Cambridge, 1882); +W. Altmann, *Die Römischen Grabaltare der Kaiserzeit* (Berlin, 1905); F. Sinn, *Stadtrömische Marmorurnen* (Mainz am Rhein, 1987).

GLENYS DAVIES

CIRCUS MAXIMUS. Roman showplace, used for chariot races and gladiatorial and hunting displays.

Traditionally the Circus Maximus was inaugurated by Romulus in the Vallis Murcia between the Palatine and Aventine hills with horse races in honor of Consus. The first assignment of places for spectators is ascribed to Tarquinius Priscus (Livy 1.35.8; Dion. Hal. 3.68.1), while the first stands for seats were built by Tarquinius Superbus (Livy 1.56.2; Dion.Hal. 4.44.1). The first *carceres,* or starting barriers for the chariots, are dated by Livy (8.20.2) to 329 B.C. These all seem to have been impermanent wooden constructions. The stream that runs down this valley must have been channeled very early to prevent flooding, probably at least as early as the time of Tarquinius Superbus, but it was not culverted in antiquity. It was bridged where the racetrack crossed it and at intervals along its length, and down it was installed a collection of monuments, of which the most important were the *metae,* groups of three elongated cones, at either end, the platforms carrying seven large wooden eggs (179 B.C.; cf. Livy 41.27.6) and seven dolphins (33 B.C.; cf. Cassius Dio 49.43.2) with which the laps were recorded, an obelisk brought from Heliopolis by Augustus (Pliny, *NH* 36.71) and a statue of the Magna Mater mounted on a rampant lion (Tertullian, *De spect.* 8). Julius Caesar installed a second euripus, ten feet wide and ten feet deep, running between the arena and the spectators to protect the latter from the

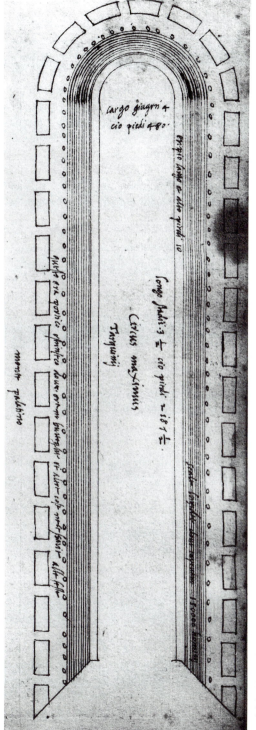

Reconstructed plan of the *Circus Maximus*, Rome, drawing by Fra Giocondo (d. 1515), St. Petersburg, Hermitage, Library. (Deutsches Archäologisches Institut, Rome. Inst. Neg. 42.214.)

wild beasts used in the games (Dion. Hal. 3.68). This was later filled in by Nero (Pliny, *NH* 8.21).

The stands of the Circus were subject to fire, and after a severe fire in 31 B.C. (Cassius Dio 50.10.3), Augustus seems to have restored it and built the first permanent *pulvinar,* a box for the gods whose attendance was invoked, on the Palatine side (*RG* 4.19), but Pliny (*NH* 36.102) credits Julius Caesar with giving the Circus its final form. At this time it was three and a half stadia long (621m) and four plethra wide (118m). The seats were in three sections, masonry in the lowest, wooden in the two upper ones. The seating capacity was put at 150,000. The outer arcades on which the seating was supported and through which passages and stairs gave access to the seats were a warren of shops and squatters of every description, especially those of questionable character, and these establishments were apt to fuel any fire that broke out. Here the great fire of Nero started (Tacitus, *Ann.* 15.38). The circus was repeatedly restored and enlarged and was regarded by Dionysios and Pliny as one of the most beautiful buildings in Rome (Dion. Hal. 3.68; Pliny, *NH* 36.102). Embellishment continued as late as the time of Constantius, who in 357 had the tallest obelisk in the world brought there from Egypt and erected on the *spina* (Amm. Marc. 17.4.12–16).

The *carceres,* twelve in number, built on a curve to equalize the competitors' chances, came to be very elaborate, with a box for the presiding magistrate above the middle and towers at each end, so that it had something of the appearance of a walled town and was nicknamed the *oppidum* (Varro, *Ling.* 5.153; Festus 201L). The opposite end, or *sphendone,* was curved and pierced by an archway that was rebuilt as a triple arch in honor of Titus's triumph in A.D. 80/81 (*CIL* 6.944). The Circus seems to have always been part of the triumphal route, giving a maximum number of people an optimum view of the procession. In the Republican period it was also used for gladiatorial shows and *venationes,* or hunts, but gradually races came to replace most other sorts of shows, though never entirely. The last games recorded here were in A.D. 550 (Procopius, *Bell. Goth.* 3.37.4).

Parts of the southeast end of the Circus Maximus are represented on the Marble Plan (*Forma urbis Romae), but little is left today except poor remains of the concrete substructures of the *cavea* on the north side of the *sphendone.* The Circus and the games given there, however, were a constant inspiration for artists in almost every medium. It survives today especially on coins that commemorate work there and on mosaics, notably mosaics at Piazza Armerina, Barcelona and Lyons. Although it was plundered for building material in the Renaissance, only trial trenches and limited samplings have been carried out in a scientific way, and the great majority of the Circus lies buried at a depth of about 12m. In the Renaissance the Circus was given to the Jewish community of Rome for their cemetery, as a place attainted by the martyrdom of Christians. Today it is a park in which the main features of the ancient complex are broadly indicated. The two obelisks of the *spina* were removed by *Sixtus V in 1587–88 and reerected in Piazza del Popolo and Piazza S. Giovanni in Laterano.

BIBLIOGRAPHY
P. Mingazzini, "Il pulvinar ad Circum Maximum," *BullCom* 72 (1946–48), 27–32; G. Lugli, *Roma antica: il centro monumentale* (Rome, 1946), 599–606, G. Forni, s.v. "Circo e ippodromo," *EAA* 2 (1959), 647–55; J. H. Humphrey, *Roman Circuses: Arenas for Chariot Racing* (London, 1986), 56–294.

L. RICHARDSON, JR

CIRIACO (CYRIACUS) OF ANCONA (1391–ca. 1452). Merchant, traveler, occasional statesman and diplomat, autodidact and protoarchaeologist.

Ciriaco de' Pizzicolli was born in Ancona in 1391 and died, possibly ca. 1452, in Cremona. A zealous convert to humanism, he spent his life traversing not only Italy but the lands and islands of the Levant in search of the physical remains of classical antiquity.

His notebooks (*commentaria*), which ultimately filled six volumes, contained Latin diaries of his journeys, often illustrated by drawings. They included copies of more than a thousand inscriptions, many of which no longer exist, as well as drafts of letters, poems and *opuscula*. These notebooks, except for a fragment, are gone, but before they perished, both Ciriaco and others had made excerpts from them ranging from single items (inscriptions, drawings, letters) to whole sections of diary. Since these excerpts were sometimes revised by Ciriaco himself and were often copied and recopied by others, the tangled skein of texts that has come down to us in some 135 manuscripts has so far defied definitive editing. About 125 extant letters, many of which contain information about antiquities, are found either in the diary fragments or in separate traditions.

Ciriaco's life until early 1435 is chronicled in a *Vita* assembled by his friend and compatriot, Francesco Scalamonti. Based largely on Ciriaco's lost diaries, it is our only evidence for these years apart from two early letters. According to Scalamonti, early mercantile journeys took Ciriaco to *Alexandria (1412), Taormina and *Palermo (1415), Constantinople (*Byzantium) and Pola (1418–19). In 1421–23, while serving as financial officer for the restoration of the port of Ancona, he won the friendship of Cardinal Gabriel Condulmer, later Pope Eugenius IV. During this time he learned Latin by reading Vergil with an itinerant scholar and developed his interest in ancient monuments, occasioned by a study of the *Arch of Trajan, which stands on the harbor mole. In December–January 1424–25, as guest of Condulmer in Rome, he studied the antiquities for forty days, taking careful notes—the beginnings of his *commentaria*. Having decided that "the stones themselves afford . . . much more information about historical events than is to be found in books," he dedicated himself to searching out and recording the scattered and crumbling monuments of antiquity before they perished "through the passage of time and the carelessness of man."

To this end he chose a commercial assignment that would place him in the Levant as representative of a kinsman's interests in Cyprus (1428–31). During these years he learned the rudiments of Greek in Constantinople, saw Christian antiquities in Damascus, bought Greek manuscripts in Nicosia and ancient sculptures in *Rhodes, studied Roman law in Famagusta and followed lectures on Homer and Hesiod in Adrianople. From the spoils of recently sacked *Thessaloniki (1430), he purchased a copy of Ptolemy's *Geography,* and at Philippi he noted down inscriptions in the appropriate margin of an Ovid's *Fasti* that he himself had copied in 1427.

When Condulmer became pope, Ciriaco cleared himself of his commercial obligations and reconnoitered Turkish-held cities near the Asian coast, taking in at the same time the antiquities of Kyzikos, Nikaia, Mytilene, *Pergamon and *Smyrna before hurrying to Rome to urge on Eugenius a council of union with the Greek church and a crusade against the Turks. Near Rome he also visited *Hadrian's Villa, *Tivoli, *Ostia and other monuments. At Siena, Ciriaco presented emperor-elect Sigismund with a gold coin of Trajan as an exemplar of a good emperor and argued for the crusade. In Rome after the coronation (May 1433) he toured the antiquities with Sigismund and pointedly deplored the burning of ancient marbles into lime. It may have been at this time that he saw the *Belvedere *Torso.*

Traveling through Northern Italy (1433–34), he was welcomed by Cosimo de' Medici's (*Medici family) circle of artists and humanists in Florence, where *Niccoli showed him his collection of manuscripts, coins, gems and sculptures in return for a report on the antiquities in the Levant. Early in 1435 he was back in Ancona.

Thus far our information comes from Scalamonti. Late the same year begins a section of diary that has survived in several editions and groups of excerpts covering journeys through Dalmatia, northwest Greece, *Delphi, Athens, *Corinth and the Peloponnesos (1435–37), including Greek and Latin inscriptions and numerous drawings. An undated visit to Egypt, from which we have drawings of an elephant and a giraffe and reports on the antiquities of Alexandria and on the pyramids, probably occurred in September 1436.

Active unofficially in the Council of Florence (1438–39), Ciriaco then served on a commission to renegotiate a treaty between Ancona and Ragusa (1440). Remaining in and around Florence (where the papal court continued to reside) from March 1441 to October 1442 he afterward made a second journey through Northern Italy (October 1442 to February 1443), which is recorded in a surviving diary excerpt that includes many inscriptions and drafts of letters to princes, prelates and humanists.

Numerous letters and some fragmentary diaries survive from 1443–48, when he was continually in the Levant combining antiquarian exploration with diplomatic activity. The diary-excerpts record, with illustrations, journeys through the Propontis (Kyzikos, Perinthos), islands of the northern Aegean (Imbros, *Samothrace, *Thasos), the Thracian coast (Ainos, Maroneia) and Mt. Athos, where he examined and purchased manuscripts (July–December 1444); a visit to some of the Cyclades (Mykonos, *Delos, *Naxos, *Paros, Andros, April 1445), also illustrated; and Crete (July–November 1445). The letters report antiquities in Constantinople (drawings of S. Sophia may come from this time),

Chios, *Samos, *Miletos, *Didyma, *Ephesos, Lesbos, *Magnesia, *Sardis, Thyatira, and Pergamon. The only portion of diary surviving in Ciriaco's own hand recounts his travels in the Peloponnesos from July 1447 to April 1448. This fragment, twenty-five folios, contains numerous illustrations in his hand. The places visited include the Tainaron peninsula, *Sparta, Mistra (where he spent the winter at the court of Constantine Paleologus) and Corinth. He returned to Italy via Arta in December 1448 and is last heard from on 31 August 1449 (letter to Genoese authorities requesting a safe-conduct for travel to the west and south). A manuscript note says he died in 1452, at Cremona.

BIBLIOGRAPHY

+B. Ashmole, "Cyriac of Ancona," *ProcBrAc* 45 (1959), 25–41. E. W. Bodnar, *Cyriacus of Ancona and Athens* (Brussels, 1960), with full bib. to 1960, C. Mitchell, "Ciriaco d'Ancona: Fifteenth-Century Drawings and Descriptions of the Parthenon," in *The Parthenon,* ed. V. Bruno (New York, 1974), 111–23; +E. W. Bodnar—C. Mitchell, *Cyriacus of Ancona's Journeys in the Propontis and the Northern Aegean, 1444–1445* (Philadelphia, 1976); E. W. Bodnar, "Ciriaco d'Ancona and the Crusade of Varna: A Closer Look," *Mediaevalia* 14 (1988, pub. 1991), 253–80; +C. Mitchell—E. W. Bodnar, *Vita . . . Kyriaci Anconitani by Francesco Scalamonti,* forthcoming.

E. W. BODNAR

CIVITA CASTELLANA. See FALERII VETERES.

CLARKE, EDWARD DANIEL (1769–1822). English mineralogist and traveler.

Born in Willingdon, Sussex, Clarke became a minister in the Church of England in 1805 and was named the first professor of mineralogy at Cambridge in 1808. He published his accounts of his *Travels in Various Countries of Europe, Asia and Africa* in six volumes between 1810 and 1823. He had toured England, Italy, Scandinavia, Finland, Russia, Siberia and Greece, as well as Egypt, Asia Minor and the Holy Land. Everywhere he collected minerals, as well as maps and relevant manuscripts. In the Greek lands he also collected ancient coins, vases and statues and has left many lively and pertinent comments about Greek archaeological sites he visited, for example, the theater at *Epidauros, the *Parthenon, the portico of the temple of Dionysos at *Naxos. In anticipation of *Schliemann, he placed Homeric *Troy near Hissarlık.

Clarke is remembered especially for his excavation of the colossal statue of "Demeter" at *Eleusis in 1801. The battered sculpture of a goddess with a basket on her head, suggesting the abundance of fruits from the earth, had been seen half-buried at Eleusis by many travelers. But the inhabitants regarded the idol as a protectress of their fields and fiercely resisted any efforts to remove it. Clarke's campaign to secure the piece was retarded by an ox that interrupted the work by rushing up to butt at the statue; the atmosphere in which it was finally extracted and put on board ship was made gloomy by the prophecy that the boat would go down. It did sink on the way back to England, but the great statue was subsequently recovered. Identified today as a caryatid similar to those of the *Erechtheion, the piece resides in the *Fitzwilliam Museum, Cambridge, along with Clarke's other antiquities. His mineral collection also went to Cambridge, and his manuscripts went to the Bodleian Library, Oxford, after his death in 1822. His coin collection was sold in 1810 to Richard Payne *Knight.

BIBLIOGRAPHY

Tsigakou, *Rediscovery* 24, 104, 122, 177; *Porträtarchiv,* no. 114; Stoneman, *Land of Lost Gods,* 151–55, 158–60, 268.

CLAUDE LORRAINE (CLAUDE GELLÉE; 1600–82). French painter, known for his pastoral landscapes, often featuring classical themes and buildings.

Claude Gellée, born in a village in Lorraine, seems to have arrived in 1613 in Rome, there becoming part of the household of the painter Agostino Tassi, who was known for his close imitation of Roman landscape painting. Except for brief trips Claude remained the rest of his life in Rome.

Archaeological renderings of specific monuments are not numerous in the oeuvre of Claude (etching of the *Forum Romanum, 1636; *Pastoral Caprice with the *Arch of Constantine,* 1651, Collection of the Duke of Westminster, London; *Landscape with the Temple of the Sibyl at *Tivoli,* ca. 1635, National Gallery of Victoria, Melbourne). But the number and range of his paintings of classical subjects with reconstructions of ancient architecture are remarkable. His imaginative depictions of ancient cities and sites include the unusual harbor scenes in a *View of *Carthage with Dido and Aeneas* (1675; Hamburger Kunsthalle) and the *Port of *Ostia with the Embarkation of St. Paula* (1630s; Prado, Madrid) and two treatments of the *Sanctuary of Apollo at *Delphi* (1650; Galleria Doria-Pamphili, Rome, and 1673; Art Institute of Chicago). He is often linked with *Poussin as one of the creators of classical landscape in the seventeenth century, although his approach was neither as archaeological nor as intellectual as Poussin's.

Though Claude is said to have been unable to read Latin, his paintings frequently feature Latin inscriptions, including his own signature.

BIBLIOGRAPHY

M. Kitson, "Claude and Carthage," *Apollo* 77 (March 1963), 226–27; I. G. Kennedy, "Claude and Architecture," *JWarb* 35 (1972), 260–83; +H. D. Russell, *Claude Lorraine, 1600–1682* (Washington, DC, 1982).

CLEMENT XIV (GIOVANNI VINCENZO GANGANELLI; 1705–74). Pope, initiator of the papal museum of antiquities known as the Museo Pio-Clementino.

Born in Rimini, G. V. Ganganelli entered a Franciscan convent there in 1723. Vowing to devote himself to learning all branches of knowledge, he studied at Pesaro and Reconati, then became a popular teacher of philosophy and theology,

Portrait of *Pope Clement XIV*, engraving by A. A. Beck, 1769. (Westfälisches Landesmuseum für Kunst und Kulturgeschichte, Münster, Porträtarchiv Diepenbroick. Photo: R. Wakonigg.)

traveling from place to place. Called to Rome in 1740 by Benedict XIV, he was made cardinal in 1759 and elected as pope in 1769.

Clement XIV introduced many reforms in the papacy, curbing expenditures and opposing clerical abuses. In 1773 he made the highly controversial decision to dissolve the Jesuit order, creating a new climate in Rome and Italy. He promoted the arts and the study of antiquity and, in line with these policies, attempted to put a stop to the flow of antiquities out of Italy into the hands of English and French collectors. Advised by his treasurer Giannangelo Braschi, the future *Pius VI, and by his commissioner of antiquities (*Commissario delle Antichità), G. B. *Visconti, he acquired antiquities that had come onto the market as the result of the breaking up of long-established family collections and initiated a new museum at the *Vatican, called the Clementinum. The Barberini candelabra from *Hadrian's Villa, the *Meleager* of Skopas and antiquities from the *Mattei family collection were among the acquisitions. Visconti initiated systematic campaigns of excavation directed by the sculptor and restorer Gaspare Sibilla and with Venceslao Pezolli as inspector, in order to acquire further material.

The new museum was developed in the Palazzetto of the Belvedere, the fifteenth-century villa of Innocent VIII. New galleries were created for statues, portrait busts and animal sculptures—the Gallerie delle Statue, the Sala dei Busti, the Sala degli Animali—and the old courtyard of the Belvedere was redesigned into an octagon, displaying in a new setting the *Laocoon, the *Belvedere Apollo and other long-cherished pieces. Clement also refurbished the Vatican Library, decorating the floor and walls with colored marbles and the ceiling with an allegorical painting by Anton Raphael *Mengs of the founding of the Museo Clementino. Development of the Vatican displays of antiquities continued under Pius VI, resulting in the eventual change of the name of the museum to the Museo Pio-Clementino.

BIBLIOGRAPHY

E. Rota, "Clemente XIV," *EI* 10 (1931), 573–74; C. Pietrangeli, *I Musei Vaticani, Cinque secoli di storia,* ch. 4, "Clemente XIV e la fondazione del Museo Clementino (1769–1774)" (Rome, 1985).

"CLEOPATRA" (ARIADNE; SLEEPING NYMPH). Sculpture in (probably Greek) marble of a reclining female figure, believed created in the second century A.C. after a Hellenistic original of the third or second century B.C.

The figure is shown clad with one breast exposed; she reclines in a slightly upright posture with her right arm across her head as if in an uneasy sleep. She wears a serpent bracelet on her left arm that led to the popular Renaissance identification of her as Cleopatra committing suicide with the asp. Iconographical traditions in Renaissance art imply that she was also equated with Venus and with the typical sleeping nymph that guarded a sacred fountain. In the late eighteenth century, E. Q. *Visconti identified the figure as *Ariadne,* an interpretation generally accepted today. She has frequently been compared with a sculptured variant of the theme, a sleeping figure formerly in the Villa Medici in Rome (until 1787) and now in the *Florence Archaeological Museum. Ridgway notes that this image of Ariadne should be classed with other figures in a restless sleep (*Barberini *Faun* and *Borghese *Hermaphrodite*) and the original may date to the third century B.C.

The *"Cleopatra"* was in the *Maffei collection in Rome in the early sixteenth century and then was purchased by *Julius II, who placed it in the Vatican collection by 1512. It was installed in the northeast corner of the Belvedere statue court (*Vatican Museums) with a fountain flowing from its base and reportedly on top of a sarcophagus "with the deeds of the emperor Trajan." The impression that the figure was a fountain nymph was enhanced in the 1530s, when the surrounding niche was decorated as a rocky grotto. A drawing by Leonardo da Vinci is the earliest known representation of the figure (ca. 1515), but it does not show the architectural setting, as does a drawing of 1538/39 by *Francisco d'Ollanda. The statue was moved in the early 1550s to a room adjoining the courtyard and in the eighteenth century to the Galleria delle Statue in the Museo Pio-Clementino. In 1798 it was seized by *Napoleon and taken to Paris, eventually returning to Rome by 1816. The piece stands today in the

Galleria delle Statue, placed on top of a sarcophagus (discovered in 1748) with a relief of a Gigantomachy.

The *"Cleopatra"* was one of the most famous statues in Rome during the Renaissance and seventeenth century and gave rise to numerous imitations and copies (e.g., for Francis I of France and Philip IV of Spain). Among the artists influenced by it were *Raphael, *Dürer, Marcantonio *Raimondi and (possibly) Giorgione. Many poets of the sixteenth and seventeenth centuries celebrated her in verse, most notably, Baldassare Castiglione and Agostino Favoriti. The statue began to decline in prestige in the eighteenth century (*Winckelmann did not care for it) and today is widely ignored by classical archaeologists.

BIBLIOGRAPHY

Bieber, 145–46; Helbig 4th ed., I, 109–10; +H. H. Brummer, *The Statue Court in the Vatican Belvedere* (Stockholm, 1970), 154–84; Haskell—Penny, 184–87; Ridgway, *Hellenistic Sculpture* I, 330–32.

CLITUMNUS. River in Umbria, Italy.

Pliny (*Ep.* 8.8) describes the springs of the Clitumnus as a place of remarkable beauty, the water cold and extraordinarily clear, the vicinity wooded with cypress, mountain ash and poplar. An ancient temple contained a statue of the river god, depicted standing, wearing the *toga praetexta;* and the shrine was oracular, with *sortes.* A number of other *sacella* or shrines nearby were dedicated to the divinities of individual springs. Each of these was covered with inscriptions celebrating the spring and its god. Above a bridge where the multiple streams from individual springs merged to form the river, it was not permitted to swim, only to sail. The site in the Imperial period belonged to the colony of Hispellum, given it as a gift by Augustus.

The little church of the Savior now standing on the right bank of the Clitumnus about 1km from its sources may incorporate material from some of these buildings and may owe something to their design. It has the form of a Corinthian temple, with four columns in antis, raised on a very high podium with an arched opening in the front. Two of the columns are fluted spirally and addorsed to the antae, two finished with scale pattern. The back of the temple tails into the steep slope of the bank, the little apse almost disappearing. The pronaos was always approached at the back by lateral stairs leading to deep, symmetrical porches, each with two columns. The church has long been regarded as a jewel of Early Christian architecture, but its date is disputed, dates of fourth–fifth centuries (Salmi, Toesca) and eighth century (Deichmann) having been advanced. It was studied and drawn in careful detail by *Palladio.

BIBLIOGRAPHY

P. Frutaz, ''Il tempietto del Clitunno in un editto del card. Carlo Rezzonico,'' *RACrist* 18 (1941), 245–64; C. Pietrangeli, ''Clitunno, Tempietto del,'' *EAA* 2 (1959), 723.

L. RICHARDSON, JR

CLUNY MUSEUM (MUSÉE DE CLUNY; MUSÉE DES THERMES ET DE L'HÔTEL DE CLUNY), Paris. French museum developed on the site of a Gallo-Roman bath and a Late Gothic (fifteenth-century) residence, the Hôtel de Cluny.

The baths, built for public use, have been dated to the late second or early third century A.C. Constructed of brick, stone and mortar, they contained a huge *frigidarium* (14.5m high), a *tepidarium* and a *caldarium,* all still accessible today. The ruins were known to exist in the Middle Ages, when private houses were built against the walls. The Benedictine order of Cluny owned the baths and adjacent property in the early 1300s and shortly after 1485 built the Hôtel de Cluny against the baths.

Confiscated from the religious order in 1789 and sold to a private citizen, the baths were acquired by the state in 1819, and the remains, believed then to be the palace of the emperor Julian, were partially excavated. The site was sold in 1837 to the city of Paris and in 1843 was joined with the adjacent Gothic mansion to form the Musée des Thermes et de l'Hôtel de Cluny. Excavations were carried out again in 1946–56.

The museum is known for its outstanding collection of French medieval art. Since the baths themselves provide important testimony about the nature of Roman civilization near *Paris, it is appropriate that the museum also houses some fragments of monuments excavated on the Ile-de-la-Cité. Most interesting are the reused stone fragments of a pillar with a dedication to Jupiter found beneath Notre Dame Cathedral, dating to the first century A.C. (reign of Tiberius). The pillar was orginally erected by a company of Paris shipbuilders, who may have also financed the baths.

BIBLIOGRAPHY

M. Fleury, s.v. "Lutetia Parisiorum," *PECS,* 534–35; S. H. Whitney, s.v. "Cluny Museum," *Art Museums of the World,* ed. V. Jackson (New York, 1987), 248–56.

CLUVERIUS, PHILIPPE (PHILIPP CLÜVER; 1580–1622). German geographer, the founder of European historical geography.

Born in Danzig to a German family, Cluverius became a soldier and traveled all over Europe. He explored on foot the whole of Italy and Sicily, among other countries, and under the influence of *Scaliger he dedicated himself for a lifetime to the subject of geography, especially in the historical sense. By studying carefully the geographical information in classical authors, he was able to chart ancient geography. His work *Germanae antiquae* in three volumes (Leiden, 1616) was for a long time the basic handbook on Germany in antiquity. He was the first to attempt to identify the Osning mountain chain as the Teutoburg Forest, site of the disastrous Roman defeat in A.D. 9.

Cluverius subsequently published a study of the ancient geography of Sicily, Corsica, Sardinia and Italy (*Italia cum insulis,* 1619–24). His works long remained standard and were much praised by the great geographer *Kiepert in the nineteenth century.

BIBLIOGRAPHY

Stark, 122; Sandys, II, 313; *Porträtarchiv,* no. 32.

CNIDOS. See KNIDOS.

COCK, HIERONYMUS (ca. 1510–70). Flemish painter, engraver and art dealer.

Born in Antwerp, Hieronymus Cock was received as a painter in the local guild in 1545 and soon traveled to Italy, probably between 1546 and 1548. As a result of his trip to Rome, he produced a series of twenty-six plates of views of Roman monuments with a title page, *Praecipua aliquot romanae antiquitatis ruinarum monumenta* in 1551, and a second series of twenty-one plates in 1561, *Operum antiquorum romanorum reliquiae.* Included in the prints, regarded as the masterpieces of his engraved works, are the Forum of Nerva, the *Colosseum, *Palatine Hill and views of statuary collections. Cock's engraving of a lost drawing by van *Heemskerck showing the Della *Valle family collection in the courtyard of the palace is a significant document of the location and condition of the Della Valle *Marsyas, Minerva, Apollo Citharoedus* and other sculptures.

BIBLIOGRAPHY

C. Hülsen—H. Egger, *Die Römischen Skizzenbuch von Marten van Heemskerck* (Berlin, 1913–16, repr. 1975), II, 14, 26–30, 34, etc.; Bober—Rubinstein, esp. 455.

COCKERELL, CHARLES ROBERT (1788–1863). English architect and archaeologist.

Cockerell was born in London and was trained as an architect by his father, Samuel Pepys Cockerell, and Robert Smirke (the architect of the *British Museum). In 1810 he went on a *Grand Tour of the Continent that lasted for seven years. He spent much of this time in the Ottoman Empire and Southern Italy and *Sicily, observing the niceties of Greek and Roman architecture, which he was to incorporate into the buildings he later designed.

He made several important archaeological discoveries. He was the first to record the *entasis* on the columns of the *Parthenon, he discovered the Centauromachy frieze at the temple of Apollo at *Bassai (the Ionic order and frieze of which he later used as decorative motifs on the new *Ashmolean Museum in Oxford [1845]), and (with *Haller von Hallerstein) was responsible for unearthing the pedimental sculpture from *Aigina. His aim as a practicing architect was to combine the "richness of rococo & the breadth and merit of the Greek." Like Vitruvius he believed that architects should have a deep knowledge of history. In his mature work he drew on *Palladio, Wren and Hawksmoor and was responsible for establishing the practice of placing a classical façade on bank buildings.

BIBLIOGRAPHY

+C. R. Cockerell, *Antiquities of Athens and Other Places of Greece, Sicily, etc.* (London, 1830); +Idem, *The Temples of Jupiter Panhellenius at Aegina, and of Apollo Epicurius at Bassae near Phigeleia at Arcadia* (London, 1860); S. P. Cockerell (ed.), *Travels in*

Southern Europe and the Levant, 1810–1817, The Journal of C. R. Cockerell, RA (London, 1903); +D. Watkin, *The Life and Work of C. R. Cockerell* (London, 1974).

MICHAEL VICKERS

CODEX COBURGENSIS. Manuscript at Veste Coburg (Coburg Castle, cod. Hz 2), dating to around 1550 and containing drawings of antiquities, especially reliefs from sarcophagi, altars and funerary cippi.

The collection of drawings is closely related to the Codex Pighianus, a manuscript assembled by the Dutch antiquarian Stephanus *Pighius. The two codices reproduce a number of the same monuments and contain numerous drawings from the same hand. They show an objectivity in reproducing monuments, for the drawings consistently indicate which parts of the reliefs are fragmentary or missing.

The drawings in the Coburgensis seem to have been prepared within the antiquarian circle of Cardinal Marcello Cervini in Rome. Included are antiquities that belonged to Cardinal Rodolfo Pio da *Carpi, the Della *Valle family and other collections in and around Rome. The drawings may have been intended as illustrations for a proposed corpus of antiquities sponsored by the Vitruvian Academy. A letter of Claudio Tolomei (1542), founder of the academy, describes Books 11 and 13 of the corpus as being devoted to relief sculpture and mythological themes.

BIBLIOGRAPHY

+Bober—Rubinstein, esp. 455; +H. Wrede—R. Harprath, *Der Codex Coburgensis, Der erste systematische Archäologiebuch, Römische Antiken Nachzeichnungen aus der Mitte des 16. Jahrhunderts,* ed. J. Kruse (Coburg, 1986); M. D. Davis, ''Zum Codex Coburgensis: frühe Archäologie und Humanismus im Kreis des Marcello Cervini,'' *Antikenzeichnung und Antikenstudium in Renaissance und Frühbarock, Akten des internationalen Symposions, Coburg, 8–10 September 1986,* ed. R. Harprath—H. Wrede (Mainz am Rhein, 1989), 185–99.

CODEX EINSIDLENSIS. See EINSIEDELN ITINERARY.

CODEX ESCURIALENSIS. Sketchbook of drawings after the antique in the Escorial, Madrid (Cod. 28-II-12).

H. Egger believed that this collection of drawings after the antique was made in the late fifteenth century in the Florentine workshop of *Ghirlandaio and was, in effect, a series of copies made after the master's originals; the copyism is evident in the inclusion of misunderstood details in many of the drawings.

The sketchbook, with eighty-two folios in three discernible sections, shows a variety of techniques, with different inks and a wide range of color for the washes. The first segment (folios 1–11) contains a mix of drawings of minor antiquities, views of Rome and details from the *Domus Aurea and relief sculpture, while the third section is almost all architectural (69–82). The central section (12–68) includes views of the best-known monuments of Rome—the *Arch of Septimius Severus, the *Arch of Constantine, the *Pantheon, the *Pyramid of Cestius, the *Arch of Titus, the *Column of Trajan and the *Column of Marcus—along with famed sculptures such as the *Belvedere *Apollo*, the **Mar-cus Aurelius* Equestrian Figure and the *Nile* river god in the Capitoline. There is also a group of drawings after the Domus Aurea.

J. Shearman argued that drawings in the important central section were copies of drawings of the early sixteenth century by *Raphael, rather than from the Ghirlandaio workshop. In any case, the drawings cannot be later than 1508, when the sketchbook was carried to Spain by Don Rodrigo de Mendoza, to be consulted for architectural forms used in his fortess La Calaharra, near Granada.

BIBLIOGRAPHY

+H. Egger, with C. Hülsen—A. Michaelis, *Codex Escurialensis, Ein Skizzenbuch aus der Werkstatt Domenico Ghirlandaios* 1–2 (Vienna 1905–6; repr. 1975); J. Shearman, "Raphael, Rome and the Codex Escurialensis," *Master Drawings* 15 (1977), 107–46; +Bober—Rubinstein, esp. 456.

COLA DI RIENZO (1313–54). Italian political revolutionary; tribune of Rome; responsible for program for reform emphasizing the revival of ancient Roman institutions.

Cola was formed in the desolate climate prevailing in Rome during the period when it had been abandoned by the papacy (1305–1417). Inspired by his zealous reading of classical authors (Cicero, Seneca, Valerius Maximus, Livy), he conceived a passionate vision of the ancient city, which in his day lay in ruins, built over by the forts and towers of the Roman nobility.

As an envoy to Pope Clement VI in Avignon (1343), Cola became close friends with *Petrarch, who shared his antiquarian dream to see Rome strong and free. Cola returned to Rome to lead an uprising of the poor against the corrupt nobles who had long made the city the arena for their feuds. He assumed the title of tribune (*Tribunus Augustus;* 1347), thus reviving the ancient Roman office that served the popular cause. He was able to read ancient Latin inscriptions, a rare skill in fourteenth-century Rome, and incorporated into his political program information thus obtained. In 1346 or 1347 he rediscovered in St. John Lateran a bronze tablet recording Vespasian's *Lex de imperio* (*Epigraphy, Roman), and used it as the text for a political speech in which he asserted that the supreme power wielded by Roman emperors was only delegated to them by the Roman people.

His short-lived success was followed by a period of exile and imprisonment by Charles IV in Prague and by the pope in Avignon. When Clement VI died in 1352, his successor, Innocent VI, freed Cola and returned him to Rome. A second bid for power ended in Cola's being murdered on the Capitol in 1354. But he had brought into Rome a remarkable new spirit, blending antiquarian and political interests and presaging the rebirth of Rome in the following century.

BIBLIOGRAPHY
I. Origo, *Tribune of Rome, A Biography of Cola di Rienzo* (London, 1938); Weiss, *RDCA,* 38–42; J.-C. M. Vigueur, "Cola di Rienzo," *DBI* 26 (1982), 662–75.

COLLECTING (TO 1500). The collecting of art in classical antiquity began as early as the seventh century B.C. in connection with the dedication of statues, paintings and other objects at temples and sanctuaries.

At some sites (e.g., the sanctuary of Apollo, *Delphi) the depositing of votive objects was so common that special chapels or treasuries were built by participating cities to accommodate the valuable dedications. The accumulation of votives occurred through the Greek and Roman world; especially well-documented examples are the *Temple of Hera at Olympia, the temple of Apollo at *Delos, for which extensive records reveal the contents of the collection and its management, and the temple of the Deified Augustus near the Roman Forum (*Forum Romanum). Such sites as these were frequented by tourists as well as the faithful, much as Christian churches of the Middle Ages or Renaissance are visited by sightseers today.

Private collecting of art seems to have begun in the Hellenistic period. The Attalids at *Pergamon, expecially Attalus II (160–139 B.C.), purchased works by "Old Masters" in sculpture and painting, or had copies made (e.g., of works by Pheidias and Polygnotos) when the originals were unattainable. Their pieces were displayed in the famed library of Pergamon and throughout the palace. Roman generals, emperors, and other prominent citizens followed their lead, acquiring works of art by conquest (e.g., Marcellus at Syracuse, 212 B.C.; Sulla in Greece, 80s B.C.); by extortion or confiscation (e.g., Verres in Sicily, 73–1 B.C.), or by legitimate purchase. There were numerous art dealers' shops in Rome, along the Via Sacra and in the Saepta Julia, as well as frequent public auctions announced by posters and preceded by exhibitions. The objects obtained might be displayed in one's villa, townhouse, or palace (e.g., *Hadrian's Villa at Tivoli, *Villa of the Papyri at Herculaneum). But there was a widespread sentiment that the public deserved access to famous Greek masterpieces, and magnanimous leaders like Agrippa arranged for their display in fora, baths, porticoes, gardens, sanctuaries, and theaters. In addition to sculpture and painting, many collected minor objects such as cameos and gems (Julius Caesar dedicated six collections of precious gems in the temple of Venus Genetrix) and statuettes and dishes made of Corinthian bronze. Etruscan sculpture was valued as well, and in fact had come to Rome as booty as early as the sack of Veii in 396 B.C.

Collecting of a sort was continued by the Church in the Middle Ages. The Church treasuries contained a variety of objects, from Church furnishings and relics to curious and precious items donated by the faithful. Roman gems and cameos often decorated ecclesiastical vessels after they had been blessed and "converted"; their inclusion may have been considered to demonstrate the continuity and universality of Church history. The medieval Church treasury, with its assortment of religious and pagan objects and natural curiosities, was the prototype of the North European *Kunst- und Wunderkammer.*

Toward the end of the Gothic period, individuals again enjoyed collecting ancient art. The most famous of these is the Duc Jean de Berry. An inventory of his collection by Robert d'Estampes in 1416 informs us of the princely richness and variety of his holdings, which included antiquities from Italy among the paintings, manuscripts and silver tableware.

Specialized collecting of antiquities in the early Renaissance reflected the contemporary perception of Rome as belonging to a separate and distinct historical era. Roman coins were valued by many humanists for their historical interest. Some humanists also appreciated the aesthetic value of ancient art. The collection of *Ciriaco of Ancona specialized in small statuary and gems that he gathered in his travels in Italy and Greece. *Poggio Bracciolini, another eager collector, was especially fond of antique statues, which he spent years gathering for the garden of his villa in the Valdarno. The extraordinary extent and variety of Lorenzo de' Medici's collection, which nurtured the young Michelangelo, is still being uncovered by scholars.

Popes of the fifteenth century took an interest in the collecting of antiquities and conservation of ancient monuments. *Pius II, though he was not himself a collector, showed his appreciation of Rome's antiquities by forbidding the reuse of stone or marble from classical buildings. *Paul II collected coins, gems and cameos. *Sixtus IV passed an edict forbidding the exploitation of antiquities and was responsible, in 1471, for the founding of the world's first public museum, in the Palazzo dei Conservatori (*Capitoline Museums).

The humanist Nicolo dei *Niccoli collected antiquities in addition to writings by ancient authors. Vespasiano da Bisticci describes Nicolo's buying a chalcedony, "engraved with a figure by the hand of Polykleitos," off the neck of a boy he saw in the street. Nicolo owned a range of antiquities: medals in bronze, silver and gold; bronze figurines and marble statues, vases and inscriptions. At the table he drank from antique goblets made of precious stone. Nicolo was perhaps able to collect more extensively than other humanists through the munificence of Cosimo de' Medici (*Medici family).

Artists of the Renaissance gathered specimens of antique sculpture to serve as models in their workshops and for their beauty. Filarete saw ancient works of art in the workshops of *Donatello and *Ghiberti in Florence. Some of these may have been the same relief fragments found in Ghiberti's studio at his death in 1455. The 1494 will of the Venetian painter Gentile Bellini (*Bellini family) lists a torso of *Venus* and a bust of *Plato* among his possessions.

The house of Andrea *Mantegna in Mantua was designed to house his important collection of antiquities. The domed, central room recalled the *Pantheon, and the niches in the wall and large cornices held statues and portrait busts such as that of the empress *Faustina,* coveted by Isabella d'*Este.

Powerful aristocrats, for example, Leonello d'Este (*Este family) and Cosimo de' Medici, followed the lead of the humanists and artists, adding antiquities to their stores of valuable and rare examples of enamel, metalwork, and other small antiquities. They strove to create collections that were encyclopedically complete to show themselves as being "universal in all things."

But such Renaissance men showed pervading interest in richness, variety and value. Filarete says of Piero de' Medici: "[W]orthy and magnanimous man that he is, of many virtues and accomplishments, he delights in every strange and worthy thing and does not note the expense." The collection of the Este in 1494 lists shields and salt cellars with figures of saints, ornate vessels and the usual assemblage of small antiquities, coins, medals and gems. The 1492 inventory of the Medici, where every item is valued in florins, and the Este inventory mentioned before, which records each item's weight, demonstrate these collections' dual worth, monetary and aesthetic. The bulk of these collections was stored in the *guardaroba,* while choice pieces were displayed in the lord's private *studiolo.* Some, including Cosimo de' Medici and Federigo da *Montefeltro, collected books as well, thereby founding the great libraries of the Renaissance.

BIBLIOGRAPHY

E. Bonnaffé, *Les Collectionneurs de l'ancienne Rome* (Paris, 1867); E. Müntz, *Les Collections des Médicis au XVe siècle* (Paris, 1888); W. S. Heckscher, "Relics of Antiquity in Medieval Settings," *JWarb* 1 (1937–38), 204–20; G. Bazin, *The Museum Age* (New York, 1967); R. Weiss, *RDCA,* ch. 13.

CHRISTINE SPERLING

COLLECTING (AFTER 1500). A change in attitudes about collecting took place around the end of the fifteenth century, quite parallel to the change in the visual arts seen in the transition from the Early to the High Renaissance.

The large scale—both in individual antiquities and in regard to a collection as a whole—became very important, and a new grandeur was sought in the ensemble. This approach is obvious in the display of the Belvedere court of the *Vatican, graced by the heroic *Laocoon,* and in the new collection on the *Capitoline Hill, where the monumental bronze *Marcus Aurelius* Equestrian Statue was placed as centerpiece (1538; *Capitoline Museums); both of these collections, however, are better studied as *museums. For private collections, one of the best examples in the sixteenth century is that of the *Farnese family, installed in the grand Palazzo Farnese, designed by Antonio da *Sangallo the Younger and fully appropriate for the colossal marbles of the *Farnese *Herakles* and the *Farnese *Bull,* among the many amassed by *Paul III and his grandson Alessandro Farnese. Small and precious antiquities were not neglected. In 1538 the family acquired through the marriage of Ottavio Farnese to Margaret of Austria (widow of Alessandro de' Medici) the highly important collection of cameos and gems that had belonged to the *Medici family, of which the *Farnese Cup was the prize piece. With Fulvio *Orsini as librarian and antiquarian, the Farnese also had his collection of coins, gems and inscriptions at their disposal and available for curious and learned visitors.

Outside Rome, the *Gonzaga family of Mantua and the *Este family of Ferrara acquired fine antiquities with the help of agents in Italy and Greece. Isabella d'*Este, who formed an exquisite collection of smaller antiquities, especially coins and gems, is the rare example of the successful female collector in Renaissance Italy. In Florence, the Medici transferred from the old quattrocento palace on the Via Larga to the Palazzo Vecchio, the Pitti Palace and the *Uffizi, steadily rebuilding the collection that had been dispersed in earlier political misfortunes. As with the Farnese, the magnificence of the collections undoubtedly represented political power, but in Tuscany the message was enriched by the Etruscan background; when Cosimo I acquired the bronze *Chimaera of Arezzo (1553), the Etruscan masterpiece made a patriotic reference to Florence's antique glory, which rivaled the Roman past of the popes and nobility of Rome. The Medici had their own base in Rome, too, in the Villa Medici (acquired 1576), filled with impressive sculpture, particularly in the garden, where the walls were inlaid with marble reliefs (e.g., from the *Ara Pacis), and the courtyard displayed the imposing *Niobe Group.

Among the Medici we also find evidence of a very different approach to collecting, in the studiolo of Francesco I in Palazzo Vecchio, created in the 1570s. The small, windowless chamber contained numerous cupboards for the items in the collection, arranged by material. Precious objects of gold, silver and gems were included along with objects of natural science, and the cupboards were covered with paintings that referred to the subject matter of the various drawers, the whole creating a compendium of knowledge about the universe and a quite sumptuous example of the Kunst- und Wunderkammer. Hundreds of cabinets of such objects of art and nature were created during the Renaissance, both north and south of the Alps. At Bologna, the naturalist and philosopher *Aldrovandi maintained a celebrated museum; at Prague the Holy Roman Emperor Rudolf II had his collection (*Hapsburg family). Classical antiquities were not always included, though carved gems were a popular item; Rudolf kept the *Gemma Augustea along with mandrake roots and bezoar stones from the stomachs of goats.

The Medici collections reached a crescendo with the creation of the Tribuna in the Uffizi, a luxuriously appointed octagonal chamber hung with Renaissance masterpieces on velvet walls and having a cupola faced with mother-of-pearl. Though begun in 1584 as a kind of Kunst- und Wunderkammer, it reached its full expression only in 1680, when several celebrated classical statues were transferred from the Villa Medici in Rome, the *Medici Venus, the *Arrotino and the pair of Wrestlers. The room combined ancient and modern, natural and man-made and monumental and small-scale items in a rich and elegantly designed setting and thus represented a most gracious blending of the sculpture gallery and the curiosity chamber.

The garden and courtyard type of display continued to flourish in the seventeenth century, in the great villas and collections of the *Borghese family and the *Ludovisi family. Excavations in search of ancient sculptures had been carried out with great vigor in the sixteenth century, and these continued apace, as enormous collections were created to satisfy aesthetic as well as political needs of the wealthy princes, cardinals and popes of Rome. Smaller collections created earlier were now swallowed up by the great ones; Scipione *Borghese, for example, had items from the old *Savelli, da *Carpi and *Ceoli collections.

This is the period in which collectors became more and more unscrupulous and greedy in their acquisitions, watching like hawks for the deaths of rivals that might release coveted items onto the market and profiting from the plunder of war. The monarchs of Europe were among the eager buyers; *Louis XIV acquired antiquities from Italy and from France (e.g., the *Venus* from Arles). Much of what Queen *Christina of Sweden owned was plunder, especially the treasures of the Hapsburgs taken by Swedish troops at the sack of Prague in 1648. When her thirst for culture led her across Europe, she took along her collections in tow in her baggage train all the way to Rome, where she established herself as a formidable competitor for the available prizes. In 1627 Charles I of England obtained some of the Gonzaga marbles at the time when he purchased the great paintings of *Raphael, *Titian and *Mantegna, which were his real interest. The Earl of *Arundel represents English collecting with a genuine passion for antiquity, so intense that it meant the dispatch of agents to Greece and Turkey. Arundel himself in his travels in Italy was allowed to conduct excavations in the ruins of Rome to augment his fine collection, which he displayed as the first gallery of ancient sculpture in England.

Later English collectors flocked to Italy on the *Grand Tour in the eighteenth century, bringing back their souvenirs and their ornaments for grand country houses. "Never forget that the most valuable acquisition a man of refined taste can make is a piece of fine Greek sculpture," Charles *Townley was advised by Gavin *Hamilton, who was one of the leading dealers for such trade in Rome, along with Thomas *Jenkins and Bartolommeo *Cavaceppi. For many collectors, such as Henry *Blundell, the quality of the piece was not nearly so important as the apparent wholeness of the statue, because it was sought as decor rather than as an antiquity to be studied for its own sake. There was thus a great demand for restoration, resulting in the pastiches of sculpture that graced many country houses. If such "originals" were not available, casts would do, and so would smaller antiquities such as urns, coins, cameos, bronzes and vases. An explosion of interest in ancient *Greek vases (widely thought of as Etruscan) took place in the eighteenth century, leading to great collections such as those of Sir William *Hamilton, English ambassador to the court of Naples.

The Neapolitan area was a hotbed of archaeological and collecting activity, above all because of the excavations newly initiated at *Herculaneum (1709, 1738) and *Pompeii (1748). The finds at these sites were strictly controlled by the royal *Bourbon family, however, and did not pass on to the market. The Bourbon collection itself was closely guarded from the public and was visited by only a few select visitors. In addition, having acquired the Farnese collection through inheritance, the Bourbons undertook to move it to Naples between 1787 and 1800, to the great dismay of art lovers in Rome.

In fact, the exodus of marbles from Rome had a lengthy history and had reached crisis proportions much earlier, when the Medici removed important works from the Villa Medici in the late seventeenth century. Although permits were required for the exportation of such material, regulations were not rigorously enforced. The popes attempted to staunch the flow of this lifeblood of the city with a strategy of supporting and augmenting museums. They sought to provide permanent places in the Vatican and the Capitoline collections for newly excavated items and for the pieces that were crisscrossing from one collection to another and were being pounced upon by rapacious dealers. A major move in this direction was made by Pope Clement IX Albani when he acquired a large part of the *Albani family collection for the Capitoline in 1733. Cardinal Alessandro Albani continued to collect and was one of the last of the Roman connoisseurs to assemble a collection of the style of the Ludovisi, Borghese and Farnese.

A new interest in travel to Greece in the eighteenth century also opened up a new source for antiquities. The ruling Turkish government had no interest in ancient marbles beyond the lime kiln, and with negotiations and bribery, a number of travelers were able to bring back choice pieces. The most celebrated case is that of Lord *Elgin and the *Parthenon marbles, which were eventually acquired by the *British Museum. Also quite important was the purchase in 1815 of the pedimental sculptures from *Aigina, by *Ludwig I of Bavaria for his *Antikensammlung in Munich. Ludwig's discriminating collecting activities in both Greece and Italy make him one of the most important figures in the history of classical collections in Germany.

But the days of the great private collections were coming to a close. Collecting was becoming an institutional activity, and, more and more, major acquisitions were made by museums rather than individuals. One of the few famous collectors of the nineteenth century, the Marchese *Campana, came to a disastrous end through overspeculating. He had permits to excavate at various sites in Rome and at Etruscan localities, but he did not manage well the enormous numbers of antiquities that he acquired and ended up "borrowing" money against their value. The scandal of his embezzlement broke in 1857, and soon Campana's collection of vases, marbles, terracottas and bronzes had to be sold to various museums (included were the Capitoline, the British Museum and especially the *Louvre, Paris) to pay his debts. Various other great collections also ended up in museums: the Borghese in the Louvre, the Ludovisi in the *Terme Museum and the Farnese in the *Museo Nazionale Archeologico of Naples.

In the twentieth century major antiquities on the market have normally been purchased by museums, while private collectors have confined themselves to purchasing small antiquities of fine quality. Inflated prices on the art market have meant that millionaires like J. Paul *Getty have had the greatest success.

One category of collector is the art investor who buys important objects and then donates them to nonprofit museums for the sake of a tax exemption. But the private collectors as well as antiquities dealers have been under fierce attack in a period when the antiquities regulations of the relevant countries command the utmost respect. Greece has had a strong prohibition of the export of antiquities from its earliest years as a new nation (1834), and Italy has attempted to enforce strictly its long-standing regulations. Other lands with classical antiquities have legislation in place, and the United Nations has attempted to contain the problem with the UNESCO Draft Convention on the Means of Prohibiting and Preventing the Illicit Import, Export and Transfer of Cultural Property. Thus, the private collector is frequently in the position of purchasing objects that have been smuggled out of their country of origin, or else are clever *forgeries, and so purchasing is often done in secret or not at all.

BIBLIOGRAPHY

F. H. Taylor, *The Taste of Angels: A History of Art Collecting from Rameses to Napoleon* (Boston, 1948); J. Alsop, *The Rare Art Traditions: The History of Art Collecting and Its Linked Phenomena* (London, 1982); +*The Treasure Houses of Britain, Five Hundred Years of Private Patronage and Art Collecting,* catalog of exhibition (New Haven, CT, 1985); +O. Impey—A. MacGregor, eds., *The Origins of Museums, The Cabinet of Curiosities in Sixteenth- and Seventeenth-Century Europe* (Oxford, 1985).

COLLIGNON, LÉON-MAXIME (1849–1917). French archaeologist, known especially for his work on Greek sculpture.

Collignon studied in Paris and Athens and lived a year in Rome before embarking with Louis Duchesne on a study voyage in 1876 that provided the material for *Notes d'un voyage en Asie Mineur* (1897) with illustrations by his own hand. On his return to France in 1876, a chair of Greek and Latin antiquities was created for him at Bordeaux. The appointment was followed within the year with the publication of his *Essai sur les monuments grecs et romains relatifs au mythe de Psyche.* A chair at the Sorbonne (1883) and acceptance into the Académie des inscriptions (1884) followed. He participated in excavations at *Pergamon and *Delphi and wrote extensively and well. Important among his works are *Histoire de la céramique grecque* (1888), *L'Archéologie classique* (1913), *L'Histoire de la sculpture grecque* (1892–7), *Le Parthenon* (1914) and *Pergame* (1900).

BIBLIOGRAPHY

T. Homolle, *M. Collignon* (1919); R. d'Amat, "Collignon, Léon-Maxime," *DBF* 9 (1961), cols. 281–82.

SHARON WICHMANN

COLOCCI, ANGELO (1474–1549). Italian humanist bishop of Nocera; the sixteenth-century successor of Pomponio *Leto as prime mover of the Roman Academy.

An aristocratic native of Iesi in the western Marches of Italy, Angelo Colocci followed a humanist uncle first to Naples and then to Rome. There he settled more or less permanently in the 1490s to make a successful career as a curial humanist. The range of Colocci's studies was broad even for a man of the Renaissance: Romance lyric, Greek, siege warfare, metrology. He was renowned for his library, his collection of antiquities and his learned garden parties, which took place at Pomponio Leto's property on the Quirinal and in his own garden by the Trevi Fountain. His energy, genial temperament and personal wealth made him the de facto successor to Leto as leader of the Roman Academy and, in a larger sense, of Rome's scholarly community. His expertise on ancient weights and measures was supreme in his own day; he owned an extensive collection of these, including two sculpted exemplars of the Roman foot and a list of Roman *Fasti*. The sculpted reclining nymph who oversaw his garden, however, was a contemporary work, down to its archaizing inscription.

His bureaucratic duties and his devotion to the good life reduced Colocci's scholarly writing to fragmentary notes (mostly preserved in the Vatican Library), but the impact of his company on his contemporaries was profound. His influence can be seen in such early sixteenth-century antiquarian works as Andrea Fulvio's textual study, the *Antiquitates urbis* of 1527, and Jacopo Mazzocchi's pictorial *Simulachrum antiquae urbis Romae* of the same year. He advised *Raphael in the latter's studies of Vitruvius and ancient Rome, acting as scribe and consultant for the vernacular Vitruvius executed for Raphael by Marco Fabio Calvo and for the final extant draft of Raphael's letter to Pope *Leo X. After the death of his wife in 1518, he took holy orders, eventually serving as bishop of Nocera. His gardens and library suffered cruelly in the 1527 Sack of Rome.

BIBLIOGRAPHY

V. Fanelli—F. Ubaldini, eds., *La Vita di Mons. Angelo Colocci (Barb. Lat. 4882), Studi e Testi* 257 (Vatican City, 1969); *Atti del Convegno di Studi su Angelo Colocci* (Iesi, 1972); V. Fanelli, *Ricerche su Angelo Colocci e sulla Roma cinquecentesca, Studi e Testi* 283 (Vatican City, 1979).

INGRID ROWLAND

COLOGNE (COLONIA AGRIPPINENSIS). Roman settlement, originally tribal capital of the Ubii (founded 38 B.C.); site of a fortress for two Roman legions; raised to the status of a colony by Claudius (A.D. 50) in honor of his wife Agrippina, who was born there.

The history of excavation in Cologne follows closely the history of building in the city. For example, the leveling off of the Platz in front of the Rathaus in 1561 led to the first in a series of discoveries at the site that would culminate in the exposure of the *praetorium* (governor's palace) when a new Rathaus was being built to replace one badly damaged during World War II. Likewise, the construction of an air-raid shelter (1941) and then of a subterranean parking ramp (1970), both near the cathedral, occasioned the discovery of the remains of sumptuously decorated houses (including the famous Dionysos mosaic) and the remains of the legionary fortress. Throughout the nineteenth century Roman remains were coming to light through finds of this sort, and much of the material has been published in the *Bonner Jahrbücher* (beginning in 1842).

An important figure in the postwar history of the city's archaeology was Otto Doppelfeld (1907–79). He participated in excavations and was a key figure in the establishment of a separate home for the Römisch-Germanisches Museum (formerly a section of the Wallraf-Richartz Museum), which opened its doors in 1974 to critical acclaim.

BIBLIOGRAPHY

O. Doppelfeld, s.v. "Colonia Agrippinensis," *PECS*, 231–32; J. von Elbe, s.v. "Köln," *Roman Germany*, 2nd ed. (Mainz, 1977), 183–226; O. Doppelfeld, *Vom unterirdischen Köln* (Cologne, 1979).

ELIZABETH C. TEVIOTDALE

COLONNA, FRANCESCO (1433/34–1527). Renaissance author and antiquarian.

Born in Venice, Colonna spent much of his life there as a Dominican friar in the monastery of SS. Giovanni e Paolo. Surviving records suggest that he lived a tempestuous and rebellious life as a monk, frequently incurring censure from his superiors. He died in Venice in 1527.

Colonna is chiefly remembered as the author of the dream romance *Hypnerotomachia Poliphili,* dedicated to Duke Guidobaldo of Urbino and first published in a lavish edition in 1499 by Aldus Manutius. Originally an unsigned work, it was noticed as early as 1512 that an acrostic given by the first letter of each chapter reveals the author's name: POLIAM FRATER FRANCISCUS COLUMNA PERAMAVIT ("Fra Francesco Colonna loved Polia completely"). The *Hypnerotomachia* is a work in the form of the traditional medieval romance, like the *Roman de la Rose,* but is based more directly on *Boccaccio's *Amorosa visione.* It differs from the latter in that the romantic wanderer has become a Renaissance antiquarian. The hero, Poliphilus, pursues his beloved Polia through a world of mysterious hieroglyphs and overgrown ruins, fallen columns, broken sculpture, temples, triumphs and dancing nymphs. The language used was a strange mixture of Italian, Latin and Greek that attempted to give the common tongue a bit of classical dignity.

The 1499 edition of Manutius has been called the most beautiful publication of the Renaissance, because of the many fine woodcuts that illustrate the classical motifs of the text. These engravings have been studied more closely than the text; to some they were supposed to hold the key to the ancient art of alchemy, and to others they offered a glimpse of the magnificence of classical antiquity. The French edition of Jean Martin, published in 1546 as *Le Songe de Poliphile,* exerted a great influence on the classical trend in French architecture. The 1592 English translation, called *The Strife of Love in a Dream,* fed the growing Elizabethan love for art and artifice and provided writers with a rich collection of imagery and material.

Colonna's most enduring influence is in his promotion of the love of classical things. His version of classicism, however, is basically romantic; unlike the Florentine rationalists, he is uninterested in systems of philosophy. His approach is guided not by reason but by imagination. Colonna was content to reconstruct the broken pieces of antiquity into an Ovidian paradise.

The *Hypnerotomachia* has at no time been considered a literary masterpiece, and Colonna has none of the archaeological passion of a man like *Alberti, but his detailed descriptions of fantastic classical art and architecture provided Renaissance writers, artists and architects (including Giorgione, *Titian, *Pietro da Cortona, *Bernini) with a wealth of imagery and symbolism to draw upon.

BIBLIOGRAPHY

M. T. Casella—G. Pozzi, *Francesco Colonna: Biografia e opere* (Padua, 1959); A. Blunt, *Artistic Theory in Italy, 1450–1600* (Oxford, 1962), 39–43; L. Gent, *Hypnerotomachia: The Strife of Love in a Dream* (New York, 1973); G. Pozzi, s.v. "Colonna, Francesco," *DBI* 27 (1982), 299–303.

DAVID FUNK

COLONNA FAMILY. Italian noble family known for its collections of antiquities in the fifteenth and sixteenth centuries.

The Colonna were among the first Renaissance antiquarians in Rome, beginning with Cardinal PROSPERO COLONNA (d. 1463), who was the first recorded owner of the *Belvedere *Torso*. He also possessed the well-known Late Hellenistic version of the *Three Graces,* now in the Piccolomini Library of Siena Cathedral, and a copy of the Lysippan *Hercules* of the *Farnese type (now in the Villa Borghese), both of which were acquired by Cardinal Francesco Piccolomini after Prospero's death. These treasures had been kept, it is presumed, in the Colonna family house or in the new palace erected near SS. Apostoli on the Quirinal Hill in the early fifteenth century.

Prospero was a friend and adviser to Flavio *Biondo while the latter was writing his *Italia illustrata* and was generally interested in topography and the locating of antiquities. He was the sponsor, around 1450, of what may be called the first underwater excavation. Perhaps acting on advice from Biondo, he commissioned *Alberti to raise the Roman ships sunk in the lake of *Nemi, an area of which Prospero was overlord. The papal court came out to Nemi to watch the exciting operation, in which Alberti used divers and machinery brought from Genoa. Unfortunately, the rotted wood did not allow for the lifting of the ships, and the project had to be abandoned.

The old Colonna house was burned in 1484, and it was in the loggia of the courtyard of the newly rebuilt house that the famous statues of two captive barbarians (*Farnese *Captives*) were first installed. These were taken by Pope Paul III when he seized the possessions of ASCANIO COLONNA, ca. 1540. A copy of a drawing by van *Heemskerck shows them in place, revealing that they were used as architectural supporting figures replacing columns, probably under the inspiration of the description of such figures by Vitruvius (1.1.6).

BIBLIOGRAPHY
Lanciani, *Storia degli scavi* I (1902), 107, 114; Weiss, *RDCA* 108, 113–4; M. Cristo-fani—B. Sangineto, "Le Tre Grazie," in *Siena: Le Origini* (Florence, 1979), 126–34; Bober—Rubinstein, 70, 96–97, 473.

COLOSSEUM (FLAVIAN AMPHITHEATER, COLISEUM). Roman Imperial amphitheater, used for gladiatorial and hunting games.

Probably no monument in Rome more eloquently symbolizes the Eternal City in its vicissitudes than the Flavian Amphitheater, known as the Colosseum. The latter name was given to the structure either because of its massive size or because it stood next to the colossal statue of the sun god, formerly the statue of Nero, on the site of whose lake the Colosseum was built. The Venerable Bede in the eighth century was probably referring to the amphitheater by its descriptive name when he wrote: "As long as the Coliseum stands, Rome will stand; When the Coliseum falls, Rome will fall; When Rome falls, the whole world will also fall." Rebuilt after lightning, fire and earthquake, robbed of its metal, used as a quarry for stone, the vast structure now stands solemn and majestic, probably more dignified in its ruined state than when it was used as an arena for the games.

The amphitheater incorporated the best elements in Roman architectural design and engineering in a building intended to gratify the worst elements in Roman taste and character. It fulfilled its function efficiently in a structure designed to accommodate the 45–50,000 spectators who came to watch the games: gladiatorial contests and staged animal hunts (*venationes*). The gladiatorial games pitted against each other condemned criminals or enslaved prisoners of war. The *venationes* altered the fauna of North Africa, as its shores were scoured for exotic beasts to be hunted to death in the arena. In A.D. 80 Titus dedicated the amphitheater with one hundred days of games; on one day alone 5,000 animals were exhibited.

Construction was begun by the Flavian emperor Vespasian (reigned A.D. 69–79), an opportune political move, restoring to the people land that had been appropriated by Nero for the lavish *Domus Aurea, the Golden House. Vespasian drained Nero's artificial lake, which had occupied the valley between the Caelian, the Velian and the Oppian hills. Using the already excavated cavity of the drained lake with its lithoid tufa as bedrock support, the engineers laid a cement foundation twenty-five feet deep. Three immense concentric travertine rings formed the outer walls. A road from Tibur (*Tivoli) was constructed to haul the travertine, 242,000 cartloads for the façade alone. Vespasian witnessed its inauguration in 79 but died before the dedication by his son Titus in 80 with the one hundred days of games.

The building, designed by an unknown architect, was a gigantic ellipse of breathtaking proportions, measuring 620 by 512 feet, 159 feet in height from its two-step base, decorated with ceremonial arches at the four main axes. The 286-by-178-foot arena (from *harena,* sand, strewn on its surface) was also an

Interior of the *Colosseum*, with chapels for the Stations of the Cross, anonymous painting, ca. 1789. (Statens Museum for Kunst, Copenhagen.)

ellipse, surrounded by the seating area (*cavea*), which measured a uniform 167 feet all around. The interior consisted of eighty radial walls like spokes of an enormous flattened wheel. On tufa bases, these walls of brick-faced concrete supported sloping barrel vaults on which rested the tiers of marble seats. A section of these seats has been restored on the east lower deck.

The eighty exterior arches on the first three levels were separated by engaged columns with a progression from bottom to top of Doric (Tuscan), Ionic and Corinthian capitals, an architectural style anticipated in the *Theater of Pompey and *Theater of Marcellus, ultimately derived from the Tabularium. Marble sculpture may have decorated each arch above the first arcade. The fourth-level attic consisted of solid walls between Corinthian-capped pilasters, every other space containing a rectangular window. Gilt-bronze shields (*clipea*) decorated the alternate spaces, said to have been added by Domitian. Between each of the pilasters are still visible three stone corbels with matching holes in the cornice to support the 240 wooden masts from which a giant sunscreen was deployed to protect the audience from the hot sun. At ground level, ringing the building was a fifty-seven foot apron of travertine, near the edge of which were 160 stone slabs or "bollards" which may have been involved both in crowd control and in raising the rope web on which the sails (*vela*) for the immense awning (*velarium*) were extended. Sailors from the naval base at Misenum were quartered nearby to handle the awning because of their expertise with ropes and cloth.

Crowds were admitted to a double ambulatory through numbered arches (I–LXXVI), excluding the four decorated arches on the main axes—one for the emperor, one for dignitaries, an entrance for gladiators and an exit, *Porta Libitinaria,* for the dead. The seats were divided into decks (*maeniana*), with a private box for the emperor and his party on the podium. A bronze fence decorated with ivory tusks and a gilded mesh net protected the senators and officials in the first rows from any animals or from gladiators who might have tried to scale the eighteen-foot wall separating the arena from the podium (*pulvinar*). In the first deck sat the nobles and priests, and farther up sat the knights; separated from these in the second deck sat the *populus:* merchants and freedmen; the poorest (*pullati*) climbed to high-up seats. Women were relegated to the topmost wooden seats (*summum maenianum in lignis*) under the portico whose roof formed the platform from which the giant awning could be maneuvered. Seats were assigned by arch, section and number so that ticket holders could enter through numbered arches to exact location identified by wedge-shaped section (*cuneus*) and deck, the social classes all skillfully separated from one another. Stairways and ramps (*vomitoria*) connected the ambulatory corridors to the *cavea* and also provided control for a potentially unruly crowd.

Mock naval battles (*naumachia*) may have been staged in the flooded arena, but only in the early years. After the elaborate substructures were built for animal cages, lifts and scenery storage, the naval games could no longer have been staged in the amphitheater. Excavation of the underground areas on the west side (site of the present Colosseum Museum) has revealed complex passageways for moving scenery from storage depots nearby. The underground passage on the east extended to the Ludus Magnus.

There is no direct evidence of any mass executions of Christians martyred in the arena. Christians, condemned as enemies of the state, could have been forced into the arena; some may have gone voluntarily, as in the unsubstantiated legend of St. Ignatius from Asia Minor at the time of Trajan. The Christian regard for life, working against the inhumane acts in the amphitheater, might have caused the emperor Constantine to ban the games in A.D. 325, although his decision was more likely the result of the urging of the Council of Nicaea in that year. The ban seems not to have been effective. St. Augustine in the late fourth century describes a fellow Christian, Alypius, who visited the games unwillingly but who, seduced by the shouts of the crowd and the carnage, watched in fascination the events he had come to condemn.

The games gradually died out, not so much from Christian conscience as from lack of funds to keep them going. Considered gifts to the people (*munera*), the games took an enormous amount of money to produce. The emperors had considered it money well spent, by themselves or wealthy nobles. At the end of the fourth century Symmachus, a learned pagan Roman, used his son's praetorship to stage one of the last games, finally held in 401. This extravaganza, with Sicilian charioteers, Spanish horses, lions and crocodiles from Africa and German captives as gladiators, went amiss when many of the animals died in transit, and the resentful Germans strangled each other the night before the games. In 414 a shocking event occurred that curtailed the games. A young priest named Telemachus from Asia Minor, who entered the arena to separate two gladiators, was stoned to death by the mob. Thereafter the emperor Honorius abolished the gladiatorial contests, but the *venationes* continued on a limited scale.

The building had been damaged by earthquakes during the early centuries, particularly by a severe one with lightning in 217, but it had been rebuilt by Elagabalus and Alexander Severus in 222–23 (with a miscellaneous variety of stones near the cornice). An elaborate restoration by Gordian III (238–40) is recorded on a coin, as well as rebuilding in 425–50 and again in 508. In 847, however, when the building no longer served a function, earthquake damage was not repaired, and in 855 space inside was leased to artisans for stone-breaking and stone-burning limekilns.

In the eleventh century the Colosseum became the fortress of the powerful Frangipani family. After the Romans had driven out the feudal families in 1144, it was appropriated as communal property with hopes to restore it. But by 1159 it was back in the hands of the Frangipani, who took it as the noble symbol of their arms, as did also Frederick Barbarossa in the following century. But the damage continued. In 1231 the southwest façade collapsed; its exterior arches became a pile of stones. In 1312 it was presented to the Senate and the people by Henry VII. *Petrarch was shocked in 1349 to see how it had suffered from the earthquakes. By 1362 the Frangipani, the Romans and the legate of the pope were all quarreling over the profits from the sale of fallen stone.

Part of the structure was awarded to the charitable Confraternity of the Salvatore in 1386, an act inscribed above the sixty-third arch, but that did not prevent the stones from being carted away. Pagan buildings had been abandoned; only those converted to new uses were protected from pillage. Under *Nicholas V (1452) one contractor alone took away 2,522 cartloads of travertine from the Colosseum, and Pope Alexander VI leased it as a quarry to share in the profits. Thieves burrowed into the walls for metal; the iron cramps by which the blocks of travertine had been fastened in lead were burned out with sulphur, leaving the travertine pitted, as it appears today. The bronze fittings, the fence, the net, the rings, the shields had vanished long before. When no longer under the protection of the feudal families, the building was left with no protectors at all.

A German traveler in 1497 reported passion plays produced in the arena amid the ruins, including scenes of flagellation and crucifixion. Myths were attached to the building that, because of its geometric perfection, in antiquity it had been a temple to the sun with a gilded dome or that it was the seat of the devil from which spirits of the dead could be evoked. Beggars, robbers and undesirables lurking beneath the arches enhanced the latter image. Benvenuto *Cellini (1532) describes how he used the Colosseum as a setting for a midnight rendezvous with occult spirits. Studies by *Brunelleschi and *Alberti were made of its harmonious proportions, but all the while it was being lauded and used as an inspirational model for Renaissance architecture, it served as a quarry, sometimes for the very buildings it inspired. The steps and a loggia of St. Peter's, the Palazzo Venezia and San Marco, the rebuilt Pons Aemilius in 1557 (Ponte Rotto), the Palazzo Barberini, the Porto di Ripetta, and the Capitoline Museum—all were built in part with stones from the Colosseum.

Pope *Sixtus V (1585–90) had conflicting designs for the building, first to convert it into a church and, that failing, to transform it into a textile factory with quarters for the weavers, the latter plan abandoned only at the death of the pope. *Bernini had been commissioned to design a church for the Colosseum, his grandiose plans including a new façade and appropriate Christian decorations and high altar. The plans were never realized; in the seventeenth century Pope Clement IX used the building to store manure for saltpeter to be used in a neighboring gunpowder factory. Roots of plants, shrubs and trees growing inside split further apart the cracks in the walls. In 1682 Antoine *Desgodetz published in Paris his detailed drawings of the buildings of Rome, including thirty pages (246–77) devoted to the Colosseum, one complete with shrubbery.

Sacred and profane uses of the building continued. John Evelyn, the diarist, describes in 1644 a small chapel, Santa Maria della Pietà nel Colosseo, erected inside over the vaults, but in 1697 quarry rights were given to Domenico Ponsiani to triturate the stone on the site for street macadam. Published posthumously in 1725, the illustrated folio text of Carlo Fontana, L'Anfiteatro flavio descritto e delineato, contains an accurate study of the monument with careful engravings, including plans to construct an interior Martyrs' Church for the jubilee year 1700. Lack of funds prevented the project of Fontana, who would have become the protector of the site; stones were still being hauled away, and all the while the building was being revered as a holy shrine of martyrdom, real or imagined. Finally, in 1744 Pope Benedict XIV forbade any further removal of stone. In 1754 he consecrated the ruin to the Christian martyrs, planting a cross in the center of the arena and erecting stations of the cross all around at appropriate intervals.

Travelers, artists and authors of the eighteenth and nineteenth centuries came to admire the picturesque, romantic ruin, part of every *Grand Tour, somber and melancholy, particularly when viewed at night. *Goethe (1787) described it with smoke rising from beggars' fire inside; *Byron conjured up dead heroes by moonlight in his poetry; Madame de Staël and Stendhal visited it by night.

Nathaniel Hawthorne described it during the moonlight tour of the four friends at the beginning of *The Marble Faun* (1860; cf. *Capitoline *Faun*), complete with Christian shrines, and Henry James in 1878 seated Daisy Miller in it at night, a prelude to her fever. The wealthy had portraits of themselves painted with the Colosseum in the background.

Between 1810 and 1814 the French under *Napoleon excavated the lower floor and a portion of the arena and began the removal of the vegetation. That abundant flora was the subject of several studies, one in 1813 and again in 1855, by which time 420 plants had been identified, some rare and exotic, which increased the allure for the romantic poets.

In 1825 Pope Leo XII added the massive triangular buttresses at the western wall, and the early archaeologists of the 1840s, *Canina, Folchi and Poletti, began its restoration, rebuilding the inner walls. An inscription in 1845 records the beneficence of Pope *Gregory XVI toward this work. In 1871 the chapel, Christian shrines and vegetation were removed by the archaeologist Pietro Rosa, laying bare the interior ribs. Guido Baccelli freed it from surrounding buildings in 1893–96. In the 1920s the Fascists further dramatized the Colosseum's central location by removing the remaining buildings and gardens surrounding it. They provided an uncluttered access and view from the Piazza Venezia by building the Street of the Imperial Fora in 1933. Thereafter all crosstown traffic circled the structure, further endangering the walls. Restoration work resumed in 1973. Only in 1981 did the excavation of the Meta Sudens block off traffic on the southwest, providing a boon to wall preservation. The exterior wall on the north side is intact with numbered arches XXIII–LIV still visible. Traffic continues around the northeast area but is closed on the southwest.

In 1984 an exhibit was held in the amphitheater using the monument as a setting for a view of Italian economy in the 1920s and 1930s. For this exhibit, executed by Cinecittà, a spectacular reconstruction of a slice of the building was mounted on the exterior and interior to show its original form and function. Re-created was a section of the external ring in wood, metal sheeting and stretched fabric along with the interior arcades. A matching section of the tiers of seats was installed extending down toward the arena floor level. There a metal walkway was built over the excavated substructures to a wide wooden exhibition platform re-creating a section of the floor of the arena across its diameter on the long axis. A heated controversy arose between architectural preservationists who opposed the use of the monument for any but its own didactic and historical exhibits and defenders of the exhibit who cited the 50,000 visitors in the first two weeks. The latter argued that entrance fees would more than offset the $1.7 million expended for the reconstruction and will help finance continued preservation. The preservationists seem to have prevailed.

The Colosseum still stands, along with Rome and the world, visited by an onslaught of tourists, who are shown the podium with its sober black cross marking a platform from which the emperor could have viewed the spectacles in antiquity. It was a time when crowds of all social levels came together on the days of the games to witness carnage, the "gift" of the Flavian emperors to the people of Rome, in a structure that ironically combined the worst in depraved appetite with the best in Roman architecture. Vespasian's architect and construction crews have left a lasting testimony of Roman ability to handle dressed stone and to stabilize enormous weight over a vast space in one of the most impressive monuments of antiquity, imitated throughout the Roman world but unequaled in its massive size, its splendid symmetry and its technical ingenuity.

BIBLIOGRAPHY

+C. Fontana, L'Anfiteatro flavio descritto e delineato (The Hague, 1725); P. Colagrossi, L'Anfiteatro flavio (Florence, 1913); +P. Quennell, The Colosseum (New York, 1971); +J. Pearson, Arena (New York, 1973); Coarelli, 166–74.

NORMA GOLDMAN

COLOSSUS OF BARLETTA. Bronze colossal statue (5.11m high) representing a standing emperor, originally holding an orb and scepter.

The identity of the emperor has been much disputed (dates in the fourth, fifth and sixth centuries A.C. have all been proposed), but it is agreed that the *Colossus* is one of the masterpieces of Late Antique sculpture.

The piece was taken by Venetians from an unknown eastern city in the thirteenth century and abandoned on the beach near Barletta, on the Adriatic Sea, after a shipwreck. In 1309 the Dominicans of Manfredonia used the bronze of the legs in casting bells; but the legs as well as the arms were remade in 1491 by the sculptor Fabio Alfano of Naples. At that time the statue was transported from the port to the marketplace of Barletta, next to the church of S. Sepulcro, where it has remained until the present. Affectionately named Saint Hercules by the citizens of Barletta, the *Colossus* was admired by *Ciriaco from nearby Ancona and by others.

BIBLIOGRAPHY

+H. Kluge—K. Lehmann-Hartleben, Grossbronzen der römischen Kaiserzeit (Berlin, 1927), 56–58, 67–71; "Barletta, colosso di," EAA 1 (1958), 980–81; S. Doeringer—D. G. Mitten—A. Steinberg, Art and Technology, A Symposium on Classical Bronzes (Cambridge, MA, 1970), 248; V. Bracco, L'Archeologia nella cultura occidentale (Rome, 1979), 64.

COLOSSUS OF RHODES. Colossal bronze statue of the sun god, Helios, erected at *Rhodes; one of the Seven Wonders of the World.

The sculpture was created by Chares of Lindos, a pupil of Lysippos, using the 300 talents obtained from the sale of the siege-engines of Demetrios Poliorcetes, abandoned outside the city in 304 B.C. The *Colossus,* seventy cubits high (ca. 32m), took twelve years to build (292–280 B.C.). Though Chares had taken elaborate care to stabilize the structure with a marble base and an iron scaffolding, it toppled at the knees in an earthquake in 227/6 B.C.

An oracle prevented the rebuilding of the *Colossus,* and it lay in fragments for many centuries. ("Few men can clasp the thumb in their arms, and its fingers are larger than most statues. Where the limbs are broken asunder, vast caverns are seen yawning" Pliny, *NH* 34.18). In A.D. 653, the Arab general Mavias finished pulling the sculpture down and sold the pieces to a Jewish merchant, who reportedly carried them off on 900 or more camels.

The idea that the *Colossus* stood astride the harbor at Rhodes and that ships sailed between its legs has no ancient authority; it seems to have been formulated in the late fifteenth century by Vigémère or Fabri. In modern times A. Gabriel conjectured that it may have stood on the promontory of the Fort St. Nicholas; H. Maryon suggested that it was erected in the district now known as the Castle.

BIBLIOGRAPHY

H. Maryon, "The Colossus of Rhodes," *JHS* 76 (1956), 68–86; L. Laurenzi, s.v. "Colosso di Rodi," *EAA* 2 (1959), 773–74.

JOHN McK. CAMP II

COLUMBARIA. Tombs characterized by numerous small niches (*loculi*) in the walls to hold the urns (*ollae*) containing the ashes of the dead; the term "columbarium" is used because of the similarity to a dovecote.

Columbaria of Hellenistic date are known in S. Etruria, but this type of tomb is particularly associated with Rome. Many large columbaria have been found over the centuries near the *Via Appia. The earliest recorded discovery was in 1469–70, a columbarium of the freedmen and servants of Nero Drusus the Elder. Others were excavated under Pius IV (1559–65), and one of these, of the *gens Pompeia,* was drawn by *Ligorio and later published by *Bartoli. The years 1726–33 saw the discovery of more columbaria. One of the most impressive was the huge columbarium of the freedmen of Livia, excavated in 1726 and published by *Bianchini in detail and with good illustrations soon afterward.

Such illustrations no doubt influenced d'*Hancarville's imaginary tomb of *Winckelmann, which imitates a columbarium. Early antiquarians were particularly interested in the inscriptions such tombs yielded and in collectible small finds: the structure of the tomb was often destroyed after looting (as happened to the columbarium of the freedmen of Livia) or allowed to decay (cf. *Piranesi's illustration of the columbarium of the freedmen of Augustus, then being used as a storeroom; today it houses a picturesque restaurant). A few columbaria excavated at a later date have fared rather better, for example, the small columbarium of Pomponius Hylas (found in 1831) and the three columbaria of the Vigna Codini (excavated 1840–53), all of which can be visited today.

BIBLIOGRAPHY

Lanciani, *The Ruins and Excavations of Ancient Rome,* 329–35, +Nash II, 324–26; 333–39; 346–48; +H. Kammerer Grothaus, "Camere sepolcrale de' liberti e liberte di Livia Augusta ed altri Caesari," *MEFRA* 91 (1979), 315–42.

GLENYS DAVIES

COLUMN OF ANTONINUS PIUS, Rome. Red granite column, originally crowned by a portrait statue, set up in the Campus Martius after the emperor's death in A.D. 161.

By the Renaissance only about six meters of the column remained visible above ground on Monte Citorio. In 1703 excavations uncovered the entire shaft and its decorated pedestal, and between 1706 and 1708 the pedestal sculptures were restored by Felici and Napoleoni. The column was badly damaged by fire in 1759, and in 1789 the pedestal was installed in the Giardino della Pigna of the Vatican. A new restoration was undertaken in 1841 by Giuseppe De Fabris. In 1979 the pedestal was moved to the Cortile delle Corazze of the Musei Vaticani. The monument is well documented in a series of prints by *Bianchini (1703), Vignoli (1705), *Piranesi (1762), *Visconti (1796) and De Fabris (1846). The pedestal reliefs depicting the apotheosis of Antoninus and his wife, Faustina, and the funerary *decursio* in their honor have long been considered by historians of Roman art as one of the key documents of the dissolution of the classical style in relief sculpture.

BIBLIOGRAPHY

+L. Vogel, *The Column of Antoninus Pius* (Cambridge, MA, 1973); R. Turcan, "Le piédestal de la colonne antonine," *RA* (1975), 305–18; D.E.E. Kleiner—F. S. Kleiner, "The Apotheosis of Antoninus and Faustina," *RendPontAcc* 51–52 (1978–80), 389–400.

FRED S. KLEINER

COLUMN OF MARCUS AURELIUS, Rome. Freestanding monumental Roman column, erected in honor of the emperor Marcus Aurelius.

Named officially *columna centenaria Divorum Marci et Faustinae* ("the hundred-foot column of the divine Marcus and Faustina"), it dominated an architectural setting in the *Campus Martius off the Via Flaminia analogous to the earlier Forum Traiani. The sculptured frieze of Luna marble winds around the shaft twenty-one times and depicts the German and Sarmatian campaigns of A.D. 172–73 and 174–75. Including a bronze statue (or statues, if Faustina, wife of Marcus, was shown) and the leveling course of travertine, its total height reached 175 Roman feet (51.95m); the column proper measured 100 Roman feet (29.6m). The pedestal is now two-thirds hidden below the level of the Piazza Colonna.

The column was begun at the end of Marcus's reign (A.D. 180) and must have been completed by 193, when its official custodian, a freedman named Adrastus, petitioned Septimius Severus for the right of building a guardhouse in its neighborhood where he and his successors could more easily attend their duty. The application was granted, and Adrastus caused the official correspondence about this business to be engraved, word by word, on the doorposts of his guardhouse. These documents, dated from 6 August to 9 September 193, were discovered in situ in 1777 in the Piazza di Monte Citorio and were removed to the Museo Pio-Clementino (*CIL* VI, 1585).

The Regional Catalogues of the fourth century A.C. list the "Temple Antonius and the spiral column 175 feet high, 203 steps inside, 56 windows.'' The column was included in the tour of Rome given to Emperor Constantius II in 357.

In the Middle Ages the column became the property of the monks of S. Silvestro (SS. Dionysii et Silvestri in Catapauli). An inscription in the vestibule of the present church, dated 1119, states that both the column and the little church of S. Nicholai de Columna (which stood close to it) were leased annually to the highest bidder by the monks. The column was evidently rented on account of the profit that could be derived from pilgrims and tourists wishing to ascend it.

The column is depicted on the Golden Bull of Louis the Bavarian (1328). The vignettes of *Lafréry (1550), Gamucci (1565), *Du Pérac (1573) and *Cavalieri (1585) and the frescoes in the Vatican Library show to what an insecure state the column was reduced toward the end of the sixteenth century. In 1589 *Sixtus V spent 9,284 scudi on repairing the monument. His architect, Domenico *Fontana, restored part of the bas-reliefs using marble from the *Septizodium. ''Having expurgated this column of all impiety,'' Sixtus had a statue of St. Paul installed on top. Recently a new and ambitious program of cleaning and restoration was carried out on the column (1981–87).

BIBLIOGRAPHY

Lanciani, *Ruins and Excavations of Ancient Rome*, 505–8; +G. Becatti, *Colonna di Marco Aurelio* (Milan, 1957); Idem, *La Colonna coclide istoriata* (Rome, 1960); Kleiner, *Roman Sculpture*, 295–301, 314.

PETER HOLLIDAY

COLUMN OF TRAJAN, Rome. Freestanding monumental Roman column, erected in the Forum of Trajan (cf. *Imperial Fora), completed A.D. 113.

The base of the Column of Trajan served as the emperor's tomb, and its sculptured frieze, winding around the shaft twenty-three times, depicts his two Dacian wars of A.D. 101–2 and 105–6. Including the gilded bronze statue of the emperor on top, it rose some 143 feet.

In Rome it soon found a companion in the *Column of Marcus Aurelius (A.D. 180–93), and Constantinople (*Byzantium), the second Rome, received its own two columns of similar type from Theodosius (A.D. 386) and Arcadius (A.D. 402).

In the medieval period, the column remained one of the marvels of the city. The *Einsiedeln Itinerary (ca. 800) lists it twice. Far to the north, it was probably the model for Bishop *Bernward's twelve-foot-high bronze column dedicated in the cathedral of Hildesheim, in the eleventh century, with its spiral frieze showing scenes from the life of Christ. The *Mirabilia (twelfth century) praises the column for its height, beauty and sculptured frieze. By the tenth-eleventh centuries, a church of St. Nicholas stood *sub columna Traiani* (''under the Column of Trajan''). Though technically the property of the church of the SS. Apostoli, by 1162 the column had been placed under the direct surveillance of the Senate. In views of the city such as that on the seal from the Golden Bull of Louis the Bavarian (1328)—more ideal than realistic—the column appears together with the *Pantheon, *Colosseum and other ancient and later monuments. From the quattrocento onward, the column awakened the interest of artists, city planners and scholars alike.

The earliest drawings from the column in our possession date from 1467 and stem from a probably unsuccessful attempt to reproduce the frieze in its entirety. *Ripanda is said to have made a complete set of drawings of the reliefs sometime before 1506. Other Renaissance artists selected specific scenes for their artistic value. The earliest complete series of drawings extant was done by Girolamo Muziano; these were engraved and published in 1576. Motifs from the frieze, such as soldiers and barbarians, scenes of building and so on, appear in countless works of art from the quattrocento onward.

In 1536 *Paul III demolished the church of St. Nicholas and freed the monument for the visit of Charles V. A decade later, houses were destroyed, and a depression was excavated around it to isolate it better. In 1558 *Michelangelo designed more adequate surroundings ''in keeping with the beauty of the monument,'' but nothing came of his plans. Later, Gregory XIII (1572–85) squared off the depression and gave it terracing walls. The bronze statue of St. Peter was placed on top of the column on 26 September 1588, under *Sixtus V.

In the sixteenth century scholars also began to direct their interest to the column. The engravings of Muziano were provided with a learned commentary by Alonso *Chacón (1576). Through such works as Giovanni Pietro *Bellori's *La Colonna Traiana,* with illustrations by Pietro Santi *Bartoli (Rome, 1667) and Antonio Francesco *Gori's *Columna Traiana,* illustrated by Andrea Morellio (Amsterdam, 1683), knowledge of the monument and its frieze spread throughout Europe. The sixteenth century also saw the first plaster casts of portions of the frieze, commissioned by Francis I in 1541.

A fascinating interpretation of the ancient monument is found in the Karlskirche in Vienna designed by Fischer von Erlach and built (1716–39) for the Hapsburg emperor Charles VI. Two 108-foot-high columns functioning as bell towers were intended to reflect the pillars of Hercules that Charles V had chosen more than two centuries earlier as a symbol of his rule. On the frieze that winds around the columns are scenes from the life of San Carlo Borromeo, the patron saint of the emperor.

Very close to its Roman prototype, by contrast, is the neoclassical colonne Vendôme in Paris, built 1806–10 for *Napoleon. It is revetted with bronze from German and Austrian cannon captured at Austerlitz. On its frieze band are depicted campaigns of the emperor.

The column attracted renewed interest in the second half of the nineteenth century. A new set of plaster casts was commissioned by Napoleon III, and the first complete series of photographs from these casts appeared in Guillaume Froehner's *La Colonne Trajane* (Paris, 1872–74), where the first attempt is made to reconstruct the history of the Dacian wars from the frieze. Conrad *Cichorius's *Die Reliefs der Trajanssäule* (1896–1900), also reproducing the entire frieze in photographs, introduced the system by which we refer to the individual scenes today. Because of its painstakingly objective description of the reliefs, it remains the foundation for scholarship today.

BIBLIOGRAPHY

Lanciani, *Storia degli scavi* 2 (1903), 122–9; +K. Lehmann-Hartleben, *Die Trajanssäule* (Berlin, 1926); Platner—Ashby s.v. "Columna Traiani"; R. Krautheimer, *Rome, Profile of a City, 312–1308* (Princeton, NJ, 1980), 36, 67, 187, 198, 233; +S. S. Frere—F. A. Lepper, *Trajan's Column* (Gloucester, NH, 1988).

GERHARD M. KOEPPEL

COMMISSARIO DELLE ANTICHITÀ (Commissioner of Antiquities). The office of antiquarian to the pope; the position was established by Paul III in 1534 and continued until 1870 and the overthrow of the Papal States, when it was replaced by the Soprintendenza per gli scavi e la conservazione dei monumenti (Superintendancy for Excavations and the Preservation of Monuments) and the Direzione Generale delle Antichità e Belle Arti (Directorate-General of Antiquities and Fine Arts).

The main duties of the commissioner were to protect all classical monuments in Rome and throughout the Papal States (in the areas outside Rome, through agents); to oversee all excavations and control the issuing of licenses; to control all exports of art, both ancient and modern, again issuing licenses, after assessing the value of the pieces and deciding whether they were important enough to remain in Rome; to act as guide for any important state visitors; to draft inscriptions for restored classical monuments and public works; and to advise his superior, the Camerlengo (papal chamberlain), on new laws to tighten control over protection of the monuments, excavations and exports.

The commissioners were as follows: Latino Giovenale Manetti (1534–53), diplomat and poet; Mario Frangipani (1556?–69), noble; Pietro Tedellini (1570–84), noble; Orazio Boario (1585–1601); Mario Arconio (1601–20), painter and architect; Lodovico Compagno (1620–37), antiquarian; Niccolo Menghini (1638–55), sculptor; Leonardo *Agostini (1655–70), antiquarian; Giovanni Pietro *Bellori (1670–94), antiquarian and art historian; Pietro Santi *Bartoli (1694–1700), engraver; Francesco Bartoli (1700–33), engraver; Francesco Palazzi (1733–44), antiquarian; Ridolfo Venuti (1744–63), antiquarian; Johann *Winckelmann (1763–68), art historian; Giovanni Battista *Visconti (1768–84), antiquarian; Filippo Aurelio Visconti (1784–99), numismatist and antiquarian; Carlo *Fea (1800–36), lawyer and antiquarian; Pietro Ercole Visconti (1836–70), antiquarian.

The only non-Italian was Winckelmann, also arguably the most famous of the commissioners. The longest serving and probably the most influential in drawing up the legal arguments for the protection of the classical heritage was Fea.

BIBLIOGRAPHY
R. T. Ridley, "To Protect the Monuments: The Commissario delle Antichità, 1534–1870," *Xenia Antiqua* 1 (1992), 117–54.

                                                                    R. T. RIDLEY

COMMODUS. See HERCULES AND TELEPHUS.

COMPUTERS IN CLASSICAL ARCHAEOLOGY. Computers are used by archaeologists to automate a variety of tasks, most commonly, recording catalog information, aiding with surveying and making drawings and performing statistical procedures.

More complex uses of computers include the storing of all the information about the excavation itself, that is, information about excavation units, strata, personnel, photographs, drawings and so on, the making of three-dimensional computer models of sites or structures and the making of computer maps, complete with information about topography, temperature, rainfall, vegetation, and water courses.

Huge quantities of data can now be kept in inexpensive computers, and transmitting the data from one computer to another is quick, easy and inexpensive. Once the data have been stored, a wide variety of analytical procedures may be performed on them. Those processes may include rather simple ones, such as extracting items with certain characteristics from a list, or very complex ones, such as seriation.

Computers were first used by archaeologists in the 1950s to carry out statistical procedures that were otherwise too laborious. They required infinite patience, since data entry and analysis involved making coded cards that carried the data and other coded cards that carried the computer instructions. The slightest error could be critical, and each process had to be individually coded for the computer. As computer technology evolved, the requirements for effective use became less onerous, and the benefits became more significant. Nonetheless, only after the appearance and commercial success of the so-called personal computer (introduced by IBM in 1981) was it possible for archaeologists to begin to use computer technologies without major assistance from computer specialists who were familiar with large systems and could write complex computer code.

As computers were evolving, new programs that virtually eliminated the need for coding individual projects were being developed. Systems for handling large quantities of data (database management systems or DBMS) were created commercially and steadily gained in power and sophistication while also becoming easier to use. Similarly, statistical packages to perform almost any relevant operation were developed. Meanwhile, computer-assisted drafting and design programs (CAD) were devised for making three-dimensional models of complex objects, and geographic information systems (GIS) were created to permit data about geography to be manipulated and analyzed very effectively. (The systems make extensive use of aerial and satellite photographs to obtain information about the geographic, topographic and climate conditions.) Although the early personal computers were not powerful enough for these complex programs, current models are, and the programs can be used by archaeologists with little computer training.

The advances in the utility of computers were the results of commercial activity. With a few exceptions, archaeologists have not written programs or provided systems for themselves; instead, they have adopted and adapted commercial products for their own use. (One notable exception is the making of the Ibycus system by David Packard. He designed a computer and associated programs specifically to deal with Greek text. Although very specialized, it was successfully used in many institutions. Eventually, however, other programs based on standard computers became available, and the Ibycus was discontinued.)

The computers and the programs for them are now so sophisticated that an archaeologist can use computers for making three-dimensional models of the site itself, collecting topographic and survey information about the surrounding area, storing all excavation information (catalogs, excavation units, photographs, personnel and so on) and performing virtually any analysis involving the collected data. Few sites use computers so extensively, but all the pieces are available.

The increasing dependence upon computers has coincided with the rise in the use of many scientific tools (C_{14}, pollen analysis, tree-ring dating); indeed, the quantity of data used for those scientific operations often requires computers. The effect of the enormous quantity of data, however, can be suffocating, and new ways for dealing with the data are required. For instance, the three-dimensional models of sites must be connected to the data about artifacts from the sites, and site models must be related to geographic and topographic information from the surrounding countryside (both technologies are available but not widely used).

As computer technologies have become widely used, scholars have learned that they have new analytic possibilities open to them. Questions that would once have gone unasked—not because they were not recognized as important but because they seemed impossible to answer—can now be asked and answered. For example, a scholar confronted with interconnected hill forts was able to predict where the connecting roads were by using the computer to determine an optimum path if the builders wished both to avoid steep gradients and to make the paths visible from the forts. But such analyses require full and complete data; so new demands are often placed on excavators to measure and record more information with more precision.

The use of computers is so new to archaeology that it is not possible to predict what is yet to come. One may say with certainty only that computers will be used more extensively and that processes as yet unknown to us will be common in the years ahead. For instance, plans already exist to provide computer-based archiving of excavation records, both to preserve them and to make them available to scholars through an electronic network.

BIBLIOGRAPHY

Newsletter of the Center for the Study of Architecture (quarterly; 1988–93); *Archaeological Computing Newsletter* (quarterly; 1984–93); *Computer and Quantitative Methods in Archaeology* (annual; 1989–91).

HARRISON EITELJORG II

CONCA. See SATRICUM.

CONSTANTINE I. Colossal seated statue of Emperor Constantine I (A.D. 306–37), of which the marble head and fragments of limbs survive, now in the *Capitoline Museums.

Originally measuring over thirty feet high, the statue once stood in the west apse of the Basilica of Constantine (*Basilica of Maxentius) in Rome. The fragments include a right arm and hand, grasping a (missing) staff; the right leg from the knee downward, including the foot; the left leg below the knee and the left foot. A marble fragment of the shoulder and bare chest of the statue, discovered in 1951, remains behind the apse on the site. A metal diadem (now lost) was used to crown the head and was attached to the brow. The statue had a brick core, and the body was made of wood covered with bronze while Pentelic marble was used to portray the exposed areas of flesh of the figure. The height of the head is eight feet six inches, and it weighs between eight and nine tons.

Evidently, the first mention of the statue is in Eusebius (*Hist. eccl.* 9.9–11; fourth century), who described a statue that many believe to be the Capitoline colossus. The next information comes in 1486 with the rediscovery of the statue, during the pontificate of Innocent VIII, in the Basilica of Constantine. Between April and September of that year, the head and fragments were moved to the Palazzo dei Conservatori on the Capitoline. The *Constantine* was rendered in a sketch by van *Heemskerck, with the head and body parts shown scattered on the ground. In the sixteenth century the head served for a time as a decoration for the *Marforio* fountain; then in the seventeenth century all the parts of the statue were collected and displayed in the courtyard of the Conservatori, where they remain today. The displayed head, foot and hand can be seen in a seventeenth-century drawing from the Tessin Collection in the Stockholm National Museum.

The identification of the head remained uncertain until 1906, when E. *Petersen recognized it as Constantine. The discovery of the head inside the basilica begun by Maxentius and completed by Constantine has led scholars to link this portrait to Constantine's capture of Rome and the building of the *Arch of Constantine, 313–15. The style of the portrait, however, closely conforms to the new types of coins issued at the *vicennalia* of 326 and also to a likeness of the mid-320s. The probable dating of the statue, therefore, is in the 320s. (See also *Constantius II.)

BIBLIOGRAPHY
Helbig, 4th ed., II, 252–54; +H. Brummer, *The Statue Court in the Vatican Belvedere* (Stockholm, 1970), 243–47; R. Calza, *Iconografia romana imperiale da Carausio a Giuliano* (Rome, 1972), 228–31; +H. P. L'Orange, *Das Spätantike Herrscherbild von Diokletian bis zu den Konstantin-Söhnen* (Berlin, 1984), 70–77; Kleiner, *Roman Sculpture,* 438–40, 464.

CONSTANTINOPLE. See BYZANTIUM.

CONSTANTIUS II (CONSTANTINE I). Colossal Roman bronze head (1.85m high), believed to represent either Constantine I (A.D. 306–37) or his son, Constantius II (A.D. 337–61), now in the *Capitoline Museums.

The head is believed to be part of a colossal bronze image consciously modeled after the marble colossus of *Constantine I found in the Basilica of Constantine (*Basilica of Maxentius). The original bronze statue is thought to have stood over thirty feet high. A colossal bronze hand holding a globe, also now in the Capitoline, seems to have been part of the sculpture. In the Late Antique head, Roman traits of individuality are noticed in the prominent aquiline nose, the pursed mouth and strong jutting chin. The top of the head is missing but may have been adorned with a crown of some sort.

The head, hand and globe are mentioned in the *Mirabilia* (ca. 1140) as located in the Lateran, having come from the *Colosseum. Rabbi Benjamin van Tudela (ca. 1170) identified the figure as Samson, while Magister *Gregorius noted that some believed it to be the *Sun,* and others, the spirit of Rome. He describes the parts of the colossus as displayed on two columns near the Lateran. A drawing of the Lateran courtyard attributed to *Marcanova (ca. 1450) shows (probably fancifully) the statue parts displayed on the two ends of a structure like a triumphal arch. Along with the *Capitoline *Wolf,* the *Spinario,* and the *Capitoline *Camillus,* the colossus was donated on 15 December 1471 by *Sixtus IV to the new museum in the palace of the Conservatori. It can be seen displayed on the Capitoline Hill in a drawing made by van *Heemskerck. It was next moved to the courtyard of the Conservatori and mounted on an elaborate socle (shown in a drawing from the Tessin Collection, Stockholm National Museum). At the beginning of the twentieth century, the bronze head was moved inside the Conservatori to the Hall of Bronzes, where it now rests.

The identity of the figure has been controversial. Stuart *Jones was the first to recognize the Late Antique period in which the colossus was made. L'Orange and Delbrück both believed the statue was Constantius II, but *Kähler, Cecchelli and M. Alföldi argued that it is Constantine. Both sides have argued on numismatic evidence and by comparison with the colossal Constantine marble, but no definitive identification has been made. The identification as Constantius II seems to be held more widely today.

BIBLIOGRAPHY

W. S. Heckscher, *Sixtus IIII aeneas insignes statuas romano populo restituendas censuit* (Utrecht, 1955); +H. Brummer, *The Statue Court in the Vatican Belvedere* (Stockholm, 1970), 241–45; +R. Calza, *Iconografia romana imperiale da Carausio a Giuliano* (Rome, 1972), 231–33; G.M.A. Hanfmann, *Roman Art* (New York, 1975), 102; Kleiner, *Roman Sculpture* 441.

CONZE, ALEXANDER CHRISTIAN LEOPOLD (1831–1914). German archaeologist; excavator and administrator.

Born at Hanover, son of a cavalry officer, Conze began law at Göttingen but turned to classics and completed his dissertation under *Gerhard at Berlin (1855). He visited Paris and London, where the Elgin marbles (*Elgin, Lord) created a lasting impression. He preferred finding new material to studying old and, like Ludwig *Ross, traveled through the Greek islands. In 1863 he became associate professor (*Extraordinarius*) for archaeology in Halle; in 1869 he became full professor at Vienna, where he founded the archaeological-epigraphical department. From 1873 to 1875 he commenced excavation at *Samothrace, intending, as *Newton at the *Mausoleum of Halikarnassos, to excavate the whole site. The move from Vienna prevented that. His talent was more administrative than pedagogical, and in 1877 he succeeded the unexceptional Karl Bötticher as director of the antiquities collection at Berlin, at the instigation of Schöne, who had followed him at Halle.

He resigned to become secretary-general of the *German Archaeological Institute (1887–1905). With *Humann and *Dörpfeld he excavated *Pergamon (1878–86, 1900–2), realizing his dream of uncovering a whole city and its surroundings. The *Great Altar, now in Berlin, remains the most significant find. He reorganized the Institute and founded the Roman-Germanic Commission in Frankfurt/Main. He initiated the scientific publication of *corpora:* on Melian vases—*Melische Tongefässe* (1902) and on Attic grave stelai—*Die attische Grabreliefs* (1893–1911). Ironically, the cost of the beautiful Pergamon reports and the fact that the political importance of the site never equaled its art denied his masterpiece its expected influence.

BIBLIOGRAPHY

F. Goethert, "Conze, Alexander Christian Leopold," *NDB* 3 (1957), 348; U. von Wilamowitz-Moellendorff, *Kleine Schriften* 6 (Berlin, 1972), 59–65.

WILLIAM M. CALDER III

COOK, ARTHUR BERNARD (1868–1952). Folklorist and classical archaeologist.

A. B. Cook, fellow of Queens' College, Cambridge, and from 1931 the first Laurence professor of classical archaeology in Cambridge, was one of the most learned men of his day. Although his scholarly production included dozens of articles, his reputation rests on his magnum opus, *Zeus* (five volumes in three parts, 1914–40). In this huge study Cook brought together literally everything that was then known about the lord of Olympos: his nature, his history, his cult, his iconography. The work, a monument of a kind of comparative and historical scholarship no longer seen, is virtually unreadable as an argument but remains immensely valuable today as a vast storehouse of facts and references.

Although Cook was one of the *Cambridge Ritualists, and some of the first part of *Zeus* may fairly be seen as advancing their thesis that the forms of tragedy and comedy derived ultimately from prehistoric agricultural ceremonial, his adherence to the tenets of the group was a sometime thing. He came to feel increasingly uncomfortable as the classical basis of their work became more and more only a jumping-off point for an ambitious reconstruction of ''primitive'' psychology and religion, and he should not be identified with the group's more venturesome theoretical constructions.

BIBLIOGRAPHY

C. Seltman, ''Arthur Bernard Cook, 1868–1952,'' *ProcBrAc* 38 (1952), 295–302.

ROBERT ACKERMAN

COPENHAGEN, DANISH NATIONAL MUSEUM (NATIONALMU-SEET).

Leading Danish museum, with the largest collection of Near Eastern and classical antiquities in Scandinavia.

The National Museum houses different collections: Danish prehistorical and historical collections, anthropology, Near Eastern and classical antiquities and coins. Formed in 1892, the museum contains many items, particularly the classical antiquities, that go back to the Royal Cabinet of Curiosities (from 1653 onward). From 1851 these were joined with the archaeological collection of King Christian VIII (1839–48), which mainly contained recently acquired Greek vases. (These still form the nucleus of the vase collection.) Acquisitions are still occasionally made through donations, primarily from the Carlsberg Foundation.

In the Greek department, the main section is the collection of Greek vases, especially the outstanding black- and red-figured vases from the sixth and fifth centuries B.C., though all periods and styles are represented by fine specimens. Partly because so many of the vases were acquired early in the nineteenth century, the condition of the vases is generally better than average. Many painters are represented, including black-figure artists such as the Gorgon Painter, the Amasis Painter, the Theseus Painter and Psiax and red-figure painters such as the Kleophrades Painter, the Pan Painter and the Achilles Painter.

Danish excavations on the island of Rhodes (1902–4) yielded a number of items (reliefs, inscriptions, pottery) now in the museum. Of importance are the two inscriptions containing the temple chronicle from the sanctuary of Athena Lindia by Timachidas (from 99 B.C.) and a list of the annually elected priests of the sanctuary (375 B.C.–A.D. 27, with gaps). Sculpture is less well represented in the collection, but two fragments stand out: the heads of a Lapith and centaur from one of the *Parthenon metopes (no. 4 on the south side), bought by a Danish sea captain in *Peiraeus in 1688.

The department of Italic-Roman antiquities contains objects acquired, on the whole, during the nineteenth century. Pre-Roman and Etruscan items are better represented than Roman art. Of special significance are a number of complete finds from Faliscan and Etruscan tombs of the seventh and sixth centuries B.C. and some twenty Etruscan bronze objects, including mirrors acquired in the nineteenth century. From the Early Imperial period is a unique monument in the shape of a column with the text of a hymn, interspersed with musical notations. The department of prehistoric Danish antiquities contains further objects from the Roman period, found in Denmark: many silver and some gold coins, bronze and silver vessels, bronze statuettes and many fine pieces of glassware. The contents of the tomb of a wealthy person in Hoby in southern Denmark (first century A.C.) are remarkable. Of particular interest are the silver "Hoby Cups," signed by Cheirosophos, with representations of Priam before Achilles and two scenes of the myth of Philoktetes; both cups bear the name of Silius (cf. Tacitus, *Annales* 1.31). The tomb was discovered by chance in 1920, by a farmer.

In the coin department there is an exquisite collection of Greek and Roman coins from the earliest to the latest period.

BIBLIOGRAPHY

CVA Danemark, 8 fasc. (Copenhagen, 1924–63); *Sylloge Nummorum Graecorum, The Royal Collection of Coins and Medals, Danish National Museum,* 43 fasc. (1942–79); +N. Breitenstein, *Antik-Cabinettet 1851* (Copenhagen, 1951); J. Jensen, *Thomsens Museum, Historien om Nationalmuseet* (Copenhagen, 1992).

J. MEJER

CORCYRA. See KORKYRA.

CORFU. See KORKYRA.

CORINTH (KORINTHOS). Major Greek and Roman city, located on the south coast of the Gulf of Corinth, ca. 9km west of the Isthmos of Corinth; it was served by the harbor towns of Lechaion and *Kenchreai.

There is evidence of human occupation at Corinth from the Neolithic period, but significant architectural remains do not appear until ca. 700 B.C. In the seventh century the city flourished under the Bacchiad family and became known for its commerce and industry, especially in the famed Corinthian pottery and bronzes.

An early temple on the "Temple Hill" that dominates the central area of the city was replaced ca. 560–540 B.C. by the Archaic *Temple of Apollo, Corinth's best-known monument. In the fifth and fourth centuries B.C., civic and commercial installments (stoas, baths, racecourse) were constructed in the area of the temple; to the east was the fountainhouse of the spring Peirene, the city's chief public water supply. Fortifications of the city may go back to the sixth century, but they reached their fullest extent in the fourth century, with walls enclosing an area from the high fortress of Akrokorinthos down around the main city (total circuit more than six miles). Long walls also extended down to Le-chaion.

During the sixth and fifth centuries, Corinth lost its foreign markets to Athens, and the city experienced a decline. But soon it rebounded and was once more populous and prosperous in the period from ca. 350 to 250 B.C. To this time belongs the construction of a huge stoa (length 165m) well to the south of the Temple of Apollo and Peirene and perhaps meant to define the southern limit of a market area (the Roman forum later occupied this site). With a bank of thirty-three shops or taverns in the rear, the south stoa has been hypothesized (O. *Broneer) to have been ordered by Philip II after the Battle of Chaironeia (338 B.C.) to accommodate meetings in Corinth of the Hellenic League he founded.

North of this central area of the city, a temple to Asklepios was erected (fourth century B.C.), with adjoining banquet rooms and water supply (the Lerna) for the cult. On the road from the Asklepieion toward the center was situated a theater with stone seats (capacity ca. 15,000) laid out in the late fifth or early fourth century B.C. Many small sanctuaries lay on the outskirts of town, as noted by Pausanias in his visit to Corinth ca. A.D. 175. Excavations have brought to light one of these on the road leading up to Akrokorinthos, the shrine of Demeter and Kore, yielding fine terracotta sculptures of the sixth–third centuries B.C.

Corinth was sacked in 146 B.C. by a Roman army under L. Mummius, and the city lay in waste for nearly a century. Under Julius Caesar a Roman colony was founded in 44 B.C. (Laus Julia Corinthiensis), to be the capital of the province of Achaia. The city experienced a dynamic period of rebuilding and new growth and became once again a major Mediterranean city. The Temple of Apollo, the fountain of Peirene, the south stoa, the theater, the Asklepieion—all show reconstruction and reusage in Roman Corinth. In the area of the forum new constructions included a series of basilicas and a speaker's platform, called *rostra* in a Roman inscription and probably identical with the *bema* at which St. Paul appeared before the Roman governor (*Acts* 18.12). An odeion begun in the first century A.C. was reconstructed in the second century at the expense of Herodes Atticus, patron of Roman Corinth. The Roman city had three great public bath complexes and at least four other small ones.

Earthquakes (A.D. 367, 375, 522, 551) and invasion (by the Herulians, 267; by Alaric, 395) took their toll on Corinth. In the Middle Ages the city was a Byzantine capital and archbishopric until it was sacked by the Normans in 1147. Strategic for the fortress on Akrokorinthos, it changed hands frequently in the ensuing centuries, becoming Turkish in 1715 and finally a part of independent Greece (1829). Yet another ruinous earthquake devastated the town of Corinth in 1858, and the inhabitants moved away.

A number of travelers noted ancient remains still standing. *Ciriaco of Ancona visited Corinth in 1436 and described a temple "of Juno" with thirteen columns standing, evidently the Temple of Apollo. It would be the principal feature described by subsequent travelers, who gave it varying names and who conflicted in their count of the number of columns still standing. Along with the temple, Roman remains (evidently of the great bath on the Lechaion Road) were noted by *Spon and *Wheler (1676), *Chandler (1776), *Leake and Dodwell (1801–6). In 1766 *Stuart made excellent drawings of the temple.

W. *Dörpfeld excavated at the temple in 1886, but sustained investigations at Corinth did not begin until 1896, when the *American School of Classical Studies mounted a joint expedition with the *Archaeological Institute of America. Funds were secured, in addition, from a number of patrons, including Mr. and Mrs. J. Montgomery Sears and Phoebe Hearst. Corinth was to become for the American School what *Olympia was for the *German Archaeological Institute and *Delphi for the *French School at Athens—an ongoing excavation of a major Greek site conducted by leading archaeologists and serving as the training ground for generations of promising young scholars.

In the early years (1896–1915) under the supervision of R. B. Richardson, T. W. Heermance and B. H. *Hill, the team explored the Temple of Apollo, the theater and odeion and the fountains of Peirene and Glauke. Also discovered were part of the propylaia of the market area, the south stoa and other buildings in this zone. An impressive series of portraits of members of the Julio-Claudian family came to light with the uncovering of the "Julian Basilica." The position of the ancient roads to Lechaion and Kenchreai was ascertained, and the cemetery on the northwest side of the city was opened.

All work ceased during World War I and was not resumed until 1925. During this period, portions of the final report began to be prepared under the leadership of Richard *Stillwell, with a flurry of volumes appearing in 1930–32. When excavations began again, work was carried out in the theater (T. L. *Shear), the odeion (O. *Broneer), the Asklepieion and Lerna (under the Dutch scholar F. J. De Waele) and the potters' quarter (Agnes Newhall Stillwell). Carl *Blegen was active at Akrokorinthos and in other projects in the area of Corinth. Further excavation took place around the Roman forum and the northwest cemetery. In 1932, a museum was created at the site (enlarged 1950), with funding provided by Ada Small-Moore, to house almost all finds from the excavations.

Under successive directors Broneer, Henry Robinson and Charles Williams (from 1966), excavation and publication have continued. Recent work includes the sanctuary of Demeter and Kore (R. Stroud, 1961–75) and the great baths of the Lechaion Road (W. Biers and J. Biers, 1965–68).

BIBLIOGRAPHY
Reports in *AJA* (1896 ff.) and *Hesperia* (1960 ff.); *Corinth, Results of Excavations Conducted by the American School of Classical Studies at Athens* 1–18 (1929–90); *Corinth, A Brief History of the City and a Guide to the Excavations,* rev. ed. (1969); H. S. Robinson, s.v. "Corinth," *PECS,* 240–43; D. Engels, *Roman Corinth* (Chicago, 1990).

CORNETO. See TARQUINIA.

CORSINI THRONE. Rounded marble chair with relief decoration, dating to the first century B.C.

The throne was found under the Cappella Corsini at San Giovanni in Laterano in Rome in 1732; since then it has been in the Galleria Corsini (now the Galleria Nazionale). Often drawn, by *Gori, among others, it was attributed somewhat vaguely to "an early period of art." Ducati (1916) first studied it in detail, assigning it to the fourth-century B.C. and an Etruscan origin, a judgment followed by his successors. Giglioli even planned to move it to the Etruscan museum of the *Villa Giulia; but nothing came of this plan. Ducati recognized the similarity of the scenes represented to those of "situla art," such as the sixth-century B.C. Certosa Situla from Bologna.

The most recent research shows that the throne is a Roman monument of the Late Republic (the use of Pentelic marble confirms a date in the first century B.C.), with a decoration fitting in with a consciously archaizing period of Roman culture. Some of the nonfigurative motifs are close to those of neo-Attic reliefs, while the source for the figured friezes is northern "situla art," which may have been encountered by Caesar's armies during his Gallic campaigns (mid-first century B.C.). The shape of the chair goes back to models of the seventh century B.C. and later that were found in the tombs of Etruria and Latium. The Corsini Throne thus exemplifies Roman antiquarianism of the Late Republic and Early Empire.

BIBLIOGRAPHY

P. Ducati, "Sedia Corsini," *MonAnt* 24 (1916), 401–58; G. de Luca, *I Monumenti antichi di Palazzo Corsini* (Rome, 1976), 93–100; +L. Bonfante, *Out of Etruria,* BAR S103 (Oxford, 1981), 79–91.

LARISSA BONFANTE

CORTONA (CURTUN). Etruscan city.

Modern Cortona is a picturesque town spilled down the slope of a steep hill that looks east over the Val di Chiana. Its towered medieval walls are based on those of the Etruscan city, huge rectangular blocks of local stone set in irregular courses without mortar. Nothing else remains of the ancient city, once one of the most prominent in Etruria.

There are tombs on the slope below the walls and in the plain beyond. Three tumuli (called *meloni,* "melons") cover stone-built chambers with false vaults; one, the Melone di Camucia, contains two chambers, one excavated in 1842 by Alessandro *François, the other not till 1964. Investigation of the Tomba Melone del Sodo II, first excavated in 1929 by A. Minto, has recently been resumed (1987), with the discovery of a remarkable altar platform attached to the tumulus, decorated with Archaic stone sculpture of warriors battling fantastic creatures. These and the tombs in the other tumuli were used for long periods; the oldest object found is a bronze ash urn of the seventh century; the latest finds are Attic potsherds of the fourth century. Two Hellenistic tombs, the Tanella di Pitagora and the Tanella Angori, are round, stone-built chambers on round bases, once covered with earth mounds. The first is illustrated by Anton Francesco *Gori in his *Museum Etruscum* III.

Fine bronzes have been found in the neighborhood; four, found at Montecchio in 1748, are now in Leiden; a small figure of a boy dedicated to *muantrns* (otherwise unknown), also from Montecchio, is still at Cortona, with the magnificent hanging lamp from a tomb excavated at Fratta in 1840, and the small bronze base of a statue dedicated to Uni (Juno), whose inscription gives us the Etruscan name of the city, Curtun. But most of the ancient material in Cortona's museum, the Palazzo Casali, was collected by zealous antiquarian members of the *Accademia Etrusca, founded in 1727 for the specific purpose of studying Etruscan antiquities and inscriptions firsthand.

BIBLIOGRAPHY
G. Dennis, *Cities and Cemeteries of Etruria,* 2nd ed. (London, 1878), II, 394–412; A. Neppi Modona, *Cortona etrusca e romana nella storia e nell'arte* (Florence, 1925); +P. Barocchi—D. Gallo, eds., *L'Accademia etrusca* (Milan, 1985); +S. Haynes, *Etruscan Bronzes* (London, 1985), 108–10; P. Zamarchi Grassi, ed., *La Cortona dei principes,* (Cortona, 1992).

                                                    EMELINE HILL RICHARDSON

COS. See KOS.

COSA (ANSEDONIA). Latin colony.

Cosa was founded in 273 B.C. on a rugged and waterless promontory, the southern anchor of the Tuscan archipelago, in territory that had belonged to *Vulci. After the Punic Wars it flourished as a port on the sea routes to Spain and France but suffered a devastating catastrophe that left it sacked and in ruins about 60 B.C. Partially rebuilt under Augustus, it survived until the second quarter of the third century. Thereafter there were revivals of life there in the mid-fourth and tenth centuries.

Excavations by the *American Academy in Rome, 1948–54, 1965–72, mainly under the direction of Frank E. *Brown, have revealed the city plan and the design of the port (cf. *Portus Cosanus) and uncovered the arx with its temples (1948–50, 1966–67), the forum with the surrounding buildings (1951–54, 1968–72), and a selection of houses (1965–69). The fortifications of polygonal masonry are of terrace type with rectangular towers at regular intervals where the slope was gentle and at points of danger. The three main gates are of inner-court plan with arched outer openings provided with portcullises. The town plan is regular, with long rectangular blocks, except where the terrain demanded adjustment. There are two main heights crowned by temples with a saddle between them where the forum was located. The arx on the higher height held the triple-cella capitolium of ca. 150 B.C., a small single-cella temple of a generation earlier and traces of an earlier temple that the capitolium replaced. The temples are of Tuscan type with painted terracotta revetments and sculptures.

The forum is a long rectangle entered on its long axis by a main street from the northwest gate and framed on two sides by streets from the other gates. On three sides it was lined with colonnades in front of offices and shops. On the long northeast side were the chief public buildings, the *comitium/curia* complex (273–250 B.C.) on the short axis of the forum, a single-cella temple (ca. 175), the *carcer* (prison) and a basilica of 150–125 B.C., rebuilt as an odeum in A.D. 50–55.

The houses of the early colony are small, with garden plots behind. Instead of an atrium, there seems to have been a transverse central hall on which other rooms opened front and back. Later houses are larger, of atrium plan and freer design.

The importance of Cosa is in its wealth of Republican architecture of the third and second centuries, both public and private, archaeologically in excellent state.

BIBLIOGRAPHY

+F. E. Brown, *Cosa, the Making of a Roman Town* (Ann Arbor, 1980); F. E. Brown—E. H. Richardson—L. Richardson, jr, *Cosa 3, The Buildings of the Forum, Memoirs of the American Academy in Rome* 37 (1993).

L. RICHARDSON, JR

COSMATI. Marble workers (*marmorari*) in Rome and Latium in the twelfth and thirteenth centuries; known for their reuse and imitation of ancient Roman stone architectural elements.

The Cosmati, whose art embellished architectural features and furniture with marble, may be grouped in at least three large families, each lasting several generations. The family of Paulus was active for most of the twelfth century in Rome and Latium; that of Ranucius (Rainerius), in the second half of the twelfth and early thirteenth centuries, primarily in northern Latium; and that of Laurentius, in the later twelfth and early thirteenth centuries, in Rome and Latium. The name of the grandson of Laurentius, Cosma (or Cosmas or Cosmatus), one of the last of the marble workers in the tradition, was adopted to refer to the whole group; his signature occurs at S. Maria, Anagni and S. Scholastica, Subiaco, but it is not possible to define his work or style in more than a general way.

The abundant fine building stone used in Roman architecture was "quarried" by the Cosmati and cut up into geometric slabs or cubes to create the rich, incrusted surfaces of altars, tombs, pulpits, candlesticks and ciboria, as well as larger architectural elements such as walls, colonnades, portals and pavements. Colorful effects were achieved with the favored stones of white marble, green serpentine, purple porphyry and *giallo antico* (predominantly yellow). The practices of seeking and cutting up columns, panels and blocks of stone from Roman architecture and of dismantling mosaics over an extended period of time no doubt destroyed a great deal of the embellishment of surviving Roman monuments. At the same time, the Cosmati have a place in the revival of Roman antiquity, in their imitation of Roman mosaic and of the techniques and designs of *opus sectile,* in which colored stones were cut up into geometric shapes to create richly patterned pavements. Finally, it is evident that these *marmorari* handled antique sculptures as well, evidently selling them, for occasionally their names may be found engraved on surviving statuary.

BIBLIOGRAPHY
+E. Hutton, *The Cosmati, The Roman Marble Workers of the XIIth and XIIIth Centuries* (London, 1950); Weiss, *RDCA,* 9; +D. F. Glass, *Studies on Cosmatesque Pavements,* BAR International Series 82 (Oxford, 1980); Greenhalgh, *Survival,* 164–65.

COTTON, MARY AYLWIN (1902–84). British archaeologist and benefactor of Mediterranean studies.

A qualified medical practitioner, "Molly" Cotton was an early diploma student at the London University Institute of Archaeology founded in 1937 by the *Wheelers, whose close friend and colleague in British archaeology she became. Dr. Cotton lived permanently in Rome from 1965, playing a crucial role in the British School's projects in South Italy, Latium and Etruria until her death. Her own pioneer excavations (1962–66) of the *villae rusticae* at *Posto* (published 1979) and *San Rocco* (1984) in the Ager Falernus of northern Campania demonstrated the potential of the working farms of Roman Italy as prime sources of social and economic information.

The Dr. M. Aylwin Cotton Foundation came into being in 1971; the vision and warm generosity of its founder are commemorated in its continuing annual awards.

BIBLIOGRAPHY
Personal acquaintance (1965–84); E. F. Macnamara, Memorial Service Address given at the University Church, London (November 1984).

DAVID RIDGWAY

COYSEVOX, ANTOINE (1640–1720). French sculptor, member of the Royal Academy of Painting and Sculpture.

After an early period in his native Lyons, Coysevox moved to Paris in 1678 and became the leading royal sculptor after the eclipse of *Girardon. Although he never visited Rome, Coysevox knew the ancient sculpture in Italian collections through plaster casts housed at the French Academy in Paris. When the royal sculptural team was engaged in making copies of the greatest groups to decorate the king's gardens, Coysevox was assigned the *Medici *Venus* (1683–85; lost), the *Nymph with a Shell* of the Borghese Collection (1683–85; Louvre), the *Crouching Venus* (after the Medici Collection version? 1684–86; Louvre) and *Castor and Pollux* after the Ildefonso Group (1685–1712; Versailles). Substantial alterations were made to complete the *Crouching Venus,* of which a bronze cast occupies the original location in the gardens of Versailles, opposite a cast of the so-called *Arrotino* (*Scythian Slave* from the Medici Collection). Coysevox provided the ancient torso with a fully modern head and depicted the goddess seated on a tortoise. A Greek inscription, "From Pheidias to the people of Elis," suggests the ancient fragment has been interpreted as the famous "Chaste Venus" described by Pausanias.

Coysevox's masterpieces, the equestrian groups of *Fame* and *Mercury* (1700–2; originally at Marly, now Place de la Concorde, Paris), are apparently intended

Crouching Venus, copy by A. Coysevox, 1684–86, Paris, Louvre. (Photo: © R.M.N., Paris.)

to rival the accomplishments of ancient sculptors; signed in Latin, with the information that Coysevox was the Royal Sculptor and from Lyons, the groups were described by his contemporaries as each carved from a single block of marble, including the trumpet of *Fame*. Coysevox is also the author of numerous portraits of the king inspired by ancient models, including a lost equestrian monument and standing and bust-length effigies.

BIBLIOGRAPHY

+G. Keller-Dorian, *Antoine Coysevox* (Paris, 1920); L. Benoist, *Coysevox* (Paris, 1930); +F. Souchal, *French Sculptors of the 17th and 18th Centuries, The Reign of Louis XIV, A–F* (Oxford, 1977), 176–224.

BETSY ROSASCO

CRETE. Largest of the Aegean islands, center of ancient Minoan Bronze Age culture.

From east to west the island is 245km (156 miles), and at its widest point from north to south it is 58km (36 miles). Three groups of mountains form a chain across the island, contributing to its magnificent scenery.

Crete has a long and complex history. It already had residents by the Stone Age but flourished especially in the Bronze Age, with Minoan civilization reaching its acme in the second millennium B.C. By the later Bronze Age (fifteenth century B.C. and following), it was a part of the Mycenaean sphere of influence (*Mycenae; *Mycenaeans). Dorian Greek was spoken in the Iron Age and in the Classical and Roman periods. When the Roman Empire was divided in A.D. 324, Crete became part of the Byzantine Empire. An interim of Arab rule (823–962) was followed by a return to the Byzantine state, a situation that lasted until the capture of Constantinople (*Byzantium) by Crusaders in 1204. Crete was then sold to Venice, remaining a part of Venetian holdings until the Turkish invasion of the late seventeenth century. Turkish soldiers withdrew in 1898, and Crete became independent; it joined Greece in 1913.

The historical and archaeological investigation of Crete has been largely a concern of the late nineteenth and twentieth centuries. In the Venetian and Turkish periods, ancient monuments were seen primarily as sources of raw materials. A few fragments were incorporated into monuments like the Bembo Fountain (1588) or the church of St. Mark in Herakleion (original date 1239 but renewed many times), which used columns from ancient *Knossos, but most ancient works were simply burned to make lime. A number of travelers from other parts of Europe made efforts to recognize the ancient sites and monuments, and some wrote accounts of their efforts. Among the most important travelers were C. *Buondelmonti, F. Sieber, R. Pashley, J. de Tournefort, L. Thenon and T.A.B. Spratt. A perennial fascination of these travelers was the *"Labyrinth" of Gortyn, actually a stone quarry of the Roman period.

More serious work began in the 1860s and the 1870s. The Kamares Cave was discovered in 1864, and prehistoric polychrome pottery of great beauty, which is named "Kamares Ware" for the site, was unearthed, stimulating additional research. Minos Kalokairinos, an amateur antiquary from Herakleion, excavated at the palace of Knossos in 1878–79. His discoveries, including ten pithoi from the west magazine, were taken to Herakleion, but most of his discoveries were destroyed in the revolution of 1897.

In 1884 Federico *Halbherr discovered an inscription recording the late sixth-
to early fifth-century B.C. law code of *Gortyn. In collaboration with several
colleagues, he worked in Crete for the next several years, visiting the Idean
Cave, the Kamares Cave, Knossos, *Phaistos, *Hagia Triada, Axos, Gortyn and
many other sites.

Also in 1884, Joseph Hazzidakis and Halbherr excavated in the Idaean Cave
and the Cave of Eileithyia at *Amnisos. A large number of objects were found,
dating from the Minoan to the Roman periods.

Crete secured its independence in 1898, and full-scale excavations were soon
initiated. Beginning in 1900, the Italian Archaeological Mission (*Italian School
of Archaeology), under the direction of Halbherr, concentrated its efforts in
central and south-central Crete. Excavations were made at the Minoan sites of
Phaistos and Hagia Triada as well as at the later sites of Lebena, Gortyn and
Prinias. At Gortyn, the major city of Crete during the Roman period, a series
of major architectural monuments was discovered. Among the most important
buildings were the temple of Apollo, the odeion and the temple of Isis and
Serapis. Luigi *Pernier, who directed the excavations at Phaistos, uncovered an
important palace of the Minoan period. Nearby Hagia Triada was also a noteworthy Minoan settlement. Significant contributions were made at other sites as
well.

British excavations at the Minoan palace of Knossos began in 1900 under the
direction of Arthur *Evans. The vast architecture of the buildings held a great
wealth of artistic and historical masterpieces, including wall paintings, miniature
sculptures in many materials, pottery, stone vases, seals, ivories and inscribed
tablets. As the largest Bronze Age site in Crete, Knossos would soon become
the cornerstone of Minoan archaeology. A British team under D. G. *Hogarth
excavated at the Dictaean Cave, where offerings had been made from the Minoan to the Roman period, and at *Zakros, where several prehistoric houses and
tombs were excavated. The town of *Palaikastro was unearthed by R. C. Bos-
anquet and R. M. Dawkins and several colleagues. In addition to an important
Minoan town, Palaikastro also had a Greek temple dedicated to Dictaean Zeus.
An inscription with a hymn to the god was found in the temple's ruins. Bos-
anquet and Dawkins also worked at Praisos, discovering Classical remains including inscriptions of the Eteo-Cretans, written in Greek characters but in a
still-undeciphered language.

An American team began working at the early Iron Age site of Kavousi in
1900, under the direction of Harriet Boyd (*Hawes). She also excavated the
Minoan town of *Gournia, and when she married Charles Hawes and retired
from fieldwork, excavations were continued by Richard *Seager, who directed
the work at the Minoan sites of Vasilike, *Pseira, *Mochlos and Pacheia Am-
mos, and by Edith Hall (*Dohan), who supervised the excavation of the Geometric town at Vrokastro.

The Greek archaeologist Stephanos *Xanthoudides directed a long series of
excavations that uncovered Minoan and Iron Age remains. His work in exca-

vating tombs, particularly the rich tholos tombs of the Minoan periods in southern Crete, preserved many objects from looting and destruction. These circular chambers, used for burials over many centuries, contained a great inventory of weapons, tools, ornaments and votive gifts.

Many other excavations took place in this important period in Cretan history. Caves with Minoan finds at Kamares, Psychro and Arkalochori were explored by Dawkins, Hogarth and Hazzidakis. Hazzidakis also worked at Gazi and at Gournes, two important Minoan cemeteries. At Chamaizi, in eastern Crete, Xanthoudides excavated a peculiar Middle Minoan elliptical building with interior partition walls.

After Crete joined Greece in 1913, excavations were greatly slowed by World War I, but work increased after the armistice was signed. The Italian and British teams continued their work, with many new discoveries. Hazzidakis discovered a Minoan palace at *Malia, and its excavation was given to a team of French archaeologists. A Minoan villa at Nirou Chani, excavated by Xanthoudides, held an unusual assortment of religious objects, including forty–fifty offering tables stored in a single room.

The periods between the Bronze Age and the Classical era now received new attention. John *Pendlebury uncovered a Sub-Minoan town at Karphi, a ''refuge site'' where some of the inhabitants of this part of Crete took shelter in the dangerous period at the close of the second millennium B.C. Geometric and Orientalizing tombs at Arkades were excavated by Doro *Levi, revealing a sequence of pottery from the Geometric to the early Archaic period that helped to document the history of Crete during this little-known period.

In the late 1920s and 1930s, excavations were made at both old and new sites. Spyridon *Marinatos, who now became ephor of antiquities, excavated at a long series of settlements and cemeteries. Among these, a Minoan villa at Amnisos stands out for the high quality of its floral wall paintings. Nicolas Platon excavated at the Poros Cave, east of Herakleion, at a Minoan town at Prassa and at several other sites. Evans and his successor, John Pendelbury, worked at Knossos, and a number of French scholars, including F. Chapouthier and P. Demargne, worked at Malia.

After the interruption of World War II, additional work continued until the present day. New excavations were begun at Phaistos, under the direction of Doro Levi, and work continued also at Gortyn under the direction of Antonio Di Vita and at Hagia Triadha under V. La Rosa.

At Knossos, Sinclair Hood continued the work pioneered by Evans, exploring a series of sites in the vicinity of the great palace. Hood, Hector Catling, John Coldstream and others also excavated a large number of tombs in Knossian territory, including important burial places from the first millennium B.C. John D. Evans explored Neolithic Knossos. British teams uncovered other sites as well, including the Early Minoan town at Myrtos, excavated by Peter Warren, and the nearby Late Minoan villa at Pyrgos, excavated by Gerald Cadogan. The

Palaikastro excavations were renewed by Hugh Sackett and Merwyn Popham and later by J. A. MacGillivray.

Malia continued to be excavated under a series of French scholars, including Pierre Demargne, H. Chevallier, Henri van Effenterre, Jean-Claude Poursat, Jean-Pierre Olivier, Claude Burain, Colette Verlinden and Pascai Darcque. The palace and its surrounding town emerged as an important center for this part of Crete.

Many Greek scholars worked in Crete. Stylianos Alexiou excavated Katsambas, the harbor for Knossos. A small Minoan community at Vathypetro was excavated by Marinatos. Platon excavated at a newly discovered Minoan palace at Zakros, in eastern Crete. Yannis Sakellarakis uncovered important tombs and a rich settlement at *Archanes, dating from the Minoan period and still important in Late Minoan III. He also renewed work at the Idean Cave and excavated an important villa at Zominthos. Western Crete was now explored in detail for the first time, thanks largely to the efforts of Costis Davaras and Yannis Tzedakis, and later to the work of Maria Vlasaki. A cult center at Kato Syme with continuous use from the Bronze Age until the first millennium B.C. was uncovered under the direction of Angeliki Lebessi and Polymnia Muhly. Antonios Vasilakis discovered an Early Minoan town at Trypiti, while Athanasia Kanta excavated an important Middle Minoan site at Monastiraki and George Rethemiotakis discovered a new Late Minoan I palace at Galatas. A Minoan sanctuary on Mt. Juktas was excavated by Alexandra Karetsou. A project that revealed a Minoan road and fort system in eastern Crete was directed by Stella Chryssoulaki in collaboration with Tzedakis. Nota Rethemiotakis discovered important Minoan tombs at Poros, near Herakleion, and Petros Themelis uncovered Iron Age tombs at Eleftherna near Rethymno.

Other countries participated in the exploration of the island. A Greek-Swedish collaboration, jointly directed by Yannis Tzedakis and Eric Hallager, excavated at Chania in western Crete, where inscribed tablets suggested the location of yet another Minoan palatial seat. A Canadian excavation, directed by Joseph W. Shaw, excavated the Minoan town and Classical sanctuary at *Kommos, in southern Crete. A joint American-Greek team under the direction of Philip Betancourt and Costis Davaras renewed work at Pseira, where a Minoan town and Byzantine monastery were uncovered. An American team led by Geraldine Gesell, Leslie Preston Day and William Coulson has pursued research at the Iron Age site of Kavousi. The young English scholar Ian Sanders prepared a much-needed survey of Roman Crete before his untimely death from cancer at the age of twenty-eight.

BIBLIOGRAPHY

N. Platon, "A Short History of Excavations in Crete," *A Guide to the Archaeological Museum of Heraclion* (Herakleion, 1962), 15–26; W. Schiering, *Fund auf Kreta* (Göttingen, 1976); C. Davaras, *Guide to Cretan Antiquities* (Park Ridge, NJ, 1976); Antonio Di Vita et al., *Creta antica* (Rome, 1984).

PHILIP P. BETANCOURT

CROUCHING VENUS (APHRODITE). Greek Hellenistic sculpture type known in numerous Roman versions (in marble, bronze and terracotta), often with variations in the arms, the goddess is shown as if intruded upon at her bath, crouching down with her arms gracefully extended around her nude body.

The type was known in Italy in the sixteenth century, perhaps through a version now in the *Prado, thought to have been in the Massimi collection ca. 1500. Leonardo da Vinci evidently was influenced by the *Venus* in his first studies (1501–3) for his *Leda*. The identification of the crouching figure as Leda may have been general; *Aldrovandi, for one, identifies the type thus. (Later, Helen of Troy was also suggested.) Another version was recorded in the late sixteenth century at the Villa Medici in Rome, identified as Venus (perhaps identical with the one in the *Uffizi today). The contrapposto of the figure was especially admired by artists, and many drew, engraved, painted or sculpted versions of a crouching female figure: van *Heemskerck (from a version owned by the Farnese, now in Naples); *Raimondi (his engraving adds a Cupid); Fra Bartolommeo (drawing in the Fogg Art Museum, Cambridge, Massachusetts); P. P. *Rubens (after the version at the Gonzaga court, Mantua; painting of *Venus, Bacchus and Ceres* in Kassel); and *Titian (painting with figure of a nymph in his *Diana and Acteon,* Edinburgh). The finest of the numerous sculptured imitations is probably the marble done for Versailles by *Coysevox (1686), signed with the name of Pheidias as well as his own.

Unlike many of the canonical antique sculptures of the Renaissance, the *Crouching Venus* has continued to interest scholars greatly in the twentieth century. The reason may be that no single copy was ever exalted to the highest rank, thereby dooming it to fall when critics took a closer look and made comparisons with other versions (cf. *Belvedere *Antinous*).

Today the version in the *Terme, with part of its original head (excavated at *Hadrian's Villa, Tivoli), and the one in the *Louvre (found at Vienne) are considered the best copies. Ridgway has recently reviewed the scanty evidence that has made the *Crouching Venus* an anthology piece associated with the name of Doidalsas of Bithynia, a sculptor of the third century B.C., on the basis of an emended passage in Pliny (*NH* 36.21). If the highly dubious connection with Doidalsas is eliminated, the piece moves stylistically into the second century B.C.

BIBLIOGRAPHY
R. Lullies, *Die Kauernde Aphrodite* (Munich, 1954); Bieber, 82–83; Sheard, nos. 42–43; Haskell—Penny, 321–23; Ridgway, *Hellenistic Sculpture,* I, 230–32.

CUMAE (KYME). The northernmost and traditionally the oldest Greek colony in Italy, although antedated by a Greek settlement on Ischia (*Pithekoussai) founded by about 750 B.C. by Euboians.

The colony consisted of a small tufa acropolis on the sea with a lagoon port, now completely silted up, and a considerable lower city landward. The Greek city prospered, fighting successfully against the Etruscans in 524 and 505 and, in cooperation with *Syracuse, crushing a combined Etruscan and Carthaginian fleet in 474 B.C., a major victory. It probably once extended its power over the whole Bay of Naples but in 421/20 fell to the Samnites. As a Samnite town, though it declined in importance, it was granted *civitas sine suffragio* by Rome in 338 and successfully resisted Hannibal in 215. It became a municipium toward the end of the Republic and was included in Agrippa's great naval base around Misenum, with attendant rebuilding and enlargement of its port facilities. Thereafter it faded into obscurity.

The naturally strong acropolis is improved in places by terracing, believed to be of the fifth century. On the acropolis are remains of two temples, both reduced to their foundations. The lower temple of Apollo, excavated in 1912, under the direction of E. Gabrici, a triple-cella Ionic building of Augustan date over older remains, was converted into a Christian basilica in the sixth or seventh century, and the floor pitted with burials. The larger and higher temple of Jupiter (?), excavated in 1927–28 under the direction of A. *Maiuri, superintendent from 1924 to 1961, is entirely Roman in its present form, with brick-faced arcades around a long, narrow cella. It was converted into a five-naved Christian basilica in the fifth or sixth century, and a presbytery and baptistery were added.

The most impressive remains are the "Cave of the Sibyl," a long, narrow, trapezoidal gallery leading to a vaulted inner chamber carved in the tufa, excavated in 1932, and the "Crypta," a vast tunnel that pierces the hill of the acropolis connecting the lower town and the port, excavated in 1925–30, probably intended as a continuation of the "Tunnel of Cocceius," a gallery about a kilometer long running straight through Monte Grillo connecting the lower town of Cumae with the shore of Lake Avernus. The last was broad enough that wagons traversing it could pass one another, and it housed an aqueduct as well as the road. It was excavated in the mid-nineteenth century.

The long, narrow forum of the lower city has been only partially explored (1938–51). Along the long sides ran tufa porticoes. On the west side is the grandiose podium temple of the Capitoline triad of three cellae built over a peripteral temple of Iuppiter Flazzus. There are also a large hall of Sullan date and a second podium temple of the first century A.C. At a little distance from the forum are ruins of two bath complexes, while an amphitheater, in part dug into the side of a hill, lies on the south edge of the city. One of the most dramatic antiquities of Campania is the Arco Felice, a brick-faced bridge spanning the deep cut in Monte Grillo through which the Via Domitiana runs on its way to Puteoli.

The cemeteries of Cumae have been plundered repeatedly since the beginning of the seventeenth century and have yielded a rich harvest of grave goods. That to the north is especially important. The tombs are of every period from the eighth century on, and both inhumation and cremation appear, the latter usually with richer offerings. Among the chamber tombs, one of mid-fourth century was decorated with important paintings now in the *Museo Nazionale, Naples. Scientific excavations in the necropolis were carried out by Pellegrini and Gabrici at the beginning of this century.

BIBLIOGRAPHY

W. Johannowsky, "Cuma," *EAA* 2 (1959), 970–73; *I Campi Flegrei nell'archeologia e nella storia, Atti dei Convegni Lincei* 33 (Rome, 1977), 130–80; (G. Buchner, "Cuma nell'VIII secolo a. C. osservata dalla prospettiva di Pithecusa," 130–48; F. Sartori, *"I Praefecti Capuam Cumas,"* 149–71; G. Pugliese Caratelli, "Problemi della storia di Cuma arcaica," 173–80); +P. Amalfitano—G. Camodeca—M. Medri, eds., *I Campi Flegrei* (Venice, 1990), 215–315.

L. RICHARDSON, JR

CUMONT, FRANZ VALERY MARIE (1868–1947). Belgian classical scholar, known for his study of astrology and the role of Oriental religions in Roman paganism, through texts and monuments.

Cumont was born at Alost and trained at Gand, as well as at Bonn, Berlin, Vienna and Paris. He gave especial attention to texts and manuscripts relevant to the study of astrology in the ancient world and moved beyond pure philology to a synthesis of philological, epigraphical and iconographical materials. He was a collaborator with F. Boll, W. Kroll and A. Olivieri in the ambitious *Catalogus Codicum Astrologorum Graecorum,* eleven volumes, 1898–1912. A distillation of his knowledge on the subject was made in the little work *Astrology and Religion Among the Greeks and Romans* (New York, 1912). His contribution to the study of Mithraism was significant (*Les Mystères de Mithra,* 1900). Cumont's archaeological research culminated in his interpretation of astrological and other symbolism in Roman funerary monuments: *Recherches sur le symbolisme funéraire des romains* (Paris, 1942).

Having served as professor of ancient history at Gand (1892–1910) and as Conservateur at the Musée du Cinquantenaire, Brussels (1899–1912), Cumont lived thereafter mainly in Paris and Rome.

BIBLIOGRAPHY

A. D. Nock, "Franz Valery Marie Cumont," *AJA* 51 (1947), 432–33; A. J. Festugière, "Franz Cumont+," *Gnomon* 21 (1949), 272–74.

CUPER (CUYPERS), GISBERT (1644–1716). Dutch classical scholar; historian and antiquarian; statesman.

Cuper was a pupil of J. F. Gronovius (*Gronovius family) at Leiden and also traveled to Paris to meet the leading scholars before he was called to Deventer as professor of history (1668). He was to remain at this post until his death; he also served as Burgermeister of Deventer and accepted other political assignments.

His publications are praised for lucidity and clever usage of comparisons as well as for solidity of research. His first important work dealt with some emendations of ancient texts and the explication of rituals along with coins and inscriptions (*Observationum libri tres, in quibus multi auctorum loci explicantur et emendatur, varii ritus eruuntur et nummi elegantissimi illustrantur,* Utrecht, 1670; the fourth book was issued at Deventer, 1678). His monograph on *Harpocrates* (Utrecht, 1676; 2nd. ed., 1687) was based on a silver statuette of Harpocrates in the possession of Joannes Smetius. Here he included various unpublished items found in the region, especially at Nijmegen, and in local collections. Cuper was the first to explicate in detail the *Apotheosis of Homer,* the marble relief found at Bovillae, Italy (now in the *British Museum), which had been published earlier by A. *Kircher.

The archives of Cuper's papers are in The Hague.

BIBLIOGRAPHY

Delaulnaye, "Cuper, Gisbert," *BU* 10 (1813), 365–66; Stark, 122–23; Sandys, II, 331.

CURTIUS, ERNST (1814–96). German archaeologist, historian and museum director.

Son of the mayor of Lübeck, brother of the philologist, Georg Curtius (1820–85), grandfather of the literary historian Ernst Robert Curtius (1886–1956), Ernst Curtius studied classics under F. G. *Welcker at Bonn, K. O. *Müller at Göttingen, whose comprehensive approach to antiquity molded his own, and August *Boeckh at Berlin. He was from 1837 to 1840 in Greece as tutor to the children of C. A. Brandis and there gained a lifelong interest in topography and monuments. He accompanied K. O. Müller on his fatal trip to *Delphi and arranged his burial on Colonnus in 1840. He returned to Berlin in 1842 and in 1844 became tutor to the crown prince of Prussia, later, Kaiser Friedrich III (1831–88), who owed his enthusiasm for archaeology to Curtius.

On 10 January 1852 Curtius delivered at the Singakademie in Berlin his famous oration on *Olympia in the presence of the royal family. This marked the first step toward excavating Olympia. After considerable delay due to the Turko-Russian War, excavations commenced in 1874. The scholarly agreement between the German and Greek governments in which the Germans promised to leave all finds in Greece, signed by Curtius at Athens on 25 April 1874, was a landmark in the history of archaeology and has been frequently imitated since.

In 1851 Curtius became member of the Berlin Academy and editor of the *Corpus Inscriptionum Graecarum.* From 1853 to 1867 he was professor of classical philology at Göttingen. His *Griechische Geschichte* (1857–61), although often naively moral, was the first Greek history written in German. In 1868 he succeeded *Gerhard as professor of archaeology at Berlin and director of the Old Museum and Antiquarium. His imperial connections eased his convincing the government to nationalize the *German Archaeological Institute and found its Athenian branch. Aged sixty, Curtius began to excavate at Olympia and soon uncovered the sculptures of the Zeus Temple and the *"*Hermes* of Praxiteles." In 1892 appeared his *Die Stadtgeschichte von Athen.* Wilamowitz succeeded him at Berlin.

An eloquent orator, Curtius's impassioned love for Hellas in the tradition of *Winckelmann and *Goethe and dislike of scientific specialization inspired men like F. Paulsen and G. P. Gooch but struck A. Erman and *Wilamowitz as sentimental or silly. Undeniably, he was a key figure in turning archaeology from treasure hunting into both a science and a cooperative supranational enterprise. Olympia remains his enduring monument.

BIBLIOGRAPHY

F. Curtius, *Ernst Curtius: Ein Lebensbild in Briefen* (Berlin, 1903); H. Kähler, "Curtius," *NDB* 3 (1957), 446–47; B. Fellmann, "Die Geschichte der deutschen Ausgrabung," *100 Jahre deutsche Ausgrabung in Olympia,* ed. B. Fellmann—H. Scheyhing (Munich, 1972), 37–48; A. Borbein, "Klassische Archäologie in Berlin vom 18. zum 20. Jahrhundert," *Berlin und die Antike: Aufsätze,* ed. W. Arenhövel—C. Schreiber (Berlin, 1979), 99–150; M. Chambers, "Ernst Curtius," in Briggs—Calder, 37–42.

                                                                    WILLIAM M. CALDER III

CURTIUS, LUDWIG (1874–1954). German archaeologist and art historian; specialist in Roman portraiture and wall painting.

A prosperous physician's son, Curtius studied at Munich under H. von *Brunn and A. *Furtwängler. His dissertation (1903) concerned the ancient Herm. In 1907 he produced his second, larger dissertation (*Habilitationschrift*) and the next year began teaching at Erlangen, where he became full professor (*Ordinarius*) in 1913. After serving in World War I, he accepted a post in 1918/19 at Freiburg im Breisgau, which he left in 1920 for Heidelberg; among his students there was O. J. *Brendel. In 1928 he became director of the *German Archaeological Institute in Rome. Because he did not approve National Socialism, he was early retired.

The center of Curtius's work was the hermeneutics of iconography, especially sculpture and wall painting. His most influential book is *Die Wandmalerei Pompejis* (1929; repr. 1960). His interests were broad and include studies of *Winckelmann and *Goethe. Many of his writings are collected in *Torso* (1958). His memoirs, *Deutsche und Antike Welt* (1950; repr. 1956), are justly famous. He was the rare archaeologist who received the honor of Knight of the Order *Pour le mérite.* Curtius resided in Rome during the last fifteen years of his life and died there in 1954.

BIBLIOGRAPHY

M. Bieber, "Ludwig Curtius†," *AJA* 59 (1955), 64–65; R. Lullies, in *Archäologenbildnisse,* 186–87; R. Lullies, *Schriften von Ludwig Curtius (1874–1954), Eine Bibliographie* (Mainz, 1979).

                                                                    WILLIAM M. CALDER III

CYCLADES. Island group in the south Aegean Sea and an administrative district of modern Greece; natural stepping-stones among Crete, the Greek mainland and Asia Minor.

Obsidian from Franchthi Cave in the Argolid documents travel to *Melos already in the Mesolithic period. There is a long tradition of multidisciplinary archaeological research in the Cyclades: by the turn of the century *Hiller von Gaertringen had produced a four-volume study of *Thera, including excavation reports, critical analyses of epigraphical and literary testimonia and studies of climate, vegetation and geological resources.

Bent (1884), Köhler (1884), Dümmler (1886) and others produced early studies of prehistoric marble anthropomorphic figures and other finds; there followed more rigorous explorations of Early Bronze Age settlements and cemeteries by *Tsountas (1898–99), who popularized the term "Cycladic Civilization" to describe the material culture of the islands ca. 3300–2000 B.C. Excavations at Phylakopi in Melos (1896–99) first established a relative chronology for the entire Cycladic Bronze Age (now much refined, particularly by work at Ayia Irini on *Keos). Between 2000 and 1450 B.C. the Cyclades may have been colonized by Minoans from Crete. At Akrotiri on Thera, spectacular wall paintings and other well-preserved remains of this period were excavated (1967–74) by *Marinatos; Fouqué and others (1866–70) had found similar discoveries sealed beneath layers of volcanic ash quarried for construction of the Suez Canal.

After the Bronze Age the islands played only minor roles in the political history of Greece, generally as members of externally controlled alliances. Among the more important post-Bronze Age sites are those of Grotta-Palati on *Naxos (extensively investigated by Kontoleon and others since World War II); Xobourgo on Tenos (dug in 1949–58 by Kontoleon); Paroikia on *Paros (explored by Rubensohn at the turn of the century); Kastro on Siphnos (examined by Brock and Macworth Young, 1934–37); the sanctuary of Poseidon and Amphitrite on Tenos (studied first by Demoulin and Graindor, 1901–3); and the Geometric town at Zagora on Andros (uncovered in the 1960s by Cambitoglou, Zapheiropoulos and Kontoleon). In addition, antiquarians have left valuable descriptions of classical and Roman monuments, including epigraphical texts (many subsequently lost or destroyed): accounts by Tournefort (1717), *Ross (1840, 1851) and Bent (1884, 1885) are particularly comprehensive, while those of much earlier travelers, such as *Buondelmonti (1408), though sketchy, can shed light on the early history of sculpture and buildings after the Latin conquest of the archipelago in the thirteenth century A.C.

Many artifacts of the Archaic and Classical periods have been studied in detail by historians of ancient art and architecture—for example, large storage jars with elaborate stamped or impressed figural scenes by Shäfer (1957) or the *Siphnian Treasury at Delphi by de la Coste Messelière (1936)—while, since 1968, Gruben, Schuller and their colleagues have vigorously investigated the development of the Doric order on Naxos, Paros and Keos. There are isolated fortification towers on some islands; remains of ancient mining, metallurgy and marble quarrying are extensive.

BIBLIOGRAPHY

+C. Rougement—G. Rougemont, eds., *Les Cyclades: Matériaux pour une étude de géographie historique* (Paris, 1983); K. Simopoulos, *Xenoi taxidiotes stin ellada* (Athens, 1984–85); +W. Ekschmitt, *Kunst und Kultur der Kykladen* (Mainz, 1986); +R. Barber, *The Cyclades in the Bronze Age* (London, 1987); J. L. Davis, "Review of Aegean Prehistory I: The Islands of the Aegean," *AJA* 96 (1992), 699–756.

JACK L. DAVIS

CYPRUS. Island located 70km south of Turkey and 103km west of Syria, measuring 222km east to west, with a maximum width of 95km and a total area of 9,251km. The copper deposits, which give Cyprus its name, occur in the Troodos Mountains, in the west.

While human habitation began in the Neolithic, the island flourished during the Bronze Age due to its copper and agricultural resources. The period ended in the eleventh century B.C. with destruction, by the Sea Peoples or earthquakes. Migrations from the Aegean followed, accompanied by the founding of the Greek-Cypriot kingdoms. Phoenician colonists arrived from Tyre in the midninth century, founding Kition. Cyprus became part of the empires of Assyria, (ca. 707–650 B.C.), Egypt (ca. 570–545 B.C.) and Persia (545–330 B.C.), although its dominant culture was Hellenic. It remained under Persia until Alexander's conquests, when it passed to Ptolemy. The island was annexed by Rome 58 B.C. and in A.D. 395 became part of the Byzantine Empire. Richard I took possession in 1191, en route to the Third Crusade, then sold Cyprus to the Knights Templar, who gave it to a Frankish Lusignan dynasty, which ruled from 1196 to 1489. It was held by Venice until 1571, when it fell to the Ottoman Turks. The island was ceded to Great Britain in 1878 and granted independence in 1960.

In the sixteenth century, travelers such as E. de Lusignan and F. Bustrone recorded visits to ancient sites. R. Pococke arrived in 1738 and described several sites, including Soli and Salamis, as did Le Bas and Waddington early in the next century. Archaeological excavation on Cyprus began with Vogüé's at Golgoi and Idalion in 1862. From 1865 to 1877, L. *Cesnola, then American and Russian consul, plundered numerous sites, amassing a collection of nearly 35,000 artifacts, most of which were purchased by the *Metropolitan Museum of Art. Legislation in 1878 limited the removal of antiquities, and the establishment of the Cyprus Museum in 1883 helped control the plundering and demolition of ancient and medieval sites.

M. Ohnefalsch-Richter began government-authorized excavations in 1878. British excavations, sponsored by the Cyprus Exploration Fund, founded in 1887, and by the British Museum were conducted at numerous sites. In the 1930s, after a two-decade hiatus, important excavations at various sites were conducted by the *Swedish Cyprus Expedition, under the direction of E. Gjerstad, by C.F.A. Schaeffer at *Enkomi and by the University of Pennsylvania at Lapethos and *Kourion. The Cyprus Department of Antiquities was founded in 1935, with A.H.S. Megaw as its first director. Its next director, P. Dikaios, excavated important prehistoric sites at Erimi, Sotira, Khirokitia and the Late Bronze Age city of Enkomi. Although work in the period around World War II was limited, A. *Furumark excavated a Late Bronze Age settlement at Sinda, while J. B. Hennessy excavated a cemetery at Stephania, and J. Du Plat Taylor excavated a Late Bronze Age sanctuary at Myrtou-Pigadhes.

In the last few decades, there has been an enormous increase in archaeological activity on Cyprus, due largely to the efforts of Dikaios's successor, V. Karageorghis. These excavations have illuminated the important role played by Cyprus during many periods, particularly the Late Bronze Age, when it played a pivotal role in the international exchanges of the fourteenth and thirteenth centuries B.C. Karageorghis excavated numerous important Late Bronze and Iron Age sites, including *Kition, Maa-Palaekastro, Pyla-Kokkinokremos, the Salamis necropolis and the Alaas cemetery. Foreign involvement continues, with American, British, French, German, Polish and Swedish projects under way. The many fine regional museums encourage pride in the antiquities and stimulate worldwide scholarly research.

BIBLIOGRAPHY

J. L. Myres—M. Ohnefalsch-Richter, *A Catalogue of the Cyprus Museum, with a Chronicle of Excavations Undertaken Since the British Occupation and Introductory Note on Cypriote Archaeology* (Oxford, 1899); C. D. Cobham, *Excerpta Cypria, Materials for a History of Cyprus* (New York, 1969, repr. of 1908 edition); V. Karageorghis, *Cyprus from the Stone Age to the Romans* (London, 1982); V. Karageorghis, ed., *Archaeology in Cyprus 1960–1985* (Nicosia, 1985).

ROBERT B. KOEHL

CYRENAICA. A narrow coastal strip in modern eastern Libya, comprising the Greek cities Cyrene, Apollonia, Ptolemais, Arsinoë and Berenice.

The zone was organized as a Roman province from 74 B.C.; in Imperial times it was part of a joint province with *Crete.

From 1705 until 1897 European travelers like M. Lemaire (1705) sought out the remains of ancient Cyrenaica. Explorers visited Cyrene and its port Apollonia most (P. Della Cella, 1816; F. W. and H. W. Beechey, 1821/22; J.-R. Pacho, 1822–24; H. Barth, 1845–49; J. Hamilton, 1852; D. G. *Hogarth, 1904), but also Arsinoë (Beecheys), Ptolemais and Berenice (J. Bruce, 1768; Beecheys; Barth). The first records of the specific ruins then visible at Cyrene are from the early nineteenth century: columns, bases and remains of a large building with a colonnade in the agora (Della Cella, Beecheys); a general plan of the city, including the agora (Beecheys). The ruins of Apollonia are likewise detailed in the notes of early travelers: the theater (Della Cella, Pacho, Barth), Roman aqueduct (Della Cella), churches (Pacho, Barth, Hamilton), minor buildings (Barth) and fortifications (Hamilton). The Beecheys drew a plan of Apollonia; Pacho mapped Cyrene, noting the Caesareum and its alignment with the agora temple of Apollo. C. Clermont-Ganneau visited only Berenice (1895), where he gathered documents and antiquities for the *Louvre.

In first excavations at Cyrene, J. Vattier de Beauville explored a necropolis and Apollo's sanctuary (1848). M. Smith and E. A. Porcher excavated near the agora (1860), and much magnificent sculpture was sent to the *British Museum. H. Weld-Blundell in the first photograph of the site showed the Caesareum and, behind it, the agora and foot of the acropolis (1895). An American team directed by R. Norton (1910–11), under the auspices of the *Archaeological Institute of America, succumbed to the region's dangers during the Italo-Turkish War, when H. F. De Cou was shot to death by Arab assassins; his grave near the team's camp looks westward from the face of the Cyrene plateau.

Italian archaeologists benefited from Italy's occupation of Libya (1914–35). F. *Halbherr had come from Crete on a survey mission, from Berenice to Derna (1910–11). Italian interests were galvanized, however, by the chance discovery of the *Venus* of Cyrene (1913; now in the *Terme Museum, Rome) and the base of a great statue to Zeus (1915). E. Ghislanzoni, superintendent of antiquities based at Berenice (1914–22), excavated at Apollonia and in Cyrene's agora. The north side of the agora, flanked by the Augusteum, was carefully explored even while military fortifications were built in the region. Ghislanzoni's successor, G. Oliverio (1923–35), established the Italian Archaeological Mission, moved the superintendency to Cyrene, and focused Italian efforts on the agora and the sanctuary of Apollo, which was completely excavated by the outbreak of World War II. Activity in the region between 1935 and 1949 was limited to G. Caputo's protection of Ptolemais's monuments (1935–42) and exploration of Cyrene's Roman forum, including the Caesareum (1935–40).

After the war the Libyan Antiquities Department (particularly under R. G. Goodchild's supervision and counsel, 1953–58, 1959–66), the Italian Mission (especially under D. *Levi, 1957–62) and English, American and French excavators have explored the pentapolis of Cyrenaica. Roughly contemporary campaigns examined Apollonia (1958–62) and Cyrene's agora (1957–62). Italian excavators have studied systematically not only the north side of the agora, with its stoas and Augusteum, but also the west side with its Portico of Emperors and temple of Apollo; the south side marked by the Road of Battos, capitolium, prytaneum and houses of Jason Magnus and Hesychius; and the east side with its tomb of Battos. Ptolemais (1954–58) and Arsinoë (1954–56, 1959–62, 1963–67, 1974) have also been opened to exploration. More recent excavations continue at Apollonia (1965–67, 1976), Ptolemais (1971, 1978–79) and Berenice (1971–75). While Italian scholars publish their half century of excavations at cyrene, an American team has discovered an extramural sanctuary of Demeter and Persephone south of the city (1973–83).

BIBLIOGRAPHY

C. H. Kraeling, *Ptolemais: City of the Libyan Pentapolis* (Chicago, 1962), 30–32; S. Stucchi, *L'Agorà di Cirene* (Rome, 1965), 15–29; R. G. Goodchild, *Cyrene and Apollonia,* 3rd ed. (Tripoli, 1970), 35–36; R. G. Goodchild, et al., *Apollonia, The Port of Cyrene: Excavations by the University of Michigan 1965–67* (Tripoli, 1976), 25–28. J. A. Lloyd et al., *Excavations at Sidi Khrebish, Benghazi (Berenice)* 1 (Tripoli, 1977), 1–10.

MARTHA W. BALDWIN BOWSKY

D

DACIAN PRISONERS. See FARNESE CAPTIVES.

DAMA DE ELCHE ("Lady from Elche"). Lifesize polychrome stone bust of a noble lady or princess, regarded by many as the masterpiece of art from ancient Spain (Iberia).

The sculpture, in excellent condition, features a mantle and stylized folds and huge necklaces, as well as a high headdress with massive circular ornaments at the sides of the head. Dates for the sculpture range from the fifth century B.C. to the second century A.C. It is, in fact, difficult to place the bust because of its Archaic or archaizing drapery, its face of Classical fifth-century type and its jewelry, which compares, on one hand, to examples in fourth-century sculpture from Latium and Etruria, and, on the other, to jewelry on funerary busts from Palmyra of Roman Imperial date (second century A.C.).

The work was discovered near Elche in August 1897 at La Alcudia, the farm of Dr. Manuel Campello Antón, who sold the bust to the *Louvre for a handsome sum. (It later returned to Spain and is now in the *Museo Archeológico Nacional, Madrid.) While the *Dama de Elche* has always been accepted as authentic in the past and has been elevated to the status of a national treasure (lavishly praised by Generalísimo Francisco Franco, it was even reproduced in 1948 on a Spanish banknote), the work is currently under challenge as a forgery. The eclecticism and the remarkably good condition of the bust are consistent with the hypothesis that it is a forgery, and the date of the appearance of the work relates it to other notorious, learned counterfeits of the late nineteenth century, such as the *Praenestine Fibula and the *Tiara of Saitaphernes. The artist, who may have been Francisco Pallas y Puig (1859–1926), the most successful and artistically satisfying forger of his time and place, could have based the work on smaller Iberian sculptures from Cerro de los Santos, and Llano de la

Consolación that had recently been published, along with a wide variety of sculptures from other places and dates.

BIBLIOGRAPHY

A. García y Bellido, *La Dama de Elche* (Madrid, 1943); J. F. Moffitt, *Art Forgery: The Case of the Lady of Elche* (Gainesville, 1995).

J. F. MOFFITT

DANCING FAUN. Small bronze statue of a Satyr from *Pompeii (Museo Nazionale, Naples; height 0.71m), found in 1830 in a large and elaborate house (''Casa del Fauno'') that was built in the second century B.C. and maintained until A.D. 79; often identified as a copy of a lost Hellenistic work of the third century B.C.

The *Dancing Faun,* largely unrestored, balances lightly on its toes and pivots to its right, turning its head back to the left. The energy and ecstasy of the figure are magnificently expressed in the wildly tousled hair and beard, the wide eyes, the smiling open mouth and the flip of the tail. The flicking wrists and the outstretched fingers suggest that the Satyr is marking the rhythm of its dance.

Soon after its discovery, the *Faun* was compared with the prestigious *Barberini *Faun* and was heralded as the finest bronze to have been excavated at Pompeii. It has been much copied for display in gardens and interiors and remains popular in this regard today.

BIBLIOGRAPHY

Beazley—Ashmole, 82–83; +Bieber, 170; Robertson, 477–78; Haskell—Penny, 208–9.

CAROL MATTUSCH

DANTE ALIGHIERI (1265–1321). Italy's greatest poet; ardent continuator of the classical tradition.

In both *The Divine Comedy* and his minor works, Dante echoes, cites or alludes to numerous ancient texts. Some ninety years ago Edward Moore noted the frequency of Dante's references to the classics: ''Aristotle is quoted or referred to more than 300 times, Virgil about 200, Ovid about 100, Cicero and Lucan about 50 each, Statius and Boethius between 30 and 40 each, Horace, Livy and Orosius between 10 and 20 each; with a few scattered references, probably not exceeding 10 in the case of any one author, to Plato, Homer, Juvenal, Seneca.'' Not all of Dante's knowledge of these authors was direct; some he obviously culled from secondary sources. For example, Homer was little more than a name to Dante, yet he places him at the head of the ancient poets in *Inferno* IV and elsewhere quotes from his work. Dante found these passages in Aristotle (whom he knew in Latin translation) and Horace and the details of the Troy story in medieval summaries. However, given the choice between referring to the original or to a reworking of it, Dante inevitably opts for the former: thus, he cites Horace's *Ars Poetica* and Statius's *Thebaid* rather than their medieval imitations.

It is not the extent of Dante's knowledge of classical antiquity (not uncommon for his times) but the depth of his understanding of it that distinguishes him from his contemporaries. Dante's penetrating reading of the classics, Vergil's *Aeneid,* in particular, allows him to re-create an image of the classical world— its myths, laws, customs, history—that, if not entirely accurate, nonetheless feels accurate. The pagan world is absorbed into Dante's Christian vision without being robbed of its distinctiveness. Dante handles his classical sources in such a way that he manages to preserve the spirit of the original passage's inner meaning, even while he is creatively and radically transforming it. This sensitivity gives Dante's works, especially *The Divine Comedy,* a classical flavor and coloring.

Occasionally, Dante refers to specific classical antiquities that were known to him; the giant pinecone of St. Peters, the *Belvedere *Pigna,* is mentioned in a simile (*Inferno* XXXI. 58–59), and he alludes to an equestrian statue of Mars that stood in Florence. But he has no interest in describing the visual heritage of antiquity for its own sake. Unlike Petrarch and subsequent humanists, Dante did not perceive the classical tradition as lost and hence in need of rediscovery. Thus, his interest in it is neither antiquarian nor philological. Rather, he sees the classical tradition as a source of images and ideas with which to nourish his mind and discourse. Seen from this perspective, his reading of the classics defies classification: it is neither typically medieval nor humanistic.

BIBLIOGRAPHY

E. Moore, *Studies in Dante, First Series: Scripture and Classical Authors in Dante* (Oxford, 1896; repr. New York, 1968); E. Paratore, ''L'eredità classica in Dante,'' in *Dante e Roma* (Firenze, 1965), 3–50; G. Martellotti, ''Dante e i classici,'' *Cultura e Scuola* 4 (1965), 125–37; M. Pastore Stocchi, ''Classica, Cultura,'' *Enciclopedia Dantesca* (Rome, 1970), II, 30–36; A. Iannucci, ed., *Dante e la ''bella scola'' della poesia: autorità e sfida poetica* (Ravenna, 1993).

AMILCARE A. IANNUCCI

DAVID, JACQUES-LOUIS (1748–1825). French painter, enthusiast of ancient Rome and classical antiquity; major participant of the social and political uprising in eighteenth-century France that accompanied the increased popularity of the new style, neoclassicism.

Born in Paris on 30 August 1748 to a middle-class family, David studied initially with the renowned rococo painter, François Boucher. By 1760, David had begun to favor a more monumental style, prompting Boucher to refer his pupil to Joseph Marie *Vien, a painter who was partisan to the new classical reaction. Under the guidance of Vien, David studied the writings of *Winckelmann. He was encouraged to eliminate any traces of the rococo manner and to adopt the style of masters in the classical tradition such as *Michelangelo, *Raphael and *Poussin.

In 1774, David won the coveted Prix de Rome and traveled to the Italian capital the following year. At that time, the influence of Wincklemann was at its height, and the enthusiasm over the recent excavations at *Pompeii continued.

Overwhelmed by the artistic climate in Rome and by the wealth of ancient sculpture and architecture he saw, David temporarily abandoned painting in order to sketch and study ancient Roman objects visible throughout the city. His investigation and study of ancient art powerfully influenced his style. A solidity and gravity of forms began to pervade his art, and this new feeling for mass and volume was well received by his Parisian patrons upon his return to Paris. The *Grief of Andromache over the Body of Hector* (1783) embodies all of the characteristics of his new classicism. The painting was a critical success with the members of the Academy of Painting and Sculpture and secured his position in the prestigious institution.

The lure of the ancients drew David back to Rome in 1784. He shut himself in his Roman studio to absorb the effects of the ancient marbles and to seek inspiration from the works of Raphael. He sought to immerse himself in antiquity in order to imbue his canvas with the spirit of the ancients. The resulting work, the powerful *Oath of the Horatii* (1785), was based upon the last act of Corneille's play *Horace*. It caused an immediate sensation in both Rome and Paris and quickly became a prime example for the budding neoclassical style.

The works that followed developed the theme of heroism, using his favorite subjects from the writings of Homer and from the histories of Greece and Rome. The *Death of Sokrates* (1787) and the *Lictors Bringing Back the Bodies of the Sons of Brutus* (1789) conveyed David's desire to paint a subject with a classical theme in a grandiose and noble style. He used direct reference to antiquity in the figure of Brutus by quoting from the *Capitoline *Brutus*.

In France, these paintings were understood to have underlying political themes of antiroyal sentiments. The ideals of the ancient Greeks and Romans as portrayed by David were viewed as powerful political statements that promoted a new France. Consequently, his involvement with revolutionary politics led to his new role in French society as a national spokesman for the French Revolution. By 1790, David was known as the "pageant master of the Republic."

His subsequent works, the *Death of Marat* (1793) and the *Death of Bara* (1794), were vital tools for the revolutionaries but simultaneously revealed the beginnings of his departure from the purity of neoclassicism. At the same time, his role as pageant master provided an outlet for his continuing fascination with antiquity. David's stage and costume designs made fashionable the ancient garb and furnishings from which the Empire style evolved.

With the notable exception of the *Rape of the Sabine Women* (1799), after the revolution David returned only occasionally to subjects of the ancient past. The *Sabine Women* reestablished David's position and fame with the new ruling class, and he became court painter under the reign of *Napoleon. His paintings now became tools for the aggrandizement of Napoleon, and he subsequently lost his fervor for those early lessons in antiquity. In 1815 the fall of Napoleon forced David to flee to Brussels. Ironically, he returned to the rococo aesthetics which he so fervently denounced in the 1780s. David died in exile in December 1825.

BIBLIOGRAPHY
D. Dowd, *Pageant Master of the Republic* (Lincoln, NE, 1948); +W. Friedlaender, *David to Delacroix* (New York, 1972); R. Rosenblum, *Transformations in Late Eighteenth Century Art* (Princeton, NJ, 1974); +*David e Roma,* Accademia di Francia a Roma (Rome, 1981).

CHERYL SUMNER

DEL MONTE VASE. See PORTLAND VASE.

DELOS. Small island in the Aegean Sea, one of the most important sanctuaries of the Ionian Greeks.

Birthplace of Apollo and Artemis and boasting an altar of goats' horns fashioned by Apollo himself, Delos was so sacred that no one was allowed to be born or to die there.

The island was first inhabited in the third millennium B.C. and again in the Late Bronze Age, when it was clearly prosperous, if we may judge by a rich "treasure" of Mycenaean gold and ivory objects found under the Artemesion by Vallois (1928) and Gallet de Santerre and Tréheux (1946); whether the cult goes back to Mycenaean times is uncertain. After a period of quiescence, in the Dark Ages, the sanctuary flourished in the Archaic period, showing strong Naxian influence in the seventh century, then Athenian and Samian influence in the sixth century. In the fifth century the Delian league took its name from the island where its treasury was kept, though Delos itself was, in fact, controlled by Athens throughout the fifth and fourth centuries. From 314 to 166 Delos was a prosperous, independent island, and the sanctuary was the recipient of numerous benefactions by Hellenistic kings. In 166 the island was given back to Athens by the Roman Senate and, under Athenian administration, remained a great international commercial center. Siding with Rome in the Mithridatic wars, Delos was plundered by the troops of Mithridates in 88 B.C. and again by his pirate ally, Athenodoros, in 69 B.C. Though the legate Triarius built a new fortification wall to protect part of the city, a gradual decline set in; nevertheless, the site remained inhabited throughout the Roman period.

Christian activity is attested as early as the third century A.C. Ravaged by Leo the Isaurian in 727, by the Slavs in 769 and by the Saracens in 821, the island was in ruins and totally abandoned throughout the Middle Ages. Travelers, including *Buondelmonti and *Ciriaco of Ancona, visited the island as early as the fifteenth century. Ciriaco has left an interesting description (1445), as have *Spon and *Wheler (1675), J. Pitton de Tournefort (1700/2), Drummond (1744), *Cockerell (1810) and Saint-Vincent and *Blouet (1829). Excavations were undertaken by the *French School at Athens starting in 1873 under the direction of Lebégue and *Homolle, from 1904 to 1914 under Holleaux, and from 1958 to 1975 under various scholars. A museum on the island houses most of the rich finds from these excavations.

The excavations have brought to light numerous important areas. Most significant is the sanctuary of Apollo itself, which was first laid out in monumental form in the late seventh and early sixth centuries B.C. It was originally approached from the north, along a sacred way lined on the west by a row of marble lions. Within the sanctuary proper there was an early building, perhaps a temple, called officially an *oikos,* along with a stoa and a colossal kouros, all built by the Naxians. Also within the sanctuary was an Artemesion of the seventh century, where several Archaic *korai* (*korai* and *kouroi*) were found, including the earliest known, that of Nikandre, also from *Naxos. Three temples of Apollo dating to the second half of the sixth century, first half of the fifth century and second half of the fifth century have been found, as well as a series of treasury-like buildings referred to in the accounts as *oikoi.* Also within the Archaic/Classical sanctuary have been uncovered a well-preserved fountain-house (Minoa), the *prytaneion,* an *ekklesiasterion* and the base of the large bronze palm tree dedicated by Nikias (Plutarch, *Nikias* 3).

By Hellenistic times the main entrance to the sanctuary was from the south, lined by two stoas of the third century B.C., the western one dedicated by Philip V of Macedon. Other Macedonian offerings stood within the sanctuary: a large building designed to hold a ship and a long Doric stoa built by Antigonos Gonatas along the north side.

In addition to the great sanctuary of Apollo, other sanctuaries were founded in the Archaic period: a Letoon, the Archegesion, a Dodecatheon, a Dioskoureion and a Heraion. This last, on the slopes of Mt. Kynthos, has produced a particularly fine collection of seventh-century Cycladic Orientalizing pottery, much of it on display in the site museum.

In Hellenistic times a prosperous town grew up on either side of the Apollo sanctuary. The French excavations have uncovered dozens of very well preserved houses of the third to first centuries B.C., many containing some of the finest mosaic floors known. The international character of the city is reflected in the sanctuaries that flourished in this period: a Dionysion, an Aphrodision, a Philadelpheion, an Asklepieion, three separate shrines of the Egyptian gods, one to the Syrian gods, several to Eastern deities on Mt. Kynthos and one of the earliest synagogues in Greece. An agora of the Italians and a business association from Beirut remind us that commerce was the great attraction for all these foreigners; trading was especially active in slaves and grain. A recent discovery of hundreds of stamped clay sealings from an archive room promises to shed more light on the life of the city.

BIBLIOGRAPHY

École Française d'Athènes, *Exploration archéologique de Délos,* 1–23 (Paris, 1909–80); W. A. Laidlaw, *A History of Delos* (Oxford, 1933); P. Bruneau—J. Ducat, *Guide de Délos,* 3rd ed. (Paris, 1983).

                                                        JOHN McK. CAMP II

DELPHI, Greece. Greek city and highly important sanctuary, located north of the Gulf of Corinth on the picturesque slopes of Mt. Parnassos; the monuments are disposed beneath the twin peaks of the Phaidriades, on either side of the Kastalian Spring; Delphi's temple of Apollo was world-famous for its oracle.

The site of Delphi was settled no earlier than the Late Bronze Age, when it seems to have been sacred to Athena and the oracular goddess Mother Earth. In the eighth century B.C. appears the first archaeological evidence of the cult of Apollo, who slew Python—the dragon who guarded the place—and seized the oracle for himself. In the seventh century was built the first masonry temple to Pythian Apollo. Delphi soon became so prosperous that it was the object of fierce contention; the first of four Sacred Wars was fought (600–586 B.C.), resulting in the control of Delphi as a federal sanctuary by the twelve Greek tribes of the Amphictyonic League.

After a fire the temple was rebuilt by the Alkmaionidai of Athens (513–505 B.C.) with funds from around and even outside the Greek world, and Delphi and its Pythian oracle achieved international status; the sacred place well deserved its reputation as the *omphalos* or "navel" of the world. The Archaic temple of Apollo, a great Doric structure with six columns on each end and fifteen down the sides, had an inner chamber, the adyton, which contained a cleft in the earth over which was placed the sacred tripod of Apollo; here his priestess, the Pythia, sat to deliver oracular messages.

The sanctuary was flanked by a series of terraces cut into the mountainside, which were eventually covered with offerings to the god and with the special houses or treasuries built by Greek states to hold such offerings. Along the Sacred Way that ascends to the temple were built the *Siphnian Treasury (ca. 525 B.C.), the *Athenian Treasury (after 490 B.C.) and a number of other Greek repositories, as well as even a treasury of the Etruscan city of Caere (*Cerveteri). Hundreds of statues—of bronze, marble, silver, gold and ivory—lined the route or stood on walls and rooftops, creating a dazzling effect. The *Charioteer* of Delphi (ca. 470 B.C.) belonged to one such group, and the gilt bronze serpent column with tripod commemorating the Battle of Plataia (479 B.C.) was erected in front of the temple of Apollo. Where the Sacred Way passes the temple of Apollo is visible a wall of the temple terrace faced with a finely jointed polygonal masonry, covered with over 800 inscriptions dating from the second century B.C. to the first century A.C. At the top of the Sacred Way was located a theater (third–second centuries B.C.), and above that was the stadium that served as a focal point for the Pythian games held every four years.

The fourth century was a period of great building activity, with a new temple of Apollo built on the foundations of the Archaic building, which was destroyed by earthquake and fire in 373 B.C. On the east side of the Kastalian Spring, in the area known as Marmaria, the temple of Athena Pronaia (Pronoia) had a similar sequence, though the new temple was not built on the site of the ruined structure. The first building (early fifth century B.C.), a Doric structure with six columns on each end and twelve on each side, had been hit by a rockslide in 480 B.C. and was completely ruined in the earthquake of 373. To the west was erected the new Doric temple of Athena Pronaia. In the space between the two was built, in the early fourth century, the splendid round tholos, a structure made of Pentelic marble, surrounded by twenty slender Doric columns.

Delphi was in the hands of history from this point. After the third and fourth Sacred Wars (356–346 B.C.; 340–338 B.C.), Philip II of Macedon, whose intervention settled the quarrels, took a seat in the Amphictyonic League and assumed control of the site. In 279 B.C. the Gauls attempted their notorious assault on Delphi but were repulsed, and in 191 B.C. the Romans became masters of the sanctuary.

The 400 years of Roman rule were punctuated by alternately dreary and encouraging periods as Delphi slowly drifted into decline, with the oracle losing its prestige. Sulla sacked the sanctuary in 86 B.C.; Augustus reorganized the Amphictyony, and under Hadrian and the Antonines Delphi had a particularly glorious period. (Pausanias described the site in the second century A.C.) Constantine carried away many of the treasures to his new capital at Constantinople (e.g., the Plataia monument; see *Byzantium), but Theodosius finally abolished the oracle around A.D. 385.

Ravaged by Slavic invaders in the Middle Ages, Delphi sank into obscurity, its name lost as the rural village of Kastri rose over its ruins. In 1436, *Ciriaco of Ancona recognized that this was the site of the ancient oracle and was able to identify the "hippodrome" (stadium) and "amphitheater" (theater), though his search for the temple of Apollo led him to a "rotunda." Remaining for six days, he made drawings and copied inscriptions. *Wheler and *Spon visited in 1676 and made a plan of the area, attempting to correlate the text of Pausanias with the ruins. They visited the Kastalian Spring, where a fountainhouse of Hellenistic or Roman date was visible. The long list of travelers who followed (skillfully compiled by Marie-Christine Hellmann) includes *Stuart and *Revett, who came to Delphi with Dawkins and *Wood; *Chandler and *Pars and L.F.S. *Fauvel (all the preceding in the eighteenth century); and *Clarke, *Dodwell and *Gell visited in the early nineteenth century; all made drawings of the Kastalian Spring, while Gell drew various other views of the ruins. *Byron and *Hobhouse were unimpressed by Delphi but took the trouble to carve their names above the Kastalian fount.

After the liberation of Greece in 1829, as national attention turned to the preservation of the archaeological heritage, there was much discussion of the possibility of excavating Delphi. The French archaeologist P. Foucart made the first soundings in the area of the temple of Apollo in 1860. But progress was hindered by the presence of the village of Kastri spreading over the hillside. An earthquake in 1873 caused great damage to the houses, and the time seemed appropriate for removing the village to another spot. But some of the inhabitants stubbornly resisted, and the settlement rebounded. The *French School at Athens, now directed by Foucart, expressed its interest in undertaking the excavation, and soon the American Charles Eliot *Norton sought to purchase the land at Delphi, first through the *American School of Classical Studies, then through the *Archaeological Institute of America. The competition reached the point of intervention by the governments of the countries involved before the French finally were awarded the concession in 1891. The French were asked to pay the bulk of the expense for moving Kastri to its new site about 1km west of the sanctuary, and the excavation was officially inaugurated in October 1892.

In the ten years of the Great Excavation ("La Grande Fouille") under the direction of Théophile *Homolle, the French could claim to have uncovered the two sanctuaries of Apollo and of Athena Pronaia and many of the most important monuments of Delphi. In 1893 the Athenian Treasury came to light, and in 1894, that of the Siphnians; nearby were found the two *kouros* figures now known as Kleobis and Biton (1893–94). In 1896 were uncovered the stadium, the podium of the temple of Apollo and, near it, the bronze *Charioteer*. The area of Marmaria, with the tholos and temples to Athena, was excavated between 1900 and 1903. Thousands of inscriptions were brought to light during the campaign. Homolle took advantage of new technology to record the excavation, making extensive use of photography from the beginning. For the carrying away of soil the French laid 1,500m of rails and utilized fifty-seven open wagons to transport earth to the spoil heap.

Reconstruction of the Athenian Treasury was carried out promptly (1906), and much later the great polygonal wall was restored (1936). Three columns of the Doric tholos were reerected in 1938, creating a scenic effect against the sharply descending mountainsides. The temple of Apollo was restored in 1938–39 and 1941. These restorations were a part of the immense labor of sorting the thousands upon thousands of fragments of monuments and finds pertaining to sculpture, epigraphy and ceramics that were unearthed during the Grande Fouille. As successor to Homolle in the study of the sculpture of Delphi, P. de la Coste-Messelière played a leading role while G. Daux and R. Flacelière studied the epigraphical material. Excavations were renewed in 1934, resulting in an expansion of the total area known and in digging down to bedrock around key monuments. To the northeast of the sanctuary of Apollo, L. Lerat enlarged evidence of Bronze Age Mycenaean habitation. P. Amandry and J. Bousquet worked in various points around the temple of Apollo, making soundings down to bedrock and on the Sacred Way. The most spectacular result of these later excavations was the discovery (1939) of a sacred deposit in which were dumped thousands of objects or fragments of gold, ivory, bronze, iron and terracotta. These included ivory parts of three Archaic lifesize chryselephantine statues (heads, hands, feet), as well as some of the gold decoration, and a bronze incense burner supported by a female statuette, considered one of the finest bronzes of the mid-fifth century. All in all, the newer excavations (1934–49) resulted in a more detailed plan of the sanctuaries and a finer chronology.

Excavation and efforts at preservation at Delphi are ongoing. The splendid sculptures and other finds from Delphi are housed in the modern museum adjacent to the site, a rebuilding (1959–61) of the museum previously set up by the Greek government. Publication of the results at Delphi has been issued in the form of final reports in the *Fouille de Delphes,* initiated by Homolle in 1902 to publish the topography and architecture (vol. 2), epigraphy (vol. 3), the sculpture (vol. 4) and the smaller finds (vol. 5). (Vol. 1 has not appeared.)

BIBLIOGRAPHY

+P. de la Coste-Messelière, *Au Musée de Delphes* (Paris, 1936); +J.-F. Bommelaer, *Guide de Delphes, le site* (Athens, 1991); +*Guide de Delphes, le Musée* (Paris, 1991); +*La Redécouverte de Delphes* (Paris, 1992).

DEMPSTER, SIR THOMAS (1579–1625). Scottish philologist and historian, regarded as the founder of the discipline of Etruscology.

Dempster was born at Cliftbog, Aberdeenshire, the twenty-fourth in a family of twenty-nine children. He was a precocious child and says in his autobiography that he learned the alphabet perfectly in one hour at the age of three. After obtaining his early education at Aberdeenshire, Dempster then studied at Cambridge, Paris, Louvain and Rome. He taught at various French universities, including Toulouse, Nîmes and Paris, but found it necessary to change his residence repeatedly because of his quarrels with colleagues and authorities. Dempster was, in fact, one in a long line of Scottish scholars who were as famous for their public duels as they were for their private studies.

After one such dispute, Dempster, who was Catholic, finally went to Italy and became a professor of civil law at Pisa. Later, he was appointed to the most distinguished post in the most famous university on the Continent, professor of humanities at the University of Bologna. He began his greatest work, *De Etruria regali libri septem,* in 1616 while at Pisa, under the patronage of Cosimo II, Grand Duke of Tuscany (*Medici family). The manuscript was handed over to the duke upon completion, but it was not published until over a hundred years later, in 1723.

De Etruria regali libri septem (Seven Books Concerning Etruria of the Kings) is a masterpiece of early scholarship in which the author attempted to assemble for the first time all known information on the Etruscans. His investigations, based mostly on the writings of the ancient authors, covered the subjects of the origins, language and customs of the Etruscans. Dempster's integration of Etruscan language, history, religion and art into one study is still appropriate today, since the aim of modern scholarship is, as was Dempster's, to understand Etruscan culture as a whole.

In the early seventeenth century the Etruscan sites known to us had not yet been rediscovered, so Dempster had practically no archaeological material on which to base his work, but he came to know the antiquities in private collections, and from these he studied sample Etruscan inscriptions. Although his training as a classicist helped him to recognize the differences between Etruscan and the other classical languages, he, like other early students of the language, assigned its origin to Hebrew (cf. Luigi *Lanzi). One of Dempster's greatest contributions to Etruscan studies was his realization that certain customs and institutions that had always been attributed to the Romans, like the *fasces,* the triumph, the military trumpet, the toga and the gladiatorial games, had, in fact, been created by the Etruscans. Dempster also included the geography of Etruria in *De Etruria regali,* providing the locations of cities based on the literary sources, but he never explored the landscape for Etruscan remains.

Dempster's scholarship also included two other works of importance in the field of classical antiquity, namely, his edition of Rosinus's *Antiquitatum romanorum corpus absolutissimum* and his edition of Accolti's *De bello a Christianis contra barbaros.* His best-known historical work was *Historia ecclesiastica gentis Scotorum,* but this work was affected by his tendency to exaggerate in matters of his homeland.

Although his study of the Etruscans was also affected by his powerful imagination, this work was nonetheless of monumental importance in providing a basis for all subsequent studies of ancient Etruria. Dempster was the first in a series of British explorers, like Sir Richard Burton, George *Dennis and D. H. Lawrence, who would travel to Italy and write about Etruria.

BIBLIOGRAPHY

"Thomas Dempster," *DNB* 5 (1922), 785–90. "Thomas Dempster," *EI* 12 (1931), 609. M. Cristofani, "Sugli inizi dell' 'Etruscheria': La pubblicazione del *De Etruria regali* di Thomas Dempster," *MEFRA* 90 (1978), 577–625.

CHERYL L. SOWDER

DENNIS, GEORGE (1814–98). English government official, traveler and archaeologist; author of *Cities and Cemeteries of Etruria,* a classic work on the Etruscans.

George Dennis was born in London on 21 July 1814, the son of an employee of the Government Excise Office. Little is known of his schooling except that he is recorded as having been at Charterhouse in 1828.

In 1829, at the age of fifteen, he started on a long career of government service—often frustrating, boring and unsatisfying. He worked in his father's office (which he hated) until 1848, when he joined the Colonial Service. From 1849 to 1863 he served in Guiana, at first as the personal secretary to the governor, later as inspector of schools. During his term in Guiana he married Nora (maiden name unknown), probably around 1860. He became vice-consul in Benghazi, during which period he was able to start some archaeological work in Tripolitania, time, work and workers permitting. He spent a short time in *Smyrna in 1868 and eventually became consul, a promotion, first in *Crete and then in *Palermo. He was consul in Palermo from 1870, returning to Smyrna in 1879. All along he found his work unsatisfactory and never paying enough salary. He begged for promotions, raises and changes of venue, and, happily, at last, he found a friendly patron in Henry (later Sir Henry) Layard, excavator of Nineveh and himself in the Colonial Service. Dennis's love of Sicily and his continued interest in the Lydians were finally satisfied in the last twenty years of his professional life, which included nine years as consul in Palermo and a total of ten years in Smyrna.

As with so many people, Dennis managed to survive because he early learned the joys of travel and, in spite of stringent financial circumstances, was able to do so. He came from an adventurous family and started traveling when he was eighteen. His letters from Scotland at the age of twenty already show his rare gift of descriptive writing. By 1839 not only had he traveled to Spain and Portugal, but he had published, anonymously, a book about them—*A Summer in Andalucia.* All through his life he never lost his love of travel nor his ability to convey the look and atmosphere of these places in his letters and in his other writings.

In 1842, during one of those leaves of absence that he seemed to have been able to obtain quite easily, he set forth for Central Italy and discovered the Etruscans. He and his traveling companion, the artist Samuel *Ainsley, were in Italy at a time when many Etruscan sites were first being discovered, recorded (after a fashion) and usually exploited. They arrived at a time of great excitement as a result of these new discoveries. The two made three tours together over a fourteen-month period, and Dennis returned subsequently twice, busily engaged in writing his book. The first edition of *Cities and Cemeteries of Etruria,* the result of these travels, was published by John Murray in 1848.

Dennis's interest in archaeological research and, in particular, in the Etruscans never dimmed. Even his determination, in the face of all kinds of official and unofficial deterrents, to dig in Lydia, was based on this. While at the Smyrna consulate he hoped to be able to dig in several sites, including *Sardis, where he sought to find clinching evidence of the Etruscan origins. (One tradition, based on the work of Herodotos, puts their provenance in Lydia, a matter still not settled over one hundred years later.) While consul in Palermo, from 1870, Dennis was able to make side trips to Etruria, pressured by his need to bring his book up-to-date. Much had happened in the interim, not the least of which was the establishment of the Italian state. More work had been done in Etruscan sites, and the material was housed in new public museums.

The second edition of the book, dedicated to Layard, was published in 1878 and reprinted in 1883. More maps, pictures and descriptive material were included.

Dennis's wife, of whom we hear very little, died in 1888. They had had no children. He retired in that same year but continued to travel and give lectures until his death on 15 November 1898 at the age of eighty-four. During his life Dennis also wrote several learned articles on a variety of subjects, a book on El Cid and a handbook to Sicily, but he was never able to persuade Murray to publish his critical social histories. His renown, which deserves to be greater, rests on the *Cities and Cemeteries of Etruria.*

The book is a classic and still remains one of the best single books on Etruria. His maps are rarely bettered; and his descriptions of both topography and Etruscan finds are full and thorough. A lengthy introduction to the Etruscans and their culture leads into a site-by-site survey of Etruria. For each site he gives a topographical description based almost completely on his own visits, including all the visible ancient remains. He gives a historical background based on the works of ancient authors and, where available, descriptions of material found at the site. Dennis's knowledge of ancient writers was extensive; in spite of his apparent lack of formal education, he nevertheless read Latin and Greek and spoke several modern languages. He also (which gives the book its charm) tells the reader about his travels in search of the sites and even how to get there.

The historical background, which he gives for each site, could not, of course, take into account the results of increasingly scientific and well-published excavation done since his time. These results have revealed the extensive occupation of Etruria prior to the Etruscans. Apennine Bronze Age peoples were followed by Iron Age Villanovans, whose culture appears to merge into the Etruscan.

This book is certainly not a boring topographical description with cultural and historical overlays. Dennis takes us along, guiding our footsteps—literally, in places—and indulging in superb flights of descriptive eloquence. Because of his thoroughness, accuracy and the breadth of his coverage, the volumes remain a mine of information. Much has changed since he last wrote, more sites have been excavated and more public museums make more new material accessible. Much, on the other hand, has gone, leaving us with Dennis often as our sole source of reference. He also remains an enchanting traveling companion.

As Dennis E. Rhodes, in his excellent biography, said of George Dennis: "(He) is surely still our best guide to one of the most perplexing and fascinating civilizations in history."

BIBLIOGRAPHY

D. E. Rhodes, *Dennis of Etruria, The Life of George Dennis* (London, 1973); G. Dennis, *The Cities and Cemeteries of Etruria,* abridged, ed. P. Hemphill (Princeton, NJ, 1985), with list of editions, p. lxi.

PAMELA HEMPHILL

DENTE, MARCO (MARCO DA RAVENNA; ca. 1493–1527). Italian engraver.

Little is known of the life of the artist Marco Dente, except that he was a native of Ravenna and that he worked in Rome, in the orbit of Marcantonio *Raimondi and *Raphael. He died in Rome during the sack of the city in 1527. Marco is known for his engravings of antiquities, especially sculptures. He created reproductions of the "Throne of Neptune" in Ravenna and the *Seated Daphnis* in Florence (*Uffizi), as well as the *Marcus Aurelius* Equestrian Statue and the *Spinario* in Rome. His most significant print is that of the *Laocoon,* made soon after the discovery of the statue in 1506 and before the right arm of Laocoon was restored, thus showing it in its original condition.

BIBLIOGRAPHY

A. Bartsch, *Le Peintre-graveur*, 14, *Oeuvres de Marc-Antoine et de ses deux principaux élèves, Augustin de Venise et Marc de Ravenne* (Leipzig, 1867); Sheard, no. 60; Bober—Rubinstein, esp. 455.

DE ROSSI, GIOVANNI BATTISTA (1822–94). Italian archaeologist, specialist in the Early Christian period.

Born at Rome, De Rossi studied at the Collegio Romano, receiving his law degree in 1843. Hired as a scribe at the Vatican Library, he began his systematic study of the Early Christian catacombs, which had received little new examination since *Bosio's labors in the seventeenth century.

His discoveries began with the exploration of the catacomb of Praetextatus (1847–50); then followed that of Callixtus, as well as the sepulchres of Pope Cornelius, Caecilia, Saint Eusebius and others. The fruit of these investigations, his three-volume classic on underground Christian cemeteries, *Roma sotteranea,* appeared in 1864, 1867 and 1877.

De Rossi also worked and published on Roman topography and Early Christian epigraphy. Recognized by *Mommsen for his distinguished epigraphical ability, De Rossi was invited by the Berlin Academy to participate in the corpus of Latin inscriptions (*Corpus Inscriptionum Latinarum*). He was entrusted with the publication of the collected works of the epigrapher B. *Borghesi and for thirty years was sole editor of the *Bullettino di Archeologia Cristiana.*

BIBLIOGRAPHY
P. Pelagatti, "De Rossi, Giovanni Battista," *EAA* 3 (1960), 78–79.

DESGODETS (DESGODETZ), ANTOINE (1653–1728). French architect.

Born in Paris, as a young architect Desgodets was named a pensioner of the *French Academy in Rome in 1674. On his way to Italy he was taken captive by Algerians but finally was released and continued to Rome in 1676.

There he spent six months carefully measuring and studying the great buildings of the city. Upon returning to Paris, he published—at the behest of the powerful Colbert and at the expense of Louis XIV—the results of his studies, *Les Édifices antiques de Rome dessinés et mesurés très exactement* (Paris, 1682), a folio volume with sumptuous illustrations by Leclerc, Lepautre and other well-known engravers. The work, of enduring influence, was reprinted in 1779 and translated into English in 1795.

In Paris Desgodets was made a member of the academy of architecture (1699) and finally professor of the academy (1719), a post that he exercised until his death in 1728.

BIBLIOGRAPHY
A--s, "Desgodets, Antoine," *BU* 2 (1814), 178; Stark, 136, 149.

DEVOTO, GIACOMO (1897–1974). Italian linguist, historian and prehistorian.

Born in Genoa, Devoto followed his father to Pavia and Milan, where he pursued his studies at the Liceo Giuseppe Parini. In 1916 he entered the University of Pavia, receiving his degree in linguistics in 1920. After brief years of teaching at Cagliari, Florence and Padua, he settled in Florence, where he taught from 1935 to 1967. Eminent as a scholar and as a citizen of Florence, Devoto received many honors, such as election to the *Accademia dei Lincei, the

*German Archaeological Institute and many other international academies and honorary degrees from the Sorbonne, Berlin, Cracow, Lima.

Known essentially as a linguist, Devoto considered himself a historian. Certainly most of his linguistic work had an historical purpose. In the sphere of archaeology, his contributions are associated especially with early Italic languages and their relationship to prehistoric cultures. In his *Gli Antichi italici* (Florence, 1931), he attacked the treasured linguistic theory of "Italic unity" and argued that Latin speakers, using copper and practicing inhumation, came to Italy ca. 2000 B.C., while Osco-Umbrian speakers (whom he called Italics) entered about 1,000 years later and used iron and cremation. He also argued that language gave evidence for a revolutionary democratic social movement among Indo-European cremating peoples.

Among other significant publications by Devoto are *Storia delle lingue di Roma* (1939) and *Origini indoeuropee* (1962). In the climate of interest in the Etruscans created by his Florentine colleagues, Devoto participated in the formation of the new institute for Etruscan studies (Istituto di Studi Etruschi, founded 1932) and its early conventions and publications; he published a number of studies that illuminate Etruscan inscriptions and language.

BIBLIOGRAPHY

A. L. Prosdocimi, "Devoto, Giacomo," *DBI* 39 (1991), 605–12.

                                                              GIULIANO BONFANTE

DE VRIENDT. See FLORIS, FRANS.

DIANA OF GABII (DIANE DE GABIES). Lifesize marble statue of a young woman adjusting her clothing, perhaps the goddess Diana (Artemis).

The sculpture is thought by some to be a later Roman copy of a Greek cult statue of Artemis Brauronia, created by Praxiteles in the fourth century B.C. The original statue stood in the goddess's sanctuary in Athens but took its iconography from ritual at *Brauron, where clothing was a regular offering to Athena.

The sculpture was excavated by Gavin *Hamilton at Gabii in 1792 on the property of Prince Borghese (cf. *Borghese family) and displayed subsequently in the gardener's house at the Villa Borghese. It was purchased by *Napoleon in 1807, taken to Paris between 1808 and 1811 and put on display in 1820 in the *Louvre, where it remains today. The statue, praised lavishly by E. Q. *Visconti, enjoyed a high reputation in the nineteenth century. Scholars of the twentieth century have connected the work with Praxiteles, but otherwise it is regarded as of minor importance today.

BIBLIOGRAPHY

G. E. Rizzo, *Prassitele* (Milan, 1932), 63, 116; Bieber, 21; Robertson, *Greek Art,* 396; Haskell—Penny, 198–99.

DIANE CHASSERESSE. See ARTEMIS OF VERSAILLES.

DIDYMA (BRANCHIDAE). Greek city in Ionia (western Asia Minor), 18km south of *Miletos.

The site housed the sanctuary and oracle of Apollo, founded as a fountain cult in the eighth or seventh century B.C. Didyma was destroyed in 494 B.C. during the Persian retaliation against the Ionian revolt led by Miletos. The oracle was reinstituted in 331 B.C. and continued until A.D. 285. Throughout its history Didyma was closely associated with Miletos, to which led a processional Sacred Way.

The principal monument of Didyma is the great Hellenistic temple of Apollo (begun after the reinstating of the cult; preceded on the site by the first temple, eighth–seventh centuries B.C., and the second temple of the Archaic period). The colossal third temple possessed several unusual features, including a large inner chamber or adyton that was open to the sky (hypaethral), within which was a small temple possibly containing the cult image. Also preserved at Didyma are Roman baths and a stadium that was presumably used for the sacred games held in connection with the religious festivals.

The oracle ceased to function around A.D. 390–400. In the Middle Ages the adyton of the temple was turned into a Christian basilica, and the temple proper was turned into a fortress. In 1446, *Ciriaco of Ancona visited Didyma and saw the temple of Apollo still standing. An earthquake (1493) threw the temple down and left only three columns upright. In 1765, the *Society of Dilettanti sent Richard *Chandler to study the monuments and take their measurements, and with him went the artist William *Pars, who made handsome watercolor views (now in the *British Museum). Didyma was also visited by *Gell (1812), *Cockerell (1812) and *Texier (1835).

In 1857–58, C. T. *Newton made excavations along the Sacred Way and collected the great Archaic seated figures known as the "Branchidai" and sent them to the British Museum. The French made excavations at the Apollo temple (1872–73, 1895–96) but were hindered by a great windmill that sat atop the rubble of the east end. In 1905, a German team under T. *Wiegand bought the windmill and removed it, then proceeded to excavate. The *German Archaeological Institute has continued to excavate at Didyma periodically throughout this century.

BIBLIOGRAPHY

+E. Pontremoli—B. Haussollier, *Didymes: fouilles de 1895 et 1896* (Paris, 1904); +T. Wiegand—H. Knackfuss, *Didyma*, 1, *Die Baubeschreibung* (Berlin, 1941); J. Fontenrose, *Didyma, Apollo's Oracle, Cult and Companions* (Berkeley, 1988), 25–27; L. Haselberger, "Werkzeichnungen am Jüngeren Didymeion, Vorbericht," *IstMitt* 30 (1983), 191–215; idem, "Bericht über die Arbeit am Jüngeren Apollontempel von Didyma," *IstMitt* 33 (1983), 90–123; S. Pülz, *Untersuchungen zu kaiserzeitlichen Bauornamentik von Didyma, IstMitt* Beiheft 35 (1989).

ANN C. GUNTER

DINSMOOR, WILLIAM BELL (1886–1973). American archaeologist; historian of Greek architecture.

Born in Windham, New Hampshire, Dinsmoor received a B.S. from Harvard College in 1906. In 1908, he began a long association with the *American School of Classical Studies in Athens as student, excavator and restorer. From 1919 to 1963, Dinsmoor taught at Columbia University. He was president of the *Archaeological Institute of America (1936–45) and in 1970 received that institute's Gold Medal for Distinguished Archaeological Achievement. During World War II, Dinsmoor was chairman of the Committee for the Protection of Cultural Treasures in War Areas and worked closely with British and Inter-Allied commissions for the preservation of important European monuments.

During his long career, Dinsmoor focused his scholarly attention on Periklean buildings in Athens. His ability to relate these buildings to their historical and cultural context and to illuminate the personalities of their architects has been greatly admired. Dinsmoor's best-known book is *The Architecture of Ancient Greece* (1950), internationally acclaimed as the most authoritative reference work in the field.

BIBLIOGRAPHY
"Bibliography of William Bell Dinsmoor," *Hesperia* 35 (1966), 87–92; *AJA* 74 (1970), 185; "W. B. Dinsmoor, 87, An Archaeologist," *New York Times,* 3 July 1973.

ANN M. NICGORSKI

DIOSCURI. See QUIRINAL HORSE TAMERS.

DISKOBOLOS. Greek sculpture of an athlete throwing the discus, originally created in bronze by Myron, ca. 440 B.C.

Discus throwing in contests was noted as early as Homer; the discus motif appears in vase paintings, gems, reliefs and figurines from the Archaic age onward, and it became a subject for major sculptures of the Classical age—by Pythagoras (?), ca. 460 B.C. (*Terme); by Polykleitos, ca. 440 B.C. (Wellesley); and by Naukides, ca. 400 B.C. (*Vatican). None were as memorable or famous as the work of Myron.

Myron posed his athlete with the arms open and curving like a drawn bow, the torso leaning into and pointing in the direction of the toss, the legs bent forward, impelling the body and missile, dragging the skin of the feet, and the head turned back to watch the disc begin its trajectory. As comparisons with sequential photographs of living athletes show, Myron's brilliant naturalistic invention is an abstract construction fitted into a shallow, relieflike plane in which abrupt turns present the body in clear and explanatory silhouettes. The scheme preserves remnants of Archaic formulas, found in other Severe Style action sculpture. The face, without grimace or distortion, and the body, delicately poised in a radial pattern, also present an ideal and stabilizing Classical symmetry.

Marble torso fragments of ancient copies of the Myronian *Diskobolos* (Capitoline, Uffizi, Bowood), which influenced Renaissance and later notions of strong contrapposto posing, were variously restored until modern times, serving as vehicles for virtuoso interpretations of dramatic classical stories. The ancient statue type was not identified until 1781, when a near-intact version was found on the Massimo estate, and the archaeologists G. B. *Visconti and Carlo *Fea linked it to the work described by Lucian (*Philopseudes* 18) and Quintilian (2.13.8). It remained obscure in the family's Lancellotti palace, where a great reputation and mystery grew up about it. The *Townley version of Myron's statue (*British Museum), discovered in 1791, was perversely restored with an alien head looking forward (giving it two Adam's apples); another copy (Vatican), found with it, was similarly restored, with a modern head. *Napoleon wanted to have the Lancellotti statue in the *Louvre; *Hitler succeeded in acquiring it for the Munich *Glyptotek; it is now in the Terme, Rome. A modern reconstruction of the figure in reinforced and painted plaster (Museum of Casts, Rome) combines parts of several copies, without the supporting struts and stump; it simulates the free and open effect of the bronze original.

BIBLIOGRAPHY

+E. Paribeni, *Sculture greche del V secolo, Museo Nazionale Romano* (Rome, 1953), 20–23; +S. Howard, ''Some Eighteenth-Century Restorations of Myron's 'Discobolos,' '' *JWarb* 25 (1962), 330–34; +Richter, *Sculpture and Sculptors* 161, 194, 252; Haskell—Penny, 199–202.

S. HOWARD

DODWELL, EDWARD (1767–1832). Irish artist and traveler.

A gentleman of private means, Dodwell, following graduation from Cambridge, made two trips to Greece, the first in 1801, the second in 1805–6. Returning to Rome and later marrying, Dodwell made Italy his home. In 1819 he published a two-volume account of his Greek travels, but his lasting accomplishment was as an artist. His *Views in Greece,* a series of colored engravings that appeared in 1821, brilliantly illustrated not only the country, its people and monuments but also Dodwell's ability to be faithful to architectural detail yet create scenes alive with light and color.

BIBLIOGRAPHY

''Dodwell, Edward,'' *DNB* 15 (1888), 178–79; H. Tregaskis, *Beyond the Grand Tour* (London, 1979), 57–65.

C.W.J. ELIOT

DOHAN, EDITH HAYWARD HALL (1877–1943). American archaeologist, remembered for her work on Bronze Age Greece and Etruscan Italy; one of the first women field archaeologists.

Born Edith Hayward Hall in New Haven, Connecticut, Dohan studied at Smith College and Bryn Mawr College. In 1903, she received from Bryn Mawr a fellowship to the *American School of Classical Studies, Athens, where she was soon invited to join an expedition to *Gournia under the direction of Harriet Boyd *Hawes. An additional stipend, from the Hoppin family—''to lift the restrictions on women in the study of archaeology''—allowed her to extend her stay until 1905.

Returning to Bryn Mawr, she wrote her dissertation on *The Decorative Art of Crete in the Bronze Age* and received her doctorate in 1908. She was hired at Mount Holyoke College (1908–12) and, at the same time, worked in the field for the Museum of the University of Pennsylvania at Sphoungaras (1910) and at Vrokastro (1910, 1912), where she was in full charge.

Edith Hall worked for many years at the University Museum, first as an assistant curator (1912–15) and then, after her marriage to Joseph Dohan (1915) and the birth of two children, as associate curator (from 1920) and curator of the Mediterranean section (from 1942). While engaged in publishing the collection, she turned to Italian materials in the University Museum and cataloged in a masterly way a chaotic mass of Etruscan and Faliscan artifacts from *Vulci, Pitigliano and Narce. She reconstructed twenty-nine original tomb groups in an exhibition that is recorded in her *Italic Tomb Groups in the University Museum* (1942), a pioneer study in Etruscan and Italic archaeology.

BIBLIOGRAPHY

G.M.A. Hanfmann, rev. of *Italic Tomb Groups, AJA* 48 (1944), 114–16; D. B. Thompson, "Dohan, Edith Hayward Hall," *Notable American Women, 1607–1950, A Biographical Dictionary* (Cambridge, MA, 1971), I, 496–97.

DOMENICHINO (DOMENICO ZAMPIERI; 1581–1641). Italian painter of the Baroque period, known for his classical style.

Born in Bologna, Domenichino was trained in the academy of the *Carracci family; by 1602 he had moved to Rome and joined in the work of the Bolognese school there at the Palazzo Farnese under the direction of Annibale Carracci. He was patronized by Monsignor G. B. Agucchi, who is known for articulating a theory of ideal classicism based on the study of *Raphael and antiquity that is manifest in the art of Domenichino.

Domenichino painted numerous scenes from classical myth (best known is his *Diana with Nymphs,* 1616–17, Galleria Borghese, Rome) and quoted from ancient statuary such as the *Laocoon (e.g., in the muscular Jerome in the *Temptation of St. Jerome,* 1604–5, Sant'Onofrio, Rome), the *Crouching Venus (Eve in the *Original Sin,* ca. 1621–22, Galleri Pallavicini, Rome) and the *Dead Giant* in the *Farnese family collection (the dying male martyr in the *Martyrdom of St. Agnes,* ca. 1619–22/25, Pinacoteca Nazionale, Bologna). But he is not known for the kind of archaeological reconstruction practiced by *Poussin, nor has he left study drawings of antiquities such as those of *Pietro da Cortona and others.

Domenichino's most studious work is the unusual scene of a funeral of a Roman emperor (1634–36, Prado, Madrid), commissioned by the viceroy of Naples, Manuel de Guzmán, for a series of "glorious deeds of the ancient Romans" for Philip IV of Spain. It shows a four-story funeral pyre in a setting that includes the *Pantheon and perhaps the *Theater of Marcellus (rather than the *Colosseum) and may thus be intended to show the *Campus Martius, the

customary location for such funerals. Antiquarian details of the gladiatorial contests and chariots circling the pyre suggest that the artist may have consulted
classical authors (e.g., Dio Cassius, Herodian). A little-known painting of a
Triumphal Arch of St. John the Baptist (ca. 1609, Prado, Madrid) also shows
an archaeological bent, as the structure of the monument closely resembles the
*Arch of Titus and the similar *Arch of Trajan at Beneventum, though Do-
menichino's creation is more elongated, and the Christian scenes in relief on it
are disposed in an original way.

BIBLIOGRAPHY

+R. E. Spear, *Domenichino* (New Haven, CT, 1982).

DOMUS AUREA (Golden House of Nero), Rome. Roman Imperial palace of
Nero built to replace the Domus Transitoria destroyed in the great fire of A.D.
64.

The palace is described by Tacitus (*Ann.* 15.42) as remarkable especially for
its parklands and ornamental waters, woods, lawns and vistas. Suetonius (*Nero*
31.1–2) adds that these were populated with every sort of animal, both domes-
ticated and wild. One dining pavilion was especially noteworthy, a rotunda that
rotated continuously, day and night. The baths were supplied with both seawater
and sulphur water.

The palace covered most of the *Palatine Hill, all the Velia, the end of the
Caelian and most of the Oppius, with the valleys between. The chief engineers
were Severus and Celer, who delighted in overcoming natural obstacles.

Its chief architectural features seem to have been an entrance complex leading
from the *Forum Romanum to the top of the Velia, an artificial lake in the basin
where the *Colosseum now stands and a residence on the Oppius. The Palatine
was not lavishly rebuilt at this time, and the Gardens of Maecenas may have
kept their identity, although they must have formed an annex.

The entrance complex began just beyond the Regia. Broad, arcaded walks
flanked the Sacra Via, now widened and laid out at a higher level, and branched
along the Clivus Palatinus. Behind these lay porticus buildings, their roofs supported on forests of uniform arcading that lent themselves to subdivision and
multiple use. At the top of the Velia stood the bronze colossus of Nero, 120
feet high, in a *vestibulum* that probably took the form of a colonnaded court.
Below, in the bowl of the Colosseum, was the great *stagnum,* its shores surrounded by buildings to the likeness of a city (Suetonius, *Nero* 31.2), fed probably by cascades from a nymphaeum built along the northeast flank of the
platform of the temple of the Deified Claudius. The residence on the Oppius
was an archetypal portico villa in at least two stories, the lower story, in large
part, a work of terracing along the brow of the hill now known to have been
essentially symmetrical, the central member a domed octagon with radiating
dependencies that was flanked by reentrant trapezoidal courts, probably, in turn,
flanked by large rectangular peristyles surrounded by banks of interconnecting
rooms. The upper story stepped back somewhat from this and extended over

Ceiling paintings from the *Domus Aurea*, Rome, watercolor copy, Codex Escurialensis, before 1508, Madrid, Escorial. (Deutsches Archäologisches Institut, Rome. Inst. Neg. 1935.764.)

the crown of the hill. The parts overlying the lower story show remarkable independence of design from it, with colonnaded fronts and colonnaded courts in the interior. At the time of Nero's death the palace had not been completed.

The *stagnum* was destroyed by Vespasian to make way for the Colosseum; he also then completed the temple of the Deified Claudius. Part of the Oppius was taken by Titus for his public baths, and the northeast part of the entrance complex along the Sacra Via was rebuilt by Domitian as warehouses (the Horrea Piperataria). In A.D. 104 a fire destroyed much of the Oppius complex, and Trajan took the opportunity to rebuild this as a vast bath complex, leveling and burying what was left of Nero's palace there in the terracing for this. Hadrian in 121 completed the destruction by moving the colossus to a place near the Amphitheatrum Flavium to make way for the temple of Venus and Roma.

The ruins were discovered in the Early Renaissance, when the painted decorations of the ceilings excited much interest, were copied and gave rise to the "grotesque style" of decoration at the end of the fifteenth century (*grottesche). First descents into the buried chambers seem to have been made about 1480, at which time the complex was called the "Terme di Tito" and "Palazzo di Tito." First excavations were carried out beginning in 1774 by L. Mirri, who unearthed sixteen rooms and published engravings and descriptions of these in *Le Antiche camere delle Terme di Tito e le loro pitture* (Rome, 1776). In 1811–14 the architect De Romanis excavated most of the west wing and produced a useful and surprisingly accurate plan of the Oppius complex. Excavation has continued intermittently to the present. Since the palace was deliberately destroyed in antiquity, little in the way of sculpture or ornament that could be salvaged has survived, and the various works of art that have been assigned to it in the past, such as the *Laocoon* group, can be reassigned with confidence to the *Baths of Trajan.

BIBLIOGRAPHY

F. Weege, "Das goldene Haus des Nero," *JdI* 28 (1913), 127–244. N. Dacos, *La Découverte de la Domus Aurea et la formation des grotesques à la renaissance* (London, 1969); L. Fabbrini, "Domus Aurea: il piano superiore del quartiere orientale," *MemPontAcc* 14 (1982), 5–24; A. M. Colini, "Considerazioni su la Velia da Nerone in poi," and L. Fabbrini, "Domus Aurea: una nuova lettura planimetrica del palazzo sul colle Oppio," *Città e architettura nella Roma imperiale, Analecta Romana* suppl. 10 (Odense, 1983), 129–45, 169–85.

L. RICHARDSON, JR

DONATELLO (DONATO DI NICCOLÒ DA BETTO BARDI; 1386–1464).

Early Renaissance Florentine sculptor whose fame rests securely on innovative works in bronze, stone and wood.

Donatello's experimentation with form, interpretation and technology has consistently evoked a response of "first" from the critics, with "rival of nature" as a parallel theme. From the Renaissance forward, all writers on Donatello give at least a perfunctory nod to his awareness of classical antiquity. Although this specific interest is a given intellectual ingredient of the Early Renaissance, the effect of ancient Rome on Donatello's work is unusually profound and is supported by reports that he studied ancient remains.

His hollow cast bronzes are among the first since Roman times to demonstrate success with the technique on a large scale. Holes and crude mending in the bronze skin of the *David* (Museo Nazionale, Florence) and failure in casting an arm of the *Baptist* for Siena Cathedral bear witness to his experimentation with the process. As assistant in the goldsmith shop of Lorenzo *Ghiberti, he learned contemporary techniques of working with metal relief, gilding and casting large bronzes, but his own examination of the surviving hollow-cast bronzes of antiquity spurred his efforts to make that process viable once more.

Because so many of his sculptures incorporate elements absorbed from a study of the past, illustration of types of borrowings is the most direct method of demonstrating Donatello's debt to the antique world. Most obvious is his use of decorative detail, as in the Roman helmet on the severed head of Goliath at the feet of the bronze *David*. A small relief "triumph" based on an antique cameo enlivens the helmet, while the boy and the head both rest on a Roman victor's wreath. The marble *St. George* (Museo Nazionale, Florence) wears Roman armor while the enthroned Virgin from the high altar of the Santo in Padua wears a classical mural crown.

A different kind of appropriation is the conscious use of an ancient monument type in a related modern context, as in the bronze horse and rider honoring Erasmo da Narni, Il Gattamelata, in Padua. The ancient Romans honored military heroes by erecting equestrian monuments to their lasting fame. Two such large bronze monuments were to be seen in fifteenth century Italian cities, the **Regisole* in Pavia and the **Marcus Aurelius* at the Lateran in Rome. The artist acknowledges its ancient purpose by choosing an equestrian sculpture to perpetuate the fame of an individual who led his soldiers in the successful defense of Venice. He also refers to ancient types when the subject is drawn from biblical antiquity, as illustrated by the general appropriation of dress and pose from Etruscan and Roman orator statues for the marble prophet figures on the campanile of Florence cathedral.

The only straightforward representation of ancient subjects in the sculptor's extant work occurs in decorative figural and architectural detail. There is no agreement about the meaning of the "*Atys-Amorino*" (Museo Nazionale, Florence). The chubby, smiling child has winged feet and a small tail but wears a contemporary Tuscan vintner's belt and protective leggings. A convincing interpretation of the bronze *David* must eventually incorporate the suggestion that the artist made conscious reference to the antique "nude idol" raised on a pedestal familiar from contemporary paintings. The reconstruction of a lost Donatello sculpture representing *Dovizia (Abundance)* or the Roman civic virtue of *Alimenta* comes closest to illustrating the artist's literal repetition of an antique form to express an ancient meaning. Made for the Commune of Florence, it was, like its ancient predecessor, freestanding and larger than lifesize and stood on an ancient column in the old market square in Florence.

Roman and, earlier, Greek sculptors had studied the human body and represented it as a reflection of the natural world, and the ancient sculptures available to interested Renaissance thinkers and artists demonstrated idealization as well as intense naturalism. The explicit surface description of emaciated limbs and hallucinatory facial expression so overpowering in the polychromed wood *Baptist* for the Frari church in Venice can be seen as a conscious reflection of Hellenistic sculpture in form and in psychological intent, while the abstract beauty of *Angel and Annunciate* in the Cavalcanti Tabernacle for Santa Croce in Florence turns to the idealized solutions of classical sculpture and their embodiment of divine perfection.

BIBLIOGRAPHY
+H. W. Janson, *The Sculpture of Donatello* (Princeton, NJ, 1957); Idem, "Donatello and the Antique," *Donatello e il suo tempo, Atti dell'VIII Convegno Internazionale* (Milan, 1968), 61–76; M. Greenhalgh, *Donatello and His Sources* (London, 1982); D. Wilkins, "Donatello's Lost *Dovizia* for the *Mercato Vecchia:* Wealth and Charity as Florentine Civic Virtues," *ArtB* 65 (1983), 401–23; B. Bennet—D. Wilkins, *Donatello* (Mt. Kisco, NY, 1984).

PATRICIA A. ROSE

DONDI, GIOVANNI "DELL' OROLOGIO" (d. 1384). Italian humanist and physician.

A Paduan, Dondi was a companion of *Petrarch until the latter's death in 1374 and was accustomed to humanist studies. With Domenico Bandini, he inaugurated a long line of humanist physicians in Italy. He composed verse in Latin and Italian and built a remarkable library of classical manuscripts, and his transcriptions preserved much of the Latin poetry of early humanists of Padua, as well as *Boccaccio's biography of Petrarch.

His letters reveal a fascination with ancient art and architecture that culminated with his journey to Rome in 1375. His accounts of that journey show an archaeologist's instinct to note down ancient monuments at Rimini, Cagli and Spello; in Rome he took copious notes on the monuments, which he later edited and copied into a volume in his library. This work is not a random study of remarkable monuments nor the itinerary of an antiquarian, but the interests and instinct of the antiquarian are clearly present, and the work concentrates on the monuments of the pagan rather than the Christian city. Furthermore, Dondi, whose library contained one of the few copies of Vitruvius in private hands at that time, showed his knowledge of it by taking measurements of ancient buildings in addition to describing them in his notes. While the measurements are frequently inaccurate, the fact of his taking them at all remains significant and may mark the beginning of detailed archaeological inquiry among the Italian humanists. His knowledge of Vitruvius also led Dondi to speculate on the structure and engineering of ancient buildings; he also copied inscriptions throughout the city. Among the monuments he measured and studied were the *Pantheon, the *Column of Trajan, the obelisk at St. Peter's, (*Obelisks), the *Colosseum and the *Arch of Constantine and *Arch of Severus. After Dondi, antiquarians of the fifteenth century in Italy frequently followed his methods of measuring and of describing the details of architecture. He was also instrumental in promoting knowledge of Vitruvius among later humanists. He died at Padua in 1384.

BIBLIOGRAPHY
Valentini—Zucchetti, IV, 65–73; V. Bellemo, *Jacopo e Giovanni de Dondi dell' Orologio* (Chioggia, 1894); L. Ciapponi, "Il 'De Architectura' di Vitruvio nel primo umanesimo," *Italia Medioevale e Umanistica* 3 (1960), 59–99; Weiss, *RDCA,* 49–53.

JAMES C. ANDERSON, JR.

DÖRPFELD (DOERPFELD), WILHELM (1853-1940). German architect and archaeologist.

After studying architecture at the Berlin Bauakademie (1873–76), Dörpfeld was sent by his teacher and future father-in-law, *Adler, to the excavation at *Olympia in 1877. Assuming responsibility for the technical side (1878), he continued to work at Olympia till 1881, when *Schliemann visited the site and offered to employ his services. Though he accepted the post of architect at the *German Archaeological Institute, Athens (1882–85), later becoming second secretary (1886–87) and finally director (1887–1912), his appointment permitted other employment. Thus, he worked for the Greeks at *Epidauros, *Eleusis and on the *Akropolis, Athens, for Schliemann at *Troy (1882, 1890), *Tiryns (1884–85) and *Orchomenos (1886) and for Schliemann's widow at Troy (1893–94).

Later his interest focused on Olympia; the topography of Athens, particularly the buildings of the Agora and Akropolis and the *Theater of Dionysos; Leukas, which he held to be Homer's Ithaca; and *Pergamon. His excavations in Leukas, funded, like those in Corfu (*Korkyra), by Kaiser Wilhelm II, incurred the disapproval of *Wilamowitz and the Berlin German Archaeological Institute. After his retirement his intolerance of views other than his own alienated younger scholars. His later books, particularly *Alt-Ithaka* (Munich, 1927) and *Alt-Olympia* (Berlin, 1935), reflect his tenacious adherence to discredited theories and his isolation from the scholarly mainstream. His contributions to the Olympia excavation report and to Schliemann's *Tiryns* and *Troja,* his *Das Griechische Theater* (Athens, 1895) and, above all, *Troja und Ilion* (Athens, 1902) have proved to be of more lasting value.

Dörpfeld's crucial role in bringing the insights of an architectural training to bear on archaeological problems is beyond dispute. He applied the more sophisticated methods developed at Olympia to Schliemann's excavations, bringing sense to the stratigraphy at Troy and discovering the megaron at *Tiryns. He also identified Troy VI rather than Troy II as the Homeric level. These were signal achievements. They earned him the sobriquets of "illuminator of Troy" (*Lichtbringer nach Troja*) and "Schliemann's finest find" (*Schliemann's schönste Fund*). His archaeological vision, however, was narrow. First and foremost an architect, he never fully appreciated the importance of pottery for chronology. Like Schliemann, as Percy *Gardner observed in 1891, Dörpfeld was lacking in "critical sobriety of judgment," though this was often disguised by the apparently objective tone of his lucid prose. Stubborn and romantic to the last, he died in Leukas, largely ignored by contemporary scholarship.

BIBLIOGRAPHY

AA 65–66 (1950–51), 381ff., with bib.; +P. Goessler, *Wilhelm Dörpfeld* (Stuttgart, 1951); A. v. Gerkan, *Gnomon* 24 (1952), 166–68; G. v. Lücken, "Dörpfeld," *NDB* 4 (1959), 35–36; H. Döhl, *Heinrich Schliemann: Mythos und Ärgernis* (Munich, 1981), 55–61; P. Gardner, *Macmillan's Magazine* 63 (April 1891), 479.

                                                            DAVID A. TRAILL

DOSIO (DOSIUS), GIOVANNI ANTONIO (1533–ca. 1610). Italian architect and sculptor; known for his rich production of drawings after antiquities.

A native of San Gimignano, Dosio was in Rome by ca. 1548. Minor commissions included the repair of marble sculptures at the *Vatican Belvedere, where Pirro *Ligorio was building the Casino of Pius IV (1559–65). He lived in an environment created by a feverishly active group of antiquarians, including *Panvinio, *Pighius, *Smetius, *Boissard, *Agustín. During this period the first fragments of the marble plan of Rome were discovered (1562; *Forma Urbis Romae), and Dosio was evidently present for the find. He made a number of drawings of key fragments, now in the Vatican (Cod. Vat. Lat. 3439, fol. 13–23).

At the same time Dosio was creating an archive of antiquities of Rome (1560–65). The leaves of the sketchbook, known conventionally as the "Libro delle antichità," are now divided in collections in Berlin (Codex Berolenensis) and in the *Uffizi; included are drawings of sarcophagi and other relief sculptures and views of Rome spotlighting key monuments (*Arch of Constantine, *Arch of Septimius Severus, *Baths of Diocletian, *Forum Romanum, markets of Trajan, forum of Nerva, *Septizodium, *Temple of Fortuna Virilis). For his friend Bernardo Gamucci, Dosio created a series of picturesque views of Rome, showing ancient monuments embedded in the contemporary fabric of Rome, to be engraved and published in Gamucci's *I Libri quattro dell'antichità,* published at Venice in 1565. The engravings were picked up and used in later editions of guides to Rome (by *Fulvio, *Marliani and others), without citing, however, the name of the artist.

Dosio was receiving commissions for sculpture for funerary monuments in churches of Rome (e.g., for Annibal *Caro, d. 1566, at S. Lorenzo in Damaso). At the same time he was becoming involved in other publishing schemes. In 1569, G. B. de' *Cavalieri published *Le Antichità di Roma,* dedicated to Grand Duke Cosimo I (*Medici family), and he filled the work with engravings based on drawings by Dosio, some from his early sketchbooks, others from the Gamucci group and still others made specifically for the publication. The new drawings depict the arch of Janus, the *Column of Marcus, the *Pantheon, the *Temple of Castor, the *Temple of Vesta and the *Tomb of Caecilia Metella. These drawings are praised for a slightly poetic touch that make them very appealing (not preserved by Cavalieri), combined with an archaeological accuracy.

Dosio has also left a series of finely detailed architectural studies of individual buildings (many in the Uffizi), made ca. 1574 for a treatise on architecture that he never finished. These show an objectivity and a conscientious attempt to show what parts of the building existed and what parts were reconstructed. Dosio was again involved in minor architectural and sculptural commissions in Rome and in Florence, until his departure ca. 1589 for Naples, where he became an engineer of the royal court. He remained mostly in Naples for the final twenty years of his life.

BIBLIOGRAPHY
+C. Hülsen, *Das Skizzenbuch des Giovannantonio Dosio im Staatlichen Kupferstich-kabinett zu Berlin* (Berlin, 1933); F. Borsi et al., eds., +*Roma antica e i disegni di architettura agli Uffizi di Giovanni Antonio Dosio* (Rome, 1976); Bober—Rubinstein, esp. 456–57.

DOSSENA, ALCEO (1878–1937). Italian sculptor, the "King of Forgers," who set a norm in modern practice, Dossena began his career making decorative masonry and marble restorations at or near Cremona.

In Rome, from 1913 to 1928, Dossena reportedly made the sundry notorious counterfeit pastiche sculptures (or improvisatory creations, in his view) then sold to various museums and collectors in Europe and the United States through dealers whom he afterward exposed when he was impoverished by meager payments and the expenses of his wife's illness. Dossena worked in Late Gothic and Early Renaissance styles as well as in his *antico* manner, simulating the appearance of Greek Archaic *kore* figures better known to archaeologists. He produced works in stone, terracotta, wood and metal and developed sophisticated "ancient patinas" by distressing the surfaces with breaks, abrasions, chemicals, bakings and general sullying. In comparison with accomplished predecessors like the pseudo-Renaissance sculptor Giovanni Bastianini (1830–68) and better-informed and equipped recent technicians, Dossena produced crude and unconvincing fakes whose inflated reputations seem more attributable to journalistic notoriety than to merit. After Dossena's death, his son, under the name Lusetti, published an apologia for his father's work, illustrating many of the sculptures.

BIBLIOGRAPHY
W. Lusetti, *Alceo Dossena scultore* (Rome, 1955); F. Arnau, *The Art of the Faker,* tr. J. M. Brownjohn (Boston, 1961), 249–67; S. Howard, "A Dossenesque 'Double Herm' in California," *California Studies in Classical Antiquity* 4 (1971), 182–98.

S. HOWARD

DROYSEN, JOHANN GUSTAV (1808–84). German historian of classical and early modern times.

Droysen, the son of an army chaplain, was born in Pomerania (from 1815, part of Prussia). At the university of Berlin he encountered the two scholars who most profoundly influenced his development: August *Böckh in classical philology and G.W.F. Hegel in the philosophy of history. After publishing translations of Aischylos and Aristophanes, he issued his history of Alexander the Great (*Geschichte Alexanders des Grossen,* 1833). Though this work did not use the results of excavations, it catapulted Droysen into the first rank of historians and was significant in several ways. First, it broke with the classical tradition that closed the study of Greek history with the decline of Athens in the age of Demosthenes (d. 322 B.C.). Droysen saw the victory of Macedon over the Greek city-states not as the end but as the beginning of a mighty epoch: the conquest of the Oriental world by Hellenic culture and the preparation for the coming of Christianity. Second, the influence of Hegel is visible in Droysen's conception of irresistible forces fulfilling themselves in political events: for him, Alexander was the tool of history. Third, Droysen expressed that fascination with power and conquest that often recurs in German historians, especially in historians of Alexander. He later expanded his work into a three-volume *Geschichte des Hellenismus,* in which he included the successors of Alexander (1877–78; new edition, 1952–53). He is thus the discoverer of the "Hellenistic Age" (ca. 323–30 B.C.). (The universally used name actually rests on a misunderstanding of *Hellenistai,* "speakers of Greek," in the New Testament.) The term and concept have been incorporated into art history and archaeology and remain of fundamental importance today.

As professor of history in Kiel (1840–51), he was active in politics, supporting the movement for Prussian supremacy. He returned to Berlin as professor in 1859 and devoted himself to a monumental *Geschichte der preussischen Politik* (14 volumes, 1855–86). Just as Philip and Alexander fulfilled their historical mission, so, for Droysen, did the statesmen who shaped Prussian policy in a single line of development: an interpretation consistent with his Hegelian conviction that history is something beyond facts and sources, a process with ethical meaning and direction.

BIBLIOGRAPHY

M. Duncker, *Johann Gustav Droysen, ein Nachruf* (Berlin, 1885); O. Hintze, "Droysen," *Allgemeine deutsche Biographie* 48 (1903), 82–114; Gustav Droysen, *Johann Gustav Droysen,* pt. 1 (Leipzig, 1910).

MORTIMER CHAMBERS

DU BELLAY, JEAN. See BELLAY, JEAN DU.

DUCATI, PERICLE (1880–1944). Italian archaeologist and art historian.

After studies under G. Carducci and E. *Brizio (in Bologna), E. Löwy, L. *Pigorini and R. *Lanciani (in Rome) and a brief appointment (1909) as Ispettore ai Musei e Scavi, Ducati held chairs of classical archaeology in Catania (1912), in Turin and finally (1920 onward) in his native *Bologna, combining his duties there with the direction, rearrangement and cataloging of the Museo Civico. He wrote extensively for the educated public as well as for students and scholars on classical art and Etrusco-Italic matters, where he made a decisive contribution to modern views. Tragically, this retiring and inoffensive scholar was killed by political adversaries.

BIBLIOGRAPHY

P. Ducati, *L'Arte classica* (Turin, 1920); Idem, *Storia dell'arte etrusca* (Florence, 1927); Idem, *Pontische Vasen* (Berlin, 1932); G. Q. Giglioli, "Commemorazione del Socio P. Ducati," *RendPontAcc* 27 (1951–52), 111–35, with bib.

F. R. SERRA RIDGWAY

DUHN, FRIEDRICH CARL VON (1851–1930). German archaeologist, specialist in Roman and Italic archaeology.

Born in Lübeck, an eminent judge's son (his father had heard K. O. *Müller), named after his godfather, F. K. von Savigny, he studied at Bonn under Bücheler, *Kekulé and Usener. Von Duhn traveled widely in Italy, *Sicily and Greece, publishing in 1879 *Über einige Basreliefs,* a work crucial for the reconstruction of the *Ara Pacis Augustae. It made his reputation overnight. After one semester at Göttingen, he became professor of archaeology (1880) at Heidelberg, where he remained. *Pompeii: eine hellenistische Stadt in Italien* appeared in 1906; *Italische Gräberkunde,* two volumes, in 1924–39. He worked particularly in Italic prehistory.

A man of aristocratic savoir faire, von Duhn was loved by the Italians, and Farnell called him "one of the very few Germans I have ever known who was in every sense a gentleman." R. Pagenstecher, C. Schuchhardt, B. Schweitzer, H. Winnefeld, O. Weinreich and R. Zahn were among his students.

BIBLIOGRAPHY

L. R. Farnell, *An Oxonian Looks Back* (London, 1934), 278; D. von Velsen, *Im Alter die Fulle: Erinnerungen* (Tübingen, 1956); O.-W. von Vacano, "von Duhn," *NDB* 4 (1959), 180; T. Hölscher, in *Archäologenbildnisse,* 100–101.

WILLIAM M. CALDER III

DU JON. See JUNIUS, FRANCISCUS, THE YOUNGER.

DUMAS PÈRE, ALEXANDRE (1802–70). French novelist and dramatist.

Abandoning a proposed Mediterranean tour in 1860, Dumas joined Garibaldi's expedition in Palermo and accompanied it to Naples. For his services as a tireless publicist and as purchaser of arms for the revolution, Dumas was appointed by Garibaldi honorary director of excavations in *Pompeii (15 September 1860) without displacing the titular director, Domenico Spinelli, Principe di San Giorgio. Dumas proposed to continue the excavations from the baths and temple of Isis to the amphitheater, to restore houses and to charge an admission fee. His post ended with the Piedmontese takeover and the appointment of Giuseppe *Fiorelli as inspector (7 December).

BIBLIOGRAPHY

R. T. Ridley, "Dumas père, Director of Excavations," *Pompeii Herculaneum Stabiae* 1 (1983), 259–88.

R. T. RIDLEY

DUNBABIN, THOMAS JAMES (1911–55). Anglo-Australian archaeologist.

Fellow of All Souls College from 1937 and S. *Casson's successor as reader in classical archaeology at Oxford from 1945, Dunbabin proceeded from Sydney via Oxford and Magna Graecia to Athens, where he was appointed assistant director of the *British School in 1936 and assumed practical responsibility for the publication of the *Perachora* material excavated by H. Payne: 1 (1940) and 2 (1962). In this, he drew on earlier (1933 onward) acquaintance with south

Italy and *Sicily, the direct result of which was held back until 1948: *The Western Greeks,* a pioneer synthesis in which Dunbabin achieved the union of historical and archaeological method advocated by his Oxford teacher A. Blakeway. At the time of his death, Dunbabin was planning a corresponding account of the relationship between Greece and the Near East in the Geometric and Archaic periods; the lectures out of which it would have grown were published posthumously in 1957.

BIBLIOGRAPHY

M. R[obertson], "Thomas James Dunbabin," *BSA Annual Report 1954–55,* 19–20; T. J. Dunbabin, *The Greeks and Their Eastern Neighbours* (London, 1957; repr. Westport, CT, 1979; ed. J. Boardman, with bibl.).

DAVID RIDGWAY

DU PÉRAC, ÉTIENNE (1525/35–1604). French engraver and architect.

Du Pérac was born in Paris (not Bordeaux, as sometimes stated). Nothing seems to be known of him before his appearance in Rome ca. 1559. He was appointed papal architect in 1572. He also worked in the studio of the noted engraver *Lafréry and contributed to the *Speculum romanae magnificentiae.*

Du Pérac published a "bird's-eye view" plan of Rome in 1573 and the *Urbis Romae sciographia* (1574; sheets 1.5m × 1m), showing restorations of the ancient monuments and dedicated to Charles IX of France. In the preface he stated that he had been studying the monuments of Rome for fifteen years and that he had been helped by Alessandro Farnese (*Farnese family).

His best-known work, *Vestigi dell'antichità di Roma,* appeared in 1575, published by Laurent de la Vacherie and dedicated to Giacomo Buoncompagni, commander in chief of the papal army. This consists of thirty-nine plates, beginning with the *Forum Romanum and *Palatine, proceeding to the *Baths of Caracalla, the Aventine Hill, the *Porta Maggiore, the Esquiline, Viminal and Quirinal hills, the *Campus Martius and moving back around to Tiber Island and concluding with the Circus of Maxentius on the *Via Appia. The plates were later pirated by Sadeler of Prague and copied by Canaletto.

Another work of 1575 was the *Illustration des fragments antiques.* In 1577, Du Pérac published another bird's-eye view of Rome, dedicated to Henry III of France (published by Ehrle). Thomas *Ashby attributed to Du Pérac a fine manuscript entitled *Disegni de le ruine di . . . Roma e come anticamente erano,* discovered in the library of C.W.D. Perrins (Malvern, England), featuring part of a text and plates of sites in Rome in their contemporary condition and how they might have appeared in antiquity. The handsome, unpublished work was dated by Ashby to 1581 but has recently been dated earlier by Wittkower (finished by ca. 1575).

Du Pérac returned to France in 1581 or 1582 and was appointed architect to the Duc d'Aumale, for whom he designed the gardens of Anet, and then in 1595 he became royal architect, working on the castle of Saint-Germain, doing paintings in the bathroom and gardens of Fontainebleau and completing the Pavillon Bullant at the Tuileries.

Du Pérac died in Paris in 1604.

BIBLIOGRAPHY

F. Ehrle, *Roma prima di Sisto V, La Pianta di Roma du Pérac—Lafréry del 1577* (Rome, 1908); T. Ashby, "Le diverse edizioni dei *Vestigi dell'antichità di Roma,*" *Bibliofilia* 16 (1915), 401–21; T. Ashby, *Topographical Study in Rome in 1581, A Series of Views by E. Du Pérac* (London, 1916); R. Wittkower, *Le Antiche rovine di Roma nei disegni di Du Pérac* (Milan, 1990).

R. T. RIDLEY

DURA-EUROPOS. Hellenistic-Oriental city in eastern Syria.

Founded and settled by Macedonian Greeks ca. 300 B.C. on the eastern edge of the Syrian desert, overlooking the Middle Euphrates, this walled city was important as a trading post and military station. It came under Parthian rule ca. 113 B.C., was conquered by L. Verus (A.D. 164/5) and remained a Roman stronghold until stormed and depopulated by the Persians (A.D. 256). The two ancient references by Isidorus of Charax (*Parthian Stations,* first century A.C.) and in the Ka'bah of Zoroaster inscription of Shapur I (third century A.C.) left the deserted ruin unidentified, known only by the modern name of Salihiyeh. The site was noticed by nineteenth-century travelers, but Friedrich Sarre and Ernst Herzfeld first (1912) recorded its Hellenistic character. Bivouacking British troops accidentally found some wall paintings (1920), which were then uncovered by James Henry Breasted, who discovered the ancient name of the city. Franz *Cumont began excavations for the French Academy (1922–23), which were followed by ten campaigns (1928–37) by Yale University, under the supervision of Michael *Rostovtzeff and led by the successive field directors Maurice Pillet, Clark Hopkins and Frank *Brown.

The city is protected by a circuit wall and is laid out on a gridiron plan of residential blocks with a central agora and government quarters on the citadel. The city served the major caravan routes from the Mediterranean to the East and southward to India, additionally garrisoning Parthian and Roman troops who policed the frontier. Its mixed population of Syrians, Macedonians, Parthians and Romans has left the most complete record of ancient daily life known from this 600-year period in western Asia. A rich variety of parchments, papyri, and graffiti documents its legal and commercial activities. Temples with paintings and sculpture are dedicated to deities of the Semites (Azzanathkona, Atargatis, Iarhibol, Bel, Hadad), Iranians (Mithra) and Graeco-Romans (Zeus, Jupiter, Artemis); particularly outstanding are a Christian baptistery with wall paintings and a synagogue covered with a brilliant cycle of murals. Dura's artworks and other archaeological finds are divided between the Damascus Museum and Yale University Art Gallery.

BIBLIOGRAPHY

P.V.C. Baur—M. I. Rostovtzeff—A. R. Bellinger et al., eds., *The Excavations at Dura-Europos, Preliminary Reports* (New Haven, CT, 1929–52); *The Excavations at Dura-*

Synagogue of Dura-Europos, west wall *in situ* before removal to the Damascus National Museum, 1934. In foreground (*l. to r.*): Comte Du Mesnil du Buisson; Hans Lietzmann, M. I. Rostovtzeff, Sophie Rostovtzeff, Frank Brown; in middle ground: Henry Pearson with Mary Sue Hopkins. (Photo: B. Goldman.)

Europos, Final Reports (New Haven, CT, 1943–77); A. Perkins, *The Art of Dura-Europos* (Oxford, 1973); C. Hopkins, *The Discovery of Dura-Europos* (New Haven, CT, 1979).

                                                           BERNARD GOLDMAN

DÜRER, ALBRECHT (1471–1526). German High Renaissance artist who won international recognition for his woodcuts, engravings and paintings.

Godson of Nuremberg's leading publisher and close friend of the scholar Willibald *Pirckheimer, Dürer belonged to his native city's humanist circles. A desire to study in Italy was fostered by the appeal of ancient art that he knew through engravings reflecting Italian fascination with antiquity and by the knowledge of ancient literature that he knew through his humanist friends. Tantalizing hints of a method for achieving perfection in art were given to him by an Italian artist working in Wittenberg, and during two sojourns in Venice he sought to uncover the "secrets." His search led him to fifteenth-century Italian methods for determining perfect human proportions and to the canon of Vitruvius, Roman architect of the first century B.C. and author of the only treatise on art to survive from the ancient world. He also sought theoretical explanations of the workshop formula for single-point perspective, a formula patterned after Euclid's proof for the tenth theorem. In treatises completed during the last years of his life, geometry, mathematical theory and a canon of perfect proportions still occupied his thoughts.

Antiquity is seen most clearly in his drawings and engravings. He drew after late fifteenth-century Italian engravings by tracing the contours and then paraphrasing the interior hatching with curling pen strokes. From Roman sculpture he learned the look of nude figures, sometimes in violent action, and from Roman relief he learned the look of restricted depth; all are seen in his copy of the right half of *Mantegna's *Battle of the Sea Gods* (Albertina, Vienna). Dürer mastered the new forms while modifying them in his own vigorous manner. A study sheet from his first Venetian stay (Albertina, Vienna) includes a clothed *Apollo* adapted from an *Eros* figure attributed to Lysippos (Roman copy in Capitoline Museum, Rome) and a lively *Rape of Europa* with kneeling female nude taken from Roman variations on the Hellenistic *Crouching Venus.* Numerous drawings from the following years return to themes of ancient myth with an ever surer and freer hand.

Engravings intended for learned customers incorporate his study of ancient art and literature. In the *Sea Monster* (B. 71), the figure of Syme modifies a nude in the earlier Mantegna *Battle of the Sea Gods,* while the whole scene recreates the myth of her abduction by Glaucus based on an ancient painting described by Philostratos, a description Dürer knew from Pirckheimer. The model for a nude woman abducted by a sea creature has been identified in a Roman cameo picturing a *Triton and Nereid* (*Museo Nazionale, Naples). Other motifs such as a *Centaur Suckling Her Young* in a drawing formerly at Veste

Coburg may also be direct reflections of antique gems and cameos collected or copied by his humanist friends.

Renaissance portraiture is based on Roman prototypes, and Dürer created six engraved portraits consciously modeled on ancient Roman funerary monuments. The bust-length portrait placed behind a low stone parapet carved with Latin inscriptions had been used a century earlier by Flemish artists, but in a handful of Venetian portraits by Giorgione and others painted between 1504 and 1515, the Roman character of the image was made more explicit. Dürer was in Venice for part of this time, and the engravings he made some years later are even closer to ancient reliefs, including the look of stone. The careful Roman lettering of the inscriptions, the subject of Book III of his treatise on measurement, includes several archaeologically correct conventions.

Some engravings reflect Roman models in the context of Christian morality, such as Venus in the dream of the slothful professor (B. 76) or *Adam and Eve* in the biblical temptation (B. 1). More than a mere transposition of the *Belvedere *Apollo* into Adam and a transformation of the *Knidian *Aphrodite* into Eve, the two biblical figures reveal the divine beauty and perfection they enjoyed before the Fall through their analogy with the two ancient divinities having perfect beauty.

In addition to drawings and engravings, specific references to classical antiquity are found in the woodcut with Pausanias's story of Hercules killing Molione's Siamese twin sons (B. 127); in the woodcut *Triumphal Arch* for Maximilian I, with its antique figural and architectural detail, including a Renaissance version of ancient hieroglyphics; and in the painting on linen of *Hercules Killing the Stymphalean Birds* (Germanische Nationalsmuseum, Nuremberg).

BIBLIOGRAPHY

+A. Dürer, *Underweysung der Messung* (Nuremberg, 1525) and *Vier Bücher von Menschlicher Proportion* (Nuremberg, 1528); E. Panofsky, *The Life and Art of Albrecht Durer*, 2nd rev. ed. (Princeton, NJ, 1945); +E. Simon, "Das Werk: Die Rezeption der Antike," *Albrecht Dürer 1471–1971*, catalog of exhibition, Germanischen Nationalsmuseum, Nuremberg (Munich, 1971); C. Mesenzeva, "Zum Problem: Dürer und die Antike," *ZfK* 46, no. 2 (1983), 187–201.

PATRICIA A. ROSE

DYING TRUMPETER (DYING GAUL; DYING GLADIATOR; MYRMILLO).

Lifesize statue made of Asiatic marble (length of plinth, 1.865m), of a nude, dying warrior; the torque around his neck and the rough texture of the hair on the head have led to the now universal conclusion that the figure represents a Gaul.

The curved musical instrument (*tuba*) on the plinth suggests a connection with the passage in Pliny (*NH* 34.88) referring to a bronze sculpture of a *Trumpeter* by Epigonos. This artist worked for the Attalid kings of *Pergamon, who commissioned various monuments with representations of Gauls, at some time after the first victories of Attalos I over the barbarians (i.e., after 233 B.C.). The piece is often thought to be a copy of a lost bronze original of the late third or early second century B.C. It has some minor restorations made by I. Buzzi soon after its discovery, including a portion of the trumpet.

The place and date of discovery of the *Trumpeter* are unknown. It is first mentioned in the inventory of the *Ludovisi family collections in 1623 as a *Dying Gladiator*. Some have conjectured that this statue and the *Ludovisi *Gaul Killing Himself and His Wife* were discovered together and that the site was the *Gardens of Sallust, occupying the extensive zone on the outskirts of Rome stretching between the Porta Salaria and the Porta Pinciana, where Cardinal Ludovico Ludovisi bought up a series of *vigne* in 1621–23. The sculpture was displayed in the Palazzo Grande of the Villa Ludovisi, until it was seized by Don Livio Odescalchi in payment of a debt. (He took possession in 1696.) Returned briefly to the Ludovisi in 1715/16, the *"Gladiator"* was acquired by Pope Clement XII, ca. 1737, for the *Capitoline Museums. It was among the war spoils taken by *Napoleon under the Treaty of Tolentino and was in Paris from 1798 to 1816. It was then returned to Rome and restored to display in the Capitoline.

The *Dying Trumpeter,* who, like the Ludovisi *Gaul,* suffers a noble and moving death, has enjoyed an enduring popularity. For two centuries he was usually identified as a gladiator (sometimes with the Latin term *Myrmillo,* indicating a certain kind of gladiator). *Winckelmann concocted a theory, largely ignored, that he was a dying herald (various Greek candidates were proposed), while E. Q. *Visconti sensibly noted that the ethnic qualities of the figure suggested that the was a Gaul or German who died heroically; he further suggested that the statue could have adorned a monument with the Ludovisi *Gaul,* perhaps a monument erected for Julius Caesar or Germanicus.

By the end of the nineteenth century H. *Brunn had convincingly argued that these were examples of the art of Pergamon. Excavations at the site soon produced bases, both round and rectangular, upon which the dedications may have rested. In addition, the evidence for a monument to the Attalids at Athens has been adduced (Pausanias 1.25.2), and numerous other statues have been candidates for these monuments commemorating victories over the Gauls. (Cf. *Grimani family.)

The *Trumpeter* was much copied (for the king of Spain, the *French Academy, the king of France and many others) and was celebrated in *Byron's *Childe Harold* as a tragic Dacian gladiator. Unlike so many of the famous antiquities of the Renaissance and later, it has suffered no loss of prestige and, if anything, has excited even more interest among scholars who have continued to debate its original usage in antiquity. F. Coarelli has recently theorized that the Capitoline *Trumpeter* and the Ludovisi *Gaul* are copies made at Pergamon for a Roman patron to commemorate Caesar's triumph over Gaul (46–44 B.C.), a suggestion approved by B. Palma. B. Ridgway, in a recent review of the Attalid problem, has stressed the need to recognize a Roman repertory of Gallic sculpture, though she regards the *Trumpeter* as the most likely candidate for a real

Pergamene inspiration. (The *Dying Trumpeter* graces the jacket of her *Hellenistic Sculpture* I, *ca. 331–200 B.C.,* Madison, Wisconsin, 1990.) J. Marszal subsequently noted that the trumpet is of a type never used by the Gauls, and that it is therefore unlikely that the statue copies a Pergamene original.

BIBLIOGRAPHY

Haskell—Penny, 224–27; B. Palma, *Museo Nazionale Romano, Le Sculture,* I, 4, *I Marmi Ludovisi: Storia della collezione* (Rome, 1983), ed. A. Giuliano, 1–4; Idem, I, 6, *I Marmi Ludovisi dispersi* (Rome, 1986), 93–96; Ridgway, *Hellenistic Sculpture,* I, 284–96.

E

ECHINUS. See ERIZZO.

ECKHEL, JOSEPH HILARIUS (1737–98). Austrian priest and numismatist.

As a youth Eckhel studied with the Jesuits in Vienna, where he mastered Greek, Latin, Hebrew, philosophy, mathematics and theology. In 1565 he taught Latin at the Theresianum in Vienna, then later, grammar and rhetoric in Steyer. From 1768 until 1771 he taught poetry at the gymnasium in Vienna.

Eckhel was introduced to coins by the priests Froelich and Khell, whom he succeeded as keeper of the Jesuit coin cabinet in Vienna. Having obtained permission to travel to Italy, he began his meticulous study of antiquity and *numismatics. He made the acquaintance of E. Cocchi, the keeper of the coin cabinet of Florence, who introduced Eckhel to Leopold, duke of Tuscany. Eckhel was invited by Leopold to rearrange completely the duke's extensive coin cabinet, a task that allowed him to develop a new system of classification. Before Eckhel, the standard means of arranging non-Roman coins and medals was by alphabetical grouping without regard to chronology. This system would not allow for comparative study, nor would stylistic changes be evident. Eckhel proposed that the non-Roman coins be classified geographically, a system that had been used previously by the French collector Joseph Pellerin but was never widely accepted. This system essentially was the foundation of the modern study of Greek numismatics.

On his return from Italy and after the suppression of the Jesuit order, Eckhel was named director of the Imperial Coin Cabinet in Vienna (1774) on recommendation by Leopold to his mother, the Empress Marie-Theresa. He was also appointed professor of antiquities at the University of Vienna. His first publication appeared in 1775, a catalog of the Viennese and Italian collections he had visited and helped arrange, as well as a full accounting of his travels: *Nummi*

Portrait of *J. Eckhel*, at work in the Coin Cabinet, Vienna, engraving by D. Klemi-Bonati. (Westfälisches Landesmuseum für Kunst und Kulturgeschichte, Münster, Porträtarchiv Diepenbroick. Photo: R. Wakonigg.)

veteres anecdocti ex museis Caesareo Vindobonensi, Florentino magni ducis Etruriae, Granelliano, nunc Caesareo, Vitzaiaco, Festeticziano, Savorgnano, Veneto aliisque (Vienna). Other publications included *Catalogus Musaei Caesarei Vindobonensis nummorum veterum . . .* (Vienna, 1779), a work arranged in the geographical system tried out in Florence; *Descriptio nummorum Antiochae Syriae* (Vienna, 1786); *L'Explication d'un choix des pierres gravées du Cabinet Imperiale des antiques* (Vienna, 1788), written in French at the request of his friend Baron Loccella.

Although these writings began to reveal his revolutionary methods, upon his *Doctrina nummorum veterum,* published in eight volumes between 1792 and 1799 in Vienna, rests the modern science of numismatics. In this massive opus, Eckhel weeded out faulty interpretations, identified probable forgeries and criticized past scholarship. He employed strict analytical methods. The first volume served as an introduction to the discipline, where metals, mint techniques, weight systems and the history of past scholarship were all included. The next three volumes consisted of Greek coinage, while the last four were devoted to Roman coins. His breadth of vision and descriptive clarity gave Eckhel the title of "father of ancient numismatics."

BIBLIOGRAPHY

E. Visconti, "Eckhel (Joseph-Hilaire)," *BU* 12 (1814), 463–67; P. R. Franke, "Eckhel, Joseph Hilarius," *NDB* 4 (1957), 302–3; A. Durand, *Médailles et jetons des numismates* (Geneva, 1965), 60–64; *Porträtarchiv,* no. 117.

MICHAEL HOFF

ÉCOLE FRANÇAISE D'ATHÈNES. See FRENCH SCHOOL AT ATHENS.

ÉCOLE FRANÇAISE DE ROME. See FRENCH SCHOOL AT ROME.

EGNATIA. See GNATHIA.

EINSIEDELN ITINERARY (ANONYMOUS EINSIDLENSIS; CODEX EINSIDLENSIS; ca. 800). Early medieval text comprising some eleven "itineraries" or routes through the city of Rome as well as a detailed description of the various sections of the city's walls.

The Einsiedeln Itinerary is known from a single manuscript, formerly in the monastery at Pfäfers (canton of St. Gall) and now in the library at Einsiedeln (Ms. 326). The codex has five parts, each by a different hand, of which the fourth (fols. 67–97) comprises a sylloge of Latin inscriptions, both secular and Christian, from Rome and Pavia; the Itinerary and the description of the walls; the liturgy of the Roman rite for Holy Week; and an anthology of Latin verse. On the basis of tomb epitaphs contained in this anthology, it appears that the manuscript, or the original it copies, was written at Reichenau in the ninth or tenth century. The compilation of the Itinerary may be placed after the reign of Pope Paul I (757–67) since the mention of a church of St. Silvester near the Antonine column must refer to Paul's foundation of S. Silvestro in Capite. A *terminus ante quem* is provided by Pope Leo IV's fortification of the "Leonine city" around St. Peter's (848–52), a project not mentioned in the description of the walls, and by a reference to the church of S. Maria Antiqua, thought to have been abandoned after the earthquake of A.D. 847. Thus, it may be loosely assigned to the age of *Charlemagne.

Apart from various Christian churches, monasteries and cemeteries, the Itinerary is the first of the medieval guides to make frequent reference to the buildings and monuments of ancient Rome. Among these are the *Pantheon, the *Temple of Minerva, the *Theater of Pompey, the *Colosseum, the triumphal *arches of Titus, Septimius Severus and Constantine, the *Columns of Trajan and Marcus Aurelius, the equestrian monument of Constantine in the Forum, the Umbilicus, the Dioscuri (*Quirinal *Horse Tamers*), the *Baths of Constantine, Trajan and Diocletian and numerous aqueducts. The abbreviated and at times confused nature of the listings, as well as the frequent indications of left and right, have led some scholars (*De Rossi, *Lanciani) to suggest that the text represents captions taken from a city plan. However, the occasional notes and comments lend credence to *Hülsen's proposal that the text is a summary of a more detailed itinerary, perhaps accompanying a map. (See also *guide-books to Rome [to 1500].)

BIBLIOGRAPHY

G. B. De Rossi, *La Roma sotterranea cristiana* 1 (Rome, 1864); R. Lanciani, "L'itiner-ario di Einsiedeln e l'ordine di Benedetto Canonico," *MonAnt* 1 (1891), 438–552; C. Huelsen, "La pianta di Roma dell'anonimo Einsidlense," *Dissertazioni della Pontificia Accademia Romana di Archeologia* ser. 2, vol. 9 (Rome, 1907), 379–424; Valentini—Zucchetti, II, 155–207.

JOHN OSBORNE

ELEUSIS. Greek sanctuary of Demeter, which lay by the sea some fourteen miles west of Athens.

By far the most important sanctuary of Demeter in the ancient world, the site was associated with the myth of the Rape of Persephone as related in the Ho-meric Hymn to Demeter. According to the legend, Demeter herself directed the foundation of the cult on the spot, in 1409 B.C., if one believes the *Marmor Parium. Thereafter, the Mysteries, one of the best-kept secrets of antiquity, were celebrated at the sanctuary into late Roman times.

The site was located in the eighteenth century by early travelers, and parts were excavated by *Gell, Gandy and Redford for the *Society of the Dilettanti in 1812. E. D. *Clarke carried off a colossal statue of "Demeter" (actually a battered caryatid) in 1801. Further work was carried out by Charles *Lenormant in 1860. The *Greek Archaeological Society undertook excavations in 1882, and these have continued sporadically ever since under Philios (1882–92), Skias (1894–1907), Kourouniotes (1917–45), A. *Orlandos, G. *Mylonas and J. Trav-los.

The sanctuary was protected by fortification walls as early as the sixth century B.C., which were thereafter expanded in Classical and Hellenistic times. A large courtyard outside the sanctuary proper had several monuments of the second century A.C., indicating the considerable interest in the cult in the Roman period: two triumphal arches, a fountainhouse, a temple of Artemis and a monumental propylon that closely imitates the *Propylaia of Athens. Once within the pro-pylon we are somewhat in the dark, as Pausanias, our usually reliable guide, was prevented by a dream from describing the sanctuary proper (1.38.7). In-scriptions that preserve inventories or building accounts shed some light on the remains, but a complete correlation of epigraphic evidence and architecture has not yet been achieved. Inside the inner propylon was an earlier elegant one built in the first century B.C. by Appius Claudius Pulcher. From here a processional way led to the great hall of Mysteries, the Telesterion, where the initiates gath-ered for the rites. The earliest finds here date to the Mycenaean period, though

there is no clear evidence of cult activity on the spot until the eighth century
B.C. The Telesterion, a large hypostyle hall that eventually grew to measure 56m
× 66m, had a long and complicated history with up to ten different building
phases recognizable. Several of these date to the fifth century B.C., and two were
carried out under the architects Iktinos (according to Strabo and Vitruvius) and
Koroibos (according to Plutarch). In the fourth century a large porch or prostoon
was added under the direction of the architect Philo (*IG* II, 2, 1673 and Vitruvius).

The deme of Eleusis, which was incorporated into the Athenian state at an
early date, lay to the west of the sanctuary, and the remains of a stadium and
theater have been recognized to the south.

BIBLIOGRAPHY

F. Noack, *Eleusis, die baugeschichtliche Entwicklung des Heiligtumes* (Berlin, 1927); K.
Kourouniotes, *Eleusiniaka* 1 (Athens, 1932); G. Mylonas, *Eleusis and the Eleusinian
Mysteries* (Princeton, NJ, 1961); J. Travlos, "Eleusina," *DOME* 5 (1970), 269–74; D.
Ziro, *Ê Kuria Eisodos tou Ierou stê Eleusinos* (Athens, 1991).

JOHN McK. CAMP II

ELGIN, LORD (THOMAS BRUCE; 1766–1841). Seventh Earl of Elgin, British diplomat and antiquarian, best known for his acquisition of marbles from
the *Parthenon, now in the *British Museum.

After an education in England and Paris, Elgin began the career open to
members of the aristocracy, serving first in the military and then in political and
diplomatic posts. After several minor appointments in Europe, he was made
ambassador to the Sublime Porte at Constantinople and resolved, at the urging
of the architect Thomas Harrison, that his time in service there would be devoted
to the improvement of the arts in England. He requested government funds to
finance his plans to make drawings and casts of the monuments on the *Akropolis in Athens but was refused. Undaunted, Elgin financed the project with
personal funds. Artists in England, including J.M.W. Turner, were interviewed
for participation in the project, but he found their salary requests too high and
instead assembled a team from Italy headed by G. B. *Lusieri, a Neapolitan
topographical painter. Also hired (in Rome) were an artist from Russia named
Feodor Ivanovitch (nicknamed "Lord Elgin's Calmuck"), two architecture specialists and two molders of casts.

Elgin proceeded to Constantinople, and Lusieri began his work in Athens
under difficult conditions. Local Turkish authorities charged fees to the team
for simply entering the Akropolis and refused to allow anything but drawings
to be done. After April 1801, Lusieri was refused further access until a *firman,*
or official order, from Constantinople was presented. Though Elgin originally
intended only to seek casts and drawings of the monuments, he was convinced
by his chaplain, Dr. Philip Hunt, to secure a *firman* that would allow him to
remove marbles from the site. Sculptures and inscriptions had been vandalized,
burned for lime, incorporated into other structures on the Akropolis and other-

Portrait of *Thomas Bruce, 7th Earl of Elgin*, by G. P. Harding. London, British Museum. (Museum.)

wise abused. At the same time the French agent *Fauvel, who had had considerable success in securing antiquities in Athens, was constantly on the alert to acquire parts of the Parthenon. Elgin later justified his actions by observing that removal of the marbles appeared the only way of preserving what remained.

Negotiations with the Turkish authority in Constantinople were successful, due, in part, to British military successes in the region against Napoleon, and permission was secured to remove anything that did not interfere with the structural stability of the fortification. From July 1801 to the beginning of 1804, Lusieri directed operations, collecting sculpture from the building itself as well as pieces buried in the rubble surrounding the Parthenon. The saws he used to remove stones from the building were inferior, and the work was sometimes clumsy, resulting in breakage of some of the sculptures. Lusieri himself referred to the "barbarisms" he committed. He removed 247 feet of the Parthenon frieze, fourteen sculptured metopes, seventeen pedimental figures, four slabs from the *Temple of Athena Nike and one caryatid from the *Erechtheion, as well as various architectural features from the *Propylaia and Parthenon. Molds were made of remaining parts of the frieze and metopes. During this entire period, Elgin himself visited Athens only once.

The crated marbles were transferred by ship to London, though forty cases remained in Peiraeus while England and Turkey were at war, and one shipload of seventeen crates, taken on Elgin's brig, the *Mentor,* sank at Cythera. All pieces were soon salvaged but at a cost of £5,000 to Elgin. By 1812, all the marbles were in England. Elgin's own route home was difficult. Returning from Constantinople, he was in France when war was declared against England in 1803, and the English diplomat was taken and held prisoner for three years.

Before his imprisonment, Elgin had stopped in Rome and consulted *Canova concerning restoration of the marbles; Canova responded by saying that "it would be a sacrilege for any man to touch them with a chisel." Though Canova's opinion carried great weight, Elgin still considered restoration. John *Flaxman was consulted in London, and Canova's opinion was seconded by the British sculptor, who would consent only to being a "repairman" for the marbles, reattaching broken limbs and other fragments.

The marbles were housed in a shed built for the purpose, and from 1807, selected artists were allowed to view the works of art. Their reactions were effusively enthusiastic; Benjamin Robert Haydon, for example, declared, "I felt as if a divine truth had blazed inwardly upon my mind." The marbles were moved several times in London, and artists continued to draw them.

Elgin, financially pressed, began to lobby the government to purchase the collection. E. Q. *Visconti had viewed them in 1814 and had written glowing reports of their value, which Elgin intended to use to support his case for state purchase of the marbles. He was dealt a setback, however, when the Board of Trustees of the British Museum appointed Richard Payne *Knight to conduct the negotiations. Payne Knight, as head of the *Society of Dilettanti, argued that the sculptures of the pediments were not as valuable as Elgin claimed; he believed them to be from the time of Hadrian and not from the hand of Pheidias. Before a Select Committee of Parliament, this question and many others were debated. (Should the marbles be restored? What were they really worth? Were they as fine as the *Laocoon and the *Belvedere *Apollo?* Had Elgin acted legally?) Ultimately, the purchase was made (7 June 1816) through a bill introduced in the House of Commons, and Elgin was paid £35,000, substantially less than he had requested. The hearings on the purchase also served to vindicate Elgin's claims that the marbles were acquired legitimately and that they were indeed works of the fifth century B.C.

The marbles were first shown at the British Museum in 1817. Almost ironically, they served the altruistic purpose first envisioned by Elgin, as students thronged the museum, and casts of the marbles were shipped to other museums around the land and in Europe. *Goethe raved of the necessity of German sculptors to see them in person. *Keats wrote a sonnet "On Seeing the Elgin Marbles"; Benjamin *West imitated them in his *Conversion of St. Paul,* Flaxman in his *Mrs. Siddons.* The French aesthetician *Quatremère de Quincy rhapsodized over the lifelike quality of the horses and humans and over the delicacy of the drapery.

Elgin himself attempted to return to public life but was never able to recover from his debts; eventually he withdrew to France to escape his creditors. He died in Paris in 1841. Controvery continues to be associated with his removal of the marbles from Greece; the Greeks themselves plead to have them returned to Athens, to be seen with the monument they adorned.

BIBLIOGRAPHY

W. St. Clair, *Lord Elgin and the Marbles* (London, 1967); J. Rothenberg, "The Acquisition of the Elgin Marbles," in *The Parthenon, Norton Critical Studies in Art History* (New York, 1974), 128–70; B. F. Cook, *The Elgin Marbles* (Cambridge, MA, 1984); C. Hitchens, *The Elgin Marbles: Should They Be Returned to Greece?* (London, 1987).

SHARON WICHMANN

ELMALI. City and upland plain in Lycia (southwestern Asia Minor), ca. 120km west of Antalya.

During the excavation of prehistoric remains at Karataş-Semayük and Bağbaşı conducted by Bryn Mawr College, under the direction of Machteld Mellink, two burial mounds of Classical date were discovered in 1969–70. Both tumuli, which had been disturbed in antiquity, contained built stone burial chambers with painted interior decoration.

The earlier tomb at Kızılbel (ca. 525 B.C.) included an exterior entrance lined with orthostats; the tomb chamber was closed by a stone portcullis. The painted scenes in friezes of uneven height include subjects from the Greek mythological repertoire (Gorgons, Medusa, birth of Chrysaor and Pegasos) as well as ceremonial scenes (warrior's departure; deer hunt; boar hunt in marshes; sea voyage; processions of soldiers, horses, attendants; banquet). Floor and ceiling also bear painted ornament. A limestone *kline* (couch) stood along the west wall, and a stone table stood in the northeast corner.

In front of the later tomb located at Karaburun (ca. 470 B.C.) stood a limestone platform 5m in length, probably to support carved stone doors or relief sculpture. Fragments of lion sculptures that may have formed additional entrance decoration were found nearby. Here the principal painted decoration depicts a Persianizing scene of the tomb owner on a couch, with his wife and servants. On the other walls are a funeral cortège with chariots and a battle scene. A stone *kline* supported the burial, and a table stood in the opposite corner. The tomb paintings of both monuments are dated principally via comparisons with Archaic East Greek and Graeco-Persian art, respectively, but represent a local tradition.

BIBLIOGRAPHY
+M. J. Mellink, annual reports in *AJA* 74–80 (1970–76); +Idem, "Local, Phrygian, and Greek Traits in Northern Lycia," *RA* (1976), 21–34.

ANN C. GUNTER

EMPORION (EMPORIAE, AMPURIAS). Greek colony and Roman town; the most important and best-preserved Greek site in Spain.

Founded by Phokaian colonists from Massalia (*Marseilles) around 600 B.C. on an island off the northeast coast of Spain (referred to as Palaiopolis), Emporion expanded and developed from a trading post to a flourishing city-state on the mainland (referred to as Neapolis). It was fortified by the fourth century B.C. and minted its own coins.

The arrival of the Romans during the second Punic War (218 B.C.) brought about long-term changes. On a plateau overlooking Neapolis was built the Roman town, with an orthogonal plan as well as walls, an amphitheater, a forum and capitol. In the Augustan period, the Roman town, Neapolis and a native settlement, Indika, were merged to form a *municipium* with the plural name of Emporiae.

The Roman town was ruined by the invasion of the Franks in A.D. 265. Occupation at Neapolis persisted in the form of a small church surrounded by burials of the fourth century A.C.; cemeteries at Estruch, Castellet and Martí testify to the local importance of Emporiae in later antiquity. A small fortified center was built at Palaiopolis in the early sixth century A.C. In the Middle Ages the town was the site of an episcopal see.

The location of Emporion has been known since Renaissance times, since it gave its names to an entire district, the Ampuridan. Excavation began at the site in 1908. Excavations in the twentieth century have revealed the enclosure of the Greek town along with a temple area and a marketplace. Hellenistic houses contained remains of mosaics and wall paintings. Finds are in the local museum and in the Barcelona Archaeological Museum.

BIBLIOGRAPHY
M. Almagro, *Las Necropolis de Ampurias* (Barcelona, 1953–55); P. MacKendrick, *The Iberian Stones Speak* (New York, 1969), 45–58; J. Maluquer de Motes, "Emporion," *PECS* 303; E. Sanmartí—J. M. Nolla, *Empúries, Guia Itineraria* (Barcelona, 1988).

SIMON KEAY

ENKOMI. Late Bronze Age town in northeast *Cyprus (locality Ayios Iakovos).

Enkomi was first investigated by the *British Museum in 1896, when tombs containing rich grave goods, including gold jewelry, ivory objects and Mycenaean pottery, were recorded. Before that date, the cemetery had been known to tomb robbers and had suffered from considerable looting. After a short British campaign in 1913, the *Swedish Cyprus Expedition excavated over twenty more tombs with many offerings. However, it was not until the French archaeologist C. Schaeffer, who previously had worked at Ugarit/Ras Shamra, began excavations in 1934 that the extensive urban settlement at Enkomi was discovered. In 1948 a joint project with Schaeffer and P. Dikaios of the Cypriot Department of Antiquities was initiated and continued until 1958. Thereafter the French continued to work at the site until just before the Turkish invasion of 1974. The French archaeologist J.-C. Courtois and other experts continue to analyze the material from the site.

The earliest finds date to the Middle Bronze Age. Later the town became a major copper-processing center and trade emporium for the eastern Mediterranean. After destructions by fire and perhaps an earthquake, the town was finally abandoned around 1050 B.C. Among the significant structures of this settlement, laid out on a grid plan, are the massive fortification wall; Building 18 (Bâtiment 18), the first ashlar building discovered on Cyprus; and several religious structures. Important finds, in addition to the objects from the tombs, include the bronze figures of the *Horned God* and the *Ingot God* and Cypro-Minoan documents.

Enkomi, identified with the ''Alasia'' of ancient texts by many scholars, was the first major Late Bronze Age town to be explored on Cyprus. It was important for establishing a chronology of events during a critical phase of the island's history, namely, the period when mainland Greeks first arrived as settlers. Many of the original historical conclusions have been questioned, but the sequence of levels at Enkomi remains the standard by which the chronologies of other Cypriot Late Bronze Age sites are determined.

BIBLIOGRAPHY
C.F.A. Schaeffer, *Missions en Chypre* (Paris, 1936); Idem, *Enkomi-Alasia* 1 (Paris, 1952); +P. Dikaios, *Enkomi Excavations* 1–3 (Mainz, 1969–71); J.-C. Courtois—J. Lagarce—E. Lagarce, *Enkomi et le bronze récent à Chypre* (Nicosia, 1986).

PAMELA J. RUSSELL

EPHESOS. Ionian Greek city on west coast of Asia Minor.

The city shifted from its original site during the reign of Kroisos to the area of the *Temple of Artemis. Because of silting in the harbor, Lysimachos rebuilt the city on higher ground between the Panayir-dağı and the Bülbül-dağı in ca. 290 B.C. The greatest city of Asia Minor in the Roman and Late Antique periods, Ephesos was destroyed in A.D. 614.

*Ciriaco of Ancona, in 1446–47, was the first of many visitors. J. T. Wood, from the *British Museum, excavated in the odeion and the theater, then in the sanctuary of Artemis (1863–74, 1883–84). A second mission from the British Museum, under D. G. *Hogarth, returned to the Artemision (1904–5). Meanwhile, Austrian archaeologists led by O. *Benndorf arrived in 1895; after one season in the Artemision, they moved to the Hellenistic-Roman city, excavating the Harbor Gymnasium and Arcadiane (1896–1901), theater (1897–1900), lower agora (1901–7), Celsus library (1903–4), church of St. Mary (1904–7, 1912), stadium (1911), Serapeion (1911, 1913) and around the official agora (*Staatsmarkt;* 1908). When Benndorf became head of the new Austrian Archaeological Institute in 1898, R. Heberdey directed the excavations (1898–1913).

During the Greek occupation after World War I, G. A. Sotiriou excavated at the church of St. John (1921–22). Austrians resumed work under J. Keil (1925–35) with exploration of Geometric-Archaic levels north of Panayir-dağı, the Mother-Goddess sanctuary (1926) and the Seven Sleepers' Grotto (1926–28). *Bädergrabungen* (1927–31) included the Vedius, theater and East Gymnasia, and excavations were conducted at the church of St. John (1927–31), the "rock-fissure temple" (1927), the temple of Domitian (1930) and the Belevi mausoleum (1931, 1933, 1935).

After World War II, F. Miltner (1954–58) led investigations of the thermae of Scholastikia, the prytaneion and Imperial-period houses (*Hanghäuser*) south of Kouretes Street. Excavations cleared structures along Kouretes Street to the *Staatsmarkt* and in Domitian Square. The distinguished Austrian restorations began with Miltner's rebuilding of Hadrian's temple, the church of St. John and others. F. Eichler (1960–69) continued exploring the prytaneion and the *Hanghäuser*. Excavations moved southward along Domitian Street, then east along Magnesian Street. A sixth-century B.C. necropolis was found in the *Staatsmarkt*. Investigation of the Belevi tumulus and Bammer's excavations of the Artemision began in 1965. Under H. Vetters (1969–86), work continued at the *Hanghäuser;* other areas of excavation were the Varius baths (1969–75), the *Staatsmarkt,* the Magnesian gate (1977–86), a church near the East Gymnasium (1983–5), the Olympieion under the church of Mary (1983–6) and around the Celsus library. In the lower agora, soundings have revealed pre-Lysimachan buildings and the old processional way, lined with Archaic tombs. Splendid rebuildings of the Celsus library (1972–8) and the adjacent gate of Mazaeus and Mithridates (1980–7) are complete, and restoration of Hadrian's gate and the Neronic stoa proceeds. Langmann became director in 1987, with plans for underwater exploration of the silted harbor.

Turkish excavations and restorations at the church of St. John have been in progress since the 1960s and at the stadium-theater road in the 1980s, most recently under S. Erdemgil and E. Akurgal.

BIBLIOGRAPHY

+Oesterreichische Archäologische Institut, *Forschungen in Ephesos* 1–9 (Vienna, 1906–81); +H. Vetters et al., "Grabungen in Ephesos von 1960–1969 bzw. 1970," *ÖJh* 50 (1972–75); Beiblatt, 225–558; C. Foss, *Ephesus After Antiquity: A Late Antique, Byzantine, and Turkish City* (Cambridge, 1979); A. Bammer, *Ephesos, Stadt an Fluss und Meer* (Graz, 1987).

JANE BURR CARTER

EPIDAUROS. Ancient Greek town on the east coast of the Peloponnese famed for its sanctuary of Asklepios.

A small theater and some inscriptions have been found on the ancient acropolis that juts out into the Saronic Gulf. Some five miles inland lies the sanctuary of Asklepios, the principal healing deity of the Greeks; almost every city had an Asklepieion, but the sanctuary at Epidauros was his most important center. The earliest votives on the site go back to ca. 500 B.C., though the buildings are to be dated to the fourth and third centuries B.C. These include a Doric peripteral temple, a dormitory (*abaton*) for the sick and the tholos, an ornate and enigmatic round building of the Doric order that apparently served some cult function. Though the structures are poorly preserved, building accounts on stone permit a detailed restoration of these monuments.

Other buildings served the needs of visitors to the sanctuary and the games: a stadium, gymnasium, stoa, banqueting hall, baths and hostel (*katagogeion*); best known and best preserved is the great theater, designed by Polykleitos and admired by Pausanias (2.27.5), which seated about 14,000 people. The sanctuary flourished throughout the Hellenistic period and was favored in Roman times as well, especially during the second century, when various buildings were built or repaired by the Roman senator Antoninus. The cult of Asklepios was very popular and among the last to give way to Christianity; at Epidauros the change is represented by a large Early Christian basilica built just north of the sanctuary.

Excavations were carried out by the *Greek Archaeological Society under the direction of P. *Kavvadias from 1881 to 1928; these exposed all the buildings of the sanctuary, and little additional work has been done since, though several studies on individual buildings have appeared.

On the slopes above, a small sanctuary of Apollo Maleatas has been excavated by Kavvadias, J. Papademetriou (1948–51) and, most recently, by B. Lambrinoudakis (1974–). The site had extensive Bronze Age habitation and a Mycenaean open-air altar; after a break in the Dark Ages, cult activity resumed in the eighth century B.C., appreciably earlier than in the lower sanctuary. The architectural remains date to the fourth and third centuries B.C., with extensive additions in the Roman period.

BIBLIOGRAPHY

P. Kavvadias, *To Ieron tou Asklēpiou en Epidaurō* (Athens, 1900); F. Robert, *Thymélè* (Paris, 1939); A. Burford, *The Greek Temple Builders of Epidauros* (Liverpool, 1969); R. A. Tomlinson, *Epidauros* (Austin, 1983).

JOHN McK. CAMP II

EPIGRAPHY, GREEK. The study of Greek inscriptions on stone, metal and clay (incised and painted), as opposed to writing on perishable materials.

In most cases the inscription is an integral part of the monument on which it stands, a work of art, a dedication, a tombstone, a building; it must be studied not as a text but as a three-dimensional object with an archaeological context.

The study of Greek inscriptions is the result of Greek literacy in Hellenic

times (cf. *Linear A and Linear B) and goes back to the earliest inscriptions—
verses and brief notes scratched or painted on pottery in the eighth century B.C.
and the inscribed stone monuments of the late seventh century B.C. The earliest
historians (Herodotos and Thucydides) made use of inscriptions, quoting them
on occasion, and so did the orators (e.g., Demosthenes) in their political and
private speeches. With the rise of learning and scholarship at Alexandria under
the influence of Aristotle, collections of epigrams and of politically important
inscriptions were made by Philochoros, Krateros, Polemon and others; none of
their works are preserved, but they have been used by historians, commentators
and encyclopedists whose books did survive.

While the interest in Latin inscriptions never faded in the West, Greek became
a foreign language there long before the fall of Constantinople in 1453 closed
the Greek lands to Western scholars and undermined Greek learning at home.
Just before that, early in the fifteenth century, *Ciriaco of Ancona was able to
travel in the East and make his fine drawings of monuments and inscriptions.
He not only preserved the knowledge of antiquity but also encouraged others
to follow in his footsteps, as his manuscripts were circulated among humanist
scholars. While the study of Latin inscriptions flourished in these circles (cf.
*epigraphy, Latin), it was several centuries until scholars devoted themselves to
the systematic collection of Greek inscriptions. One of the most notable discoveries of this period, made on the island of *Paros, was a chronicle of Greek
history, originally acquired for *Peiresc but eventually secured in 1627 for the
Earl of *Arundel (*Marmor Parium).

Before the Greek War of Independence came to an end (1830), such travelers
as *Wheler, *Fauvel and the controversial *Fourmont collected and copied inscriptions in Greece, and German scholars began their dedicated pursuit of this
branch of archaeology. Among the Greeks, K. Pittakis diligently copied and
commented on Attic inscriptions, and his publications are still valuable. F. *Halbherr and E. Fabricius made a major discovery later in the century (1884) at
*Gortyn, where they found the remains of the famous Gortyn Law Code, some-
times referred to as the "queen of inscriptions."

Greek epigraphy as a scholarly discipline was developed within the German
(formerly, the Prussian) Academy of Berlin by August *Boeckh, the author of
the first two volumes of the *Corpus Inscriptionum Graecarum* (IG), conceived
in 1815 and actually published in 1828 and 1843. The work auspiciously undertaken on the *IG* in Berlin has been carried forward by scholars from other
countries, including A. Wilhelm (Vienna), L. Robert (Paris) and M. Guarducci
(Rome).

When excavations by the *American School of Classical Studies were undertaken in the *Agora, Athens, producing many inscriptions, several distinguished epigraphists (B. D. Meritt, S. Dow, J. A. Oliver) created a new trend
in the study of Greek inscriptions, "architectural epigraphy," which considers
the inscription as part of a three-dimensional monument and insists on supplying

photographs of all sides, not just the inscribed part. Recently, this trend has been blended with the traditional approach in the publication of the third edition of the Berlin Academy's corpus of Attic inscriptions dating from before the official adoption of the Ionic alphabet in 403/2 B.C. (*IG,* I, 3rd ed., edited by David M. Lewis of Oxford). A new handbook of Greek epigraphy, with general introduction and generously selected and illustrated examples of all types of Greek inscriptions, has been published by Guarducci in four volumes (Rome, 1967–80).

BIBLIOGRAPHY

G. Klaffenbach, *Griechische Epigraphik* (Göttingen, 1957); A. G. Woodhead, *The Study of Greek Inscriptions* (Cambridge, 1959); G. Pfohl, *Das Studium der griechischen Epigraphik, eine Einführung* (Darmstadt, 1977); H. R. Immerwahr, *Attic Script, A Survey* (Oxford, 1990); L. H. Jeffery, *The Local Scripts of Archaic Greece,* 2nd ed., with suppl. by A. W. Johnston (Oxford, 1990).

ANTONY RAUBITSCHEK

EPIGRAPHY, LATIN. The study of Latin inscriptions, normally on stone, bronze or other durable surfaces.

Inscriptions are classified into two major types according to their content: formal, legal documents (*acta*) and records of individuals and their deeds (*tituli*). Recorded *acta* include laws of the Republic and the Empire, as well as the calendars and the *Fasti* of consuls and triumphing emperors, which help to clarify the chronology of Roman history. Epitaphs, a form of *tituli,* make up the largest single group of inscriptional types. Other forms of *tituli* are dedicatory inscriptions and *elogia,* inscriptions on public works and inscriptions on portable objects. Among the most famous *tituli* is the *Res Gestae* of the emperor Augustus, which was inscribed on two bronze tablets before the *Mausoleum of Augustus. These have been lost, but the text was largely recovered in 1555, when a copy was found on the walls of a mosque, once a temple to Augustus and Rome, in Ancyra, Galatia (*Monumentum Ancyranum).

Roman inscriptions were not entirely ignored in the Middle Ages. The earliest written collection or sylloge of inscriptions, in the *Einsiedeln Itinerary, was compiled in the ninth century as part of a description of Rome's antiquities. In the Late Middle Ages and Early Renaissance, epigraphical studies began in earnest when humanists recognized in inscriptions valuable information concerning the history, language and physical appearance of antique Rome. Quite naturally, these studies centered around the ancient city. A modest sylloge of Roman inscriptions was composed in the fourteenth century by Giovanni *Dondi. In 1346, *Cola di Rienzo identified the *Lex de imperio Vespasiani* inscribed on a bronze tablet used to build an altar in St. John *Lateran (now in the *Capitoline Museums).

*Poggio Bracciolini also examined the ancient remains of Rome and recorded their inscriptions. In 1417, he discovered four pages of inscriptions from the Einsiedeln Itinerary and included these in his collection (completed 1429). Poggio's sylloge and that of Nicola Signorili (1409) formed the foundation of the important collections of inscriptions from Rome and around Italy by *Ciriaco of Ancona, *Marcanova and *Felice Feliciano.

Soon afterward, Bartolommeo *Fonzio compiled a sylloge in the late fifteenth century that was richly illustrated but still had the random arrangement employed by earlier scholars. Fra *Giocondo improved upon the rather haphazard organization of the earlier sylloges, using a topographical sequence, and also distinguished between inscriptions that he had copied personally and those known to him secondhand. Andreas *Alciati prepared a sylloge of inscriptions from Milan and the surrounding area (1518–19), which was of the highest quality but was never published.

The first sylloge to be printed, by Desiderio Spreti, was on the inscriptions of Ravenna (1489). German printers, inspired by the epigraphical interests of the Italian humanists, published the Roman inscriptions of Augsburg (Konrad *Peutinger, 1505) and Mainz (Johann Hüttlich, 1520 and 1525). In 1521, Jacopo Mazzocchi published the first printed collection of inscriptions in Rome. He depended on sylloges by Signorili, Poggio, Fra Giocondo and Francesco *Albertini and was probably assisted by Mario Maffei, Mariangelo Accursio and Andrea *Fulvio.

The *Fasti Consulares* were known from only a few fragments until 1546, when thirty fragments of the *Fasti* and twenty-six of the *Acta Triumphorum* were unearthed in the *Forum Romanum. (Originally, these inscriptions probably formed part of the wall of the Regia, rebuilt in 36 B.C.). A few years later *Michelangelo had them moved to the Palazzo Conservatori on the Capitoline, where they are today. The *Fasti Capitolini* were published first by *Marliani in 1549.

A calendar of Roman festivals from 8 B.C. to A.D. 3 (*Fasti Anni Iuliani* or *Fasti Maffeiani*) was discovered in Rome in 1547. Paulus Manutius published it for the first time as an appendix to Sigonius's publication of the *Fasti Capitolares* (1555).

Northern scholars appear to have been particularly attracted to the idea of a *corpus absolutissimum.* Petrus Apianus and Bartholomaeus Amantius printed the first corpus of inscriptions, arranged geographically, in Ingolstadt (1534). *Panvinio conceived a grand scheme for the publication of all Latin inscriptions in the Roman world. His large collection, though lost, is partially represented in a corpus by Martinus *Smetius, published in Antwerp in 1588 by *Lipsius. The organization of the inscriptions by subject was continued in later corpora. J. J. *Scaliger also planned such a grand corpus and entrusted the task to Janus *Gruter. It was published in Heidelberg in 1602 with twenty-four indexes by Scaliger.

In the eighteenth century, a new critical attitude led to the rejection of forgeries, such as had been disseminated as early as the sixteenth century by the notorious falsifiers *Annio da Viterbo and Pirro *Ligorio. Scipione *Maffei initiated the critical examination of corpora when he detected many inaccuracies and forgeries among the transcriptions in Ludovico Muratori's carelessly prepared sylloge of 1739. In the nineteenth century, Bartolomeo *Borghesi and Marini made major advances toward a critical and scientific method. The greatest of all Latin epigraphers, Theodor *Mommsen, having studied under Borghesi, initiated and organized the monumental *Corpus Inscriptionum Latinarum* (CIL). Sponsored by the Berliner Akademie der Wissenschaft, publication of the *CIL* continues to this day in the preparation of supplements and indexes.

In the late nineteenth century, scholarly attention turned to archaic Latin, as some of the earliest-known inscriptions were discovered or turned up in or near Rome: the Duenos vase, found in 1880; the *Lapis Niger, found in 1899; and the *Praenestine Fibula. Until recently the Praenestine Fibula was considered by many to be the most ancient of these inscriptions, but its authenticity is now in the gravest doubt. Wolfgang *Helbig and Ferdinand Dummler presented the fibula at a meeting of the *German Archaeological Institute in Rome in 1887 and published it the same year, with Helbig's claiming to have acquired the fibula from an unnamed friend who had bought it in Palestrina in 1871. The recent research of Maria Guarducci convinced many leading authorities, such as A. E. Gordon, who had already had suspicions, that the fibula is a forgery and that the inscription was concocted by Helbig himself.

BIBLIOGRAPHY

R. Cagnat, *Cours d'epigraphie latine,* 4th ed. (Paris, 1914); P. Lehmann, "Two Roman Reliefs in Renaissance Disguise," *JWarb* 4–5 (1941–42), 47–66; +A. E. Gordon, *Album of Dated Latin Inscriptions* (Berkeley, 1958–65); Weiss, *RDCA,* ch. 11; Sheard, no. 3; +A. E. Gordon, *Illustrated Introduction to Latin Epigraphy* (Berkeley, 1983).

CHRISTINE SPERLING

ERECHTHEION (ERECHTHEUM), Athens. Greek temple, situated on the north side of the *Akropolis, Athens, begun in 421 B.C. and completed in 406 B.C.

The structure housed several chthonic cults, including the city's chief cult, to Athena Polias. Although the name "Erechtheion" is rarely used by ancient sources, scholars have no doubt about the building's identity. The architect is unknown, but *Dörpfeld speculated that it was Mnesikles, the architect of the *Propylaia, because of the complexity of the design of the Erechtheion.

According to Pausanias (1.26-27), writing in the second century A.C., within the temple could be found the altar and statue of Athena Polias, an altar of Poseidon/Erechtheus and altars of Boutes and Hephaistos. There were also a well of seawater and marks on the bedrock of the Akropolis caused by Poseidon's trident during his contest with Athena. Pausanias also mentions an adjoining shrine of Pandrosos (probably west of the Erechtheion) in which was located the sacred olive tree given by Athena in the contest. The north porch sheltered a mark on the rock caused by Zeus's thunderbolt.

Due to cult requirements and topographical irregularities, the ground plan of the Erechtheion is unusual, featuring internal divisions in the cella. Nevertheless the temple demonstrates a successful unity in design. The main block of the cella was entered on the east through a hexastyle façade. On the north and south sides were placed monumental porches. Because of the slope of the Akropolis, the columnar north porch is considerably lower than the one on the south. The latter is famous for its six female caryatid figures supporting the superstructure. One caryatid was removed by Lord *Elgin in 1803 and taken to London (it is now in the *British Museum), and, in recent restorations, all of the remaining caryatids were removed and replaced with copies. The originals are now in the *Akropolis Museum.

The Erechtheion underwent various repairs and alterations in its later history. During the reign of Augustus repairs were made to the structure, which had been damaged by a fire that may have occurred during the siege of Sulla in 86 B.C. Later, most likely in the seventh or eighth century A.C., the interior of the temple was converted into an aisled Christian basilica, involving the removal of the interior cross-walls.

During the Turkish period, the Erechtheion served as a residence for the ruling Turks who occupied the Akropolis. As a result of the explosion in the *Parthenon in 1687 and the ensuing fire, the building was severely damaged. Its ruins were often admired by travelers and drawn or painted by artists (*Stuart and *Revett, H. W. "Grecian" *Williams, Ippolito *Caffi).

Further damage occurred in 1827, during the Greek War of Independence. Cleaning and restoration of the building took place between 1837 and 1843 and, later, between 1902 and 1909, under N. Balanos. The temple recently underwent new restorations (1979–87) to correct problems associated with the earlier restorations.

BIBLIOGRAPHY
G. P. Stevens—J. M. Paton, *The Erechtheum* (Cambridge, MA, 1927); W. Dörpfeld—H. Schleif, *Erechtheion* (Berlin, 1942); N. M. Kontoleon, *To Erechtheion hos oikodomema chthonias latreias* (Athens, 1949); Ridgway, *Fifth Century Styles in Greek Sculpture,* 105–8; +Tsigakou, *Rediscovery of Greece,* 32, 123, 125, 137, 203a; +Travlos, 213–14.

MICHAEL HOFF

ERETRIA. Greek city on the south coast of the island of Euboia, 18km southeast of its rival *Chalkis, with the most extensive preserved remains of any site on the island.

A leader, along with Chalkis, in Greek colonizing efforts in the eighth century B.C., Eretria seems to have experienced an early prosperity but may have suffered a decline as a result of the Lelantine War with Chalkis. An important Archaic temple with Doric columns on all sides was erected to Apollo Daphnephoros in the sixth century B.C. but was razed during a Persian sack of the city in 490 B.C. In the fourth century, Eretria flourished again. The Eretrians constructed their well-known theater, remarkable for its underground passage dug under the orchestra and featuring steps connecting the stage with the center of the orchestra. The city was destroyed once again in 198 B.C. by a Rome-Pergamon coalition and thereafter fell prey to quarrying of its quality building stone.

In 1436 *Ciriaco of Ancona made drawings of some of the city walls and the theater, the most recognizable parts of the ancient town. Much later, after the liberation of Greece, an attempt was made by the Greeks to found a new city, and Bavarian architects drew up a city plan, never realized, but recording all the remains of ancient walls known at that time (1830).

Between 1890 and 1895, the *American School of Classical Studies cleared the theater and excavated two gymnasia and a temple of Dionysos. Excavations at the end of the nineteenth century by K. Kourouniotis for the *Greek Archaeological Society exposed the foundations of the temple of Apollo and unearthed the well-known pedimental sculpture of *Theseus and Antiope* (found in 1900 and now in the Chalkis Museum). In the 1960s, wide-scale investigation was conducted by C. Davaras for the *Greek Archaeological Service, with K. Schefold overseeing a Swiss team. The Swiss have systematically published the results in *Eretria, Ausgrabungen und Forschungen* (Bern, 1968).

BIBLIOGRAPHY

+K. Schefold, "The Architecture of Eretria," *Archaeology* 21 (1968), 272–81; P. Auberson—K. Schefold, *Führer durch Eretria* (Bern, 1972); T. W. Jacobsen, "Eretria," *PECS,* 315–17.

ERICHIUS. See ERIZZO.

ERIM, KENAN TEVFIK (1929–90). Turkish American archaeologist, excavator of *Aphrodisias in Caria, Turkey.

Born in Istanbul, Kenan Erim spent his childhood in Geneva—his father was a diplomat with the League of Nations—and studied at New York University, where he later was professor of classics (1958–71). His doctorate was from Princeton (1958), where he identified, from coins, the excavation at Sierra Orlando in Sicily as ancient *Morgantina. From 1961 on he devoted himself to the discovery of the archaeological wealth of Aphrodisias; for its publication his collaborators were Joyce Reynolds (inscriptions), Martha Joukowsky (prehistoric Aphrodisias) and R.R.R. Smith (Julio-Claudian sculpture of the Sebasteion). The National Geographic Society long supported the excavation and awarded him its Centennial Medal (1988); New York City awarded him the Liberty Medal (1986). He died in Ankara in 1990.

BIBLIOGRAPHY

G. W. Bowersock, "Kenan Tevfik Erim," *AJA* 95 (1991), 281–83.

LARISSA BONFANTE

ERIZZO (ERICHIUS; ECHINUS), SEBASTIANO (1525–85). Venetian antiquarian, numismatist and philosopher.

Erizzo studied at Padua, where he acquired a knowledge of Greek and Latin that enabled him to develop a fascination for ancient philosophy. Upon returning to Venice, he became a senator and quickly rose in civic ranks, being elected to the ruling Council of Ten.

His literary achievements were many and varied. Among his publications were a treatise on ancient inventors and a comparative discussion of ancient and contemporary republican governments. His philosophical works included some of the first Italian translations of Plato's dialogues, which were published in 1574. Connected with his interest in ancient philosophy was his active involvement with antiquities, particularly coins. His coin cabinet was among the finest in Europe and after his death was published by Lorenzo Tiepolo, the civil administrator of San Marco.

Roman Imperial coin with portrait of Augustus, engraving from S. Erizzo, *Discorso sopra le medaglie*, (1559).

Erizzo's only publication on antiquities, *Discorso sopra le medaglie degli antichi con la dichiarazione delle monete consulari e delle medaglie degli imperatori romani* (Venice, 1559), had an immediate impact on the nascent science of numismatics. The appeal was such that it was reprinted in 1568 and again in 1571 (a fourth, more complete edition is without date). Erizzo's work addressed the question whether ancient coins were actually money or commemorative medallions designed to perpetuate the memory of an event or person illustrated, a problem that had plagued scholars in the Renaissance. Although Erizzo erroneously argued that coins were simple medals, his catalog was more complete and more methodical than that of his contemporary rival Enea *Vico, and his study demonstrated a keen awareness and understanding of ancient numismatics.

BIBLIOGRAPHY

Ginguené, "Erizzo (Sebastien)," *BU* 13 (1815), 251–53; A. de Lacaze, "Erizzo (Sebastien)," *NBG* 16 (Paris, 1858), 259; E. Babelon, *Traité des monnaies grecques et romaines,* pt. 1: *Theorie et doctrine* 1 (Paris, 1901), 112.

MICHAEL HOFF

ESTE, ISABELLA D' (1474–1539). Marchioness of Mantua, one of the few women in Renaissance Italy to have built up a major art collection in fulfillment of "lo insatiabile desiderio nostro de cose antique" (our insatiable desire for antiquities).

The foundation of this collection was laid shortly after Isabella arrived in Mantua in 1490 as the bride of the Marquis Francesco II Gonzaga (*Gonzaga family). After his death in 1519, the contents of her Studiolo—Grotta were transferred from the castle to new quarters, the Appartamento della Grotta, in the Corte Vecchia of the Ducal Palace. Years later, in the 1570s, her grandson Duke Guglielmo defended the preservation of this state treasure, which was identified as paramount to "the reputation of the house." Accordingly, it is not surprising that the Grotta was singled out in most travelogues published in the 16th century, including those by Leandro *Alberti and Heinrich Schickhardt.

As the wife of a ruler of a small North Italian state, Isabella had neither the mandate nor the need to enter into a field traditionally dominated by men, and she did not possess the financial means to support this interest. She was, furthermore, unable to look for encouragement (although this problem has been exaggerated out of all proportion) from her husband, who once confessed to knowing more about the breeding of horses than about engraved gems. Nonetheless, Isabella made the most of what was available to her, using the Mantuan ambassadors and orators, family friends and retainers to further her single-minded and lifelong obsession with the decoration of her private apartments. By 1497 she had begun to collect antiquities in quantity, and Isabella was still actively adding to her holdings the year before her death, at which time *Giulio Romano recorded her purchase of a small collection of cameos.

The extent of the influence exerted on Isabella by the cultural milieu of her native Ferrara and by her father, Duke Ercole d'Este, remains to be assessed. It must, nonetheless, have been of paramount importance. In 1498, pitting her interests against those of her father, Isabella ordered an agent in Venice to ship to Mantua, on approval, Domenico de' Piero's antiquities so that Duke Ercole would not see them.

Isabella was not ill disposed to the occasional outlay of sizable sums. Thus, in 1506 she paid 115 ducats for an onyx vase that may be identical to the small cameo object now in the Herzog Anton Ulrich-Museum in Brunswick. More frequently, however, it was through gifts that the collection was augmented. In 1515 Isabella obtained title from the Duke of Milan to the collection of the Sforza of Pesaro. Similarly, she had relied years earlier (in 1501), on the generosity of Cesare Borgia when she came into possession of the Montefeltro treasures. In addition to a *Venus,* about which little is known, Isabella acquired at this time the *Cupid* by *Michelangelo. Together with the version attributed to Praxiteles, which arrived in Mantua in 1506, it became the premier piece in the Grotta; the two statuettes were placed in facing cupboards on either side of the window. Various antique bronzes as well as statuettes by *Antico were displayed along the moldings in the room. A collection of cameos and *pietre dure* vases were housed together with *naturalia* (including branches of coral) in cabinets on the back wall of the Grotta. Three antique busts, including a notable one of *Octavian,* and a unicorn horn completed the decoration of this façade of the room.

Unlike the Grotta, the adjacent Studiolo was designed primarily to set off a series of allegorical pictures and to house a small collection of books. It was, however, under the window in the Studiolo that Isabella placed the large fragment of a *Proserpina* sarcophagus her son had received as a gift from Pope Hadrian VI. Although most of the collection was disbanded at the time of the sale to Charles I and during the subsequent sack of Mantua, this fragment is still in the Ducal Palace, together with a relief of two Satyrs. A bust of *Faustina* acquired from *Mantegna is also in the Ducal Palace. Other pieces, such as the Antico *Hercules and Antaeus,* ended up in the Kunsthistorisches Museum in Vienna while the allegorical pictures are now in the *Louvre in Paris. The celebrated cameo portraits of *Augustus and Livia,* like the twin Cupids, can no longer be identified.

In addition to the generous archival evidence found in Isabella d'Este's correspondence files for a wide range of negotiations (of special interest are letters from her agents Cristoforo Romano and Fra Sabba da *Castiglione), an inventory drawn up in 1542 documents the full extent of the contents of the Studiolo and the Grotta. Leaving aside a large number of handsomely mounted chalcedony, jasper and plasma cups and vases and the 110 medallions mounted on twenty-two plaques, Isabella owned a total of some 1,200 gold, silver and bronze medallions. Accordingly, it was not without reason that the learned Cardinal Pietro *Bembo, himself a knowledgeable collector, wrote favorably of Isabella's efforts, as did Paolo Giovio.

BIBLIOGRAPHY

+S. Béguin, ed., *Le Studiolo d'Isabella d'Este* (Paris, 1975); +C. M. Brown, "New Documents on Isabella d'Este's Collection of Antiquities," *Cultural Aspects of the Italian Renaissance—Essays in Honour of Paul Oskar Kristeller,* ed. C. Clough (Manchester, 1976), 324–53; idem, "The Grotta of Isabella d'Este," *GBA* (May–June 1977), 155–71, (February 1978), 72–82; idem, *La Grotta di Isabella d'Este—Un simbolo di continuità dinastica per i duchi di Mantova* (Mantua, 1985); L. Ventura, ed., *Isabella d'Este: I luoghi del collezionismo* (Modena, 1994); idem, "Isabella d'Este's Apartments in the Corte Vecchia of the Ducal Palace in Mantua," in *The Court of the Gonzaga in the Age of Mantegna, 1450–1550,* ed. R. Oresko et al., forthcoming.

CLIFFORD M. BROWN

ESTE FAMILY. Rulers of the North Italian city-state of Ferrara from the thirteenth century.

Ferrara became a major cultural force in Italy during the reign of LEONELLO (1407–50), who was himself one of the earliest collectors of ancient gems. A similar interest in ancient art was evidenced by his successors, as is shown by the inventory drawn up in 1494 during the time of ERCOLE I (1431–1505). Father to both Isabella (d'*Este) and Alfonso (themselves among the leading collectors of their time), Ercole encouraged a love of the antique in his children. It is uncertain, however, whether or not he succeeded in negotiating the purchase of Pope *Paul II's collection of antique bronze statuettes that was offered to him in 1486 through the Venetian jeweler Domenico de' Piero.

ALFONSO I (1474–1534) directed his main efforts toward the decoration of his *camerino* in the Via Coperta, where Federico Gonzaga (*Gonzaga family) saw a collection of both modern and ancient vases and statues. Alfonso's main interests seem to have lain, however, in other areas. According to Celio Calcagnini, the duke proposed a method whereby both the obverse and the reverse of mounted medallions could be seen. The extent of the family's holdings in 1540 is known from the scholarly inventory drawn up for ERCOLE II (1508–59). The fifty-six *tabulae* may correspond not only to the mounts but also to the drawers in the cabinet in which this collection was housed.

That a scholarly interest in antique medallions remained a matter of special interest to the Este is known from the fact that ALFONSO II (1533–97) obtained the loan of Cesare Gonzaga's medallion cabinet in 1564. Presumably, the task of inspecting its contents was left to the court antiquarian Enea *Vico, who was responsible in 1565 for negotiating the purchase of three major collections of medallions at a total cost of over 3,000 scudi.

Letters from the ducal archaeological agent in Rome, Alessandro de Grandi (1565–72), document the growth of the Estense collection under Alfonso II, for whom Pirro *Ligorio built a library and museum (*antiquarium*) on the southeast side of the Castello. In addition to negotiations for the antiquities of Rodolfo Pio da *Carpi, a license was received in 1571 for the removal from Rome of fourteen busts; an additional six, together with marbles, departed the following February. Ten years later, Claudio Ariosto negotiated in Venice the purchase of over one hundred statues and busts, while the inventory of the collection is dated to 1584. An equally important catalog of the Este holdings is found among the Aldrovandi papers in Bologna (143, III, cc. 18v-23).

After the death of Alfonso II, CESARE (1567–1628) surrendered the government of Ferrara to the pope and left for Modena. Presumably at this time, he removed many of the Este treasures, including the celebrated collections of medallions.

Of the other members of the Este family, the brothers of the rulers of Ferrara, Cardinal IPPOLITO II (1509–72) was most passionately commited to ancient art; his collections were divided between Rome and his villa at Tivoli.

BIBLIOGRAPHY

Documenti inediti per servire alla storia dei musei d'Italia (Florence, 1879), II iv–ix, 100–155; G. Gruyer, *L'Art ferrarais a l'époque des princes d'Este* (Paris, 1897); D. Coffin, "Pirro Ligorio and Decoration of the Late 16th Century at Ferrara," *ArtB 37* (1955), 167–85; Idem, *The Villa d'Este at Tivoli* (Princeton, NJ, 1960); D. Goodgal, "The Camerino of Alfonso I d'Este," *Art History* 1 (1978), 162–90; E. Corradini, "Le raccolte estensi di antichità," in *L'Impresa di Alfonso II,* ed. J. Bentini—L. Spezzaferro (Bologna, 1987), 163–92.

CLIFFORD M. BROWN

ETRUSCAN TOMBS. Etruscan burials, especially in underground, rock-cut chambers in use from the seventh to the first centuries B.C. in ancient Etruria (in Tuscany, Umbria and Latium of modern Italy).

A great percentage of our knowledge of the Etruscans comes from their burials. It is clear that their tombs were known and entered from the Middle Ages onward. At Tarquinia, the Tomba Bartoccini contains inscriptions of the Late Gothic period showing that the tomb was used as a place of Christian worship. The twelfth-century chronicle of *William of Malmesbury preserves accounts of visits to underground chambers, probably Etruscan, in Italy.

During the Renaissance an Etruscan tomb was opened in 1466 at *Volterra, containing—as described by Antonio Ivano of Sarzano—what was obviously Etruscan pottery and stone ash urns of a type commonly found there. It has been suggested that *Michelangelo may have known such sculptured urns, since his *Pietà* in Florence (before 1555; Museo del Opera del Duomo) shows a dead Christ in a pose similar to that of Patroklos on Volterran ash urns with the *Death of Patroklos.* Michelangelo's drawing of a bearded male in a wolf-skin cap (Casa Buonarroti, Florence) is almost certainly based on an Etruscan tomb painting of

the underworld deity *Aita* (Hades). Michelangelo is one of many major Renaissance artists—*Donatello, *Brunelleschi, Leonardo, *Cellini, *Vasari—who seem to have had knowledge of Etruscan antiquities. *Alberti's interest in Etruscan architecture led him to attempt a reconstruction of the (lost) tomb of Lars Porsenna of *Chiusi (described by Pliny the Elder, *NH* 26.91).

In the early sixteenth century, *Annio of *Viterbo evidently excavated tombs in the area of his home city (although his treatment of the material was untrustworthy). About one hundred years later Athanasius *Kircher made a tour of Etruria and visited rock-cut chambers at *Bomarzo that must have been like the tombs at *Cerveteri, with beds, chairs and other furniture carved out of the living rock. Kircher reports (1659) the local belief that the chambers were built for habitation by cave-dwelling troglodytes like those of Malta. There is also evidence from the sixteenth and seventeenth centuries that antiquities were being extracted from Etruscan burials and collected and studied. Cassiano dal *Pozzo ordered drawings recording Etruscan bronzes (Windsor Castle), and *Poussin has left a drawing of an Etruscan mirror as well as paintings that seem to show the influence of such objects.

An explosion of interest in the Etruscans, the *Etruscheria of the eighteenth century, went hand in hand with the discovery of new tombs. Purposeful searching in and around Volterra led to the discovery of many Hellenistic tombs and the collection of pottery and ash urns. Mario *Guarnacci carried out systematic excavation to secure finds for his Etruscan museum (later, the Museo Etrusco Guarnacci, Volterra), and Pietro Bucelli ardently collected such materials; his heirs later immured some one hundred urns into the façade of Palazzo Bucelli at Montepulciano. The indefatigable *Gori, who toured northern Etruria to visit collectors and sites, in 1728 supervised excavations of a number of tombs on the property of P. Franceschini at Volterra and made a vivid record of the event. In his *Museum Etruscum* (1737) he published the plan and elevation of the Caecina Tomb, showing the locations of some forty ash urns.

Later in the eighteenth century, Corneto (i.e., *Tarquinia) began to attract attention, and because of its painted decoration it became and has remained the single most exciting locale of Etruscan tombs. Thomas *Jenkins conducted excavation there (1761), and James *Byres gave guided tours and commissioned copies of some of the frescoes. Between 1828 and 1833, some ten new tombs were discovered in the Monterozzi necropolis at Tarquininia. The *Hyperboreans, led by *Stackelberg, took a great interest and explored the newly discovered sepulchres, such as the Tomb of the Baron, Tomb of the Inscriptions and Tomb of the Chariot (Tomba delle Bighe), of which Stackelberg made beautiful watercolor copies. The painter Carlo *Ruspi soon arrived, commissioned first by E. *Gerhard for the *Instituto di Corrispondenza Archeologica (*German Archaeological Institute) to make copies of the Querciola Tomb. Ruspi conceived the idea of making tracings as preparatory drawings for actual-size facsimiles of Etruscan tomb paintings. His first facsimiles were made for the *Vatican and were displayed in the new Museo Gregoriano Etrusco; others were then made for *Ludwig I of Bavaria through commission from his agent Martin von *Wagner. These would adorn Ludwig's Room of the Vases in his Pinacotheka at Munich. The copies made included the Querciola and the Tombs of the Triclinium, of the Inscriptions, of the Chariots, of the Dead Man and of the Baron.

In this same period the rock-cut tombs of *Cerveteri were under exploration; in 1836 was discovered the incomparable *Regolini-Galassi Tomb, an Orientalizing burial with spectacular grave goods (now in the Vatican). The Marchese *Campana excavated the Tomb of the Reliefs (1846–47) and the "Sarcophagus of the Spouses," now in the *Louvre, as well as the Campana Tomb at Veii (1842/43). At *Perugia, the Tomb of the Volumni was found in 1840; at *Vulci, *Francois discovered the remarkable François Tomb (1857), and the *Campanari family excavated tombs for Pope *Gregory XVI (1834). Lucien Bonaparte, Prince of *Canino, removed a staggering number of Greek vases from his personal estate, setting the tone for the plundering of Etruscan tombs for vases that persists to the present (cf. *Metropolitan Museum of Art). An important event that brought Etruscan tombs to a wider public was the exhibition of the Campanari in London, in which they created captivating reconstructions of Etruscan tombs.

The great publications of Etruscan tombs began to appear. Mrs. Hamilton Gray's *Tour to the Sepulchres of Etruria in 1839* was followed by Byres's *Hypogaei or Sepulchral Caverns of Tarquinia, The Capital of Ancient Etruria* (in 1842, long after his death). The masterpiece of George *Dennis, *Cities and Cemeteries of Etruria,* first published in 1848, gathered together a vast amount of information about Etruscan tombs.

In the twentieth century, Etruscan tombs have been excavated in untold numbers up and down the length and breadth of Etruria and contiguous regions, ranging in date from the Iron Age (ninth–eighth centuries B.C.) to the Hellenistic period (third–first centuries B.C.). Plundering and treasure hunting continued at the same time that improved techniques of excavation and ethical considerations promoted scientific research to secure more data for the understanding of the archaeological contexts. At *Populonia, A. Minto discovered numerous monumental stone tombs of the Archaic period after the removal (begun in 1908) of heaps of incompletely processed iron slag that had been dumped over the necropolis in antiquity. At Tarquinia the *Lerici Foundation discovered some 6,000 tombs through geophysical prospection (1955–62), of which the most important painted ones are the Tomb of the Jugglers and the Tomb of the Hunter. Among most recent finds at the Tarquinian necropoleis are the Tomb of the Aninas Family in the Scataglini area and the Tomb of the Blue Demons, discovered in 1985 during work on a highway next to the Monterozzi; it contains the earliest-known representations of the terrifying devils that populate late Etruscan tomb painting and sculpture. Investigations at Cortona, beginning in 1987, unearthed a funerary altar attached to the Tomba Melone del Sodo II (originally excavated by Minto, 1928–29), decorated with Archaic stone sculptures of lionesses (or sphinxes) attacking humans.

BIBLIOGRAPHY
+F. Weege, *Etruskische Malerei* (Halle, 1921); +M. Moretti, *New Monuments of Etruscan Painting,* tr. D. Kiang (University Park, PA, 1970); +*Pittura etrusca, disegni e documenti del XIX secolo dell'Archivio dell'Instituto Archeologico Germanico di Roma* (Rome, 1986); +N. T. de Grummond, "Rediscovery," in *Etruscan Life and Afterlife* (Detroit, 1986), 18–46; +*Les Étrusques et l'Europe* (Paris, 1992).

ETRUSCHERIA. Passion for Etruscan art and civilization that spread through Europe in the eighteenth century.

Although Etruscan tombs, inscriptions and objects were identified and studied at least as early as the fifteenth century (cf. *Etruscan tombs), in the eighteenth century Etruscan antiquities became enormously popular.

Both a symptom and a cause of *Etruscheria* was the publication in 1723–26 of Thomas *Dempster's *De Etruria regali,* resurrected from a seventeenth-century manuscript by Thomas Coke and published with notes by F. *Buonarroti and attractive copperplate illustration. The vogue for Etruscan things led to the founding of an academy, the *Accademia Etrusca at Cortona (1726); exploration and excavations at a number of old Etruscan cities—*Volterra, Siena, *Arezzo, *Cortona, *Tarquinia; and the formation of collections (e.g., the *Guarnacci antiquities at Volterra). A surge of interest in the language led to dramatic progress in its interpretation, especially by Luigi *Lanzi.

The mania for the Etruscans led to the attribution of Greek vases (found in abundance in Etruscan tombs) to Etruscan artists, a development that explains why Josiah *Wedgwood could call "Etruria" the factory where his magnificent classicizing vases were produced. Interiors were decorated in the "Etruscan taste" by Robert Adam (e.g., the Etruscan Room at Osterley park, 1775–77), who drew inspiration from Greek vases and Pompeian painting (*Adam family). G. B. *Piranesi, with his engravings and publications, was perhaps the most visible of the Etruscan partisans, who were prone to attribute to the Etruscans the invention of a number of elements of civilization, including architecture, law, navigation, science. The Etruscan (or Tuscan) form of the Doric order, with the column sitting on its own base and with its narrow capital, became popular throughout Europe and today is more widespread in England and America than the Greek Doric.

BIBLIOGRAPHY
M. Cristofani, *La Scoperta degli etruschi, Archeologia e antiquaria nel '700* (Rome, 1983); F. Borsi, ed., *Fortuna degli etruschi,* catalog of exhibition (Milan, 1985); N. T. de Grummond, "Rediscovery," in *Etruscan Life and Afterlife,* ed. L. Bonfante (Detroit, 1986), 37–40; *Les Étrusques et l'Europe* (Paris, 1992), esp. 275–321.

EVANS, SIR ARTHUR JOHN (1851–1941). English archaeologist, the excavator of *Knossos in *Crete and discoverer of Minoan civilization.

The son of Sir John Evans (1823–1908), the eminent naturalist, authority on prehistoric remains and numismatist, Arthur grew up amid wealth and scientific

Photograph of (*l. to r.*) *Arthur Evans, Duncan Mackenzie, and Theodore Fyfe* at Knossos. (The Ashmolean Museum, Oxford.)

study. As a small child he began his own collection of coins and ancient objects. He was always extraordinarily nearsighted but was gifted with a remarkably clear vision of exceedingly minute details.

Neither at Harrow nor at Brasenose College, Oxford, did Evans distinguish himself. In 1871, however, he published his first paper on numismatics and began his peregrinations in the Balkans, which led to his book *Through Bosnia and the Herzegovina on Foot* (1877), his position as political writer for the *Manchester Guardian* and his residence and later (1882) his imprisonment at Ragusa (Dubrovnik). In 1878 he had married Margaret Freeman, daughter of the historian E. A. Freeman, whose four-volume *History of Sicily* Evans completed after Freeman's death in 1892; she died the year after her father.

Evans, keeper of the *Ashmolean Museum since 1884, then turned his attention to the early systems of writing in Europe. Interest in engraved gems and seals led him to Crete in 1894, and Crete remained Evans's scholarly focal point for the rest of his long life. In 1900 he began excavating at Knossos, a site that he had privately bought. Within five years the remains of the great palace were brought to light and provided the basis for a complete reevaluation of Aegean prehistory. Evans had continued publishing steadily: *Cretan Pictographs and Pre-Phoenician Script* (1896), *Mycenaean Tree and Pillar Cult* (1901), *Prehistoric Tombs of Knossos* (1905) and the epochal *Scripta Minoa* (1909), among others.

In 1911 his great contribution to knowledge was recognized by the award of knighthood, but his crowning work, *The Palace of Minos,* yet lay in the future. Volume I was published in 1921; volume II, parts 1 and 2, in 1928; volume III, in 1930; volume IV, parts 1 and 2, in 1935; and the index (in collaboration with his half-sister, the art historian Joan Evans) in 1936. *The Palace of Minos* is a far broader synthesis of the Minoan world than its title implies, and it remains fundamental in Aegean Bronze Age studies. The restorations carried out in the palace and its dependencies by Evans, largely at his own expense, represent the style of an earlier age of archaeological technique than the present and were always controversial, but they have contributed immeasurably to public interest in and support of archaeology. As Carl W. *Blegen wrote of him at the time of his death:

It is the great achievement of Evans, founded on his observation of the stratification discovered at Knossos and on his knowledge of the related material, to have created an orderly comprehensive synthesis from the scattered and uncoordinated evidence at hand, and to have drawn up the first systematic outline of early history in the Aegean. His division of the Cretan Bronze Age into three periods, Early, Middle and Late, proved to be applicable in general terms (though with minor differences in the subdivisions) to the whole of the Aegean area, and he thus laid an enduring foundation for all later work in this field. His recognition of the creative role played by Minoan Crete in the origin and evolution of the earliest European civilization will stand unchallenged; while his recovery and brilliant reconstruction of a culture long buried and completely lost will remain a lasting memorial to his genius. (*AJA* 45 [1941], 612–13)

BIBLIOGRAPHY
J. Evans, *Time and Chance, The Story of Arthur Evans and His Forebears* (London, 1943); S. L. Horowitz, *The Find of a Lifetime: Sir Arthur Evans and the Discovery of Knossos* (New York, 1981).

W. W. DE GRUMMOND

EXCAVATIONS AND EXPEDITIONS. As early as the eleventh century monks of St. Albans excavated antiquities of Roman Britain during a search for building materials at ancient *Verulamium. A similar situation resulted in the discovery of ancient pottery and sarcophagi at Nogent in northern France in the early twelfth century. The abbot of Nogent, *Guibert, described the find in careful detail and was led to conclude that the materials were pre-Christian. Such excavation, attested numerous times in the history of sites rich in reusable marble or limestone, was not archaeological in purpose, but the modest scholarship sometimes associated with it may be linked with the kind of salvaging and recording of information made during projects of clearing and excavation that attend urban renewal or construction.

Purposeful travel to archaeological sites in order to make records begins in 1375 with Giovanni *Dondi, who left his native Padua to visit Rome, where he took abundant notes, copied inscriptions and made measurements of classical monuments. In 1415–16 *Buondelmonti traveled to *Crete, the Greek islands and Constantinople (*Byzantium) and on his travels made maps of the cities he visited, including indications of ancient ruins, with other topographical features. He was followed by *Ciriaco of Ancona, whose travels in the 1420s and 1430s ranged widely in Italy, Greece and the Levant. Ciriaco's diaries contained descriptions and drawings of antiquities and copies of over 1,000 inscriptions. A similar instinct to search out antiquities and inscriptions is seen in the survey around Lake Garda made by *Mantegna, *Felice Feliciano, *Marcanova and Samuele da Tradate (1464) and the trips of numerous artists and tourists who went underground to see the ruins of the *Domus Aurea (beginning around 1480).

As the demand for antiquities burgeoned, entrepreneurs began to dig specifically for the purpose of finding portable and marketable antiquities. In this case the finds were not accidental but extracted in accordance with a plan. Nevertheless, the plan was a quite simple one, involving what may only be called treasure hunting, a practice that has a very long and unfortunate history, especially in the city of Rome. *Alberti's fascinating attempt to carry out *underwater excavation and raise the Roman ships at *Nemi (1446–48), though it featured systematic preparation and an interest in truly historical material, is not far removed from this kind of search for objects. The so-called excavation by *Annio of Viterbo, in which he salted a tomb and pretended to discover it for the first time in the presence of Pope Alexander VI (1493), is a shameful episode in the history of excavation.

There must have been many attempts in the sixteenth century to clear ancient ruins so that they could be mapped. Numerous surviving drawings and engravings by a variety of architects reveal an impulse to measure and record the plans and elevations of ancient buildings. *Palladio has left plans and sections of such monuments, including baths in Rome and the *Temple of Fortuna at Praeneste. There is debate over his accuracy, but the basic methodology is rational and archaeological. Pirro *Ligorio is a more elusive, controversial figure, difficult to evaluate because of the sheer enormity of his writings and drawings and because he had a tendency to ''complete'' imaginatively an artifact or building he was drawing. He did reconstructions of a number of buildings of Rome and excavated at *Hadrian's Villa to locate ancient sculptures for his patron, Cardinal Ippolito d'Este (*Este family).

The mapping of sites, especially of Rome, was a significant archaeological pastime in the sixteenth century. Annio da Viterbo was a pioneer, but once again he brings embarrassment—this time because of his forgery of a map of the

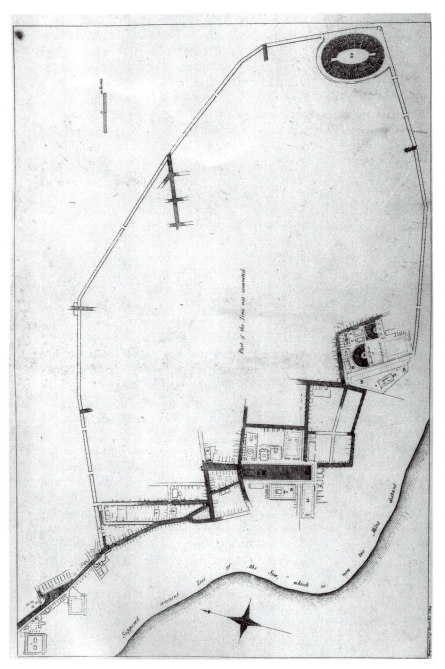

Plan of excavated portions of Pompeii, lithograph by J. D. Harding, from W. Light, *Views of Pompeii* (1828). (Deutsches Archäologisches Institut, Rome. Inst. Neg. 92.878.)

ancient city, which he attributed to the early Roman writer Fabius Pictor. Annio depicted the city as shaped like a bow, with the Tiber as its chord, and divided the city into four squared sections. A far more reputable project was that of *Raphael, who was commissioned by Pope *Leo X to prepare a map of ancient Rome. Making a survey of the city with A. *Fulvio, he devised a way to place the monuments according to their listing in the Late Antique regionary catalogs of the city. Raphael died before he made his map, but there may be some reflection of it in the engraved plates made by Marco Fabio Calvo in 1532 (*Antiquae urbis Romae cum regionibus simulacrum*); the city of Rome is shown as round, with sixteen equal sectors (two are added to the ancient fourteen regions). In each of the slices of the pie are represented the major monuments of the region. A totally different approach was that of L. Bufalini (1551), who laboriously measured the entire circuit of the contemporary city and inserted the ancient monuments into the two-dimensional street plan. *Marliani created a map of the ancient city only, with fortifications, hills and plans of some of the key monuments, likewise two-dimensional. Ligorio also made maps of Rome, his masterpiece being a great, panoramic bird's-eye view of the city in 1561. Antonio Tempesta created the most splendid map of this type, a panorama in twelve separate sheets (total size, 109 × 245cm), which was done with great accuracy and artistic sense (1593).

In the seventeenth century began a new exploration of Greece, as agents for scholars and princes searched for appropriate antiquities in the 1620s. *Peiresc yearned for Greek inscriptions, and *Arundel had Petty and *Roe scouring Turkey and the Aegean for marbles, with considerable success. *Nointel visited the *Akropolis in Athens and had priceless drawings made, recording the *Parthenon sculptures before their removal (1674), and the faithful travelers *Spon and *Wheler visited and identified many sites in Greece (1675–76), making highly schematic bird's-eye maps, plans and elevations and writing descriptions that would be immensely useful to later topographers. These were but a prelude to the numerous expeditions to follow in the eighteenth and nineteenth centuries. An organization now sponsored expeditions for the retrieval of archaeological knowledge in Greece, the *Society of Dilettanti in London. It sent *Stuart and *Revett to Athens (1751–53), where they produced an excellent plan and views of the city, as well as plans, elevations, details and views of numerous monuments, all of remarkable beauty and accuracy. Also for the Dilettanti, an expedition was dispatched to Asia Minor, led by *Chandler, with *Pars and *Revett as artists. *Elgin and his agents dismantled and carried away many of the marbles of the *Parthenon and other monuments on the Athenian Akropolis (1801–4); although the undertaking involved searching in the rubble of the Akropolis, it could scarcely be called an excavation. Nevertheless, Elgin is justified in his claim that the project was not looting but an attempt to save classical antiquities; thus, it counts as an attempt at archaeological preservation. Only slightly more purposeful were the excavations of C. R. *Cockerell and *Haller von Hallerstein, the leaders of an international group of young architects and scholars with a heart for adventure. They supervised the excavation of the temples at *Aigina (1811) and at *Bassai (1811–12; joined by *Stackelberg) and made exquisite architectural drawings. Their hauls of sculpture were sold to *Ludwig I of Bavaria and to the *British Museum.

In Italy, excavations had begun at *Herculaneum (1709) and *Pompeii (1748) for the *Bourbon family. It is customary to vilify the early excavations at Pompeii, largely as a result of the scathing criticisms made by *Winckelmann (1762), who, having been snubbed by the royal court, had motivation for his bitter remarks. It is true that treasures were extracted, as in the past, with insufficient regard for the context and that the excavation strategy was haphazard. But excellent plans were made of the buildings that were excavated, and an interesting innovation was made in regard to publication. For the multivolume work on Herculaneum, an organized committee held regular meetings at which they pooled their knowledge, discussing the finds to reach a consensus (*Academia Herculanensis).

The efforts of Etruscan scholars were less conspicuous, and their motives less suspect. They, too, formed a group to foster their research, the *Accademia Etrusca (1727), where they might deliver and receive news of the latest discoveries. Insufficiently recognized is the remarkable work of *Buonarroti and *Gori, who made surveys and undertook excavation for the increase of knowledge rather than for the acquisition of antiquities, which were, in general, an unglamorous lot. Buonarroti made a survey of tombs around Civita Castellani (*Falerii Veteres) in 1691 and systematically recorded the exterior of the tombs, the structure of the interiors, the inscriptions and the finds, which included some painted but modest ash urns. His discussion of his work, published in his notes to *Dempster's *De Etruria regali* (1723), is comparable to modern excavation reports. Gori supervised the excavation of tombs at *Volterra (1728 and following) and recorded in great and objective detail the finds, including urns and pottery, plans and elevations and even a top map showing the location of the urns. Measurements of some of the urns and tombs were included. The successors in Etruria of Gori and Buonarroti were the explorers at the painted tombs of *Tarquinia of the late eighteenth and early nineteenth centuries. *Byres secured copies of some of the frescoes (1760s), followed by Stackelberg and his companions (1827), who opened and recorded the spectacular painted tombs there (*Etruscan tombs).

Work continued at Pompeii in the nineteenth century, with the finest results achieved when Giuseppe *Fiorelli was put in charge in 1860. Fiorelli's approach was scientific; he had a careful strategy for uncovering the city on a measured scheme, dividing it into regions and blocks (*insulae*) and giving each house a code number. One of Fiorelli's most ingenious ideas was a system of taking plaster casts of organic materials, especially human, that had been encapsulated by the volcanic ash and had thus left a hollow cavity in the earth. By pumping wet plaster into the empty cavities, he created the casts of bodies that still may be seen around the site of Pompeii. The diametric opposite of the scrupulous, professional Fiorelli was the Marchese *Campana, an adventurer who discovered and excavated numerous sites and carried away many works of art for his collection or for sale. His disastrous misuse of funds at his bank led to the sensational sale of his antiquities in 1861.

In the eighteenth and nineteenth centuries, British and American archaeologists made significant contributions to fieldwork. The *Society of Antiquaries of London, officially founded in 1707, provided a haven for those interested in the antiquities of Britain—whether prehistoric, Roman or medieval—and encouraged exploration in the field. William *Stukely (d. 1765) copied inscriptions and made plans of Roman and other sites; he was among the first to realize that the growth patterns of crops on the surface of the earth reflected monuments underneath. Thomas *Jefferson is credited with being the first to understand that strata of earth on an archaeological site could give clues to the sequence of activities. Though he was an avid student of classical architecture, his observations were, in fact, made in reference to native American mounds on his estate in Virginia (1784). The insights of this colonial archaeologist were without immediate successors. Yet another figure who remains somewhat isolated is Richard Pullan, whose expedition to *Priene for the Society of Dilettanti (1868–69) included the earliest-known use of a two-dimensional grid of trenches and also one of the first attempts to record excavation through photography. Soon afterward, General *Pitt-Rivers developed his celebrated rigorous field methods, in excavations privately financed at his own estate of Cranborne Chase (1884–90). Including Romano-British sites in his investigations, he utilized gridding and careful stratigraphical excavation, noting the relationship of objects to their context and recording the cross-sections of earth in the balks of his trenches. He was a pioneer in the observation of faunal remains in an archaeological context.

Excavation in Greece had a totally different character after the liberation of the country from the Turks. The *Greek Archaeological Society, founded in 1837, undertook responsible excavations immediately in the *Theater of Dionysos in Athens and soon afterward in the Odeion of Herodes Atticus, the *Tower of the Winds and the *Agora, as well as on the *Akropolis. The nineteenth century also saw the beginning of exploration under the aegis of foreign institutions that were able to secure the funding for increasingly expensive labors. The *Expédition scientifique de Morée sponsored by the French government was a multidisciplinary project, well in advance of its time, that investigated the ancient ruins of the Greek Peloponnese along with its geography and natural history (1829–31). The French were also the first to found a school in Athens as a base for archaeologists and their students (1846; *French School at Athens); their major excavations, continuing into the twentieth century, were at *Delos (begun 1877) and *Delphi (from 1892). They were followed by the *German Archaeological Institute at Athens (founded 1874), with ongoing missions at *Olympia (from 1876) and the *Kerameikos Excavations in Athens (from 1907). The *American School of Classical Studies opened its doors in 1882 and provided a base for American scholars doing research at *Corinth (from 1896) and

in the *Agora at Athens (from 1930). The next school to be founded was the
*British School at Athens (1886); it sponsored many excavations but is espe-
cially associated with the continuation of the work of Sir Arthur *Evans at
Knossos (from 1900). The Italians were among the earliest to work on *Crete
(at *Gortyn, 1884), though they did not create the *Italian School of Archae-
ology in Athens until 1909. From this base they excavated on the islands of
Lemnos (from 1919) and *Rhodes (from 1929), as well as continuing work at
Gortyn.

The movement to found such archaeological institutes actually began in Italy,
with the *Instituto di Corrispondenza Archeologica, created in 1827. Originally
an international body, with cooperation among scholars of Italy, France, Germany and other nations, it gradually became the province of the Germans and
ultimately was transformed into the *German Archaeological Institute (officially
founded in 1871). The foreign schools in Italy did not focus so closely on one
or two particular sites as did their Greek counterparts but became involved with
a variety of projects. The *French School in Rome (founded in 1873) did not
begin its well-known campaigns at *Bolsena until 1946. The *British School at
Rome (founded 1899) developed its involvement with North Africa and southern
Etruria especially under the direction of J. B. *Ward-Perkins (1946–74). The
*American Academy in Rome, officially founded in 1905, sponsored excava-
tions at *Cosa (from 1948) and in the *Forum Romanum (from 1964). Italian
excavators often working for the government made important strides in the excavation of the city of Rome, for example, Giacomo *Boni, who is noted for
having employed stratigraphical analysis in the Forum Romanum (1898 and
following), and Rodolfo *Lanciani, who worked in a number of places in the
city. Lanciani's greatest achievement lay in his fundamental archaeological map
of Rome, the *Forma Urbis Romae,* issued in forty-six sheets. Italian archaeology
in the twentieth century has come to be conducted under the umbrella of a
national ministry (Ministero per i Beni Culturali e Ambientali), with supervision
by the appropriate superintendents and inspectors in each region of Italy.

The period of the founding of the great archaeological schools was contemporary with that of the magnificent private archaeologists, Sir Arthur *Evans
and Heinrich *Schliemann. (The plunderer of *Cyprus, General *Cesnola, did
not make a significant contribution to the history of excavation.) With their own
wealth they were able to sponsor the kind of large-scale excavations that were
otherwise being carried out by institutes. Evans at Knossos (from 1900) and
Schliemann at *Troy (from 1871), *Mycenae (from 1876), *Tiryns (from 1876)
and other sites developed strategies for moving enormous amounts of earth. By
means of excavation they revealed a culture that was almost totally unknown
before, that of Bronze Age Aegean Greece. This was an area that would prove
to be very fruitful in the twentieth century, with numerous new sites to occupy
both foreign and Greek archaeologists.

Like the schools, Evans and Schliemann began to use a more sophisticated
division of tasks, so that an excavation would base itself on the labor of local

men and women, would have experts in architecture, restoration, mapping and photography and would have an individual to keep a daybook, often the director. Schliemann is credited with calling in outside experts for consultation and thus having a multidisciplinary approach to archaeological sites.

The excavation of classical (and other) sites in the twentieth century has become a well-organized industry. Universities, museums and foundations have joined the national bureaus and schools in Greece, Italy and other nations with classical antiquities, in providing funding and staffing for excavations far too numerous to list. These projects normally adhere to excavation techniques and principles that have evolved steadily to the point that they have become part of standard procedure in the field. Among the regular features of a well-conceived excavation in the twentieth century are the preliminary survey and formulation of strategy, the establishment of an accurate grid, the use of good photography and recording in the field, appropriate techniques for cleaning, restoration and conservation, efficient cataloging, photography and drawing for retrieval and study of finds and timely dissemination of the results of excavation. Many believe in the multidisciplinary ideal, in which visiting specialists are consulted, though few plan an excavation from the beginning to have a balanced interdisciplinary strategy (as did the *Minnesota Messenia Expedition). Compared with the total picture of excavations of previous centuries, it is clear that a significant evolution has taken place. Increasing reliance on the resources of modern science and the techniques of New World anthropologists now suggest that a revolution is at hand. To the familiar surveying instruments and microscopes are added computers, not only for organizing data but also for mapping and simulation of monuments (*computers in archaeology). Innovators debate the usage of new technology not only for excavation but also for the avoiding of excavation. Acutely aware that excavation means destruction of evidence, many advocate the employment of surveys and remote sensing that allow the accumulation of data without the time, expense and destruction involved in full-scale excavation, or at least they wish to supplement excavation with such nondestructive techniques. One of the most successful applications of geophysical prospection was that of the *Lerici Foundation used in the 1960s to locate thousands of tombs in Etruria. Periscopic cameras allowed the investigators to determine which tombs should actually be excavated. Aerial photography became a method for locating sites as a result of reconaissance missions during World War II (*Bradford) and has found its continuation in the balloon photography of Julian and Eunice Whittlesey utilized at numerous sites and of J. Wilson and Eleanor Myers on Bronze Age Aegean sites on Crete. Satellite photography can also assist in the locating of sites and the analysis of the use of farmlands and other resources. (See also *underwater archaeology.)

BIBLIOGRAPHY
Michaelis; G. E. Daniel, *A Short History of Archaeology* (London, 1981); Stoneman, *Land of Lost Gods;* Weiss, *RDCA;* B. Trigger, *A History of Archaeological Thought* (Cambridge, 1989).

Frontispiece, engraving from A. Blouet et al., *Expédition scientifique de Morée* (1831–38). (Deutsches Archäologisches Institut, Rome. Inst. Neg. 68.5323.)

EXPÉDITION SCIENTIFIQUE DE MORÉE (Scientific Expedition to the Morea).

French research expedition to the Peloponnese (Morea) and the Cyclades led by the naturalist J.-B. Bory de Saint-Vincent.

A French government resolution of 1828 founded the Expédition, whose motivation, "to render homage to the glorious country that the armed might of France has set free," was at once romantic and nationalistic. Its purpose, however, was scientific: to explore and describe the land, its geology, its natural history and to record its ancient monuments. Bory was further enjoined to extend his research beyond these subjects to include "places and men"—what would today be called human geography.

The Expédition consisted of two parts: Bory was charged with the supervision of the physical sciences, and the architect and antiquarian *Blouet (1795–1853) with the supervision of the recording of ancient monuments.

From 1829 until 1831, Bory and his brigades of topographers, geologists, botanists, zoologists, entomologists, antiquarians, artists, draftsmen and epigraphers conducted an exhaustive survey of the Peloponnese and the Cyclades, collecting specimens, mapping, drawing and recording. Such a collaboration among scientists and antiquarians was unprecedented. The resulting publication, a finely illustrated and thorough study of the landscape, its monuments and natural history, continues to serve as a basic source for Peloponnesian research of all periods.

BIBLIOGRAPHY

M. Bory de Saint-Vincent et al., *Expédition (Commission) Scientifique de Morée, Section des sciences physiques* (Paris, 1832–36), 3 vols. in 5 and atlas; A. Blouet et al., *Expédition Scientifique de Morée, ordonée par le gouvernement français: Architecture, sculptures, inscriptions et vues du Péloponnèse, des Cyclades et de l'Attique* (Paris, 1831–38); A. Lecroix, "Notice historique sur Bory de Saint-Vincent," *Mémoires de l'Académie Nationale des Sciences* 54 (1902), i–lxxv.

S. L. PETRAKIS

F

FABRETTI, RAFFAELO (1619–1700). Italian archaeologist and epigrapher.

Born at Urbino, Fabretti worked in Rome for popes and cardinals, including service on a diplomatic mission to Spain. Under Innocent XI he was made keeper of the archives at Castel Sant'Angelo, a post he held until his death. Fabretti spent much time in Rome and Latium investigating aqueducts and their sources. His results were published in a full account of Roman aqueducts, *De aquis et aquaeductibus veteris Romae dissertationes tres* (Rome, 1680). As he pursued the courses of aqueducts, he indefatigably recorded Latin inscriptions in and around Rome. It is reported that he was aided in his discoveries by a unique assistant: his horse, named Marco Polo, had the remarkable habit of standing stock-still when he came near an antiquity and in some manner pointing toward the find. Fabretti published inscriptions he had personally collected in his *Inscriptionum antiquarum quae in aedibus paternis asservantae descriptio* (Rome, 1699). His collection of inscriptions and other antiquities became part of the holdings of the Palazzo Ducale, Urbino.

Fabretti also produced a publication (a folio edition) on the *Column of Trajan, *De columna Trajani syntagma* (Rome, 1683), which contained as well an early treatment of the *Tabula Iliaca, used to advantage by *Beger. Fabretti had a running quarrel with Jacob Gronovius (*Gronovius family) over the interpretation of Livy, and he corresponded with *Spon, *Mabillon and other learned antiquarians of his time.

BIBLIOGRAPHY

S.v. "Fabretti, Raphael," *NBG* 16 (1858), cols. 942–43; Stark, 116, 142, 143, 258, 280; Sandys, II, 280.

FACELLUS. See FAZELLO.

FAESULAE. See FIESOLE.

FALERII VETERES (CIVITA CASTELLANA; FALERIA). Faliscan/
Etruscan city.

Falerii Veteres, 54km north of Rome, on a narrow ridge between the Filetto
and the Maggiore rivers, considered itself Etruscan, though its inhabitants spoke
and wrote an Italic language not unlike Latin. Its tombs line the cliffs below
the city and along the rivers; the oldest are cremation burials of the seventh
century, and the latest are chamber tombs of the third century. In 241 B.C. Rome
conquered the Faliscans; the city was abandoned, but its temples were still visited.

Investigations were made at Civita Castellana in the late seventeenth century
by *Buonarroti. In the late nineteenth century four temple complexes were discovered, the first, at Celle north of Falerii on the Maggiore, in 1886. Pasqui
identified this, probably correctly, with Ovid's temple of Juno Curritis (*Amores*
3.13). Votive material dates from the Bronze Age; temple terracottas from the
fifth to the second centuries. Cozza uncovered a second temple in 1887 at Lo
Scasato within the city. Its beautiful terracottas may be as late as the second
century. Inscriptions from two other temples, one found in 1894 at Sassi Caduti
outside the city, and the other in 1896 at Vignale, on the arx, suggest that the
first was dedicated to Mercury (*mercui*), and the second to Apollo (*apolonos*).

The inhabitants of Falerii Veteres were transferred in 241 B.C. to a site 4.8km
west of the old, on the left bank of the Rio Purgatorio. Falerii Novi (Santa Maria
di Falleri) is in open country, quite unlike the earlier city, but it is defended by
a magnificent towered wall (a novelty in Italy in the third century) with arched
gateways. The city must have been more Roman than Etruscan in style; there
are the remains of a theater, apparently Augustan, inside the walls, and the
system of fortification is like, but more elaborate than, that of the Latin colony
of *Cosa, founded in 273 B.C.

BIBLIOGRAPHY

G. Dennis, *Cities and Cemeteries of Etruria,* 2nd ed. (London, 1878), I, 87–114; L. R.
Taylor, *Local Cults in Etruria, Papers and Monographs of the American Academy in
Rome* (Rome, 1923), 60–96; L. Banti, *Il Mondo degli etruschi* (Rome, 1960), 50–53; G.
Colonna, ed., *Santuari d'Etruria* (Milan, 1985) 85–8, 110–13.

EMELINE HILL RICHARDSON

FARNESE, ALESSANDRO I. See PAUL III.

FARNESE BULL (PUNISHMENT OF DIRCE). Colossal, freestanding group
(height 3.70m) showing a rocky landscape with a bull and a number of figures.

The group has been massively restored as a scene of the *Punishment of Dirce,*
as she is being tied to a bull, an act performed by Zethus and Amphion. Pliny
(*NH* 36.33–34) mentions such a group created by Apollonius and Tauriskos,
adopted Rhodians of the first century B.C., which could be seen in Rome in his

The Farnese *Bull*, small bronze copy by A. Susini, Rome, Galleria Borghese, ca. 1625. (Deutsches Archäologisches Institut, Rome. Inst. Neg. 80.2869.)

day. The Farnese *Bull* may be a copy of this work, created in the early third century A.C. for the *Baths of Caracalla.

The work was discovered in the course of excavations for Pope *Paul III (see also *Farnese family) in the Baths of Caracalla in 1545. It may have been discovered at the same time as the *Farnese *Hercules*. The restoration, made with advice from *Michelangelo, was evidently a slow process. When *Aldrovandi saw the work in 1550 in the Palazzo Farnese (second courtyard), it had only the bull and one of the male figures (which Aldrovandi identified as Hercules). By 1585 the restoration was complete, as may be seen in the engraving of the group published that year by G. B. de' *Cavalieri. By this time the subject had been identified as the *Punishment of Dirce*.

The influence of the group was great. It has been recognized in the *Rape of Europa* (1559–1662) by *Titian and the *Rape of the Daughters of Leucippus* (ca. 1618) by P. P. *Rubens. The painter Federico Zuccaro described the Farnese *Bull* as a "marvellous mountain of marble" and ranked it as the greatest ancient sculpture surviving, along with the *Laocoon*. This opinion is astonishing in the light of the near obscurity of the work today, but, in fact, until the nineteenth century, many who saw it had a similar evaluation. Louis XIV was among those who admired the *Bull;* he tried, unsuccessfully, to buy it in 1665.

In the eighteenth century, *Ficoroni deduced that the Farnese *Bull* was a Roman copy, an astute observation for the time, but *Winckelmann denied this, declaring, instead, that it was Greek, of the period after Alexander the Great. There was much debate over the degree of restoration of the sculpture, with a corresponding vacillation in critical reaction. Eventually, by the ninteenth century, the Farnese *Bull* had suffered a serious devaluation. Recently F. Heger has voiced the remarkable opinion that the Farnese sculpture is the very work mentioned by Pliny.

The statue was moved to Naples in 1786 and stands today in the *Museo Nazionale in Naples, facing the Farnese *Hercules.*

BIBLIOGRAPHY

Bieber, 134; Haskell—Penny, 165–67; M. Marvin, "Freestanding Sculptures from the Baths of Caracalla," *AJA* 87 (1983), 367–68; *LIMC* III, 635–36, 641–44 (F. Heger); +*Il Toro Farnese: la "montagna di marmo" tra Roma e Napoli* (Naples, 1991).

FARNESE CAPTIVES (THE KING OF ARMENIA AND THE KING OF PARTHIA; DACIAN PRISONERS). Two over-lifesize Roman marble figures, believed to have adorned originally the Forum of Trajan (A.D. 107–16; cf. *Imperial Fora); they are dressed as barbarians, with long tunic, trousers and cloak, bearded countenances and soft peaked cap, and assuming poses of submission.

The statues originally belonged to the *Colonna family, whose house they adorned as architectural supporting figures, probably through the inspiration of a passage in Vitruvius (*De archit.* 1.1.6) telling how statues of captive Persians had been used by the Spartans to support an entablature in place of columns. The statues were later seized from the Colonna family by Pope *Paul III (*Farnese family) and eventually installed (by 1594) at the top of the main staircase of the Palazzo Farnese. In 1790 the two statues were transferred to Naples and are today in the *Museo Nazionale. A number of other specimens of similar captives were known during the Renaissance, including the eight on the attic of the *Arch of Constantine. (These were, unfortunately, "decapitated" in the sixteenth century; new heads were attached in the eighteenth century.)

Flaminio *Vacca first suggested that the statues had come from Trajan's Forum, and later scholars identified them as Dacians. (Some called them the King of Parthia and the King of Armenia.) There is extensive evidence now to confirm this hypothesis. M. Waelkens reviewed the known specimens of Dacian captives (some of which were clearly recorded as excavated in the Forum of Trajan) and cataloged forty-five of them, made of varying stones and in varying sizes. Two main poses of captives have been recognized, with hands crossed below the waist and with arms across the chest; the Farnese captives represent these two known types. Waelkens hypothesizes that the Dacians were part of the façades

facing onto the forum but probably did not actually support any architectural elements.
BIBLIOGRAPHY
Haskell—Penny, 169–72; M. Waelkens, "From a Phrygian Quarry: The Provenance of the Dacian Prisoners in Trajan's Forum at Rome," *AJA* 89 (1985), 641–53; Bober—Rubinstein, 197–98.

FARNESE CUP (TAZZA FARNESE). Large, honey-brown Indian sardonyx (diameter 20cm) belonging to the Hellenistic period (second or first century B.C.), carved in the shape of a cup.

The exterior has a representation of the head of Medusa, while the interior is carved with a fertility theme that seems to have originated in Ptolemaic Egypt. The identity of the principal figures, a mythological triad, is hotly disputed.

The cup first appears in recorded history in the early part of the fifteenth century, when it was seen at Herat or Samarkand and drawn by the artist Mohammed al-Khayyām. Soon afterward the stone went to Italy; it has been speculated that it was taken as a tribute piece by the Byzantine emperor John VIII Palaiologos to the Ecumenical Council at Ferrara in 1438 or that it was brought in after the fall of Constantinople in 1453. It has been suggested that it passed into the collection of Pope *Paul II, and then Lorenzo de' Medici (*Medici family) acquired it from *Sixtus IV; the stone was assessed as worth the grand sum of 10,000 florins. The cup passed in 1538 to the *Farnese family, from whom it takes its name, and then in the eighteenth century it went, along with the other family treasures, to Naples and eventually into the *Museo Nazionale di Napoli. The Tazza Farnese suffered from a sad and shocking assault in 1925, when a guard at the Museo Nazionale, in a fit of madness, used an umbrella to strike the case in which it was displayed, breaking it into a number of pieces. The cup has been restored twice (1925 and 1951) and has, on the whole, its original appearance. At some unknown date, a hole was bored crudely in the center of the cup.

Scipione *Maffei was the first to publish the Farnese Cup, but modern study of the iconography begins with E. Q. *Visconti, who saw the three principal figures as the Nile, Isis and Horus. Others have substituted Graeco-Roman deities (e.g., Hades, or Dionysos, and Demeter and Triptolemos) and argued, in addition, that the figures are allegorical portraits of Ptolemaic rulers. The Isis figure, for example, has been identified as Cleopatra I, II, III or VII; the Triptolemos as Ptolemy VI or X and so on. Recently, E. J. Dwyer, developing an idea of R. Merkelbach, has argued that the scene is a Ptolemaic work of the earlier part of the first century B.C., showing an archetypal depiction of creation, including representations of constellations and planets. J. Pollini dates the cup to the reign of Augustus (31 B.C.–A.D. 14) and sees the scene as a representation of Saturnus and Gallus with allusions to Augustus's victory at Actium and the inauguration of a Golden Age.

BIBLIOGRAPHY
H. Blanck, "Eine persische Pinselzeichnung nach der Tazza Farnese," *AA* 79 (1964), 307–12; D. B. Thompson, "The Tazza Farnese Reconsidered," *Das Ptolemaische Ägypten,* ed. H. Maehler—V. M. Strocka (Mainz, 1977), 113–22; +U. Pannuti et al., *Il Tesoro di Lorenzo il Magnifico, Repertorio delle gemme e dei vasi* (Florence, 1980), I, 69–72; +E. J. Dwyer, "The Temporal Allegory of the Tazza Farnese," *AJA* 96 (1992), 255–82; J. Pollini, "The Tazza Farnese: *Augusto Imperatore "Redeunt Saturnia Regna!"* *AJA* 96 (1992), 283–300.

BABETTE E. ARTHUR

FARNESE FAMILY. Italian family, long established in Lazio, which rose rapidly to the ranks of the great European families, becoming rulers of the duchy of Parma and Piacenza under the Farnese pope, *Paul III (ALESSANDRO FARNESE).

The family amassed a veritable museum of classical antiquities that was without equal among the private collections of Rome during the sixteenth century. Most of the contents were housed in Palazzo Farnese, but antiquities belonging to the family were also to be seen in the Farnesina, in the Orti Farnesiani on the Palatine and in the Villa Madama.

The fine collection begun by Paul III was considerably enlarged by his grandson, Cardinal ALESSANDRO FARNESE (1520–89). A most important patron of contemporary art, Alessandro avidly acquired classical works, too. He actively promoted excavations in Rome in the *Forum Romanum and in the *Baths of Caracalla, where the *Farnese *Bull* and the *Farnese *Hercules* were found, and at *Hadrian's Villa in Tivoli, of which he was made governor in 1535. After Paul's death, throughout the reigns of *Julius III (1550–55) and Pius IV (1555–59), Alessandro was frequently absent from Rome for political reasons, and his collecting was therefore temporarily halted, but once he had returned permanently to Rome, he resumed the purchase of classical sculpture, coins and gems on a grand scale. In 1562, for example, he paid Paolo del Bufalo (*Bufalo family) 1,575 scudi for ten antique pieces, including the *Atlas* now at Naples. The cardinal's influence enabled him to obtain important, newly discovered works: thus, when, sometime before 1568, a large group of portrait busts of Roman emperors was unearthed, he acquired many of them to display in the Gallery of the Palazzo Farnese; on another occasion, when a great number of statues of ancient philosophers and emperors were excavated, Alessandro apparently selected the best for his collection.

Alessandro and his brother, Cardinal RANUCCIO (1530–65), assembled around them an important circle of antiquarians and were generous in supporting their studies. The group included the eccentric Pirro *Ligorio, Onofrio *Panvinio, who published the Consular and Triumphal *Fasti,* the fragments of which Alessandro had rescued from the Forum, Annibal *Caro, a particular authority on ancient coins, and Fulvio *Orsini. The latter spent almost his entire life in Farnese service and acquired many classical antiquities for his patrons. These

Marble bust of *Homer*,
in the Farnese collec-
tion; engraving from J.
Gronovius, *Thesaurus
antiquitatum graeco-
rum*, 2 (1694–1703).
(The Warburg Institute,
University of London.)

he arranged in a studio next to the library of the Palazzo Farnese, since Alessandro wished to make the collection available to scholars.

The family's collections had been substantially augmented in 1538, when
another of Paul III's grandsons, OTTAVIO (1525–86), later Duke of Parma,
married Margaret of Austria. She was the widow of Alessandro de' Medici.
Included in her dowry were a number of important *Medici family antiquities,
among them the Naples copies of the Pergamene group that comprises a *Dying
Warrior,* a *Persian,* an *Amazon* and a *Giant,* as well as the *Dionysos and Eros,*
now also at Naples. In addition she brought many classical gems and cameos,
including the celebrated Tazza Farnese (*Farnese Cup). Ottavio Farnese himself
collected antique sculpture: in 1546 he purchased from the *Sassi family col-

lection a bust of *Pompey,* a *Roma Triumphans,* a *Hermaphrodite* and several other works.

The Farnese "Museum" received its last major addition in 1600, when Fulvio Orsini left his collection to his current patron, Cardinal ODOARDO FARNESE (1573–1626), Alessandro's nephew. Besides contemporary paintings and drawings, this comprised many classical coins, engraved gems, inscriptions, portrait busts and herms with portraits.

The majority of these antiquities remained in Rome throughout the seventeenth and eighteenth centuries, although the Farnese, who came increasingly to live in Parma and rarely to use the palace in Rome, removed the pictures in 1649. The ducal line eventually died out with ANTONIO FARNESE in 1731. The entire Farnese property then passed to Don Carlos of Bourbon (*Bourbon family), who was the son of Philip V of Spain and ELISABETTA FARNESE (1692–1766), Antonio's niece, and who later became king of Naples. His son Ferdinand started to move the Farnese sculptures from Rome around 1786–87. Cardinal Alessandro's will of 1589 had decreed that the antiquities should remain intact in Palazzo Farnese in perpetuity, and there was, in any case, considerable opposition to the export of such a large portion of Rome's heritage, but eventually *Pius VI was persuaded to license the removal. The painter Philip Hackert and Domenico Venuti were put in charge of the transfer, and the statues were extensively restored by Carlo *Albacini before being shipped to Naples. There they were at first divided mainly between the royal villas at Capodimonte and Caserta, but in 1816 Ferdinand decided to establish the Museo Borbonico, now the *Museo Nazionale, Naples, where the Farnese collection was given its final home, together with the antiquities excavated from *Pompeii and *Herculaneum.

BIBLIOGRAPHY

R. Lanciani, *Storia degli scavi,* 2 (1903), 149 ff.; F. de Navenne, *Rome, le Palais Farnèse et les Farnèse* (Paris, 1914), 431–86; A. de Franciscis, "Per la storia del Museo Nazionale di Napoli," *Archivio storico per le provincie napoletane* n.s. 30 (1944–46), 169–200; +A. de Franciscis, *Il Museo Nazionale di Napoli* (Naples, 1963), 32–40; +R. Ajello—F. Haskell—C. Gaspari, *Classicismo d'età romana; la Collezione Farnese* (Naples, 1988).

CLARE ROBERTSON

FARNESE FLORA. Colossal marble sculpture (3.42m) considered a classicizing creation of Roman art, or a Roman copy of a Greek sculpture, perhaps of Aphrodite, created during the fourth century B.C.

The standing female figure is dressed in a form-revealing, clinging chiton with a belt at the hips added by the copyist. The figure shows major restorations, including the head and the proper left hand.

The sculpture was not discovered in the Baths of Caracalla, as is sometimes stated, but became a part of the *Farnese family collections before excavations were undertaken there for *Paul III in 1545–46. It was drawn by van *Heemskerck between 1532 and 1536 and was noted by *Aldrovandi in 1550 in the Palazzo Farnese, still in an unrestored condition. It was displayed along with another female statue identified as a *Flora,* which perhaps inspired the restoration of this work as *Flora.* The work as restored was engraved by *Cavalieri in 1561 (who labeled it, however, as *Spes,* or *Hope*). Philip *Rubens included it in his *Electorum libri II* (1608), along with an engraved illustration by his brother, Peter Paul (*Rubens). The latter imitated the pose and clinging garment in an allegorical figure in his painting of the *Capture of Jülich* in the Maria de' Medici series (1620s).

In the eighteenth century the restoration of the statue as *Flora* was criticized, and other identifications were suggested: a *Muse* or a *Hora* (*Winckelmann), *Hope* (E. Q. *Visconti). In 1787 the sculpture was removed from the Palazzo Farnese and sent for new restoration to the studio of C. *Albacini, where the identity as *Flora,* however, was reaffirmed. The sculpture was then sent to Naples and may be seen today in the *Museo Nazionale.

Among the replicas of the Farnese *Flora* may be noted a fine small bronze of the fifteenth or sixteenth centuries (Florence, private collection), which omits the attributes of Flora, and a number of marble copies of lifesize scale created in the seventeenth and eighteenth centuries (e.g., one by M. Rysbrack for the Pantheon at Stourhead).

BIBLIOGRAPHY

+M. Bieber, *Ancient Copies, Contributions to the History of Greek and Roman Art* (New York, 1977), 47; Sheard, no. 24; Haskell—Penny, 217–19; M. Marvin, ''Freestanding Sculptures from the Baths of Caracalla,'' *AJA* 87 (1983), 376–77.

FARNESE HERCULES (HERAKLES). Colossal marble statue (3.17m high) of Hercules, resting after the Labor of the Golden Apples.

The sculpture, signed on the rocky base by Glykon of Athens, is a work of the late second or early third centuries A.C. that probably reflects an original created by Lysippos in the fourth century B.C. The piece once stood in the central hall of the *Baths of Caracalla, between a column and a wall, with only its front and back clearly visible.

It was recorded as standing in that spot in 1545 by Antonio Sangallo the Younger, during the course of excavations ordered by Pope *Paul III (see *Farnese family); the director of the work was possibly Mario Maccarone. After the discovery, the *Hercules* was restored by Guglielmo della Porta, who was recommended for the job by *Michelangelo. He supplied a left hand and two legs for the figure, as well as many patches where there were minor damages. Fifteen years later, the original legs of the *Hercules* were found in a well three miles from the original site, but they were not to replace the della Porta legs until the end of the eighteenth century.

The sculpture was installed in the first courtyard of the Palazzo Farnese, where it was seen by *Aldrovandi in 1550. It was much admired and considered one of the greatest of all sculptures surviving from antiquity. Among the artists influenced by it were Perino del Vaga, Annibale *Carracci, who imitated it in the decorations for the Farnese Gallery, and P. P. *Rubens. Hendrick *Goltzius made a beautiful engraving of the back view of the statue (published 1617), bringing out the impressive size of the *Hercules* by showing a view with only the heads of two small spectators looking up at the statue.

In 1787, the *Hercules* was removed from the Palazzo Farnese and restored again, then taken to Naples along with the other Farnese treasures. *Napoleon coveted the piece but failed to secure it; it remained in Naples and may be seen today in the *Museo Nazionale.

Many replicas were made through the centuries, including small Renaissance bronzes, full-scale copies in stone and a remarkable copper copy over 9m high, by the Augsburg goldsmith J. J. Anthoni (between 1713 and 1717). An astonishing and powerful modern version of the Farnese *Hercules* was created out of soldered Volkswagen bumpers by Jason Seley of Cornell University (now in the Cornell University Museum).

BIBLIOGRAPHY

J. R. Martin, *The Farnese Gallery* (Princeton, NJ, 1965); S. Boorsch in Sheard, no. 100; Haskell—Penny, 229–32; M. Marvin, ''Freestanding Sculptures from the Baths of Caracalla,'' *AJA* 87 (1983), 347–84; Ridgway, *Roman Copies,* 82; D. Krull, *Der Herakles vom Typ Farnese, Kopienkritische Untersuchung eines Schöpfung des Lysipp* (Frankfurt, 1985).

FARNESE VENUS (CALLIPYGIAN VENUS; APHRODITE KALLIPY-GOS). Lifesize marble statue (1.52m) of a female found in the *Domus Aurea in Rome, part of the *Farnese family collection by 1594.

The statue has been identified as the type of the Hellenistic Aphrodite Kallipygos whose temple stood in *Syracuse. According to Athenaios (12.554c–d), the statue was the dedication of two daughters who had a contest to determine which had a more shapely derriere. The contest resulted in marriage for both and led to their making this offering to Aphrodite.

The sculpture depicts a female wearing a chiton tied under her breasts and slipping off her right shoulder so that her right breast is revealed. With her left hand she lifts the back of the garment above her shoulder, baring her buttocks and legs as she looks backward at the result. The gesture, that of a dancer, would be appropriate for the beauty contests that were part of the cult.

The Farnese *Venus* was restored by C. *Albacini before 1792, at which time it was moved to Naples with the rest of the Farnese collection (today in the *Museo Nazionale, Naples). Copies of the statue in various media exist from antiquity, and the type became immensely popular in the seventeenth and eighteenth centuries, when it was widely copied, particularly in bronze. The story of Athenaios was often cited with approbation, although some critics registered moral disapproval.

BIBLIOGRAPHY
A. Giuliano, "L'Afrodite Callipyge di Siracusa," *ArchCl* 5 (1953), 210–4; G. Säflund, *Aphrodite Kallipygos* (Stockholm, 1963); Haskell—Penny, 316–18; *LIMC*, II, 85–86.

MARY ELLEN SOLES

FASCISM, ARCHAEOLOGY UNDER. Fascism and the Fascist Party were the opportunistic invention of Benito Mussolini after he left the Socialist Party over the issue of Italian intervention in World War I.

Fascism, named for the *fasces,* the ancient Roman bundle of rods that symbolized political power, achieved its classic formulation in Mussolini's contribution to the article, "Fascismo: dottrina," in the *Enciclopedia Italiana* 14 (1932), 847–51. The product of an inspired journalist, Fascism offered the state, informed by the Fascist Party, as a substitute for family and church, holding out meaning and community to the individual. It appealed to artists, such as Marinetti and Pound, but it also had a use for scholarship.

As founder of the Second Roman Empire, Mussolini sponsored many significant archaeological excavations and other research, especially during the 1930s. Roman pleasure barges from the time of Caligula, known since the Renaissance, were rescued through a spectacular engineering feat from Lake *Nemi and restored. (Vengeful soldiers burned them while retreating in 1944.) The *Forum Romanum was regularized and excavated down to a consistent Late Republican level. From 1938 to 1942 most of *Ostia was laid bare in an impressive, if hurried, series of campaigns. The imperial cities of *Sabratha and *Leptis Magna in Libya were excavated and, in part, restored.

The building of a major thoroughfare from the *Colosseum to the Piazza Venezia in 1932 permitted excavation and investigation of the *Imperial Fora. In the path of the Via dell'Impero (today, Via dei Fori Imperiali) lay the Flavian Forum of Peace. (Unfortunately, the official schedule gave scholars all too short a time to conduct their research before it was covered over.)

A tour de force of archaeology and engineering was the recovery and restoration of the *Ara Pacis Augustae, which lay buried beneath the Palazzo Fiano off Rome's busy Via del Corso. The whole was reconstructed near the *Mausoleum of Augustus on the Tiber, with the text of the *Res Gestae* of Augustus (*Monumentum Ancyranum) as a final touch. The unity of ideology and archaeology made a statement about both ancient and modern Rome.

The positive side of the Fascist devotion to Italy's imperial past lay in the large amounts of money and attention given to scholarship, especially archaeology. But this attention was aimed at propaganda, and from this flowed the negative side. Haste and publicity were often more important than scholarly precision. It has been lamented that Ostia was uncovered too rapidly and that the Forum of Peace was covered over with too little time for proper study. The reconstructed theater at Sabratha is more suited to tourist admiration than scholarly research.

BIBLIOGRAPHY
R. de Felice, *Mussolini il fascista: L'Organizzazione dello stato fascista* (Turin, 1968); Idem, *Mussolini il duce: Gli Anni di Consenso* (Turin, 1974); M. Cagnetta, *Antichisti e impero fascista* (Bari, 1979); R. T. Ridley, *"Augusti manes volitant per auras*: The Archaeology of Rome under the Fascists," *Xenia* 11 (1986), 19–46.

E. C. KOPFF

FAUN WITH KID (QUEEN OF SWEDEN'S FAUN). Under-lifesize (1.36m) marble statue of a youthful faun or Satyr, looking up at a goat he carries on his shoulders; Roman copy of a Greek bronze original, perhaps of the early third century B.C.

The statue is heavily restored, including both arms and one foot. It was discovered in Rome ca. 1674 near the Chiesa Nuova and was soon afterward restored by Ercole Ferrata. Acquired by Queen *Christina of Sweden, it went the route of many of her other antiquities after her death—to Cardinal Azzolini, then to the *Odescalchi family and finally, in 1724, to Philip V of Spain. It remains in the *Prado today.

The statue, almost totally ignored in modern scholarship, was amazingly popular in the seventeenth and eighteenth centuries. It was copied for Versailles and for Peter the Great, for the *French Academy in Rome and for the Royal Academy in London, as well as for many less influential displays. Besides marble, bronze and plaster, it was copied in lead (full-scale, at Chatsworth), in gilded bronze and in biscuit de Sèvres.

BIBLIOGRAPHY
A. Blanco, *Museo del Prado: Catálogo de la Scultura* 1 *Esculturas clasicas* (Madrid, 1957), 33; *Christina, Queen of Sweden: A Personality of European Civilization* (Stockholm, 1966), 433–34, 438; Haskell—Penny, 211–12.

FAUVEL, LOUIS-FRANÇOIS-SÉBASTIEN (1753–1838). French artist, scholar, excavator, collector and diplomat.

Trained as an artist, Fauvel traveled from Paris to Greece in 1780, hired by Comte de *Choiseul-Gouffier to gather illustrative material for the second volume of *Voyage pittoresque de la Grèce.* In 1784 he was rehired by the count as one of the ambassador's retinue in Constantinople. For eight years he journeyed throughout Greece taking casts and acquiring antiquities, and, among other ventures, he discovered *Bassai and excavated at *Marathon and on the *Akropolis at Athens. He made two trips to Egypt (1789 and 1792), giving special attention to the antiquities of *Alexandria. In 1792 Choiseul-Gouffier lost his post, and Fauvel lost his patron. Settling in Athens, Fauvel found support by lending money and selling antiquities. He also engaged in research, particularly of Athens and its environs. *Napoleon's invasion of Egypt, however, led to his house arrest (1799) and return to France (1801).

In 1803 Fauvel returned to Athens as vice-consul and devoted himself to the study of antiquities, with frequent excavations of tombs, keeping savants informed of major discoveries through his writings. Shortly after the outbreak of the Greek War of Independence, Fauvel proceeded to *Smyrna, where, largely forgotten, he died in poverty on 12 March, 1838. Today he is remembered as the urbane host and cicerone in whose steps *Byron and other travelers to Athens followed.

BIBLIOGRAPHY

P. E. Legrand, "Biographie de Louis-François-Sébastien Fauvel," *RA* 30 (1897), 41–66, 185–201, 385–404, and 31 (1897), 94–103, 185–223; *DBF* fasc. 76 (1973), cols. 805–6; H. Tregaskis, *Beyond the Grand Tour* (London, 1979), 12–20; L. Beschi, "L. S. Fauvel ed Alessandria," *Alessandria e il mondo ellenistico-romano, studi in onore di Achille Adriani,* ed. N. Bonacasa—A. Di Vita, 4 (Rome, 1983), 3–12.

C.W.J. ELIOT

FAYUM PORTRAITS. Paintings of the face, bust or full-length body, buried with the mummified dead in cemeteries located mainly in the Fayum oasis region of Roman Egypt.

Usually, Fayum portraits are painted on wood panels and show a facial or bust-length image. Prior to burial, the panel was wrapped into the mummy with the portrait left exposed to view. Less frequently, the paintings were executed on cloth, sometimes on large shrouds showing the deceased at full length and wrapped around the mummy. Whether on wood or cloth, at first the portraits were painted in the wax-based encaustic medium; later, they were done mainly in egg-based tempera. They seem to have been produced from the first half of the first century into the mid-fourth century A.C. Beyond technical aspects of these paintings evident from visual inspection, details of their production remain mysterious, for we have not a single artist's signature nor an excavated workshop nor any reference to this art form in the writings of ancient Roman authors. Although many of the paintings show a high level of technical excellence, especially the early examples in encaustic, the majority of them are more properly considered the products of craftsmen than great artists. The portraits as a whole, more than 800 of which survive in museums and private collections the world over, constitute a precious survival of an art form that is otherwise virtually lost: ancient panel painting.

Less than two dozen Fayum portraits are known to have been recovered prior to 1887, the earliest of these being painted shrouds covering two mummies acquired at Sakkara in 1615 by Pietro della Valle and now in Dresden. In 1887, however, a large number of portraits began to be acquired at the Er-Rubayat necropolis in the Fayum oasis by agents of Theodor Graf, a Viennese antiquities dealer. Numbering in the hundreds, these subsequently were sold, either by Graf himself during his lifetime or by his heirs, at auction, after his death. More portraits, numbering 146 in all, were recovered by Sir W. M. Flinders Petrie in excavations at the Hawara necropolis, also in the Fayum region, during 1888 and 1911. The largest group of mummy paintings found outside the Fayum oasis was excavated between 1896 and 1911 at Antinoopolis, in Middle Egypt, by Albert Gayet.

BIBLIOGRAPHY
K. Parlasca, *Mumienporträts und verwandte Denkmäler* (Wiesbaden, 1966); A. F. Shore, *Portrait Painting from Roman Egypt,* rev. ed. (London, 1972); D. L. Thompson, *Mummy Portraits in the J. Paul Getty Museum* (Malibu, 1982).

DAVID L. THOMPSON

FAZELLO (FAZELLI; FACELLUS), TOMMASO (1498–1570). Historian from *Sicily.

Fazello, born at Sciacca in Sicily, studied at Palermo and entered the Dominican order. He next studied at Rome and at Padua, where he received his doctorate. At Rome, he became friends with the humanist scholar Paolo Giovio, who encouraged him to write a history of Sicily.

Returning to Palermo, Fazello undertook to teach philosophy and at the same time kept up his religious exercises. He so devoted himself to his studies that eventually he gave up all but one meal a day and reduced the number of hours he slept each night. His history of Sicily, *De rebus siculis decades duae* (Palermo, 1558), which was his only publication, included material on the ancient history and antiquities of Sicily, showing an immense personal knowledge of topography that allowed him to identify, on the basis of ancient authors, many of the major sites of Sicily. His work is still considered fundamental for the study of ancient Sicily.

BIBLIOGRAPHY
Weiss, "Fazelli, Thomas," *BU* 14 (1815), 239–41; B. Pace, *Studi e ricerche archeologiche di Sicilia, RendAcLinc,* cl. sc. morali 25 (1917); E. Librino—B. Pace, "Fazello, Tommaso," *EI* 14 (1932), 919.

FEA, CARLO (1753–1836). Italian archaeologist.

Fea was a law graduate of the University of Rome who attained fame and turned to antiquities with his edition of *Winckelmannn's *Storia delle Arti* (1783–84), which contained his own "Dissertation on the Ruins of Rome." He edited two volumes of invaluable archival documents, *Miscellanea filologica* (1790, 1836) and began his excavating career at Ardea (1791). In the upheavals of the time of *Napoleon, he was exiled and imprisoned a number of times but was finally triumphantly vindicated by his appointment as commissioner of antiquities (*Commissario delle Antichità) in 1800, which post he held until his death; he was the longest incumbent. In 1801 he was appointed president of the *Capitoline Museum (until 1809) and prefect of the Chigiana Library.

As commissioner he had to authorize all excavations and art exports. He was responsible for the antiquities regulations of 1802 and stimulated the new wave of archaeological clearings in Rome (*Arch of Constantine, *Arch of Septimius Severus and the *Colosseum), carrying out his own investigations of the *Pantheon with *Valadier (1804). During the French occupation (1809–14) he worked with Valadier on the *Domus Aurea and the *Temple of Vesta. He suggested that this temple belonged to Hercules.

Portrait of *Carlo Fea*,
Rome, Deutsches Ar-
chäologisches Institut
(German Archaeological
Institute). (Deutsches Archäologisches Insti-
tut, Rome. Inst. Neg.
76.1820.)

The uncovering of the *Colosseum arena in 1812 provoked him to many
bitter debates. With the Duc de *Blacas, he cleared and identified the *Temple
of Castor (1816) and, with the Count of Funchal, discovered the Clivus Capitolinus and the Temple of Concord (1817). He published a guide to Rome
(*Nuova descrizione de' monumenti antichi,* 1819) and was a major drafter of
the Pacca edict on antiquities (1820), as well as the leading expert on the history
and law of aqueducts.

Fea was the only Italian among the founding members of the *Instituto di
Corrispondenza Archeologica (1829). He was the dominant figure in Roman
archaeology for nearly forty years and an indefatigable protector of the monuments.

BIBLIOGRAPHY

Notizie della vita e delle opere degli scrittori romani (Rome, 1880), I, 115–24, (with bibl.); E. Re, "Brumaio dell'abate Fea," *Nuova antologia* (16 September 1928), 216–31; G. d'Angelis d'Ossat, "Carlo Fea e lo studio di monumenti romani," *Bolletino della Deputazione di Storia Patria per la Liguria* 2 (1936), 315–28; R. Ridley, "Carlo Fea," *DBI* (forthcoming).

R. T. RIDLEY

FELICIANO, FELICE (1433–79). Italian Renaissance scribe, antiquary (self-styled *Felix antiquarius*), amateur humanist, poet, printer, alchemist; notorious in his day as a down-at-the-heels eccentric.

Feliciano was born in Verona and died probably in or near Rome. He modestly collected antique coins and drawings by his artist friends and is famous for an amusing trip round Lake Garda in 1464 to inspect antique inscriptions in company with *Mantegna, Samuele da Tradate and Giovanni *Marcanova, a rich doctor, bibliophile, antiquarian writer and epigraphist. For Marcanova in Bologna, in 1465, he transcribed classical, medieval and humanistic texts and almost single-handedly executed the most gorgeously written, illuminated and illustrated fifteenth-century corpus of classical inscriptions that exists (Modena, Bibl. Estense α.L.5.15). He composed (1459 or 1460) a pattern-book of the Latin alphabet based on Pythagorean geometric principles and Roman lapidary models (Vat. Lat. 6852; ed. Mardersteig, 1960).

Since before 1457 he was a passionate disciple of *Ciriaco of Ancona, the much-traveled father of scientific classical epigraphy, and probably met Marcanova ca. 1457–60 when the latter was getting his first Ciriacesque epigraphic sylloge transcribed (Bern, Stadtbibl, B.42). Feliciano is cardinally important in archaeology because so many of Ciriaco's fugitive papers, which he copiously copied, passed through his hands. When antique epigraphs and Ciriaco's records of them are lost, Feliciano is sometimes the earliest, occasionally the sole, witness to their original wording. But though he journeyed about Italy—never in Greek lands—his independent finds were relatively few: his essential epigraphical work was done in his scriptorium. The fullest (Verona, Bibl. Capit. 269: a copy) of his five identified epigraphic manuscripts is dedicated to Mantegna and dated 1463; depending on Ciriaco, it combines predominantly Italian inscriptions with others from elsewhere in the Mediterranean world.

Concerning his fidelity, his characteristic style (e.g., Modena, cod. cit.) was fancifully to enliven monuments and to enframe prominent inscriptions in brightly colored sham-antique settings of his own devising with scant regard to line divisions and so on. Occasionally, however (e.g., Faenza, Bibl.Com.7: his autograph copy of Ciriaco's typically accurate lost record, rich in Veronensia, of inscriptions he surveyed in North Italy in 1433), he would faithfully stick to his exemplar in imagery, letter forms and line divisions. Like Ciriaco, he positively relished occasional, innocently amusing or evocative modern fake-antique inscriptions.

BIBLIOGRAPHY
G. B. de Rossi, *Inscriptiones christianae urbis Romae* 2 (Rome, 1888), 391–93; L. Pratilli, "Felice Feliciano alla luce dei suoi codici," *Atti del Reale Istituto Veneto* 99 (1939–40), 33–105; +F. Feliciano, *Alphabetum romanum,* ed. G. Mardersteig (Verona, 1960); +C. Mitchell, "Felice Feliciano Antiquarius," *ProcBrAc* 47 (1961), 197–221, with biog. and checklist of manuscripts.

CHARLES MITCHELL

FELIX GEM. Sard intaglio gem, 2.7cm × 3.5cm, carved in the late first century B.C. or early first century A.C.

Greek inscriptions on the gem name the artist, Felix, and the owner (probably), Calpurnius Severus. The scene depicted is *The Theft of the Palladium by Diomedes and Odysseus.*

The gem was recorded in 1457 in the collection of Cardinal Pietro Barbo (*Paul II) and in 1483 in that of Cardinal Francesco Gonzaga (*Gonzaga family). It was known to *Mantegna, serving as a source of inspiration for motifs in his engraving of the *Battle of the Sea Gods* and his paintings of *Parnassus* and the *Triumph of Caesar.* It was subsequently in the *Arundel and Marlborough collections, among others, and today is in the *Ashmolean Museum, Oxford.

BIBLIOGRAPHY
Sheard, nos. 7–8; M. Vickers, "The Felix Gem in Oxford and Mantegna's Triumphal Programme," *GBA,* ser. 6, 101 (1983), 97–102; C. M. Brown, "Cardinal Francesco Gonzaga's Collection of Antique Intaglios and Cameos," *GBA,* ser. 6, 101 (1983), 102–3.

FELLOWS, CHARLES (1799–1860). English traveler, explorer and archaeologist.

A Nottingham worthy, Fellows spent much of his life in travel. Arriving at *Smyrna in 1838, he proceeded to Turkey's southwest corner and was the first European to explore Lycia and to write of the ruins and antiquities of *Xanthos and of neighboring cities such as *Side. These discoveries, extended by further journeys in 1839, provoked such interest in England that in 1841–42 and 1844 he led expeditions that secured for the *British Museum over a hundred cases of architecture and sculpture. Of the several monumental tombs so collected (e.g., the Archaic Lion Tomb and the fourth-century Tomb of Payava), the Nereid Monument (ca. 380 B.C.) is not only the largest but also the richest in the quality, variety and importance of its sculpture. In 1845 Fellows was knighted, rightly so, because his published travels and researchers mark him as a scholar, no less than an explorer, of rare distinction.

BIBLIOGRAPHY
"Fellows, Charles," *DNB* 6 (repr. 1937–38), 1166–67.

C.W.J. ELIOT

FIANO, FRANCESCO DA (ca. 1355–ca. 1425). Roman humanist and curial official.

Francesco da Fiano held a variety of curial appointments in Rome, including papal *scriptor* (1379 and 1381), papal *computator* (1387), Vatican registrar of documents (1389). Sometime between 1399 and 1404 he was appointed *cancellarius* of Rome by Pope Boniface IX. With the return of the Curia to Rome from Viterbo in 1406, he came to be regarded as a fount of knowledge on the city of Rome and led most of the early fifteenth-century humanists around the ruins of the classical city. These tours are described by Bartolomeo Bayguera in his poem *Itinerarium.* So closely did Francesco become associated with the ruins of ancient Rome in the minds of curial officials that it was to him that Cencio Rustici appealed, from the Council of Constance in 1416, for an invective against those who were destroying the ancient remains. He died in Rome, on or before 1425.

BIBLIOGRAPHY

F. Novati, *La Giovinezza di Coluccio Salutati* (Turin, 1888), 91–5; L. Bertalot, ''Cincius Romanus und seine Briefe,'' *Quellen und Forschungen aus italienischen Archiven und Bibliotheken* 21 (1929–30), 222–25; H. Baron, *The Crisis of the Early Renaissance* 2 (Princeton, NJ, 1955), 401–8.

JAMES C. ANDERSON, JR.

FICORONI, FRANCESCO DE' (1664–1747). Italian collector, dedicated student of antiquity and its artifacts.

Ficoroni's main interest was the acquisition of Roman and Etruscan objects—almost exclusively small, personal items. His impressive collection of inscribed mirrors, coins, tesserae, seals and bullae provided the subjects for a series of publications, including *Le Bolle de' oro* (Rome, 1732); *Dei tali ed altri strumenti lusori degli antichi* (Rome, 1734); and *I Piombi antichi* (Rome, 1740). In 1736, Ficoroni published *Le Maschere sceniche e le figure comiche degli antichi romani,* a lavishly illustrated, selective overview of ancient mask motifs that is still of value today.

His interests were not tied solely to the collectible, as is shown by his study of Roman topography, *Le Vestigia e rarità di Roma ricercate e spiegate* (1744). It is interesting that in this work he included his birthplace, Lugnano Valmontone, identified as the ancient Labico, near *Praeneste.

The much-honored Ficoroni was a member of the Royal Academy in both London and Paris and the Accademia Peloritana of Messina. Furthermore, he served as both founder and general promoter of the society known as the Colonia Esquilina degli Inculti. His name is most frequently mentioned in connection with the exquisite Praenestine cista, which he acquired in 1738 (the *Ficoroni Cista, now in the *Villa Giulia, Rome). Ficoroni refused an Englishman's generous bid for the bronze cista and, instead, presented it to the Museum Kircherianum in Rome in order that it might be always studied and admired by connoisseurs of the antique. With it Ficoroni included an inscribed mirror (erroneously identified as a patera).

At his death on 1 February 1747 in Rome, the massive collection was widely dispersed. Major pieces are now in the Villa Giulia and the *Museo Nazionale, Naples. Through his dedication to the collection and publication of ancient objects categorized by subject (e.g., comic masks) and use (e.g., game pieces), Ficoroni was a pioneer in using the approach of the systematic *corpus* pursued later by Eduard Gerhard and others.

BIBLIOGRAPHY
G. Q. Giglioli, "Francesco de' Ficoroni," *EI* 15 (1932), 225. L. Guerrini, "Ficoroni, Francesco de'," *EAA* 3 (1960), 647–48; T. Dohrn, *Die Ficoronische Ciste in der Villa Giulia in Rom* (Berlin, 1972).

JOHN A. ELLIOTT

FICORONI CISTA. Bronze cylindrical toilet box of Praenestine type—the largest and most beautiful example known—dating to the second half of the fourth century B.C. (Late Classical period).

The body of the cylinder is engraved with a mythological scene of the Argonauts visiting the land of the Bebryces, where Polydeukes defeated their king Amykos in boxing and bound him to a tree. Though the myth is Greek, recent scholarship has seen the version here as Italic. The handle features three bronze statuettes (Bacchus and two Satyrs), and the feet of the cista show a bronze relief appliqué with Herakles, Eros and perhaps Iolaus.

An inscription on the lid relates that the cista was made at Rome by a certain Novios Plautios and was given by Dindia Macolnia to her daughter. It was probably placed in the daughter's grave. The cista was excavated somewhere between *Praeneste and Labico (Lugnano) before 14 May 1738, when it was reported in the collection of Francesco de' *Ficoroni. Ficoroni later related that along with the vessel he bought a mirror showing Polydeukes and Amykos in the presence of Luna; it is usually assumed that the mirror was found in the cista. By 1745 Ficorini had donated the piece to the Museum Kircherianum (Athanasius *Kircher) so that it might be studied with other antiquities there. In 1913 the Ficoroni Cista was transferred to the *Villa Giulia Museum. It has undergone at least two restorations (unrecorded but later than 1848), involving the attachment of the ancient bronze cylinder to a modern body and floor for the cista; one of the three feet is modern, and the bronze cylinder, with its incised representation, has been cleaned and patched.

The Danish archaeologist P. O. *Brøndsted published a study of the Ficoroni Cista in 1834. Tobias Dohrn has issued the authoritative modern monograph on it.

BIBLIOGRAPHY
C. J. Contucci, *Musei Kircheriani in Romano Societatis Jesu Collegio aerea* 1 (Rome, 1863); T. Dohrn, *Die Ficoronische Ciste in der Villa Giulia in Rom* (Berlin, 1972); H. A. Weis, "The Motif of the Adligatus and Tree," *AJA* 86 (1982), 21–38.

FIESOLE (FAESULAE; VIPSUL?). Etruscan and Roman city of northern Etruria, located on a hilltop with a spectacular view of modern Florence and the valleys of the Arno and Mugnone.

Only scattered fragments suggest occupation of Fiesole in the Archaic period. In the third century B.C., the town faced the Gallic invasion (225 B.C.; Polybius 2.25) and the passage of Hannibal (217 B.C.; Polybius 3.80.82; Livy 22.3), who devastated the fertile fields of the region. The major part of the town's well-preserved fortification wall seems to date from this period. Several monumental stone tombs and an Etruscan temple (in the "Archaeological Zone") belong to this time; the latter provides a rare example of an Etruscan temple with preserved stone cella walls. The city was sacked in 90 B.C. during the Social War and was subsequently resettled by the veterans of Sulla. A large part of the visible remains at Fiesole belongs to the time of Augustus (31 B.C.–A.D. 14), including baths, a theater and a second version of the temple. In A.D. 539 Fiesole was occupied by Belisarius. The presence of a Lombard cemetery overlying the temples likewise testifies to medieval activity.

In 1792 remains of the stairway of the Roman temple were discovered but, upon examination by Luigi *Lanzi, were declared of little importance. Baron von Sherlerstein undertook excavation of the theater in 1809; he soon decided to cover the site to prevent looting of building stone. The excavations were finally resumed with government protection in 1870, and finds were stored in an embryonic civic collection, today, the splendid local Museo Archeologico. Excavation of the temples has been irregular, with campaigns in 1899–1900, 1910–12, 1954, 1958 and 1960. The baths were first investigated in 1891. In the twentieth century the buildings of the Archaeological Zone have been carefully restored, and the site has been well maintained. The stratigraphy and ceramics of the Hellenistic, Roman and medieval periods have been illuminated recently in excavations in urban Fiesole under G. De Marinis (1986–89).

BIBLIOGRAPHY

P. Bocci Pacini, s.v. "Faesulae," *PECS,* 322–23; +M. De Marco, *Comune di Fiesole, Museo Archeologico, Scavi: Guida* (Fiesole, 1981); S. Steingräber, *Città e necropoli dell'Etruria* (Rome, 1983), 45–52; *Archeologia urbana a Fiesole, lo scavo di Via Marini-Via Portigiani* (Firenze, 1990).

FIORELLI, GIUSEPPE (1823–96). Italian archaeologist.

Fiorelli was born at Naples 8 June 1823 and died there 28 January 1896. He began his career with publications on numismatics (1843, 1844, 1848, 1851) and was employed until 1848 in the administration of the excavations of *Pompeii. Imprisoned in 1848 on charges of political conspiracy, he prepared for publication the daybooks of the excavations of Pompeii from their beginning to his own time (*Pompeianarum antiquitatum historia 1748–1860,* Naples, 1860–64). Absolved of the charges against him, he became secretary to the Count of *Syracuse, brother of the king, and conducted excavations in the necropolis of *Cumae, published as *Notizia dei vasi dipinti rinvenuti a Cuma nel MDCCCLVI* (Naples, 1856). About the same time he published *Monumenta epigraphica pompeiana: inscriptionum oscarum apographa* (Naples, 1858) and, in collaboration with Carlo Sorgente, a large plan of Pompeii (Naples, 1858–60).

Fiorelli became professor of archaeology at the University of Naples in 1860 and remained there three years, when he was appointed director (*ispettore*) of the excavations of Pompeii. In this position, for the next decade he distinguished himself by the introduction of strict scientific method and regular publication of the progress of work (*Giornale degli scavi,* 1861–65; *Gli Scavi di Pompei dal 1861 al 1872,* Naples, 1873; and *Descrizione di Pompei,* Naples, 1875, the last still a basic work). He also founded a school of archaeology in Pompeii that eventually became the Scuola Italiana di Archeologia. Late in 1863 he became director of the *Museo Nazionale in Naples and superintendent of excavations and began reorganization of the collections and publication of catalogs. He also founded the museum of the Certosa di S. Martino. In 1865 he was made a senator of Italy and in 1875 general director of Antichità e Belle Arti; as such he founded the *Notizie degli scavi di antichità* in 1876.

BIBLIOGRAPHY

G. Spano, ''Fiorelli, Giuseppe,'' *EI* 15 (1932), 427; G. Fiorelli, *Appunti autobiografici* (Rome, 1939).

L. RICHARDSON, JR

FITZWILLIAM MUSEUM, Cambridge. English museum with a wide-ranging collection of works of art and artifacts, owned by the University of Cambridge; the classical antiquities form a significant component.

The museum was founded in 1816, when Richard, seventh Viscount Fitzwilliam of Merrion (1745–1816), made a bequest to the University of Cambridge to promote ''the Increase of Learning and other great Objects of that Noble Foundation.'' Viscount Fitzwilliam's collection itself contained no antiquities, and for the first half of the century very few were acquired for the museum. An exception was the important Pashley Sarcophagus (Roman, ca. 140 A.D.), showing the triumphant return of Dionysos from the East, donated by Admiral Sir Pulteney Malcolm in 1835.

In 1850, the Fitzwilliam received a major donation of Greek and Roman marbles from John Disney, a collection that had been assembled in Italy between 1748 and 1753 by Thomas Hollis and his friend and heir Thomas Brand Hollis; noteworthy pieces were a young *Pan* and a head of *Serapis.* In 1864 came another major acquisition in the purchase of the entire collection of Colonel William Martin *Leake for £5,000 (valued at twice the sum), amassed during his extensive travels in Italy and, especially, Greece. Besides a superb collection of Greek coins, there were engraved Greek and Roman gems (including a fine sapphirine chalcedony of a *Lady and Her Maid* signed by Dexamenos), Greek vases, terracottas and bronzes. Other antiquities were transferred to the Fitzwilliam during this period, such as the cabinet of coins and seals formed by Andrew Perne, master of Peterhouse, and bequeathed to the university in 1589, and the University Collection, given by Edward Daniel *Clarke and J. M. Cripps, of which the most notable piece was the caryatid excavated by Clarke at *Eleusis, believed by him to represent Ceres (i.e., Demeter).

During the period when a classical archaeologist, Sir Charles *Walston, served as director of the museum (1883–89), it acquired a number of antiquities, including an antefix from the *Parthenon. The Fitzwilliam also received during this period objects discovered during British excavations at *Naukratis and on *Cyprus. Donations of glass and Cypriote antiquities were made by Sir Henry Bulwer (1892), and in the early twentieth century various objects were given by Winifred *Lamb, honorary keeper of Greek and Roman antiquities. In 1926 the Fitzwilliam acquired the marble statuette of a ''Minoan goddess,'' now notorious as a forgery that deceived Lamb (who paid part of the purchase price), Sir Arthur *Evans and A.J.B. *Wace. The most significant body of Greek and Roman sculpture came to the museum in 1937, as a bequest of C. S. Ricketts and C. H. Shannon. Exceptional pieces were a copy of the torso of the *Apollo Sauroktonos* of Praxiteles and a colossal head of *Antinous* from *Hadrian's Villa at Tivoli.

Between 1981 and 1983, the Fitzwilliam received an enormous allocation of objects from the collection of Sir Henry Solomon Wellcome (1853–1936), well known for his contributions to medical research but also a pioneer in the archaeological use of aerial photography. The collection includes a study archive of more than 15,000 impressions of engraved gems made mostly in the eighteenth and nineteenth centuries, as well as ancient and modern original gems.

BIBLIOGRAPHY
+W. Lamb, *CVA Fitzwilliam Museum*, fasc. 1–2 (Oxford, 1930–36); +L. Budde—R. Nicholls, *A Catalogue of the Greek and Roman Sculpture in the Fitzwilliam Museum, Cambridge* (Cambridge, 1964); +D.W.J. Gill, ''The Director, the Dealer, the Goddess and Her Champions: The Acquisition of the Fitzwilliam Goddess,'' *AJA* 97 (1993), 383–401; M. Henig, *Classical Gems: Ancient and Modern Intaglios and Cameos in the Fitzwilliam Museum, Cambridge* (Cambridge, 1994).

FIUMI, ENRICO (1908–76). Italian historian and archaeologist, specializing in medieval and Etruscan studies.

Born at *Volterra, Fiumi became the outstanding historian of the city and its territory. His training as an economist led him to the study of the social and economic history of Volterra and other Tuscan cities, from modern times to antiquity. He found his material in the archives of these cities, and his publications are pioneers of their kind.

His archaeological publications include articles on Volterra's Etruscan fortifications, its cemeteries, excavations, collections and the creation of its venerable museum, the Guarnacci (Mario *Guarnacci). An important article assembles the archaeological evidence for the city's earliest period, the Iron Age, and its Archaic continuation. Others describe the Hellenistic tombs and their alabaster urns.

Fiumi was director of the Guarnacci Museum and Library for over thirty years and an honorary inspector of antiquities and the fine arts. In 1950 he began to excavate the Roman theater, revealed as one of the finest Imperial building complexes in Tuscany. His last book, published posthumously, *Volterra etrusca e romana,* is at once history, guide and catalog, an outstanding survey of the life of the ancient city.

BIBLIOGRAPHY

G. Maetzke, "Commemorazione del Professor Enrico Fiumi," in *Storia e sviluppo del Museo Guarnacci di Volterra* (Florence, 1977), 5–10; *Studi per Enrico Fiumi* (Pisa, 1979), 11–15, with bib.

EMELINE HILL RICHARDSON

FLAXMAN, JOHN (1755–1826). English sculptor, leading exponent of the neoclassical style.

Born in York, Flaxman showed precocious talent as a child in spite of fragile health, in a happy, caring family. He won modeling prizes from the age of twelve and exhibited waxes regularly from 1770 onward at the Royal Academy. Inspired by reading the classics and blessed with a vivid imagination, he was employed at twenty by *Wedgwood and Bentley to sketch portraits and cameos on classical themes. By 1780 Flaxman was engaged in designing memorial sculptures, which became his principal livelihood. Examples of his work are found in Westminster Abbey, St. Paul's Cathedral and elsewhere throughout England.

From 1787 to 1794 Flaxman and his wife resided in Rome, where he continued research while providing models as well as supervising other local artists for Wedgwood. At the time the theories of *Winckelmann had a profound influence on the shaping of taste, and Flaxman was among his disciples, drawing great inspiration from the monuments of antiquity, especially Greek vase painting. He was inspired by literary sources as well, and he produced excellent book illustrations for Homer's *Iliad* and *Odyssey,* for Aischylos, Hesiod and Ovid, as well as for Dante.

Flaxman was elected an associate of the Royal Academy in 1797 and member in 1800. Mild mannered, he nonetheless raised hackles on a visit to Paris in 1802, criticizing *Napoleon for publicly flaunting the artistic spoils he had brought back from Italian campaigns. In 1810 Flaxman was named professor of sculpture at the Royal Academy, meanwhile continuing to produce important memorial statuary. The spirit of his works is calm and sedate, approaching the classical ideal of noble perfection, but somewhat lacking in vigor.

Flaxman Hall, at University College, London, has a substantial collection of his works along with documentation of his life.

BIBLIOGRAPHY

S. Colvin, *The Drawings of Flaxman in 32 Plates with Descriptions* (London, 1876); Thieme—Becker, "Flaxman, John," 12 (1916), 79–83; S. Stephen—S. Lee, "Flaxman, John," *DNB* 7 (1973), 254–60.

J. S. TASSIE

FLORENCE, ARCHAEOLOGICAL MUSEUM (MUSEO ARCHEOLO-
GICO DI FIRENZE). Principal collection of antiquities in Florence, containing Egyptian, Etruscan, Greek and Roman objects and monuments.

The Florence Archaeological Museum was inaugurated in 1881, but the core of its holdings comes from collections amassed by the *Medici family (from the fifteenth century to 1737) and by the dukes of Lorraine (Lorena), who subsequently ruled Tuscany into the nineteenth century. Acquired in the time of Lorenzo il Magnifico was the fine bronze *Head of a Horse,* and from the sixteenth-century collection of Cosimo I came the museum's most famous pieces, a pair of monumental Etruscan bronzes: the *Chimaera,* found at Arezzo (1553), and the *Arringatore,* said to have been found near Perugia (acquired 1566). A large bronze figure of *Minerva* was also found at Arezzo, in a well (1541). In 1633 was added yet another impressive bronze, the *"Idolino"* (found at Pesaro, 1530). The latter four bronzes were subsequently placed side by side in the *Uffizi Gallery (1789), along with other antiquities collected through the centuries.

With the unification of Italy, King Victor Emmanuel II decreed that an Etruscan Museum should be founded in Florence, the capital of the new nation (1870), to display this important facet of the Italian heritage. It was combined with an Egyptian Museum founded earlier by Duke Leopold II (1832), and the collections were housed in the Cenacolo di Foligno in Via Faenza; also shown was the *François Vase, which had been acquired by Leopold in 1845. As a result of the efforts of the royal commissario, Luigi *Pigorini, the collection was moved in 1881 into new quarters, in the Palazzo della Crocetta (Via della Colonna), the present home of the Florence Archaeological Museum.

A debate ensued regarding the appropriate arrangement of the material and whether the criteria should be historical, topographical or aesthetic. Under the leadership of Luigi A. Milani (d. 1914), the topographical concept triumphed. Milani created a Museo Topografico Centrale dell'Etruria, to which he added an archaeological garden, featuring stone grave markers and even entire tombs that he had moved from *Volterra, *Vetulonia, *Orvieto and Casal Marittimo. An Antiquarium was created to hold special works of art such as the two Greek marble *kouroi* Milani had secured for the museum (known since the eighteenth century, from the collection of the Canonico Bellini of Osimo). The splendid new display was ready for the public in 1897.

After Milani's death, the museum experienced a difficult period in which it continued to acquire excavated materials, but the available space and arrangement of the displays remained unchanged. When A. Minto became superintendent of antiquities (1923–51), the museum complexes underwent a restructuring and for some time presented an organic and balanced exhibit. But the calamitous flood in Florence of 1966 did untold damage to the antiquities and the displays, occasioning yet another renovation of the collection. Under superintendent Guglielmo Maetzke, enormous restoration efforts were undertaken, continuing to the present under Francesco Nicosia. The work has been carried out in the Centro di Restauro founded by Maetzke in 1967. Among the antiquities restored and/ or provided new displays in recent years are the François Vase and almost all the objects of the topographical museum. Numerous special exhibitions have spotlighted portions of the collection (e.g., Roman portraits, Greek and Roman gems, Greek vases).

BIBLIOGRAPHY
F. Nicosia, "I Musei Archeologici," *La Città degli Uffizi* (Florence, 1982), 33–35, with bib., 33–35; +"Luigi Adriano Milani: Origine e sviluppo del Complesso Museale Archeologico di Firenze," *Studi e Materiali,* n.s. 5 (1982), 33–175; A. Romualdi—G. De Marinis, *Itinerario Laurenziano nel Museo Archeologico di Firenze* (Florence, 1992).

FLORIS, FRANS (DE VRIENDT; ca. 1519–70). Flemish painter from Antwerp; a pupil of Lambert *Lombard.

In the sketchbook in the Basel Öffentliche Kunstsammlung (Kupferstichkabinett) is what remains of the drawings after ancient sculptures that Frans Floris made during his stay in Italy (1541–ca. 46), including some autograph drawings and some copies by some of his pupils. Floris's free approach in copying his models reveals that his admiration for the ancient artists was less absolute than Lambert Lombard's. He belongs to a generation for which the cult of Greek and Roman works, the study of which was by then part of all artists' background, is replaced by admiration for contemporary Italian painters, especially, *Michelangelo. Floris treats mythological and historical subjects, which he encountered in Lombard's workshop, with a personal style more inspired by Michelangelo and Venetian painting than by the ancients. His art, widely disseminated through engravings, marks a decisive turning point in the evolution of Flemish painting due to its new iconography and forms.

BIBLIOGRAPHY
N. Dacos, *Les Peintres belges à Rome au XVIe siècle* (Brussels, 1964); +C. Van de Velde, "A Roman Sketchbook of Frans Floris," *Master Drawings,* 7 (1969), 255–86; Idem, *Frans Floris (1519/20–1570), Leven en Werken* (Brussels, 1975).

G. DENHAENE

FONTANA, DOMENICO (1543–1607). Italian architect.

Born in Melida on Lake Lugano, Domenico Fontana went to Rome ca. 1563, finding employment with Cardinal Felice Peretti, who later became Pope *Sixtus V (1585–90). Fontana aided Sixtus in his radical urban transformation of the city of Rome and in the process was involved in the clearing, movement and destruction of Roman antiquities.

Fontana is most remembered for his dramatic success (1586) in moving the great Vatican obelisk (*obelisks) from its position beside St. Peter's to the spot in front of the basilica, before an admiring crowd. As a result Fontana was ennobled; he wrote a triumphant book describing this engineering feat and other works he had undertaken for the pope. Unfortunately, he had placed the obelisk a few degrees out of the axis of *Michelangelo's St. Peter's, a problem that had to be taken into account by *Maderno in his completion of the nave. For Sixtus V, Fontana reerected four obelisks in all, including the ones at S. Maria Maggiore (1587), the Lateran (1588) and Piazza del Popolo (1589). The artist describes how Sixtus ordered the restoration of the *Column of Marcus Aurelius and the placement of a bronze statue of St. Paul on top; a corresponding image of St. Peter was placed on the *Column of Trajan. In addition, Fontana saw to the transportation and restoration of the *Quirinal *Horse Tamers*. The pope and his architect are also known for the destruction of the *Septizodium on the Palatine Hill (1589) and for pulling down parts of the *Baths of Diocletian. An amazing scheme to transform the *Colosseum into workshops and apartments for workers in a wool-spinning industry was interrupted by Sixtus's death.

Fontana's architecture in Rome for the pope and others (e.g., the Lateran palace and the Moses Fountain of the Aqua Felice) is regarded as monotonous and unimaginative, displaying a weak classicism in the Late Mannerist style.

BIBLIOGRAPHY

+*Della trasportatione dell'obelisco vaticano et delle fabriche di nostro signore papa Sisto V* (Rome, 1590); S. Giedion, *Space, Time and Architecture,* 3rd ed. (London, 1954), 75–106; T. Magnuson, *Rome in the Age of Bernini* 1 (Uppsala, 1982), 20–29.

FONZIO, BARTOLOMMEO (BARTHOLOMAEUS FONTIUS; 1445–1513).

Italian Renaissance humanist, scholar and teacher; specialist in epigraphy.

Sponsored by Lorenzo de' Medici (cf. *Medici family), Francesco Sassetti and Bernardo *Rucellai, Fonzio was on good terms with the leading humanists of his day in his native Florence and elsewhere. By 1472 he had visited Rome and in an eloquent letter lamented the ruinous condition of the monuments, while naming his favorites.

On this trip and others he assembled a significant manuscript (Codex Ashmolensis; Oxford, Bodleian) with a sylloge or collection of inscriptions that he had seen personally or that he had read about in other scholars' manuscripts. The collection included epitaphs, historical notices and a few inscriptions of sacred significance. Fonzio did not arrange these, as did some other epigraphers, in topographical or chronological schemes nor even according to subject matter, but merely placed them in a random order. His manuscript is also important because of its rich illustration with drawings in pen and wash done by an anonymous artist in a style influenced by *Botticelli. These drawings include many copied from the manuscripts of *Ciriaco of Ancona, such as those of a bust of *Aristotle,* the *Muses* (from *Samothrace), *Medusa* and the colossal temple of Hadrian at Kyzikos (now lost). There is also a drawing of the corpse of *"Tulliola," discovered in Rome in 1485.

Fonzio was evidently much consulted for his knowledge of epigraphy. He almost certainly composed the inscription on the tomb of Francesco Sassetti and his wife in Sta. Trinità, Florence, and probably also devised the Latin phrases carved on the sarcophagus and triumphal arch represented in the *Adoration of the Magi* by *Ghirlandaio in the same chapel.

BIBLIOGRAPHY

F. Saxl, "The Classical Inscription in Renaissance Art and Politics," *JWarb* 4 (1940–41), 9–45; Weiss, *RDCA* 77–78, 146, 164.

FORGERY. The production of false works of art or artifacts in imitation of genuine ones, with the specific purpose of deceiving.

The words "forgery" (a corruption of *fortis,* "strong") and "fake" (from the wonder-working religious Fakir) reveal an ambivalence toward practices condemned outright as "false" and "counterfeit." All works are, of course, unique, and many antiquarian ones have been misinterpreted as well as misrepresented after their manufacture. Intent to deceive (which is often difficult to prove), usually for motives of monetary gain or esteem, traditionally defines objects as forgeries.

Something like forgery was practiced in classical antiquity when craftsmen signed their works as by Myron, Praxiteles and other great artists to satisfy ambitious and unlettered buyers (Martial 4.35; 9.56; Phaedrus, *Fabulae Aesopiae,* 5 Prologue). Blatant examples of this shallow ruse were noted by *Winckelmann and his predecessors (e.g., *Quirinal *Horse Tamers* by "Phidias"); misleading inscription had a long history in antiquity. The first collectors of classical art, the Attalid kings of Hellenistic Pergamon, after acquiring old pieces through conquest and purchase (Aigina, sculpture by Polykleitos), commissioned copies of, and improvisations upon, renowned works (*Athena Parthenos*). They also fostered eclectic and conservative archaisms—a kind of deception, too. Kindred examples of maintaining old styles and images associated with venerated traditions were already legion in the ancient Near East (Pharaonic appropriations and stylistic revivals by Rameses II or cylinder seals, generally). In classical Greece and afterward, earlier modes continued to be reproduced, especially in honorific and decorative works (Panathenaic amphorae, architectural orders and profiles, Kritios's *Tyrannicides,* Alkamenes' *Hermes,* Praxiteles' *Dionysos*). Pottery and other minor arts were also copied, because of rivalry, admiration and tradition, sometimes provincially as well as for profit (Etrusco-Corinthian and later Italic ware); coins especially were counterfeited, often with baser metals (Celtic and, eventually, Carolingian money). In a parallel vein, damaged original works and commercial copies were commonly restored to make them appear whole again (Olympia west pediment corners, *Laocoon,* Lansdowne *Artemis*). Like the manufacture of reproductions and casts, most of these activities are not considered forgery, but fakes were surely made for Roman collectors.

The modern premium awarded originality follows naturally upon the ideals of immaculate conception, the sanctity of personal property and expression and the romance of objective scholarship. During the Middle Ages and the rule of its iconic imagery, classical representation had little appeal, and ancient work was preserved largely for its value as raw material and for its use in illustrating Christian narratives. With few exceptions, even in expanded ensembles, little effort was made to simulate the detailed appearance of classical antiquities (gem reliquaries, *Regisole* of Pavia, Campo Santo *Antinous*). This essentially material and didactic exploitation has persisted along with later attitudes.

With the rebirth of classical norms of illusion and individualism in Italy around the fourteenth century, ancient naturalism in art was increasingly prized and emulated. Classical works were avidly studied and collected for their capacity to enhance self-knowing; the self-imposed models were, however, also partially viewed as tyrants and inspired "quarrels" and competition. *Vasari records that lesser studios and great masters (*Ghiberti, *Michelangelo) simulated ancient minor arts and statuary to demonstrate their skill and for income. Much evidence exists for a budding Renaissance industry in *antico* productions, then or later peddled as ancient works. This manufacture included coins, medals, gems, jewelry, plate, plaques, statuettes, manuscripts and inscriptions (e.g., by Marmita of Parma, Cavino of Padua, Bertoldo, *Antico, Briosco; the Venetian Este relief, *Cellini silver vase and parts of the *Ciriaco of Ancona, *Medici family, *Fulvio and *Ligorio collections). Comparable objects were already hoarded for their material value and portability in medieval cabinets and treasuries.

Vasari also records the practice of fancifully restoring excavated fragments for the decoration of villas and palaces—first in Florence (*Donatello and *Verrocchio for the Medici) and then in Rome for wealthy ecclesiastical houses and papal and royal collections (Lorenzetto for della *Valle; Montorsoli at the Belvedere, *Primaticcio for Fontainebleau). These inventive restorations, innovations and copies (twelve Caesars, philosophers and so on) were an important source of income, activity and learning for young sculptors until modern times (e.g., the della Portas, *Bernini, *Algardi, Duquesnoy, *Girardon, L. S. Adam, Roubilliac, Nollekens). Some minor sculptors worked largely in making reproductions, pastiches and new or reworked *antico* pieces, as well as fakes, for an industry that quickly extended beyond Italy to supply foreign monarchs and other wealthy patrons investing in the growing art market and antiquarian craze. By the mid-eighteenth century, this tradition resulted in the almost exclusively antiquarian activities of *Cavaceppi and his circle (*Pichler, *Jenkins, *Franzoni, Gavin *Hamilton, Sibilla, *Albacini and others), who supplied their clients with massively reworked and fabricated "antiquities" that helped usher in the first modern style, neo-classicism.

Beginning with the sensational and jealously guarded discoveries at *Pompeii in the late eighteenth century, modern excavations have stimulated attempts to assimilate the exciting, new unearthed images by imitation and forgery. Pompeian murals encouraged the revival and forgery of encaustic painting (*Caylus, *Mengs, G. B. Casanova, Guerra), a genre once imitated by *Poussin. Pompeian mosaics, small bronzes and household goods spawned an industry in fakes, facsimiles and imitations of a sort that commonly develops around archaeological sites. Collections of *Greek vases (especially W. *Hamilton's), then called Etruscan (*Etruscheria), inspired patriotic and historically minded artists to ape their fabric and linear mode with imitations and *antico* production (*Piranesi, *Ingres, *Wedgwood's Etrurian, Jaspar, and Basalt ware). New imports from Greece prompted reinterpretations, especially of the *Parthenon and *Aigina sculptures, for many years (*Thorvaldsen's restorations and archaistic *Hope* are watersheds).

More clandestine antiquarian manufacture followed midcentury discoveries in the Crimea (Roushomowsky's *Tiara of Saitaphernes) and Sardinia (Sardo-Phoenician bronzes); there also was a significant modern production of Tanagra figurines and larger Etruscan terracottas, as well as small bronzes (Pennelli brothers' British Museum sarcophagus, Metropolitan *Warriors* and so on). The Minoan discoveries of *Evans resulted not only in local and international fakes but in wholesale reconstructions based upon minute fragments. These and simplified Cycladic idols and artifacts (with other esoteric and Stone Age productions) both inspired numerous forgeries and influenced the primitivism of many modern artists (Matisse, Brancusi, Modigliani and others). Archaic, Classical, and Hellenistic discoveries at the *Akropolis in Athens, *Olympia and other sites also prompted fashionable forgery and reinterpretation (Grueneisen, Moutaffof, and *Campana collections; Hildebrand, Rodin, Bourdelle, Picasso, Boccioni fragments and improvisations). Works by the specialist forger Alceo *Dossena and his ilk, who made gauche and artificially battered variations upon newly discovered and marginally understood antiquities (as well as Renaissance works), typify recent fakery in the popular imagination. Works by them and more accomplished followers figure heavily in a lucrative antiquities market. This situation, coupled with restrictions on export and suspicions concerning provenance (even archaeological sites have been salted with fakes) have significantly affected recent opinion about works with unusual pedigrees or mixed claims to authenticity (*Fayum portraits; Boston "counterpart" to the *Ludovisi Throne; Berlin *Seated Goddess*; Metropolitan *Kouros*; *Dama de Elche*).

Dealers and craftspeople have been quick to respond to discoveries and shifts in taste by manufacturing enticing tales of origin and attractive subjects as well as by adopting ever more sophisticated studio practices—with the aid of specialists, publications, reproductions and gallery studies. They also make the new seem old and consistent with their models by carefully treating surfaces with breaks, burial, baking, immersions in acid, alkali or colored stain and the like to induce an appropriate antique appearance and patina. The amateur's and collector's affection, connoisseurship and investment have, in turn, supported a growing class of agents and scholars who know ways of the studio and market and are expert in matters of style and context prerequisite for responsible decision making. Developments in science and technology, ranging from biological classification by minutiae to computerized atomic analysis, have also been employed in authenticating objects: ultraviolet, infrared and X-ray examinations now provide evidence invisible in ordinary light; carbon-14 deterioration, thermoluminescence and dendrite deposits help to determine age; and reconstructions of ancient manufacture and spectrographic, isotopic and neutron accelerator analyses can identify fabric and provenance.

BIBLIOGRAPHY
+H. Ladendorf, *Antikenstudium und Antikenkopie* (Berlin, 1958), with bib.; +D. Mustilli, s.v. "Falsificazione," *EAA* 2 (1960), 576–89, with bib.; +O. Kurz, *Fakes,* 2nd ed. (New York, 1967); +S. Howard, "A Dossenesque 'Double Herm' in California," *California Studies in Classical Antiquity* 4 (1971), 181–98, with bib.

S. HOWARD

FORMA URBIS ROMAE (MARBLE PLAN, SEVERAN MARBLE PLAN). A map of Rome carved on slabs of marble in A.D. 203–11 under Septimius Severus and Caracalla, probably on the basis of an earlier plan made under Vespasian or Domitian and, less probably, another made for Agrippa.

It is a fundamental tool for the study of the topography of ancient Rome, even in its very fragmentary state. Of 712 catalogued fragments, many composed of several pieces, less than fifty have been positively identified and located.

The first fragments were rediscovered in the spring of 1562 behind the church of SS. Cosma and Damiano outside the hall in the south corner of the Templum Pacis in an excavation made by Torquato Conti for Cardinal Alessandro Farnese (*Farnese family). The map had covered the southwest wall of this area, and some plates may still have been attached to it. *Panvinio, curator of the Farnese collections, or Cardinal Farnese may have commissioned the careful drawings of the important fragments that appear in Cod.Vat.Lat. 3439, fol. 13–23, believed to be by Antonio *Dosio; the codex later belonged to Panvinio's successor, Fulvio *Orsini, and is known as the Codex Orsinianus. The fragments were apparently kept in a ground-floor storeroom of Palazzo Farnese, where they were subsequently neglected until, at an uncertain date, workmen broke a number of them up to use as building material in walls in the "giardino segreto" on the Tiber.

Much later, in 1673, Giovanni Pietro *Bellori undertook to publish the fragments, working from both the actual fragments and the drawings in the Codex Orsinianus, occasionally correcting the latter. Presumably at this time what remained were still in the same storage place. Following this call of the plan to the attention of the learned world, in 1727 Duke Antonio Farnese was petitioned by the Senate of Rome to donate the fragments to the Campidoglio or to create for them a "campidoglio" in Palazzo Farnese. Although this initiative was slow in bearing fruit, eventually Charles III of Naples, heir of the Farnese, presented the fragments in December 1741. It was decided to exhibit them on the stair of the Museo Capitolino, using Bellori's plates as pattern and authority, and missing and mutilated fragments were restored according to this, despite problems of scale, and marked with a six-pointed star. The work was entrusted to G.-B. Nolli, the cartographer, whose men did not hesitate to trim away uninscribed portions. Twenty panels of fragments following Bellori were installed on the museum stairs, plus six of other fragments.

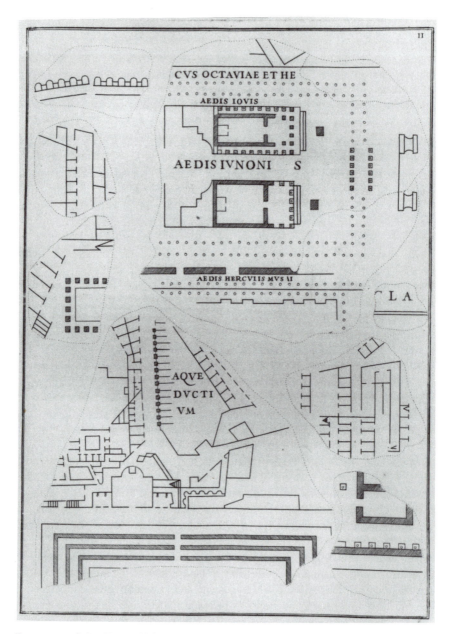

Fragments of the *Forma Urbis Romae* (Marble Plan of Rome), engraving from G. P. Bellori, *Ichnographia veteris Romae XX tabulis comprehensa* (1764). (The Warburg Institute, University of London.)

In the nineteenth century the fragments were repeatedly studied by various scholars, notably *Canina, Jordan and Trendelenburg. More fragments came to light in excavations near the Column of Phocas, behind SS. Cosma e Damiano, and near the *Temple of Castor. Then in June 1888, in connection with work on the Tiber embankment, a wall surrounding the "giardino segreto" of Palazzo Farnese was demolished, and 186 fragments were discovered used in it. Subsequently, 451 more were extracted from masonry in various points here. In 1903, after much debate and many difficulties, it was decided to remove the panels from the stair of Museo Capitolino and to reconstruct such parts of the plan as were known, on the garden wall of Palazzo dei Conservatori, within a schematic plan of the ancient city, while the unidentified fragments were consigned to storage. Unfortunately, exposure to the weather proved deleterious, and in 1928 a thorough reconsideration of the monument was undertaken. The fragments were removed to the Antiquarium Comunale on the Caelian and displayed in a room dedicated to them, and a new publication was planned. When the Antiquarium Comunale was dismantled in 1939, the Forma Urbis was sent first to Palazzo Caffarelli and then to Palazzo Farnesino dei Baullari. Finally, in 1955, the fragments were moved to Palazzo Braschi, where they were studied, cataloged, described and published by a commission of four scholars who were the heirs of a commission first formed in 1924. New joins and discoveries continue to be made, and the Forma Urbis continues to be housed in Palazzo Braschi.

BIBLIOGRAPHY

G. Carettoni et al., *La Pianta marmorea di Roma,* 1–2 (Rome, 1960); E. Rodriguez Almeida, *Forma urbis marmorea: aggiornamento generale,* 1–2. (Rome, 1981); J. C. Anderson, jr., "Post-Mortem Adventures of the Marble Plan of Rome," *The Classical Outlook* (March-April 1982), 69–72.

L. RICHARDSON, JR

FORUM BOARIUM, Rome. Roman public square, an ill-defined area along the Tiber River from the Aventine to the *Capitoline Hill, eventually running to the crest of the ridge between the *Forum Romanum and the river.

The name has been thought to indicate that the site was a cattle market, but, in fact, the area was unsuited for such use, and the name may derive, instead, from the Aiginetan bronze sculpture of a bull that marked the starting point of the city boundary (pomerium) of Romulus. It was the site of the head of the Sublician bridge and, earlier, probably the point from which a ferry across the river departed. It was throughout history a scene of intense traffic, for all traffic along and across the Tiber tended to concentrate there. It was the site of important shrines, notably, the early altar of Hercules (Ara Maxima Herculis), the temple of Portunus and the shrine of Pudicitia Patricia. Although it was subject to flooding, the Forum Boarium was heavily built up from an early date, and remains of numerous apartment houses and warehouses have been found.

A round temple, presumably that of Hercules Victor *in Foro Boario,* exca-

The *Temple of Fortuna Virilis*, Rome, elevation and cross-section, etching by G. B. Piranesi, from *Le Antichità romane* (1756). (Deutsches Archäologisches Institut, Rome. Inst. Neg. 87.435).

vated and dismantled in the time of *Sixtus IV (1471–84), is a sorry loss, though B. *Peruzzi has left a reconstruction drawing of it. Two other temples owe their excellent preservation to their having been converted to use as churches. A round one, commonly known as the *"Temple of Vesta," may be a temple of Hercules. During the Middle Ages, it became the church of S. Stefano delle Carrozze and then of S. Maria del Sole. It is Corinthian, made of Greek marble, and shows many signs of Greek workmanship. Its date is disputed, but it was probably built about 100 B.C. The ancient entablature and roof long ago vanished, having been replaced by the low conical tile roof visible today.

The other building, known as the "Temple of Fortuna Virilis," was maintained in the Middle Ages as the church of S. Maria de Gradellis, and in 1492 S. Maria Egiziaca. A rectangular Ionic temple of tufa with travertine parts, it is probably of the time of Sulla (early first century B.C.) and may be the shrine of Portunus, god of harbors. With four columns across the façade and a high podium, the temple has a frontal emphasis.

Beginning with *Dosio in the sixteenth century, one finds careful drawings of architectural members and details and interesting attempts at reconstruction of the roofing of the round temple. These temples were first the object of clearance of encumbrance and restoration in 1810–11 under *Valadier, who also published measured drawings of the round one, the first of several sets made between then and 1850. Final clearance of the rectangular temple was not accomplished until the early years of the twentieth century.

BIBLIOGRAPHY
E. Fiechter, "Der ionische Tempel am Ponte Rotto in Rom (S. Maria Egiziaca)," *RM* 21 (1906), 220–73; F. Rakob—W. D. Heilmeyer, *Der Rundtempel am Tiber in Rom* (Mainz, 1973); F. Coarelli, *Il Foro Boario* (Rome, 1988).

L. RICHARDSON, JR

FORUM ROMANUM, Rome. The principal market and public square of the Romans, located in the low area between the *Capitoline Hill and *Palatine Hill; it became the heart of Republican Rome, but in early times was marshy, except in the dry season, and subject to frequent flooding; through it ran the brook of the Cloaca, with some of its tributaries.

Under Tarquinius Superbus in the sixth century B.C., the people of Rome were coerced into work on the course of the Cloaca, which must have meant deepening the channel and building up its banks. Market activities of the forum must have been confined to an area northwest of this, running more or less perpendicular to what we now think of as the axis of the forum. On the other hand, the *Temple of Castor and the *Temple of Vesta, as well as the Regia (which was the headquarters of the Pontifex Maximus and a shrine in its own right) and a number of other sacred buildings always associated with the forum, were on the southeast side of the Cloaca.

The Comitium, which was always distinguished from the forum, would have bounded it on the northeast on a line not far from the *Lapis Niger, but to the

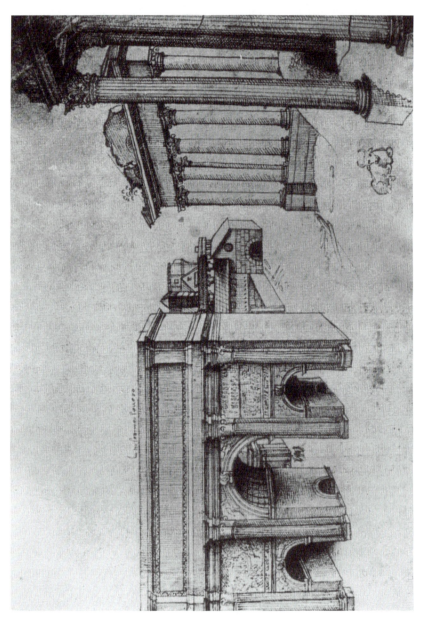

View of the *Forum Romanum*, Rome, with Arch of Septimius Severus, Temple of Vespasian and Temple of Saturn, drawing from the Codex Escurialensis, before 1508, Madrid, Escorial. (Deutsches Archäologisches Institut, Rome. Inst. Neg. 7376.)

southwest it could have included most of the area of the *Basilica Julia. Around it were a few shrines and monuments, but the open area seems to have been kept remarkably free, except for the Lacus Curtius, down to the building of the Rostra with its ships' beaks from the Battle of Antium (338 B.C.). By 310 B.C. the butchers' shops (*tabernae lanienae*) had been confined to the southwest end of the forum; the money changers' shops (*tabernae argentariae*) that burned in 210 B.C. must go back at least to this date. But by the time of the second Punic War, the food market must have been largely, if not entirely, moved to the Forum Piscarium and its adjacencies and the Velabrum.

The monumentalization of the forum begins after the second Punic War and is seen in the multiplication of porticoes and basilicas, buildings of Greek inspiration adapted to Roman purposes. The *Basilica Aemilia et Fulvia was erected on the northeast side of the forum in 179 B.C., followed in 174 by a porticus running along the shoulder of the Capitoline and then by the Basilica Sempronia in 170, which balanced the Basilica Aemilia on the opposite side of the forum. The area was now effectively framed by fine buildings. The Cloaca was culverted across the forum at a date unknown, but presumably sometime around the middle of the second century B.C.

The forum in this form, with occasional additions and restorations, lasted down to the time of Julius Caesar. He proposed to rebuild it completely, spent lavishly from the spoils of Gaul to this end and made a splendid beginning. But his untimely death left much of the work to Augustus, who gave it its familiar form with rostra at either end and an almost uninterrupted line of basilica porticoes and temple façades down either side and across either end.

It was now used almost entirely for ceremonial purposes. It kept this general appearance until the time of Diocletian, despite the addition of such features as the *Temple of Vespasian, the Equus Domitiani and the *Arch of Septimius Severus. But under Diocletian a new rostra was built at the southeast end in front of the Rostra of the temple of the Deified Julius, and lines of lofty columns crowned with honorary statues on the rostra and in front of the Basilica Julia formed a frame focusing on a larger column on a high-stepped base toward the west corner that eventually became the column of Phocas; this court of honor was soon cluttered with smaller monuments.

In the Middle Ages the forum does not seem to have been heavily built up, except at the edges. There was makeshift use of the buildings and ruins, with conversion of many of the buildings into churches, from S. Maria Antiqua and S. Martina in the sixth century to S. Lorenzo in Miranda in the eleventh century (*Temple of Antoninus and Faustina). In the sixteenth century the Forum Romanum was plundered at many points by treasure hunters, as it had been for marble and lime since the days of Theodoric and *Charlemagne. By the Early Renaissance the vicinity of the *Temple of Castor had become known as the Tre Colonne (1467), and by 1591 at least the general area was commonly known as the Campo Vaccino (Cow Pasture), although its proper identity had always been known.

Systematic excavations began only under the French in the time of *Napoleon, when *Valadier proposed to turn the forum into a vast archaeological park, with the individual major ruins dug out and freed and connected by avenues of trees. Real clearance began under Giacomo *Boni at the end of the nineteenth century. He proposed to clear the whole forum down to its last ancient level, while leaving a few later structures as documents but then continued and took the Sacra Via down to its Augustan level. He also carried out deep stratigraphic excavations at certain points, notably in the Comitium, the Sepulcretum and the Lacus Juturnae. More recent work has concentrated on completely clearing the northwest end on the lower slope of the Capitoline and straightening out the history of such buildings as the Basilica Paulli, the Regia, the temple of Vesta and the Atrium Vestae (Hall of Vesta; the quarters for the Vestal Virgins).

BIBLIOGRAPHY

G. Lugli, *Roma antica, Il Centro monumentale* (Rome, 1946), 57–242; C. F. Giuliani— P. Verduchi, *L'Area centrale del foro romano* (Florence, 1987); F. Coarelli, *Il Foro romano*, 1, *Periodo arcaico* (Rome, 1983); 2, *Periodo repubblicano e augusteo* (Rome, 1985).

L. RICHARDSON, JR

FORZETTA, OLIVIERO (1299/1300–1373). Italian moneylender, collector of manuscripts and works of art.

Oliviero Forzetta stands out in the fourteenth century as one of the few contemporaries of *Petrarch who showed a passion for antiquities and classical texts that would rival Renaissance attitudes. A native of Treviso, where he qualified as notary and held public office, Forzetta became extremely wealthy as a moneylender. Knowledge of his collecting activities is based on an elaborate memorandum he wrote in 1335, regarding his plans for a trip to Venice. He lists all the authors whose books he will seek (Ovid, Sallust, Cicero, Livy, Valerius Maximus, Seneca, along with various theologians) and the antiquities he wishes to acquire and where he will seek them. He expresses interest in paintings, coins, bronzes and reliefs, with an especial interest in "four boys in stone from Ravenna." The latter has been identified as a Roman relief showing four *putti*, dating to the first–second centuries A.C. and now in the Museo Archeologico, Venice (formerly in San Vitale, Ravenna).

At his death, the art collection of Forzetta was dispersed in accordance with his will, which asked that the pieces be sold to provide dowries for needy girls.

BIBLIOGRAPHY

Weiss, *RDCA,* 28–29; +L. Gargan, *Cultura e arte nel Veneto at tempo del Petrarca* (Padua, 1978); Sheard, no. 16; Bober—Rubinstein, 90–91.

FOSSE, GIOVANNI PIETRO DALLE. See VALERIANUS BOLZANIUS.

FOURMONT, MICHEL, Abbé (1690–1746). French linguist, specialist in Greek inscriptions.

Orphaned as a child and indigent, Fourmont was unable to receive a proper education until the age of twenty-five. He then came into his inheritance and was able to begin his studies in Paris. In the space of three years he prepared himself to teach Latin, Greek, Hebrew and Syriac. Soon afterward, he took Holy Orders and became professor of Syriac at the College Royal.

In 1728, Fourmont was sent along with the Abbé Sevin to Constantinople to determine on behalf of the king of France whether the Turks had any Greek or Latin manuscripts in the Seraglio Library that might be published. When the mission proved fruitless, Fourmont set sail for Chios and Athens, now searching for Greek inscriptions, attended by his nephew Claude Fourmont. His travels led him to *Eleusis, Megara, Salamis, *Aigina, *Sounion, Porto Rafti and *Marathon, after which he claimed to have recorded 900 inscriptions (more than 650 were from Athens and its surroundings and included Attic lists of tribes, magistrates and priests).

Next on his itinerary were *Corinth, *Epidauros, Troizen, Hermione; then followed *Nemea, *Sikyon, Nauplia, Aigos and Patras. Finally, in 1730 he visited *Sparta and Amyklai, where his quest for inscriptions became an uncontrollable mania. He now suffered from mental disturbances, which evidently had their origin in numerous illnesses he had endured in all these travels. He literally plundered Sparta, dismantling buildings to find inscriptions (''I must excavate without scruple,'' he declared), and after recording inscriptions, having the text chiseled away and obliterated! Called home from Greece at this point, he returned to Paris to reveal his discoveries.

The abbé lectured on his finds to the Académie des inscriptions et belles-lettres but failed to produce the definitive, annotated publication of all the inscriptions that he had envisioned. Claude Fourmont was unable to help him, since he was forced to tutor Greek, Hebrew and Syriac to live. The inscriptions, nevertheless, became famous and excited great interest; eventually those ''from Sparta'' were denounced as forgeries on the basis of their impossible contents and unlikely letter forms. Modern research at Sparta has vindicated some of Michel Fourmont's readings, but in general his records are used with the greatest caution.

Fourmont also worked on the Etruscan language and was named a member of the *Accademia Etrusca at Cortona (1740).

BIBLIOGRAPHY

E. Bréhaut, ''Fourmont, Michel,'' *NBG* 18 (1857), cols. 365–70; Stoneman, *Land of Lost Gods,* 95–107.

FRAIAPANE. See FRANGIPANI.

FRANCESCO DI GIORGIO MARTINI (FRANCESCO MAURIZIO DI MARTINO POLLAIUOLO; 1439–1501). Sienese painter, sculptor, architect and engineer.

Francesco di Giorgio served as consultant on water supply, fortifications, artillery and siege techniques. He was employed at the court of Urbino and later worked for the Aragonese royal family at Naples. In his final years he served the Sienese Republic in various capacities, and was appointed chief architect of the Duomo.

Francesco di Giorgio's early career in Siena was that of an artist true to the old-fashioned Gothic school. But his transfer to the humanist circles of Duke Federigo da *Montefeltre at Urbino, where he acted as engineer (1477–82), led to a sudden intellectual development. He studied texts in Latin in the famous ducal library and was inspired to try his own translation of Vitruvius (which resulted, however, in failure). In addition, he compiled his own treatise on architecture, civil engineering and military techniques with a section on the architecture of the ancients. This treatise, showing progressive polishing in the six accepted copies of it that are known, was illustrated with drawings from the artist's own hand. The Codice Saluzzo 148 in the Biblioteca Reale, Turin, with a set of drawings of Roman imperial architecture attached, is considered the final version.

Francesco di Giorgio studied the visible ruins and ancient sites to the north of Rome as well as in Rome itself—the *Palatine, the Caelian, the *Lateran and the *Baths of Caracalla. He showed an especial predilection for the *Septizodium and was interested in tombs along the *Via Appia. Travels to the Aragonese court provided the occasion for investigating the topography of ancient Casinum and the Phlegrean area, where he saw examples of Roman concrete construction. Francesco di Giorgio understood the true nature of Roman concrete structures but omitted examples from his own texts. His treatise on architecture was built on Vitruvian descriptions of an architecture that was, to a certain extent, already out of vogue in the Augustan period in which Vitruvius wrote. He may not have recognized that Late Antique buildings of the time of Maxentius and Constantine were actually ancient architecture. Though he made intelligent observations on the spot as he viewed Roman buildings, these were not necessarily consistent with his text on the canonical Greek architecture described by Vitruvius.

Of the many artists of the Renaissance and later periods who observed and sketched the splendid ruins of Rome, Francesco di Giorgio is among the earliest. A collection of architectural sketches in the Uffizi (Gabinetto dei Disegni e Stampe, nr. 318–37, 1436–37), with notes and measurements of the monuments, stands at the beginning of topographical research. Sometimes ancient elements from such studies turn up in his art as well, but they are regularly transformed and converted into fresh Renaissance forms.

BIBLIOGRAPHY

C. Promis, *Vita di Francesco di Giorgio* (Turin, 1841); A. Bartoli, *I Monumenti antichi di Roma nei disegni degli Uffizi di Firenze* 1 (Rome, 1915); S. Brinton, *Francesco di Giorgio Martini of Siena* (London, 1934); A. Weller, *Francesco di Giorgio 1439–1501* (Chicago, 1943); C. H. Ericsson, *Roman Architecture Expressed in Sketches by Francesco di Giorgio Martini, Studies in Imperial Roman and Early Christian Architecture,*

Commentationes Humanarum Litterarum 66 (Ekenas, 1980); +L. Belosi, ed., *Francesco di Giorgio e il Rinascimento a Siena* (Milan, 1993); +F. P. Fiore—M. Tafuri, eds., *Francesco di Giorgio architetto* (Milan, 1993).

CHRISTOFFER H. ERICSSON

FRANCESCO DI SAVONA. See SIXTUS IV.

FRANCESCO GIAMBERTI, GIULIANO DI. See SANGALLO, GIULIANO DA.

FRANCISCO D'OLLANDA (DE HOLLANDA; 1510–83). Portuguese artist, humanist and architect.

Born in Portugal, probably at Lisbon, Francisco d'Ollanda was sent in 1537 by King John III to Italy to bring back records of its antiquities. He passed through Spain and southern France on his way to Italy, taking note of ancient aqueducts and bridges he saw along the route and arriving in Rome in 1538. There he became friends with *Michelangelo and, through him, made other acquaintances before his departure from the city in 1540. He visited a number of other Italian cities, including Terracina, Minturno, Naples, Barletta, Ancona, Venice, Padua.

Francisco's sketchbook of monuments he had seen in his travels was presented upon his return to John III and is today in the library of the Escorial, Madrid (MS A/e ij6). It consists of fifty-four sheets with 113 drawings, mostly made with pen and ink, occasionally with black and red chalk; a few watercolors are included. He did his assignment thoroughly, bringing back to Portugal tidy drawings of the *Column of Trajan, the *Arch of Constantine, the *Arch of Titus, the *Arch of the Argentarii and numerous famed sculptures, including statues in the Belvedere (*Laocoon, *Cleopatra, *Nile, *Belvedere *Apollo*) as well as on the Capitoline (*Spinario, *Marcus Aurelius* Equestrian Figure) and in private collections (Ludovisi *Juno* from the *Cesi collection). He created a handsome watercolor of the *Domus Aurea and, in Venice, made a drawing of the **Horses* of San Marco.

BIBLIOGRAPHY

"Francisco de Hollanda," Thieme—Becker, 12 (1916), 331–33, 614; +E. Tormo, *Os Desenhos das antigualhas que vio Francisco d'Ollanda, pintor portugués* (Madrid, 1940); +Bober—Rubinstein, esp. 457.

FRANÇOIS, ALESSANDRO (1796–1857). Italian archaeologist, discoverer of the *François Vase and Tomb of the Monkey at *Chiusi and the *François Tomb at *Vulci.

Born in Florence, François traveled widely as a young man both in Italy and abroad before settling down to excavate in the territory of the ancient Etruscan cities. He worked at *Cosa from 1825 to 1828 and at *Cortona in 1843 and then excavated at *Volterra, *Fiesole, *Roselle, *Vetulonia and *Populonia, as well as at Chiusi and Vulci. He was invited to become a member of two of the leading archaeological associations of his day, the *Accademia Etrusca and the *Instituto di Corrispondenza Archaeologica.

François formed his own society for the promotion of his excavations, with the French archaeologist and epigrapher A. Noël des Vergers as his principal collaborator. He especially hoped to found a great museum with the antiquities that he had excavated; meanwhile, he kept these at his home in Livorno (where he served as a commissary of war for the Grand Duke of Tuscany). In spite of repeated attempts in Florence, he was unable to establish the museum there; he then turned to the French government but was again rebuffed. After the spectacular discovery of the François Tomb in 1857, he received great acclaim, and there was a surge of interest in his projects. But he died of an illness a few months later and was unable to ride the waves of this success.

BIBLIOGRAPHY

P. Pelagatti, "François, Alessandro," *EAA* 3 (1960), 729; F. Buranelli ed., *La Tomba François di Vulci* (Vatican City, 1987), 22–33.

FRANÇOIS TOMB, Vulci. Etruscan painted tomb, variously dated; the paintings from the walls, now believed to belong to the fourth century B.C., include the theme of Achilles sacrificing Trojan prisoners before the shade of Patroklos and Macstrna freeing Caile Vipinas as Cneve Tarchunies Rumach is slain; also depicted is the Etruscan Vel Saties, who evidently commissioned the painting of the tomb.

The spectacular discovery of the tomb was made in 1857 by Alessandro *François, working in collaboration with A. Noël des Vergers, who has left a stirring account of the opening of the chamber; he reports that much of the material in the tomb disintegrated upon contact with the air. François's own account, scarcely less emotional, was published immediately in the *Bullettino* of the *Instituto di Corrispondenza Archeologica (1857). He noted that the unplundered tomb, with its huge dromos and multiple chambers, contained some twenty-five skeletons as well as cremation burials. The grave goods included gold jewelry, carved gems, painted vases and objects of bronze.

In 1862, the owner of the property, Prince Alessandro Torlonia (*Torlonia family), had the paintings removed from the walls of the tomb, subdivided into panels by P. Succi and transferred to Rome. *Dennis reported in 1878 that the panels were on view at the Collegio Romano. Later, they were moved to the Museo Torlonia on Via della Lungara. In 1945 they went to the Istituto di Restauro in Rome and eventually to the Villa Albani, where now, scarcely legible, they may be seen by permission only. The recent restoration and exhibition of the Vel Saties panel at the Museo Gregoriano Etrusco (*Vatican Museums) were the occasion for a thorough study of the discovery of the tomb and the publication of what could be recovered from its original grave goods.

BIBLIOGRAPHY

A. Noël des Vergers, *L'Etrurie et les étrusques* (Paris, 1862–64), I, 139; II, 47; III, 16; G. Dennis, *Cities and Cemeteries of Etruria,* 2nd ed. (London, 1878) 449; N. T. de

Grummond, "Rediscovery," in *Etruscan Life and Afterlife,* ed. L. Bonfante (Detroit, 1986), 18; F. Buranelli, ed., *La Tomba François di Vulci* (Vatican City, 1987).

FRANÇOIS VASE. Attic Greek black-figured krater (mixing bowl) with volute handles, dated ca. 570 B.C.

From the time of its discovery the vase was recognized as a major monument of Greek ceramics because of its high quality, great size (height 66cm) and display of Greek mythological themes, especially from the Trojan War. Among the numerous inscriptions on the vase are found the signatures of the painter, Kleitias, and the potter, Ergotimos.

The vase was discovered in numerous fragments by Alessandro *François at Fonte Rotella near Chiusi in the area of two previously plundered tombs. He found approximately two-thirds of the vessel in 1844; encouraged by A. M. Migliarini, who recognized the significance of the find, he returned to Fonte Rotella in 1845 and located five more large pieces. The vessel, restored by G. G. Franceschi, was purchased by Leopoldo II, Grand Duke of Tuscany, for 500 zecchini and deposited in the *Uffizi. It was given initial publication by E. *Braun. Subsequently, one more piece of the vase was discovered and donated to the museum by C. Strozzi. In 1900, the magnificent volute krater was smashed into 638 pieces by a museum guard who, in a fit of vengeful anger at his superior, threw a heavy stool at the display case. The vase was again restored (by P. Zei), including the Strozzi fragment, but now lacking another piece that was stolen at the time and not returned to the museum until 1904. A final restoration of the François Vase was executed in 1973 by R. Giachetti under the direction of M. Cristofani for the Soprintendenza Archeologica della Toscana. The work included dismantling the vase, removing glue, plaster and watercolor from previous restorations and reintegrating the fragments. The vessel is currently on display in surroundings designed for its protection and study in the *Florence Archaeological Museum.

BIBLIOGRAPHY

"Materiali per servire alla storia del Vaso François," *Bolletino d'Arte* 62 (1981), ser. spec. 1.

FRANGIPANI (FRANGIPANE; FRAIAPANE) FAMILY. Baronial family of medieval and Renaissance Rome, powerful in politics and possessing significant collections of ancient inscriptions and sculptures; the *Arch of Titus was incorporated into their fortress in the twelfth century.

There were several branches of the family of importance during the fifteenth and sixteenth centuries. The ancestral house near Piazza S. Marco was visited by *Aldrovandi in the mid-sixteenth century. At that time it was held by CURZIO, who served faithfully as a deputy for the building commission on the Capitoline Hill. Another Frangipani residence, on the Palatine, was the site of excavations in the second decade of the sixteenth century. Among the antiquities probably owned by the Frangipani were a Roman sarcophagus relief with a *Judgment of Paris* and another with a *suovetaurilia.*

BIBLIOGRAPHY

Lanciani, *Storia degli scavi,* I, (1902), 171–72; II, (1903), 35–36, 69; Bober—Rubinstein, 474.

FRANZONI, FRANCESCO ANTONIO (1734–1818). Italian sculptor and restorer.

Born in Carrara, site of the famous quarries, Franzoni had a natural affinity for working in marble. By 1765 he was in Rome and was soon employed at the Vatican by *Pius VI (pope from 1775 to 1799), making ornamental decorations such as those on the clocks of St. Peter's and doing restorations of sculptures in the museum. He also worked outside the Vatican, making, for example, a chimney decoration and a coat of arms for Palazzo Braschi and the lions on the monument of Maria Flaminia Odescalchi Chigi in S. Maria del Popolo.

Franzoni is remembered, above all, for his restorations of animal sculptures, especially in the Sala degli Animali at the *Vatican Museums. Sometimes his retorations were erroneous, as in the case of a milk-cow that he made into a steer, or extravagant, as in the case of the famous *biga* (chariot) in the Sala della Biga, placed at the entrance to the Museo Pio-Clementino. Only the body of the chariot, with its acanthus relief, is ancient; Franzoni restored it (1778) as having two galloping horses, the body of one being an antiquity unrelated to the *biga* donated by Prince Borghese (*Borghese family).

Franzoni also restored the *Antinous* in the Sala Rotonda at the Vatican, as well as the huge porphyry basin in the same room. His brother, Giuseppe Franzoni, also worked in Rome but is best known for assisting *Thorvaldsen in restoring the sculptures from *Aigina.

BIBLIOGRAPHY

F. Noack, "Franzoni, Francesco Antonio," Thieme—Becker 12 (1916), 391; *The Vatican Collections: The Papacy and Art* (New York, 1982), 126–27; C. Pietrangeli, *I Musei Vaticani, cinque secoli di storia* (Rome, 1985), esp. 52.

FRAZER, SIR JAMES GEORGE (1854–1941). Scottish anthropologist and classicist.

The eldest son of Calvinist parents, Frazer was born in Glasgow and went to the university there at the age of fifteen. Despite his excellent record at Glasgow (he studied with G. G. Ramsey), he realized that his preparation was inadequate and accordingly entered Trinity College, Cambridge, in 1875. Second in the classical tripos in 1878, he gained a fellowship in 1879 with a dissertation on Platonic epistemology.

Although Frazer's major work, *The Golden Bough* (2 vols., 1890; 3 vols., 1900; 12 vols., 1911–15), has been profoundly influential in anthropology, the history of religion and literary criticism, for classics its importance derives principally from his then-novel willingness to use evidence from classical civilizations interchangeably with data from preliterate cultures in order to illustrate what he believed were the iron laws governing human spiritual evolution—from magic to religion and then to positive science. Such a yoking of classical and "primitive" marks an important step in the long undermining of the idealization of Greece and Rome.

Although (or perhaps because) he grew up immersed in Victorian Scottish piety, he seems never to have been touched by religious feeling himself. Undeniably, Frazer's underlying polemic purpose was to augment, from a seemingly historical-scientific viewpoint, the attack on religion already under way by the supporters of Darwin. Only the least attentive of his readers could fail to notice the "family resemblance" between the vegetation cults of the eastern Mediterranean and Christianity, despite Frazer's pointed silence on the latter.

In addition, Frazer did much important classical work of a more traditional kind, albeit only on texts that would profit from the folkloric and ethnographic comparisons and amplifications that were his special strength. The translation and massive commentary on Pausanias that he produced in six volumes in 1898 are noteworthy because they are based on detailed, extensive personal observation. Twice in the 1890s Frazer made the difficult journey to Greece and followed his author's itineraries, augmenting his personal observations with plans of other sites then being excavated. As a result, his work is still an eminently usable guide to Pausanias's Greece. His editions of Apollodorus, *The Library* (Loeb Library, two volumes, 1921) and Ovid's *Fasti* (five volumes, 1929) are more conventional, "armchair" scholarly productions.

BIBLIOGRAPHY

T. Besterman, *A Bibliography of Sir James George Frazer, O. M.* (London, 1939); R. R. Marett, "James George Frazer, 1854–1941," *ProcBrAc* 27 (1941), 377–91; R. Ackerman, "Frazer on Myth and Ritual," *Journal of the History of Ideas* 36 (1975), 115–34; Idem, *J. G. Frazer, His Life and Work* (Cambridge, 1987).

ROBERT ACKERMAN

FREDERICK II OF HOHENSTAUFEN (1194–1250). Holy Roman Emperor and King of Sicily.

As part of his consolidation of imperial power, Frederick promulgated an image of himself as a new Augustus and thus fostered a revival of ancient classical forms. His coinage, using the silver denarius and a gold coin called the Augustalis, is totally within the Roman imperial spirit. The Augustalis, first used in 1231 and featuring a bust of the emperor with laurel wreath (obverse) and an imperial eagle (reverse), is perhaps the most classical artifact or art object of the entire Middle Ages. An astonishing colossal head of Frederick (found south of Rome on the Via Appia, now in the *German Archaeological Institute, Rome) is stylized in a medieval way but clearly imitates the hairstyle and features of the Roman emperor Augustus.

It is clear that Frederick took a lively interest in actual Roman antiquities. He ordered Osberto Commenali to excavate near Augusta in hopes of finding in-

Portrait of *Frederick II
of Hohenstaufen*, Rome,
Deutsches Archäolo-
gisches Institute (Ger-
man Archaeological
Institute). (Deutsches
Archäologisches Institut,
Rome. Inst. Neg. 54.7.)

teresting material, and he removed from Grottaferrata a bronze group of a man
and a cow that he wished to keep at Lucera. He also spent a considerable sum
of money on a large antique onyx cup.

Frederick's building schemes echo the scale, majesty and iconography of antique imperial architecture. Most famous, before its destruction, was the splendid
marble portal at Capua, with its bridge towers, gate with true arch and ensemble
of busts and statues of classical type. Still surviving (in the local museum) are
a much-mutilated statue of Frederick, a female personification of the city of
Capua (or perhaps of Justice) and busts of two judges.

The climate created by Frederick II set the stage for the surprisingly classical
art of Nicola *Pisano, as well as for the Renaissance itself nearly 200 years
later.

BIBLIOGRAPHY

B. Rowland, Jr., ''The Augustan Revival of Frederick II,'' in *The Classical Tradition in
Western Art* (Cambridge, 1963), 128–32, 344–45; Weiss, *RDCA*, 12–13; T. C. Van Cleve,
The Emperor Frederick II of Hohenstaufen (Oxford, 1972), 333–46.

FREDERIKSEN, MARTIN WILLIAM (1930–80). Australian historian of ancient Italy.

Frederiksen was tutorial fellow in ancient history, Worcester College, Oxford University, from 1960; editor of the *Journal of Roman Studies,* 1968–74; and designated Jerome Lecturer, Ann Arbor–Rome, 1983. He proceeded from Sydney via Oxford to the *British School at Rome, where participation (1954–56) in the embryonic South Etruria survey colored his later achievements in Roman Republican history. A projected magnum opus on the interaction of native, Etruscan, Greek and Roman elements in Campania was at an advanced stage of active preparation when he died. Current Anglo-Italian rapport in the classical field owes more to Frederiksen's inspiring example than to the merely formal channels.

BIBLIOGRAPHY

P. A. Brunt, "M. W. Frederiksen 1930–80," *JRS* 70 (1980), ix; J. B. Ward Perkins—F. Zevi—R. B. Rutherford, "Martin W. Frederiksen 1930–1980," *BSR* 48 (1980), 1–5 with bib.; M. W. Frederiksen, *Campania,* ed. with additions by N. Purcell (British School at Rome, 1984).

DAVID RIDGWAY

FRENCH ACADEMY IN ROME (ACADÉMIE DE FRANCE À ROME). Academy for advanced training in the fine arts for painters, sculptors, architects and musicians; the participants chosen in Paris through competition for the Prix de Rome receive a stipend from the state to support their study.

The French Academy in Rome was founded in 1666 by Colbert, secretary of state for *Louis XIV, with Charles Errard as the first director. It had as its purpose the promotion of the fine arts but indirectly fed archaeological interests since it served as a center for studying ancient monuments and sculptures. For Louis XIV, it was a base for securing copies and casts of statuary he wished to have for Versailles, as well as a listening post for news of antiquities for sale. During the early years of the academy in Rome Louis was able to buy key pieces for sale there—the *"Germanicus"* and *"Cincinnatus"* (now in the *Louvre).

Pensioners at the French Academy in Rome were often assigned to make a marble copy or take molds to make a cast of some famous statue; while many of the pieces went back to France, eventually, the academy began to accumulate a first-class collection of plaster casts in Rome. By 1684 there were some one hundred casts, and in 1724, when the institution moved into the Palazzo Mancini on the Via del Corso, the academy was able to mount a dazzling display of most of the important sculptures known in the seventeenth and eighteenth centuries, from the *Vatican, the *Capitoline Museums, the *Farnese family collection and others. Frequently, foreign connoisseurs and even Roman visitors came to the academy to see and take casts. Later, when the academy moved again, to the Villa Medici on the Pincio in 1803 (*Medici family), the setting was especially enhancing for the casts.

Architecture students contributed to the study of classical monuments, since they were assigned projects of making drawings or reconstructions of Roman architecture. Especially from the second half of the eighteenth century and the nineteenth century survive numerous architects' projects from the French Academy, representing a wide range of monuments in the city of Rome, around the *Forum Romanum, the *Imperial Fora, the *Palatine, the *Capitoline and elsewhere. After excavations were begun at *Pompeii and *Herculaneum, these cities also provided material for students' projects. Under the directorate of *Ingres (1834–41), a course in archaeology and topography of Rome was installed for the pensioners, the first sessions of which were taught by *Nibby. The students even took part in excavations at the *Temple of Antoninus and Faustina (1809 and following) when Rome was occupied by the French under *Napoleon. The excavation unfortunately ended badly, with disagreement over whether the gaping trenches should be kept open.

Among the members of the French Academy in Rome best known for their study of classical antiquity were Hubert *Robert, whose Roman caprices testify to the fluidity with which ancient sculptures, like casts, could be moved from place to place and grouped and regrouped; Joseph-Marie Vien (director, 1775–81), who was famed for his *Cupid Seller* of 1763, a work that fooled others as a copy of a painting from Herculaneum; and Jacques-Louis *David (Prix de Rome, 1774), whose exposure in Rome to the ideas of the circle of *Winckelmann lay behind his creation of the revolutionary neoclassical painting of the *Oath of the Horatii* (1785).

BIBLIOGRAPHY

A. de Montaiglon—J. Guiffrey, eds. *Correspondance des directeurs de l'Académie de France à Rome avec les Surintendants des Batiments* 1–18 (Paris, 1887–1912); H. Lapauze, *Histoire de l'Académie de France à Rome* 1–2 (Paris, 1924); Haskell—Penny, 37–42, 62–63; +J.-P. Alaux, *Académie de France à Rome, ses directeurs, ses pensionnaires,* 1–2 (Paris, 1933); *Roma Antiqua, Forum, Colisée, Palatin,* catalog of exhibition (Rome, 1985).

FRENCH SCHOOL AT ATHENS (ÉCOLE FRANÇAISE D'ATHÈNES).

Leading French institution for the study of antiquity in Greek lands.

Founded by a decree of King Louis-Philippe dated 11 September 1846 and under the sponsorship of the Académie des inscriptions et belles lettres, the French School at Athens was the first of the foreign archaeological institutions established on Greek soil (followed by the *German Archaeological Institute, 1874). It was housed in temporary quarters until 1874, when it moved to a new, permanent location in Odos Didotou. Under the successive direction of A. Daveluy (1846–67; too long, according to C. Picard), E. Burnouf and, especially, A. Dumont (1875–78; too brief), the school flourished; among its early members were A. Grenier, E. *Beulé and N. Fustel de Coulanges.

In response to the founding of the German institute, the French school under Dumont established the Institut de correspondance hellénique, with its regular meetings and communications, which then were published annually in the *Bulletin de Correspondance Hellénique* (founded 1877). Another innovation of Dumont was the founding in 1873 of the *French School at Rome, where the scholars bound for Athens could study for a year in preparation for their stay in Greece. (Dumont himself served as director of the new Rome branch, before going to Athens.) Theses and monographs by French archaeologists, whether working in Greece or in Italy, were now published in the *Bibliothèque des Écoles d'Athènes et de Rome*.

The most notable archaeological result of the earliest years was the research of Beulé, largely at his own expense, at the Athenian *Akropolis (1852–53), where he uncovered the ancient entrance to the citadel (the ''Beulé Gate''). The young Théophile *Homolle, with a scanty sum of 1,300 francs, was sent by Dumont to *Delos, where he uncovered the sanctuary of Delian Apollo (1877–79), thereby initiating a long-term commitment of the French to the archaeology of the island. The epigraphist P. Foucart (director 1878–90) prepared the way, in an epic campaign lasting ten years, for the French school to dig at *Delphi. As director of the school, Homolle launched the Great Excavation (la Grande Fouille) at Delphi (1892–1903), which uncovered the sanctuaries of Apollo and Athena Pronaia, the *Athenian Treasury, the *Siphnian Treasury, and the *Charioteer of Delphi as well as many other sculptures and thousands of inscriptions.

The premier status of the French School was challenged by the spectacular successes of the Germans at *Olympia and elsewhere; the Greek government had noted its preference that the Germans, with their meticulous techniques, undertake the work at Delphi. (The Germans graciously declined in favor of the French.) The French archaeologists were open to criticism because they had failed to have an architect in the early campaigns at Delos, and soon their publication of Delphi was blasted for having fanciful reconstructions. In addition, Athens was becoming crowded with new schools, including the *American School of Classical Studies (founded 1881), the *British School at Athens (1886) and the *Italian School (1910). Always sensitive to the competition, the French, nevertheless, displayed a generous international spirit in inviting members from those nations that had no institution in Athens. Thus, with pensions from their own countries, Swiss, Belgian, Danish, Polish and Dutch scholars found a base at Odos Didotou, beginning in 1892.

Some prestige was recovered by the triumphant prosecution of the work at Delphi (concluded with great ceremony in 1903) and by the entry of the French into Roman and Byzantine studies at Philippi (from 1914). Especially important was the work at the Minoan palace at *Malia, begun in 1922 by C. Picard and L. Renaudin in collaboration with Greek archaeologists. (Their successors were F. Chapouthier, J. *Charbonneaux, P. Demargne and a number of other scholars, as the work continued through the twentieth century.) Excavation at Delos was renewed in 1903 under M. Holleaux, with handsome support from the Duc de Loubat, and discoveries old and new were published with great zeal. The publication of Delphi was advanced by G. Daux and P. de la Coste-Messelière. A new cycle of excavations was begun in 1934, led by P. Amandry and J. Bousquet and continuing intermittently through the century under directors of the school R. Demangel (1936–50), Daux (1950–69) and Amandry (1969–81). The French School celebrated its centenary with great fanfare under director Demangel in 1946.

BIBLIOGRAPHY

G. Radet, *L'Histoire et l'oeuvre de l'École française d'Athènes* (1901); *Le Centenaire de l'École française d'Athènes, BCH,* suppl. (1946); C. Picard, "L'Oeuvre de l'École française d'Athènes," *Revue Historique* 199 (1948), 1–21, 189–207; *La Redécouverte de Delphes* (Paris, 1992).

FRENCH SCHOOL AT ROME (ÉCOLE FRANÇAISE DE ROME).
French institution sponsoring research on ancient Italy.

Founded in 1873 in consequence of the conversion of the *Instituto di Corrispondenza Archeologica into the Prussian Archaeological Institute (*German Archaeological Institute) and the transformation of Rome into the capital of the kingdom of Italy, the École française de Rome served first as a preparatory school for the *French School at Athens, but by 1875—the official date of opening—it accepted scholars interested only in Roman antiquity. The first director was Albert Dumont, and among the first members in 1874–75 was Abbé L. Duchesne, whose editing of the *Liber Pontificalis* (1886–92) was one of the great scholarly achievements of the epoch. The school was provided with quarters in Palazzo Farnese in December 1875, and the director, A. Geffroy (1875–82, 1888–95) was provided with a sumptuous apartment, where he was expected to play a diplomatic and social role commensurate with France's national interest, a role that continues today. The French School has always looked both to the Vatican and to the Quirinal, and with the inauguration in 1881 of its publication *Mélanges d'Archéologie et d'Histoire,* its promotion of work by the international community of scholars in Rome made it a worthy rival of the German Archaeological Institute. It has always since maintained an exceptionally active program of publications.

Monsignor Duchesne became director in 1895 and held the post until his death in 1922. During his years the school counted among its members Maurice Bresnier (1896–99), Alfred Merlin (1900–3), Jérome Carcopino (1904–7), Albert Grenier (1904–7) and André Piganiol (1906–9). Although the school's interests remained rooted in Rome itself, it early began to extend its activities to Latium and Etruria and, before the turn of the century, to North Africa, where it has always been especially active.

Following the death of Monsignor Duchesne, the directorship passed to Carcopino (1922–23), then to Émile Mâle (1923–37) and back again to Carcopino (1937–40). After World War II, the French School was quick to recover under the direction of Grenier (1945–52) and to open excavations at *Bolsena in central Etruria under Raymond Bloch and at *Megara Hyblaea in Sicily under F. Villard and G. Vallet, who later became director of the school. Both sites proved rewarding; Bolsena (possibly the ancient Volsinii; cf. *Orvieto) provided excellent Republican levels, and Megara Hyblaea revealed a very early example of Greek colonial town planning, nonorthogonal but with parallel streets, evidently keyed to the survey of its territory. More recently, excavations have been undertaken in the heart of Rome—under Palazzo Farnese, around Villa Medici and in Vigna Barberini at the east corner of the *Palatine Hill.

BIBLIOGRAPHY

L'Histoire et l'oeuvre de l'École française de Rome (Paris, 1931); L'École française de Rome, 1875–1975, catalog of exhibition (Paris, 1975).

L. RICHARDSON, JR

FROTHINGHAM, ARTHUR LINCOLN, JR. (1859–1923). American archaeologist and editor.

Born to a wealthy Bostonian family, Frothingham spent his youth studying foreign languages in Rome (1868–73; 1875–81); he earned a doctorate from Leipzig in 1883. Between 1882 and 1886, he taught Semitic languages and archaeology at Johns Hopkins, then archaeology and the history of art at Princeton from 1886. He was professor of ancient history and archaeology at Princeton from 1898 to 1906.

Frothingham was a founder of the *Archaeological Institute of America, the founding editor of the *American Journal of Archaeology* (1885–96) and an associate director of the *American Academy in Rome. His work as an archaeologist seems to have been limited to that of guide and organizer rather than excavator. Acting as agent for two American museums in the 1890s, he acquired at least twenty-nine Etruscan tomb groups excavated by Francesco Mancinelli at Narce, plus numerous antiquities from other Etruscan and Roman sites in Italy.

Frothingham was well known for his wide-ranging and prolific scholarship, his editorial and administrative skills and his teaching. His work as an agent for the legal acquisition of archaeological material with specific contexts enriched several American museums.

BIBLIOGRAPHY

E. H. Dohan, Italic Tomb-Groups in the University Museum (Philadelphia, 1942); M. A. Lavin, The Eye of the Tiger: The Founding and Development of the Department of Art and Archaeology, 1883–1923, Princeton University (Princeton, NJ, 1983); A. A. Donohue, "One Hundred Years of the American Journal of Archaeology: An Archival History," AJA 89 (1985), 3–12; R. D. De Puma, Etruscan Tomb-Groups (Mainz, 1986).

RICHARD DANIEL DE PUMA

FUFLUNA. See POPULONIA.

FULVIO (FULVIUS), ANDREA (ca. 1470–1527). Italian grammarian, poet and antiquarian.

We know nothing of Fulvio's early years beyond the fact that he left his

Portrait of *M. Agrippa*, from A. Fulvio, *Illustrium imagines* (1517).

native Palestrina to receive a sound humanistic education with Pomponio *Leto in Rome. Here he acquired a deep familiarity with an impressive range of classical and Christian writers and his lifelong passion for the archaeological remains of ancient Rome. By 1510, when Francesco *Albertini published his *Opusculum* on the topography of ancient and modern Rome, Fulvio was sufficiently intimate with the material to write the laudatory epigram on the frontispiece.

His earliest archaeological work, the *Antiquaria urbis* (1513), is a tightly compressed but learned survey of ancient Roman monuments written in Latin hexameters and includes the major churches, recent papal tombs and notable contemporary buildings. Fulvio cites inscriptions more frequently than classical authors and gives precious indications of the depredation inflicted on significant monuments. He describes the traditional classes of antiquities, the gates and hills, bridges, aqueducts, temples, circuses, theaters, obelisks and columns, but his vision of Rome oscillates between the city of Romulus and the emperors and that of his patron, *Leo X. The *Antiquaria urbis* tells as much about the reception of classical antiquity during the Renaissance as about the nature of the monuments themselves.

The *Illustrium imagines* (1517), the first printed book illustrating Roman coins and medals, may have been conceived and commissioned by the printer Mazzocchi but was researched principally by Fulvio. Designed to provide an authentic iconographic collection of famous Romans, it nevertheless begins with Janus and Alexander the Great, and its 207 reproductions comprise some imaginary coins and garbled inscriptions.

Fulvio's *Antiquitates urbis,* a greatly expanded prose version of his earlier poetic description of Rome, appeared just before the Sack of Rome in 1527. Following the historical and philological approach of *Biondo and Albertini, Fulvio gives a systematic account in five books of what was still visible of ancient Rome in his day, but he again records some recent art and architecture. He succinctly recounts the foundation of Rome, then describes in the first book the gates and walls and the topography contained by the fourteen regions, using Leto's interpolated text of the *Notitia.* Book 2 lists the hills; book 3, the bridges, aqueducts, baths and forums; book 4, the arches, theaters, porticoes and a variety of secular buildings; and book 5 works through the temples of the ancient city. The preface notes that Fulvio accompanied *Raphael in archaeological surveying of Rome, perhaps acting as his scholarly guide. Fulvio had a sharp eye for topographical detail and used literary evidence with discretion, and while he was the first to locate correctly some important monuments in the *Forum Romanum, his knowledge of inscriptions and numismatics, though comparable to Albertini's, was far from scientific. In the *Imagines* we recognize the prototype of the iconographic handbooks of Roman ruler-portraits edited later by *Vico, Statius, *Orsini, Hubert *Goltzius and *Bellori. Fulvio's *Antiquitates* was widely respected by later antiquarians and was reprinted in *Graevius's *Thesaurus* in the eighteenth century. Fulvio dedicated the *Antiquitates* to his second Medici patron, Clement VII, who granted a six-year copyright to the printer Mazzocchi. However, we hear nothing more of Fulvio after the Sack of Rome in 1527, and he apparently perished in the fighting.

BIBLIOGRAPHY

R. Weiss, "Andrea Fulvio Antiquario Romano," *Annali della Scuola Normale Superiore di Pisa, Cl. di Lettere, Storia e Filosofia* 28 (1959), 1–44; I. Calabi Limentani, "Andrea Fulvio . . . autore degli *Epigrammata Antiquae Urbis?,*" *Epigraphica* 31 (1969), 205–12; Weiss, *RDCA,* 86–89, 178–79; P. Jacks, *The Antiquarian and the Myth of Antiquity* (Cambridge, 1993), 180 ff.

ROBERT W. GASTON

FUNERARY ICONOGRAPHY. Throughout antiquity various objects were made specifically for the grave and were decorated with this purpose in mind.

The total iconographic repertoire was very wide, but the actual range of motifs used varied according to time, place and type of object. Nevertheless, certain themes and motifs came to be associated specifically with a funerary purpose and remained in use over a long period: an example is the so-called funerary banquet scene popular in Greek, Etruscan and Roman funerary art. The motifs range from straightforward factual representations, for example, of funerary rites, to less obviously funerary themes, for example, mythological scenes, which have been interpreted as complex allegories of death and afterlife beliefs.

The study of funerary iconography can be divided into three interlinked branches. The first involves the publication of the monuments with accurate descriptions and illustrations. This process began with the earliest drawings and publications of monuments and antiquities, for example, the dal *Pozzo-Albani collection of drawings, or P. S. and F. *Bartoli's volume on the tomb of the Nasonii (1680; cf. *Tomb of Ovid). *Montfaucon's *L'Antiquité expliquée* (1719–24), although an uncritical account with little regard for chronology, went further in collecting evidence from a variety of sources and using it to create a picture of ancient life, including funerary customs and beliefs. The next step came at the turn of the last century with a number of large volumes that collect details of similar types of monument. A major example is the corpus of Roman sarcophagi begun by Carl *Robert in 1890, on which the work continues. There the material is grouped according to decorative theme, and this arrangement encourages another type of iconographic study, that of individual motifs. The motifs are traced through different periods, examining changes in details and significance as they spread to new areas. This approach has been pursued particularly in recent studies.

Third is the study of funerary symbolism and allegory. Even in the early descriptions of funerary monuments, attempts were made to explain why the motifs used were chosen and to interpret them as allusions to eschatological beliefs. For example, in 1698 F. *Buonarotti suggested that the Roman Nereid and Triton motif alludes to the journey of the soul to the Isles of the Blessed, an interpretation that continues to be debated in modern scholarship. Many commentators have since assumed the existence of a "funerary language" in which pictorial images represent eschatological concepts. At times such attempts at explaining funerary decoration become almost mystical, as in parts of Bachofen's *Gräbersymbolik* of 1859. Franz *Cumont, in reaction to works of this kind, asserted the need for a more scientific method in the investigation of funerary symbolism, based on an accurate assessment of contemporary religious beliefs. As a result of his wide-ranging research, a clearer understanding of the role of the Eastern mystery religions in Roman funerary art has been gained, and a new approach to the study of funerary symbolism has been established. Nevertheless, the subject remains a contentious one with many avenues still to be explored.

BIBLIOGRAPHY

J. J. Bachofen, *Versuch über die Gräbersymbolik der Alten* (Basel, 1859); +F. Cumont, *Recherches sur le symbolisme funéraire des Romains* (Paris, 1942); +K. Friis Johansen,

The Attic Grave Reliefs of the Classical Period (Copenhagen, 1951); +B. Andreae, *Studien zur römischen Grabkunst* (Heidelberg, 1963).

GLENYS DAVIES

FURTWÄNGLER, ADOLF (1853–1907). German archaeologist and museologist.

Born at Freiburg in Breisgau, son of a classical scholar and schoolmaster, Furtwängler began his university study there in 1870, continued at Leipzig under *Overbeck and wrote his dissertation at Munich under *Brunn on "Eros in der Vasenmalerei" (1874). A two-year fellowship in Italy and Greece followed. In the autumn of 1878, he joined the excavations at *Olympia and the next year published *Die Bronzefunde aus Olympia und deren Kunstgeschichtliche Bedeutung.* In the same year, with his friend *Loeschcke, he published *Mykenischen Thongefäße,* *Schliemann's new finds, followed in 1886 by their *Mykenischen Vasen,* both pioneer studies. In 1879 he habilitated under *Kekulé at Bonn and in 1880 became assistant of Ernst *Curtius in the *Berlin museum, in charge of minor art, gems, terracottas and vases, and lectured at the university. His authoritative articles (e.g., *Herakles*) in Roscher's *Lexikon* are from this period.

The freedom Curtius wisely granted Furtwängler and the variety of material with which a museum man must be concerned, joined with his brilliance and praeternatural memory, made Furtwängler the last archaeologist to achieve *Welcker's *Totalitätsideal.* He knew and read about everything from *Mycenae to Adamklissi. His great books required long gestation. Like *Beazley, he saw the need for accurate catalogs but, unlike Beazley, he saw forest as well as trees. In 1885 appeared in two volumes his *Beschreibung der Vasensammlung im Antiquarium,* where 4,220 objects were described in a manner still exemplary. In 1893 appeared his *Die Meisterwerke griechischer Plastik,* expanded and translated by Eugénie Sellers (*Strong) in 1895 as *Masterpieces of Greek Sculpture.* This work, called by Sieveking "the Book of Books" and "the Bible of the Archaeologists," reveals the author's profound familiarity with the literary, historical and stylistic aspects of his subject and has guided much subsequent research. His publication (1883–87) of the Sabouroff Collection proved his mastery of terracottas.

In 1894 Furtwängler succeeded *Brunn in the Munich chair and began his long collaboration with Paul *Arndt. In 1900 appeared his most influential work, *Die Antiken Gemmen* in three volumes. Ludwig *Curtius called it "historical writing in the grand style." In this "history of stone carving in antiquity," the author created a new discipline, the historical study of gems, dated by style. In April 1900, he reopened the excavations at the temple of Aphaia in *Aigina, publishing his results in 1906. The next year, his projected history of ancient art barely begun, he succumbed to dysentery, contracted at Aigina, and is buried, like K. O. *Müller, in Athens.

Among his Munich students were J. Sieveking, Ludwig *Curtius, Georg *Lippold, Eduard Schmidt and Ernst *Buschor. A short, passionate man, intolerant of incompetence, he enraged superiors, like *Conze and Kekulé, while being adored by students. In productivity, erudition and breadth of interest, he can be compared only with T. *Mommsen and *Wilamowitz. The famed conductor, Wilhelm Furtwängler (1886–1954), was his son.

BIBLIOGRAPHY

A. Furtwängler, *Briefe aus dem Bonner Privatdozentenjahr 1879/80 und der Zeit seiner Tätigkeit an den Berliner Museen 1880–1894*, ed. A. Greifenhagen (Stuttgart, 1965); P. Zazoff—H. Zazoff, *Gemmensammler und Gemmenforscher* (Munich, 1983), 203–43; A. E. Furtwängler, "Adolf Furtwängler," in Briggs—Calder, 84–92; R. Lullies in *Archäologenbildnisse*, 110–11.

WILLIAM M. CALDER III

FURUMARK, ARNE (1903–82). Swedish archaeologist, professor at Uppsala University, 1952–70.

Specializing in the study of the Aegean Late Bronze Age cultures, Furumark published the two parts of his magnum opus in 1941, *The Mycenaean Pottery, Analysis and Classification* and *The Chronology of Mycenaean Pottery*, ever since, the standard work on this topic. An important historical study followed in 1950, "The Settlement at Ialysos and Aegean History c. 1550–1400 B.C." (*OpArch* 6). Methodologically innovative research into the prehistory of Italy resulted in *Det Äldsta Italien* (1947). Furumark was one of the first scholars to realize the importance and correctness of Ventris's decipherment of Linear B; he published a comprehensive study of its implications and embarked himself on a serious attempt to decipher the Linear A script and to make the texts throw light on the Minoan religion. Furumark excavated in Cyprus (Sinda, 1947–48) and Italy (San Giovenale, 1962–63).

BIBLIOGRAPHY

R. Hägg, *OpAth* 8 (1968), 213–17 (bibl.); +C. Nylander, *Kungl. Vitterhets Historie och Antikvitets Akademiens Arsbok* (1983), 34–39 (obit.).

ROBIN HÄGG

G

GALASSI, VINCENZO. See REGOLINI-GALASSI TOMB.

GALLIA. See GAUL.

GAMBERELLI, BERNARDO DI MATTEO DEL BORRA. See ROSSEL-LINO, BERNARDO.

GARCÍA Y BELLIDO, ANTONIO (1903–72). Spanish archaeologist.

Born in Villanueva de los Infantes (Ciudad Real) of a wealthy family, García y Bellido pursued his first studies in San Sebastian and later attended the University of Madrid, where, as a student of Obermaier and Gomez Moreno, he received his doctorate with a thesis on the Spanish Baroque and the architecture of the Churriguera. He continued his education in various universities in France, Italy, Germany and England.

In 1931 he won the chair in classical archaeology at the University of Madrid, but he always preferred research to teaching. In 1950 he was named director of the Instituto Español de Arqueología "Rodrigo Caro." He was also president of the Sociedad Española de Estudios Clásicos, founder of the journal *Hispania Antiqua Epigraphica* and director of *Archivo Español de Arqueología*. Doctor honoris causa of various universities, he was a member of several academies and research institutions in other countries, among them the *Archaeological Institute of America and the Hispanic Society of New York.

Over the course of his life he published more than 150 works, for the most part, on ancient history and archaeology, frequently illustrated with his own drawings. Of special importance are his works on the Carthaginian and Greek colonizations, the Iberian world and Roman art and religion.

BIBLIOGRAPHY
A. García y Bellido, *Fenicios y cartagineses en Occidente* (Madrid, 1942); +Idem, *Hispania graeca* (Madrid, 1948); +Idem, *Esculturas romanas de España y Portugal* (Madrid, 1949); +Idem, *Arte romano* (Madrid, 1955).

FERNANDO FERNÁNDEZ GÓMEZ

GARDENS OF SALLUST (HORTI SALLUSTIANI). A vast estate, perhaps the finest in ancient Rome, laid out in the upper valley between the Quirinal and Pincio hills, created by the historian C. Sallustius Crispus (86–35 B.C.).

Sallust used his great wealth, amassed as governor of Numidia, in laying out the Horti, perhaps taking the gardens of Julius Caesar by the Porta Collina as a nucleus. His work was continued by his grandnephew of the same name, but the gardens had probably become an imperial property by A.D. 43. They were always a prized residence of the emperor and were sacked by the Goths in 410 and left in ruins, from which they never recovered.

The gardens' boundaries are the Porta Salaria and the Aurelian Walls on the north, the Servian Walls along the brow of the Quirinal and Piazza Barberini or Via Bissolati on the west. Their main features were a brook, a temple of Venus Hortulorum Sallustianorum, a *porticus miliarensis* built by Aurelian in which to exercise his horses and an imperial residence complete with a forum and baths, which may have included the dining pavilion with adjacencies in at least four stories of highly sophisticated architecture that is the most important part surviving today.

A drawing by Pirro *Ligorio shows the round ground plan of the temple of Venus, and L. Bufalini's plan of Rome of 1551 reveals the walls of baths, a racetrack and porticoes and the Sallustian *obelisk (a Roman copy of the one erected by Augustus in the *Circus Maximus), standing from 1789 in front of S. Trinità dei Monti. The land was purchased by the *Ludovisi family in 1621–23, and construction led to the discovery of numerous pieces of sculpture; these may have included the *Ludovisi *Gaul Killing Himself and His Wife* and the *Dying Trumpeter,* as well as a large acrolithic head of a goddess, all now in the *Terme Museum. The *Ludovisi Throne, also in the Terme, was discovered in the area of the temple of Venus in 1887. Today, parts of the Gardens of Sallust lie beneath the present buildings of the American Embassy and the *German Archaeological Institute.

BIBLIOGRAPHY
+Nash, I, 491–99; B. Palma, *Museo Nazionale Romano, Le Sculture,* I, 4, *I Marmi Ludovisi: Storia della collezione,* ed. A. Giuliano (Rome, 1983), 1–10, 19; G. Cipriani, *Horti Sallustiani,* 2nd ed. (Rome, 1983).

L. RICHARDSON, JR

GARDNER, PERCY (1846–1937). British numismatist and art historian.

Educated at Christ's College, Cambridge, Gardner was appointed in 1871 to a position in the *British Museum, where he worked on the *Catalogue of Greek*

Coins, editing the volumes on the Parthian (1877) and Samian (1882) coinage, Thrace (1877), the Seleucid kings of Syria (1878), Thessaly to Aetolia (1883) and the Peloponnese (1887). In the spring of 1877, he accompanied Charles *Newton to evaluate the finds of *Schliemann's recent excavations at *Mycenae. A founding member of the Society for the Promotion of Hellenic Studies, he served as first editor of the *Journal of Hellenic Studies* (1879–95). He held the Disney chair of archaeology at Cambridge (1880–87) while still employed at the British Museum but resigned both posts to become professor of classical archaeology at Lincoln College, Oxford (1885–1925).

Working in a field where new discoveries are constantly making good books out of date, Gardner wrote a surprising number of books that still retain their usefulness, for instance, *Types of Greek Coins* (1883); (with F. Imhoof-Blumer) *Numismatic Commentary on Pausanias* (1887); *Sculptured Tombs of Hellas* (1896). They are marked by a fine eye for detail, artistic sensitivity and plain common sense. In the combination of his talents, Gardner had few rivals among his contemporaries, and these qualities are well exemplified by his brilliant observations on Schliemann's Mycenaean discoveries (*The Academy,* 21 and 28 April 1877). He has long been underrated.

BIBLIOGRAPHY

P. Gardner, *Autobiographica* (Oxford, 1933); *Who Was Who 1929–1940;* J. Toynbee— H. Major, "Gardner, Percy," *DNB 1931–40* (1949), 306–8.

DAVID A. TRAILL

GARIMBERTO, GEROLAMO (1506–75). Italian Renaissance author and collector.

Garimberto was born in Parma but was active in Rome, where he served as bishop of Gallese and vicar at S. Giovanni in Laterano. Ulisse *Aldrovandi wrote admiringly of Garimberto's rarities and antiquities in his *Delle statue antiche* of 1550. Garimberto's collection continued to grow and to attract attention in the intervening years. Indeed, a recommendation to view it was included in all printings of *Le Cose maravigliose dell'alma città di Roma* between 1565 and 1588. An inventory drawn up ca. 1569 for *Albrecht V, duke of Bavaria (Munich, Hauptstaatsarchiv, 4853), shows that by that date Garimberto owned some forty pictures (mainly copies of famous works by Correggio and Parmigianino) in addition to 150 statues, statuettes, reliefs, marble columns, heads and busts. Engravings of twenty-five of his antique marbles were published in books 3 and 4 of Giovanni Battista de'*Cavalieri's *Antiquarum statuarum urbis Romae* (1594).

Knowledge of the range of his collection and collecting policies is further augmented by the preservation of Garimberto's extensive correspondence with a fellow collector, Cesare Gonzaga, between 1562 and 1573. The bulk of this material is in the State Archives in Parma (Raccolta Manoscritti, Busta 112 and Gonzaga di Guastalla 48[4]–49). One of the letters (2 May 1565) refers specifically to Garimberto's purchase of antique statues from the Francesco Lisca collection, while a letter dated 30 December 1564 deals with his acquisition of a *Hercules Strangling the Serpents*. As with several of the Lisca pieces, the *Hercules* can be identified on the basis of the Cavalieri engraving, and in this instance the statuette is now in the Museum of Antiquities in Turin.

Author of five modestly useful books on religious and secular matters, Garimberto was a friend and/or agent for such notable collectors as Cosimo de' Medici, (*Medici family) for whom he procured various "tavole di pietra"; he was also custodian of the antiquities of Gian Girolamo Rossi, which the Medici inherited. He also served Alfonso II d'Este and Tomasso de Cavalieri, with whom he evaluated the Paolo del Bufalo (*Bufalo family) collection for Cardinal Alessandro Farnese (*Farnese family). In addition to correspondence with the latter concerning the antiquarian Pirro *Ligorio, Garimberto was a friend of the Farnese librarian Fulvio *Orsini, who acquired and subsequently published several of his antiquities, including the statuette of the poet *Moschion* now in the *Museo Nazionale, Naples. It is, however, primarily through the survival of his correspondence with the lord of Guastalla Cesare Gonzaga (whose own holdings were built up largely on the basis of Garimberto's expertise) that his role as collector and agent for fellow collectors is most completely documented. He also played a leading role in the acquisition of statuary for Guglielmo Gonzaga's Galleria dei Mesi in the Ducal Palace in Mantua.

BIBLIOGRAPHY
I. Affo, *Memorie degli scrittori e letterati parmigiani* (Parma, 1793), IV, 135–44; +P. P. Bober, "Francesco Lisca's Collection of Antiquities," *Essays in the History of Art Presented to Rudolf Wittkower*, ed. D. Frazer et al. (New York, 1967), 119–23; C. M. Brown, "Paintings and Antiquities from the Roman Collection of Gerolamo Garimberto Offered to Duke Albrecht Vth of Bavaria in 1576," *Xenia* 10 (1985), 41–77; Idem, with A. M. Lorenzoni, *"Our Accustomed Discourse on the Antique": Cesare Gonzaga and Gerolamo Garimberto, Two Reniassance Collectors of Greco-Roman Art* (New York, 1993).

CLIFFORD M. BROWN

GAUL (GALLIA). Region inhabited by the ancient Gauls, including modern France and parts of Belgium, Germany, Switzerland and Italy.

Celtic Gaul may be divided into three main civilizations: Neolithic and (beginning 1800 B.C.) Bronze Age; Hallstatt, or Late Bronze and Iron Age (800–500 B.C.); and La Tène (500 till the Roman conquest). The Neolithic era has always attracted interest because of the prominence of its chief monuments, the megaliths and menhirs. A count taken in 1880 listed 6,192 of them in France, of which 4,747 were in Brittany and 3,450 at Carnac, the chief Breton site. The largest is 20m high, and heights of 7m are not uncommon. With Hallstatt come iron and some of the most highly worked bronze (notably, the *Vix burial), but only with La Tène do the Gauls come into regular contact with the classical world. Architecture becomes significant as the Gauls settle in *oppida* (native towns), which, in the south, often copied classical features such as the grid street plan and stone-built city walls with towers (Entremont, near Aix-en-Provence; Ensérune, near Béziers). Imports from Italy, especially wine, are extensive (as testified by amphora finds), and Gallic cities now begin striking their own coins, often imitating classical issues, sometimes (as did Vercingetorix) with original types. Gold, especially in the form of torques, is common. The best collection of small finds from these periods is in the Musée des Antiquités Nationales, St. Germain-en-Laye, Paris (and not in the *Louvre). It is housed in a thirteenth–fourteenth-century château, one of the principal royal residences, largely restored by Napoleon III.

From the founding of Massalia (*Marseilles) in 600 B.C. to the coming of Rome, a line of Greek colonies grew up along the southern shore. The chief ones were Herakles Monoikos (Monaco), Nikaia (Nice), Antipolis (Antibes), Athenopolis (St. Tropez), Olbia (near Hyères), Massalia, St. Blaise (near Fos; ancient name uncertain, possibly Mastromela), Agathe Tyche (Agde), Aphrodisia(?) (Port-Vendres); across the border in Spain is *Emporion (Ampurias); and inland are Arelate (*Arles), *Glanon (St. Rémy). Notably lacking in Greek origins are Cannes and, despite its superb harbor, Toulon. Most of these were founded by Phokaia (Ionia), either directly or as subcolonies of Massalia, and some were trading posts rather than cities proper (*poleis*). The degree of Massalia's political control over them is debated, as is the extent of its immediate territory (the *chora*), but their hellenizing influence upon the Gauls, both in trade and culture, was pervasive (*Nîmes). Excavation has been extensive at St. Blaise, Glanon and Olbia, which are in the open; elsewhere it has been inhibited by the modern city overlying the site. The best local museums are at Antibes (in the eighteenth-century Bastion St. André, built by Vauban), Nice and Marseilles.

Roman Gaul includes modern Belgium and Switzerland. The first Roman colony was Aquae Sextiae (Aix-en-Provence), founded in 123 B.C. (remains scanty); in imperial times Lugdunum (*Lyons) was the administrative capital, where an amphitheater, theater, odeon and extensive aqueduct remains survive. Well-preserved amphitheaters also exist at Arles, Nîmes, Fréjus, Nice, Saintes and Paris, and theaters exist at Vienne, Autun, Arles, Fréjus, *Orange and Vaison. *"Triumphal" arches are to be seen at Orange (*Arch at Orange), Reims, St. Rémy (*Arch at St. Rémy), Carpentras, Cavaillon, Saintes and Autun. At La Turbie, above Monaco, a great mausoleum-like monument marks the boundary of Gaul and Italy. Temples are relatively rare, the two best-preserved being that of Augustus and Livia at Vienne and the *Maison Carrée at Nîmes, as are baths, the best examples of which are the baths of Constantine at Arles and the baths of Cluny (*Cluny Museum), Paris. Unlike, for example, Britain, nearly all French cities can boast of a Roman origin, so that excavation is usually only local and restricted by modern building. Extensive "open" sites (i.e., like *Pompeii or *Delos) are therefore rare but exist at Vaison-la-Romaine (Vaucluse), Glanon (Provence) and, more recently, St. Romain-en-Gal (Vienne).

Archaeological study was given a great impulse first, by the foundation of the *French Academy in Rome (1666; open to architects, 1720) and later, by Napoleon III, who consciously identified himself with Augustus and his dominions with the Roman Empire. This led to some neglect of non-Roman (e.g., Greek) material but produced many fine reproductions and adaptations of Roman monuments; notable are the Pantheon, the Madeleine, the Arc de Triomphe and the Colonne Vendôme (which replaced an original scheme to import the *Column of Trajan from Rome), all in Paris. By comparison, interest in Greek Gaul was, for long, minimal and almost restricted to scholars in Provence. An important milestone was Michel Clerc's two-volume *Massalia* (Marseilles, 1927–29), followed by the extensive work of F. Benoît. Since 1967 the focus has shifted to the excavations of M. Euzennat and F. Salviat at Marseilles, and the claims of Greek Gaul as a whole are achieving a wider recognition. Prominent in other fields of current research are R. Chevallier's studies of the Roman road system, while Roman villas and other aspects of rural archaeology, especially in Picardy and northern France, have benefited from R. Agache's pioneer work in air photography.

BIBLIOGRAPHY

A. Grenier, *Manuel d'archéologie gallo-romaine* (Paris, 1931–60); F. Benoît, *Recherches sur l'hellénisation du Midi de la Gaule* (Aix-en-Provence, 1965; repr. Marseilles, 1980); J.-P. Morel, "Les Phocéens en Occident," *Parola del Passato* 21 (1966), 378–420; P. MacKendrick, *Roman France* (London, 1971); +S. Piggott—G. Daniel—C. McBurney, eds., *France Before the Romans* (London, 1974); A.L.F. Rivet, *Gallia Narbonensis* (London, 1988).

A. TREVOR HODGE

GELA. Greek colony in *Sicily.

The foundation of Gela is assigned to Rhodians and Cretans in 689 B.C. (Thucydides 6.4.3), although it is suggested that Rhodian colonists may have settled there prior to that date. From about the mid-seventh century, the Geloans occupied themselves with territorial expansion. They founded Akragas ca. 582 B.C. (Thucydides 6.4) and under Hippokrates at the beginning of the fifth century gained control of the Chalkidian cities of eastern Sicily (Herodotos 7.154). After Gelon transferred his rule to *Syracuse ca. 485 B.C., Gela's importance declined. In 405 B.C. the city was conquered by Carthage and abandoned. It was refounded ca. 338 B.C. under Timoleon but destroyed ca. 282 B.C., and the inhabitants were relocated at nearby Phintias (Licata). Only scattered occupation is attested until 1233, when Herakleia (popularly, Terranova) was founded above the Archaic city.

Since Schubring (1873), the site of Gela has been generally identified with that of modern Terranova (renamed Gela). Ruins were visible here throughout the Middle Ages. Tombs provided rich material for local collections, especially during the nineteenth century. Some official investigation was conducted in the necropoleis at the end of the nineteenth century, but excavations were initiated on a large scale only by P. *Orsi in 1900. Through 1908 he explored extensive areas of the site, including the acropolis and several cemeteries. Work continued intermittently until 1951, when excavations were renewed on a broad scale within the city, its suburbs and the hinterland. As a result, Gela's many sanctuaries and necropoleis are especially well known.

BIBLIOGRAPHY

P. Orsi, "Gela-Scavi del 1900–1905," *MonAnt* 17 (1906), 5–758; P. Griffo, *Gela* (Paris, 1964); P. Orlandini, "Gela-Topografia dei santuari e documentazione archeologica dei culti," *Rivista del R. Istituto d'Archeologia e Storia dell'Arte* 15 (1968), 20–66.

BARBARA A. BARLETTA

GELL, SIR WILLIAM (1777–1836). English traveler, topographer, artist, scholar.

Gell's lifelong modus operandi was already apparent in the titles he gave to the published accounts of his early travels: *The Topography of Troy and Its Vicinity, Illustrated and Explained by Drawings and Descriptions* (1804); *The Itinerary of Greece, with a Commentary on Pausanias and Strabo, and an Account of the Monuments of Antiquity at Present Existing in That Country* (1810; 2nd ed., 1827). These works made Gell the obvious leader of the second expedition sent by the *Society of Dilettanti to Asia Minor, and from 1811 he worked tirelessly on the description and illustration of the classical sites recorded in the massive volumes of the Society's *Antiquities of Ionia* (1821 onward).

In 1814, Gell reached Italy in the entourage of Princess Caroline, wife of the future king, George IV; he began work soon afterward on his account of *Pompeii, settling permanently in Italy in 1820. The Dilettanti appointed him correspondent in Naples, where his services as cicerone were eagerly sought by English visitors.

Although the excavation of Pompeii had been in progress for more than sixty years by 1814, there were few published accounts of any kind—and none that were available to the English public. Gell responded to the deficiency with skill and knowledge. His immensely successful *Pompeiana: The Topography, Edifices and Ornaments of Pompeii* came out in 1817–19; a French adaptation followed in 1827; and in 1852 a new edition incorporated the results of excavations since the first. Pompeian "edifices and ornaments" exerted a considerable influence on contemporary decorative arts in England. Perhaps more significantly, the discoveries at Pompeii furnished the public with an unprecedented opportunity to inspect the ordinary life of an ancient society at firsthand—or at least through Gell's eyes. The intellectual consequences were considerable; a lesser product was *Bulwer-Lytton's *Last Days of Pompeii* (1834: "[W]e love to feel within us the bond which unites the most distant eras").

In Rome, Gell's principal achievements were topographical. His drawings in *Le Mura di Roma* (1820) complemented a text by the young Italian archaeologist Antonio *Nibby and led to a more ambitious collaborative project: a map of the Roman Campagna by Gell, combined with a commentary by Nibby. As it turned out, each published separately: *The Topography of Rome and Its Vicinity* (with map: Gell, 1834; 2nd ed. 1846, ed. E. H. Bunbury); *Analisi storico-topografico-antiquaria* . . . (Nibby, 1837; 1848).

Gell regarded himself as no more than an accurate recorder. This in itself constituted a vital addition—spanning Troy, Greece and Rome—to the knowledge of classical lands available in the prephotographic age. Maps were still rare; Gell's work on the Roman Campagna included the basic triangulation. In Greece and Ionia, he was the heir of *Stuart and *Revett; in Italy, Gell's achievements as a topographer, no less than as a popularizer, broke new ground and heralded a new age of exegesis. In his own words (*in litt.* 1831), he showed that the events of Roman history "are really reducible to the test of locality, and are no longer Romances."

BIBLIOGRAPHY

W. W. [Wroth], "Gell, Sir William (1777–1836)," *DNB* 7 (1921–22), 994–96; E. Clay, with M. W. Frederiksen, *Sir William Gell in Italy: Letters to the Society of Dilettanti 1831–1835* (London, 1976).

DAVID RIDGWAY

GEMMA AUGUSTEA. Roman cameo of the age of Augustus (31 B.C.–A.D. 14) representing the emperor Augustus as Jupiter, being paid tribute by a general in a two-horse chariot, probably Tiberius. Standing next to Tiberius is a youth in armor, who may be Germanicus.

Augustus and Tiberius appear in the upper zone of the gem, with the goddess Roma and various allegorical personifications. A second zone, below, shows Roman soldiers and allies with their prisoners. The cameo is carved from a piece of Arabian onyx in two layers, white on dark blue, and is one of the largest ancient cameos known (19cm × 23cm).

The splendid work was first recorded in 1246 in the treasury of the Abbey of St. Sernin, Toulouse, and remained there, except for a short period between 1447 and 1453, when it was in Florence, in the house of the banker O. Castellani. Casts were made of it at that time, one of which was seen by Filarete, as he noted in his *Trattato dell'architettura*, 24. Pope *Paul II tried to acquire the Gemma Augustea from Toulouse by promising the citizens that he would build a bridge across the Garonne River, but the stone remained in the treasury of St. Sernin until 1533. At that time Francis I removed it, ostensibly to make a gift to Pope Clement VII, but was unable to part with the treasure and kept it for himself. In 1560 it was included in the royal inventory of Fontainebleau. When the palace was ransacked by the Huguenots in 1591, the Gemma Augustea disappeared. *Peiresc, who owned a painted copy of the stone, noted that he had seen the original in Venice (ca. 1602). Soon afterward it was bought by the emperor *Rudolph II for 12,000 ducats and was kept at Prague. After the death of Rudolph in 1612, the emperor Matthias had the imperial treasures moved to Vienna, where the gem remains today, in the *Kunsthistorisches Museum.

The first serious scholarship on the gem is connected with the research of

Gemma Augustea, drawing by (or after) P. P. Rubens, ca. 1622. Lübeck, Sankt-Annen Museum. (Museum.)

Peiresc and Peter Paul *Rubens, who were planning to make it one of the centerpieces of a major book on gems (never published). Rubens prepared a design for an engraving, and Peiresc studied the subject matter of the cameo, identifying it as the *Apotheosis of Augustus.* Albert *Rubens, the son of the artist, later built on the unpublished notes of Peiresc in writing his own analysis, in which he identified the figure in the chariot as Tiberius, and dated the event represented as the triumph of Tiberius in A.D. 12. His treatise was published anew with warm approval by H. Kähler (1968), who argued for an adjustment of the date to A.D. 10, when Tiberius entered Rome victorious but had to postpone his triumph. The two-horse chariot, not properly associated with a full triumph, would fit with this date. Other scholars have proposed the dates of 7 B.C. and A.D. 9.

BIBLIOGRAPHY

F. Eichler—E. Kris, *Die Kameen in Kunsthistorischen Museum Wien* (Vienna, 1927), 52–56; +H. Kähler, *Alberti Rubeni Dissertatio de Gemma Augustea* (Berlin, 1968); +M. van der Meulen, *Petrus Paulus Rubens Antiquarius* (Alphen aan den Rijn, 1975), 157–61; F. Bastet, "Der Skorpion auf der Gemma Augustea," in *Studies in Classical Art and Archaeology, A Tribute to P. H. v. Blanckenhagen* (Locust Valley, NY, 1979), 217–23; Kleiner, *Roman Sculpture,* 69–72, 117.

GEMMA TIBERIANA (GRAND CAMÉE DE FRANCE). Roman imperial carved cameo, the largest surviving example (31cm × 26.5cm).

Cut from a sardonyx of five layers, the stone is most often interpreted to represent the enthroned emperor Tiberius with his mother, Livia, seated beside him, as a young general, perhaps Germanicus, salutes him amid other family members. Above, in heaven, are Augustus and other deified members of the family; in a zone below are barbarian captives.

The remarkable cameo is first recorded as existing in 1341 in the Sainte Chapelle in Paris; but it is conjectured to have arrived there in 1247 from Constantinople as a present from the emperor Baldwin II to Louis IX. Soon after the inventory, the great gem was sent by Philippe de Valois to Pope Clement VI and remained in the possession of the popes at Avignon until its return in 1379. At this time Charles V attached a base in Gothic style to the gilded silver Byzantine mounting for the stone.

The Gemma Tiberiana lay in the treasury of the Sainte Chapelle, largely forgotten as an object of archaeological interest for centuries, until its rediscovery by *Peiresc in 1620. Excited by the find, Peiresc wrote to his friends about it, noting that it was reported to represent the Christian theme of Joseph at the court of Pharaoh; he was the first to label the figures in the stone as Tiberius and members of the Roman imperial court, and many of his identifications are still widely accepted today. Peiresc notified Peter Paul *Rubens of the important discovery, and the two men were inspired by the study of this cameo and the equally stunning *Gemma Augustea to plan a book on all the most famous gems of Europe. Though the book was not completed, Rubens did make a drawing and engraving after the stone and a handsome painting in grisaille three times the size of the original (acquired by the Ashmolean Museum, Oxford in 1990). Many of Peiresc's and Rubens's notes and drawings were then published in a treatise on the Gemma Tiberiana by the painter's son Albert *Rubens (1665). He interpreted the scene as showing Germanicus before Tiberius in triumph, an event before Germanicus's death in A.D. 19.

In 1791, the revolutionary assembly in Paris decreed the sale of objects in the Sainte Chapelle, but the Gemma Tiberiana was saved and deposited in the Cabinet des Médailles of Louis XVI. In 1864 the gem was stolen, and it lost its Byzantine/Gothic mounting, but fortunately it was retrieved and returned to the cabinet. A new mount in neoclassical style was prepared for it by A. Delafontaine.

Modern scholars have sometimes challenged the traditional identifications and proposed new theories. B. Andreae supports the theory that the stone represents Caligula before Tiberius, at the time when his brother Nero Germanicus was invested as quaestor in A.D. 26.

BIBLIOGRAPHY

E. Babelon, *Catalogue des camées antiques et modernes de la Bibiothèque Nationale* (Paris, 1897), 120–37; B. Andreae, *The Art of Rome* (New York, 1977), tr. R. E. Wolf, 147–49; Kleiner, *Roman Sculpture*, 149–51. C. White, "Rubens and the Cameo of Tiberius," *Cameos in Context, The Benjamin Zucker Lectures, 1990,* ed. M. Henig—M. Vickers (Oxford, 1993).

GENNADIUS, JOANNES (1844–1932). Greek diplomat, scholar and bibliophile.

A leader in Greek diplomacy for over sixty years, Joannes Gennadius served as chief spokesman for Greece and the Greeks in England. His patriotism found passionate expression in his library, the most comprehensive collection of books on Greece assembled by one man, including subject matter ranging from remote antiquity to his own time. In 1922 he offered his library to the *American School of Classical Studies in Athens, on condition that it be freely available to scholars of all nations in its own separate housing. The Gennadius Library was built on Mt. Lykabettos in 1923–25, initially to contain nearly 30,000 volumes donated by Gennadius. Subsequently, the number more than doubled.

The Gennadeion is outstanding for its holdings on early travelers to Greece (e.g., *Buondelmonti, *Ciriaco, *Spon, *Wheler, *Chandler, *Nointel, *Choiseul-Gouffier, *Fauvel) and on the history of Greek archaeological studies (e.g., the great illustrated works of *Stuart and *Revett, Robert *Adam, Sir William *Hamilton, E. Q. *Visconti, the *Expédition scientifique de Morée). The archival material on *Byron and *Schliemann and the collection of drawings by *Lear are of exceptional importance.

BIBLIOGRAPHY

S. H. Weber, *Voyages and Travels in Greece, the Near East and Adjacent Regions Made Previous to the Year 1801* (Princeton, NJ, 1953); +F. R. Walton, *The Gennadius Library* (Athens, 1981).

GERALD OF WALES (GIRALDUS CAMBRENSIS, GERALD DE BARRI; ca. 1146–ca. 1223).

Historian of Wales and Ireland, archdeacon of Brecknock (1175–1204) and advocate for the independence of the Welsh Church from Canterbury.

Gerald's familiarity with classical literature is apparent throughout his writings, and his contact with classical remains is recorded in the *Itinerarium Kambriae*. Accompanying Archbishop Baldwin on his travels through Wales in 1188, Gerald described the countryside and its buildings. He identified the city of Caerleon as an old Roman camp and recorded the baths, temples, aqueducts, theaters and other Roman buildings that remained in the twelfth century. In his journey through Caermardyn, he also mentioned the Roman brick walls that were still partially standing.

BIBLIOGRAPHY

Giraldus Cambrensis, *The Itinerary Through Wales and the Description of Wales,* introd. W. Llewelyn Williams (London, 1908); Antonia Gransden, ''Realistic Observation in Twelfth-Century England,'' *Speculum* 47 (1972), 29–51.

JOANNE E. SOWELL

GERASA (JERASH).

Hellenistic and Roman city located in present-day Jordan.

By the second century A.C., the Hellenistic settlement at Gerasa was transformed into an affluent city of Roman Syria, advantageously situated ca. 42km north of Amman on the major Petra–Damascus road built by Trajan. Named a Roman colony, probably under Caracalla, Gerasa declined in the third century and revived, but only briefly, in the age of Justinian. Major Roman structures include the temples of Zeus and Artemis, theaters, a hippodrome, a huge triumphal triple-arch and impressive colonnades. The style of architecture is rich and often Baroque.

Roman Gerasa, partially overbuilt by modern Jerash, was first identified in 1806 by the Arabist Ulrich Seetzen. Some clearing around the visible structures preceded the major undertakings by Yale University with the British School of Archaeology in Jersualem and the American Schools of Oriental Research (1928–34); recovery work continued after World War II by Jordanian and foreign—particularly, Italian—teams. Their main interests have been in clearing, conserving and restoring the visible architecture and establishing the urban geography of a typical Roman city in the East. Finds from Gerasa are in the Yale University Art Gallery and the archaeological museum in Jerusalem.

BIBLIOGRAPHY

C. H. Kraeling, ed., *Gerasa, City of the Decapolis* (New Haven, CT, 1938); +I. Browning, *Jerash and the Decapolis* (London, 1982); G. Gullini et al., ''Gerasa I, Report of the Italian Archaeological Expedition at Jerash, Campaigns 1977–1981,'' *Mesopotamia* 18–19 (1983–84), 5–134.

BERNARD GOLDMAN

Photograph of *F.W.E. Gerhard.* (Deutsches Archäologisches Institut, Berlin.)

GERHARD, FRIEDRICH WILHELM EDUARD (1795–1867). German archaeologist; editor and collator of corpora of ancient artworks, organizer of the *Instituto di Corrispondenza Archeologica.

Born in Posen, Gerhard studied philology at Breslau and at Berlin under A. *Böckh. His archaeological studies began with a trip to Italy (1819–20) and study at Bonn (1821). The following year, in Rome, Gerhard began to meet and study with an international group of archaeologists, among whom were eventually T. *Panofka, A. Kestner, O. M. von *Stackelberg, C. J. Bunsen, C. *Fea and B. *Thorvaldsen. With the first three he formed an organization called the

"Roman *Hyperboreans" (*Hyperboreisch-römische Gesellschaft*). His association with the group inspired him to produce the early study of the *Forum Romanum called *Della Basilica Giulia ed alcuni siti del Foro Romano* (1823), in which the precise site of the famous basilica was first established.

Gerhard and his associates had long recognized the need for the cataloging of the major archaeological collections. In 1828, with Panofka he published the first and only volume of a corpus of sculptures in the *Museo Archeologico in Naples, *Neapels antike Bildwerke,* and next helped Bunsen produce the *Beschreibung der Stadt Rom* (1829). In these same years the Hyperboreans decided that an expanded association of internationally recognized archaeologists should be formed; on 21 April 1829, the Instituto di Corrispondenza Archeologica was born (destined to become the *German Archaeological Institute in 1871).

Gerhard's "Rapporto volcente" in *Annali dell'Instituto,* 1831, was a landmark eyewitness account of the excavations at *Vulci for the Prince of *Canino and a remarkable treatment of the many *Greek vases found there. In this publication Gerhard offered an accurate account of the four major types of Greek vase decoration, an analysis that helped settle the dispute over the origins of painted vases. (L. *Lanzi had correctly argued that the vases were Greek, though found in Etruscan graves.)

Of all the Hyperboreans, the well-traveled Gerhard was most aware of the vast wealth of ancient material in need of collection and publication, and he was to devote the remainder of his life to that pursuit. In 1834 he moved to Berlin, where he published the first volume of the *Berlins antike Bildwerke,* a large work on sculpture with a projected scope of 500 plates. Again only one volume saw completion (1836). In 1843 he was made professor of archaeology at the University of Berlin, and in 1855 he became director of the sculpture collection of the *Berlin museum.

The publishing of the four volumes of vase paintings, *Auserlesene griechische Vasenbilder* (1839–58), demonstrated Gerhard's organizational skills. Simultaneously, he published the first four volumes of the corpus of Etruscan mirrors, *Etruskische Spiegel,* 1840–67 (to be completed by A. Klügmann and G. Körte, volume 5, 1897). With these works, Gerhard succeeded in formulating a new systematic and scientific approach to classical antiquity, in which the goal was the publication of a comprehensive corpus of works of a particular category. The principles of methodology set up by Gerhard were to become standard practice. His insistence upon categorical and comparative analysis for the judging of antiquities is his greatest legacy.

In 1854–55, Gerhard prepared his *Griechische Mythologie.* In this work, as in many of the corpora, he acknowledged and perhaps overemphasized the importance of iconography and subject. Today, many of his interpretations are regarded as strained.

A growing weakness and trouble with his eyesight limited his last years' work and travels. He died at Berlin in 1867.

BIBLIOGRAPHY
O. Jahn, *Eduard Gerhard* (Berlin, 1868); P. Romanelli, "Gerhard, Eduard," *EI* 16 (1932) 662; H. Sichtermann, "Gerhard, Eduard," *EAA* 3 (1960), 843–4; *Porträtarchiv,* no. 145; H. B. Jessen, in *Archäologenbildnisse,* 20–22.

JOHN A. ELLIOTT

GERKAN, ARMIN VON (1884–1969). German archaeologist and architectural historian.

Armin von Gerkan was born of German parents at Subbath on the Baltic coast. His early studies were at Riga, but during Russian political unrest in 1906 he transferred to Dresden. He returned to Riga for his diploma in 1907, then set off for his traveling experience in Greece and Asia Minor.

Wilheim *Dörpfeld arranged for von Gerkan to participate in the excavations conducted by Theodor *Wiegand for the *Berlin museum at *Miletos, *Didyma and *Samos (1908–14). The experience was to influence him for the rest of his life.

During World War I, he served first as a Russian officer and, after 1918, as a volunteer in a German military unit. In 1920 he became a research assistant at the Berlin museum, where he wrote up in three volumes the results of the excavations at Miletos. He wrote his doctoral dissertation at Greifswald on the planning of Greek cities (*Griechische Stadteanlagen*), a study that is still today basic for research on the nature of the ancient city.

Von Gerkan's career took a different direction in 1924, when he accepted the position of second secretary at the *German Archaeological Institute in Rome and began to apply himself to the study and publication of the topography and architecture of Rome and *Pompeii. In the following years, amid the vicissitudes of archaeological politics, he was to serve as first secretary of the institute branches in both Athens and Rome. In 1944 he left Rome, eventually accepting appointments at Göttingen and Bonn, then moving on to Cologne and Hamburg, where he died at the age of eighty-five. Von Gerkan is regarded as one of the most important scholars of ancient architectural history and a founder of that branch of archaeological research.

BIBLIOGRAPHY
F. W. Deichmann, "Armin von Gerkan+," *RM* 77 (1970), vii–xviii; R. Naumann in *Archäologenbildnisse,* 226–27.

GERMAN ARCHAEOLOGICAL INSTITUTE (DEUTSCHES ARCHÄOLOGISCHES INSTITUT), Rome and Athens. Major German institution for the study of archaeology in classical lands, with the central administration in Berlin and the oldest and most important branches in Athens and Rome.

A royal order signed by Wilhelm I in Versailles on 2 March 1871 initiated the conversion of the *Instituto di Corrispondenza Archeologica in Rome into the Royal Prussian Institute of Archaeology with headquarters in Berlin. The Instituto had long been dependent on Prussian royal patronage for funds, and the Franco-Prussian War brought matters to a head. In 1874 this became the German Archaeological Institute (Deutsches Archäologisches Institut [DAI]) and almost immediately undertook the establishment of a branch in Athens, and the construction of a new building for the Roman branch on the grounds of Palazzo Caffarelli on the Capitoline Hill. The conversion was completed following an order by Bismarck signed 9 May 1885, in which the official language of publications and meetings of the institute was changed from Italian to German, although other languages, especially Italian, continued to be used. The architect of the new institute was Alexander *Conze as general secretary, who continued in office to 1905; Theodor *Mommsen acted as éminence grise. The various publications of the institute were revamped into the *Antike Denkmäler,* the *Jahrbuch des Instituts* with its various subdivisions and the addition of the *Römische* and *Athenische Mitteilungen.* Branches of the DAI were subsequently founded at Istanbul and Cairo (1929), Madrid (1943) and Baghdad (1955).

Rome

The direction of the institute in Rome was initially in the hands of W. Henzen as first secretary (1856–87) and W. *Helbig as second (1865–87), and then passed to E. *Petersen as first secretary in 1887, with C. *Hülsen as second. Successive first secretaries were G. *Körte (1905–7) and R. Delbrueck (1908–19). Of equal importance were the continuance of Hülsen as second secretary until 1908 and the presence of A. *Mau, first as assistant to Henzen beginning in 1873, later as librarian until his death in 1909.

With Germany's declaration of war against Italy in August 1916 the institute was closed and put under the protection of the Swiss embassy. After the war, the building on the Capitoline, considered too significant a location to ignore, was sequestered by the Italian government in 1919, but the library, under the care of the long-term Swiss librarian Alfred Joller, was packed into cases and sealed and then stored in the Castel Sant'Angelo. The building on the Capitoline was lost, but the library was delivered back to representatives of Germany in October 1920 under Walther *Amelung's supervision. Amelung was made first secretary of the Roman branch in May 1921, and at the beginning of 1924 the institute was installed in a building in Via Sardegna belonging to the German evangelical congregation. A new library was dedicated on 30 October 1924 and opened to the public in December, thanks to the devoted efforts of Joller. Amelung then continued as first secretary until his death in 1927; he was succeeded by Ludwig *Curtius (1928–37).

Curtius inaugurated in 1929 a separate photographic archive under the direction of Hermine Speier and pushed for its expansion, especially to cover whole collections and classes of monuments, for example, portraits and sarcophagi. By the time of his departure in 1937, the collection included more than 100,000 prints and 23,000 negatives. At the same time, the library had grown to 52,100 volumes, with an annual increase of 1,700 volumes and subscriptions to 400 periodicals. Under his direction, the institute enjoyed a golden age and cosmopolitanism enriched by the presence of many promising and influential German scholars. With the triumph of National Socialism, the institute, at first an outpost of resistance to the new regime, eventually became deeply divided politically, resulting ultimately in Curtius's suspension and enforced retirement. He was succeeded by Armin von *Gerkan.

The years of World War II were naturally very difficult. At first, the institute continued work under Crous, Deichmann and Fuhrmann, although it lost members successively to the military; but in October 1943, following the landing of the Allies in Italy, orders came for the transport of the goods and library of the institute to Salzburg, which took place at the beginning of 1944. Although the cases were returned to Rome toward the end of 1945 and housed in the Museo d'Arte Moderna and in 1947 returned to the Via Sardegna and the library reopened on a limited scale, the fate of the institute and the library remained in doubt until 1953. Beginning in February 1946 it was put in the hands of an international commission, and both political and financial difficulties ensued. Persistent efforts to return it to the internationalism of the Instituto di Corrispondenza Archeologica eventually fell to the ground for lack of broad support; there were petitions for its return to Germany signed by both scholars and scholarly institutions; and in April 1953 it was finally returned to German control. Guido von *Kashnitz-Weinberg was appointed first director on *Winckelmann's birthday, 9 December 1953.

The years of Kaschnitz, 1953–56, were very productive. The *Römische Mitteilungen,* interrupted since the publication of volume 59 (1944) in Munich in 1948, was resumed with a sumptuous double volume, 60/61 (1953/54), as was the *Anzeiger;* a new edition (the fourth) of Helbig's great guide to the museums of Rome, *Führer durch die öffentlichen Sammlungen klassischer Altertumer in Rom,* was launched under the editorship of Hermine Speier (published in four volumes, Tübingen, 1963–72); the course in Pompeian archaeology was revived under von Gerkan; and plans were laid for a splendid new building to house the institute. Kaschnitz was succeeded by Reinhard *Herbig (1956–61), under whom programs of excavation at Palinuro and *Rusellae were initiated, and in October 1959 the institute moved to Palazzo Torlonia in Via Bocca di Leone to allow the complete rebuilding of its headquarters in Via Sardegna. Unfortunately, Herbig's sudden death on 29 September 1961 prevented him from seeing the fruits of his most important labors.

The new institute opened 1 October 1964, although its dedication did not take place until 8 March 1965. In 1962 Herbig had been succeeded as director by Theodor Kraus (1962–84), during whose early years a vigorous program of excavations was pursued at Policoro, *Metapontum and *Segesta, while, a little later, institute activity was extended to Tunisia, where Friedrich Rakob was first occupied with excavations at the water sanctuary of Zaghouan (1964), the quarries of Chemtou (1965) and *Carthage and later in Algeria at Lambaesis, the mausoleum of El-Souma (1973–74) and the mausoleum of Beni Rhenane (1975–77). At the same time, institute members, especially Rakob and Dieter Mertens, continued the study, recording and publication of ancient architectural monuments in Italy, especially around Rome, in Campania and in Magna Graecia and Sicily.

The heart of the institute has always been its library, now approaching a total of 140,000 volumes and 750 periodicals, and its photographic archive now contains well over 200,000 prints and 100,000 negatives.

L. RICHARDSON, JR

Athens

The branch of the German Archaeological Institute in Athens was officially opened on 9 December (Winckelmann's birthday) in 1874, with a specific mission to match in Greece the remarkable achievements of the institute in Rome. The first secretary was Otto Lüders (1874–75), followed by Ulrich Köhler (1875–86), E. *Petersen (1886–87) and W. *Dörpfeld (1887–1912). Assistants in these early years included F. von *Duhn, G. *Körte and Habbo Gerhardus Lolling. In 1887–88, permanent quarters for the Athenian branch were erected, through the financial support of *Schliemann and following architectural designs by Dörpfeld, on the corner of what later became Odos Phidiou and Odos Charilaou Trikoupi.

The first excavations by the new school were conducted at the Mycenaean tomb at Menidi in Attika (1879), followed by work at the temple of Athena, *Tegea, by A. Milchhofer (1879) and Dörpfeld (1882). Other projects were immediately initiated at Nauplion (Lolling) and the temple of Poseidon at *Sounion (Dörpfeld). In these years, excavations were also undertaken at *Olympia under the direction of E. *Curtius (1876–81), but these were not the direct responsibility of the new Athens branch; rather, they were sponsored by the royal Prussian ministry, and all the records were kept in Berlin. Students with a travel stipend to study in Greece were regularly dispatched by the Athenian institute to participate at Olympia and to write reports on the progress of the work. Similarly, a representative of the Athens branch was sent to work with Carl *Humann in the Berlin-sponsored work at *Pergamon.

The earliest monographs of the institute (1879) pertained to Mycenaean pottery (by A. *Furtwängler and G. *Loeschcke) and the excavations at Menidi. This was also the period when Lolling produced his Ur-Baedeker (see *guidebooks to Greece), and Curtius, assisted in mapping by a military unit supervised by J. Kaupert, produced his *Karten von Attika,* a fundamental work on Athenian and Attic topography.

Much of the history of the institute in the ensuing years is bound up with the prolific activity of Dörpfeld as architect, field archaeologist and administrator of the Athenian branch. Especially significant were his contributions at Olympia and, in collaboration with Schliemann, at *Troy, *Tiryns and *Orchomenos. Dörpfeld and his colleagues gave attention to the topography of Athens, including the *Theater of Dionysos (1886) and the area of the *Agora; from 1907 the Germans were involved in the *Kerameikos excavations, assuming full responsibility from 1912 to 1930. Dörpfeld articulated lofty ideals for the institute, stressing the need for practical missions in securing and publishing archaeological data through travel and excavation and for scholarly achievements in research and the instruction of young archaeologists. He also systematically developed a collection of slides and photographs and initiated the use of the slide projector for the institute's sessions of archaeological reports. To the years before and after 1900 belong many of the priceless photographic records made of the *Akropolis in this period. A rare female archaeologist at the institute, Margarete *Bieber, produced a two-volume catalog of the photographic collection (1912).

The German school began its investigations at *Thera in 1895, under the direction of *Hiller von Gaertringen, who originally began to explore the island for its inscriptions but then enlarged his scope and discovered, among other things, the first traces of Bronze Age habitation on the island. From 1900 to 1913, Dörpfeld directed the work at Pergamon (formerly, under the aegis of the Berlin museums). In 1910 the Germans began their long series of excavations on *Samos (under T. *Wiegand) and, in 1911, work on the temple of Artemis at *Korkyra (also under Dörpfeld).

Georg *Karo served the Athens branch as second secretary (1905–12) and then as first secretary (1912–20) during the difficult years of World War I. The institute closed its doors in 1916; its program of publication suffered interruption and postponement, and its personnel was scattered; Karo himself went to Asia Minor and occupied himself with the preservation of endangered sites. The institute resumed operation in 1920 under the direction of F. *Studniczka (1920–21) and then E. *Buschor (1921–29), with Karo returning in the 1930s. Work resumed at Samos (1925) and in the Kerameikos (1927), and, after Karo's return, excavation was carried on apace at a number of sites.

The director of the institute during the following years of world crisis was Walther Wrede (1937–44), a high official of the Nazi Party. Constantly occupied with political assignments, he left much of the care of the institute to young and dedicated assistants Roland Hampe, Ernst Homann-Wedeking, Ulf Jantzen and Frank Brommer. The excavations at Olympia were warmly approved by Hitler and were launched with new vigor and an annual expense account of 50,000 marks against the backdrop of the staging of the modern Olympic Games in Berlin in 1936. In grand style, part of the stadium at Olympia was excavated.

When war broke out in 1939, at first little changed at the Athenian institute. But then in the spring of 1940, the Greek government suspended all excavation. The German effort at the Kerameikos and Olympia was now concentrated on protection of the monuments. With the Nazi occupation of Greece in 1941, the institute attempted to return to full activity, but due to diminishing funds, grand plans remained mainly on paper. The German evacuation in 1944 left Hampe and Jantzen, now military officials, among the last Germans remaining in the country as they handed over the institute to Greek authorities. The library, left in boxes at Odos Phidiou, was rescued from water damage by N. Bufidis, librarian of the Athens National Archaeological Museum; some 25,000 volumes were returned to their shelves. The photo archives were taken to the National Museum under order of director Christos Karouzos.

Emil Kunze (director 1951–67) oversaw the difficult reopening of the German Archaeological Institute in Athens and the resumption of its publications. New excavation campaigns were promptly undertaken at the Heraion at Samos (from 1952, under Buschor, followed by Homann-Wedeking and H. Kyrileis), Olympia (also from 1952), the Kerameikos (from 1956, under D. Ohly, followed by F. Willemsen and U. Knigge). Jantzen excavated at Tiryns during the years in which he served as director (1967–74). His publication of the volume celebrating the centenary of the Athenian branch is fundamental for the history not only of the institute but of German archaeology.

BIBLIOGRAPHY

L. Wickert, *Beiträge zur Geschichte des Deutschen Archäologischen Instituts von 1879 bis 1929* (Mainz, 1979); K. Bittel et al., *Beiträge zur Geschichte des Deutschen Archäologischen Instituts von 1929 bis 1979* 1 (Mainz, 1979); U. Jantzen, *Einhundert Jahre Athener Institut, 1874–1974* (Mainz, 1986).

GETTY, J. PAUL (1892–1976). American billionaire; founder of the J. Paul Getty Museum in Malibu, California.

During his many years of business-related travel, Getty developed a keen interest in art collecting. In 1931 he purchased his first work of art, a seventeenth-century Dutch landscape painting. In the 1950s, Getty began adding works of ancient art to his growing collection. Among his early acquisitions were two pieces from English collections, the Elgin *Kore* and the Lansdowne *Herakles,* an especial favorite of Getty, because it came from the villa at Tivoli owned by Hadrian (*Hadrian's Villa), a great collector with whom he felt an affinity. Getty took pleasure in visiting archaeological sites when possible and read extensively on ancient art and related subjects.

In 1968, Getty decided to expand his modest museum, then located in his Los Angeles ranch home. The new building at Malibu was designed to simulate Roman architecture of the first century A.C.; the *Villa of the Papyri at Herculaneum was chosen by Getty as a prototype for the new museum complex and gardens; Norman Neuerburg acted as consultant for the building, which opened in 1974. Getty himself, having settled in England, at Sutton Place in Surrey, was never able to see the completed building before his death.

At the time of his death, Getty's collection of antiquities ranked as one of the most important in the United States. Subsequent acquisitions have further enhanced its value; it includes Greek and Roman sculpture in bronze, marble and terracotta; Attic and Italiote vases; Etruscan jewelry; Greek and Roman carved gems; and examples of Roman and Romano-Egyptian painting. Outstanding pieces in the collection are the bronze *Victorious Athlete* in the manner of Lysippos, fourth–third centuries B.C.; a marble Cycladic *Harpist,* ca. 2500 B.C.; and a marble head of *Achilles* (?) from Tegea, fourth century B.C. Critics of acquisitions made by the Getty Museum have lamented that large sums of money were spent on unprovenanced antiquities that had evidently been ripped from their archaeological context and illegally exported from their country of origin.

BIBLIOGRAPHY

J. Paul Getty, *The Joys of Collecting* (New York, 1965); + N. Neuerburg, "The New J. Paul Getty Museum," *Archaeology* 27 (1974), 175–181; "J. Paul Getty," *New York Times Biographical Service* (June 1976), VII, pt. 1, 843; "J. Paul Getty," *New York Times,* late ed., 7 June 1976, 32; "J. Paul Getty and His Museum," in *The J. Paul Getty Museum, Handbook of the Collections* (Malibu, 1986), 1–23.

SHELLIE WILLIAMS

GEVAERTS, JAN-CASPAR (GEVARS; GEVART; GEVARTIUS, JANUS CASPERIUS; 1593–1666). Flemish humanist, numismatist, historian, philologist and poet.

Gevaerts received his basic education at the Jesuit College in Antwerp and later studied literature at the Collegium in Louvain. In addition, he was in contact with the Leiden humanists, including Scriverius, Meursius and Heinsius. In 1617 he moved to Paris, where he met *Peiresc and the brothers Dupuy, but he turned down a professorship in Paris and returned to Antwerp. There he was appointed secretary to the city.

Gevaerts became an intimate friend of P. P. *Rubens, who entrusted the education of his son Albert (*Rubens) to him in 1629. Gevaerts collaborated with the artist on his decorations for the entry of Archduke Ferdinand into Antwerp in 1635, composing the Latin inscriptions and devising selected allegories, subjects and ornamental motifs, many of them based on Roman monuments and coins (published in his *Inscriptiones,* 1635, and *Pompa Introitus,* 1642). He corresponded with many Italian antiquarians, including Girolamo *Aleandro and Lorenzo Pignoria, and socialized with the great humanists of his day, *Graevius, J. F. *Gronovius and Heinsius. He owned a good humanist library and 2,000 gold, silver and bronze coins, sold after his death. He published several of his coins in his commentary on the *Silvae* of Statius (*Opera omnia,* Leiden 1616). He assisted in the posthumous publication of Albert Rubens's treatises on the *Gemma Tiberiana and *Gemma Augustea (1665; the former is sometimes incorrectly ascribed to Gevaerts). A portrait of Gevaerts by Rubens showed the secretary at his desk with a bust of Marcus Aurelius next to him.

BIBLIOGRAPHY

M. Hoc, *Étude sur J.-G. Gevaerts* (Brussels, 1922).

MARJON VAN DER MEULEN

GHIBERTI, LORENZO (LORENZO DI CIONE, LORENZO DI BARTOLUCCIO; 1378/81–1455). Italian goldsmith and sculptor.

The contest in 1401 for the commission of the Baptistery doors in Florence—often indicated as the advent of Renaissance art—marks the beginning of Ghiberti's life's work as well. The competition reliefs for the doors by Ghiberti and his rival *Brunelleschi included many figural quotations from antique artworks, such as sarcophagi and the *Spinario.

Ghiberti's well-known victory gained for him the commission for the doors now on the north side of the Baptistery. In the early reliefs for the north doors, there is little reference to ancient art, and the artist's interest seems to have ebbed. However, perhaps as the result of a trip to Rome in 1416, Ghiberti's later panels (1416–24) show a renewed observation of antiquity in the figural motifs that he applied to the reliefs quite literally. While in Rome, Ghiberti probably examined antique reliefs and statues while making drawings for future reference in his studio.

In the Porto del Paradiso (1424–52), Ghiberti's second set of doors for the Baptistery, Roman motives have been integrated so completely that, though they are used throughout, they are nearly indistinguishable from the artist's own inventions. Ghiberti's broader knowledge and deeper understanding of his sources may have resulted, as before, from a visit to Rome (between 1425 and 1430) and renewed contact with antique models. In the later doors, Ghiberti may have been influenced by written descriptions of ancient art, in addition to the surviving monuments.

Ghiberti had a rudimentary education, and his reading and use of Latin were imperfect. His *Commentarii* (ca. 1447) was written in Italian, the *volgare,* rather than humanist Latin. The format of this work, however, demonstrates a contemporary, humanistic view of history. The first portion, on the art of ancient Greece and Rome, is drawn largely from the writings of Vitruvius and Pliny. The second part describes the decline of art under Constantine and its rebirth in the Trecento and concludes with Ghiberti's autobiography. The third and final portion of the *Commentarii* is a jumble of miscellaneous notes on various subjects, some of which are theoretical (such as anatomy and optics, in which the sources are Averroes, Adhazen and others). He includes a description of a *Hermaphrodite* found in Rome in the first half of the fifteenth century and a chalcedony gem with *Diomedes and the Palladium* in the collection of *Niccoli.

Ghiberti owned a valuable collection of antiquities, which his family preserved until ca. 1530. His most famous possession was a marble relief called the "Letto di Polyklito" (*Bed of Polykleitos*). There were also torsos, of a *Satyr, Venus, Narcissus* and *Mercury;* a lifesize bronze leg; statue heads and some *Greek vases. Reliefs and gems also probably formed part of his collection. Ghiberti owned a small library as well.

BIBLIOGRAPHY

+J. von Schlosser, "Über einige Antiken Ghibertis," *JKS* 24 (1903), 125–59; Idem, ed., *Lorenzo Ghibertis Denkwürdigkeiten (I Commentarii)* (Berlin, 1912); R. Krautheimer, *Lorenzo Ghiberti* 2nd ed. (Princeton, NJ, 1982); Bober—Rubinstein, 59–60, 74, 127, 130, 156.

CHRISTINE SPERLING

GHIRLANDAIO, DOMENICO (1449–94). Italian painter of the Early Renaissance.

Born in Florence, Ghirlandaio made two trips to Rome, in 1475 and in 1481–82. According to Vasari, the artist drew many Roman monuments—arches, baths, columns, obelisks, amphitheaters, aqueducts. He did his drawings freehand but so accurately that when they were completed, one could check the measurements with a rule and find them correct. The paintings Ghirlandaio created after his second sojourn in Rome are crowded with references to antiquity that are best understood as the result of records made in his drawings in these years.

An examination of the question of Ghirlandaio's study drawings must take into account a sketchbook in the library of the Escorial, Madrid (Cod. 28-II-12; the *Codex Escurialensis), believed to contain copies of drawings made by Ghirlandaio in Rome. Some of the motifs drawn in the Escurialensis are clearly depicted in paintings by Ghirlandaio; for example, a close imitation of particular *grottesche* from the *Domus Aurea of Nero appears in paneling of the scene of the *Birth of the Virgin* in Santa Maria Novella, Florence (1488–90). The same scene contains a pilaster with an unusual Ionic capital (featuring the infant Hercules [?] between serpents) that is also drawn in the Escurialensis. If Ghirlandaio made the original drawings of these items, which were then copied in the Escurialensis, he was thus one of the earliest to make copies of the paintings in the Domus Aurea and was a leading figure in creating the rage for *grottesche* in Renaissance art.

Ghirlandaio made extensive use of the iconography of coins, sarcophagi and historical Roman relief in his frescoes, as well as references to key monuments in Rome. His *Vision of Augustus on the Capitoline Hill* in the Sassetti Chapel in Santa Trinità, Florence (1485), shows a panorama of Rome that includes the *Pantheon, a spiral column of the type of the *Column of Trajan and the *Pyramid of Cestius. His *Adoration of the Shepherds* in the same chapel shows a remarkable invention of a Roman-style triumphal arch of Pompey and a sarcophagus adorned with a garland motif also appearing in the Codex Escurialensis (from a sarcophagus in the garden of the Palazzo Caffarelli, Rome).

BIBLIOGRAPHY

+H. Egger, with C. Hülsen—A. Michaelis, *Codex Escurialensis, Ein Skizzenbuch aus der Werkstatt Domenico Ghirlandaios* 1–2 (Vienna, 1905–6; repr. 1975); +N. Dacos, ''Ghirlandaio and the Antique,'' *Bulletin de l'Institut Historique Belge de Rome* 34 (1962), 419–55; Bober—Rubinstein, esp. 458.

GIAMBOLOGNA (GIOVANNI BOLOGNA; JEAN BOULOGNE; 1529–1608). Italian sculptor.

Born in northern France in an area that was part of Flanders, the artist spent his early years in Northern Europe and arrived in Italy in 1550, probably for the occasion of the Jubilee of *Julius III. He spent at least two years studying antiquities in Rome, among other things, making numerous drawings of the group of the *Farnese *Bull*. He arrived in Florence in 1553 and, after attracting the attention of various collectors, became court sculptor to the *Medici.

Giambologna is perhaps best known for his sculptural groups on mythological themes, both lifesize and statuettes. The *Rape of a Sabine* (1581–82) and *Hercules Slaying a Centaur* (1595–1600) articulate a new integration of classicism with contemporary art. His small bronze sculptures of kneeling women bathing reflect the *Crouching Venus* discovered in Rome in the sixteenth century. *Peasant Resting on a Staff* has parallels in Roman genre sculpture, and his famous statue of *Mercury* is based on antique representations of athletes. The *Lion Attacking a Bull* demonstrates a knowledge of numismatics, and his statuettes of *Psyche, Astronomy* and *Apollo* are essays in the ultimate expression of the *figura serpentinata,* the figure twisting and turning in space, reflecting his concept of the antique as the embodiment of grace and elegance.

This ideal is displayed in the classical motif of river gods in the bronze and marble *Fountain of Neptune,* Bologna (1566). His *Fountain of Ocean,* Florence (1571–75) used figural types based on the *Farnese *Hercules,* newly discovered when he was in Rome. The *Apennine* (ca. 1583) at the Medici Villa at Pratolino, a colossal garden sculpture of a mountain god, combines living rock, brick, stone, stucco and lava in the creation of an artificial mountain. The interest in reshaping nature in the manner of the ancients forms a dominant classicizing motif of the sixteenth century.

His sculpture on mythological subjects bridged the gap between Mannerism of the early sixteenth century and the Baroque style of the seventeenth century. Precursors to the style displaying the idea of absolute rule may be found in his bronze equestrian monuments of Cosimo I de' Medici (1587–93) and Fernando I (1601–8), both in Florence, and his bronze portrait bust of Cosimo I, Florence, Uffizi Gallery (ca. 1574), inspired by Roman imperial portrait busts, looks forward to state portraits of the seventeenth century. Giambologna's mythological subjects and antique figural types, his elegant style and his multimedia set pieces influenced the next generation of sculptors in the Baroque period, most notably *Bernini.

BIBLIOGRAPHY

C. Avery—A. Radcliffe, eds., *Giambologna, Sculptor to the Medici* (London, 1978); J. Holderbaum, *The Sculptor Giovanni Bologna* (New York, 1983); C. Avery, *Giambologna: The Complete Sculpture* (Mt. Kisco, NY, 1987).

C. NAUMER

GIBBON, EDWARD (1737–94). British historian of Rome.

With the publication of the *Decline and Fall of the Roman Empire,* of which the first volume appeared in 1776, Edward Gibbon achieved a deserved and enduring reputation as one of the greatest of all historians of Graeco-Roman civilization. This monumental work, written in an incomparable style and comprehending the history of East and West from the Antonine age to the capture of Constantinople, reflects the wide reading and deep thinking of its author from the days of his adolescence. In 1753 Gibbon's father sent him to Lausanne in Switzerland to be cured of an impulsive conversion to the Roman Catholic Church while at Oxford. After a formal return to Protestantism in late 1754, the seventeen-year-old was obliged to remain in Lausanne until 1758, and during those years he acquired a thorough familiarity with French language and culture that was to make him as much a continental European as an Englishman. At Lausanne, Gibbon's reading included certain works that were ultimately to serve as important influences on the *Decline and Fall.* Among these was the biography of the emperor Julian by the Abbé de la Bletterie.

It has often been noticed that in the *Decline and Fall* Gibbon shows little interest in ancient art, antiquities, manuscripts and monuments, but formerly he had shown a keen awareness of the value of physical evidence for history. In 1763 he had returned to Lausanne, by way of Paris, and devoted himself to intensive preparation for a tour of Italy he was to make in the following year. His journals reveal careful study of the volumes of the *Bibliothèque raisonnée* as well as the works of Muratori, *Montfaucon, Mabillon and especially *Cluverius. He began the composition of a commonplace book on the regions of Italy, but the plan of the book became much more ambitious as he worked on it. This was the *Recueil géographique sur l'Italie ancienne,* of which the various sheets were collated and published after his death by Lord Sheffield under the title *Nomina gentesque Italiae antiquae.* Gibbon continued to work on the *Recueil* while in Italy in 1764–65.

The journal that Gibbon wrote during his *Grand Tour has much to say about the antiquities he saw in Italy. Unfortunately, however, it lacks any entry from Rome for the famous date of 15 October 1764, on which, as he later claimed, "the idea of writing the decline and fall of the city first started to my mind." Whether Gibbon as an older man innocently persuaded himself of this moment of inspiration "amidst the ruins of the Capitol" or whether he was actually too inspired at the time to write anything at all in his diary we shall never know. The remains of ancient Rome, among which the eminent Scottish expatriate James *Byres conducted him, clearly left a great impression. The final chapter of the *Decline and Fall* opens with an eloquent evocation of the fallen city in the fifteenth century. Nevertheless, during an excursion from Rome to Naples, Gibbon apparently failed to take advantage of the opportunity to examine the newly discovered antiquities at *Herculaneum and *Pompeii. It also appears that he took no notice of *Winckelmann, who was then resident in Rome. But by the end of his life, Gibbon's library included two copies of Winckelmann's *History of Ancient Art* in French translation, as well as a French text of the famous letters on the discoveries at Herculaneum.

BIBLIOGRAPHY

G. A. Bonnard, ed., *Le Journal de Gibbon à Lausanne, 17 August 1763–19 April 1764* (Lausanne, 1945); Idem, *Gibbon's Journey from Geneva to Rome: His Journal from 20 April to 2 October 1764* (Edinburgh, 1961); Pierre Ducrey et al., eds., *Gibbon et Rome à la lumière de l'historiographie moderne* (Lausanne, 1977); G. W. Bowersock—J. Clive—S. R. Graubard, eds., *Edward Gibbon and the Decline and Fall of the Roman Empire* (Cambridge, MA, 1977).

G. W. BOWERSOCK

GIGLIOLI, GIULIO QUIRINO (1886–1957). Italian archaeologist and art historian.

A pupil of E. Löwy and R. *Lanciani and a patriotic citizen of Rome, Giglioli discovered and promptly published the *Apollo* of *Veii while on leave from the front (1916). He combined his Rome University chairs of ancient topography (1923) and classical art history (1925 onward) with the duties of city councillor and parliamentary deputy (1935), devoting inexhaustible energy and learning to the retrieval and illustration of the (mainly) Roman and Italic past via excavation, restoration (the *Mausoleum and Forum of Augustus), exhibitions, museum work and publication, notably fascicles of the *Corpus Vasorum Antiquorum* and the basic *Arte etrusca.*

His spirit unbroken by internment after the fall of Mussolini (1943), Giglioli resumed his chair and founded the journal *Archeologia Classica* (1948). The most distinguished of his many brilliant pupils was Massimo Pallottino, the founder of "Etruscology" as an autonomous discipline within the classical area.
BIBLIOGRAPHY
G. Q. Giglioli, *L'Arte etrusca* (Milan, 1935; 2nd ed. 1949); Idem, *Mostra Augustea della Romanità: Catalogo* (Rome, 1937; 4th ed. 1958); Idem, "Religione degli Etruschi," in *Storia delle religioni,* ed. P. Tacchi Venturi (Turin, 1944; 4th ed. 1948); M. Pallottino, *Giulio Quirino Giglioli, Quaderni di Studi Romani* 19 (Rome, 1958, with bib.).

F. R. SERRA RIDGWAY

GIOCONDO, FRA GIOVANNI (FRA GIOVANNI DA VERONA; 1433–1515). Italian architect, engineer and antiquarian; especially known for his studies in Roman *epigraphy.

One of the most famous architects of his time, Fra Giocondo traveled extensively in Italy and Europe. In 1486–95, he was in Naples working for King Alfonso II. He was summoned to France in 1500 by Charles VIII. His last major commission, from Pope *Leo X in 1513 to assist *Raphael and *Bramante in the rebuilding of St. Peter's, brought him to Rome, where he died in 1515.

An early notice of Fra Giocondo dates to ca. 1480, when he was in Rome copying antique inscriptions. His surviving collection of Latin inscriptions is extensive and includes examples from Rome and all of Italy. The compiled transcriptions are meticulously accurate and in this way superior to earlier sylloges. An early copy of his sylloge, dedicated to Lorenzo de' Medici (*Medici family) in 1489, is now in the Biblioteca Capitolare in Verona. Other important copies are located in the Biblioteca Nazionale in Florence (1497–99) and the Biblioteca Marciana in Venice.

Fra Giocondo studied the appearance of Roman inscriptions, as well as their

Fragment of Cornice found in the Forum of Trajan, Rome, and carried to St. Peter's for building material, drawing by Fra Giocondo. St. Petersburg, Hermitage, Library. (Deutsches Archäologisches Institut, Rome. Inst. Neg. 42.192.)

content. The introduction of a treatise on epigraphic lettering by Fra Giocondo in Munich informs us that he designed a Roman alphabet according to ideal, geometric principles, as did also *Felice Feliciano, *Mantegna and Fra Luca de Pacioli.

Fra Giocondo's training as an architect and engineer complemented his antiquarian interests. Numerous studies of ancient monuments in Rome and Italy survive in three volumes of drawings in the Hermitage, Leningrad. These have been attributed to Fra Giocondo, though some may be copies from his drawings. The studies include detailed plans of Roman buildings, outlines of cornices with precise measurements and drawings from Roman reliefs. Some drawings investigate Roman construction methods and engineering. Others are imaginative and show fanciful views of Rome as it existed in antiquity. Similar drawings by Fra Giocondo are in the *Uffizi in Florence, the *Louvre in Paris and the Kunstgewerbe Museum in Berlin. Fra Giocondo contributed drawings to *Francesco di Giorgio's treatise on civil and military architecture in 1476.

Fra Giocondo also studied ancient literature. He published an important and popular edition of *De architectura* by Vitruvius in Venice in 1511. (It was reissued in 1513, 1522 and 1525.) Fra Giocondo also published editions of works by other Latin authors such as Sallust (1509) and Nonius Marcellus (1513).

BIBLIOGRAPHY

R. Brenzoni, *Fra Giovanni Giocondo Veronese* (Florence, 1960); +M. Gukovskj, "Ritrovamento dei tre volumi di disegni attribuiti a Fra Giocondo," *Italia Medioevale e Umanistica* 6 (1963) 263–69; L. A. Ciapponi, "A Fragmentary Treatise on Epigraphic Alphabets by Fra Giocondo da Verona," *RQ* 32 (1979), 18–40.

CHRISTINE SPERLING

GIRARDON, FRANÇOIS (1628–1715). French academic sculptor and art collector.

Born in Troyes, Girardon traveled to Rome in 1648, returning ca. 1650 and going on to Paris, where he worked closely with *Le Brun. Received into the Académie in 1657, he was soon professor; he subsequently rose to assistant rector (1672), rector (1674) and finally, chancellor of the Académie (1695).

Girardon became the principal sculptor to *Louis XIV and was the chief adviser on the planning and development of sculptural decoration for Versailles; on a second trip to Italy (1668), he investigated and gave advice on the acquisition of casts of antique sculpture for Versailles; later on, he would correct plaster casts of ancient pieces and would restore antiquities such as the *Venus* of *Arles, discovered in 1651 and brought from that city in 1684 to be set up at Versailles (now in the *Louvre, Paris).

Girardon collected for his own sake as well. An inventory made of his collection after his death in 1715 provides remarkable testimony to the number and kind of antiquities and copies of antiquities that were collected and available for study in Paris at this period. Girardon had his best pieces drawn by R. Charpentier and engraved for an anthology of the *Galerie de Girardon.* The evidence of inventory and engravings show that he owned portraits thought to be ancient of *Lykourgos, Epikouros, Diogenes, Euripides, Alexander the Great, Ptolemy, Octavius* and *Marcellus,* as well as copies in bronze of *Sokrates, Han-*

nibal, Julius Caesar, Vitellius, Seneca, Commodus, Caracalla. His *Alexander the Great,* with head in porphyry, was set by Girardon on a bust of *verde antico* marble, with a mantle of gilded bronze (now Musée de Versailles).

Girardon's own sculpture shows neither more nor less imitation of the antique than other works in the authoritarian academic style of the court in the later seventeenth century. His *Apollo Attended by Nymphs* (1662–72, Versailles), starring a variant of the *Belvedere *Apollo* in the center of the composition, shows a relish for Hellenistic-style drapery and hair.

BIBLIOGRAPHY
+F. Souchal, "La collection du sculpteur Girardon d'après son inventaire après décès," *GBA* 1973 (82), 1–98; Haskell—Penny, 38, 39, 41, 42, etc.; +F. Souchal, *French Sculptors of the 17th and 18th Centuries, The Reign of Louis XIV* 2 (Oxford, 1981), 14–83.

GIULIO ROMANO (GIULIO PIPPI or DI PIETRO DE' GIANUZZI; 1492?–1546). Italian painter and architect.

Apprenticed at an early age to *Raphael, Giulio was his favorite assistant and chief executant of his designs. His participation is evident first in the Stanza dell'Incendio in the Vatican and increasingly in Raphael's later projects, notably in the frescoes of the Loggia di Psiche in the Farnesina and of the Vatican Logge. On Raphael's death, Giulio and Giovanni Francesco Penni inherited his workshop, paintings, drawings, antiquities (probably) and the responsibility for completing commissions left unfinished at their master's death, such as the painting of the *Transfiguration* and the decoration of Villa Madama and of the Sala di Costantino in the Vatican Stanze.

In 1524, through the efforts of Baldassare Castiglione, Giulio was summoned to Mantua by the Marchese Federigo Gonzaga (*Gonzaga family). By 1526 he had become a citizen of Mantua, city architect and principal artist to the Gonzaga court. He virtually ruled there as supreme impresario of the arts for more than two decades, directing a large team of assistants and overseeing all enterprises in architecture, decoration and theatrical design that were ambitiously conceived by Federigo to both modernize and transform Mantua into a "second Rome."

Giulio was the first major Roman-born artist of the Renaissance to draw deeply and exhaustively upon the legacy of ancient monuments of his native city. Many of his paintings show the influence of classical statues and reliefs, for example, the *Laocoon, *Belvedere *Apollo,* Vatican *"*Cleopatra,*" Egyptian telamon statues (then at Tivoli), Mantuan *Apollo* and Mantuan *Venus Genetrix,* the last of which inspired the pair of Dianas on the pilasters that flank the scene of the painting of the *Baptism of Constantine.* For pose and drapery, he studied neo-Attic decorative reliefs such as the *Borghese *Dancers* (*Louvre), which inspired the powerful vase-bearing woman in the *Fire in the Borgo* fresco in the Stanza dell'Incendio, and the *Grimani Altar base, which appears as a fragmented prop in the *Madonna of the Oak.* Ruins of Roman edifices in the *Imperial Fora and elsewhere are hauntingly introduced to create a romantic mood, as in the *Stoning of St. Stephen,* in which the *Theater of

Marcellus, Temple of the Sibyl at *Tivoli and the *Column of Trajan and Marketplace of Trajan appear as menacing reminders of the pagan past in a super-
naturally lit landscape. In his S. Maria dell'Anima altarpiece, the cavernous
forms of the *Basilica of Maxentius animate the penumbral background.

Innumerable monuments fueled his antiquarian researches, yet those that
seemed to kindle his imagination most during his Roman years were Late
Imperial historical reliefs and *Roman sarcophagi of the second century A.C.
The *Columns of Marcus Aurelius and of Trajan, as Vasari emphasizes, taught
him how to depict accurately the details of Roman ritual, costume and weaponry
in his military frescoes. In the *Battle of Ostia* the expressive motif of prisoners
grasped by the hair and hustled forward is derived from details of the former
column and episodes of the latter, for example, scene XVIII. From those reliefs
he culled a wide repertory of rhetorical poses and iconographical motifs of
Roman soldiery. The familiar figures of *adlocutio* on the Column of Trajan and
on the *Arch of Constantine are transposed in the scene of Constantine's oration
in the *Vision of the True Cross* in the Sala di Costantino. In the fresco of the
Battle of the Milvian Bridge, the figure of Constantine on horseback and his
charging soldiers are modeled on the emperor and his troops attacking the Dacians in the Trajanic frieze on the Arch of Constantine. Another rich mine for
Late Imperial syntax was the corpus of Antonine mythological and battle sarcophagi, especially the latter, with their nervous rhythms, densely packed figures
and broken angular poses that hark back to the Pergamene Baroque. From them
he evolved an archaeologically correct yet dramatic narrative language, founded
on antique principles of movement and posture. His figures are robustly modeled
with a stony plasticity and arranged in a network of "interlocking action" that
evokes the entangled struggling figures, piled up and close to the plane, of
Roman sarcophagus reliefs.

Giulio's taste in collecting reflects a broader scope and a deeper sensibility
to the multiple facets of antiquity. In 1520 he purchased many of the antique
sculptures of the Giovanni *Ciampolini collection, which he later brought to
Mantua or offered to the Gonzaga. According to his will of 1524, he possessed
a substantial collection of antiquities, "marble and not marble, extant both in
the house and outside." An inventory of 1528 reveals his passion for large and
small antiquities of all media, including terracotta vases. Vasari, on his visit to
Mantua in 1541, observed that Giulio's house contained "many antiquities
brought from Rome and others received from the Duke [Federigo]." An authority also on antique medals and engraved gems, he made drawings, known
through sixteenth-century engravings, of many antique cameos.

Giulio's Mantuan paintings and stuccos disclose a discriminating response to
antiquities of diverse styles and media. The fresco of the *Marriage Feast of
Cupid and Psyche* in the Sala di Psiche, Palazzo del Te (1527–28), is a key
example; the poses of at least half of the twenty-odd figures are taken from
motifs and conventions of large- and small-scale antiquities, accessible or known

through casts to Giulio. The sources include the statues in the *Uffizi of the foot-clapping satyr with cymbals and the *Bacchus* leaning on a Satyr, the widely known *British Museum sarcophagus of a Bacchic procession, Roman state reliefs and sarcophagi of *victimarii,* a *Campana Relief of the *Seasons,* *Arretine vase reliefs of lovers and the *Gemma Augustea. In the Sala degli Stucchi (Palazzo del Te), the continuous double stucco frieze of an imperial triumph appears more pristinely classical than its source, the Column of Trajan. In the Sala di Troia in the Palazzo Ducale, his undulating cyclorama of *Iliad* episodes (1538–39) contrasts with his earlier sculpturesque treatment of the battle scene in the Sala di Costantino: the struggle for Patroklos's corpse is a poignant linear compression of the central figures of the Ciampolini frieze of a battle between Romans and Gauls (in the same room). In the salon frescoes of his house, the Casa Pippi, he celebrates the theme of *romanitas* in quoting figures of Securitas, Annona and Ceres from reverses of Neronian coins.

As an architect, Giulio proved to be even more versatile and innovative. Though he studied ruins and plans of ancient buildings, the effects he sought were primarily expressive. For the massive rustication that animates the façade of the Palazzo Maccarani (ca. 1520) in Rome and overflows the portal and pilasters of its lower story, he turned to ancient utilitarian structures, such as the *Porta Maggiore. In Mantua he built sumptuous villas and palaces for Federigo and renovated the Cathedral of Mantua and the abbey church of San Benedetto Po for Cardinal Ercole Gonzaga. His most brilliant achievement was the Palazzo del Te, a *villa suburbana* (ca. 1525–34) on the outskirts of Mantua, which widely influenced later sixteenth-century architects and Baroque ceiling painters. There, he invested elegant classical forms with startling new tensions and ambivalent functions, by introducing diverse levels of reality, endless *bizzarrie* and ingenious motifs, like the slipping triglyphs and massive keystones, and contrasting smooth wall surfaces with rough, undressed stone blocks. In this villa and in the south façade of the Cortile della Cavallerizza of the Palazzo Ducale, clashes between finished and unfinished forms and between load-bearing and decorative classical elements produce a restless, unclassical effect that has been interpreted as Giulio's expression of dynamic conflict, embodied in much of Mannerist architecture.

Recently, it has been reappraised as the product of sophisticated wit and playfulness, grounded in classical vocabulary yet calculated to amuse, delight, deceive or dismay the viewer. Giulio's archaeological learning, variety of invention and caprice led Aretino justly to characterize his art as "antiquely modern and modernly antique."

BIBLIOGRAPHY

+F. Hartt, *Giulio Romano,* 1–2 (New Haven, CT, 1958); E. H. Gombrich, "The Style 'all'antica': Imitation and Assimilation," *Norm and Form* (London, 1971), 122–28; T. Yuen, "Giulio Romano, Giovanni da Udine, and Raphael: Some Influences of the Minor

Arts in Antiquity," *JWarb* 29 (1979), 262–72; +E. H. Gombrich et al., *Giulio Romano* (Milan, 1989), 227–43.

TOBY YUEN

GIUSTINIANI, VINCENZO (1564–1637). Italian marquis, patron of artists (e.g., Caravaggio) and collector of antiquities.

The son of a Genoese banker, Giustiniani used his enormous wealth to assemble the largest collection of ancient statuary in Rome in his time. He displayed his vast array of statues, portrait busts, puteals and sarcophagi in his villa near S. Luigi dei Francesi, in another villa near S. Giovanni in Laterano and in his public garden. The sculptures were made famous by an illustrated catalog sponsored by Vincenzo and published in two volumes (*Galleria Giustiniani*, 1628 and 1631) and by the lavish praises of *Sandrart, who was an intimate friend of the family.

The collection was important for its wide repertory of subjects and themes,

Relief of a *Sacrifice*, from the Giustiniani collection, Rome, engraving from *Galleria Giustiniani* (1628–31). (Deutsches Archäologisches Institut, Rome. Inst. Neg. 1931.1400.)

though there were relatively few pieces of great quality. Most notable were the *Vestal Virgin (Hestia Giustiniani)*; a *Resting Faun* of Praxitelean type; a *Pudicitia;* a *Caryatid;* and a *Minerva.* The latter, reportedly found near the church of S. Maria sopra Minerva (or, according to an alternative version, near the *Temple of Minerva Medica), was said to be so revered by the Giustiniani and by all the youth of Rome that they would stop periodically to kiss the statue's hand. The Giustiniani *Minerva* was acquired from the family much later by Lucien Bonaparte, the Prince of *Canino, who sold it, in turn, to the pope to be displayed in the *Vatican. Many portrait busts went to Cardinal Alessandro Albani (*Albani family) and subsequently to the *Capitoline Museums, while still others (e.g., the *Vestal Virgin; Resting Faun*) were acquired by the *Torlonia family. The overall contents of the collection are known from an inventory drawn up on 3 February 1638 after Vincenzo's death.

BIBLIOGRAPHY

R. Lanciani, "Sculture antiche del palazzo Giustiniani," *BullComm* 37 (1904), 3–66; 38 (1905), 3–61; +L. Huetter, "Il Palazzo Giustiniani," *Capitolium* 5 (1929), 606–16; C. Gasparri, "Materiali per servire allo studio del Museo Torlonia di scultura antica," *MemLinc* 377 (1980), ser. 8, 24.2; Haskell—Penny, 26, 269–70.

MARJON VAN DER MEULEN

GJERSTAD, EINAR (1897–1988). Swedish archaeologist.

Born in Örebro, Einar Gjerstad received his doctorate at Uppsala in 1926. He took part in excavations at *Asine and on *Cyprus (1923–24) before becoming director of the *Swedish Cyprus Expedition (1927–31). Because of the important results of the expedition and the authoritative program of research and publication, Gjerstad became known as the "father of Cypriot archaeology." Later, from his excavations in the *Forum Romanum, Gjerstad proposed a revised (and highly controversial) chronology for the Iron Age in Rome, shifting the foundation date of the city from 753 B.C. to ca. 575 B.C.

Gjerstad was director of the *Swedish Institute in Rome (1935–40) and a member of numerous international honorary bodies (e.g., the Istituto di Studi Etruschi, the British Academy). He served as professor of classical archaeology and ancient history at the University of Lund from 1940 to 1972.

BIBLIOGRAPHY

+*The Swedish Cyprus Expedition,* 1–4 (Stockholm, 1934–72); +*Early Rome,* 1–6. (Lund, 1953–73); P. G. Gierow, "Einar Gjerstad," *Vetenskapssocietetens i Lund Årsbok* (1988), 171–76.

INGRID E. M. EDLUND

GLANON (GLANUM). Site 1km south of St-Rémy-de-Provence, occupied since very early times, with important Hellenistic and Roman phases, mentioned by Ptolemy and included in the *Tabula Peutingeriana.

Excavations, begun in 1921 under the direction of Henri Rolland, have uncovered Celtic and Roman sculptures, remains of Hellenistic houses of the Delian type and Roman baths, temples and a forum. Many of the finds from the excavations are housed in the Hôtel de Sade in St-Rémy. Glanum's greatest period of prosperity was the Augustan age; it was abandoned after the Germanic invasion of ca. A.D. 270. A few buildings were erected on the site in the Middle Ages. At the entrance to the Augustan town are an arch (*Arch at St-Remy) and a cenotaph (*Monument of the Julii); only these famous "Antiques" stood above ground when the modern excavations began. They were much admired and frequently described by antiquarians and reproduced by artists from the seventeenth century on.

BIBLIOGRAPHY

+H. Rolland, *Fouilles de Glanum, 1947–1956, Gallia* Suppl. 11 (Paris, 1958); +Idem, *Glanum, Saint Rémy de Provence* (Paris, 1960); G.-C. Picard, "Glanum et les origines de l'art romano-provençal," *Gallia* 21 (1963), 111–24; 22 (1964), 1–21; F. Salviat, *Glanum,* 2nd ed. (Paris, 1979).

FRED S. KLEINER

GLYPTICS. The practice of cutting gems, whether by engraving in intaglio or by carving in relief, as with cameos.

Classical gems were prized during the Middle Ages and were collected to adorn a variety of objects—reliquaries, crosses, book covers, rings; the subject matter of the gem could be an ancient portrait (as on the cameo of Augustus on the ninth-century Cross of Lothair at Aachen) or a mythological theme (as on a seal with Apollo used by the twelfth-century bishop Henry of Bayeaux) and thus sometimes totally inappropriate for the Christian context in which they most frequently appear; the users were evidently not disturbed by the alien subject matter.

Spectacular collections of ancient gems were assembled as early as the fifteenth century by Pope *Paul II and by Lorenzo de Medici (*Medici family) and in the sixteenth century by the *Gonzaga family. But little research was done on glyptics before the seventeenth century. Enea *Vico issued three large engraved sheets before his death (ca. 1570), and these were picked up and reworked by the French engineer P. Thomassin in thirty-three small plates at the beginning of the seventeenth century. Vico gave no information about the gems and, in fact, rarely gave the outline of the stone around the images, which sometimes got jumbled together. F. *Orsini included gems, along with coins and marbles, as sources for *portrait iconography, in his *Illustrium imagines* (1570), of which an expanded edition was issued in 1606 by J. Faber, with high-quality illustrations by T. Galle. Orsini was sometimes deceived by forgeries, and his interest in gems was limited to portraits. Rings and ring stones were studied by the physician A. Le Pois (*Discours sur les médailles et graveurs antiques, principalement romaines,* Paris, 1579) and by the Antwerp antiquarian and collector Abraham Gorlaeus (*Dactyliotheca,* Delft, 1601).

What would have been the finest of books on ancient gems in the early seventeenth century—a volume planned by P. P. *Rubens and N. C. *Peiresc—

was never completed. They intended to assemble a corpus of all the most famous cameos of Europe, including the *Gemma Augustea and the *Gemma Tiberiana (rediscovered by Peiresc in 1620), the *Great Cameo of The Hague, the *Rubens Vase and a number of other items from Rubens's personal collection and probably the cameo glass *Portland Vase. With illustrations by Rubens (condition and actual size of the stones were indicated) and notes on coloring and iconography by Peiresc, the work would have been a landmark in scholarship. The illustrations were later utilized by Albert *Rubens, whose dissertations on the Gemma Augustea and Gemma Tiberiana were published in 1665. Also unpublished was a group of engraved plates of some 2,000 gems collected in Italy by Louis Chaduc of Auvergne (d. 1638). The most influential glyptics publication of the century was Le Gemme antiche figurate, a two-volume work annotated by Leonardo *Agostini with assistance from G. P. *Bellori. The second enlarged edition (1686) contained 265 engravings of gems, almost all antique. P. A. *Maffei expanded the work still further in a four-volume edition (1707–9).

The eighteenth century was a period of enormous interest in collecting and studying carved gems. De La *Chausse opened the period with his own Le Gemme antiche figurate (Rome, 1700), considered a relatively superficial work, with engravings by *Bartoli that showed all the stones in similar borders in a similar style with a similar size (not actual size). Soon afterward, Elisabeth Sophia *Cheron published her anthology of gems in French collections, controversial because she had made the gems look like paintings, with parts omitted or added in an arbitrary way. The leading collector and scholar of gems in the first half of the eighteenth century was Baron von *Stosch, whose Gemmae antiquae caelatae of 1724 was important for its focus on seventy gems with artist's signatures and for its low percentage of forgeries. Stosch's own collection of gems was published after his death in a systematic fashion by *Winckelmann. The Italian engraver and dealer Pier Leone Ghezzi (1674–1755) has left behind two caricature drawings showing Stosch within the circle of his friends in Rome, the later of which is labeled "Congresso de migliori Antiquarij di Roma" (Congress of the Better Antiquaries of Rome; 1728, Vatican Museums). Included in the drawings are Francesco *Ficoroni, whose gems were later published by Nicolao Galeotti, and Francesco Valesio, who helped Stosch compile his signed gems.

*Gori's publications of gems in Florentine and other collections belong to this period (Museum Florentinum . . . Gemmae antiquae ex thesauro Mediceo et privatorum dactyliothecis Florentiae, 1731–32; Museum Cortonense, 1750; his Thesaurus gemmarum antiquarum astriferarum of 1750 deals with gems of astrological significance). Though Gori is criticized for publishing many forgeries from Florentine collections, he is nonetheless recognized for emphasizing the relatively ignored category of Etruscan gems. Somewhat of a cause célèbre was his opinion about an Etruscan carnelian scarab showing the myth of the Seven Against Thebes that belonged to Baron von Stosch (the "Stosch'scher Stein," now in Berlin). The scene, with five heroes, much discussed at the *Accademia

Etrusca, was correctly analyzed by Gori as having Etruscan inscriptions. (Stosch thought they were Archaic Greek.)

An enduring work on glyptics was published in Paris by P. J. Mariette in his two-volume *Traité des pierres gravées* (1750), still cited in modern bibliographies. The first volume includes an introduction to the subject, discussions of materials and technique and a full bibliography on the subject, along with a discussion of modern gem engraving, useful for the perennial problem of sorting out authentic ancient stones. The second volume contains plates (not so highly regarded, since the gems are rendered in the prevailing Rococo style). The gem engraver J.-L. Natter discussed the technique of the ancients in his *Traité de la methode de graver en pierres fines* (1754); he and a host of other artists created gems in the classical style, sometimes signing their names in Greek. The problem of forgeries continued to be enormous, as modern artists also signed ancient stones.

The history of glyptic publications in the ensuing period is punctuated by the numerous catalogs of collections, which made more and more material accessible and which evolved a format for presenting individual pieces in a systematic way. The chain of publications stretches from Galeotti's *Museum Odescalchum* (1751/52) and *Eckhel's treatment of the imperial Hapsburg collections in Vienna (1788) to the catalogs of the gems in the *British Museum (A. H. Smith, *A Catalogue of Engraved Gems in the British Museum,* with revisions by A. S. Murray, 1888) and *Babelon's magisterial work on the cameos of the Bibliothèque Nationale (*Catalogue des camées antiques et modernes de la Bibliothèque Nationale,* Paris, 1897).

An important aid to the study and appreciation of gems in the eighteenth and nineteenth centuries was the usage of casts, circulated in small groups or accumulated in enormous commercial stocks, such as that made by James *Tassie in London, published by R. E. *Raspe (1791). The number of casts of ancient and modern gems cataloged by Raspe and available to Tassie's customers ran to 15,833. The idea of the *dactyliotheca,* the collection of impressions of gems, was pioneered by Philipp Daniel Lippert (1702–85), who published a series of texts sold along with the casts, beginning in 1755. The impressions provided the student or scholar with a precise image that far surpassed the engravings in previous publications, subject as they were to the vagaries of prevailing styles in art. The advent of photography in the second half of the nineteenth century had similar advantages.

The evolution of glyptics into a modern, scientific pursuit reached its culmination with the study of Adolf *Furtwängler, *Die Antiken Gemmen,* published in three volumes in 1900. Illustrating and cataloging hundreds of gems in actual size by photography, Furtwängler dealt with the chronological development of glyptics in antiquity, including sections on the Near East and the then-novel "Mycenaean" material, as well as Greek, Roman and Etruscan gems presented by period and style. His thorough review of publications on gems before 1900 adds to the value of the work. A later, comprehensive treatment in English in the tradition of Furtwängler is the standard *Engraved Gems of the Greeks, Romans and Etruscans* by G.M.A. Richter (2 vols., London, 1968–71).

Many branches of glyptic studies have developed in the twentieth century. The numerous publications by J. Boardman and others have resulted in a codification of the study of the Greek material; Boardman's *Greek Gems and Finger Rings, Early Bronze Age to Late Classical* (1970) catalogs and illustrates over 1,000 gems, adding in a number of color plates. Engraved seals of the Aegean Bronze Age constitute a special category that was first observed in 1791 (one example was cataloged by *Raspe for Tassie). In 1843 Ludwig *Ross noted early gems on the Greek islands ("Island Gems"), especially *Melos, but it was not until the uncovering of Mycenaean and Minoan civilization by *Schliemann and *Evans that scholars began to understand the context of the pieces. Evans was a passionate collector of seals on Crete from 1894, and his searches eventually led him to the excavation of Knossos. (His superb collection of gems is in the *Ashmolean Museum.) He published numerous gems in his volumes on the Palace of Minos at Knossos. In modern scholarship the seals have been cataloged in the great corpus launched by F. *Matz, *Corpus der minoischen und mykenischen Siegel* (begun 1964). Etruscan gems have received their due from P. Zazoff (*Etruskische Skarabaen,* 1968), while Roman portrait gems of the Republic have been studied by M.-L. Vollenweider. Among her many contributions to glyptic studies is *Die Porträtgemmen der römischen Republik,* 1972–74. W.-R. Megaw produced a monograph on Roman Imperial cameos, *Kameen von Augustus bis Alexander Severus* (1987). Numerous superb catalogs have been produced as a wide variety of international scholars working on antiquity and later art-historical periods have given attention to the discipline.

BIBLIOGRAPHY

+A. Furtwängler, *Die Antiken Gemmen* (Vienna, 1900; repr. 1964–65), I, 402–35; +G.M.A. Richter, *Engraved Gems of the Greeks, Etruscans and Romans* (London, 1968–71), 20–23; P. Zazoff, *Gemmensammler und Gemmenforscher: von einer noblen Passion zur Wissenschaft* (Munich, 1983); M. Henig, *Classical Gems, Ancient and Modern Intaglios and Cameos in the Fitzwilliam Museum, Cambridge* (Cambridge, 1994), xiii–xxiii.

GLYPTOTHEK, Munich. An important German museum of Greek and Roman statuary.

The Glyptothek was the brainchild of King *Ludwig I of Bavaria, who financed both the building itself and the purchase of most of its holdings. The young crown prince became enthralled with ancient sculpture on a trip to Rome in the winter of 1804–5. During the following quarter century, he succeeded in acquiring a truly remarkable collection.

The earliest phase of collecting (until 1810) consisted of a few cautious purchases made on Ludwig's behalf by Friedrich Müller, a poet and painter, and Georg Dillis, Ludwig's gallery inspector, both residents in Rome. In 1810, Johann Martin von *Wagner, a painter and sculptor with a good eye both for quality and for authenticity, began to act as Ludwig's agent in Rome. Ludwig's letters to Rome of this period betray relentless impatience for the acquisition of "extraordinarily beautiful" antiquities. During the following few years Wagner arranged many important purchases for the Glyptothek, including a Medusa head from the Rondanini collection (Roman after a Pheidian original) and the *Boy Strangling a Goose* from the Braschi collection (Roman after a third-century B.C. original).

Ludwig prevailed upon Wagner to travel to Greece in 1812 in order to act as his agent at the auction of sculptures recently excavated at the sanctuary of Aphaia at *Aigina (ca. 500–490 B.C.). Although Wagner was in quarantine on the day of the auction, even worse confusion and misfortune befell his competitors, and he was able to finalize a contract for the purchase of the Aigina sculptures. The *Barberini *Faun* (ca. 220 B.C.), considered by both the crown prince and his agent to be the most desirable piece in Rome, was acquired in the summer of 1813. Wagner's activities as Ludwig's agent continued until 1815, when he arranged for the purchase of several pieces from the collection of Cardinal Albani (*Albani family).

The construction of the museum building designed by Leo von *Klenze began in 1816. No expense was spared in carrying out the elaborate plans for the museum; this left little capital for purchases. Furthermore, only new purchases that would serve Klenze's plan for the arrangement and content of rooms were considered acceptable. Neoclassical in style, the Glyptothek was richly outfitted with exterior sculpture and interior stucco work. Two rooms reserved as reception halls were frescoed by Peter von Cornelius with scenes of the Trojan War and deeds of the Olympian gods.

When the Glyptothek opened as a public museum in 1830, there were still some lacunae in the collection vis-à-vis Klenze's conception, especially in the Early Greek room. The *Apollo* from Tenea (560–550 B.C.; purchased in 1853) and the Munich *Kouros* (540–530 B.C.; purchased in 1919) admirably filled the gap. The acquisition of a group of Assyrian reliefs occasioned the construction in 1864 of an additional exhibition room in the interior courtyard of the museum. Also in 1864 a chair in archaeology was established at the university in Munich. Heinrich *Brunn, the first scholar to occupy the chair, was contacted by Ludwig in 1867 to write a catalog of the collection (published 1868) and a few years later became director of the Glyptothek. Adolf *Furtwängler, who took the Munich chair in archaeology and the directorship of the Glyptothek in 1894, published a new catalog of the collection in 1900.

The Bayerischer Verein der Kunstfreunde (Bavarian Society of Friends of Art), founded in 1905, lent the Glyptothek some important pieces that later came into the possession of the museum following the dissolution of the association. The museum building was transferred to the Bavarian state in 1918. The sculptures that had belonged to Ludwig became the property of the Bavarian state in 1923. In 1935, the directorship of the Glyptothek was separated from the university chair in archaeology.

The most spectacular events of the twentieth century were the acquisition and subsequent loss of the Massimi-Lancelotti *Diskobolos* (now in the *Terme Museum, Rome). The statue, which Ludwig had coveted but had not succeeded in obtaining, was purchased in 1938 by the German government from the heirs of Elisabeth Aldobrandini-Lancelotti at a very high price. It was exhibited in the Glyptothek for a year before it was removed for safekeeping at the outbreak of World War II (autumn 1939). The American occupation forces, believing that the statue had come into German hands through Hitler's personal and political connections with the Italian Fascist regime, turned the *Diskobolos* over to the Italian government in 1948.

Most of the collection survived the war, but the museum building was virtually destroyed. Between 1947 and 1956, the building was restored according to Klenze's original plans (without the Assyrian room of 1864). The opulent interiors of the nineteenth-century building were not re-created. Instead, simple architectural members articulate the interior of the reconstructed museum (work carried out 1967–71). The Glyptothek reopened to the public in 1972. The Verein der Freunde und Förderer der Glyptothek und der Antikensammlungen (Society of Friends and Patrons of the Glyptothek and the Antikensammlungen) supports public programs, conservation work and new acquisitions. A new scholarly catalog of the collection (ed. Klaus Vierneisel) began publication in 1979 (nine volumes projected).

BIBLIOGRAPHY

H. Diepolder, s.v. "Monaco," *EAA* 5 (1963), 146–49; D. Ohly, *Glyptothek München: Griechische und römische Skulpturen,* 4th ed. (Munich, 1977); K. Vierneisel—G. Leinz, eds., *Glyptothek München 1830–1980: Jubiläumsausstellung zur Entstehungs- und Baugeschichte* (Munich, 1980).

ELIZABETH C. TEVIOTDALE

GNATHIA (EGNATIA). Italic and Roman site on the east coast of Apulia, Italy.

Gnathia reveals habitation in the Bronze and Iron ages and then, development as a city of the Messapian culture in the fourth–third centuries B.C. In this period, the city was heavily fortified, and the tombs outside the city were filled with fine grave goods. Under the Romans, Gnathia prospered from its location on the road built by Trajan (A.D. 109) to link Rome with Brundisium. In Early Christian times the city had a bishopric; it was destroyed under unknown circumstances at the beginning of the Middle Ages.

Gnathia is known, above all, for the elegant pottery that was first discovered in its tombs beginning with excavation in 1848. "Gnathia ware" is a black gloss type of pottery (fourth–early third centuries B.C.) with delicate overpainting of vine and ivy sprigs in added colors of white, yellow and red; the vessels are small and often for the symposium. Although it has long been recognized that there were other significant workshops producing the pottery (e.g., at Taranto, Canosa), Gnathia ware has continued to be called by the name of the site where it was first identified.

*Mommsen visited Gnathia in the nineteenth century and saw a number of tombs, most of which are now covered over. Systematic excavations were begun in 1912 under the Superintendency of Antiquities for Puglia and have continued intermittently through the century. Most of the visible monumental remains are of the Roman period.

BIBLIOGRAPHY

C. Drago, s.v. "Gnathia," *EAA* 3 (1960), 966–71; +J. R. Green, *Gnathia Pottery in the Akademisches Kunstmuseum Bonn* (Mainz, 1976).

GOETHE, JOHANN WOLFGANG VON (1749–1832). The most distinguished German man of letters and ardent student of antiquity.

ut his life, Goethe was deeply committed to a faith in the compelling and shaping power of classical civilization. Although introduced in 1765–68, through his teacher A. F. Oeser (1717–99) in Leipzig, to the tenets of *Winckelmann's admiration of Greek culture, as well as *Lessing's *Laokoon* (1766), and sharing his father's respect for the ancient world, he was not drawn fully into the magnetism of the Greek universe of natural, aesthetic and moral reflection until his stay in Rome and Southern Italy in 1786–88. Familiar from early youth and through visits to the celebrated Electoral collection of casts at Mannheim (1769, 1771) with reproductions of such masterpieces as the Uffizi *Dancing Faun* and parts of the *Laocoon* Group, Goethe recalls in his autobiography, *Dichtung und Wahrheit* (1809f.), early impressions of the *Belvedere *Apollo,* the *Dying Trumpeter,* the Prado *Castor and Pollux* and a Corinthian capital. He acquired in his native Frankfurt reproductions of the heads of Laocoon and his sons, the daughters from the *Niobe* Group and the so-called head of *Sappho.* In Weimar, where he lived as a court official from 1775 to his death, he added to his collection the bust of the Belvedere *Apollo* and other important pieces.

His encomium in J. K. Lavater's *Physiognomische Fragmente* (1774) of the blind poet suggests that he knew a reproduction of the Naples *Homer.* A prose version of *Iphigenia* (1779) and its subsequent poetic recasting, hymnic fragments such as "Prometheus" (1774) and a number of poems of classical design testify to his fascination with Greek mythological topics during the first years at Weimar. The overwhelming encounter in Rome with the monuments of classical art was the experience that determined his unswerving preoccupation with the objects and substance of Greek culture: his reflections on aesthetic theory, his extensive collections of major and minor Greek sculpture, coins, cameos, seals and terracottas. In Rome, with a pronounced distaste for everything Baroque and more impressed by the majestic size than the design, Goethe studied the *Colosseum and the ruins of the imperial palaces on the *Palatine Hill. The *Pantheon gave him a first impression of the "greatness" of classical architecture. He returned frequently to the *Pyramid of Cestius and the *Temple of Vesta, having on his way to Rome admired the aqueduct of Spoleto, the amphitheater in *Verona and the temple of Minerva at Assisi, the first wholly preserved classical monument he saw. Among the eminent pieces of sculpture, he was most drawn to the Belvedere *Apollo*, the Ludovisi *Juno*, the *Zeus* of Otricoli, the Rondanini *Medusa*, the Giustiniani *Minerva* (*Giustiniani, Vincenzo), the *Minerva* from Velletri, the *Medici *Venus* and the Praxitelean *Venus* of *Arles, as well as the *Quirinal *Horse Tamers*.

The objects he admired in Italy were, with few exceptions, Roman copies. Greek originals he found only in seals and cameos and, especially, in coins— of which the collection of Prince Torremuzza in Palermo offered incomparable historical documents. Compared with our present knowledge of the ancient world, Goethe's was severely limited: he was familiar only with parts of Italy and Sicily and a few classical remains in the Rhine, Main and Mosel regions of Germany (e.g., the *Igel Monument).

Near Naples he saw the early Doric temple at *Paestum, which was for him the first evidence of Archaic style. In Sicily he visited Girgenti (*Akragas), *Segesta, the remains of the theater at Taormina and, on his return trip to Rome, what had at the time been uncovered of the ruins of *Pompeii and *Herculaneum and the treasures exhibited at the museum of Charles III at Portici, "the alpha and omega of all collections of antiquities" (1 June 1787). The Medici *Venus* in Florence is the last work he praised enthusiastically before returning to Weimar in 1788. Also during these years (1786–87) his friend *Tischbein created the splendid image of *Goethe in the Campagna*, a portrait that evokes movingly the poet's reverence for the ruins of antiquity.

The deep impression made by the figures of *Michelangelo intensified, in turn, his fascination with the classical rendering of the human body. Of the most lasting consequence were a few drawings of the *Parthenon sculptures, which in 1788 Sir Richard Worthley (1751–1805) showed him in Rome—"the extreme frontier of human artistic achievement"; they later sustained his interest in the published accounts of the *Elgin marbles and prepared him in 1812 and 1817– 18 for the marble figures from the temple at *Aigina, newly brought to Munich, and the Amazon frieze of the temple of Apollo at *Bassai, of which he saw the drawings in the original size by the young painter Louise Seidler (1786–1866). In 1819 he received a cast of the horse head from the east pediment of the Parthenon.

A project to compile a comprehensive work on Italian life and art, with the assistance of the Swiss archaeologist Heinrich Meyer (1759–1832), was not realized; the account of his *Italian Journey,* enriched and elaborated in retrospect, was published in 1816.

His attachment to classical values became the foundation and thrust of his subsequent life. In a periodical, *Propyläen* (1798–1800), he reiterated, with the help of Meyer (and in severe opposition to the emerging Romantic sensibility), his belief in an "objective" aesthetic theory; here Goethe published (1798) his long-delayed essay on "Laocoon" and a number of more general programmatic pieces reflecting his faith, that of Schiller (1759–1805) and of the small group of the "Weimar Friends of Art," in nonsubjective non-Romantic art. From 1800–05, he (and Meyer) commented in the same critical spirit on works submitted by young German artists for an annual exhibition in Weimar; none of these efforts had a significant effect on contemporary art. His emphasis upon a clear differentiation among the several genres of art was asserted once more in the terms he set for the Weimar Friends of Art Prize Competition of 1803. Two years later he summarized in a magisterial essay the importance for himself and his age of Winckelmann's exemplary role as an archaeologist and a human being.

In 1797, Meyer had supplied Goethe with a copy of the celebrated fresco of the *Aldobrandini *Wedding,* an example of the "chromatic delicacy" of the ancients to which he returned in later comments. Two of his most important essays on classical art with archaeological implications deal with the reconstruction of Polygnotos's paintings (1803) and those described by Philostratos (1818). Other studies offer interpretations of a grave near *Cumae (1812), with the three-part relief of a dancer's tomb, and Myron's *Cow* (1818). In his later journal, *Kunst und Alterthum* (1816–32), in miscellaneous reviews and in his extensive correspondence, Goethe continued to demonstrate to the end of his life an undiminished interest in reproductions of classical works and the scholarly discourse on archaeological topics. The chief commentaries on classical texts are his review of the translation of the poems of Lucretius by K. L. von Knebel (1822); his thoughts on Euripides' *Phaethon* (1823–27), *Kyklops* (1824) and *Bacchae* (1827); and his observations on the apotheosis of Homer (1827) and the *Poetics* of Aristotle (1827). His library contained the most important European reference works on antiquity, and he remained in constant touch with distinguished scholars in the fields of archaeology and philology, with F. A. *Wolf, A. Hirt (1759–1839), C. W. Coudray (1775–1845), G. Hermann (1772–1848), B. G. Niebuhr (1776–1831) and J. H. Voss (1751–1826).

While Goethe was never a professional archaeologist, his knowledge of historical context and specific detail was impressive, his sensual relationship to the material was exceptionally keen and his judgment was never sentimental, nostalgic or dogmatic. He kept far from the rhetoric of ideal beauty or harmony; Greek life and art offered no abstract or speculative paradigm but inexhaustible evidence of a robust faith in the coherence and productivity of a natural universe.

To his European contemporaries Goethe seemed, at times, part of a Romantic sensibility; he himself remained, in his discursive writings as well as his creative literary work, deeply, if critically, attached to classical convictions and forms. His *Römische Elegien,* written shortly after his return from Rome, was followed by groups of splendid elegiac poems ("Alexis und Dora," "Euphrosyne," "Amyntas," "Die Metamorphose der Pflanzen," etc.); he translated passages of Homer and Pindar, Sophokles and Euripides, Phaidros's and Aesop's *Fables,*

Horace and Ovid. Certain of his most accomplished plays—*Torquato Tasso* (1790); *Achilleis* (1798); *Die Natürliche Tochter* (1804); *Pandora* (1810); *Des Epimenides Erwachen* (1815)—show strong and elegant classicist features; and parts of the second *Faust*, especially the "Klassische Walpurgisnacht" and the Helena episode, offer the richest evidence of Goethe's profound understanding of the ancient heritage reflected, modified but indispensable, in a modern consciousness.

BIBLIOGRAPHY

C. Praschniker, "Goethe als Archäologe," *Archaiologike Ephemeris* (1937), 423–32; H. Trevelyan, *Goethe and the Greeks* (Cambridge, 1941); M. Wegner, *Goethes Anschauung antiker Kunst* (Berlin, 1944); E. Grumach, *Goethe und die Antike* 1–2 (Potsdam, 1949); S. Schulze, *Goethe und die Kunst* (Stuttgart, 1994).

VICTOR LANGE

GÖLBAŞI. See TRYSA.

GOLDEN HOUSE OF NERO. See DOMUS AUREA.

GOLDMAN, HETTY (1881–1972). American archaeologist.

One of the first female archaeologists to excavate in Greece, Goldman was also an early pioneer in the study of the Greek Bronze Age. Her excavation at Eutresis in Boeotia has become a benchmark in the study of the Early Bronze Age, and the resulting publication, *Excavations at Eutresis in Boeotia* (1931), continues to serve as a model for archaeological publications. Besides her investigations at the sites of Halai and Kolophon, Goldman's other major achievement was the excavation of Tarsus, where the excavated material provides the best example of culture change from the Neolithic to the Islamic period in the southern Cilician plain.

As a Harvard Norton Fellow, Goldman worked at the *American School of Classical Studies in Athens. In 1936 she was appointed to a professorship at the Institute for Advanced Study, Princeton, the first woman awarded that honor. In 1966, she received the Gold Medal for Distinguished Archaeological Achievement from the *Archaeological Institute of America.

BIBLIOGRAPHY

S. Weinberg, ed., *The Aegean and the Near East, Studies Presented to Hetty Goldman* (Locust Valley, NY, 1956); *A Symposium in Memory of Hetty Goldman* (Princeton, NJ, 1974).

MICHAEL HOFF

GOLTZIUS (GOLTZ), HENDRIK (1558–1617). Netherlandish painter and engraver.

Goltzius traveled to Florence, Naples and Rome in 1590–91, following the tradition established by *Gossaert, van *Heemskerck and other northern artists of getting a proper education in Italy by viewing the remains of classical antiquities. While in Rome, Goltzius made a number of drawings of antiquities,

Portrait of *Claudius*, after Hubert Goltzius, *Icones imperatorum romanum* (1645).

of which some fifty-four have survived; this "Roman Portfolio," containing drawings of the *Laocoon, the *Belvedere *Torso,* the *Belvedere *Antinous,* the *"Cleopatra" and other statues, was sold to the emperor Rudolf II in 1612. Three splendid engravings based on the drawings—of the *Farnese *Hercules,* the *Belvedere *Apollo* and "*Hercules and Telephos*"—were issued shortly after Goltzius's death in 1617.

BIBLIOGRAPHY

E. K. J. Reznicek, *Die Zeichnungen von Hendrik Goltzius,* 1–2 (London, 1968–71); H. H. Brummer, *The Statue Court in the Vatican Belvedere* (Stockholm, 1970); S. Boorsch in Sheard, nos. 55, 100; *Porträtarchiv,* no. 16.

GOLTZIUS (GOLTZ), HUBERT (1526–83). Netherlandish painter, engraver, antiquarian and numismatist.

Early in his life Goltzius received an education in art and the classics from his father, Rüdiger, a painter originally from Würzburg. Goltzius subsequently entered the atelier of the painter Lambert *Lombard at Antwerp, where it is said that he copied many drawings of antiquities. His penchant for classical art certainly included coins, for in 1557 Goltzius published his *Vitae omnium fere imperatorum a C. Iulio Caesare usque ad Carolum V* (Antwerp). This was an iconographical encyclopedia in the Renaissance tradition based on images from the coin collections in Antwerp, in particular, the collections of the geographer Cornelius Grapheus. Goltzius dedicated this work to Philip II of Spain, who bestowed on him the honor of court historian and painter.

In 1558, under the advice and patronage of the amateur antiquarian Mark Laurin, Duke of Waterfliet, Goltzius began traveling throughout Europe with the purpose of inspecting all the major coin cabinets. After two years of travel, he settled in Brugge to arrange his voluminous notes and drawings. The publications that resulted from his studies became the standard references on numismatics until *Eckhel in the eighteenth century. These include *C. Iulius Caesar, ex antiquis numismatibus* (Brugge, 1560); *Fasti magistratuum et triumphorum Romanorum, ex antiquis tam numismatum quam marmorum monumentis restitutae* (Brugge, 1566); *Caesar Augustus et Tiberius, ex antiquis numismatibus* (Brugge, 1574); *Thesaurus rei antiquariae huberrimus ex antiquis tam numismatum quam marmorum inscriptionibus* (Antwerp, 1579). These works were republished in separate editions during the seventeenth century. The last edition was collectively published in 1708 under the title *Huberti Goltzii De re nummaria antiqua opera* (Antwerp).

Goltzius displayed a zeal for accuracy in his publications, directing the operations of a printing press installed in his house, as well as engraving the designs of the coins himself. Goltzius's works, however, like other numismatic publications of the period, include a large number of forgeries and, in some cases, wholly imaginary pieces, as well as unattributable inscriptions; thus, the criticisms leveled at Goltzius by Eckhel nearly 200 years later are justified. For the period in which he wrote, however, Goltzius, more than anyone else, expanded the popularity of antique coins and paved the way for the more exact science of numismatics.

BIBLIOGRAPHY

A. L. Millin, "Goltzius (Hubert)," *BU* 18 (1817), 34–36; F. A. J. van Hulst, *Hubert Goltzius* (Liège, 1846); E. Gregoire, "Goltzius (Hubert)," *NBG* 21 (1858), cols. 133–35; *Porträtarchiv*, no. 12.

MICHAEL HOFF

GONZAGA, CESARE (1536–75). Italian Renaissance prince and collector.

Cesare Gonzaga, Lord of Guastalla, Duke of Ariano and Prince of Molfetta, was the son of Ferrante Gonzaga, and, like his father, he served under the banner of Philip II of Spain. As brother-in-law of Carlo Borromeo, he had further access to people in high places and as the grandson of Isabella d*Este, he inherited that love of learning and collecting to which most of his efforts were devoted. His palace in Mantua (on the site of the present Accademia Virgiliana) served as the meeting place for the Accademia degli Invaghiti and housed a collection that was admired by *Vasari, who wrote of the "very beautiful antiquarium and studio full of ancient statues and heads." The contents of his celebrated medallion cabinet were once borrowed by a fellow collector, the Duke of Ferrara.

Six years before Vasari's visit, in 1560, Cesare was in Rome, where he met Bishop Gerolamo *Garimberto, with whom he kept up a lively correspondence that is now preserved in the Parma State Archives (Raccolta Manoscritti, Busta 112; Gonzaga di Guastalla 48[4]–49). As a friend, adviser and procurer, Garimberto kept Cesare abreast of all matters pertaining to their mutual interest in, and collecting of, antiquities. Cesare's holdings were described by Ulisse *Aldrovandi, and a substantial catalog also exists to document a total of some 156 objects, the preponderance of these being antique heads displayed on marble pedestals. None can now be identified, although, like Cesi (*Cesi family) and the Medici (*Medici family), Cesare owned a nearly lifesize *Pan and Apollo*. The inventory (Parma State Archives, Gonzaga di Guastalla, Busta 5) does not contain a separate entry, however, for the contents of the medallion cabinet, which was decorated with antique and *all'antica* statuettes and colonettes of various types of marble commissioned in Rome through Garimberto.

BIBLIOGRAPHY

D. Franchini et al., eds., *La Scienza a corte* (Rome, 1979), 188–92; C. M. Brown, "Major and Minor Collections of Antiquities in Documents of the Late 16th Century," *ArtB* 66 (1984), 496–507; Idem, with A. M. Lorenzoni, *"Our Accustomed Discourse on the Antique": Cesare Gonzaga and Gerolamo Garimberto, Two Renaissance Collectors of Greco-Roman Art* (New York, 1993).

CLIFFORD M. BROWN

GONZAGA FAMILY. Rulers of Mantua from 1328 until the extinction of the main branch of the family in 1628; a number of collateral branches had control of neighboring territories; thus in addition to Mantua itself, important cultural centers existed at Gazzuolo, Guastalla and Sabbioneta.

Although the ground was laid by LUIGI (1334–82) and by FRANCESCO I (1366–1407), only with GIAN FRANCESCO (1395–1444), first Marquis of Mantua, did the city-state become a major center for humanist studies and the Ducal Palace become its principal showcase. This trend was continued by his son and heir LUDOVICO (1412–78), who brought to Mantua the learned antiquarian painter Andrea *Mantegna. In 1461 Cristoforo Geremia sent to Ludovico four antique heads, including one of the emperor Hadrian.

There is little to suggest, however, that Ludovico's ambitions as a collector

of antiquities were as elevated as those of the second-born son Cardinal FRAN-
CESCO (1444–83). In 1472 the cardinal asked his father for the aid of Mantegna
so that the artist could examine with him his recently acquired cameos and
antique bronze heads. The inventory of his holdings, which rivaled, even if they
did not equal, that formed by his mentor, Pope *Paul II, catalogs no fewer than
1,250 medallions, 150 engraved gems and nearly 500 cameos. Few of the engraved gems can now be identified, although there are several notable exceptions, including the *Felix Gem in the *Ashmolean Museum, Oxford. The two
versions of the *Fall of Phaethon* cannot, however, be securely linked to any of
the existing gems. Bronze plaques after similar gems may preserve the features
of the celebrated *Julius Caesar* carnelian that had been bequeathed to Duke
Alfonso of Aragon.

The cardinal's collection of bronzes was bequeathed to his elder brother FED-
ERICO (1441–84), whose own collection contained a variety of objects, including "figures like that of Bacchus."

During the reign of FRANCESCO II (1441–84), his wife, Isabella d'*Este,
continued the family tradition, and this enriched heritage was passed on to their
firstborn son, FEDERICO II (1500–40), under whom Mantua was elevated to
the rank of a duchy. Under the direction of *Giulio Romano, a setting for the
antique and *all'antica* bronzes and marbles was provided both in the Gabinetto
di Cesare and in the Loggia di Marmi in the Appartamento di Troia complex
of the palace. The inventory of Federico II's Antiquarium in the Castello catalogs no fewer than 1,500 antique medallions.

In the 1570s, under GUGLIELMO (1538–87), the Loggia di Marmi was transformed into the Galleria dei Mesi. With the assistance of the Rome-based collector and antiquarian Gerolamo *Garimberto, the Mantuan collection was
significantly augmented by twenty-two imperial busts, various reliefs, including
one with the legend of *Jason and Medea,* and a number of statues, among them
two lifesize statues of *Muses.*

The adjacent Galleria della Mostra was built during the reign of VINCENZO
I (1562–1612), and at this time the *Mensa Isiaca* from the Pietro *Bembo collection (now in the Museo Egizio, Turin) came to Mantua together with the
Canossa collection, which included the *Madonna della Perla* of Giulio Romano
(Madrid, Prado) as well as the Hellenistic bronze *Praying Youth,* now in Berlin.
In 1587 the so-called *Gonzaga Cameo in the *Kunsthistorisches Museum, Vienna, was acquired from the same Flemish agent who had first offered this gem,
which had been stolen from the Shrine of the Three Kings in Cologne Cathedral,
to Cardinal Alessandro Farnese (*Farnese family). In 1603 Vincenzo purchased
thirty-two busts and statues from the Peranda collection in Rome at the cost of
an annuity of 300 scudi.

Under Cardinal Duke FERNANDO (1587–1626), the archaeological holdings
of the family were further augmented. Forty-two chests of statuary left Rome

for Mantua on 11 May 1613, followed by forty statues in 1618. What portions of the Gonzaga patrimony were left over after the sale to Charles II of England in 1627–28 were appropriated as the spoils of war by the imperial forces after the general sack of 1630. Although the bulk of the antiquities ended up in various collections, a number of ancient marbles from the Gonzaga collections can still be found in the Ducal Palace.

Of the collateral branches of the family, GIAN FRANCESCO of Gazzuolo (1445–96) owned many *all'antica* statuettes made by his sculptor *Antico, who then passed into the services of Bishop LUDOVICO (1458–1511). Ludovico assembled a modest number of originals at his court of Gazzuolo, but limited resources forced him to satisfy his desire for Roman busts through gesso casts of pieces in other collections.

The Lord of Guastalla, CESARE *GONZAGA, assembled a notable collection of some 156 pieces, in addition to antique medallions, with the aid of Garimberto. The Duke of Sabbioneta, VESPASIANO (1531–91), displayed numerous antique busts and statues obtained by his father during the Sack of Rome in 1527. These were set up between 1579 and 1584 in his Antiquarium, or Galleria degli Antichi, adjoining his pleasure palace, the Casino del Giardino. Thus, while the Ducal Palace in Mantua remained the principal display case for the Gonzaga family collection of antiquities, the buildings erected by the collateral branches nevertheless boasted sizable holdings.

BIBLIOGRAPHY

A. Luzio, "Contibuto alla storia delle suppellettili del Palazzo Ducale di Mantova: II-Le Collezioni di antichità acquistate a Roma e Venezia da' duchi Guglielmo e Vincenzo I," *Atti e Memorie dell'Accademia Virgiliana* (1913), 113–41; +G. Amadei—E. Marani, *I Gonzaga a Mantova* (Milan, 1975); D. Franchini et al., eds., *La Scienza a corte* (Rome, 1979); +D. Chambers—J. Martineau, eds., *Splendours of the Gonzaga* (Milan, 1981).

CLIFFORD M. BROWN

GOORLE, ABRAHAM VAN (GOIRLE; GORLAEUS; 1549–1608). Flemish magistrate, collector and numismatist.

Born in Antwerp, van Goorle moved to Utrecht in 1570 to become counselor to the Duke of Nieuwenaer, Stadholder of Utrecht, but had to leave for political reasons. After 1596 he resided in Delft, where he was visited by Buchelius and socialized with J. *Scaliger, Vorstius and Petrus Bertius. He owned a collection of coins and ancient rings. In a letter to Jacques Cools of 13 April 1601, van Goorle discussed selling his spectacular numismatic collection, which numbered 13,260 coins: 630 gold (100 Greek, 30 consular and 500 imperial); 7,400 silver (900 Greek, 1,500 consular and 5,000 imperial); 2,000 bronze; and 230 gold and 3,000 bronze and silver "duplicates." Queen *Christina acquired part of the collection, but the bulk went to Henry, Prince of Wales, who bequeathed them to Charles I; eventually they went into the Bodleian Library, Oxford. Van Goorle's *Thesaurus numismatum romanorum* was published in 1609 in Leiden shortly after his death. His *Paralipomena numismatum* also appeared posthumously.

Much less is known about his collection of ancient rings and gems. When Buchelius visited van Goorle in Utrecht in 1595, he saw a ring with a *Marsyas* (probably a copy of the "Seal of Nero" in the *Medici family collection). He also reported that the magistrate had imitations of ancient rings made; Scaliger confirmed this. In his *Dactyliotheca sive annulorum sigillarum,* which appeared in 1601 (Nuremberg), probably many of his own rings are illustrated. Together with the second volume, *Variarum gemmarum, quibus antiquitas insignando uti solita, sculptura,* it was republished by Jacob Gronovius (*Gronovius family) in 1695. Van Goorle was a correspondent of *Peiresc. The French scholar visited him in 1606 and made notes on several of his gems.

BIBLIOGRAPHY

C. Ruelens, in *Rubens Bulletijn* 22 (1885), 47; E. Babelon, *Traité de la numismatique* (Paris, 1901), 117–18; F. M. Jaeger, "Over David van Goorle as Atomist," *Oud-Holland,* 36 (1918), 220–28.

MARJON VAN DER MEULEN

GORDION. City in Phrygia (western Asia Minor) on the Sangarios River, ca. 100km southwest of Ankara.

First inhabited in the Early Bronze Age, Gordion was a provincial outpost of the Hittite Empire but came to prominence in the ninth and eighth centuries B.C. as the capital of the Phrygian Empire. Destroyed by the Kimmerian invasion of ca. 690 B.C., the city was resettled in the seventh or sixth centuries B.C. under Lydian protection. Gordion remained under Persian rule until the arrival of Alexander in 333 B.C., when tradition records that he cut the Gordian knot. In Hellenistic times the area was inhabited by the Galatians. By 189 B.C. a Roman contingent under Manlius Volso reported the city abandoned.

Investigations at Gordion were first carried out in 1900 by an Austrian expedition. A series of campaigns from 1950 to 1973 directed by Rodney S. Young for the University of Pennsylvania exposed large areas of the habitation mound and opened a number of tumulus burials in the nearby cemetery. A new field project was undertaken in 1988. Excavations at Gordion continue under the direction of G. K. Sams.

The Phrygian city consisted of a number of large structures, including a palace composed of parallel megara, surrounded by an impressive wall of cut stone masonry. Following the destruction attributed to the Kimmerian attack, the settlement was rebuilt with a similar plan.

On high ground to the northeast of the citadel and city were cemeteries. Most of the burials contained royalty or nobility and were covered by large tumuli; they range in date from early Phrygian to Hellenistic times. The largest tumulus, attributed to King Midas or his predecessor, covered a wooden structure and contained wooden furniture, numerous bronze vessels and ornaments.

BIBLIOGRAPHY

A. Körte—G. Körte, *Gordion, Jdl,* Erg. 5 (Berlin, 1904); R. S. Young, preliminary reports in *AJA* 59–72 (1955–68); Idem, *Three Great Early Tumuli,* Gordion Excavations Final Reports I, University Museum Monograph 43 (Philadelphia, 1981); L. E. Roller, *Nonverbal Graffiti, Dipinti and Stamps,* Gordion Special Studies I, University Museum Monograph 63 (Philadelphia, 1987); A. C. Gunter, *The Bronze Age,* Gordion Excavations Final Reports III, University Museum Monograph 71 (Philadelphia, 1991).

ANN C. GUNTER

GORI, ANTONIO FRANCESCO (1691–1757). Italian archaeologist, philologist, theologian; one of the founders of systematic Etruscan studies.

Born in Florence, Gori spent his life there but continually made excursions to other cities of Tuscany. Priest (from 1717) and prior of the Baptistery of S. Giovanni (from 1746), he was also professor of history at the Liceo of Florence. He was inspired in his early years by his teacher A. M. Salvini and by the example of the great Florentine archaeologist F. *Buonarroti to develop an interest in antiquities, especially inscriptions, coins, gems and objects of the minor

Etruscan gem (the "Stosch'scher Stein") with the story of the *Seven Against Thebes,* from the collection of Baron von Stosch, engraving from A. F. Gori, *Difesa dell'antico alfabeto de Toscani* (1742).

arts. His first important publication was on classical inscriptions, *Inscriptiones graecae et latinae in Etruriae urbibus extantes* (1727). Gori also had an interest in Christian antiquities (e.g., in ivory diptychs) and in Renaissance art history.

His greatest contributions to archaeology stem from his investigations of antiquity in his beloved Tuscany. In his *Museum florentinum,* a work that eventually reached ten volumes (1731–62), mostly edited by Gori himself, he presented a comprehensive treatment of collections in Florence and nearby cities (*Arezzo, *Cortona, *Chiusi, Montepulciano, Siena, *Perugia). The work, which embraced gems, coins, statues and portraits, many previously unpublished, created a sensation in Florence, and little attention was paid to its weaknesses, namely, the mediocre quality of some of the illustrations and the uncritical acceptance of some modern forgeries.

Gori's special attraction to Etruscan antiquities was pursued in his *Museum etruscum* (Florence, 1736–43), a three-volume work that established him as a leading figure in the *Etruscheria* of the eighteenth century. Among the works published were the *Chimera* of Arezzo, the *Arringatore* and the *"Idolino,"* all now in the *Florence Archaeological Museum. He also incurred the bitter resentment and enmity of Scipione *Maffei, whose claims in the Etruscan field were prior but whose publications had not been so splashy. Maffei criticized the priest Gori for his habit of seeing the gods and religion in every statue or object, and their disagreement over the Etruscan alphabet and language escalated into one of the famous quarrels of the era.

Gori was a founder of the Società Colombaria (Academia Columbaria; 1735), Florence's answer to the *Accademia Etrusca of Cortona. The rather informal sessions of the group gave opportunities for reports on new discoveries and for displays of antiquities. Other publications by Gori include *Monumentum sive columbarium libertorum et servorum Liviae Augustae et Caesarum Romae delectum* (1727), on the columbarium for the ash urns of the servants of Livia (*columbaria); *Thesaurus gemmarum antiquarum astriferarum* (1750), on ancient gems with astral symbolism; and *Museum cortonense* (1750), on the antiquities of Cortona.

BIBLIOGRAPHY
E. Gayot, "Gori, Antoine-Francois," *NBG* 21 (1858), cols. 293–96; M. Cristofani, *La Scoperta degli etruschi, Archeologia e antiquaria nel '700* (Rome, 1983); *Porträtarchiv,* no. 61.

GORTYN. Ancient capital of the Roman province Creta-Cyrenae, located in the Messara near modern Hagii Deka (*Crete).

Early explorers C. *Buondelmonti (1415), O. Belli (1586–87) and S. *Maffei (1700) cataloged the many columns and statues, buried ruins of Hagios Titos, "larger" and Pythion theaters and amphitheater. *Buondelmonti compared Gortyn in its grandeur to his own Florence. Statuary discovered under Turkish rule (mid-eighteenth–nineteenth centuries) was taken to England: reports name statues of the *Minotaur,* a large *Bull and Europa* and *Bacchus.* L. Thenon discovered and removed to Paris the first fragment of the famous law code (1857).

But it was not until the Italian F. *Halbherr and the German E. Fabricius came to Gortyn (1884) that the law code (also called the "Great Inscription," or "Queen of Inscriptions") was discovered beneath a millstream where it had been reused in the walls of the Roman odeum. This inscription, cut into twelve stone blocks dating to the fifth century B.C., is of the greatest importance for the study of Greek law, society and language. Halbherr and Fabricius also discovered in the Pythion Temple a text of a treaty dated 170 B.C. made by *Pergamon and Gortyn, *Knossos, *Phaistos and Lyttos; they built a vault to shelter the precious law code (1887).

After such momentous explorations, the *Italian School of Archaeology established a permanent Mission on Crete for its first Cretan excavations, those at Gortyn. In the period of great excavations (1897–1935), Italian archaeologists under Halbherr, together with J. Hazzidakis and S. *Xanthoudides, excavated at the Pythion theater (1897–98), Hagios Titos (1900–1; A. *Orlandos, 1920s), amphitheater (1910), praetorium, odeum and nymphaea (1912–13), Iseum (1913–14) and baths (1914, 1919). Many of Halbherr's and other Italian finds are now in Galleries 18–20 of the *Herakleion Museum. Some, however, are still in situ, like the statue bases in the praetorium, reused Roman inscriptions and traces of an earlier temple at Hagios Titos and blocks in the Pythion theater that contain a forerunner of Halbherr's law code. Others are protected inside the Collection of Antiquities, like the monumental inscription to A. Larcius Lepidus Sulpicianus from the nymphaeum.

Though Crete was not the major focus of the Italian School of Archaeology after World War I, M. Guarducci and D. *Levi were sent there and published the abundant inscriptions of Gortyn. The Cretan Mission under L. *Pernier resumed excavations at the odeum, Iseum, nymphaeum, praetorium and Pythion theater and identified the circus (1935). Sporadic investigations have taken place on the acropolis (1954–61), in a Late Minoan country villa (1958) and in the praetorium (1970s). N. Platon mapped the extent of the ancient site (1962). The grandeur of ancient Gortyn comes not from its movable artifacts, including its many inscriptions, but from the sheer expanse of its architectural remains, still scattered beneath olive groves and not yet systematically excavated.

Since 1978, major Italian excavations have returned to Gortyn from Phaistos to investigate the Late Roman, Protobyzantine and Byzantine water supply and necropoleis and towns (1978–81), as well as the Hellenistic fortifications (1980–84).

BIBLIOGRAPHY

M. Guarducci, *Inscriptiones Creticae,* 4 (Rome, 1950), 1–13; S. Spanakis, *Crete: A Guide,* 1 (Herakleion, 1964), 104–14; Idem, *Krete: Tourismos, Historia, Archaiologia,*

3rd ed., 1 (Herakleion, 1981), 168–81; +*Creta antica: Cento anni di archeologia italiana (1884–1984),* Scuola Archeologica Italiana di Atene (Rome, 1984), 19–34, 69–116.

MARTHA W. BALDWIN BOWSKY

GOSSAERT (MABUSE), JAN (ca. 1478–ca. 1536). Flemish painter, associated with bringing the study of antiquity to Northern European artists.

A master at Antwerp by 1503, Gossaert, also called by the name Mabuse, worked for the house of Burgundy all his life. In 1508–9, he made a trip to Italy, visiting Rome, Florence and Venice. Four drawings of antiquities survive from the trip, of the *Colosseum (Kupferstichkabinett, Berlin), the *Spinario* (University Print Cabinet, Leiden), an *Apollo,* now in Naples (Accademia, Venice) and the *Standing Hercules,* now in the Palazzo dei Conservatori (London, collection of Lord Wharton). His knowledge of ancient sculptures and buildings is reflected in several paintings with erotic subject matter. The ample, sensuous nudes of *Neptune and Amphitrite* (1516; Staatliche Museen, Berlin) stand on the front porch of a Tuscan Doric building, and his *Danae* (1527; Alte Pinakothek, Munich) is seated in a round Ionic temple with columns of colored marble. His interest in anatomy, perspective and classical architecture and sculpture helped convey the discoveries of the Italian Renaissance to his Flemish contemporaries.

BIBLIOGRAPHY
J. G. van Gelder, "Jan Gossaert in Rome, 1508–1509," *Oud-Holland* 59 (1942), 1–11; H. Pauwels—H. R. Hoetink—S. Herzog, eds., *Jan Gossaert genaamd Mabuse,* catalog of exhibition (Rotterdam, 1965); Bober—Rubinstein, 459.

GOURNIA. Bronze Age Aegean site, located on the north shore of eastern *Crete, near the harbor of Sphoungaras.

The settlement at Gournia, founded in the third millennium B.C., was occupied continuously until the destruction of Minoan civilization in the Late Minoan (LM) IB period, shortly after the turn of the fifteenth century; after a short lapse it was reoccupied in the LM III period, during the Mycenaean occupation of Crete. Most remains date to the LM IB period, and the site is important because of the picture it provides of the everyday activities of ordinary people who lived at this time. It is also important because of the small palace, located near the center of the site, which provided an administrative and ceremonial center for the region around the Bay of Mirabello. In the reoccupation period, the settlement was much smaller; one of the houses, a megaron, may indicate the presence of Mycenaean Greeks on the site.

The site was excavated from 1901 to 1904 by Harriet Boyd *Hawes under the auspices of the *American School of Classical Studies in Athens. In the early 1970s, further excavation was carried out in the early cemetery under the supervision of the *Greek Archaeological Service. In the early 1990s, a team of Greek and American archaeologists surveyed the area around the site preparing for renewed excavation.

BIBLIOGRAPHY

H. B. Hawes et al., *Gournia, Vasilike, and Other Prehistoric Sites on the Isthmus of Hierapetra* (Philadelphia, 1908); J. S. Soles, "The Early Gournia Town," *AJA* 83 (1979), 149–67; Idem, "The Gournia Palace," *AJA* 95 (1991), 17–78; Idem, *Prepalatial Cemeteries at Mochlos and Gournia, Hesperia* suppl. 24 (Princeton, NJ, 1992); +*Aerial Atlas of Crete,* 186–93.

JEFFREY S. SOLES

GOZZADINI, GIOVANNI (1810–87). Italian nobleman; archaeologist, historian and politician; the discoverer of *Villanovan culture, which he believed to be an early phase of Etruscan civilization.

A lifelong student of the antiquities of his native *Bologna, Gozzadini served in numerous distinguished administrative posts, including that of the first director general of the Museo Civico of Bologna after the merger of the university and communal collections (1878). Aided by his wife, Maria Teresa, he made major discoveries in the vicinity of his property at Villanova (1853) and at *Marzabotto (1862) and published his findings promptly and with rich illustration. He has been criticized for failing to realize that Marzabotto was not a cemetery and for publishing the objects he excavated in an arrangement according to type rather than find spot or context.

Casa Gozzadini was the center of an intellectual circle of writers, scientists, politicians and archaeologists, presided over by Maria Teresa Gozzadini. Visitors included George *Dennis, A. H. Layard, *Montelius, *Schliemann.

BIBLIOGRAPHY

G. Gozzadini, *Di un sepolcreto etrusco scoperto presso Bologna* (Bologna, 1855); Idem, *Di un' antica necropoli a Marzabotto nel Bolognese* (Bologna, 1865); D. Vitali, "La scoperta di Villanova e il conte Giovanni Gozzadini," *Dalla Stanza delle Antichità al Museo Civico* (Bologna, 1984), 223–37.

GRAEVIUS, JOHANNES GEORGIUS (JOHANN GEORG GRAEVE; 1632–1703). German classical philologist, historian and archaeologist.

Graevius was born in Naumburg and studied law in Leipzig and philology at Deventer under J. F. Gronovius (*Gronovius family). He was called to Duisburg as professor of eloquence in 1656, then to Utrecht in 1656. There he attracted a large number of students by his method of studying and teaching ancient authors from more than a purely philological point of view. He was called to prestigious posts at Leiden, Heidelberg and Padua but refused to leave Utrecht.

Graevius's principal interest was in Roman literature (Cicero, Caesar, Suetonius), but he is remembered in the history of classical archaeology for his treasuries of Roman antiquities paralleling the Greek treasury of Jacob Gronovius. The *Thesaurus antiquitatum romanorum* appeared in twelve volumes (Utrecht, 1694–99), with its rich selection of more than 120 treatises by various scholars, sometimes with illustrations taken from the earlier publications by these authors. Included are *dissertationes* by *Panvinio, *Agustín, *Orsini, Albert *Rubens, *Marliani, *Nardini, *Bellori, *Bosio, *Lipsius, *Aleandro and many others. The scheme of the work embraces Roman government and law (volumes 1–2), topography of Rome (3–4), religion (5), clothing (6), families (7), the calendar, markets, marriage (8), games, amphitheaters, the triumph (9), the army (10), coins, weights and measures (11) and a miscellany on baths, banquets, lamps, tombs, items of personal adornment (12). He also published a *Thesaurus antiquitatum et historiarum Italiae,* issued as six segments in three volumes (Leiden, 1704), a work later expanded by P. Burmann into thirty-nine volumes. In addition, Graevius served as editor for the *De pictura veterum* of Franciscus *Junius.

BIBLIOGRAPHY

Stark, 110, 123, 126–27, 129, 156; Sandys, II, 327–28; *Porträtarchiv,* no. 49.

GRAND CAMÉE DE FRANCE. See GEMMA TIBERIANA.

GRANDJOUAN, CLAIREVE (1929–82). American archaeologist.

The daughter of a French diplomat, Grandjouan received a varied and unorthodox education and upbringing that included two years in the jungles of Martinique with her mother and sister. She obtained her B.A. and Ph.D. from Bryn Mawr College, spending many years along the way working at the *American School of Classical Studies at Athens. In connection with research in the Athenian Agora, she published a volume on terracottas and plastic lamps of the Roman period from the site (1961) and completed a manuscript on Hellenistic relief molds from the Agora before her untimely death in 1982. She is remembered as a brilliant lecturer and teacher at Hunter College (1967 and following) and as an inspiring leader of the *Archaeological Institute of America (AIA). Her public lectures for the AIA, the Museum of Natural History, the Smithsonian and other institutions were enormously successful, serving to create communication between archaeologist and public in a style that has rarely been equaled.

BIBLIOGRAPHY

B. S. Ridgway, "Claireve Grandjouan," *AJA* 87 (1983), 131–32; C. Grandjouan, *Hellenistic Relief Molds from the Athenian Agora,* completed by E. Markson and S. Rotroff, (Princeton, NJ, 1989).

SHELLIE WILLIAMS

GRAND TOUR. Travel on the European Continent undertaken mainly by British patricians, especially the young, for whom the tour was an essential part of their education; artists, architects and designers followed in their path.

The eighteenth-century Grand Tour of Europe, particularly of Italy, was to be of major consequence for the development of classical archaeology. It was also to prove of equal significance in the diffusion of the classical tradition throughout the visual arts and literature. While British collectors, patrons and artists had traveled abroad during the seventeenth century in search of classical antiquity (notably, Inigo Jones with the Earl of *Arundel, the first great collector of antique sculpture in Britain), the golden age of the Grand Tour was bounded chronologically by the Treaty of Utrecht in 1713 and the start of the French revolutionary wars in 1793. At its highest level the tour not only was the climax to a classical education (as described by Edward *Gibbon is his *Autobiography,* 1796) but frequently led to the formation of important collections, the design of country houses and their parkland and the promotion of archaeological inquiry. For example, Thomas Coke, later first Earl of Leicester, undertook an exceptionally long tour, from 1712 to 1718, which resulted in the creation of the majestic neo-Palladian Holkham Hall, Norfolk, its gallery of outstanding classical sculpture, its consciously Arcadian landscape and the publication of Thomas *Dempster's key manuscript, *De Etruria regali,* in 1723–26. Other tours, such as Lord Burlington's two in 1715 and 1727, introduced Roman thermal planning into contemporary architecture and led to the sponsorship of Robert Castell's reconstruction of Roman gardens in his *Villas of the Ancients Illustrated* (1728).

The *Society of Dilettanti, originally founded in 1732 as a dining club for former grand tourists, was transformed later in the century into a learned body that played a key role in the Greek Revival, mainly though the promotion and financing of archaeological expeditions. The activities of leading members ranged from acquiring classical sculpture, such as by Charles *Townley and William Weddell (whose collections are still largely intact, in the *British Museum and Newby Hall, Yorkshire, respectively); accumulating and publishing painted vases, such as by Sir William *Hamilton; and surveying and illustrating important Greek architecture, as by James *Stuart and Nicholas *Revett, through their *Antiquities of Athens* 1 (1762) and 2 (1789).

Meanwhile, archaeological studies on the tour continued to stimulate contemporary design. On returning to London, Stuart had created in 1759 the first neoclassical interior in Europe, with his Painted Room *all'antica* at Spencer House, involving wall decorations derived from *Herculaneum and integrated furniture based on a fusion of Greek and Roman prototypes. Robert *Adam, after four years traveling in Italy and Dalmatia, was to rival Stuart's ingenuity with a highly eclectic language of design, applied in an unprecedented range of media (e.g., Etruscan Dressing Room, Osterley Park, ca. 1775). In turn, the Earl of Aylesford, assisted by Joseph Bonomi, used the results of travelers' accounts of the new excavations in Southern Italy to devise the first-ever Pompeian Revival interior at Packington Hall, Warwickshire, between 1785 and 1788.

By the turn of the century, apart from restricted travel on the Continent, the decline of the Grand Tour with the shift from Rome to Greece was symbolized by the arrival of Lord *Elgin's marbles in London amid fierce controversy between 1803 and 1812. Within six years of Waterloo, in 1821, a regular steamboat service was crossing the channel; twenty years later, a network of railways was spreading throughout Europe, and the Grand Tour had been replaced by

"A Great Circular Tour of the Continent," advertised by the father of all travel agents, Thomas Cook.

BIBLIOGRAPHY

J. Lees-Milne, *Earls of Creation* (London, 1962); +B. Ford, "The Englishman in Italy," in *The Treasure Houses of Britain,* ed. G. Jackson-Stops (New Haven, CT, 1985), 40–49; C. Hibberd, *The Grand Tour* (London, 1987); J. Wilton-Ely, "Pompeian and Etruscan Tastes in the Neo-Classical Interior," in *The Fashioning and Functioning of the British Country House,* ed. G. Jackson-Stops (Washington, DC, 1989), 51–74; J. Black, *The Grand Tour in the 18th Century* (New York, 1992).

JOHN WILTON-ELY

GRAPHIA AUREAE URBIS ROMAE (ca. 1155). The "Account of the Golden City of Rome," extant in a single manuscript in Florence, Laurentiana Pluteus LXXXIX inf. XLI, written ca. 1254.

The text has been published by Schramm, and by Valentini and Zucchetti with topographical annotations. The *Graphia* has three parts: a historical introduction tracing the founding of Rome to Janus, "son of Noah"; a revised and interpolated version of the **Mirabilia Urbis Romae;* and an account of imperial offices and regalia drawn largely from the *Etymologiae* of Isidore of Seville, who may also be the source of the pretentious Greek-sounding title ("[t]he word *graphium* in Greek is *scriptorium* in Latin. For *graphia* means 'writing,' " *Etym.* 6, 9, 2). The text circulated anonymously in the Middle Ages, but Herbert Bloch has shown that the compiler, who was also the author of parts one and three, was almost certainly Petrus Diaconus of Montecassino (ca. 1107–after 1159). In its entirety, the *Graphia* is an idiosyncratic and personal fantasy of imperial Rome, but it influenced some later medieval writers who accepted it as an authentic source for early Roman history.

Petrus Diaconus rearranged the *Mirabilia Urbis Romae,* integrating the legends into the itinerary so that the text has greater topographical coherence. His changes do not add much of substance to the *Mirabilia*'s account of Roman topography, except for the important notice that Pope Anastasius IV (d. 1154) "was buried in the porphyry monument [sarcophagus] of blessed Helena." (See also *guidebooks to Rome [to 1500].)

BIBLIOGRAPHY

Valentini—Zucchetti, III, 67–110; P. E. Schramm, *Kaiser Könige und Päpste, Gesammelte Aufsätze zur Geschichte des Mittelalters* 3 (Stuttgart, 1969), 313–59; 4.1 (Stuttgart, 1970), 22–33; R. L. Benson, "Political *Renovatio:* Two Models from Roman Antiquity," *Renaissance and Renewal in the Twelfth Century,* ed. R. L. Benson and G. Constable, with C. D. Lanham (Cambridge, MA, 1982), 351–55; H. Bloch, "Der Autor der 'Graphia aureae urbis Romae,' " *Deutsches Archiv für Erforschung des Mittelalters* 40 (1984), 55–175.

DALE KINNEY

GRAVISCA (GRAVISCAE). The principal port of Etruscan *Tarquinia and later site of a Roman maritime colony (181 B.C.), on the Tyrrhenian coast ca.

fifty miles north of Rome, already marshbound and in decline by the fifth century A.C. (Rutilius Namatianus 1, 281f).

Current Italian excavations, started in 1967, have revealed a prosperous Archaic Greek sanctuary, founded and used by Greek residents within the Etruscan community, with complex building phases and rich votive offerings, Greek lamps and pottery with dedications to Aphrodite and other divinities and part of a stone anchor dedicated by one Sostratos (cf. Herodotos 4. 152) to the Aiginetan Apollo (Tarquinia National Museum).

BIBLIOGRAPHY

L. Quilici, "Graviscae," in *La Via Aurelia* (Rome, 1968), 107–20; +M. Torelli et al., "Gravisca (Tarquinia).–Scavi nella città etrusca e romana, Campagne 1969 e 1970," *NSc* (1971), 195–299; Idem, "Il santuario greco di Gravisca," *Parola del Passato,* 32 (1977), 398–458.

F. R. SERRA RIDGWAY

GREAT ALTAR, Pergamon. Hellenistic monument on the acropolis at *Pergamon, probably dedicated by the Attalid ruler Eumenes II (197–157 B.C.) to commemorate a major military victory, perhaps over marauding Gauls.

The monument is sometimes referred to as the "Altar of Zeus," but there is, in fact, no certain evidence to which god the altar was dedicated. The monument, measuring ca. 36m × 34m × 16.5m, consisted of a platform on which the altar itself stood, approached via a flight of steps and enclosed on the other three sides by a wall surrounded by an Ionic colonnade. A frieze of over-lifesize figures in high relief ran along the socle of the monument, depicting a battle of gods and giants in which the protagonists were identified by inscriptions, some of which survive. The relief is thought to symbolize Pergamene victory over its enemies or of culture over barbarism. The myth is related in great detail, suggesting to E. Simon (1975) that scholars at Pergamon may have consulted the genealogy of Hesiod's *Theogony* to identify the principals in the battle. A second frieze in lower relief was placed in an inner colonnade around the altar proper, with scenes from the life of Telephos, son of Herakles and mythical founder of Pergamon.

The monument is mentioned in only one classical source, the late Roman author Ampelius, who describes the altar as one of the wonders of the world. It is perhaps also mentioned in the book of *Revelation* (2.13) as the "throne of Satan." The Great Altar was renovated under Septimius Severus in the late second century A.C., and a protective baldachino was placed over the sacrificial altar.

Modern interest in the altar begins with the German engineer C. *Humann, who was investigating at Pergamon from 1869 and had sent to Berlin some fragments of the *Gigantomachy* he had extracted from a Byzantine wall. Heinrich *Brunn had drawn attention to the Ampelius reference to Pergamon, but there was no interest in excavating at the site until A. *Conze was put in charge of the *Berlin museum, in 1877. Conze and Humann cooperated on every point to secure the spectacular reliefs; at first, their work went basically unnoticed by the archaeological world, for all eyes were turned toward the great discoveries at *Olympia and *Schliemann's *Troy. Much of the work was done in 1878–79, involving the transporting of great blocks from the monument to the ships in the harbor of Dikili, some eighteen miles distant. The pieces were shipped to Berlin, where Otto Puchstein labored to put them together, and Hans Schrader was engaged on the restoration of the altar. The result, the partly reconstructed altar and some 75% of the *Gigantomachy,* was set up in the *Pergamon Museum in Berlin. Humann had declared that "a whole new epoch of art" was revealed, and visitors to the exhibition concurred, making comparisons with *Michelangelo and *Rubens and with the German Baroque. Others complained that the sculptures lacked the "noble simplicity and serene greatness" of the best Greek art. Later, the sculptures were to take their place as a key monument of the Hellenistic Baroque.

BIBLIOGRAPHY

Michaelis, 166–72; +H. Kähler, *Der Grossen Fries von Pergamon* (Berlin, 1948); +E. Rohde, *Pergamon, Burgberg und Altar,* 2nd ed. (Berlin, 1982); *"Wir haben eine ganze Kunstepoche gefunden!''': ein Jahrhundert Forschungen zum Pergamonaltar, Katalog der Sonderausstellung der Antikensammlung, Pergamonmuseum November 1986 bis April 1987* (Berlin, 1986); H.-J. Schalles, *Der Pergamonaltar, Zwischen Bewertung und Verwertbarkeit* (Frankfurt am Main, 1986).

ANN C. GUNTER

GREAT CAMEO OF THE HAGUE. Large, Roman, two-layered agate cameo (29cm × 21cm), showing an imperial couple in triumph, formerly in The Hague, today in the Rijksmuseum het Koninklijk Penning-Kabinet, Leiden.

The cameo was known to P. P. *Rubens, who had an engraving made of it ca. 1625. Perhaps belonging to the artist, it was shipped off to the East Indies along with the *Rubens Vase in 1628. The ship was wrecked, but the Great Cameo survived and turned up later in Persia (1664). In 1765 it was put up for sale in Europe, and in 1823 it was sold to King William I of the Netherlands, who presented it to the collection at The Hague.

The iconography has been much debated through the centuries, with identifications ranging from *Livia and Augustus* (*Cuper); to *Germanicus and Agrippina* (*Babelon); *Claudius and Messalina* (*Furtwängler); and *Constantine and His Wife* (G. *Bruns). The dating has correspondingly varied widely, from the time of Augustus (first century B.C.) to Constantine (fourth century A.C.). H. Möbius has suggested that the puzzling cameo is actually a forgery, created in the circle of Rubens in the seventeenth century.

BIBLIOGRAPHY

E. von Mercklin, *Gnomon* 23 (1951), 117; M. van der Meulen, *Petrus Paulus Rubens Antiquarius* (Aalphen an den Rijn, 1975), 139–40; W.-R. Megow, *Kameen von Augustus bis Alexander Severus* (Berlin, 1987), 84–88.

GREEK ARCHAEOLOGICAL SERVICE. Department of the Greek Ministry of Culture responsible for archaeology in Greece.

The service was originally established to prevent the theft of manuscripts and antiquities. At the beginning of the nineteenth century, Adamantios Korais was among the first in Greece to recognize the need for such protection. His efforts led to the decree of interior minister Grigoris Dikaios (Papaflessas) in 1825 regulating the collection of antiquities and providing for their protection in the schools. In 1827 a further decree forbade the sale or transport of antiquities outside Greece. In 1829, the second year of the newly constituted Greek state led by Ioannis Capodistria, a National Museum was established on *Aigina. Andreas Mustoxydis was appointed director and ephor of antiquities and remained in charge until March 1832, when he resigned after the assassination of Capodistria.

In 1832 Kyriakos Pittakis was appointed superintendent of the antiquities of Athens. Under his direction the Archaeological Service was founded in 1833 but not established by law until May 1834. The national collection was moved to Athens and entrusted first to the German scholar Ludwig *Ross, then to Georgios Gennadius and finally to Pittakis himself. The archaeological law provided for the supervision and protection of all antiquities in Greece; Byzantine remains were incorporated in a later decree of 1837.

The service was reorganized in 1899 and went through several expansions: in 1911 the founding of a Department of Restoration; in 1914 the establishment of the Byzantine and Christian Museum; and in 1915 the publication of the first volume of the *Archaiologikon Deltion.* This first issue, describing the work of the service, includes articles by those scholars who can be regarded as belonging to the first generation of Greek archaeologists: F. Versakis, K. Kourouniotis, A. *Orlandos, K. Romaios, V. Stais, G. Soteriades and C. *Tsountas.

The most important law, however, must be considered that of 1932, which regulates excavation in Greece and gives to each of the foreign archaeological schools established in Athens three excavation permits every year. By interpretation of this law in 1985, the Ministry of Culture has expanded the limitation of three permits to apply both to surface surveys and to *synergasia* (joint Greek-foreign projects). Further, permission for foreign scholars to work in any archaeological capacity in Greece must now be sought through the appropriate foreign school.

BIBLIOGRAPHY

G. Pharmakides, *The Painter Athanasios Iatrides* (Athens, 1960); A. Kokkou, *The Preservation of the Antiquities of Greece and the First Museums* (Athens, 1977); V. Petrakos, *Essay on the Archaeological Law* (Athens, 1982).

WILLIAM D. E. COULSON

GREEK ARCHAEOLOGICAL SOCIETY (ARCHAEOLOGICAL SOCIETY; ARCHAIOLOGIKĒ HETAIREIA). The foundation of the Archaeological Society in Athens, under charter from King Otho in 1837, marked the rise in the interest of Greek antiquities.

The society celebrated its 150th anniversary (1987) in the Odeion of Herodes Atticus, the very building it excavated and restored beginning in 1848. It was established under the inspiration of Konstantinos Bellios and Kyriakos Pittakis, with sixty-six founding members, for the dual purpose of working for the preservation of antiquities in Greece and conducting excavations. The society was responsible for the first modern excavations in Greece, which began in 1837 in the *Theater of Dionysos at Athens. The following year saw the initiation of an extensive excavation and restoration program on the Athenian *Akropolis. In 1840, work included the *Tower of the Winds, and in 1858 excavations began in the Athenian *Agora.

The activity of the society expanded considerably under the direction of Stephanos Koumanoudis, and excavations began at a number of sites that later came to be among the most famous in Greece. In Athens this included the *Kerameikos (1863), Asklepieion (1864) and *Roman Agora (1884). In Attika itself work began at *Eleusis (1882), the theater at Zea at the *Peiraeus (1883–84), the Amphiareion at Oropos (1884), *Rhamnous (1890) and Thorikos (1983). Outside Attika, the society was active at *Mycenae (1876) in connection with Heinrich *Schliemann, *Thera (1874), *Thebes (1880), *Epidauros (1881), *Vapheio (1889), Amyklai (1890) and Messene (1895). Restoration programs of classical buildings began at the temple of Poseidon at *Sounion (1873) and the temple of Apollo at *Bassai (1880) and of Byzantine monuments at Mistra (1895) and Meteora (1909). The society has been especially active in this century; its report for 1987 listed excavations at thirty-eight sites throughout Greece, including the work of Manolis *Andronikos at *Vergina. It also acts as a financial liaison between the Greek state and a number of excavators and restoration committees, such as those for the Akropolis and Epidauros.

The work of the society is published yearly in the *Praktika* of the Archaeological Society in Athens, whose first issue dates to 1871, and in the *Ergon* of the Archaeological Society (1837–1937; 1954–), which consists of the annual speech of the general secretary. More interpretive articles are published in the *Archaiologiki Ephemeris* (1837–), the oldest archaeological periodical in Greece.

The society is governed by a board of eleven members headed by a president, but much of the administrative detail is in the hands of the general secretary. Past secretaries have numbered some of the most distinguished Greek archaeologists: A. Rangabe (1837–51), S. Vyzantios (1851–52), K. Pittakis (1852–59), A. Koumanoudis (1859–94), P. *Kavvadias (1895–1909, 1912–20), C. *Tsountas (1910–11), I. Dragatsis (1921–23), A. Oikonomos (1924–51), A. *Orlandos (1951–79), G. *Mylonas (1979–87) and V. Petrakos (1987–). The society's premises at 22 Panepistimiou Street, Athens, contain extensive archives and library holdings.

BIBLIOGRAPHY

V. Petrakos, *The Archaeological Society in Athens, A History of 150 Years 1837–1987* (Athens, 1987).

WILLIAM D. E. COULSON

GREEK VASES. Vessels of metal and pottery produced in the Greek world during the first millennium B.C.

Nearly all the Greek vases of gold and silver of the kind we hear about in epigraphical and literary sources have long since been melted down. We are left in the main with their low-priced bronze and fictile analogues, mostly the latter. The odd fact is that what was, in effect, the unrecyclable junk from antiquity has gradually come to be endowed with characteristics it never used to possess. It was rare for painted fictile vases to be collected before the eighteenth century; their status was still as low as it had been in antiquity. Classical art was, for the most part, the pursuit of aristocrats who found that sculpture was an effective means of bolstering their social and political position. When an interest was first taken in such vases, it was widely thought that they were of Etruscan manufacture (*Etruscheria), since they were first found in abundance in Etruscan tombs. This view was refuted by *Winckelmann and *Lanzi. By the end of the eighteenth century, the supply of sculpture had diminished, and a new, nonaristocratic public for classical art emerged who sought and found different exempla in the past. The potter and his craft were self-evidently nonaristocratic, and Greek pots were readily accepted as the relics of the first European democracy. They thus became desirable objects for collectors and began to be sold for high prices by dealers such as Sir William *Hamilton and the Prince of *Canino (cf. *Gerhard). Thomas Hope used his collection to decorate the interiors of his houses; he and others began to study fictile vessels for the lessons, real or imaginary, they could impart about antiquity. Otto *Jahn wrote the first major study. Later on, some scholars (e.g., *Pfuhl, *Buschor and *Beazley), under the influence of the study of Italian primitive painting on one hand, and of the Arts and Crafts movement on the other, thought it worthwhile to identify the hands of the artisans who decorated the extant black- and red-figured pottery vessels. While this has greatly benefited the flourishing market in Greek antiquities, it has, on balance, distorted the study of ancient Greece, inasmuch as it has led to the widespread belief that decorated pottery was of primary importance in antiquity. The study of the imagery on vases has been, on the whole, a more profitable area of research.

BIBLIOGRAPHY

O. Jahn, *Beschreibung der Vasensammlungen* (Munich, 1854), ix-lxxxv; R. M. Cook, *Greek Painted Pottery,* 2nd ed. (London, 1972); D. von Bothmer, "Notes on Collectors of Vases," catalog of exhibition, Kimbell Art Museum, *Wealth of the Ancient World* (Fort Worth, 1983), 37–44; +M. Vickers—D. Gill, *Artful Crafts, Ancient Greek Silverware and Pottery* (Oxford, 1994).

MICHAEL VICKERS

GREGORIUS, MAGISTER (ca. 1200). Author of an early description of Rome.

Among the numerous medieval guides to the sights of the city of Rome, the *Narracio de mirabilibus urbis Romae,* written by an otherwise unknown "magister Gregorius," is unique in its single-minded devotion to the city's physical inheritance from classical antiquity. The author, well versed in ancient history

and with a ready command of authors such as Lucan, Ovid, Vergil and Suetonius, is presumed to be English since the only known copy of his work is
contained in a thirteenth-century manuscript now in the library of St. Catharine's
College, Cambridge (no. 3, fol. 190–203) and also because large portions of his
text are cited in Ranulph Higden's *Polychronicon,* written at St. Werburg's
abbey, Chester, in the mid-fourteenth century. A *terminus post quem* for the
Narracio is provided by the quotation of the opening lines of the poem "De
Roma" of *Hildebert of Lavardin (1057–1134).

Following a prologue in which Gregory informs us that he has been "constrained to set down on paper those things which I have seen in Rome that are
most worthy of admiration," he then proceeds to describe the city and its classical monuments in varying degrees of detail. A list of the city's gates is followed by an account of the bronze statues, the marble statues, various
"palaces," an aqueduct, the *Pantheon and a variety of triumphal arches, *obelisks and tombs. Interest in Rome's Christian monuments is conspicuous by its
absence. Gregory mentions St. Peter's only once, and then merely as a geographic reference to locate the nearby tomb of Romulus. Similarly, S. Giovanni
in Laterano is included only to locate the papal collection of classical statuary
that stood in the square outside. This collection contained many of the bronzes
that would later form the nucleus of the museum on the Capitoline Hill, including the *Spinario* and the *Lupa* (*Capitoline *Wolf*).

Despite his professed disdain for the "empty stories" (*vanas fabulas*) told by
both the pilgrims and the Roman populace, Gregory was rarely successful in his
attempts to discover the true identity of the various pieces he saw. For example,
he devotes a large portion of his text to a discussion of the bronze equestrian
statue of *Marcus Aurelius* (then standing outside the Lateran), providing two
possible interpretations, neither of which is correct. At other times he appears
singularly misinformed, for example, in his list of the names of the city's gates.
But while his explanations and identifications may be fanciful, there is no evidence to suggest that he invented any of the statues or buildings he so vividly
describes. Thus, his account supplies valuable information concerning the existence and placement of various pieces, including some of which no trace now
remains.

Perhaps more interesting than the actual objects is Gregory's attitude toward
them: a passionate curiosity that led him to wash his hands in the sulphurous
bath of Apollo, to pace off and record the width of the Pantheon and to return
three times to see a nude statue of Venus that had entranced him. With his
contemporary *Henry of Blois, he stands at the beginning of a long line of
northern antiquarians who have been captivated by the "marvels" of ancient
Rome. (See also *guidebooks to Rome [to 1500].)

BIBLIOGRAPHY

M. R. James, "Magister Gregorius de Mirabilibus urbis Romae," *English Historical
Review* 32 (1917), 531–54; G. Rushforth, "Master Gregorius de mirabilibus urbis Romae:
A New Description of Rome in the Twelfth Century," *JRS* 9 (1919), 14–58; Valentini—

Zucchetti, III, 137–67; Magister Gregorius, *Narracio de mirabilibus urbis Romae,* ed. R. Huygens (Leiden, 1970).

JOHN OSBORNE

GREGORY XVI (MAURO CAPPELARI DELLA COLOMBA; 1765–1846). Pope, creator of the Etruscan museum in the *Vatican.

A native of Belluno, Mauro Cappelari della Colomba entered the Camaldolese order at Murano. Called to Rome, he was made cardinal in 1826 by Leo XII and was elected pope in 1831 with the name of Gregory XVI. He governed in confused, difficult times and is not remembered for political success. But he had a major influence on the arts as patron and protector of artists and scholars and as restorer of many monuments. Gregory improved existing museums at the Vatican and created an important new one, named for him as the Museo Gregoriano Etrusco.

The museum was set up in the old Palazzetto del Belvedere in a suite of rooms that had been used by papal officials under the reign of Pope *Pius VI. The first wide-ranging public museum of Etruscan antiquities, it opened its doors in 1837 to display antiquities recovered in Etruria over the past 200 years but found its most immediate impetus in the excavation on papal property of the spectacular *Regolini-Galassi Tomb at Cerveteri (1836). Another major new discovery was the "*Mars" found at Todi (1835), a nearly lifesize hollow cast bronze of a warrior god in armor, displayed with a helmet supplied by *Thorvaldsen (now removed). Along with the Etruscan material were included some of the finest Greek vases known, excavated from Etruscan tombs, especially at *Vulci.

BIBLIOGRAPHY

A. M. Ghisalberti, "Gregorio XVI," *EI* 17 (1933), 940–41; P. Perali, "Il Museo Gregoriano Etrusco," in *Gregorio XVI, Miscellanea commemorativa* (Rome, 1948), 365–403; C. Pietrangeli, *I Musei Vaticani, Cinque secoli di storia* (Rome, 1985), ch. 8, "Gregorio XVI fonda nuovi musei al Vaticano e al Laterano"; +G. Rosati—F. Buranelli, *Musei Vaticani, Egizi ed etruschi,* introd. F. Roncalli (Florence, 1983).

GRIMANI ALTAR (ARA GRIMANI). Rectangular Graeco-Roman altar or candelabrum base (height 0.94m) featuring reliefs on all four sides of Satyrs and maenads making love and reveling.

The altar is first recorded in 1587, in the *Grimani family bequest to the city of Venice, but it very likely was known in the earlier part of the century, since one of the reliefs seems to have been imitated by Correggio in his painting of *Io and Jupiter* (Kunsthistorisches Museum, Vienna, ca. 1530). The altar is not mentioned in the inventory of Cardinal Domenico Grimani's collection made in Rome in 1523, but as the inventory was drawn up quickly and by no means in detail, it is possible that the altar was discovered in Rome (many of the cardinal's antiquities were found on his property on the Quirinal Hill).

The piece was displayed in the Statuario Pubblico of the Venetian Republic in the Antisala of the Biblioteca Marciana beginning in 1596, later becoming part of the modern Archaeological Museum of Venice. The Grimani Altar was dated by D. Strong to the Julio-Claudian period (first century B.C.–first century A.C.); B. Forlati Tamaro described the work as a fine Greek original of the second century B.C.

BIBLIOGRAPHY

B. Forlati Tamaro, *Il Museo Archeologico del Palazzo Reale di Venezia,* 2nd ed. (Rome, 1969), 15; E. Knauer, "Zu Correggios Io und Ganymed," *ZfK* 33 (1970), 61–67; M. Perry, "Cardinal Domenico Grimani's Legacy of Ancient Art to Venice," *JWarb* 41 (1978), 215–44; +Bober—Rubinstein, 125.

GRIMANI FAMILY. Italian noble family from Venice, well known for its art collections.

Cardinal DOMENICO GRIMANI (1461–1523) amassed an important collection of marble statues, inscriptions and other antiquities in Rome during the first quarter of the sixteenth century. The cardinal resided in the Palazzo San Marco (later Palazzo Venezia) and also owned a *vigna* on the Quirinal Hill. Possibly some of his antiquities were excavated there during the building of his villa.

By 1505 the cardinal already had a collection that astounded ambassadors from Venice who came to call. In 1514 he added at least one under-lifesize statue of a Gaul (*Gaul Falling Backwards*); there were possibly two others— *Dead Gaul; Fallen Gaul*—which were discovered at an unknown site in Rome along with five (possibly seven) other statues that are now thought to be copies from a monument dedicated by Attalos I (or II) on the *Akropolis in Athens. (The others were acquired for the *Medici family. See also *Ludovisi *Gaul.*) Amico *Aspertini recorded the Gaul statues before they were transferred to Venice. *Titian, El Greco and others admired the pose of the *Gaul Falling Backward* and adapted it for compositions in paintings.

Perhaps by this time the cardinal had also acquired the *Grimani Altar. He owned a famous bust of *Vitellius* and a colossal statue of *Agrippa* and was an avid collector of gems and coins, which were later inherited by his nephew MARINO (1488–1546), cardinal of Orvieto; some of these eventually went to the Museo Archeologico in Venice; others went to the Hermitage, St. Petersburg.

At his death in 1523, Cardinal Domenico bequeathed a large part of his art collection to the state of Venice, with the stipulation that the works (paintings and antiquities) all be arranged together in a room in honor of the donor. A selection of the finest marble busts and statues was set up in a room in the Palazzo Ducale, with an inscription about the donor originally devised by Pietro *Bembo. The pieces stayed there from 1525 to 1586. Subsequently, they became part of a collection of antiquities donated to the state (statuary, sarcophagi, reliefs, urns, altars, candelabrum bases; some Greek originals were included) by GIOVANNI GRIMANI (1500–93), nephew of Domenico, himself patriarch of Aquileia. Kept in his palazzo near S. Maria Formosa, after Giovanni's death the whole Grimani collection was installed in the new Statuario Pubblico in the

Gaul Falling Backward, sculpture once owned by Cardinal Domenico Grimani, Venice, Archaeological Museum. (Deutsches Archäologisches Institut, Rome. Inst. Neg. 82.533. With permission of the Ministero per i Beni Culturali e Ambientali.)

Marcian Library (1596). These antiquities form the core of the current Museo Archeologico of Venice, now installed in the Procuratie Nuove.

BIBLIOGRAPHY

M. Perry, ''The Statuario Pubblico of the Venetian Republic,'' *Saggi e Memorie di Storia dell'Arte* 8 (1972), 75–150; Idem, ''Cardinal Domenico Grimani's Legacy of Ancient Art to Venice,'' *JWarb* 41 (1978), 215–44; Bober—Rubinstein, 475; +G. Traversari, *La Statuaria ellenistica del Museo Archeologico di Venezia* (Rome, 1986); +L. Sperti, *Rilievi greci e romani del Museo Archeologico di Venezia* (Rome, 1988).

GRONOVIUS (GRONOV) FAMILY. German-Dutch family of classicists, of whom the most celebrated was JOHANN FRIEDRICH GRONOVIUS (1611–71), a specialist in philology, rector at Deventer and professor at Leiden.

Most of his highly influential publications have to do with Latin prose writers (Livy, Tacitus, both Senecas, Pliny the Elder, Gellius), rather than archaeology. His son JACOB GRONOVIUS (1645–1716), philologist and archaeologist, studied under him at Deventer and Leiden and then traveled to England, France, Spain and Italy. Visiting Florence, he was warmly received by Cosimo de'

Medici (*Medici family), grand duke of Tuscany, and through Medici influence became professor of Greek at the University of Pisa. In 1679 he returned to Leiden and accepted the chair in literature that had been held by his father, a position that he was to hold until his death thirty-seven years later. Though he produced various new editions of his father's texts of Tacitus, Gellius and Seneca's tragedies and his own editions of Livy and Cicero, his interests ran more to Greek authors and antiquities. His vicious polemical exchanges with Richard Bentley and other philologists tarnished his reputation but have no bearing on his place in the history of archaeology. He is remembered for his great thirteen-volume treasury of Greek antiquities, *Thesaurus antiquitatum graecarum* (1694–1703), long considered indispensable for the study of the ancient world. The first three volumes contain biographies and portrayals of famous Greek personages, both real and mythological. Book IV is on geography, V and VI on political organization. In VII is found information on religious festivals. Greek literature is the main theme of Books VIII–XI, while XII contains tombs and lamps.

Gronovius's youngest daughter died unexpectedly in 1716, driving him to despair and his own death of a broken heart a month later. The Gronovius tradition was carried on by his son ABRAHAM (1695–1775), a librarian at Leiden.

BIBLIOGRAPHY

Stark, 110, 127, 129, 182; Sandys, II, 329; *Porträtarchiv,* no. 50.

GROPIUS, GEORG CHRISTIAN (birth date unknown–d. 1845). Painter from north Germany; diplomat and agent for antiquities in Athens.

Born in Brunswick, as a youth Gropius was in the entourage of Wilhelm von *Humboldt in Paris and also traveled to Italy. At the age of about twenty-five, he was dispatched by Lord Aberdeen to be his agent in Athens. He remained there the rest of his life, serving as Austrian vice-consul (1816 ff.) and as a representative for the governments of Britain and Prussia as well (1840 ff.)

Gropius played a key role in the sale of the pedimental sculptures from *Aigina to *Ludwig of Bavaria. Acting as agent (1811 ff.) for *Cockerell and *Haller von Hallerstein, discoverers of the sculptures, he pressured Ludwig's agent, Johann Martin von *Wagner, to sign a provisional contract without seeing the marbles; upon finally seeing the pieces, Wagner immediately ratified the contract, and the purchase proceeded. Gropius also assisted Haller and his party to obtain a permit from Veli Pasha, governor of the Morea, to excavate at *Bassai, promising the Turk a share of half the treasure found.

A well-known figure in politics and the art world in Athens, Gropius was sometimes criticized for his opportunism, but, on the whole, he skillfully avoided unpopularity with rival parties and governments.

BIBLIOGRAPHY

Stark, 261, 327; Michaelis, 36; Stoneman, *Land of Lost Gods,* 191–94.

GROTTESCHE. Fanciful decorations involving mixed plant, human and animal forms, of classical origin, revived during the Renaissance.

The term *grottesche* was coined during the Renaissance to denote recently rediscovered Roman ornamental decorations in the *Domus Aurea and other buildings that were buried beneath the earth in what were thought to be caves or artificial grottoes. (Some, like Benvenuto *Cellini, knew perfectly well that they were not caves.) The surprising juxtaposition of heterogeneous elements in *grottesche,* like stems of flowers and shoots supporting roofs or sprouting human elements, contrasted with values of balance, reason and clarity associated with the classical past by Renaissance humanists.

Pirro *Ligorio, in a discourse on *grottesche,* made an impressive list of dozens of sites in and around Rome where he had seen these decorations. *Grottesche* at three important Roman sites proved influential to Renaissance artists: the stuccoed ornamentation at *Hadrian's Villa at Tivoli and at the *Colosseum and especially Famulus's painted decorations adorning the surviving vaults of Nero's Domus Aurea. European artists and scholars, amateurs on the *Grand Tour and dealers of antiquities are among those who left graffiti with the names and dates of their visits on the remaining walls of the Domus Aurea, from ca. 1480 to the nineteenth century. Among the artists' names identified are *Ghirlandaio, *Aspertini, Frans *Floris, Perino del Vaga, Giovanni da *Udine, Marten van *Heemskerck and Karel van Mander. The Spanish scholar Antonio *Agustín and the banker/collector Tiberio *Ceoli also signed.

Despite Vitruvius's well-known lamentation (*De architectura* 7.5.1–7) that these decorative monstrosities were supplanting traditional imitative frescoes, they were eagerly adopted by Renaissance artists. Among the earliest utilizations of *grottesche* were Signorelli's painted frames in the Orvieto Cathedral (ca. 1499–1504) and Filippino Lippi's *St. Philip Exorcising the Demon* in the Strozzi Chapel at Santa Maria Novella, Florence. Also at this time, Pinturicchio decorated with grotesques the vaulted ceilings of the Piccolomini Library of Siena Cathedral, the ceiling of the della Rovere palace in Rome and the Borgia apartments in the *Vatican. But the most influential of the Renaissance fresco decorations based on Nero's Domus Aurea are those applied to the walls of the Vatican "Loggetta" under the direction of *Raphael (ca. 1515).

Grottesche influenced the sculpture of *Michelangelo and Andrea *Sansovino and by the end of the sixteenth century were found on monumental architecture from Fontainebleau to the Palazzo Vecchio in Florence. The dissemination of *grottesche* throughout Europe was accomplished by artistic connections and the burgeoning print culture. Marten van Heemskerck and Giovanni da Udine made copies of the stucco decorations at the Colosseum, while Giuliano da *Sangallo and Girolamo da *Carpi reproduced those at Hadrian's Villa. Some of the earliest engravings of *grottesche* were made by Zoan Andrea from Mantua at the end of the fifteenth century and in the early sixteenth century by Enea *Vico and Etienne Delaune, for example. Flettner's *Book of Moresques* (1549) contains ornamental designs that are actually grotesques or arabesques. In the seventeenth century, Bernardo Capitelli engraved *grottesche* for Cassiano dal *Pozzo, and the discovery of more ruins at the Domus Aurea inspired engravings by P. S. *Bartoli.

Classical *grottesche* absorbed other ornamental art forms, such as late medieval drolleries and marginalia. In the sixteenth century, *grottesche* came to be synonymous with the term *sogni dei pittori*—or the "dreams of painters," as known to *Dürer. The fantastic amalgamations in Arcimboldo's allegorical portraits and Pieter Bruegel's "Elck" pictures are understood as grotesques. Still later, the term began to be associated with whatever was strange and uncanny in life as well as in art. Hence E.T.A. Hoffmann understood Jacques Callot's *Balli* illustrations as grotesques, and Edgar Allan Poe entitled a collection of his stories *Tales of the Grotesque and Arabesque*. The fusion of heterogeneous elements in the tradition of *grottesche* remains omnipresent in architectural decoration, jewelry, furniture, crafts and the fine arts.

BIBLIOGRAPHY
+W. Kayser, *The Grotesque in Art and Literature* (Bloomington, IN, 1963); +N. Dacos, "Graffiti de la Domus Aurea," *Bulletin de l'Institute Historique Belge* 38 (1967), 145–74; N. Dacos, *La Découverte de la Domus Aurea et la formation des grotesques à la Renaissance,* with appendix, text of Pirro Ligorio (Leiden, 1969); E. Kuryluk, *Salome and Judas in the Cave of Sex; The Grotesque, Origins, Iconography, Techniques* (Evanston, IL, 1987).

CATHERINE MORRIS WESTCOTT

GRUEBER, HERBERT APPOLD (1846–1927). English numismatist.

Born in Hambridge, Somerset, H. A. Grueber was privately tutored and became a leading expert on Roman numismatics in his employment at the *British Museum. As an assistant, then assistant keeper and finally keeper of the Department of Coins and Medals, he served there from 1866 until his death in 1927.

His chief contribution to archaeological studies lay in his catalog of Roman Republican coins in the British Museum, first published in 1910. The work contains issues of the mints at Rome and in Italy as well as in the provinces from the earliest specimens down into the early empire. His publication is based on the organization of the British Museum coin collection devised by John Francis William, Count de Salis (d. 1871), who labored from 1859 to 1869 to classify and augment properly the British Museum collection.

BIBLIOGRAPHY
Who's Who, 1927 1233; H. A. Grueber, *Coins of the Roman Republic in the British Museum,* 1–3. (London, 1910, repr. 1970).

GRUTER, JANUS (JAN GRUYTÈRE; 1560–1627). Dutch philologist and epigrapher.

Gruter, born at Antwerp, received his education at Cambridge and Leiden and became professor of history at Heidelberg (1592) and director of the Palatine

Library there (1602). An indefatigable worker, he normally studied late into the night, always standing upright. In addition to his numerous philological and historical studies of Roman authors, he made a major contribution to epigraphy (*epigraphy, Latin) with his monumental collection, *Inscriptiones antiquae totius orbis romani* in two volumes, published (evidently) at Heidelberg in 1603. The work was based on a collection of inscriptions published by *Smetius in 1588, which *Scaliger had seen and wanted to augment. Scaliger persuaded Gruter to do the expanded version, himself adding a number of new inscriptions. The resulting corpus was dedicated to the emperor Rudolf II (*Hapsburg family) and long held an authoritative rank in Latin epigraphical studies.

BIBLIOGRAPHY

E. Grégoire, "Gruter (Jean)," *NBG* 22 (1869), cols. 264–69.

GUARNACCI, MARIO (1701–85). Italian clergyman and scholar; one of the first to excavate Etruscan tombs.

Guarnacci was born at Volterra of a noble and wealthy family and went to Rome in 1726 as a churchman. A fine scholar, he was advanced by Popes Clement XII and Benedict XIV and had a brilliant career.

Antiquarian and collector, he spent his holidays at *Volterra, where, with his brothers Piero and Giovanni, he excavated a number of Etruscan tombs. The first excavation, in 1738, produced ten urns; he wrote to his friend Anton Francesco *Gori, "So, my museum of such things begins!"

Interest in Volterran antiquities unfortunately produced a flood of forgeries, and in 1744 Gori was asked to visit the Guarnacci "museum" to detect and discard any such. This he did, and cataloged the remainder: eighty-four urns, two covers, bronze vessels and figurines, pottery, gold, glass and Etruscan coins. On some coins the word *velathri* appears; Gori was the first to realize that this must have been the Etruscan name for Volterra.

In 1757 Guarnacci retired to Volterra; in 1761 he willed his library and museum (today, the Museo Etrusco Guarnacci) to his city; at his death, the museum contained 214 urns, two lids, two sarcophagi (the only two ever found at Volterra), 114 bronze figurines, seventy-four gold ornaments, as well as coins, pottery, glass and ivory.

BIBLIOGRAPHY

E. Fiumi, "La collezione di urne del Museo Guarnacci nel XVIII e XIX secolo," in *Urne volterrane* 2, *Il Museo Guarnacci* (Florence, 1977), reissued as *Storia e sviluppo del Museo Guarnacci di Volterra, a cura del Consorzio di gestione del Museo e della Biblioteca Guarnacci di Volterra* (Florence, 1977).

EMELINE HILL RICHARDSON

GUATTANI, GIUSEPPE ANTONIO (1748–1830). Italian scholar of archaeology and ancient art.

Born at Rome, Guattani trained as a lawyer but became interested in the arts, music and poetry. Through contact with E. Q. *Visconti and F. Piranesi, he turned to the study of antiquity. Guiding his wife, a famous singer, to concerts all over Europe, Guattani compiled his *Memorie enciclopediche,* in four volumes (1806), which contained notices of paintings and sculptures existing in the various museums he had visited. In 1804 Pius VII invited him to return from Paris to Rome, where he served as perpetual secretary of the *Pontificia Accademia Romana di Archeologia and the Accademia di S. Luca and also as supervisor of antiquities for sculpture found in Rome. At the same time, Augustus III of Poland employed Guattani as his antiquarian consultant.

Guattani's greatest contribution to scholarship was his seven-volume corpus of Roman monuments in *Monumenti antichi inediti, ovvero notizie sulle antichità e belle arti di Roma* (1784–89, 1805), a supplement to the *Monumenti inediti* of *Winckelmann. Among other things he left an authoritative description of the city of Rome, *Roma descritta ed illustrata,* two volumes (1805).
BIBLIOGRAPHY
G. Cressedi, "Guattani, Giuseppe Antonio," *EAA* 3 (1960), 1067.

GUBBIO (IGUVIUM). Italian town northeast of Perugia, inhabited by Umbrians in antiquity.

After the Social War (90 B.C.), the Umbrians were granted Roman citizenship, and Iguvium became a *municipium.* The town declined under the Roman Empire but regained some distinction as a bishopric in the Middle Ages. In 1384, Gubbio came into the hands of the counts of Urbino, and from 1631 it was included as part of papal territory.

The remains of the large Roman theater on the west side of the town were always known. Near these remains in 1444 the celebrated inscribed bronze plaques known as the Eugubine Tables (or Iguvine Tables) were discovered. They were found in an "underground chamber" paved with mosaics. Originally, there may have been nine plaques; seven were sold to the town of Gubbio by 1456, and two others are said to have been sold to Venice but to have disappeared after 1540. The seven, of three different sizes, are today in the Palazzo dei Consoli. Dating from the third–first centuries B.C., they constitute the largest body of inscriptions in the Umbrian language known today.

In the sixteenth century, Justus *Lipsius recognized that the texts were religious (1588), but the language was not yet conclusively identified. In the seventeenth and eighteenth centuries, Dutch, Old English, Old High German, Celtic, Greek and Hebrew were all suggested. Since four of the tablets are written in the Etruscan alphabet (three are in the Roman), various attempts were made to read them as Etruscan (e.g., by Thomas *Dempster), but F. *Buonarotti and, finally, K. O. *Müller laid this theory to rest. T. Aufrecht and A. Kirchhoff produced the first modern critical edition of the texts, along with a translation into Latin, *Umbrische Sprachdenkmäler,* three volumes (Berlin, 1849–51). *Devoto translated them into Italian (1948), and Poultney into English (1959).

BIBLIOGRAPHY
J. W. Poultney, *The Bronze Tablets of Iguvium,* Philological Monographs of the American
Philological Association, 28 (Baltimore, 1959); L. Richardson, jr, s.v. "Iguvium," *PECS,*
406.

GUIBERT OF NOGENT (1053–1121). French cleric, abbot of Nogent-sous-
Coucy in northern France.

Guibert describes the unearthing of an ancient cemetery in the vicinity of his
monastery at the beginning of the twelfth century. His remarkably sensitive
description reveals that he recognized that the tombs were pre-Christian, since
the sarcophagi were arranged according to a different custom, in a circle with
a single one in the middle. He also identified the pottery as antique. He could
not find any literary evidence of the existence of Nogent in antiquity but nonetheless argued from the finds that it must have been an important town. Along
with *Hildebert of Lavardin and Magister *Gregorius, Guibert reveals the existence of a humanistic interest in the visual remains of antiquity in the twelfth
century.

BIBLIOGRAPHY
Guibert of Nogent, *De vita sua,* ed. Bourgin (Paris, 1907); J. Adhémar, *Influences antiques dans l'art du Moyen Age français* (London, 1939), 17, 72, 99, 110.

GUIDEBOOKS TO GREECE. The finds of archaeology in Greece are accessible to nonspecialists through many excellent guidebooks. Alongside these, but
not identical with them, stand early travelers' accounts of their voyages. The
archaeologist Thomas Blagg has thus defined the difference between these two
kinds of books: a traveler's narrative tells you what he has seen; a guidebook
tells you what you will see. If we accept this distinction, the first guidebook is
that of Pausanias, who wrote in the 170s of our era. Indeed, we read him in the
pages of any modern guidebook, since most archaeologists accept many of his
identifications of artists and locations of sites and buildings as authoritative.

After Pausanias, there is a long gap until the writing of more books on Greek
travel. The first man of early modern times who set out to explore Greek lands
was the Florentine monk Cristoforo *Buondelmonti, who visited Rhodes about
1414–23. He wrote two historical-geographic works: *Descriptio insulae Candiae*
(1417) and *Liber insularum archipelagi* (1420). He also inspired the productive
travels of Ciriaco de' Pizzicolli (*Ciriaco of Ancona). After visiting Alexandria
in 1413, Ciriaco traveled extensively in Greece from the 1420s onward. The
original works of both these men are almost totally lost, but we have numerous
redactions and excerpts from them.

Although classical Greek authors were read in the original in Europe in the
fifteenth and sixteenth centuries, humanists showed little interest in Greece itself
or its topography. Symptomatic was the view of Athens published in Hartmann
Schedel's *Liber chronicarum* (1492), where the city was depicted as a generic
Northern European town. Voyages to Greece revived in the seventeenth and

eighteenth centuries, with the tour taken by the English naturalist George *Wheler and the French physician Jacob *Spon. The latter published an account with respectable illustrations of the *Parthenon, the *Monument of Lysikrates, the *Tower of the Winds and other monuments in his *Voyage d'Italie, de Dalmatie, de Grèce et du Levant* (1678). Wheler published his *A Journey into Greece* in 1682.

In addition, numerous, well-known publications of the eighteenth century constitute travel literature on Greece; one thinks of the publications of Robert *Wood on *Palmyra and *Baalbek, of R. *Chandler on Ionia, of *Stuart and *Revett on Athens. But though all of these may have constituted useful literature for travelers, they are not properly called guidebooks.

After the liberation of Greece from Turkish rule in the 1830s, Pausanias's modern successors began to issue books to assist the traveler. The first was *A Handbook for Travellers in the Ionian Islands, Greece, Turkey, Asia Minor and Constantinople*, edited and published by John Murray (London, 1840). He cites "the valuable and carefully prepared notes by Mr. Levinge," but he also draws on earlier travelers (Holland, *Leake, Pashley, et al.), sometimes almost reproducing their words (e.g., p. 23, on protecting children from the evil eye, taken directly from *Hobhouse). Murray divided his book into sections on the Ionian Islands, Greece and the Morea (the Peloponnese), the sections corresponding to the probable stages of the traveler's route to Greece. The guide quickly went through several much-expanded editions, reaching a seventh (little changed from the sixth) in 1900.

Meanwhile, the incomparable firm of Baedeker had entered the field. The first Baedeker pertaining to Greece was *Athens and Its Environs* (Athens, 1871; 5th ed., 1888), published by Karl Wilberg, German consul and a bookseller in Athens, in one small (now rare) volume of 127 pages with the same text in English, French and German. The text was actually only an excerpt from Baedeker's guide to Southern Italy, which contained advice for an excursion to Athens.

The first true Baedeker to Greece was mainly the work of Habbo G. Lolling (1848–94), the librarian of the *German Archaeological Institute, in Athens, and the successor to Colonel William Leake as the connoisseur of the Greek landscape. The first version of the book, a kind of Ur-Baedeker, was *Griechenland* (1878), printed by Baedeker in some ten proof copies and never actually published by the firm. It included a colossal introduction (410 pp.) on Greek geography and history, followed by 324 pages on detailed routes and sights for the traveler. The book covers only "northern" Greece, that is, Boeotia, *Thebes, *Delphi, Euboea and environs; Attica and the Peloponnese are omitted. Baedeker decided that so detailed a treatment was too long and told Lolling to compress the text. The book has been reprinted as *Reisenotizien aus Griechenland, 1876 und 1877* (Berlin, 1989).

The first regular Baedeker appeared in 1883; Lolling wrote most of it, but *Dörpfeld and Purgold contributed the part on *Olympia, where Germans had excavated since 1875. *Griechenland* had five editions in German (1883–1908), four in English (1889–1909) and one in French (1910). In successive editions new experts were brought in, for example, A.J.B. *Wace on *Sparta.

The other large series of modern guidebooks was begun by Hachette, Paris, and is known as Blue Guides or Guides Bleus. The volume on Greece descends from the *Itineraire descriptif, historique et archéologique de l'orient* by E. Isambert and A. L. Joanne (Paris, 1861, etc.), when the Hachette series was called Guides-Joanne. P. B. Joanne later became editor and issued a two-volume guide to Greece alone, written mainly by B. Haussoullier: *Athènes et ses environs* (1888) and *Grèce continentale et îles* (1891). Later editions were called simply *Grèce.* In 1955 Hachette issued the first English version, *Greece,* in the collection Hachette World Guides. A German translation of the then-current French version appeared first in 1963 as part of Hachette's Die blauen Führer.

The Hachette guides remain in print but have been rivaled in English by the Blue Guides, descending from a series also originally published by Hachette. The first Blue Guide to Greece was *Athens and Environs* (London, 1962), written by Stuart Rossiter. He later became editor of the Blue Guides and expanded his book into *Greece* (London, 1967); this guide was based partly on the work of experts treating this or that site. It has gone through several editions and editors and is generally considered the best guidebook to Greece. The sixth edition, prepared by Robin Barber, appeared in 1995.

Even more scientific is *Griechelandkunde: Ein Führer zu klassischen Statten* by E. Kirsten and W. Kraiker (Heidelberg, 1955 etc.), a two-volume study by two German professors that concentrates on archaeology and geography and omits entirely the most convenient routes, information on food, Greek customs and other suggestions for the traveler. It originated in a series of *Merkblätter* issued to German soldiers in Greece during World War II; it has a long, scholarly bibliography.

The book on Greece in the popular series Fodor's Modern Guides (London, 1960 etc.) concerns travel, shopping and customs and makes little attempt at precise archaeological coverage. The illustrated Companion Guides, in several formats, are beautifully written and evoke both history and atmosphere but also do not concentrate on detailed descriptions of sites.

BIBLIOGRAPHY

J. Morton Paton, *Chapters on Medieval and Renaissance Visitors to Greek Lands* (Princeton, NJ, 1951); Weiss, *RDCA,* Ch. 10; J.P.A. van der Vin, *Travellers to Greece and Constantinople,* 2 vols. (Leiden, 1980); D. Constantine, *Early Greek Travellers and the Hellenic Ideal* (Cambridge, 1984); Stoneman, *Land of Lost Gods;* R. Eisner, *Travelers to an Antique Land, The History and Literature of Travel to Greece* (Ann Arbor, 1991).

MORTIMER CHAMBERS

GUIDEBOOKS TO ROME (TO 1500). Early in Rome's history as center of the Catholic Church and trustee of its many sacred relics, guidebooks were needed to assist the pilgrims who came to the city from all of Europe. Today these guidebooks are an important source for the study of Roman topography.

A typical early guide is the *Notitia ecclesiarum urbis Romae* from the time of Pope Honorius I (625–638). It led pilgrims to the city's station churches (where papal masses were regularly held), the lesser churches and the cemeteries, ending with a description of the wonders of St. Peter's. The *Einsiedeln Itinerary from the ninth century includes descriptions of the ancient monuments and their inscriptions, with the usual itinerary of churches.

The most important and influential of all guidebooks was the *Mirabilia urbis Romae*. Its original appearance in the mid-twelfth century may be connected with the renovation of the Senate in 1143–44. The name of the Canon Benedict is sometimes given as its author. In the *Mirabilia,* Rome's pagan history and Christian history are combined and confused, reflecting the dual nature of the city itself. The guidebook begins with a bare listing of monuments organized according to type: bridges, temples, palaces, baths, *obelisks, *"triumphal" arches and so on. The latter portion recounts fantastic legends about Christian martyrs and ancient Romans, often erasing the distinction between the two periods. One legend, for example, tells of the appearance of the Virgin Mary and the Christ child to Augustus on the Capitoline; at this location the church of S. Maria in Aracoeli was built. The translation of the *Mirabilia* into Italian, *Le Miracole di Roma* in the thirteenth century, is an early example of the written *volgare.*

The *Graphia aureae urbis Romae,* from the twelfth century, is a more extensive guidebook than the *Mirabilia.* It is made up of three parts: the first tells of Rome from the arrival of Noah in Italy to the foundation of the city by Romulus; the second repeats the *Mirabilia,* improved somewhat by reference to nearby monuments to locate the sites of miracles and legends; the third portion, the *Libellus de ceremoniis aule imperatoris,* discusses old Roman law, customs and administration.

Most later guidebooks rely heavily on the *Mirabilia* as a model. These guidebooks, however, become increasingly better organized and easier to use; the accounts of legends become more integrated with the locations of their occurrence, and the monuments are often identified by both their antique and contemporary names. Examples of such "improved" *Mirabilia* are *De mirabilibus civitatis Romae* by Nicolas Rosell (ca. 1360) and the *Tractatus de rebus antiquis et situ Romae,* written by a native Roman in the early fifteenth century.

Pilgrims probably used guides like the *Notitia,* giving the locations of churches, their relics and indulgences, in conjunction with the *Mirabilia* and the *Graphia.* There were also available detailed guides to individual churches. In the latter part of the twelfth century, guides were written—perhaps in rivalry— to St. Peter's and St. John Lateran (*Descriptio Basilicae Vaticanae* and *Descriptio Lateranensis Ecclesiae*).

Discussion of the monuments of ancient Rome, divorced from Christian references, occupies the more historically minded authors and increases in number in the thirteenth, fourteenth and fifteenth centuries. Magister *Gregorius, who wrote *De mirabilibus urbis Romae* (ca. 1200), shows a keen appreciation of ancient art in his warm, vivid descriptions. Most of the scholarly works on the appearance of the city were not intended as practical guides but are, instead, attempts to understand the topography of the monuments and their history. Among the most important of these descriptions are those by *Petrarch, Giovanni *Dondi, Nicola Signorili, *Poggio Bracciolini, Flavio *Biondo and *Alberti.

The *Mirabilia* was the earliest and most-often printed guidebook in fifteenth-century Italy. One of the first editions was printed by Giovanni da Reno, ca. 1475. The *Mirabilia* and the *Indulgentiae ecclesiarum urbis Romae,* listing the churches, the relics and indulgences of the principal churches, were often published together and were translated into German, Italian and French.

The humanists of the fifteenth century made dramatic progress in the description of the monuments of Rome. *Poggio Bracciolini's *De varietate fortunae* (1448) is not truly a guidebook, but in assigning Rome a place as the chief example of the instability of fortune, Poggio took the opportunity to describe the city in terms that demonstrate that he took a fresh look at the monuments. He read inscriptions anew and turned to a wide range of ancient authors, Greek and Roman, to illuminate the antiquities. The *Roman instaurata* (composed 1444–46) of Flavio *Biondo was an exceptionally comprehensive and detailed archaeological handbook in its time, not superseded until *Marliani (*guidebooks to Rome, after 1500). The works of Pomponio *Leto and Bernardo *Rucellai bring a new source into topographical studies, with their editions of the early regionary catalog of Rome, the *Notitia regionum urbis,* ascribed to Publius Victor. The *De urbe Roma* of Rucellai, composed a little after 1495, was a full and careful commentary on Leto's interpolated text of the *Notitia* and made use of the latest evidence unearthed in the city.

BIBLIOGRAPHY

H. Jordan, *Topographie der Stadt Rom in Altertum* 2 (Berlin, 1871); O. Pollak, *Le Guide di Roma, Materialen zu einer Geschichte der römischen Topographie,* ed. L. Schudt (Vienna, 1930); Valentini—Zucchetti; F. Castagnoli, *Topografia di Roma antica* (Turin, 1980), 1, 5, 31, etc.; Weiss, *RDCA,* 64–84.

CHRISTINE SPERLING

GUIDEBOOKS TO ROME (AFTER 1500). The countless guidebooks to Rome written after 1500 are of several different types. Guides for pilgrims and travelers' accounts continue to be written, often with poetical or fanciful content. Most important for the history of classical archaeology are works that examine Roman topography and antiquarian questions.

The early sixteenth century saw the publication of an up-to-date treatment of the marvels of Rome by F. *Albertini, whose *Opusculum de mirabilibus novae et veteris urbis Romae* (1510) describes the ancient monuments and civic improvements of the Renaissance popes Nicholas V, *Sixtus IV and *Julius II and contains information about excavations and recent discoveries. The well-documented work featuring inscriptions, coins and citations from ancient and

Renaissance authors was an immediate success (it went through five editions between 1510 and 1523) and greatly influenced sixteenth-century literature on the city. It was surpassed, however, by the great work of A. *Fulvio, who had been schooled by *Leto and collaborated with *Raphael in trying to do a reconstruction of the ancient city. His *Antiquitates urbis,* published just before the Sack of Rome in 1527, shows the results of a lifetime of studying the monuments.

Known for his seriousness and solidity, B. *Marliani published his *Antiquae urbis Romae topographiae* in 1534, a topographical work that quickly appeared in new editions and was eventually translated into Italian and English. It follows a typical format for Renaissance guidebooks, beginning with a description of the hills, gates and walls of Rome and then proceeding to discuss certain areas of the town, such as the *Capitoline Hill and adjacencies, the *Palatine Hill, with the *Imperial Fora, the Aventine Hill, the *Campus Martius, the Tiber. In contrast to Marliani, P. *Ligorio has been criticized for his fanciful ideas (*Delle antichità di Roma,* 1553) and negative influence on O. *Panvinio and others. *Palladio issued a brief guide to antiquities, *L'Antichità di Roma* (1554), that was immensely popular and went through edition after edition and translation into French and Spanish. In 1750 it was still being reprinted and was sometimes combined with one of the dozens of *Cose maravigliose* turned out well into the eighteenth century to guide pilgrims to churches. B. Gamucci produced *I Libri quattro dell'antichità* (Venice, 1565), utilizing views of ancient Rome by *Dosio.

Modest progress was made in topography in the seventeenth century, with the works of the Sienese Jesuit Alessandro Donati (*Roma vetus ac recens,* 1638) and F. *Nardini (*Roma antica,* 1665). A new breed of guide was in use—well illustrated, combining ancient and modern elements and drawing wholesale from previous topographical and ecclesiastical texts. These guides were assembled by family publishing houses such as Franzini and De' Rossi. Girolamo Franzini of Venice moved his family to Rome sometime before 1600 to start the family firm there; his son Antonio carried the business forward. An example of their mature publications is the *Descrizione di Roma antica e moderna* (1643), "in which are contained churches, monasteries, hospitals, companies, colleges and seminaries, temples, theaters, amphitheaters, naumachiae, circuses, forums, curias, palaces and statues, libraries, museums, paintings and artists' names, [with] Index of the most important popes, emperors and dukes." Successors to these were the immensely popular guides of Fioravante Martinelli, *Roma ricercata* (first published 1644) and Pietro Rossini, the *Mercurio errante* (first published 1693). Martinelli intended his guide to be concise and to help the tourists find their way through all the riches of Rome in a ten-day planned itinerary. In the eighteenth century, the Vasi family carried on this tradition. The engraver Giuseppe Vasi, in whose workshop the young *Piranesi worked, was celebrated for his great ten-volume compendium of engravings, *Delle magnificenze di Roma, antica e moderna* (1747–61). But to the category of handbooks he contributed the *Itinerario istruttivo* (1763), with an eight-day plan to see ancient and modern Rome. The text gave references to the illustrations of the *Magnificenze*, but later editions put out by his son Mariano were to include the quietly detailed and appealing engravings of Giuseppe.

An era of great erudition in topography was initiated with A. *Nibby. His *Itinerario di Roma* in two volumes (1827) could take into account the enormous amount of information about ancient Rome revealed by the French excavations of Roman monuments under *Napoleon and by his own work in the *Temple of Venus and Roma and in the *Basilica of Maxentius, which he succeeded in identifying properly after it had long been called the temple of Peace. He paid careful attention to medieval accounts of Rome in his analysis of topography in his time. His rival was C. *Fea, whose *Nuova descrizione di Roma antica e moderna* in three volumes (1820) had a fairly standard treatment of monuments but included much information on collections of antiquities at the *Vatican and the *Capitoline Museums. An increasing number of special guides or catalogs of individual collections, villas and monuments were being issued, such as Fea's own book on the *Pantheon, *L'Integrità del Panteon di M. Agrippa* (1837).

L. *Canina's *Indicazione topografica di Roma antica* (1837) used an organizing principle based on the early regionary catalogs of Rome, as had been done by Leto in the fifteenth century (*guidebooks to Rome, [to 1500]). *Lanciani noted this in his review of topographical guides of the nineteenth century, and he observed that others pursued a chronological arrangement, as in T. H. Dyer's *A History of the City of Rome: Its Structure and Monuments* (1865), while yet another approach was the architectural, with emphasis on classes of famous buildings (all the baths, all the theaters, and so on). Here belongs L. *Canina's *Edifizi di Roma antica* (six volumes, 1848–56), not a guidebook, but revealing a new attitude toward the ancient monuments, with its bold reconstructions of ruined buildings, still of value. The German school, beginning with the *Beschreibung Roms* of C. Bunsen and others and continuing with W. A. Becker and H. Jordan, followed a "mixed" system, in which the three methods—by region, chronology, and famous buildings—were blended as appropriate for a given topic. This is the system of Lanciani's own masterly guide, *The Ruins and Excavations of Ancient Rome,* with subtitle *A Companion Book for Student and Travelers,* a learned work that, nevertheless, is meant to be quite readable for nonspecialists.

The twentieth century has seen dramatic contrasts in the available guides to the monuments of Rome. On the truly scholarly side, a new achievement is found in the topographical dictionaries of *Platner and *Ashby and L. Richardson, jr, with the monuments arranged in alphabetical order; not intended as guidebooks to carry about the city, these works, nevertheless, provide superb descriptions of monuments and sites along with appropriate ancient and modern bibliographical citations. Their illustrated counterpart is the *Pictorial Dictionary* *of Ancient Rome* by E. Nash (2 vols., rev. ed. 1968), with 1,338 photos. Numerous works by G. *Lugli are of importance for the study of Roman topography and the techniques by which the buildings were constructed; his *Itinerario di Roma antica* (1975) belongs in the guide category. On the other extreme there is a proliferation of highly commercial popular guides, bright with colored photographs and low in price. Among the ubiquitous guides available in and out of Italy, the Fodor series is popular, with its itineraries and up-to-the-minute tips on travel; and the guides of the Touring Club Italiano (*Roma e dintorni,* in many editions) are informative and authoritative. Booklets on individual monuments issued by the Ministry of Public Instruction in Italian, French, German and English (an example is *L'Ara Pacis Augustae* by G. Moretti), with their concise descriptions and small but useful photographs make handy guides on site and in the library. The leading portable comprehensive guide to ancient Rome is F. Coarelli's *Guida archeologica di Roma,* with plans, color photos, bibliography and study helps (3rd ed., 1980).

BIBLIOGRAPHY

O. Pollak, *Le Guide di Roma, Materialen zu einer Geschichte der römischen Topographie,* ed. L. Schudt (Vienna, 1930); F. Castagnoli, *Topografia di Roma Antica* (Turin, 1980), esp. 1–7; Weiss, *RDCA,* passim; Richardson, *New Topographical Dictionary,* xxiii–xxvi.

GUSTAV III'S MUSEUM OF ANTIQUITIES, Stockholm. The first publicly owned art museum outside Italy.

This museum, consisting of the king's private collection of antique sculpture, was opened in 1794, according to a wish expressed by King Gustaf III (*GUSTAVUS III, d. 1792). It was housed in two galleries in neoclassical style in the Royal Palace at Stockholm (restored in the original arrangement in 1992). The collection of sculpture had been acquired by the king himself, partly during his journey to Italy with the sculptor J. T. Sergel (1783–84); in all it comprised 182 items, among them fine works like the *Endymion* and the *Apollo* but also heavily restored copies and forgeries. Among the sellers were Giovanni Volpato and Francesco Piranesi. The king also collected ancient vases, some of which were bought from Sir William *Hamilton in Naples; a selection is now exhibited in the museum.

BIBLIOGRAPHY

+*Gustav III:s antikmuseum* (Stockholm, 1992).

ROBIN HÄGG

GUSTAVUS III (GUSTAF III, GUSTAV III) (1746–92). King of Sweden.

During the reign of Gustavus III, Sweden experienced interior turmoil due to dissension between the political parties and the lack of leadership within the House of Parliament. The king succeeded in obtaining his goals by strengthening the role of the monarch at the expense of the aristocracy, but a conspiracy among members of the nobility led to his assassination at the Opera House in Stockholm in 1792 (an event known from Verdi's *The Masked Ball*).

Outside the scope of Swedish history, King Gustavus is known as a patron of the arts, and he himself wrote plays on historical topics. His fascination with classical art and architecture was expressed in the many public buildings erected in Stockholm during his reign and in the decoration of his residences outside the city, but he also formed a collection of antiquities then (and now) housed in the Royal Palace in Stockholm.

The origin of this collection goes back to 1783–84, when the king, during his travels in Italy, visited famous sites such as Vesuvius (cf. *Pompeii, *Herculaneum) and *Hadrian's Villa at Tivoli and also had the opportunity to admire the sculpture galleries in the *Vatican shown to him by Pope *Pius VI. Through the son of G. B. *Piranesi, Francesco Piranesi, the king acquired a large number of statues, of which many were reported to have been found at Tivoli, whereas others came from private collections in Rome. Among the most famous pieces were *Apollo and the Nine Muses* and an *Endymion,* which, according to some scholars, is an eighteenth-century creation, although it, too, was supposed to have come from Hadrian's Villa. In addition to the marble sculptures bought in Italy, the collection included statues originally brought to Sweden by Queen *Christina and a number of Greek vases (mostly South Italian of the fourth century B.C.), acquired from Sir William *Hamilton, the English minister in Naples.

The main importance of this collection lies in the history of its foundation, and it serves as a reflection of how the era of Gustavus III in this concrete way gained inspiration from the cultural heritage of Italy. (See also *Gustav III's Museum of Antiquities, Stockholm.)

BIBLIOGRAPHY

R. N. Bain, *Gustavus III and His Contemporaries* (London, 1904); O. Antonsson, *Antik konst* (Stockholm, 1958); A. Andrén, ''Ur antiksamlandets historia,'' *Stockholm. Nationalmuseum, Antiken* (Stockholm, 1967), 19–32; +*Stockholm. Nationalmuseum, Gustaf III* (Stockholm, 1972); +*Gustav III:s antikmuseum* (Stockholm, 1992).

INGRID E. M. EDLUND

GUSTAVUS VI ADOLPHUS (GUSTAF VI ADOLF, GUSTAV VI ADOLF) (1882–1973). King of Sweden, lifelong devotee of archaeology.

Following his principle that archaeology is a ''key to the unknown,'' King Gustav VI Adolf participated in excavations in Sweden as a student. He became a highly respected participant in the Swedish excavations at *Asine in Greece in 1922 and on *Cyprus as a member of the *Swedish Cyprus Expedition (1927–31), directed by Einar *Gjerstad. In Italy he took part in the American-Swedish excavations at *Morgantina in Sicily (begun in 1955) and played an active role in the Swedish excavations at San Giovenale (begun in 1956) and *Acquarossa (begun in 1966) in Etruria.

BIBLIOGRAPHY

+A. Boëthius et al., *Etruscan Culture. Land and People* (Malmö, 1962); +E. W. Wetter et al., *Med kungen på Acquarossa* (Malmö, 1972); E. Gjerstad, "Konung Gustaf VI Adolf," *Kungl. Fysiografiska Sällskapets årsbok* (1972–73), 83–89; +C. Nylander, "Gustavo VI Adolfo, il 're archeologo,' " *Gli Etruschi e l'Europa* (Milan, 1992), 462–67.

INGRID E. M. EDLUND

H

HADRIAN'S VILLA, near Tivoli. The largest and most famous of ancient villas, designed for the emperor Hadrian between A.D. 120 and 138, this vast retreat was spread over more than a hundred hectares of gently contoured land.

Of avant-garde design, the villa consisted of a profusion of pavilions, casinos and pools, all reflecting the fascination architecture had for the intellectual autocrat. Many of the original elements of construction stand today, though shorn of their mosaics, waterworks and marbles (many of the last-named can be seen in the museums of Rome, particularly, the *Vatican). The exact extent of the place is unknown, and only now is the scientific study of the remains going forward.

The villa was hardly ever used after Hadrian's death in 138. In due time olive groves appeared between the wrecks of the pavilions and casinos, making it the most romantic of sights. Early on, humanists recognized its importance, and from time to time important works of art, chiefly sculpture, were found. Pirro *Ligorio, the designer of the neighboring Villa d'Este, first explored parts of the villa more or less scientifically in the mid-sixteenth century. More casual attacks were made by scores of predators who took away large amounts of booty; the lack of knowledge as to where, in the sprawling fabric of the villa, this material came from is a considerable hindrance to the overall artistic and archaeological study of the site. Englishmen on the *Grand Tour tramped through it, buying objects now seen in great country houses and museums of Great Britain. Visitors such as Gavin *Hamilton excavated a considerable number of statues.

In the eighteenth century, G. B. *Piranesi and his son Francesco carefully made a large-scale map of the remains that was duly published by the latter; it is still the basis for our knowledge of some of the outlying structures. A more modern plan was made at the turn of the present century by Italian engineers, for the government had obtained title to the central part of the villa (that part the visitor sees today), and proper conservation and some methodical investigation were begun. Of great importance were the visits to the site, from Ligorio's time onward, by major architects, for whom the buildings—baths, theaters, halls, scenic fountains and the like—were a revelation because most of them were unrelated to Vitruvius's conservative prescriptions and therefore to those of the Renaissance as well. *Palladio, Borromini, Rainaldi probably, Piranesi and a host of Beaux Arts architects spent time at the villa, and in the present century such masters as LeCorbusier and Louis Kahn fell under its spell. *Kähler's study of the villa is good but necessarily incomplete; Clark's is readable and very evocative; and Aurigemma's is well illustrated. More such works, as well as a complete modern survey, are needed, and the study of the provenance and history of objects known to have been found at the villa could profitably be pursued.

BIBLIOGRAPHY

H. Kähler, *Hadrian und seine Villa bei Tivoli* (Berlin, 1950); E. Clark, *Rome and a Villa* (New York, 1952); S. Aurigemma, *Villa adriana* (Rome, 1961); W. L. MacDonald—B. M. Boyle, "The Small Baths at Hadrian's Villa," *JSAH* 39 (1980), 5–27; W. L. MacDonald—J. A. Pinto, *Hadrian's Villa and Its Legacy* (New Haven, CT, 1995).

WILLIAM L. MacDONALD

HAGIA PHOTIA. Bronze Age site in eastern *Crete, with remains of the Early Minoan (EM) period.

In 1971, C. Davaras discovered at Hagia Photia one of the largest and most important cemeteries of Bronze Age Crete, consisting of more than 260 tombs of the EM I/II periods. The tombs, of a type previously unknown in Cretan archaeology, featured a small, primitive chamber cut in the soft bedrock, with a rudimentary antechamber, actually a shaft to provide access in the manner of the dromos in later tombs. The chamber was closed with a large upright stone slab to facilitate reopening of the tomb for subsequent burials. Finds included more than 1,500 clay vases and a remarkable series of obsidian blades. The influence of the culture of the Cyclades is so strong that one may describe this site as a Cycladic colony in Crete.

Some 150m west of the cemetery, M. Tsipopoulou excavated in 1984–85 an unusual rectangular building with thirty-six rooms and a central court (dating to Middle Minoan IA or IB), a possible forerunner of the great Minoan palaces.

BIBLIOGRAPHY

C. Davaras, "Protominoikon nekrotapheion Aghias Photias Siteias," *AAA* 4 (1971), 392–97; *Hagios Nikolaos Museum* (Athens, 1982); M. Tsipopoulou, *Archaeological Survey of Aghia Photia, Siteia, Studies in Mediterranean Archaeology and Literature,* pocketbook no. 76 (Partille, 1989); *Aerial Atlas of Crete,* 66–69.

COSTIS DAVARAS

HAGIA TRIADHA (AYIA TRIADA; HAGHIA TRIADA), Crete. Chiefly Minoan site (Early Minoan–Late Minoan III) in the Mesara Valley in central *Crete.

Excavation was begun by the *Italian School of Archaeology in 1902, under the direction of Federico *Halbherr and Roberto Paribeni. They exposed a luxurious Late Minoan (LM) I complex of storage and residential suites furnished with alabaster floors and dados, one room of which, probably a shrine, was richly decorated with wall painting depicting a landscape containing at least one woman. The complex was interpreted as a "summer palace" for the *Phaistos royalty, but a recent analysis of it as two separate residences makes that theory less likely.

It was destroyed in the LM IB burning also found elsewhere on Crete, resulting here in the abandonment of a hoard of copper ingots as well as the preservation of the largest group discovered of still-undeciphered Linear A tablets (*Linear A and B). In LM IIIA2 there was a revival of the town, with ambitious construction of a temple, a vast stoa, probably connected with commerce, and what may have been an administrative building (the "megaron"). Recent careful study by Vincenzo La Rosa has clarified dating and architectural details for all periods.

The famous Hagia Triadha sarcophagus, a limestone larnax dating to LM III (fourteenth century B.C.) was found in a tomb northeast of the residential area.

BIBLIOGRAPHY

C. Long, *The Hagia Triadha Sarcophagus*, Studies in Mediterranean Archaeology 49 (Göteborg, 1974); F. Halbherr—E. Stefani—L. Banti, *Haghia Triada nel periodo tardopalaziale*, ASAtene 55 (1977); L. V. Watrous, "Ayia Triada: A New Perspective on the Minoan Villa," *AJA* 88 (1984), 123–24; V. La Rosa, "Nouvelles données du Bronze Moyen au Bronze Récent à Haghia Triada," *Aegaeum, Annales d'Archéologie Égéene de l'Université de Liège,* 3 (1989), 81–92.

JOSEPH W. SHAW

HALBHERR, FEDERICO (1857–1930). Italian archaeologist.

Halbherr, one of the first archaeologists to explore and excavate on *Crete, was founder of the *Italian School of Archaeology in Athens and discoverer of the great inscription with the Law Code at *Gortyn and of many Cretan sites, including Minoan *Phaistos, *Hagia Triadha and Archaic Prinias. Halbherr first went to Crete to search for Archaic Greek inscriptions upon the suggestion of his teacher, Domenico Comparetti, in 1884. His discovery of the Gortyn Code, a series of regulations dealing chiefly with property and still the longest single Greek inscription known, was followed by numerous discoveries by him, his students and colleagues throughout Crete, but especially in the area of the Mesara Plain. His early explorations include caves (Idaean Cave of Zeus; Psychro in the Mountains of Dikti) and Graeco-Roman settlement sites (Prinias, Kourtes, Praesos, Axos, Lebena). In the Mesara he was responsible for initiating the excavation of the large Late Minoan I palace at Phaistos and the sumptuous buildings at nearby Hagia Triadha, as well as both the odeum (which contained the Law Code) and the temple of Apollo at *Gortyn.

An indefatigable explorer, Halbherr, whose contributions often remain unrecognized, is nonetheless remembered for his modesty and generosity and his insatiable desire to learn.

BIBLIOGRAPHY
A. della Seta, ''Federico Halbherr,'' *ASAtene* 13–14 (1930–31), 1–8; A. Di Vita et al., eds., *Ancient Crete, A Hundred Years of Italian Archaeology (1884–1984)* (Rome, 1984); V. La Rosa, ''Federico Halbherr e Creta,'' *L'Archeologia italiana nel Mediterraneo* (Catania, 1986), 53–72.

JOSEPH W. SHAW AND GIULIANA BIANCO

HALIKARNASSOS (HALICARNASSUS). City in Caria (southwestern Asia Minor), located at modern Bodrum on the north coast of the gulf of Kos.

One of its eminent citizens, the historian Herodotos, recorded that the city was settled by Dorians. A member of the Dorian hexapolis, Halikarnassos came under Persian domination in the sixth century B.C. and was ruled by native Carian dynasts. The city rose to prominence in the fourth century B.C. under the Hekatomnid dynasty. Mausolos, satrap of Caria from ca. 377 to 353 B.C., moved the capital of the satrapy to Halikarnassos and initiated a number of monumental building projects. Halikarnassos resisted Alexander in 334 B.C., surrendering after a siege. The city was under Ptolemaic domination until 190 B.C. and was then granted autonomy.

Halikarnassos was famed in antiquity for the tomb of Mausolos, or *Mausoleum, one of the Seven Wonders of the World, built by his widow, Artemisia. The original appearance of the tomb is disputed, but it apparently stood on a podium that carried freestanding sculptures and was crowned by a chariot group.

Few ancient structures are now preserved, most having been destroyed or reused during subsequent construction, such as in the castle of the Knights of St. John built in the fifteenth century. Excavations at the site of the mausoleum were carried out in the nineteenth century by C. T. *Newton. More recently, a Danish expedition (between 1964 and 1977) studied the area around the tomb, ascertaining that it was surrounded by a large peribolos wall and that it stood in an area already used as a monumental nekropolis.

BIBLIOGRAPHY
+C. T. Newton, *A History of Discoveries at Halicarnassus, Cnidus and Branchidae* (London, 1863); K. Jeppesen—K. Flemming Højlund—K. Aaris-Sørenson, *Reports of the Danish Archaeological Expedition to Bodrum* 1–3 (Copenhagen, 1981–91).

ANN C. GUNTER

HALLER VON HALLERSTEIN, CARL CHRISTOPH, BARON (1774–1817). German architect and archaeologist, remembered for the great precision of his drawings and his systematic approach to excavation at an early date.

Born near Nuremberg to a noble family, Haller studied architecture at Stuttgart and Berlin (where the neoclassical architects F. *Schinkel and Leo von *Klenze were also pupils). In 1808 he set out for Italy to spend two years drawing views of the city of Rome and studying ancient and early Christian architecture.

Joining P. O. *Brøndsted, Otto Magnus von *Stackelberg, Georg Koes and Jacob Linckh, he sailed for Greece, arriving in Athens in 1810. The group soon met C. R. *Cockerell, who quickly became their leader. Haller and Cockerell were close friends who shared a love of measuring and drawing; their talents were well employed in their excavation at *Aigina (1811), where they made careful drawings of the temple of Aphaia (they thought it a temple of Zeus) and discovered the famous pedimental sculptures, later sold to Crown Prince *Ludwig of Bavaria.

Further dramatic discoveries awaited the friends at *Bassai (1811–12), where Haller directed the work (1812; Cockerell was in Sicily). The sculptured frieze with a Centauromachy and an Amazonomachy that they discovered ultimately found its way to the *British Museum. Haller made a drawing of the famous Corinthian capital from Bassai, the earliest complete example known.

Tragically, Haller died of a fever in 1817 in Thessaly. He was buried there and later was probably transferred to the Protestant cemetery in the *Hephaisteion in Athens. Cockerell eventually published many of Haller's drawings in *The Temple of Jupiter Panhellenius at Aegina, and of Apollo Epicurius at Bassae near Phigaleia in Arcadia* (London, 1860).

BIBLIOGRAPHY

Stark, 260–62; Tsigakou, *Rediscovery of Greece* 22, 192c; H. Haller von Hallerstein, *Und die Erde gebar ein Lacheln, Der erste deutsche Archäologe in Griechenland, Carl Haller von Hallerstein, 1774–1817* (Munich, 1983); H. Bankel, in *Archäologenbildnisse*, 16–17.

HAMILTON, GAVIN INGLIS (1723–98). Scottish painter; excavator and dealer in antiquities.

Born in Lanarkshire and educated at Glasgow University, Gavin Hamilton trained as a painter in Rome. He returned to Scotland in 1751 and established himself as a portrait painter but stayed only five years before returning to Rome with the intention of making his reputation as a history painter. Brief visits to his native country apart, he spent the rest of his life in Italy.

His interest in classical archaeology was demonstrated in his earliest years as a painter. A portrait of the Jacobite exile William Hamilton of Bangour, painted in 1748, depicts the sitter (a poet and classical scholar who translated the *Iliad* into English blank verse) laurel-wreathed against a grisaille ground above a bas-relief frieze. The large-scale *Dawkins and Wood Discovering Palmyra* of 1758 (on loan to Glasgow University), commissioned by James Dawkins's brother Henry as a posthumous tribute to his brother's achievement, shows Hamilton's interest in contemporary archaeology and his growing enthusiasm for the classical world, in spite of the rather odd combination of Roman togas and Turkish slippers in which he dresses the principal figures.

Contemporary with this work was a *Paris and Helen* painted for Nathaniel

Self-Portrait, drawing by Gavin Hamilton. Edinburgh, National Gallery of Scotland, Scottish National Portrait Gallery. (National Gallery of Scotland.)

Curzon of Kedleston. It was the artist's first treatment of a subject that was to inspire him with his "great plan in life"—a series of paintings telling the story of Paris and "my sweet Helen." This project was envisaged as a series of six small canvases for the Earl of Shelburne, but the earl declined Hamilton's proposal, and the scheme was finally realized ten years later, on a larger scale and with an increased number of paintings—now eight—in the Villa Borghese, commissioned by Prince Marcantonio Borghese in 1782.

Hamilton meanwhile had achieved considerable success and earned much contemporary esteem for a series of six large paintings of scenes from the *Iliad*. Commissioned by various aristocratic patrons, they reached a much wider public and enjoyed considerable popularity via Cunego's engravings. In addition, Hamilton painted *The Death of Lucretia* (Drury Lane Theatre) and *Agrippina Landing with the Ashes of Germanicus* (Tate Gallery), together with a number of smaller-scale subjects—*Muses,* a *Juno,* a *Hebe* and so on—and the occasional portrait. His reputation was thus established as the foremost history painter of his age, leader of the community of British painters living in Rome and a more thoroughgoing neoclassicist than even *Mengs.

He was, however, a slow and not always very diligent painter, largely because from 1769 onward, his energies were diverted into organizing archaeological excavations. In writing to one of his patrons, Charles *Townley, he urged, "[N]ever forget that the most valuable acquisition a man of refined taste can make is a piece of Greek sculpture." Hamilton tried to ensure that as many of his patrons as possible should benefit from such valuable acquisitions. He excavated first at *Hadrian's Villa, between 1769 and 1771, at Tor Colombaro on the Via Appia from the autumn of 1771 and during the following years at Albano, Grottaferrata, Genzano, *Nemi, Monte Cagnuolo between Genzano and Civita Lavinia, Castel di Guido (the ancient Lorium), *Ostia and Gabii.

From about 1773, export licenses became increasingly hard to obtain, as Pope *Clement XIV and his successor, *Pius VI, grew alarmed at the extensive traffic in the export of antiquities from Italy. Consequently, many of Hamilton's later finds made their way into the new Pio-Clementino museum (*Vatican Museums). In his last years virtually none of his finds reached his British clients, for he was employed by Prince Marcantonio Borghese (*Borghese family) at Gabii expressly to find items for his own collection. (Most of these finds are now in the *Louvre.) Hamilton recorded finding, on this site, fragments of about 200 statues, and "twenty-two that are good and worth restoring. All go to the Prince Borghese, who builds a place for their reception at the Villa."

Many of Hamilton's finds did end up in the sculpture galleries of great houses in England. The Earl of Egremont at Petworth obtained a *Satyr Pouring Wine* that Hamilton dug up in the Campagna; Thomas Mansell-Talbot, at Margam Abbey in Wales, bought a statue and two busts excavated from Hadrian's Villa by Hamilton, together with a statue of a Satyr that Hamilton purchased on his behalf from the Barberini collection; Smith-Barry at Marbury Hall, Cheshire, acquired three statues found by Hamilton; the Warwick Vase, found at Hadrian's Villa in 1769, was sold by Gavin Hamilton to Sir William *Hamilton, who, in turn, gave it to the Earl of Warwick. But the cream of Hamilton's finds went to the Earl of Shelburne (the Marquess of Lansdowne; 1737–1805) and to Charles Townley. Shelburne's "truly aristocratic collection" included statues of *Cincinnatus* (also identified as *Jason*), *Marcus Aurelius* and a *Meleager,* which "Mengs and some others think . . . may be a young Hercules" (but it was also identified as *Antinous* and, finally, as *Hermes*). There was also a *Diomedes,* who

"holds the Palladium in one hand while he defends himself with the right holding a dagger . . . it would be to the last degree absurd to suppose it anything
else." (It was later identified as a *Diskobolos* after Myron.) As with so many
pieces, this was a restoration ("the legs and arms are modern, but restored in
perfect harmony with the rest"). As for Townley's collection, now in the *British Museum, this extensive group of statues, busts, reliefs and vases contained,
as crown of the collection, a *Venus* that *Canova thought "the finest female
statue he had seen in England" and that Payne *Knight later described as
"worth more than any two articles in Lord Elgin's collection"; a *Dog and Bitch*
at play (a similar group found with it at Monte Cagnuolo went to the Museo
Pio-Clementino); a magnificent marble vase from the same site; a *Cupid* bending
his bow, found in 1775 at Castel di Guido; and many other items that contributed
toward making Townley's one of the most admired collections of its time.
(Many of the objects Hamilton excavated are illustrated in Zoffany's painting
of Townley's Library in Park Street.)

Hamilton enjoyed a reputation for honesty rare among his contemporaries. At
a time when much highly dubious restoration was undertaken, and Thomas
Jenkins's workshops in the Colosseum, producing "antique" cameos and intaglios for tourists, were notorious, "not the least suspicion of any unfair or even
questionable transaction has ever fallen upon Hamilton in connection with his
dealings in antiques." Restoration of antiquities was considered perfectly legitimate in the eighteenth century, and Hamilton never pretended that his finds
were other than reconstructions of fragments. *Canova, grateful for Hamilton's
interest and encouragement, wrote of him as "a sincere man with a very intelligent understanding of the best style, and an excellent painter."

BIBLIOGRAPHY

+Sir Henry Ellis, *The Townley Gallery,* 1–2 (London, 1846); A.T.F. Michaelis, *Catalogue of the Ancient Marbles at Lansdowne House,* ed. A. H. Smith (London, 1889);
+D. Irwin, "Gavin Hamilton, Archaeologist, Painter and Dealer," *ArtB* 44 (1962), 87–
102; B. Skinner, *Scots in Italy in the 18th Century* (Edinburgh, 1966); Haskell—Penny,
66–68, 142, 152, 182–84, 200.

SERENA Q. HUTTON

HAMILTON, SIR WILLIAM (1730–1803). Diplomat, vulcanologist and collector.

Although descended from a noble family, Hamilton had little money of his
own, and after a decade in the army as a young man he married an heiress,
Catherine Barlow, in 1758. In 1764 he was appointed envoy extraordinary to
the court of Naples by George III, whom he had known from boyhood. His
diplomatic duties not being onerous, he devoted much time to the study of
Vesuvius and other volcanoes and to archaeology, especially the excavations at
*Pompeii and *Herculaneum. His house, the Palazzo Sessa, became a well-
known center of cultural life. The Hamiltons entertained many royal and other
visitors to Naples and were enlightened patrons of music and the arts.

Lord and Lady Hamilton attend the excavation of a tomb at Nola, watercolor by C. H. Kniep, 1790. (Deutsches Archäologisches Institut, Rome. Inst. Neg. 1938.149.)

He also collected paintings and antiquities, largely as an investment for his retirement. The heavy expense of publishing d'*Hancarville's four folio volumes in 1766–67 forced him to begin to sell earlier. In 1772 his first collection of antiquities was purchased by the *British Museum with a parliamentary grant of £8,400. It included over 700 vases, 175 terracottas, 150 ivories, 600 bronzes, 150 gems, 300 objects of glass and 100 of gold and about 6,000 coins.

Other objects that passed through Hamilton's hands included the large marble bowl restored by *Piranesi from fragments found in *Hadrian's Villa (the Warwick Vase, now in the Burrell Collection, Glasgow) and the Barberini or *Portland Vase, acquired by him from James *Byres for £1,000 and later sold to the Dowager Duchess of Portland (now in the British Museum).

After the death of his first wife, he took under his protection the beautiful but shallow-minded ''Emma Hart,'' formerly the mistress of his nephew Charles Greville. She used to entertain Hamilton and his guests (including *Goethe in 1787) by impersonating classical heroines in a variety of dress and posture (''Lady Hamilton's Attitudes''). In 1791 Hamilton actually married Emma, who, in view of her history, was not received at court and later became even more notorious as the mistress of Lord Nelson.

The plates for the publication of Hamilton's second collection of antiquities were prepared under the supervision of Wilhelm *Tischbein. In the text of the first volume (1791), Hamilton propounded the then-extraordinary theory that many so-called Etruscan vases should, on the evidence of inscriptions and provenance, be considered Greek. In 1796 he attempted to sell the collection, comprising over 1,000 vases, about half of them figured, to the King of Prussia for £7,000, but without success. When the Neapolitan court had to be evacuated to Palermo during the war with France, part of the collection was put on board HMS *Colossus,* which was wrecked off the Isles of Scilly in 1798. A few vases recovered at the time have since been lost, but between 1975 and 1979 many thousands of small fragments were salvaged and deposited in the British Museum.

After his recall from Naples in 1800, Hamilton had his paintings auctioned and sold his remaining vases to Thomas Hope for £4,000. Following the sale of the Hope vases in 1917, Hamilton's second collection has been scattered around the world.

BIBLIOGRAPHY

D'Hancarville (P. F. Hugues), *Collection of Etruscan, Greek and Roman Antiquities from the Cabinet of the Hon. W. Hamilton,* 1–4 (Naples, 1776–77); W. Hamilton, *Collection of Engravings from Ancient Vases . . . Published by W. Tischbein,* 1–3. (Naples, 1791–95); B. Fothergill, *Sir William Hamilton, Envoy Extraordinary* (London, 1969); *Porträtarchiv,* no. 100; N. H. Ramage, ''Sir William Hamilton as Collector, Exporter and Dealer: The Acquisition and Dispersal of His Collections,'' *AJA* 94 (1990), 469–80; Idem, ''Goods, Graves and Scholars: 18th-Century Archaeologists in Britain and Italy,'' *AJA* 96 (1992), 653–61.

B. F. COOK

HANCARVILLE, PIERRE-FRANÇOIS HUGUES, COMTE D' (1719–1805). Prominent French adventurer, antiquarian and art historian.

Born in Nancy, son of a cloth merchant, endowed with energy, imagination and intelligence, Hancarville acquired a considerable reputation thanks to solid studies in the classics, history and languages. After military service with Prince Ludwig of Mecklenberg, Hancarville roamed most of Western Europe, making various useful contacts on the strength of his personal charm. These wanderings were punctuated by periods in prison for debts and for unrealistic projects proposed under various noble aliases. The final, permanent identity assumed was that of le Comte d'Hancarville.

In Naples in the 1760s he struck up a meaningful friendship based on mutual antiquarian interests with Sir William *Hamilton, the new British ambassador. Hancarville's erudition and artistic talent led Hamilton to entrust him with preparing and illustrating the lavish bilingual catalog entitled *Collection of Etruscan, Greek and Roman Antiquities from the Cabinet of the Hon.ble Wm. Hamilton* in four volumes (1767–76). At this same time, Hancarville established a cordial, if wary, relationship with the most famous German archaeologist in Italy, J. J. *Winckelmann.

The decade of the 1780s was spent in England and France, during which he published two volumes for which he was accused of pornography: *Monuments de la vie privée des douze Césars* (1780) and its sequel, *Monuments du culte secret des dames romaines* (1784); the erotic illustrations here were mainly pseudoantiques of Hancarville's own invention.

His crowning achievement was the publication in London in 1785 of a speculative study of art history and comparative mythology, *Recherches sur l'origine, l'esprit et le progrès des arts de la Grèce; sur leur connexion avec les arts et la religion des plus anciens peuples connus.*

Hancarville died in Padua in 1805.

BIBLIOGRAPHY

H. de la Porte, ''Hancarville (Pierre-François Hugues, dit d'),'' *BU* 18 (1873), 415–16; Guyot de Fère, ''Hancarville (Pierre-François Hugues, dit d'),'' *NBG* 23 (1861), cols. 286–87; F. Haskell, ''The Baron d'Hancarville: An Adventurer and Art Historian in Eighteenth-Century Europe,'' in *Oxford, China and Italy,* ed. E. Chaney—N. Ritchie (Florence, 1987), 177–91.

J. S. TASSIE

HANFMANN, GEORGE MAXIM ANOSSOV (1911–86). American archaeologist; excavator of *Sardis (1958–76).

Born in St. Petersburg, Russia, Hanfmann studied under G. *Rodenwaldt in Berlin, receiving his D.Phil. there with a dissertation on early Etruscan sculpture (1934). He earned the Ph.D. from Johns Hopkins University (1935) and went immediately as a junior fellow to Harvard University, with which he was to be associated until his retirement in 1982, as teacher, as curator of ancient art at the Fogg Museum and as director of the Sardis excavations.

In 1951 Hanfmann's book on *The Seasons Sarcophagus at Dumbarton Oaks* established his international reputation. There followed numerous publications on Sardis and on holdings and exhibitions at the Fogg, as well as his classic text on *Roman Art* (1964; 2nd ed., 1975). Noted for his sensitive and lively use of the English language and his versatility and productivity as a scholar and organizer, Hanfmann was awarded the Gold Medal for Distinguished Archaeological Achievement, the highest honor of the *Archaeological Institute of America, in 1978.

BIBLIOGRAPHY
Studies Presented to George M. A. Hanfmann (Mainz, 1971); D. G. Mitten, "George Maxim Anossov Hanfmann, 1911–1986," *AJA* 91 (1987), 259–63; J. Bloom, "Appendix: Bibliography of George M. A. Hanfmann," *AJA* 91 (1987), 264–66.

SHELLIE WILLIAMS

HAPSBURG (HABSBURG) FAMILY. Royal family ruling in Germany and Austria and at various times in many other European political units; in the fifteenth century, the Hapsburgs unified a number of kingdoms under the control of the Holy Roman Emperor; in connection with the title they stressed their classical forebears along with their Christian heritage and made frequent references to the Argonauts and the quest for the Golden Fleece, as well as to the Trojan hero Aeneas, founder of the Roman people, and to Roman rulers such as Julius Caesar and Augustus. The title of Holy Roman Emperor remained in the family until 1806.

MAXIMILIAN I (1459–1519) and his grandson CHARLES V (1500–58) seem to have had little genuine interest in classical monuments themselves, and their artists only occasionally referred to ancient themes to enhance the traditional imperial rhetoric. *Dürer's huge woodcut *Triumphal Arch of Maximilian* depicts a complex and elaborate monument that resembles a Gothic church more than a Roman classical arch, and *Titian's famous portrait of *Charles V on Horseback* (1548; Madrid, Prado) scarcely justifies the claim that it is based on the *Marcus Aurelius* Equestrian Statue. Charles's sister, MARY, QUEEN OF HUNGARY, who ruled the Netherlands from 1531 to 1555, sought to secure casts of famous sculptures for her castle at Binche. Encouraged by her counselor, Charles's minister Granvelle (*Perrenot de Granvelle), she accepted the suggestion of court artist Leone Leoni that they attempt to secure the molds of statues that had been used by *Primaticcio to decorate Fontainebleau. By 1550, a series of plaster copies had been made, of which the *"*Cleopatra*" and the *Nile* from the *Vatican Belvedere are specifically named.

Of the many members of the Hapsburg family celebrated for their art collections, perhaps most notable for his inclusion of classical antiquities was *ALBRECHT V (1528–79), Duke of Bavaria, who displayed his collection in the Antiquarium at the Stadtresidenz in Munich (begun 1563). Albrecht and his brother Archduke FERDINAND II (1529–95), as well as their nephew, the Holy Roman Emperor RUDOLF II (1552–1612), belong among the princes who developed *Kunst- und Wunderkammern,* that is, collections of a wide range of art objects and curiosities. Ferdinand II had no interest in classical antiquities (he did own casts of the *Laocoon* Group), but his castle at Ambras near Innsbruck was renowned for its spectacular variety of collectibles. Along with arms and armor, scientific instruments and ethnographical items (from Turkey, North Africa, Asia, the New World) were objects of varying materials, some quite exotic, such as coral, glass, feathers, ivory, wood, bronze, silver and gold. The gold *Saltcellar* made by Benvenuto *Cellini and given to Ferdinand by King Charles IX of France was probably the most famous piece at Schloss Ambras. Specimens of natural science were included, such as plants, animals, bones, horns and minerals. The archduke also had an enormous numismatic collection, the precise contents of which are not known.

The collection of Rudolf was even more diverse and encyclopedic; not merely a cabinet of curiosities, it is thought to represent a systematic gathering of objects from nature and the arts, showing the emperor's control of knowledge and, therefore, power. Eccentric, unpopular and of poor health, Rudolf retired soon after his election in 1576 to Hradschin Castle in Prague, where he devoted himself to arcane learning and to patronage of the arts. The contents of his *Kunstkammer,* inventoried between 1607 and 1611, embraced an astonishing array of *naturalia* and *artificialia,* with an even wider geographical range than that of the collection of Ferdinand. Rudolf's interest in the occult no doubt explains the selection of some of the objects; of particular interest are the precious stones with magic properties, of which the *Gemma Augustea (now in the *Kunsthistorisches Museum, Vienna) was undoubtedly his most admired piece; he also owned a fine cameo with a double portrait of a king and queen, perhaps of Ptolemaic date (perhaps also in Vienna, or else in the Hermitage, St. Petersburg; its provenance is entangled with that of the double-portrait gem known as the Gonzaga Cameo). As for ancient marbles, he had relatively few; worth noting are a fine torso of a youth, one of the sons from the *Niobe* Group and a marble relief, perhaps the original Roman sculpture known as the *Bed of Polykleitos* (probably really *Cupid and Psyche*).

During the course of the Thirty Years' War (1618–48), the collections of Rudolf at Prague were pillaged several times and sadly dispersed; the culmination was the sack of Prague in 1648, when the Hapsburg treasures were seized for the crown of Sweden. Many items went to the collection of Queen *Christina, although some pieces remained in the imperial collection and passed to the Kunsthistorisches Museum.

Much of Christine's collection ended up later in the royal collections of Spain and thus joined the antiquities and casts that had been assembled by the Spanish Hapsburgs. PHILIP II (1527–98) owned some portraits of Roman emperors and a bronze copy of the *Spinario* that had been given to him by Cardinal Ricci. These holdings were augmented by his grandson PHILIP IV (1605–65). When Philip converted the fortess of the Alcazar into a palace, among the adornments he sought for it were casts and copies of the most beautiful statuary in Rome. *Velazquez made his well-known trip to Rome (1650), from which he returned with plaster casts of the *Farnese *Flora* and the *Farnese *Hercules,* as well as a bronze copy of the *Borghese *Hermaphrodite* (now in the Prado, Madrid).

There is evidence to indicate that the *"Cleopatra," Laocoon, *Venus Felix* and *Nile* from the Belvedere were among a number of other casts Velazquez secured.

The collection of Christina came to Spain during the reign of PHILIP V (1683–1746). Having passed to the *Odescalchi family in 1692, it was purchased by Philip in 1724. Among the statues were the *Castor and Pollux, *Faun with Kid* and *Muses,* which are today in the Prado.

BIBLIOGRAPHY

E. Harris, "La Mision de Velazquez in Italia," *ArchEspArt* 33 (1960), 109–36; R. Bauer—H. Haupt, "Das Kunstkammerinventar Kaiser Rudolfs II, 1607–11," *Jahrbuch der Kunsthistorischen Sammlungen in Wien* 72 (1976); H. Trevor–Roper, *Princes and Artists, Patronage and Ideology at Four Habsburg Courts* (New York, 1976); E. Scheicher, *Die Kunst- und Wunderkammer der Habsburger* (Vienna, 1979); B. Boucher, "Leone Leoni and Primaticcio's Moulds of Ancient Sculpture," *BurlMag* 123 (1981), 23–25; O. Impey—A. MacGregor, eds., *The Origins of Museums, The Cabinet of Curiosities in Sixteenth and Seventeenth-Century Europe* (Oxford, 1985), 29–53.

HARE, AUGUSTUS JOHN CUTHBERT (1834–1903). English artist, traveler and author of guidebooks.

Born in Rome, nephew of Julius Hare and Augustus Hare, by whose widow he was adopted, Hare graduated from University College, Oxford, in 1857. A timid celibate, he lived much of his adult life in Italy with his adoptive mother. A prolific writer and artist in watercolor, he is famous for a revealing, witty and indiscreet autobiography in six volumes (1896–1900) and many highly personal guidebooks, the most famous his *Walks in Rome* (1871; 17th ed., 1905), imitated by Georgina Masson, *The Companion Guide to Rome* (1965). His leisurely anecdotal style and power of observation enhance their charm.

BIBLIOGRAPHY

A.J.C. Hare, *Memorials of a Quiet Life,* 1–3 (1872–76); Idem, *The Story of My Life,* 1–6 (1896–1900); S. E. Fryer, "Hare, Augustus John Cuthbert," *DNB,* 2nd. Suppl., 2 (1912), 212–13.

WILLIAM M. CALDER III

HARRISON, JANE ELLEN (1850–1928). English classicist, specializing in Greek drama and religion.

After strenuous efforts to secure an education, Jane Ellen Harrison, the daughter of well-to-do Nonconformist parents, became one of the first generation of English university women, entering Newnham College, Cambridge, in 1875. After she took her degree, she supported herself as a writer and lecturer on classical subjects and made a trip to Greece; there she met *Dörpfeld, whose theories she would later champion. She returned to Newnham as a research fellow in 1898 and in the years before World War I established herself as an innovative and controversial scholar with a series of publications, most notably, *Prolegomena to the Study of Greek Religion* (1903) and *Themis* (1912). In these, working closely with her friends A. B. *Cook, F. M. Cornford and Gilbert Murray (*Cambridge Ritualists) and drawing upon *Frazer, Durkheim and Bergson, she attempted an imaginative reconstruction of the social and psychological basis of pre-Olympian Greek religion. She and the other Ritualists are associated with the theory that the forms of Greek drama derive from the structure of Dionysian ritual performed in preclassical times. With the possible exception of Eugénie *Strong, she was the premier female classical scholar of her time.

BIBLIOGRAPHY
J. Stewart, *Jane Ellen Harrison: A Portrait in Letters* (London, 1959); R. Ackerman, "Jane Ellen Harrison: The Early Work," *GRBS* 13 (1972), 209–31; R. Schlesier, "Jane Ellen Harrison," in Briggs—Calder, 127–41.

ROBERT ACKERMAN

HAWES, HARRIET BOYD (1871–1945). American archaeologist, one of the first women to direct an excavation.

While attending the *American School of Classical Studies in Athens, Hawes organized the first American excavation on the island of *Crete. Encouraged by British archaeologists Sir Arthur *Evans and D. G. *Hogarth and using the modest funds available through an Agnes Hoppin Memorial Fellowship from Smith College, she journeyed to Crete in 1900. She first visited Evans at *Knossos (where she witnessed the discovery of the famous throne from the Palace of Minos), then traveled by mule to her chosen site, Kavousi. The place turned out to be rich in Submycenaen and Geometric remains. The following year she began work at the Bronze Age site of *Gournia, sponsored by the American Exploration Society of Philadelphia, and continued there in 1903 and 1904.

Hawes became an instructor at Smith College from 1900 to 1906. Between 1906 and 1920 she worked on the publication of Gournia, and during this same period she wrote, along with her husband, Charles, *Crete, The Forerunner of Greece* (published 1909). She returned to teaching in 1920, at Wellesley College, where she remained until 1936.

BIBLIOGRAPHY
"Harriet Boyd Hawes," *Washington Post,* 1 April 1945, sec. 3, p. 6; H. B. Hawes, "Memoirs of a Pioneer Excavator on Crete," *Archaeology* 18 (1965), 94–101, 268–76; P. W. Lehmann, Introduction to *A Land Called Crete: A Symposium in Memory of Harriet Boyd Hawes* (Smith College, Northampton, MA, 1967), 11–14; M. Allsebrook, *Born to Rebel: The Life of Harriet Boyd Hawes* (Oxford, 1992).

SHELLIE WILLIAMS

HEEMSKERCK, MAERTEN (MARTEN) VAN (MARTINUS HEMS-KERIC; 1498–1574). Dutch painter and print designer, famed for his drawings of Roman antiquities.

Aside from the few anecdotal remarks that Carel van Mander makes in his *Schilder-boeck* (1604) about Heemskerck's early years, we know almost nothing about the artist's youth and early adulthood. Heemskerck's first teacher, Cornelis Willemsz. of Haarlem, is well documented but has no authenticated oeuvre; his second teacher, Jan Lucasz. of Delft, is mentioned only twice in the documents and is today an artistic nonentity. Heemskerck himself has no known juvenilia.

Photograph of *Harriet Boyd Hawes*, 1892. (J. Soles.)

Portrait of *Marten van Heemskerck* on a column base, etching by P. Galle; from *Memorabiliores Judaeae gentis clades* [1570?]. (Westfälisches Landesmuseum für Kunst und Kulturgeschichte, Münster, Porträtarchiv Diepenbroick. Photo: R. Wakonigg.)

Thus, we cannot say if either of his two teachers introduced him to antique art. From the general appearance of early sixteenth-century art in Haarlem and Delft, we may presume, however, that both Willemsz. and Lucasz. were thoroughly Late Gothic painters who had no taste for things classical (though van Mander does mention that Willemsz.'s sons visited Rome).

We might assume that things changed for Heemskerck when he joined the Haarlem atelier of Jan van Scorel ca. 1527, for Scorel had already studied in Rome in 1522–24 and had served as curator of the Belvedere (*Vatican Museums) under the Dutch pope, Adrian VI. Scorel, however, seems to have had less interest in the antique than is usually thought. Except for a few *vedute* featuring vaguely classical-looking and probably imaginary monuments, no drawings of antiquities by his hand have survived; aside from his *Lucretia* and *Cleopatra,* not one of his extant paintings illustrates a classical subject; and only a handful of his painted figures is based upon classical models. Possibly the puritanical Adrian, who condemned classical sculpture as ''the effigies of heathen idols'' and even closed the Belvedere during Scorel's tenure as caretaker, discouraged Scorel from making an intensive study of the antique. In any case, in the paintings that Heemskerck made during his association with Scorel (ca. 1527–30) and the brief period of independent Haarlem activity following it (ca.

1530–May 1532), allusions to the antique are few and imprecise. For example, the pose of the angel in the 1532 *St. Luke Painting the Virgin* (Frans Hals Museum, Haarlem) recalls only in a general way the customary stance of Bacchic thyrsus-bearers.

All of this changed quite suddenly in May 1532, when Heemskerck departed Haarlem for his own study sojourn in Rome. There he diligently sketched antiquities, making innumerable drawings of the city's classical statues, reliefs, architectural ruins, sculptural fragments and ornament. Eighty-seven sheets of these sketches (executed in pen and brown ink or in red or black chalk) are contained in two sketchbooks in the Kupferstichkabinett in Berlin. It is largely upon these celebrated Roman drawings that the artist's present fame rests. In many of the sketches Heemskerck's approach seems remarkably objective, lending to the drawings a quality of archaeological exactness. Others are much more dramatically and consciously "composed" and are marked by sharp foreshortenings, eccentric viewpoints and abrupt juxtapositions of near and distant objects. Though van Mander states that Heemskerck remained in Rome only three years, modern scholars have argued more convincingly for a longer stay of four to five years. There is evidence that Heemskerck worked with Francesco Salviati and others on the festival decorations for the triumphal entry of Charles V into Rome in April 1536. Also, Heemskerck's early post-Roman paintings were clearly influenced by the Roman high Maniera style of Jacopino del Conte and Salviati, a style that did not begin to crystallize until 1537. In any event, Heemskerck is not mentioned again in the Netherlands before November 1537.

Heemskerck could easily have encountered the young Salviati on his daily sketching expeditions, for both Salviati and Giorgio *Vasari—one of the first of Heemskerck's Roman acquaintances—were busily drawing the city's antiquities in the weeks immediately following Heemskerck's arrival in Rome. Salviati may have encouraged and, perhaps, even helped supervise Heemskerck's early sketching campaign.

Heemskerck consulted his study drawings repeatedly as he composed his post-Roman paintings and print designs. Many of his painted landscapes and interiors are studded with classical "accessories" culled from his sketches. One thinks, for example, of the colossal foot in the *Triumph of Bacchus* (Kunsthistorisches Museum, Vienna) or the statue court in the second *St. Luke Painting the Virgin* (Musée des Beaux-Arts, Rennes). His favorite classical figurative model was the *Laocoon;* Heemskerck was temperamentally drawn to this dramatic *exemplum doloris,* and he lent its shape to his many post-Roman images of the suffering Christ and crucified thieves (*Crucifixion* and *Flagellation,* Cathedral, Linköping; *Crucifixion,* Museum, Ghent; etc.) and to the struggling Israelites in his *Brazen Serpent* (Frans Hals Museum, Haarlem).

BIBLIOGRAPHY

+C. Hülsen—H. Egger, *Die Römischen Skizzenbücher von Marten van Heemskerck,* 1–2 (Berlin, 1913–16); +M.H.L. Netto-Bol, *The So-Called Maarten de Vos Sketchbook of Drawings After the Antique* (The Hague, 1976); I. M. Veldman, "Notes Occasioned by the Publication of the Facsimile Edition of . . . *Die römischen Skizzenbücher von Marten van Heemskerck,*" 9 (1977), 106–13; +R. Grosshans, *Maerten van Heemskerck-Die Gemälde* (Berlin, 1980).

JEFFERSON C. HARRISON

HELBIG, WOLFGANG (1839–1915). German archaeologist and philologist.

A pupil of F. Ritschl and O. *Jahn, Helbig reached the *German Archaeological Institute in Rome as a scholarship holder from Bonn in 1862; and Rome was his base for the rest of his life.

While assistant director of the institute (1865–87), Helbig contributed to three very different fields of archaeological research. *Untersuchungen über die campanische Wandmalerei* and related works (1868–73) explored the Hellenistic affinities of the Pompeian wall paintings. *Die Italiker in der Po-ebene* (1879) underpinned and secured a wide currency for the ''*Pigorini hypothesis,'' which saw the *terramara* area of North Italy as the prehistoric cradle of Italic civilization (cf. *Brizio).

The considerable *Homerische Epos aus den Denkmälern erläutert* (1884; 2nd ed., 1887) compared the civilization described in the allegedly ninth-century Homeric poems with the material newly (1876) revealed by *Schliemann's finds in the Shaft Graves at Mycenae, regarding both as indispensable to the proper understanding of the culture that the Greeks brought to Italy. "His essay became the standard text-book" (*Myres), and its effect was not wholly positive, although Helbig's differentiation between Homeric and classical times was an important step. Helbig saw much that was Phoenician in the new pre-Hellenic culture: he continued to see it long after the essentially Aegean affinities of the Mycenaeans were generally accepted. Meanwhile, the West was utilized as a reasonable pointer to the probable cultural state of Homer's Ionian homeland. But Helbig's hypothetical Ionia, though widely acclaimed, did not survive the impact of excavation at *Samos (1894: J. Boehlau), *Miletos (1899: T. *Wiegand) and *Ephesos (1904: D. G. *Hogarth).

From an early stage in his official career in Rome, Helbig also acted as academic adviser and go-between to those desirous of buying and selling antiquities; and it is clear that he continued this necessarily discreet activity after his withdrawal from the institute. An important (but not always fortunate) client from ca. 1885 was Carl *Jacobsen, founder of the *Ny Carlsberg Glyptothek in Copenhagen, of which the Etruscan section was eventually christened "Helbig Museum" *honoris causa.* What amounted to Helbig's partnership with the eccentric but talented restorer, gem cutter and dealer Francesco Martinetti (1833–95) extended to the addition of incised mythological scenes to genuine (originally plain) Praenestine cistae. There can be no reasonable doubt that Helbig and Martinetti were responsible for forging the inscribed so-called *Praenestine Fibula (*CIL* 1²: 2, no. 3: Manios) and for a well-orchestrated attempt to append it to the contents of the *Bernardini Tomb.

Of more lasting value is the detailed guide to classical collections in Rome

Photograph of *Wolfgang Helbig* (*seated, r.*) and his wife the Principessa Nadina Schakowskoy (*seated, beside him*), with family and associates at the Deutsches Archäologisches Institut (German Archaeological Institute), Rome, 1884–85. (Deutsches Archäologisches Institut, Rome. Inst. Neg. 76.864.)

that Helbig published in 1892: *Führer durch die öffentlichen Sammlungen klassischer Altertümer in Rom* (latest revision in 4 vol.: 1963–72).

BIBLIOGRAPHY
Madame [N.] Helbig, *Sketches from Trastevere* (Aberdeen, 1914); Sir John L. Myres, *Homer and His Critics,* ed. D. Gray (London, 1958), 150–55; M. Guarducci, "La cosidetta Fibula Prenestina: Antiquari, eruditi e falsari nella Roma dell'ottocento," *MemLinc,* ser. 8, 24 (1980), 415–574; Eadem, *MemLinc* 28 (1984), 127–77; M. Moltesen, *Wolfgang Helbig, Brygger Jacobsens agent i Rom* (Copenhagen, 1987); H. Lehman, "Wolfgang Helbig (1839–1915) an seinem 150. Geburtstag," *RM* 96 (1989), 7–86; S. Fuscagni, *Il Profilo culturale di Wolfgang Helbig attraverso "Die Italiker in der Po-ebene"* (Città di Castello, 1992); M. Pearce—E. Gabba, "Dalle terremare a Roma: Wolfgang Helbig e la teoria delle origini degli Italici," *Rivista Storica Italiana* 107 (1995), 119–32.

DAVID RIDGWAY

HELLENISTIC "RULER." Over-lifesize bronze statue, dating to the second or first century B.C., now in the Museo Nazionale delle *Terme, Rome.

The sculpture depicts a powerfully muscled nude male, standing in a relaxed pose leaning on a spear, his body turning gently in space. The head, turned toward the proper right, features short, tousled hair and a highly individualized countenance with a lightly indicated beard. The statue is in excellent condition, having only minor repairs, with the spear added in modern times (height of the statue is 2.44m). The once-inlaid eyes are now missing. Latin inscriptions of the Republican period, little understood, appear on the belly and thigh of the figure.

The Hellenistic *"Ruler"* was discovered in 1885 in Rome in the *Baths of Constantine, during construction of the now-demolished Teatro Drammatico Nazionale. Described by J. J. Pollitt as "the one large-scale and complete original Greek portrait statue that has come down to us," it is a key monument of the Hellenistic period. Not all have seen it as Greek, however; for some scholars, it is a work of Roman Late Republican art.

Since its discovery, most discussions about the *"Ruler"* have hinged on identifying the compelling personality represented. He lacks a diadem on his head and thus, properly speaking, need not be called a ruler; this point has not deterred scholars from searching albums of Hellenistic coinage for a convincing royal comparison. Among the many suggestions are Perseus of Macedon (F. *Studniczka, 1896), Antiochus II Theos (W. Klein, 1907), Demetrius I of Syria (R. Delbrueck, 1912) and Alexander I Balas (H. von Heintze). On the Roman side, proposed identifications have included Agrippa (J. Six, 1898), Lucullus (R. *Carpenter, 1927), Sulla (Carpenter, 1945). P. Williams (1945) argued that the *"Ruler"* was part of a group with the seated Bronze *Boxer* in the Terme, also found in the Baths of Constantine, and that he would have had a twin, thus creating a group of Castor and Pollux (with King Amycus, whom Pollux defeated in a boxing match).

BIBLIOGRAPHY
P. Williams, "Amykos and the Dioskouroi," *AJA* 49 (1945), 330–47; +L. de Lachenal, in *Museo Nazionale Romano, Le Sculture,* ed. A. Giuliano, I, 1 (Rome, 1979), 198–201; Pollitt, *Art in the Hellenistic Age,* 72–73; R.R.R. Smith, *Hellenistic Royal Portraits* (Oxford, 1988), 84–86; N. Himmelmann, *Herscher und Athlet* (Milan, 1989), 126–49.

HEMSKERIC, MARTINUS. See HEEMSKERCK, MAERTEN VAN.

HENRY OF BLOIS (ca. 1098–1171). English bishop; an early collector of classical antiquities.

Henry had important royal connections, being the nephew of King Henry I and a brother of Stephen of Blois, who later succeeded Henry I when he became king. He was brought up at Cluny in France but came to England in 1126 and quickly rose to powerful and important positions in the Church. He became bishop of Winchester by 1129. His ambition to become papal legate was satisfied between 1139 and 1143; this involved him in many journeys to Rome. A contemporary, John of Salisbury, noted that during one of these sojourns Henry bought up "old statues" and had them taken back to Winchester. He was mocked for "buying up idols carefully made by the heathen in the error of their hands rather than their minds," but Henry stoutly defended his purchases by saying that he was removing the old statues to prevent the Romans from falling victim to their innate avarice and the dangers of renewed idol worship.

While in Rome, Henry must have developed a taste for colored marble. He obtained a font of Tournai marble from Belgium for his own cathedral at Winchester and so started a fashion for using various polished marbles as architectural features in England. His collection of classical sculptures has vanished without trace or record, although one medieval source says that he was buried under a slab of Roman marble bearing the inscription "Hic portat lapides quas portavit ab Urbe" (He bears stones that he bore from the City).

BIBLIOGRAPHY
J. Adhémar, *Influences antiques dans l'art du Moyen Age français* (London, 1939), 97; Weiss, *RDCA,* 9; J. C. Turquet, "Henry of Blois, Patron of Sculpture," unpublished M. A. thesis, Courtauld Institute of Art, London, 1974; G. Zarnecki, "Henry of Blois as a Patron of Sculpture," in *Art and Patronage in the English Romanesque,* ed. S. Macready—F. H. Thompson (London, 1986), 159–72.

ELEANOR A. ROBBINS

HEPHAISTEION, Athens. Classical temple above the Athenian *Agora.

Popularly known as the "Theseum," the building is the best-preserved example of a Doric temple in Greece. Lying almost literally in the shadow of the *Parthenon, it has received far less attention than if it were found anywhere else. The identification of the temple as that of Hephaistos and Athena is generally, but not universally, accepted. Pausanias's reference to the Hephaisteion as "above the kerameikos (Agora) and the stoa called Basileios" and the concentration of metalworking establishments in the area favor the identification.

The "Theseum" *(Hephaisteion)*, Athens, engraving from A. Blouet et al., *Expédition scientifique de Morée* (1831–38). (Deutsches Archäologisches Institut, Rome. Inst. Neg. 1937. 1168.)

The temple is built largely of Pentelic marble, except for the bottom step, which is of limestone, and parts of the ceiling, trim and sculpture, which are of island marble. It was a peripteral temple with 6 by 13 columns, measuring 13.70m × 31.77m. The interior consisted of pronaos, cella and opisthodomos. A colonnade of superimposed Doric columns is usually restored within the cella, though the number of columns and their arrangement are a matter of some controversy. In addition, the temple has one of the most elaborate sculptural programs of any Greek temple. The Doric frieze at the east end carried the *Labors of Herakles,* while the *Labors of Theseus* were depicted on the four easternmost metopes of the south and north flanks. A combat scene with gods looking on decorated a continuous "Ionic" frieze over the pronaos, while the opisthodomos carried a scene of *Lapiths and Centaurs* in battle. There were pedimental groups as well, of which some fragments survive, along with cuttings on the pediment floor. The roof seems to have been adorned with figural akroteria.

On the basis of pottery and the style of the architecture, the start of construction of the temple is usually dated to around the middle of the fifth century B.C. From the architecture it appears as though the building took some time to complete, and according to an inscription (*IG* I² 370/1) the cult statues, done by Alkamenes (Cicero *De nat.deo.* 1.30; Valerius Maximus 8.11 ext 3), were not installed until 421–415 B.C.

Excavations by D. B. Thompson (1936) showed that in the Hellenistic period the temenos was landscaped; large planting pits indicated the positions of rows of shrubs along the north, west and south sides of the temple.

The temple was converted into a Christian church early in the seventh century A.C., shortly after the Slavic invasion, according to the latest study (A. Frantz). The conversion required a reorientation of the temple; a door was cut through the back wall of the cella, and an apse was built at the east end. A major rebuilding was done in the middle Byzantine period (before 1300). This required the removal of the pronaos columns and their replacement by an arch, the removal of the cella door-wall and the interior colonnades and the construction of the great barrel vault that still roofs the building today. As the church of St. George, the building was used as a burial ground. Sepulchral inscriptions date from 896 to 1103, and sixty-five graves were uncovered, the majority dating from the twelfth to the fourteenth centuries. The temple was used as a Protestant cemetery in the nineteenth century. Occupants of interest include John Tweddell (d. 1799), who was buried in the center of the building by *Fauvel in a vain attempt to locate and recover the bones of Theseus; George Watson (d. 1810), whose Latin epitaph was written by *Byron; *Haller von Hallerstein (d. 1817); and Marius Wohlgemuth (d. 1822), a Philhellene who died in the siege of the *Akropolis. The temple ceased to be used as a church in 1834 and for a time was used as a museum and center for the storage of antiquities.

BIBLIOGRAPHY

W. B. Dinsmoor, *Observations on the Hephaisteion, Hesperia Suppl.* 5 (1941); H. Koch, *Studien zum Theseustempel in Athen* (Berlin, 1955); H. A. Thompson—R. E. Wycherley, *The Agora of Athens, The Athenian Agora,* 14 (Princeton, NJ, 1972), 140–49; E. B. Harrison, "Alkamenes' Sculptures for the Hephaisteion," *AJA* 81 (1977), 137–78, 265–87, 411–26.

JOHN McK. CAMP II

HERAION. See TEMPLE OF HERA.

"HERA" OF CHERAMYES. Archaic Greek marble statue (ca. 570–60 B.C.).

The sculpture was found by a native of *Samos about 1875, 10m north of the northeast corner of the temple of Hera, and acquired for the *Louvre by Paul Girard. An over-lifesize standing female figure (preserved height with plinth about 1.92m) wearing Ionic chiton, diagonal himation and veil, the statue is missing its head and left hand, which was holding an object at the breast. A vertical inscription along the himation border down the left leg identifies her as a dedication to Hera by Cheramyes, an otherwise unknown Samian.

Inscription, find spot, size, veil and shape (cylindrical lower body) originally suggested a representation of the goddess Hera, whose cult image at Samos is known from ancient testimonia and coins. The columnar shape on the round plinth was compared by some to *xoana*, wooden statues attested in ancient literature as the earliest Greek sculpture; others associated the shape with cast bronze statues, a technique attributed to two Samian sculptors, Rhoikos and Theodoros, or with Near Eastern influence. Most saw an early stage of Greek sculpture in the Samian Hera and compared her with the more primitive Nikandre of *Delos discovered two years earlier. Hera was recognized as an Ionian type familiar from *Newton's finds at *Miletos and as the ancestor of the Archaic marble *korai* (**korai* and *kouroi*) uncovered on the Akropolis of Athens in 1886.

German excavations on *Samos since 1900 have produced three other dedications by the same Cheramyes, including an identical female figure found in 1984. Thus, the Louvre "Hera" may be a votive *kore* from a group on a single base, like the dedication by Geneleos.

BIBLIOGRAPHY

+P. Girard, "Statue de style archaïque trouvée dans l'ile de Samos," *BCH* 4 (1880), 483–93; +E. Buschor, *Altsamische Standbilder* (Berlin, 1935), II, 25–26; +G. Richter, *Korai: Archaic Greek Maidens* (New York, 1968), 46, no. 55; J. Pedley, *Greek Sculpture of the Archaic Period: The Island Workshops* (Mainz, 1976), 52–53, no. 46; H. Kyrieleis, "Neue archaische Skulpturen aus dem Heraion von Samos," in *Archaische und klassische griechische Plastik* (Mainz, 1986).

SARAH P. MORRIS

HERAKLEION MUSEUM, HERAKLEION, Crete. One of the largest Greek museums, an almost exclusive repository of the movable goods of the Minoans of ancient *Crete.

The original Syllogos was founded (1883) by the Society of Friends of Education, under J. Hazzidakis's presidency and located in two rooms near Hagios Minas, Herakleion. The initial collection comprised antiquities donated by many individual owners, both Turkish and Greek. M. Kalokairinos had begun to explore *Knossos (1878), and F. *Halbherr to work at *Gortyn, the Idaean Cave and the Cave of Eileithyia (1884). Hazzidakis began collecting Cretan antiquities lest they disappear to Constantinople (1883).

After the Cretan revolution, the collection was moved to the old Turkish barracks (1898), and plans to relocate it to the Venetian Loggia were abandoned (1900). Instead, the Khounkiar mosque (old church of St. Francis) housed the collection. Hazzidakis and S. *Xanthoudides founded the Greek Archaeological Service on Crete and the first Herakleion Museum, which was financed by G.

A. Jeanti and planned by W. *Dörpfeld and P. *Kavvadias (1904–12). This building was destroyed by earthquake (1926), and a new building was erected (1936–40). During World War II, Herakleion was bombed and used for several military purposes by Italian forces, but the museum's contents were stored safely in its basement.

The present, earthquake-proof structure was built after 1951. N. Platon classified the stored artifacts and opened sixteen galleries. S. Alexiou completed and extended the museum. A north wing with four galleries (5–8) was added, and Room 17 was used to house the Giamalakis collection, acquired by the Greek state from the Herakleiote doctor (1962).

Exhibits are in chronological order and further grouped by site, so that the visitor walks through finds from the Neolithic period and then the Minoan First, New and Final Palatial periods (third and second millennia, Galleries 1–10, 13–16). Galleries 12 and 18–20 take one into the first millennium, showing an uninterrupted flow of culture after the Minoans into the Geometric, Orientalizing and Archaic periods (Galleries 11–12, 19) and on into the Classical, Hellenistic and Roman (18, 20). Materials from Halbherr's earliest sites are now in Rooms 1 (Cave of Eileithyia), 18–20 (Gortyn) and 19 (Idaean Cave). Goods from *Knossos dominate Galleries 1–2 and 4–6, including such famous finds as the *Town* Mosaic (2), the *Snake Goddess,* Ivory *Acrobat* and *Bull's Head* Rhyton (4). *Phaistos fills Galleries 3–4 and 6, with the Phaistos Disk in 3. *Hagia Triadha goods, particularly the *Harvester* Vase, *Boxer* Vase and *Chieftain* Cup, can be found in Gallery 7; finds from *Zakro are in 8. The *Octopus* Flask from Palaikastro is on display in Gallery 9, and the *Poppy Goddess* from Gázi, west of Herakleion, is in 10. Gallery 12 contains the many new finds from the Sanctuary of Hermes Dendrites at Symi, while a Roman copy of the Archaic Hymn to Zeus Diktaios from Palaikastro is in the exhibit of Archaic monumental art (19). Upstairs galleries 14–16 display the painted sarcophagus of *Hagia Triadha and frescoes from Knossos.

BIBLIOGRAPHY

S. Spanakis, *Crete: A Guide,* 1 (Herakleion, 1964), 138–39; S. Alexiou, *Odegos Archaiologikou Mouseiou Herakleiou* (Athens, 1973), 3–6; S. Spanakis, *Krete: Tourismos, Historia, Archaiologia,* 3rd ed., 1 (Herakleion, 1981), 238; +S. Logiadou-Platonos—N. Marinatos, *Crete* (Athens, 1986), 87.

MARTHA W. BALDWIN BOWSKY

HERBIG, REINHARD (1898–1961). German archaeologist; versatile and prolific scholar of Etruscan, Roman and Greek art and archaeology.

Reinhard Herbig was born in Munich, the son of the Etruscologist Gustav Herbig. After serving in World War I (in which he was wounded), he studied at Rostock, Breslau and then Heidelberg. There he wrote his dissertation on windows in ancient architecture (*Das Fenster in der Architektur des Altertums,* Athens, 1929). After travels in Italy and Greece, he was called to the universities of Jena (1933), Würzburg (1936) and Heidelberg (from 1941 to 1956). He was then named first director of the *German Archaeological Institute in Rome, a post he held until his death five years later.

Herbig's publications were wide-ranging. Most remembered are his contributions to Etruscan studies, such as his corpus of Etruscan stone sarcophagi (*Die jungeretruskischen Steinsarcophage,* Berlin, 1952) and his volume on the gods and demons of Etruria (*Götter und Dämonen der Etrusker,* 2nd ed., ed. E. Simon, 1965). But he also published significant studies in the areas of Roman painting; Greek architecture, myth and religion; and Renaissance painting.
BIBLIOGRAPHY
O. Brendel, ''Reinhard Herbig,'' *AJA* 67 (1963), 81; W. Fuchs, in *Archäologenbildnisse,* 274–75.

HERCULANEUM. A small Roman seaport on the Bay of Naples, on the western slopes of Vesuvius almost opposite *Pompeii.

The site is a naturally strong one on a headland between the gullies of two torrents. It seems always to have been a minor center, though believed to have been founded by Hercules. Strabo (5.4.8) says it was occupied successively by Oscans, Tyrrhenians and Pelasgians and then by Samnites, but only the last have left their mark. It was taken by Minatius Magius and T. Didius in the Social War (Vell.Pat. 2.16.2) and became a *municipium* after it. It was severely hit by the earthquake of A.D. 62 and obliterated by the eruption of Vesuvius in 79, which poured a torrent of mud over a first stratum of looser volcanic debris. This did much damage but solidified to the consistency of tufa, sealing and preserving much perishable organic material.

It was rediscovered in 1709 by a farmer digging a well who happened to hit the theater, from which he extracted some marble architectural members. These were brought to the attention of Maurice, Prince d'Elboeuf, an Austrian cavalry officer who was building himself a villa nearby. Enlargement of the excavation by tunneling produced two statues of women in excellent state, the *Grande Herculanèse* and the *Petite Herculanèse* (the ''Large'' and ''Small'' Herculaneum Women), which d'Elboeuf sent to Vienna; they went eventually into the Antikensaal at Dresden.

In 1738, after the marriage of Maria Amalia, daughter of Augustus, Elector of Saxony, to Charles III of Naples, it was decided to build a royal residence at Portici and to reopen and pursue the excavations. The work was entrusted to a Spanish military engineer, Alcubierre, who excavated by tunneling, using workers of whom many were convicts in chain gangs. He was fortunate in having the assistance of a young Swiss engineer, Karl Weber, who made excellent plans of the buildings under very difficult circumstances.

The excavators were lucky. The first building attacked, the theater, a small but very elegant building, produced a rich harvest of sculptures, both bronze and marble, and also architectural marbles. Work here continued until 4 March 1780. The theater was followed almost immediately (by 12 September 1739) by the discovery of the ''Basilica'' (probably rather a public porticus), with not only two marble equestrian statues of M. Nonius Balbus and statues of several members of his family but also several of the finest paintings ever recovered from the buried cities. The entrance to this structure, flanked by quadrifrontal arches to either side, crosses the Decumanus Maximus and supports the notion that Herculaneum had no forum, its place being taken by a concentration of buildings along this broad street, which is, in part, colonnaded.

The next important discovery was the *Villa of the Papyri or Villa dei Pisoni, a suburban villa of great extent at Portici, across the western gully from Herculaneum. Excavation began with the discovery in June 1750 of a round belvedere with a fine marble pavement and continued until February 1761, when work was suspended because of noxious fumes in the tunnels. In the course of this excavation was recovered an important collection of bronze and marble sculptures of every size, including numerous busts of philosophers, poets and orators—many of them labeled—copies of some famous classical pieces and some excellent Roman portraits, as well as many graceful decorative pieces and fountain figures. As important, if not more so, was the discovery of a library and smaller quantities of rolls of papyrus at four other points. Martini's catalog of these reaches 1,806 items, many of which are presumably fragments of the same rolls, but many others were destroyed in the process of excavation. The number of rolls is put by De Petra at probably less than 1,000, but there is every likelihood that many more still lie buried.

Work in the tunnels of Herculaneum was suspended in March 1780. Excavation in an open trench was begun 9 January 1828 and continued until 12 April 1837. It was resumed in July 1850 and pursued in desultory fashion until the end of April 1855; it was resumed again in February 1869 and continued until 1 March 1876, after which work of repair and restoration with a reduced staff continued for another year. During this period of almost half a century, fractions of only four blocks, Insulae II, III, V and VI, parts of half a dozen houses and the public baths were brought to light. Despite public interest in the proceedings and royal patronage at intervals, work was then suspended indefinitely because of the difficulty and expense entailed.

Despite various efforts, some of them international, to get work on the ancient city under way again, it was not resumed until 16 May 1927, but it has continued with only temporary interruptions since then. Excavations under A. *Maiuri began with the completion of Insula III (1927–29) and continued with Insula IV (1929–32). The baths and lower half of Insula V were cleared in 1931–34, and the west front of the Insula Orientalis, in 1933–37. Insula V was completely excavated in 1937–38, and Insula VI, except for the northwest corner, in 1939–40. The seafront under the city was addressed in 1939–42, but work was interrupted by the war. In 1952 excavation of the eastern palaestra was resumed, as well as excavation in the Terme Suburbane and Area Suburbana. All these excavations were duly reported by Maiuri in a magisterial publication of 1958. Since then, work has progressed with the completion of the excavation of the northwest corner of Insula VI and excavation of the beach below the Area

Suburbana. The latter has been especially informative, for whereas it was previously thought that the general absence of skeletons indicated that Herculaneum had been almost entirely evacuated in the first morning of the eruption of 79, it is now known that scores perished on the beach.

It is clear that Herculaneum was never a wealthy or important city. The city plan is exceptionally regular, with long, narrow blocks and rectangular building lots that show few irregularities, unlike Pompeii. But the only houses that are truly luxurious are a single row of half a dozen along the seafront and the suburban villas, obviously the houses of a small aristocracy, possibly none of whom was in year-round residence here. The other houses are all modest and unpretentious. The Terme del Foro are low-ceilinged, dark and oppressive, though the Terme Suburbane are handsomer and more spacious. Industry of any importance is conspicuously lacking. A few public buildings, the Palaestra, the "Basilica" and the theater, all probably the gifts of beneficent individuals, attest to the presence of wealth in the neighborhood, but the absence of a real forum and of venerable temples shows that the town was a dependency on the economy of others, especially Naples, rather than an entity in its own right.

The influence of Herculaneum on the world of art and archaeology is inestimable. The publication of *Le Antichità di Ercolano* (1757–92), following Ottavio Bayardi's notoriously inept catalog of the collections of the royal museum at Portici in 1754, electrified the world. It consisted of five large volumes of paintings, two volumes of bronzes and one of lamps and candelabra, with handsome engravings and excellent descriptions of the objects by the members of the *Academia Herculanensis. Thereafter, in whole and in part, this was repeatedly copied and imitated in other parts of Italy and foreign countries and set the "Pompeian" style of the late eighteenth century.

The first open-trench excavations of Herculaneum made little impression on the world, as they were eclipsed by the steady stream of important discoveries at Pompeii. But the reminder of the splendid statuary and furniture found in the first excavations, which in quantity and quality far outshone what Pompeii produced, in part, because Pompeii had been, to a great extent, systematically plundered by the survivors after the eruption, kept alive hope that the resumption of excavations would bear rich fruit. When money and the technical means to deal with the bank of tufa covering Herculaneum were made available in 1927, Maiuri lost no time in undertaking the challenge. In fact, the treasure of Herculaneum proved rather different, a wealth of carbonized wooden structural members, fittings and furniture, as well as comestibles and other perishable material.

BIBLIOGRAPHY

+A. Maiuri, *Ercolano: i nuovi scavi (1927–1958)*, 1–2 (Rome, 1958); +T. Kraus—L. von Matt, *Pompeii and Herculaneum* (New York, 1975), 116–49; A. de Vos—M. de Vos, *Pompei Ercolano Stabia* (Rome, 1982), 259–306.

L. RICHARDSON, JR

HERCULES AND TELEPHUS (COMMODUS). Roman copy or adaptation of a Greek original (bronze) of the fourth century B.C.

The over-lifesize statue (2.12m) shows Hercules wearing his lion skin, supporting a child on his left arm. The right arm hangs down and has been restored (probably correctly; probably by Montorsoli) as holding the club that is the regular attribute of Hercules. The club itself is a still-later restoration.

The statue was discovered in Rome in the Campo dei Fiori on 15 May 1507. The pope, Julius II, immediately had the piece taken to the Belvedere courtyard (*Vatican Museums), where it took its place near the entrance. In 1536 it was set in a niche between the statues of the *Belvedere *Apollo* and the *"*Cleopatra.*" It was removed from the Belvedere for *Napoleon and sent to France in 1798. Upon its return in 1816, it was not restored to its niche in the Belvedere but was soon set up in the Sala Rotonda of the Vatican, where it may be seen today.

The statue was demoted from the Belvedere as a result of a decline in popularity. At the time of its discovery, it was a rare example of ancient monumental statuary in extremely good condition. Adding to interest in it was the fact that Tommaso Inghirami, prefect of the Vatican Library, identified the statue as the sensationally profligate emperor Commodus. *Boissard later reported the idea that the child was Commodus's minion. *Winckelmann argued that the statue showed Hercules with the child Ajax, while E. Q. *Visconti interpreted the pair as Hercules with his son Telephus, an identification that has stood the test of time. The recognition that the work is a copy of a Greek original meant that the *Hercules,* like so many other former favorites, has fallen in esteem and now attracts relatively little attention.

BIBLIOGRAPHY

+H. Brummer, *The Statue Court in the Vatican Belvedere* (Stockholm, 1970), 132–38; Haskell—Penny, 188–89; Bober—Rubinstein, 166.

HERMES, SEATED. Bronze statue of the first century B.C., probably a Roman copy of a Greek original, discovered in 1758 in the peristyle of the *Villa of the Papyri at *Herculaneum and now in the *Museo Nazionale, Naples (height 1.15m).

The statue is generally placed within the stylistic tradition of Lysippos, although it has also been called an independent creation of the Hellenistic period. A number of small bronzes (e.g., one found in Feurs, southern France) represent the same type. The long-legged boy sits on a (modern) rock, leaning forward and turning to his right. Strapped to each ankle are two small wings, one original and the rest restored. The head, extensively restored soon after discovery and again in the twentieth century, has short, curly hair, prominent ears, projecting chin and an unrevealing expression.

One of the most celebrated antique statues at the time of its discovery, the *Seated Hermes* has often been analyzed and reproduced. *Winckelmann noted that the caduceus was missing and inferred that the god had been transported from Greece, losing his attribute in the process. Vivant Denon coveted the piece for the museum of *Napoleon, but the statue never went to Paris. It was probably stored in Palermo during this crucial period (1798–1816) and went to the Museo Borbonico (later Museo Nazionale) by 1819. The Germans did capture the *Hermes* during World War II, but it was returned to Naples in 1947.

BIBLIOGRAPHY

+Bieber, 41–42; D. Pandermalis, "Zur Programm der Statuenausstellung in der Villa dei Papiri," *AM* 86 (1971), 200–201; Haskell—Penny, 267–69; M. R. Wojcik, *La Villa dei Papiri ad Ercolano* (Rome, 1986), 120–23.

CAROL MATTUSCH

HERMES OF PRAXITELES. Over-lifesize (2.15m) sculpture of Parian marble, representing Hermes carrying the infant Dionysos.

The *Hermes* lacks his right arm and is restored below the knees (the right foot is original) but otherwise is in excellent condition; the sculpture is generally regarded to be of the highest quality.

The *Hermes* was discovered in 1877 at Olympia during German excavations in the *Temple of Hera. Immediately, it was related to a passage in Pausanias (5.17.3) citing a dedication in the temple of a *Hermes with the Infant Dionysos* by, or in the manner of, Praxiteles (fourth century B.C.). Through the years the work has aroused constant controversy over whether it is a rare original by one of the greatest Greek masters or a copy of a later date. Gustav *Hirschfeld, director of the excavations at the time, declared it a copy; he has been followed by twentieth-century scholars who have made a special examination of the sculptural technique of the work, such as Blumel, R. *Carpenter and Sheila Adam. They believe the technique, the supporting tree and strut and the highly realistic drapery could not belong to a fourth-century B.C. original. On the opposite side are *Bieber, *Richter and *Dinsmoor, who argue that the work is too fine to be a copy. Recently, B. Ridgway has concluded that the work has a strongly eclectic character, with a formulaic body known in another example, from Elis (first century B.C.), and an idealized head type seen also in the *Oilpourer* in Munich. The footwear, believed by K. Dohan to be impossible before the second century B.C., is seen as part of this eclecticism.

BIBLIOGRAPHY

Symposium: "Who Carved the Hermes of Praxiteles?" *AJA* 35 (1931), 249–97; Bieber, 16–17; R. Carpenter, "A Belated Report on the Hermes Controversy," *AJA* 73 (1969), 465–68; Ridgway, *Roman Copies,* 85–86.

HERMITAGE, St. Petersburg (formerly Leningrad). Premier museum of Russia, known for its vast collections of painting, sculpture and luxury objects, including important classical antiquities.

The Hermitage takes its name from the building erected for the Empress

Catherine II the Great in 1764–65, next to the imperial Winter Palace, as a place of retreat and a repository for her art collection. Now called the Small Hermitage, this structure is one of five buildings along the Neva River that make up the Hermitage proper—along with the Winter Palace, the Old Hermitage, the New Hermitage and the Hermitage Theater. Portions of the complex were opened as a public museum in 1852, and the galleries were greatly expanded after the Revolution of 1917. With the exception of a period during World War II (1941–45), the museum was kept open through the Soviet period and remains today a public museum of overwhelming importance.

The archaeological collections had their beginning in the reign of Peter I the Great (1696–1725), who acquired ancient golden objects excavated in the kurgans (mound tombs) of Siberia, to be placed in his European-style *Kunstkammer*. Eager to reserve such pieces for himself, in 1718 he passed a decree ordering the "collection from earth and water of old inscriptions, ancient weapons, dishes, and everything old and unusual." Archaeology then became a specific interest of the Imperial Academy of Science, and soon the splendid Scythian tombs of the Black Sea were investigated as well (beginning in the Ukraine in 1763). Often overlapping in style and iconography with Greek art, Scythian treasures have been excavated at numerous sites, continuing to the present day. Among the Hermitage's prize pieces are magnificent grave goods of gold and other precious metals from Kul Oba (Kerch, excavated 1830), Chertomlyk (1863), the Great Bliznitsa (1864–68), the "Seven Brothers" mounds (1875 ff.), Solokha (1912 ff.) and Tolstaya Mogila (1971).

Numerous Greek vases excavated in Scythian tombs, along with antiquities from various Greek colonies along the Black Sea (cf. *Olbia, *Bosporus Cimmerius), form a significant category of the collection of classical antiquities of the Hermitage. The prestige of the collection of Greek ceramics is doubly enhanced by the acquisitions made in 1860–62 from the breakup of the Italian collections of the Marchese *Campana; there were well-preserved Greek vases from South Italy, including a splendid hydria from *Cumae, decorated with gilded relief and known as the Regina Vasorum ("Queen of Vases"), as well as Etruscan bucchero. Roman portraits from the Campana sale of 1860–62 combined with others acquired earlier in 1787 and 1852 from the L. Brown and Laval collections to create an important gallery of works ranging from the second century B.C. to Late Antiquity (the bust of *Philip the Arab* is notable). Of large scale statuary, the nude *Taurian Venus* (a fine Roman copy of a Hellenistic type) is of particular interest as the first classical statue to be acquired for the Russian collections; it was given to Peter the Great by Pope Clement XI in 1720. An assemblage of Tanagra-style terracotta statuettes was purchased from the collection of the Russian ambassador to Berlin, P. A. Saburov, in the early twentieth century.

The superb glyptic collection, rivalling those of Vienna and Paris, was begun by Catherine the Great, who gathered items from the collections of de Breteuil, *Byres and *Mengs (1780–82) and especially from Louis-Philippe, duke of

Orléans. What Catherine herself called "cameo fever" led her to amass eventually some 10,000 gems. The masterpiece of ancient glyptics at the Hermitage is the "Gonzaga" Cameo, acquired in 1814, when it was given to Emperor Alexander I by the wife of Napoleon. The large cameo carving (15.7 × 11.8cm.), probably of Hellenistic date and featuring royal portraits of a male and female, has sometimes been identified with a double portrait cameo listed in inventories of the *Gonzaga family collection in the sixteenth century (though the real "Gonzaga Cameo" is probably a very similar piece in the *Kunsthistorisches Museum, Vienna, described quite precisely by *Peiresc in the seventeenth century as being in the Gonzaga cabinet).

BIBLIOGRAPHY

"Leningrado," *EAA* 4 (1961) 545–56; +O. Neverov, *Antichnye Kamei v sobranii gosudarstvennogo Ermitazha* (Leningrad, 1971); +S. P. Boriskovskaia—E.N. Khodza, *Hermitage Museum: Antichnaia Koroplastika*, catalog of exhibition (Leningrad, 1976); +*From the Land of the Scythians*, catalog of exhibition (New York, 1975), 26–31; B. Piotrovsky, *The Hermitage—Its History and Collections* (Leningrad, 1982).

HILDEBERT OF LAVARDIN (ca. 1056–1133). French scholar, poet and archbishop of Tours (1125–33).

Born in Lavardin and educated at Le Mans, where he was subsequently appointed bishop (1096–1125), Hildebert was a cultivated scholar whose achievements mark him as a major precursor of the twelfth-century literary renaissance. His mastery of classical poetic form and diction represents the high-water mark of medieval classicism. His visit to Rome in 1100–1 probably inspired his twin elegies on that city, of which the first, *Par tibi, Roma, nihil, cum sis prope tota ruina* ("Nothing equals you, Rome, though you are almost totally in ruins"; *Carmina minora* 36), is unrivaled as a nostalgic tribute to Rome's former greatness. The poem was quoted at length by *William of Malmesbury, and the opening lines were cited enthusiastically by Magister *Gregorius, along with poetry of Lucan, Vergil and Ovid.

In evoking this past glory from the contemplation of Rome's ruined buildings and broken statuary, Hildebert gives early expression to that ntiquarian sensibility that was to play such a powerful role in the later history of the West.

BIBLIOGRAPHY

M. Manitius, *Geschichte der lateinischen Literatur des Mittelalters* 3 (Munich, 1931), 853–65; P. van Moos, *Hildebert von Lavardin* (Stuttgart, 1965); Hildebert, *Carmina minora,* ed. A. Scott (Leipzig, 1969); W. Jackson, "Hildebert of Lavardin," *Dictionary of the Middle Ages,* ed. J. R. Strayer, 6 (1985), 225–27.

DAVID A. TRAILL

HILL, BERT HODGE (1874–1958). American archaeologist, excavator and administrator.

Born in Bristol, Vermont, Bert Hill received the M.A. from Columbia University (1900) and attended the *American School of Classical Studies (ASCS) in Athens (1900–1903). For the following three years he was assistant curator of classical antiquities at the *Museum of Fine Arts, Boston. In 1906 he became director of the ASCS, a post he held until 1927. He next served as director of excavations on Cyprus for the University of Pennsylvania, conducting campaigns at Lapithos and *Kourion.

Hill's publications were relatively few; perhaps his best-known contribution was his study of the springs at Corinth (*The Springs—Peirene, Sacred Spring, Glauke,* Princeton, NJ, 1964). He is remembered as an excellent administrator and a superlative teacher. He received much recognition in the form of honorary degrees (University of Vermont, University of Salamanca) and foreign memberships (*German Archaeological Institute, Society for the Promotion of Hellenic Studies, Archaeological Society of Athens and others). In 1936–37 he held the distinguished appointment of Charles Eliot Norton Lecturer for the *Archaeological Institute of America.

BIBLIOGRAPHY

C. W. Blegen, "Bert Hodge Hill," *AJA* 63 (1959), 193–94.

HILLER VON GAERTRINGEN, FRIEDRICH FREIHERR (1864–1947).

German archaeologist, specializing in Greek epigraphy.

Born at Reppersdorf in Silesia of an old Prussian aristocratic family, Hiller studied under Alfred von Gutschmid at Tübingen, under T. *Mommsen and Carl *Robert at Berlin and under *Wilamowitz, whose eldest daughter he married, at Göttingen. Early inheritor of great wealth, he soon decided to become a gentleman-scholar. His accidental discovery in 1890 at Nysa of the Chairemon monument with the two letters of Mithridates (*SIG* II³. 741) won Hiller for epigraphy. He next excavated the theater at *Magnesia-on-the-Maeander at his own expense. At Wilamowitz's suggestion he edited for *Inscriptiones Graecae* (IG) the inscriptions of Rhodes (1895). He excavated at his own expense *Thera (1896–1902) and published the results in four volumes (1899–1909). *IG* became the center of his work: the Doric islands from Syme to *Melos (1898); the *Cyclades (1903, 1909); Arcadia (1913); pre-Euclidean Attica (1924); *Epidauros (1929). He edited the inscriptions of *Priene in 1906 and with colleagues revised Dittenberger's *Sylloge* in four volumes (1915–24).

Hiller contributed frequently to the *Realencyclopädie* (e.g., Rhodes, Miletos, Thera, Thessaly). He was honorary professor at Berlin (1917–33) and was active in the Prussian Academy. He frequently visited Greece to inspect the original monuments. His estates and enormous library were lost in World War II. He died in poverty and blind.

BIBLIOGRAPHY

F. Hiller von Gaertringen, "Erinnerungen und Betrachtungen eines alten Epigraphikers," *Neue Jahrbucher für Antike und Deutsche Bildung* (1942), 108–12; G. Klaffenbach, "Friedrich Freiherr Hiller von Gaertringen," *Gnomon* 21 (1949), 274–77; K. Hallof, "Bibliographie Friedrich Freiherr Hiller von Gaertringen," *Klio* 69 (1987), 573–98.

WILLIAM M. CALDER III

HIMERA. Greek settlement in *Sicily.

Himera represents the northwestern limit of Greek colonization in Sicily. It was established ca. 648 B.C. (Diod. 13. 62. 4) by a mixed population of Zankleans (Strabo 6. 2. 6) and Myletidai, presumably refugees from *Syracuse (Thucydides 6. 5. 1). About 483 B.C., Theron of *Akragas expelled the local tyrant, who, in appealing to *Carthage, provoked the Battle of Himera in 480 B.C. (Herodotos 7. 165–66). It remained under Akragan control until after 461 B.C. but was destroyed by Carthage in 409. Survivors were resettled at nearby Thermae Himeraeae by the Carthaginians in 408/7 B.C. (Cic. *Verr* 2. 35. 86).

Largely covered by earth and later constructions, the site was, nevertheless, identified by scholars and travelers since *Fazello (*De rebus siculis*) through a combination of ancient sources, local tradition and topography. A complete topographical study that included exploration of the western cemetery was carried out by Mauceri in 1877. Brief campaigns in subsequent years included examination of the eastern cemetery in 1926–27 and Marconi's excavations in the temenos of the temple of Victory (1929–30). Only in 1963 did extensive investigation of ancient Himera begin under the Archaeological Institute of the University of Palermo. Through 1975, work concentrated in the plain of Himera located on the more eastern of Himera's two hills. Both sacred and habitation areas were found there. Exploration also focused on some of the surrounding cemeteries and the temenos of the temple of Victory.

BIBLIOGRAPHY

P. Marconi, *Himera, lo scavo del tempio della Vittoria e del temenos* (Rome, 1931); A. Adriani, "Scavi di Himera (1963–67)," *Kokalos* 13 (1967), 216–32; N. Bonacasa, "Himera: A Greek City of Sicily," *Archaeology* 29 (1976), 42–51.

BARBARA A. BARLETTA

HIRSCHFELD, GUSTAV (1847–95). German archaeologist.

Hirschfeld, born in Pyritz to a Jewish merchant family, studied at Berlin with E. *Curtius and at Tübingen and Leipzig. With a traveler's stipend from the *German Archaeological Institute (1871–73), he toured Italy, Greece and Asia Minor. His publication record for these early years is strong, showing that he worked in Etruscan Italy (*Marzabotto, the Certosa in *Bologna), as well as Geometric Greece (the Dipylon at Athens). At *Olympia he took part in the first German campaigns (1875, 1877) and was directing excavations at the time of the discovery of the *Hermes* of Praxiteles. After travels to London and Paris, Hirschfeld returned to Leipzig to pass his qualifying stage and then received a call to Königsberg (1878), where he would remain until his untimely death in 1895. Named after him are the Hirschfeld Krater, a Geometric vase excavated at the Dipylon (now in the *National Archaeological Museum, Athens), which he was the first to publish, and the Hirschfeld Painter, designated as the artist of the krater and other Geometric vases.

BIBLIOGRAPHY
F. W. Goethert, "Hirschfeld, Gustav," *NDB* 9 (1972), 225; R. Lullies, in *Archäologen-bildnisse*, 88–89; +J. N. Coldstream, *Greek Geometric Pottery* (London, 1968), 41–44.

HITLER, ADOLF (1889–1945). Dictator of Germany and leader (Führer) of the National Socialist (Nazi) Party; strongly influenced by classical antiquity in his political propaganda and state architecture.

Hitler's attitude toward the Greeks was in the tradition of *Winckelmann, showing reverence for the "purity" of the Greeks and their history and culture. He never visited Greece, though he expressed a wish to see the *Parthenon, and his government supported the German excavations at *Olympia in connection with the staging of the Olympic games at Berlin in 1936. But his greatest admiration went to the monuments of imperial Rome, and he sought to have these emulated in monuments created for him by his architects, chief of whom was Albert Speer. In a trend reacting against the modern architecture of Gropius's Bauhaus, Hitler's architects designed triumphal arches, baths, vast assembly places (e.g., the Kongresshalle for Nuremberg, recalling the *Colosseum), and a great hall of the people (Volkshalle) for Berlin, based on the *Pantheon.

Hitler's most striking encounter with classical archaeology came in his visit to Italy in May 1938. Mussolini, who himself passionately sought to revive the Roman Empire (*Fascism, archaeology under), spared no expense in preparations for the visit of the Führer. A "triumphal" entry route was prepared that took Hitler past the *Pyramid of Cestius, the *Baths of Caracalla, the *Arch of Constantine, the Colosseum and the *Imperial Fora. His visit included a tour of the spectacular Augustan exhibition, the Mostra Augustea della Romanità, a scheduled event that lasted only one hour and that left Hitler begging for more. Rainy weather the next day allowed him to return; with G.Q. *Giglioli as his guide on both visits, Hitler especially admired a copy of the *Res Gestae* of Augustus (*Monumentum Ancyranum), Roman antiquities from Germany, and Italo Gismondi's stunning models of ancient buildings and of the entire city of Rome. He also visited the tomb of Hadrian (*Castel Sant'Angelo) with *Bianchi Bandinelli as his guide, the *Capitoline Museums, the Pantheon, and the *Ara Pacis Augustae, and viewed the garden frescoes from the *Villa of Livia at Prima Porta. Before his departure, he was presented with a large painted vase, a red-figure krater of the fourth century B.C., and a silver replica of the *Capitoline *Wolf.* Overwhelmed by the magnitude and power of Roman antiquity, he later exclaimed, "Rome completely bowled me over!"

An aftereffect of Hitler's journey was his success in purchasing the Roman copy of the *Diskobolos* attributed to Myron in the *Terme Museum. Galeazzo Ciano, Italian minister of foreign affairs, sold the piece against the wishes of many for the sum of five million lire, and it arrived in Germany by 1938, to go on display at the Munich *Glyptothek. After the death of Hitler the *Diskobolos* was returned to Italy.

BIBLIOGRAPHY
Haskell—Penny, 199–200; +A. Scobie, *Hitler's State Architecture, the Impact of Classical Antiquity* (University Park, PA, 1990).

HITTORFF (HITTORF), JACQUES IGNACE (1792/3–1867). German architect, archaeologist and architectural historian.

Hittorff was born at Cologne and worked as a stonecutter in his youth. In 1810 he went to Paris, where he received academic training in architecture and, eventually, royal patronage. Then, given leave by Louis XVIII, he made a journey to the south of France, Italy, and Sicily (1822–24) and returned to Paris with a rich portfolio of designs and notes on buildings he had seen.

Accompanied by his pupils Ludwig Zanth and Wilhelm Stier, he had made a striking discovery in Sicily. His study of the architecture of *Agrigento, *Segesta and *Syracuse led him to the conclusion, novel at the time, that Greek architecture was painted. His conclusions were presented definitively in *L'Architecture polychrome chez les grecs, ou restitution du temple d'Empédocle à Agrigente* (1851), in which he illustrated for the first time a reconstruction of a Greek temple adorned with full coloring, with its mural paintings and votive offerings, its altars and sculptures, likewise colored. Though disputed in details, Hittorff's revolutionary conclusion was to find general acceptance.

Among his many commissions in Paris, Hittorff was charged with the embellishment of the Place de la Concorde, where he disposed candelabra, statues and fountains to magnificent effect, and with the development of the Champs-Élysées, where he built fountains and the rotunda of the Panorama, which had a covering the exact diameter of the *Pantheon in Rome.

BIBLIOGRAPHY
J. I. Hittorff—L. Zanth, *Architecture antique de la Sicile* (Paris, 1827?); E. Breton, "Hittorff, Jacques-Ignace," *NBG* 24 (1859), cols. 807–11; Michaelis, 47; *Porträtarchiv*, no. 159.

HOBHOUSE, JOHN CAM (BROUGHTON DE GYFFORD), BARON (1786–1869). English politician and traveler, lifelong friend of Lord *Byron.

Hobhouse and Byron met at Trinity College, Cambridge, and decided to travel together on a *Grand Tour that was to focus on Greece and Turkey (1809–10). More disciplined and more serious about the archaeological sites they visited together, Hobhouse "would potter with a map and compass" and with a copy of Pausanias's ancient guide to the sites in his hand, while Byron would ride off in search of adventures. Hobhouse had his own archaeological thrills, participating, for example, in the opening of tombs in the Troad.

Hobhouse's description of their travels was published in 1813 as *A Journey Through Albania and Other Provinces of Turkey in Europe and Asia to Constantinople During the Years 1809 and 1810*. At this period, as Hobhouse notes, "Attica . . . swarms with tourists." Along with many useful travel tips, he includes eloquent descriptions of monuments, such as the *Temple of Olympian

Zeus in Athens, and records remarkable local superstitions about the monuments. ''A curious notion prevailing among the common Athenians, with respect to the statues, is that they are real bodies mutilated and enchanted with their present state of petrification by magicians who will have power over them as long as the Turks are masters of Greece.''

Hobhouse and Byron combined later for a second trip on the Continent, including Italy and Rome (1816–17), after which Hobhouse returned to England for a long and respectable political career.

BIBLIOGRAPHY

Stoneman, *Land of Lost Gods,* 175, 181; R. Eisner, *Travellers to an Antique Land, The History and Literature of Travel to Greece* (Ann Arbor, 1991), 105–11.

HOGARTH, DAVID GEORGE (1862–1927). English archaeologist, excavator and administrator.

Hogarth's apprenticeship included travels with Sir William Ramsay in Asia Minor from 1887 and excavation in *Cyprus (*Paphos) and Egypt. While director of the *British School at Athens (1897–1900), he excavated on *Melos (Phylakopi), *Crete (*Zakro), and *Naukratis. Returning to Asia Minor, Hogarth explored the *Temple of Artemis at Ephesos on behalf of the *British Museum, for which he also planned and started the excavation of Carchemish. Hogarth was keeper of the *Ashmolean Museum from 1908; during World War I he was in Cairo and coordinated the activities of a former member of his Carchemish team, T. E. Lawrence ''of Arabia.''

BIBLIOGRAPHY

D. G. Hogarth, *Accidents of an Antiquary's Life* (London, 1910); idem, *The Wandering Scholar* (London, 1925); A. H. Sayce, ''David George Hogarth 1862–1927,'' *ProcBrAc* 13 (1927), 379–83.

DAVID RIDGWAY

HOLLAR, WENZEL (1607–77). Bohemian artist and engraver.

Born in Prague, Hollar worked in Germany, England and the Low Countries. In 1636 he entered the service of Thomas Howard, Earl of *Arundel, who employed him (with Hendrick van Borcht the Younger) to prepare illustrations of paintings and sculpture with a view to publishing them in a ''Galleria Arundelliana.'' The English Civil War meant that his work never appeared, but Hollar published engravings of items in the Arundel collection independently. His main source of income was as a book illustrator, and he engraved topographical views, notably of London both before and after the Great Fire of 1666.

BIBLIOGRAPHY

G. Parthey, *Wenzel Hollar: beschreibendes Verzeichnis seiner Kupferstiche* (Berlin, 1853); K. S. van Eerde, *Wenceslaus Hollar, Delineator of His Time* (Charlottesville, VA, 1970); M. Vickers, ''Hollar and the Arundel Marbles,'' *Stadel Jahrbuch,* n.s. 7 (1979), 126–32; R. Pennington, *A Descriptive Catalogue of the Etched Work of Wenceslaus Hollar, 1607–1677* (Cambridge, 1982).

MICHAEL VICKERS

HOMOLLE, THÉOPHILE (1848–1925). French archaeologist and administrator.

Born in Paris, Homolle was educated at the École Normale (1869–71) and studied at Rome, doing research on the history and ruins of *Ostia. Continuing to Greece, he was soon sent by the *French School at Athens to *Delos, where he conducted many campaigns of excavation.

Homolle held the chair in Greek epigraphy at the Collège de France from 1884 until 1891, when he was called to be director of the French School at Athens. The well-known and highly important French excavations at *Delphi were carried on while he was director of the school (1891–1904, 1912–13). Returning to France, he was next made director of the National Museums but was relieved of his post when the *Mona Lisa* of Leonardo da Vinci was stolen from the *Louvre (though Homolle was in no way at fault). Much admired for his tact and leadership, he was subsequently made director of the Bibliothèque Nationale.

The publications of Homolle are almost all articles or excavation reports in journals.

BIBLIOGRAPHY

S. Reinach, *RA* 22 (1925), 136–39; F. H. Heffner, "Théophile Homolle," *AJA* 30 (1926), 339.

HOORN, GERARD VAN (1881–1969). Dutch philologist and archaeologist.

Born in Amsterdam, where he studied classical languages, van Hoorn continued his studies in Bonn, Germany; thereafter he traveled to Greece and Italy. He obtained his doctor's degree in 1909, with the dissertation *De vita atque cultu puerorum monumentis antiquis explanatio* (University of Amsterdam). In 1918 he was appointed lecturer and, later, professor of archaeology at the universities of Utrecht and Groningen, where he taught upon his retirement in 1951. He founded the library and archaeological collection of the Archaeological Institute of Utrecht, at that time part of the Institute of Art History. He gave his collection of ancient *choes* (jugs) in permanent loan to the collection. Van Hoorn also served as conservator of the Museum of Antiquities (PUG) of Utrecht from 1918 to 1957. He participated in excavations at the Roman *castra* at Utrecht (1935 and 1943) and at De Meern (1940).

BIBLIOGRAPHY

R. C. Engelberts, "In Memoriam Gerard van Hoorn," *BABesch* 45 (1970), 2–3; J. J. C. van Hoorn-Groneman, Bibliography, *BABesch* 45 (1970), 4–11.

MARJON VAN DER MEULEN

HOROLOGION OF ANDRONIKOS. See TOWER OF THE WINDS.

HORSES OF SAN MARCO, Venice. Monumental, gilded bronze sculptural group of four horses; displayed for many centuries on the façade of San Marco in Venice.

The horses are made of hollow-cast bronze, measuring 2.35m high × 2.5m long with the heads and bodies cast separately. No other equestrian monument with comparable anatomical and stylistic characteristics has been discovered from antiquity. Among the most frequently studied monuments, the group is variously described as Greek, dating to the fourth century B.C., as late Roman, dating to the fourth century A.C. and points in between. Originally, the horses formed part of a quadriga group, but both their date and place of origin are unknown.

Taken as war booty by Doge Enrico Dandolo, the horses came to Venice from Constantinople in 1204 following the conquest of that city in the Fourth Crusade; they may have once graced the Hippodrome in Constantinople (*Byzantium). They were in place on the façade of the Basilica San Marco by around the middle of the thirteenth century, there to remain until 1797, when *Napoleon's army removed them and carried them to Paris. In 1807–8 they were dramatically displayed atop the Arc de Triomphe du Carrousel, drawing a golden chariot. After Napoleon's defeat, the horses were returned to Venice in 1815.

In 1902 they were removed to the courtyard of the Ducal Palace for restoration, and again, during World War I, they were removed, for safekeeping, to the Ducal Palace and then to *Castel Sant'Angelo in Rome. After the war they were put on display in the Palazzo Venezia, before undergoing further restoration (1919) and being returned to Venice. The horses were again stored for safety from 1942 to 1945. Recent concern for their preservation, enhanced by a major exhibition in Europe and America, 1979–80, led to their removal from the façade; henceforth they are to be displayed indoors.

Due to their unique nature and their popularity, the horses have been described frequently and have had an impact on a wide variety of viewers. They are first mentioned in a letter of *Petrarch dated 1364. In the fifteenth century, *Ciriaco reported that the horses were made by Pheidias and had once adorned the temple of Janus in Rome. From the sixteenth century onward, they were frequently attributed to Lysippos, on the basis of a passage in Pliny mentioning a bronze quadriga made by the artist for the Rhodians (*NH* 34.63). *Winckelmann thought they dated to the age of Nero; Lord *Byron described the horses in *Childe Harold's Pilgrimage*. Artists frequently depicted them or imitated them, as in maps of Venice by Jacopo de' *Barbari and views of the city by Gentile Bellini (*Bellini family), Guardi and Canaletto. Vincenzo Chilone recorded the ceremony welcoming the horses back from Paris. Perhaps of greater importance is their influence on equestrian monuments and representations, such as *Donatello's *Gattamelata,* Verrocchio's *Colleone* and *Canova's monument of Charles III. Leonardo's equine studies and the engravings of Dürer (*The Knight, Death and the Devil,* 1513) also show the inspiration of the *Horses* of San Marco.

BIBLIOGRAPHY
E. Vittoria, *I Cavalli di Venezia* (Venice, 1972); +*The Horses of San Marco, Venice,* Metropolitan Museum of Art (New York, 1977); Haskell—Penny, 236–40.

ELIZABETH R. MEANEY

HORTI SALLUSTIANI. See GARDENS OF SALLUST.

HOUSE OF LIVIA (CASA DI LIVIA), Rome. Roman house of the Late Republic/Early Empire on the Palatine Hill, sometimes thought to belong to Livia, wife of the emperor Augustus.

The house has yielded a number of important paintings in the Second Pompeian style, dated to ca. 30 B.C. Of the four rooms where paintings are preserved, one features fruit garlands suspended illusionistically from painted columns; above is a landscape frieze painted in yellow, generally regarded as the crowning achievement of Roman monochrome painting. An adjoining room has large mythological paintings of Polyphemus and Galatea and of Io and Argus, set in the tripartite illusionistic walls (here, predominantly red) of the Second Pompeian style.

The house was discovered in 1869 during excavations ordered by Napoleon III, who had acquired a large area of the Palatine (the Orti Farnesiani) from the Bourbons of Naples. The extensive excavations were directed by Pietro Rosa, who unfortunately left meager reports of his results. The discovery of lead pipes for bringing water to the house inscribed with the name of Julia Aug[usta], that is, the name of Livia after the death of Augustus, led to the designation of the residence as the House of Livia. Some have argued that the house is the one purchased by Augustus from the Hortensii and have seen the house as simply part of the entire complex of the House of Augustus on the Palatine, though these may, indeed, have been the quarters of the empress.

BIBLIOGRAPHY
+G. E. Rizzo, *La Pittura della "Casa di Livia" (Palatino), MonPit* sec. 3, fasc. 3 (Rome, 1936); Nash, I, 310–15; R. Ling, *Roman Painting* (Cambridge, 1991), 37–38, etc.; Richardson, *New Topographical Dictionary,* 73–74.

HÜLSEN, CHRISTIAN KARL FRIEDRICH (1858–1935). German archaeologist; prolific writer on Roman topography and epigraphy and on Italian sketchbooks of ancient monuments.

Born and educated in Berlin, Hülsen studied classical philology, ancient history and archaeology with E. *Curtius, J. G. *Droysen, E. Hübner, J. Vahlen and T. *Mommsen. With a stipend from the *German Archaeological Institute, he was sent to Rome by Mommsen to assist in the corpus of Latin inscriptions from the city of Rome (*CIL* VI). He was soon made second secretary for the institute, a post he held for over two decades (1887–1909). To his interest in inscriptions was added a new specialty, topography of the city of Rome, and in this period he published his well-known study *Das Forum Romanum* (1904; 2nd

Photograph of *Christian Hülsen*, ca. 1905. (Deutsches Archäologisches Institut, Berlin.)

ed., 1905), translated into a number of languages (e.g., *The Roman Forum*, tr. J. B. Carter, 1909). His crowning achievement in Roman topography was his publication in 1907 of the third volume of the *Topographie der Stadt Rom in Alterthum* (initiated by H. Jordan), harvesting the fruits of his twenty years of research in the city.

Embittered because he was passed over twice for the post of first secretary, Hülsen moved to Florence and remained there, with the exception of five years at the University of Heidelberg, until the end of his life in 1935. During this period he added a third difficult specialty to his scholarly repertory, as he produced a number of studies on the drawings, engravings and other records of antiquity made during the Renaissance by G. da *San Gallo, Marten van *Heemskerck, G. *Dosio and others. Another monumental publication of this period was his study of the churches of Rome during the Middle Ages (*Le Chiese di Roma nel Medio Evo,* 1927).

Hülsen was much celebrated during his lifetime, with honorary degrees from Oxford, Erlangen and New York and memberships in the academies of Berlin, Munich, Paris and Rome (*Accademia dei Lincei and *Pontificia Accademia).
BIBLIOGRAPHY
L. Curtius, "Christian Hülsen, Gedächtnisworte," *RM* 50 (1935), 355; H. G. Kolbe, in *Archäologenbildnisse,* 126–27.

HUMANN, CARL (1839–1896). German engineer, field archaeologist and topographer.

Humann never studied archaeology, took a doctorate or held a university post. But he excavated for Germany the greatest monument of Hellenistic art to have survived, the *Great Altar of *Pergamon, now in Berlin. Like *Schliemann and *Dörpfeld, he was the self-made man. Born at Essen-Steele into an innkeeper's family, he trained to become an engineer. Forced by tuberculosis in 1861 to live in a southern climate, he began as a surveyor for the Turkish government for rail and highway construction. The job familiarized him with the topography and ruins of Asia Minor.

Humann began excavating with Pergamon, which, supported secretly by *Conze, he excavated 1878–86. In 1882, at the request of *Mommsen, he obtained a squeeze of the *Monumentum Ancyranum (*Res gestae Divi Augusti*). His excavations brought modern attention to Tralles (1888), *Magnesia-on-the-Maeander (1890–93), *Priene (1895) and even *Ephesos (1895). He became an expert topographer whose work was incorporated into H. *Kiepert's maps of Asia Minor.

Humann was buried in the Catholic cemetery in Smyrna, but his remains were removed to the site of Pergamon in 1967.
BIBLIOGRAPHY
C. Schuchhardt—T. Wiegand, eds., *Der Entdecker von Pergamon Carl Humann: Ein Lebensbild* (Berlin, 1931); F. Karl—E. Dörner, "Von Pergamon zum Nemrud Dag, Die archäologischen Entdeckungen Carl Humanns," *Kulturgeschichte der Antiken Welt* 40 (Mainz, 1991).

WILLIAM M. CALDER III

HUMBOLDT, KARL WILHELM VON, BARON (1767–1835). German scholar and diplomat; patron of the arts and lover of antiquity.

Humboldt, best known as a brilliant linguist and as brother of the great German naturalist, Alexander von Humboldt, became a central figure in intellectual circles in Rome when he served on a diplomatic mission to the papal court, 1802–08. At his home on the Pincio Hill he united German, Swiss and

Danish artists and scholars such as F. *Welcker, Angelika *Kauffmann, *Zoëga and *Thorvaldsen.

Humboldt's love of Greek and Roman antiquity was manifest in his poems on Rome (he felt that the city was "the sum of all life and all history") and on some of its well-known statues (the *Ludovisi *Ares,* the Ludovisi *Juno,* the *Nymph Anchirroe*). He acquired a number of pieces of original sculptures as well as casts, which he took back to his castle at Tegel, near Berlin. Prince Luigi Boncompagni Ludovisi, in a reversal of the *Ludovisi family policy of not allowing casts of their sculptures, gave Humboldt copies of the *Ares,* the *Ludovisi *Gaul Killing Himself and His Wife* and the "Papirius" group, all of which are still to be seen at Tegel. Humboldt's love of Greek culture surpassed even his devotion to Rome; he regarded the Greek genius as synonymous with pure humanity and is said to have died with verses from Homer on his lips.

After the downfall of Napoleon (1815), Humboldt helped with the negotiations for the return of antiquities from Paris to the Vatican. He also played an important part on the commission for the establishment of an art museum in Berlin, preparing a long and masterful report with recommendations on the display of antiquities (1830).

BIBLIOGRAPHY
Stark, 273–78; P. O. Rave, *Wilhelm von Humboldt und das Schloss zu Tegel* (Berlin, 1973); P. R. Sweet, *Wilhelm von Humboldt, A Biography,* 1–2. (Columbus, OH, 1978–80).

HYPERBOREANS (ROMAN HYPERBOREANS). Four Northern European scholars of the early nineteenth century who formed a union in Rome, the *Hyperboreisch-römische Gesellschaft,* to study classical antiquity.

The group, formed in 1823, consisted of Eduard *Gerhard, from Posen, Theodor *Panofka of Silesia and the noblemen August Kestner of Hanover and Otto Magnus von *Stackelberg of Livonia.

Together, the young men read Pausanias, Sophokles, Philostratos, Hyginus and other authors and engaged in adventurous investigations of classical antiquity in Rome, Latium and Etruria. Kestner and Stackelberg visited newly opened *Etruscan tombs at *Tarquinia (the Tomb of the Baron is named for Kestner). The society promoted publications, including the preparation of the engravings, with text, for two volumes of *Monumenti inediti* (1826).

Kestner was especially interested in the aesthetic aspects of ancient art, while Gerhard was inclined toward the systematic study and cataloging of artifacts and works of art. Stackelberg, an artist of great sensitivity and skill, was the mystic of the group. Panofka, regarded as unmethodical in his scholarship, was appreciated for his charm and for his ability to attract others to the circle. As scholars from various nations joined them (Carlo *Fea, the Duc de *Luynes, B. *Thorvaldsen, C. J. Bunsen), the union evolved, in 1829, into the *Instituto di Corrispondenza Archeologica.

BIBLIOGRAPHY
Stark, 285–86; Michaelis, 57–62; F. Eckstein, s.v. "Iperborei," *EAA* 4 (1961), 176–78.

I

IDOLINO (APOLLO; BACCHUS; GANYMEDE, etc.). Bronze statue, approximately lifesize (height 1.50m), of a slender, nude boy.

The well-preserved bronze shows a youth resting gracefully on his right leg, with his right arm raised to give or receive an offering and his left arm dangling by his side. The pose and the Classical style of the face and hair are reminiscent of the *Doryphoros* of Polykleitos and once led to the suggestion that the work is an original by the master dating to the fifth century B.C. (*Furtwängler and others). But the delicate proportions are often thought to show a later development, and the piece is judged to be a Roman variant in the Polykleitan style. It could be a "functional" statue—a *lychnonchos* (lamp support), a type of sculpture popular among the Romans. A copy of the head in basalt is also known.

The "Little Idol," as it came to be called and as it is still known today, was discovered in 1530 at Pesaro by Alessandro Borignano, during building operations. He presented the piece to Francesco Maria delle Rovere, whose property eventually came down to Vittoria delle Rovere, wife of Ferdinand II of the *Medici family. The statue was in Florence by 1630 and is recorded in the *Uffizi by 1646–47. Removed from Florence to escape the invading French, 1800–3, it returned to the Uffizi and was exhibited there until ca. 1889. By 1897 it was on display as one of the showpieces of the Museo Archeologico of *Florence and has remained there since.

The earliest descriptions of the statue called it Bacchus, but a number of other suggestions have been made through the centuries (*Apollo, Ganymede, Mercury*; *Winckelmann and *Gori called it a *Genius*). No attempt is made today to identify the youth.

BIBLIOGRAPHY
R. Kekulé, *Über die Bronzestatue des sogenannten Idolino* (Berlin, 1889); M. Cristofani, "Per una storia del collezionismo archeologico nella Toscana granducale, I: I grandi bronzi," *Prospettiva* 17 (1979), 4–15; Haskell—Penny, 240–41.

IGEL MONUMENT. Roman funerary monument erected around A.D. 250 in the village of Igel, near *Trier.

The monument, 23m high and built of red and red-gray sandstone, was erected by the Secundinii, a Celtic family of cloth merchants, and carries reliefs with scenes of mythology and the daily life and work of the Secundinii.

The monument was already protected in the early Middle Ages because of its imagined connection with St. Helena. (It was regarded as a memorial of the wedding of Helena and Constantius Chlorus.) The medieval Latin word *agulia,* meaning "obelisk," was applied to the monument and thus gave rise to the name of the location. The Igel monument was frequently studied, beginning with *Pirckheimer and Petrus Apianus, who copied the inscription in the sixteenth century. Shortly afterward, *Mansfeld attempted to move the towering structure to his palace outside Luxembourg but was unsuccessful. It was drawn and described by A. Wiltheim (*Wiltheim family) in the seventeenth century and by W. *Pars a century later. *Goethe was among those keenly interested in the Igel monument and has left frequent and lengthy references in his diary and letters.

BIBLIOGRAPHY
H. Dragendorff—E. Kruger, *Das Grabmal von Igel* (Trier, 1924), 6–38; E. Grumach, *Goethe und die Antike* 1 (Berlin, 1949), 463–71; E. Zash, s.v. "Igel," *PECS,* 405.

IGUVIUM. See GUBBIO.

ILIAC TABLET. See TABULA ILIACA.

IMPERIAL FORA, Rome. Complex of four fora and a temple precinct adjoining the *Forum Romanum, constructed over a period of 150 years during the Late Roman Republic and Early Empire; they comprise the Forum of Caesar, Forum of Augustus, Temple of Peace, Forum of Nerva (Forum Transitorium) and Forum of Trajan.

The five areas, known collectively (though erroneously) as the Imperial Fora, adjoin the east side of the Forum Romanum and the *Capitoline Hill. They were constructed with the purpose of relieving pressure on the Roman Forum, which became progressively more inadequate for the needs of the expanding city. All five are parallel or perpendicular to the same axis and form a distinct unit. They have overall dimensions of 600m × 200m and form one of the largest architectural complexes in the Roman Empire.

Parts of the Imperial Fora remained aboveground throughout the Middle Ages.

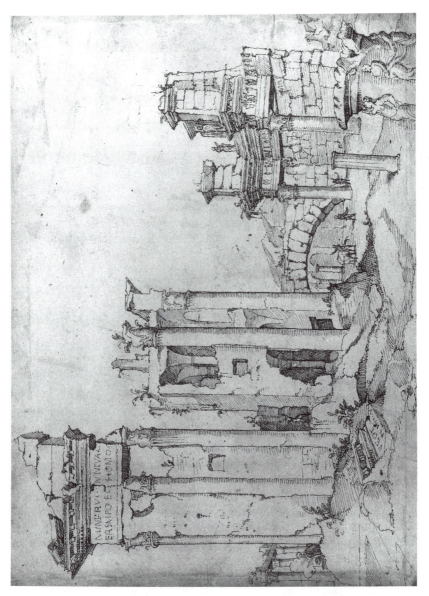

The Forum of Nerva ("Forum Transitorium"), with temple of Minerva, part of the Imperial Fora, drawing by M. van Heemskerck, Berlin, Kupferstichkabinett. (© Bildarchiv Preussicher Kulturbesitz, Berlin, 1994. Photo: J. P. Anders, 79 D2.)

The fora of Trajan, Augustus and Nerva are all mentioned in the twelfth-century *Mirabilia*. Drawings by Marten van *Heemskerck (1534) indicate what was still standing during the sixteenth century. *Giulio Romano was among the artists influenced by the remains. In the late sixteenth century, the area was developed by the Sovereign Order of the Knights of Malta. It was crowded with buildings when, in 1904, authorities proposed to drive a new road through the area to connect Piazza Venezia and Via Cavour. Seven years later, Corrado *Ricci published an archaeological analysis of the Fora, in which he called for minimal demolition of existing buildings and maximum exposure of the ancient monuments. Excavations began in 1924, first in the Forum of Augustus and then in the Forum of Trajan. In 1931, much of the area was leveled to make way for Mussolini's Via dell'Impero, which was opened in the following year (*fascism, archaeology under). In this period, Italo Gismondi prepared his splendid architectural models of buildings of the Imperial Fora.

The individual components of the complex may be reviewed as follows. The Forum Iulium (Forum of Caesar), begun in 54 B.C. and dedicated in 46, was not completed until after Caesar's death; it was restored by Trajan and Domitian. The forum consisted of a long, narrow piazza (160m × 75m), with the sides flanked by double porticoes and with the temple of Venus Genetrix on the east end, dominating the complex. Enough of the forum remained in the fifteenth century to provide plunder for the restoration of the apostolic palace by Pope Eugenius IV. *Pius II took more building materials for the construction of the Loggia of Benediction at St. Peter's. The whole of the temple of Venus and about one-half of the southwest colonnade were excavated by Ricci (1930–33).

The Forum of Augustus, begun in 42 B.C. and completed in 2 B.C., followed the basic design of its predecessor. It was a squarish piazza measuring 125 × 118m, overlooked by the temple of Mars Ultor ("Mars the Avenger," i.e., of the murder of Caesar). From the fourth century A.C., the complex was known as the forum of Mars. The piazza was flanked by colonnaded halls, beyond which were small, semicircular courtyards. Prior to the systematic excavations of Ricci in 1924 and 1926, the temple of Mars was opened up in 1838–42 by the removal of the Romanesque tower of SS. Annunziata, clearing of a part of the podium and enclosure of the zone with a wall. Excavations in the 1930s and 1970s revealed cemeteries underlying the forum, dating back to the Iron Age.

The "Forum of Peace" was actually a temple precinct, vowed by Vespasian in A.D. 71 to celebrate the capture of Jerusalem and to identify the new dynasty with peace and prosperity, after a period of war. The temple of Peace was destroyed by fire in 192 and rebuilt by Septimius Severus. Our knowledge of the plan is derived not from excavation but almost entirely from the *Forma Urbis Romae, the third-century marble map of Rome that was once displayed in a hall adjoining the temple. The precinct measured 110m × 135m and was laid out as a formal garden with porticoes on three sides. The temple, which was aligned with the short axis of the complex, stood in the center of the far side. Together with adjoining rooms, it contained booty from the sack of Jerusalem and a notable collection of Greek paintings and sculpture of an earlier date. The relics from Jerusalem remained in the temple until the fifth century, when they were carried off by Vandals. The temple of Peace was mentioned in medieval itineraries, but with evident confusion about which building it was.

The Forum of Nerva, measuring 120m × 45m, was constructed in the space between the fora of Caesar and Augustus and the temple of Peace. Begun by Domitian and opened by Nerva in 97 A.D., it contained the *Temple of Minerva. Columns of the forum wall with a frieze of Minerva (called Arca Noe in the Middle Ages, and later Le Colonnacce) were visible in the sixteenth century, and the Temple of Minerva survived in part at that time, as may be seen in the Heemskerck view. Clement VII (1592–1605) took away thirty-five cartloads of building materials for the construction of St. Peter's, and then Paul V (1605–21) leveled the temple and carried away the stone to build the Acqua Paola on the Janiculum Hill. The Colonnacce survived; under Ricci (1930–33) the structure was more fully excavated, along with the Temple of Minerva. It was restored in 1987–88.

The Forum of Trajan, the final and most ambitious extension to the Imperial Fora, was financed with booty from Trajan's Dacian War; it was begun in A.D. 107 and inaugurated in 112. In order to create sufficient level space, a ridge of high ground connecting Quirinal and Capitoline hills was demolished. The rectangular piazza, approached through a convex façade, was flanked by porticoes, the central sections of which were broken outward to form semicircular exedrae. At the far end stood a large, transverse basilica, the Basilica Ulpia, 120m × 60m, with apses at both ends. Beyond the basilica was the *Column of Trajan, the height of which (38m) recorded the height of the ground demolished to level the site. On either side of the column was a library, and at the end of the forum stood a colonnaded enclosure containing a temple, erected in honor of Trajan by his successor, Hadrian. To the northeast of the forum stood the market of Trajan, including a hall with more than 150 shops, cut into the Quirinal Hill in a series of terraces. While the market and the libraries were constructed of brick and brick-faced concrete, no expense was spared in the selection of colored marble for the forum and basilica. The Forum of Trajan was, as Ammianus Marcellinus observed in the fourth century, "a construction unique under the heavens." Still in use for the declamations of poets in the seventh century, the forum was mentioned in the *Einsiedeln Itinerary, ca. 800, but by the fourteenth century the quarter was abandoned. Though the Column of Trajan continued to stand and be a familiar monument, the forum was covered over and was not cleared until the French operations of 1812–14. G. *Boni excavated the semicircular exedra on the northeast side, and in 1928–34 major clearance was undertaken in the forum by Ricci, in connection with the construction of the Via dell'Impero (now Via dei Fori Imperiali).

BIBLIOGRAPHY

G. Fiorani, "Problemi architettonii del Foro di Cesare," *Quaderni dell'Istituto di Topografia* 5 (1968), 91; +P. Zanker, *Forum Augustum* (Tübingen, 1968); P. Zanker, "Das

Trajansforum als Monument imperialer Selbstdarstellung,'' *AA* (1970), 499–544; J. C. Anderson, *The Historical Topography of the Imperial Fora,* Collection Latomus, 182 (Brussels, 1984); +R. Meneghini, *Il Foro di Nerva* (Rome, 1991).

INGRES, JEAN-AUGUSTE-DOMINIQUE (1780–1867). French painter, dominant figure of nineteenth-century French neoclassicism.

Born and initially trained in provincial France, Ingres entered Jacques-Louis *David's Paris atelier in 1797. This artistic milieu provided Ingres with models, including antique sculpture and casts, and access to texts like the classical iconographical studies of E. Q. *Visconti and Antoine Mongez; *Winckelmann's *Monumenti inediti;* catalogs of engraved gems and cameos by J. *Tassie and R. E. *Raspe; and Sir William *Hamilton's publications of his collections of Greek vases.

Ingres laid the foundations for his classicism during the years he spent in Italy, beginning in 1806 as a winner of the Prix de Rome. He remained in Rome until 1820, when he moved to Florence; he finally returned to Paris in 1824. Ingres's later years in Italy were spent as director of the *French Academy in Rome (1834–41), during which time he revised the academic curriculum, founded an archaeology course and added a library, as well as antique and Renaissance casts for the galleries.

The classical past informs Ingres's work in regard to poses, themes, compositions and accoutrements. From the beginning, Ingres borrowed poses from classical statuary for his paintings, as in the *Envoys to Achilles from Agamemnon,* the painting that won the Prix de Rome for him (1801). Here the artist utilized the Vatican *Ganymede* for the graceful hip-shot pose of Achilles' companion Patroklos and the Vatican "*Phocion*" for the cloaked figure of Odysseus. In his *Jupiter and Thetis* (1811), Ingres's sources for the figures include Greek vases, as known through drawings by John *Flaxman and other copies, and, for the base of the throne, an antique cameo in the Naples museum that he knew from either Winckelmann or Tassie—Raspe. Ingres aggrandized contemporary history through classical themes, as with *Romulus, Conqueror of Acron* (1812), which commemorated *Napoleon's triumphal entrance into Rome in the manner of Plutarch's Romulus.

His imitation of the antique might take on an archaeological objectivity, as in the many versions he created of *Vergil Reading the Aeneid to Augustus,* beginning as early as 1811 (e.g., the fragmented composition with the central group only, in Brussels, ca. 1819; the Pradier engraving of 1832; the watercolor of 1850 in the Fogg Museum). The portraits of Augustus and Agrippa were done with uncanny accuracy, based on the latest research, and may easily be identified by iconographers today. Portraits of Livia, Octavia and Vergil were also carefully studied. Using recent publications on *Herculaneum, Ingres attempted to reproduce a Roman interior with authentic furniture. One may footnote almost every detail in this "magpie-like variety of borrowings" (Mongan).

Contemporaries, especially from the rival Romantic tradition, criticized him fiercely for his imitations. Theophile Silvestre thought Ingres shameless: "[H]ow unscrupulously he pillages statues, reliefs, engraved gems, antique cameos, frescos, vases, antique implements, paintings, prints, mosaics and Italian tombs!" (1855).

But Ingres never wavered in his approach to antiquity. With his carefully chosen and researched subject matter, his imitation of classical prototypes and his intellectual stress of line over color, he consistently viewed himself as heir of the classical tradition.

BIBLIOGRAPHY
+I. Blum, "Ingres, Classicist and Antiquarian," *Art in America* 24 (January 1936), 3–11; +A. Mongan, "Ingres and the Antique," *JWarb* 10 (1947), 1–13; +R. Rosenblum, *The International Style of 1800: A Study in Linear Abstraction* (New York, 1976); +P. Condon, *The Pursuit of Perfection: The Art of J.-A.-D. Ingres,* J. B. Speed Art Museum, catalog of exhibition (Louisville, KY, 1983).

CATHERINE MORRIS WESTCOTT

INSTITUTO DI CORRISPONDENZA ARCHEOLOGICA. International association of classical archaeologists, the first to be organized.

Formed in Rome in 1829 on the initiative of C. J. Bunsen, E. *Gerhard, A. Kestner, C. *Fea and B. *Thorvaldsen and with the early support of C. *Lenormant and the Duke of *Luynes, representing France, the Instituto di Corrispondenza Archeologica was a loose successor to the Hyperboreisch-römische Gesellschaft (*Hyperboreans), with a very different purpose. Its mission was to promote publication of news of archaeological excavation and discoveries, information about collections of antiquities and the results of archaeological investigations.

The first president was the elder Duke of *Blacas d'Aulps, but real responsibility lay with a network of scholar secretaries scattered through Western Europe radiating from Rome and Paris. Thanks to the authority of the founders and noble patronage, support and assurance of privileged information were won from both the Vatican superintendency of antiquities and the court of Naples, and membership grew very rapidly in the early years.

From the beginning it was envisaged to have three publications: the *Bullettino,* a monthly report of news; the *Monumenti inediti,* an annual large folio of the most important discoveries of any sort; and the *Annali* to accompany the *Monumenti,* with explanations of the plates and disquisitions on their subjects. The languages accepted were Italian, French and, occasionally, Latin; the material considered was Roman, Etruscan and Greek, rarely Egyptian or Near Eastern.

The first eight years of the institute were both productive and difficult. Gerhard was originally in charge of all publications, but a deluge of material had led to launching of a fourth series, the *Memorie,* and dissatisfaction with the *Monumenti* and *Annali* executed in Rome had led almost at once to their transference to Paris and the editing of T. *Panofka. With Panofka's move to Berlin, difficulties with Paris ensued. But in 1834 Gerhard had brought Emil *Braun

Casa Tarpeia on the Capitoline Hill, Rome, original seat of the Instituto di Corrispondenza Archeologica, engraving from *Monumenti inediti* 2 (1834–38). (Deutsches Archäologisches Institut, Rome. Inst. Neg. 38.575.)

to Rome and had him appointed librarian and instituted courses of archaeological lectures, the fees for which were invested for the benefit of the library, which soon became one of the institute's great assets. Eventually, by 1837 everything had been ironed out, and all the institute's activities were again concentrated in Rome, with Bunsen, Braun and R. Lepsius effectively in charge.

The years of Braun, 1837–56, were golden years. Despite political and economic upheaval throughout Europe, archaeological discoveries and studies abounded, not only in Italy but in Greece, Asia Minor and Egypt, and the institute's contributors worked feverishly. Following the death of Blacas, Metternich became president in May 1841, and Frederick William IV of Prussia, as patron of the institute, beginning in 1842, assured it of a substantial annual subvention. Braun also began to expand the institute's activities in teaching and, beginning in 1838 with Otto *Jahn, tutored young scholars in archaeology. The institute's quarters, early established in Palazzo Caffarelli, then soon became a mecca for students, among them Wilhelm Henzen, who became Braun's associate as editor for many years, and Heinrich *Brunn. The list is studded with important names.

After the death of Braun, Brunn came from Bonn to become secretary with Henzen. Then, in 1858, after years of economic uncertainty, the royal subvention from Prussia was more than trebled and the next year was made the object of a *Ministerialrescript* calling for a central direction in Berlin, funds for the library and publications and stipends for young Prussian students of archaeology at the institute. Now assured of patronage and with an enlarged mission, it grew and burgeoned in every direction, especially in epigraphical studies, excavations and catalogs of collections. In 1865 Wolfgang *Helbig succeeded Brunn as secretary. Finally, in 1871, Kaiser Wilhelm began the transformation, completed in 1874, of the private institute with royal patronage into the public *German Archaeological Institute with multiple branches in many countries.

BIBLIOGRAPHY
A. Michaelis, *Geschichte des Deutschen Archäologischen Instituts 1829–1879* (Berlin, 1879); G. Carettoni et al., *L'Istituto di Corrispondenza Archeologica* (Rome, 1980).

L. RICHARDSON, JR

ISTHMIA. Modern geographical designation for the ancient Greek site of the Isthmian Festival, which was held biennially in honor of the hero Palaimon at the sanctuary of Poseidon on the Isthmus of Corinth.

The site was associated with the cult of Poseidon from an early date, with the first temple—a Doric structure—erected in the first half of the seventh century B.C. This Archaic temple was destroyed by fire in 470 B.C. and replaced by a new Doric structure, which itself was damaged by fire in 390 B.C. and then restored. Adjacent to the precinct of Poseidon was the early stadium (Archaic period), overlaid by the cult area of the hero Palaimon (of Roman date), in whose honor the Isthmian games were celebrated. The later stadium was erected in the Hellenistic period, ca. 250m away from the precinct of Poseidon. The theater of Isthmia, northeast of the sanctuary, was built ca. 400 B.C. with a trapezoidal orchestra; with rebuildings it continued in use into Roman times.

Adjacent to the temple of Poseidon was erected a small temple to Palaimon, as part of a surge of Roman construction at Isthmia in the second century A.C., but thereafter the cult ceased to function, and the temples were abandoned. A great fortress was erected in Early Christian times to the east of the temples, probably in the fourth century A.C., partially utilizing stone from the earlier buildings.

Early investigations were conducted at Ischia by P. Monceaux (1883), whose misleading and erroneous conclusions included the idea that the late fortress was the precinct of Poseidon and Palaimon. He was followed by H. N. Fowler and C. A. Robinson, Jr., in their survey of ancient sites in the Corinthia (1925). In 1932 R. J. H. Jenkins and A. H. S. Megaw of the *British School at Athens excavated in the Isthmian region and corrected some of the errors of earlier publications. A major expedition to excavate Isthmia was mounted by the University of Chicago, in collaboration with the *American School of Classical Studies and under the direction of O. *Broneer. He excavated the sanctuary of Poseidon (1952–60), while the theater was unearthed under the supervision of E. R. Gebhard (1959–62). In 1967 the Isthmia excavations were entrusted to the University of California at Los Angeles (director, P. A. Clement), in a campaign to excavate the Early Christian fortress. Gebhard resumed direction for the University of Chicago in 1976. Campaigns of study and excavation (1985–89) by Gebhard and F. Hemans have generated a new plan of the temple and a refinement of the chronology. M. Sturgeon has completed a study of the sculpture excavated by Broneer between 1952 and 1967, including a remarkable marble basin (perirrhanterion) dating ca. 660–650 B.C.

BIBLIOGRAPHY

+O. Broneer, *Isthmia* 1–3 (Princeton, NJ, 1971–77); +E. Gebhard, *The Theater at Isthmia* (Chicago, 1973); O. Broneer, "The Isthmian Sanctuary of Poseidon," *Neue Forschungen in griechische Heiligtumer,* ed. U. Jantzen (Tübingen, 1976); +M. Sturgeon, *Isthmia* 4 *Sculpture I: 1952–1967* (Princeton, NJ, 1987); E. Gebhard—F. Hemans, "University of Chicago Excavations at Isthmia, 1989: I," *Hesperia* 61 (1992), 1–77.

ITALIAN SCHOOL OF ARCHAEOLOGY (SCUOLA ARCHEOLOGICA ITALIANA DI ATENE), Athens.

Principal center for Italian study and research into the Bronze Age and classical civilizations of Greece.

The Italian School of Archaeology at Athens was founded in 1909 through the initiative of Domenico Comparetti and Federico *Halbherr as a natural consequence of the work carried out earlier by the Italian Archaeological Mission to *Crete (Missione Archeologica Italiana di Creta; founded 1899). The school opened for the purpose of providing a program to train Italian students on Greek soil, in the presence of Hellenic monuments and inscriptions and with opportunities to visit excavations and collections. The program was interdisciplinary, open to archaeologists and architects as well as to philologists, epigraphers and historians.

The first director of the school was Luigi *Pernier, long associated with work on Crete from his excavations at *Phaistos. Pernier sought out new avenues for Italian research in Greece, carrying out explorations in Euboia and identifying new themes, such as classical sculpture, for the participating students. The school continued to excavate on Crete, and many students honed their skills at *Gortyn. Reports on Gortyn soon appeared in the first issues of the school's *Annuario,* founded in 1914 to demonstrate the scientific commitment of the new Italian institution.

Under the directorship of A. Della Seta (from 1919), the school began research on the island of Lemnos, an appropriate site for an Italian team in light of the well-known association of the island with the "Tyrrhenians" (possibly Etruscans). After long diplomatic negotiations, work began in 1925 at Vrokastro and then in 1926 at Hephaistia and Myrina. Among the members of the team were G. Caputo, A. Adriani, F. Magi, L. Laurenzi and D. Mustilli. The results included the uncovering of the Tyrrhenian necropolis of the seventh–sixth centuries B.C. as well as some of the habitation quarter, revealing a culture totally unknown before. They also excavated the cemetery of the Attic colony of the fifth–fourth centuries B.C. Della Seta could claim to have retrieved at least some of the context of the famous stele from Kaminia (found in 1885), inscribed in a language resembling Etruscan. There followed excavations at Kaminia itself and then at the prehistoric settlement of Poliochni, lasting until 1936. The results of Poliochni were finally and authoritatively published by L. Bernabò Brea, in *Poliochni* 1–2 (Rome, 1964–76).

In 1938, in line with the notorious racial laws in Italy in that period, Della Seta was recalled from the directorship of the school. His replacement, G. Libertini, introduced the project, aimed to satisfy Fascist imperial designs, of excavating to find Roman roots at Pallanteon in Arcadia; he discovered only two Christian basilicas.

During these years Italian archaeologists conducted significant explorations in the Dodecanese islands (occupied by Italy beginning in 1912), particularly at *Rhodes and *Kos. The Missione Archeologica Italiana there was under the direction of A. *Maiuri from 1924; work was carried out parallel to, but also sometimes in cooperation with, that of the school in Athens. The extensive excavations at Ialysos in Rhodes were published in the volumes of *Clara Rhodos,* 1–9 (1928–49). Della Seta directed work on the island of Kos, with help from Doro *Levi, followed by L. Laurenzi, who from 1928 to 1933 planned and executed a systematic investigation of the entire island.

Laurenzi served as director of the school in Athens from 1941 until he was imprisoned by the Germans in 1943, resulting in a severe interruption of the work of the institution. With the advent of Levi in 1948, the school returned to full activity, with special emphasis on the work on Crete, particularly at Phaistos, and on Minoan–Mycenaean sites at Iasos (1960–75).

BIBLIOGRAPHY
+A. Di Vita Gafà "L'archeologia italiana in Grecia," *Il Veltro* 27 (1983), 267–81; L. Becchi, "L'archeologia italiana in Grecia (1909–1940)," *L'Archeologia italiana nel Mediterraneo fino alla seconda querra mondiale,* ed. V. La Rosa (Catania, 1986), 107–20.

ITALICA (SANTIPONCE). City of Roman Spain on the banks of the Guadalquivir, founded in 205 B.C. by Scipio; the village of Santiponce covers part of its ruins and is being progressively dislodged as ongoing excavation of the ancient city proceeds.

Cited by Strabo and Pliny as among the most important cities of Baetica, Italica, from the reign of Augustus, coined money bearing the titles *Municipium Italic(ense)* and *Iulia Augusta Mun(icipium) Italic(ensium).* Its greatest development, however, took place over the course of the second century A.C., when it was favored by the emperors Trajan and Hadrian, the former having been born in the city (in A.D. 53). Hadrian honored it with the title of *Colonia Aelia Augusta Italica* and beside the old city raised a *nova urbs* endowed with impressive public services and majestic buildings from which has surfaced a great quantity of sculpture, inscriptions and architectural remains, currently preserved in situ or in the provincial Archaeological Museum of Seville, established in 1867 and housed since 1946 in the "Pabellón Renacimiento" of the Plaza de América.

Italica survived into the Visigothic period but languished progressively and was finally abandoned (tenth century) after the Arab conquest. The ruins, never completely covered and known in the Renaissance as "old Seville," were identified as Italica by the Sevillan humanist Rodrigo Caro (1573–1617). Archaeological excavations began in the eighteenth century and continue today.

BIBLIOGRAPHY
+A. García y Bellido, *Colonia Aelia Augusta Italica* (Madrid, 1945); J. M. Luzón, *La Itálica de Adriano* (Seville, 1975); *Itálica (Santiponce, Sevilla), Excavaciones arqueológicas en España* 121 (1982); P. Leon, *Traianeum de Itálica* (Seville, 1988).

FERNANDO FERNÁNDEZ GÓMEZ

ITHAKA (ITHAKI). Greek island in the Ionian Sea, generally identified with the homeland of Odysseus.

Despite minor difficulties, present-day Ithaki fits Homer's description of Odysseus's Ithaca remarkably well. Particularly after 1810, when Ithaki fell under British rule, it was visited by a series of learned travelers, eager to pinpoint the site of Odysseus's palace, Eumaeus's hut, the cave of the nymphs and so on. Murray's *Handbook for Travellers in Greece* (1854), which describes the island at length and discusses rival theories, demonstrates the remarkable contemporary interest. Mt. Aetos, on the isthmus between the two sections of the island, might seem the natural site for the king's palace. The ruins on the summit and col, however, are Archaic and Classical, too late to support their traditional association with Odysseus, though some Late Helladic III shards have been found there. *Schliemann excavated here rather casually in 1868 and more seriously in 1878, both times with little success. *Leake argued that Odysseus's palace should be sought near Polis Bay. British excavations there have revealed evidence of settlements dating to Late Helladic III. The most sensational finds, however, have been the thirteen bronze tripod-cauldrons, discovered in a cave-shrine in Polis Bay, dating to the ninth or eighth century B.C. These presumably inspired or, more probably, were inspired by the thirteen bronze tripods that Odysseus received from the Phaiakians (*Od.* 8.387–91; 13.13–16) and hid in the Cave of the Nymphs (*Od.* 367–70). The identification of Ithaca with Leucas, advocated by *Dörpfeld, has found few followers.

BIBLIOGRAPHY

+W. Gell, *The Geography and Antiquities of Ithaca* (London, 1807); W. M. Leake, *Travels in Northern Greece* (London, 1835), III, 24–50; H. Schliemann, *Ithaque, le Péloponnèse et Troie* (Paris, 1869), 14–83; +A.J.B. Wace—F. H. Stubbings, *A Companion to Homer* (London, 1962), 398–421.

                                                                             DAVID A. TRAILL

IZMIR. See SMYRNA.

J

JACOBSTHAL, PAUL (1880–1957). German archaeologist, specialist in Greek and Celtic archaeology.

Born in Berlin, Paul Jacobsthal first studied there, then at Göttingen and Bonn, where he wrote his dissertation under G. *Loeschcke. In 1912 he published his catalog, *Göttinger Vasen,* initiating his career as an expert on Greek vases, a study that he shared through the years with J. D. *Beazley. In the same year he became professor (*Ordinarius*) at Marburg, there to raise the quality of the archaeology department, introducing a prehistoric section. Constrained to emigrate in 1935, Jacobsthal moved to England, becoming lecturer at Christ Church College, Oxford, in 1937 and university reader in Celtic archaeology in 1947. Collaborating with Beazley, he supervised the two series *Bilder griechischer Vasen* and Oxford Monographs in Classical Archaeology.

Jacobsthal was versatile, publishing on a variety of topics. His most important book on the Celts, *Early Celtic Art* (1944; repr. 1969), explored relationships with the Greeks. His ability to range over a wide geographical area was demonstrated in his *Greek Pins and Their Connections with Europe and Asia,* which appeared in 1956. Jacobsthal died the following year in Oxford.

BIBLIOGRAPHY

H. Möbius, "Paul Jacobsthal," *Gnomon* 29 (1957), 637–38; K. Schefold, in *Archäologenbildnisse,* 204–5.

JACQUES, PIERRE (1516/20–96). French sculptor.

Some of Jacques's work is in Reims (cathedral and museum). Of great importance for Roman architecture and sculpture are his ninety-seven folia of sketches (Bibliothèque Nationale, Paris) after statues, reliefs and architectural fragments done in Rome (1572–77). He often noted the location (*Theater of Marcellus, *Mausoleum of Augustus) or collection (della *Valle, *Cesi, *Carpi,

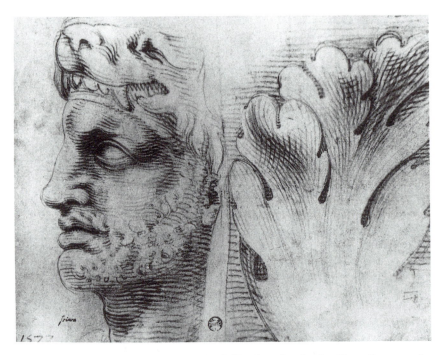

Standard Bearer in relief from the Arch of Claudius, drawing by Pierre Jacques, after
S. Reinach, *L'Album de Pierre Jacques* (1902). (G. Koeppel.)

*Bufali, *Farnese) where a piece was drawn, sometimes adding the date of the
sketch. Pierre Jacques drew for his own interest and study, often selecting only
details of a larger work, such as heads from the *Column of Trajan.
BIBLIOGRAPHY
+S. Reinach, *L'Album de Pierre Jacques* (Paris, 1902); H. Vollmer, ''Jacques, Pierre,''
in Thieme—Becker, 28 (1925), 310–11.

                                                        GERHARD M. KOEPPEL

JAHN, OTTO (1813–69). German archaeologist and philologist.

Born in Kiel, son of a well-to-do lawyer, musically gifted, Jahn attended
Schulpforte. At Kiel he studied under Nitzsch and Classen, at Leipzig under
Gottfried Hermann, whose narrow ''word-philology'' he rejected and at Berlin
under *Böckh and Lachmann, who taught him exactitude and method. He took
his doctorate under Nitzsch at Kiel (1836) with a dissertation on Palamedes. He
visited collections at Copenhagen, Paris, Switzerland and Rome, where he
learned from Emil *Braun. He met Otfried *Müller in Florence. In his first class
at Kiel (1839) he taught T. *Mommsen; in his last at Bonn (1869), *Wilamowitz. In 1842 he became associate professor (*Extraordinarius*) for classical philology and archaeology at Greifswald. In 1847 Jahn succeeded W. A. *Becker

Portrait of *Otto Jahn*,
steel engraving by A.
Weger. (Westfälisches
Landesmuseum für Kunst
und Kulturgeschichte,
Münster, Porträtarchiv
Diepenbroick. Photo: R.
Wakonigg.)

as professor of archaeology at Leipzig, where he became colleague of Haupt
and Mommsen. In April 1851 all three were dismissed for political reasons.

Jahn survived as a freelance writer until 1855. His *Florus* appeared in 1851
and in 1853, the influential catalog of Ludwig I's vase collection at Munich. He
next began the work for which he is most remembered, his four-volume life of
Mozart (1856–60). He became (1855) professor of classics and director of the
university art museum at Bonn. Bad luck ever dogged Jahn—his mad wife, an
illegitimate son, loss of the Leipzig chair and finally the epic struggle with
Ritschl over Sauppe that sent him to an early grave. His life of Beethoven,
Juvenal commentary and handbook of archaeology were casualties.

Jahn turned German archaeology permanently from the mystical absurdities
of *Gerhard, *Panofka and Creuzer to a rational, precise positivism. He restricted mythological exegesis of monuments to ancient literature and founded
*"Monumental Philology" (see especially his Pausanias and Pliny work).
Through students like *Michaelis (his nephew), *Robert and Wilamowitz, he
exerted enormous influence.

BIBLIOGRAPHY

A. Michaelis—E. Petersen, *Otto Jahn in seinen Briefen mit einem Bilde seines Lebens*
(Leipzig, 1913); L. Wickert, *Theodor Mommsen—Otto Jahn: Briefwechsel 1842–1868*
(Frankfurt am Main, 1962); G. Luck—E. Langlotz, "Otto Jahn 1813–1869," *150 Jahre
Rheinische Friedrich-Wilhelms-Universität zu Bonn 1818–1968: Bonner Gelehrte Bei-*

träge zur Geschichte der Wissenschaften in Bonn: Philosophie und Altertumswissenschaften (Bonn, 1968), 144–64, 221–26; W. M. Calder III—H. Cancik—B. Kytzler, eds., *Otto Jahn (1813–1868) [sic]: Ein Geisteswissenschaftler zwischen Klassizismus und Historismus,* (Stuttgart, 1991).

WILLIAM M. CALDER III

JEFFERSON, THOMAS (1743–1826). American statesman, scientist, inventor and architect; great proponent of the classical tradition in America.

Jefferson was born at Shadwell, his father's estate in Virginia. At the age of nine he began the study of Latin and Greek at boarding school; from 1760 to 1762 he was enrolled in the school of philosophy at the College of William and Mary and completed his formal education with a five-year study of the law under George Wythe, who also encouraged his interest in classical languages. He was introduced to Roman architecture when, in reading the works of Robert Morris and James Gibbs, his attention was directed to *Palladio's Four Books of Architecture,* a work all but unknown at that time in America.

Not until the spring of 1787, however, did Jefferson have the chance to examine Roman ruins firsthand. While serving as minister to France, he made a three-month trip through Southern France and Northern Italy and set down careful descriptions of the monuments he saw. At Vienne, for example, he made notes (now lost) on the Praetorian palace and wrote to Madame de Tessé: "I am glad you were not there; for you would have seen me more angry than I hope you will ever see me. The Pretorian palace, as it is called, comparable for its fine proportions to the Maison quarrée [cf. *Maison Carrée], totally defaced by the Barbarians who have converted it to its present purpose." It was being used at that time as a church and school. Jefferson was obviously familiar with the available publications dealing with the antiquities of the region, for at Vienne he also measured and made detailed notes on the "sepulchral pyramid" (*L'Aiquille,* a monument that once stood atop the center of the spina of a circus that had already disappeared), noting that the monument was "inedited." At Orange he admired the *Arch but was outraged at finding the circular wall of the amphitheater being pulled down in order to pave a road. At *Nimes he described the amphitheater and the Maison Carrée as "two of the most superb remains of antiquity which exist," finding in the latter a model for the Virginia Capitol building. At Bordeaux he measured the bricks in the Roman circus and was so impressed by their quality and durability that later, when he was secretary of state, he recommended that the federal Capitol building be constructed in brick rather than stone.

If Jefferson had done nothing else, he would be remembered as the chief proponent of the Roman Revival style in American architecture, a style that he believed expressed the ideals of the young republic. His greatest architectural achievement, the University of Virginia, was inspired by the layout of a Roman villa; its pavilions are decorated with façades copied from ancient buildings, and the Rotunda is modeled on the *Pantheon, though simplified and reduced to one-half the scale of the original.

While still a young man preparing drawings for his mansion at Monticello, a Roman-Palladian villa, Jefferson had acquired a sophisticated knowledge of the famous sculptures and paintings regarded as canonical in European taste. Around 1771, he drew up a plan, never realized, to acquire copies of some of the traditional models of excellence—the *Medici *Venus,* the *Farnese *Herakles,* the *Belvedere *Apollo,* the *Spinario,* the *Arrotino,* the *Dying Trumpeter.* He did eventually acquire a copy of the *"Cleopatra" in the Vatican, though it was not on his original list.

Jefferson was a revolutionary in the field of archaeology. In the process of excavating an Indian barrow (see Query XI of his *Notes on Virginia*), he employed the method of stratigraphical examination a hundred years before it became common practice.

He died at Monticello on 4 July 1826.

BIBLIOGRAPHY

K. Lehman, *Thomas Jefferson, American Humanist,* 2nd impression (Chicago, 1965); W. H. Adams, ed., *Jefferson and the Arts: An Extended View* (Washington, DC, 1976); S. Howard, "Thomas Jefferson's Art Gallery for Monticello," *ArtB* 59 (1977), 583–600; M. Reinhold, *Classica Americana* (Detroit, 1984).

JOHN SVARLIEN

JENKINS, THOMAS (1722–98). English artist, antiquarian and archaeological entrepreneur.

Jenkins was born in Rome, but trained as a painter in England, under Thomas Hudson. When Jenkins returned to his native city in 1763 with the landscapist Richard Wilson, he soon became one of its most powerful antiquarian art dealers and financiers. His academy memberships in Rome and Florence speak for his established reputation in the world of art, achieved as a dealer-agent, banker-host and unofficial envoy and spy for Hanoverian England at the Holy See, while it was host to the court of the Pretender.

His influence with Pope *Clement XIV, a local anti-Jesuitical antiquarian society and émigré artists, milords and other Transalpines on the *Grand Tour was as legendary and as notorious as were his sharp and seductive practices in art trading. His subsidizing the manufacture of fake gems in the *Colosseum (reported by Nollekens), pepping up worthless statuary fragments with extravagant restoration and advertisement for princes of state and commerce and sale and resale of distressed collectors' (e.g., *Barberini, *Mattei, Lante, Altieri), artists' and dealers' goods, often of marginal quality or authenticity, were comparably infamous—and successful—enterprises. He underwrote excavations in Rome, the Campagna and *Hadrian's Villa, at times with the better-reputed Gavin *Hamilton and James *Byres, to enrich his stores, and he supplied many of the major collections in contemporary England and elsewhere with classical antiquities, along with paintings, drawings and other art objects. His own snap-

Portrait of *Thomas Jenkins* by A. von Maron, Rome, Academia di S. Luca, ca. 1792. (Deutsches Archäologisches Institut, Rome. Inst. Neg. 66.751.)

shotlike drawings of antiquities then for sale (probably made with a copying device), preserved in the Townley and Lyde Browne collection albums at the *British Museum, are important but now little-known archaeological and art-historical documents that also speak for the character of his artistic ability. His collection and much of his fortune were confiscated during Napoleon's occupation of Rome, and Jenkins died, broken, while fleeing to a large estate he had purchased in Devon.

BIBLIOGRAPHY

A. Michaelis, *Ancient Marbles in Great Britain,* tr. C.A.M. Fennell (Cambridge, 1882), 74ff., 96ff., passim; T. Ashby, "Thomas Jenkins in Rome," *PBSR* 6 (1913), 487–511; S. Howard, "An Eighteenth-Century Handlist and Beginnings of the Pio-Clementino," *Eighteenth-Century Studies* 7 (1973), 40–61; B. Ford, "Six Notable English Patrons in Rome, 1750–1800," *Apollo* 99 (1974), 408–61.

S. HOWARD

JERASH. See GERASA.

JOHNSON, JOTHAM (1905–67). American archaeologist, administrator and editor.

Born in Newark, New Jersey, Jotham Johnson was educated at Princeton (A.B., 1926), the *American School of Classical Studies in Athens (fellow, 1927–28) and the University of Pennsylvania (Ph.D., 1931). He taught at the University of Pittsburgh (1937–46) and at New York University (NYU) (1946 and following), where he was for many years chair of the Classics Department (from 1948). Johnson served as field director of the University of Pennsylvania excavations at Minturnae (1931–34) and later as general director of NYU excavations at *Aphrodisias.

His own publications were few, but Johnson served as editor of *Classical Weekly* (1938–42), as archaeological editor of *Classical Journal* (1946–50) and as the founding editor of *Archaeology* magazine (1948–51), the immensely popular publication of the *Archaeological Institute of America (AIA), intended to interpret the discoveries and research of scholars for a wider public. Johnson was honored by the AIA as Charles Eliot Norton lecturer (1950–51) and as president (1961–64). His sudden death at the age of sixty-one (he was attending a meeting of department heads at NYU) was lamented by associates, who remembered him as a warm, jovial colleague and collaborator.

BIBLIOGRAPHY

New York Times, 9 February 1958, 39; "Jotham Johnson, 1905–1967," *AJA* 71 (1967), 221; S.v. "Johnson, Jotham," *Who Was Who in America* 4 (1968), 498.

JONES, SIR HENRY STUART- (1867–1939). English historian, lexicographer and administrator.

Educated at Balliol College, Oxford, Henry Stuart-Jones served as director of the *British School at Rome (1903–5). He became general editor of the cataloging of ancient sculpture from Roman municipal collections, issuing volumes on the *Capitoline and Conservatori museums (1912, 1926).

The majority of his publications are historical and include the Oxford Classical Text of Thucydides (1898–1900), a *Companion to Roman History* (1912) and chapters in the *Cambridge Ancient History.* But he is best known for his heroic revision, carried out from 1911 until his death in 1939, of Liddell and Scott's *Greek-English Lexikon,* subsequently known as Liddell-Scott-Jones or LSJ.

Stuart-Jones was Camden professor of ancient history at Oxford (1919–27) and later rose to be vice-chancellor of the University of Wales (1929–31). He was knighted in 1933.

BIBLIOGRAPHY

H. Stuart Jones, *A Catalogue of the Ancient Sculptures Preserved in the Municipal Collections of Rome,* 1, *The Sculpture of the Museo Capitolino* (Oxford, 1912); 2, *Palazzo dei Conservatori* (Oxford, 1926; repr. Rome 1968); *New York Times,* 30 June 1939, 19; "Jones, Sir Henry Stuart-," *Concise DNB* 2 (1982), 370.

JONGKEES, JAN HENDRIK (1913–67). Dutch philologist and numismatist.

Born in Bussum, the Netherlands, Jongkees studied classical languages and archaeology at the University of Utrecht under C. W. Vollgraff and G. van *Hoorn. He showed an interest in numismatics at an early age and ultimately obtained his doctor's degree in 1941 with a thesis in this area, *The Kimonian Dekadrachms.* His wide-ranging interests encompassed the classical archaeology of Asia Minor as well as Mediterranean, national and Early Christian archaeology; in addition, he pursued church history and the history of humanism.

Jongkees served as assistant to van Hoorn from 1941 to 1945 and also worked as an assistant at the Royal Numismatic Cabinet at The Hague. He was a delegate to the Dutch Historical Institute in Rome, returning to Utrecht in 1947.

His excavation experience included work at the Roman *castra* in Utrecht (1935 and 1943), as well as at De Meern (1940). He directed excavations at De Meern in 1957 and 1960. He succeeded van Hoorn as professor *extraordinarius* in 1951 and became *ordinarius* in 1959 of the Archaeological Institute of the University of Utrecht. Under his guidance the library became one of the best in the Netherlands; he also acquired important works of art for the collection of the Archaeological Institute. He founded the institute's series, *Archeologica Traiectina,* in which he published three volumes himself. Among the numerous publications listed in his bibliography are articles on the *Great Cameo of The Hague, S. W. *Pighius, Fulvio *Orsini's *Imagines* and Reinier van der Wolff.

BIBLIOGRAPHY

C. Isings, "In Memoriam Jan Hendrik Jongkees," *BABesch* 42 (1967), 2–3; M. F. Jongkees-Vos, Bibliography, *BABesch* 42 (1967), 4–9.

MARJON VAN DER MEULEN

JULIUS II (GIULIANO DELLA ROVERE; 1443–1513). Renaissance pope, patron of the arts and collector of antiquities; he began the Belvedere collection at the *Vatican.

Born at Albisola near Savona, Giuliano della Rovere was elevated to the cardinalate in 1471 by his uncle *Sixtus IV. The pope heaped bishoprics, abbeys and benefices on the young cardinal, and he became accustomed to acquiring and holding power. When elected as pope himself in 1503, he made his chief goal the restoration of the Papal States, which had gone to ruin under his predecessor, Alexander VI. With a keen sense of timing in military and political affairs, Julius II was able to recover lost papal property (Perugia and Bologna) and drive the menace of France out of Italy.

As much as for his abilities as a fierce and canny leader, Julius was admired for his adventurous taste and patronage in art. Some of the greatest works of the Italian Renaissance were commissioned by Julius from *Michelangelo and *Raphael. He developed an interest in ancient art that led to the founding of a museum of sculpture at the Vatican, at the time a quite unusual idea that was to have immense influence. Julius himself evidently owned one of the most famous ancient statues known in the Renaissance, the *Belvedere *Apollo.* He had the piece moved to the Vatican, to be displayed in the Belvedere courtyard along with, soon, a number of other great sculptures he secured. The whole ensemble was intended to, and did, bring great prestige to the papacy.

When new pieces were discovered, the pope would move aggressively to acquire them. In 1506 he outmaneuvered his competitors for the *Laocoon, and he soon added other memorable works to the Belvedere, either from excavations or from previously existing collections: the *Commodus as Hercules* (*Hercules and Telephus*), *"Cleopatra," *Venus Felix, Hercules and Antaeus* and the *Tiber* river god (*Nile and Tiber). Before he became pope, Julius had already demonstrated his sense of the potential importance of antique images when he salvaged a marble eagle of the period of Trajan and had it installed in the portico of the church of SS. Apostoli in Rome. The eagle is framed by an oak wreath, which must have appealed to Julius since the Rovere coat of arms featured an oak tree.

In spite of such interests, Julius II did little to protect endangered monuments in the city of Rome, and the sad tradition of destruction seen in the fifteenth century continued during his pontificate.

BIBLIOGRAPHY

Pastor, *History of the Popes,* VI, esp. 485–92; Haskell—Penny, esp. 6–10; Bober—Rubinstein, 219–20; +Lanciani, *Storia degli scavi* 1 (1989), 181–221.

JULIUS III (GIOVANNI MARIA DE' CIOCCHI DE MONTE or DEL MONTE; 1487–1555). Pope, patron of the arts and ardent admirer of classical culture.

Born in Rome, Giovanni Maria De Monte became Pope Julius III in 1550. During his short reign of five years, he was occupied with church reform, with replenishing the papal treasury and with providing food for the Roman populace. He sponsored the creation of the Collegium Germanicum and improvements of the university at Rome and patronized a number of well-known artists, including *Vasari, *Michelangelo, Ammanati, Prospero Fontana, *Vignola.

As a lover of classical antiquity, he identified with Julius Caesar (as had *Julius II) and upon his election commissioned a series of twelve canvases for public display depicting admirable deeds of Caesar. A longing to live in the style of the ancients is implied by his construction of the *Villa Giulia in a family *vigna* (vineyard and pleasure garden) outside Rome, beyond the Porta del Popolo. The palazzetto, with its exterior façade and interior hemicycle overlooking a courtyard, was designed by Vignola. Beyond this, a loggia and nymphaeum were constructed by Ammanati. The layout of the villa, reflects the descriptions of ancient villas in the letters of Pliny the Younger (2.17; 5.6); included in the painted decorations by Fontana are scenes based on ancient paintings described by Philostratos (*Imagines* 1.6, the *Feast of the Cupids,* in the "South Room"; 1.29, the *Feast of the Andrians,* in the "North Room"). Numerous classical subjects were chosen for the frescoes throughout the villa, and classical statuary was abundant. A statue of Venus crowned the fountain in

Residence of Julius III, the *Villa Giulia*, Rome, view of hemicycle court. (Deutsches Archäologisches Institut, Rome. Inst. Neg. 66.2239.)

the first courtyard, while a Venus-Nymph graced the sunken fountain in the second courtyard.

A letter of Ammanati gives a detailed account of the villa and its antiquities in 1555. The *vigna* was also fully described by the Frenchman J. J. *Boissard, who visited there before 1559; his *Romanae urbis topographia,* volume 3 (1597), includes numerous full-page engravings by Theodoor de Bry, of herms, altars, reliefs and statues. The collection attracted humanists (S. W. *Pighius, M. *Smetius) as well as artists (G. da *Carpi, G. B. Franco), whose sketchbooks contain valuable information. After the death of the pope, an inventory of the sculptures bequeathed to his brother was drawn up, listing no fewer than 300 marbles.

Julius III took little interest in the statue court of the Belvedere in the *Vatican created by Julius II and, in fact, even gave away the Belvedere statue of *Mercury* to Cosimo I de' Medici (statue now in the *Uffizi). He also removed the *"*Cleopatra*" from its niche in the Belvedere court and replaced it with a modern figure of a river god; upon the advice of Vasari, the *Cleopatra* was then placed in a new square room flanking the statue court, where it served as the crowning figure of a fountain.

Portrait of *Franciscus Junius*, by G. Vertue after A. van Dyck, from F. Junius, *Etymologicum Anglicanum* (1743). (Westfälisches Landesmuseum für Kunst und Kulturgeschichte, Münster, Porträtarchiv Diepenbroick. Photo: R. Wakonigg.)

BIBLIOGRAPHY
C. H. Smyth, "The Sunken Courts of the Villa Giulia and the Villa Imperiale," *Essays in Memory of Karl Lehmann* (New York, 1964), 304–13; T. Falk, "Studien zur Topographie und Geschichte der Villa Giulia in Rom," *Römisches Jahrbuch für Kunstgeschichte* 13 (1971), 101–78; A. Nova, *The Artistic Patronage of Pope Julius III (1550– 1555), Profane Imagery and Buildings for the De Monte Family in Rome* (New York, 1988).

JUNIUS (DU JON), FRANCISCUS, THE YOUNGER (1591–1677). Dutch humanist, known for his study of ancient art, especially painting.

Franciscus Junius the Younger was dedicated equally to the study of German philology (of which he was one of the founding fathers) and the reconstruction from texts of the history, criticism and theory of the visual arts in classical antiquity. His father, Franciscus Junius the Elder, a French Huguenot refugee, was a noted theologian and Hebraist who held professorships in Heidelberg, where Junius was born, and Leiden, where he grew up and studied. The major influence on his formation as a scholar was his brother-in-law, Johannes Gerardus Vossius, who informed and inspired him through his lectures and books on the history of classical rhetoric and literature.

Junius spent the decisive years of his life (1621–42) at the court of Thomas Howard, Earl of *Arundel, as his librarian and the educator of his children and grandchildren. Arundel was an outstanding patron of the arts and, next to Charles I, the greatest collector of works of art, books and classical antiquities in Britain. At Arundel's behest, Junius began his great work on the arts of antiquity soon after his arrival in Britain. He reviewed all of classical, biblical and early medieval literature (what was available to him) for passages that, in one way or another, pertain to the arts of painting, sculpture, architecture and the mechanical arts in the ancient world. He never abandoned this activity during his long life, forever improving and enlarging the contents of the two books into which he cast the results of his literary expeditions.

Junius's first book, *De pictura veterum,* appeared in Amsterdam in 1637 with a dedication to Charles I as a promoter of the arts. For Junius, *pictura* included all the visual arts that depict nature. But the art of classical painting, which could be recovered only through literature and which in antiquity magisterially demonstrated the life, the dignity and the charm of *pictura,* lay naturally at the heart of his work. *De pictura veterum* is composed of three books that treat respectively the origins, the progress, and the perfection of the arts as they were comprehended and commented upon in antiquity itself. Junius's text is almost entirely composed of quotations from ancient sources, which, as Hugo Grotius pointed out in a *laudatio* of the work, are fitted together like the individual *tesserae* of a mosaic to give a complete picture of his subject.

Reading the book is like entering classical literature itself. There are voices from the entire range of classical civilization in Latin and in Greek (the latter accompanied by their translations into Latin), reporting on, debating, evaluating and refining the vocabulary and rhetorical grammar of critical judgment and the art of describing works of art. Junius's founding principle is, as it was for the writers of antiquity, that all arts are one, that poetry paints as it sings, rhetoric and history paint as they report, describe and debate and pictures speak and act. In consequence, Junius liberally uses texts that are concerned with the perfection of the verbal arts and applies them to the elucidation of the guiding principles and *exempla* of the visual arts. His far-ranging book defines, within the framework of archaeology, the place of the arts in the humanities. Junius's praise of *pictura* is also a defense of the fine arts against their detractors (in his days, the Puritans) and their abuse by luxury and commerce.

At the request of Lady Arundel, Junius also prepared an English translation, *The Painting of the Ancients* (London, 1638), omitting large passages chiefly of interest to antiquarians and philologians and adding new quotations, including excerpts from modern poets, most notably, Sir Philip Sydney. The translation was destined especially to benefit British painters and their patrons. On his own, Junius also prepared a Dutch translation for his compatriots, again revised in parts, *De Schilderkonst der Oude* (Middelburgh, 1641).

The second book into which Junius cast his vast collection of excerpts from ancient literature is an encyclopedia, in alphabetical order, of the lives and works of the artists of antiquity and of anonymous works of art and the crafts, the *Catalogus adhuc ineditus, architectorum, mechanicorum, sed praecipue pictorum, statuariorum, caelatorum.* It appeared posthumously, seen through the press by *Graevius, together with a new and vastly enlarged edition of *De pictura veterum* in 1694 (Rotterdam; and with a different title page, London).

Together the two books contain the largest treasure of literary sources on the history of ancient art and its theory ever assembled. During the nineteenth century, Junius's argument, the *tout-ensemble* of his mosaic and even the relevance of many of his sources—for example, the *Imagines* of Philostratos—were challenged and sometimes derided as merely literary or fantastic by protagonists of an ever more self-assured spade-and-object-oriented science of archaeology. *Overbeck's widely influential collection of literary sources on Greek art, *Die antiken Schriftquellen* (1868), is a slim volume carved out of Junius's two books that contains only what Overbeck thought was of use to a modern archaeologist. Junius's contributions to the history of art and archaeology are again being studied and reevaluated, with new editions and translations available.

BIBLIOGRAPHY

D. Howarth, *Lord Arundel and His Circle* (New Haven, CT, 1985); F. Junius, *The Literature of Classical Art* 1, *The Painting of the Ancients;* 2, *A Lexicon of Artists and Their Works,* ed. K. Aldrich—P. Fehl—R. Fehl (Berkeley, 1991); Rolf H. Bremmer, Jr., ed., *Franciscus Junius and His Circle* (forthcoming).

PHILIPP FEHL

K

KABBADIAS, PANAGHIOTIS. See KAVVADIAS, PANAYIOTIS.

KÄHLER, HEINZ (1905–74). German art historian and archaeologist.

Born in Tetenbüll, Heinz Kähler studied classical archaeology, ancient history, philology and art history at Freiburg im Breisgau, completing his dissertation under H. Dragendorff in 1929. With a travel stipend from the *German Archaeological Institute, he toured France, Spain, Portugal, Italy, Greece and Asia Minor (1930–31). Kähler then worked as an assistant at the *Pergamon Museum (1936–37) and in Munich in the museum of casts of ancient sculpture with E. *Buschor (1937–41). He ultimately settled at Cologne, the successor to A. *Rumpf at the Institut für Klassische Archäologie of the university (1960–73).

Kähler published on a wide range of subjects in architecture and architectural sculpture, from Archaic Greece to Rome and Byzantium. On Greek art he contributed a study of the sculptures of the *Great Altar of Pergamon (1942). Founding the series Monumenta Artis Romanae with J. Morear, he himself produced monographs on monuments of Roman art: the *Gemma Augustea (1968, in which he republished the seventeenth-century treatise of A. *Rubens) and the *Augustus* of Prima Porta (1959). He published articles or book-length studies on other Roman monuments: *Hadrian's Villa (1950), the *Arch of Constantine (1953), the *Temple of Fortuna Primigenia at Praeneste (1958), the Aemilius Paullus monument at *Delphi (1965), the Villa of Maxentius at *Piazza Armerina (1973). Kähler's general study of Roman art, Rom und sein Imperium (Baden-Baden, 1962) was translated into English as the popular survey for students, The Art of Rome and Her Empire (New York, 1963).

BIBLIOGRAPHY
C. Schwingenstein, in Archäologenbildnisse, 293–94.

KARO, GEORG(E) (1872–1963). German archaeologist, specialist in Aegean civilization.

Karo was born in Venice; he studied in Munich under W. Christ and E. Woelfflin and in Bonn under G. *Loeschcke. In Rome from 1896 to 1901, he was a protégé of W. *Helbig, who interested him in the chronological and other aspects of Etruscan Orientalizing. In 1905, he began his association with the *German Archaeological Institute in Athens, where he served first under W. *Dörpfeld, then as director himself until 1919 and again from 1930 to 1936. From 1922, he synthesized the emerging Minoan and Mycenaean worlds for the *Pauly-Wissowa Real-Encyclopädie*. Karo's greatest contribution to scholarship lies in the same field: *Die Schachtgräber von Mykenai* (1930–33), the definitive publication of the material found by *Schliemann in the Shaft Graves at *Mycenae (Circle A). Karo lived in the United States from 1939 until 1952; his Martin Classical Lectures at Oberlin College were published as *Greek Personality in Archaic Sculpture* (1948).

BIBLIOGRAPHY

G. Karo, *Fünfzig Jahre aus dem Leben eines Archäologen* and *Greifen am Thron: Erinnerungen an Knossos* (Baden-Baden, 1959); F. Matz, "Georg Karo," *Gnomon* 36 (1964), 637–40; D. Ridgway, "Manios Faked?" *BICS* 24 (1977), 17–30.

DAVID RIDGWAY

KARTEROS. See AMNISOS.

KASCHNITZ-WEINBERG, GUIDO VON (1890–1958). Austrian art historian, archaeologist and theorist.

At the University of Vienna, where he studied and took his degree, Kaschnitz came into contact with the *Wiener Schule* (Vienna School) of art history (F. *Wickhoff, A. *Riegl, M. Dvoràk). When, after World War I, he was employed at the *German Archaeological Institute at Rome, he published a review in which he emphasized the difference between his own views and those of the *Wiener Schule*. Though he acknowledged the value of stylistic criteria in classifying a work of art, he also stressed the need of an analysis of its structure. By "structure" he meant the principles that gave rise to such a work of art. He used this method of approach, which he called *Strukturforschung,* in his books and articles on the prehistoric art of Italy, Sicily, Sardinia and Malta, as well as on portrait sculpture in Etruria and ancient Rome.

He was married in 1925 to Marie-Luise Kaschnitz, a distinguished writer. In 1932 Kaschnitz, became professor at Königsberg, in 1937 at Marburg and in 1940 at Frankfurt am Main. From 1953 till 1955 he was director at the German Archaeological Institute at Rome. After his death, his *Ausgewählte Schriften* were published in three volumes by H. von Heintze with the collaboration of G. Kleiner (Berlin, 1965). His history of Roman architecture and art (*Römische Kunst*) appeared, also posthumously, in four paperback volumes (Hamburg, 1961–63). The influence of his theory on classical archaeology is apparent in the later writings of F. *Matz and in those of R. *Bianchi-Bandinelli. In ethnology, the meaning of the term "structuralisme," coined by C. Lévi-Strauss, is not far removed from the views of Kaschnitz.

BIBLIOGRAPHY

Review of A. Riegl, *Spätrömische Kunstindustrie, Gnomon* 5 (1929), 195–213; R. Bianchi Bandinelli, *Storicità dell'arte classica* (Firenze, 1950); E. Homann-Wedeking, "Guido von Kaschnitz-Weinberg," *Paideuma* 7 (1959), 11–18; C. Schwingenstein, "Guido von Kaschnitz-Weinberg," *NDB* 11 (1977), 312–13.

E. HOMANN-WEDEKING

KAUFFMANN, MARIA ANNA CATHERINA ANGELICA (1741–1807). Swiss-born painter and engraver, one of the earliest members of the neoclassical movement in art.

The child prodigy of a painter father, Angelica Kauffmann worked most of her life in Italy and England. Multilingual, warm and persuasive, she moved in the highest professional, fashionable and intellectual circles, where she was in demand for her sensitive portraits, although also acclaimed in her own time for her paintings of classical subjects. In 1763, she arrived in Rome, where she became friends with *Mengs and *Winckelmann (whose portrait she painted), at the time when he was constructing his history of ancient art. Angelica had the opportunity to study firsthand the most famous classical antiquities, including the painting of the *Aldobrandini *Wedding,* the *Farnese family collections and many other works. She was elected to the artists' association of the Academy of St. Luke in 1764.

In England by 1766, Kauffmann was admired by Sir Joshua Reynolds, David Garrick and Henry Fuseli and was one of two women artists among the founding members of the English Royal Academy. She shared with Benjamin *West popularity as the leading painter in England of classical subjects. Among her numerous works on classical themes (in England as well as later in Italy) were *Cornelia, Mother of the Gracchi* (Virginia Museum of Art, Richmond); *Pliny the Younger and His Mother at Misenum* (the Art Museum, Princeton) and a series of themes on ancient artists, drawn especially from anecdotes in the *Natural History* of Pliny the Elder: *Zeuxis Choosing the Models for the Painting of Helen of Troy* (Annmary Brown Memorial, Providence, Rhode Island, 1770s); *Alexander, Apelles and Kampaspe* (Landeshaupt, 1782–83); and *Praxiteles Showing Phryne the Statue of Cupid* (Museum of Art, Rhode Island School of Design, 1794). Her paintings frequently revealed her study of antiquities in Rome, as in the allegorical painting of *Design* on the ceiling of the Central Hall of the Royal Academy, where a female artist is depicted practicing drawing before the *Belvedere *Torso.* Angelica worked extensively with the *Adam family in their re-creation of the classical ambience in art and architecture.

At her father's death, the newly married Kauffmann returned to Rome (1780s), where followed her friendship with *Goethe and others in his circle, as well as continued production of portraits and classical paintings. Her funeral, arranged by *Canova, was said to rival *Raphael's and involved the entire Academy of St. Luke. She was buried beside her husband, the painter Antonio Zucchi, at S. Andrea delle Fratte, but her fame also warranted a place in the *Pantheon: on the first anniversary of her death a memorial bust was unveiled in this monument of the antiquity she had loved.

BIBLIOGRAPHY

+V. Manners—G. Williamson, *Angelica Kauffmann, R. A., Her Life and Works* (London, 1924); L. R. Eddy, "An Antique Model for Kauffmann's *Venus Persuading Helen to Love Paris,*" *ArtB* 58 (1976), 571–73; W. W. Roworth, "The Gentle Art of Persuasion: Angelica Kauffmann's *Praxiteles and Phryne,*" *ArtB* 65 (1983), 488–92; A. Rosenthal, "Angelica Kauffmann Ma(s)king Claims," *Art History* 15 (1992), 38–59.

B. UNDERWOOD DURETTE

KAVVADIAS, PANAYIOTIS (PANAGHIOTIS KABBADIAS; 1849–1928).
Greek archaeologist.

Born in Cephalonia, Kavvadias studied classics at Athens and attended courses at Munich and Paris, led by *Brunn and Foucart, respectively. While pursuing an academic career at the University of Athens, he was appointed ephor of the antiquities of the Islands (1879). His excavation at *Epidauros (1881–85 and later intervals through 1909), which brought to light the greatest part of the sanctuary of Asklepios, won him wide recognition. He promptly published and provided with a commentary the inscriptions from the shrine. His appointment in 1885 as general ephor of Greece resulted in the first systematic excavation of the *Akropolis in Athens, in collaboration with G. Kawerau (1885–91).

Gifted with an administrative talent, Kavvadias reorganized and enlarged the Akropolis and the *National Archaeological Museum in Athens. He wrote in Greek the first catalog of the sculptures in the museum. In 1895 he became secretary of the Archaiologikē Hetaireia (*Greek Archaeological Society). He initiated the publication of the *Archaiologikon Deltion,* which aimed at the prompt publication of new finds, and he wrote an account of the history of the Hetaireia up to 1900. He undertook excavations in Athens, the Peloponnese and the Islands, and he founded several regional museums, in particular, the museum at Epidauros, in which he partly restored several of the buildings. He became professor at the University of Athens, where he taught history of ancient art and epigraphy (1904–22). In 1926 he was elected a member of the Academy at Athens.

BIBLIOGRAPHY

Fouilles d' Epidaure (Athens, 1893); *To Ieron tou Asklepiou en Epidauro* (Athens, 1900); *Die Ausgrabung der Akropolis vom Jahre 1885 bis zum Jahre 1890* (Athens, 1906).

ANGELIKI PETROPOULOU

KEA. See KEOS.

KEATS, JOHN (1795–1821). English Romantic poet, whose knowledge of the art of classical antiquity was shaped by holdings in British collections and reproductions in engravings and paintings.

Keats was introduced to the *Elgin marbles in 1817 by B. R. Haydon, who had led the campaign to have the *Parthenon sculptures installed in the *British Museum. Keats's sonnet "On Seeing the Elgin Marbles" explores his response to the permanence of their grandeur in contrast to the brief futility of man's existence. His enthusiasm for the marbles may have inspired his "Ode on a Grecian Urn," written in 1819. Recent scholarship asserts, however, that Keats drew from a variety of sources, which include the *Townley vase (British Museum) and the *Borghese and Sosibios vases (*Louvre). The poet would have known the Paris urns from G. B. *Piranesi's *Vasi, candelabri, cippi* (Rome, 1778). The Sosibios vase was also illustrated in the engravings of *Les Monuments antiques du Musée Napoléon* (Paris, 1804–6); in fact, Keats's own drawing of the Sosibios vase may have been based on this source.

Keats's trip to Italy, planned for health reasons, occurred too late to exert any influence on his poetry. His last volume was published in July 1820; he left for Italy in September. From letters it is known that Keats traveled from Naples to Rome via Gaeta and Terracina and that he saw the *Forum Romanum and the *Colosseum on his entry into the city. Further sightseeing was strictly forbidden by Keats's doctor to prevent the poet from becoming overly excited, but to no avail. The poet died in 1821 and was buried in the Protestant cemetery in Rome.

BIBLIOGRAPHY

W. J. Bate, *John Keats* (New York, 1966); +J. Dickie, "The Grecian Urn: An Archaeological Approach," *Bulletin of the John Rylands Library* 52 (1969), 1–19; S. Colvin, *John Keats* (New York, 1970); D. Hewlett, *A Life of John Keats* (London, 1970).

DEBRA L. MURPHY

KEKULÉ VON STRADONITZ, REINHARD (1839–1911). German art historian and museum director.

Born in Darmstadt, nephew of the great chemist, Kekulé studied at Erlangen under Friedrichs, at Berlin under *Gerhard, *Droysen and *Böckh and at Rome under Heinrich *Brunn, to whom he owed most. In 1870 he succeeded *Jahn at Bonn. In 1889 at the personal wish of Kaiser Wilhelm II, Kekulé advanced to Berlin as director of the antiquities collections. In 1890 he succeeded Carl *Robert as professor at the university, a post he held simultaneously with the directorship. With the emperor's permission he assumed the title von Stradonitz. He did much to expand the museum's collections by deft purchases and arranging of excavations, in which he was later ably helped by *Wiegand. His beautifully phrased lectures attracted large audiences. He found cataloging uncongenial, and his aperçus are often dated today. His role in the history of the discipline was crucial. He early abandoned the *"monumental philology" of Jahn and, influenced by Brunn, in the sense of *Winckelmann, but tempered by careful scholarship, he stressed the beauty of the object itself, the *ars gratia artis* of the fin de siècle, and became, in *Langlotz's words, "the founder of modern iconology." His student *Wilamowitz attests his lasting influence.

BIBLIOGRAPHY
H. Schrader, "Reinhard Kekulé von Stradonitz," *BiogJahr* 35 (1913), 1–40; U. von Wilamowitz-Moellendorff, *Erinnerungen 1848–1914,* 2nd ed. (Leipzig, 1929), 93–94; E. Langlotz, "Reinhard Kekulé 1839–1911," *150 Jahre Rheinische Friedrich-Wilhelms-Universität zu Bonn 1818–1968: Bonner Gelehrte Beiträge zur Geschichte der Wissenschaften in Bonn Philosophie und Altertumswissenschaften* (Bonn, 1968), 227–32; A. H. Borbein, "Klassische Archäologie in Berlin vom 18. bis zum 20. Jahrhundert," *Berlin und die Antike: Aufsätze,* ed. W. Arenhövel—C. Schreiber (Berlin, 1979), 99–150; W. Schiering, in *Archäologenbildnisse,* 73–74.

WILLIAM M. CALDER III

KELSEY, FRANCIS WILLEY (1858–1927). American archaeologist.

Francis Kelsey was born in Ogden, New York, and received his Ph.D. from the University of Rochester in 1886. From 1889 until his death of heart trouble at the age of sixty-nine, he served as professor of Latin language and literature at the University of Michigan (Ann Arbor). For the university, he organized excavations at Karanis, a Graeco-Roman town in Egypt (1920s), and also conducted excavations at Pisidian Antioch (1924) and at *Carthage (1924–25). He played a key role in purchasing papyri and manuscripts abroad and in making papyrology a subject of interest in America. He secured for the university a wide variety of antiquities either from excavations or by purchase, creating a museum that would eventually be named for him, The Francis W. Kelsey Museum of Ancient and Medieval Archaeology (contents today, ca. 84,000 items). The museum also contains a rich archive of Kelsey's papers and correspondence.

Kelsey was elected president of both the American Philological Association (1906–7) and the *Archaeological Institute of America (1907–12). He is remembered especially for his translation from the German of the great classic on *Pompeii written by August *Mau, *Pompeii—Its Life and Art* (New York, 1899).

BIBLIOGRAPHY
D. M. Robinson, "Francis Willey Kelsey," *AJA* 31 (1927), 357–58; "Kelsey, Francis Willey," *Who Was Who in America,* 1 (1942), 664; "Unearthing the Past: The Expeditions of the Kelsey Museum," *Research News,* University of Michigan, 23.5 (November 1972), 5–6.

KENCHREAI. Eastern port of *Corinth on the Saronic Gulf, 11km east of the city, important from the first to fifth centuries A.C.

Kenchreai is mentioned by Paul in the Epistle to the Romans as an early center for Christianity. It also is loosely described in Apuleius's *Metamorphoses,* in which the sanctuary of Isis is named as the place where the hero of the tale is transformed from an ass into a man. The site declined after major earthquakes in A.D. 365 and 375. The ecclesiastical complex constructed over the sanctuary of Isis functioned until the sixth century. Structural remains have always been visible.

Kenchreai was excavated between 1963 and 1966 by the *American School of Classical Studies, along with the universities of Chicago and Indiana, under the direction of Robert Scranton. The work was conducted using a combination of conventional and underwater techniques to reconstruct the port in its different phases. The harbor was found to be artificially improved by the construction of two huge moles (now submerged) of broken rock and earth. During the excavation, one hundred colored cut-glass panels (in *opus sectile*) were discovered in packing crates. The panels, now in the Isthmia Museum, are dated ca. A.D. 370 and are thought to be from Egypt. They display a variety of plant motifs, decorative patterns, birds, human figures, literary figures, harbors and seaside buildings.

The Kenchreai excavation was one of the first American explorations of a Roman harbor. Site publications address the complex architectural and artistic remains in different volumes, providing detailed description and analysis of data.

BIBLIOGRAPHY

R. Scranton—E. Ramage, "Investigations at Corinthian Kenchreai," *Hesperia* 36 (1967), 124–86; R. Brill—L. Ibrahim—R. Scranton, *Kenchreai: Eastern Port of Corinth,* 2, *The Panels of Opus Sectile in Glass* (Leiden, 1976); R. Scranton, s.v. "Kenchreai," *PECS,* 446.

JOHN L. KISSINGER

KEOS (KEA, TZIA). Nearest of the *Cyclades to the Greek mainland, home of an important Bronze Age "Temple" discovered by J. L. *Caskey in 1960 at Ayia Irini.

Keos has been well explored by recent surface surveys. Neolithic finds from Kephala were also excavated by Caskey and colleagues (1960–67). Proximity to silver, lead and copper may have promoted prosperity at Ayia Irini; the freestanding "Temple" with its large terracotta figures of women in Minoan dress and posture, imposing houses and wall paintings leave no doubt that the site lay on major Aegean trade routes in the second millennium B.C.

In Classical times, Keos supported four city-states: Koressos (briefly renamed Arsinoe in the third century B.C.), Ioulis, Karthaia and Poieessa. J. Pitton de Tournefort visited the ruins of Ioulis and Karthaia in 1700; P. O. *Brøndsted dug at Karthaia in 1812 and in 1826 correctly identified the locations of all four poleis. Since World War II, the *Greek Archaeological Service and the University of Athens have excavated at Karthaia, Poieessa and Koressos (where a well-known *kouros* was recovered in the 1930s). The states later merged, and in medieval times only Ioulis survived as Chora, its fortifications destroyed in 1647 by the Venetian captain Morosini. A monumental reclining lion of Archaic date is carved in bedrock at Ioulis; not far away, one of the best-preserved ancient fortification towers in Greece stands within the ruins of the monastery of Ayia Marina.

BIBLIOGRAPHY

+P. O. Brøndsted, *Voyages dans la Grèce* (Paris, 1826); I. N. Psyllas, *Istoria tes nesou Keas* (Athens, 1921); +*Keos,* 1–8 (Princeton, NJ, 1977–92); +J. F. Cherry—J. L. Davis—E. Mantzourani, *Landscape Archaeology as Long-Term History, Northern Keos in the Cycladic Islands* (Los Angeles, 1991); K. Manthos, *Archaiologia kai istoria tes nesou Keas,* ed. L. Mendoni (Athens, 1991).

JACK L. DAVIS

KERAMEIKOS EXCAVATIONS, Athens. Investigations in present-day Athens in an area of the city including, but not identical with, the ancient Kerameikos district.

The district, crossed by converging roads from *Peiraeus, *Eleusis and Boiotia, is noted for its city walls and gates (the Dipylon Gate, the Sacred Gate) and its ancient cemeteries with graves beginning in the twelfth century B.C. The excavation site occupies much of the city block bounded by the modern streets Ermou, Peiraios, Salaminos, Psaramilingou, Asomaton and Melidoni.

Sporadic excavations in the first half of the nineteenth century by L.F.S. *Fauvel, Lord Strangford and K. Pittakis gave way to systematic excavations by the *Greek Archaeological Society after a landowner dug a ditch and came down on the impressive grave monument of Dexileos (fourth century B.C.) and others in situ. Over a hundred grave monuments were then found between 1863 and 1870. In 1870, excavations were conducted with the specific aim of finding the Dipylon Gate, the main gate of the ancient city (fourth century B.C.), which had been buried under successive huge dumps. Along the edge of the road leading to the Dipylon and to the Academy of Plato, an original boundary stone of the Kerameikos was found. Excavations continued in 1873–74 in the area of the Dipylon Gate and were conducted as well at the Themistoklean city wall, the Sacred Gate and graves in a mound south of the church of Hagia Triadha.

From 1907 to 1912, A. Brückner directed the Kerameikos excavations for the Greek Archaeological Society and then from 1912 to 1930 for the *German Archaeological Institute. The main discoveries in this productive period were the Sacred Way, the Street of Tombs and the Dipylon-Academy Road, as well as burials from the Late Geometric period to the fourth century B.C. in the mound at Hagia Triadha. The latter included the great finds of Proto-Attic pottery. Among other discoveries were the Dipylon head and hand of a *kouros,* quantities of material from late Roman kilns—pottery, lamps, terracotta figurines—and the Dipylon hoard of 598 coins (the latest A.D. 578). Here, as elsewhere, excavations directed by E. *Buschor were destructive.

In the second half of the twentieth century, investigations by the German Archaeological Institute were resumed under the direction of D. Ohly, producing new evidence for the history of the Dipylon Gate and fountainhouse, for Classical and post-Classical houses northeast of the Dipylon, for the city wall and for the grave precinct of the Street of Tombs. From 1978 onward, new excavations have been opened up in the area bounded by present-day Ermou Street, the Themistoklean city wall, the Sacred Gate and Melidoni Street, in which stratified deposits of the fifth century B.C.–sixth century A.C., conscientiously recorded, have yielded rich new information and remarkable finds of pottery, terracotta figurines, metalwork, sculpture, lamps and loom weights.

BIBLIOGRAPHY

A. Brückner, *Der Friedhof am Eridanos bei der Haghia Triada zu Athen* (Berlin, 1909); U. Knigge, *The Athenian Kerameikos,* tr. J. Binder (Athens, 1991).

JUDITH BINDER AND NANCY T. DE GRUMMOND

KIEPERT, HEINRICH (1818–99). German topographer and cartographer of the ancient world.

August Meineke won Kiepert for classics as a schoolboy. A Berliner, he studied classics, history and geography there under *Böckh, von Ranke and Karl Ritter. After a journey to Asia Minor (1841), he became, in 1845, director of cartography at the Geographisches Institut in Weimar and, in 1852, director at the publishing house Reimer in Berlin. In 1855 he became member of the Akademie der Wissenschaften; in 1859, associate professor (*Extraordinarius*) at Berlin for geography; and in 1874, full professor. He traveled widely in classical lands. Schuchhardt preserves a memorable account of his visit to Asia Minor in 1886. A friend of Theodor *Mommsen, he drew many maps for the *Corpus Inscriptionum Latinarum.*

His specialty remained the historical geography of classical antiquity. He based his exact work on the critical examination of ancient literary sources, the monuments and reports of ancient and modern travelers. His great works are *Topographisch-historische Atlas von Hellas und der hellenischen Kolonien* (1841–46); *Atlas antiquus,* 6th ed. (1887–89); and *Lehrbuch der alten Geographie* (1878). The Puget Sound controversy between Britain and the United States, referred to Wilhelm II, was settled by Kiepert.

BIBLIOGRAPHY

E. G. Sihler, *From Maumee to Thames and Tiber* (New York, 1930), 68; C. Schuchhardt, *Aus Leben und Arbeit* (Berlin, 1944), 118–24; W. Unte, ''Berliner klassische Philologen im 19. Jahrhundert,'' *Berlin und die Antike: Aufsätze,* ed. W. Arenhövel—C. Schreiber (Berlin, 1979), 40; R.J.A. Talbert, ''Mapping the Classical World: Major Atlases and Map Series, 1872–1990,'' *JRA* 5 (1992), 5–38.

WILLIAM M. CALDER III

KING OF ARMENIA. See FARNESE CAPTIVES.

KING OF PARTHIA. See FARNESE CAPTIVES.

KIRCHER, ATHANASIUS (1601–80). Jesuit priest; German polymath and antiquarian, one of the first to study Egyptian obelisks and hieroglyphics.

Kircher entered the Jesuit order at Paderborn and successively resided at Münster, Cologne, Koblenz, Mainz, Würzburg, Avignon and Vienna before settling in Rome sometime after 1635. His studies during these years included theology, physics, mathematics, astronomy, natural history and Oriental languages.

Portrait of *Athanasius Kircher*, engraving by C. Bloemaert, from A. Kircher, *Mundus subterraneus*, (1664). (Westfälisches Landesmuseum für Kunst und Kulturgeschichte, Münster, Porträtarchiv Diepenbroick. Photo: R. Wakonigg.)

In Provence he met *Peiresc, with whom he shared a multitude of interests and who encouraged him in Egyptian studies. Upon arriving in Rome, Kircher had an introduction to the *Barberini family from Peiresc and was appointed at the Jesuit Collegio Romano as professor of mathematics, physics and Oriental languages. After eight years he was released from the post and was able to spend the rest of his life engaged in studying, collecting and publishing in the many areas that aroused his curiosity. His publications embraced Syriac and Coptic sacred texts, the culture of China and the Far East, alchemy, theology and many scientific questions (e.g., magnetism, optics, sundials). He wrote a guidebook to Latium (1669) and has left an early description of Etruscan tombs near Bomarzo, though a projected *Iter Hetruscum* never saw the light. His great work on Egyptology, *Oedipus aegypticus,* in three volumes, was published at Rome, 1652–55. Kircher was the first to publish the sculpture of the *Apotheosis of Homer* by Archelaos of Priene (1658), newly discovered at Bovillae, Italy.

Kircher invented scientific instruments (such as his *pantometrum* for practical geometry) and collected such instruments, along with weights and ancient bronzes. His collection formed the core of the Museum Kircherianum at the Collegio Romano, to which later were added objects from Praeneste such as mirrors, the famous *Ficoroni Cista and finds from the *Bernardini Tomb, as well as prehistoric and ethnographic collections assembled by *Pigorini. The holdings of the museum have since been dispersed to the *Villa Giulia (proto-

historic materials), Museo Nazionale delle *Terme (classical and Christian), Palazzo Venezia (medieval) and the Museo Pigorini (prehistoric and ethnographic).
BIBLIOGRAPHY
F. Bonanni, *Musaeum Kircherianum* (Rome, 1790); E. Gayot., "Kircher, Athanase," *NBG* 27 (1861), cols. 769–76; F. Krafft, "Kircher, Athanasius," *NDB* 11 (1977), 641–45; *Porträtarchiv,* no. 35.

KIRCHNER, JOHANNES (1859–1940). German expert on Greek epigraphy.

Born in Tallin, Estonia, Kirchner spent his youth in St. Petersburg, where his father was a civil servant. Like *Wilamowitz, he attended the elite school at Schulpforte (where he is buried) and the University of Bonn; decisive in his training was study under Dittenberger, the expert on Greek inscriptions, in Halle. Kirchner taught at the Friedrich-Wilhelms-Gymnasium, Berlin, 1884–1924. Archaeology gave him the basis for his work in the area of Greek inscriptions. His *Prosopographia Attica* (2 vols., 1901–3), a biographical register with full references of all known Athenians, has not been superseded. In 1906 Wilamowitz enlisted him for the reediting of all Athenian inscriptions after 403 B.C.; this huge work became volumes 2–3, in the second edition ("editio minor") of the standard corpus, *Inscriptiones Graecae* (1913–40). Among his other works is *Imagines Inscriptionum Atticarum,* photographs of inscriptions (ed. 2, 1948).
BIBLIOGRAPHY
G. Klaffenbach, "Johannes Kirchner," *Gnomon* 16 (1940), 429–32; S. Dow, "Johannes Kirchner," *AJA* 46 (1942), 127–28.

MORTIMER CHAMBERS

KITION (LARNACA). Greek and Phoenician city.

Ancient Kition, located on the east coast of *Cyprus, was an important commercial and religious center during the Late Bronze Age and the subsequent Archaic and Classical periods. *Cesnola began his archaeological explorations of Cyprus in Larnaca in 1866, where he uncovered, according to his own account, over 3,000 tombs of Classical, Hellenistic and Roman date. Kition was known to be a Phoenician settlement of the ninth century B.C. from historical documents, and nineteenth-century excavations uncovered inscriptions relating to the Phoenician temple of Astarte. In 1929–30, the *Swedish Cyprus Expedition excavated a sanctuary of Herakles-Melkarth on the acropolis of Kition.

The discovery of Late Bronze Age remains in 1959 has radically changed the understanding of the development of the town. While there exists some evidence of Early and Middle Bronze Age settlement at Kition, the earliest major occupation dates to the thirteenth century B.C. In a large religious precinct with a sacred garden and rectangular pool, temples constructed of ashlar masonry were identified, as well as an industrial quarter with workshops for the smelting of copper. The proximity of these industrial rooms to the religious area has led the excavator, V. Karageorghis, to suggest that the copper industry was organized under the direct protection of patron deities. In a separate settlement area, a number of Late Bronze Age tombs were found that yielded numerous pots, bronze vessels, objects of ivory and gold and a remarkable polychrome faience rhyton with a hunting scene.

Kition can be considered the first Western colony established by the Phoenicians. Their arrival on Cyprus is placed around 850 B.C. Excavations by Karageorghis between 1963 and 1981 demonstrated that the Late Bronze Age religious precinct was modified by the Phoenicians but continued to be used for cult purposes; the largest temple of Astarte in the Phoenician world was built on the foundations of a Late Bronze Age shrine.

BIBLIOGRAPHY

K. Nicolaou, s.v. "Kition," *PECS,* 456–58; V. Karageorghis, *Kition: Mycenaean and Phoenician Discoveries in Cyprus* (London, 1976); V. Karageorghis et al., *Excavations at Kition* (Nicosia, 1974–85).

PAMELA J. RUSSELL

KLENZE, LEO VON (1784–1864). German neoclassical architect.

Born at Schladen near Brunswick, Leo von Klenze studied architecture in Berlin with Friedrich Gilly and from 1816 served as court architect to the kings of Bavaria, Maximilian I and *Ludwig I. In 1834 he was sent to the newly liberated Greece by Ludwig I; during a three-month stay in Athens, he assisted with the renewal of the city, supervising the restoration of the *Parthenon and reporting the results in an emotional outburst to the new king Otho. He also reviewed and simplified a plan of Athens that had been devised by the architects S. Kleanthis and E. Schaubert and made a thorough study concerning the protection of the antiquities of the city. Klenze was one of the first to note the asymmetry of the *Propylaia and the *Erechtheion.

The architect designed in 1844 the neoclassical jewel of the church of St. Dionysius Areopagites in Athens, but the structure was not begun until 1858 and was finished only in 1888. In Munich his most important works in the Greek Revival style are the Ionic *Glyptothek (1816–30), which served for the display of Ludwig's sculptures from *Aigina and the rest of his collection, and the Doric Propylaean (1846–63). For St. Petersburg he designed the new Hermitage Museum (1842–51) in neoclassical terms.

The capricious Ludwig held a competition among fifty-one architects (including Klenze, *Haller von Hallerstein and *Schinkel) to build for him a national monument of German heroes, a Walhalla, with the designs being submitted in 1814–16; no winner was ever announced, but in 1819 he commissioned his favorite Klenze to make new designs for the project. Under the influence of buildings they had seen on a trip to *Paestum and *Sicily (1817–18), Klenze and Ludwig chose the form of a Greek temple for the monument erected near Regensburg overlooking the Danube River, completed in 1842. Resembling the Parthenon on the *Akropolis, the Walhalla features a gigantic system of stepped terraces and diagonal staircases supporting an octastyle Doric temple. A rich polychrome marble "cella" inside is decorated with an Ionic frieze by Martin von *Wagner showing the early history of Germany. Figures of Valkyries supporting the upper entablature of the chamber resemble caryatids, except that they are dressed in northern bearskins.

As an author, Klenze left behind a commentary on his travels in Greece, *Aphoristische Bemerkungen gesammelt auf seiner Reise nach Griechenland* (Berlin, 1838).

BIBLIOGRAPHY

Tsigakou, *Rediscovery,* esp. 203; +D. Watkin—T. Mellinghoff, *German Architecture and the Classical Ideal, 1740–1840* (London, 1987), ch. 6, "Leo von Klenze."

KNIDIAN APHRODITE (CNIDIAN APHRODITE; CNIDIA; KNIDIA). Greek statue, one of the most famous sculptures of antiquity.

This mid–fourth-century B.C. work by Praxiteles stood in an enclosure on *Knidos that was open to view on all sides. The statue was the first nude sculpture of the goddess, and with it Praxiteles canonized the representation of the goddess at her bath, raising it to the level of cult and making acceptable the intimacy of her nudity. The goddess was shown dropping her mantle onto a water jar at her left, while the right hand, in a seemingly unconscious gesture of modesty, was held before the pudenda. The type is known through the description and extravagant praise heaped upon it by ancient writers (e.g., Pliny, *NH* 36. 20–22; Lucian, *Eikones* 6), and excellent physical testimony exists among the coins of Knidos and numerous Roman copies. The best-known and most complete example is in the *Vatican Museums ("Colonna" copy), although a female head in the *British Museum, excavated on Knidos by C. *Newton, has been claimed as the statue's original.

The fame of the statue made Knidos a popular tourist stop and caused King Nikomedes of Bithynia to offer to forgive the city's enormous debt in exchange for the statue, but the citizens refused the offer. The influence of this statue on subsequent Hellenistic variations on the theme of the nude goddess places it in a critical position for the development of the female nude in Western art.

A replica of the type was in the collection of Prospero Santacroce in Rome in the late fifteenth century (now in Munich, *Glyptothek), but far more attention came to an over-lifesize replica that was in the papal collection at the Belvedere statue court by 1536. Placed adjacent to the *Laocoon and the *Belvedere Apollo,* it drew the praises of artists, poets and travelers. Jonathan *Richardson, Sr. and Jr., first pointed out the likelihood (1728) that the statue might be a copy of the Knidia. A statue of the same type was presented to Pius VI (1775–99) by Conestabile Colonna, a work that soon eclipsed the Belvedere statue, which, in any case, for some time had been covered with a prudish stucco drapery. The Colonna copy (itself having suffered for a time with a whitewashed lead cloak around the legs, removed in 1932), came to be regarded as the most important of numerous replicas identified by C. S. Blinkenberg and others.

BIBLIOGRAPHY

J. J. Bernoulli, *Aphrodite, Ein Baustein zur Griechische Kunstymythologie* (Leipzig, 1873), 206–12; C. Blinkenberg, *Knidia, Beitrage zur Kenntnis der Praxitelischen Aph-

rodite (Copenhagen, 1983); Haskell—Penny, 330–31; +LIMC, II, 49–52; Bober—Rubinstein, 61.

MARY ELLEN SOLES

KNIDOS. Dorian Greek city at the extremity of the long peninsula that extends westward at the southwest corner of modern Turkey between the islands of Kos and Simi.

The site climbs from the sea to a lofty acropolis and occupies as well the island opposite, to which it is connected by an isthmus with a harbor on each side. The legendary founder of the city was Triopis, a Thessalian, but Herodotos (1.174) says the colonists were Lakonians. Knidos with *Halikarnassos, *Kos, and Kameiros, Lindos and Ialysos on *Rhodes formed the Dorian Hexapolis, which became the Pentapolis when Halikarnassos was excluded before the fifth century B.C.; the assembly and the games honoring Triopian Apollo were held at Knidos.

The *Society of Dilettanti in 1812 noted well-preserved city walls, a long Doric stoa (possibly the *pensilis ambulatio* of Sostratos), two theaters, baths, a temple, perhaps dedicated to Dionysos, the sanctuary of Demeter, a Corinthian temple of the Roman period, a Roman odeum and an extensive necropolis. C. *Texier (1833–37) drew several of the funerary structures. Charles *Newton excavated extensively from 1857 to 1859 and dispatched 384 crates of sculpture and other antiquities to the *British Museum; these included the marble lion, ten feet long, from the Lion Tomb and the fourth-century B.C. Demeter of Parian marble. After surface explorations in 1949–50. G. Bean and J. M. Cook concluded that the city had originally been located 40km to the east at Burgaz (Datça) and had moved to the present site in the fourth century B.C. American excavations under Iris C. Love (1967–77) recovered earlier pottery to disprove that theory and revealed the round podium of the temple that housed Praxiteles' *Knidian *Aphrodite,* a monumental altar on the terrace below, a Hellenistic house with wall paintings, the temple of Apollo Karneios and five Byzantine churches. Middle Minoan pottery was found near the small harbor. Excavations were recommenced by Ramazan Özgen in 1987 and continue.

BIBLIOGRAPHY

Society of Dilettanti, *Antiquities of Asia Minor* 3 (London, 1840); C. T. Newton, *A History of Discoveries at Halicarnassus, Cnidus, and Branchidae* 2 (London, 1863); +I. C. Love, reports in *AJA,* 72–74 (1968–70); 76–79 (1972–75); 79 (1975); 81–82 (1977–78; N. C. Stampolidis, ''Der 'Nymphenaltar' in Knidos und der Bildhauer Theon aus Antiochia,'' *AA* (1984), 113–27.

JANE BURR CARTER

KNIGHT, RICHARD PAYNE (1750–1824). English art historian and connoisseur.

A major figure in epigraphy, textual criticism and art history, Richard Payne Knight dominated his day as a critic of ancient art. A good scholar but an arrogant autodidact, Payne Knight acquired his position by his standing in the *Society of Dilettanti, which he joined in 1781. In 1786 he published his study of Priapus, in which he shocked contemporaries by the emphasis he placed on the god's role in ancient religion. In 1791 he questioned the authenticity of Abbé *Fourmont's inscriptions from Lakonia. He himself published the "Elean Inscription" (Boeckh, *CIG* i.11). In 1808 he published a discussion of the text of Homer and the place of the digamma in the epic language. In 1820 he republished his discussion with a full text of *Iliad* and *Odyssey,* inserting the digamma at all possible—and many impossible—positions, along with many other drastic textual innovations. Although extreme, the work remains of value. His negative review of Falconer's *Strabo* in the *Edinburgh Review* for 1809 provoked a controversy.

His greatest triumphs and most crushing humiliation lay in art history. He possessed, displayed in his house on Soho Square, a remarkable collection of coins and small bronzes, acquired in many youthful visits to Italy. His knowledge of work in metal enabled him to detect a marble sculptor's imitation of bronze. His discussions of ancient sculpture, especially his text for the catalog *Specimens of Antient Sculpture,* published by the Dilettanti in 1809, set the standard of art criticism. He discussed the possibility that many works of art were Roman copies. They included the *Belvedere *Torso* and *Farnese *Hercules,* the *Medici *Venus,* the *Belvedere *Apollo,* the *Niobe* group, the *Borghese *Gladiator* and the *Dying Trumpeter.* He always believed in the authenticity of the *Laocoon.*

He was also an important figure in convincing the public that Roman art was inferior to Greek. Indeed, he regarded the "prodigious superiority of the Greeks over every other nation, in all works of real taste and genius" as one of the "most curious moral phaenomena in the history of man." The period of Roman dominance he regarded as little different from the arrival of the Dark Ages.

When Lord *Elgin brought his sculptures from Athens, Payne Knight told him he had wasted his energy, for the sculptures were Roman and artistically inferior. In 1816 Payne Knight testified before a select committee of the House of Commons against the nation's purchasing the Elgin marbles. In the ensuing controversy Elgin suffered financial loss, while Payne Knight suffered the loss of his reputation as a critic of Greek art.

BIBLIOGRAPHY

R. P. Knight, *An Account of the Remains of the Worship of Priapus* (London, 1786); Idem, *An Analytical Essay on the Greek Alphabet* (London, 1791); Idem, *An Inquiry into the Symbolical Language of Ancient Art and Mythology* (London, 1818); M. Clarke—N. Penny, *The Arrogant Connoisseur: Richard Payne Knight, 1751–1824* (Manchester, 1982).

E. C. KOPFF

KNOSSOS. Site on the hill of Kephala, in the north-central part of the island of *Crete, famed as the mythological domain of King Minos and as the location of the most important Bronze Age palace of Crete.

Though Knossos has yielded evidence of habitation from a quite early date (before 7000 B.C.) and from Hellenic Greek and Roman times, it is most important for its Minoan Bronze Age material. Excavations have revealed two major periods, of the Old Palace and the New Palace; since Minoan chronology, in particular, and the chronology of Aegean civilization, in general, remain highly controversial, it is safest to say that the two palatial periods belong roughly to a time frame from ca. 1900 B.C. to the fourteenth century B.C., though the end of the palace may have come considerably earlier. The developed palace is recognized as a labyrinthine structure, covering about two hectares, that stood in the heart of the surrounding town. Among the other structures explored in the area are the House of the Frescoes, the Little Palace, the Royal Villa, the Caravanserai and various houses, tombs and cemeteries on the periphery of the town.

The palace featured a central court running north–south, and rooms serving a wide variety of purposes ranged along the west (major entrance, storage magazines, theatral area, throne room, chamber associated with religion) and the east (residential and industrial quarter). Rising up to four stories in places, the palace featured construction of timber and rubble, with the walls often faced with frescoes or reliefs and with architectural details picked out in gypsum or alabaster. Winding passages, monumental staircases, light wells and stone-lined tanks in the floors (''lustral basins'') gave the palace a dynamic character. The repeated use of the downward-tapering column and a motif in stone shaped like the horns of a bull were also distinctive elements.

At some time not yet agreed upon and through a cause much debated, the palace suffered destruction. The finding of archives of tablets written in Linear B (*Linear A and B) in the final habitation layers suggests the palace had been taken over by *Mycenaens.

Postpalatial Knossos reveals fluctuations of population in the surrounding town and countryside. The Sub-Minoan period and Early Iron Age are represented (eleventh to eighth centuries B.C.), but the Orientalizing (seventh century B.C.), earlier Archaic (sixth century B.C.) and Classical periods are little known. Hellenistic Knossos was a site of some importance, known from literature as the principal city of Crete at the time. As a Roman colony it was heavily populated from around the time of Augustus (27 B.C. and following); aqueducts and well-appointed villas and houses, as well as a civil basilica and temples, have been discovered.

After the Early Christian and Byzantine periods (surviving remains indicate basilicas of the fifth-sixth centuries A.C.), Knossos was once again deserted. With the Arab conquest of 827, nearby *Herakleion became the more important site. During Venetian occupation (1204–1669), Knossos yielded statuary that was taken away to Venice.

In the nineteenth century, several campaigns of exploration suggested that the site housed a Bronze Age palace. Minos Kalokairinos excavated in the west wing of the palace (1878–79) and extracted diagnostic pottery, including great

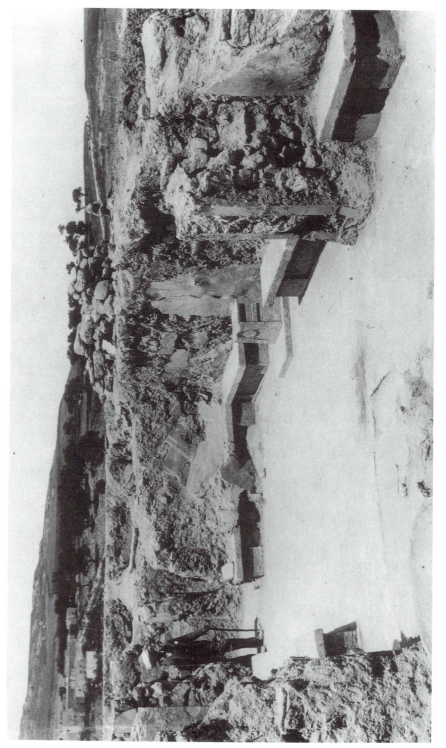

Throne room at the *Palace of Minos, Knossos*, before reconstruction. (The Ashmolean Museum, Oxford.)

ceramic storage jars (*pithoi*). In 1881, W. J. Stillman reported to the *Archaeological Institute of America that at Knossos he had viewed the remains of
ancient walls with huge blocks of hewn stone incised with signs. Arthur *Evans,
encouraged by F. *Halbherr, visited the island for the first time in 1894, in
search of evidence of Bronze Age writing and images, especially on sealstones.
He was led to Knossos as the principal source for these stones and was able to
acquire the site and secure excavation permits in 1900. Aided by J. L. *Myres
and Duncan Mackenzie, in a five-year period he completed most of the excavation of the palace and made considerable progress in exploring its environs.
He named the astonishing culture he unearthed after King Minos and utilized
the name for a chronological scheme of Early, Middle and Late Minoan, closely
related to the Egyptian system of Old, Middle and New Kingdom.

Soon after excavation began, Evans observed the rapid deterioration in the
throne room and other newly excavated areas, and he determined to roof and,
concomitantly, to restore the palace. To this end he employed the architect
Theodore Fyfe (1900–4) and, later, Christian Doll. Their reconstructions and
those done later by Piet de Jong were ambitious and sometimes highly speculative. Though the site became a showplace, the validity of the reconstructions
remains a controversial point. For the restoration of frescoes, Evans relied on
the Swiss artist Emile Gilliéron and his son Edouard. From 1906 the dig headquarters were at the Villa Ariadne, a residence near the palace built for Evans
by Doll.

Evans spent a great deal of his personal fortune on the purchase of the site,
as well as on the materials and labor for its reconstruction and the building of
the Villa Ariadne. In addition, there were crowds of local workers to pay—both
men and women—sometimes numbering as many as 300. Visitors were constantly coming to see the site, and they had to be entertained hospitably. Among
these were leading archaeologists, many of whom joined in dialogue with Evans
on the interpretation of the site, such as the Italian Luigi *Pernier, the German
*Dörpfeld and, from the *British School at Athens, Ernest Gardner and Alan
*Wace. The American Harriet Boyd (*Hawes) was present in 1900 during the
excavation of the palace throne, which Evans referred to at the time as the
"Throne of Ariadne."

The work of publishing and publicizing Knossos came to consume Evans. He
published on the scripts first, as was natural since this material was at the heart
of his first investigations. His *Scripta Minoa* began to appear in 1909 (the first
volume dealt with the hieroglyphic-type script), but at his death over thirty years
later he still had not brought out the majority of the material. It is clear that he
himself had hoped to decipher the two scripts Linear A and B, and so he did
not publish the tablets and give others a chance to compete with him. The
posthumous second volume of *Scripta Minoa* (1952) provided key material that
helped Michael *Ventris to decipher Linear B.

The volumes of his great comprehensive report, *The Palace of Minos,* began
to appear in 1921 and were completed, with index, in 1936. Fully covered in

the five-volume work are the architecture, frescoes, pottery and seals of the palace and its dependencies. *The Palace of Minos* is imbued with Evans's passionate and partisan belief that the civilization he excavated was the dominant force in the Aegean and that Mycenaean culture was basically marginal and dependent, a position that has been adamantly denied by specialists working on mainland Greece of the Bronze Age.

After the first grand campaigns of 1900–5 and 1907–10, Evans continued to carry out minor excavations and tests and make restorations at Knossos from time to time (1913, 1922–31). The British School then assumed the direction of the work, first under J.D.S. *Pendlebury, who was curator from 1930 to 1934 and published *A Handbook to the Palace of Minos at Knossos* (1933; new ed., 1954). In succeeding years, numerous projects have been undertaken to enlarge the picture of the town that surrounded the palace and refine the chronology of the site. Of the many distinguished British archaeologists who have guided work at Knossos, R. W. Hutchinson (1935–40) and M.S.F. Hood (1950–61) had especially long tenures. Excavations in the area of a Minoan mansion discovered by Evans but left unexplored have been carried out in several campaigns (1967–68, 1971–73, 1977) under M. Popham (Minoan remains) and L. H. Sackett (later material). The "Unexplored Mansion" site has yielded the best chronological sequence so far from the post-Minoan periods, including frescoed Roman houses containing fragments of plaster sculptures (second century A.C.). In another area by the Stratigraphical Museum of Knossos, excavations by P. Warren in a building of Late Minoan IB have unearthed the bones of some four children showing butchering marks; these have been interpreted as showing ritual cannibalism.

BIBLIOGRAPHY

+A. Brown, *Arthur Evans and the Palace of Minos* (Oxford, 1983); W. A. McDonald—C. G. Thomas, *Progress into the Past, the Rediscovery of Mycenean Civilization,* 2nd ed. (Bloomington, IN, 1990); +*Aerial Atlas of Crete,* 124–47; L. H. Sackett, *Knossos, from Greek City to Roman Colony, Excavations at the Unexplored Mansion II,* 1–2 (Oxford, 1992).

KOLDEWEY, ROBERT (1855–1925). German excavator and historian of architecture.

Like *Dörpfeld, Koldewey was an outsider who never held a university post. He studied architecture, archaeology and art history at Berlin, Munich and Vienna. He never took a doctorate and owed little to his studies. He learned, rather, from field experience. Francis H. Bacon of Boston, the son-in-law of Frank *Calvert, the adviser of *Schliemann, invited Koldewey to participate in his excavation of *Assos in 1882–83. There Koldewey learned to excavate and perfected his remarkable talent for architectural drawing. He survived from excavations assigned him by the *German Archaeological Institute. He excavated for them in Lesbos (1885–86); and in 1887 he first turned to Mesopotamia, excavating Surghul, ancient Nine and at El Hibba, the ancient Lagasch. In 1889 he excavated Neandria, a Greek site, where he discovered the "Aeolian capital."

In 1890–91 and 1894 he aided F. Luschan in excavating the Late Hellenistic city of Schamal. In 1890–91 with Otto Puchstein he gathered material for their *Die Griechische Tempel in Unteritalien und Sizilien,* two volumes (1899). The famous drawings are by Koldewey. From 1895 to 1898 he taught school in Görlitz but was rescued by Puchstein, who convinced Richard Schöne to arrange a survey of Mesopotamia by Koldewey, to whom in 1898 he entrusted Babylon.

Koldewey's excavations for the Berlin Museum continued until the English captured Baghdad in 1917. He was the discoverer of Babylon as Schliemann was of Troy. The Procession Street and the Ishtar Gate, now in the *Pergamon Museum, Berlin are his most spectacular finds. A bitter, lonely misogynist who despised scholars, Koldewey founded the modern archaeology of the Near East. The Koldewey Society commemorates his services to architectural history.

BIBLIOGRAPHY

W. Andrae, *Babylon: Die Versunkene Weltstadt und ihr Ausgräber Robert Koldewey* (Berlin, 1952); O. Reuther, "Erinnerungen an Robert Koldewey," *Festschrift zum 80. Geburtstag von Ernst Walter Andrae* (Karlsruhe, 1952), 31–34. B. Hrouda, "Koldewey, Robert," *NDB* 12 (1979), 459–60; J. Renger, "Die Geschichte der Altorientalistik und der vorderasiatischen Archäologie in Berlin von 1875–1945," *Berlin und die Antike: Aufsätze,* ed. W. Arenhövel—C. Schreiber (Berlin, 1979), 151–92.

WILLIAM M. CALDER III

KOMMOS, Crete. Minoan and Greek site.

Kommos is the modern toponym for a sandy shoreside area at the south end of the shoreline of the Mesara Plain on the Libyan Sea. It gave its name to a Minoan-Greek site slightly to the north, discovered by Sir Arthur *Evans (1924), who thought of it as the harbor terminus of a road leading south from *Knossos. The first actual excavation began in 1976 with the direction of J. W. Shaw and M. C. Shaw under the auspices of the University of Toronto and the *Royal Ontario Museum, with the cooperation of the *American School of Classical Studies and the Greek Antiquities Service.

During two decades of exploration were discovered moderate-sized houses of a Minoan town (Middle Minoan I–Late Minoan III) and, to the south, unexpectedly large ashlar buildings of a civic character. Structure T, the largest, is of Late Minoan I date and of palatial form, with a large court bordered by colonnaded stoas on the north and south; originally it was perhaps 6,000m^2. Structure P, reusing part of T, consisted of six long galleries open to the west and perhaps used to shelter ships during the winter months.

Built above the northwestern part of these Minoan buildings is an unusually well-preserved Greek sanctuary with clear stratification, used from ca. 1050 B.C.–A.D. 200. During that time three Greek temples were built, one upon the other. The first, A, established in the Sub-Minoan/Protogeometric period, was a small rectangular, roofed structure, open on the east. The second, B, built upon the first about 800 B.C., was also open on the east, with a central pillar at the entrance. It featured a bench along its north wall and a Phoenician-inspired shrine on its axis. Temple B was deserted around 600 B.C. After a long hiatus, it was replaced ca. 375 B.C. by Temple C, which had a formal cult statue base as well as wall benches. Its plan, with a central hearth between two columns set on the longitudinal axis, is based upon a tradition beginning at least as early as the Geometric temple of Apollo at Dreros. C, with its exterior altars and attendant buildings, flourished during the Hellenistic period. It was probably dedicated to Zeus and Athena.

BIBLIOGRAPHY

J. Shaw, "Excavations at Kommos (Crete) During 1986–92," *Hesperia* 62 (1993), 129–90; *Kommos,* 1: *The Kommos Region and Houses of the Minoan Town,* ed. J. W. Shaw—M. C. Shaw (part 1, Princeton, NJ, 1995; part 2 in press); 2: ed. P. Betancourt, *The Final Neolithic Through Middle Minoan III Pottery* (Princeton, NJ, 1990); 3: ed. L. V. Watrous, *The Late Bronze Age Pottery* (Princeton, NJ, 1992).

JOSEPH W. SHAW

KORAI AND KOUROI. Greek sculptured figures dating to the Orientalizing and Archaic periods (ca. 660–ca. 480 B.C.).

The *korai* (sing., *kore,* "maiden") belong to a female figure type represented dressed (usually) and in a frontal pose, with legs sometimes together, sometimes apart, and with arms in varied poses. The *kouroi* (sing., *kouros,* "youth") belong to a male type represented as nude or nearly so, frontal, with arms down by the side and left leg (usually) advanced. Though the colossal marble *kouros* at *Delos drew attention as early as the visit of *Buondelmonti in 1416, the great majority of *kouroi* were first discovered or acquired or received attention in the nineteenth or early twentieth century. The *Piombino *Apollo* (now regarded as archaizing rather than truly Archaic) was discovered in the early nineteenth century off the coast of Italy. Especially important were the finds at the sanctuary of Ptoan Apollo near *Thebes in Boeotia, where excavations in 1885–86 and 1903 turned up a large number of significant examples. In 1932, the *Metropolitan Museum of Art acquired its fine Attic *Kouros.* A notorious case was that of the well-preserved marble figure excavated at Anavysos in 1936, which was smuggled out of the country and brought back from Paris by Greek police; it is today in the *National Archaeological Museum, Athens. Another well-known discovery was made in 1959 at the port of *Peiraeus (*Peiraeus Bronzes), when a rare bronze *kouros* was found with a cache of bronzes of different periods gathered together for export in Roman times. The *Kritios *Boy* and the *Blond *Boy* found on the *Akropolis, Athens, in the nineteenth century are also studied as part of the *kouros* tradition.

The male statues were at first all thought to represent Apollo (as, in fact, some of them do), but V. I. Leonardos realized that the identification did not apply in every case and in 1895 proposed the use of the generic Greek term *kouros.* W. Deonna decided to use quotation marks for his *Les "Apollons archaïques"* (1895), while G.M.A. *Richter made the word *kouros* canonical with her authoritative study of the statue type, *Kouroi, Archaic Greek Youths* (1st ed., 1942; 3rd ed., 1970).

The *korai,* like the *kouroi,* first began to be studied as a group in the nineteenth century. Interest in the figures leaped in 1886 with the excavation of some fourteen of the finest examples found packed together in a hole northwest of the *Erechtheion on the *Akropolis at Athens. Further striking examples were the *Hera of Cheramyes, discovered on Samos in 1875, and the *Auxerre *Lady,* transferred to the *Louvre in 1908.

The term *kore* was well established for the sculpture type by the time of the cataloging of the Akropolis by Dickins in 1912; *Langlotz produced a masterly catalog of the Akropolis figures in 1939. Richter published her companion volume for the *kouroi,* called *Korai, Archaic Greek Maidens* in 1968. More recently, E. Guralnick studied the proportions of both *kouroi* and *korai* with statistical tables executed by computer; she found that certain key examples of early *kouroi* and *korai* were significantly similar to Egyptian statues of the "second canon."

BIBLIOGRAPHY

G. Dickins, *Catalogue of the Acropolis Museum* (Cambridge, 1912); +H. Payne—G. M. Young, *Archaic Marble Sculpture from the Acropolis,* 2nd ed. (London, 1950); B. S. Ridgway, *The Archaic Style in Greek Sculpture* (Princeton, NJ, 1977), 45–119; E. Guralnick, "The Proportions of *Kouroi,*" *AJA* 82 (1978), 461–72; eadem, "Proportions of *Korai,*" *AJA* 85 (1981), 269–80.

KORINTHOS. See CORINTH.

KORKYRA (KORFU). Greek island in the Ionian Sea opposite the Greek-Albanian border.

Excavation has documented the Corinthian colony of ca. 734 B.C. on the Palaiopolis peninsula midway along the east coast. French military engineers, fortifying the peninsula in 1813–14, noted antiquities. In 1822, British engineers discovered the Archaic Kardaki temple. Lechat (*French School at Athens) and Karapanos excavated terracotta Artemis votives in 1889 at Kanoni, on the southern tip of Palaiopolis peninsula. Farmers found the pediment of the great Artemis temple in 1910 and the ephor Versakis excavated it (April 1911). Kaiser Wilhelm II, then on the island, obtained permission to continue the work and summoned W. *Dörpfeld. Dörpfeld, with the ephor K. A. Rhomaios, completed the excavation (1911–14, 1920). The Doric temple, ca. 580 B.C., is the earliest known Greek peripteral temple constructed entirely of stone. With eight columns on the ends and seventeen on the flanks, the length was only slightly greater than twice the width (ca. 23.5m × 49m). Dörpfeld and Rhomaios also excavated at the Kardaki Temple (1912, 1914) and at another sanctuary within the royal estate of Mon Repos (1914).

Ephors have conducted most subsequent excavations. J. Papademetriou examined the Early Christian basilica at Palaiopolis (1936, 1939) and a fifth-century B.C. temple on the north coast at Roda (1939–40). B. Kallipolitis continued excavations of the Palaiopolis basilica from 1955 to 1959, found a

Roman bath at the Olive Institute just north of the basilica in 1959 and unearthed Archaic burials in the necropolis at Garitsa in 1961. G. Dontas, with P. Kalligas, excavated the important Archaic-Classical sanctuary (Heraion) briefly investigated by Dörpfeld at Mon Repos (1962–67), Archaic-Hellenistic houses on the Evelpides property (1962, 1964–65), and installations at the ancient Alkinoos Harbor (1965–66).

Since 1970, the *Greek Archaeological Service has exposed a Late Archaic pediment from a probable Dionysos sanctuary at Kanoni on the Giovani-Kolla properties (1973–74, 1977–78), a fifth-century altar and temple near the Artemis temple (1973, 1979), large Roman structures at Kassopi in the northeast (1970–71) and other antiquities. Dontas returned, with A. Mallwitz of the *German Archaeological Institute, to the Kardaki temple in 1976–78.

New excavations by the Belgian Catholic University of Leuven and Brown University have uncovered Roman bathing facilities at Kasfiki near the Palaipolis basilica (1987–89).

Prehistoric material, Paleolithic to Bronze Age, has been found by Dörpfeld (1913), Bulle (1930), Dontas (1964) and Sordinas (1965–66) on many parts of the island.

BIBLIOGRAPHY

+G. Rodenwaldt ed., *Korkyra, Archaische Bauten und Bildwerke,* 1: *Der Artemistempel* (Berlin, 1940); 2: *Die Bildwerke des Artemistempels* (Berlin, 1939); G. Dontas, *Odegos Archaiologikou Mouseiou Kerkyras* (Athens, 1970); W. B. Dinsmoor, Jr., "The Kardaki Temple Reexamined," *AM* 88 (1973), 165–74; G. Dontas, *Ergon* (1977), 81–88; *Ergon* (1978), 36–37.

JANE BURR CARTER

KÖRTE, GUSTAV (1852–1917). German archaeologist, one of the leading Etruscan scholars of his generation.

Born in Berlin, Gustav Körte studied in Göttingen, Munich (under Heinrich *Brunn), and Berlin. He was at the *German Archaeological Institute in Athens from 1877 to 1879 and then, after appointments in Berlin and Göttingen, held the chair for classical archaeology in Rostock from 1881 to 1905. After two years as director of the *German Archaeological Institute in Rome, he became professor of classical archaeology in Göttingen, a post he held until his death.

Körte's early work focused on Greek vase painting and sculpture. Travels in Turkey led to an interest in ancient Phrygia and the first excavations at *Gordion in 1900, with his brother Alfred Körte. His principal contributions concern the influence of the Greeks on Etruscan art. He completed *Gerhard's work on Etruscan mirrors and Brunn's study of Etruscan relief urns and also published material from *Orvieto, *Tarquinia, *Volsinii and *Perugia.

BIBLIOGRAPHY

G. Körte—A. Körte, *Gordion, Ergebnisse der Ausgrabung* (Berlin, 1904); G. Körte, "Etrusker," *RE* 6 (1907), cals. 730–70; idem, *Das Volumniergrab bei Perugia* (Berlin, 1909); C. Schwingenstein, in *Archäologenbildnisse,* 102.

LYNN E. ROLLER

KOS (COS). Greek island off the southwest coast of Turkey; the principal city of the island (ancient and modern) is also named Kos.

The remains at Kos that have been excavated include temples, theaters, an agora and a gymnasium (from the Greek period) and an odeum, baths and large villas (from the Roman period).

The principal site on the island is that of the temple of Asklepios, located outside the city of Kos. Pilgrims to the god of healing made Kos a flourishing health resort; it was an important center of early medicine, whose most prominent representative was the great physician Hippokrates of Kos (d. 399 B.C.). The complex was begun in the middle of the fourth century B.C. and in its fully developed form featured a grand complex of four terraces joined by stairways. On the second terrace were an altar and small Ionic temple to Asklepios, and on the fourth was a large Doric temple to the god, enclosed by porticoes for the pilgrims, created in the second century B.C.

The island is subject to earthquakes, one of which, in A.D. 554, leveled the city and the sanctuary of Asklepios. By 1331, there was a monastery on the site of the Asklepieion. Cristoforo *Buondelmonti visited Kos in the fifteenth century and recounted a legend believed at that time that the ghost of Hippokrates' daughter was prone to appearances in the town.

In modern times the site of the Asklepieion was recognized by the epigraphist R. Paton. Excavations were begun there in 1900–4 by the Germans under R. Herzog, and in 1912 the island was occupied by Italy. Excavations resumed from 1922 to 1943, largely on the part of the *Italian School of Archaeology, with L. Laurenzi directing.

BIBLIOGRAPHY

R. Herzog, *Koische Forschungen und Funde* (Leipzig, 1899), P. W. Lehmann, "The Setting of Hellenistic Temples," *JSAH* 13.4 (1954), 15–20; M. G. Picozzi, s.v. "Kos," *PECS*, 465–67, S. M. Sherwin White, *Ancient Cos, An Historical Study from the Dorian Settlement to the Imperial Period* (Göttingen, 1978).

KOURION. Hellenistic and Graeco-Roman town on the south coast of *Cyprus.

Kourion reached its fullest development during the Roman and Early Christian periods, although occupation in the area (at Sotira and Kandou) goes back to Neolithic times. As a result of extensive archaeological exploration in the region, the domain of the ancient kingdom of Kourion contains many of the most impressive remains visible on the island. On the site of the Hellenistic city, on a dramatic bluff overlooking the Mediterranean, are located Roman structures with mosaics of mythological and gladiatorial scenes, a bath complex, a theater erected in the Hellenistic period and an Early Christian basilica. Kourion was the site of a bishopric that lasted until the abandonment of the city as a result of Arab raids in A.D. 647.

The Kourion area was extensively explored by *Cesnola in the 1870s; among his presumed discoveries was the "Treasure of Kourion," a collection of gold and silver objects of various periods. Kourion was first systematically excavated by G. McFadden and B. H. *Hill for the University Museum of the University of Pennsylvania between 1933 and 1954. In the 1970s A.H.S. Megaw cleared the basilica. Since 1964 the Cypriot Department of Antiquities has carried out excavations in the town center. Dramatic evidence for the town's destruction by an earthquake in A.D. 365 has been uncovered by D. Soren in his excavations, begun in 1984, of a house within the settlement.

Neighboring areas explored by McFadden and Hill include the Bronze Age settlement of Bamboula, the early Iron Age cemetery at Kaloriziki, the Sanctuary of Apollo Hylates and the late Hellenistic cemetery at Ayios Ermoyenis. The Sanctuary of Apollo Hylates has more recently been investigated by D. Soren and D. Buitron, a project that led to the 1986 reconstruction of the Roman temple of Apollo Hylates by the Cypriot Department of Antiquities.

BIBLIOGRAPHY

K. Nicolaou, s.v. "Kourion," *PECS,* 467–68; H. W. Swing, ed., *An Archaeological Guide to the Ancient Kourion Area and the Akrotiri Peninsula* (Nicosia, 1982); D. Soren—J. James, *Kourion, The Search for a Lost Roman City* (New York, 1988).

PAMELA J. RUSSELL

KOUROI. See *KORAI* AND *KOUROI.*

KRAAY, COLIN (1918–82). British expert in Greek and Roman numismatics.

Kraay served as keeper in the coin room of the *Ashmolean Museum, Oxford, from 1975 until his death, simultaneously holding the post of university lecturer at Oxford. He published numerous articles and books of distinction, including *Archaic and Classical Greek Coins* (1976) and the series of Ashmolean fascicles for the *Sylloge Nummorum Graecorum.* He is especially remembered for articles dealing with problems of Greek numismatics in the sixth and fifth centuries B.C.

Kraay's preeminence in the field was recognized when he was elected president of the Royal Numismatic Society (1970–74) and of the Centro Internazionale di Studi Numismatici at Naples (1974–79); he was also chosen as a fellow of the British Academy. In addition, he received the Barclay Head Prize in ancient numismatics (1948) and the honorary medal of the American Numismatic Society.

BIBLIOGRAPHY

"Dr. Colin Kraay," *London Times,* 28 January 1982, 14; *Who's Who* (New York, 1982), 1254.

SHELLIE WILLIAMS

KRITIOS (KRITIAS) BOY. Greek Archaic sculpture of a youth, made of Parian marble (height 1.167m), found on the *Akropolis, Athens (now in the *Akropolis Museum).

Both arms below the elbow, the right leg below the knee and the left foot are missing. The torso, heralded because it shows clear weight shift and thus breaks with Archaic formulas for the *kouros* (*korai* and *kouroi*), was discovered southeast of the *Parthenon, probably in 1865–66 and matched with the head, unearthed in a different area of the Akropolis in 1888. It was frequently noted that the style of the figure and the fine condition of the marble suggested that it was made just before the Persian sack of the Akropolis in 480 B.C., but Hurwit has demonstrated that the statue was not found in Persian debris and that some surfaces of the statue show considerable evidence of weathering.

Before the discovery of the head, *Furtwängler advised restoration with another head (Akropolis 699) found along with the torso but later judged alien and removed. The true head, improperly restored in the 1950s or 1960s, was recently reattached more cleanly (1987), revealing that the head was turned to the youth's right more than had been realized.

The statue with alien head was connected with the bronze sculptor Kritios by Furtwängler, who pointed out its resemblance to the Harmodios group of Kritios and his school (erected 477 B.C.; the correct spelling of Kritios is attested by inscriptions). The likelihood that the statue reflects the influence of bronze sculpture is widely admitted, though it is not possible to confirm the attribution to Kritios in the absence of any originals by his hand.

The subject of the sculpture has normally been identified as a victorious boy athlete. Hurwit supported an earlier argument for *Theseus.*

BIBLIOGRAPHY

G. Dickins, *Catalogue of the Acropolis Museum* (Cambridge, 1912), 264–66; +H. Payne—G. M. Young, *Archaic Marble Sculpture from the Acropolis* (New York, 1950), pl. 109–12; +G. M. A. Richter, *Kouroi, Archaic Greek Youths,* 3rd ed. (London, 1970), 149; J. M. Hurwit, "The Kritios Boy: Discovery, Reconstruction and Date," *AJA* 93 (1989), 41–80.

SHARON WICHMANN

KUNSTHISTORISCHES MUSEUM, Vienna. Major art-historical museum of Austria, containing a rich collection of classical antiquities.

The nucleus of the antiquities collection of the Kunsthistorisches Museum was formed in the eighteenth century, when the existing coin cabinet of the *Hapsburgs was merged with the carved gems and other antiquities. Franz de Paula Neumann was made curator of the combined coin and antiquities cabinet in 1798, and he began to consolidate the collection of marble sculptures, inscriptions and bronzes in the same way the coins and gems had been gathered together previously. The collection of gems, including the spectacular *Gemma Augustea and a handsome Hellenistic double portrait cameo (possibly the piece known in the seventeenth century as the Gonzaga Cameo), had received attention from the time of Rudolf II (d. 1612). A bronze tablet with a Senate decree of 186 B.C. on Bacchic rituals was in the imperial collection by 1727.

A number of antiquities, gathered together from the imperial palaces, were combined with recent local discoveries of Roman and barbarian antiquities and with objects from long-established private collections (e.g., bronzes from the collection of J. de France, 1808; more than 600 Italic and Greek vases from the collection of Franz Anton Graf Lamberg, 1815).

In 1806 the statue of a nude *Youth* from Magdalensberg was added to the collection; this over-lifesize bronze (183.5m) is now believed to be a cast from the original found in 1502 at Magdalensberg (formerly Helenenberg) by a peasant during plowing. The piece, described in a letter to the emperor Maximilian I and probably studied by Albrecht *Dürer on his trip to Italy in 1505, featured a Latin inscription naming the dedicants that was published by Petrus Apianus and Bartholomeus Amantius (1534). The piece became the property of the archbishop of Salzburg but disappeared and remained known only in the cast.

The existing collections were augmented significantly in the late nineteenth century by finds from the Austrian archaeological expeditions to *Samothrace (1873, 1875) and *Ephesos (1895–1906) and to the Heroon of *Trysa. In 1891 the Kunsthistorisches Museum was inaugurated in its present location on Maria Theresien Platz in Vienna, but sufficient space for proper display of the finds from Trysa and Ephesos was not secured until the opening in 1978 of the Ephesos-Museum in the annex of the Neue Burg.

BIBLIOGRAPHY

+F. Eichler—E. Kris, *Die Kameen im Kunsthistorischen Museen* (Vienna, 1927); F. Eichler, s.v., ''Vienna,'' *EAA* 7 (1966), 1164–65; R. Wünsche, ''Der Jungling von Magdalensberg: Studien zur römische Idealplastik,'' *Festschrift für Luitpold Dussler* (Munich, 1972), 45–80; +*Guss + Form: Bronzen aus der Antikensammlung, Kunsthistorischen Museum, Wien* (Vienna, 1986); A. Bernhard-Walcher et al., ''Antikensammlung,'' in *Kunsthistorisches Museum, Wien, Führer durch die Sammlungen* (Vienna, 1988), 59–119.